D0608555

Oxford
Mini
School
German
Dictionary

Editorial Manager: Valerie Grundy
New Edition: Nicholas Rollin
with the assistance of Marie-Louise Wasmeier

OXFORD
UNIVERSITY PRESS

OXFORD
UNIVERSITY PRESS

Great Clarendon Street, Oxford OX2 6DP

Oxford University Press is a department of the University of Oxford.
It furthers the University's objective of excellence in research,
scholarship, and education by publishing worldwide in

Oxford   New York

Auckland   Cape Town   Dar es Salaam   Hong Kong   Karachi
Kuala Lumpur   Madrid   Melbourne   Mexico City   Nairobi
New Delhi   Shanghai   Taipei   Toronto

With offices in

Argentina   Austria   Brazil   Chile   Czech Republic   France   Greece
Guatemala   Hungary   Italy   Japan   Poland   Portugal   Singapore
South Korea   Switzerland   Thailand   Turkey   Ukraine   Vietnam

Oxford is a registered trade mark of Oxford University Press
in the UK and in certain other countries

British Library Cataloguing in Publication Data available

ISBN-10: 0-19-911207-X
ISBN-13: 978-0-19-911207-4

10 9 8 7 6 5 4

Printed in Italy by Legoprint

INTRODUCTION

This dictionary has been specially written for students who are in their first years of learning German all the way through to preparing for exams. We have paid particular attention to making the dictionary user-friendly. With the help of bold headwords, alphabet tabs, easy-to-follow signposts and examples, the right translation can quickly be found. The things students need to know about words in German are clearly shown. These include main parts of irregular verbs, noun plurals, and the case taken by prepositions.

Throughout the writing of this dictionary we have worked in close consultation with students, teachers, and examining boards. We gratefully acknowledge the examining boards AQA (formerly NEAB and SEG), OCR, and EDEXCEL, who have read and commented on the dictionary text.

Since the first edition of this dictionary there have been many changes in German life. Not least has been the introduction of the euro. This new edition of the dictionary takes full account of these changes and many new words and examples have been included in order to provide the best possible learner's dictionary of German at this level.

HOW A BILINGUAL DICTIONARY WORKS

A bilingual dictionary contains two languages. When you look up a word in one of the languages, it gives the translation for that word in the other language. This dictionary is divided into two halves which are separated by a section of dark-edged pages. In the first half you look up German words, which are in alphabetical order, to find out what they mean in English and in the second half you look up English words, also in alphabetical order, to find out how to say them in German.

At the entry, you will find not only **translations** but also other information that will help you get the right word and use it correctly. Here is a guide to the different things you will find in an entry:

headword	a word you look up in the dictionary
translation	translations are the only things that are in 'ordinary' type in the dictionary. They are always typed like this, and something which is typed in a different way can never be a translation
noun	word class (part of speech): tells you whether the word you are looking up is a noun, a verb, an adjective, or some other part of speech. A headword can be more than one part of speech. For instance, book can be a noun (she was reading a book) or a verb (I've booked the seats)
(*signpost*)	helpful information: to guide you to the right translation, to show you how to use the translation, or to give you extra information about either the headword or the translation
example	a phrase or sentence using the word you have looked up. You should read through them carefully to see if they are close to what you want to understand or say
der/die/das	gender: after a German noun to tell you whether it is masculine (der), feminine (die), or neuter (das)
(PL *die........*)	shows the plural form of a German noun
●	indicates a phrasal verb such as to carry on
★	shows an idiomatic expression such as over the moon
[27]	verb number – tells you which verb pattern to look at in the dark-edged of the dictionary
✧	indicates an irregular German verb
SEP	indicates that a German verb is separable such as ablenken (PERF lenkt ab)

USING THE DICTIONARY

To find out what a German word means

Suppose you want to find out what the German word **Tor** means. You need to use the first half of the dictionary to find the German word that you are looking for. To help you do this, the guide words at the top of each page show the alphabetical range of words on the pages you have open. You will know that all German nouns start with a capital letter. Notice that this makes no difference to the alphabetical order, nor do accented letters like **ü**.

When you find the entry for **Tor** you will find the translation but you will also see what the gender of **Tor** is. Nouns in German are either masculine, feminine, or neuter. These are shown in the dictionary as *der*, *die*, or *das*. You can see that **Tor** says *das* so it is neuter.

However, it often happens that a German word has more than one translation in English so you will see that the translation for **Tor** is divided into sections numbered **1** and **2**.

Tor das (PL die **Tore**) **1** gate; **2** goal;
 mit 3 zu 2 Toren gewinnen to win
 by 3 goals to 2.

The first translation is **gate** and the second is **goal**. You will need to look at both translations and see which fits best in the German sentence you are trying to understand, so:

Uli hat das Tor geöffnet means Uli opened the gate

BUT

Uli steht im Tor means Uli's in goal

In English, the plural of most nouns is formed by adding -s. In German there are quite a lot of ways of forming the plural and these are not always easy to recognize. To help you with this, we show the plural form after every noun headword. For instance, if you are trying to find out what the German word **Häuser** means, you can see immediately that it is the plural of **Haus** and so it means **houses**.

Haus das (PL die **Häuser**) **1** house;
 2 nach Hause home; **zu Hause** at
 home.

German like English has certain words that you would use when chatting with friends but not in more formal situations. German words like this are marked (*informal*) like **flitzen** here:

flitzen verb (*informal*) (PERF **ist**
 geflitzt) **1** to dash; **2** to whizz.

You can think of a dictionary entry as being made out of different sorts of building bricks. In the entries below you can see how they fit together to help you find what you need. The more you use your dictionary the more confident you will feel about finding your way around it.

GERMAN-ENGLISH

headword in bold for easy look-up

word class (part of speech)

main forms of iregular verbs

gender

noun plurals in bold for easy look-up

typical examples to show German in context

abergläubisch *adjective* superstitious.

abfahren ⋄*verb* (PRES **fährt ab**, IMPERF **fuhr ab**, PERF **ist abgefahren**) to leave; **Peter fährt morgen ganz früh ab** Peter is leaving very early tomorrow morning; **wann fährt der Zug nach Berlin ab?** when does the Berlin train leave?

Abfahrt *die* (PL *die* **Abfahrten**) **1** departure; **2** run (*on a ski slope*); **3** exit (*on a motorway*).

Abfall *der* (PL *die* **Abfälle**) rubbish.

Abfalleimer *der* (PL *die* **Abfalleimer**) rubbish bin.

abfliegen ⋄*verb* (IMPERF **flog ab**, PERF **ist abgeflogen**) **1** to take off; **die Maschine ist mit zehn Minuten Verspätung abgeflogen** the plane took off ten minutes late; **2** to leave (*by plane*); **ich fliege um elf Uhr ab** my plane leaves at 11 o'clock.

Abflug *der* (PL *die* **Abflüge**) departure.

ENGLISH-GERMAN

case governed by German preposition

based *adjective* **1 to be based on** basieren auf (+ DAT); **the film is based on a true story** der Film basiert auf einer wahren Geschichte; **2 to be based in** wohnen in (+ DAT); **he's based in Bristol** er wohnt in Bristol.

essential structures for expression in German

basement *noun* Kellergeschoss *das* (PL die Kellergeschosse).

plural form

irregular verb

bear *noun* Bär *der* (PL die Bären).

bear *verb* **1** ertragen ◇; **I can't bear the idea** ich kann den Gedanken nicht ertragen; **2 to bear something in mind** an etwas (ACC) denken; **I'll bear it in mind** ich denke daran.

case of 'etwas' shown in translation of example

gender

blush *verb* erröten (PERF *sein*).

perfect formed with 'sein'

bolt *noun* (on a door) Riegel *der* (PL die Riegel).

bolt *verb* **1** (lock) verriegeln; **2** (gobble down) runterschlingen ◇ SEP (informal).

seperable verb

informal word or expression

◇ IRREGULAR VERB: See the verb tables in the centre of the dictionary

Finding an English word and how to say it in German

You can see that it is quite easy once you know how the dictionary works to look up a German word and find out what it means. Students usually find it harder to use the dictionary to find out how to say something in German. This dictionary is written specially to help you do this and to make it easy to find the right way of saying things in German.

Suppose you want to know how to say **garden** in German. Look up the word in the second part of the dictionary. If you follow the same method of going through the alphabetical order of the headwords as you did when you were looking up a German word, you will find **garden** on page 434.

garden *noun* Garten *der* (PL *die* Gärten).

Now you can see that the German word for **garden** is **Garten**. But if you want to make a sentence using a noun like **Garten** you need to know its gender. The dictionary shows you that it is *der* **Garten** so in the garden will be **im Garten**. It is not always as easy as this to know which German word you need. Sometimes there will be more than one German word for the English word you are looking up. When the dictionary entry gives you more than just one translation, it is very important to take the time to read through the whole entry. If you look up plug the entry looks like this:

plug *noun* **1** (*electrical*) Stecker *der* (PL *die* Stecker); **2** (*in a bath or sink*) Stöpsel *der* (PL *die* Stöpsel); **to pull out the plug** den Stöpsel herausziehen.

You can see that **1** tells you that the German word for an electrical plug is **Stecker** and **2** tells you that the word for a **plug** in a bath or a sink is **Stöpsel**. Remember that information which is either in brackets or italics or both is there to help you, but it will never be the translation itself.

Wherever there is more than one translation, depending on what meaning of the English word you are looking for, the dictionary will always help you to choose the right one. Often it is not enough to find the translation of one word.

In the case of more common words the dictionary also gives you a selection of phrases you will often want to use. In the entry for **hair** below you can find out how to use the translation **Haare** in different expressions:

hair *noun* **1** Haare (*plural*); **to comb your hair** sich (DAT) die Haare kämmen; **to wash your hair** sich (DAT) die Haare waschen; **to have your hair cut** sich (DAT) die Haare schneiden lassen; **she's had her hair cut** sie hat sich die Haare schneiden lassen; **2 a hair** ein Haar.

Note on the German Spelling Reform

The German spelling reform was adopted by German-speaking countries in July 1996. You will find all the new spellings in this dictionary. However, since you may come across old spellings if you are reading pre-reform German material, we have also given all the most frequent old spellings as headwords to help you locate the entry. These are cross-referred to the new spellings. Thus **As** is cross-referred to **Ass** but the old spelling of **Ausschuss** (**Ausschuß**) is not shown.

Aa

Aal *der* (PL die **Aale**) eel.

ab *preposition* (+ DAT) from; **ab Montag** from Monday; **Kinder ab sechs Jahren** children from the age of six.

ab *adverb* **1** off; **der Henkel ist ab** the handle has come off; **ab ins Bett!** (*informal*) off (you go) to bed!; **2 ab und zu** now and again.

abbiegen ⬦*verb* (IMPERF **bog ab**, PERF **ist abgebogen**) **1** to turn off; **nach rechts abbiegen** to turn off to the right; **2 biegen Sie an der Ampel (nach) links ab** turn left at the lights.

Abbildung *die* (PL die **Abbildungen**) illustration.

abbrechen ⬦*verb* (PRES **bricht ab**, IMPERF **brach ab**, PERF **hat abgebrochen**) **1** to break off (*a branch, negotiations*); **Ruth brach ein paar Zweige ab** Ruth broke off a few branches; **2** to pull down (*a building*); **3** to cut short; **leider mussten wir unsere Ferien vorzeitig abbrechen** unfortunately we had to cut short our holidays; **er hat sein Studium aus finanziellen Gründen abgebrochen** he left university for financial reasons; **4** (PERF **ist abgebrochen**) **der Ast ist abgebrochen** the branch has broken off.

Abend *der* (PL die **Abende**) evening; **am Abend** in the evening; **heute Abend** this evening, tonight; **gestern Abend** yesterday evening,

last night; **wann esst ihr zu Abend?** when do you have dinner?

Abendbrot *das* evening meal.

Abendessen *das* (PL die **Abendessen**) supper, dinner (*in the evening*); **was gibt es zum Abendessen?** what are we having for supper?

Abendkurs *der* (PL die **Abendkurse**) evening course.

abends *adverb* in the evening.

Abenteurfilm *der* (PL die **Abenteuerfilme**) adventure film.

Abenteuer *das* (PL die **Abenteuer**) adventure.

aber *conjunction* but; **es ist zwar nützlich, aber zu teuer** it's useful, but too expensive.

aber *adverb* really; **das ist aber sehr nett von dir** that's really nice of you; **du bist aber groß!** aren't you tall!; **aber ja!** but of course!; **jetzt ist aber Schluss!** that's it now!

abergläubisch *adjective* superstitious.

abfahren ⬦*verb* (PRES **fährt ab**, IMPERF **fuhr ab**, PERF **ist abgefahren**) to leave; **Peter fährt morgen ganz früh ab** Peter is leaving very early tomorrow morning; **wann fährt der Zug nach Berlin ab?** when does the Berlin train leave?

Abfahrt *die* (PL die **Abfahrten**) **1** departure; **2** run (*on a ski slope*); **3** exit (*on a motorway*).

Abfall *der* (PL die **Abfälle**) rubbish.

Abfalleimer *der* (PL die **Abfalleimer**) rubbish bin.

a b c d e f g h i j k l m n o p q r s t u v w x y z

abfliegen ◇*verb* (IMPERF **flog ab**, PERF **ist abgeflogen**) **1** to take off; **die Maschine ist mit zehn Minuten Verspätung abgeflogen** the plane took off ten minutes late; **2** to leave (*by plane*); **ich fliege um elf Uhr ab** my plane leaves at 11 o'clock.

Abflug *der* (PL *die* **Abflüge**) departure.

Abflussrohr *das* (PL *die* **Abflussrohre**) outlet, drain.

abfragen *verb* (PERF **hat abgefragt**) **1** to test; **sie fragt ihn Vokabeln ab** she's testing him on his vocabulary; **2** to call up (*on a computer*); **Adressen am Computer abfragen** to call up addresses on the computer.

Abgase (*plural noun*) exhaust fumes.

abgeben ◇*verb* (PRES **gibt ab**, IMPERF **gab ab**, PERF **hat abgegeben**) **1** to hand in (*homework, an application, lost property*); **2** to pass (*in football*); **den Ball abgeben** to pass the ball; **3 sich mit etwas abgeben** to spend time on something; **mit solchen Typen würde ich mich nicht abgeben** I wouldn't associate with blokes like that; **4 jemandem etwas abgeben** to give someone something; **gib mir ein Stück von deiner Schokolade ab** give me a piece of your chocolate; **5 er wird einen guten Lehrer abgeben** he'll make a good teacher.

abgelegen *adjective* remote.

abgemacht *adjective* agreed.

Abgeordnete *der/die* (PL *die* **Abgeordneten**) member of parliament.

abgießen *verb* (IMPERF **goss ab**, PERF **hat abgegossen**) **1** to pour away; **2** to drain (*vegetables*).

Abhang *der* (PL *die* **Abhänge**) slope.

abhängen[1] ◇*verb* (IMPERF **hing ab**, PERF **hat abgehangen**) **von jemandem abhängen** to depend on somebody; **von etwas abhängen** to depend on something; **es hängt vom Wetter ab, ob wir am Wochenende nach Wales fahren** whether or not we are going to Wales at the weekend depends on the weather.

abhängen[2] *verb* (PERF **hat abgehängt**) **1** to unhitch (*a trailer*); **2** to uncouple (*a train carriage*); **3** (*informal*) to shake off; **die Einbrecher hängten die Polizei schnell ab** the burglars soon shook off the police.

abhängig *adjective* dependent.

abheben ◇*verb* (IMPERF **hob ab**, PERF **hat abgehoben**) **1** to lift off; **2** to withdraw (*money*); **3** to answer the phone; **ich habe schon zweimal angerufen, aber niemand hat abgehoben** I've rung twice before, but nobody answered.

abholen *verb* (PERF **hat abgeholt**) **1** to collect; **2** to pick up; **ich hole dich am Bahnhof ab** I'll pick you up at the station.

Abitur *das* (PL *die* **Abiture**) A levels (*German students usually take Abitur at 19, sitting exams in four subjects, which they have to pass to* go on to university); **sein Abitur machen** to do your A levels.

Abiturient *der* (PL die Abiturienten) A-level student.

Abiturientin *die* (PL die Abiturientinnen) A-level student.

Abkommen *das* (PL die Abkommen) agreement.

abkürzen *verb* (PERF hat abgekürzt) **1** to abbreviate; **wie kürzt man das Wort ab?** how do you abbreviate that word?; **2 den Weg abkürzen** to take a short cut.

Abkürzung *die* (PL die Abkürzungen) **1** abbreviation; **die Abkürzung für Europäische Union is EU** the abbreviation for European Union is EU; **2** short cut.

abladen ◊*verb* (PRES lädt ab, IMPERF lud ab, PERF hat abgeladen) to unload.

ablaufen ◊*verb* (PRES läuft ab, IMPERF lief ab, PERF ist abgelaufen) **1** to expire (*passport, contract*); **2** to drain off; **das Badewasser ablaufen lassen** to let the bathwater out; **3** to go off; **wie ist die Besprechung abgelaufen?** how did the meeting go?

Ablaufdatum *das* (PL die Ablaufdaten) expiry date.

ablegen *verb* (PERF hat abgelegt) **1** to take off; **2 abgelegte Kleidung** cast-offs.

ablehnen *verb* (PERF hat abgelehnt) **1** to turn down (*a position, money, an invitation*); **2** to reject (*an applicant, a suggestion*).

ablenken *verb* (PERF hat abgelenkt) **1** to distract; **jemanden von seiner Arbeit ablenken** to distract somebody from their work; **2 jemanden von seinen Sorgen ablenken** to take somebody's mind off their worries; **3** to divert (*attention, suspicion*); **vom Thema ablenken** to change the subject.

abliefern *verb* (PERF hat abgeliefert) **1** to deliver; **2** to hand in (*an essay, a form, lost property*); **3** to drop off; **die Kinder abliefern** to drop the children off.

abmachen *verb* (PERF hat abgemacht) **1** to take off; **kannst du den Deckel abmachen?** can you take off the lid?; **2** to agree; **wir müssen noch einen Termin für unser nächstes Treffen abmachen** we still have to agree on a date for our next meeting; **abgemacht!** agreed!; **3** to sort out; **das müsst ihr untereinander abmachen** you'll have to sort that out amongst yourselves.

Abmachung *die* (PL die Abmachungen) agreement.

abnehmen ◊*verb* (PRES nimmt ab, IMPERF nahm ab, PERF hat abgenommen) **1** to take off (*remove*); **2 kann ich dir etwas abnehmen?** (*carry*) can I take something (for you)?; (*help*) can I do anything for you?; **3 jemandem etwas abnehmen** to take something off somebody; **sie nehmen einem schnell zwanzig Euro ab** they'll soon take 20 euros off you; **4** to buy; **5** to decrease (*in* number); **6** to diminish; **7** to lose weight; **er hat schon vier Kilo abgenommen** he's already lost four kilos; **8** to answer the phone; **9 das nehme ich dir nicht ab** (*informal*) I don't buy that.

Abonnement das (PL die **Abonnements**) subscription.

abonnieren verb (PERF **hat abonniert**) to subscribe to.

abraten ◇verb (PRES **rät ab**, IMPERF **riet ab**, PERF **hat abgeraten**) **jemandem von etwas abraten** to advise somebody against something.

abräumen verb (PERF **hat abgeräumt**) to clear away; **den Tisch abräumen** to clear the table.

abreagieren verb (PERF **hat abreagiert**) **1 seine Wut an jemandem abreagieren** to take your anger out on somebody; **2 sich abreagieren** to calm down.

Abreise die departure.

abreisen verb (PERF **ist abgereist**) to leave.

abreißen ◇verb (IMPERF **riss ab**, PERF **hat abgerissen**) **1** to tear down (*a poster, notice*); **2** to demolish (*a building*); **3** (PERF **ist abgerissen**) to come off (*a button, for example*).

Absage die (PL die **Absagen**) refusal.

absagen verb (PERF **hat abgesagt**) **1** to cancel; **2 eine Einladung absagen** to turn down an invitation.

Absatz der (PL die **Absätze**) **1** heel (*of a shoe*); **2** paragraph.

abschaffen verb (PERF **hat abgeschafft**) **1** to abolish (*a regulation, capital punishment*); **2** to get rid of; **wir haben unseren Hund abgeschafft** we got rid of our dog.

abscheulich adjective horrible.

abschicken verb (PERF **hat abgeschickt**) to send off.

Abschied der (PL die **Abschiede**) **1** parting; **2** farewell; **3 Abschied nehmen** to say goodbye.

Abschleppdienst der breakdown service.

abschleppen verb (PERF **hat abgeschleppt**) **1** to tow away; **2 sich mit den Koffern abschleppen** (*informal*) to struggle along with the suitcases; **3 jemanden abschleppen** (*informal*) to pick somebody up.

Abschleppwagen der (PL die **Abschleppwagen**) breakdown truck.

abschließen ◇verb (IMPERF **schloss ab**, PERF **hat abgeschlossen**) to lock.

Abschlussprüfung die (PL die **Abschlussprüfungen**) final exam.

abschneiden ◇verb (IMPERF **schnitt ab**, PERF **hat abgeschnitten**) **1** to cut off; **ich schneide dir eine Scheibe Brot ab** I'll cut you a slice of bread; **2 gut/ schlecht abschneiden** to do well/ badly.

abschrecken verb (PERF hat abgeschreckt) to deter.

abschreiben ◇verb (IMPERF schrieb ab, PERF hat abgeschrieben) to copy.

Abseilen das abseiling.

abseits adverb 1 far away; **etwas abseits** a little way away; 2 offside (in soccer).

Absender der (PL die Absender) sender.

absetzen verb (PERF hat abgesetzt) 1 to take off (your hat, glasses); 2 to put down (a bag, suitcase); 3 to drop off; **ich setze euch am Bahnhof ab** I'll drop you off at the station; 4 **die Pille absetzen** to stop taking the pill.

Absicht die (PL die Absichten) intention.

absichtlich adverb intentionally.

absolut adjective absolute.

absolut adverb absolutely; **das ist absolut unmöglich** that's absolutely impossible.

abspülen verb (PERF hat abgespült) 1 to rinse, to rinse off; 2 to do the washing up.

Abstand der (PL die Abstände) 1 distance; **in zwanzig Meter Abstand** at a distance of 20 metres; **Abstand halten** to keep your distance; 2 interval.

abstauben verb (PERF hat abgestaubt) to dust.

abstellen verb (PERF hat abgestellt) 1 to turn off (the radio, a tap); 2 to put down (a suitcase, the shopping); 3 to park (the car).

Abstimmung die (PL die Abstimmungen) vote.

abstreiten ◇verb (IMPERF stritt ab, PERF hat abgestritten) to deny.

abstürzen verb (PERF ist abgestürzt) 1 to fall; 2 to crash (a plane).

Abszess der (PL die Abszesse) abscess.

abtauen verb (PERF hat abgetaut) to defrost (the fridge).

Abteil das (PL die Abteile) compartment.

abteilen verb (PERF hat abgeteilt) 1 to divide up; 2 to divide off.

Abteilung die (PL die Abteilungen) department.

Abtreibung die (PL die Abtreibungen) abortion.

abtrocknen verb (PERF hat abgetrocknet) 1 to dry up; 2 **sich abtrocknen** to dry yourself.

abwägen verb (IMPERF wog ab, PERF hat abgewogen) to weigh up.

abwärts adverb down.

Abwasch der washing-up.

abwaschen ◇verb (PRES wäscht ab, IMPERF wusch ab, PERF hat abgewaschen) 1 to wash up (the dishes); 2 to wash off (dirt, marks).

Abwasser das (PL die Abwässer) sewage.

Abwechslung die (PL die Abwechslungen) change; **zur Abwechslung** for a change.

abwerten verb (PERF hat abgewertet) to devalue.

abwertend adjective pejorative.

b c d e f g h i j k l m n o p q r s t u v w x y z

abwesend *adjective* absent.

Abwesenheit die absence.

abwischen *verb* (PERF **hat abgewischt**) to wipe.

abzählen *verb* (PERF **hat abgezählt**) to count.

Abzeichen das (PL die **Abzeichen**) badge.

abziehen ⋄*verb* (IMPERF **zog ab**, PERF **hat abgezogen**) **1** to take off (*a sheet, backing*); **die Betten abziehen** to strip the beds; **2** to take out (*a key*); **3** to deduct, to take away; **4** to withdraw (*troops*); **5** (PERF **ist abgezogen**) to escape (*steam or smoke, for example*); **6** (PERF **ist abgezogen**) **sie sind gleich nach dem Essen abgezogen** (*informal*) they pushed off straight after the meal.

abzielen *verb* (PERF **hat abgezielt**) **etwas zielt auf etwas ab** something is aimed at something.

Abzweigung die (PL die **Abzweigungen**) turning.

ach *exclamation* oh!

Achsel die (PL die **Achseln**) shoulder.

Acht[1] die (PL die **Achten**) eight; **eine Acht schreiben** to write an eight.

Acht[2] die **1 Acht geben** to pay attention; **er sollte in der Schule besser Acht geben** he should pay more attention at school; **2 auf etwas/jemanden Acht geben** to look after something/somebody; **3 gib Acht!** watch out!; **4 sich in Acht nehmen** to be careful;

5 etwas außer Acht lassen to disregard something.

acht *number* eight; **um acht (Uhr)** at eight (o'clock); **um halb acht** at half past seven.

Achtel das (PL die **Achtel**) eighth.

achten *verb* (PERF **hat geachtet**) **1** to respect (*a person, an opinion*); **2 auf etwas achten** to pay attention to something; **3 auf jemanden achten** to look after somebody; **4 achte nicht darauf!** don't take any notice of it!

achter, achte, achtes *adjective* eighth; **jede achte Kiste** every eighth crate; **mein achter Geburtstag** my eighth birthday; **sie ging als Achte durchs Ziel** she finished eighth.

Achterbahn die (PL die **Achterbahnen**) roller coaster.

achtgeben SEE **Acht**[2].

achthundert *number* eight hundred.

achtmal *adverb* eight times.

Achtung die **1** respect; **Achtung vor jemandem haben** to have respect for somebody; **2 Achtung!** look out!; **Achtung, fertig, los!** on your marks, get set, go!; 'Achtung Stufe' 'mind the step'.

achtzehn *number* eighteen.

achtzig *number* eighty.

Acker der (PL die **Äcker**) field.

addieren *verb* (PERF **hat addiert**) to add.

Ader die (PL die **Adern**) vein.

Adjektiv das (PL die **Adjektive**) adjective.

Adler der (PL die **Adler**) eagle.

adoptieren verb (PERF hat **adoptiert**) to adopt.

Adoption die (PL die **Adoptionen**) adoption.

Adoptiveltern plural noun adoptive parents.

Adoptivkind das (PL die **Adoptivkinder**) adopted child.

Adresse die (PL die **Adressen**) address.

adressieren verb (PERF hat **adressiert**) to address; **an wen soll ich den Brief adressieren?** who shall I address the letter to?

Advent der Advent.

Adventskalender der (PL die **Adventskalender**) Advent calendar.

Adventskranz der (PL die **Adventskränze**) Advent wreath.

Adverb das (PL die **Adverbien**) adverb.

Aerobic das aerobics.

Affe der (PL die **Affen**) 1 monkey; 2 ape.

Afrika das Africa; **aus Afrika** from Africa; **nach Afrika** to Africa.

Afrikaner der (PL die **Afrikaner**) African.

Afrikanerin die (PL die **Afrikanerinnen**) African.

afrikanisch adjective African.

AG[1] die (PL die **AGs**) (Aktiengesellschaft) Plc (Public limited company).

AG[2] die (PL die **AGs**) 1 work group; 2 school club.

Agentur die (PL die **Agenturen**) agency.

aggressiv adjective aggressive.

ähneln verb (PERF hat **geähnelt**) 1 to resemble; **er ähnelt seinem Vater sehr** he's very like his father; 2 **sich ähneln** to be alike.

ahnen verb (PERF hat **geahnt**) 1 to know; **das konnte ich wirklich nicht ahnen** I had no way of knowing that; **wer soll denn ahnen, dass ...?** who would know that ...?; 2 to suspect; **so etwas habe ich doch schon geahnt** I did suspect something like that.

ähnlich adjective 1 similar; 2 **jemandem ähnlich sein** to be like somebody; **jemandem ähnlich sehen** to look like somebody; 3 **ähnlich wie** like; 4 **das sieht dir ähnlich!** (informal) that's just like you!

Ähnlichkeit die (PL die **Ähnlichkeiten**) similarity.

Ahnung die 1 idea; **hast du eine Ahnung, wie er heißt?** have you got any idea what he's called?; 2 **keine Ahnung!** no idea!; **er hat von Mode absolut keine Ahnung** he doesn't know a thing about fashion; 3 premonition.

ahnungslos adjective unsuspecting.

Ahorn der (PL die **Ahorne**) maple.

Aids das Aids.

Akademiker der (PL die **Akademiker**) university graduate.

Akademikerin die (PL die **Akademikerinnen**) university graduate.

akademisch adjective academic.

Akkusativ der (PL die **Akkusative**) accusative.

Akne die acne.

Akte die (PL die **Akten**) file.

Aktentasche die (PL die **Aktentaschen**) briefcase.

Aktion die (PL die **Aktionen**) 1 action; **in Aktion treten** to go into action; 2 campaign.

Aktiv das active.

aktiv adjective active.

Aktualisierung die (PL die **Aktualisierungen**) 1 up-date; 2 updating.

aktuell adjective 1 topical; **ein aktuelles Thema** a topical issue; 2 **nicht mehr aktuell** no longer relevant; 3 current; **eine aktuelle Sendung** a current-affairs programme.

Akzent der (PL die **Akzente**) 1 accent; **mit starkem Akzent sprechen** to speak with a strong accent; 2 accent (on a letter); 3 stress; **den Akzent auf etwas legen** to stress something.

albern adjective silly.

albern adverb in a silly way.

Albtraum der (PL die **Albträume**) nightmare.

Album das (PL die **Alben**) album.

Algebra die algebra.

Alkohol der alcohol.

alkoholfrei adjective non-alcoholic.

Alkoholiker der (PL die **Alkoholiker**) alcoholic.

Alkoholikerin die (PL die **Alkoholikerinnen**) alcoholic.

alkoholisch adjective alcoholic.

All das space; **einen Satelliten ins All schicken** to send a satellite into space.

alle SEE **aller**.

Allee die (PL die **Alleen**) avenue.

allein adjective, adverb alone 1 **sie waren allein im Zimmer** they were alone in the room; **jemanden allein lassen** to leave somebody alone; 2 on your own; **sie hat das ganz allein gezeichnet** she drew it all on her own; 3 **von allein** by yourself, by itself (automatically); 4 **allein stehend** single; 5 **eine allein erziehende Mutter** a single mother; **der/die allein Erziehende** single parent; 6 **nicht allein** not only; 7 **allein der Gedanke** the mere thought.

alleinerziehend, alleinstehend SEE **allein**.

aller, alle, alles pronoun 1 all; **alle meine Freunde** all my friends; **alles Geld** all the money; **alle miteinander** all together; 2 **alle Jungen in der Schule** all the boys in the school; **alle Bewohner der Stadt sind dagegen** all the people of the town are against it; **alles Gute!** all the best!; **Getränke aller Art** all kinds of drinks; 3 **alle** (plural) all; **alle waren da** they were all there; **wir alle** all of us; **wir**

haben alle gesehen we saw all of them; **4 ohne allen Grund** without any reason; **5 alle beide** both of them; **6** every; **alle Tage** every day; **alle fünf Minuten** every five minutes; **7 alles** everything, everybody (*people*).

alle *adjective* **alle sein** (*informal*) to be all gone.

allerbester, allerbeste, allerbestes *adjective* **1** very best; **2 am allerbesten** best of all.

allerdings *adverb* **1** though; **das Essen ist gut, allerdings ziemlich teuer** the food's good, though rather expensive; **2** certainly (*yes*); **'tut das weh?' – 'allerdings!'** 'does it hurt?' – 'it certainly does!'.

Allergie *die* (PL *die* **Allergien**) allergy.

allergisch *adjective* allergic.

Allerheiligen *das* All Saints' Day.

allerlei *adjective* all sorts of; **allerlei Ausreden** all sorts of excuses.

allerletzter, allerletzte, allerletztes *adjective* very last.

alles SEE **aller**.

allgemein *adjective* **1** general; **2 im Allgemeinen** in general.

allgemein *adverb* **1** generally; **2 es ist allgemein bekannt, dass** ... it is common knowledge that ....

allmählich *adjective* gradual.

allmählich *adverb* gradually; **wir sollten allmählich gehen** it's time we got going.

Alltag *der* **1** daily routine; **2** weekday.

alltäglich *adjective* everyday (*event, sight*).

alltags *adverb* on weekdays.

Alpen *plural noun* **die Alpen** the Alps.

Alphabet *das* (PL *die* **Alphabete**) alphabet.

alphabetisch *adjective* alphabetical.

als *conjunction* **1** when; **als meine Freundin hier war** when my friend was here; **erst als** only when; **2** than (*as a comparison*); **er ist jünger als sie** he's younger than her; **3 lieber … als** … rather … than …; **ich würde lieber ins Kino gehen, als zum Essen** I'd rather go to the cinema than for a meal; **4** as; **als Frau kann ich das verstehen** as a woman, I can sympathize; **gerade als ich gehen wollte** just as I was about to leave; **5 als ob** as if; **als ob ich das nicht wüsste** as if I didn't know that!

also *adverb, conjunction* **1** so; **ich konnte ihn telefonisch nicht erreichen, also habe ich ihm ein Fax geschickt** I couldn't get through to him on the phone, so I sent him a fax; **2** then; **also kommst du mit?** you're coming too, then?; **also gut** all right then; **3** well; **also, wie gesagt** well, as I said before; **4 na also!** there you are!

alt *adjective* **1** old; **wie alt bist du?** how old are you?; **alt werden** to grow old; **2 alles beim Alten lassen** to leave everything as it was.

a b c d e f g h i j k l m n o p q r s t u v w x y z

Altar der (PL die **Altäre**) altar.

Alter das (PL die **Alter**) 1 age; **in deinem Alter** at your age; **im Alter von zwanzig** at the age of twenty; **2** old age; **im Alter** in old age.

älter adjective 1 older; **mein Rad ist älter als deins** my bike is older than yours; **2** elder; **mein älterer Bruder** my elder brother; **3** elderly.

altern verb (PERF **ist gealtert**) to age.

Alternative die (PL die **Alternativen**) alternative.

Altersgenosse der (PL die **Altersgenossen**) person of one's own age.

Altersgenossin die (PL die **Altersgenossinnen**) person of one's own age.

Altersgrenze die (PL die **Altersgrenzen**) age limit.

Altersheim das (PL die **Altersheime**) old people's home.

ältester, älteste, ältestes adjective 1 oldest; 2 eldest; **der älteste Sohn** the eldest son.

Altglas das used glass.

Altglascontainer der (PL die **Altglascontainer**) bottle bank.

altmodisch adjective old-fashioned.

Altpapier das waste paper.

Altstadt die (PL die **Altstädte**) old town.

Alufolie die tin foil.

Aluminium das aluminium.

am = **an dem**; 1 **am Freitag** on Friday; **2 am besten** the best; **3 am**

teuersten (the) most expensive; 4 **am höchsten** the highest; **5 am Abend** in the evening.

Ameise die (PL die **Ameisen**) ant.

Amerika das America.

Amerikaner der (PL die **Amerikaner**) American.

Amerikanerin die (PL die **Amerikanerinnen**) American.

amerikanisch adjective American.

Ampel die (PL die **Ampeln**) traffic lights.

Amsel die (PL die **Amseln**) blackbird.

Amt das (PL die **Ämter**) 1 office; 2 exchange (telephone).

amtlich adjective official.

amüsant adjective amusing.

amüsieren verb (PERF **hat amüsiert**) 1 to amuse; 2 **sich amüsieren** to enjoy oneself; **amüsier dich gut!** enjoy yourself!; 3 **sich über etwas amüsieren** to find something funny.

an preposition (+ DAT or + ACC) (the dative is used when talking about position; the accusative shows movement or a change of place) 1 at; **an der Spitze** at the top; **sich an den Tisch setzen** to sit down at the table; **er arbeitet an der Schule** he works at the school; 2 on (attached to, when talking about time); **das Bild hängt an der Wand** the picture is on the wall; **an dem Tag** on that day; **ich habe am fünften März Geburtstag** my birthday is on the fifth of March;

3 to; **einen Brief an jemanden schicken** to send a letter to somebody; **4 an einer Krankheit sterben** to die of a disease; **5 an jemanden denken** to think of somebody; **6 sich an etwas erinnern** to remember something; **7 an (und für) sich** actually; **an sich ist das kein Problem** actually, it's no problem; **8 es liegt an dir, jetzt etwas zu unternehmen** it's up to you to do something now.

an adverb **1** on; **das Licht ist an** the light's on; **2 ohne etwas an** with nothing on; **3 an die dreißig Euro** about thirty euros; **4 von heute an** from today.

analysieren verb (PERF **hat analysiert**) to analyse.

Ananas die (PL die **Ananas**) pineapple.

Anästhetikum das (PL die **Anästhetika**) anaesthetic.

anbieten ◇verb (IMPERF **bot an**, PERF **hat angeboten**) to offer; **Anna bot mir an, mich nach Hause zu bringen** Anna offered to take me home.

Anblick der (PL die **Anblicke**) sight.

anbrennen ◇verb (IMPERF **brannte an**, PERF **ist angebrannt**) to burn; **das Essen ist angebrannt** the food's burnt.

Andenken das (PL die **Andenken**) **1** souvenir; **2 zum Andenken an unsere Ferien** to remind us of our holiday.

anderer, andere, anderes adjective **1** other; **ich nehme das andere T-Shirt** I'll have the other T-shirt; **2** different; **3 ein anderer/ eine andere/ ein anderes** another; **ein anderes Mal** another time.

andere pronoun **1** der/die/das **andere** the other one; **nicht dieses Buch, sondern das andere** not that book, but the other one; **die anderen** the others; **die anderen kommen später** the others are coming later; **2 andere** other ones (things, toys, etc.); **3 ein anderer/ eine andere/ein anderes** a different one (thing), someone else (person); **4 kein anderer** no one else; **5 unter anderem** among other things; **6 etwas anderes** something else; **7 alles andere** everything else.

andererseits adverb on the other hand.

andermal adverb **ein andermal** another time.

ändern verb (PERF **hat geändert**) **1** to change; **2** to alter (a garment); **3 sich ändern** to change; **sie hat sich sehr geändert** she's changed a lot.

anders adverb **1** differently; **2 anders aussehen** to look different; **3 niemand anders** nobody else; **jemand anders** somebody else; **4 anders als** different from; **du bist ganz anders als ich** you're quite different from me; **5 irgendwo anders** somewhere else.

anderthalb number one and a half.

Anerkennung die **1** appreciation; **2** recognition (of a king, state).

Anfall der (PL die **Anfälle**) fit.

Anfang der (PL die **Anfänge**)
1 beginning, start; **am Anfang** at
the beginning; **von Anfang an** from
the start; **zu Anfang** at first.

anfangen ◇verb (PRES **fängt an**,
IMPERF **fing an**, PERF **hat
angefangen**) 1 to begin, to start;
die Schule fängt um acht an
school starts at eight; **mit etwas
anfangen** to start (on) something;
2 bei einer Firma anfangen to
start working for a firm; **3 was soll
ich damit anfangen?** what am I
supposed to do with that?; **4 damit
kann ich nichts anfangen** that's no
good to me (*it's no use*), it doesn't
mean anything to me (*I don't
understand it*).

Anfänger der (PL die **Anfänger**)
beginner.

Anfängerin die (PL die
Anfängerinnen) beginner.

anfassen verb (PERF **hat
angefasst**) 1 to touch; 2 to tackle
(*a problem, a task*); 3 to treat (*a
person*); **4 mit anfassen** to lend a
hand; **5 sich anfassen** to feel; **es
fasst sich weich an** it feels soft;
6 jemanden anfassen to take
somebody's hand; **sie hat ihre
Mutter angefasst** she took her
mother's hand; **fasst euch an!** hold
hands!

anfragen verb (PERF **hat
angefragt**) to enquire, to ask.

anfreunden verb (PERF **hat sich
angefreundet**) 1 **sich anfreunden**
to make friends; **sie freundet sich
mit allen möglichen Leuten an** she

makes friends with all sorts of
people; **2 sich anfreunden** to
become friends; **wir haben uns
angefreundet** we've become
friends.

Anführungszeichen plural
noun inverted commas.

Angabe die (PL die **Angaben**)
1 piece of information; 2 serve (*in
tennis*); 3 showing off; **das ist nur
Angabe** he is/she is/they are only
showing off.

angeben ◇verb (PRES **gibt an**,
IMPERF **gab an**, PERF **hat
angegeben**) 1 to give (*your name, a
reason*); 2 to show off; 3 to indicate
(*on a map*); 4 to serve (*in tennis*).

Angeber der (PL die **Angeber**)
show-off.

Angeberin die (PL die
Angeberinnen) show-off.

Angebot das (PL die **Angebote**)
offer.

angehen ◇verb (IMPERF **ging an**,
PERF **ist angegangen**) 1 to come on
(*a radio, heating, a light*); 2 to
concern; **das geht auch dich
etwas an** it concerns you too; **das
geht dich nichts an** it's none of
your business; 3 (PERF **hat
angegangen**) to tackle (*problems,
difficulty, work*).

Angehörige der/die (PL die
Angehörigen) relative.

Angel die (PL die **Angeln**) fishing
rod.

Angelegenheit die (PL die
Angelegenheiten) 1 matter;

2 business; **das ist meine Angelegenheit** that's my business.

angeln verb (PERF **hat geangelt**) **1** to fish; **angeln gehen** to go fishing; **2** to catch (a fish).

Angelrute die (PL die **Angelruten**) fishing rod.

angemessen adjective adequate.

angenehm adjective pleasant.

angenehm exclamation pleased to meet you! (when introduced to somebody).

Angestellte der/die (PL die **Angestellten**) employee.

angewiesen adjective dependent; **auf etwas angewiesen sein** to be dependent on something; **auf jemanden angewiesen sein** to be dependent on somebody.

angewöhnen verb (PERF **hat angewöhnt**) **1** jemandem etwas **angewöhnen** to get somebody used to something; **2** sich etwas **angewöhnen** to get into the habit of doing something; **ich habe es mir angewöhnt, früh aufzustehen** I've got into the habit of getting up early.

Angewohnheit die (PL die **Angewohnheiten**) habit.

angreifen ✧verb (IMPERF **griff an**, PERF **hat angegriffen**) **1** to attack; **2** to affect (your health, voice).

Angriff der (PL die **Angriffe**) attack.

Angst die (PL die **Ängste**) **1** fear; **2** Angst haben to be afraid; **vor jemandem Angst haben** to be afraid of somebody; **mir ist Angst** I'm afraid; **3** jemandem Angst

machen to frighten somebody; **4** Angst vor einer Prüfung haben to be worried about an exam; **Angst um jemanden haben** to be worried about somebody.

ängstlich adjective **1** nervous; **2** frightened; **3** anxious.

anhaben ✧verb (informal) (PRES **hat an**, IMPERF **hatte an**, PERF **hat angehabt**) to have on; **sie hat heute das neue Kleid an** she's got her new dress on today.

anhalten ✧verb (PRES **hält an**, IMPERF **hielt an**, PERF **hat angehalten**) **1** to stop; **2** den Atem **anhalten** to hold your breath; **3** to last; **das schöne Wetter wird nicht lange anhalten** the nice weather won't last long; **4** jemanden zur Arbeit anhalten to urge somebody to work.

Anhalter der (PL die **Anhalter**) hitchhiker; **per Anhalter fahren** to hitchhike.

Anhalterin die (PL die **Anhalterinnen**) hitchhiker.

Anhang der (PL die **Anhänge**) appendix.

Anhänger der (PL die **Anhänger**) **1** supporter; **2** trailer; **3** label (on a suitcase); **4** pendant; **5** loop (for hanging up).

Anhängerin die (PL die **Anhängerinnen**) supporter.

anhören verb (PERF **hat angehört**) **1** to listen to (music, a CD); **sich etwas anhören** to listen to something; **ich kann ihn mir nicht länger anhören** I can't listen to

a b c d e f g h i j k l m n o p q r s t u v w x y z

him any longer; **2 sich anhören** to sound; **sich gut anhören** to sound good; **3 jemandem etwas anhören** to hear something in somebody's voice; **man hörte ihr die Verzweiflung an** you could hear the despair in her voice.

anklagen *verb* (PERF **hat angeklagt**) to accuse.

Ankleidekabine die (PL die **Ankleidekabinen**) changing cubicle.

anklicken *verb* (PERF **hat angeklickt**) **etwas anklicken** to click on something; **das Icon anklicken** to click on the icon.

ankommen ◇*verb* (IMPERF **kam an**, PERF **ist angekommen**) **1** to arrive; **gut ankommen** to arrive safely; **2 (bei jemandem) gut ankommen** (*informal*) to go down well (with somebody); **3 ankommen auf** to depend on; **es kommt ganz darauf an** it all depends; **4 es drauf ankommen lassen** (*informal*) to take a chance; **5 auf ein paar Minuten kommt es nicht an** a few minutes don't matter.

ankündigen *verb* (PERF **hat angekündigt**) to announce.

Ankunft die (PL die **Ankünfte**) arrival.

Ankunftstafel die (PL die **Ankunftstafeln**) arrivals board.

Ankunftszeit die (PL die **Ankunftszeiten**) time of arrival.

Anlage die (PL die **Anlagen**) **1** gardens; **2** investment; **das Haus**

ist eine gute Anlage the house is a good investment; **3** plant (*industrial, for recycling, for example*); **4** enclosure; **als Anlage** enclosed; **5** system (*music, loudspeakers, etc.*); **6** installation (*military*).

Anlass der (PL die **Anlässe**) **1** cause; **der Anlass ihres Streits** the cause of their row; **Anlass zu etwas geben** to give cause for something; **2** occasion; **ein festlicher Anlass** a festive occasion; **aus Anlass ihres Geburtstags** on the occasion of her birthday.

Anleitung die (PL die **Anleitungen**) instructions.

anmachen *verb* (PERF **hat angemacht**) **1** to turn on (*the light, radio, TV*); **2** to light (*a fire*); **3** to dress (*salad*); **4** (*informal*) to chat up (*a person*).

Anmeldeformular das (PL die **Anmeldeformulare**) registration form.

anmelden *verb* (PERF **hat angemeldet**) **1** to register (*a car, change of address*); **2 jemanden anmelden** to enrol somebody; **3 jemanden anmelden** to make an appointment for somebody; **sind Sie angemeldet?** do you have an appointment?; **4 ein Gespräch anmelden** to book a call (*on the phone*); **5 sich anmelden** to say that you're coming; **6 sich anmelden** to register your new address (*in Germany a change of address has to be registered at the 'Einwohnermeldeamt'*); **sich**

polizeilich anmelden to register with the police; **7 sich anmelden** to make an appointment; **sich beim Arzt anmelden** to make an appointment with the doctor; **8 sich anmelden** to check in (*at a hotel*); **9 sich anmelden** to enrol; **sich zu einem Abendkurs anmelden** to enrol for an evening course.

Anmeldung die (PL die Anmeldungen) **1** registration; **2** appointment.

annehmbar adjective acceptable.

annehmen ✧ verb (PRES nimmt an, IMPERF nahm an, PERF hat angenommen) **1** to accept (*an invitation, help, a verdict*); **2** to take (*a call, name*); **3** to adopt (*a child, habit*); **4** to assume; **angenommen, dass** ... assuming that ...; **5** to suppose.

Annonce die (PL die Annoncen) (small) ad.

Anorak der (PL die Anoraks) **1** anorak; **2** cagoule.

anordnen verb (PERF hat angeordnet) **1** to arrange; **2** to order.

anpassen verb (PERF hat sich angepasst) **sich anpassen** to adapt.

anpassungsfähig adjective adaptable.

anprobieren verb (PERF hat anprobiert) to try on.

Anruf der (PL die Anrufe) (phone) call.

Anrufbeantworter der (PL die Anrufbeantworter) answering machine.

anrufen ✧ verb (IMPERF rief an, PERF hat angerufen) **1** to ring, to phone; **ich rufe schnell mal meine Mutter an** I'll just quickly ring my mother; **2** to call to (*a passer-by*).

ans = **an das**; **ans Telefon gehen** to answer the phone.

Ansage die (PL die Ansagen) announcement.

Ansager der (PL die Ansager) announcer.

Ansagerin die (PL die Ansagerinnen) announcer.

anschalten verb (PERF hat angeschaltet) to switch on.

anschauen verb (PERF hat angeschaut) **1** to look at; **2 sich etwas anschauen** to look at something, to watch something (*on TV*); **sie schauten sich den neuen Film an** they saw the new film.

anscheinend adverb apparently.

Anschlag der (PL die Anschläge) **1** notice; **2** attack; **ein Anschlag auf den Präsidenten** an attack on the president.

Anschlagbrett das (PL die Anschlagbretter) notice board.

anschlagen ✧ verb (PRES schlägt an, IMPERF schlug an, PERF hat angeschlagen) **1** to put up (*a notice, an announcement*); **2** to chip.

anschließen ✧ verb (IMPERF schloss an, PERF hat angeschlossen) **1** to connect;

b
c
d
e
f
g
h
i
j
k
l
m
n
o
p
q
r
s
t
u
v
w
x
y
z

2 sich an etwas anschließen to follow something; **an den Vortrag schließt sich eine Diskussion an** the talk will be followed by a discussion; **3 sich jemandem anschließen** to join somebody; **sich einer Gruppe anschließen** to join a group.

anschließend *adverb* **1** afterwards; **2 anschließend an das Essen** after the meal.

Anschluss *der* (PL die **Anschlüsse**) **1** connection; **2 Anschluss finden** to make friends; **3 den Anschluss verlieren** to lose contact; **4 im Anschluss an** after.

anschnallen *verb* (PERF **hat sich angeschnallt**) **sich anschnallen** to fasten your seat belt.

Anschrift *die* (PL die **Anschriften**) address.

Anschuldigung *die* (PL die **Anschuldigungen**) accusation.

ansehen ◇*verb* (PRES **sieht an**, IMPERF **sah an**, PERF **hat angesehen**) **1** to look at; **sie sah mich nicht an** she didn't look at me; **2 sich etwas ansehen** to look at something(*on TV*) to watch something; **sich einen Film ansehen** to see a film; **3 sich eine Stadt ansehen** to look round a town; **4** to regard; **ich sehe ihn als meinen Freund an** I regard him as a friend.

Ansehen *das* **1** respect; **2** reputation.

Ansicht *die* (PL die **Ansichten**) view; **meiner Ansicht nach** in my view.

Ansichtskarte *die* (PL die **Ansichtskarten**) picture postcard.

ansprechen ◇*verb* (PRES **spricht an**, IMPERF **sprach an**, PERF **hat angesprochen**) **1** to speak to; **2** to appeal to; **die Musik spricht mich an** the music appeals to me; **3** to mention; **er hat den Skandal, in den sie verwickelt war, angesprochen** he mentioned the scandal she was involved in; **4 auf etwas ansprechen** to respond to something (*a treatment, for example*).

Anspruch *der* (PL die **Ansprüche**) **1** demand; **keine Ansprüche stellen** to make no demands; **2** claim (*for compensation*); **3 Anspruch auf etwas haben** to be entitled to something; **4 viel Zeit in Anspruch nehmen** to take up a lot of time; **5 etwas in Anspruch nehmen** to take advantage of something (*an offer, for example*).

anständig *adjective* **1** decent; **2** respectable.

anstarren *verb* (PERF **hat angestarrt**) to stare at.

anstatt *preposition* (+ GEN) instead of.

anstatt *conjunction* **anstatt zu arbeiten** instead of working.

ansteckend *adjective* infectious.

anstelle *preposition* (+ GEN) instead of.

anstellen *verb* (PERF **hat angestellt**) **1** to employ; **2** to turn on (*the TV, radio*); **3** (*informal*) to do; **was stellt ihr heute Abend noch an?** what are you doing tonight?; **wie kann ich es nur anstellen, dass ...?** what can I do to ...?; **4 sich anstellen** to queue; **5 sich anstellen** to make a fuss; **stell dich nicht so an!** don't make such a fuss!

Anstieg der (PL die **Anstiege**) **1** increase; **2** way up, ascent.

anstreichen ♦ verb (IMPERF **strich an**, PERF **hat angestrichen**) to paint.

anstrengen verb (PERF **hat angestrengt**) **1** to tire; **ihr Besuch hat mich sehr angestrengt** their visit tired me out; **2 sich anstrengen** to make an effort.

anstrengend adjective tiring.

Anstrengung die (PL die **Anstrengungen**) effort.

Antarktis die **die Antarktis** the Antarctic.

Anteil der (PL die **Anteile**) **1** share; **mein Anteil an dem Gewinn** my share of the profit; **2 Anteil nehmen** to sympathize; **3 Anteil nehmen an** to take an interest in.

Antenne die (PL die **Antennen**) aerial.

Antibiotikum das (PL die **Antibiotika**) antibiotic.

antik adjective antique.

Antiquitäten plural noun antiques.

Antiseptikum das (PL die **Antiseptika**) antiseptic.

Antivirenprogramm das (PL die **Antivirenprogramme**) anti-virus software.

Antrag der (PL die **Anträge**) application; **einen Antrag stellen** to make an application.

Antragsformular das (PL die **Antragsformulare**) application form.

Antwort die (PL die **Antworten**) answer, reply; **jemandem eine Antwort geben** to give somebody an answer.

antworten verb (PERF **hat geantwortet**) to answer, to reply; **auf etwas antworten** to answer something; **jemandem antworten** to reply to somebody.

Anwalt der (PL die **Anwälte**) lawyer.

Anwältin die (PL die **Anwältinnen**) lawyer.

Anweisung die (PL die **Anweisungen**) instruction.

anwenden verb (PERF **hat angewendet**) **1** to use (a method, process, medicine); **2** to apply (a rule, law).

anwesend adjective present.

Anwesenheit die presence; **er gab es in meiner Anwesenheit zu** he admitted it in my presence.

Anzahl die number.

anzahlen verb (PERF **hat angezahlt**) to pay a deposit; **hundert Euro anzahlen** to pay a deposit of a hundred euros; **ein Auto anzahlen** to pay a deposit on a car.

Anzahlung die (PL die **Anzahlungen**) deposit.

Anzeichen das (PL die **Anzeichen**) sign.

b c d e f g h i j k l m n o p q r s t u v w x y z

Anzeige die (PL die **Anzeigen**)
1 advertisement; 2 report (*to the police*); (eine) **Anzeige gegen jemanden erstatten** to report somebody to the police.

anzeigen verb (PERF **hat angezeigt**) 1 to report; **jemanden anzeigen** to report somebody to the police; 2 to show (*the time, a date*).

anziehen ✧verb (IMPERF **zog an**, PERF **hat angezogen**) 1 to attract; 2 to put on (*clothes, the brakes*); 3 to dress (*a child or doll*); **gut angezogen** well dressed; 4 to tighten (*a knot, a screw*); 5 **sich anziehen** to get dressed; 6 **was soll ich anziehen?** what shall I wear?

Anzug der (PL die **Anzüge**) suit.

anzünden verb (PERF **hat angezündet**) to light.

Apfel der (PL die **Äpfel**) apple.

Apfelsaft der (PL die **Apfelsäfte**) apple juice.

Apfelsine die (PL die **Apfelsinen**) orange.

Apotheke die (PL die **Apotheken**) chemist's, pharmacy.

Apotheker der (PL die **Apotheker**) chemist, pharmacist.

Apothekerin die (PL die **Apothekerinnen**) chemist, pharmacist.

Apparat der (PL die **Apparate**) 1 set (*TV, radio*); 2 camera; 3 phone; **am Apparat!** speaking!; 4 gadget.

Appartement das (PL die **Appartements**) flat.

Appetit der appetite; **guten Appetit!** enjoy your meal!

Aprikose die (PL die **Aprikosen**) apricot.

April der April; **am ersten April** on the first of April; **April, April!** April fool!; **jemanden in den April schicken** to play an April fool trick on somebody.

Aquarium das (PL die **Aquarien**) 1 aquarium; 2 tank (*for fish*).

Äquator der equator.

Araber der (PL die **Araber**) Arab.

Araberin die (PL die **Araberinnen**) Arab.

arabisch adjective 1 Arab; **die arabischen Länder** the Arab countries; 2 Arabian; 3 Arabic (*number*); **die arabische Sprache** Arabic.

Arbeit die (PL die **Arbeiten**) 1 work; **viel Arbeit haben** to have a lot of work; **von der Arbeit kommen** to come from work; 2 job; 3 test (*at school*); 4 **sich viel Arbeit machen** to go to a lot of trouble.

arbeiten verb (PERF **hat gearbeitet**) to work.

Arbeiter der (PL die **Arbeiter**) worker.

Arbeiterin die (PL die **Arbeiterinnen**) worker.

Arbeitgeber der (PL die **Arbeitgeber**) employer.

Arbeitnehmer der (PL die **Arbeitnehmer**) employee.

Arbeitsamt das (PL die **Arbeitsämter**) job centre.

arbeitslos adjective unemployed.

Arbeitslose der/die (PL die Arbeitslosen) unemployed person; **die Arbeitslosen** the unemployed.

Arbeitslosigkeit die unemployment.

Arbeitsplatz der (PL die Arbeitsplätze) 1 job; 2 desk.

Arbeitspraktikum das (PL die Arbeitspraktika) work experience.

Arbeitsstunde die (PL die Arbeitsstunden) working hour.

Arbeitszimmer das (PL die Arbeitszimmer) study.

Architekt der (PL die Architekten) architect.

Architektin die (PL die Architektinnen) architect.

Architektur die architecture.

Ärger der 1 annoyance; 2 trouble; **Ärger mit dem Auto haben** to have trouble with the car.

ärgerlich adjective 1 annoying; 2 annoyed; **er war darüber sehr ärgerlich** he was very annoyed about it.

ärgern verb (PERF hat geärgert) 1 to annoy; 2 sich ärgern to be annoyed, to get annoyed; **ich habe mich darüber geärgert** I was annoyed about it; **sich über jemanden ärgern** to get annoyed with somebody.

Arktis die Arktis the Arctic; **in der Arktis** in the Arctic.

Arm der (PL die Arme) arm; **jemanden auf den Arm nehmen** (informal) to pull somebody's leg.

arm adjective poor.

Armband das (PL die Armbänder) bracelet.

Armbanduhr die (PL die Armbanduhren) wrist-watch.

Armee die (PL die Armeen) army.

Ärmel der (PL die Ärmel) sleeve.

Ärmelkanal der (English) Channel.

Armut die poverty.

arrangieren verb (PERF hat arrangiert) 1 to arrange; 2 sich arrangieren to come to an arrangement.

Art die (PL die Arten) 1 way; **auf diese Art** in this way; **auf seine Art** in his own way; 2 kind; **diese Art (von) Buch** this kind of book; **Bücher aller Art** books of all kinds; 3 species; **eine gefährdete Art** an endangered species; 4 nature; **es ist nicht seine Art, das zu tun** it's not (in) his nature to do that.

Arterie die (PL die Arterien) artery.

artig adjective well-behaved.

Artikel der (PL die Artikel) article; **der bestimmte/unbestimmte Artikel** the definite/indefinite article.

Arznei die (PL die Arzneien) medicine.

Arzneimittel das (PL die Arzneimittel) drug.

Arzt der (PL die Ärzte) doctor.

Ärztin die (PL die Ärztinnen) doctor.

ärztlich adjective medical.

ärztlich adverb **sich ärztlich behandeln lassen** to have medical treatment.

a
b
c
d
e
f
g
h
i
j
k
l
m
n
o
p
q
r
s
t
u
v
w
x
y
z

As SEE **Ass.**

Asche die (PL die **Aschen**) ash.

Aschenbecher der (PL die **Aschenbecher**) ashtray.

Aschermittwoch der Ash Wednesday.

Asiat der (PL die **Asiaten**) Asian.

Asiatin die (PL die **Asiatinnen**) Asian.

asiatisch adjective Asian.

Asien das Asia; **nach Asien** to Asia.

Ass das (PL die **Asse**) ace.

aß SEE **essen.**

Assistent der (PL die **Assistenten**) assistant.

Assistentin die (PL die **Assistentinnen**) assistant.

Ast der (PL die **Äste**) branch.

Asthma das asthma.

Astrologie die astrology.

Astronaut der (PL die **Astronauten**) astronaut.

Astronomie die astronomy.

Asyl das **1** asylum; **um politisches Asyl bitten** to apply for political asylum; **2** hostel (for the homeless).

Asylant der (PL die **Asylanten**) asylum-seeker.

Atelier das (PL die **Ateliers**) (artist's) studio.

Atem der breath; **außer Atem sein** to be out of breath.

atemlos adjective breathless.

Atemlosigkeit die breathlessness.

Athlet der (PL die **Athleten**) athlete.

Athletin die (PL die **Athletinnen**) athlete.

Atlantik der der **Atlantik** the Atlantic (Ocean); **im Atlantik** in the Atlantic.

Atlas der (PL die **Atlanten**) atlas.

atmen verb (PERF **hat geatmet**) to breathe.

Atmosphäre die (PL die **Atmosphären**) atmosphere.

Atom das (PL die **Atome**) atom.

atomar adjective atomic.

Atombombe die (PL die **Atombomben**) atomic bomb.

Atomwaffen plural noun nuclear weapons.

atomwaffenfrei adjective nuclear-free.

attraktiv adjective attractive.

ätzend adjective **1** corrosive; **2** caustic (wit, remark).

au exclamation **1** ouch!; **2** oh! (when surprised or enthusiastic); **au ja!** oh yes!

auch adverb **1** also, too; **Sophie war auch dabei** Sophie was also there, Sophie was there too; **ich auch** me too; **nicht nur ... sondern auch** ... not only ... but also ...; **2** 'ich gehe jetzt' – 'ich auch' 'I'm going now' – 'so am I'; **'er schläft'** – **'sie auch'** 'he's asleep' – 'so is she'; **3** 'ich bin nicht müde' – 'ich auch nicht'** I'm not tired'–'neither am I'; **das weiß ich auch nicht** I don't know either; **4 auch wenn** even if; **5 wann auch** whenever; **was auch** whatever; **wo auch** wherever; **wer auch** whoever; **6 wie dem auch sei**

however that may be; **7 lügst du auch nicht?** you're not lying, are you?

auf preposition (+ DAT or + ACC) (the dative is used when talking about position; the accusative shows movement or a change of place) **1** on; **das Buch liegt auf dem Tisch** the book's on the table; **er hat das Buch auf den Tisch gelegt** he put the book on the table; **2 ich war auf der Party** I was at the party; **ich gehe auf eine Party** I'm going to a party; **ich war auf der Post** I was at the post office; **er ist auf die Post gegangen** he went to the post office; **3 auf der Straße** in the street; **auf diese Art** in this way; **auf Deutsch** in German; **5** for (indicating time or distance); **er ist auf ein paar Tage verreist** he's gone away for a few days; **6 auf seinen Rat hin** on his advice; **7 auf Wiedersehen!** goodbye!

auf adverb **1** open; **die Tür ist auf** the door is open; **Mund auf!** open your mouth!; **2 auf** (out of bed); **auf sein** to be up; **er ist schon auf** he's already up; **3 auf einmal** suddenly; **4 auf einmal** at once (at the same time); **5 auf und ab** up and down; **6 sich auf und davon machen** to make off.

aufbekommen ◇ verb (IMPERF **bekam auf**, PERF **hat aufbekommen**) **1** to get open; **2 Hausaufgaben aufbekommen** to be given homework.

aufbewahren verb (PERF **hat aufbewahrt**) to keep.

aufblasen ◇ verb (PRES **bläst auf**, IMPERF **blies auf**, PERF **hat aufgeblasen**) to blow up.

aufbleiben ◇ verb (IMPERF **blieb auf**, PERF **hat aufgeblieben**) **1** to stay open; **wie lange bleiben die Geschäfte auf?** how long do the shops stay open?; **2** to stay up (not go to bed).

aufbringen ◇ verb (IMPERF **brachte auf**, PERF **hat aufgebracht**) **1** to raise (money); **2** to find (patience, strength); **3** to open; **ich bringe die Tür nicht auf** I can't open the door; **4 jemanden aufbringen** to make somebody angry; **5 Verständnis für etwas aufbringen** to be able to understand something.

aufeinander adverb **1** one on top of the other; **die Bretter aufeinander legen** to put the planks one on top of the other; **2 aufeinander liegen** to lie on top of each other; **3 aufeinander folgen** to follow one another; **4 aufeinander warten** to wait for each other; **5 aufeinander schießen** to shoot at each other; **6 aufeinander fahren** to collide with each other.

Aufenthalt der (PL die **Aufenthalte**) **1** stay; **2** stop (pause in a journey); **zehn Minuten Aufenthalt haben** to stop for ten minutes.

Aufenthaltsraum der (PL die **Aufenthaltsräume**) **1** lounge; **2** recreation room.

Auffahrt die (PL die **Auffahrten**) **1** drive; **2** slip road.

auffallend adjective striking.

a
b
c
d
e
f
g
h
i
j
k
l
m
n
o
p
q
r
s
t
u
v
w
x
y
z

auffangen ◇*verb* (PRES **fängt auf**, IMPERF **fing auf**, PERF **hat aufgefangen**) to catch.

aufführen *verb* (PERF **hat aufgeführt**) 1 to perform (*a play*); 2 to list (*words, items*); 3 **sich aufführen** to behave.

Aufführung *die* (PL *die* **Aufführungen**) performance.

auffüllen *verb* (PERF **hat aufgefüllt**) 1 to fill up; 2 to stock up.

Aufgabe *die* (PL *die* **Aufgaben**) 1 task; 2 exercise (*at school*); 3 question (*in a test or an exam*); 4 **Aufgaben** homework.

aufgeben ◇*verb* (PRES **gibt auf**, IMPERF **gab auf**, PERF **hat aufgegeben**) 1 to give up; **ich gebe auf!** I give up!; 2 to post; 3 to check in (*luggage*); 4 to place (*an advertisement, order*); 5 **Hausaufgaben aufgeben** to set homework.

aufgehen ◇*verb* (IMPERF **ging auf**, PERF **ist aufgegangen**) 1 to open (*of a door or flower, for example*); 2 to come undone (*of a knot or zip, for example*); 3 to rise (*of the sun, moon*); 4 to realize; **es ist mir aufgegangen, dass ...** I've realized that ...; 5 to work out (*in maths*); **zehn durch drei geht nicht auf** three into ten won't go.

aufgeregt *adjective* excited.

aufgeschlossen *adjective* open-minded.

aufgrund *preposition* (+ GEN) 1 because of; 2 on the strength of.

aufhaben ◇*verb* (PRES **hat auf**, IMPERF **hatte auf**, PERF **hat aufgehabt**) 1 to have on (*a hat*); 2 **den Mund aufhaben** to have your mouth open; 3 **etwas aufhaben** to have homework to do; **viel aufhaben** to have a lot of homework; 4 to be open; **der Laden hat abends auf** the shop is open in the evening.

aufhalten ◇*verb* (PRES **hält auf**, IMPERF **hielt auf**, PERF **hat aufgehalten**) 1 to hold open (*a door*); 2 to hold up, to keep (*somebody from doing something*); 3 **die Hand aufhalten** to hold out your hand; 4 **die Augen aufhalten** to keep your eyes open; 5 to check (*inflation, an advance, unemployment*); 6 **sich aufhalten** to stay; 7 **sich mit etwas aufhalten** to spend your time on something.

aufhängen *verb* (PERF **hat aufgehängt**) 1 to hang up (*washing*); 2 **sich aufhängen** to hang yourself.

aufheben ◇*verb* (IMPERF **hob auf**, PERF **hat aufgehoben**) 1 to pick up (*from the ground*); 2 to keep; 3 to abolish (*a law*); 4 **gut aufgehoben sein** to be well looked after.

aufheitern *verb* (PERF **hat aufgeheitert**) 1 to cheer up; 2 **sich aufheitern** to brighten up (*of the weather*).

aufhören *verb* (PERF **hat aufgehört**) to stop; **aufhören zu arbeiten** to stop working.

aufklären *verb* (PERF **hat aufgeklärt**) to solve (*a crime*);

2 to explain (*an event, incident*); **3** ein Kind aufklären to tell a child the facts of life; **4** sich aufklären to be solved (*a misunderstanding or mystery*); **5** sich aufklären to clear up; das Wetter klärt sich auf the weather is clearing up.

Aufkleber der (PL die **Aufkleber**) sticker.

auflegen verb (PERF hat aufgelegt) **1** to put on; **2** to hang up (*when phoning*); **3** to lay; noch ein Gedeck auflegen to lay another place (*at table*); **4** to publish; ein Buch neu auflegen to reprint a book.

auflösen verb (PERF hat aufgelöst) **1** to dissolve; **2** to close (*an account*); **3** sich auflösen to dissolve; **4** sich auflösen to break up (*of a crowd, demonstration*); **5** der Nebel hat sich aufgelöst the fog has lifted; **6** in Tränen aufgelöst sein to be in floods of tears.

aufmachen verb (PERF hat aufgemacht) **1** to open; **2** jemandem aufmachen to open the door to somebody; **3** to undo (*a zip, knot*); **4** sich aufmachen to set out.

aufmerksam adjective **1** attentive; **2** auf etwas aufmerksam werden to notice something; **3** jemanden auf etwas aufmerksam machen to draw somebody's attention to something.

aufmuntern verb (PERF hat aufgemuntert) to cheer up.

Aufnahme die (PL die **Aufnahmen**) **1** photograph; **2** recording; **3** admission (*to hospital, to a club*); **4** welcome.

Aufnahmeprüfung die (PL die **Aufnahmeprüfungen**) entrance exam.

Aufnahmetaste die (PL die **Aufnahmetasten**) record button.

aufnehmen ✧verb (PRES nimmt auf, IMPERF nahm auf, PERF hat aufgenommen) **1** to receive (*guests*); **2** to take up (*an idea, activity, a theme*); **3** to admit (*to hospital, to a club*); **4** to photograph; **5** to film; **6** to record (*a song, a programme, a film*); **7** es mit jemandem aufnehmen können to be a match for somebody; **8** to take (*food, news*); etwas gelassen aufnehmen to take something calmly.

aufpassen verb (PERF hat aufgepasst) **1** to pay attention; **2** to watch out; **3** auf jemanden aufpassen to look after somebody; **4** auf etwas aufpassen to keep an eye on something; pass auf meine Tasche auf keep an eye on my bag.

aufräumen verb (PERF hat aufgeräumt) to tidy up.

aufrecht adjective upright.

aufregen verb (PERF hat aufgeregt) **1** to excite; **2** to annoy; **3** sich aufregen to get worked up.

aufregend adjective exciting.

aufs = auf das.

Aufsatz der (PL die **Aufsätze**) essay.

a b c d e f g h i j k l m n o p q r s t u v w x y z

aufschieben ⬦*verb* (IMPERF **schob auf**, PERF **hat aufgeschoben**) **1** to put off (*an arrangement*); **2** to slide open.

aufschlagen *verb* (PRES **schlägt auf**, IMPERF **schlug auf**, PERF **hat aufgeschlagen**) to open.

aufschließen ⬦*verb* (IMPERF **schloss auf**, PERF **hat aufgeschlossen**) to unlock.

Aufschnitt *der* sliced cold meat and cheese.

aufschreiben ⬦*verb* (IMPERF **schrieb auf**, PERF **hat aufgeschrieben**) to write down.

aufsehen ⬦*verb* (PRES **sieht auf**, IMPERF **sah auf**, PERF **hat aufgesehen**) to look up.

Aufsehen *das* sensation, stir; **Aufsehen erregen** to cause a stir.

Aufseher *der* (PL *die* **Aufseher**) **1** supervisor; **2** warder (*in a prison*); **3** attendant (*in a museum*).

Aufseherin *die* (PL *die* **Aufseherinnen**) **1** supervisor; **2** warder (*in a prison*); **3** attendant (*in a museum*).

aufsetzen *verb* (PERF **hat aufgesetzt**) **1** to put on; **2** to draft; **3** **sich aufsetzen** to sit up.

Aufsicht *die* **1** supervision; **2** supervisor.

Aufstand *der* (PL *die* **Aufstände**) rebellion.

aufstehen ⬦*verb* (IMPERF **stand auf**, PERF **ist aufgestanden**) **1** to get up; **2** (PERF **hat aufgestanden**) to be open.

aufstellen *verb* (PERF **hat aufgestellt**) **1** to put up; **2** to set up (*skittles, chess pieces*); **3** **eine Mannschaft aufstellen** to pick a team; **4** **eine Liste aufstellen** to draw up a list; **5** **sich aufstellen** to line up.

auftauen *verb* (PERF **ist aufgetaut**) **1** to thaw; **2** to defrost; **die Erdbeeren sind aufgetaut** the strawberries have defrosted; **3** (PERF **hat aufgetaut**) to defrost; **ich habe die Erbeeren aufgetaut** I've defrosted the strawberries.

aufteilen *verb* (PERF **hat aufgeteilt**) to divide up.

Auftrag *der* (PL *die* **Aufträge**) **1** job; **2** order (*in business*); **etwas in Auftrag geben** to order something; **3** instructions; **einen Auftrag ausführen** to carry out an instruction; **4** **im Auftrag von** on behalf of.

auftreten ⬦*verb* (PRES **tritt auf**, IMPERF **trat auf**, PERF **ist aufgetreten**) **1** to appear (*on stage*); **2** to arise (*a problem, difficulty*); **3** to behave; **4** to tread.

aufwachen *verb* (PERF **ist aufgewacht**) to wake up.

aufwachsen ⬦*verb* (PRES **wächst auf**, IMPERF **wuchs auf**, PERF **ist aufgewachsen**) to grow up.

aufwecken *verb* (PERF **hat aufgeweckt**) to wake up.

aufziehen ⬦*verb* (IMPERF **zog auf**, PERF **hat aufgezogen**) **1** to wind up (*a clock or toy*); **2** to draw (*curtains*); **3** **jemanden aufziehen** (*informal*) to tease somebody; **4** to bring up (*a child*).

Aufzug *der* (PL die **Aufzüge**) lift; **ich fahre mit dem Aufzug runter** I'm going down in the lift.

Auge *das* (PL die **Augen**) **1** eye; **2 unter vier Augen** in private.

Augenarzt *der* (PL die **Augenärzte**) ophthalmologist.

Augenärztin *die* (PL die **Augenärztinnen**) ophthalmologist.

Augenblick *der* (PL die **Augenblicke**) moment; **im Augenblick** at the moment.

Augenbraue *die* (PL die **Augenbrauen**) eyebrow.

August *der* August.

aus *preposition* (+ DAT) **1** out of; **er hat es aus dem Fenster geworfen** he threw it out of the window; **2** from; **aus Spanien** from Spain; **aus Erfahrung** from experience; **3** made of; **aus Holz** made of wood; **4 aus Spaß** for fun; **5 aus der Mode** out of fashion; **6 aus Versehen** by mistake; **7 aus welchem Grund?** for what reason?; **8 aus ihr ist eine gute Rechtsanwältin geworden** she made a good lawyer; **aus ihm ist nichts geworden** he never made anything of his life.

aus *adverb* **1** off (*of a TV, radio*); **das Licht ist aus** the light is off; **Licht aus!** lights out!; **2** finished; **wenn das Spiel aus ist** when the game has finished; **3 von mir aus** as far as I'm concerned; **4 von sich aus** of your own accord.

ausbauen *verb* (PERF **hat ausgebaut**) **1** to extend (*a building*); **2** to build up.

ausbeuten *verb* (PERF **hat ausgebeutet**) to exploit.

ausbilden *verb* (PERF **hat ausgebildet**) to train.

Ausbildung *die* **1** training; **2** education.

ausbreiten *verb* (PERF **hat ausgebreitet**) **1** to unfold; **2** to spread; **3** to stretch (*one's arms etc*).

ausbuhen *verb* (PERF **hat ausgebuht**) to boo; **die Menge buhte den Schiedsrichter aus** the crowd booed the referee.

ausdehnen *verb* (PERF **hat ausgedehnt**) **1** to extend, to prolong; **2** to expand.

Ausdruck[1] *der* (PL die **Ausdrücke**) expression; **etwas zum Ausdruck bringen** to express something.

Ausdruck[2] *der* (PL die **Ausdrucke**) print-out.

ausdrucken *verb* (PERF **hat ausgedruckt**) to print out.

ausdrücken *verb* (PERF **hat ausgedrückt**) **1** to squeeze (*oranges, lemons*); **2** to express; **3 sich ausdrücken** to express oneself.

auseinander *adverb* **1** apart; **etwas auseinander nehmen** to take something apart; **auseinander halten** to tell apart; **auseinander gehen** to part; **2 auseinander schreiben** to write as separate words; **3 auseinander schreiben** to write as separate words; **4 sich mit einem Problem auseinander setzen** to come to

...ps with a problem; **5 sich mit ...mandem auseinander setzen** to ...ave it out with somebody.

Ausfahrt *die* (PL *die* **Ausfahrten**)
1 exit; **2 'Ausfahrt freihalten'** 'keep clear'.

Ausfall *der* (PL *die* **Ausfälle**)
1 result; **2** failure, breakdown;
3 loss (*of hair, teeth*);
4 cancellation.

ausfallen ◇*verb* (PRES **fällt aus**,
IMPERF **fiel aus**, PERF **ist ausgefallen**) **1** to be cancelled;
etwas ausfallen lassen to cancel something; **2** to fall out (*hair*); **3** to fail (*an engine, brakes, a signal*);
4 to break down (*a machine, a car, heating*); **5** to turn out; **gut ausfallen** to turn out well.

Ausflug *der* (PL *die* **Ausflüge**)
outing, trip; **einen Ausflug machen** to go on an outing.

Ausfuhr *die* export.

ausführen *verb* (PERF **hat ausgeführt**) **1** to carry out (*a plan*);
2 to export (*goods*); **3** to take out; **er hat seine Freundin zum Essen ausgeführt** he took his girlfriend out for a meal; **4 den Hund ausführen** to take the dog for a walk.

ausführlich *adjective* detailed.

ausführlich *adverb* in detail.

ausfüllen *verb* (PERF **hat ausgefüllt**) **1** to fill in; **ein Formular ausfüllen** to fill in a form; **2 ihr Beruf als Lehrerin füllt sie ganz aus** teaching gives her great satisfaction.

Ausgabe *die* (PL *die* **Ausgaben**)
1 edition; **2** issue; **3 Ausgaben** expenditure.

Ausgang *der* (PL *die* **Ausgänge**)
1 exit; **'kein Ausgang'** 'no exit';
2 end, ending; **3** result (*of a game, discussion*).

ausgeben ◇*verb* (PRES **gibt aus**,
IMPERF **gab aus**, PERF **hat ausgegeben**) **1** to spend; **2** to hand out; **3 Fahrkarten ausgeben** to issue tickets; **4** to serve (*food*);
5 sich ausgeben als to pretend to be; **6 einen ausgeben** (*informal*) to treat everybody (*to a round of drinks for example*).

ausgebucht *adjective* fully booked.

ausgehen ◇*verb* (PRES **geht aus**,
IMPERF **ging aus**, PERF **ist ausgegangen**) **1** to go out; **mit Freunden ausgehen** to go out with friends; **2** to run out (*of supplies*);
3 to end; **schlecht ausgehen** to end badly; **4 davon ausgehen, dass ...** to assume that ...

ausgerechnet *adverb*
1 ausgerechnet heute today of all days; **2 ausgerechnet sie** she of all people.

ausgeschlossen *adjective* out of the question.

ausgestorben *adjective* **1** dead;
2 extinct.

ausgewogen *adjective* balanced.

ausgezeichnet *adjective* excellent.

ausgleichen *verb* (IMPERF **glich aus**, PERF **hat ausgeglichen**) to equalize; **sie haben in der letzten Minute ausgeglichen** they equalized in the last minute.

aushalten ◇*verb* (PRES **hält aus**, IMPERF **hielt aus**, PERF **hat ausgehalten**) **1** to stand; **2 es ist nicht zum Aushalten** it's unbearable.

Aushilfe *die* (PL *die* **Aushilfen**) temporary assistant, temp.

aushöhlen *verb* (PERF **hat ausgehöhlt**) to hollow out.

auskennen ◇*verb* (IMPERF **kannte sich aus**, PERF **hat sich ausgekannt**) **1** sich auskennen to know your way around; **2 sich gut mit etwas auskennen** to know a lot about something.

auskommen ◇*verb* (IMPERF **kam aus**, PERF **ist ausgekommen**) **1** to manage; **mit fünfzig Euro auskommen** to manage on fifty euros; **2 mit jemandem gut auskommen** to get on well with somebody.

Auskunft *die* (PL *die* **Auskünfte**) **1** information; **2** information desk; **3** enquiries (*when phoning*).

auslachen *verb* (PERF **hat ausgelacht**) to laugh at.

ausladen ◇*verb* (PRES **lädt aus**, IMPERF **lud aus**, PERF **hat ausgeladen**) **1** to unload; **2 jemanden ausladen** (*informal*) to put somebody off.

Ausland *das* **im Ausland** abroad; **ins Ausland reisen** to travel abroad.

Ausländer *der* (PL *die* **Ausländer**) foreigner.

Ausländerin *die* (PL *die* **Ausländerinnen**) foreigner.

ausländisch *adjective* foreign.

Auslandsgespräch *das* (PL *die* **Auslandsgespräche**) international call.

ausleeren *verb* (PERF **hat ausgeleert**) to empty.

ausleihen ◇*verb* (IMPERF **lieh aus**, PERF **hat ausgeliehen**) **1** to lend; **2 sich etwas ausleihen** to borrow something.

ausmachen *verb* (PERF **hat ausgemacht**) **1** to turn off; **2** to put out; **3** to arrange; **wir haben ausgemacht, dass wir uns heute Abend treffen** we've arranged to meet up this evening; **4 das macht mir nichts aus** I don't mind; **macht es Ihnen etwas aus, wenn ...?** would you mind if ...?; **5 viel ausmachen** to make a great difference.

Ausnahme *die* (PL *die* **Ausnahmen**) exception.

ausnutzen *verb* (PERF **hat ausgenutzt**) **1** to use; **2** to take advantage of; **3** to exploit.

auspacken *verb* (PERF **hat ausgepackt**) to unpack.

Auspuff *der* (PL *die* **Auspuffe**) exhaust.

ausrechnen *verb* (PERF **hat ausgerechnet**) to work out.

Ausrede *die* (PL *die* **Ausreden**) excuse.

ausreichend adjective
1 sufficient; 2 fair, pass (as a mark at school).

Ausreise die (PL die Ausreisen) departure (from a country).

ausrichten verb (PERF hat ausgerichtet) jemandem etwas ausrichten to tell somebody something.

ausrufen verb (IMPERF rief aus, PERF hat ausgerufen) 1 to call out; 2 to call, to declare; allgemeine Wahlen ausrufen to call a general election.

Ausrufezeichen das (PL die Ausrufezeichen) exclamation mark.

ausruhen verb (PERF hat sich ausgeruht) sich ausruhen to have a rest.

ausrüsten verb (PERF hat ausgerüstet) to equip.

Ausrüstung die equipment.

ausschalten verb (PERF hat ausgeschaltet) 1 to switch off; 2 to eliminate.

ausschneiden ◇verb (IMPERF schnitt aus, PERF hat ausgeschnitten) to cut out.

Ausschuss der (PL die Ausschüsse) committee.

aussehen ◇verb (PRES sieht aus, IMPERF sah aus, PERF hat ausgesehen) to look.

Aussehen das appearance.

außen adverb 1 (on the) outside; von außen from the outside; 2 nach außen outwards.

Außenminister der (PL die Außenminister) Foreign Secretary, Foreign Minister.

außer preposition (+ DAT) 1 apart from, except (for); alle außer ihm everyone except (for) him; 2 out of; außer Sicht out of sight; außer Betrieb out of order; 3 außer Haus out; 4 außer sich sein to be beside yourself.

außer conjunction 1 except; außer sonntags except Sundays; 2 außer wenn unless.

außerdem adverb 1 as well; 2 besides.

äußerer, äußere, äußeres adjective 1 external (injury, circumstances); 2 outer (layer, circle); 3 outward (appearance, effect).

außergewöhnlich adjective unusual.

außerhalb preposition (+ GEN) outside.

außerhalb adverb außerhalb wohnen to live out of town.

Außerirdische der/die (PL die Außerirdischen) alien (from outer space).

äußerlich adjective 1 external; 2 outward (appearance).

außerordentlich adjective extraordinary.

äußerst adverb extremely.

Äußerung die (PL die Äußerungen) remark.

Aussicht die (PL die Aussichten) 1 prospect; etwas in Aussicht haben to have the prospect of

Auswand ... **rer**

something; **keine Aussichten auf Erfolg haben** to have no chance of success; **2** view; **ein Zimmer mit Aussicht aufs Meer** a room with a view of the sea.

Aussprache die (PL die Aussprachen) **1** pronunciation; **2** talk.

aussprechen ⋄verb (PRES **spricht aus**, IMPERF **sprach aus**, PERF **hat ausgesprochen**) **1** to pronounce; **2** to express; **3 lassen Sie ihn aussprechen** let him finish (speaking); **4 sich aussprechen** to talk; **sich mit jemandem aussprechen** to have a talk with somebody; **5 sich gegen etwas aussprechen** to come out against something; **sich für etwas aussprechen** to come out in favour of something; **6 sich lobend über jemanden aussprechen** to speak highly of somebody.

aussteigen ⋄verb (IMPERF **stieg aus**, PERF **ist ausgestiegen**) **1** to get out; **2** to get off.

ausstellen verb (PERF **hat ausgestellt**) **1** to display (in a shop); **2** to exhibit; **3** to make out (a certificate, bill); **4** to issue (a passport); **5** to switch off.

Ausstellung die (PL die Ausstellungen) exhibition.

ausstreichen ⋄verb (IMPERF **strich aus**, PERF **hat ausgestrichen**) to cross out.

aussuchen verb (PERF **hat ausgesucht**) **1** to choose; **2 sich etwas aussuchen** to choose something.

Austausch der exchange.

austauschen verb (PERF **hat ausgetauscht**) **1** to exchange; replace; **3** to substitute (a pl...)

Auster die (PL die Austern) o... er).

austragen ⋄verb (PRES **trägt** ... IMPERF **trug aus**, PERF **hat ausgetragen**) **1** to deliver ... aus, newspapers); **2** to hold (a race ...

Australien das Australia ... **Australien from Australia** ...

Australier der (PL die Au... Australian.

Australierin die (PL die Australierinnen) Austral...

australisch adjective Austral...

austreten ⋄verb (PRES **tritt aus**, IMPERF **trat aus**, PERF **hat ausgetreten**) **1** to stamp out (a cigarette or fire); **2** to wear out (a shoes); **3** (PERF **ist ausgetreten**) **aus einem Klub austreten** to leave a club; **ich trete aus** I'm leaving; **4** (informal) (PERF **ist ausgetreten**) to go to the loo.

austrinken ⋄verb (IMPERF **trank aus**, PERF **hat ausgetrunken**) to drink up.

Ausverkauf der (PL die Ausverkäufe) sale.

ausverkauft adjective **1** sold out; **2 ein ausverkauftes Haus** a full house (at the cinema or theatre).

Auswahl die (PL die Auswahlen) choice, selection; **wenig Auswahl haben** to have a limited selection.

Auswanderer der (PL die Auswanderer) emigrant.

a b c d e f g h i j k l m n o p q r s t u v w x y z

Auswanderin

Auswanderin die (PL die Auswanderinnen) emigrant.

auswandern verb (PERF ist ausgewandert) to emigrate; nach Amerika auswandern to emigrate to America.

Auswanderung die emigration.

auswärts adverb 1 away (in sport); auswärts spielen to play away; 2 auswärts essen to eat out; 3 sie arbeitet auswärts she doesn't work locally.

Auswärtsspiel das (PL die Auswärtsspiele) away game.

Ausweg der (PL die Auswege) way out.

Ausweis der (PL die Ausweise) 1 identity card; 2 card (for students or members); 3 pass.

auswendig adverb by heart.

auswirken verb (PERF hat sich ausgewirkt) sich auf etwas auswirken to have an effect on something.

ausziehen ◊verb (IMPERF zog aus, PERF hat ausgezogen) 1 to take off (clothes); 2 to undress; 3 sich ausziehen to get undressed; 4 (PERF ist ausgezogen) to move out (move house); wir ziehen nächste Woche aus we're moving out next week.

Auszubildende der/die (PL die Auszubildenden) trainee.

Auto das (PL die Autos) car; Auto fahren to drive; das Auto waschen to wash the car.

Autobahn die (PL die Autobahnen) motorway.

Autobahnraststätte die (PL die Autobahnraststätten) motorway service area.

Autofahrer der (PL die Autofahrer) motorist.

Autogramm das (PL die Autogramme) autograph.

Automat der (PL die Automaten) machine.

automatisch adjective automatic.

Autor der (PL die Autoren) author.

Autorin die (PL die Autorinnen) authoress.

Autorität die authority.

Autoskooter der (PL die Autoskooter) bumper car, dodgem car.

Autostopp der per Autostopp fahren to hitchhike.

Autotelefon das (PL die Autotelefone) car phone.

Autounfall der (PL die Autounfälle) car accident.

Autoverleih der (PL die Autoverleihe) car hire (firm).

Axt die (PL die Äxte) axe.

Bb

Baby das (PL die Babys) baby.

Babysitting das babysitting; Babysitting machen to babysit.

Bach der (PL die Bäche) stream.

Backe die (PL die Backen) cheek.

backen ◇*verb* (PRES **bäckt**, IMPERF **backte**, PERF **hat gebacken**) to bake.

Bäcker der (PL die **Bäcker**) 1 baker; 2 beim **Bäcker** at the baker's.

Bäckerei die (PL die **Bäckereien**) baker's.

Backofen der (PL die **Backöfen**) oven.

Backpflaume die (PL die **Backpflaumen**) prune.

Bad das (PL die **Bäder**) 1 bath; 2 bathroom; 3 pool (*for swimming*).

Badeanzug der (PL die **Badeanzüge**) swimsuit.

Badehose die (PL die **Badehosen**) swimming trunks.

Bademeister der (PL die **Bademeister**) swimming-pool attendant.

Bademeisterin die (PL die **Bademeisterinnen**) swimming-pool attendant.

Bademütze die (PL die **Bademützen**) bathing cap.

baden *verb* (PERF **hat gebadet**) 1 to have a bath; 2 to bathe (*in the sea*); 3 to bath (*wash somebody*).

Badetuch das (PL die **Badetücher**) bath towel.

Badewanne die (PL die **Badewannen**) bath (*tub*).

Badezimmer das (PL die **Badezimmer**) bathroom.

Bahn die (PL die **Bahnen**) 1 railway; 2 train; mit der **Bahn** fahren to go by train; 3 tram; 4 track (*in sport*); 5 lane (*on a track*); 6 path; auf die

schiefe **Bahn** geraten to go off the rails.

Bahnhof der (PL die **Bahnhöfe**) (railway) station.

Bahnsteig der (PL die **Bahnsteige**) platform.

Bahnübergang der (PL die **Bahnübergänge**) level crossing.

bald *adverb* 1 soon; bis **bald**! see you soon!; 2 wird's **bald**! (*informal*) get a move on!; 3 almost; ich hätte **bald** vergessen, ihn anzurufen I almost forgot to ring him.

baldig *adjective* speedy.

Balken der (PL die **Balken**) beam.

Balkon der (PL die **Balkons**) balcony.

Ball der (PL die **Bälle**) 1 ball; **Ball** spielen to play ball; 2 ball; auf dem **Ball** at the ball.

Ballett das (PL die **Ballette**) ballet.

Balletttänzer der (PL die **Balletttänzer**) ballet dancer.

Balletttänzerin die (PL die **Balletttänzerinnen**) ballet dancer.

Ballon der (PL die **Ballons**) balloon.

Banane die (PL die **Bananen**) banana.

Band[1] das (PL die **Bänder**) 1 ribbon; 2 tape (*for recording*); etwas auf **Band** aufnehmen to tape something; 3 production line; am **Band** arbeiten to work on the production line; 4 am laufenden **Band** (*informal*) nonstop.

Band[2] der (PL die **Bände**) volume.

Band[3] die (PL die **Bands**) band.

band SEE **binden**.

Bank¹ *die* (PL *die* **Bänke**) bench.

Bank² *die* (PL *die* **Banken**) bank; **ich muss erst zur Bank gehen** I have to go to the bank first.

Bankkauffrau *die* (PL *die* **Bankkauffrauen**) bank clerk.

Bankkaufmann *der* (PL *die* **Bankkaufleute**) bank clerk.

Bankkonto *das* (PL *die* **Bankkonten**) bank account.

Banknote *die* (PL *die* **Banknoten**) banknote.

bankrott *adjective* bankrupt; **bankrott gehen/machen** to go bankrupt.

Bär *der* (PL *die* **Bären**) bear.

Bar *die* (PL *die* **Bars**) bar.

bar *adjective* (in) cash.

Bardame *die* (PL *die* **Bardamen**) barmaid.

barfuß *adjective* barefoot.

Bargeld *das* cash.

Barkeeper *der* (PL *die* **Barkeeper**) barman.

Barren *der* (PL *die* **Barren**) 1 bar; 2 parallel bars.

Bart *der* (PL *die* **Bärte**) beard.

bärtig *adjective* bearded.

Basel *das* Basle.

Basis *die* (PL *die* **Basen**) basis.

Bass *der* (PL *die* **Bässe**) bass.

basta *exclamation* and that's all!

basteln *verb* (PERF **hat gebastelt**) 1 to make (*things*); 2 **sie bastelt gern** she likes making things.

bat SEE **bitten**.

Batterie *die* (PL *die* **Batterien**) battery.

Bau *der* (PL *die* **Bauten**) 1 construction; **im Bau sein** to be under construction; 2 building; 3 building site; **auf dem Bau arbeiten** to work on a building site.

Bauarbeiten *plural noun* building work.

Bauarbeiter *der* (PL *die* **Bauarbeiter**) builder.

Bauarbeiterin *die* (PL *die* **Bauarbeiterinnen**) builder.

Bauch *der* (PL *die* **Bäuche**) stomach, belly.

Bauchschmerzen *plural noun* stomachache.

bauen *verb* (PERF **hat gebaut**) 1 to build; 2 **einen Unfall bauen** (*informal*) to have an accident.

Bauer *der* (PL *die* **Bauern**) 1 farmer; 2 pawn (*in chess*).

Bäuerin *die* (PL *die* **Bäuerinnen**) 1 farmer; 2 farmer's wife.

Bauernhof *der* (PL *die* **Bauernhöfe**) farm.

Baum *der* (PL *die* **Bäume**) tree.

Baumwolle *die* cotton.

Bausparkasse *die* (PL *die* **Bausparkassen**) building society.

Baustelle *die* (PL *die* **Baustellen**) building site.

Bayer *der* (PL *die* **Bayern**) Bavarian.

Bayerin *die* (PL *die* **Bayerinnen**) Bavarian.

Bayern *das* Bavaria; **aus Bayern** from Bavaria.

bay(e)risch *adjective* Bavarian.

beabsichtigen verb (PERF hat beabsichtigt) to intend.

beachten verb (PERF hat beachtet) **1** to take notice of; **beachte ihn einfach nicht** just don't take any notice of him; **2** to observe; **3** to follow (a rule, advice); **4** to obey; **die Verkehrsregeln beachten** to obey traffic regulations.

Beamte der (PL die **Beamten**) **1** civil servant (in Germany all public employees, such as teachers and policemen, are 'Beamte'); **2** official.

Beamtin die (PL die **Beamtinnen**) **1** civil servant; **2** official.

beanspruchen verb (PERF hat beansprucht) **1** to claim (benefit); **2** to take up (time, space); **jemanden beanspruchen** to take up somebody's time; **3** to demand (energy, attention); **die Arbeit beansprucht sie sehr** her work is very demanding; **4** to take advantage of (hospitality, services, help); **ich möchte Ihre Geduld nicht zu sehr beanspruchen** I don't want to try your patience.

Beanstandung die (PL die **Beanstandungen**) complaint.

beantragen verb (PERF hat beantragt) to apply for.

beantworten verb (PERF hat beantwortet) to answer.

bearbeiten verb (PERF hat bearbeitet) **1** to deal with; **einen Antrag bearbeiten** to deal with an application; **2** to adapt (a play); **3** to treat (wood, for example); **er hat die Oberfläche mit Wachs bearbeitet** he's treated the surface with wax; **4** jemanden bearbeiten, dass er etwas macht (informal) to work on somebody so that he does something (persuade).

beaufsichtigen verb (PERF hat beaufsichtigt) to supervise.

Becher der (PL die **Becher**) **1** beaker, mug; **2** pot, carton (of yoghurt, cream).

Becherglas das (PL die **Bechergläser**) tumbler.

Becken das (PL die **Becken**) **1** basin; **2** pool (for swimming); **3** pelvis.

bedanken verb (PERF hat sich bedankt) **sich bedanken** to say thank you; **vergiss nicht, dich zu bedanken** don't forget to say thank you; **ich habe mich bei ihm bedankt** I thanked him.

Bedarf der **1** need; **2** bei Bedarf if required; **3** demand; **je nach Bedarf** according to demand.

bedauerlicherweise adverb unfortunately.

bedauern verb (PERF hat bedauert) **1** to regret; **ich bedaure kein Wort** I don't regret a single word; **2** ich bedaure sehr, dass du nicht kommen kannst I'm very sorry that you can't come; **bedaure!** sorry!; **3** jemanden bedauern to feel sorry for somebody.

bedecken verb (PERF hat bedeckt) to cover.

a
b
c
d
e
f
g
h
i
j
k
l
m
n
o
p
q
r
s
t
u
v
w
x
y
z

bedeckt *adjective* **1** covered; **2** overcast (*weather*); **gestern war es den ganzen Tag bedeckt** it was overcast all day yesterday.

bedenken ◇*verb* (IMPERF **bedachte**, PERF **hat bedacht**) to consider.

Bedenken *plual noun* **1** doubts; **Bedenken haben** to have doubts; **2 ohne Bedenken** without hesitation.

bedenklich *adjective* **1** worrying; **die Situation ist sehr bedenklich** the situation is very worrying; **2** dubious; **er hat bedenkliche Mittel angewendet, um sein Ziel zu erreichen** he's used dubious methods to achieve his aims; **3** serious.

bedeuten *verb* (PERF **hat bedeutet**) to mean.

bedeutend *adjective* **1** important; **2** considerable.

Bedeutung *die* (PL die **Bedeutungen**) **1** meaning; **2** importance.

bedienen *verb* (PERF **hat bedient**) **1** to serve; **hier wird man sehr schnell bedient** you get served very quickly here; **2** to operate; **3 sich bedienen** to help oneself.

Bedienstete *der/die* (PL die **Bediensteten**) servant.

Bedienung *die* (PL die **Bedienungen**) **1** service; **Bedienung inbegriffen** service included; **2** waiter, waitress; **3** shop assistant; **4** operation (*of a machine*).

Bedingung *die* (PL die **Bedingungen**) condition; **nur unter der Bedingung, dass du mitkommst** only on condition that you're coming with us.

bedrohen *verb* (PERF **hat bedroht**) to threaten.

bedroht *adjective* endangered.

Bedrohung *die* (PL die **Bedrohungen**) threat.

beeilen *verb* (PERF **hat sich beeilt**) **sich beeilen** to hurry (up); **beeilt euch!** hurry up!

beeindrucken *verb* (PERF **hat beeindruckt**) to impress.

beeinflussen *verb* (PERF **hat beeinflusst**) to influence.

beenden *verb* (PERF **hat beendet**) to end.

Beerdigung *die* (PL die **Beerdigungen**) funeral.

Beere *die* (PL die **Beeren**) berry.

Beet *das* (PL die **Beete**) **1** bed (*of flowers*); **2** patch (*of vegetables*).

befahl SEE **befehlen**.

Befehl *der* (PL die **Befehle**) **1** order; **2** command; **den Befehl über etwas haben** to be in command of something.

befehlen ◇*verb* (PRES **befiehlt**, IMPERF **befahl**, PERF **hat befohlen**) **1 jemandem befehlen, etwas zu tun** to order somebody to do something; **2** to give orders.

befestigen *verb* (PERF **hat befestigt**) **1** to fix; **etwas an der Wand befestigen** to fix something to the wall; **2** to fasten.

befinden ◇*verb* (IMPERF **befand sich**, PERF **hat sich befunden**) **sich befinden** to be; **sie befindet sich zur Zeit in Deutschland** she's in Germany at the moment.

befolgen *verb* (PERF **hat befolgt**) to follow.

befördern *verb* (PERF **hat befördert**) **1** to carry (*people by bus or train*); **2** to transport (*goods by train or lorry*); **3** to promote; **er ist zum Kommissar befördert worden** he's been promoted to superintendent.

befragen *verb* (PERF **hat befragt**) to question.

befreien *verb* (PERF **hat befreit**) **1** to free; **2** to exempt; **jemanden vom Wehrdienst befreien** to exempt somebody from military service; **3 sich befreien** to free oneself.

Befreiung *die* liberation.

befreunden *verb* (PERF **hat sich befreundet**) **sich befreunden** to make friends.

befreundet *adjective* **mit jemandem befreundet sein** to be friends with somebody; **wir sind schon lange gut befreundet** we've been close friends for a long time.

befriedigen *verb* (PERF **hat befriedigt**) to satisfy.

befriedigend *adjective* satisfactory.

Befugnis *die* (PL *die* **Befugnisse**) authority.

begabt *adjective* gifted, talented.

Begabung *die* gift, talent.

begann SEE **beginnen**.

begegnen *verb* (PERF **ist begegnet**) **1 jemandem begegnen** to meet somebody; **etwas begegnen** to meet something; **2 sich begegnen** to meet (each other).

Begegnung *die* (PL *die* **Begegnungen**) meeting.

begehen ◇*verb* (IMPERF **beging**, PERF **hat begangen**) to commit.

begeistern *verb* (PERF **hat begeistert**) **1 jemanden für etwas begeistern** to fill somebody with enthusiasm for something; **2 sich begeistern** to get enthusiastic.

begeistert *adjective* enthusiastic.

Begeisterung *die* enthusiasm.

Beginn *der* beginning; **zu Beginn** at the beginning.

beginnen ◇*verb* (IMPERF **begann**, PERF **hat begonnen**) to begin, to start.

begleiten *verb* (PERF **hat begleitet**) to accompany; **jemanden begleiten** to accompany somebody; **er hat mich nach Hause begleitet** he took me home.

beglückwünschen *verb* (PERF **hat beglückwünscht**) to congratulate.

begonnen SEE **beginnen**.

begraben ◇*verb* (PRES **begräbt**, IMPERF **begrub**, PERF **hat begraben**) to bury.

begreifen ◇*verb* (IMPERF **begriff**, PERF **hat begriffen**) to understand.

begrenzen verb (PERF **hat begrenzt**) to limit.

Begriff der (PL die **Begriffe**) 1 concept; **davon kann ich mir keinen Begriff machen** I can't imagine that; 2 term; **ein Begriff aus der Malerei** a painting term; 3 **im Begriff sein, etwas zu tun** to be about to do something; 4 **für meine Begriffe** to my mind; 5 **schwer von Begriff** (*informal*) slow on the uptake.

Begründung die (PL die **Begründungen**) reason.

begrüßen verb (PERF **hat begrüßt**) 1 to greet; 2 to welcome.

Begrüßung die welcome.

begünstigen verb (PERF **hat begünstigt**) to favour.

behaart adjective hairy.

behaglich adjective cosy.

behalten ◇verb (PRES **behält**, IMPERF **behielt**, PERF **hat behalten**) 1 to keep; **du kannst die CD behalten** you can keep the CD; 2 to remember (*a name*).

Behälter der (PL die **Behälter**) container.

behandeln verb (PERF **hat behandelt**) 1 to treat; **er ist sehr schlecht behandelt worden** he's been treated very badly; **einen Patienten behandeln** to treat a patient; 2 to deal with (*a subject, question*).

Behandlung die (PL die **Behandlungen**) treatment.

behaupten verb (PERF **hat behauptet**) 1 to claim; 2 **sich behaupten** to assert oneself.

Behauptung die (PL die **Behauptungen**) claim.

beherrschen verb (PERF **hat beherrscht**) 1 to rule over (*a country, people*); 2 to control; 3 to know; 4 **sich beherrschen** to control oneself.

behilflich adjective **jemandem behilflich sein** to help somebody.

behindert adjective disabled, handicapped; **ist er behindert?** does he have a disability?

Behinderte der/die (PL die **Behinderten**) disabled person, handicapped person.

Behindertenheim das (PL die **Behindertenheime**) home for handicapped people.

Behinderung die 1 obstruction; 2 handicap, disability.

Behörde die (PL die **Behörden**) authority, authorities.

behüten verb (PERF **hat behütet**) to protect.

bei preposition (+ DAT) 1 near; **die Diskothek beim Bahnhof** the disco near the station; 2 at (*indicating a place or time*); **bei mir** at my place; **beim Arzt** at the doctor's; **bei Beginn** at the beginning; 3 **bei seinen Eltern wohnen** to live with your parents; 4 **bei uns in der Firma** in our firm; **bei guter Gesundheit** in good health; 5 **bei einem Verlag arbeiten** to work for a publisher; 6 **bei Regen** if it rains;

bei Nebel in fog; **bei Tag** by day; **7 etwas bei sich haben** to have something on you; **8 bei Morris** c/o Morris; **9 sich bei jemandem entschuldigen** to apologize to somebody; **10 bei der hohen Miete** with the high rent; **11 beim Fahren** while driving; **beim Lesen sein** to be reading; **beim Frühstück** at breakfast; **12 bei der Ankunft** on arrival.

beibringen ⬦ *verb* (PRES **bringt bei**, IMPERF **brachte bei**, PERF **hat beigebracht**) **jemandem etwas beibringen** to teach somebody something.

Beichte *die* (PL *die* **Beichten**) confession.

beichten *verb* (PERF **hat gebeichtet**) to confess.

beide *adjective, pronoun* **1** both; **ihr beide** both of you; **er hat seine beiden Eltern verloren** he has lost both his parents; **2 die ersten beiden** the first two; **eins von beiden** one of the two; **3 keiner von beiden** neither (of them); **4 beides** both; **er kann beides - Klavier und Gitarre spielen** he can do both · play the piano and the guitar; **5 dreißig beide** thirty all (*in tennis*).

beieinander *adverb* together.

Beifahrer *der* (PL *die* **Beifahrer**) passenger.

Beifahrerin *die* (PL *die* **Beifahrerinnen**) passenger.

Beifall *der* applause.

Beil *das* (PL *die* **Beile**) axe.

Beilage *die* (PL *die* **Beilagen**) **1** supplement (*to a paper*); **2** side-dish; **als Beilage Reis und Spinat** served with rice and spinach.

beiläufig *adjective* casual.

beilegen *verb* (PERF **hat beigelegt**) to enclose.

Beileid *das* condolences; **jemandem sein Beileid aussprechen** to offer your condolences to somebody.

beiliegen ⬦ *verb* (PRES **liegt bei**, IMPERF **lag bei**, PERF **hat beigelegen**) to be enclosed; **ein Scheck liegt bei** please find enclosed a cheque.

beiliegend *adjective* enclosed.

beim = **bei dem**.

Bein *das* (PL *die* **Beine**) leg.

beinahe *adverb* almost.

Beinbruch *der* (PL *die* **Beinbrüche**) broken leg; **das ist doch kein Beinbruch** (*informal*) it's not the end of the world.

beisammen *adverb* together.

beiseite *adverb* **1** aside; **etwas beiseite schieben** to push something aside; **2 etwas beiseite legen** to put something by; **3 das Geld beiseite schaffen** to hide the money away.

Beispiel *das* (PL *die* **Beispiele**) example; **zum Beispiel** for example; **mit gutem Beispiel vorangehen** to set a good example.

beispielsweise *adverb* for example.

beißen ⬦ *verb* (IMPERF **biss**, PERF **hat gebissen**) **1** to bite; **2** to sting (*of* smoke, for example); **3 sich beißen** to clash; **die Farben beißen sich** the colours clash.

Beitrag der (PL die **Beiträge**)
1 contribution; **2** subscription; **3** premium (*insurance fee*); **4** article (*in a newspaper*).

beitragen ◇verb (PRES **trägt bei**, IMPERF **trug bei**, PERF **hat beigetragen**) **zu etwas beitragen** to contribute to something.

beitreten ◇verb (PRES **tritt bei**, IMPERF **trat bei**, PERF **ist beigetreten**) to join; **ich trete dem Fußballverein bei** I'm joining the football club.

bekam SEE **bekommen**.

bekämpfen verb (PERF **hat bekämpft**) **1** to fight; **2 sich bekämpfen** to fight.

bekannt adjective **1** well known; **2** familiar; **das kommt mir bekannt vor** that seems familiar; **3 mit jemandem bekannt sein** to know somebody; **4 für etwas bekannt sein** to be (well) known for something; **5 jemanden bekannt machen** to introduce somebody; **6 das ist mir bekannt** I know that; **7 etwas bekannt geben/machen** to announce something; **sie gab ihre Verlobung bekannt** she announced her engagement; **8 bekannt werden** to become known.

Bekannte der/die (PL die **Bekannten**) **1** acquaintance; **2** friend.

bekannt geben verb (PRES **gibt bekannt**, IMPERF **gab bekannt**, PERF **hat bekannt gegeben**) to announce SEE **bekannt**.

bekanntlich adverb **Rauchen ist bekanntlich schädlich** as you know, smoking is bad for you.

beklagen verb (PERF **hat sich beklagt**) **sich beklagen** to complain.

Bekleidung die clothes, clothing.

bekommen ◇verb (IMPERF **bekam**, PERF **hat bekommen**) **1** to get; **Angst bekommen** to get frightened; **2** to catch (*a cold, the train*); **3 ein Kind bekommen** to have a baby; **4 was bekommen Sie?** (*in a shop*) can I help you? (*in a restaurant*) what would you like?; **5 was bekommen Sie dafür?** how much is it?; **6** (PERF **ist bekommen**) **fettes Essen bekommt mir nicht** fatty food doesn't agree with me; **7** (PERF **ist bekommen**) **die Ferien sind mir gut bekommen** the holiday did me good.

Belag der (PL die **Beläge**) **1** covering; **2** coating; **3** topping (*on bread*); **4** lining (*of brakes*).

belasten verb (PERF **hat belastet**) **1** to burden; **2** to put weight on (*foot*); **3** to pollute (*the atmosphere*); **4** to debit (*an account*); **5** to incriminate.

belästigen verb (PERF **hat belästigt**) **1** to bother; **2** to harass.

Belastung die **1** strain; **2** load; **3** burden; **4** pollution.

belaufen ◇verb (PRES **beläuft**, IMPERF **belief**, PERF **belaufen**) **sich auf etwas belaufen** to amount to something; **die Rechnung beläuft sich auf fünfhundert Euro** the bill amounts to five hundred euros.

belegen *verb* (PERF **hat belegt**) **1** to cover; **2 eine Scheibe Brot mit Käse belegen** to put some cheese on a slice of bread; **3** to enrol for (*a course*); **4** to reserve (*a seat*); **5 den ersten Platz belegen** to come first; **6** to prove (*facts*).

belegt *adjective* **1** occupied; **2 der Platz ist belegt** this seat is taken; **3 ein belegtes Brot** an open sandwich; **4 die Nummer ist belegt** (*when phoning*) the number's engaged.

beleidigen *verb* (PERF **hat beleidigt**) to insult.

Beleidigung *die* (PL *die* **Beleidigungen**) insult.

Beleuchtung *die* lighting.

Belgien *das* Belgium.

Belgier *der* (PL *die* **Belgier**) Belgian.

Belgierin *die* (PL *die* **Belgierinnen**) Belgian.

belgisch *adjective* Belgian.

Belichtung *die* exposure.

beliebig *adjective* any; **eine beliebige Zahl** any number you like.

beliebig *adverb* **beliebig lange** as long as you like; **beliebig viele** as many as you like.

beliebt *adjective* popular.

Beliebtheit *die* popularity.

bellen *verb* (PERF **hat gebellt**) to bark.

belohnen *verb* (PERF **hat belohnt**) to reward.

Belohnung *die* (PL *die* **Belohnungen**) reward.

belügen *verb* (IMPERF **belog**, PERF **hat belogen**) to lie to.

bemerkbar *adjective* **sich bemerkbar machen** to attract attention, to become noticeable.

bemerken *verb* (PERF **hat bemerkt**) **1** to notice; **2** to remark; **3 nebenbei bemerkt** by the way.

Bemerkung *die* (PL *die* **Bemerkungen**) remark.

bemitleiden *verb* (PERF **hat bemitleidet**) to pity.

bemühen *verb* (PERF **hat sich bemüht**) **1 sich bemühen** to try; **sich sehr bemühen** to try hard; **er bemüht sich um eine Stelle** he's trying to get a job; **2 sich um jemanden bemühen** to try to help somebody; **3 bitte, bemühen Sie sich nicht** please don't trouble yourself.

Bemühung *die* (PL *die* **Bemühungen**) effort.

benachrichtigen *verb* (PERF **hat benachrichtigt**) **1** to inform; **2** to notify (*officially*).

benachteiligt *adjective* disadvantaged.

benehmen ◇*verb* (PRES **benimmt sich**, IMPERF **benahm sich**, PERF **hat sich benommen**) **sich benehmen** to behave; **benimm dich!** behave yourself!

Benehmen *das* behaviour.

beneiden verb (PERF hat beneidet) to envy; **jemanden um etwas beneiden** to envy somebody something.

benoten verb (PERF hat benotet) to mark.

benutzen verb (PERF hat benutzt) to use.

Benutzer der (PL die Benutzer) user.

Benutzerin die (PL die Benutzerinnen) user.

Benutzung die use.

Benzin das petrol.

beobachten verb (PERF hat beobachtet) to observe, to watch; **Vögel beobachten** to watch birds.

bequem adjective 1 comfortable; 2 **machen Sie es sich bequem** make yourself at home; 3 lazy; 4 easy; **eine bequeme Lösung finden** to find an easy way out.

beraten ◇verb (PRES berät, IMPERF beriet, PERF hat beraten) 1 to advise; 2 **jemanden gut/schlecht beraten** to give somebody good/bad advice; 3 **sich beraten lassen** to get advice; 4 **gut beraten sein** to be well advised; 5 to discuss (a plan, matter); 6 **sich über etwas beraten** to discuss something.

Berater der (PL die Berater) adviser.

Beratung die (PL die Beratungen) 1 advice; 2 discussion; 3 consultation (with a doctor).

berauben verb (PERF hat beraubt) to rob.

berechnen verb (PERF hat berechnet) 1 to charge; **jemandem zehn Euro für etwas berechnen** to charge somebody ten euros for something; 2 **jemandem zu viel berechnen** to overcharge somebody; 3 to calculate.

berechtigen verb (PERF hat berechtigt) **jemanden berechtigen, etwas zu tun** to give someone the right to do something.

berechtigt adjective justified.

Bereich der (PL die Bereiche) 1 area; 2 field (in a profession); **im Bereich Tourismus** in the field of tourism.

bereit adjective ready.

bereiten verb (PERF hat bereitet) 1 to make (coffee, tea); 2 to cause (trouble, difficulty); **leider hat es uns Schwierigkeiten bereitet** unfortunately it caused us some trouble; 3 to give (a surprise, pleasure).

bereits adverb already.

bereuen verb (PERF hat bereut) to regret.

Berg der (PL die Berge) 1 mountain; 2 hill.

bergab adverb downhill.

Bergarbeiter der (PL die Bergarbeiter) miner.

bergauf adverb uphill.

bergen ◇verb (PRES birgt, IMPERF barg, PERF hat geborgen) to rescue.

Bergsteigen das mountaineering.

Bergsteiger der (PL die Bergsteiger) mountaineer, climber.

Bergsteigerin die (PL die Bergsteigerinnen) mountaineer, climber.

Bergwacht die mountain rescue.

Bergwerk das (PL die Bergwerke) mine.

Bericht der (PL die Berichte) report.

berichten verb (PERF hat berichtet) 1 to report; die Zeitungen haben nichts davon berichtet the newspapers didn't report anything about it; 2 jemandem über etwas berichten to tell somebody about something; er hat mir über seine Ferien in Amerika berichtet he told me about his holiday in America.

berücksichtigen verb (PERF hat berücksichtigt) to take into account.

Beruf der (PL die Berufe) 1 occupation; 2 profession; ich bin Lehrerin von Beruf I'm a teacher by profession; 3 trade; 4 was sind Sie von Beruf? what do you do for a living?

beruflich adjective 1 professional; 2 vocational (training).

beruflich adverb 1 beruflich erfolgreich sein to be successful in your career; 2 viel beruflich unterwegs sein to be away a lot on business.

Berufsberatung die careers advice.

Berufsschule die (PL die Berufsschulen) technical college.

berufstätig adjective working.

Berufsverkehr der rush-hour traffic.

beruhigen verb (PERF hat beruhigt) 1 to calm down; 2 to reassure; 3 sich beruhigen to calm down.

Beruhigungsmittel das (PL die Beruhigungsmittel) sedative, tranquillizer.

berühmt adjective famous.

berühren verb (PERF hat berührt) 1 to touch; 2 to touch on (a topic, an issue); 3 to affect; ihre Geschichte berührte ihn seltsam he was strangely affected by her story; 4 sich berühren to touch.

besaß SEE besitzen.

beschädigen verb (PERF hat beschädigt) to damage.

Beschädigung die (PL die Beschädigungen) damage; der Sturm verursachte zahlreiche Beschädigungen the storm caused considerable damage.

beschaffen[1] verb (PERF hat beschafft) to get; kannst du mir nicht einen Job beschaffen? can't you get me a job?

beschaffen[2] adjective so beschaffen sein, dass ... to be such that ...

beschäftigen verb (PERF hat beschäftigt) 1 to occupy (keep busy); 2 to employ (people); 3 sich beschäftigen to occupy yourself; 4 ich beschäftige mich mit den

a
b
c
d
e
f
g
h
i
j
k
l
m
n
o
p
q
r
s
t
u
v
w
x
y
z

a
b
c
d
e
f
g
h
i
j
k
l
m
n
o
p
q
r
s
t
u
v
w
x
y
z

Kindern I'm busy with the children; **5 sich mit einem Fall beschäftigen** to deal with a case; **sein Aufsatz beschäftigt sich mit der Umweltverschmutzung** his essay deals with environmental pollution.

beschäftigt adjective 1 busy; 2 employed.

Beschäftigung die (PL die Beschäftigungen) 1 occupation; 2 activity.

Bescheid der (PL die Bescheide) 1 information; 2 jemandem Bescheid sagen to let somebody know; 3 über etwas Bescheid wissen to know about something.

bescheiden adjective modest.

Bescheinigung die (PL die Bescheinigungen) 1 certificate; eine Bescheinigung des Arztes a doctor's certificate; 2 (written) confirmation.

beschimpfen verb (PERF hat beschimpft) to abuse.

beschlagnahmen verb (PERF hat beschlagnahmt) to confiscate.

beschleunigen verb (PERF hat beschleunigt) 1 to speed up; 2 to accelerate; **der Lastwagen hinter uns hat plötzlich beschleunigt** the lorry behind us suddenly accelerated.

beschließen ◇verb (IMPERF beschloss, PERF hat beschlossen) to decide.

Beschluss der (PL die Beschlüsse) decision.

beschränken verb (PERF hat beschränkt) to limit.

beschränkt adjective 1 narrow-minded; 2 dim; **sie ist ein bisschen beschränkt** she's a bit dim.

beschreiben ◇verb (IMPERF beschrieb, PERF hat beschrieben) to describe.

Beschreibung die (PL die Beschreibungen) description.

beschuldigen verb (PERF hat beschuldigt) to accuse.

Beschuldigung die (PL die Beschuldigungen) accusation.

beschützen verb (PERF hat beschützt) to protect.

Beschwerde die (PL die Beschwerden) complaint.

beschweren verb (PERF hat sich beschwert) sich beschweren to complain; **ich habe mich bei den Nachbarn über ihn beschwert** I've complained to the neighbours about him.

beschwipst adjective tipsy.

beseitigen verb (PERF hat beseitigt) to remove.

Besen der (PL die Besen) broom.

besetzen verb (PERF hat besetzt) 1 to occupy; 2 to fill (a post, role); 3 to trim, to edge (with lace or fur).

besetzt adjective 1 occupied; 2 besetzt sein to be engaged (a phone, toilet); 3 taken (a table, seat); **der Platz ist besetzt** this seat is taken; 4 full (of a train, bus); **der Zug ist voll besetzt** the train is full up.

Besetztzeichen das (PL die Besetztzeichen) engaged tone.

Besetzung die (PL die Besetzungen) 1 cast; 2 team; 3 occupation.

besichtigen verb (PERF hat besichtigt) 1 to look round (a town, museum); 2 to see (sights, a house).

Besichtigung die (PL die Besichtigungen) visit.

besinnungslos adjective unconscious.

Besitz der 1 property; 2 im Besitz einer Sache sein to be in possession of something.

besitzen ◇verb (IMPERF besaß, PERF hat besessen) 1 to own; sie besitzen ein Haus in Italien they own a house in Italy; 2 to have (talent, a quality).

Besitzer der (PL die Besitzer) owner.

Besitzerin die (PL die Besitzerinnen) owner.

besonderer, besondere, besonderes adjective 1 special; unter besonderen Umständen in special circumstances; 2 particular; ohne besondere Begeisterung without any particular enthusiasm; 3 keine besonderen Kennzeichen no distinguishing features.

Besonderheit die (PL die Besonderheiten) 1 special feature; 2 peculiarity.

besonders adverb particularly.

besorgen verb (PERF hat besorgt) to get; ich kann dir Karten besorgen I can get you tickets.

besorgt adjective worried.

besprechen ◇verb (PRES bespricht, IMPERF besprach, PERF hat besprochen) 1 to discuss; ich muss es erst mit meinen Eltern besprechen I'll have to discuss it with my parents first; 2 to review (a book, film).

Besprechung die (PL die Besprechungen) 1 meeting (at work); 2 discussion; 3 review (of a film, play).

besser adjective, adverb better; alles besser wissen to know better.

Besserung die 1 improvement; 2 gute Besserung! get well soon!

beständig adjective 1 constant; 2 settled (weather).

Bestandteil der (PL die Bestandteile) component.

bestätigen verb (PERF hat bestätigt) 1 to confirm; 2 to acknowledge (receipt); 3 sich bestätigen to be confirmed, to prove to be true.

beste SEE bester.

bestechen ◇verb (PRES besticht, IMPERF bestach, PERF hat bestochen) 1 to bribe; 2 to win over.

Bestechung die (PL die Bestechungen) bribery.

Besteck das (PL die Bestecke) cutlery.

bestehen ◇*verb* (IMPERF **bestand**, PERF **hat bestanden**) **1** to exist; **2 es besteht die Gefahr, dass** ... there is a danger that ...; **noch besteht die Hoffnung, dass** ... there is still hope that ...; **3** to pass; **eine Prüfung bestehen** to pass an exam; **4 auf etwas bestehen** to insist on something; **5 aus etwas bestehen** to consist of something; **6 aus etwas bestehen** to be made of something.

bestellen *verb* (PERF **hat bestellt**) **1** to order (*goods*); **2** to reserve (*tickets*); **3** to tell; **jemandem etwas bestellen** to tell somebody something; **4 bestell ihm schöne Grüße** give him my regards; **5 kann ich etwas bestellen?** can I take a message?; **6** to send for; **jemanden zu sich bestellen** to send for somebody.

Bestellung die (PL die **Bestellungen**) **1** order (*for goods*); **2** reservation (*for tickets*).

bestens *adverb* very well; **das hat ja bestens geklappt** that worked out very well.

bester, beste, bestes *adjective* **1** best; **sein bestes Buch** his best book; **2 ich halte es für das Beste, wenn** ... I think it would be best if ...; **sein Bestes tun** to do your best; **3 einen Witz zum Besten geben** to tell a joke; **4 jemanden zum Besten halten** to pull somebody's leg.

am besten *adverb* best; **du bleibst am besten zu Hause** you'd best stay at home; **es ist am besten, wenn wir gleich anfangen** it's best if we get started straight away.

bestimmen *verb* (PERF **hat bestimmt**) **1** to fix (*a time, price*); **2** to decide (on); **etwas allein bestimmen** to decide (on) something on your own; **er bestimmt immer, was wir machen** he always decides what we're going to do; **3** to be in charge; **4 für jemanden bestimmt sein** to be meant for somebody; **5 für etwas bestimmt sein** to be intended for something (*a donation for a good cause, for example*).

bestimmt *adjective* **1** certain; **zu einer bestimmten Zeit** at a certain time; **2** particular; **suchen Sie etwas Bestimmtes?** are you looking for anything in particular?; **3** definite.

bestimmt *adverb* **1** certainly, definitely; **ich komme ganz bestimmt** I'm definitely coming; **2 er hat es bestimmt vergessen** he's bound to have forgotten; **3 du weißt es doch bestimmt noch** surely you must remember it.

Bestimmung die (PL die **Bestimmungen**) regulation.

bestrafen *verb* (PERF **hat bestraft**) to punish.

bestreiten ◇*verb* (IMPERF **bestritt**, PERF **hat bestritten**) **1** to deny; **2** to dispute; **das möchte ich nicht bestreiten** I'm not disputing it; **3** to pay for.

bestürzt *adjective* upset.

Besuch der (PL die Besuche)
1 visit; **2** attendance (at school);
3 Besuch haben to have visitors/a
visitor; **4** bei Freunden zu Besuch
sein to be staying with friends; zu
Besuch kommen to be visiting.

besuchen verb (PERF hat besucht)
1 to visit; **2** to go to (an exhibition,
the theatre); die Schule besuchen
to go to school; **3** to attend (a
lecture).

Besucher der (PL die Besucher)
visitor.

Besucherin die (PL die
Besucherinnen) visitor.

betätigen verb (PERF hat betätigt)
1 to operate; **2** die Bremse
betätigen to apply the brakes;
3 sich politisch betätigen to be
involved in politics; **4** sich
künstlerisch betätigen to do art;
5 sich als Reporter betätigen to
work as a reporter.

Betäubungsmittel das (PL die
Betäubungsmittel) anaesthetic.

Bete die Rote Bete beetroot.

beteiligen verb (PERF hat
beteiligt) **1** to give a share to;
jemanden mit zehn Prozent an
einem Geschäft beteiligen to give
somebody a ten percent share of a
business; **2** sich an etwas
beteiligen to take part in
something; **3** kann ich mich an
eurem Spiel beteiligen? can I join
in your game?

beten verb (PERF hat gebetet) to
pray.

Beton der concrete.

betonen verb (PERF hat betont) to
stress.

Betonung die (PL die Betonungen)
stress.

Betrag der (PL die Beträge)
amount.

betragen ◇verb (PRES beträgt,
IMPERF betrug, PERF hat betragen)
1 to amount to, to come to; **2** sich
betragen to behave; haben sich die
Kinder gut betragen? did the
children behave well?

Betragen das behaviour.

betreffen ◇verb (PRES betrifft,
IMPERF betraf, PERF hat betroffen) to
concern; was mich betrifft as far as
I'm concerned.

betreten ◇verb (PRES betritt,
IMPERF betrat, PERF hat betreten)
1 to enter; **2** 'Betreten verboten'
'keep out', 'keep off' (the grass, for
example).

Betrieb der (PL die Betriebe)
1 business, firm; **2** activity; es war
viel Betrieb it was very busy; **3** in
Betrieb sein to be working (of a
machine); **4** außer Betrieb sein to
be out of order; **5** eine Maschine in
Betrieb setzen to start up a
machine.

Betriebsferien plural noun
firm's holiday; 'Betriebsferien'
'closed for the holidays'.

Betriebspraktikum das (PL die
Betriebspraktika) training course.

betrinken ◇verb (IMPERF betrank
sich, PERF hat sich betrunken) sich
betrinken to get drunk.

betrog SEE betrügen.

a

b

c

d

e

f

g

h

i

j

k

l

m

n

o

p

q

r

s

t

u

v

w

x

y

z

Betrug der 1 deception; 2 fraud; **was für ein Betrug** what a swindle!

betrügen ◇verb (IMPERF **betrog**, PERF **hat betrogen**) 1 to cheat; **jemanden um tausend Euro betrügen** to cheat somebody out of a thousand euros; 2 to be unfaithful to, to cheat on; **sie hat ihren Mann betrogen** she's been unfaithful to her husband.

betrunken adjective drunk.

Bett das (PL die **Betten**) bed; **ins Bett gehen** to go to bed; **das Bett machen** to make the bed.

Bettbezug der (PL die **Bettbezüge**) duvet cover.

betteln verb (PERF **hat gebettelt**) to beg.

Bettlaken das (PL die **Bettlaken**) sheet.

Bettler der (PL die **Bettler**) beggar.

Bettlerin die (PL die **Bettlerinnen**) beggar.

Bettwäsche die bed linen.

Bettzeug das bedding.

beugen verb (PERF **hat gebeugt**) 1 to bend; 2 to decline, to conjugate (in grammar); 3 **sich nach vorn beugen** to bend forwards; **sich über etwas beugen** to bend over something; 4 **sich aus dem Fenster beugen** to lean out of the window; 5 **sich beugen** to submit.

Beule die (PL die **Beulen**) 1 bump; 2 lump; 3 dent.

beurteilen verb (PERF **hat beurteilt**) to judge.

Beutel der (PL die **Beutel**) bag.

Bevölkerung die (PL die **Bevölkerungen**) population.

bevor conjunction 1 before; 2 **bevor nicht** until; **bevor er nicht unterschrieben hat** until he has signed.

bevorzugen verb (PERF **hat bevorzugt**) to prefer.

bewachen verb (PERF **hat bewacht**) to guard.

bewaffnen verb (PERF **hat bewaffnet**) to arm.

bewahren verb (PERF **hat bewahrt**) **jemandem vor etwas bewahren** to protect someone from something.

bewaffnet adjective armed.

bewährt adjective 1 reliable; 2 proven (method, design); 3 **ein bewährtes Rezept** a well-tried recipe.

bewegen[1] verb (PERF **hat bewegt**) 1 to move; 2 **sich bewegen** to take exercise; 3 **sich bewegen** to move.

bewegen[2] ◇verb (IMPERF **bewog**, PERF **hat bewogen**) **jemanden dazu bewegen, etwas zu tun** to persuade somebody to do something.

bewegt adjective eventful.

Bewegung die (PL die **Bewegungen**) 1 movement; 2 exercise; 3 **eine Maschine in Bewegung setzen** to start (up) a machine; 4 **sich in Bewegung setzen** to start to move.

Beweis der (PL die **Beweise**) 1 proof; 2 **belastende Beweise**

incriminating evidence; **3** token, sign.

beweisen ◇verb (IMPERF **bewies**, PERF **hat bewiesen**) **1** to prove; **2** to show.

bewerben ◇verb (PRES **bewirbt sich**, IMPERF **bewarb sich**, PERF **hat sich beworben**) **sich bewerben** to apply; **sich um eine Stelle bewerben** to apply for a job.

Bewerber der (PL die **Bewerber**) applicant.

Bewerberin die (PL die **Bewerberinnen**) applicant.

Bewerbung die (PL die **Bewerbungen**) application.

bewohnen verb (PERF **hat bewohnt**) to live in.

Bewohner der (PL die **Bewohner**) **1** resident; **2** inhabitant (of a region).

Bewohnerin die (PL die **Bewohnerinnen**) **1** resident; **2** inhabitant (of a region).

bewölkt adjective cloudy.

Bewölkung die clouds.

bewundern verb (PERF **hat bewundert**) to admire.

Bewunderung die admiration.

bewusst adjective **1** conscious; **2** deliberate; **3 sich etwas bewusst sein** to be aware of something; **ich war mir der Folgen bewusst** I was aware of the consequences.

bewusstlos adjective unconscious.

Bewusstsein das **1** consciousness; **2 bei vollem Bewusstsein sein** to be fully conscious; **3 mir kam zu(m) Bewusstsein, dass** ... I realized that ....

bezahlbar adjective affordable.

bezahlen verb (PERF **hat bezahlt**) **1** to pay; **für etwas 10 Euro bezahlen** to pay 10 euros for something; **2** to pay for (goods, food); **er hat das Essen bezahlt** he paid for the meal.

Bezahlung die payment.

bezeichnend adjective typical.

beziehen ◇verb (IMPERF **bezog**, PERF **hat bezogen**) **1** to cover; **2 das Bett frisch beziehen** to put clean sheets on the bed; **3** to move into; **wann kannst du die neue Wohnung beziehen?** when will you be able to move into the new flat?; **4** to get (goods, a pension); **5** to take (a newspaper); **6 sich auf etwas/jemanden beziehen** to refer to something/somebody; **7 es bezieht sich** it's clouding over.

Beziehung die (PL die **Beziehungen**) **1** connection; **2** relationship; **3 Beziehungen** contacts; **Anna hat gute Beziehungen** Anna has good contacts; **4 diplomatische Beziehungen** diplomatic relations; **5 in dieser Beziehung** in this respect; **6 eine Beziehung zu etwas haben** to be able to relate to something (to art, pop music, for example).

beziehungsweise conjunction **1** or rather; **2** respectively.

Bezirk der (PL die **Bezirke**) district.

a
b
c
d
e
f
g
h
i
j
k
l
m
n
o
p
q
r
s
t
u
v
w
x
y
z

Bezug der (PL die Bezüge) **1** cover
(of a cushion, duvet, etc.);
2 connection; **keinen Bezug zu
etwas haben** to be unable to relate
to something; **3 auf etwas Bezug
nehmen** to refer to something; **4 in
Bezug auf** regarding; **5 mit Bezug
auf Ihr Angebot** with reference to
your offer.

bezweifeln verb (PERF **hat
bezweifelt**) to doubt.

BH der (PL die BHs) bra.

Bibel die (PL die Bibeln) bible; **die
Bibel** the Bible.

Bibliothek die (PL die
Bibliotheken) library.

Bibliothekar der (PL die
Bibliothekare) librarian.

Bibliothekarin die (PL die
Bibliothekarinnen) librarian.

biegen ◇verb (IMPERF **bog**, PERF **hat
gebogen**) **1** to bend; **2 sich biegen**
to bend; **3** (PERF **ist gebogen**) to
turn; **um die Ecke biegen** to turn
the corner.

Biene die (PL die Bienen) bee.

Bier das (PL die Biere) beer.

Bierdeckel der (PL die Bierdeckel)
beer mat.

bieten ◇verb (IMPERF **bot**, PERF **hat
geboten**) **1** to offer; **2** to bid (at an
auction); **3 es bietet sich die
Möglichkeit** there is a possibility;
4 to present (a sight); **5 das lasse
ich mir nicht bieten!** I won't put up
with it!

Bikini der (PL die Bikinis) bikini.

Bild das (PL die Bilder) **1** picture;
jemanden ins Bild setzen to put
somebody in the picture; **2** scene.

bilden verb (PERF **hat gebildet**) **1** to
form; **2 sich bilden** to form; **3 sich
bilden** to educate yourself.

Bildschirm der (PL die
Bildschirme) screen.

bildschön adjective (very)
beautiful.

Bildung die **1** formation;
2 education.

billig adjective cheap.

Billion die (PL die Billionen) billion
(a million million); **drei Billionen
Euro** three Billion euros.

bin SEE sein.

Binde die (PL die Binden) **1** bandage;
2 sanitary towel.

binden ◇verb (IMPERF **band**, PERF
hat gebunden) **1** to tie; **2** to bind (a
book); **3** to make up (a bouquet);
4 to thicken (a sauce); **5 sich
binden** to commit oneself.

Bindestrich der (PL die
Bindestriche) hyphen.

Bindfaden der (PL die Bindfäden)
(piece of) string.

Bindung die (PL die Bindungen)
1 tie; **2** relationship; **3** binding (on
a ski).

Biokost die health food.

Biologie die biology.

biologisch adjective biological.

Birke die (PL die Birken) birch tree.

Birne die (PL die Birnen) **1** pear;
2 bulb.

bis *preposition* (+ ACC) **1** as far as; **dieser Zug fährt nur bis Passau** this train only goes as far as Passau; **2** up to; **Kinder bis zehn zahlen die Hälfte** children up to ten pay half; **bis jetzt** up to now; **bis zu** up to; **3** until, till (*with time*); **4** by; **bis dahin** by then; **5 bis auf** except for; **alle sind durchgefallen bis auf die zwei Mädchen** everyone failed except for the two girls; **6 bis bald!** see you soon!; **7 von München bis Salzburg** from Munich to Salzburg; **von Montag bis Freitag** from Monday to Friday; **zwei bis drei Euro** two to three euros.

bis *conjunction* until, till; **sie bleibt, bis es dunkel wird** she's staying until it gets dark.

Bischof *der* (PL die **Bischöfe**) bishop.

bisher *adverb* so far.

bisherig *adjective* previous.

Biss *der* (PL die **Bisse**) bite.

biss SEE **beißen**.

bisschen *pronoun* **1 ein bisschen** a bit; ; **ein bisschen Brot** a bit of bread; **2 kein bisschen** not a bit.

bissig *adjective* **1** vicious; **'Vorsicht bissiger Hund!'** 'beware of the dog!'; **2** cutting (*remark, tone*).

bist SEE **sein**.

Bitte *die* (PL die **Bitten**) request.

bitte *adverb* **1** please; **'möchten Sie Kuchen?' – 'ja bitte'** 'would you like some cake?' – 'yes please'; **2** you're welcome (*in reply to thanks*); **3** come in (*after a knock on the door*); **4** (*in a shop*) **bitte?** yes, please?; **5 wie bitte?** sorry?

bitten ◇*verb* (IMPERF **bat**, PERF **hat gebeten**) to ask; **jemanden um etwas bitten** to ask somebody for something.

bitter *adjective* bitter.

blamieren *verb* (PERF **hat blamiert**) **1** to disgrace; **2 jemanden blamieren** to embarrass somebody; **3 sich blamieren** to make a fool of yourself.

Blase *die* (PL die **Blasen**) **1** bubble; **2** blister; **3** bladder.

blasen ◇*verb* (PRES **bläst**, IMPERF **blies**, PERF **hat geblasen**) to blow.

Blasinstrument *das* (PL die **Blasinstrumente**) wind instrument.

Blaskapelle *die* (PL die **Blaskapellen**) brass band.

blass *adjective* pale.

Blatt *das* (PL die **Blätter**) **1** leaf; **2** sheet; **ein Blatt Papier** a sheet of paper; **3** page; **4** newspaper.

blau *adjective* **1** blue; **ein blau gestreiftes Kleid** a dress with blue stripes; **2 ein blaues Auge haben** to have a black eye; **3 ein blauer Fleck** a bruise; **4 blau sein** (*informal*) to be tight; **5 eine Fahrt ins Blaue** a mystery tour.

Blech *das* (PL die **Bleche**) **1** sheet metal; **2** tin; **3** baking tray; **4** brass (*in music*).

Blei *das* lead.

a
b
c
d
e
f
g
h
i
j
k
l
m
n
o
p
q
r
s
t
u
v
w
x
y
z

bleiben ⋄*verb* (IMPERF **blieb**, PERF **ist geblieben**) **1** to stay, to remain; **2** to be left; **3 bleiben Sie am Apparat** hold the line; **4 bei etwas bleiben** to stick to something; **5 ruhig bleiben** to keep calm; **6 wo bleibt er so lange?** where has he got to?; **7 etwas bleiben lassen** to not do something; **wenn du nicht mitkommen willst, dann lass es eben bleiben** if you don't want to come, then don't.

bleich *adjective* pale.

Bleichmittel *das* (PL **die Bleichmittel**) bleach.

bleifrei *adjective* unleaded.

Bleistift *der* (PL **die Bleistifte**) pencil.

Bleistiftspitzer *der* (PL **die Bleistiftspitzer**) pencil sharpener.

blenden *verb* (PERF **hat geblendet**) **1** to dazzle; **2 es geht mir blendend** I feel great; **wir haben uns blendend amüsiert** we had a great time.

blendend *adjective* **1** marvellous; **2 es geht mir blendend** I feel great; **wir haben uns blendend amüsiert** we had a great time.

Blick *der* (PL **die Blicke**) **1** look; **2** glance; **3 auf den ersten Blick** at first sight; **4** view; **ein Zimmer mit Blick aufs Meer** a room with a sea view.

blicken *verb* (PERF **hat geblickt**) **1** to look; **2 sich blicken lassen** to show your face.

blieb SEE **bleiben**.

blies SEE **blasen**.

blind *adjective* blind.

Blinddarm *der* (PL **die Blinddärme**) appendix.

Blinddarmentzündung *die* (PL **die Blinddarmentzündungen**) appendicitis.

Blinde *der/die* (PL **die Blinden**) blind person, blind man/woman.

blinken *verb* (PERF **hat geblinkt**) **1** to flash; **2** to indicate (*of a car*).

Blinker *der* (PL **die Blinker**) indicator.

blinzeln *verb* (PERF **hat geblinzelt**) to blink.

Blitz *der* (PL **die Blitze**) **1** (flash of) lightning; **2** flash.

blitzen *verb* (PERF **hat geblitzt**) **1** to flash; **2** to sparkle; **3 es hat geblitzt** there was a flash of lightning.

Block *der* (PL **die Blöcke**) **1** pad (*for writing on*); **2** (PL **die Blocks**) block (*of flats*).

Blockflöte *die* (PL **die Blockflöten**) recorder.

blöd *adjective* stupid.

Blödsinn *der* nonsense.

blond *adjective* blonde, fair-haired.

bloß *adverb* **1** only; **es kostet bloß fünf Euro** it's only five euros; **2 warum hat er das bloß gemacht?** why on earth did he do it?; **3 was mache ich bloß?** whatever shall I do?; **4 fass das bloß nicht an!** don't touch it!

bloß *adjective* **1** bare (*feet*); **mit bloßem Auge** with the naked eye; **2** mere (*words, suspicion*); **der bloße Gedanke daran** the mere thought of it.

Blume *die* (PL **die Blumen**) flower.

Blumenkohl *der* cauliflower.

Bluse die (PL die **Blusen**) blouse.

Blut das blood.

Blutdruck der blood pressure.

Blüte die (PL die **Blüten**) blossom.

bluten verb (PERF **hat geblutet**) to bleed.

Blutgefäß das (PL die **Blutgefäße**) bloodvessel.

Blutprobe die (PL die **Blutproben**) blood test.

Blutwurst die (PL die **Blutwürste**) black pudding.

Bock der (PL die **Böcke**) 1 buck; 2 billy-goat; 3 ram; 4 **Bock auf etwas haben** (informal) to fancy something; 5 **einen Bock schießen** (informal) to make a blunder.

Bockwurst die (PL die **Bockwürste**) frankfurter.

Boden der (PL die **Böden**) 1 ground; 2 floor; 3 bottom (of a container); 4 loft, attic.

Bodensee der Lake Constance.

bog SEE **biegen.**

Bogen der (PL die **Bögen**) 1 curve; 2 arch; 3 turn (in skiing).

Bohne die (PL die **Bohnen**) bean.

bohren verb (PERF **hat gebohrt**) to drill.

Bohrer der (PL die **Bohrer**) drill.

Bohrinsel die (PL die **Bohrinseln**) oil rig.

Bohrmaschine die (PL die **Bohrmaschinen**) electric drill.

Bombe die (PL die **Bomben**) bomb.

Bonbon der (PL die **Bonbons**) sweet.

Boot das (PL die **Boote**) boat.

Bord[1] das (PL die **Borde**) shelf.

Bord[2] der an **Bord** on board; über **Bord** overboard.

Bordkarte die (PL die **Bordkarten**) boarding card.

borgen (PERF **hat geborgt**) 1 to borrow; 2 **sich etwas borgen** to borrow something; **ich habe es mir von ihr geborgt** I borrowed it from her; 3 **jemandem etwas borgen** to lend somebody something; **Evi hat mir ihr Buch geborgt** Evi lent me her book.

Börse die (PL die **Börsen**) stock exchange.

Börsenmakler der (PL die **Börsenmakler**) stock broker.

Borste die (PL die **Borsten**) bristle.

böse adjective 1 bad; 2 wicked; 3 naughty (child); 4 angry; **böse werden** to get angry; **ich bin mit ihm böse** I'm angry with him; 5 **auf jemanden böse sein** to be cross with somebody.

boshaft adjective malicious.

bot SEE **bieten.**

Bote der (PL die **Boten**) messenger.

Botin die (PL die **Botinnen**) messenger.

Botschaft die (PL die **Botschaften**) 1 message; 2 embassy; **die britische Botschaft** the British Embassy.

Botschafter der (PL die **Botschafter**) ambassador.

Botschafterin die (PL die **Botschafterinnen**) ambassador.

Bowle die (PL die **Bowlen**) punch
(*for drinking*).

boxen *verb* (PERF **hat geboxt**) **1** to
box; **2** to punch.

Boxer der (PL die **Boxer**) boxer.

brach SEE **brechen**.

brachte SEE **bringen**.

Branche die (PL die **Branchen**) (line
of) business.

Branchenverzeichnis das (PL
die **Branchenverzeichnisse**)
classified directory.

Brand der (PL die **Brände**) fire.

Brandung die surf.

brannte SEE **brennen**.

Brasilianer der (PL die
Brasilianer) Brazilian.

Brasilianerin die (PL die
Brasilianerinnen) Brazilian.

braten ⋄*verb* (PRES **brät**, IMPERF
briet, PERF **hat gebraten**) **1** to fry;
2 to roast.

Braten der (PL die **Braten**) **1** roast;
2 joint.

Brathähnchen das (PL die
Brathähnchen) roast chicken.

Bratkartoffeln *plural noun* fried
potatoes.

Bratpfanne die (PL die
Bratpfannen) frying pan.

Bratwurst die (PL die **Bratwürste**)
fried sausage.

Brauch der (PL die **Bräuche**)
custom.

brauchbar *adjective* **1** usable;
2 useful.

brauchen *verb* (PERF **hat
gebraucht**) **1** need; **ich brauche
eine neue Birne für meine Lampe**
I need a new bulb for my light; **du
brauchst nur auf den Knopf zu
drücken** all you need to do is press
the button; **du brauchst nicht zu
gehen** you needn't go; **2 sie
braucht es nur zu sagen** she only
has to say; **3** to take (*time*); **wie
lange brauchst du mit dem Auto?**
how long does it take you by car?;
4 ich könnte es gut brauchen I
could do with it.

brauen *verb* (PERF **hat gebraut**) to
brew.

Brauerei die (PL die **Brauereien**)
brewery.

braun *adjective* **1** brown; **2 braun
werden** to get a tan; **braun
(gebrannt) sein** to be tanned.

Bräune die tan.

Brause die (PL die **Brausen**) fizzy
drink.

Braut die (PL die **Bräute**) bride.

Bräutigam der (PL die **Bräutigame**)
bridegroom.

Brautjungfer die (PL die
Brautjungfern) bridesmaid.

Brautpaar das (PL die **Brautpaare**)
bride and groom.

brav *adjective* good.

BRD die (*Bundesrepublik
Deutschland*) FRG (*Federal
Republic of Germany*).

brechen ⋄*verb* (PRES **bricht**, IMPERF
brach, PERF **hat gebrochen**) **1** to
break (*an agreement, a record*) to
break; **2 sich den Arm brechen** to break

your arm; **3** to vomit; **4** (PERF **ist gebrochen**) to break; **der Ast ist gebrochen** the branch broke.

breit *adjective* **1** wide; **2** broad; **3 die breite Masse** the general public.

Breite die (PL die **Breiten**) width.

Bremse die (PL die **Bremsen**)
1 brake; **2** horsefly.

bremsen *verb* (PERF **hat gebremst**) **1** to brake; **2** to slow down (*development, production*); **3** jemanden bremsen (*informal*) to stop somebody; **er ist nicht mehr zu bremsen** there's no stopping him.

Bremslicht das (PL die **Bremslichter**) brake light.

Bremspedal das (PL die **Bremspedale**) brake pedal.

brennen ◇*verb* (IMPERF **brannte**, PERF **hat gebrannt**) **1** to burn; **2** to be on (*of a light*); **das Licht brennen lassen** to leave the light on; **3** to sting (*of a wound or sore*); **4 das Haus brennt** the house is on fire; **es brennt!** fire!; **5 darauf brennen, etwas zu tun** to be dying to do something.

Brennnessel die (PL die **Brennnesseln**) stinging nettle.

Brennpunkt der (PL die **Brennpunkte**) focus.

Brett das (PL die **Bretter**) **1** board; **2** plank; **3** shelf.

Brezel die (PL die **Brezeln**) pretzel.

bricht SEE **brechen**.

Brief der (PL die **Briefe**) letter.

Brieffreund der (PL die **Brieffreunde**) pen friend.

Brieffreundin die (PL die **Brieffreundinnen**) pen friend.

Briefkasten der (PL die **Briefkästen**) **1** letterbox; **2** postbox.

Briefmarke die (PL die **Briefmarken**) stamp.

Brieftasche die (PL die **Brieftaschen**) wallet.

Briefträger der (PL die **Briefträger**) postman.

Briefträgerin die (PL die **Briefträgerinnen**) postwoman.

Briefumschlag der (PL die **Briefumschläge**) envelope.

Briefwechsel der correspondence.

briet SEE **braten**.

Brillant der (PL die **Brillanten**) diamond.

Brille die (PL die **Brillen**) glasses, spectacles.

bringen ◇*verb* (IMPERF **brachte**, PERF **hat gebracht**) **1** to bring; **2** to take; **Peter bringt dich nach Hause** Peter will take you home; **3 die Kinder ins Bett bringen** to put the children to bed; **4 einen Film im Fernsehen bringen** to show a film on television; **5** to publish (*an article*); **6** to yield (*interest, a profit*); **7** jemanden dazu bringen, etwas zu tun to get somebody to do something; **8 mit sich bringen** to entail; **9** etwas hinter sich bringen to get something over and done with; **10** es so weit bringen to go far;

a b c d e f g h i j k l m n o p q r s t u v w x y z

11 **jemanden auf eine Idee bringen** to give somebody an idea; 12 **es zu nichts bringen** to get nowhere; 13 **das bringt's nicht!** (*informal*) that's no use!

Brise die (PL die **Brisen**) breeze.

Brite der (PL die **Briten**) Briton; **die Briten** the British.

Britin die (PL die **Britinnen**) Briton.

britisch adjective British.

Brokkoli der broccoli.

Brombeere die (PL die **Brombeeren**) blackberry.

Brosche die (PL die **Broschen**) brooch.

Broschüre die (PL die **Broschüren**) brochure.

Brot das (PL die **Brote**) 1 bread; **ein Brot** a loaf of bread; 2 **ein Brot** a slice of bread.

Brötchen das (PL die **Brötchen**) roll.

Bruch der (PL die **Brüche**) 1 break; 2 fracture; 3 hernia; 4 fraction.

Bruchteil der (PL die **Bruchteile**) fraction.

Brücke die (PL die **Brücken**) bridge.

Bruder der (PL die **Brüder**) brother.

Brühe die (PL die **Brühen**) 1 broth; 2 stock (*for cooking*).

Brühwürfel der (PL die **Brühwürfel**) stock cube.

brüllen verb (PERF hat **gebrüllt**) to roar.

brummen verb (PERF hat **gebrummt**) 1 to buzz; 2 to growl (*of a bear*); 3 to hum (*of an engine*).

Brunnen der (PL die **Brunnen**) 1 well; 2 fountain.

Brüssel das Brussels.

Brust die (PL die **Brüste**) 1 chest; 2 breast.

Brustschwimmen das breaststroke.

brutto adverb gross.

BSE das (*bovine spongiforme Enzephalopathie*) BSE.

Bub der (PL die **Buben**) boy.

Buch das (PL die **Bücher**) book.

Buche die (PL die **Buchen**) beech.

buchen verb (PERF hat **gebucht**) to book.

Bücherei die (PL die **Büchereien**) library.

Bücherregal das (PL die **Bücherregale**) bookcase.

Buchhalter der (PL die **Buchhalter**) accountant, bookkeeper.

Buchhalterin die (PL die **Buchhalterinnen**) accountant, bookkeeper.

Buchhandlung die (PL die **Buchhandlungen**) bookshop.

Büchse die (PL die **Büchsen**) tin, can.

Büchsenöffner der (PL die **Büchsenöffner**) tin opener.

Buchstabe der (PL die **Buchstaben**) letter (*of the alphabet*); **ein großer Buchstabe** a capital letter; **ein kleiner Buchstabe** a small letter.

buchstabieren verb (PERF hat **buchstabiert**) to spell.

Bucht die (PL die **Buchten**) bay.

Buchung die (PL die **Buchungen**) booking, reservation.

bücken (PERF **hat sich gebückt**) **sich bücken** to bend down.

Buddhismus der Buddhism.

Bude die (PL die **Buden**) **1** hut; **2** stall; **3 meine Bude** (*informal*) my room, my pad.

Büfett das (PL die **Büfetts**) buffet.

Bügel der (PL die **Bügel**) hanger.

Bügeleisen das (PL die **Bügeleisen**) iron.

bügeln *verb* (PERF **hat gebügelt**) to iron.

Bühne die (PL die **Bühnen**) stage.

Bulle der (PL die **Bullen**) **1** bull; **2** (*informal*) cop.

Bummel der (PL die **Bummel**) stroll (*around town*).

bummeln *verb* (PERF **ist gebummelt**) **1** to stroll; **wir sind durch die Stadt gebummelt** we strolled around town; **2** (PERF **hat gebummelt**) to dawdle.

Bund[1] der (PL die **Bünde**) **1** association; **2** waistband.

Bund[2] das (PL die **Bunde**) bunch.

Bundesbürger der (PL die **Bundesbürger**) German citizen.

Bundeskanzler der (PL die **Bundeskanzler**) Federal Chancellor.

Bundesland das (PL die **Bundesländer**) (federal) state.

Bundesliga die (German) national football league.

Bundesrat der Upper House (*of the German Parliament*).

Bundesrepublik die Federal Republic.

Bundesstraße die (PL die **Bundesstraßen**) A road, major road.

Bundestag der Lower House (*of the German Parliament*).

Bundeswehr die (German) Army.

Bungalow der (PL die **Bungalows**) bungalow.

bunt *adjective* colourful.

Buntstift der (PL die **Buntstifte**) coloured pencil.

Burg die (PL die **Burgen**) castle.

Bürger der (PL die **Bürger**) citizen.

Bürgerin die (PL die **Bürgerinnen**) citizen.

Bürgermeister der (PL die **Bürgermeister**) mayor.

Bürgersteig der (PL die **Bürgersteige**) pavement.

Büro das (PL die **Büros**) office.

Büroklammer die (PL die **Büroklammern**) paper clip.

Bürste die (PL die **Bürsten**) brush.

bürsten *verb* (PERF **hat gebürstet**) to brush.

Bus der (PL die **Busse**) bus; **ich fahre mit dem Bus** I'm going by bus.

Busbahnhof der (PL die **Busbahnhöfe**) bus station.

Busch der (PL die **Büsche**) bush.

Busen der (PL die **Busen**) bosom.

Busfahrer der (PL die **Busfahrer**) bus driver.

a b c d e f g h i j k l m n o p q r s t u v w x y z

Busfahrerin die (PL die Busfahrerinnen) bus driver.

Busfahrkarte die (PL die Busfahrkarten) bus ticket.

Bushaltestelle die (PL die Bushaltestellen) bus stop.

Buslinie die (PL die Buslinien) bus route.

Bussard der (PL die Bussarde) buzzard.

Bußgeld das (PL die Bußgelder) fine.

Büstenhalter der (PL die Büstenhalter) bra.

Busverbindung die (PL die Busverbindungen) **1** bus connection; **2** bus line.

Butter die butter.

Butterbrot das (PL die Butterbrote) sandwich, bread and butter.

bzw. SEE beziehungsweise.

Cc

Café das (PL die Cafés) cafe.

Cafeteria die (PL die Cafeterias) cafeteria.

campen verb (PERF hat gecampt) to camp.

Camper der (PL die Camper) camper.

Camperin die (PL die Camperinnen) camper.

Camping das camping.

Campingbus der (PL die Campingbusse) camper (vehicle).

Campingkocher der (PL die Campingkocher) camping stove.

Campingplatz der (PL die Campingplätze) campsite.

CD die (PL die CDs) CD.

CD-Spieler der (PL die CD-Spieler) CD player.

Cello das (PL die Cellos) cello.

Cent der (PL die Cents) cent (in euro and dollar systems); **25 Cent** 25 cents.

Champignon der (PL die Champignons) mushroom.

Chance die (PL die Chancen) chance.

Chaos das chaos.

chaotisch adjective chaotic.

Charakter der (PL die Charaktere) character.

charmant adjective charming.

Charterflug der (PL die Charterflüge) charter flight.

Chatroom der (PL die Chatrooms) chatroom.

Chauvinist der (PL die Chauvinisten) chauvinist.

Chef der (PL die Chefs) **1** head (of a firm); **2** boss.

Chefin die (PL die Chefinnen) **1** head (of a firm); **2** boss.

Chemie die chemistry.

Chemikalie die (PL die Chemikalien) chemical.

Chemiker der (PL die Chemiker) chemist.

Chemikerin die (PL die **Chemikerinnen**) chemist.

chemisch adjective **1** chemical; **2 chemische Reinigung** dry-cleaning, dry-cleaner's.

Chicorée der chicory.

China das China.

Chinese der (PL die **Chinesen**) Chinese; **die Chinesen** the Chinese.

Chinesin die (PL die **Chinesinnen**) Chinese.

chinesisch adjective Chinese.

Chipkarte die (PL die **Chipkarten**) smart card.

Chips plural noun crisps.

Chirurg der (PL die **Chirurgen**) surgeon.

Chirurgin die (PL die **Chirurginnen**) surgeon.

Chlor das chlorine.

Chor der (PL die **Chöre**) choir.

Christ der (PL die **Christen**) Christian.

Christentum das Christianity.

Christin die (PL die **Christinnen**) Christian.

christlich adjective Christian.

Christus der Christ.

circa adverb approximately.

Clown der (PL die **Clowns**) clown.

Cola™ die (PL die **Colas**) Coke™.

Comic der (PL die **Comics**) cartoon.

Comicheft das (PL die **Comichefte**) comic.

Computer der (PL die **Computer**) computer; **ich spiele am**
Computer I'm playing on the computer.

Computerprogramm das (PL die **Computerprogramme**) computer program.

Computerspiel das (PL die **Computerspiele**) computer game.

Container der (PL die **Container**) **1** container; **2** skip.

Cordsamt der corduroy.

Couch die (PL die **Couchs**) sofa.

Couchtisch der (PL die **Couchtische**) coffee table.

Cousin der (PL die **Cousins**) cousin.

Cousine die (PL die **Cousinen**) cousin SEE **Kusine.**

Creme die (PL die **Cremes**) **1** cream; **2** cream dessert.

Curry das **1** curry; **2** curry powder.

Currywurst die (PL die **Currywürste**) curried sausage.

Cursor der (PL die **Cursors**) cursor.

Dd

da adverb **1** there; **da draußen** out there; **da drüben** over there; **da sein** to be there; **man muss pünktlich da sein** you have to be there on time; **2 ist noch Brot da?** is there any bread left?; **3** here; **sind alle da?** is everyone here?; **da sind deine Handschuhe** here are your gloves; **4 ist Sabine da?** is Sabine about?; **5 von da an** from then on; **6 ich bin wieder da** I'm back; **7** so (therefore); **der Bus war**

a b c d e f g h i j k l m n o p q r s t u v w x y z

weg, da bin ich gelaufen the bus had gone, so I walked; **8 da kann man nichts machen** there's nothing you can do about it; **9 da, wo die Straße nach Stuttgart abzweigt** at the turning for Stuttgart.

da conjunction as, since; **da es gerade regnet** as it's raining.

dabei adverb **1** (included or next to) with it/him/her/them; **sie hatten die Kinder dabei** they had the children with them; **2 dicht dabei** close by; **3** (referring to something already mentioned) about it; **das Wichtigste dabei** the most important thing about it; **4** at the same time; **er malte ein Bild und sang dabei** he painted a picture and sang at the same time; **5** during this; **6 jemandem dabei helfen, etwas zu tun** to help somebody do something; **7 was hast du dir denn dabei gedacht?** what were you thinking of?; **8 dabei sein** to be there; **er ist dabei gewesen** he was there; **9 was ist denn dabei?** so what?; **10 dabei sein, etwas zu tun** to be just doing something; **ich war gerade dabei zu gehen** I was just about to leave; **11 dabei bleiben** to stick with it (an opinion, for example); **12** and yet, even though.

dabeibleiben ◇ verb (IMPERF **blieb dabei**, PERF **ist dabeigeblieben**) **1** to stay on (at an organisation); **2 er hat mit dem Training begonnen, ist aber nicht dabeigeblieben** he started training, but didn't keep it up.

dabeisein SEE **dabei**.

Dach das (PL die **Dächer**) roof.

Dachboden der (PL die **Dachböden**) loft, attic.

Dachgeschoss das (PL die **Dachgeschosse**) attic.

Dachrinne die (PL die **Dachrinnen**) gutter (on roof edge).

dachte SEE **denken**.

Dackel der (PL die **Dackel**) dachshund.

dadurch adverb **1** through it/them; **das Wasser muss dadurch gelaufen sein** the water must have run through it; **2** as a result; **3** in this way; **ich nehme die U-Bahn, dadurch bin ich eine halbe Stunde eher da** I'll take the tube, that way I'll be there half an hour earlier.

dadurch conjunction **dadurch, dass** because.

dafür adverb **1** for it/them; **dafür kriegt man nicht viel** you won't get much for it/them; **2** instead; **wenn er schon nicht auf die Party gehen will, kann er dich dafür zum Essen einladen** if he doesn't want to go to the party he can take you for a meal instead; **3** but then (on the other hand); **4 dafür, dass** considering (that); **5 ich kann nichts dafür** it's not my fault.

dagegen adverb **1** against it/them; **ich bin dagegen** I'm against it; **2** for it/them (when swapping); **3** into it; **das Auto ist dagegen gefahren** the car drove into it; **4** by comparison; **5 hast du was**

dagegen? do you mind?;
6 however.

daheim adverb at home.

daher adverb 1 from there; 2 that's why.

dahin adverb 1 there; 2 bis dahin (in the past) until then, (in the future) by then; 3 jemanden dahin bringen, dass er etwas tut to get somebody to do something.

dahinten adverb over there.

dahinter adverb 1 behind it/them; 2 dahinter kommen to get to the bottom of it; ich bin endlich dahinter gekommen I finally got to the bottom of it.

dalassen ✧verb (PRES lässt da, IMPERF ließ da, PERF hat dagelassen) to leave there.

damals adverb at that time, then; wir wohnten damals in Berlin we were then living in Berlin.

Dame die (PL die Damen) 1 lady; 2 queen (in chess or cards); 3 draughts.

Damenbinde die (PL die Damenbinden) sanitary towel.

damit adverb 1 with it/them; ich will damit spielen I want to play with it; hör auf damit! stop it!; 2 by it; was meinst du damit? what do you mean by that?; 3 damit hat es noch Zeit there's no hurry (about that); 4 therefore, because of that; sie hat den zweiten Satz verloren und damit das Spiel she lost the second set and because of it the match.

damit conjunction so that; ich habe es aufgeschrieben, damit du es nicht vergisst I wrote it down so that you won't forget.

Damm der (PL die Dämme) 1 dam; 2 embankment.

dämmern verb (PERF hat gedämmert) es dämmert it is getting light, it is getting dark.

Dämmerung die 1 dawn; 2 dusk.

Dampf der (PL die Dämpfe) steam.

dämpfen verb (PERF hat gedämpft) 1 to steam (in cooking); 2 to muffle (a sound); 3 to dampen (somebody's enthusiasm).

dampfen verb (PERF hat gedampft) to steam.

Dampfer der (PL die Dampfer) steamer.

danach adverb 1 after it/them; 2 afterwards; kurz danach shortly afterwards; 3 danach suchen to look for it/them; 4 danach riechen to smell of it; 5 accordingly; 6 es sieht danach aus it looks like it.

Däne der (PL die Dänen) Dane.

daneben adverb 1 next to it/them; 2 by comparison.

Dänemark das Denmark.

Dänin die (PL die Däninnen) Dane.

dänisch adjective Danish.

Dank der 1 thanks; mit Dank zurück thanks for the loan; 2 vielen Dank thank you very much.

dank preposition (+ GEN or + DAT) thanks to.

a
b
c
d
e
f
g
h
i
j
k
l
m
n
o
p
q
r
s
t
u
v
w
x
y
z

a b c d e f g h i j k l m n o p q r s t u v w x y z

dankbar *adjective* **1** grateful; **2** rewarding.

danke *exclamation* thank you, thanks; **danke schön** thank you very much; **(nein) danke** no thank you, no thanks.

danken *verb* (PERF **hat gedankt**) **1** to thank; **2 nichts zu danken** don't mention it.

dann *adverb* then.

daran *adverb* **1** on it/them; **2 daran denken** to think of it/them; **3 dicht daran** close to it/them; **4 nahe daran sein, etwas zu tun** to be on the point of doing something; **5** about it/them; **daran ist nichts zu machen** there is nothing you can do about it; **6 es liegt daran, dass** ... it is because ...; **7 er ist daran gestorben** he died of it.

darauf *adverb* **1** on it/them; **2 darauf warten** to wait for it; **3 darauf antworten** to reply to it; **4** after that; **kurz darauf** shortly after that; **5 am Tag darauf** the day after; **6 am darauf folgenden Tag** the following day; **7 es kommt darauf an, ob** ... it depends whether ....

daraufhin *adverb* as a result.

daraus *adverb* **1** out of it/them, from it/them; **2 was ist daraus geworden?** what has become of it/them?; **3 mach dir nichts daraus** don't worry about it.

darf, darfst SEE **dürfen**.

darin *adverb* **1** in it/them; **2** in that respect; **der Unterschied liegt**

darin, dass ... the difference is that ...

Darm *der* (PL **die Därme**) intestine(s).

darstellen *verb* (PERF **hat dargestellt**) **1** to represent; **2** to portray; **dieses Gemälde stellt Szenen aus dem Bürgerkrieg dar** this painting portrays scenes from the civil war; **3** to describe; **er stellt es so dar, als sei es meine Schuld** the way he describes it, it's all my fault; **4** to play (*in the theatre*).

Darsteller *der* (PL **die Darsteller**) actor.

Darstellerin *die* (PL **die Darstellerinnen**) actress.

darüber *adverb* **1** over it/them; **2** about it; **darüber sprechen** to talk about it; **3** more; **dreißig Euro oder darüber** thirty euros or more.

darum *adverb* **1** round it/them; **2 darum bitten** to ask for it; **3** that's why; **darum komme ich nicht** that's why I'm not coming; **4 ich sorge mich darum** I worry about it; **5 es geht darum, zu gewinnen** the main thing is to win; **6 darum geht es nicht** that's not the point; **7** because of that; **darum, weil** because.

darunter *adverb* **1** under it/them; **2 im Stock darunter** on the floor below; **3** among them; **mehrere Schüler, darunter zwei Zehnjährige** a number of pupils, among them two ten year olds; **4** less; **dreißig Euro oder darunter** thirty euros or less; **5** was

verstehen Sie darunter? what do you understand by that?

das *article (neuter)* **1** the; **das Haus** the house; **2** that; **das Mädchen war es** it was that girl; **das da** that one.

das *pronoun* **1** which, that; **das Kleid, das ich im Schaufenster gesehen habe** the dress which I saw in the window; **2 das mit der Spitze** the one with the lace; **3** who; **das Mädchen, das gegenüber wohnt** the girl who lives opposite; **4** that; **das wusste ich nicht** I didn't know that; **das geht** that's all right.

Dasein *das* existence.

dasein SEE da.

dass *conjunction* **1** that; **ich freue mich, dass** ... I'm very pleased that ...; **2 ich verstehe nicht, dass Karin ihn mag** I don't understand why Karin likes him.

dasselbe *pronoun* the same, the same one.

Daten *plural noun* data.

Datenbank *die* (PL die **Datenbanken**) database.

Datenverarbeitung *die* data processing.

datieren *verb* (PERF **hat datiert**) to date.

Dativ *der* (PL die **Dative**) dative.

Datum *das* (PL die **Daten**) date.

Dauer *die* **1** duration; **2** length; **3 für die Dauer von fünf Jahren** for (a period of) five years; **4 von Dauer sein** to last; **5 auf die Dauer** in the long run; **auf Dauer** permanently.

Dauerkarte *die* (PL die **Dauerkarten**) season ticket.

dauern *verb* (PERF **hat gedauert**) **1** to last; **2 lange dauern** to take a long time; **es hat vier Wochen gedauert, bis der Brief hier ankam** it took four weeks for the letter to arrive.

dauernd *adjective* constant.

dauernd *adverb* constantly.

Dauerwelle *die* (PL die **Dauerwellen**) perm.

Daumen *der* (PL die **Daumen**) thumb.

Daunendecke *die* (PL die **Daunendecken**) duvet.

davon *adverb* **1** from it/them; **2** about it; **ich weiß nichts davon** I don't know anything about it; **3** of it/them; **die Hälfte davon** half of it/them; **4 das kommt davon** (*informal*) it serves you right; **5 was habe ich davon?** what's the point?; **6 abgesehen davon** apart from that.

davor *adverb* **1** in front of it/them; **2** beforehand; **3 Angst davor haben** to be frightened of it/them; **4 kurz davor sein, etwas zu tun** to be on the point of doing something.

dazu *adverb* **1** to it/them; **2** in addition; **noch dazu** in addition (to it); **3 wit it; was isst du dazu?** what are you having with it?; **4 ich habe keine Lust dazu** I don't feel like it; **5 jemanden dazu bringen, etwas zu tun** to get somebody to do

a b c d e f g h i j k l m n o p q r s t u v w x y z

something; **6 ich bin nicht dazu gekommen** I didn't get round to it; **7 er ist nicht dazu bereit** he's not prepared to do it.

dazugeben *verb* (PRES **gibt dazu**, IMPERF **gab dazu**, PERF **hat dazugegeben**) to add.

dazugehören *verb* (PERF **hat dazugehört**) **1** to belong to it/them; **2** to go with it/them (*of accessories*); **alles, was dazugehört** everything that goes with it.

dazukommen *verb* (IMPERF **kam dazu**, PERF **ist dazugekommen**) **1** to arrive; **2** to be added; **3 kommt noch etwas dazu?** would you like anything else?

dazwischen *adverb* **1** in between; **2** between them; **der Unterschied dazwischen** the difference between them.

dazwischenkommen *verb* (PRES **kommt dazwischen**, IMPERF **kam dazwischen**, PERF **ist dazwischengekommen**) to crop up.

DB *die* (*Deutsche Bundesbahn*) German railways.

DDR *die* (*Deutsche Demokratische Republik*) GDR, East Germany; **in der ehemaligen DDR** in the former East Germany.

Debatte *die* (PL *die* **Debatten**) debate.

Decke *die* (PL *die* **Decken**) **1** blanket, cover; **2** (table)cloth; **ich habe eine neue Decke aufgelegt**

I've put on a new tablecloth; **3** ceiling.

Deckel *der* (PL *die* **Deckel**) **1** lid; **2** top.

decken *verb* (PERF **hat gedeckt**) **1** to cover; **2 ein Tuch über etwas decken** to spread a cloth over something; **3 den Tisch decken** to lay the table; **4 jemanden decken** to cover up for somebody; **5 einen Spieler decken** to mark a player (*in sport*).

definieren *verb* (PERF **hat definiert**) to define.

Definition *die* (PL *die* **Definitionen**) definition.

dehnbar *adjective* elastic.

dehnen *verb* (PERF **hat gedehnt**) to stretch.

dein *adjective* your.

deiner, deine, deins *pronoun* yours; **meine Uhr ist kaputt, kann ich deine haben?** my watch is broken, can I take yours?

deinetwegen *adverb* **1** because of you; **2** for your sake.

deins SEE **deiner**.

deklinieren *verb* (PERF **hat dekliniert**) to decline.

Delfin *der* (PL *die* **Delfine**) dolphin.

Delle *die* (PL *die* **Dellen**) dent.

Delphin *der* (PL *die* **Delphine**) dolphin.

dem *article* (*dative*) **1** (to) the; **2 es liegt auf dem Tisch** it's on the table.

dem *pronoun* **1** to him; **gib es dem** give it to him; **2** to it, to that one;

3 to whom; **der Mann, dem ich das Geld gegeben habe** the man I gave the money to; **4** which; **das Messer, mit dem ich Zwiebeln schneide** the knife that I cut onions with.

demnächst *adverb* shortly.

Demokratie *die* (PL *die* **Demokratien**) democracy.

demokratisch *adjective* democratic.

Demonstrant *der* (PL *die* **Demonstranten**) demonstrator.

Demonstrantin *die* (PL *die* **Demonstrantinnen**) demonstrator.

Demonstration *die* (PL *die* **Demonstrationen**) demonstration.

demonstrieren *verb* (PERF **hat demonstriert**) to demonstrate.

den *article* (accusative) **1** the; **2 ich habe mir den Arm gebrochen** I've broken my arm.

den *pronoun* **1** him; **kennst du den?** do you know him?; **2** it, that one; **den kannst du gerne haben** you're welcome to it; **ich nehme den** I'll take that one; **who(m)**; **4** which; **der Mantel, den ich mir gekauft habe** the coat I bought.

denen *pronoun* (dative plural) **1** (to) them; **2** that, (to) whom; **die Menschen, denen sie geholfen hat** the people she helped.

denkbar *adjective* conceivable.

denken ✧ *verb* (IMPERF **dachte**, PERF **hat gedacht**) **1** to think; **ich denke oft an dich** I often think of you;

2 das kann ich mir denken I can imagine.

Denkmal *das* (PL *die* **Denkmäler**) monument.

denn *conjunction* **1** because, for; **2 mehr denn je** more than ever.

denn *adverb* **1 wo denn?** where?; **2 was ist denn los?** so what's the matter?; **3 warum denn nicht?** why ever not?; **4 es sei denn** unless.

dennoch *conjunction* nevertheless.

deprimierend *adjective* depressing.

deprimiert *adjective* depressed.

der *article* **1** (masculine) the; **der Mann** the man; **2** (feminine and plural genitive) of the; **die Katze der Frau** the woman's cat; **der Ball der Kinder** the children's ball; **3** (dative) (to) the; **ich gab es der Frau** I gave it to the woman.

der *pronoun* **1** who; **der Mann, der hier wohnt** the man who lives here; **2** which; **der Regenschirm, der mir gehört** the umbrella which is mine; **3 der da** that one; **4** him, he.

deren *pronoun* **1** their; **die Kinder und deren Hund** the children and their dog; **2** whose; **3** of which.

derselbe *pronoun* the same, same one.

des *article* **1** (masculine and neuter genetive singular) of the; **das Klingeln des Telefons** the ringing of the phone; **2 der Ball des Jungen** the boy's ball.

a b c d e f g h i j k l m n o p q r s t u v w x y z

deshalb *adverb* **1** therefore;
2 that's why.

Desinfektionsmittel *das* (PL die
Desinfektionsmittel) disinfectant.

desinfizieren *verb* (PERF **hat
desinfiziert**) to disinfect.

dessen *pronoun* **1** his; **2** its;
3 whose; **der Junge, dessen
Mutter weint** the boy whose
mother is crying; **4** of which.

desto *adverb* the; **je mehr, desto
besser** the more the better.

deswegen *conjunction*
1 therefore; **2** that's why.

Detektiv *der* (PL die Detektive)
detective.

deutlich *adjective* clear.

deutlich *adverb* **ich konnte ihn
deutlich sehen** I could clearly see
him.

Deutsch *das* German; **auf
Deutsch** in German; **fließend
Deutsch sprechen** to speak fluent
German.

deutsch *adjective* German.

Deutsche *der/die* (PL die
Deutschen) German; **er ist
Deutscher** he's German.

Deutschland *das* Germany; **nach
Deutschland** to Germany.

Devisen *plural noun* foreign
currency.

Dezember *der* December; **am
ersten Dezember** on the first of
December; **im Dezember** in
December.

Dezimalzahl *die* (PL die
Dezimalzahlen) decimal (number).

d. h. (*das heißt*) i.e.

Dia *das* (PL die Dias) slide.

Diagnose *die* (PL die Diagnosen)
diagnosis.

diagonal *adjective* diagonal.

Diagramm *das* (PL die Diagramme)
diagram.

Dialekt *der* (PL die Dialekte) dialect.

Dialog *der* (PL die Dialoge) dialogue.

Diamant *der* (PL die Diamanten)
diamond.

Diät *die* (PL die Diäten) diet;
jemanden auf Diät setzen to put
somebody on a diet.

dich *pronoun* **1** you; **2** yourself.

dicht *adjective* **1** thick (*fog*);
2 dense; **3** watertight; **4** airtight;
5 **er ist nicht ganz dicht**
(*informal*) he's off his head.

dicht *adverb* **1** densely; **2** tightly;
3 close; **geh nicht so dicht an den
Käfig** don't go so close to the cage;
dicht bei close to.

Dichter *der* (PL die Dichter) poet.

Dichterin *die* (PL die Dichterinnen)
poet.

Dichtung *die* (PL die Dichtungen)
1 poetry; **2** seal, washer.

dick *adjective* **1** thick; **2** swollen
(*ankle, tonsils*); **3** fat (*person*).

Dickkopf *der* (PL die Dickköpfe)
1 stubborn person; **2** **einen
Dickkopf haben** to be stubborn.

die *article (feminine and plural)*
the; **die Frau** the woman; **die
Bücher** the books.

die *pronoun (feminine and plural)*
1 who; **die Frau, die hier wohnt**

the woman who lives here; **die Frau, die ich kenne** the woman I know; **die Kinder, die ich gefragt habe** the children I asked; **2** which; **die Tasche, die ich gekauft habe** the bag I bought; **3** she, her; **4** them; **ich meine die** I mean them; **5 die da** that one, (*plural*) those.

Dieb *der* (PL die **Diebe**) thief.

Diebin *die* (PL die **Diebinnen**) thief.

Diebstahl *der* (PL die **Diebstähle**) theft.

Diele *die* (PL die **Dielen**) **1** hall; **2** floorboard.

dienen *verb* (PERF **hat gedient**) to serve.

Dienst *der* (PL die **Dienste**) service; **Dienst haben** to work, to be on duty (*of a soldier or doctor*).

Dienstag *der* (PL die **Dienstage**) Tuesday; **am Dienstag** on Tuesday.

dienstags *adverb* on Tuesdays.

dienstfrei *adjective* **1** ein **dienstfreier Tag** a day off; **2 dienstfrei haben** to have time off, to be off duty.

dienstlich *adverb* on business.

Dienstreise *die* (PL die **Dienstreisen**) business trip.

diese SEE **dieser**.

Diesel *der* diesel.

dieselbe *pronoun* the same, the same one.

dieser, diese, dieses *adjective* **1** this; **2** these; **diese Äpfel** these apples.

dieses *pronoun* **1** this one; **mir gefällt dieses am besten** I like this one best; **2** these ones.

diesmal *adverb* this time.

Digitaluhr *die* (PL die **Digitaluhren**) **1** digital watch; **2** digital clock.

Diktat *das* (PL die **Diktate**) dictation.

Ding *das* (PL die **Dinge**) thing; **vor allen Dingen** above all; **das war ein Ding** (*informal*) that was quite something.

Dings *das* (PL die/das thingummy.

Dinosaurier *der* (PL die **Dinosaurier**) dinosaur.

Diplom *das* (PL die **Diplome**) diploma.

dir *pronoun* **1** you, to you; **sie hat es dir gegeben** she gave it to you; **ich verspreche dir, dass** ... I promise you that ...; **2 Freunde von dir** friends of yours; **3** yourself.

direkt *adjective* direct.

direkt *adverb* direct; **der Bus fährt direkt zum Flughafen** the bus goes direct to the airport.

Direktor *der* (PL die **Direktoren**) **1** director; **2** headmaster, principal; **3** manager (*of a bank, theatre*).

Direktorin *die* (PL die **Direktorinnen**) **1** director; **2** headmistress, principal; **3** manager (*of a bank, theatre*).

Direktübertragung *die* (PL die **Direktübertragungen**) live transmission.

Dirigent *der* (PL die **Dirigenten**) conductor.

a b c d e f g h i j k l m n o p q r s t u v w x y z

dirigieren verb (PERF **hat dirigiert**) to conduct.

Diskette die (PL die **Disketten**) floppy disk.

Diskettenlaufwerk das (PL die **Diskettenlaufwerke**) disk drive.

Disko die (PL die **Diskos**) disco.

Diskothek die (PL die **Diskotheken**) disco, discotheque.

Diskriminierung die discrimination; **die Diskriminierung von Frauen** discrimination against women.

Diskussion die (PL die **Diskussionen**) discussion; **zur Diskussion stehen** to be under discussion.

diskutieren verb (PERF **hat diskutiert**) to discuss.

Disziplin die (PL die **Disziplinen**) discipline.

DJH die (*Deutsche Jugendherberge*) German youth hostel (association).

DM die (*Deutsche Mark*) DM, Deutschmark SEE **Mark.**

D-Mark die (PL die **D-Mark**) Deutschmark, German mark SEE **Mark.**

doch adverb 1 yes (*when you are contradicting somebody*); **'hast du keinen Hunger?' – 'doch!'** 'aren't you hungry?' – 'yes, I am!'; 2 after all; **sie hat ihn doch eingeladen** she invited him after all; **sie ist doch nicht gekommen** she hasn't come after all; 3 **er hat doch meinen Brief bekommen?** he did get my letter, didn't he?; **sie kommt doch?** she's coming, isn't

she?; 4 anyway; **du hörst ja doch nicht auf mich** you won't listen to me anyway; 5 **pass doch auf!** do be careful!.

doch conjunction but.

Doktor der (PL die **Doktoren**) doctor; **den Doktor machen** to do a doctorate.

Dokument das (PL die **Dokumente**) document.

Dokumentarfilm der (PL die **Dokumentarfilme**) documentary.

Dokumentarsendung die (PL die **Dokumentarsendungen**) documentary (programme).

dolmetschen verb (PERF **hat gedolmetscht**) to interpret.

Dolmetscher der (PL die **Dolmetscher**) interpreter.

Dolmetscherin die (PL die **Dolmetscherinnen**) interpreter.

Dom der (PL die **Dome**) cathedral.

Donau die Danube.

Donner der thunder.

donnern verb (PERF **hat gedonnert**) to thunder.

Donnerstag der (PL die **Donnerstage**) Thursday; **am Donnerstag** on Thursday.

donnerstags adverb on Thursdays.

doof adjective (*informal*) stupid.

Doppel das (PL die **Doppel**) 1 duplicate; 2 doubles (*in sport*).

Doppelbett das (PL die **Doppelbetten**) double bed.

Doppelfenster das (PL die **Doppelfenster**) double-glazed window; **wir haben Doppelfenster** we've got double glazing.

Doppelhaus das (PL die **Doppelhäuser**) semi-detached house.

Doppelklick der (PL die **Doppelklicks**) double-click (*with mouse*).

Doppelpunkt der (PL die **Doppelpunkte**) colon.

doppelt adjective **1** double; **2 in doppelter Ausführung** in duplicate; **3 die doppelte Menge** twice the amount.

doppelt adverb **1** doubly; **2** twice; **doppelt so viel** twice as much; **sich doppelt anstrengen** to try twice as hard.

Doppelzimmer das (PL die **Doppelzimmer**) double room.

Dorf das (PL die **Dörfer**) village.

Dorn der (PL die **Dornen**) thorn.

dort adverb there; **dort drüben** over there.

dorther adverb from there.

dorthin adverb there; **geht ihr jetzt dorthin?** are you going there now?

Dose die (PL die **Dosen**) tin, can.

dösen verb (PERF hat **gedöst**) to doze.

Dosenöffner der (PL die **Dosenöffner**) tin opener.

Dosierung die (PL die **Dosierungen**) dose.

Dosis die (PL die **Dosen**) dose.

Dotter der (PL die **Dotter**) yolk.

Dozent der (PL die **Dozenten**) lecturer.

Dozentin die (PL die **Dozentinnen**) lecturer.

Drache der (PL die **Drachen**) dragon.

Drachen der (PL die **Drachen**) kite.

Drachenfliegen das hang-gliding; **Drachenfliegen gehen** to go hang-gliding.

Draht der (PL die **Drähte**) **1** wire; **2 er ist auf Draht** (*informal*) he's on the ball.

Drama das (PL die **Dramen**) drama.

Dramatik die drama.

dran adverb SEE **daran 1 ich bin dran** it's my turn; **wer ist dran?** whose turn is it?; **2 gut dran sein** to be well off; **3 arm dran sein** to be in a bad way; **4 spät dran sein** to be late.

drängen verb (PERF hat **gedrängt**) **1** to push; **2** to press, to urge (*somebody*); **3 sich drängen** to crowd; **die Leute drängten sich vor der Kasse** people crowded around the box-office.

drankommen ✧verb (IMPERF kam **dran**, PERF ist **drangekommen**) to have your turn; **wer kommt dran?** whose turn is it?

drauf adverb SEE **darauf 1 drauf und dran sein, etwas zu tun** to be on the point of doing something; **2 gut drauf sein** (*informal*) to be in a good mood.

draußen adverb outside.

Dreck der dirt.

a
b
c
d
e
f
g
h
i
j
k
l
m
n
o
p
q
r
s
t
u
v
w
x
y
z

a
b
c
d
e
f
g
h
i
j
k
l
m
n
o
p
q
r
s
t
u
v
w
x
y
z

dreckig *adjective* dirty, filthy.

Drehbuch *das* (PL *die* Drehbücher)
1 screenplay; 2 script.

drehen *verb* (PERF hat gedreht)
1 to turn; **an etwas drehen** to turn
something; 2 to shoot (*a film*);
3 **sich drehen** to turn; 4 **sich im
Kreis drehen** to rotate; 5 **es dreht
sich um ihr Taschengeld** it's about
her pocket money.

Drei *die* (PL *die* Dreien) three.

drei *number* three.

Dreieck *das* (PL *die* Dreiecke)
triangle.

dreieckig *adjective* triangular.

dreifach *adjective* triple.

dreihundert *number* three
hundred.

dreimal *adverb* three times.

Dreirad *das* (PL *die* Dreiräder)
tricycle.

dreißig *number* thirty.

drei viertel *number* three-
quarters.

Dreiviertelstunde *die* (PL *die*
Dreiviertelstunden) three-
quarters of an hour.

dreizehn *number* thirteen.

drin *adverb* SEE **darin**; **drin sein** to
be inside.

dringend *adjective* urgent.

drinnen *adverb* 1 inside;
2 indoors.

dritt *adverb* **sie sind zu dritt** there
are three of them.

dritte SEE **dritter**.

Drittel *das* (PL *die* Drittel) third.

drittens *adverb* thirdly.

dritter, dritte, drittes *adjective*
third; **zum dritten Mal** for the third
time; **ein Dritter** a third person;
jeder Dritte, der mitwollte every
third person who wanted to come;
die Dritte Welt the Third World.

Droge *die* (PL *die* Drogen) drug.

drogenabhängig *adjective*
addicted to drugs.

Drogenabhängige *der/die* (PL *die*
Drogenabhängigen) drug addict.

Drogenabhängigkeit *die* drug
addiction.

drogensüchtig *adjective*
addicted to drugs.

Drogensüchtige *der/die* (PL *die*
Drogensüchtigen) drug addict.

Drogerie *die* (PL *die* Drogerien)
chemist's.

Drogist *der* (PL *die* Drogisten)
chemist.

Drogistin *die* (PL *die* Drogistinnen)
chemist.

drohen *verb* (PERF hat gedroht) to
threaten; **jemandem drohen** to
threaten somebody.

Drohung *die* (PL *die* Drohungen)
threat.

Drossel *die* (PL *die* Drosseln)
1 thrush (*bird*); 2 throttle.

drüben *adverb* over there.

Druck *der* 1 pressure; **jemanden
unter Druck setzen** to put
pressure on somebody; 2 printing;
3 (PL *die* Drucke) print.

drücken *verb* (PERF hat gedrückt)
1 to press; 2 **an der Tür drücken** to

push the door; **'bitte drücken'** 'push'; **3** to hug; **4** to pinch (*of shoes*); **5 die Preise drücken** to force down prices; **6 sich vor etwas drücken** (*informal*) to get out of something; **du hast dich mal wieder vor dem Aufräumen gedrückt** you've got out of tidying up again.

drucken *verb* (PERF **hat gedruckt**) to print.

Drucker der (PL die **Drucker**) printer.

Druckknopf der (PL die **Druckknöpfe**) press stud.

Druckluftmesser der (PL die **Druckluftmesser**) pressure gauge.

Drucksache die (PL die **Drucksachen**) printed matter.

Druckschrift die (PL die **Druckschriften**) **1** block letters; **2** type; **3** pamphlet.

Drüse die (PL die **Drüsen**) gland.

Dschungel der (PL die **Dschungel**) jungle.

du *pronoun* **1** you; **2 du sagen** to say 'du' (to each other); **per du sein** to be on familiar terms (*'du' is used when talking to family members, close friends, or people of your own age; otherwise 'Sie' is used*).

Dudelsack der (PL die **Dudelsäcke**) bagpipes.

Duft der (PL die **Düfte**) fragrance, scent.

duften *verb* (PERF **hat geduftet**) to smell; **nach Lavendel duften** to smell of lavender.

dumm *adjective* **1** stupid; **2 das wird mir jetzt zu dumm** (*informal*) I've had enough of it; **3 so etwas Dummes!** how annoying!; **4 der Dumme sein** to draw the short straw.

dummerweise *adverb* stupidly.

Dummheit die (PL die **Dummheiten**) **1** stupidity; **2** stupid thing; **mach keine Dummheiten** don't do anything stupid.

Dummkopf der (PL die **Dummköpfe**) fool.

Dünger der (PL die **Dünger**) fertilizer.

dunkel *adjective* **1** dark; **ein dunkler Anzug** a dark suit; **2 im Dunkeln** in the dark; **3** vague (*idea*); **4** shady (*business*); **5** deep (*voice*).

Dunkelheit die darkness, dark; **bei Einbruch der Dunkelheit** at dusk.

dünn *adjective* **1** thin; **2** weak (*coffee, tea*).

Dunst der (PL die **Dünste**) haze.

Duo das (PL die **Duos**) duet.

durch *preposition* (+ ACC) **1** through; **er ist durch das Fernsehen bekannt geworden** he's become famous through television; **2** by; **durch Boten** by courier; **3 acht durch zwei ist vier** eight divided by two is four; **4** due to.

durch *adverb* **1** through; **die ganze Nacht durch** all through the night; **2 den Winter durch** throughout the winter; **3 durch und durch** completely; **4 es war acht Uhr**

a b c d e f g h i j k l m n o p q r s t u v w x y z

a
b
c
d
e
f
g
h
i
j
k
l
m
n
o
p
q
r
s
t
u
v
w
x
y
z

durch (*informal*) it was gone eight o'clock.

durcharbeiten *verb* (PERF **hat durchgearbeitet**) **1** to work through; **die Nacht durcharbeiten** to work through the night; **2 sich durch etwas durcharbeiten** to work your way through something.

durchaus *adverb* absolutely.

durchblicken *verb* (PERF **hat durchgeblickt**) **1** (*informal*) to understand; **durchblicken lassen, dass** ... to hint that ....

durchbrechen ◇*verb* (PRES **bricht durch,** IMPERF **brach durch,** PERF **hat durchgebrochen**) **1** to snap, to break in two; **2** (PERF **ist durchgebrochen**) **das Brett ist durchgebrochen** the board has snapped.

Durcheinander *das* **1** muddle; **2** mess; **in der Wohnung herrschte ein fürchterliches Durcheinander** the flat was a terrible mess; **3** confusion; **im allgemeinen Durcheinander** in the general confusion.

durcheinander *adverb* **1** in a mess; **mein Zimmer ist durcheinander** my room is (in) a mess; **2 die Akten durcheinander bringen** to muddle up the files; **Karl hat ihre Namen durcheinander gebracht** Karl got their names mixed up; **3** confused; **bring mich nicht durcheinander** don't confuse me; **4 sie haben alle durcheinander geredet** they all talked at once.

durcheinanderbringen SEE **durcheinander.**

durchfahren ◇*verb* (PRES **fährt durch,** IMPERF **fuhr durch,** PERF **ist durchgefahren**) **1** to drive through; **2** to go through; **3 der Zug fährt (in Stuttgart) durch** the train doesn't stop (in Stuttgart).

Durchfall *der* diarrhoea.

durchfallen ◇*verb* (PRES **fällt durch,** IMPERF **fiel durch,** PERF **ist durchgefallen**) **1** to fall through; **2** to fail (*an exam*).

durchführen *verb* (PERF **hat durchgeführt**) to carry out.

Durchgang *der* (PL **die Durchgänge**) **1** passage; **2 'Durchgang verboten'** 'no entry'; **3** round (*in sport*).

Durchgangsverkehr *der* through traffic.

durchgehen ◇*verb* (IMPERF **ging durch,** PERF **ist durchgegangen**) **1** to go through; **2** (*informal*) to escape; **3 jemanden etwas durchgehen lassen** to let somebody get away with something.

durchkommen ◇*verb* (IMPERF **kam durch,** PERF **ist durchgekommen**) **1** to come through; **2** to get through (*on the phone, in an exam*); **3** to pull through (*after an illness*).

durchlassen ◇*verb* (PRES **lässt durch,** IMPERF **ließ durch,** PERF **hat durchgelassen**) **1** to let through; **2** to let in.

durchmachen verb (PERF **hat durchgemacht**) **1** to go through; **2** to work through (your lunch break, for example); **3 wir haben die Nacht durchgemacht** we made a night of it.

Durchmesser der (PL die **Durchmesser**) diameter.

durchnehmen ◇verb (PRES **nimmt durch**, IMPERF **nahm durch**, PERF **hat durchgenommen**) to do (a topic at school).

durchs = durch das.

Durchsage die (PL die **Durchsagen**) announcement.

Durchschnitt der (PL die **Durchschnitte**) average; **im Durchschnitt** on average.

durchschnittlich adjective average.

durchschnittlich adverb on average.

durchsetzen verb (PERF **hat durchgesetzt**) **1** to carry through; **2 sich durchsetzen** to assert yourself; **3 sich durchsetzen** to catch on (of a fashion, an idea).

durchsichtig adjective transparent.

durchstreichen ◇verb (IMPERF **strich durch**, PERF **hat durchgestrichen**) to cross out.

Durchzug der draught.

dürfen ◇verb (PRES **darf**, IMPERF **durfte**, PERF **hat gedurft** or **hat dürfen**) **1** to be allowed; **sie darf das nicht** she's not allowed to do that; **er hat nicht gedurft** he wasn't allowed to; **2 Klaus hat sie im** Krankenhaus besuchen dürfen Klaus was allowed to visit her in hospital; **3 darf ich?** may I?; **4 das dürfen Sie nicht vergessen** you mustn't forget that; **du darfst es nicht alles so ernst nehmen** you mustn't take it all so seriously; **5 du darfst froh sein, dass sonst nichts passiert ist** you should be glad that nothing else happened; **das darf einfach nicht passieren** that just shouldn't happen; **das dürfte nicht schwierig sein** that shouldn't be difficult; **6 das darf nicht wahr sein!** I don't believe it!; **7 was darf es sein?** can I help you?; **8 das dürfte der Grund sein** that's probably the reason.

durfte, durften, durftest, durftet SEE **dürfen**.

dürftig adjective poor, meagre.

Dürre die (PL die **Dürren**) drought.

Durst der thirst; **Durst haben** to be thirsty.

durstig adjective thirsty.

Dusche die (PL die **Duschen**) shower.

duschen verb (PERF **hat geduscht**) **1** to have a shower; **2 sich duschen** to have a shower.

Düsenflugzeug das (PL die **Düsenflugzeuge**) jet (plane).

düster adjective **1** gloomy (future, thoughts); **2** dark.

Dutzend das (PL die **Dutzende**) dozen.

duzen verb (PERF **hat geduzt**) to call somebody 'du'; **wollen wir uns duzen?** shall we say 'du' to each other? ('*du*' is used when talking to family members, close friends, or people of your own age).

dynamisch *adjective* dynamic.

D-Zug *der* (PL die **D-Züge**) fast train, express.

Ee

Ebbe *die* (PL die **Ebben**) low tide; **es ist Ebbe** the tide is out.

eben *adjective* **1** flat; **2** level.

eben *adverb* **1** just; **Gabi war eben hier** Gabi was just here; **eben noch** just now; **2 eben!** exactly!

Ebene *die* (PL die **Ebenen**) **1** plain; **2** level; **3** plane (*in geometry*).

ebenso *adverb* just as; **Ulla hat den Film ebenso oft gesehen wie du** Ulla's seen the film just as often as you; **ich habe ebenso viel Arbeit wie du** I've got just as much work as you.

Echo *das* (PL die **Echos**) echo.

echt *adjective* real, genuine; **die Kette ist aus echtem Gold** the necklace is real gold.

echt *adverb* (*informal*) really; **das ist echt gut** that's really good.

Eckball *der* (PL die **Eckbälle**) corner (kick).

Ecke *die* (PL die **Ecken**) corner; **um die Ecke** round the corner.

eckig *adjective* square.

Edelstein *der* (PL die **Edelsteine**) precious stone.

EDV *die* (*elektronische Datenverarbeitung*) electronic data processing, EDP.

Efeu *der* (PL die **Efeus**) ivy.

Effekt *der* (PL die **Effekte**) effect.

effektiv *adjective* effective.

effektiv *adverb* really, actually.

EG *die* (*Europäische Gemeinschaft*) EC.

egal *adjective* **1 das ist mir egal** it's all the same to me; **2 egal, wie groß** no matter how big; **egal, ob er es will oder nicht** (it doesn't matter) whether he wants to or not.

egoistisch *adjective* selfish.

Ehe *die* (PL die **Ehen**) marriage.

ehe *conjunction* before; **ehe ich nicht weiß, was er will, mache ich nichts** I won't do anything before I know what he wants.

Ehefrau *die* (PL die **Ehefrauen**) wife.

ehemalig *adjective* former.

Ehemann *der* (PL die **Ehemänner**) husband.

Ehepaar *das* (PL die **Ehepaare**) married couple.

eher *adverb* **1** earlier, sooner; **je eher, desto besser** the sooner the better; **2** rather; **eher gehe ich zu Fuß, als Geld für ein Taxi auszugeben** I'd rather walk than pay for a taxi; **3** more; **das ist schon eher möglich** that's more likely.

Ehre *die* (PL die **Ehren**) honour.

ehrenamtlich *adjective* honorary.

Ehrgeiz *der* ambition.

ehrgeizig *adjective* ambitious.

ehrlich *adjective* honest.

Ehrlichkeit *die* honesty.

Ei *das* (PL die **Eier**) egg.

Eiche *die* (PL die **Eichen**) oak.

Eichhörnchen *das* (PL die **Eichhörnchen**) squirrel.

Eid *der* (PL die **Eide**) oath.

Eidechse *die* (PL die **Eidechsen**) lizard.

Eidotter *das* (PL die **Eidotter**) egg yolk.

Eierbecher *der* (PL die **Eierbecher**) egg-cup.

Eierschale *die* (PL die **Eierschalen**) eggshell.

Eifer *der* eagerness.

Eifersucht *die* jealousy.

eifersüchtig *adjective* jealous; **auf jemanden eifersüchtig sein** to be jealous of somebody.

eifrig *adjective* eager.

Eigelb *das* (PL die **Eigelb(e)**) egg yolk.

eigen *adjective* own; **sie ist erst siebzehn und hat schon ihr eigenes Auto** she's only seventeen and she's already got her own car.

Eigenart *die* (PL die **Eigenarten**) peculiarity.

eigenartig *adjective* peculiar.

Eigenschaft *die* (PL die **Eigenschaften**) 1 quality; 2 characteristic.

eigensinnig *adjective* obstinate.

eigentlich *adjective* actual.

eigentlich *adverb* actually; **eigentlich habe ich keine Lust, heute ins Kino zu gehen** actually I don't fancy going to the cinema today.

Eigentum *das* property.

Eigentümer *der* (PL die **Eigentümer**) owner.

eignen *verb* (PERF **hat sich geeignet**) **sich eignen** to be suitable.

Eile *die* hurry.

eilen *verb* 1 (PERF **ist geeilt**) to hurry; 2 (PERF **hat geeilt**) to be urgent; **das eilt nicht** it's not urgent.

eilig *adjective* 1 urgent; 2 hurried; 3 **es eilig haben** to be in a hurry.

Eilzug *der* (PL die **Eilzüge**) fast stopping train.

Eimer *der* (PL die **Eimer**) bucket.

ein, eine, ein *article* a, an; **ein Haus** a house; **eine Allergie** an allergy; **ein bisschen mehr** a bit more; **was für ein Kleid hast du gekauft?** what sort of dress did you buy?

ein *adjective* 1 one; **sie haben nur ein Kind** they've got just one child; **eines Abends** one evening; 2 **einer Meinung sein** to be of the same opinion; 3 **ein für alle Mal** once and for all.

einander *pronoun* each other, one another.

Einbahnstraße *die* (PL die **Einbahnstraßen**) one-way street.

Einband *der* (PL die **Einbände**) cover.

a b c d e f g h i j k l m n o p q r s t u v w x y z

einbauen verb (PERF **hat eingebaut**) **1** to fit; **2** to install.

Einbauküche die (PL die **Einbauküchen**) fitted kitchen.

einbiegen ✧verb (IMPERF **bog ein**, PERF **ist eingebogen**) to turn; **der Radfahrer bog langsam in die Seitenstraße ein** the cyclist turned slowly down the side street.

einbilden verb (PERF **hat sich eingebildet**) **1** sich einbilden to imagine; **das bildest du dir nur ein** you're only imagining it; **2** Till bildet sich viel ein Till is very conceited.

Einbildung die imagination; **das ist alles nur Einbildung** it's all in the mind.

einbrechen ✧verb (PRES **bricht ein**, IMPERF **brach ein**, PERF **ist eingebrochen**) to break in; **in unserem Haus sind Diebe eingebrochen** thieves broke into our house; **bei unseren Nachbarn ist eingebrochen worden** our neighbours have been burgled.

Einbrecher der (PL die **Einbrecher**) burglar.

einbringen verb (IMPERF **brachte ein**, PERF **hat eingebracht**) to bring in; **die Ernte einbringen** to gather in the harvest.

Einbruch der (PL die **Einbrüche**) **1** burglary; **2** vor Einbruch der Dunkelheit before it gets dark; **3** bei Einbruch der Nacht at nightfall.

einchecken verb (PERF **hat eingecheckt**) **am Flughafen**

einchecken to check in at the airport.

eindeutig adjective **1** clear; **2** definite (proof).

Eindruck der (PL die **Eindrücke**) impression; **einen guten Eindruck auf jemanden machen** to make a good impression on somebody.

eindrucksvoll adjective impressive.

eine SEE ein, einer.

eineinhalb number one and a half.

einer, eine, ein(e)s pronoun **1** one; **einer von uns** one of us; **wie soll das einer wissen?** how is one supposed to know?; **2** somebody; **3** kaum einer** hardly anyone; **4** you; **das macht einen müde** it makes you tired.

einerseits adverb on the one hand; **einerseits sagt sie, dass sie kein Geld hat, andererseits kauft sie sich dauernd neue Sachen** on the one hand she claims to have no money, on the other hand she's constantly buying new things.

eines SEE einer.

einfach adjective **1** simple; **2** easy; **3** single (ticket, knot).

einfach adverb simply.

Einfachheit die simplicity.

Einfahrt die (PL die **Einfahrten**) **1** entrance; **2** arrival (of a train); **3** slip road (on a motorway).

Einfall der (PL die **Einfälle**) idea.

einfallen ✧verb (PRES **fällt ein**, IMPERF **fiel ein**, PERF **ist eingefallen**) **1** jemandem einfallen to occur to somebody; **2** ihr Name fällt mir

nicht ein I can't think of her name; **3 was fällt dir eigentlich ein?** what do you think you're doing?; **4 sich etwas einfallen lassen** to think of something.

Einfamilienhaus das (PL die Einfamilienhäuser) detached family house.

Einfluss der (PL die Einflüsse) influence.

einfrieren ⬦verb (IMPERF fror ein, PERF ist eingefroren) **1** to freeze; **2** (PERF hat eingefroren) to freeze (food in the freezer).

Einfuhr die (PL die Einfuhren) import.

einführen verb (PERF hat eingeführt) **1** to import; **2** to introduce.

Einführung die (PL die Einführungen) introduction.

Eingabe die input (of data).

Eingang der (PL die Eingänge) entrance.

Eingangshalle die (PL die Eingangshallen) hallway.

eingeben ⬦verb (PRES gibt ein, IMPERF gab ein, PERF hat eingegeben) **1** to hand in; **2** to input, to key in.

eingebildet adjective **1** conceited; **2** imaginary (illness).

Eingeborene der/die (PL die Eingeborenen) native.

eingehen ⬦verb (IMPERF ging ein, PERF ist eingegangen) **1** to shrink (of clothes); **2** to die (of plants); **3** to arrive (of goods); **4** auf etwas eingehen to go into something; sie

ging näher darauf ein she went into it in more detail; **5 auf etwas nicht eingehen** to ignore something; **6 auf etwas eingehen** to agree to something; **Oliver ist auf unseren Plan eingegangen** Oliver agreed to our plan; **7 ein Risiko eingehen** to take a risk.

eingeschrieben adjective registered; **ein eingeschriebener Brief** a registered letter.

eingestellt adjective **1 auf etwas eingestellt sein** to be prepared for something; **2 fortschrittlich eingestellt sein** to be progressively minded.

eingewöhnen verb (PERF hat sich eingewöhnt) **sich eingewöhnen** to settle in.

eingießen ⬦verb (IMPERF goss ein, PERF hat eingegossen) to pour.

Eingriff der (PL die Eingriffe) **1** intervention; **2** operation (surgical).

einheimisch adjective **1** native; **2** local.

Einheit die (PL die Einheiten) **1** unity; **2** unit (of drink, soldiers).

Einheitspreis der (PL die Einheitspreise) **1** standard price; **2** flat fare.

einholen verb (PERF hat eingeholt) **1** to catch up with; **2** to make up (time, a delay); **3** to buy; **einholen gehen** to go shopping.

einhundert number one hundred.

einige SEE einiger.

einigen verb (PERF hat sich geeinigt) **sich einigen** to come to

a
b
c
d
e
f
g
h
i
j
k
l
m
n
o
p
q
r
s
t
u
v
w
x
y
z

an agreement; **sich auf etwas einigen** to agree on something.

einiger, einige, einiges *adjective, pronoun* 1 some; **vor einiger Zeit** some time ago; 2 several; 3 **nur einige waren noch da** there were only a few left; 4 **einiges** quite a lot; **wir haben einiges gesehen** we saw quite a lot (of things); 5 **einiges** some things; **einiges hat uns nicht gefallen** there were some things we didn't like.

einigermaßen *adverb* 1 fairly; 2 fairly well; 3 '**wie geht es dir?**'– '**einigermaßen**' 'how are you?' – 'so-so'.

einiges SEE **einiger**.

Einigung die agreement.

Einkauf der (PL die **Einkäufe**) 1 purchase; 2 shopping; **Einkäufe machen** to do some shopping.

einkaufen *verb* (PERF **hat eingekauft**) 1 to buy; **ich habe vergessen Milch einzukaufen** I forgot to buy milk; 2 to shop; **wir kaufen meist im Supermarkt ein** we usually shop at the supermarket; **einkaufen gehen** to go shopping.

Einkaufsbummel der (PL die **Einkaufsbummel**) shopping spree.

Einkaufswagen der (PL die **Einkaufswagen**) shopping trolley.

Einkaufszentrum das (PL die **Einkaufszentren**) shopping centre.

Einkommen das (PL die **Einkommen**) income.

einladen ✧*verb* (PRES **lädt ein**, IMPERF **lud ein**, PERF **hat eingeladen**)

1 to invite; **jemanden zum Abendessen einladen** to invite somebody for dinner; 2 **jemanden ins Kino einladen** to take sombody to the cinema; 3 to treat; **ich lade euch ein** I'll treat you; 4 to load (*goods*).

Einladung die (PL die **Einladungen**) invitation.

einleben *verb* (PERF **hat sich eingelebt**) **sich einleben** to settle down.

Einleitung die (PL die **Einleitungen**) introduction.

einlösen *verb* (PERF **hat eingelöst**) to cash.

einmal *adverb* 1 once (*in the past*); **es war einmal ...** once upon a time ...; 2 one day (*in the future*); 3 **auf einmal** suddenly; 4 **auf einmal** at the same time; **sie kamen alle auf einmal** they all came at the same time; 5 **nicht einmal** not even; 6 **noch einmal** again; 7 **es geht nun einmal nicht** it's just not possible.

einmalig *adjective* 1 unique; 2 fantastic; 3 single, one-off (*payment*).

einmischen *verb* (PERF **hat sich eingemischt**) **sich einmischen** to interfere.

Einmündung die (PL die **Einmündungen**) 1 junction (*of roads*); 2 confluence (*of rivers*).

einordnen *verb* (PERF **hat eingeordnet**) 1 to put in order; 2 **sich einordnen** to fit in (*with* *other people*); **3 sich einordnen** to get in lane (*when driving*).

einpacken *verb* (PERF **hat eingepackt**) **1** to pack; **2** to wrap.

einreichen *verb* (PERF **hat eingereicht**) to hand in.

Einreise *die* (PL die **Einreisen**) entry.

einreisen *verb* (PERF **ist eingereist**) to enter a country; **er reiste nach Italien ein** he entered Italy.

einrichten *verb* (PERF **hat eingerichtet**) **1** to furnish; **2** to set up (*an organisation*); **3** to arrange; **kannst du es so einrichten, dass du vormittags da bist?** can you arrange to be here in the morning?; **4 sich einrichten** to furnish your home; **5 sich einrichten** to economize; **6 sich auf etwas einrichten** to prepare for something.

Einrichtung *die* (PL die **Einrichtungen**) **1** furnishing; **2** furnishings; **3** setting up; **4** institution; **staatliche Einrichtungen** state institutions.

Eins *die* (PL die **Einsen**) one.

eins *number* one; **eins zu eins** one all; **es ist eins** it's one o'clock.

eins *pronoun* SEE **einer**

eins *adjective* **mir ist alles eins** it's all the same to me.

einsam *adjective* lonely.

einsammeln *verb* (PERF **hat eingesammelt**) to collect.

Einsatz *der* **1** use; **2** stake (*when betting*).

einschalten *verb* (PERF **hat eingeschaltet**) **1** to switch on (*a radio, TV*); **2 sich einschalten** to intervene.

einschlafen ◇*verb* (PRES **schläft ein**, IMPERF **schlief ein**, PERF **ist eingeschlafen**) to go to sleep.

einschließen ◇*verb* (IMPERF **schloss ein**, PERF **hat eingeschlossen**) **1** to lock in; **2** to include; **3 sich einschließen** to lock yourself in.

einschließlich *preposition* (+ GEN) including; **einschließlich der Unkosten** including expenses.

einschließlich *adverb* inclusive.

einschränken *verb* (PERF **hat eingeschränkt**) **1** to restrict; **2** to cut back; **3 sich einschränken** to economize.

einschreiben ◇*verb* (IMPERF **schrieb ein**, PERF **hat sich eingeschrieben**) **1 sich einschreiben** to enrol (*at university*); **2 sich einschreiben** to put your name down.

Einschreiben *das* (PL die **Einschreiben**) registered letter, registered parcel; **per Einschreiben** registered.

einsehen ◇*verb* (PRES **sieht ein**, IMPERF **sah ein**, PERF **hat eingesehen**) **1** to realize; **2** to see; **das sehe ich nicht ein** I don't see why.

einseitig *adjective* one-sided.

einsenden ◇*verb* (IMPERF **sendete ein/sandte ein**, PERF **hat**

a b c d e f g h i j k l m n o p q r s t u v w x y z

a
b
c
d
e
f
g
h
i
j
k
l
m
n
o
p
q
r
s
t
u
v
w
x
y
z

eingesendet/hat eingesandt) to send in.

einsetzen *verb* (PERF hat eingesetzt) 1 to put in (*a missing part*) to insert; 2 to use; **während der Weltmeisterschaft wurden Sonderzüge eingesetzt** special trains were put on during the World Cup; 3 to stake (*money*); 4 to start (*of rain, snow*); 5 **sich für jemanden einsetzen** to support somebody.

Einsicht *die* 1 insight; 2 sense; 3 **zu der Einsicht kommen, dass** ... to come to realize that ....

einsperren *verb* (PERF hat eingesperrt) to lock up.

Einspruch *der* (PL die **Einsprüche**) objection.

einst *adverb* 1 once; 2 one day (*in the future*).

einstecken *verb* (PERF hat eingesteckt) 1 to put in (*a coin*); 2 **einen Brief einstecken** to post a letter; 3 to plug in; 4 **etwas einstecken** to put something in your pocket or bag, to take something; 5 (*informal*) to take (*insults*).

einsteigen ◇*verb* (IMPERF stieg ein, PERF ist eingestiegen) 1 to get in; 2 to get on (*a bus or train*).

einstellen *verb* (PERF hat eingestellt) 1 to employ (*in a job*); 2 to adjust (*a machine*); 3 to focus (*a camera*); 4 to tune into (*a radio station*); 5 to stop; 6 **sich auf etwas einstellen** to prepare yourself for something; 7 **sich schnell auf eine**

neue Situation einstellen to adjust quickly to a new situation.

Einstellung *die* (PL die **Einstellungen**) 1 employment; 2 adjustment; 3 stopping; 4 take (*of a film*); 5 attitude; **seine politische Einstellung** his political views.

Einstieg *der* (PL die **Einstiege**) entrance.

einstürzen *verb* (PERF ist eingestürzt) to collapse.

einstweilen *adverb* 1 for the time being; 2 meanwhile.

eintausend *number* one thousand.

einteilen *verb* (PERF hat eingeteilt) 1 to divide up; 2 **sich seine Zeit gut einteilen** to organize your time well.

Eintopf *der* (PL die **Eintöpfe**) stew.

Eintrag *der* (PL die **Einträge**) entry.

eintragen ◇*verb* (PRES trägt ein, IMPERF trug ein, PERF hat eingetragen) 1 to enter, to write; 2 **sich eintragen** to put your name down.

einträglich *adjective* profitable.

eintreffen ◇*verb* (PRES trifft ein, IMPERF traf ein, PERF ist eingetroffen) 1 to arrive; 2 to come true.

eintreten ◇*verb* (PRES tritt ein, IMPERF trat ein, PERF ist eingetreten) 1 to enter; 2 **in einen Klub eintreten** to join a club; 3 **für jemanden eintreten** to stand up for somebody.

Eintritt der **1** entrance; **2** admission; **'Eintritt frei'** 'admission free'.

Eintrittskarte die (PL die **Eintrittskarten**) (admission) ticket.

Eintrittspreis der (PL die **Eintrittspreise**) admission charge.

einverstanden adjective **1 einverstanden sein** to agree; **einverstanden! okay!**; **2 mit jemandem einverstanden sein** to approve of somebody.

Einwand der (PL die **Einwände**) objection.

Einwanderer der (PL die **Einwanderer**) immigrant.

Einwanderin die (PL die **Einwanderinnen**) immigrant.

einwandern verb (PERF ist **eingewandert**) to immigrate; **nach Europa einwandern** to immigrate into Europe.

Einwanderung die immigration.

einwärts adverb inwards.

einweichen verb (PERF hat **eingeweicht**) to soak (washing).

einwerfen ◇verb (PRES **wirft ein**, IMPERF **warf ein**, PERF hat **eingeworfen**) **1** to post; **2** to put in (a coin, money); **3** to throw in; **4** to smash.

Einwohner der (PL die **Einwohner**) inhabitant.

Einzahl die singular.

einzahlen verb (PERF hat **eingezahlt**) to pay in.

Einzel das (PL die **Einzel**) singles (in sport).

Einzelheit die (PL die **Einzelheiten**) detail.

Einzelkarte die (PL die **Einzelkarten**) single ticket.

Einzelkind das (PL die **Einzelkinder**) only child.

einzeln adjective **1** single; **2** individual; **3** odd (sock, for example).

einzeln adverb **1** individually; **2** separately, one at a time; **bitte einzeln eintreten** please enter one at a time.

Einzelne der/die/das (PL die **Einzelnen**) **1 der/die Einzelne** the individual; **2 Einzelne** some; **3 ein Einzelner/eine Einzelne/ein Einzelnes** a single one; **jeder/jede/ jedes Einzelne** every single one; **4 im Einzelnen** in detail; **ins Einzelne gehen** to go into detail.

Einzelzimmer das (PL die **Einzelzimmer**) single room.

einziehen ◇verb (IMPERF **zog ein**, PERF **hat eingezogen**) **1** to collect (payment); **2** to draw in (its feelers, claws); **3 den Kopf einziehen** to duck; **4** (PERF **ist eingezogen**) to move in; **wann zieht ihr in die neue Wohnung ein?** when are you moving into your new flat?; **5** (PERF **ist eingezogen**) to soak in.

einzig adjective only; **ein einziges Mal** only once.

Einzige der/die/das (PL die **Einzigen**) **1 der/die/das Einzige** the only one; **2 ein Einziger/eine Einzige/ein**

Einziges a single one; **kein Einziger/keine Einzige/kein Einziges** not a single one; **3 das Einzige, was mich stört** the only thing that bothers me.

Eis das **1** ice; **2** ice cream.

Eisbahn die (PL die **Eisbahnen**) skating rink.

Eisbär der (PL die **Eisbären**) polar bear.

Eisbecher der (PL die **Eisbecher**) ice-cream sundae.

Eisdiele die (PL die **Eisdielen**) ice-cream parlour.

Eisen das iron.

Eisenbahn die (PL die **Eisenbahnen**) railway.

eisern adjective iron.

Eishockey das ice hockey.

eisig adjective icy.

eiskalt adjective **1** ice-cold (drink); **2** freezing cold.

Eislaufen das ice-skating.

Eisläufer der (PL die **Eisläufer**) skater (on ice).

Eisläuferin die (PL die **Eisläuferinnen**) skater (on ice).

Eisportionierer der (PL die **Eisportionierer**) scoop.

Eiswürfel der (PL die **Eiswürfel**) ice cube.

Eiszapfen der (PL die **Eiszapfen**) icicle.

eitel adjective vain.

Eitelkeit die vanity.

Eiter der pus.

Eiweiß das **1** egg-white; **2** protein.

Ekel der disgust.

ekelhaft adjective disgusting.

ekeln verb (PERF **hat sich geekelt**) **sich vor etwas ekeln** to find something disgusting.

eklig adjective disgusting.

Ekzem das (PL die **Ekzeme**) eczema.

Elefant der (PL die **Elefanten**) elephant.

elegant adjective elegant, stylish.

Elektriker der (PL die **Elektriker**) electrician.

elektrisch adjective electrical.

Elektrizität die electricity.

Elektroherd der (PL die **Elektroherde**) electric cooker.

Elektronik die electronics.

elektronisch adjective electronic.

Elektrorasierer der (PL die **Elektrorasierer**) electric razor.

Elend das misery.

elend adjective **1** miserable; **2** terrible.

elf number eleven.

Elfe die (PL die **Elfen**) fairy.

Elfmeter der (PL die **Elfmeter**) penalty (in soccer).

Ellbogen der (PL die **Ellbogen**) elbow.

Eltern plural noun parents.

Email das (PL die **Emails**) enamel.

E-Mail die (PL die **E-Mails**) email.

empfahl SEE **empfehlen**.

Empfang der (PL die **Empfänge**)
1 reception; 2 receipt (of goods or a
letter).

empfangen ◇verb (PRES
empfängt, IMPERF **empfing**, PERF **hat
empfangen**) to receive.

Empfängnisverhütung die
contraception.

Empfangsdame die (PL die
Empfangsdamen) receptionist.

empfehlen ◇verb (PRES
empfiehlt, IMPERF **empfahl**, PERF **hat
empfohlen**) to recommend.

empfindlich adjective 1 sensitive;
2 delicate; 3 touchy.

empfing SEE **empfangen**.

empfohlen SEE **empfehlen**.

empört adjective indignant.

Ende das (PL die **Enden**) 1 end; Ende
April at the end of April; am Ende
der Straße at the end of the road;
2 am Ende in the end; 3 ending (of
a film, novel); 4 zu Ende sein to be
finished, to be over; 5 Ende gut,
alles gut all's well that ends well.

enden verb (PERF **hat geendet**) to
end.

endgültig adjective 1 final
(consent, decision); 2 definite.

Endivie die (PL die **Endivien**)
endive.

endlich adverb finally, at last; na
endlich! at last!

endlos adjective endless.

Endspiel das (PL die **Endspiele**)
final.

Endstation die (PL die
Endstationen) terminus.

Endung die (PL die **Endungen**)
ending.

Energie die energy.

energisch adjective energetic.

eng adjective 1 narrow; 2 tight;
3 close; **eng befreundet sein** to be
close friends.

Engel der (PL die **Engel**) angel.

England das England; aus
England from England.

Engländer der (PL die **Engländer**)
Englishman.

Engländerin die (PL die
Engländerinnen) Englishwoman.

englisch adjective English.

Englisch das English; auf
Englisch in English.

Enkel der (PL die **Enkel**) grandson.

Enkelin die (PL die **Enkelinnen**)
granddaughter.

Enkelkind das (PL die **Enkelkinder**)
grandchild.

entdecken verb (PERF **hat
entdeckt**) to discover.

Entdeckung die (PL die
Entdeckungen) discovery.

Ente die (PL die **Enten**) duck.

entfernen verb (PERF **hat entfernt**)
to remove.

entfernt adjective 1 distant;
2 zehn Kilometer entfernt ten
kilometres away.

entfernt adverb entfernt
verwandt sein to be distantly
related.

Entfernung die (PL die
Entfernungen) distance.

a
b
c
d
e
f
g
h
i
j
k
l
m
n
o
p
q
r
s
t
u
v
w
x
y
z

a **entführen** verb (PERF **hat entführt**)
1 to kidnap; **2** to hijack.

b
Entführer der (PL die **Entführer**)
c **1** hijacker; **2** kidnapper.

d **Entführerin** die (PL die
Entführerinnen) **1** hijacker;
e **2** kidnapper.

f **Entführung** die (PL die
Entführungen) **1** hijacking;
g **2** kidnapping.

h **entgegen** preposition (+ DAT)
contrary to.

i
entgegengesetzt adjective
j **1** opposite; **2** opposing (views).

k **entgegenkommen** ✧verb
(IMPERF **kam entgegen**, PERF **ist**
l **entgegengekommen**) **1** to come
m towards; **2** jemandem
entgegenkommen to come to meet
n somebody; **3** jemandem auf
halbem Wege **entgegenkommen**
o to meet somebody halfway;
p **4** jemandem freundlich
entgegenkommen to be
q accommodating towards
somebody.

r
entgegenkommend adjective
s **1** obliging; **2** der
entgegenkommende Verkehr the
t oncoming traffic.

u **Entgelt** das payment.

v **Enthaarungsmittel** das (PL die
Enthaarungsmittel) hair remover,
w depilatory.

x **enthalten** ✧verb (PRES **enthält**,
IMPERF **enthielt**, PERF **hat enthalten**)
y **1** to contain; **2** sich einer Sache
enthalten to abstain from
z something; sich der Stimme

enthalten to abstain; **3** (PERF **ist
enthalten**) in etwas **enthalten
sein** to be included in something;
im Preis enthalten included in the
price.

entkommen ✧verb (IMPERF
entkam, PERF **ist entkommen**) to
escape.

entlang preposition (+ ACC or + DAT)
along; die Straße **entlang** along
the road; am Fluss **entlang** along
the river.

entlanggehen ✧verb (IMPERF
ging entlang, PERF **ist
entlanggegangen**) to walk along.

entlanglaufen ✧verb (PRES **läuft
entlang**, IMPERF **lief entlang**, PERF **ist
entlanggelaufen**) to run along.

entlassen ✧verb (PRES **entlässt**,
IMPERF **entließ**, PERF **hat entlassen**)
1 to dismiss (from a job); **2** to
discharge (from hospital); **3** to
release (from prison).

Entlassung die (PL die
Entlassungen) **1** dismissal;
2 discharge; **3** release.

entmutigen verb (PERF **hat
entmutigt**) to discourage.

entschädigen verb (PERF **hat
entschädigt**) to compensate.

Entschädigung die
compensation.

entscheiden ✧verb (IMPERF
entschied, PERF **hat entschieden**)
1 to decide (on); **2** sich
entscheiden to decide.

entscheidend adjective decisive,
crucial.

Entscheidung die (PL die Entscheidungen) decision.

Entschiedenheit die decisiveness.

entschließen ◇ verb (IMPERF entschloss sich, PERF hat sich entschlossen) 1 sich entschließen to decide; 2 sich anders entschließen to change your mind; **Karl hat sich anders entschlossen** Karl has changed his mind.

entschlossen adjective determined.

Entschluss der (PL die Entschlüsse) decision.

entschuldigen verb (PERF hat entschuldigt) 1 to excuse; **entschuldigen Sie bitte** excuse me; 2 sich entschuldigen to apologize; **ich habe mich bei Michi entschuldigt** I apologized to Michi.

Entschuldigung die (PL die Entschuldigungen) 1 apology; 2 jemanden um Entschuldigung bitten to apologize to somebody; 3 **Entschuldigung!** sorry!; 4 **Entschuldigung** (with a question or request) excuse me; **Entschuldigung, können Sie mir sagen, wie ich zum Bahnhof komme?** excuse me, could you tell me the way to the station?; 5 excuse.

Entsetzen das horror.

entsetzlich adjective 1 horrible; 2 terrible.

entsetzt adjective horrified.

entspannen verb (PERF hat sich entspannt) 1 sich entspannen to relax; 2 sich entspannen to ease (of a situation).

entspannend adjective relaxing.

entsprechen ◇ verb (PRES entspricht, IMPERF entsprach, PERF hat entsprochen) 1 den Anforderungen entsprechen to meet the requirements; 2 einer Sache entsprechen to correspond to something; 3 to agree with (the truth, a description); 4 to comply with (certain standards).

entsprechend adjective 1 corresponding; 2 appropriate.

entsprechend preposition (+ DAT) in accordance with.

entstehen ◇ verb (IMPERF entstand, PERF ist entstanden) 1 to develop; 2 to result (of damage).

enttäuschen verb (PERF hat enttäuscht) to disappoint.

Enttäuschung die (PL die Enttäuschungen) disappointment.

entweder conjunction either; **entweder heute oder morgen** either today or tomorrow.

entwerten verb (PERF hat entwertet) 1 to devalue; 2 to punch (a ticket in a machine found on trains, trams, buses, and on the platform; you have to punch your ticket before each journey).

Entwerter der (PL die Entwerter) ticket-punching machine (these machines are found on trains, trams, buses, and on the platform;

you have to punch your ticket before each journey).

entwickeln *verb* (PERF **hat entwickelt**) **1** to develop; **2** to display *(ability, a characteristic)*; **3 sich entwickeln** to develop.

Entwicklung *die* (PL *die* **Entwicklungen**) **1** development; **2** developing.

Entwicklungsland *das* (PL *die* **Entwicklungsländer**) developing country.

Entwurf *der* (PL *die* **Entwürfe**) **1** design; **2** draft.

entzückend *adjective* delightful.

entzünden *verb* (PERF **hat entzündet**) **1** to light *(a fire, match)*; **2 sich entzünden** to become inflamed; **3 sich entzünden** to ignite.

Entzündung *die* (PL *die* **Entzündungen**) inflammation.

Enzian *der* (PL *die* **Enziane**) gentian.

Epidemie *die* (PL *die* **Epidemien**) epidemic.

er *pronoun* **1** he; **2** it; **'wo ist mein Mantel?' – 'er liegt auf dem Stuhl'** 'where's my coat?' – 'it's on the chair'; **3** him *(stressed)*; **er war es** it was him.

erben *verb* (PERF **hat geerbt**) to inherit.

erblich *adjective* hereditary.

Erbschaft *die* (PL *die* **Erbschaften**) inheritance.

Erbse *die* (PL *die* **Erbsen**) pea.

Erdbeben *das* (PL *die* **Erdbeben**) earthquake.

Erdbeere *die* (PL *die* **Erdbeeren**) strawberry.

erbrechen *verb* (PRES **erbricht**, IMPERF **erbrach**, PERF **hat erbrochen**) **1** to brng up *(food)*; **2 sich erbrechen** to be sick.

Erde *die* **1** earth, soil; **2** ground; **auf der Erde** on the ground; **3** Earth; **4** earth *(for electricity)*.

Erdgeschoss *das* (PL *die* **Erdgeschosse**) ground floor; **im Erdgeschoss** on the ground floor.

Erdkunde *die* geography.

Erdnuss *die* (PL *die* **Erdnüsse**) peanut.

ereignen *verb* (PERF **hat sich ereignet**) **sich ereignen** to happen.

Ereignis *das* (PL *die* **Ereignisse**) event.

erfahren ◇*verb* (PRES **erfährt**, IMPERF **erfuhr**, PERF **hat erfahren**) **1** to hear, to learn; **2** to experience.

erfahren *adjective* experienced.

Erfahrung *die* (PL *die* **Erfahrungen**) experience.

erfinden ◇*verb* (IMPERF **erfand**, PERF **hat erfunden**) to invent.

Erfindung *die* (PL *die* **Erfindungen**) invention.

Erfolg *der* (PL *die* **Erfolge**) **1** success; **Erfolg haben** to be successful; **2 Erfolg versprechend** promising; **3 viel Erfolg!** good luck!

erfolglos *adjective* unsuccessful.

erfolgreich *adjective* successful.

erfolgversprechend SEE **Erfolg.**

erforderlich *adjective* necessary.

erforschen *verb* (PERF hat erforscht) **1** to explore; **2** to investigate.

erfreulicherweise *adverb* happily.

erfreut *adjective* pleased.

Erfrischung *die* (PL *die* Erfrischungen) refreshment.

Erfrischungsgetränk *das* (PL *die* Erfrischungsgetränke) soft drink.

erfüllen *verb* (PERF hat erfüllt) to fulfil; **sich erfüllen** to come true.

Ergebnis *das* (PL *die* Ergebnisse) result.

ergreifen ✧*verb* (IMPERF ergriff, PERF hat ergriffen) **1** to seize, to grab; **2** to take (*measures, an opportunity*); **3** to take up (*a job, career*); **4** to move; **die Nachricht von ihrem Tod hat uns tief ergriffen** the news of her death moved us deeply; **5 die Flucht ergreifen** to flee.

ergreifend *adjective* moving.

erhalten ✧*verb* (PRES erhält, IMPERF erhielt, PERF hat erhalten) **1** to receive; **2** to preserve.

erhältlich *adjective* obtainable.

Erhaltung *die* **1** preservation; **2** conservation; **3** maintenance.

erheben ✧*verb* (IMPERF erhob, PERF hat erhoben) **1** to raise; **2** to charge (*a fee*); **3 Protest erheben** to protest; **4 sich erheben** to rise up (*in a rebellion*).

erheblich *adjective* considerable.

erheitern *verb* (PERF hat erheitert) to amuse.

erhitzen *verb* (PERF hat erhitzt) to heat.

erhöhen *verb* (PERF hat erhöht) **1** to increase; **2 sich erhöhen** to rise.

Erhöhung *die* (PL *die* Erhöhungen) increase.

erholen *verb* (PERF hat sich erholt) **1 sich erholen** to have a rest; **ich habe mich in den Ferien gut erholt** I had a good rest on holiday; **2 sich von einer Krankheit erholen** to recover from an illness.

erholsam *adjective* restful.

Erholung *die* rest; **Iris ist zur Erholung in die Berge gefahren** Iris went to the mountains for a rest.

erinnern *verb* (PERF hat erinnert) **1** to remind; **2 sich erinnern** to remember.

Erinnerung *die* (PL *die* Erinnerungen) **1** memory; **2** souvenir.

erkälten *verb* (PERF hat sich erkältet) **1 sich erkälten** to catch a cold; **2 erkältet sein** to have a cold; **Ben ist erkältet** Ben has a cold.

Erkältung *die* (PL *die* Erkältungen) cold.

erkennbar *adjective* recognizable.

erkennen ✧*verb* (IMPERF erkannte, PERF hat erkannt) **1** to recognize; **2** to realize.

erklären *verb* (PERF hat erklärt) **1** to explain; **2** to declare; **3 sich zu etwas bereit erklären** to agree to something.

Erklärung die (PL die **Erklärungen**)
1 explanation; 2 declaration;
3 eine öffentliche Erklärung a
public statement.

erkundigen verb (PERF hat sich
erkundigt) 1 sich erkundigen to
enquire; ich werde mich nach den
Zügen erkundigen I'm going to
enquire about the trains; 2 to ask
about; Susi hat sich nach dir
erkundigt Susi was asking about
you.

Erkundigung die (PL die
Erkundigungen) enquiry.

erlauben verb (PERF hat erlaubt)
1 to allow; jemandem etwas
erlauben to allow somebody to do
something; 2 sich etwas erlauben
to allow yourself something; 3 sich
alles erlauben to do as you please;
4 erlauben Sie mal! (informal) do
you mind!

Erlaubnis die permission.

erleben verb (PERF hat erlebt) 1 to
experience; 2 to have (a
disappointment, an experience);
eine Überraschung erleben to
have a surprise; 3 er hat die
Geburt seines Enkels nicht mehr
erlebt he didn't live to see the birth
of his grandson.

Erlebnis das (PL die **Erlebnisse**)
experience.

erledigen verb (PERF hat erledigt)
to deal with, to do.

erledigt adjective 1 settled;
2 (informal) worn out.

Erleichterung die relief.

erleiden ◇verb (IMPERF erlitt, PERF
hat erlitten) to suffer.

Erlös der (PL die **Erlöse**) proceeds.

erloschen adjective 1 out,
extinguished; 2 extinct.

ermäßigen verb (PERF hat
ermäßigt) to reduce.

Ermäßigung die (PL die
Ermäßigungen) reduction.

ermorden verb (PERF hat
ermordet) to murder.

ermutigen verb (PERF hat
ermutigt) to encourage.

ernähren verb (PERF hat ernährt)
1 to feed; 2 sich von Nudeln
ernähren to live on pasta; 3 to
support (a family).

Ernährung die 1 diet; eine
gesunde Ernährung a healthy
diet; 2 nutrition.

erneuern verb (PERF hat erneuert)
to renew.

erneut adjective renewed.

erneut adverb once again.

Ernst der 1 seriousness; 2 im Ernst
seriously; 3 ist das dein Ernst?
are you serious?

ernst adjective serious.

ernsthaft adjective serious.

ernstlich adjective serious.

Ernte die (PL die **Ernten**) harvest;
die Ernte einbringen to gather in
the harvest.

ernten verb (PERF hat geerntet) to
harvest.

erobern verb (PERF hat erobert) to
conquer.

a
b
c
d
e
f
g
h
i
j
k
l
m
n
o
p
q
r
s
t
u
v
w
x
y
z

Eroberung die (PL die Eroberungen) conquest.

eröffnen (PERF hat eröffnet) to open.

Eröffnung die (PL die Eröffnungen) opening.

erraten ◇verb (PRES errät, IMPERF erriet, PERF hat erraten) to guess.

erregen verb (PERF hat erregt) 1 to arouse; 2 to cause; sie erregte viel Aufsehen she caused a sensation.

Erreger der (PL die Erreger) germ.

Erregung die excitement.

erreichen verb (PERF hat erreicht) 1 to reach; 2 den Zug erreichen to catch the train; 3 to achieve (a goal, aim); 4 Irene ist telefonisch zu erreichen Irene can be contacted by phone.

erröten verb (PERF ist errötet) to blush.

Ersatz der replacement, substitute.

Ersatzmann der (PL die Ersatzmänner) substitute (in sport).

Ersatzmittel das (PL die Ersatzmittel) substitute (material, ingredient).

Ersatzreifen der (PL die Ersatzreifen) spare tyre.

Ersatzteil das (PL die Ersatzteile) spare part.

erschaffen verb (IMPERF erschuf, PERF erschaffen) to create.

erscheinen ◇verb (IMPERF erschien, PERF ist erschienen) to appear.

erschöpft adjective exhausted.

erschrecken verb 1 (PERF hat erschreckt) to scare; 2 (◇PRES erschrickt, IMPERF erschrak, PERF ist erschrocken) to get a fright.

erschreckend adjective alarming.

erschrocken adjective 1 frightened; 2 startled.

ersetzen verb (PERF hat ersetzt) to replace; jemandem einen Schaden ersetzen to compensate somebody for damages.

Ersparnisse plural noun savings.

erst adverb 1 first; erst einmal first of all; 2 only; eben erst only just; 3 not until; erst nächste Woche not until next week; Oma war erst zufrieden, als die ganze Familie da war granny was not happy until all the family were there.

erstatten verb (PERF hat erstattet) to reimburse.

Erstattung die (PL die Erstattungen) reimbursement.

erstaunen verb (PERF hat erstaunt) to astonish.

erstaunlich adjective astonishing.

erstaunt adjective amazed; über etwas erstaunt sein to be amazed about something.

Erste der/die/das (PL die Ersten) 1 der/die Erste the first (one); das Erste the first (thing); 2 Dirk kam als Erster Dirk arrived first; Marianne ging als Erste Marianne left first; 3 als Erster/Erste etwas tun to be the first to do something;

a 4 **als Erstes** first of all; **5 fürs Erste** for the time being.

b **erstens** *adverb* firstly.

c **erster, erste, erstes** *adjective* first; **mein erstes Rad war rot** my first bike was red; **der erste April** the first of April; **erste Hilfe** first aid.

d

e **erstklassig** *adjective* first-class.

f **erstmals** *adverb* for the first time.

g **erteilen** *verb* (PERF **hat erteilt**) to give (*advice, information*).

h **ertragen** ◇*verb* (PRES **erträgt**, IMPERF **ertrug**, PERF **hat ertragen**) to bear.

i

j **ertrinken** ◇*verb* (IMPERF **ertrank**, PERF **ist ertrunken**) to drown; **sie ertrank im See** she drowned in the lake.

k

l **erwachsen** *adjective* grown-up.

m **Erwachsene** der/die (PL die **Erwachsenen**) adult, grown-up.

Erwachsenenbildung die adult education.

n

o **erwähnen** *verb* (PERF **hat erwähnt**) to mention.

p **erwarten** *verb* (PERF **hat erwartet**) to expect.

q **Erwartung** die (PL die **Erwartungen**) expectation.

r **erwürgen** *verb* (PERF **hat erwürgt**) to strangle.

s

t **erzählen** *verb* (PERF **hat erzählt**) to tell.

u **Erzählung** die (PL die **Erzählungen**) story.

v

w **Erzeugnis** das (PL die **Erzeugnisse**) product.

x

y

z

erziehen ◇*verb* (IMPERF **erzog**, PERF **hat erzogen**) **1** to bring up; **2** to educate.

Erzieher der (PL die **Erzieher**) teacher.

Erzieherin die (PL die **Erzieherinnen**) teacher.

Erziehung die **1** upbringing; **2** education.

es *pronoun* **1** it; **es regnet** it is raining; **2 es gibt** there is, there are; **3 'wo ist das Baby?' - 'es schläft'** 'where's the baby?' - 'he's/she's asleep'.

Esel der (PL die **Esel**) donkey.

essbar *adjective* edible.

essen ◇*verb* (PRES **isst**, IMPERF **aß**, PERF **hat gegessen**) to eat; **iss keine Bonbons** don't eat sweets.

Essen das **1** meal; **2** food.

Essig der vinegar.

Essiggurke die (PL die **Essiggurken**) gherkin.

Esskastanie die (PL die **Esskastanien**) sweet chestnut.

Esszimmer das (PL die **Esszimmer**) dining room.

Etage die (PL die **Etagen**) floor; **in der zweiten Etage** on the second floor.

Etagenbett das (PL die **Etagenbetten**) bunk beds.

ethnisch *adjective* ethnic.

Etikett das (PL die **Etikett(e)n**) label.

Etui das (PL die **Etuis**) case.

etwa *adverb* **1** about; **er ist etwa so groß wie du** he's about as tall as you; **2** for example; **3** nicht etwa, dass ... not that ...; **4** hat Klaus etwa Angst gehabt? Klaus wasn't scared, was he?

etwas *pronoun, adverb*
1 something; **2** anything; sonst noch etwas? anything else?; **3** some; etwas von dem Geld some of the money; noch etwas Kaffee? (some) more coffee?; **4** a little; nur etwas Zucker only a little sugar; etwas lauter singen to sing a little louder.

EU die (*Europäische Union*) EU.

euch *pronoun* **1** you; ich habe euch eingeladen I've invited you; **2** to you; Eva hat es euch geschenkt Eva gave it to you; **3** (*reflexive*) yourselves.

euer *adjective* your.

Eule die (PL die Eulen) owl.

eurer, eure, eures *pronoun* yours.

Euro der (PL die Euros) euro; ein Euro hat hundert Cent the euro is divided into a hundred cents; es kostet 3 Euro it costs 3 euros.

Eurocent der (PL die Eurocents) cent; 50 Eurocent 50 cents.

Euroland das eurozone.

Europa das Europe.

Europäer der (PL die Europäer) European.

Europäerin die (PL die Europäerinnen) European.

europäisch *adjective* European.

Eurostar der Eurostar; mit dem Eurostar fahren to go by Eurostar.

Eurostück das (PL die Eurostücke) one-euro coin.

evangelisch *adjective* Protestant.

eventuell *adjective* possible.

eventuell *adverb* possibly.

ewig *adjective* eternal.

ewig *adverb* forever.

Ewigkeit die eternity.

Examen das (PL die Examen) examination, exam.

Exemplar das (PL die Exemplare) **1** copy; **2** specimen.

existieren *verb* (PERF hat existiert) to exist.

Expedition die (PL die Expeditionen) expedition.

explodieren *verb* (PERF ist explodiert) to explode.

Explosion die (PL die Explosionen) explosion.

Export der (PL die Exporte) export.

exportieren *verb* (PERF hat exportiert) to export; Russland exportiert viel Öl und Holz Russia exports a lot of oil and timber.

extra *adverb* **1** separately; **2** extra; **3** specially; **4** (*informal*) on purpose.

extrem *adjective* extreme.

Ff

fabelhaft *adjective* fabulous, fantastic.

Fabrik die (PL die Fabriken) factory.

a
b
c
d
e
f
g
h
i
j
k
l
m
n
o
p
q
r
s
t
u
v
w
x
y
z

Fach das (PL die **Fächer**)
1 compartment; 2 drawer;
3 subject (at school).

Facharzt der (PL die **Fachärzte**)
specialist.

Fachärztin die (PL die
Fachärztinnen) specialist.

Fachfrau die (PL die **Fachfrauen**)
expert.

Fachmann der (PL die **Fachleute**)
expert.

fade adjective tasteless.

Faden der (PL die **Fäden**) thread.

fähig adjective 1 capable; 2 able.

Fähigkeit die (PL die **Fähigkeiten**)
ability.

Fahne die (PL die **Fahnen**) flag.

Fahrausweis der (PL die
Fahrausweise) ticket.

Fahrbahn die (PL die **Fahrbahnen**)
1 carriageway; 2 road.

Fähre die (PL die **Fähren**) ferry.

fahren ⬦verb (PRES **fährt**, IMPERF
fuhr, PERF **ist gefahren**) 1 to go; mit
dem Zug nach Wien fahren to go
to Vienna by train; ich bin mit dem
Auto gefahren I went by car; ; 2 to
drive; Hanna ist sehr schnell
gefahren Hanna drove very fast;
3 to ride (of a cyclist); 4 to run (of a
train, bus); der Zug fährt nicht an
Sonn- und Feiertagen the train
doesn't run on Sundays and public
holidays; 5 to leave; wann fahrt
ihr?; 6 was ist in sie gefahren? (informal)
what's got into her?; 7 (PERF **hat
gefahren**) to drive; er hat Doris
nach Hause gefahren he drove

Doris home; ich habe das Auto in
die Garage gefahren I drove the
car into the garage.

Fahrer der (PL die **Fahrer**) driver.

Fahrerflucht die hit-and-run
driving; **Fahrerflucht begehen** to
be involved in a hit-and-run.

Fahrerin die (PL die **Fahrerinnen**)
driver.

Fahrgast der (PL die **Fahrgäste**)
passenger.

Fahrkarte die (PL die **Fahrkarten**)
ticket.

Fahrkartenausgabe die ticket
office.

Fahrkartenautomat der (PL die
Fahrkartenautomaten) ticket
machine.

Fahrkartenschalter der (PL die
Fahrkartenschalter) ticket office.

fahrlässig adjective negligent.

Fahrlehrer der (PL die **Fahrlehrer**)
driving instructor.

Fahrplan der (PL die **Fahrpläne**)
timetable.

Fahrpreis der (PL die **Fahrpreise**)
fare.

Fahrprüfung die (PL die
Fahrprüfungen) driving test; die
Fahrprüfung machen to take your
driving test.

Fahrrad das (PL die **Fahrräder**)
bicycle.

Fahrradfahrer der (PL die
Fahrradfahrer) cyclist.

Fahrradfahrerin die (PL die
Fahrradfahrerinnen) cyclist.

Fahrradweg der (PL die Fahrradwege) cycle lane.

Fahrschein der (PL die Fahrscheine) ticket.

Fahrschule die (PL die Fahrschulen) driving school.

Fahrstuhl der (PL die Fahrstühle) lift.

Fahrt die (PL die Fahrten) 1 journey; gute Fahrt! have a good journey!; 2 trip; 3 drive; 4 in voller Fahrt at full speed.

Fahrzeug das (PL die Fahrzeuge) vehicle.

fair adjective fair.

Faktor der (PL die Faktoren) factor.

Falke der (PL die Falken) falcon.

Fall der (PL die Fälle) 1 case; in diesem Fall in this case; auf alle Fälle, auf jeden Fall in any case; für alle Fälle just in case; 2 auf jeden Fall definitely; 3 auf keinen Fall on no account; 4 fall.

Falle die (PL die Fallen) trap.

fallen ✧ verb (PRES fällt, IMPERF fiel, PERF ist gefallen) 1 to fall; 2 etwas fallen lassen to drop something; wir haben den Plan fallen lassen we've dropped the idea; 3 eine Bemerkung fallen lassen to make a comment.

fällen verb (PERF hat gefällt) to fell, to cut down (trees).

fallenlassen SEE fallen.

fällig adjective due.

falls conjunction 1 if; 2 in case.

Fallschirm der (PL die Fallschirme) parachute.

falsch adjective 1 wrong; du hast ihn falsch verstanden you got him wrong; 2 false (teeth, etc.); 3 forged.

fälschen verb (PERF hat gefälscht) to forge.

Fälschung die (PL die Fälschungen) 1 fake; 2 forgery.

Falte die (PL die Falten) 1 fold; 2 crease; 3 pleat; 4 wrinkle.

falten verb (PERF hat gefaltet) to fold.

faltig adjective 1 wrinkled; 2 creased.

familiär adjective familiar.

Familie die (PL die Familien) family.

Familienname der (PL die Familiennamen) surname.

Fan der (PL die Fans) fan.

fand SEE finden.

Fantasie die 1 imagination; 2 Fantasien (plural) fantasies.

fantasievoll adjective imaginative.

fangen ✧ verb (PRES fängt, IMPERF fing, PERF hat gefangen) to catch.

Fantasie die 1 imagination; 2 Fantasien (plural) fantasies.

fantasievoll adjective imaginative.

fantastisch adjective fantastic.

Farbe die (PL die Farben) 1 colour; 2 paint; 3 dye; 4 suit (in playing cards).

farbecht adjective colour fast.

färben verb (PERF hat gefärbt) 1 to dye; 2 sich die Haare färben to dye your hair; **3 das Sweatshirt färbt** this sweatshirt runs.

farbenblind *adjective* colour blind.

Farbfernsehen *das* colour television.

Farbfilm *der* (PL die **Farbfilme**) colour film.

farbig *adjective* coloured.

farblos *adjective* colourless.

Farbstift *der* (PL die **Farbstifte**) coloured pencil.

Farbstoff *der* (PL die **Farbstoffe**) **1** dye; **2** colouring *(for food)*.

Farbton *der* (PL die **Farbtöne**) shade.

Fasan *der* (PL die **Fasane**) pheasant.

Fasching *der* (PL die **Faschinge**) carnival.

Faser *die* (PL die **Fasern**) fibre.

Fass *das* (PL die **Fässer**) barrel; **Bier vom Fass** draught beer.

fassen *verb* (PERF **hat gefasst**) **1** to grasp; **2 einen Dieb fassen** to catch a thief; **3** to hold *(of a container)*; **4** to understand; **5 nicht zu fassen** unbelievable; **6 sich fassen** to compose yourself; **7 einen Entschluss fassen** to make a decision; **8 sich kurz fassen** to be brief.

Fassung *die* (PL die **Fassungen**) **1** version; **2** composure; **3 jemanden aus der Fassung bringen** to throw somebody, to upset somebody; **4** setting *(for gems)*.

fassungslos *adjective* speechless.

Fastfood *das* fast food.

fast *adverb* **1** almost; **2 fast nie** hardly ever.

Fastenzeit *die* (PL die **Fastenzeiten**) Lent.

Fastnacht *die* carnival.

faul *adjective* **1** lazy; **2** rotten; **3 eine faule Ausrede** a lame excuse; **4 an der Sache ist etwas faul** *(informal)* there's something fishy about it.

faulen *verb* (PERF **ist gefault**) to rot.

faulenzen *verb* (PERF **hat gefaulenzt**) to laze about.

Faust *die* (PL die **Fäuste**) **1** fist; **2 auf eigene Faust** off your own bat.

Fax *das* (PL die **Fax(e)**) fax.

faxen *verb* (PERF **hat gefaxt**) to fax; **ich faxe Ihnen die Liste** I'll fax you the list.

Februar *der* February.

fechten ✧*verb* (PRES **ficht**, IMPERF **focht**, PERF **hat gefochten**) to fence.

Feder *die* (PL die **Federn**) **1** feather; **2** spring; **3** nib *(of a pen)*.

Federball *der* (PL die **Federbälle**) **1** badminton; **2** shuttlecock.

Federhalter *der* (PL die **Federhalter**) fountain pen.

Federmäppchen *das* (PL die **Federmäppchen**) pencil case.

Fee *die* (PL die **Feen**) fairy.

fegen *verb* (PERF **hat gefegt**) to sweep.

fehl *adjective* **fehl am Platz** out of place.

fehlen verb (PERF **hat gefehlt**) **1** to be missing; **2** to be lacking; **3** to be absent (*from school*); **4 mir fehlt die Zeit** I haven't got the time; **es fehlt ihnen einfach das Geld für ein neues Auto** they simply haven't got the money for a new car; **5 was fehlt dir?** what's the matter?; **6 Rudi fehlt mir** I miss Rudi.

Fehler der (PL die **Fehler**) **1** mistake; **2** fault.

Feier die (PL die **Feiern**) **1** party; **2** celebration.

Feierabend der (PL die **Feierabende**) **1** finishing time; **2 nach Feierabend** after work.

Feierlichkeiten plural noun festivities.

feiern verb (PERF **hat gefeiert**) to celebrate.

Feiertag der (PL die **Feiertage**) **1** holiday; **ein gesetzlicher Feiertag** a public holiday; **2 am ersten Feiertag** on Christmas Day; **der zweite Feiertag** Boxing Day.

Feige die (PL die **Feigen**) fig.

feige adjective cowardly; **du bist feige** you're a coward.

Feigenbaum der (PL die **Feigenbäume**) fig tree.

Feigling der (PL die **Feiglinge**) coward.

Feile die (PL die **Feilen**) file.

fein adjective **1** fine; **2** delicate; **3** refined; **4 sich fein machen** to dress up.

Feind der (PL die **Feinde**) enemy.

feindlich adjective hostile.

Feld das (PL die **Felder**) **1** field; **2** pitch; **3** box (*on a form*); **4** square (*on a board game*).

Fell das (PL die **Felle**) fur, skin.

Fels der rock.

Felsen der (PL die **Felsen**) cliff.

feminin adjective feminine.

Feminist der (PL die **Feministen**) feminist.

Feministin die (PL die **Feministinnen**) feminist.

Fenster das (PL die **Fenster**) window.

Fensterladen der (PL die **Fensterläden**) shutter.

Ferien plural noun holidays; **Ferien haben** to be on holiday.

Ferienhaus das (PL die **Ferienhäuser**) holiday home.

fern adjective **1** distant; **2 sich fern halten** to keep away; **jemanden von etwas fern halten** to keep somebody away from something.

fern adverb far away.

Fernbedienung die remote control.

Ferngespräch das (PL die **Ferngespräche**) long-distance call.

ferngesteuert adjective remote-controlled.

Fernglas das (PL die **Ferngläser**) binoculars.

fernhalten SEE **fern**.

Fernost das Far East.

Fernrohr das (PL die **Fernrohre**) telescope.

Fernsehapparat der (PL die Fernsehapparate) television set.

fernsehen ◇verb (PRES **sieht fern**, IMPERF **sah fern**, PERF **hat ferngesehen**) to watch television.

Fernsehen das television; **im Fernsehen** on television.

Fernseher der (PL die Fernseher) television (set).

Fernsehsendung die (PL die Fernsehsendungen) television programme.

Fernsehturm der (PL die Fernsehtürme) television tower.

Fernsprecher der (PL die Fernsprecher) telephone.

Ferse die (PL die Fersen) heel.

fertig adjective **1** finished; **mit den Hausaufgaben fertig werden** to finish your homework; **fertig sein** to be finished; **2 mit jemandem fertig werden** (informal) to be through with somebody; **3 völlig fertig sein** to be completely worn out; **4 mit etwas fertig werden** to cope with something (problems, for example); **5** ready; **das Essen ist fertig** food's ready; **6 etwas fertig machen** (prepare) to get something ready; (complete) to finish something; **sich fertig machen** to get ready; **7 jemanden fertig machen** to wear somebody out, to wear somebody down; **der ständige Stress macht mich fertig** this constant stress is wearing me down; **8 es fertig bringen, etwas zu tun** to bring yourself to do something; **ich**

bringe es einfach nicht fertig I just can't bring myself to do it.

fertig adverb **fertig essen** to finish eating.

fertigbringen SEE **fertig**.

Fertiggericht das (PL die Fertiggerichte) ready-to-serve meal.

fertigmachen SEE **fertig**.

Fest das (PL die Feste) **1** party; **2** celebration; **3** festival.

fest adjective **1** firm; **2** fixed (salary, address); **3** solid; **feste Nahrung** solids; **4 fest werden** to harden.

fest adverb **1 fest schlafen** to be fast asleep; **2 fest befreundet sein** to be close friends; **3 fest angestellt sein** to be in permanent employment.

festbinden ◇verb (IMPERF **band fest**, PERF **hat festgebunden**) to tie (up).

festhalten ◇verb (PRES **hält fest**, IMPERF **hielt fest**, PERF **hat festgehalten**) **1** to hold on to; **2 sich festhalten** to hold on; **halt dich an mir fest** hold on to me.

Festigkeit die strength.

festlegen verb (PERF **hat festgelegt**) **1** to fix; **2 sich auf etwas festlegen** to commit yourself to something.

Festlegung die (PL die Festlegungen) establishment.

festlich adjective festive.

festmachen verb (PERF **hat festgemacht**) **1** to fix; **ich mache**

gleich einen Termin fest I'll fix a date straight away; **2** to fasten.

Festnahme die (PL die **Festnahmen**) arrest.

festnehmen ⬦ verb (PRES **nimmt fest**, IMPERF **nahm fest**, PERF **hat festgenommen**) to arrest.

Festplatte die (PL die **Festplatten**) hard disk.

feststehen ⬦ verb (IMPERF **stand fest**, PERF **hat festgestanden**) to be certain; **eins steht fest, Daniel lade ich nicht mehr ein** one thing's certain, I'm not going to invite Daniel again.

feststellen verb (PERF **hat festgestellt**) **1** to establish; **2** to notice.

Fete die (PL die **Feten**) party.

Fett das (PL die **Fette**) **1** fat; **2** grease.

fett adjective **1** fat (person); **2** greasy, fatty (food); **3** bold (type).

fettarm adjective low-fat; **fettarme Milch** skimmed milk.

fettig adjective greasy.

Fetzen der (PL die **Fetzen**) **1** scrap; **2** rag.

feucht adjective **1** damp; **2** humid.

Feuchtigkeit die **1** moisture; **2** humidity.

Feuer das **1** fire; **2 hast du Feuer?** have you got a light?

Feuerlöscher der (PL die **Feuerlöscher**) fire extinguisher.

Feuermelder der (PL die **Feuermelder**) fire alarm.

Feuertreppe die (PL die **Feuertreppen**) fire escape.

Feuerwehr die (PL die **Feuerwehren**) fire brigade.

Feuerwehrauto das (PL die **Feuerwehrautos**) fire engine.

Feuerwehrmann der (PL die **Feuerwehrleute**) fireman.

Feuerwerk das fireworks.

Feuerzeug das (PL die **Feuerzeuge**) lighter.

ficht SEE **fechten**.

Fieber das (high) temperature, fever; **(hohes) Fieber haben** to have a (high) temperature.

fiel SEE **fallen**.

fies adjective (informal) nasty.

Figur die (PL die **Figuren**) **1** figure; **2** character.

Filiale die (PL die **Filialen**) branch.

Film der (PL die **Filme**) film.

filmen verb (PERF **hat gefilmt**) to film.

Filter der (PL die **Filter**) filter.

Filzstift der (PL die **Filzstifte**) felt pen.

Finale das (PL die **Finale**) final.

finanziell adjective financial.

finanzieren verb (PERF **hat finanziert**) to finance.

finden ⬦ verb (IMPERF **fand**, PERF **hat gefunden**) **1** to find; **2** to think; **wie findest du das?** what do you think of it?; **findest du?** do you think so?; **3 ich finde nichts dabei** I don't mind.

fing SEE **fangen**.

Finger der (PL die **Finger**) finger.

a
b
c
d
e
f
g
h
i
j
k
l
m
n
o
p
q
r
s
t
u
v
w
x
y
z

Fingernagel der (PL die Fingernägel) fingernail.

Finne der (PL die Finnen) Finn.

Finnin die (PL die Finninnen) Finn.

Finnland das Finland.

finster adjective 1 dark; im Finstern in the dark; 2 sinister.

Finsternis die darkness.

Firma die (PL die Firmen) firm, company.

Fisch der (PL die Fische) 1 fish; 2 Fische Pisces; Helmut ist Fisch Helmut is Pisces.

Fischer der (PL die Fischer) fisherman.

fit adjective fit; er hält sich durch Jogging fit he keeps fit by jogging.

Fitnesstraining das keep fit.

fix adjective 1 quick; 2 fix und fertig all finished, all ready; 3 ich bin fix und fertig (informal) I'm shattered.

flach adjective 1 flat; 2 low; 3 shallow; die Erdbeeren kommen in die flache Schüssel the strawberries go into the shallow bowl.

Fläche die (PL die Flächen) 1 surface; 2 area.

flackern verb (PERF hat geflackert) to flicker.

Flagge die (PL die Flaggen) flag.

Flamme die (PL die Flammen) flame.

Flasche die (PL die Flaschen) bottle.

Flaschenöffner der (PL die Flaschenöffner) bottle opener.

flauschig adjective 1 fluffy; 2 fleecy.

Fleck der (PL die Flecken) 1 stain; 2 spot; 3 ein blauer Fleck a bruise.

fleckig adjective 1 stained; 2 blotchy (skin).

Fledermaus die (PL die Fledermäuse) bat.

Fleisch das 1 meat; 2 flesh.

Fleischer der (PL die Fleischer) butcher.

Fleischerei die (PL die Fleischereien) butcher's.

Fleiß der hard work.

fleißig adjective hard-working.

flicken verb (PERF hat geflickt) to mend.

Flicken der (PL die Flicken) patch (for mending).

Fliege die (PL die Fliegen) 1 fly; 2 bow tie.

fliegen ◇verb (IMPERF flog, PERF ist geflogen) 1 to fly; 2 ich bin geflogen (informal) I fell; 3 Manfred ist geflogen (informal) Manfred has been fired; 4 (PERF hat geflogen) to fly (a plane).

fliehen ◇verb (IMPERF floh, PERF ist geflohen) to flee.

Fliese die (PL die Fliesen) tile.

Fließband das (PL die Fließbänder) 1 conveyor belt; 2 assembly line.

fließen ◇verb (IMPERF floss, PERF ist geflossen) to flow.

fließend adjective 1 running; 2 fluent; fließendes Deutsch fluent German; 3 moving (traffic).

Flitterwochen *plural noun* honeymoon; **sie fahren nach Ägyten für ihre Flitterwochen** they're going to Egypt for their honeymoon.

flitzen *verb* (*informal*) (PERF **ist geflitzt**) 1 to dash; 2 to whizz.

Flocke *die* (PL die **Flocken**) flake.

flog SEE **fliegen**.

Floh *der* (PL die **Flöhe**) flee.

floh SEE **fliehen**.

Flohmarkt *der* (PL die **Flohmärkte**) flea market.

floss SEE **fließen**.

Flosse *die* (PL die **Flossen**) 1 fin; 2 flipper.

Flöte *die* (PL die **Flöten**) flute.

fluchen *verb* (PERF **hat geflucht**) to curse.

Flüchtling *der* (PL die **Flüchtlinge**) refugee.

Flug *der* (PL die **Flüge**) flight.

Flugbegleiter *der* (PL die **Flugbegleiter**) flight attendant.

Flugbegleiterin *die* (PL die **Flugbegleiterinnen**) flight attendant.

Flugblatt *das* (PL die **Flugblätter**) pamphlet.

Flugdienstleiter *der* (PL die **Flugdienstleiter**) air-traffic controller.

Flugdienstleiterin *die* (PL die **Flugdienstleiterinnen**) air-traffic controller.

Flügel *der* (PL die **Flügel**) 1 wing; 2 grand piano.

Fluggast *der* (PL die **Fluggäste**) (air) passenger.

Fluggesellschaft *die* (PL die **Fluggesellschaften**) airline.

Flughafen *der* (PL die **Flughäfen**) airport.

Fluglotse *der* (PL die **Fluglotsen**) air-traffic controller.

Fluglotsin *die* (PL die **Fluglotsinnen**) air-traffic controller.

Flugplatz *der* (PL die **Flugplätze**) 1 airport; 2 airfield.

Flugzeug *das* (PL die **Flugzeuge**) aeroplane; **mit dem Flugzeug fliegen** to go by air.

Fluor *das* fluoride.

Flur *der* (PL die **Flure**) 1 hall; 2 corridor.

Fluss *der* (PL die **Flüsse**) river.

flüssig *adjective* liquid.

Flüssigkeit *die* (PL die **Flüssigkeiten**) liquid.

flüstern *verb* (PERF **hat geflüstert**) to whisper.

Flut *die* (PL die **Fluten**) 1 high tide; **bei Flut** at high tide; 2 flood (*of letters, complaints*).

Flutlicht *das* floodlight.

focht SEE **fechten**.

Föhn *der* (PL die **Föhne**) hair drier.

föhnen *verb* (PERF **hat geföhnt**) to blow-dry.

Folge *die* (PL die **Folgen**) 1 consequence; 2 episode; 3 **etwas zur Folge haben** to result in something; 4 **an den Folgen eines**

a b c d e f g h i j k l m n o p q r s t u v w x y z

Unfalls sterben to die as the result of an accident.

folgen *verb* (PERF **ist gefolgt**) **1** to follow; **daraus folgt, dass** ... it follows that ...; **ich kann dir nicht folgen** I can't follow what you're saying; **2** (PERF **hat gefolgt**) to obey.

folgend *adjective* **1** following; **2 Folgendes** the following.

Folgerung die (PL die **Folgerungen**) conclusion.

folgsam *adjective* obedient.

Folie die (PL die **Folien**) foil.

Folienkartoffel die (PL die **Folienkartoffeln**) jacket potato.

Folterkammer die (PL die **Folterkammern**) torture chamber.

Fön™ SEE **Föhn**.

fönen SEE **föhnen**.

fördern *verb* (PERF **hat gefördert**) **1** to promote; **2** to sponsor.

fordern *verb* (PERF **hat gefordert**) to demand.

Forderung die (PL die **Forderungen**) **1** demand; **2** claim.

Forelle die (PL die **Forellen**) trout.

Form die (PL die **Formen**) **1** shape; **2** form; **in Form sein** to be on form; **3** tin (*for baking*).

Format das (PL die **Formate**) format.

formatieren *verb* (PERF **hat formatiert**) to format.

formen *verb* (PERF **hat geformt**) **1** to form; **2 sich formen** to take shape.

förmlich *adjective* formal.

förmlich *adverb* **1** formally; **2 jemanden förmlich zwingen, etwas zu tun** to positively force somebody to do something; **ich hätte förmlich schreien können** I really could have screamed.

Formular das (PL die **Formulare**) form.

Forscher der (PL die **Forscher**) **1** researcher, research scientist; **2** explorer.

Forschung die (PL die **Forschungen**) research.

Forst der (PL die **Forste(n)**) forest.

Förster der (PL die **Förster**) forester.

fort *adverb* **1** away; **2 fort sein** to have gone; **3 und so fort** and so on; **4 in einem fort** on and on.

fortbewegen *verb* (PERF **hat fortbewegt**) **1** to move; **2 sich fortbewegen** to move.

fortfahren ◇*verb* (PRES **fährt fort**, IMPERF **fuhr fort**, PERF **ist fortgefahren**) **1** to leave; **wann fährt ihr fort?** when are you leaving?; **2** to continue.

fortgeschritten *adjective* advanced.

Fortpflanzung die (PL die **Fortpflanzungen**) **1** reproduction; **2** propagation.

Fortschritt der (PL die **Fortschritte**) progress; **Fortschritte machen** to make progress.

fortsetzen *verb* (PERF **hat fortgesetzt**) to continue.

Fortsetzung die (PL die Fortsetzungen) **1** continuation; **2** instalment.

Foto das (PL die Fotos) photo.

Fotoapparat der (PL die Fotoapparate) camera.

Fotograf der (PL die Fotografen) photographer.

Fotografie die (PL die Fotografien) **1** photography; **2** photograph.

fotografieren verb (PERF hat fotografiert) **1** to photograph, to take a photograph of; **2** to take photographs.

Fotografin die (PL die Fotografinnen) photographer.

Fotokopie die (PL die Fotokopien) photocopy.

fotokopieren verb (PERF hat fotokopiert) to photocopy.

Fracht die (PL die Frachten) freight, cargo.

Frage die (PL die Fragen) question; **eine Frage stellen** to ask a question; **etwas in Frage stellen** to question something; **das kommt nicht in Frage** that's out of the question.

Fragebogen der (PL die Fragebogen) questionnaire.

fragen verb (PERF hat gefragt) **1** to ask; **2 sich fragen** to wonder.

Fragezeichen das (PL die Fragezeichen) question mark.

fraglich adjective doubtful.

Franken[1] der (PL die Franken) (Swiss) franc.

Franken[2] das Franconia.

Frankreich das France.

Franzose der (PL die Franzosen) Frenchman.

Französin die (PL die Französinnen) Frenchwoman.

Französisch das French.

französisch adjective French.

fraß SEE fressen.

Frau die (PL die Frauen) **1** woman; **2** wife; **3** Mrs, Ms ('*Frau*' is usually used to address both married and unmarried women).

Fräulein das (PL die Fräulein) **1** young lady; **2** Miss; **Fräulein Schmidt** Miss Schmidt.

frech adjective cheeky.

Frechheit die (PL die Frechheiten) **1** cheek; **2** cheeky remark.

Frechheit die (PL die Frechheiten) **1** cheeky remark; **2** cheekiness.

frei adjective **1** free; **2** freelance; **3 ist dieser Platz frei?** is this seat taken?; **4 ein freier Tag** a day off; **sich frei nehmen** to take a day off; **5 'Zimmer frei'** 'vacancies'.

Freibad das (PL die Freibäder) open-air swimming pool.

Freie das **im Freien** in the open air.

freigebig adjective generous.

Freiheit die (PL die Freiheiten) **1** freedom; **2** liberty; **sich Freiheiten erlauben** to take liberties.

freimachen verb (PERF hat freigemacht) **1** to take time off; **2 sich freimachen** to take time off.

Freistoß der (PL die Freistöße) free kick.

Freistunde die (PL die Freistunden) free period.

Freitag der (PL die Freitage) Friday.

freitags adverb on Fridays.

freiwillig adjective voluntary.

Freizeit die 1 spare time; 2 leisure.

Freizeitkleidung die leisure wear, casual clothes.

fremd adjective 1 foreign; 2 strange; **fremde Leute** strangers; **ich bin hier fremd** I'm a stranger here.

Fremde der/die (PL die Fremden) 1 foreigner; 2 stranger.

Fremdenverkehr der tourism.

Fremdenverkehrsbüro das (PL die Fremdenverkehrsbüros) tourist office.

Fremdenzimmer das (PL die Fremdenzimmer) room (to let).

Fremdsprache die (PL die Fremdsprachen) foreign language.

fressen ◇verb (PRES frisst, IMPERF fraß, PERF hat gefressen) to eat.

Freude die (PL die Freuden) 1 joy; 2 pleasure; **mit Freuden** with pleasure; 3 **an etwas Freude haben** to be delighted with something; 4 **jemandem eine Freude machen** to please somebody.

freuen verb (PERF hat sich gefreut) 1 **sich freuen** to be pleased; **sich über etwas freuen** to be pleased about something; 2 **sich auf etwas freuen** to look forward to something.

Freund der (PL die Freunde) 1 friend; 2 boyfriend.

Freundin die (PL die Freundinnen) 1 friend; 2 girlfriend.

freundlich adjective 1 friendly; 2 kind.

freundlicherweise adverb kindly.

Freundlichkeit die friendliness.

Freundschaft die (PL die Freundschaften) friendship; **mit jemandem Freundschaft schließen** to make friends with somebody.

Frieden der peace.

Friedhof der (PL die Friedhöfe) cemetery.

friedlich adjective peaceful.

frieren ◇verb (IMPERF fror, PERF hat gefroren) 1 to be cold; **frierst du?** are you cold?; 2 **es friert** it's freezing, it's frosty; 3 (PERF ist gefroren) to freeze.

Frikadelle die (PL die Frikadellen) rissole.

frisch adjective fresh; **sich frisch machen** to freshen up.

frisch adverb freshly; **'frisch gestrichen'** 'wet paint'.

Friseur der (PL die Friseure) hairdresser.

Friseuse die (PL die Friseusen) hairdresser.

frisieren verb (PERF hat frisiert) 1 **jemanden frisieren** to do somebody's hair; 2 **sich frisieren** to do your hair.

frisst SEE **fressen**.

Frisur die (PL die **Frisuren**) hairstyle, hairdo.

froh adjective **1** happy; **frohe Weihnachten!** happy Christmas!; **2 über etwas froh sein** to be glad about something.

fröhlich adjective cheerful.

Fröhlichkeit die cheerfulness.

fromm adjective devout.

fror SEE **frieren**.

Frosch der (PL die **Frösche**) frog.

Frost der (PL die **Fröste**) frost.

frostig adjective frosty.

Frottee das (PL die **Frottees**) towelling.

Frottiertuch das (PL die **Frottiertücher**) towel.

Frucht die (PL die **Früchte**) fruit.

fruchtbar adjective fertile.

Fruchtsaft der (PL die **Fruchtsäfte**) fruit juice.

früh adjective, adverb **1** early; **von früh auf** from an early age; **2 heute früh** this morning.

Frühe die **in aller Frühe** at the crack of dawn.

früher adjective **1** earlier; **2** former.

früher adverb **1** earlier; **2** formerly; **3 früher war sie ganz anders** she used to be quite different; **das war früher ein Blumengeschäft** it used to be a florist's.

frühestens adverb at the earliest.

Frühjahr das (PL die **Frühjahre**) spring; **im Frühjahr** in spring.

Frühling der (PL die **Frühlinge**) spring; **im Frühling** in spring.

Frühstück das (PL die **Frühstücke**) breakfast.

frühstücken verb (PERF **hat gefrühstückt**) to have breakfast.

frühzeitig adjective early.

Fuchs der (PL die **Füchse**) fox.

fühlen verb (PERF **hat gefühlt**) **1** to feel; **2 sich krank fühlen** to feel ill.

fuhr SEE **fahren**.

führen verb (PERF **hat geführt**) **1** to lead; **sie führt mit fünf Punkten** she is five points in the lead; **unsere Mannschaft führt** our team's winning; **2** to run (a shop or business); **3** to show round; **4** to keep (a diary, list); **5 ein Telefongespräch führen** to make a phone call.

Führer der (PL die **Führer**) **1** leader; **2** guide.

Führerschein der (PL die **Führerscheine**) driving licence; **den Führerschein machen** to take your driving test.

Führung die (PL die **Führungen**) **1** leadership; **2** guided tour; **3** management (of a shop); **4 in Führung** in the lead.

Führungsposition die (PL die **Führungspositionen**) **1** top position; **2** pole position.

füllen verb (PERF **hat gefüllt**) **1** to fill; **2** to stuff (a turkey, peppers); **3 sich füllen** to fill (up).

Füller der (PL die **Füller**) fountain pen.

a
b
c
d
e
f
g
h
i
j
k
l
m
n
o
p
q
r
s
t
u
v
w
x
y
z

Füllfederhalter der (PL die Füllfederhalter) fountain pen.

Füllung die (PL die Füllungen) filling.

Fundament das (PL die Fundamente) foundations.

Fundbüro das (PL die Fundbüros) lost property office.

fünf number five.

fünfhundert number five hundred.

Fünftel das (PL die Fünftel) fifth.

fünfter, fünfte, fünftes adjective fifth.

fünfzehn number fifteen.

fünfzig number fifty.

Funkausstellung die (PL die Funkausstellungen) radio and television exhibition.

Funke der (PL die Funken) spark.

funkeln verb (PERF hat gefunkelt) 1 to sparkle; 2 to twinkle (of a star).

funktionieren verb (PERF hat funktioniert) to work.

für preposition (+ ACC) 1 for; 2 was für ein ...? what sort of ... ?; 3 für sich by yourself; jetzt habe ich das Haus ganz für mich now I've got the house to myself; 4 das Für und Wider the pros and cons.

Furcht die fear.

furchtbar adjective terrible.

fürchten verb (PERF hat gefürchtet) 1 to fear; 2 sich fürchten to be afraid; ich fürchte mich vor ihm I'm afraid of him; ich fürchte, das geht nicht I'm afraid that's not possible.

fürchterlich adjective dreadful.

füreinander adverb for each other.

fürs = für das.

Fürsorge die 1 care; 2 welfare; 3 (informal) social security.

Fuß der (PL die Füße) 1 foot; zu Fuß on foot; zu Fuß gehen to walk; 2 base.

Fußabdruck der (PL die Fußabdrücke) footprint.

Fußball der (PL die Fußbälle) football.

Fußballplatz der (PL die Fußballplätze) football pitch.

Fußballspiel das (PL die Fußballspiele) football match.

Fußballspieler der (PL die Fußballspieler) footballer.

Fußboden der (PL die Fußböden) floor.

Fußgänger der (PL die Fußgänger) pedestrian.

Fußgängerzone die (PL die Fußgängerzonen) pedestrian precinct.

Fußweg der (PL die Fußwege) footpath.

Futter das 1 feed; ich habe dem Hund schon Futter gegeben I've already given the dog his food; 2 lining (of clothes).

füttern verb (PERF hat gefüttert) 1 to feed; den Hund und die Katze füttern to feed the dog and the cat; 2 to line.

Futur das (PL die Future) future (tense).

Gas

Gg

gab SEE **geben.**

Gabel die (PL die **Gabeln**) fork.

gähnen verb (PERF **hat gegähnt**) to yawn.

Galerie die (PL die **Galerien**) gallery.

galoppieren verb (PERF **ist galoppiert**) to gallop.

Gammler der (PL die **Gammler**) drop-out.

Gammlerin die (PL die **Gammlerinnen**) drop-out.

Gang der (PL die **Gänge**) 1 walk; 2 errand; 3 corridor; 4 **ein Platz am Gang** an aisle seat; 5 course (of a meal); 6 gear (of a car); 7 **in Gang setzen** to get going; 8 **im Gange** in progress.

gängig adjective 1 common; 2 popular (goods).

Gans die (PL die **Gänse**) goose.

Gänseblümchen das (PL die **Gänseblümchen**) daisy.

Gänsehaut die goose pimples.

ganz adjective 1 whole 1 **ganz Deutschland** the whole of Germany; 2 **im Großen und Ganzen** on the whole; 3 **eine ganze Menge** quite a lot; 4 all; **mein ganzes Geld** all my money; **die ganzen Leute** all the people; 5 **etwas wieder ganz machen** to mend something.

ganz adverb 1 quite; **es war ganz gut** it was quite good; 2 **ganz und**

gar completely; 3 **ganz und gar nicht** not at all.

ganztägig adjective, adverb 1 full-time; 2 all-day; **ganztägig geöffnet** open all day.

ganztags adverb 1 full time; 2 all day.

Ganztagsschule die (PL die **Ganztagsschulen**) 1 all-day school; 2 all-day schooling.

gar adjective done, cooked.

gar adverb 1 **gar nicht** not at all; **gar nichts** nothing; 2 **oder gar** or even.

Garage die (PL die **Garagen**) garage.

Garantie die (PL die **Garantien**) guarantee.

garantieren verb (PERF **hat garantiert**) to guarantee.

Garderobe die (PL die **Garderoben**) cloakroom; **wir können die Mäntel an der Garderobe abgeben** we can leave the coats in the cloakroom.

Gardine die (PL die **Gardinen**) curtain.

Garn das (PL die **Garne**) thread.

Garnele die (PL die **Garnelen**) 1 shrimp; 2 prawn.

Garten der (PL die **Gärten**) garden.

Gärtner der (PL die **Gärtner**) gardener.

Gärtnerin die (PL die **Gärtnerinnen**) gardener.

Gas das (PL die **Gase**) 1 gas; 2 **Gas geben** to accelerate.

a b c d e f g h i j k l m n o p q r s t u v w x y z

a

Gasherd der (PL die **Gasherde**) gas cooker.

b

Gaspedal das (PL die **Gaspedale**) accelerator.

c

Gasse die (PL die **Gassen**) lane.

d

Gast der (PL die **Gäste**) 1 guest; **wir haben heute Abend Gäste** we've got guests tonight; **2 bei jemandem zu Gast sein** to be staying with somebody.

e

f

g

Gastarbeiter der (PL die **Gastarbeiter**) foreign worker, guest worker.

h

Gästezimmer das (PL die **Gästezimmer**) 1 (hotel) room; 2 spare room.

i

j

k

gastfreundlich adjective hospitable.

l

Gastfreundschaft die hospitality.

m

Gastgeber der (PL die **Gastgeber**) host.

n

Gastgeberin die (PL die **Gastgeberinnen**) host.

o

Gasthaus das (PL die **Gasthäuser**) inn.

p

q

Gasthof der (PL die **Gasthöfe**) inn.

Gaststätte die (PL die **Gaststätten**) restaurant.

r

s

Gauner der (PL die **Gauner**) crook.

t

Gebäck das 1 pastries; 2 biscuits.

u

gebären ◇verb (IMPERF gebar, PERF hat geboren) 1 to give birth to; 2 geboren werden to be born.

v

w

Gebäude das (PL die **Gebäude**) building.

x

y

geben ◇verb (PRES gibt, IMPERF gab, PERF hat gegeben) 1 to give; 2 to

z

deal (cards); 3 to teach (at school); 4 geben Sie mir bitte Frau Scheck please put me through to Mrs Scheck; 5 es gibt there is, there are; es gibt viele gute Restaurants in München there are lots of good restaurants in Munich; was gibts or gibt's im Kino? what's on at the cinema?; was gibt es zum Mittagessen? what are we having for lunch?; 6 was gibts or gibt's Neues? what's the news?, what's new?; 7 sich geschlagen geben to admit defeat; 8 das gibt sich wieder it'll get better; 9 das gibts or gibt's doch nicht! I don't believe it!

Gebet das (PL die **Gebete**) prayer.

gebeten SEE bitten.

Gebiet das (PL die **Gebiete**) 1 area; 2 field.

gebildet adjective educated.

Gebirge das (PL die **Gebirge**) mountain range; im Gebirge in the mountains.

Gebiss das (PL die **Gebisse**) 1 teeth; 2 false teeth, dentures.

gebissen SEE beißen.

geblieben SEE bleiben.

geboren verb SEE gebären.

geboren adjective 1 born; 2 née; Frau Hahn, geborene Müller Mrs Hahn, née Müller.

geborgen adjective safe.

geboten SEE bieten.

gebracht SEE bringen.

gebraten adjective fried.

Gebrauch der (PL die **Gebräuche**)
1 use; **vor Gebrauch schütteln**
shake before use; 2 custom.

gebrauchen verb (PERF **hat
gebraucht**) to use.

Gebrauchsanweisung die (PL
die **Gebrauchsanweisungen**)
instructions (for use).

gebraucht adjective used, secondhand.

Gebrauchtwagen der (PL die
Gebrauchtwagen) second-hand
car.

gebrochen SEE **brechen**.

Gebühr die (PL die **Gebühren**) fee,
charge.

gebührenfrei adjective free (of
charge).

gebührenpflichtig adjective
1 subject to a charge; 2 **eine
gebührenpflichtige Straße** a toll
road.

gebunden SEE **binden**.

Geburt die (PL die **Geburten**) birth.

Geburtenregelung die birth
control.

Geburtsdatum das (PL die
Geburtsdaten) date of birth.

Geburtsort der (PL die
Geburtsorte) place of birth.

Geburtstag der (PL die
Geburtstage) birthday.

Geburtsurkunde die (PL die
Geburtsurkunden) birth
certificate.

gedacht SEE **denken**.

Gedächtnis das (PL die
Gedächtnisse) memory.

Gedanke der (PL die **Gedanken**)
1 thought; **in Gedanken
versunken sein** to be lost in
thought; 2 **sich Gedanken
machen** to worry; 3 **jemanden auf
andere Gedanken bringen** to take
somebody's mind off things.

gedankenlos adjective
thoughtless.

gedankenlos adverb without
thinking.

Gedeck das (PL die **Gedecke**)
1 place setting; 2 set meal.

Gedicht das (PL die **Gedichte**)
poem.

Geduld die patience.

geduldig adjective patient.

gedurft SEE **dürfen**.

geehrt adjective 1 honoured;
2 **Sehr geehrte Frau Ross** Dear
Mrs Ross.

geeignet adjective 1 suitable;
2 right.

Gefahr die (PL die **Gefahren**)
1 danger; **außer Gefahr** out of
danger; 2 **auf eigene Gefahr** at
your own risk; **Gefahr laufen,
etwas zu tun** to run the risk of
doing something.

gefährdet adjective at risk,
endangered; **eine gefährdete Art**
an endangered species.

gefährlich adjective dangerous.

gefallen[1] SEE **fallen**.

gefallen[2] ◇verb (PRES **gefällt**,
IMPERF **gefiel**, PERF **hat gefallen**)
1 **es gefällt mir** I like it; **es hat mir
sehr gut gefallen** I liked it a lot;

a

2 sich etwas gefallen lassen to put up with something.

b

c

Gefallen[1] der (PL die **Gefallen**) favour.

d

Gefallen[2] das pleasure; **dir zu Gefallen** to please you.

e

f

Gefangene der/die (PL die **Gefangenen**) prisoner.

Gefängnis das (PL die **Gefängnisse**) prison.

g

h

Gefäß das (PL die **Gefäße**) container.

i

gefasst adjective **1** calm, composed; **2 auf etwas gefasst sein** to be prepared for something.

j

k

gefiel SEE **gefallen**.

l

geflogen SEE **fliegen**.

geflossen SEE **fließen**.

m

Geflügel das poultry.

n

gefochten SEE **fechten**.

o

gefräßig adjective (informal) greedy.

p

q

gefrieren ⬦verb (IMPERF **gefror**, PERF **ist gefroren**) to freeze.

r

Gefrierfach das (PL die **Gefrierfächer**) freezer (compartment).

s

t

gefroren adjective frozen.

u

Gefühl das (PL die **Gefühle**) **1** feeling; **2 etwas im Gefühl haben** to have a feel for something.

v

gefüllt adjective stuffed (peppers, for example).

w

x

gefunden SEE **finden**.

gegangen SEE **gehen**.

y

gegeben SEE **geben**.

z

gegebenenfalls adverb if need be.

gegen preposition (+ ACC) **1** against; **2 gegen die Mauer fahren** to drive into the wall; **3 ein Mittel gegen Grippe** a cure for flu; **4** towards; **gegen Abend** towards evening; **5 gegen vier Uhr** around four o'clock; **6** compared with; **7** versus (in sport).

Gegend die (PL die **Gegenden**) **1** area; **2** neighbourhood.

gegeneinander adverb against each other, against one another.

Gegenmittel das (PL die **Gegenmittel**) **1** remedy; **2** antidote.

Gegensatz der (PL die **Gegensätze**) **1** contrast; **2** opposite; **3 im Gegensatz zu mir** unlike me.

gegenseitig adjective mutual.

gegenseitig adverb **sich gegenseitig helfen** to help each other.

Gegenstand der (PL die **Gegenstände**) **1** object; **2** subject (in grammar or of a discussion).

Gegenteil das (PL die **Gegenteile**) **1** opposite; **2 im Gegenteil** on the contrary.

gegenüber preposition (+ DAT) **1** opposite; **Susi saß mir gegenüber** Susi sat opposite me; **2** compared with; **3** towards; **jemandem gegenüber freundlich sein** to be friendly towards somebody.

gegenüber *adverb* opposite; **meine Freundin wohnt gegenüber** my friend lives opposite.

Gegenwart *die* 1 present; 2 presence.

gegessen SEE **essen**.

Gegner *der* (PL *die* **Gegner**) opponent.

Gegnerin *die* (PL *die* **Gegnerinnen**) opponent.

gegrillt *adjective* grilled.

Gehackte *das* mince.

Gehalt *das* (PL *die* **Gehälter**) salary.

gehässig *adjective* spiteful.

geheim *adjective* secret.

Geheimnis *das* (PL *die* **Geheimnisse**) secret.

geheimnisvoll *adjective* mysterious.

gehen ✧*verb* (IMPERF **ging**, PERF **ist gegangen**) 1 to go; **schlafen gehen** to go to bed; 2 to walk; 3 **über die Straße gehen** to cross the road; 4 **es geht ihr gut** she's well; **wie geht es Ihnen?** how are you?; **es geht** it's not too bad; 5 **das geht nicht** that's impossible; 6 **um etwas gehen** to be about something; **worum gehts** *or* **geht's hier?** what's it all about?; 7 **die Uhr geht falsch** the clock's wrong.

Gehirn *das* (PL *die* **Gehirne**) brain.

Gehirnerschütterung *die* (PL *die* **Gehirnerschütterungen**) concussion.

gehoben SEE **heben**.

geholfen SEE **helfen**.

Gehör *das* hearing.

gehorchen *verb* (PERF **hat gehorcht**) to obey.

gehören *verb* (PERF **hat gehört**) 1 to belong; **es gehört mir** it belongs to me; 2 **dazu gehört Mut** that takes courage; 3 **es gehört sich nicht** it isn't done.

gehorsam *adjective* obedient.

Gehsteig *der* (PL *die* **Gehsteige**) pavement.

Geier *der* (PL *die* **Geier**) vulture.

Geige *die* (PL *die* **Geigen**) violin.

Geisel *die* (PL *die* **Geiseln**) hostage.

Geist *der* (PL *die* **Geister**) 1 mind; 2 ghost; 3 wit.

geistesabwesend *adjective* absent-minded.

Geisteskrankheit *die* (PL *die* **Geisteskrankheiten**) mental illness.

Geisteswissenschaften (*plural noun*) arts, humanities.

geistig *adjective* mental.

geistreich *adjective* witty, clever.

geizig *adjective* mean.

gekannt SEE **kennen**.

gekonnt SEE **können**.

Gel *das* (PL *die* **Gele**) gel.

Gelächter *das* (PL *die* **Gelächter**) laughter.

geladen SEE **laden**.

gelähmt *adjective* paralysed.

Gelände *das* (PL *die* **Gelände**) 1 ground; 2 area.

Geländer *das* (PL *die* **Geländer**) 1 banister(s); 2 railing(s).

a
b
c
d
e
f
g
h
i
j
k
l
m
n
o
p
q
r
s
t
u
v
w
x
y
z

gelangweilt *adjective* bored.

gelassen *verb* SEE lassen

gelassen *adjective* calm.

geläufig *adjective* 1 common; 2 das ist mir nicht geläufig I'm not familiar with it.

gelaunt *adjective* gut gelaunt sein to be in a good mood.

gelb *adjective* yellow.

Geld *das* (PL die Gelder) money.

Geldautomat *der* (PL die Geldautomaten) cash dispenser.

Geldbörse *die* (PL die Geldbörsen) purse.

Geldschein *der* (PL die Geldscheine) banknote.

Geldstrafe *die* (PL die Geldstrafen) fine.

Geldwechsel *der* 1 bureau de change; 2 currency exchange.

gelegen SEE liegen.

Gelegenheit *die* (PL die Gelegenheiten) 1 opportunity; 2 occasion.

gelegentlich *adverb* occasionally.

Gelenk *das* (PL die Gelenke) joint.

Geliebte *der/die* (PL die Geliebten) lover.

geliehen SEE leihen.

gelingen ◇*verb* (IMPERF gelang, PERF ist gelungen) to succeed; es ist mir gelungen, sie zu überreden I succeeded in persuading her.

gelten ◇*verb* (PRES gilt, IMPERF galt, PERF hat gegolten) 1 to be valid; 2 to apply (*of a rule*); 3 jemandem

gelten to be directed at somebody; 4 sein Wort gilt viel his word is worth a lot; 5 das gilt nicht that doesn't count; 6 als etwas gelten to be regarded as something.

gelungen *verb* SEE gelingen

gelungen *adjective* successful.

Gemälde *das* (PL die Gemälde) painting.

gemein *adjective* mean.

Gemeinde *die* (PL die Gemeinden) 1 community; 2 congregation.

gemeinsam *adjective* 1 common; 2 joint.

gemeinsam *adverb* together; gemeinsam essen to eat together.

Gemeinschaft *die* (PL die Gemeinschaften) community.

gemischt *adjective* mixed.

gemocht SEE mögen.

Gemüse *das* (PL die Gemüse) vegetables.

Gemüsehändler *der* (PL die Gemüsehändler) greengrocer.

Gemüseladen *der* (PL die Gemüseläden) greengrocer's shop.

gemusst SEE müssen.

gemustert *adjective* patterned.

gemütlich *adjective* 1 cosy; 2 mach es dir gemütlich make yourself comfortable.

genannt SEE nennen.

genau *adjective* 1 exact; 2 accurate (*scales, description*); 3 meticulous; 4 ich weiß nichts Genaues I don't know any details.

genau adverb 1 exactly; **sich etwas genau ansehen** to look at something carefully; 2 **genau genommen** strictly speaking.

Genauigkeit die accuracy.

genauso adverb 1 just the same; 2 **genauso gut** just as good; **genauso viel** just as much, just as many; **genauso lange** just as long.

Genehmigung die (PL die Genehmigungen) 1 permission; 2 permit; licence.

Generation die (PL die Generationen) generation.

Generator der (PL die Generatoren) generator.

generell adjective general.

Genetik die genetics.

Genf das Geneva.

Genfer See der Lake Geneva.

genial adjective brilliant.

Genick das (PL die Genicke) (back of the) neck.

Genie das (PL die Genies) genius.

genießbar adjective edible.

genießen ◇ verb (IMPERF genoss, PERF hat genossen) to enjoy.

genommen SEE nehmen.

genug adverb enough.

genügen verb (PERF hat genügt) to be enough.

genügend adjective 1 enough; 2 sufficient.

Genuss der (PL die Genüsse) 1 enjoyment; 2 consumption (of alcohol).

geöffnet adjective open.

Geometrie die geometry.

Gepäck das luggage.

Gepäckaufbewahrung die (PL die Gepäckaufbewahrungen) left-luggage office.

Gepäckausgabe die left-luggage office.

Gepäckträger der (PL die Gepäckträger) 1 porter; 2 roof rack; 3 carrier (on a bike).

gerade adjective 1 straight; 2 **etwas gerade biegen** to straighten something; 3 upright; 4 **eine gerade Zahl** an even number.

gerade adverb 1 just; **gerade erst** only just; 2 **es war nicht gerade billig** it wasn't exactly cheap.

geradeaus adverb straight ahead.

geradebiegen SEE gerade.

gerannt SEE rennen.

Gerät das (PL die Geräte) 1 appliance; 2 set (TV or radio); 3 tool; 4 gadget; 5 **die Geräte** apparatus (in gymnastics).

geraten ◇ verb (PRES gerät, IMPERF geriet, PERF ist geraten) 1 to get (somewhere, the wrong side of the road etc.); **in etwas geraten** to get into something; **in Wut geraten** to get angry; 2 **an den Richtigen geraten** to come to the right person; 3 **gut/schlecht geraten** to turn out well/badly; 4 **nach jemandem geraten** to take after somebody.

Gerätetauchen das scuba diving.

geräuchert *adjective* smoked.

geräumig *adjective* spacious.

Geräusch *das* (PL die **Geräusche**) noise.

gerecht *adjective* 1 just; 2 fair.

Gerechtigkeit *die* justice.

Gerede *das* gossip.

Gericht *das* (PL die **Gerichte**) 1 court; 2 dish.

gerieben SEE **reiben**.

gering *adjective* 1 small (*amount*); 2 low (*value*); 3 short (*time, distance*).

Gerippe *das* (PL die **Gerippe**) skeleton.

gerissen *adjective* crafty.

geritten SEE **reiten**.

gern(e) *adverb* 1 gladly; 2 **jemanden gern haben** to like somebody; **etwas gern tun** to like doing something; **ich tanze gern** I like dancing; **ich hätte gerne einen Kaffee** I'd like a coffee; **welchen Belag hättest du gerne?** which topping would you like?; 3 **ja, gern!** yes, I'd love to!; 4 **das glaube ich gern** I can well believe that.

Gerste *die* barley.

Geruch *der* (PL die **Gerüche**) smell.

Gerücht *das* (PL die **Gerüchte**) rumour.

Gerümpel *das* junk.

gesalzen *verb* SEE **salzen**.

gesalzen *adjective* 1 salted; 2 **gesalzene Preise** (*informal*) steep prices.

gesamt *adjective* 1 whole; 2 **die gesamten Kosten** the total cost; 3 **die gesamten Werke** the complete works.

Gesamtschule *die* (PL die **Gesamtschulen**) comprehensive school.

gesandt SEE **senden**.

Geschäft *das* (PL die **Geschäfte**) 1 shop; 2 business; 3 deal.

Geschäftsführer *der* (PL die **Geschäftsführer**) manager.

Geschäftsführerin *die* (PL die **Geschäftsführerinnen**) manageress.

Geschäftszeiten *plural noun* business hours.

geschehen ◇*verb* (PRES **geschieht**, IMPERF **geschah**, PERF **ist geschehen**) to happen.

gescheit *adjective* clever.

Geschenk *das* (PL die **Geschenke**) present, gift.

Geschichte *die* (PL die **Geschichten**) 1 story; 2 history; 3 **mach bloß keine große Geschichte daraus** don't make such a thing of it.

Geschick *das* 1 skill; 2 fate.

geschickt *adjective* 1 skilful; 2 clever.

geschieden *verb* SEE **scheiden**.

geschieden *adjective* divorced; **meine Eltern sind geschieden** my parents are divorced.

geschienen SEE **scheinen**.

Geschirr *das* 1 crockery; 2 dishes.

gewissermaßen *adverb* **1** more or less; **2** as it were.

Gewitter *das* (PL die **Gewitter**) thunderstorm.

gewittrig *adjective* thundery.

gewöhnen *verb* (PERF **hat gewöhnt**) **1** jemanden an etwas gewöhnen to get somebody used to something; **2** an etwas gewöhnt sein to be used to something; **3** sich an etwas gewöhnen to get used to something.

Gewohnheit *die* (PL die **Gewohnheiten**) habit.

gewöhnlich *adjective* **1** usual; **2** ordinary.

gewöhnlich *adverb* usually; wie gewöhnlich as usual.

gewohnt *adjective* **1** usual; **2** etwas gewohnt sein to be used to something; Renate ist es nicht gewohnt, früh aufzustehen Renate isn't used to getting up early.

gewollt SEE **wollen**.

gewonnen SEE **gewinnen**.

geworden SEE **werden**.

geworfen SEE **werfen**.

Gewürz *das* (PL die **Gewürze**) spice.

gewusst SEE **wissen**.

Gezeiten *plural noun* tides.

gezogen SEE **ziehen**.

gezwungen SEE **zwingen**.

gibt SEE **geben**.

gierig *adjective* greedy.

gießen ◇*verb* (IMPERF **goss**, PERF **hat gegossen**) **1** to pour; es gießt it's pouring; **2** to water; vergiss nicht, die Blumen zu gießen don't forget to water the flowers.

Gießkanne *die* (PL die **Gießkannen**) watering can.

Gift *das* (PL die **Gifte**) poison.

giftig *adjective* **1** poisonous; **2** toxic.

Gigabyte *das* (PL die **Gigabytes**) gigabyte; eine Festplatte mit 20 Gigabyte Speicherkapazität a twenty gigabyte hard disk.

ging SEE **gehen**.

Gipfel *der* (PL die **Gipfel**) **1** peak, summit; **2** der Gipfel der Geschmacklosigkeit the height of bad taste.

Gips *der* plaster.

Giraffe *die* (PL die **Giraffen**) giraffe.

Girokonto *das* (PL die **Girokonten**) current account.

Gitarre *die* (PL die **Gitarren**) guitar.

Gitarrist *der* (PL die **Gitarristen**) guitarist, guitar player.

Gitter *das* (PL die **Gitter**) **1** grid; **2** bars.

glänzen *verb* (PERF **hat geglänzt**) to shine.

glänzend *adjective* **1** shining; **2** brilliant; ein glänzender Erfolg a brilliant success.

Glas *das* (PL die **Gläser**) **1** glass (*the material*); **2** glass (*for a drink*); **3** jar.

Glasscheibe *die* (PL die **Glasscheiben**) pane (of glass).

Glasur *die* **1** icing; **2** glaze.

glatt *adjective* **1** smooth; **2** slippery; **3** eine glatte Absage a flat refusal.

glatt *adverb* **1** smoothly; **2** flatly; etwas glatt ablehnen to flatly reject something; **3** das ist glatt gelogen that's a downright lie; **4** ich habe ihren Geburtstag glatt vergessen I totally forgot about her birthday.

Glatteis *das* (black) ice.

Glatze *die* (PL die Glatzen) eine Glatze haben to be bald; eine Glatze bekommen to go bald.

glauben *verb* (PERF hat geglaubt) **1** to believe; an Gott glauben to believe in God; **2** to think; **3** nicht zu glauben! incredible!

gleich *adjective* **1** same; **2** identical; **3** gleich bleibend constant; **4** das ist mir gleich it's all the same to me; ganz gleich, wer anruft no matter who calls.

gleich *adverb* **1** the same; **2** equally; **3** immediately; gleich danach immediately afterwards; gleich neben right next to; ich komme gleich I'm coming (right away); er ist gleich fertig he'll be ready in a minute.

gleichartig *adjective* similar.

gleichberechtigt *adjective* equal.

Gleichberechtigung *die* equality.

gleichbleibend SEE gleich.

gleichen ✧*verb* (IMPERF glich, PERF hat geglichen) **1** to be like; **2** sich gleichen to be alike.

gleichfalls *adverb* **1** also; **2** danke gleichfalls! the same to you!

Gleichgewicht *das* balance.

gleichgültig *adjective* indifferent; das ist doch gleichgültig it's not important.

gleichwertig *adjective* **1** equivalent; **2** of the same value; **3** of the same standard.

gleichzeitig *adverb* at the same time.

Gleis *das* (PL die Gleise) **1** track, line; **2** platform; Gleis vier platform four.

glich SEE gleichen.

Glied *das* (PL die Glieder) **1** limb; **2** link.

glitschig *adjective* slippery.

glitzern *verb* (PERF hat geglitzert) to glitter.

global *adjective* global, general; der globale Temperaturanstieg global warming.

Glocke *die* (PL die Glocken) bell.

Glück *das* **1** luck; viel Glück! good luck!; Glück haben to be lucky; zum Glück luckily; **2** happiness.

glücklich *adjective* **1** lucky; es war ein glücklicher Zufall, dass ich ihn heute in der Stadt getroffen habe it was a lucky coincidence that I met him in town today; **2** happy.

glücklicherweise *adverb* luckily, fortunately.

Glückwunsch *der* (PL die Glückwünsche) congratulations;

herzlichen Glückwunsch zum Geburtstag! happy birthday!

Glückwunschkarte die (PL die Glückwunschkarten) greetings card.

Glühbirne die (PL die Glühbirnen) light bulb.

glühen verb (PERF hat geglüht) to glow.

Gokart der (PL die Gokarts) go-kart; **Gokart gehen** to go karting.

Gold das gold.

golden adjective 1 gold; 2 golden.

Goldfisch der (PL die Goldfische) goldfish.

Golf[1] der (PL die Golfe) gulf.

Golf[2] das golf.

Golfplatz der (PL die Golfplätze) golf course.

Golfschläger der (PL die Golfschläger) golf club.

Golfspieler der (PL die Golfspieler) golfer.

Golfspielerin die (PL die Golfspielerinnen) golfer.

Gorilla der (PL die Gorillas) gorilla.

goss SEE gießen.

Gosse die (PL die Gossen) gutter (in street).

Gott der (PL die Götter) god.

Gottesdienst der (PL die Gottesdienste) service.

Göttin die (PL die Göttinnen) goddess.

Grab das (PL die Gräber) grave.

graben verb (PRES gräbt, IMPERF grub, PERF hat gegraben) to dig.

Grad der (PL die Grade) degree.

Grafik die (PL die Grafiken) graphics.

Gramm das (PL die Gramme) gram.

Grammatik die (PL die Grammatiken) grammar.

grammatikalisch adjective grammatical; **ein grammatikalischer Fehler** a grammatical error.

grantig adjective grumpy.

Gras das (PL die Gräser) grass.

grässlich adjective horrible.

Gräte die (PL die Gräten) (fish)bone.

gratis adverb free of charge.

gratulieren verb (PERF hat gratuliert) 1 to congratulate; 2 **ich habe Gabi zum Geburtstag gratuliert** I wished Gabi happy birthday; 3 **wir gratulieren!** congratulations!

grau adjective grey.

Gräuel der horror.

grauen verb (PERF hat gegraut) **mir graut es davor** I dread it.

grauenvoll adjective 1 grim; 2 horrific.

grauhaarig adjective grey-haired.

grausam adjective cruel.

Grausamkeit die cruelty.

graziös adjective graceful.

greifen ⋄verb (IMPERF griff, PERF hat gegriffen) 1 to take hold of; 2 to catch; 3 **nach etwas greifen** to reach for something; 4 **um sich greifen** to spread (of fire).

a
b
c
d
e
f
g
h
i
j
k
l
m
n
o
p
q
r
s
t
u
v
w
x
y
z

grell adjective **1** glaring; **2** garish; **3** shrill.

Grenze die (PL die **Grenzen**)
1 border; **2** boundary; **3** limit.

grenzen verb (PERF **hat gegrenzt**)
an etwas grenzen to border on something.

Greuel SEE **Gräuel**.

Grieche der (PL die **Griechen**)
Greek.

Griechenland das Greece.

Griechin die (PL die **Griechinnen**)
Greek.

griechisch adjective Greek.

Griff der (PL die **Griffe**) **1** grasp;
2 handle.

griff SEE **greifen**.

griffbereit adjective handy; **sie
hat den Korkenzieher immer
griffbereit** she always keeps the
corkscrew handy.

Grill der (PL die **Grills**) **1** grill;
2 barbecue.

Grille die (PL die **Grillen**) cricket (*the
insect*).

grillen verb (PERF **hat gegrillt**) **1** to
grill; **2** to have a barbecue.

Grillfest das (PL die **Grillfeste**)
barbecue.

grinsen verb (PERF **hat gegrinst**) to
grin.

Grippe die (PL die **Grippen**) flu.

grob adjective **1** coarse; **2** rough;
3 rude; **4 ein grober Fehler** a bad
mistake.

Groschen der (PL die **Groschen**)
1 groschen (*one hundredth of a
Schilling in the former Austrian*

currency) SEE **Schilling**;
2 (*informal*) **der Groschen ist
gefallen** the penny's dropped.

groß adjective **1** big; **2** great;
Gisela hatte große Angst Gisela
was very frightened; **3** tall; **4 ein
großer Buchstabe** a capital letter;
5 groß werden to grow up; **6 die
großen Ferien** the summer
holidays; **7 im Großen und
Ganzen** on the whole; **8 Groß und
Klein** young and old.

groß adverb **was soll man da
schon groß machen?** what are
you supposed to do?

großartig adjective great.

Großbritannien das Great
Britain.

Großbuchstabe der (PL die
Großbuchstaben) capital (letter).

Größe die (PL die **Größen**) **1** size;
2 height; **3** greatness.

Großeltern plural noun
grandparents.

großenteils adverb largely.

Großmarkt der (PL die
Großmärkte) hypermarket.

Großmutter die (PL die
Großmütter) grandmother.

großschreiben ◇verb (IMPERF
großschrieb, PERF **hat
großgeschrieben**) **ein Wort
großschreiben** to write a word
with a capital.

Großstadt die (PL die **Großstädte**)
city.

Großvater der (PL die **Großväter**)
grandfather.

großzügig adjective generous.

grub SEE **graben**.

grün *adjective* **1** green; **2 im Grünen** in the country; **3 die Grünen** the Greens.

Grund *der* (PL **die Gründe**) **1** ground; **2** bottom; **3** reason; **aus diesem Grund** for this reason; **4 im Grunde genommen** basically.

gründen *verb* (PERF **hat gegründet**) **1** to set up, to found; **2 sich auf etwas gründen** to be based on something.

Grundlage *die* (PL **die Grundlagen**) basis.

gründlich *adjective* thorough.

grundsätzlich *adjective* **1** fundamental; **2** basic.

grundsätzlich *adverb* **1** basically; **2** on principle.

Grundschule *die* (PL **die Grundschulen**) primary school.

Grundstück *das* (PL **die Grundstücke**) plot (of land).

Gruppe *die* (PL **die Gruppen**) group.

Gruß *der* (PL **die Grüße**) greeting; **einen schönen Gruß an Lars** give my regards to Lars; **mit herzlichen Grüßen** with best wishes.

grüßen *verb* (PERF **hat gegrüßt**) **1** to greet; **2** to say hello; **3 grüß Gott!** hello; **4 grüße Thomas von mir** give Thomas my regards; **Gisela lässt grüßen** Gisela sends her regards.

gucken *verb* (PERF **hat geguckt**) to look.

gültig *adjective* valid.

Gültigkeit *die* validity.

Gummi *der* (PL **die Gummis**) rubber.

Gummiband *das* (PL **die Gummibänder**) rubber band.

Gummistiefel *der* (PL **die Gummistiefel**) wellington (boot).

günstig *adjective* **1** favourable; **2** convenient.

Gurgel *die* (PL **die Gurgeln**) throat.

gurgeln *verb* (PERF **hat gegurgelt**) to gargle.

Gurke *die* (PL **die Gurken**) **1** cucumber; **2** gherkin.

Gürtel *der* (PL **die Gürtel**) belt.

Gürteltasche *die* (PL **die Gürteltaschen**) bum bag.

gut *adjective* **1** good; **2 guten Appetit!** enjoy your meal!; **3 schon gut** that's all right; **also gut** all right; **4 im Guten** amicably; **5 alles Gute!** all the best!.

gut *adverb* **1** well; **2 gut schmecken** to taste good; **3 gut zwei Stunden** good two hours; **4 uns geht's gut** we're fine; **ihm geht es nicht gut** he's not well.

Gut *das* (PL **die Güter**) **1** property; **2** estate; **3** (*plural*) goods, freight.

Güte *die* **1** goodness; **du meine Güte!** my goodness!; **2** quality.

Güterzug *der* (PL **die Güterzüge**) goods train.

gutgehen SEE **gut**.

gutmütig *adjective* good-natured.

Gutschein *der* (PL **die Gutscheine**) **1** voucher; **2** coupon.

a
b
c
d
e
f
g
h
i
j
k
l
m
n
o
p
q
r
s
t
u
v
w
x
y
z

Gymnasium das (PL die Gymnasien) grammar school.

Gymnastik die 1 gymnastics; 2 keep-fit (exercises).

Hh

Haar das (PL die Haare) 1 hair; **sich die Haare waschen** to wash your hair; 2 **um ein Haar** (informal) very nearly.

Haarbürste die (PL die Haarbürsten) hairbrush.

haarig adjective hairy.

Haarschnitt der (PL die Haarschnitte) haircut.

Haarwaschmittel das (PL die Haarwaschmittel) shampoo.

haben ◇verb (PRES hat, IMPERF hatte, PERF hat gehabt) 1 to have (got); **ich habe ein neues Auto** I have (I've got) a new car; **etwas gegen jemanden haben** to have something against somebody; 2 (used with another verb, like 'have' in English, to form past tenses) **ich habe Werners Adresse verloren** I've lost Werner's address; **ich habe deine Mutter gestern angerufen** I rang your mother yesterday; 3 **Angst haben** to be frightened; **Hunger haben** to be hungry; **Husten haben** to have a cough; 4 **heute haben wir Mittwoch** it's Wednesday today; 5 **die Kinder haben Ferien** the children are on holiday; 6 **was hat sie?** what's the matter with her?;

7 **ich hätte gern** ... I'd like ...; **ich hätte ihr geholfen** I would have helped her; 8 **sich haben** (informal) to make a fuss.

Habicht der (PL die Habichte) hawk.

hacken verb (PERF hat gehackt) 1 to chop (up); 2 to peck (of a bird).

Hackfleisch das minced meat.

Hacksteak das (PL die Hacksteaks) beefburger (without bread).

Hafen der (PL die Häfen) harbour.

Haferflocken plural noun porridge oats.

haftbar adjective **für etwas haftbar sein** to be liable for something.

haften verb (PERF hat gehaftet) 1 to stick; 2 **für etwas haften** to be responsible for something.

Hagel der hail.

hageln verb (PERF hat gehagelt) to hail.

Hagelschauer der (PL die Hagelschauer) hailstorm.

Hahn der (PL die Hähne) 1 cock; 2 tap.

Hähnchen das (PL die Hähnchen) chicken.

Hai der (PL die Haie) shark.

Haken der (PL die Haken) 1 hook; 2 tick; 3 catch; **da muss ein Haken dran sein** there must be a catch.

halb adjective half; **zum halben Preis** at half price; **halb eins** half past twelve.

Halbbruder der (PL die Halbbrüder) half-brother.

Halbfinale das (PL die Halbfinale) semi-final.

halbieren verb (PERF hat halbiert) to halve.

Halbkreis der (PL die Halbkreise) semicircle.

Halbpension die half board.

Halbschwester die (PL die Halbschwestern) half-sister.

halbtags adverb part-time.

halbwegs adverb 1 half-way; 2 more or less.

Halbzeit die (PL die Halbzeiten) 1 half; 2 half-time; **während der Halbzeit** during half-time.

half SEE helfen.

Hälfte die (PL die Hälften) half; **zur Hälfte** half.

Halle die (PL die Hallen) 1 hall; 2 foyer.

Hallenbad das (PL die Hallenbäder) indoor swimming pool.

hallo exclamation hello!

Hals der (PL die Hälse) 1 neck; 2 throat; **mir tut der Hals weh** I've got a sore throat; 3 **aus vollem Hals schreien** to shout at the top of your voice; 4 **Hals über Kopf** in a rush.

Halsband das (PL die Halsbänder) collar.

Halsschmerzen plural noun sore throat; **Paul hat Halsschmerzen** Paul's got a sore throat.

Halstuch das (PL die Halstücher) scarf.

Halt der 1 hold; **jetzt hat es einen besseren Halt** it holds better now; 2 **Halt machen** to stop!

halt exclamation stop!

haltbar adjective 1 hard-wearing; 2 durable; 3 **mindestens haltbar bis** ... best before ....

halten ✧verb (PRES hält, IMPERF hielt, PERF hat gehalten) 1 to hold; 2 to keep; **sein Versprechen halten** to keep your promise; **warm halten** to keep warm; 3 to stop; **der Bus hält direkt vor seiner Haustür** the bus stops right outside his door; 4 to save (in sport); 5 to take (a paper, magazine); 6 **ich habe ihn für deinen Bruder gehalten** I took him for your brother; 7 **viel von jemandem halten** to think a lot of somebody; **jemanden für ehrlich halten** to think somebody is honest; 8 **zu jemandem halten** to stand by somebody; 9 **eine Rede halten** to make a speech; 10 **sich halten** to keep (of milk, fruit, etc.); 11 **sich links/rechts halten** to keep left/right; 12 **sich gut halten** to do well; 13 **sich an etwas halten** to keep to something.

Haltestelle die (PL die Haltestellen) stop.

haltmachen SEE Halt.

Haltung die (PL die Haltungen) 1 posture; 2 attitude; 3 composure.

Hammelfleisch das mutton.

Hammer der (PL die Hämmer) hammer.

a b c d e f g h i j k l m n o p q r s t u v w x y z

hämmern *verb* (PERF hat gehämmert) to hammer.

Hamster der (PL die Hamster) hamster.

Hand die (PL die Hände) hand; **jemandem die Hand geben** to shake hands with somebody.

Handarbeit die (PL die Handarbeiten) 1 handicraft; 2 hand-made article.

Handball der handball.

Handbremse die (PL die Handbremsen) handbrake; **die Handbremse ziehen** to pull the handbrake.

Handbuch das (PL die Handbücher) manual.

Handel der 1 trade; 2 deal; 3 **in den Handel kommen** to come on the market.

handeln *verb* (PERF hat gehandelt) 1 to trade, to deal; 2 **mit jemandem handeln** to bargain with somebody; 3 to act; 4 **von etwas handeln** to be about something; 5 **es handelt sich um ...** it's about ...; **worum handelt es sich?** what's it about?

Handelsschule die (PL die Handelsschulen) business school, vocational college.

Handfläche die (PL die Handflächen) palm.

Handgelenk das (PL die Handgelenke) wrist.

Handgepäck das hand luggage.

handhaben *verb* (PERF hat gehandhabt) to handle.

Händler der (PL die Händler) dealer.

handlich *adjective* handy.

Handlung die (PL die Handlungen) 1 act; 2 action; 3 plot.

Handschellen (*plural noun*) handcuffs.

Handschrift die (PL die Handschriften) handwriting.

Handschuh der (PL die Handschuhe) glove.

Handtasche die (PL die Handtaschen) bag.

Handtrommel die (PL die Handtrommeln) tambourine.

Handtuch das (PL die Handtücher) towel.

Handwerker der (PL die Handwerker) 1 craftsman; 2 workman.

Handwerkszeug das tools.

Handy das (PL die Handys) mobile (phone).

Hang der (PL die Hänge) slope.

Hängematte die (PL die Hängematten) hammock.

hängen[1] *verb* (PERF hat gehängt) 1 to hang; **Florian hat das Bild an die Wand gehängt** Florian hung the picture on the wall; **sie hängte ihren Mantel in den Schrank** she hung her coat up in the cupboard; 2 **sie haben den Wohnwagen an das Auto gehängt** they attached the caravan to the car; 3 **sich an jemanden hängen** to latch on to somebody.

hängen[2] ✧ *verb* (IMPERF hing, PERF hat gehangen) 1 to hang; **mein**

Bild hat immer hier gehangen my picture used to hang here; **2 an seinen Eltern hängen** to be attached to your parents; **sie hängt sehr an ihrer Mutter** she's very attached to her mother; **3 an etwas hängen bleiben** to catch on something, to stick to something; **ich bin mit dem Ärmel am Zaun hängen geblieben** I got my sleeve caught on the fence.

hängenbleiben SEE **hängen²**.

Hansaplast™ das plaster.

Happen der (PL die **Happen**) mouthful; **ich habe heute keinen Happen gegessen** I haven't had a bite to eat all day.

Harfe die (PL die **Harfen**) harp.

Harke die (PL die **Harken**) rake.

harmlos adjective harmless.

hart adjective **1** hard; **2** harsh.

hart gekocht adjective hard-boiled.

Häschen das (PL die **Häschen**) bunny rabbit.

Hase der (PL die **Hasen**) hare.

Haselnuss die (PL die **Haselnüsse**) hazelnut.

Hass der hatred.

hassen verb (PERF **hat gehasst**) to hate.

hässlich adjective **1** ugly; **sie hat ein hässliches Gesicht** she's got an ugly face; **2** nasty; **das war sehr hässlich von dir** that was very nasty of you.

hast SEE **haben**.

hastig adjective hasty.

hat, hatte, hatten, hattest, hattet SEE **haben**.

Haube die (PL die **Hauben**) **1** bonnet; **2** cap.

hauen ◇verb (PRES **haut**, IMPERF **haute**, PERF **hat gehauen**) **1** to beat; **2** to thump, to bang; **3 sich hauen** to fight; **4 jemanden übers Ohr hauen** (informal) to cheat somebody.

Haufen der (PL die **Haufen**) **1** heap; **2** crowd (of people); **3 ein Haufen** (informal) heaps of; **ein Haufen Geld** heaps of money.

haufenweise adverb heaps of; **Gabi hat haufenweise CDs** Gabi has heaps of CDs.

häufig adjective frequent.

Häufigkeit die frequency.

Hauptbahnhof der (PL die **Hauptbahnhöfe**) main station.

Hauptgericht das (PL die **Hauptgerichte**) main course.

Hauptrolle die (PL die **Hauptrollen**) lead.

Hauptsache die (PL die **Hauptsachen**) main thing.

hauptsächlich adjective main.

hauptsächlich adverb mainly.

Hauptschule die secondary school.

Hauptstadt die (PL die **Hauptstädte**) capital.

Hauptstraße die (PL die **Hauptstraßen**) main road.

Hauptverkehrszeit die (PL die **Hauptverkehrszeiten**) rush hour.

a b c d e f g h i j k l m n o p q r s t u v w x y z

Hauptwort das (PL die Hauptwörter) noun.

Haus das (PL die Häuser) **1** house; **2 nach Hause** home; **zu Hause** at home.

Hausarbeit die (PL die Hausarbeiten) **1** housework; **die Kinder müssen bei der Hausarbeit helfen** the children have to help with the housework; **2** homework.

Hausaufgaben plural noun homework; **hast du deine Hausaufgaben gemacht?** have you done your homework?

Hausfrau die (PL die Hausfrauen) housewife.

Haushalt der (PL die Haushalte) **1** household; **2 den Haushalt machen** to do the housework; **im Haushalt helfen** to help with the housework; **3** budget.

Haushaltswarengeschäft das (PL die Haushaltswaren-geschäfte) hardware shop.

Hausmeister der (PL die Hausmeister) caretaker.

Hausnummer die house number.

Hausschlüssel der (PL die Hausschlüssel) front-door key.

Hausschuh der (PL die Hausschuhe) slipper.

Haustier das (PL die Haustiere) pet.

Haustür die (PL die Haustüren) front door.

Haut die (PL die Häute) skin; **aus der Haut fahren** (informal) to go up the wall.

Hebamme die (PL die Hebammen) midwife.

Hebel der (PL die Hebel) lever.

heben ◇verb (IMPERF hob, PERF hat gehoben) **1** to lift; **2 sich heben** to rise.

Hecke die (PL die Hecken) hedge.

Heer das (PL die Heere) army.

Hefe die (PL die Hefen) yeast.

Heft das (PL die Hefte) **1** exercise book; **2** issue (of a magazine).

heften verb (PERF hat geheftet) **1** to pin; **2** to tack (by sewing); **3** to clip; **4** to staple.

heftig adjective **1** violent; **2** heavy (snow, rain).

Heftklammer die (PL die Heftklammern) staple.

Heftpflaster das (PL die Heftpflaster) sticking plaster.

Heftzwecke die (PL die Heftzwecken) drawing pin.

Heide die heath.

Heidekraut das heather.

Heidelbeere die (PL die Heidelbeeren) bilberry.

heilen verb (PERF hat geheilt) **1** to cure; **2** to heal.

heilig adjective **1** holy; **2 heilig halten** to hold sacred; **3 der heilige Franz von Assisi** Saint Francis of Assisi.

Heiligabend der (PL die Heiligabende) Christmas Eve.

Heilige der/die (PL die Heiligen) saint.

Heilmittel das (PL die **Heilmittel**) remedy.

Heim das (PL die **Heime**) **1** home; **2** hostel.

heim adverb home.

Heimat die (PL die **Heimaten**) **1** home; **2** native land.

Heimatstadt die home town.

Heimfahrt die (PL die **Heimfahrten**) **1** journey home; **2** way home.

heimgehen ◇verb (IMPERF **ging heim**, PERF **ist heimgegangen**) to go home.

heimlich adjective secret.

heimlich adverb secretly.

Heimspiel das (PL die **Heimspiele**) home game.

Heimweg der (PL die **Heimwege**) way home.

Heimweh das homesickness; **Heimweh haben** to be homesick.

Heirat die (PL die **Heiraten**) marriage.

heiraten verb (PERF **hat geheiratet**) to marry.

heiser adjective hoarse.

heiß adjective hot.

heißen ◇verb (IMPERF **hieß**, PERF **hat geheißen**) **1** to be called; **wie heißt du?** what's your name?; **2** to mean; **3** das heißt that is; **4** es heißt it is said; **5** wie heißt 'dog' auf Deutsch? what's the German for 'dog'?

heiter adjective **1** bright; **2** cheerful.

heizen verb (PERF **hat geheizt**) **1** to heat (a room); **2** to put the heating on; **3** to have the heating on.

Heizung die heating.

hektisch adjective hectic.

Held der (PL die **Helden**) hero.

Heldin die (PL die **Heldinnen**) heroine.

helfen ◇verb (PRES **hilft**, IMPERF **half**, PERF **hat geholfen**) **1** to help; **Lisa hilft mir** Lisa is helping me; **2** es hilft nichts it's no good; **3** sich zu helfen wissen to know what to do; **ich weiß mir nicht zu helfen** I don't know what to do.

Helfer der (PL die **Helfer**) **1** helper; **2** assistant.

Helferin die (PL die **Helferinnen**) **1** helper; **2** assistant.

hell adjective **1** light (colour); **2** bright; **3** eine helle Stimme a clear voice; **4** helles Bier lager; **5** da ist heller Wahnsinn (informal) that's sheer madness.

hellwach adjective wide awake.

Helm der (PL die **Helme**) helmet.

Hemd das (PL die **Hemden**) **1** shirt; **2** vest.

Henkel der (PL die **Henkel**) handle.

Henne die (PL die **Hennen**) hen.

her adverb **1** here; **komm her** come here; **2** vor jemandem her in front of somebody; **3** hinter etwas her sein to be after something; **4** von der Farbe her as far as the colour is concerned; **5** wo bist du her? where do you come from?; **6** wo hat Klaus das her? where did Klaus

a
b
c
d
e
f
g
h
i
j
k
l
m
n
o
p
q
r
s
t
u
v
w
x
y
z

get it from?; **7 her damit!**
(*informal*) give it to me!; **8** ago; **das ist schon lange her** it was a long time ago; **das ist drei Tage her** it was three days ago.

herab *adverb* down.

herablassend *adjective* condescending.

herabsetzen *verb* (PERF **hat herabgesetzt**) **1** to reduce; **2** to belittle.

heran *adverb* **1 an etwas heran** close to something, right up to something; **bis an die Wand heran** up to the wall; **2 immer heran!** come closer!

herankommen ⋄*verb* (IMPERF **kam heran**, PERF **ist herangekommen**) **1** to come near; **2 herankommen an** to come up to; **3 ich komme nicht heran** I can't get at it.

herauf *adverb* up.

heraufkommen ⋄*verb* (IMPERF **kam herauf**, PERF **ist heraufgekommen**) to come up.

heraus *adverb* out.

herausbekommen ⋄*verb* (IMPERF **bekam heraus**, PERF **hat herausbekommen**) **1** to get out; **2** to find out; **3** to solve; **4 Geld herausbekommen** to get change.

herausbringen *verb* (IMPERF **brachte heraus**, PERF **hat herausgebracht**) **1** to publish (*a book*); **2** to release (*an album*); **3** to launch.

herausfinden ⋄*verb* (IMPERF **fand heraus**, PERF **hat herausgefunden**)

1 to find out; **2** to find your way out.

herausgeben ⋄*verb* (PRES **gibt heraus**, IMPERF **gab heraus**, PERF **hat herausgegeben**) **1** to hand over; **2** to bring out.

herauskommen ⋄*verb* (IMPERF **kam heraus**, PERF **ist herausgekommen**) to come out.

herausnehmen ⋄*verb* (PRES **nimmt heraus**, IMPERF **nahm heraus**, PERF **hat herausgenommen**) **1** to take out; **sie hat ihren Lippenstift aus der Tasche herausgenommen** she took her lipstick out of the bag; **2 sich die Mandeln herausnehmen lassen** to have your tonsils out; **3 es sich herausnehmen, etwas zu tun** to have the nerve to do something; **du nimmst dir zu viel heraus** you're going too far.

herausstellen *verb* (PERF **hat herausgestellt**) **1** to put out; **2 sich herausstellen** to turn out; **es stellte sich heraus, dass ... it** turned out that ...

herausziehen ⋄*verb* (IMPERF **zog heraus**, PERF **hat herausgezogen**) **1** to pull out.

herb *adjective* **1** sharp; **2** dry (*wine*).

herbei *adverb* over (here); **kommt herbei!** come over here!

Herberge *die* (PL **die Herbergen**) hostel.

Herbergsmutter *die* (PL **die Herbergsmütter**) warden (*in a youth hostel*).

Herbergsvater der (PL die Herbergsväter) warden (*in a youth hostel*).

herbringen ⬦*verb* (IMPERF **brachte her**, PERF **hat hergebracht**) to bring (here).

Herbst der (PL die Herbste) autumn; **im Herbst** in autumn.

Herd der (PL die Herde) cooker.

Herde die (PL die Herden) **1** herd; **2** flock.

herein *adverb* in; **herein!** come in!

hereinfallen ⬦*verb* (PRES **fällt herein**, IMPERF **fiel herein**, PERF **hereingefallen**) to be taken in; **auf einen Betrüger hereinfallen** to be taken in by a swindler.

hereinkommen ⬦*verb* (IMPERF **kam herein**, PERF **ist hereingekommen**) to come in.

hereinlassen ⬦*verb* (PRES **lässt herein**, IMPERF **ließ herein**, PERF **hat hereingelassen**) to let in; **Max lässt mich nicht ins Zimmer herein** Max won't let me into the room.

Herfahrt die (PL die Herfahrten) **1** journey here; **2** way here.

hergeben ⬦*verb* (PRES **gibt her**, IMPERF **gab her**, PERF **hat hergegeben**) **1** to hand over; **gib die Tasche her!** hand over the bag!; **2** to give away; **3** sich für etwas **hergeben** to get involved in something; **dazu gebe ich mich nicht her** I won't have anything to do with it.

Hering der (PL die Heringe) herring.

herkommen ⬦*verb* (IMPERF **kam her**, PERF **ist hergekommen**) to come (here); **wo kommt das her?** where does it come from?

Herkunft die (PL die Herkünfte) **1** origin; **2** background.

Heroin das heroin.

Herr der (PL die Herren) **1** gentleman; **2 Herr Huber** Mr Huber; **3 Sehr geehrte Herren** Dear Sirs (*in a letter*); **4 meine Herren!** gentlemen!; **5** master; **6 der Herr** the Lord.

herrichten *verb* (PERF **hat hergerichtet**) to get ready, to prepare; **sie richtet die Betten für die Gäste her** she's getting the beds for the guests ready.

herrlich *adjective* marvellous.

herrschen *verb* (PERF **hat geherrscht**) **1** to rule; **2** to be; **es herrschte große Aufregung** there was great excitement.

herstellen *verb* (PERF **hat hergestellt**) to manufacture, to make; **in Deutschland hergestellt** made in Germany.

Herstellung die (PL die Herstellungen) manufacture, production.

herüber *adverb* over (here).

herum *adverb* **um … herum** round; **falsch herum** the wrong way round; **im Kreis herum** in a circle.

herumdrehen *verb* (PERF **hat herumgedreht**) **1** to turn (over or round); **2 sich herumdrehen** to turn round.

a b c d e f g h i j k l m n o p q r s t u v w x y z

herumführen *verb* (PERF hat herumgeführt) to show around.

herumgehen ◇*verb* (IMPERF ging herum, PERF ist herumgegangen) 1 to go round; 2 to walk around; im Park herumgehen to walk around the park; 3 to pass (*of time*).

herunter *adverb* down; die Treppe herunter down the stairs.

herunterfallen ◇*verb* (PRES fällt herunter, IMPERF fiel herunter, PERF ist heruntergefallen) 1 to fall down; 2 to fall off.

herunterkommen ◇*verb* (IMPERF kam herunter, PERF ist heruntergekommen) 1 to come down; 2 (*informal*) to go to rack and ruin.

herunterlassen ◇*verb* (PRES lässt herunter, IMPERF ließ herunter, PERF hat heruntergelassen) to let down, to lower.

hervor *adverb* out.

hervorragend *adjective* outstanding.

hervorragend *adverb* outstandingly well.

hervorrufen ◇*verb* (IMPERF rief hervor, PERF hat hervorgerufen) to cause.

Herz *das* (PL die Herzen) 1 heart; 2 hearts (*in cards*).

Herzanfall *der* (PL die Herzanfälle) heart attack.

Herzinfarkt *der* (PL die Herzinfarkte) heart attack.

herzlich *adjective* 1 warm; 2 sincere; 3 herzlichen Dank

many thanks; 4 herzliche Grüße best wishes; 5 herzlichen Glückwunsch! congratulations!; 6 herzlich willkommen in Passau! welcome to Passau!

herzlos *adjective* heartless.

Herzschlag *der* (PL die Herzschläge) 1 heartbeat; 2 heart failure; er hat einen Herzschlag bekommen he had a heart attack.

heterosexuell *adjective* heterosexual.

Heterosexuelle *der/die* (PL die Heterosexuellen) heterosexual.

Heu *das* hay.

heulen *verb* (PERF hat geheult) 1 to howl; 2 (*informal*) to cry.

Heuschnupfen *der* hayfever; ich habe Heuschnupfen I suffer from hayfever.

heute *adverb* today; heute Abend this evening; heute Morgen this morning.

heutig *adjective* 1 today's; 2 in der heutigen Zeit nowadays.

heutzutage nowadays; heutzutage sind sie häufig they're common nowadays.

Hexe *die* (PL die Hexen) witch.

Hexenschuss *der* lumbago.

hielt SEE halten.

hier *adverb* here.

hierher *adverb* here; komm sofort hierher! come here immediately!

hierhin *adverb* here.

hiesig *adjective* local.

hieß SEE heißen.

Hilfe die (PL die Hilfen) **1** help; **2** aid.

hilflos adjective helpless.

hilfsbereit adjective helpful.

hilft SEE **helfen.**

Himbeere die (PL die Himbeeren) raspberry.

Himmel der (PL die Himmel) **1** sky; **2** heaven.

himmlisch adjective heavenly.

hin adverb **1** there; **hin und zurück** there and back; **2** hin und wieder now and again; **3** hin und her back and forth, to and fro; **4** auf meinen Rat hin on my advice; **auf Ihren Brief hin** in reply to your letter; **5** wo ist Dominik hin? where's Dominik gone?; **6** es ist nicht mehr lange hin it's not long to go; **7** ich bin hin (informal) I'm worn out.

hinauf adverb up; **die Straße hinauf** up the road.

hinaufgehen ◇verb (IMPERF ging hinauf, PERF ist hinaufgegangen) to go up.

hinaus adverb **1** out; **2** auf Jahre hinaus for years to come.

hinausbringen ◇verb (IMPERF brachte hinaus, PERF hat hinausgebracht) **1** to see out (a person); **2** to take out; **den Abfall hinausbringen** to take the rubbish out.

hinausgehen ◇verb (IMPERF ging hinaus, PERF ist hinausgegangen) **1** to go out; **2** über etwas hinausgehen to exceed something; **3** das Zimmer geht nach Norden hinaus the room faces north.

hindern verb (PERF hat gehindert) to stop; **jemanden daran hindern, etwas zu tun** to stop somebody from doing something.

Hindernis das (PL die Hindernisse) obstacle.

hinduistisch adjective Hindu.

hindurch adverb **1** through it/them; **2** das ganze Jahr hindurch throughout the year.

hinein adverb **1** in; **2** in etwas hinein into something.

hineingehen ◇verb (IMPERF ging hinein, PERF ist hineingegangen) **1** to go in; **2** in etwas hineingehen to go into something.

hinfahren ◇verb (PRES fährt hin, IMPERF fuhr hin, PERF ist hingefahren) **1** to go/drive there; **2** (PERF hat hingefahren) to take/drive there.

Hinfahrt die (PL die Hinfahrten) **1** journey there, way there; **2** outward journey.

hinfallen ◇verb (PRES fällt hin, IMPERF fiel hin, PERF ist hingefallen) to fall over.

hing SEE **hängen.**

hingehen ◇verb (IMPERF ging hin, PERF ist hingegangen) **1** to go there; **wo geht ihr hin?** where are you going?; **2** to go by (of time).

hinken verb (PERF hat/ist gehinkt) to limp.

hinkommen ◇verb (IMPERF kam hin, PERF ist hingekommen) **1** to get there; **2** to go; **wo kommt das Buch hin?** where does the book go?; **3** mit etwas hinkommen

a
b
c
d
e
f
g
h
i
j
k
l
m
n
o
p
q
r
s
t
u
v
w
x
y
z

(*informal*) to manage (with something).

hinlegen *verb* (PERF **hat hingelegt**)
1 to put down; **leg die Zeitung unten hin** put the paper down there; **2 sich hinlegen** to lie down.

hinsetzen *verb* (PERF **hat sich hingesetzt**) **sich hinsetzen** to sit down; **Petra setzte sich neben ihm hin** Petra sat down next to him.

hinten *adverb* at the back; **von hinten** from behind.

hinter *preposition* (+ DAT *or* + ACC)
1 behind; **2 etwas hinter sich bringen** to get something over with.

hintere SEE **hinterer**.

hintereinander *adverb* **1** one behind the other; **2** one after the other; **dreimal hintereinander** three times in a row.

hinterer, hintere, hinteres *adjective* **1** back; **2 am hinteren Ende** at the far end.

Hintergrund *der* (PL *die* **Hintergründe**) background.

hinterher *adverb* afterwards.

Hintern *der* (PL *die* **Hintern**) bottom.

Hinterrad *das* (PL *die* **Hinterräder**) back wheel.

hinters = **hinter das**.

hinüber *adverb* **1** over (there), across (there); **2 das Radio ist hinüber** (*informal*) the radio has had it.

hinübergehen *⋄verb* (IMPERF **ging hinüber**, PERF **ist**

hinübergegangen) to go over, to go across.

hinunter *adverb* down.

Hinweg *der* (PL *die* **Hinwege**) way there; **auf dem Hinweg** on the way there.

Hinweis *der* (PL *die* **Hinweise**)
1 hint; **das war ein deutlicher Hinweis, dass er lieber allein fährt** it was an obvious hint that he prefers to go on his own; **2** reference; **3 Hinweise zur Bedienung** operating instructions.

hinweisen *⋄verb* (IMPERF **wies hin**, PERF **hat hingewiesen**) to point; **jemanden auf etwas hinweisen** to point something out to somebody.

Hirn *das* (PL *die* **Hirne**) brain.

Hirnhautentzündung *die* meningitis.

Hirsch *der* (PL *die* **Hirsche**) **1** deer; **2** stag; **3** venison.

Hirt *der* (PL *die* **Hirten**) shepherd.

Hirtin *die* (PL *die* **Hirtinnen**) shepherd.

Historiker *der* (PL *die* **Historiker**) historian.

historisch *adjective* historical.

Hitze *die* heat.

hitzefrei *adjective* **hitzefrei haben** to be sent home early from school because of hot weather.

Hitzewelle *die* (PL *die* **Hitzewellen**) heatwave.

Hitzschlag *der* (PL *die* **Hitzschläge**) heatstroke.

hob SEE **heben**.

Hobby das (PL die Hobbys) hobby.

Hoch das (PL die Hochs) 1 cheer; **ein dreifaches Hoch für das Geburtstagskind** three cheers for the birthday girl/boy; 2 high (pressure).

hoch adjective (with endings 'hoch' becomes 'hoher/hohe/hohes') 1 high; **der Zaun ist zu hoch** the fence is too high; **ein hoher Zaun** a high fence; 2 deep (snow); 3 great (age, weight).

hoch adverb 1 highly; **hoch begabt** highly gifted; 2 **die Treppe hoch** up the stairs.

hochachtungsvoll adverb **Hochachtungsvoll** Yours faithfully.

hochhackig adjective high-heeled; **hochhackige Schuhe** high-heeled shoes.

Hochhaus das (PL die Hochhäuser) high-rise building.

hochheben ◇verb (IMPERF **hob hoch**, PERF **hat hochgehoben**) to lift up; **sie hob das Kind hoch** she lifted up the child.

hochnäsig adjective stuck-up.

Hochschule die (PL die Hochschulen) university, college.

Hochsprung der high jump.

höchst adverb extremely.

höchstens adverb 1 at most; 2 except perhaps.

höchster, höchste, höchstes adjective highest; **der Mount Everest ist der der höchste Berg der Welt** Mount Everest is the

highest mountain in the world; **es ist höchste Zeit** it is high time.

Höchstgeschwindigkeit die maximum speed.

höchstmöglich adjective highest possible; **die höchstmögliche Geschwindigkeit** the highest possible speed.

Höchsttemperatur die (PL die Höchsttemperaturen) maximum temperature.

Hochzeit die (PL die Hochzeiten) wedding.

Hochzeitstag der (PL die Hochzeitstage) 1 wedding day; 2 wedding anniversary.

Hocker der (PL die Hocker) stool.

Hockey das hockey.

Hockeyschläger der (PL die Hockeyschläger) hockey stick.

Hof der (PL die Höfe) 1 yard; 2 farm.

hoffen verb (PERF **hat gehofft**) to hope; **auf etwas hoffen** to hope for something.

hoffentlich adverb hopefully; **hoffentlich nicht** I hope not.

Hoffnung die (PL die Hoffnungen) hope.

hoffnungslos adjective hopeless.

höflich adjective polite.

Höflichkeit die (PL die Höflichkeiten) politeness, courtesy.

Höhe die (PL die Höhen) 1 height; 2 **das ist die Höhe!** (informal) that's the limit!

hoher, hohe, hohes SEE **hoch**.

höher adjective 1 higher; 2 deeper.

a b c d e f g h i j k l m n o p q r s t u v w x y z

a **hohl** *adjective* hollow.

b **Höhle** die (PL die **Höhlen**) 1 cave;
2 den.

c **holen** *verb* (PERF **hat geholt**) 1 to
get, to fetch; 2 **jemanden holen**
lassen to send for somebody;
3 **sich etwas holen** to get
something.

Holland das Holland.

g **Holländer** der (PL die **Holländer**)
Dutchman.

Holländerin die (PL die
Holländerinnen) Dutchwoman.

holländisch *adjective* Dutch.

Hölle die (PL die **Höllen**) hell.

Holz das (PL die **Hölzer**) wood.

Holzkohle die charcoal.

m **homöopathisch** *adjective*
homeopathic.

homosexuell *adjective*
homosexual.

Homosexuelle der/die (PL die
Homosexuellen) homosexual.

Honig der (PL die **Honige**) honey.

horchen *verb* (PERF **hat gehorcht**)
1 to listen; 2 to eavesdrop.

hören *verb* (PERF **hat gehört**) 1 to
hear; 2 to listen (to); **Musik hören**
to listen to music.

Hörer der (PL die **Hörer**) 1 listener;
2 receiver (*of a phone*).

Hörerin die (PL die **Hörerinnen**)
listener.

Hörgerät das (PL die **Hörgeräte**)
hearing aid.

Horizont der (PL die **Horizonte**)
horizon.

horizontal *adjective* horizontal.

Horn das (PL die **Hörner**) horn.

Horoskop das (PL die **Horoskope**)
horoscope.

Horrorfilm der (PL die **Horrorfilme**)
horror film.

Hose die (PL die **Hosen**) trousers.

Hosenträger *plural noun* braces.

Hotdog das or der (PL die **Hotdogs**)
hot dog.

Hotel das (PL die **Hotels**) hotel.

Hotelverzeichnis das (PL die
Hotelverzeichnisse) list of hotels.

hübsch *adjective* 1 pretty; 2 nice.

Hubschrauber der (PL die
Hubschrauber) helicopter.

Huf der (PL die **Hufe**) hoof.

Hufeisen das (PL die **Hufeisen**)
horseshoe.

Hüfte die (PL die **Hüften**) hip.

Hügel der (PL die **Hügel**) hill.

Huhn das (PL die **Hühner**) 1 chicken;
2 hen.

Hummel die (PL die **Hummeln**)
bumble-bee.

Hummer der (PL die **Hummer**)
lobster.

Humor der humour; **Humor haben**
to have a sense of humour.

Hund der (PL die **Hunde**) dog; **den**
Hund ausführen to take the dog for
a walk.

Hundehütte die (PL die
Hundehütten) kennel.

hundemüde *adjective* (*informal*)
dog-tired.

Hundepension die (PL die Hundepensionen) kennels (for boarding).

hundert number a hundred, one hundred.

Hunger der hunger; **Hunger haben** to be hungry.

hungrig adjective hungry.

Hupe die (PL die Hupen) horn.

hurra exclamation hooray!.

Husten der cough.

husten verb (PERF hat gehustet) to cough.

Hut der (PL die Hüte) hat.

hüten verb (PERF hat gehütet) **1** to look after (a child, children); **2 sich hüten** to be on your guard; **3 sich hüten, etwas zu tun** to take care not to do something.

Hütte die (PL die Hütten) hut.

Hygiene die **1** hygiene; **2** health care.

hygienisch adjective hygienic.

hypnotisieren verb (PERF hat hypnotisiert) to hypnotize.

Hypothek die (PL die Hypotheken) mortgage.

hysterisch adjective hysterical.

Ii

ich pronoun I.

Icon das (PL die Icons) icon; **das Icon anklicken** to click the icon.

IC-Zug der (PL die IC-Züge) (Intercityzug) intercity train.

ideal adjective ideal.

Idee die (PL die Ideen) idea.

identifizieren verb (PERF hat identifiziert) to identify.

identisch adjective identical.

Idiot der (PL die Idioten) idiot.

idiotisch adjective idiotic.

idyllisch adjective idyllic.

Igel der (PL die Igel) hedgehog.

ihm pronoun **1** him, to him; **2** it, to it.

ihn pronoun **1** him; **2** it.

ihnen pronoun them, to them.

Ihr adjective your; **Ihr Sohn hat mir geschrieben** your son wrote to me.

ihr pronoun **1** you (plural); **2** her, to her; **3** (standing for an object) it, to it.

ihr adjective **1** her; **2** its; **3** their; **sie haben ihr Auto verkauft** they sold their car.

ihrer, ihre, ihr(e)s pronoun **1** hers; **mein Rad ist rot, ihrs ist blau** my bike is red, hers is blue; **2** theirs; **das ist nicht ihre Katze, ihre ist schwarz** that's not their cat, theirs is black.

Ihrer, Ihre, Ihr(e)s pronoun yours; **mein Job ist nicht so interessant wie Ihrer** my job's not as interesting as yours.

ihretwegen adverb **1** for her sake; **2** for their sake; **3** because of her; **4** because of them.

Ihretwegen adverb **1** for your sake; **2** because of you.

Illusion die (PL die Illusionen) illusion.

Illustration 132 GERMAN · ENGLISH

a

Illustration die (PL die Illustrationen) illustration.

b

Illustrierte die (PL die Illustrierten) magazine.

c

im = in dem; was läuft im Kino? what's on at the cinema?; im August in August.

d

Imbiss der (PL die Imbisse) 1 snack; 2 snack bar.

e

f

Imbissstube die (PL die Imbissstuben) snack bar.

g

Imitator der (PL die Imitatoren) mimic, impressionist.

h

imitieren verb (PERF hat imitiert) to imitate.

i

immer adverb 1 always; 2 immer wieder again and again; 3 immer mehr more and more; immer dunkler darker and darker; 4 immer noch still; 5 immer, wenn er anruft every time he rings; 6 wo/wer/wann immer wherever/whoever/whenever; 7 für immer for ever.

j

k

l

m

n

immerhin adverb at least.

o

immerzu adverb all the time.

Imperfekt das imperfect; 'ich schlug' steht im Imperfekt 'ich schlug' is in the imperfect.

p

q

Impfausweis der (PL die Impfausweise) vaccination certificate.

r

s

impfen verb (PERF hat geimpft) to vaccinate.

t

u

Impfung die (PL die Impfungen) vaccination.

v

w

x

y

z

imponieren verb (PERF hat imponiert) to impress; jemandem imponieren to impress somebody.

Import der (PL die Importe) import.

Importeur der (PL die Importeure) importer.

importieren verb (PERF hat importiert) to import.

imprägniert adjective waterproof.

imstande adverb imstande sein, etwas zu tun to be able to do something; er ist nicht imstande, seine Hausaufgaben allein zu machen he's not able to do his homework on his own.

in preposition (+ DAT or + ACC) (the dative is used when talking about position; the accusative shows movement towards something) 1 in; es ist in der Küche it's in the kitchen; 2 into, in; ich habe es in meine Tasche gesteckt I've put it in my bag; 3 in die Schule gehen to go to school; 4 Susi ist in der Schule Susi is at school; 5 in diesem Jahr this year; 6 in sein to be in; Rap ist in rap is in.

inbegriffen adjective included; Essen ist inbegriffen food is included.

indem conjunction 1 while; 2 by.

Inder der (PL die Inder) Indian.

Inderin die (PL die Inderinnen) Indian.

Indianer der (PL die Indianer) (American) Indian, native American.

Indianerin die (PL die Indianerinnen)(American)Indian, native American.

indianisch adjective (American) Indian, native American.

Indien das India.

indisch adjective Indian.

indiskutabel adjective out of the question.

individuell adjective individual.

Individuum das (PL die Individuen) individual.

Industrie die (PL die Industrien) industry.

industriell adjective industrial.

Infektion die (PL die Infektionen) infection.

Infinitiv der (PL die Infinitive) infinitive.

infizieren verb (PERF hat infiziert) 1 to infect; 2 sich bei jemandem infizieren to be infected by somebody.

Inflation die (PL die Inflationen) inflation.

infolge preposition (+ GEN) as a result of.

infolgedessen adverb consequently.

Informatik die computer science.

Informatiker der (PL die Informatiker) computer scientist.

Informatikerin die (PL die Informatikerinnen) computer scientist.

Information die (PL die Informationen) (piece of) information.

Informationsbüro das (PL die Informationsbüros) (tourist) information office.

informieren verb (PERF hat informiert) 1 to inform; 2 informiert sein to be aware; da bist du falsch informiert you've been wrongly informed; 3 sich über etwas informieren to find out about something; ich habe mich darüber genau informieren lassen I found out all about it.

Ingenieur der (PL die Ingenieure) engineer.

Ingenieurin die (PL die Ingenieurinnen) engineer.

Ingwer der ginger.

Inhaber der (PL die Inhaber) 1 owner (of a shop); 2 holder (of an office).

Inhaberin die (PL die Inhaberinnen) 1 owner (of a shop); 2 holder (of a position).

Inhalt der (PL die Inhalte) 1 contents; den Inhalt der Dose mit etwas Wasser verdünnen dilute the contents of the tin with a little water; 2 content (of a story, film); er hat den Inhalt der Geschichte kurz für uns zusammengefasst he gave us a quick summary of the content of the story; 3 volume; 4 area (of a rectangle, circle, etc.).

Initiative die (PL die Initiativen) initiative; die Initiative ergreifen to take the initiative.

inklusive preposition (+ GEN) including.

inklusive *adverb* inclusive.

innen *adverb* inside; **nach innen** inwards.

Innenstadt *die* (PL *die* **Innenstädte**) town centre, city centre.

Innere *das* **1** interior; **2** inside.

innerer, innere, inneres *adjective* **1** inner; **2** inside; **3** internal (*injuries*).

innerhalb *preposition* (+ GEN) **1** within; **2** during.

innerhalb *adverb* **innerhalb von** within.

innerlich *adjective* **1** internal; **2** inner.

innerlich *adverb* **1** internally; **2** inwardly.

ins = **in das**; **ins Theater gehen** to go to the theatre.

Insekt *das* (PL *die* **Insekten**) insect.

Insel *die* (PL *die* **Inseln**) island.

Inserat *das* (PL *die* **Inserate**) advertisement.

inserieren *verb* (PERF **hat inseriert**) to advertise.

insgesamt *adverb* in all.

Instinkt *der* (PL *die* **Instinkte**) instinct.

instinktiv *adjective* instinctive.

Instrument *das* (PL *die* **Instrumente**) instrument; **ein Instrument spielen** to play an instrument.

intelligent *adjective* intelligent.

Intelligenz *die* intelligence.

Intensivpflege *die* intensive care.

Intensivstation *die* (PL *die* **Intensivstationen**) intensive care unit.

Intercityzug *der* (PL *die* **Intercityzüge**) intercity train.

interessant *adjective* interesting.

Interesse *das* (PL *die* **Interessen**) interest; **Interesse für jemanden/etwas haben** to be interested in somebody/something.

interessieren *verb* (PERF **hat interessiert**) **1** to interest; **2 sich für etwas interessieren** to be interested in something.

Internat *das* (PL *die* **Internate**) boarding school.

international *adjective* international.

Internet *das* Internet.

Internetcafé *das* (PL *die* **Internetcafés**) Internet cafe; **wo gibt es hier ein Internetcafé?** where is there an Internet cafe?

Interview *das* (PL *die* **Interviews**) interview.

inzwischen *adverb* in the meantime, meanwhile.

Ire *der* (PL *die* **Iren**) Irishman; **die Iren** the Irish.

irgend *adverb* **1** at all; **wenn irgend möglich** if at all possible; **wenn du irgend kannst** if you could possibly manage it; **2 irgend so ein Idiot** some such idiot.

irgendein *adjective* **1** some; **2** any; **3 irgendein anderer** someone else, anyone else.

a
b
c
d
e
f
g
h
i
j
k
l
m
n
o
p
q
r
s
t
u
v
w
x
y
z

irgendeiner, irgendeine, irgendein(e)s *pronoun* **1** any one; **'welche möchten Sie?' - 'irgendeine'** 'which one would you like?' - 'any one'; **2** somebody, someone; **3** anybody, anyone; **hat irgendeiner angerufen?** has anybody phoned?

irgendetwas *pronoun*
1 something; **2** anything.

irgendjemand *pronoun*
1 somebody; **2** anybody, anyone.

irgendwann *adverb* **1** some time, at some time; **2** any time, at any time.

irgendwas (*informal*) SEE **irgendetwas**.

irgendwie *adverb* somehow.

irgendwo *adverb* **1** somewhere; **2** anywhere.

Irin *die* (PL *die* **Irinnen**) Irishwoman.

irisch *adjective* Irish.

Irisch *das* Irish (*language*).

Irland *das* Ireland.

ironisch *adjective* ironic.

irre *adjective* **1** mad; **2** (*informal*) incredible, fantastic (*party, song*).

irre *adverb* **irre gut** incredibly good.

irren *verb* (PERF **ist geirrt**) **1** to wander (about) (*when lost*); **2** (PERF **hat sich geirrt**) **sich irren** to be mistaken, to be wrong.

irrsinnig *adjective* **1** mad; **2** (*informal*) incredible.

Irrtum *der* (PL *die* **Irrtümer**) mistake.

Islam *der* Islam.

isst SEE **essen**.

ist SEE **sein**.

Italien *das* Italy.

Italiener *der* (PL *die* **Italiener**) Italian.

Italienerin *die* (PL *die* **Italienerinnen**) Italian.

italienisch *adjective* Italian.

Jj

ja *adverb* **1** yes; **2 ich glaube ja** I think so; **3 du kommst doch, ja?** you'll come, won't you?; **es passt doch, ja?** it fits, doesn't it?; **4 sag's ihm ja nicht!** don't (you dare) tell him, whatever you do!; **seid ja vorsichtig!** do be careful!; **5 es ist ja noch früh** it's still early; **ich kann ihn ja mal fragen, ob er mitkommen will** I could always ask him if he wants to come.

Jacht *die* (PL *die* **Jachten**) yacht.

Jacke *die* (PL *die* **Jacken**) **1** jacket; **2** cardigan.

Jackett *das* (PL *die* **Jacketts**) jacket.

Jagd *die* (PL *die* **Jagden**) **1** hunt; **2** hunting.

jagen *verb* (PERF **hat gejagt**) **1** to hunt; **2** to chase; **drei Polizisten jagten den Einbrecher, aber er hängte sie schnell ab** three policemen chased the burglar, but he soon shook them off; **meine Mutter hat mich aus dem Bett gejagt** (*informal*) my mother chased me out of bed; **3 jemanden**

aus dem Haus jagen to throw somebody out of the house; **4 damit kannst du mich jagen** (*informal*) I can't stand that.

Jäger der (PL die **Jäger**) **1** hunter; **2** fighter (*aircraft*).

jäh *adjective* sudden.

Jahr das (PL die **Jahre**) **1** year; **in den sechzigen Jahren** in the sixties; **Kinder bis zu zwölf Jahren** children up to the age of twelve; **2 ein freiwilliges soziales Jahr (FSJ)** gap year (*during which socially useful work is done for subsistence payment*).

jahrelang *adverb* for years.

Jahrestag der (PL die **Jahrestage**) anniversary.

Jahrestag der (PL die **Jahrestage**) anniversary.

Jahreszeit die (PL die **Jahreszeiten**) season.

Jahrgang der (PL die **Jahrgänge**) **1** year; **2** vintage.

Jahrhundert das (PL die **Jahrhunderte**) century.

-jährig *adjective* **eine dreißigjährige Frau** a woman aged thirty; **eine zweijährige Verspätung** a two-year delay.

jährlich *adjective, adverb* yearly; **zweimal jährlich** twice a year.

Jahrmarkt der (PL die **Jahrmärkte**) fair.

Jahrtausend das (PL die **Jahrtausende**) millennium.

Jahrzehnt das (PL die **Jahrzehnte**) decade.

jähzornig *adjective* hot-tempered.

jammern *verb* (PERF **hat gejammert**) to moan.

Januar der January.

Japan das Japan.

Japaner der (PL die **Japaner**) Japanese.

Japanerin die (PL die **Japanerinnen**) Japanese.

japanisch *adjective* Japanese.

jawohl *adverb* **1** yes; **2** certainly.

je *adverb* **1** ever; **besser denn je** better than ever; **2** each; **sie kosten je zwanzig Euro** they are twenty euros each; **3 seit eh und je** always; **4 je nach** depending on.

je *preposition* (+ ACC) per.

je *conjunction* **1 je mehr, desto besser** the more the better; **2 je nachdem** it depends.

Jeans *plural noun* jeans.

jede SEE **jeder**.

jedenfalls *adverb* in any case.

jeder, jede, jedes *adjective* **1** every; **jedes Mal** every time; **2** each; **3** any; **ohne jeden Grund** without any reason.

jedes *pronoun* **1** everybody, everyone; **2** each one; **3** anybody, anyone; **das kann jeder** anybody can do that.

jedermann *pronoun* everybody, everyone.

jederzeit *adverb* at any time.

jedes SEE **jeder**.

jedesmal SEE **jeder**.

jedoch *adverb* however.

jemals *adverb* ever.

jemand *pronoun* **1** somebody, someone; **jemand hat das für dich abgegeben** sombody left this for you; **2** anybody, anyone; **hat jemand angerufen?** did anybody call?

jener, jene, jenes *adjective* (*used in elevated language and in literature*) **1** that; **2** those (*plural*).

jenes *pronoun* **1** that one; **2** those (*plural*).

jenseits *preposition* (+ GEN) (on) the other side of.

Jetlag *der* jet lag.

jetzt *adverb* now.

Job *der* (PL die **Jobs**) job.

jobben *verb* (*informal*) (PERF **hat gejobbt**) to work.

joggen *verb* (PERF **ist gejoggt**) to jog.

Jogginganzug *der* (PL die **Jogginganzüge**) tracksuit.

Joghurt *der* (PL die **Joghurt(s)**) yoghurt.

Johannisbeere *die* (PL die **Johannisbeeren**) **1 rote Johannisbeeren** redcurrants; **2 schwarze Johannisbeeren** blackcurrants.

Journalist *der* (PL die **Journalisten**) journalist.

Journalistin *die* (PL die **Journalistinnen**) journalist.

Joystick *der* (PL die **Joysticks**) joystick (*for computer games*).

jubeln *verb* (PERF **hat gejubelt**) to **1** cheer; **2 Beifall jubeln** to applaud.

Jubiläum *das* (PL die **Jubiläen**) **1** anniversary; **2** jubilee.

Jude *der* (PL die **Juden**) Jew.

Judentum *das* Judaism.

Jüdin *die* (PL die **Jüdinnen**) Jew.

jüdisch *adjective* Jewish.

Jugend *die* youth.

Jugendherberge *die* (PL die **Jugendherbergen**) youth hostel.

Jugendklub *der* (PL die **Jugendklubs**) youth club.

Jugendliche *der/die* (PL die **Jugendlichen**) **1** young man/woman; **2 die Jugendlichen** youth, young people.

Jugendzentrum *das* (PL die **Jugendzentren**) youth centre.

Jugoslawien *das* Yugoslavia.

jugoslawisch *adjective* Yugoslavian.

Juli *der* July.

jung *adjective* **1** young; **2 Jung und Alt** young and old.

Junge¹ *der* (PL die **Jungen**) boy.

Junge² *das* (PL die **Jungen**) young (*animal*).

Jungfrau *die* (PL die **Jungfrauen**) **1** virgin; **2** Virgo.

jüngster, jüngste, jüngstes *adjective* **1** youngest; **2** latest (*news, developments*); **3 in jüngster Zeit** recently.

Juni *der* June.

Jury *die* (PL die **Jurys**) **1** jury; **2** judges (*in sport*).

a
b
c
d
e
f
g
h
i
j
k
l
m
n
o
p
q
r
s
t
u
v
w
x
y
z

a

Juwelier der (PL die **Juweliere**) jeweller.

b

Jux der (*informal*) laugh; **aus Jux** for a laugh.

c

d

Kk

e

f

g

Kabel das (PL die **Kabel**) 1 cable; 2 wire.

h

Kabelfernsehen das cable television.

i

Kabeljau der (PL die **Kabeljaus**) cod.

j

k

Kabine die (PL die **Kabinen**) 1 cabin; 2 cubicle (*for changing*); 3 car (*of a cable car*).

l

Kachel die (PL die **Kacheln**) tile.

m

Käfer der (PL die **Käfer**) beetle.

n

Kaffee der (PL die **Kaffee(s)**) coffee; **zwei Kaffee mit Milch bitte** two white coffees please.

o

Kaffeekanne die (PL die **Kaffeekannen**) coffee-pot.

p

Käfig der (PL die **Käfige**) cage.

q

kahl *adjective* 1 bald (*head*); 2 bare (*tree, walls*).

r

Kahn der (PL die **Kähne**) 1 barge; 2 rowing boat.

s

Kaiser der (PL die **Kaiser**) emperor.

t

Kaiserin die (PL die **Kaiserinnen**) empress.

u

Kakao der (PL die **Kakao(s)**) cocoa; **zwei Kakao bitte** two cups of cocoa please.

v

w

Kakerlak der (PL die **Kakerlaken**) cockroach.

x

y

z

Kaktus der (PL die **Kakteen**) cactus.

Kalb das (PL die **Kälber**) 1 calf; 2 veal.

Kalbfleisch das veal.

Kalender der (PL die **Kalender**) 1 calendar; 2 diary.

Kalk der 1 lime; 2 limescale; 3 calcium.

Kalorie die (PL die **Kalorien**) calorie.

kalorienarm *adjective* low-calorie, low in calories.

kalorienreich *adjective* high-calorie, rich in calories.

kalt *adjective* cold; **ist dir kalt?** are you cold?; **stell die Heizung an, den Kindern ist kalt** put on the heating, the children are cold; **abends essen wir kalt** we have a cold meal in the evening; **den Wein kalt stellen** to chill the wine.

Kälte die 1 cold; 2 coldness; 3 **fünf Grad Kälte** five degrees below zero.

kam SEE **kommen**.

Kamel das (PL die **Kamele**) camel.

Kamera die (PL die **Kameras**) camera.

Kamerad der (PL die **Kameraden**) friend.

Kameradin die (PL die **Kameradinnen**) friend.

Kameramann der (PL die **Kameramänner**) cameraman.

Kamin der (PL die **Kamine**) fireplace; **wir saßen am Kamin** we sat by the fire.

Kamm der (PL die **Kämme**) 1 comb; 2 ridge (*of a mountain*).

kämmen *verb* (PERF hat gekämmt)
1 to comb; 2 sich kämmen to comb
your hair.

Kammer die (PL die Kammern)
1 store room; 2 chamber.

Kampagne die (PL die
Kampagnen) campaign.

Kampf der (PL die Kämpfe) 1 fight;
2 contest; 3 struggle.

kämpfen *verb* (PERF hat gekämpft)
to fight.

Kanada das Canada.

Kanadier der (PL die Kanadier)
Canadian.

Kanadierin die (PL die
Kanadierinnen) Canadian.

kanadisch *adjective* Canadian.

Kanal der (PL die Kanäle) 1 canal;
2 channel (radio, TV); 3 der Kanal
the (English) Channel; 4 sewer,
drain.

Kanalinseln *plural noun* Channel
Islands.

Kanalisation die sewers, drains.

Kanarienvogel der (PL die
Kanarienvögel) canary.

Kandidat der (PL die Kandidaten)
candidate.

Kandidatin die (PL die
Kandidatinnen) candidate.

Känguru das (PL die Kängurus)
kangaroo.

Kaninchen das (PL die Kaninchen)
rabbit.

kann SEE können.

Kännchen das (PL die Kännchen)
1 pot; ein Kännchen Kaffee bitte a
pot of coffee please; 2 jug (of milk).

Kanne die (PL die Kannen) 1 pot (for
coffee, tea); 2 jug (for water); 3 can
(for oil); 4 churn (for milk);
5 watering can.

kannst SEE können.

kannte SEE kennen.

Kante die (PL die Kanten) edge.

Kantine die (PL die Kantinen)
canteen; wir essen immer in der
Kantine zu Mittag we always have
lunch in the canteen.

Kanu das (PL die Kanus) canoe;
Kanu fahren to go canoeing.

Kapelle die (PL die Kapellen)
1 chapel; 2 (brass) band.

kapieren *verb* (informal) (PERF hat
kapiert) to understand; er hat es
mir schon dreimal erklärt, aber
ich kapier es einfach nicht he's
already explained it to me three
times, but I still don't get it.

Kapital das capital.

Kapitalismus der capitalism.

Kapitän der (PL die Kapitäne)
captain.

Kapitel das (PL die Kapitel) chapter.

Kappe die (PL die Kappen) cap.

kaputt *adjective* 1 broken; 2 an
meinem Computer ist etwas
kaputt there's something wrong
with my computer; 3 ich bin
kaputt (informal) I'm shattered.

kaputtgehen ◇*verb* (informal)
(IMPERF ging kaputt, PERF ist
kaputtgegangen) 1 to break; 2 to
pack up; mein Fernseher ist
mitten im Fußballspiel
kaputtgegangen the television

a b c d e f g h i j k l m n o p q r s t u v w x y z

packed up in the middle of the football match; **3** to wear out (*of clothing*); **4** to break up (*of a marriage or friendship*).

kaputtmachen *verb* (*informal*) (PERF **hat kaputtgemacht**) **1** to break; **er macht alle seine Spielsachen kaputt** he breaks all his toys; **2** to ruin (*clothes, furniture*); **3** to finish off (*a person*); **die viele Arbeit macht mich ganz kaputt** all this work is wearing me out; **4 sich kaputtmachen** to wear yourself out.

Kapuze *die* (PL **die Kapuzen**) hood.

Karamell *der* (PL **die Karamells**) caramel.

Karfreitag *der* Good Friday.

Karibik *die* **die Karibik** the Caribbean.

karibisch *adjective* Caribbean.

kariert *adjective* **1** check; **ein karierter Rock** a check skirt; **2** squared (*paper*).

Karneval *der* (PL **die Karnevale**) carnival.

Karo *das* (PL **die Karos**) **1** square; **2** diamonds (*in cards*).

Karotte *die* (PL **die Karotten**) carrot.

Karpfen *der* (PL **die Karpfen**) carp.

Karriere *die* (PL **die Karrieren**) career; **Karriere machen** to get to the top.

Karte *die* (PL **die Karten**) **1** card; **ich schicke euch eine Karte aus Italien** I'll send you a card from Italy; **2** card (*for playing*); **wir haben den ganzen Abend Karten** gespielt we played cards all evening; **gute/schlechte Karten haben** to have a good/bad hand; **3** ticket; **gibt es noch Karten für das Popfestival?** can you still get tickets for the pop festival?; **4** menu; **5** map; **ich kann Oberammergau nicht auf der Karte finden** I can't find Oberammergau on the map; **6** alles auf eine Karte setzen to put all your eggs in one basket.

Kartenspiel *das* (PL **die Kartenspiele**) **1** card game; **2** pack of cards.

Kartoffel *die* (PL **die Kartoffeln**) potato.

Kartoffelbrei *der* mashed potatoes.

Kartoffelchips *plural noun* potato crisps.

Karton *der* (PL **die Kartons**) **1** cardboard; **2** cardboard box.

Karussell *das* (PL **die Karussells**) merry-go-round; **Karussell fahren** to go on the merry-go-round.

Käse *der* cheese.

Käsekuchen *der* (PL **die Käsekuchen**) cheesecake.

Kaserne *die* (PL **die Kasernen**) barracks.

Kasse *die* (PL **die Kassen**) **1** till; **2** checkout; **an der Kasse zahlen** pay at the checkout; **3** cash desk (*in a bank*); **4** box-office; **Sie können die Karten an der Kasse abholen** you can collect the tickets from the box office; **5** ticket office (*at a sports stadium*); **Sie müssen sich**

an der Kasse anstellen you have to queue at the ticket office; **6** health insurance; **7 knapp bei Kasse sein** (*informal*) to be short of money; **gut bei Kasse sein** (*informal*) to be in the money.

Kassenzettel der (PL die **Kassenzettel**) receipt.

Kassette die (PL die **Kassetten**) **1** cassette, tape; **ich habe den neuen Song auf Kassette aufgenommen** I've taped the new song; **2** box (*for money, jewellery*).

Kassettenrekorder der (PL die **Kassettenrekorder**) cassette recorder.

kassieren verb (PERF **hat kassiert**) **1** to collect the money; **2** to collect the fares; **3 wie viel hat er kassiert?** how much did he charge me?; **4 darf ich bei Ihnen kassieren?** would you like to pay now? (*your bill in a restaurant*); **5** (*informal*) to take away (*a driving licence, for example*).

Kassierer der (PL die **Kassierer**) cashier.

Kassiererin die (PL die **Kassiererinnen**) cashier.

Kastanie die (PL die **Kastanien**) chestnut.

Kasten der (PL die **Kästen**) **1** box; **2** crate; **ein Kasten Bier** a crate of beer; **3** bin; **4** letter-box; **5 was auf dem Kasten haben** (*informal*) to be brainy.

Katalog der (PL die **Kataloge**) catalogue.

Katalysator der (PL die **Katalysatoren**) catalytic converter.

katastrophal adjective, adverb **1** catastrophic; **2 sie hat katastrophal schlecht abgeschnitten** she came out terribly badly.

Katastrophe die (PL die **Katastrophen**) catastrophe.

Kategorie die (PL die **Kategorien**) category.

Kater der (PL die **Kater**) **1** tom-cat; **2 einen Kater haben** (*informal*) to have a hangover.

Kathedrale die (PL die **Kathedralen**) cathedral.

Katholik der (PL die **Katholiken**) Catholic.

Katholikin die (PL die **Katholikinnen**) Catholic.

katholisch adjective Catholic.

Kätzchen das (PL die **Kätzchen**) kitten.

Katze die (PL die **Katzen**) cat.

kauen verb (PERF **hat gekaut**) to chew.

kauern verb (PERF **hat gekauert**) to crouch.

Kauf der (PL die **Käufe**) **1** purchase; **2 ein guter Kauf** a bargain; **3 etwas in Kauf nehmen** to put up with something.

kaufen verb (PERF **hat gekauft**) to buy.

Käufer der (PL die **Käufer**) buyer.

Käuferin die (PL die **Käuferinnen**) buyer.

a
b
c
d
e
f
g
h
i
j
k
l
m
n
o
p
q
r
s
t
u
v
w
x
y
z

Kauffrau die (PL die **Kauffrauen**) businesswoman.

Kaufhaus das (PL die **Kaufhäuser**) department store.

Kaufmann der (PL die **Kaufleute**) businessman.

Kaugummi der (PL die **Kaugummis**) chewing gum.

Kaulquappe die (PL die **Kaulquappen**) tadpole.

kaum adverb hardly, scarcely.

Kaution die (PL die **Kautionen**) 1 deposit; 2 bail.

Kegel der (PL die **Kegel**) 1 cone; 2 skittle.

Kegelbahn die skittle alley.

kegeln verb (PERF **hat gekegelt**) to play skittles.

Kehle die (PL die **Kehlen**) throat.

Keim der (PL die **Keime**) 1 shoot; 2 germ.

kein adjective 1 no; **auf keinen Fall** on no account; **2 ich habe keine Zeit** I haven't got any time; **er hat kein Geld** he hasn't got any money; **3 keine zehn Minuten** less than ten minutes.

keiner, keine, kein(e)s pronoun 1 nobody, no one; 2 none, not one; **3 von diesen Kleidern gefällt mir keins** I don't like any of these dresses; **4 keiner von beiden** neither (of them).

keinesfalls adverb on no account.

keineswegs adverb by no means.

keinmal adverb not once.

keins SEE **keiner**.

Keks der (PL die **Kekse**) biscuit.

Keller der (PL die **Keller**) cellar.

Kellergeschoss das (PL die **Kellergeschosse**) basement.

Kellner der (PL die **Kellner**) waiter.

Kellnerin die (PL die **Kellnerinnen**) waitress.

kennen ◇verb (IMPERF **kannte**, PERF **hat gekannt**) 1 to know; **2 kennen lernen** to get to know; **sich kennen lernen** to get to know each other; **3 kennen lernen** to meet; **ich habe Ulrike in London kennen gelernt** I met Ulrike in London; **wo habt ihr euch kennen gelernt?** where did you meet?

kennenlernen SEE **kennen**.

Kenntnis die (PL die **Kenntnisse**) 1 knowledge; **2 etwas zur Kenntnis nehmen** to take note of something.

Kennzeichen das (PL die **Kennzeichen**) 1 mark; 2 characteristic; 3 registration (number) (of a vehicle).

Kerl der (PL die **Kerle**) 1 bloke; **2 Eva ist ein netter Kerl** Eva's a nice girl.

Kern der (PL die **Kerne**) 1 pip; 2 stone (of an apricot, peach); 3 kernel (of a nut).

Kernenergie die nuclear power.

Kernkraftwerk das (PL die **Kernkraftwerke**) nuclear power station.

Kernwaffen plural noun nuclear weapons.

Kerze die (PL die **Kerzen**) candle.

Kerzenhalter der (PL die **Kerzenhalter**) candlestick.

Kessel der (PL die **Kessel**) **1** kettle; **2** boiler.

Kette die (PL die **Ketten**) chain.

Keule die (PL die **Keulen**) **1** club; **2** leg (of lamb); **3** drumstick (of chicken).

kichern verb (PERF hat **gekichert**) to giggle.

Kiefer[1] der (PL die **Kiefer**) jaw.

Kiefer[2] die (PL die **Kiefern**) pine tree.

Kiefernzapfen der (PL die **Kiefernzapfen**) cone.

Kieselstein der (PL die **Kieselsteine**) pebble.

Kilo das (PL die **Kilo(s)**) kilo.

Kilogramm das (PL die **Kilogramme**) kilogram.

Kilometer der (PL die **Kilometer**) kilometre.

Kind das (PL die **Kinder**) child.

Kindergarten der (PL die **Kindergärten**) nursery school.

Kindergeld das child benefit.

Kinderkrippe die (PL die **Kinderkrippen**) crèche.

kinderleicht adjective very easy; das ist kinderleicht it's child's play.

Kindertagesstätte die (PL die **Kindertagesstätten**) day nursery.

Kinderwagen der (PL die **Kinderwagen**) pram.

Kindheit die childhood.

kindisch adjective childish.

Kinn das (PL die **Kinne**) chin.

Kino das (PL die **Kinos**) cinema.

Kiosk das (PL die **Kioske**) kiosk (for newspapers or snacks).

kippen verb (PERF hat **gekippt**) **1** to tip; **2** (PERF ist **gekippt**) to topple.

Kirche die (PL die **Kirchen**) church.

Kirsche die (PL die **Kirschen**) cherry.

Kissen das (PL die **Kissen**) **1** cushion; **2** pillow.

Kiste die (PL die **Kisten**) **1** crate; **2** box.

kitzeln verb (PERF hat **gekitzelt**) to tickle.

kitzlig adjective ticklish.

Kiwi die (PL die **Kiwis**) kiwi fruit.

klagen verb (PERF hat **geklagt**) to complain.

Klammer die (PL die **Klammern**) **1** peg (for washing); **2** grip (for hair); **3** bracket.

Klammeraffe die (PL die **Klammeraffen**) at, @ (in email addresses); dieter-punkt-schmidt-Klammeraffe-einfachkom-punkt-com dieter-dot-schmidt@einfachkom-dot-com.

Klamotten plural noun gear (clothes).

Klang der (PL die **Klänge**) sound.

klang SEE klingen.

Klappe die (PL die **Klappen**) **1** flap; **2** clapperboard; **3** (informal) trap (mouth); halt die Klappe! shut up!

klappen verb (PERF hat **geklappt**) **1** nach vorne klappen to tilt forward; **2** nach hinten klappen to tip back; **3** nach oben klappen to lift up; **4** nach unten klappen to

a
b
c
d
e
f
g
h
i
j
k
l
m
n
o
p
q
r
s
t
u
v
w
x
y
z

put down; **5** to work out;
hoffentlich klappt es I hope it'll
work out.

Klappstuhl der (PL die
Klappstühle) folding chair.

klar adjective **1** clear (water,
answer); **klar werden** to become
clear; **2 jetzt ist mir alles klar** now
I understand; **3 sich klar werden**
to make up your mind; **4 sich über
etwas im Klaren sein** to realize
something.

klar adverb clearly; **na klar!**
(informal) of course!

klären verb (PERF **hat geklärt**) **1** to
clarify; **2** to sort out; **3** to purify
(sewage); **4 sich klären** to clear (of
the weather or the sky); **5 sich
klären** to resolve itself, to be
settled.

Klarinette die (PL die **Klarinetten**)
clarinet.

klarwerden SEE klar.

Klasse die (PL die **Klassen**) **1** class;
erster Klasse reisen to travel first
class; **2** year; **in die sechste
Klasse gehen** to be in year six.

klasse adjective (informal) great,
smashing.

Klassenarbeit die (PL die
Klassenarbeiten) (written) test.

Klassenbuch das register (kept
by the teacher, it also contains notes
about students' achievements)

Klassenfahrt die (PL die
Klassenfahrten) school trip.

Klassenkamerad der (PL die
Klassenkameraden) class-mate.

Klassenkameradin die (PL die
Klassenkameradinnen) class-
mate.

Klassensprecher der (PL die
Klassensprecher) class
representative.

Klassensprecherin die (PL die
Klassensprecherinnen) class
representative.

Klassenzimmer das (PL die
Klassenzimmer) classroom.

klassisch adjective classical.

Klatsch der gossip.

klatschen verb (PERF **hat
geklatscht**) **1** to clap; **jemandem
Beifall klatschen** to clap
somebody, to applaud somebody;
2 to slap; **3** to gossip.

klauen verb (informal) (PERF **hat
geklaut**) to pinch.

Klavier das (PL die **Klaviere**) piano.

kleben verb (PERF **hat geklebt**) **1** to
stick; **2** to glue; **3 jemandem eine
kleben** (informal) to belt somebody
one.

klebrig adjective sticky.

Klebstoff der (PL die **Klebstoffe**)
glue.

Klebstreifen der (PL die
Klebstreifen) sticky tape.

Klecks der (PL die **Kleckse**) stain.

Kleid das (PL die **Kleider**) **1** dress;
**Uschi hat sich zwei neue Kleider
gekauft** Uschi bought two new
dresses; **2 Kleider** clothes.

Kleiderbügel der (PL die
Kleiderbügel) coat hanger.

Kleiderschrank der (PL die **Kleiderschränke**) wardrobe.

Kleidung die clothes, clothing.

klein adjective **1** small, little; **etwas klein schneiden** to cut something up small; **2** short; **Peter ist kleiner als Klaus** Peter is shorter than Klaus.

Kleingarten der (PL die **Kleingärten**) allotment (used mainly as garden).

Kleingeld das change.

Klempner der (PL die **Klempner**) plumber.

klettern verb (PERF **ist geklettert**) to climb.

Klick der (PL die **Klicks**) click (with mouse).

Klicken das click (noise).

Klient der (PL die **Klienten**) client.

Klientin die (PL die **Klientinnen**) client.

Klima das (PL die **Klimas**) climate.

Klimaanlage die (PL die **Klimaanlagen**) air conditioning.

Klinge die (PL die **Klingen**) blade.

Klingel die (PL die **Klingeln**) bell.

klingeln verb (PERF **hat geklingelt**) to ring; **es klingelt** there's a ring at the door.

klingen ◇verb (IMPERF **klang**, PERF **hat geklungen**) to sound.

Klinik die (PL die **Kliniken**) clinic.

Klinke die (PL die **Klinken**) handle.

Klippe die (PL die **Klippen**) rock.

Klo das (informal) (PL die **Klos**) loo.

klopfen verb (PERF **hat geklopft**) **1** to knock; **2** to beat.

Klosett das (PL die **Klosetts**) lavatory.

Kloß der (PL die **Klöße**) dumpling.

Kloster das (PL die **Kloster**) **1** monastery; **2** convent.

Klotz der (PL die **Klötze**) block.

Klub der (PL die **Klubs**) club.

klug adjective **1** clever; **2 ich werde daraus nicht klug** I don't understand it.

Klugheit die cleverness.

Klumpen der (PL die **Klumpen**) lump.

knabbern verb (PERF **hat geknabbert**) to nibble.

Knäckebrot das (PL die **Knäckebrote**) crispbread.

knacken verb (PERF **hat geknackt**) to crack.

Knall der (PL die **Knalle**) bang.

knallen verb (PERF **hat geknallt**) **1** to go bang; **2** to pop (of a cork); **3** to slam (of a door); **4** to crack (of a whip).

knapp adjective **1** scarce; **2** tight (skirt, top); **3 knapp bei Kasse sein** to be short of money; **4 mit knapper Mehrheit** by a narrow majority; **5** just; **eine knappe Stunde** just under an hour; **sie haben knapp verloren** they only just lost; **6 das war knapp** (informal) that was a close shave.

knarren verb (PERF **hat geknarrt**) to crack.

Knauf der (PL die **Knäufe**) knob.

a
b
c
d
e
f
g
h
i
j
k
l
m
n
o
p
q
r
s
t
u
v
w
x
y
z

a **knautschen** verb (PERF hat geknautscht) **1** to crumple; **2** to crease.

b

c **kneifen** ◇verb (IMPERF **kniff**, PERF hat **gekniffen**) **1** to pinch; **2** (informal) to chicken out; **sie hat mal wieder gekniffen und nichts gesagt** she's chickened out yet again and didn't say anything.

d

e

f

Kneipe die (PL die **Kneipen**) pub.

g

kneten verb (PERF hat geknetet) to knead.

h

i **knicken** verb (PERF hat geknickt) **1** to bend; **2** to fold.

j

Knie das (PL die **Knie**) knee.

k

knien verb (PERF hat gekniet) **1** to kneel; **2 sich knien** to kneel down.

l

m **kniff** SEE **kneifen**.

knipsen verb (PERF hat geknipst) (to photograph) to take a snap, to take snaps.

n

o

Knoblauch der garlic.

p

Knoblauchzehe die (PL die **Knoblauchzehen**) clove of garlic.

q

r **Knöchel** der (PL die **Knöchel**) **1** ankle; **2** knuckle; **Mario hat sich beim Jogging den Knöchel verstaucht** Mario sprained his ankle when jogging.

s

t

u **Knochen** der (PL die **Knochen**) bone.

v

Knopf der (PL die **Knöpfe**) button.

w

x **Knoten** der (PL die **Knoten**) **1** knot; **2** bun (as a hairstyle); **3** lump.

y

z **Knüller** der (PL die **Knüller**) scoop (in journalism).

knurren verb (PERF hat geknurrt) **1** to growl; **2** to rumble; **3** to grumble.

knusprig adjective crisp, crusty (bread).

Koalabär der (PL die **Koalabären**) koala bear.

Koch der (PL die **Köche**) **1** cook; **2** chef.

Kochbuch das (PL die **Kochbücher**) cookery book.

kochen verb (PERF hat gekocht) **1** to cook; **2** to boil; **das Wasser kocht** the water's boiling.

Köchin die (PL die **Köchinnen**) cook.

Kochtopf der (PL die **Kochtöpfe**) saucepan.

Koffer der (PL die **Koffer**) suitcase.

Kofferkuli der (PL die **Kofferkulis**) baggage trolley.

Kofferraum der (PL die **Kofferräume**) boot.

Kohl der **1** cabbage; **2** (informal) rubbish; **rede keinen Kohl** don't talk rubbish.

Kohle die (PL die **Kohlen**) coal.

Kohlrübe die (PL die **Kohlrüben**) swede.

Kokain das cocaine.

Kokosnuss die (PL die **Kokosnüsse**) coconut.

Kollege der (PL die **Kollegen**) colleague.

Kollegin die (PL die **Kolleginnen**) colleague.

Köln das Cologne.

Kölnischwasser das eau de cologne.

Kombination die (PL die Kombinationen) combination.

Komfort der comfort.

Komiker der (PL die Komiker) comedian.

komisch adjective funny.

Komma das (PL die Kommas) 1 comma; 2 decimal point; **zwei Komma fünf** two point five.

kommen ◇verb (IMPERF **kam**, PERF **ist gekommen**) 1 to come; 2 to get; **wie komme ich zur U-Bahn?** how do I get to the tube station?; **kommt gut nach Hause!** have a safe journey home!; 3 **etwas kommen lassen** to send for something; 4 **wie kommst du darauf?** what gave you that idea?; 5 **hinter etwas kommen** to find out about something; 6 **zur Schule kommen** to start school; 7 to go; **die Gabeln kommen in die Schublade** the forks go in the drawer; **ins Krankenhaus kommen** to go to hospital; 8 **wer kommt zuerst?** who's first?; **du kommst an die Reihe** it's your turn; 9 **wie kommt das?** why is that?; 10 **zu etwas kommen** to acquire something; 11 **wieder zu sich kommen** to come round (after fainting or anaesthetic); 12 **dazu kommen, etwas zu tun** to get round to doing something; **ich komme einfach nicht zum Einkaufen** I just can't get round to doing the shopping; 13 **das kommt davon!** see what happens!

Kommissar der (PL die Kommissare) superintendent.

Kommode die (PL die Kommoden) chest of drawers.

Kommunismus der communism.

Kommunist der (PL die Kommunisten) communist.

Kommunistin die (PL die Kommunistinnen) communist.

kommunizieren verb (PERF hat kommuniziert) to communicate.

Komödie die (PL die Komödien) comedy.

Kompass der (PL die Kompasse) compass.

komplett adjective complete.

Kompliment das (PL die Komplimente) compliment.

kompliziert adjective complicated.

Komponist der (PL die Komponisten) composer.

Komponistin die (PL die Komponistinnen) composer.

Kompott das (PL die Kompotte) stewed fruit.

Kompromiss der (PL die Kompromisse) compromise; **einen Kompromiss schließen** to compromise.

Konditional das (verb tense) conditional.

Konditorei die (PL die Konditoreien) patisserie, cake shop.

Kondom das (PL die Kondome) condom.

a
b
c
d
e
f
g
h
i
j
k
l
m
n
o
p
q
r
s
t
u
v
w
x
y
z

Konfektion die ready-made clothes.

Konferenz die (PL die Konferenzen) conference.

Konflikt der (PL die Konflikte) conflict.

König der (PL die Könige) king.

Königin die (PL die Königinnen) queen.

königlich adjective royal.

Königreich das (PL die Königreiche) kingdom.

Konjunktion die (PL die Konjunktionen) conjunction.

Konkurrent der (PL die Konkurrenten) competitor.

Konkurrentin die (PL die Konkurrentinnen) competitor.

Konkurrenz die competition.

können ◇verb (PRES **kann**, IMPERF **konnte**, PERF **hat gekonnt**) **1** can; **kann ich Ihnen helfen?** can I help you?; **kannst du Auto fahren?** can you drive?; **kannst du Deutsch?** can you speak German?; **ich konnte nicht früher kommen** I couldn't come any earlier; **das kann ich nicht** I can't do that; **2 etwas können** to be able to do something; **er wird es vor Dienstag nicht machen können** he won't be able to do it before Tuesday; **3 das kann gut sein** that may well be so; **es kann sein, dass … it may be that …; 4 ich kann nichts dafür** it's not my fault.

Können das ability.

Könner der (PL die Könner) expert.

könnt SEE **können**.

konnte, konnten, konntest, konntet SEE **können**.

Konrektor der (PL die Konrektoren) deputy headteacher, deputy headmaster.

Konrektorin die (PL die Konrektorinnen) deputy headteacher.

Konserven plural noun tinned food.

Konsonant der (PL die Konsonanten) consonant.

Konstruktion die (PL die Konstruktionen) construction (in grammar).

Konsul der (PL die Konsuln) consul.

Konsulat das (PL die Konsulate) consulate.

konsultieren verb (PERF hat konsultiert) to consult.

Kontakt der (PL die Kontakte) contact.

Kontaktlinse die (PL die Kontaktlinsen) contact lens.

Kontinent der (PL die Kontinente) continent.

Konto das (PL die Konten) account.

Kontrolle die (PL die Kontrollen) **1** check; **2** control.

Kontrolleur der (PL die Kontrolleure) inspector.

kontrollieren verb (PERF hat kontrolliert) **1** to check; **2** to control.

konzentrieren verb (PERF hat konzentriert) **1** to concentrate;

2 sich konzentrieren to concentrate.

Konzert das (PL die **Konzerte**) **1** concert; **2** concerto.

Kopf der (PL die **Köpfe**) **1** head; **2 sich den Kopf zerbrechen** to rack your brains; **3 seinen Kopf durchsetzen** to get your own way; **4 sich den Kopf waschen** to wash your hair; **5 auf dem Kopf** upside down; **6 ein Kopf Salat** a lettuce.

köpfen verb (PERF **hat geköpft**) **1** to head (in football); **2** to behead.

Kopfhörer der (PL die **Kopfhörer**) headphones.

Kopfkissen das (PL die **Kopfkissen**) pillow.

Kopfsalat der (PL die **Kopfsalate**) lettuce.

Kopfschmerzen plural noun headache.

Kopie die (PL die **Kopien**) copy.

kopieren verb (PERF **hat kopiert**) **1** to copy; **2** to photocopy.

Kopiergerät das (PL die **Kopiergeräte**) photocopier.

Korb der (PL die **Körbe**) **1** basket; **2 jemandem einen Korb geben** to turn somebody down.

Kork der (PL die **Korke**) cork.

Korken der (PL die **Korken**) cork.

Korkenzieher der (PL die **Korkenzieher**) corkscrew.

Korn das (PL die **Körner**) **1** corn (in general); **2** grain (a seed).

Körper der (PL die **Körper**) body.

körperbehindert adjective disabled.

Körpergeruch der (PL die **Körpergerüche**) body odour.

körperlich adjective physical.

Korrektur die (PL die **Korrekturen**) correction.

korrigieren verb (PERF **hat korrigiert**) to correct.

Korsika das Corsica.

koscher adjective kosher.

Kosmetik die (PL die **Kosmetika**) **1** cosmetics; **2** beauty care.

Kost die food.

kostbar adjective precious.

Kosten plural noun **1** cost; **2** expenses.

kosten verb (PERF **hat gekostet**) **1** to cost; **2 wie viel kostet es?** how much is it?; **3** to taste.

kostenlos adjective free (of charge).

köstlich adjective **1** delicious; **2** funny.

Kostüm das (PL die **Kostüme**) **1** suit; **2** costume.

Kotelett das (PL die **Koteletts**) chop.

Krabbe die (PL die **Krabben**) **1** crab; **2** shrimp.

krabbeln verb (PERF **ist gekrabbelt**) to crawl.

Krach der **1** row; **2** noise; **3** crash.

krachen verb (PERF **hat gekracht**) **1** to crash; **2** (PERF **ist gekracht**) to crack; **er ist gegen die Mauer gekracht** he crashed into the wall.

krächzen verb (PERF **hat gekrächzt**) to croak.

a
b
c
d
e
f
g
h
i
j
k
l
m
n
o
p
q
r
s
t
u
v
w
x
y
z

Kraft die (PL die **Kräfte**) **1** strength; **er hat nicht viel Kraft** he's not very strong; **2** force; **in Kraft treten** to come into force; **3 geistige Kräfte** mental powers; **4** worker.

kräftig adjective **1** strong; **2** nourishing.

kräftig adverb **1** strongly; **2** hard; **kräftig schütteln** shake hard.

Kraftwerk das (PL die **Kraftwerke**) power station.

Kragen der (PL die **Kragen**) collar.

Krähe die (PL die **Krähen**) crow.

Kralle die (PL die **Krallen**) claw.

Kram der stuff; **mach deinen Kram allein!** (informal) do it yourself!

kramen verb (PERF **hat gekramt**) to rummage about.

Krampf der (PL die **Krämpfe**) cramp.

Kran der (PL die **Kräne**) crane (machine).

Kranich der (PL die **Kraniche**) crane (bird).

krank adjective ill, sick; **krank werden** to fall ill.

Kranke der/die (PL die **Kranken**) patient.

kränken verb (PERF **hat gekränkt**) to hurt.

Krankenhaus das (PL die **Krankenhäuser**) hospital; **sie haben ihn gestern ins Krankenhaus eingeliefert** he was taken to hospital yesterday.

Krankenkasse die health insurance; **bei welcher Krankenkasse sind Sie versichert?** what health insurance have you got?

Krankenpfleger der (PL die **Krankenpfleger**) (male) nurse.

Krankenpflegerin die (PL die **Krankenpflegerinnen**) nurse.

Krankenschwester die (PL die **Krankenschwestern**) nurse; **Ulrike ist Krankenschwester** Ulrike is a nurse.

Krankenversicherung die (PL die **Krankenversicherungen**) medical insurance.

Krankenwagen der (PL die **Krankenwagen**) ambulance.

Krankheit die (PL die **Krankheiten**) illness, disease.

kratzen verb (PERF **hat gekratzt**) to scratch.

Kratzer der (PL die **Kratzer**) scratch.

kraus adjective frizzy.

Kraut das (PL die **Kräuter**) **1** herb; **2** sauerkraut; **3** cabbage.

Kräutertee der (PL die **Kräutertees**) herbal tea.

Krawall der (PL die **Krawalle**) **1** riot; **2** row.

Krawatte die (PL die **Krawatten**) tie.

kreativ adjective creative.

Krebs der (PL die **Krebse**) **1** crab; **2** cancer; **3** Cancer.

Kredit der (PL die **Kredite**) **1** loan (by a bank); **auf Kredit** on credit; **2** credit (reputation).

Kreditkarte die (PL die **Kreditkarten**) credit card.

Kreide die (PL die **Kreiden**) chalk.

kreieren verb (PERF hat kreiert) to create.

Kreis der (PL die **Kreise**) 1 circle; 2 district.

Kreislauf der 1 cycle; 2 circulation.

Kreuz das (PL die **Kreuze**) 1 cross; 2 (small of the back); 3 intersection (of a motorway); 4 clubs (in cards).

kreuzen verb (PERF hat gekreuzt) 1 to cross; 2 sich kreuzen to cross.

Kreuzfahrt die (PL die **Kreuzfahrten**) 1 cruise; eine Kreuzfahrt machen to go on a cruise; 2 crusade.

Kreuzung die (PL die **Kreuzungen**) 1 crossroads; 2 cross (of plants, animals).

Kreuzworträtsel das (PL die **Kreuzworträtsel**) crossword (puzzle).

kriechen ⋄verb (IMPERF kroch, PERF ist gekrochen) to crawl.

Krieg der (PL die **Kriege**) war.

kriegen verb (informal) (PERF hat gekriegt) 1 to get; 2 ein Kind kriegen to have a baby.

Krimi der (PL die **Krimis**) thriller.

Kriminalroman der (PL die **Kriminalromane**) crime novel.

kriminell adjective criminal.

Kriminelle der/die (PL die **Kriminellen**) criminal.

Krippe die (PL die **Krippen**) 1 manger; 2 crib; 3 crèche.

Krise die (PL die **Krisen**) crisis.

Kristall[1] der (PL die **Kristalle**) crystal.

Kristall[2] das (glass) crystal.

kritisch adjective critical.

kritisieren verb (PERF hat kritisiert) 1 to criticize; 2 to review.

kroch SEE kriechen.

Krokodil das (PL die **Krokodile**) crocodile.

Krone die (PL die **Kronen**) crown.

Kröte die (PL die **Kröten**) toad.

Krücke die (PL die **Krücken**) crutch.

Krug der (PL die **Krüge**) 1 jug; 2 mug.

Krümel der (PL die **Krümel**) crumb.

krümelig adjective crumbly.

krumm adjective 1 bent; 2 crooked.

Kruste die (PL die **Krusten**) crust.

Küche die (PL die **Küchen**) 1 kitchen; 2 cooking; die italienische Küche Italian cooking; 3 warme Küche hot food.

Kuchen der (PL die **Kuchen**) cake.

Kuckuck der (PL die **Kuckucke**) cuckoo.

Kugel die (PL die **Kugeln**) 1 ball; 2 bullet; 3 sphere; wieviele Kugeln Eis möchtest du? how many scoops of ice-cream would you like?

Kugelschreiber der (PL die **Kugelschreiber**) ballpoint pen, biro.

Kuh die (PL die **Kühe**) cow.

kühl adjective cool.

kühlen verb (PERF hat gekühlt) 1 to cool, to chill; 2 to refrigerate.

Kühler der (PL die **Kühler**) radiator.

Kühlerhaube die (PL die Kühlerhauben) bonnet.

Kühlschrank der (PL die Kühlschränke) fridge.

Kühltruhe die (PL die Kühltruhen) freezer.

Küken das (PL die Küken) chick.

Kuli der (PL die Kulis) biro.

Kultur die (PL die Kulturen) 1 culture; 2 civilization.

Kulturbeutel der (PL die Kulturbeutel) toilet bag.

kulturell adjective cultural.

Kummer der 1 sorrow; 2 worry; 3 trouble.

kümmern verb (PERF hat gekümmert) 1 to concern; 2 sich um jemanden kümmern to look after somebody; sich um den Garten kümmern to look after the garden; 3 sich darum kümmern, dass ... to see to it that ...; 4 kümmere dich um deine eigenen Angelegenheiten mind your own business.

Kunde der (PL die Kunden) 1 customer; 2 client.

Kundendienst der 1 customer services (department); 2 after-sales service.

kündigen verb (PERF hat gekündigt) 1 to cancel; 2 to give notice; die Firma hat ihm gekündigt the company gave him his notice; 3 seine Stellung kündigen to hand in your notice.

Kundin die (PL die Kundinnen) 1 customer; 2 client.

Kundschaft die customers.

Kunst die (PL die Künste) 1 art; 2 skill.

Kunstausstellung die (PL die Kunstausstellungen) art exhibition.

Künstler der (PL die Künstler) artist.

Künstlerin die (PL die Künstlerinnen) artist.

künstlerisch adjective artistic.

künstlich adjective artificial.

Kunststoff der (PL die Kunststoffe) plastic.

Kunststück das (PL die Kunststücke) 1 trick; 2 feat.

Kunstwerk das (PL die Kunstwerke) work of art.

Kupfer das copper.

Kupplung die (PL die Kupplungen) 1 clutch (of a car); 2 coupling.

Kürbis der (PL die Kürbisse) pumpkin.

Kurier der (PL die Kuriere) courier (delivery person).

Kurierdienst der (PL die Kurierdienste) courier service.

Kurort der (PL die Kurorte) health resort.

Kurs der (PL die Kurse) 1 course; 2 exchange rate; 3 price (of shares).

Kurve die (PL die Kurven) 1 curve; 2 bend.

kurz *adjective* **1** short; **vor kurzem** a short time ago; **2 zu kurz kommen** to get less than your fair share, to come off badly.

kurz *adverb* **1** shortly; **2** briefly; **3 kurz gesagt** in a word.

Kurzarbeit *die* short-time working.

kurzärmelig *adjective* short-sleeved.

kürzen *verb* (PERF **hat gekürzt**) **1** to shorten; **2** to cut.

kurzfristig *adjective* short-term.

kurzfristig *adverb* at short notice.

kürzlich *adverb* recently.

kurzsichtig *adjective* short-sighted.

Kurzwaren *plural noun* haberdashery.

Kusine *die* (PL die **Kusinen**) cousin.

Kuss *der* (PL die **Küsse**) kiss.

küssen *verb* (PERF **hat geküsst**) **1** to kiss; **2 sich küssen** to kiss.

Küste *die* (PL die **Küsten**) coast.

Kuvert *das* (PL die **Kuverts**) envelope.

LI

Labor *das* (PL die **Labors**) laboratory.

Lache *die* (PL die **Lachen**) pool.

lächeln *verb* (PERF **hat gelächelt**) to smile.

lachen *verb* (PERF **hat gelacht**) to laugh.

lächerlich *adjective* ridiculous.

Lachs *der* (PL die **Lachse**) salmon.

Lack *der* (PL die **Lacke**) **1** varnish; **2** paint.

lackieren *verb* (PERF **hat lackiert**) **1** to varnish; **2** to spray (*with paint*).

laden ✧*verb* (PRES **lädt**, IMPERF **lud**, PERF **hat geladen**) **1** to load; **wir haben die Möbel in den Möbelwagen geladen** we loaded the furniture into the removal van; **2 eine Batterie laden** to charge a battery; **3** to summon; **mein Bruder wurde als Zeuge geladen** my brother was summoned as a witness.

Laden *der* (PL die **Läden**) **1** shop; **wann macht der Laden zu?** when does the shop close?; **2** shutter; **wenn es heiß ist, lassen wir die Läden den ganzen Tag zu** when it's hot we keep the shutters closed all day.

Ladendieb *der* (PL die **Ladendiebe**) shoplifter.

Ladung *die* (PL die **Ladungen**) **1** cargo; **2** charge (*of dynamite or shot*); **3** summons; **4** load.

lag SEE **liegen**.

Lage *die* (PL die **Lagen**) **1** situation; **nicht in der Lage sein, etwas zu tun** not be in a position to do something; **2** layer.

Lager *das* (PL die **Lager**) **1** camp; **2** warehouse; **3** stock; **etwas auf Lager haben** to have something in stock; **4** stock-room; **5** bearing (*in a machine*).

a b c d e f g h i j k l m n o p q r s t u v w x y z

lagern verb (PERF hat gelagert)
1 to store; 2 to camp.

lahm adjective lame.

lähmen verb (PERF hat gelähmt) to paralyse.

Lähmung die paralysis.

Laib der (PL die Laibe) loaf.

Laken das (PL die Laken) sheet.

Lakritze die liquorice.

Lamm das (PL die Lämmer) lamb.

Lampe die (PL die Lampen) lamp.

Lampenschirm der (PL die Lampenschirme) lampshade.

Lancieren das launch (of product).

Land das (PL die Länder) 1 country; auf dem Land in the country; 2 land; 3 state (there are 16 Länder in Germany).

Landebahn die (PL die Landebahnen) runway.

landen verb (PERF ist gelandet) 1 to land; 2 im Krankenhaus landen (informal) to end up in hospital.

Landkarte die (PL die Landkarten) map.

Landkreis der (PL die Landkreise) district.

ländlich adjective rural.

Landschaft die (PL die Landschaften) 1 countryside; 2 landscape.

Landschaftsschutzgebiet das (PL die Landschaftsschutzgebiete) conservation area.

Landstraße die (PL die Landstraßen) country road.

landswirtschaftlich adjective agricultural.

Landtag der state parliament.

Landwirtschaft die agriculture, farming.

lang adjective 1 long; seit langem for a long time; 2 tall.

lang adverb eine Woche lang for a week.

langärmelig adjective long-sleeved.

Länge die (PL die Längen) 1 length; 2 longitude.

lange adverb 1 a long time; lange nicht not for a long time; 2 so lange wie möglich as long as possible; 3 er ist lange nicht so reich he's nowhere near as rich.

langen verb (PERF hat gelangt) 1 to be enough; das Geld langt nicht (informal) it's not enough money; mir langt's (informal) I've had enough; 2 to reach; nach etwas langen to reach for something; 3 jemandem eine langen (informal) to slap somebody's face.

Langlauf der cross-country (in skiing).

langsam adjective, adverb slow; die Musik geht mir langsam auf die Nerven the music is slowly getting on my nerves.

längst adverb 1 a long time ago; das habe ich schon längst gemacht I did it a long time ago; 2 for a long time; er weiß es schon längst he's known it for a long time; **3 längst nicht** nowhere near, not nearly.

längster, längste, längstes *adjective* longest; **Marion hat den längsten Aufsatz geschrieben** Marion wrote the longest essay.

langweilen *verb* (PERF **hat gelangweilt**) **1** to bore; **2 sich langweilen** to be bored.

langweilig *adjective* boring.

Lappen *der* (PL die **Lappen**) cloth, rag.

Laptop *der* (PL die **Laptops**) laptop.

Lärm *der* noise; **sich über den Lärm beschweren** to complain about the noise.

las SEE **lesen**.

Laser *der* (PL die **Laser**) laser.

Laserdrucker *der* (PL die **Laserdrucker**) laser printer.

Laseroperation *die* laser surgery.

Laserstrahl *der* (PL die **Laserstrahlen**) laser beam.

lassen ◇*verb* (PRES **lässt**, IMPERF **ließ**, PERF **hat gelassen**) **1** to let; **jemanden schlafen lassen** to let somebody sleep; **lass uns jetzt gehen** let's go now; **2 jemandem etwas lassen** to let somebody have something; **3** to leave; **die Kinder zu Hause lassen** to leave the children at home; **lass mich!** leave me!; **4 jemanden warten lassen** to keep somebody waiting; **5 etwas reparieren lassen** to have something repaired; **6 lass das!** stop it!; **7 die Tür lässt sich leicht öffnen** the door opens easily; **das**

lässt sich alles machen that can all be arranged.

lässig *adjective* casual.

Last *die* (PL die **Lasten**) **1** load; **2 jemandem zur Last fallen** to be a burden on somebody.

lästig *adjective* troublesome.

Lastwagen *der* (PL die **Lastwagen**) lorry, truck.

Latein *das* Latin.

Laterne *die* (PL die **Laternen**) **1** lantern; **2** street lamp.

Laub *das* leaves.

Lauch *der* leek(s).

Lauf *der* (PL die **Läufe**) **1** run; **2** course; **im Laufe der Zeit** in the course of time; **im Laufe der Jahre** over the years; **3** race; **4** barrel (*of a gun*).

Laufbahn *die* (PL die **Laufbahnen**) career.

laufen ◇*verb* (PRES **läuft**, IMPERF **lief**, PERF **ist gelaufen**) **1** to run; **sie kann viel schneller laufen als ihr Bruder** she can run much faster than her brother; **2** to walk; **du kannst nach Hause laufen oder mit dem Bus fahren** you can walk home or go on the bus; **3** to roll; **4 Ski laufen** to ski; **5** to be on (*of a film, programme, or machine*).

laufend *adjective* **1** running; **2** current (*issue, month*); **3 auf dem Laufenden sein** to be up to date; **Anita hält mich auf dem Laufenden** Anita keeps me up to date.

laufend *adverb* continually, constantly.

a b c d e f g h i j k l m n o p q r s t u v w x y z

Läufer der (PL die **Läufer**) 1 runner; 2 rug; 3 bishop (*in chess*).

Läuferin die (PL die **Läuferinnen**) runner.

Laufmasche die (PL die **Laufmaschen**) ladder (*in your tights*).

Laufwerk das (PL die **Laufwerke**) drive (*on a computer*).

Laune die (PL die **Launen**) mood.

launisch adjective moody.

Laus die (PL die **Läuse**) louse.

Laut der (PL die **Laute**) sound.

laut adjective 1 loud; 2 noisy.

laut adverb 1 loudly; 2 **laut lesen** to read aloud; 3 **lauter stellen** to turn up.

laut preposition (+ GEN or + DAT) according to.

lauten verb (PERF **hat gelautet**) 1 to be; 2 to go.

läuten verb (PERF **hat geläutet**) to ring.

lauter adjective nothing but.

Lautsprecher der (PL die **Lautsprecher**) (loud)speaker.

Lautstärke die volume.

lauwarm adjective lukewarm.

Lavendel der lavender.

Lawine die (PL die **Lawinen**) avalanche.

Leben das (PL die **Leben**) life; **am Leben sein** to be alive; **ums Leben kommen** to lose your life.

leben verb (PERF **hat gelebt**) 1 to live; 2 to be alive; 3 **leb wohl!** farewell!

lebend adjective living.

lebendig adjective 1 living; 2 **lebendig sein** to be alive; 3 lively.

Lebensgefahr die mortal danger; **sein Vater ist in Lebensgefahr** his father is critically ill.

lebensgefährlich adjective 1 extremely dangerous; 2 critical; **lebensgefährlich verletzt** critically injured.

Lebenshaltungskosten plural noun cost of living.

lebenslänglich adjective life.

lebenslänglich adverb for life.

Lebenslauf der (PL die **Lebensläufe**) CV.

Lebensmittel plural noun food, groceries.

Lebensmittelgeschäft das (PL die **Lebensmittelgeschäfte**) grocer's (shop).

Lebensmittelvergiftung die (PL die **Lebensmittelvergiftungen**) food poisoning.

Lebensunterhalt der livelihood; **seinen Lebensunterhalt verdienen** to earn one's living.

Leber die (PL die **Lebern**) liver.

Leberfleck der (PL die **Leberflecke**) mole.

Leberwurst die liver sausage.

Lebewesen das (PL die **Lebewesen**) living being, living thing.

lebhaft adjective 1 lively; 2 vivid (*idea, colour*).

Lebkuchen der (PL die Lebkuchen) gingerbread.

leblos adjective lifeless.

Leck das (PL die Lecks) leak.

lecken verb (PERF hat geleckt) 1 to lick; **die Katze leckte ihre Jungen** the cat licked the kittens; **an etwas lecken** to lick something; 2 to leak.

lecker adjective delicious.

Leder das (PL die Leder) leather.

ledig adjective single.

lediglich adverb merely.

leer adjective empty; **leer machen** to empty.

leeren verb (PERF hat geleert) 1 to empty; 2 **ein leeres Blatt Papier** a blank sheet of paper; 3 **sich leeren** to empty.

Leerlauf der neutral (gear).

Leerung die (PL die Leerungen) collection.

legal adjective legal.

legen verb (PERF hat gelegt) 1 to put; 2 to lay; 3 **sich legen** to lie down; 4 **sich legen** to die down (of a storm, noise); **unsere Begeisterung hat sich gelegt** our enthusiasm has worn off.

leger adjective, adverb casual; **leger gekleidet sein** to be casually dressed.

Lehm der clay.

Lehne die (PL die Lehnen) 1 back (of a chair); 2 arm (of a sofa or chair).

lehnen verb (PERF hat gelehnt) 1 to lean; 2 **sich an etwas lehnen** to lean against something.

Lehrbuch das (PL die Lehrbücher) textbook.

lehren verb (PERF hat gelehrt) to teach.

Lehrer der (PL die Lehrer) 1 teacher; 2 instructor.

Lehrerin die (PL die Lehrerinnen) 1 teacher; 2 instructor.

Lehrerzimmer das (PL die Lehrerzimmer) staffroom.

Lehrling der (PL die Lehrlinge) 1 apprentice; 2 trainee.

Lehrplan der (PL die Lehrpläne) syllabus.

Lehrstelle die (PL die Lehrstellen) apprenticeship, trainee post.

Leibwächter der (PL die Leibwächter) bodyguard.

Leiche die (PL die Leichen) (dead) body, corpse.

leicht adjective 1 light; 2 easy; **jemandem leicht fallen** to be easy for somebody; **es ist ihm nicht leicht gefallen** it wasn't easy for him; **Markus macht es sich immer leicht** Markus always takes the easy way out; 3 **ein leichter Akzent** a slight accent.

Leichtathletik die athletics.

leichtfallen SEE **leicht**.

Leichtsinn der 1 carelessness; 2 recklessness.

leichtsinnig adjective 1 careless; 2 reckless.

Leid das 1 sorrow; 2 harm; 3 **es tut mir Leid** I'm sorry; **Andreas tut mir Leid** I feel sorry for Andreas.

a
b
c
d
e
f
g
h
i
j
k
l
m
n
o
p
q
r
s
t
u
v
w
x
y
z

leid *adjective* **jemanden leid sein** to be fed up with somebody; **etwas leid sein** to be fed up with something.

leiden ◇*verb* (IMPERF **litt**, PERF **hat gelitten**) **1** to suffer; **2 jemanden gut leiden können** to like somebody; **3 ich kann Erika nicht leiden** I can't stand Erika.

leider *adverb* **1** unfortunately; **2 leider ja** I'm afraid so; **leider nicht** I'm afraid not.

leihen ◇*verb* (IMPERF **lieh**, PERF **hat geliehen**) **1** to lend; **2 sich etwas leihen** to borrow something; **ich habe mir das Buch von Alex geliehen** I borrowed the book from Alex.

Leihgabe die (PL die **Leihgaben**) loan (*by a bank*).

Leihwagen der (PL die **Leihwagen**) hire car.

Leim der (PL die **Leime**) glue.

Leine die (PL die **Leinen**) **1** rope; **2** line (*for washing*); **3** lead (*for a dog*).

Leinen das (PL die **Leinen**) linen.

Leinwand die (PL die **Leinwände**) screen (*in a cinema*).

leise *adjective* quiet.

leise *adverb* **1** quietly; **2 die Musik leiser stellen** to turn the music down.

leisten *verb* (PERF **hat geleistet**) **1** to achieve; **2 jemandem Hilfe leisten** to help somebody; **3 jemandem Gesellschaft leisten** to keep somebody company; **4 sich etwas leisten** to treat yourself to

something; **5 sich etwas leisten können** to be able to afford something; **ich kann mir kein neues Auto leisten** I can't afford a new car.

Leistung die (PL die **Leistungen**) **1** achievement; **2** performance; **3 Leistungen** payment.

Leistungskurs der (PL die **Leistungskurse**) main subject.

leiten *verb* (PERF **hat geleitet**) **1** to lead; **2** to direct; **3** to manage, run (*a business*); **4** to conduct.

Leiter[1] die (PL die **Leitern**) ladder.

Leiter[2] der (PL die **Leiter**) **1** leader; **2** head; **3** manager; **4** director; **5** conductor (*of an orchestra or electricity*).

Leiterin die (PL die **Leiterinnen**) **1** leader; **2** head; **3** manageress; **4** director.

Leitung die (PL die **Leitungen**) **1** direction; **2** management; **3** (*phone*) line; **4** (*electric*) lead; **5** cable; **6** pipe; **7 unter der Leitung von** conducted by.

Leitungswasser das tap water.

Lektion die (PL die **Lektionen**) lesson.

lenken *verb* (PERF **hat gelenkt**) **1** to steer; **2** to guide; **3 den Verdacht auf jemanden lenken** to throw suspicion on somebody.

Lenkrad das (PL die **Lenkräder**) steering wheel.

Lenkstange die (PL die **Lenkstangen**) handlebars.

lernen verb (PERF **hat gelernt**) **1** to learn; **schwimmen lernen** to learn to swim; **2** to study.

lesbisch adjective lesbian.

lesen ⬦verb (PRES **liest**, IMPERF **las**, PERF **hat gelesen**) to read.

Leser der (PL die **Leser**) reader.

Leseratte die (PL die **Leseratten**) bookworm.

Leserin die (PL die **Leserinnen**) reader.

Letzte der/die/das (PL die **Letzten**) **1** der/die **Letzte** the last (one); das **Letzte** the last (thing); **2** Boris kam als **Letzter** Boris arrived last.

letzte SEE letzter.

letztens adverb **1** recently; **2** lastly.

letzter, letzte, letztes adjective **1** last; **zum letzten Mal** for the last time; **das letzte Mal** the last time; **2** latest (news, information); **3** in **letzter Zeit** recently.

leuchten verb (PERF **hat geleuchtet**) to shine.

Leuchter der (PL die **Leuchter**) candlestick.

Leuchtreklame die neon sign.

Leuchtturm der (PL die **Leuchttürme**) lighthouse.

leugnen verb (PERF **hat geleugnet**) to deny.

Leukämie die leukaemia.

Leute plural noun people.

Lexikon das (PL die **Lexika**) **1** encyclopaedia; **2** dictionary.

Licht das (PL die **Lichter**) light.

Lichtbild das (PL die **Lichtbilder**) photograph.

Lichtschalter der (PL die **Lichtschalter**) light switch.

Lid das (PL die **Lider**) (eye)lid.

Lidschatten der (PL die **Lidschatten**) eye shadow.

lieb adjective **1** dear; **liebe Gabi** dear Gabi; **2** nice; **das ist lieb von euch** that's nice of you; **3** jemanden lieb haben to be fond of somebody; **4** es wäre mir lieber, wenn ... I'd prefer it if ...; **5** ihr liebstes Spielzeug her favourite toy.

Liebe die (PL die **Lieben**) love.

lieben verb (PERF **hat geliebt**) to love.

liebenswürdig adjective kind.

lieber adverb **1** rather; **2** lieber mögen to like better; **3** lass das lieber you'd better not do that; **4** ich trinke lieber Kaffee I prefer coffee.

Liebesbrief der (PL die **Liebesbriefe**) love letter.

Liebesfilm der (PL die **Liebesfilme**) romantic film.

Liebeskummer der **Liebeskummer haben** to be lovesick.

liebevoll adjective loving.

liebhaben SEE lieb.

Liebling der (PL die **Lieblinge**) **1** darling; **2** favourite.

Lieblings- prefix favourite.

liebster, liebste, liebstes adjective **1** dearest; **2** favourite.

a
b
c
d
e
f
g
h
i
j
k
l
m
n
o
p
q
r
s
t
u
v
w
x
y
z

liebstes adverb am liebsten best (of all); **ich mag Max am liebsten** I like Max best.

Lied das (PL die **Lieder**) song.

lief SEE **laufen**.

liefern verb (PERF **hat geliefert**) **1** to deliver; **2** to supply.

Lieferung die (PL die **Lieferungen**) delivery.

Lieferwagen der (PL die **Lieferwagen**) (delivery) van.

liegen ✧verb (IMPERF **lag**, PERF **hat gelegen**) **1** to lie; **der Brief liegt auf dem Tisch** the letter is on the table; **es liegt viel Schnee** there's lots of snow; **2** to be, to be situated; **3 liegen bleiben** to stay (in bed); **er ist liegen geblieben** he didn't get up; **4 etwas bleibt liegen** something is left behind; **die Arbeit ist liegen geblieben** the job was left undone; **5 der Schnee bleibt liegen** the snow is settling; **6 liegen lassen** to leave; **7 es liegt mir nicht** it doesn't suit me; **8 an etwas liegen** to be due to something; **9 das liegt an ihm** it's up to him.

liegenbleiben, liegenlassen SEE **liegen**.

Liegestuhl der (PL die **Liegestühle**) deckchair.

Liegewagen der (PL die **Liegewagen**) couchette (car).

ließ SEE **lassen**.

liest SEE **lesen**.

Lift der (PL die **Lifte**) lift.

Liga die (PL die **Ligen**) league.

lila adjective **1** purple; **2** mauve.

Limo die (PL die **Limo(s)**) SEE **Limonade**.

Limonade die (PL die **Limonaden**) **1** fizzy drink; **2** lemonade.

Limone die (PL die **Limonen**) lime.

Lineal das (PL die **Lineale**) ruler.

Linie die (PL die **Linien**) **1** line; **2** route (of a bus); **Linie 6** number 6.

Linienflug der (PL die **Linienflüge**) scheduled flight.

Linke die **1** left; **zu meiner Linken** on my left; **2** left hand; **3** left side; **4 die Linke** the left (in politics).

linker, linke, linkes adjective **1** left; **2** left-wing.

links adverb **1** on the left; **links fahren** to drive on the left; **links abbiegen** to turn left; **nach links** left; **von links** from the left; **2 links sein** to be left-wing; **3 zwei links, zwei rechts stricken** to purl two, knit two; **4** (clothing) inside out.

Linkshänder der (PL die **Linkshänder**) left-hander.

Linkshänderin die (PL die **Linkshänderinnen**) left-hander.

Linse die (PL die **Linsen**) **1** lens; **2** lentil.

Lippe die (PL die **Lippen**) lip.

Lippenstift der (PL die **Lippenstifte**) lipstick.

Liste die (PL die **Listen**) list.

listig adjective cunning.

Liter der (PL die **Liter**) litre.

Literatur die literature.

litt SEE **leiden**.

Livesendung die (PL die Livesendungen) live programme.

Lizenz die (PL die Lizenzen) licence.

Lkw der (PL die Lkws) (*Lastkraftwagen*) lorry, truck.

Lob das praise.

loben verb (PERF hat gelobt) to praise.

Loch das (PL die Löcher) hole.

Locke die (PL die Locken) curl.

locken verb (PERF hat gelockt) 1 to tempt; 2 to curl.

locker adjective 1 loose; 2 slack (*rope*); 3 relaxed (*atmosphere, person*).

lockerlassen ◇verb (PRES lässt locker, IMPERF ließ locker, PERF hat lockergelassen) **nicht lockerlassen** (*informal*) not to let up.

lockig adjective curly.

Löffel der (PL die Löffel) 1 spoon; 2 ein Löffel Mehl a spoonful of flour.

log SEE lügen.

Logik die logic.

logisch adjective 1 logical; 2 ja, logisch! yes, of course!

Lohn der (PL die Löhne) 1 wages; 2 reward.

lohnen verb (PERF hat sich gelohnt) sich lohnen to be worth it.

Lokal das (PL die Lokale) 1 bar; 2 restaurant.

Lokomotive die (PL die Lokomotiven) locomotive, engine.

Lorbeerblatt das (PL die Lorbeerblätter) bay leaf.

Los das (PL die Lose) 1 (lottery) ticket; 2 das große Los ziehen to hit the jackpot; 3 lot.

los adjective 1 der Hund ist los the dog is off the lead; 2 die Schraube ist los the screw's loose; 3 es ist viel los there's a lot going on; 4 etwas los sein to be rid of something; 5 was ist los? what's the matter?.

los adverb 1 los! go on!; 2 Achtung, fertig, los! ready, steady, go!

losbinden ◇verb (IMPERF band los, PERF hat losgebunden) to untie.

löschen verb (PERF hat gelöscht) 1 to put out; 2 seinen Durst löschen to quench your thirst; 3 to delete, to cancel; 4 to erase.

lose adjective loose.

lösen verb (PERF hat gelöst) 1 to solve; 2 to undo; 3 to buy; eine Fahrkarte lösen to buy a ticket; 4 to release; 5 to remove; 6 sich lösen to come undone; 7 sich lösen to be solved (*of a puzzle or mystery*); sich von selbst lösen to be resolved (*of a problem*); 8 sich in Wasser lösen to dissolve in water.

losfahren ◇verb (PRES fährt los, IMPERF fuhr los, PERF ist losgefahren) 1 to set off; 2 to drive off.

losgehen ◇verb (IMPERF ging los, PERF ist losgegangen) 1 to set off; 2 to come off (*of a button*); 4 to go off (*of a bomb*); 5 auf jemanden losgehen to go for somebody.

a
b
c
d
e
f
g
h
i
j
k
l
m
n
o
p
q
r
s
t
u
v
w
x
y
z

loslassen ◇verb (PRES **lässt los**, IMPERF **ließ los**, PERF **hat losgelassen**) **1** to let go of; **2** to let go.

Lösung die (PL die **Lösungen**) solution.

Losung die (PL die **Losungen**) **1** slogan; **2** password; **die Losung nennen** to give the password.

loswerden ◇verb (PRES **wird los**, IMPERF **wurde los**, PERF **ist losgeworden**) to get rid of.

Lotterie die (PL die **Lotterien**) lottery.

Lotto das (PL die **Lottos**) (national) lottery.

Löwe der (PL die **Löwen**) **1** lion; **2** Leo; **Wilhelm ist Löwe** Wilhelm's a Leo.

Loyalität die loyalty.

Lücke die (PL die **Lücken**) gap.

Luft die (PL die **Lüfte**) **1** air; **2** die **Luft anhalten** to hold your breath; **3** in die **Luft gehen** (informal) to blow your top; **4** jemanden wie **Luft behandeln** to ignore somebody.

Luftballon der (PL die **Luftballons**) balloon.

Luftdruck der air pressure.

Luftmatratze die (PL die **Luftmatratzen**) air-bed.

Luftpost die airmail; **per Luftpost** by airmail.

Luftverschmutzung die air pollution.

Luftwaffe die air force.

Lüge die (PL die **Lügen**) lie.

lügen ◇verb (IMPERF **log**, PERF **hat gelogen**) to lie.

Lügner der (PL die **Lügner**) liar.

Lügnerin die (PL die **Lügnerinnen**) liar.

Lunge die (PL die **Lungen**) lungs.

Lungenentzündung die pneumonia.

Lupe die (PL die **Lupen**) magnifying glass.

Lust die **1** pleasure; **2** Lust haben, etwas zu tun to feel like doing something; **ich habe keine Lust** I don't feel like it; **Lust auf etwas haben** to feel like something.

lustig adjective **1** jolly; **2** funny; **3** Dieter hat sich über mich lustig gemacht Dieter made fun of me.

lutschen verb (PERF **hat gelutscht**) to suck.

Lutscher der (PL die **Lutscher**) lollipop.

Luxemburg das Luxembourg.

Luxus der luxury.

Mm

machen verb (PERF **hat gemacht**) **1** to make; **2** to do; **was machst du da?** what are you doing?; **3** was **macht die Arbeit?** how's work?; **was macht Karin?** how's Karin?; **4** sich an die Arbeit machen to get down to work; **5** schnell machen to hurry; **6** das macht nichts it doesn't matter; **7** to come to; **das macht fünf Euro** that comes to five euros; **8 sich nichts aus etwas machen** to not be very keen on something; **Gisela macht sich nichts aus Schokolade** Gisela isn't keen on chocolate.

Macht die (PL die **Mächte**) power; **an die Macht kommen** to come to power.

Mädchen das (PL die **Mädchen**) girl.

Mädchenname der (PL die **Mädchennamen**) maiden name.

Made die (PL die **Maden**) maggot.

mag SEE **mögen**.

Magazin das (PL die **Magazine**) magazine.

Magen der (PL die **Mägen**) stomach.

Magenschmerzen plural noun stomach-ache.

mager adjective **1** thin; **2** lean; **3** low-fat.

Magie die magic.

Magnet der (PL die **Magnete(n)**) magnet.

magnetisch adjective magnetic.

magst SEE **mögen**.

Mahagoni das mahogany.

mähen verb (PERF **hat gemäht**) to mow; **den Rasen mähen** to mow the lawn.

mahlen ◇verb (PERF **hat gemahlen**) to grind.

Mahlzeit die (PL die **Mahlzeiten**) meal; **Mahlzeit!** enjoy your meal!

Mai der May; **der Erste Mai** May Day.

Maiglöckchen das (PL die **Maiglöckchen**) lily of the valley.

Mais der maize.

Majonäse die mayonnaise.

Majoran der marjoram.

Makkaroni (plural noun) macaroni.

Makler der (PL die **Makler**) estate agent.

Makrele die (PL die **Makrelen**) mackerel.

Mal das (PL die **Male**) **1** time; **nächstes Mal** next time; **zum ersten Mal** for the first time; **2** mark; **3** mole.

mal adverb **1** times; **zwei mal drei** two times three; **2** by (with measurements); **3** sometime (in the future); **ich möchte mal nach Brasilien fahren** I'd like to go to Brazil sometime; **4** schon mal ever; **5 ich war schon mal da** I've been once before; **6 nicht mal** not even; **7 komm mal her!** come here!

malen verb (PERF **hat gemalt**) to paint.

Maler der (PL die **Maler**) painter.

Malerei die painting.

Malerin die (PL die **Malerinnen**) painter.

Mallorca das Majorca.

Mama die (PL die **Mamas**) mum.

Mami die (PL die **Mamis**) mummy.

man pronoun **1** you, one; **wie macht man das?** how do you do it?; **man kann ja nie wissen** one can never tell; **2** they, people; **man**

sagt they say; **3 man hat mir gesagt** I was told.

mancher, manche, manches *adjective* **1** many a; **so manchen Tag** many a day; **2 manche** (*plural*) some; **an manchen Tagen** some days.

manches *pronoun* **1** many a person; **2 manche** (*plural*) some people; **3 manches** some things.

manchmal *adverb* sometimes.

Mandarine die (PL die **Mandarinen**) mandarin.

Mandel die (PL die **Mandeln**) **1** almond; **2** tonsil.

Mandelentzündung die tonsillitis.

Mangel der (PL die **Mängel**) **1** lack; **2** shortage; **3** defect, fault.

mangelhaft *adjective* **1** faulty; **2** unsatisfactory (*school mark*).

Manie die (PL die **Manien**) mania.

Manieren *plural noun* manners; **er hat keine Manieren** he's got no manners.

Mann der (PL die **Männer**) **1** man; **2** husband.

Männchen das (PL die **Männchen**) male (*animal*).

Mannequin das (PL die **Mannequins**) model.

männlich *adjective* **1** male; **2** manly; **3** masculine.

Mannschaft die (PL die **Mannschaften**) **1** team; **2** crew.

Manschette die (PL die **Manschetten**) cuff.

Mantel der (PL die **Mäntel**) coat.

Mappe die (PL die **Mappen**) **1** folder; **2** briefcase; **3** bag.

Märchen das (PL die **Märchen**) fairy tale.

Margarine die margarine.

Marienkäfer der (PL die **Marienkäfer**) ladybird.

Marine die (PL die **Marinen**) navy.

Mark die (PL die **Mark**) mark (*German currency until replaced by the euro; one hundred marks =* h*51.13 euros*).

Marke die (PL die **Marken**) **1** make, brand; **meine Mutter fährt seit Jahren die gleiche Marke** my mother has been driving the same make of car for years; **Adidas ist eine führende Marke** Adidas is a leading brand; **2** tag; **3** stamp (*for letters*); **4** coupon.

markieren *verb* (PERF **hat markiert**) **1** to mark; **2** to fake.

Markt der (PL die **Märkte**) market; **auf den Markt bringen** to launch (*a product*).

Marktplatz der (PL die **Marktplätze**) market-place.

Marmelade die (PL die **Marmeladen**) jam.

Marmor der marble.

Marokko das Morocco.

Marsch der (PL die **Märsche**) march.

März der March.

Masche die (PL die **Maschen**) **1** stitch; **2** mesh; **3** (*informal*) trick; **die Masche raushaben** to know how to do it; **das is die neueste Masche** that's the latest thing.

Maschine die (PL die **Maschinen**) 1 machine; 2 plane; 3 typewriter; **Maschine schreiben** to type.

Masern plural noun measles.

Maske die (PL die **Masken**) mask.

maskieren verb (PERF **hat sich maskiert**) 1 **sich maskieren** to dress up; 2 **sich maskieren** to disguise yourself.

Maß[1] das (PL die **Maße**) 1 measure; 2 measurement; 3 extent; **in hohem Maße** to a high degree; 4 **Maß halten** to show moderation.

Maß[2] die (PL die **Maß**) litre (of beer).

maß SEE messen.

Masse die (PL die **Massen**) 1 mass; **eine Masse Arbeit** masses of work; 2 crowd; 3 mixture (in cooking).

massenhaft adjective masses of.

Massenvernichtungswaffen plural noun weapons of mass destruction.

massieren verb (PERF **hat massiert**) to massage.

mäßig adjective moderate.

Maßnahme die (PL die **Maßnahmen**) measure.

Maßstab der (PL die **Maßstäbe**) 1 standard; 2 scale.

Mast der (PL die **Masten**) 1 mast; 2 pole; 3 pylon.

Material das (PL die **Materialien**) 1 material; 2 materials.

Mathe die (informal) maths.

Mathematik die mathematics.

Matratze die (PL die **Matratzen**) mattress.

Matrose der (PL die **Matrosen**) sailor.

Matsch der 1 mud; 2 slush.

matschig adjective 1 muddy; 2 slushy.

matt adjective 1 weak; 2 matt; 3 dull; 4 **matt!** checkmate!

Matte die (PL die **Matten**) mat.

Mauer die (PL die **Mauern**) wall.

Maul das (PL die **Mäuler**) mouth; **halt's Maul!** (informal) shut up!

Maulkorb der (PL die **Maulkörbe**) muzzle.

Maulwurf der (PL die **Maulwürfe**) mole.

Maulwurfshügel der (PL die **Maulwurfshügel**) molehill.

Maurer der (PL die **Maurer**) bricklayer.

Maus die (PL die **Mäuse**) mouse.

Maximum das (PL die **Maxima**) maximum.

Mayonnaise die mayonnaise.

Mechaniker der (PL die **Mechaniker**) mechanic.

Mechanikerin die (PL die **Mechanikerinnen**) mechanic.

mechanisch adjective mechanical.

meckern verb (PERF **hat gemeckert**) 1 to bleat; 2 to grumble.

Medaille die (PL die **Medaillen**) medal.

Medien plural noun media.

a
b
c
d
e
f
g
h
i
j
k
l
m
n
o
p
q
r
s
t
u
v
w
x
y
z

Medikament das (PL die Medikamente) medicine, drug.

Medizin die (PL die Medizinen) medicine.

Meer das (PL die Meere) sea.

Meeresfrüchte plural noun seafood.

Meerschweinchen das (PL die Meerschweinchen) guinea pig.

Megabyte das (PL die Megabytes) megabyte.

Mehl das flour.

mehr adverb, pronoun more; **nichts mehr** no more; **nie mehr** never again.

mehrere pronoun several.

mehreres pronoun several things.

mehrfach adjective 1 multiple, many; 2 repeated.

mehrfach adverb several times.

Mehrheit die (PL die Mehrheiten) majority.

mehrmalig adjective repeated.

mehrmals adverb several times.

Mehrwertsteuer die value added tax.

Mehrzahl die 1 majority; 2 plural.

meiden ◇verb (IMPERF mied, PERF hat gemieden) to avoid.

Meile die (PL die Meilen) mile.

mein adjective my.

meine SEE meiner.

meinen verb (PERF hat gemeint) 1 to think; 2 to mean; **es gut meinen** to mean well; 3 to say.

meiner, meine, mein(e)s pronoun mine.

meinetwegen adverb 1 for my sake; 2 because of me; 3 as far as I'm concerned; **'kann ich das Auto haben?' – 'meinetwegen'** 'can I take the car?' – 'I don't mind'.

meins SEE meiner.

Meinung die (PL die Meinungen) opinion.

meist adverb 1 mostly; 2 usually.

meiste adjective, pronoun der/die/das meiste most; die meisten most; **am meisten** most, the most.

meistens adverb 1 mostly; 2 usually.

Meister der (PL die Meister) 1 master; 2 champion.

Meisterin die (PL die Meisterinnen) champion.

Meisterschaft die (PL die Meisterschaften) championship.

Meisterstück das (PL die Meisterstücke) 1 masterpiece; 2 masterstroke.

Meisterwerk das (PL die Meisterwerke) masterpiece.

melden verb (PERF hat gemeldet) 1 to report; 2 to register; 3 **sich melden** to report, (on the phone) to answer; **Luise hat sich gemeldet** (in school) Luise put up her hand; 4 **sich bei jemandem melden** to get in touch with somebody.

Melodie die (PL die Melodien) melody, tune.

Melone die (PL die Melonen) 1 melon; 2 bowler (hat).

a
b
c
d
e
f
g
h
i
j
k
l
m
n
o
p
q
r
s
t
u
v
w
x
y
z

Menge die (PL die **Mengen**)
1 quantity; **eine Menge Geld** a lot
of money; 2 crowd; 3 set (in maths).

Mensch der (PL die **Menschen**)
1 human being; 2 person; **kein
Mensch** nobody; **jeder Mensch**
everybody; 3 **die Menschen**
people; **wie viele Menschen?** how
many people? 4 (as an
exclamation) **Mensch!** (informal)
wow!, hey!; **Mensch, hab ich mich
geärgert!** (informal) I was damn
annoyed.

menschenleer adjective
deserted.

Menschenverstand der
gesunder Menschenverstand
common sense.

Menschheit die mankind.

menschlich adjective 1 human;
2 humane.

Mentalität die (PL die
Mentalitäten) mentality.

Menü das (PL die **Menüs**) 1 set menu
(in restaurant); 2 menu (of
computer program).

merken verb (PERF hat gemerkt)
1 to notice; 2 **sich etwas merken**
to remember something.

Merkmal das (PL die **Merkmale**)
feature.

merkwürdig adjective strange,
odd.

Messe die (PL die **Messen**) 1 mass;
2 trade fair.

messen ◇verb (PRES **misst**, IMPERF
maß, PERF **hat gemessen**) 1 to
measure; (bei jemandem) **Fieber
messen** to take somebody's

temperature; 2 **sich mit
jemandem messen können** to be
as good as somebody.

Messer das (PL die **Messer**) knife.

Messing das brass.

Metall das (PL die **Metalle**) metal.

Meter der (PL die **Meter**) metre.

Metermaß das (PL die **Metermaße**)
tape measure.

Methode die (PL die **Methoden**)
method.

metrisch adjective metric.

Metzger der (PL die **Metzger**)
butcher.

Metzgerei die (PL die **Metzgereien**)
butcher's (shop).

Mexiko das Mexico.

miauen verb (PERF **hat miaut**) to
miaow.

mich pronoun 1 me; 2 myself.

mied SEE **meiden**.

Miete die (PL die **Mieten**) 1 rent; **zur
Miete wohnen** to live in rented
accommodation; 2 hire charge.

mieten verb (PERF **hat gemietet**)
1 to rent; 2 to hire.

Mieter der (PL die **Mieter**) tenant.

Mieterin die (PL die **Mieterinnen**)
tenant.

Mietshaus das (PL die
Mietshäuser) block of rented flats.

Mietvertrag der (PL die
Mietverträge) lease.

Mietwagen der (PL die **Mietwagen**)
hire car.

Migräne die (PL die **Migränen**)
migraine.

a **Mikrochip** der (PL die **Mikrochips**) microchip.

b **Mikrofon** das (PL die **Mikrofone**) microphone.

c **Mikroskop** das (PL die **Mikroskope**) microscope.

d **Mikrowellenherd** der (PL die **Mikrowellenherde**) microwave oven.

f **Milch** die milk.

g **Milchshake** der (PL die **Milchshakes**) milk shake.

h **mild** adjective mild.

i **Militär** das army.

j **militärisch** adjective military.

k **Milliarde** die (PL die **Milliarden**) thousand million, billion; **zwei Milliarden Euro** two billion euros.

l **Millimeter** der (PL die **Millimeter**) millimetre.

Million die (PL die **Millionen**) million.

n **Millionär** der (PL die **Millionäre**) millionaire.

o **Millionärin** die (PL die **Millionärinnen**) millionairess.

p **Minderheit** die (PL die **Minderheiten**) minority.

q **minderjährig** adjective under age.

r **mindestens** adverb at least.

s **mindester, mindeste, mindestes** adjective least.

t **mindestes** pronoun **1** der/die/das **Mindeste** the least; **zum Mindesten** at least; **2 nicht im Mindesten** not in the least.

Mine die (PL die **Minen**) **1** mine; **2** lead (in a pencil); **3** refill (for a ball-point).

Mineralwasser das (PL die **Mineralwässer**) mineral water.

Minirock der (PL die **Miniröcke**) miniskirt.

Minister der (PL die **Minister**) minister.

Ministerin die (PL die **Ministerinnen**) minister.

Ministerium das (PL die **Ministerien**) ministry, department.

minus adverb minus.

Minute die (PL die **Minuten**) minute.

mir pronoun **1** me, to me; **2** myself.

mischen verb (PERF hat gemischt) **1** to mix; **2 die Karten mischen** to shuffle the cards; **3 sich mischen** to mix.

Mischung die (PL die **Mischungen**) **1** mixture; **2** blend.

miserabel adjective (informal) **1** hopeless; **2** dreadful.

missbilligen verb (PERF hat missbilligt) to disapprove.

Missbrauch der abuse.

missbrauchen verb (PERF hat missbraucht) to abuse.

Misserfolg der (PL die **Misserfolge**) failure.

Missgeschick das (PL die **Missgeschicke**) **1** misfortune; **2** mishap.

misshandeln verb (PRES hat misshandelt) to ill-treat.

misslingen ◇*verb* (IMPERF **misslang**, PERF **ist misslungen**) to fail; **es misslang ihr** she failed.

misst SEE **messen**.

Misstrauen *das* 1 mistrust; 2 distrust.

misstrauen *verb* (PERF **hat misstraut**) **jemandem misstrauen** to mistrust somebody.

misstrauisch *adjective* suspicious.

Missverständnis *das* (PL *die* **Missverständnisse**) misunderstanding.

missverstehen ◇*verb* (IMPERF **missverstand**, PERF **hat missverstanden**) to misunderstand.

Mist *der* 1 manure; 2 (*informal*) rubbish.

Mistel *die* (PL *die* **Misteln**) mistletoe.

mit *preposition* (+ DAT) 1 with; **2 mit der Bahn fahren** to go by train; **mit dem Boot fahran** to go by boat; **3 mit sechs Jahren** at the age of six; **4 mit jemandem sprechen** to speak to somebody; **5 mit Bleistift** in pencil; **6 mit lauter Stimme** in a loud voice.

mit *adverb* as well, too; **warst du mit dabei?** were you there too?

Mitarbeiter *der* (PL *die* **Mitarbeiter**) 1 colleague; 2 employee.

Mitarbeiterin *die* (PL *die* **Mitarbeiterinnen**) 1 colleague; 2 employee.

mitbringen ◇*verb* (IMPERF **brachte mit**, PERF **hat mitgebracht**) to bring, to bring along; **ich bringe den Kindern Schokolade mit** I'm taking the children some chocolate.

miteinander *adverb* with each other, with one another.

Mitesser *der* (PL **Mitesser**) blackhead.

mitfahren ◇*verb* (PRES **fährt mit**, IMPERF **fuhr mit**, PERF **ist mitgefahren**) **1 mit jemandem mitfahren** to go with somebody; **die Kinder fahren mit uns mit** the children are coming with us; **2 bei jemandem mitfahren** to get a lift with somebody; **jemanden mitfahren lassen** to give somebody a lift.

mitgeben ◇*verb* (PRES **gibt mit**, IMPERF **gab mit**, PERF **hat mitgegeben**) to give.

Mitglied *das* (PL *die* **Mitglieder**) member.

mithalten ◇*verb* (PRES **hält mit**, IMPERF **hielt mit**, PERF **hat mitgehalten**) to keep up.

mitkommen ◇*verb* (IMPERF **kam mit**, PERF **ist mitgekommen**) 1 to come too; 2 to keep up.

Mitleid *das* pity; **kein Mitleid mit jemandem haben** not to feel any sympathy for somebody.

mitmachen *verb* (PERF **hat mitgemacht**) 1 to join in; **hast du Lust, bei dem Spiel mitzumachen?** do you want to join in the game?; 2 to take part in; 3 to go through (*experiences, troubles*):

a b c d e f g h i j k l m n o p q r s t u v w x

sie hat viel mitgemacht she's gone through a lot.

mitnehmen ◇*verb* (PRES **nimmt mit**, IMPERF **nahm mit**, PERF **hat mitgenommen**) 1 to take, to take along; **Anni hat die Kinder auf den Spielplatz mitgenommen** Anni has taken the children to the playground; 2 to give a lift to; 3 to affect (badly); 4 **zum Mitnehmen** to take away.

Mitschüler *der* (PL *die* **Mitschüler**) schoolfriend.

Mitschülerin *die* (PL *die* **Mitschülerinnen**) schoolfriend.

mitsingen *verb* (IMPERF **sang mit**, PERF **hat mitgesungen**) to sing along.

mitspielen *verb* (PERF **hat mitgespielt**) 1 to play; **wer spielt bei dem Fußballspiel mit?** who's playing in the football match?; **willst du mitspielen?** do you want to join in?; 2 **in einem Film mitspielen** to be in a film.

Mittag *der* (PL *die* **Mittage**) 1 midday; 2 lunch; **zu Mittag essen** to have lunch; 3 lunch-break.

Mittagessen *das* (PL *die* **Mittagessen**) lunch; **beim Mittagessen** at lunch.

mittags *adverb* 1 at lunchtime, at midday; 2 **um zwölf Uhr mittags** at noon.

Mittagspause *die* (PL *die* **Mittagspausen**) lunch-break.

Mitte *die* (PL *die* **Mitten**) 1 middle; 2 centre.

Mitteilung *die* (PL *die* **Mitteilungen**) 1 announcement; 2 communication.

Mittel *das* (PL *die* **Mittel**) 1 means; 2 **ein Mittel gegen Husten** a cough remedy; 3 **öffentliche Mittel** public funds.

Mittelalter *das* Middle Ages.

Mitteleuropa *das* Central Europe.

mittelgroß *adjective* medium-sized.

mittelmäßig *adjective* mediocre.

Mittelmeer *das* Mediterranean.

Mittelpunkt *der* (PL *die* **Mittelpunkte**) centre; **im Mittelpunkt stehen** to be the centre of attention.

Mittelstand *der* middle class.

Mittelstürmer *der* (PL *die* **Mittelstürmer**) centre-forward.

mitten *adverb* **mitten in/auf** in the middle of; **mitten in der Nacht** in the middle of the night.

Mitternacht *die* midnight.

mittlerer, mittlere, mittleres *adjective* 1 middle; 2 medium (quality, size); 3 average.

mittlerweile *adverb* 1 meanwhile; 2 by now.

Mittwoch *der* (PL *die* **Mittwoche**) Wednesday.

mittwochs *adverb* on Wednesdays.

Mixer *der* (PL *die* **Mixer**) liquidizer.

Möbel *plural noun* furniture.

Möbelwagen *der* (PL *die* **Möbelwagen**) removal van.

Mobiltelefon das (PL die Mobiltelefone) mobile phone.

möbliert adjective furnished.

mochte, möchte SEE mögen.

Mode die (PL die Moden) fashion.

Modell das (PL die Modelle) model.

Moderator der (PL die Moderatoren) presenter (on TV).

Moderatorin die (PL die Moderatorinnen) presenter (on TV).

modern adjective modern.

modernisieren verb (PERF hat modernisiert) to modernize.

modisch adjective fashionable.

Mofa das (PL die Mofas) moped.

mogeln verb (PERF hat gemogelt) to cheat.

mögen ◇verb (PRES mag, IMPERF mochte, PERF hat gemocht) 1 to like; **ich mag ihn nicht** I don't like him; **ich möchte** I'd like; **ich möchte gern wissen** I'd like to know; **möchtest du nach Hause?** would you like to go home?; 2 **lieber mögen** to prefer; **ich möchte lieber Tee** I would prefer tea; 3 **etwas nicht tun mögen** not to want to do something; **ich mag nicht fragen** I don't want to ask; **ich mag nicht mehr** I've had enough; 4 **das mag sein** maybe; 5 **was mag das sein?** whatever can it be?

möglich adjective possible; **alles Mögliche** all sorts of things.

möglicherweise adverb possibly.

Möglichkeit die (PL die Möglichkeiten) possibility.

möglichst adverb if possible; **möglichst früh** as early as possible.

Möhre die (PL die Möhren) carrot.

Mokka der (PL die Mokkas) mocca.

Molekül das (PL die Moleküle) molecule.

Moment der (PL die Momente) moment; **im Moment** at the moment; **Moment (mal)!** just a moment!

momentan adjective 1 temporary; 2 current.

momentan adverb 1 temporarily; 2 at the moment.

Monat der (PL die Monate) month.

monatelang adverb for months.

monatlich adjective, adverb monthly.

Mönch der (PL die Mönche) monk.

Mond der (PL die Monde) moon.

Mondschein der moonlight; **im Mondschein** by moonlight.

Montag der (PL die Montage) Monday.

montags adverb on Mondays.

Moped das (PL die Mopeds) moped.

Moral die 1 moral; 2 morale; 3 morals.

moralisch adjective moral.

Mord der (PL die Morde) murder.

Mörder der (PL die Mörder) murderer.

Mörderin die (PL die Mörderinnen) murderer.

Morgen der (PL die Morgen) morning; **am Morgen** in the morning; **heute Morgen** this morning; **guten Morgen!** good morning!

morgen adverb tomorrow; **morgen Abend** tomorrow evening.

morgens adverb in the morning.

Moschee die (PL die Moscheen) mosque.

Mosel die (River) Moselle.

Moskau das Moscow.

Moslem der (PL die Moslems) Muslim.

moslemisch adjective Muslim.

Moslenin die (PL die Mosleninnen) Muslim.

Motiv das (PL die Motive) **1** motive; **2** motif.

Motivation die motivation.

Motor der (PL die Motoren) engine, motor.

Motorrad das (PL die Motorräder) motorcycle, motorbike.

Mousse die (PL die Mouses) mousse.

Möwe die (PL die Möwen) seagull.

Mücke die (PL die Mücken) **1** midge; **2** mosquito.

müde adjective tired.

Müdigkeit die tiredness.

Mühe die (PL die Mühen) **1** effort; **sich Mühe geben** to make an effort; **2** trouble; **machen Sie sich keine Mühe** don't go to any trouble; **3 mit Müh und Not** only just.

Mühle die (PL die Mühlen) **1** mill; **2** grinder (for coffee).

mühsam adjective laborious.

Müll der rubbish.

Müllabfuhr die refuse collection.

Mülleimer der (PL die Mülleimer) rubbish bin.

Mülltonne die (PL die Mülltonnen) dustbin.

Mumps der mumps.

München das Munich.

Mund der (PL die Münder) mouth; **halt den Mund!** (informal) shut up!

Mundharmonika die (PL die Mundharmonikas) mouth organ.

mündlich adjective oral.

Münster das (PL die Münster) cathedral.

Münze die (PL die Münzen) coin.

Münzfernsprecher der (PL die Münzfernsprecher) payphone.

murmeln verb (PERF hat gemurmelt) to mumble.

mürrisch adjective surly.

Muschel die (PL die Muscheln) **1** mussel; **2** (sea) shell; **3** mouthpiece (of a phone).

Museum das (PL die Museen) museum.

Musik die music.

Musikal das (PL die Musikals) musical.

musikalisch *adjective* musical.

Musiker *der* (PL *die* Musiker) musician.

Musikerin *die* (PL *die* Musikerinnen) musician.

Muskat *der* nutmeg.

Muskel *der* (PL *die* Muskeln) muscle.

Müsli *das* muesli.

muss SEE **müssen**.

müssen ◇*verb* (PRES **muss**, IMPERF **musste**, PERF **hat gemusst**)
1 etwas tun müssen to have to do something; **sie muss es tun** she's got to do it, she must do it; **muss ich?** do I have to?; **muss das sein?** is that necessary?; **2 Sie müssten es mal versuchen** you should try it; **3 sie müssen gleich hier sein** they'll be here at any moment; **4 ich muss mal** (*informal*) I need (to go to) the loo.

Muster *das* (PL *die* Muster)
1 pattern; **2** sample.

Mut *der* courage; **jemandem Mut machen** to encourage somebody.

mutig *adjective* courageous.

Mutter[1] *die* (PL *die* Mütter) mother.

Mutter[2] *die* (PL *die* Muttern) nut.

Muttersprache *die* (PL *die* Muttersprachen) mother tongue, native language.

Muttertag *der* (PL *die* Muttertage) Mother's Day.

Mutti *die* (PL *die* Muttis) mum.

Mütze *die* (PL *die* Mützen) cap.

MwSt. (*Mehrwertsteuer*) VAT.

Mythos *der* (PL *die* Mythen) myth.

Nn

na *exclamation* well; **na und?** so what?; **na gut** all right then.

Nabel *der* (PL *die* Nabel) navel.

nach *preposition* (+ DAT) **1** to; **nach Hause gehen** to go home; **nach oben** up; **nach hinten** back; **nach rechts abbiegen** to turn right; **2** after; **nach Ihnen** after you; **zehn nach eins** ten past one; **nach etwas greifen** to reach for something; **3** according to; **meiner Meinung nach** in my opinion.

nach *adverb* **nach und nach** bit by bit, gradually; **nach wie vor** still.

nachahmen *verb* (PERF **hat nachgeahmt**) to imitate.

Nachbar *der* (PL *die* Nachbarn) neighbour.

Nachbarin *die* (PL *die* Nachbarinnen) neighbour.

Nachbarschaft *die* neighbourhood.

nachdem *conjunction* **1** after; **2 je nachdem** it depends; **je nachdem, wie schnell du damit fertig wirst** it depends on how quickly you can finish it.

nachdenken ◇*verb* (IMPERF **dachte nach**, PERF **hat nachgedacht**) to think; **über etwas nachdenken** to think about something; **ich habe lange über ihr Angebot nachgedacht und mich schließlich dagegen entschieden** I've thought a long time about her offer and finally decided against it.

a b c d e f g h i j k l m n o p q r s t u v w x y z

nachdenklich *adjective* thoughtful.

nacheinander *adverb* one after the other; **die Bewerber kamen nacheinander herein** the applicants came in one after the other.

Nachfrage *die* (PL *die* **Nachfragen**) demand; **es besteht keine Nachfrage** there's no demand for it.

nachgehen ◇*verb* (IMPERF **ging nach**, PERF **ist nachgegangen**) 1 to be slow; **meine Uhr geht nach** my watch is slow; 2 **jemandem nachgehen** to follow somebody; **einer Sache nachgehen** to look into something.

nachher *adverb* afterwards; **erst gehen wir ins Kino und nachher könnten wir essen gehen** we go to the cinema first and afterwards we could go for a meal; **bis nachher!** see you later!

nachholen *verb* (PERF **hat nachgeholt**) 1 to catch up on; **ich hatte Grippe und muss jetzt viel Mathe nachholen** I've had flu and now I've got a lot of maths to catch up on; 2 to make up for (*something missed*); 3 **eine Prüfung nachholen** to do an exam at a later date.

nachkommen ◇*verb* (IMPERF **kam nach**, PERF **ist nachgekommen**) 1 to come later, to follow; 2 **ich komme nicht nach** I can't keep up; 3 **einem Versprechen nachkommen** to carry out a promise; **seinen Verpflichtungen**

nachkommen to meet your commitments.

nachlassen ◇*verb* (PRES **lässt nach**, IMPERF **ließ nach**, PERF **hat nachgelassen**) 1 to ease; **meine Zahnschmerzen lassen langsam nach** my toothache is getting better; 2 to let up; **sobald die Kälte nachlässt** as soon as it gets warmer; 3 to deteriorate; 4 **etwas vom Preis nachlassen** to take something off the price; **jemandem zwanzig Euro nachlassen** to give somebody twenty euros off.

nachlässig *adjective* careless.

nachlaufen ◇*verb* (PRES **läuft nach**, IMPERF **lief nach**, PERF **ist nachgelaufen**) **jemandem nachlaufen** to run after somebody; **Philipp läuft allen Mädchen nach** (*informal*) Philipp chases all the girls.

nachmachen *verb* (PERF **hat nachgemacht**) to copy.

Nachmittag *der* (PL *die* **Nachmittage**) afternoon.

nachmittags *adverb* in the afternoon.

Nachnahme *die* **per Nachnahme** cash on delivery.

Nachname *der* (PL *die* **Nachnamen**) surname.

nachprüfen *verb* (PERF **hat nachgeprüft**) to check; **er prüft nach, ob es stimmt** he's going to check if it is correct.

Nachricht *die* (PL *die* **Nachrichten**) 1 news; **ich warte noch immer auf eine Nachricht von ihm** I'm still waiting for news of him; **eine Nachricht hinterlassen** to leave a message; **2 die Nachrichten** the news; **das kam in den Nachrichten** it was on the news.

Nachrichtensprecher der (PL die Nachrichtensprecher) newsreader.

Nachrichtensprecherin die (PL die Nachrichtensprecherinnen) newsreader.

nachschlagen ⋄verb (PRES schlägt nach, IMPERF schlug nach, PERF hat nachgeschlagen) to look up.

nachsehen ⋄verb (PRES sieht nach, IMPERF sah nach, PERF hat nachgesehen) **1** to check; **sieh nach, wer da ist** go and see who's there; **2** to look up; **3 jemandem etwas nachsehen** to let somebody get away with something.

nachsitzen ⋄verb (IMPERF saß nach, PERF hat nachgesessen) to be in detention; **Jan muss nachsitzen** Jan has detention.

Nachspeise die (PL die Nachspeisen) dessert, pudding.

nächste SEE **nächster**.

nächstens adverb shortly.

nächste, nächste, nächstes adjective **1** next; **2** nearest; **am nächsten sein** to be nearest; **3 in nächster Nähe** close by.

nächstes pronoun der/die/das Nächste (the) next; **als Nächstes** next.

Nacht die (PL die Nächte) night.

Nachteil der (PL die Nachteile) disadvantage.

Nachtfalter der (PL die Nachtfalter) moth.

Nachthemd das (PL die Nachthemden) nightdress, nightshirt.

Nachtigall die (PL die Nachtigallen) nightingale.

Nachtisch der (PL die Nachtische) dessert, pudding.

Nachtklub der (PL die Nachtklubs) night club.

Nachtleben das nightlife.

nachträglich adjective **1** subsequent; **2** belated.

nachträglich adverb **1** later; **2** belatedly.

nachts adverb at night; **um zwei Uhr nachts** at two o'clock in the morning.

Nacken der (PL die Nacken) neck.

nackt adjective **1** naked; **2** bare.

Nacktschnecke die (PL die Nacktschnecken) slug.

Nadel die (PL die Nadeln) **1** needle; **2** pin.

Nagel der (PL die Nägel) nail.

Nagelbürste die (PL die Nagelbürsten) nailbrush.

Nagelfeile die (PL die Nagelfeilen) nailfile.

Nagellack der (PL die Nagellacke) nail varnish.

nagelneu adjective brand-new.

Nagelschere die (PL die Nagelscheren) nail scissors.

a b c d e f g h i j k l m n o p q r s t u v w x y z

Nähe die **1** proximity; **2** in der Nähe der Kirche near the church; ganz in der Nähe nearby; **3** aus der Nähe close up.

nahe, nah *adjective, adverb* **1** near, nearby; der Nahe Osten the Middle East; nahe daran sein, etwas zu tun to nearly do something; **2** close; nahe bei close to; nahe verwandt sein to be closely related; **3** jemandem nahe legen, etwas zu tun to urge somebody to do something; **4** nahe liegend obvious.

nah *preposition* (+ DAT) near, close to.

nahelegen, naheliegend SEE nahe.

nähen *verb* (PERF hat genäht) **1** to sew; **2** to stitch (*a wound*).

näher *adjective* **1** closer; **2** nähere Einzelheiten further details; **3** shorter (*way, road*).

näher *adverb* **1** closer; näher kommen to come closer; **2** more closely; **3** Näheres further details.

nähern *verb* (PERF hat sich genähert) sich nähern to approach; wir näherten uns dem Dorf we were approaching the village.

Nähgarn das cotton.

nahm SEE nehmen.

Nähmaschine die (PL die Nähmaschinen) sewing machine.

Nahrung die food.

Naht die (PL die Nähte) seam.

Nahverkehrszug der (PL die Nahverkehrszüge) local train.

Name der (PL die Namen) name; im Namen von on behalf of; ich rufe im Namen von Herrn und Frau Schmidt an I'm calling on behalf of Mr and Mrs Schmidt.

nämlich *adverb* **1** because; **2** namely; **3** das war nämlich ganz anders it was quite different actually.

nannte SEE nennen.

nanu *exclamation* well, well!

Narbe die (PL die Narben) scar.

Narr der (PL die Narren) fool.

Närrin die (PL die Närrinnen) fool.

Nase die (PL die Nasen) nose; die Nase voll haben (*informal*) to have had enough.

Nasenbluten das nosebleed.

Nashorn das (PL die Nashörner) rhinoceros.

nass *adjective* wet.

Nation die (PL die Nationen) nation.

Nationalhymne die (PL die Nationalhymnen) national anthem.

Nationalität die (PL die Nationalitäten) nationality.

Natur die **1** nature; von Natur aus by nature; **2** die freie Natur the open countryside.

Naturlehrpfad der (PL die Naturlehrpfade) nature trail.

natürlich *adjective* natural.

natürlich *adverb* of course, naturally.

Natürlichkeit die naturalness.

Naturschützer der (PL die Naturschützer) conservationist.

Naturschützerin der (PL die Naturschützerinnen) conservationist.

Naturschutzgebiet das (PL die Naturschutzgebiete) nature reserve.

Naturwissenschaft die natural science.

Nebel der (PL die Nebel) **1** fog; **2** mist.

nebelig adjective SEE **neblig**.

neben preposition (+ DAT or + ACC with movement towards a place) **1** next to; **er hat neben mir gesessen** he sat next to me; **er hat sich neben mich gesetzt** he sat down next to me; **2** apart from.

nebenan adverb next door.

nebenbei adverb **1** as well, at the same time; **er liest die Zeitung und hört nebenbei Musik** he reads the newspaper and listens to music at the same time; **2** on the side; **nebenbei arbeite ich noch in einem Blumengeschäft** I work in a florist's on the side; **das mache ich so nebenbei** (informal) that's just a sideline; **3** in passing; **nebenbei bemerkt** by the way.

nebeneinander adverb next to each other.

nebenhergehen ◇ verb (IMPERF ging nebenher, PERF ist nebenhergegangen) to walk alongside.

neblig adjective **1** foggy; **2** misty.

necken verb (PERF hat geneckt) to tease.

Neffe der (PL die Neffen) nephew.

Negativ das (PL die Negative) negative.

negativ adjective negative.

nehmen ◇ verb (PRES nimmt, IMPERF nahm, PERF hat genommen) **1** to take; **2 ich nehme eine Suppe** I'll have soup; **3 was nehmen Sie dafür?** how much do you want for it?; **4 jemanden zu sich nehmen** to have somebody live with you; **5 sich etwas nehmen** to take something; **nimm dir ein Stück Kuchen** help yourself to a piece of cake.

Neid der envy, jealousy.

neidisch adjective envious, jealous.

nein adverb no.

Nelke die (PL die Nelken) carnation.

nennen ◇ verb (IMPERF nannte, PERF hat genannt) **1** to call; **2** to name; **3 ihr Name wurde nicht genannt** her name wasn't mentioned; **4 sich nennen** to call yourself.

Nerv der (PL die Nerven) nerve; **Gabi geht mir auf die Nerven** Gabi gets on my nerves.

nervig adjective nerve-wracking.

nervös adjective nervous.

Nervosität die nervousness.

Nessel die (PL die Nesseln) nettle.

Nest das (PL die Nester) **1** nest; **2** little place (a village).

nett adjective nice.

netto adverb net.

Netz das (PL die Netze) **1** net; **2** network; **3** string bag; **4** (spider's) web.

a
b
c
d
e
f
g
h
i
j
k
l
m
n
o
p
q
r
s
t
u
v
w
x
y
z

Netzkarte die (PL die Netzkarten) unlimited travel ticket (*over a transport network*).

Netzwerk das (PL die Netzwerke) network.

neu *adjective* 1 new; **wie neu** as good as new; **neue Sprachen** modern languages; 2 **seit neuestem** recently; 3 **die neueste Mode** the latest fashion; **das Neueste** the latest news; **das Neueste an Audioausrüstung** the latest in audio equipment; 4 **das ist mir neu** that's news to me.

neu *adverb* 1 newly; 2 only just; **es ist neu eingetroffen** it has only just come in; 3 **etwas neu schreiben** to rewrite something.

neuartig *adjective* new; **ein neuartiger Flaschenöffner** a new kind of bottle opener.

neuerdings *adverb* recently.

Neugier die curiosity.

neugierig *adjective* curious, inquisitive.

Neuigkeit die (PL die Neuigkeiten) piece of news; **gibt es irgendwelche Neuigkeiten?** is there any news?

Neujahr das New Year, New Year's Day.

neulich *adverb* the other day.

neun *number* nine.

neunter, neunte, neuntes *adjective* ninth.

neunzehn *number* nineteen.

neunzig *number* ninety.

Neuseeland das New Zealand.

nicht *adverb* 1 not; **ich kann nicht** I can't; **Iris hat nicht angerufen** Iris didn't ring; **bitte nicht** please don't; **nicht!** don't!; **nicht berühren!** don't touch!; 2 **'ich mag das nicht' – 'ich auch nicht'** 'I don't like it' – 'neither do I'; 3 **nicht (wahr)?** isn't he/she/it?; **du kennst ihn doch, nicht?** you know him, don't you?; 4 **gar nicht** not at all; 5 **nicht mehr** no more.

Nichte die (PL die Nichten) niece.

Nichtraucher der (PL die Nichtraucher) non-smoker.

Nichtraucherabteil das (PL die Nichtraucherabteile) no-smoking compartment.

Nichtraucherin die (PL die Nichtraucherinnen) non-smoker.

nichts *pronoun* 1 nothing; 2 **ich habe nichts gewusst** I didn't know anything; 3 **nichts mehr** no more; 4 **das macht nichts** it doesn't matter; 5 **nichts ahnend** unsuspecting.

nichtsahnend SEE nichts.

Nichtschwimmerbecken das (PL die Nichtschwimmerbecken) shallow swimming pool (*for non-swimmers and learners*).

nicken *verb* (PERF hat genickt) to nod.

Nickerchen das (PL die Nickerchen) nap; **ein Nickerchen machen** to have a nap.

nie *adverb* never.

nieder *adjective* low.

nieder *adverb* down.

Niederlage die (PL die Niederlagen) defeat.

Niederlande plural noun die Niederlande the Netherlands.

Niederländer der (PL die Niederländer) Dutchman; die Niederländer the Dutch.

Niederländerin die (PL die Niederländerinnen) Dutchwoman.

niederländisch adjective Dutch.

niedlich adjective sweet.

niedrig adjective 1 low; 2 base.

niemals adverb never.

niemand pronoun nobody; **wir haben niemand** or **niemanden gesehen** we didn't see anybody.

Niere die (PL die Nieren) kidney.

nieseln verb (PERF hat genieselt) to drizzle; **es nieselt** it's drizzling.

niesen verb (PERF hat geniest) to sneeze.

Nil der der Nil the River Nile.

Nilpferd das (PL die Nilpferde) hippopotamus.

nimmt SEE nehmen.

nirgends, nirgendwo adverb nowhere.

Niveau das (PL die Niveaus) 1 level; 2 standard.

noch adverb 1 still; **immer noch** still; 2 even; **noch besser** even better; 3 **noch nicht** not yet; **noch nie** never; 4 **gerade noch** only just; 5 **wer war noch da?** who else was there?; **was noch?** what else?; 6 **noch einmal** again; 7 **noch ein Bier** another beer; **noch etwas Kaffee?** (would you like some)

more coffee?; 8 **noch gestern** only yesterday; 9 **noch und noch Geld** loads of money.

noch conjunction nor; **weder ... noch** neither ... nor.

nochmals adverb again.

Nominativ der (PL die Nominative) nominative.

Nonne die (PL die Nonnen) nun.

Nordamerika das North America.

Nordamerikaner der (PL die Nordamerikaner) North American.

Nordamerikanerin die (PL die Nordamerikanerinnen) North American.

nordamerikanisch adjective North American.

Norden der north.

Nordirland das Northern Ireland.

nördlich adjective 1 northern; 2 northerly (direction).

nördlich adverb, preposition (+ GEN) **nördlich von Wien** to the north of Vienna; **nördlich der Stadt** north of the town.

Nordosten der north-east.

Nordpol der North Pole.

Nordsee die North Sea.

Nordwesten der north-west.

nörgeln verb (PERF hat genörgelt) to grumble.

Norm die (PL die Normen) 1 norm; 2 standard.

normal adjective normal.

normalerweise adverb normally.

a **Norwegen** das Norway.

b **Norweger** der (PL die **Norweger**) Norwegian.

c **Norwegerin** die (PL die **Norwegerinnen**) Norwegian.

d **norwegisch** adjective Norwegian.

e **Not** die (PL die **Nöte**) 1 need; **zur Not** if necessary, at a pinch; **mit knapper Not** only just; 2 hardship.

f **Notaufnahme** die (PL die **Notaufnahmen**) accident & emergency (hospital department).

g

h **Notausgang** der (PL die **Notausgänge**) emergency exit.

i **Notdienst** der **Notdienst haben** to be on call.

j

k **Note** die (PL die **Noten**) 1 note; **Noten lesen** to read music; 2 mark.

l **Notfall** der (PL die **Notfälle**) emergency.

m **notfalls** adverb if need be.

n **notieren** verb (PERF **hat notiert**) 1 to note down; 2 **sich etwas notieren** to make a note of something.

o **nötig** adjective necessary.

p **nötig** adverb urgently.

q **Notiz** die (PL die **Notizen**) 1 note; 2 **keine Notiz von etwas nehmen** to take no notice of something; 3 item (in a newspaper).

r

s

t **Notizblock** der (PL die **Notizblöcke**) notepad.

u

v **Notizbuch** das (PL die **Notizbücher**) notebook.

w

x

y

z

Notlage die (PL die **Notlagen**) crisis.

Notruf der (PL die **Notrufe**) 1 emergency call; 2 emergency number.

notwendig adjective necessary.

November der November.

nüchtern adjective 1 sober; **wieder nüchtern werden** to sober up; 2 **auf nüchternen Magen** on an empty stomach; 3 down-to-earth.

Nudeln plural noun 1 noodles; 2 pasta.

Null die (PL die **Nullen**) 1 zero, nought; 2 failure.

null number 1 nought; **unter null** below zero; 2 nil; **zwei zu null** two nil; 3 love (in tennis); 4 **null Fehler haben** to have no mistakes; **ich habe null Ahnung** (informal) I haven't got a clue; 5 **in null Komma nichts** (informal) in less than no time.

numerieren SEE **nummerieren**.

Nummer die (PL die **Nummern**) 1 number; 2 issue (of a magazine); 3 size (of clothing); 4 act; 5 **auf Nummer sicher gehen** to play safe.

nummerieren verb (PERF **hat nummeriert**) to number.

Nummernschild das (PL die **Nummernschilder**) number plate.

nun adverb now.

nun exclamation well; **nun ja …** well, yes ….

nur adverb 1 only; 2 **was sollen wir nur tun?** what on earth are we going to do?; **sie soll es nur**

versuchen! just let her try!; **3 nur zu!** go ahead!

Nürnberg das Nuremberg.

Nuss die (PL die **Nüsse**) nut.

Nutzen der benefit; **von Nutzen sein** to be useful.

nutzen, nützen verb (PERF hat genutzt/genützt) **1** to use; **etwas nutzen** to take advantage of something; **2** to be useful; **3 nichts nutzen** to be no use; **das nutzt mir nichts** that won't help me; **4 das nutzt ja doch nichts** it's pointless.

nützlich adjective useful.

nutzlos adjective useless.

Oo

ob conjunction **1** whether; **wissen Sie, ob heute noch ein Zug nach Freising fährt?** do you know if there is another train to Freising today?; **2 ob Alex noch anruft?** I wonder if Alex will ring; **3 und ob!** you bet!

obdachlos adjective homeless.

Obdachlose der/die (PL die **Obdachlosen**) homeless person; **die Obdachlosen** the homeless.

oben adverb **1** on top; **oben auf** on top of; **die Vase steht oben auf dem Schrank** the vase is on top of the cupboard; **2** at the top; **von oben bis unten** from top to bottom; **er hat uns von oben bis unten gemustert** he looked us up and down; **3** upstairs; **4 nach oben up,** upstairs; **er ist nach oben in sein Zimmer gegangen** he went up into his room; **geht der Fahrstuhl nach oben?** is the lift going up?; **hier oben** up here; **da oben** up there; **5 siehe oben** see above (on a page); **6 oben erwähnt** above mentioned; **6 oben ohne** (informal) topless.

obenerwähnt SEE oben.

Ober der (PL die **Ober**) waiter; **Herr Ober!** waiter!

oberer, obere, oberes adjective upper, top.

Oberfläche die (PL die **Oberflächen**) surface.

oberflächlich adjective superficial.

Oberhaupt das (PL die **Oberhäupter**) head.

Oberhemd das (PL die **Oberhemden**) shirt.

Oberschenkel der (PL die **Oberschenkel**) thigh.

Oberschule die (PL die **Oberschulen**) secondary school.

oberster, oberste, oberstes adjective top.

Oberstufe die (PL die **Oberstufen**) upper school.

Oberweite die (PL die **Oberweiten**) chest measurement, bust measurement.

Objekt das (PL die **Objekte**) object.

Objektiv das (PL die **Objektive**) lens.

objektiv adjective objective.

Oboe die (PL die **Oboen**) oboe; **Oboe spielen** to play the oboe.

Obst das fruit.

Obstbaum der (PL die **Obstbäume**) fruit tree.

Obstsalat der (PL die **Obstsalate**) fruit salad.

obszön adjective obscene.

obwohl conjunction although.

öde adjective 1 desolate; 2 dreary; **das ist so ein furchtbar öder Job** it's such terribly dull job.

oder conjunction 1 or; 2 **du kennst sie doch, oder?** you know her, don't you?

Ofen der (PL die **Öfen**) 1 oven; 2 stove; 3 heater.

offen adjective 1 open; **offen haben** to be open; **Tag der offenen Tür** open day; 2 frank; 3 vacant; **eine offene Stelle** a vacancy; 4 **offen bleiben** to stay open; 5 **offen bleiben** to remain open (of a question, possibility).

offen adverb 1 openly; 2 frankly; **offen gesagt** frankly.

offenbar adjective obvious.

offenbar adverb 1 apparently; 2 **da hast du dich offenbar geirrt** you seem to have made a mistake; **sie hat offenbar den Zug verpasst** she must have missed the train.

offenbleiben SEE **offen**.

offensichtlich adjective obvious.

öffentlich adjective public.

Öffentlichkeit die public; **in aller Öffentlichkeit** in public.

offiziell adjective official.

Offizier der (PL die **Offiziere**) officer.

öffnen verb (PERF **hat geöffnet**) to open; **jemandem die Tür öffnen** to open the door for somebody.

Öffner der (PL die **Öffner**) opener.

Öffnung die (PL die **Öffnungen**) opening.

Öffnungszeiten plural noun opening times.

oft adverb often.

öfter, öfters adverb quite often; **ich habe ihn öfters mal getroffen** I used to meet him quite often.

ohne preposition (+ ACC) 1 without; **ohne mich** count me out; 2 **ohne weiteres** easily; 3 **oben ohne** (informal) topless; 4 **das ist nicht ohne** (informal) it's not bad.

ohne conjunction without; **ohne zu überlegen** without thinking.

Ohnmacht die **in Ohnmacht fallen** to faint.

ohnmächtig adjective 1 unconscious; 2 **ohnmächtig werden** to faint; **Gisela ist ohnmächtig** Gisela's fainted.

Ohr das (PL die **Ohren**) ear.

Ohrenschmerzen plural noun earache.

Ohrring der (PL die **Ohrringe**) earring.

oje exclamation oh dear!

Ökoladen der (PL die **Ökoläden**) health-food shop.

Ökologie die ecology.

ökologisch adjective ecological.

Oktober der October.

Öl das (PL die Öle) oil.

Ölfarbe die (PL die Ölfarben) oil-paint.

Ölgemälde das (PL die Ölgemälde) oil painting.

ölig adjective oily.

Olive die (PL die Oliven) olive.

Olivenöl das (PL die Olivenöle) olive oil.

Ölteppich der (PL die Ölteppiche) oil slick.

Olympiade die (PL die Olympiaden) Olympic Games; **die Olympiade findet alle vier Jahre statt** the Olympic Games take place every four years.

olympisch adjective Olympic.

Oma die (PL die Omas) granny.

Omelett das (PL die Omeletts) omelette.

Omi die (PL die Omis) granny.

Onkel der (PL die Onkel) uncle.

Opa der (PL die Opas) grandpa.

Oper die (PL die Opern) opera.

Operation die (PL die Operationen) operation.

Operationssaal der (PL die Operationssäle) operating theatre.

operieren verb (PERF hat operiert) 1 to operate on; **sich operieren lassen** to have an operation; **sie wurde am Magen operiert** she had a stomach operation; 2 to operate.

Opfer das (PL die Opfer) 1 sacrifice; 2 victim; **das Erdbeben forderte viele Opfer** the earthquake claimed many victims.

Optiker der (PL die Optiker) optician.

Optikerin die (PL die Optikerinnen) optician.

Optimist der (PL die Optimisten) optimist.

optimistisch adjective optimistic.

Orange die (PL die Orangen) orange.

orange adjective orange.

Orangensaft der (PL die Orangensäfte) orange juice.

Orchester das (PL die Orchester) orchestra.

ordentlich adjective 1 tidy; 2 respectable; 3 proper (meal, job, salary); 4 **eine ordentliche Tracht Prügel** (informal) a good hiding.

ordentlich adverb 1 tidily; **ordentlich schreiben** to write neatly; 2 respectably; 3 properly; 4 **ordentlich feiern** (informal) to have a really good celebration; **wir sind ordentlich nass geworden** (informal) we got soaked.

ordinär adjective vulgar.

ordnen verb (PERF hat geordnet) 1 to arrange; 2 to put in order.

Ordner der (PL die Ordner) file.

Ordnung die 1 order; **Ordnung halten** to keep order; 2 **Ordnung machen** to tidy up; **die Wohnung in Ordnung bringen** to tidy up the flat; 3 **mit der Waschmaschine ist etwas nicht in Ordnung** there's something wrong with the washing

a

machine; **4 etwas in Ordnung bringen** to put something right; **die Waschmaschine in Ordnung bringen** to repair the washing machine; **5 in Ordnung!** okay!; **6 er ist in Ordnung** he's all right.

Organ das (PL die **Organe**) **1** organ; **2** (informal) voice.

Organisation die (PL die **Organisationen**) organization.

organisch adjective organic.

organisieren verb (PERF **hat organisiert**) **1** to organize; **2** (informal) to get (hold of).

Orgel die (PL die **Orgeln**) organ.

orientieren verb (PERF **hat sich orientiert**) **1 sich orientieren** to get your bearings; **2 sich über etwas orientieren** to inform yourself about something.

Orientierung die **1** orientation; **die Orientierung verlieren** to lose your bearings; **2 zu Ihrer Orientierung** for your information.

Orientierungsjahr das (PL die **Orientierungsjahre**) gap year.

Orientierungspunkt der (PL die **Orientierungspunkte**) landmark, reference point.

Orientierungsrennen das orienteering.

Orientierungssinn der sense of direction.

originell adjective original.

Orkan der (PL die **Orkane**) hurricane.

Ort der (PL die **Orte**) **1** place; **an Ort und Stelle** on the spot; **2** (small) town.

Orthografie, Orthographie die spelling.

örtlich adjective local.

Ortschaft die (PL die **Ortschaften**) village.

Ortsgespräch das (PL die **Ortsgespräche**) local call.

Ossi der (informal) (PL die **Ossis**) East German.

Osten der east.

Osterei das (PL die **Ostereier**) Easter egg.

Ostern das Easter.

Österreich das Austria.

Österreicher der (PL die **Österreicher**) Austrian.

Österreicherin die (PL die **Österreicherinnen**) Austrian.

österreichisch adjective Austrian.

östlich adjective **1** eastern; **2** easterly.

östlich adverb, preposition (+ GEN) **östlich von Wien** to the east of Vienna; **östlich der Stadt** east of the town.

Ostsee die Baltic (Sea).

oval adjective oval.

Ozean der (PL die **Ozeane**) ocean.

Ozon das ozone.

Ozonschicht die ozone layer.

Pp

Paar das (PL die Paare) **1** pair; **ein Paar Schuhe** a pair of shoes; **2** couple.

paar pronoun **ein paar** a few; **ein paar Mal** a few times; **alle paar Tage** every few days.

paarmal SEE paar.

paarweise adjective in pairs; **die Kinder stellten sich paarweise auf** the children lined up in pairs.

Päckchen das (PL die Päckchen) **1** package, packet; **2** small parcel.

packen verb (PERF hat gepackt) **1** to pack; **ich muss jetzt meinen Koffer packen** I must pack my case now; **2** to grab (hold of); **von Furcht gepackt** seized with fear.

Packung die (PL die Packungen) packet, pack.

Pädagoge der (PL die Pädagogen) **1** educationalist; **2** teacher.

pädagogisch adjective educational.

Paddel das (PL die Paddel) paddle.

paddeln verb **1** (PERF hat gepaddelt) to paddle (a canoe); **2** (PERF ist gepaddelt) to paddle (along a lake, river).

Paket das (PL die Pakete) **1** parcel; **Gabi hat mir ein Paket geschickt** Gabi sent me a parcel; **2** packet; **kaufe bitte ein Paket Waschpulver für mich** can you please buy a packet of washing powder for me.

Pakistan das Pakistan.

Pakistaner der (PL die Pakistaner) Pakistani.

Pakistanerin die (PL die Pakistanerinnen) Pakistani.

pakistanisch adjective Pakistani.

Palast der (PL die Paläste) palace.

Palme die (PL die Palmen) palm (tree).

Pampelmuse die (PL die Pampelmusen) grapefruit.

Panik die panic; **in Panik geraten** to panic.

Panne die (PL die Pannen) **1** breakdown; **wir haben auf dem Rückweg eine Panne gehabt** we had a breakdown on the way back; **2** mishap; **uns ist eine Panne passiert** we had a mishap.

Panzer der (PL die Panzer) tank (military).

Papa der (PL die Papas) daddy.

Papagei der (PL die Papageien) parrot.

Papier das (PL die Papiere) paper.

Papierkorb der (PL die Papierkörbe) waste-paper basket.

Papiertüte die (PL die Papiertüten) paper bag.

Pappe die (PL die Pappen) cardboard.

Paprika der (PL die Paprikas) **1** pepper; **2** paprika.

Papst der (PL die Päpste) pope.

Parabolantenne die (PL die Parabolantennen) satellite dish.

Paradies das paradise.

a
b
c
d
e
f
g
h
i
j
k
l
m
n
o
p
q
r
s
t
u
v
w
x
y
z

Paragraph der (PL die Paragraphen) **1** section; **2** clause.

parallel adjective parallel.

Pärchen das (PL die Pärchen) couple.

Parfüm das (PL die Parfüms) perfume.

Park der (PL die Parks) park.

Parkanlage die (PL die Parkanlagen) park.

parken verb (PERF hat geparkt) to park.

Parkett das (PL die Parkette) **1** (in a theatre) stalls; **2** parquet floor.

Parkhaus das (PL die Parkhäuser) multi-storey car park.

Parklücke die (PL die Parklücken) parking space.

Parkplatz der (PL die Parkplätze) **1** car park; **2** parking space.

Parkschein der (PL die Parkscheine) car-park ticket.

Parkuhr die (PL die Parkuhren) parking meter.

Parkverbot das 'Parkverbot' 'no parking'; in der Innenstadt ist Parkverbot you can't park in the town centre.

Parlament das (PL die Parlamente) parliament.

Parole die (PL die Parolen) slogan.

Partei die (PL die Parteien) **1** party; **2** für jemanden Partei ergreifen to side with somebody.

Parterre das (PL die Parterres) ground floor.

Partie die (PL die Partien) **1** part; **2** game (of tennis, chess).

Partner der (PL die Partner) partner.

Partnerin die (PL die Partnerinnen) partner.

Partnerstadt die (PL die Partnerstädte) twin town.

Party die (PL die Partys) party.

Pass der (PL die Pässe) **1** passport; **2** pass.

Passage die (PL die Passagen) **1** shopping arcade; **2** passage (of text); **3** sequence (of music, film).

Passagier der (PL die Passagiere) passenger.

Passant der (PL die Passanten) passer-by.

Passantin die (PL die Passantinnen) passer-by.

passen (PERF hat gepasst) **1** to fit; jemandem passen to fit somebody; **2** to suit; jemandem passen to suit somebody; Freitag passt mir nicht Friday doesn't suit me; seine Art passt mir nicht I don't like his manner; **3** zu etwas passen to go with something; zu jemandem passen to be right for somebody.

passend adjective **1** suitable; **2** matching.

passieren verb (PERF ist passiert) to happen.

Passiv das passive.

passiv adjective passive.

Passkontrolle die passport control.

Passwort das (PL die Passwörter) password (in computing); das

Passwort eingeben to give the password.

Paste die (PL die **Pasten**) paste.

Pastete die (PL die **Pasteten**) pie.

Pate der (PL die **Paten**) godfather.

Patenkind das (PL die **Patenkinder**) godchild.

patent adjective capable, clever.

Patentante die (PL die **Patentanten**) godmother.

Patient der (PL die **Patienten**) patient.

Patientin die (PL die **Patientinnen**) patient.

Patin die (PL die **Patinnen**) godmother.

patschnass adjective soaking wet.

pauken verb (informal) (PERF hat **gepaukt**) to swot.

pauschal adjective all-inclusive.

Pauschalreise die (PL die **Pauschalreisen**) package tour.

Pause die (PL die **Pausen**) 1 break; 2 pause; 3 interval.

Pazifik der der **Pazifik** the Pacific (Ocean).

PC der (PL die **PCs**) PC.

Pech das 1 bad luck; **Pech haben** to be unlucky; 2 pitch.

Pedal das (PL die **Pedale**) pedal.

peinlich adjective 1 embarrassing; **es war mir sehr peinlich** I felt very embarrassed about it; 2 awkward; 3 meticulous.

Peitsche die (PL die **Peitschen**) whip.

Pelle die skin.

Pelz der (PL die **Pelze**) fur.

pendeln verb 1 (PERF ist **gependelt**) to commute; 2 (PERF hat **gependelt**) to swing.

Pendelverkehr der 1 commuter traffic; 2 shuttle service.

Pendler der (PL die **Pendler**) commuter.

penetrant adjective 1 overpowering (odour, perfume); 2 pushy (person).

Penis der (PL die **Penisse**) penis.

pennen verb (informal) (PERF hat **gepennt**) to sleep, to kip.

Pension die (PL die **Pensionen**) 1 guesthouse; 2 volle Pension full board; 3 pension; **eine schöne Pension haben** to get a good pension; **in Pension gehen** to retire.

pensioniert adjective retired.

per preposition (+ ACC) 1 by; **per Luftpost** by airmail; 2 per.

Perfekt das (PL die **Perfekte**) perfect.

perfekt adjective perfect.

Periode die (PL die **Perioden**) period.

Perle die (PL die **Perlen**) 1 pearl; 2 bead.

Person die (PL die **Personen**) person; **für vier Personen** for four people; **ich für meine Person** personally.

Personal das staff, personnel.

Personalausweis der (PL die **Personalausweise**) identity card.

a
b
c
d
e
f
g
h
i
j
k
l
m
n
o
p
q
r
s
t
u
v
w
x
y
z

a **Personenzug** der (PL die Personenzüge) stopping train.

b **persönlich** *adjective* personal.

c **persönlich** *adverb* 1 personally; 2 in person.

d **Persönlichkeit** die (PL die Persönlichkeiten) personality.

e **Perücke** die (PL die Perücken) wig.

f **Pessimist** der (PL die Pessimisten) pessimist.

g **pessimistisch** *adjective* pessimistic.

h **Petersilie** die parsley.

i **Petroleum** das paraffin.

j **Pfad** der (PL die Pfade) path.

k **Pfadfinder** der (PL die Pfadfinder) (Boy) Scout.

l **Pfadfinderin** die (PL die Pfadfinderinnen) (Girl) Guide.

m **Pfand** das (PL die Pfänder) 1 forfeit; 2 deposit (*on a bottle*); 3 pledge.

n **Pfandflasche** die (PL die Pfandflaschen) returnable bottle.

o **Pfanne** die (PL die Pfannen) (frying) pan.

p **Pfannkuchen** der (PL die Pfannkuchen) pancake.

q **Pfarrer** der (PL die Pfarrer) 1 vicar; 2 priest.

r **Pfau** der (PL die Pfauen) peacock.

s **Pfauhenne** die (PL die Pfauhennen) peahen.

t **Pfeffer** der pepper.

u **Pfefferkorn** das (PL die Pfefferkörner) peppercorn.

v **Pfefferkuchen** der gingerbread.

Pfefferminzbonbon der (PL die Pfefferminzbonbons) mint.

Pfefferminze die peppermint.

Pfeffermühle die (PL die Pfeffermühlen) peppermill.

Pfeife die (PL die Pfeifen) 1 whistle; 2 pipe.

pfeifen ◇*verb* (IMPERF pfiff, PERF hat gepfiffen) to whistle.

Pfeil der (PL die Pfeile) arrow.

Pfeiler der (PL die Pfeiler) 1 pillar; 2 pier.

Pfennig der (PL die Pfennige) pfennig (*one hundredth of a mark in the former German currency*) **ich habe keinen Pfennig mehr** I haven't got a penny left SEE **Mark**.

Pferd das (PL die Pferde) horse.

Pferderennen das (PL die Pferderennen) horse race.

Pferdeschwanz der (PL die Pferdeschwänze) ponytail.

pfiff SEE **pfeifen**.

Pfingsten das (PL die Pfingsten) Whitsun.

Pfirsich der (PL die Pfirsiche) peach.

Pflanze die (PL die Pflanzen) plant.

pflanzen *verb* (PERF hat gepflanzt) to plant; **pflanze mehr Bäume** plant more trees.

Pflaster das (PL die Pflaster) 1 pavement; 2 plaster.

Pflaume die (PL die Pflaumen) plum.

Pflege die 1 care; 2 nursing; 3 ein Kind in Pflege nehmen to foster a child.

Pflegeeltern plural noun foster parents.

Pflegeheim das (PL die Pflegeheime) nursing home.

Pflegekind das (PL die Pflegekinder) foster child.

pflegeleicht adjective easy-care (fabric).

pflegen verb (PERF hat gepflegt) 1 to look after, to care for; eine Freundschaft pflegen to foster a friendship; 2 to nurse.

Pfleger der (PL die Pfleger) (male) nurse.

Pflicht die (PL die Pflichten) duty; Pflicht sein to be compulsory.

pflichtbewusst adjective conscientious.

Pflichtfach das (PL die Pflichtfächer) compulsory subject.

pflücken verb (PERF hat gepflückt) to pick.

Pflug der (PL die Pflüge) plough.

pflügen verb (PERF hat gepflügt) to plough.

Pforte die (PL die Pforten) gate.

Pförtner der (PL die Pförtner) porter.

Pfosten der (PL die Pfosten) post.

Pfote die (PL die Pfoten) paw.

pfui exclamation ugh!

Pfund das (PL die Pfund(e)) pound.

Pfütze die (PL die Pfützen) puddle.

Phantasie die SEE Fantasie.

phantasievoll adjective SEE Fantasievoll.

phantastisch adjective fantastic.

Philosoph der (PL die Philosophen) philosopher.

Philosophie die (PL die Philosophien) philosophy.

Photo das (PL die Photos) SEE Foto.

Phrase die (PL die Phrasen) 1 phrase; 2 cliché.

Physik die physics.

Physiker der (PL die Physiker) physicist.

Physikerin die (PL die Physikerinnen) physicist.

Pickel der (PL die Pickel) spot, pimple.

Picknick das (PL die Picknicks) picnic.

Pik das spades (in cards).

pikant adjective spicy.

Pille die (PL die Pillen) pill.

Pilot der (PL die Piloten) pilot.

Pilotin die (PL die Pilotinnen) pilot.

Pilz der (PL die Pilze) 1 mushroom; 2 fungus.

Pinguin der (PL die Pinguine) penguin.

pinkeln verb (informal) (PERF hat gepinkelt) to pee.

Pinnwand die (PL die Pinnwände) noticeboard.

Pinsel der (PL die Pinsel) brush.

Pinzette die (PL die Pinzetten) tweezers.

Pirat der (PL die Piraten) pirate.

a
b
c
d
e
f
g
h
i
j
k
l
m
n
o
p
q
r
s
t
u
v
w
x
y
z

Piste die (PL die **Pisten**) 1 run, piste;
2 track; 3 runway.

Pizza die (PL die **Pizzas**) pizza.

Pkw der (PL die **Pkws**)
(*Personenkraftwagen*) car.

plagen verb (PERF hat geplagt) 1 to
bother, to torment; 2 to pester;
3 sich plagen to struggle; sich in
der Schule plagen to struggle at
school; er muss sich plagen he has
to work hard.

Plakat das (PL die **Plakate**) poster.

Plan der (PL die **Pläne**) 1 plan;
2 map.

planen verb (PERF hat geplant) to
plan.

Planierraupe die (PL die
Planierraupen) bulldozer.

planmäßig adjective scheduled.

planmäßig adverb 1 according to
plan; alles läuft planmäßig
everything is going according to
plan; 2 on schedule; der Zug ist
planmäßig abgefahren the train
left on schedule.

Plastik¹ das plastic.

Plastik² die (PL die **Plastiken**)
sculpture.

Plastiktüte die (PL die
Plastiktüten) plastic bag.

Platin das platinum.

platt adjective flat; platt sein
(*informal*) to be flabbergasted.

plattdeutsch adjective low
German.

Platte die (PL die **Platten**) 1 plate;
2 dish; kalte Platte cold meats and
cheeses; 3 hotplate; 4 record;

5 board (*made of wood*); 6 slab
(*made of stone*); 7 sheet (*made of
metal or glass*); 8 top (*of a table*).

Plattenspieler der (PL die
Plattenspieler) record player.

Platz der (PL die **Plätze**) 1 place; viel
Platz haben to have a lot of room;
Platz lassen to leave room; auf die
Plätze, fertig, los! on your marks,
get set, go!; 2 seat; Platz nehmen to
take a seat; 3 square (*in a town*);
4 ground, pitch; einen Spieler
vom Platz stellen to send a player
off; 5 court (*for tennis*); 6 course
(*for golf*).

Plätzchen das (PL die **Plätzchen**)
1 biscuit; 2 spot.

platzen verb (PERF ist geplatzt)
1 to burst; 2 der Plan ist geplatzt
(*informal*) the plan fell through;
3 vor Neugier platzen to be
bursting with curiosity.

plaudern verb adverb 1 to chat.

plaudern verb (PERF hat
geplaudert) to chat.

pleite adjective (*informal*) broke.

Plombe die (PL die **Plomben**) filling.

plombieren verb (PERF hat
plombiert) to fill.

plötzlich adjective sudden.

plötzlich adverb suddenly.

plump adjective 1 plump;
2 clumsy.

Plural der (PL die **Plurale**) plural.

Plus das 1 plus; 2 profit;
3 advantage.

plus adverb plus.

PLZ SEE Postleitzahl.

Po der (*informal*) (PL die **Pos**) bottom.

a
b
c
d
e
f
g
h
i
j
k
l
m
n
o
p
q
r
s
t
u
v
w
x
y
z

Poesie die poetry.

Pokal der (PL die **Pokale**) **1** cup; **2** goblet.

Pokalspiel das (PL die **Pokalspiele**) cup-tie.

Pole der (PL die **Polen**) Pole.

Polen das Poland.

polieren verb (PERF **hat poliert**) to polish.

Polin die (PL die **Polinnen**) Pole.

Politik die **1** politics; **2** policy.

Politiker der (PL die **Politiker**) politician.

Politikerin die (PL die **Politikerinnen**) politician.

politisch adjective political.

Politur die (PL die **Polituren**) polish.

Polizei die police.

polizeilich adjective police.

polizeilich adverb by the police; **sich polizeilich anmelden** to register with the police.

Polizeiwache die (PL die **Polizeiwachen**) police station.

Polizist der (PL die **Polizisten**) policeman.

Polizistin die (PL die **Polizistinnen**) policewoman.

polnisch adjective Polish.

Pommes frites plural noun chips, French fries.

Pony[1] das (PL die **Ponys**) pony.

Pony[2] der (PL die **Ponys**) fringe.

Popmusik die pop music.

poppig adjective bright; **Natalie hat immer poppige Socken an** Natalie always wears bright socks.

Porree der (PL die **Porrees**) leek; **eine Stange Porree** a leek.

Portemonnaie das SEE **Portmonee.**

Portier der (PL die **Portiers**) porter.

Portion die (PL die **Portionen**) portion; **möchtest du eine zweite Portion?** would you like a second helping?

Portmonee das (PL die **Portmonees**) purse.

Porto das postage.

Porträt das (PL die **Porträts**) portrait.

Portugal das Portugal.

Portugiese der (PL die **Portugiesen**) Portuguese.

Portugiesin die (PL die **Portugiesinnen**) Portuguese.

portugiesisch adjective Portuguese.

Posaune die (PL die **Posaunen**) trombone.

Post die **1** post; **mit der Post** by post; **2** post office.

Postamt das (PL die **Postämter**) post office.

Postbote der (PL die **Postboten**) postman.

Poster das (PL die **Poster**) poster.

Postkarte die (PL die **Postkarten**) postcard.

Postleitzahl die (PL die **Postleitzahlen**) postcode.

Pracht die splendour.

prächtig adjective splendid.

prahlen *verb* (PERF **hat geprahlt**) to boast.

praktisch *adjective* 1 practical; **praktische Erfahrung** practical experience; 2 handy; 3 **ein praktischer Arzt** a general practitioner.

praktisch *adverb* 1 practically; 2 in practice.

Praline die (PL die **Pralinen**) chocolate.

Präposition die (PL die **Präpositionen**) preposition.

Präsens das present (tense).

Präservativ das (PL die **Präservative**) condom.

Präsident der (PL die **Präsidenten**) president.

Präsidentin die (PL die **Präsidentinnen**) president.

Pratikum das (PL die **Praktika**) practical training.

Praxis die (PL die **Praxen**) 1 practice; 2 practical experience; 3 surgery.

Preis der (PL die **Preise**) 1 price; **um keinen Preis** not at any price; 2 prize.

Preisausschreiben das (PL die **Preisausschreiben**) competition.

Preiselbeere die (PL die **Preiselbeeren**) cranberry.

preiswert *adjective* reasonable, cheap.

Prellung die (PL die **Prellungen**) bruise.

Premierminister der (PL die **Premierminister**) prime minister.

Presse die press.

Priester der (PL die **Priester**) priest.

prima *adjective* (*informal*) brilliant.

Prinz der (PL die **Prinzen**) prince.

Prinzessin die (PL die **Prinzessinnen**) princess.

Prise die (PL die **Prisen**) pinch; **eine Prise Salz** a pinch of salt.

privat *adjective* private.

Privileg das (PL die **Privilegien**) privilege.

pro *preposition* (+ ACC) per.

Probe die (PL die **Proben**) 1 test; **jemanden auf die Probe stellen** to test somebody; **ein Auto Probe fahren** to test-drive a car; 2 sample; 3 rehearsal.

probefahren SEE Probe.

probieren *verb* (PERF **hat probiert**) 1 to try; 2 to taste.

Problem das (PL die **Probleme**) problem.

Produkt das (PL die **Produkte**) product.

Produzent der (PL die **Produzenten**) producer.

produzieren *verb* (PERF **hat produziert**) to produce.

Profi der (PL die **Profis**) pro.

Profil das (PL die **Profile**) 1 profile; 2 tread (*of a tyre*).

Programm das (PL die **Programme**) 1 programme; 2 program (*in computing*); 3 channel (*on TV*).

programmieren verb (PERF hat programmiert) to program.

Programmierer der (PL die Programmierer) programmer.

Programmiererin die (PL die Programmiererinnen) programmer.

Projekt das (PL die Projekte) project.

Promille das (PL die Promille) alcohol level; **zuviel Promille haben** to be over the limit.

Pronomen das (PL die Pronomen) pronoun.

Prospekt der (PL die Prospekte) brochure.

prost exclamation cheers!

Protein das (PL die Proteine) protein.

Protest der (PL die Proteste) protest.

protestantisch adjective Protestant.

protestieren verb (PERF hat protestiert) to protest.

Protokoll das (PL die Protokolle) 1 minutes, transcript; 2 record (in court); 3 protocol.

protzen verb (PERF hat geprotzt) to show off; **Klaus protzt mit seinem neuen Auto** Klaus is showing off with his new car.

Proviant der provisions.

Prozent das (PL die Prozente) 1 per cent; **zehn Prozent** ten per cent; 2 **Prozente bekommen** (informal) to get a discount.

Prozentsatz der (PL die Prozentsätze) percentage.

Prozess der (PL die Prozesse) 1 court case; **einen Prozess gewinnen** to win a case; 2 trial; 3 process.

Prozession die (PL die Prozessionen) procession.

prüfen verb (PERF hat geprüft) 1 to test, to examine (at school); 2 to check; **hast du die Reifen geprüft?** have you checked the tyres?

Prüfung die (PL die Prüfungen) 1 examination, exam; **eine Prüfung bestehen** to pass an examination; **sie ist durch die Prüfung gefallen** she failed the exam; 2 check.

Prügel der (PL die Prügel) 1 stick; 2 **Prügel bekommen** to get a beating.

Prügelei die (PL die Prügeleien) fight.

prügeln verb (PERF hat geprügelt) 1 to beat; 2 **sich prügeln** to fight; **sich um etwas prügeln** to fight for something.

Psychiater der (PL die Psychiater) psychiatrist.

Psychiaterin die (PL die Psychiaterinnen) psychiatrist.

psychisch adjective psychological.

Psychologe der (PL die Psychologen) psychologist.

Psychologie die psychology.

Psychologin die (PL die Psychologinnen) psychologist.

a
b
c
d
e
f
g
h
i
j
k
l
m
n
o
p
q
r
s
t
u
v
w
x
y
z

a

b

c

d

e

f

g

h

i

j

k

l

m

n

o

p

q

r

s

t

u

v

w

x

y

z

Publikum das **1** audience, crowd; **2** public.

Pudding der (PL die **Puddinge**) **1** blancmange; **2** pudding (steamed).

Pudel der (PL die **Pudel**) poodle.

Puder der (PL die **Puder**) powder.

Puffmais der popcorn.

Pulli der (PL die **Pullis**) pullover.

Pullover der (PL die **Pullover**) pullover.

Puls der (PL die **Pulse**) pulse; **der Arzt maß meinen Puls** the doctor took my pulse.

Pult das (PL die **Pulte**) desk.

Pulver das (PL die **Pulver**) powder.

Pulverkaffee der instant coffee.

Pumpe die (PL die **Pumpen**) pump.

pumpen verb (PERF **hat gepumpt**) **1** to pump; **2** (informal) to lend; **jemandem Geld pumpen** to lend somebody money; **3** (informal) to borrow; **sich etwas pumpen** to borrow something.

Punker der (PL die **Punker**) punk.

Punkerin die (PL die **Punkerinnen**) punk.

Punkt der (PL die **Punkte**) **1** dot, spot; **Punkt sechs Uhr** at six o'clock on the dot; **2** full stop; **3** point; **nach Punkten siegen** to win on points.

pünktlich adjective punctual.

Puppe die (PL die **Puppen**) **1** doll; **2** puppet.

pur adjective **1** pure; **2** Whisky pur neat whisky.

Purzelbaum der (PL die **Purzelbäume**) somersault.

pusten verb (PERF **hat gepustet**) to blow.

Pute die (PL die **Puten**) turkey.

putzen verb (PERF **hat geputzt**) **1** to clean; **putz dir die Zähne** clean your teeth; **putzen gehen** to work as a cleaner; **2 sich die Nase putzen** to blow your nose.

Putzfrau die (PL die **Putzfrauen**) cleaning lady, cleaner.

putzig adjective cute.

Puzzle das (PL die **Puzzles**) jigsaw (puzzle).

Pyjama der (PL die **Pyjamas**) pyjamas.

Pyramide die (PL die **Pyramiden**) pyramid.

Pyrenäen (plural noun) die **Pyrenäen** the Pyrenees.

Qq

Quadrat das (PL die **Quadrate**) square.

quadratisch adjective square.

Quadratmeter der (PL die **Quadratmeter**) square metre.

quaken verb (PERF **hat gequakt**) **1** to quack; **2** to croak (of a frog).

Qual die (PL die **Qualen**) **1** torment; **2** agony; **es war eine Qual, das ansehen zu müssen** it was agony to watch.

quälen verb (PERF **hat gequält**) **1** to torment; **2** to torture; **3** to pester; **4 sich quälen** to suffer; **5 sich mit etwas quälen** to struggle with something; **sich durch ein Buch quälen** to struggle (your way) through a book.

Quälgeist der (informal) (PL die **Quälgeister**) pest.

Qualifikation die (PL die **Qualifikationen**) qualification.

qualifizieren verb (PERF **hat qualifiziert**) **sich qualifizieren** to qualify; **sie haben sich für die dritte Runde qualifiziert** they qualified for the third round.

Qualität die (PL die **Qualitäten**) quality.

Qualle die (PL die **Quallen**) jellyfish.

Qualm der thick smoke.

qualmen verb (PERF **hat gequalmt**) to give off clouds of smoke; **sie qualmt wie ein Schlot** (informal) she smokes like a chimney.

Quarantäne die quarantine.

Quark der (curd cheese) quark.

Quartett das (PL die **Quartette**) quartet.

Quartier das (PL die **Quartiere**) **1** accommodation; **2** quarters.

quasseln verb (informal) (PERF **hat gequasselt**) to natter.

Quatsch der (informal) rubbish.

quatschen verb (informal) (PERF **hat gequatscht**) to chat.

Quelle die (PL die **Quellen**) **1** source; **2** spring.

quer adverb **1** across; **2** crosswise; **3** diagonally; **quer gestreift** with diagonal stripes; **4 quer durch** straight through.

quergestreift SEE quer.

Querstraße die (PL die **Querstraßen**) side street; **die erste Querstraße rechts** the first turning on the right.

quetschen verb (PERF **hat gequetscht**) **1** to crush; **2** to squash; **3 ich habe mich in meine Jeans gequetscht** I squeezed into my jeans.

Quetschung die (PL die **Quetschungen**) bruise.

quietschen verb (PERF **hat gequietscht**) to squeak.

quitt adjective quits.

Quittung die (PL die **Quittungen**) receipt.

Quiz das (PL die **Quiz**) quiz.

Rr

Rabatt der (PL die **Rabatte**) discount.

Rache die revenge.

rächen verb (PERF **hat gerächt**) **1** to avenge; **2 sich an jemandem rächen** to take revenge on somebody; **3 das wird sich rächen** you'll have to pay for it.

Rad das (PL die **Räder**) **1** wheel; **2** bike; **Julia ist mit dem Rad gekommen** Julia came by bike; **3 Rad fahren** to cycle.

a
b
c
d
e
f
g
h
i
j
k
l
m
n
o
p
q
r
s
t
u
v
w
x
y
z

Radar der radar.

Radarschirm der (PL die Radarschirme) radar screen.

radeln verb (PERF ist geradelt) to cycle; **Max ist ins Dorf geradelt** Max cycled into the village.

radfahren SEE **Rad**.

Radfahrer der (PL die Radfahrer) cyclist.

Radfahrerin die (PL die Radfahrerinnen) cyclist.

Radfahrweg der (PL die Radfahrwege) cycle lane.

Radiergummi der (PL die Radiergummis) rubber.

Radieschen das (PL die Radieschen) radish.

Radio das (PL die Radios) radio.

radioaktiv adjective radioactive.

Radiosendung die (PL die Radiosendungen) radio broadcast.

Radler der (PL die Radler) cyclist.

Radlerin die (PL die Radlerinnen) cyclist.

Radrennen das **1** cycle race; **Maria hat das Radrennen gewonnen** Maria won the cycle race; **2** cycle racing.

Radweg der (PL die Radwege) cycle path.

raffiniert adjective crafty.

Rahm der cream.

Rahmen der (PL die Rahmen) **1** frame; **2** framework; **3** limits; **im Rahmen des Möglichen** within the bounds of possibility.

rahmen verb (PERF hat gerahmt) to frame (a picture).

Rakete die (PL die Raketen) rocket.

ran (informal) SEE **heran**.

Rand der (PL die Ränder) **1** edge; **2** rim; **der Rand der Tasse war angeschlagen** the rim of the cup was chipped; **3** ring, mark; **4** margin (of a page); **du musst einen Rand für die Korrekturen lassen** you must leave a margin for the corrections; **5** outskirts (of a town); **6** etwas am Rande erwähnen to mention something in passing; **7** am Rande der Pleite sein to be on the verge of bankruptcy; **8** außer Rand und Band geraten (informal) to go wild.

Randstreifen der (PL die Randstreifen) hard shoulder.

Rang der (PL die Ränge) **1** rank; **2** (in a theatre) circle.

rannte SEE **rennen**.

rasch adjective quick.

Rasen der (PL die Rasen) lawn, grass.

rasen verb (PERF ist gerast) to tear along, to rush; **gegen eine Mauer rasen** to career into a wall.

Rasenmäher der (PL die Rasenmäher) lawnmower.

Rasierapparat der (PL die Rasierapparate) **1** shaver; **2** razor.

Rasiercreme die (PL die Rasiercremes) shaving cream.

rasieren verb (PERF hat rasiert) **1** to shave; **2** sich rasieren to shave.

Rasierklinge die (PL die Rasierklingen) razor blade.

Rasierwasser das aftershave.

Rasse die (PL die Rassen) 1 race; 2 breed; **ich weiß nicht, was für eine Rasse unser Hund ist** I don't know what breed our dog is.

Rassenhass der racial hatred.

rassisch adjective racial.

Rassismus der racism.

Rassist der (PL die Rassisten) racist.

Rassistin die (PL die Rassistinnen) racist.

rassistisch adjective racist.

rasten verb (PERF hat gerastet) to rest.

Rastplatz der (PL die Rastplätze) picnic area (on a motorway).

Raststätte die (PL die Raststätten) services (on a motorway).

Rat der 1 advice; **ein Rat** a piece of advice; **jemanden zu Rate ziehen** to ask somebody's advice; 2 **sich keinen Rat wissen** not to know what to do; 3 council.

Rate die (PL die Raten) instalment; **in monatlichen Raten abzahlen** to pay in monthly instalments.

raten ✧ verb (PRES rät, IMPERF riet, PERF hat geraten) 1 **jemandem raten** to advise somebody; **was rätst du mir?** what do you advise me to do?; 2 to guess; **richtig raten** to guess right.

Rathaus das (PL die Rathäuser) town hall.

rationell adjective efficient.

ratlos adjective helpless; **Emma hat mich ratlos angesehen** Emma gave me a helpless look; **ratlos sein** not to know what to do.

ratsam adjective advisable; **es wäre ratsam, früher zu fahren** it would be advisable to leave earlier.

Ratschlag der (PL die Ratschläge) piece of advice, advice; **deine klugen Ratschläge kannst du dir sparen** you can keep your advice to yourself.

Rätsel das (PL die Rätsel) 1 puzzle; 2 mystery.

rätselhaft adjective mysterious.

Ratte die (PL die Ratten) rat.

rau adjective 1 rough; 2 harsh; 3 **eine raue Stimme** a husky voice; 4 **einen rauen Hals haben** to have a sore throat.

Raub der robbery.

Raubdruck der (PL die Raubdrucke) pirated edition.

Räuber der (PL die Räuber) robber.

Rauch der smoke.

rauchen verb (PERF hat geraucht) to smoke; **'Rauchen verboten'** 'no smoking'.

Rauchen das smoking; **passives Rauchen** passive smoking.

Raucher der (PL die Raucher) smoker.

Raucherin die (PL die Raucherinnen) smoker.

Räucherlachs der smoked salmon.

räuchern verb (PERF hat geräuchert) to smoke (fish, meat).

a
b
c
d
e
f
g
h
i
j
k
l
m
n
o
p
q
r
s
t
u
v
w
x
y
z

a

b

c

d

e

f

g

h

i

j

k

l

m

n

o

p

q

r

s

t

u

v

w

x

y

z

rauf (*informal*) SEE **herauf, hinauf.**

rauh *adjective* SEE **rau.**

Raum der (PL die **Räume**) **1** room; das Haus hat sehr große Räume the house has very big rooms; **2** space; wir brauchen mehr Raum we need more space; **3** die Rakete ist im Raum explodiert the rocket exploded in space; **4** area; im Raum Berlin in the area of Berlin.

räumen *verb* (PERF hat **geräumt**) **1** to clear; das Geschirr vom Tisch räumen to clear away the dishes; **2** die Hemden in den Schrank räumen to put the shirts in the cupboard; seine Sachen beiseite räumen to put your things to one side; die Akten aus dem Schrank räumen to take the files out of the cabinet; **3** to vacate.

Raumfahrt die space travel.

Raumschiff das (PL die **Raumschiffe**) space ship.

Räumungsverkauf der closing-down sale.

Raupe die (PL die **Raupen**) caterpillar.

raus (*informal*) SEE **heraus, hinaus.**

Rauschgift das (PL die **Rauschgifte**) drug; Rauschgift nehmen to take drugs.

Rauschgiftsüchtige der/die (PL die **Rauschgiftsüchtigen**) drug addict.

rauskriegen *verb* (*informal*) (PERF hat **rausgekriegt**) **1** to get out; **2** ein Geheimnis rauskriegen to find out a secret; **3** ich kann die

Aufgabe nicht rauskriegen I can't do the exercise.

räuspern *verb* (PERF hat sich **geräuspert**) sich räuspern to clear your throat.

reagieren *verb* (PERF hat reagiert) to react.

Reaktion die (PL die **Reaktionen**) reaction.

realisieren *verb* (PERF hat realisiert) **1** to realize; **2** to implement.

Reality-Show die (PL die **Reality-Shows**) reality show.

Realschule die (PL die **Realschulen**) secondary school.

rebellieren *verb* (PERF hat rebelliert) to rebel.

Rechen der (PL die **Rechen**) rake.

Recherche die (PL die **Recherchen**) investigation.

rechnen *verb* (PERF hat gerechnet) **1** to do arithmetic; Peter kann gut rechnen Peter's good at arithmetic, Peter's good at figures; **2** to reckon; mit etwas rechnen to reckon with something; **3** er wird zu den besten Schauspielern gerechnet he's reckoned to be one of the best actors; **4** to count; jemanden zu seinen Freunden rechnen to count somebody as a friend; **5** mit etwas rechnen to expect something; **6** auf jemanden rechnen to count on somebody.

Rechner der (PL die **Rechner**) **1** calculator; **2** computer.

Rechnung die (PL die Rechnungen) 1 bill; 2 invoice; **die Rechnung liegt bei** the invoice is enclosed; 3 calculation.

Recht das (PL die Rechte) 1 law; **nach deutschem Recht** under German law; 2 right; **Recht haben** to be right; **im Recht sein** to be in the right; **Recht bekommen** to be proved right; 3 **jemandem Recht geben** to agree with somebody; 4 **mit Recht** rightly; **du hast dich mit Recht beschwert** you were right to complain.

recht adjective 1 right; **jemandem recht sein** to be all right with somebody; **wenn es dir recht ist** if it's all right with you; 2 **der/die Rechte** the right man/woman; 3 **das Rechte** the right thing; **etwas Rechtes** something proper; **ich habe nichts Rechtes gegessen** I haven't had a proper meal; **etwas Rechtes lernen** to learn something useful; 4 real; **ich habe keine rechte Lust** I don't really feel like it.

recht adverb 1 correctly; 2 quite; **recht einfach** quite simple; 3 really; 4 **recht vielen Dank** many thanks; 5 **das geschieht dir recht!** (it) serves you right!; 6 **man kann es nicht allen recht machen** you can't please everyone.

Rechte die 1 right (side); **zu meiner Rechten** on my right; 2 right hand; 3 **die Rechte** the right (in politics).

rechte SEE **rechter**.

Rechteck das (PL die Rechtecke) rectangle.

rechteckig adjective rectangular.

rechter, rechte, rechtes adjective 1 right; **auf der rechten Seite** on the right; 2 right-wing.

rechtfertigen verb 1 (PERF **hat gerechtfertigt**) to justify; 2 **sich rechtfertigen** to justify yourself.

rechtlich adjective legal.

rechts adverb on the right; **nimm die dritte Abzweigung rechts** take the third turning on the right; **von rechts** from the right; **rechts abbiegen** to turn right.

Rechtsanwalt der (PL die Rechtsanwälte) lawyer.

Rechtsanwältin die (PL die Rechtsanwältinnen) lawyer.

Rechtschreibprogramm das (PL die Rechtschreibprogramme) spell checker.

Rechtschreibung die spelling.

Rechtshänder der (PL die Rechtshänder) **Klaus ist Rechtshänder** Klaus is right-handed.

Rechtshänderin die (PL die Rechtshänderinnen) **Beate ist Rechtshänderin** Beate is right-handed.

rechtzeitig adjective timely.

rechtzeitig adverb in time; **wir sind gerade noch rechtzeitig angekommen** we got there just in time.

Redakteur der (PL die Redakteure) editor.

a
b
c
d
e
f
g
h
i
j
k
l
m
n
o
p
q
r
s
t
u
v
w
x
y
z

Redakteurin die (PL die Redakteurinnen) editor.

Rede die (PL die Reden) **1** speech; **eine Rede halten** to make a speech; **2 nicht der Rede wert** not worth mentioning; **davon kann keine Rede sein** it's out of the question; **jemanden zur Rede stellen** to take somebody to task.

reden verb (PERF hat geredet) **1** to talk; **2** to speak; **mit jemandem reden** to speak to somebody; **3 sie hat kein Wort geredet** she didn't say a word; **4 mir ist egal, was über mich geredet wird** I don't care what people say about me.

Redewendung die (PL die Redewendungen) idiom, expression.

redigieren verb (PERF hat redigiert) to edit.

redlich adjective honest.

Redlichkeit die honesty.

Redner der (PL die Redner) speaker.

Rednerin die (PL die Rednerinnen) speaker.

reduzieren verb (PERF hat reduziert) to reduce.

reflexiv adjective reflexive.

Reformhaus das (PL die Reformhäuser) health-food shop.

Regal das (PL die Regale) **1** shelf; **2** shelves, bookcase.

Regel die (PL die Regeln) **1** rule; **in der Regel** as a rule; **2** period (menstruation).

regelmäßig adjective regular.

regeln verb (PERF hat geregelt) **1** to regulate; **2** to direct (the traffic); **3** to settle (a matter); **wir haben die Sache so geregelt, dass ...** we've arranged things so that ...; **4 sich von selbst regeln** to sort itself out.

Regelung die (PL die Regelungen) **1** regulation; **2** settlement.

Regen der rain.

Regenbogen der (PL die Regenbogen) rainbow.

Regenmantel der (PL die Regenmäntel) raincoat.

Regenschirm der (PL die Regenschirme) umbrella.

Regenwurm der (PL die Regenwürmer) earthworm.

regieren verb (PERF hat regiert) **1** to govern; **2** to rule, to reign.

Regierung die (PL die Regierungen) **1** government; **2** reign.

Regisseur der (PL die Regisseure) director.

Regisseurin die (PL die Regisseurinnen) director.

Register das (PL die Register) **1** index; **2** register.

regnen verb (PERF hat geregnet) to rain.

regnerisch adjective rainy.

Reh das (PL die Rehe) deer.

reiben ◇ verb (IMPERF rieb, PERF hat gerieben) **1** to rub; **2** to grate.

reibungslos adjective smooth.

reich adjective rich.

Reich das (PL die **Reiche**) **1** empire; **das Römische Reich** the Roman Empire; **2** kingdom, realm.

reichen verb (PERF **hat gereicht**) **1** to hand, to pass; **2** to be enough; **mit dem Geld reichen** to have enough money; **3 bis zu etwas reichen** to reach up to something; **er reicht seinem Vater bis zur Schulter** he comes up to his father's shoulder; **die Felder reichen bis zum Wald** the fields extend as far as or up to the forest; **4 mir reichts!** (informal) I've had enough!

reichlich adjective **1** large; **2** ample (space).

reichlich adverb plenty of.

Reichtum der (PL die **Reichtümer**) wealth.

Reichweite die **1** reach; **außer Reichweite** out of reach; **2** range.

reif adjective **1** ripe; **2** mature.

Reife die maturity; **mittlere Reife** exams taken after five years of secondary schooling.

Reifen der (PL die **Reifen**) **1** tyre; **2** hoop.

Reifendruck der tyre pressure.

Reifenpanne die (PL die **Reifenpannen**) puncture.

Reihe die (PL die **Reihen**) **1** row; **2** series; **eine Reihe von Ereignissen** a series of events; **3 der Reihe nach** in turn; **außer der Reihe** out of turn; **du bist an der Reihe** it's your turn.

Reihenfolge die (PL die **Reihenfolgen**) order; **in der**

richtigen Reihenfolge in the right order.

Reihenhaus das (PL die **Reihenhäuser**) terraced house.

Reim der (PL die **Reime**) rhyme.

reimen verb (PERF **hat gereimt**) **1** to rhyme; **2 sich reimen** to rhyme.

rein[1] adjective **1** pure; **2** clean; **3** sheer (madness); **4 etwas ins Reine schreiben** to make a fair copy of something; **etwas ins Reine bringen** to sort something out.

rein adverb **1** purely; **2** absolutely; **rein gar nichts** absolutely nothing.

rein[2] (informal) SEE **herein, hinein.**

reinigen verb (PERF **hat gereinigt**) to clean.

Reinigung die (PL die **Reinigungen**) **1** cleaning; **2** cleaner's.

Reis der rice.

Reise die (PL die **Reisen**) **1** journey, trip; **gute Reise!** have a good journey!; **auf meinen Reisen** on my travels; **2** voyage.

Reiseandenken das (PL die **Reiseandenken**) souvenir.

Reisebüro das (PL die **Reisebüros**) travel agency.

Reisebus der (PL die **Reisebusse**) coach.

Reiseführer der (PL die **Reiseführer**) **1** guidebook; **2** (travel) guide.

a b c d e f g h i j k l m n o p q r s t u v w x y z

reisekrank *adjective* travel-sick; **reisekrank werden** to get travel-sick.

Reiseleiter *der* (PL *die* **Reiseleiter**) (travel) guide.

Reiseleiterin *die* (PL *die* **Reiseleiterinnen**) tourist guide.

reisen *verb* (PERF **ist gereist**) to travel.

Reisende *der/die* (PL *die* **Reisenden**) traveller.

Reisepass *der* (PL *die* **Reisepässe**) passport.

Reisescheck *der* (PL *die* **Reiseschecks**) traveller's cheque.

Reiseziel *das* (PL *die* **Reiseziele**) destination.

reißen ◇*verb* (IMPERF **riss**, PERF **hat gerissen**) 1 to tear; 2 to snatch; 3 to pull; **an etwas reißen** to pull at something; 4 **mit sich reißen** to sweep away; 5 **etwas an sich reißen** to snatch something; **die Macht an sich reißen** to seize power; 6 **Witze reißen** to crack jokes; 7 **sich um etwas reißen** to fight for something; 8 (PERF **ist gerissen**) **hin und her gerissen sein** to be torn; 9 (PERF **ist gerissen**) to tear, to break.

Reißverschluss *der* (PL *die* **Reißverschlüsse**) zip.

Reißzwecke *die* (PL *die* **Reißzwecken**) drawing pin.

reiten ◇*verb* (IMPERF **ritt**, PERF **hat/ ist geritten**) to ride.

Reiter *der* (PL *die* **Reiter**) rider.

Reiterin *die* (PL *die* **Reiterinnen**) rider.

Reitschule *die* (PL *die* **Reitschulen**) riding school.

Reiz *der* (PL *die* **Reize**) 1 attraction, appeal; 2 charm.

reizen *verb* (PERF **hat gereizt**) 1 to appeal to, to tempt; **das reizt mich sehr** it's very tempting; 2 to annoy; **jemanden zum Zorn reizen** to provoke somebody to anger; 3 to irritate (*the skin, eyes*); 4 to bid (*when playing cards*).

reizend *adjective* charming.

reizvoll *adjective* attractive.

Reklame *die* (PL *die* **Reklamen**) 1 advertisement, advert; **für etwas Reklame machen** to advertise something; 2 commercial (*on TV*).

Rekord *der* (PL *die* **Rekorde**) record.

Rektor *der* (PL *die* **Rektoren**) 1 head (*of a school*); 2 vice-chancellor (*of a university*).

Religion *die* (PL *die* **Religionen**) religion.

religiös *adjective* religious.

Rendezvous *das* (PL *die* **Rendezvous**) date.

Rennbahn *die* (PL *die* **Rennbahnen**) racetrack.

rennen ◇*verb* (IMPERF **rannte**, PERF **ist gerannt**) to run.

Rennen *das* (PL *die* **Rennen**) race.

Rennfahrer *der* (PL *die* **Rennfahrer**) racing driver.

Rennwagen *der* (PL *die* **Rennwagen**) racing car.

renovieren *verb* (PERF **hat renoviert**) to renovate, to redecorate.

rentabel *adjective* profitable.

Rente *die* (PL *die* **Renten**) pension; **in Rente gehen** to retire.

Rentner *der* (PL *die* **Rentner**) pensioner.

Rentnerin *die* (PL *die* **Rentnerinnen**) pensioner.

Reparatur *die* (PL *die* **Reparaturen**) repair.

reparieren *verb* (PERF **hat repariert**) to repair.

Reportage *die* (PL *die* **Reportagen**) 1 report; 2 live commentary.

Reporter *der* (PL *die* **Reporter**) reporter.

Reporterin *die* (PL *die* **Reporterinnen**) reporter.

Reptil *das* (PL *die* **Reptile**) reptile.

Republik *die* (PL *die* **Republiken**) republic.

Reservat *das* (PL *die* **Reservate**) reservation.

Reserverad *das* (PL *die* **Reserveräder**) spare wheel.

reservieren *verb* (PERF **hat reserviert**) to reserve.

Reservierung *die* (PL *die* **Reservierungen**) reservation.

Reservoir *das* (PL *die* **Reservoirs**) reservoir.

Respekt *der* respect.

respektieren *verb* (PERF **hat respektiert**) to respect.

Rest *der* (PL *die* **Reste**) 1 rest, remainder; 2 left-over; **zum Mittagessen gibts die Reste** we're having the leftovers for lunch; 3 **die Reste** the remains.

Restaurant *das* (PL *die* **Restaurants**) restaurant.

restlich *adjective* remaining.

restlos *adjective* complete.

Resultat *das* (PL *die* **Resultate**) result.

retten *verb* (PERF **hat gerettet**) 1 to save, to rescue; **jemandem das Leben retten** to save somebody's life; 2 **sich retten** to escape.

Rettich *der* (PL *die* **Rettiche**) radish.

Rettung *die* rescue.

Rettungsboot *das* (PL *die* **Rettungsboote**) life boat.

Rettungsring *der* (PL *die* **Rettungsringe**) lifebelt.

Rettungsschwimmer *der* (PL *die* **Rettungsschwimmer**) lifeguard; **gibt es einen Rettungsschwimmer im Schwimmbad?** is there a lifeguard at the pool?

Rettungsschwimmerin *die* (PL *die* **Rettungsschwimmerinnen**) lifeguard.

Rettungswagen *der* (PL *die* **Rettungswagen**) ambulance.

Rezept *das* (PL *die* **Rezepte**) 1 prescription; 2 recipe.

Rezeption *die* (PL *die* **Rezeptionen**) reception; **bitte geben Sie Ihren Schlüssel an der Rezeption ab** please leave your key at reception.

R-Gespräch *das* (PL *die* **R-Gespräche**) reverse-charge call.

Rhabarber *der* rhubarb.

Rhein *der* Rhine.

Rheuma *das* rheumatism.

a b c d e f g h i j k l m n o p q r s t u v w x y z

Rhythmus der (PL die **Rhythmen**) rhythm.

richten verb (PERF **hat gerichtet**) 1 to direct, to point (a torch, telescope, gun); 2 **eine Frage an jemanden richten** to put a question to somebody; 3 to address (a letter, remarks); 4 to prepare (a meal, room); 5 **sich auf etwas richten** to be directed towards something; 6 **sich nach jemandem richten** to fit in with somebody's wishes; **sich nach den Vorschriften richten** to follow the rules; 7 **sich nach etwas richten** to depend on something.

Richter der (PL die **Richter**) judge.

richtig adjective 1 right; 2 **das Richtige** the right thing; **der/die Richtige** the right man/woman; 3 real, proper.

richtig adverb 1 correctly; **hast du das Formular richtig ausgefüllt?** have you filled in the form correctly?; 2 really; 3 **richtig stellen** to put right; **die Uhr geht richtig** the clock is telling the right time.

Richtlinie die (PL die **Richtlinien**) guideline.

Richtung die (PL die **Richtungen**) 1 direction; 2 trend.

rieb SEE **reiben**.

riechen ◇verb (IMPERF **roch**, PERF **hat gerochen**) 1 to smell; 2 **ich kann ihn nicht riechen** (informal) I can't stand him.

rief SEE **rufen**.

Riegel der (PL die **Riegel**) 1 bolt; 2 **ein Riegel Schokolade** a bar of chocolate.

Riemen der (PL die **Riemen**) strap.

Riese der (PL die **Riesen**) giant.

riesengroß adjective gigantic.

riesig adjective gigantic, huge; **ein riesiger Lastwagen** a gigantic lorry.

riet SEE **raten**.

Rind das (PL die **Rinder**) 1 ox; 2 cow; **Rinder** cattle; 3 beef.

Rinde die (PL die **Rinden**) 1 bark; 2 rind; 3 crust.

Rinderbraten der (PL die **Rinderbraten**) roast beef.

Rindfleisch das beef.

Ring der (PL die **Ringe**) ring.

Ringbuch das (PL die **Ringbücher**) ring binder.

Ringen das wrestling.

Rinne die (PL die **Rinnen**) 1 gutter; 2 drainpipe, channel.

Rippe die (PL die **Rippen**) rib.

Risiko das (PL die **Risiken**) risk.

riskant adjective risky.

riskieren verb (PERF **hat riskiert**) to risk, to put at risk.

Riss der (PL die **Risse**) 1 tear; 2 crack.

riss SEE **reißen**.

ritt SEE **reiten**.

Rivale der (PL die **Rivalen**) rival.

Rivalin die (PL die **Rivalinnen**) rival.

Robbe die (PL die **Robben**) seal.

Roboter der (PL die **Roboter**) robot.

roch SEE **riechen.**

Rock der (PL die **Röcke**) skirt.

Roggen der rye.

roh adjective **1** raw; **2** rough; **3** brutal.

Rohr das (PL die **Rohre**) **1** pipe; **2** reed; **3** cane.

Rohstoff der (PL die **Rohstoffe**) raw material.

Rolladen SEE **Rollladen.**

Rolle die (PL die **Rollen**) **1** roll; **2** reel; **3** role, part; **4 es spielt keine Rolle** it doesn't matter.

rollen verb (PERF **hat gerollt**) **1** to roll; **2** (PERF **ist gerollt**) to roll.

Roller der (PL die **Roller**) scooter.

Rollkragen der (PL die **Rollkrägen**) polo neck.

Rollladen der (PL die **Rollläden**) shutter.

Rollschuh der (PL die **Rollschuhe**) roller-skate.

Rollschuhfahrer der (PL die **Rollschuhfahrer**) skater (on rollerskates).

Rollschuhfahrerin die (PL die **Rollschuhfahrerinnen**) skater (on rollerskates).

Rollschuhlaufen das roller-skating.

Rollstuhl der (PL die **Rollstühle**) wheelchair.

Rolltreppe die (PL die **Rolltreppen**) escalator.

Rom das Rome.

Roman der (PL die **Romane**) novel.

romantisch adjective romantic.

Römer der (PL die **Römer**) Roman.

Römerin die (PL die **Römerinnen**) Roman.

röntgen verb (PERF **hat geröntgt**) to X-ray.

rosa adjective pink.

Rose die (PL die **Rosen**) rose.

Rosenkohl der (Brussels) sprouts.

Rosine die (PL die **Rosinen**) raisin.

Rosmarin der rosemary.

Rosskastanie die (PL die **Rosskastanien**) horse-chestnut, conker.

Rost der (PL die **Roste**) **1** rust; **2** grate, grill.

rösten verb (PERF **hat geröstet**) **1** to roast; **2** to toast.

rosten verb (PERF **ist gerostet**) to rust.

rostig adjective rusty.

Röstkartoffeln plural noun roast potatoes.

rot adjective red.

Röteln plural noun German measles.

rothaarig adjective red-haired.

Rotkehlchen das (PL die **Rotkehlchen**) robin.

Rotkohl der red cabbage.

Rotwein der (PL die **Rotweine**) red wine.

Routine die routine.

rüber adverb (informal) over; **komm zu uns rüber** come over to us.

Rückblende die (PL die **Rückblenden**) flashback.

a b c d e f g h i j k l m n o p q r s t u v w x y z

Rücken der (PL die **Rücken**) 1 back; 2 spine (of a book).

rücken verb (PERF hat gerückt) to move; **kannst du ein wenig rücken?** can you move over a bit?

Rückfahrkarte die (PL die **Rückfahrkarten**) return ticket; **eine Rückfahrkarte nach München** a return ticket to Munich.

Rückfahrt die return journey; **auf der Rückfahrt** on the way back.

Rückgabe die (PL die **Rückgaben**) return.

Rückgang der (PL die **Rückgänge**) decrease; **ein Rückgang in der Anzahl der Unfälle** a decrease in the number of accidents.

rückgängig adjective **etwas rückgängig machen** to cancel something.

Rückhand die backhand (in tennis).

Rückkehr die return.

Rückreise die return journey.

Rucksack der (PL die **Rucksäcke**) rucksack.

Rückseite die (PL die **Rückseiten**) back.

Rücksicht die consideration.

rücksichtslos adjective 1 inconsiderate; **ein rücksichtsloser Fahrer** a reckless driver; 2 ruthless.

rücksichtsvoll adjective considerate.

Rücksitz der (PL die **Rücksitze**) back seat.

rückwärts adverb backwards.

Rückwärtsgang der (PL die **Rückwärtsgänge**) reverse (gear).

Rückweg der (PL die **Rückwege**) 1 way back; 2 return journey.

Rückzahlung die (PL die **Rückzahlungen**) refund, repayment.

Ruder das (PL die **Ruder**) 1 oar; 2 rudder.

Ruderboot das (PL die **Ruderboote**) rowing boat.

rudern verb (PERF ist gerudert) 1 to row; **ich bin über den See gerudert** I rowed across the lake; 2 (PERF hat gerudert) to row; **ich habe Monika über den See gerudert** I rowed Monika across the lake.

Rudern das rowing; **du bist mit dem Rudern dran** it's your turn to row.

Ruf der (PL die **Rufe**) 1 call, shout; 2 reputation; 3 phone number.

rufen ◇verb (IMPERF **rief**, PERF hat **gerufen**) to call; **den Arzt rufen** to send for the doctor.

Rufnummer die (PL die **Rufnummern**) phone number.

Ruhe die 1 silence; **Ruhe bitte!** quiet please!; 2 rest; 3 peace; **jemanden in Ruhe lassen** to leave somebody in peace; **in aller Ruhe** calmly; 4 **sich nicht aus der Ruhe bringen lassen** to not get worked up; 5 **sich zur Ruhe setzen** to retire.

ruhen verb (PERF hat geruht) to rest; **hier ruht ...** here lies ....

Ruhestand der im Ruhestand retired.

Ruhetag der (PL die Ruhetage) closing day; 'Dienstag Ruhetag' 'closed on Tuesdays'.

ruhig adjective 1 quiet; 2 peaceful; 3 calm.

ruhig adverb 1 quietly; sich ruhig verhalten to keep quiet; 2 calmly; ruhig bleiben to remain calm; 3 sehen Sie sich ruhig um you're welcome to look around; du kannst es ihm ruhig sagen it's OK, you can tell him.

Ruhm der fame.

Rührei das scrambled eggs.

rühren verb (PERF hat gerührt) 1 to move; 2 to stir; 3 sich rühren to move; 4 an etwas rühren to touch, to touch on.

Ruine die (PL die Ruinen) ruin.

ruinieren verb (PERF hat ruiniert) to ruin.

rülpsen verb (PERF hat gerülpst) to belch.

Rum der rum.

Rumänien das Romania.

rumänisch adjective Romanian.

Rummel der 1 hustle and bustle; 2 fuss; 3 fair.

Rummelplatz der (PL die Rummelplätze) fairground.

rund adjective round.

rund adverb about; rund um around.

Runde die (PL die Runden) 1 round; 2 lap; 3 circle, group; 4 über die Runden kommen (informal) to get by.

Rundfahrt die (PL die Rundfahrten) tour.

Rundfrage die (PL die Rundfragen) poll.

Rundfunk der radio; im Rundfunk on the radio.

rundherum adverb all around.

Rundkurs der (PL die Rundkurse) (motor racing) circuit.

runter adverb (informal) SEE herunter, hinunter; runter da! get off!

runzlig adjective wrinkled.

Rüsche die (PL die Rüschen) frill.

Russe der (PL die Russen) Russian.

Rüssel der (PL die Rüssel) trunk.

Russin die (PL die Russinnen) Russian.

russisch adjective Russian.

Russland das Russia.

Rüstung die (PL die Rüstungen) 1 armament; 2 arms; 3 (suit of) armour.

Rutschbahn die (PL die Rutschbahnen) slide.

rutschen verb (PERF ist gerutscht) 1 to slide; 2 to slip; 3 rutsch mal! move over!

rutschig adjective slippery.

rütteln verb (PERF hat gerüttelt) to shake; an der Tür rütteln to rattle at the door.

a b c d e f g h i j k l m n o p q **r** s t u v w x y z

Ss

Saal der (PL die **Säle**) hall.

Saatkrähe die (PL die **Saatkrähen**) rook.

Sabbat der (PL die **Sabbate**) Sabbath.

Sache die (PL die **Sachen**) 1 matter; **das ist eine andere Sache** that's a different matter; 2 business; **das ist seine Sache** that's his business; 3 thing; **meine Sachen** my things (*clothing*); **sie räumt nie ihre Sachen weg** she never puts away her things; 4 **zur Sache kommen** to get to the point; 5 **das ist so 'ne Sache** (*informal*) it's a bit tricky.

Sachgebiet das (PL die **Sachgebiete**) field, area.

sachlich adjective 1 objective; 2 factual.

sächlich adjective neuter.

Sachsen das Saxony.

Sack der (PL die **Säcke**) 1 sack; 2 bag.

Sackgasse die (PL die **Sackgassen**) dead end, cul-de-sac.

Saft der (PL die **Säfte**) 1 juice; 2 sap.

saftig adjective juicy.

Säge die (PL die **Sägen**) saw.

Sägemehl das sawdust.

sagen verb (PERF hat gesagt) 1 to say; **man sagt, dass ...** it's said that ...; 2 **was ich noch sagen wollte** by the way; **unter uns gesagt** between you and me; 3 to tell; **jemandem etwas sagen** to tell somebody something; **sag mal** tell me; **was sagen Sie dazu?** what do you think about it?; 4 to mean; **das hat nichts zu sagen** it doesn't mean anything; 5 **zu jemandem Tante sagen** to call somebody aunt; 6 **ihr Gesicht sagte alles** it was written all over her face.

sägen verb (PERF hat gesägt) to saw.

sagenhaft adjective 1 legendary; 2 (*informal*) brilliant.

sah SEE **sehen**.

Sahne die cream.

Saison die (PL die **Saisons**) season.

Saite die (PL die **Saiten**) string.

Sakko das (PL die **Sakkos**) jacket.

Salami die (PL die **Salamis**) salami.

Salat der (PL die **Salate**) 1 lettuce; **ein grüner Salat** a lettuce; 2 salad.

Salatsoße die (PL die **Salatsoßen**) salad dressing.

Salbe die (PL die **Salben**) ointment.

Salbei der sage.

salopp adjective casual, informal.

Salz das salt.

salzen verb (PERF hat gesalzen) to salt.

salzig adjective salty.

Salzkartoffeln plural noun boiled potatoes.

Salzwasser das 1 salt water; 2 salted water (*for cooking*).

Samen der (PL die **Samen**) 1 seed; 2 sperm, semen.

Sammelalbum das (PL die **Sammelalben**) scrapbook.

sammeln verb (PERF hat gesammelt) **1** to collect; **Martin sammelt Briefmarken** Martin collects stamps; **2** to gather; **3 sich sammeln** to gather; **seine Gedanken sammeln** to gather your thoughts.

Sammler der (PL die **Sammler**) collector.

Sammlerin die (PL die **Sammlerinnen**) collector.

Sammlung die (PL die **Sammlungen**) collection; **eine Sammlung für einen guten Zweck** a collection for a good cause.

Samstag der (PL die **Samstage**) Saturday.

samstags adverb on Saturdays.

Samt der (PL die **Samte**) velvet.

samt preposition (+ DAT) (together) with; **Mimi kam samt Puppen und Katze** Mimi arrived with her dolls and cat.

sämtlicher, sämtliche, sämtliches adjective all the; **meine sämtlichen Bücher** all my books.

Sand der sand.

Sandale die (PL die **Sandalen**) sandal.

sandig adjective sandy.

Sandpapier das (PL die **Sandpapiere**) sandpaper.

sandte SEE **senden**.

sanft adjective gentle; **eine sanfte Stimme** a soft voice.

sang SEE **singen**.

Sänger der (PL die **Sänger**) singer.

Sängerin die (PL die **Sängerinnen**) singer.

sank SEE **sinken**.

Sardelle die (PL die **Sardellen**) anchovy.

Sardine die (PL die **Sardinen**) sardine.

Sarg der (PL die **Särge**) coffin.

Sarkasmus der sarcasm.

sarkastisch adjective sarcastic.

SARS das SARS (the disease).

saß SEE **sitzen**.

Satellit der (PL die **Satelliten**) satellite.

Satellitenfernsehen das satellite television.

satt adjective **1** full (up); **bist du satt geworden?** have you had enough to eat?; **sich satt essen** to eat as much as one wants; **satt machen** to be filling; **2 etwas satt haben** (informal) to be fed up with something.

Sattel der (PL die **Sättel**) saddle.

Satteltasche die (PL die **Satteltaschen**) saddlebag.

Satz der (PL die **Sätze**) **1** sentence; **2** set (of things or in tennis); **ein Satz Reifen** a set of tyres; **3** movement (in music); **4** rate (of tax, interest); **5** leap.

sauber adjective **1** clean; **2** neat; **3** (informal) fine (expressing irony); **4 sauber machen** to clean.

Sauberkeit die cleanliness, cleanness.

saubermachen SEE **sauber**.

a
b
c
d
e
f
g
h
i
j
k
l
m
n
o
p
q
r
s
t
u
v
w
x
y
z

Sauce die (PL die Saucen) SEE Soße.

sauer adjective **1** sour; **2** pickled; **3** acid; **saurer Regen** acid rain; **4 sauer sein** (informal) to be annoyed; **ich bin sauer auf Eva** I'm annoyed with Eva.

Sauerei die (informal) (PL die Sauereien) **1** mess; **2** disgrace, scandal; **3** obscenity.

Sauerstoff der oxygen.

saufen ◇verb (informal) (PRES **säuft**, IMPERF **soff**, PERF **hat gesoffen**) to drink, to booze.

saugen verb (PERF **hat gesaugt**) **1** to suck; **2** to vacuum, to hoover.

Säugetier das (PL die Säugetiere) mammal.

Säugling der (PL die Säuglinge) baby, infant.

Säule die (PL die Säulen) column, pillar.

Saum der (PL die Säume) hem.

Säure die (PL die Säuren) acid.

Saxofon das (PL die Saxofone) saxophone.

S-Bahn die (PL die S-Bahnen) city and suburban railway.

Scanner der (PL die Scanner) scanner.

schäbig adjective shabby.

Schach das chess; **Schach!** check!

Schachbrett das (PL die Schachbretter) chessboard.

Schachfigur die (PL die Schachfiguren) chess piece.

Schachtel die (PL die Schachteln) box.

schade adjective **1 schade sein** to be a pity; **schade!** (what a) pity!; **2 zu schade für jemanden sein** to be too good for somebody.

Schädel der (PL die Schädel) skull.

Schaden der (PL die Schäden) **1** damage; **2** disadvantage.

schaden verb (PERF **hat geschadet**) **1** to damage; **das hat seinem Ruf geschadet** it damaged his reputation; **2 jemandem schaden** to harm somebody; **3 das schadet nichts** it doesn't matter.

schädlich adjective harmful.

Schaf das (PL die Schafe) sheep.

Schäfer der (PL die Schäfer) shepherd.

Schäferhund der (PL die Schäferhunde) sheepdog.

schaffen[1] ◇verb (IMPERF **schuf**, PERF **hat geschaffen**) to create; **wie geschaffen für** made for.

schaffen[2] verb (PERF **hat geschafft**) **1** to manage; **es schaffen, etwas zu tun** to manage to do something; **2 eine Prüfung schaffen** to pass an exam; **3 jemandem zu schaffen machen** to cause somebody trouble; **4 geschafft sein** (informal) to be worn out.

Schaffner der (PL die Schaffner) **1** conductor; **2** (ticket) inspector.

Schaffnerin die (PL die Schaffnerinnen) **1** conductress; **2** (ticket) inspector.

Schakal der (PL die Schakale) jackal.

Schal der (PL die Schals) scarf.

Schale die (PL die Schalen) **1** skin; **2** peel; **3** shell; **4** dish, bowl; **eine Schale Obst** a bowl of fruit.

schälen verb (PERF hat geschält) **1** to peel; **er hat ihr eine Orange geschält** he peeled an orange for her; **2 sich schälen** to peel; **mein Rücken schält sich** my back's peeling.

Schall der sound.

Schallplatte die (PL die Schallplatten) record.

schalten verb (PERF hat geschaltet) **1** to switch; **auf etwas schalten** to turn to something; **2** to change gear; **3 schnell schalten** (informal) to catch on quickly.

Schalter der (PL die Schalter) **1** switch; **2** counter.

Schaltjahr das (PL die Schaltjahre) leap year.

schämen verb (PERF hat sich geschämt) **sich schämen** to be ashamed.

Schampon das (PL die Schampons) SEE Shampoo.

Schande die **1** disgrace; **2** shame.

scharf adjective **1** sharp; **2** hot (food); **ein scharfer Wind** a biting wind; **3** fierce (dog, frost); **4 scharf nachdenken** to think hard; **5** (in photography) **scharf sein** to be in focus; **scharf einstellen** to focus; **6 scharf schießen** to fire live ammunition; **7 scharf auf etwas sein** (informal) to be really keen on something; **sie ist scharf auf Bernd** (informal) she fancies Bernd.

Schaschlik der (PL die Schaschliks) kebab.

Schatten der (PL die Schatten) **1** shadow; **2** shade.

schattig adjective shady.

Schatz der (PL die Schätze) **1** treasure; **2** darling.

Schätzchen das (PL die Schätzchen) darling.

schätzen verb (PERF hat geschätzt) **1** to estimate; **2** to value; **3** to reckon, to guess; **schätz mal!** guess!; **4 etwas zu schätzen wissen** to appreciate something.

Schau die (PL die Schauen) show.

schauen verb (PERF hat geschaut) **1** to look; **2** to watch; **Fernsehen schauen** to watch television.

Schauer der (PL die Schauer) shower.

Schauergeschichte die (PL die Schauergeschichten) horror story.

Schaufel die (PL die Schaufeln) **1** shovel; **2** dustpan.

Schaufenster das (PL die Schaufenster) shop window.

Schaukel die (PL die Schaukeln) swing.

schaukeln verb (PERF hat geschaukelt) to swing.

Schaukelstuhl der (PL die Schaukelstühle) rocking chair.

Schaum der **1** foam; **2** froth; **3** lather.

schäumen verb (PERF hat geschäumt) **1** to foam; **2** to froth (up).

a
b
c
d
e
f
g
h
i
j
k
l
m
n
o
p
q
r
s
t
u
v
w
x
y
z

Schauplatz der (PL die Schauplätze) scene.

Schauspiel das (PL die Schauspiele) 1 play; 2 spectacle.

Schauspieler der (PL die Schauspieler) actor.

Schauspielerin die (PL die Schauspielerinnen) actress.

Schauspielkunst die dramatic art, acting.

Scheck der (PL die Schecks) cheque.

Scheckbuch das (PL die Scheckbücher) chequebook.

Scheckkarte die (PL die Scheckkarten) cheque card.

Scheibe die (PL die Scheiben) 1 pane (of a window, car); 2 slice; eine Scheibe Schinken a slice of ham; die Salami in Scheiben schneiden to slice the salami; du könntest dir eine Scheibe von ihr abschneiden (informal) you could take a leaf out of her book; 3 disc.

Scheibenwischer der (PL die Scheibenwischer) windscreen wiper.

scheiden ◇verb (IMPERF schied, PERF hat geschieden) 1 to separate; sich scheiden lassen to get divorced; sie haben sich im Juli scheiden lassen they got divorced in July; 2 geschieden sein to be divorced.

Scheidung die (PL die Scheidungen) divorce.

Schein der (PL die Scheine) 1 light; 2 appearance; etwas nur zum Schein machen to only pretend to do something; 3 certificate; 4 note (money).

scheinbar adverb apparently.

scheinen ◇verb (IMPERF schien, PERF hat geschienen) 1 to shine; 2 to seem; mir scheint it seems to me.

Scheinwerfer der (PL die Scheinwerfer) 1 headlamp, headlight; 2 floodlight, spotlight.

Scheitel der (PL die Scheitel) parting (in your hair).

scheitern verb (PERF ist gescheitert) to fail.

Schenkel der (PL die Schenkel) thigh.

schenken verb (PERF hat geschenkt) 1 to give; etwas geschenkt bekommen to be given something; 2 sich etwas schenken to give something a miss; 3 das ist ja geschenkt! (informal) it's a gift!

Schere die (PL die Scheren) 1 (pair of) scissors; 2 shears; 3 claw (of a crab).

scheren verb (informal) (PERF hat geschert) to bother; sich nicht um etwas scheren not to care about something; scher dich um deine eigenen Angelegenheiten! mind your own business!; scher dich zum Teufel! go to hell!

Scherz der (PL die Scherze) joke.

scheu adjective shy.

scheuern verb (PERF hat gescheuert) 1 to scrub; 2 to rub.

Scheune die (PL die Scheunen) barn.

scheußlich *adjective* horrible.

Schi *der* (PL *die* **Schi(er)**) SEE **Ski**.

Schicht *die* (PL *die* **Schichten**)
1 layer; 2 class; 3 shift.

Schicht *die* (PL *die* **Schichten**)
1 stratum; 2 section; 3 shift (*in factory etc*).

schick *adjective* 1 stylish, smart;
2 (*informal*) great.

schicken *verb* (PERF **hat geschickt**) to send.

Schicksal *das* (PL *die* **Schicksale**) fate.

Schiebedach *das* (PL *die* **Schiebedächer**) sunroof.

schieben ◇*verb* (IMPERF **schob**, PERF **hat geschoben**) 1 to push;
2 **etwas auf etwas schieben** to blame something for something; **die Schuld auf jemanden schieben** to put the blame on somebody.

schied SEE **scheiden**.

Schiedsrichter *der* (PL *die* **Schiedsrichter**) referee, umpire.

schief *adjective* crooked; **ein schiefer Blick** a funny look.

schief *adverb* 1 **das Bild hängt schief** the picture is not straight;
2 **schief gehen** to go wrong.

Schiefer *der* slate.

schiefgehen SEE **schief**.

schielen *verb* (PERF **hat geschielt**) to squint.

schien SEE **scheinen**.

Schienbein *das* (PL *die* **Schienbeine**) shin.

Schiene *die* (PL *die* **Schienen**)
1 rail; 2 splint.

schießen ◇*verb* (IMPERF **schoss**, PERF **hat geschossen**) 1 to shoot; **auf jemanden schießen** to shoot at somebody; **ein Tor schießen** to score a goal; 2 (PERF **ist geschossen**) to shoot (along); **Andrea ist in die Höhe geschossen** Andrea's shot up (*has got a lot taller*).

Schiff *das* (PL *die* **Schiffe**) ship; **ein Schiff zu Wasser lassen** to launch a ship.

Schifffahrt *die* (PL *die* **Schifffahrten**) boat trip.

schikanieren *verb* (PERF **hat schikaniert**) to bully.

Schikoree *der* SEE **Chicorée**.

Schild[1] *das* (PL *die* **Schilder**) 1 sign;
2 badge; 3 label.

Schild[2] *der* (PL *die* **Schilde**) shield.

Schildkröte *die* (PL *die* **Schildkröten**) 1 tortoise; 2 turtle.

Schilling *der* (PL *die* **Schilling(e)**) Schilling (*the currency of Austria until replaced by the euro; 100 Schillings* = h7.26 *euros*).

Schimmel *der* (PL *die* **Schimmel**)
1 mould; 2 white horse.

Schimpanse *der* (PL *die* **Schimpansen**) chimpanzee.

schimpfen *verb* (PERF **hat geschimpft**) 1 to tell off; 2 to grumble.

Schinken *der* (PL *die* **Schinken**) ham; **ein Schinkenbrötchen** a ham roll.

a b c d e f g h i j k l m n o p q r **s** t u v w x y z

Schirm der (PL die **Schirme**)
1 umbrella; 2 sunshade; 3 shade
(of a lamp); 4 peak (of a cap).

Schlaf der sleep.

Schlafanzug der (PL die
Schlafanzüge) pyjamas.

Schlafcouch die (PL die
Schlafcouchs) sofa bed.

schlafen ◇verb (PRES **schläft**,
IMPERF **schlief**, PERF **hat
geschlafen**) 1 to sleep; 2 to be
asleep; **das Baby schläft** the baby's
asleep; 3 **schlafen gehen** to go to
bed.

schlaff adjective 1 slack (rope);
2 limp (handshake, body);
3 lethargic.

schläfrig adjective sleepy; **ich bin
schläfrig** I'm sleepy.

Schlafsaal der (PL die **Schlafsäle**)
dormitory.

Schlafsack der (PL die
Schlafsäcke) sleeping bag.

Schlafwagen der (PL die
Schlafwagen) sleeper.

Schlafzimmer das (PL die
Schlafzimmer) bedroom.

Schlag der (PL die **Schläge**) 1 blow,
punch; **Schläge kriegen** to get a
beating; 2 stroke; 3 (electric) shock;
4 **Schlag auf Schlag** in quick
succession; **auf einen Schlag** all at
once.

schlagen ◇verb (PRES **schlägt**,
IMPERF **schlug**, PERF **hat
geschlagen**) 1 to hit; **einen Nagel
in die Wand schlagen** to knock a
nail into the wall; 2 to beat; 3 to
bang; **mit dem Kopf gegen etwas**
schlagen to bang your head
against something; 4 to strike (of a
clock); 5 to whip (cream); 6 **sich
schlagen** to fight; 7 **sich
geschlagen geben** to admit defeat.

Schlager der (PL die **Schlager**) hit.

Schläger der (PL die **Schläger**)
1 racket (in tennis); 2 bat (in
baseball); 3 club (in golf); 4 stick
(in hockey); 5 thug.

Schlägerei die (PL die
Schlägereien) fight.

Schlagsahne die 1 whipping
cream; 2 whipped cream.

Schlagzeile die (PL die
Schlagzeilen) headline.

Schlagzeug das (PL die
Schlagzeuge) drums.

Schlagzeuger der (PL die
Schlagzeuger) drummer.

Schlamm der mud.

schlampen verb (PERF **hat
geschlampt**) to be sloppy.

Schlamperei die (PL die
Schlampereien) 1 sloppiness;
2 mess.

schlampig adjective sloppy.

Schlange die (PL die **Schlangen**)
1 snake; 2 queue; **Schlange
stehen** to queue.

schlank adjective slim.

Schlankheitskur die (PL die
Schlankheitskuren) diet; **eine
Schlankheitskur machen** to be on a
diet.

schlapp adjective worn out, tired
out.

schlau *adjective* 1 crafty; 2 clever; **ich werde nicht schlau daraus** I can't make head nor tail of it.

Schlauch *der* (PL die **Schläuche**) hose.

schlauchlos *adjective* tubeless.

schlecht *adjective* 1 bad; **schlecht werden** to go bad; 2 **mir ist schlecht** I feel sick; 3 **jemanden schlecht machen** to run somebody down.

schlecht *adverb* 1 badly; **schlecht gelaunt** in a bad mood; 2 **es geht ihm schlecht** he's not well.

schleichen ◇*verb* (IMPERF **schlich**, PERF **ist geschlichen**) 1 to creep; 2 to crawl (*in traffic*); 3 **sich schleichen** to creep.

Schleife *die* (PL die **Schleifen**) 1 bow; 2 loop.

Schlepper *der* (PL die **Schlepper**) 1 tug; 2 tractor.

Schleuder *die* (PL die **Schleudern**) 1 catapult; 2 spin-dryer.

schleudern *verb* (PERF **hat geschleudert**) 1 to hurl; 2 to spin (*washing*); 3 (PERF **ist geschleudert**) to skid.

schlich SEE **schleichen**.

schlicht *adjective* plain, simple.

schlief SEE **schlafen**.

schließen ◇*verb* (IMPERF **schloss**, PERF **hat geschlossen**) 1 to close, to shut; 2 to close down; 3 to lock; 4 to conclude; **aus etwas schließen, dass** ... to conclude from something that ...; 5 **einen Vertrag schließen** to enter into a contract;

6 **Freundschaft mit jemandem schließen** to make friends with somebody; 7 **sich schließen** to close.

Schließfach *das* (PL die **Schließfächer**) locker.

schließlich *adverb* 1 finally; 2 after all; **er hat sie schließlich doch eingeladen** he's invited her after all.

schlimm *adjective* bad.

schlimmstenfalls *adverb* if the worst comes to the worst.

Schlips *der* (PL die **Schlipse**) tie.

Schlitten *der* (PL die **Schlitten**) sledge; **Schlitten fahren gehen** to go sledging.

Schlittschuh *der* (PL die **Schlittschuhe**) skate; **Schlittschuh laufen** to skate.

Schlittschuhlaufen *das* ice-skating.

Schlitz *der* (PL die **Schlitze**) 1 slit; 2 flies (*in trousers*); 3 slot.

Schloss *das* (PL die **Schlösser**) 1 lock; 2 castle.

schloss SEE **schließen**.

Schluck *der* (PL die **Schlucke**) 1 mouthful; 2 gulp.

Schluckauf *der* hiccups.

schlucken *verb* (PERF **hat geschluckt**) to swallow.

schlug SEE **schlagen**.

Schlüpfer *der* (PL die **Schlüpfer**) knickers.

Schluss *der* (PL die **Schlüsse**) 1 end, ending; **zum Schluss** in the end; **Schluss machen** to stop; **mit**

a jemandem Schluss machen to finish with somebody; **2** conclusion.

Schlüssel der (PL die Schlüssel) **1** key; **2** spanner.

Schlussverkauf der sales.

schmal adjective **1** narrow; **2** thin (face, nose); **3** sie ist schmäler geworden she's lost weight.

schmecken verb (PERF hat geschmeckt) to taste; die Suppe schmeckt gut the soup tastes good; das schmeckt mir nicht I don't like it; das Eis schmeckt nach Zitrone the ice cream tastes of lemon.

schmeicheln verb (PERF hat geschmeichelt) to flatter; jemandem schmeicheln to flatter somebody.

schmeißen ◇verb (informal) (IMPERF schmiss, PERF hat geschmissen) to chuck; mit etwas schmeißen to chuck something.

schmelzen ◇verb (PRES schmilzt, IMPERF schmolz, PERF ist geschmolzen) **1** to melt; der Schnee ist geschmolzen the snow has melted; **2** (PERF hat geschmolzen) to melt (snow, ice); **3** (PERF. hat geschmolzen) to smelt (ore).

Schmerz der (PL die Schmerzen) **1** pain; **2** grief.

schmerzen verb (PERF hat geschmerzt) to hurt; mein Kopf schmerzt my head is aching.

schmerzhaft adjective painful.

schmerzlos adjective painless.

Schmerzmittel das (PL die Schmerzmittel) painkiller.

Schmerzschwelle das (PL die Schmerzschwellen) painthreshold.

Schmetterling der (PL die Schmetterlinge) butterfly.

schmettern verb (PERF hat geschmettert) **1** to hurl; **2** to smash (in tennis); **3** to blare out (music, orders).

schmieren verb (PERF hat geschmiert) **1** to lubricate; **2** to spread (butter, jam); Brote schmieren to spread slices of bread; jemandem eine schmieren (informal) to clout somebody; **3** to scrawl; **4** to smudge.

schmilzt SEE schmelzen.

Schminke die make-up.

schminken verb (PERF hat geschminkt) **1** to make up; **2** sich schminken to put on make-up.

schmiss SEE schmeißen.

schmolz SEE schmelzen.

Schmuck der **1** jewellery; **2** decoration.

schmücken verb (PERF hat geschmückt) to decorate.

schmuggeln verb (PERF hat geschmuggelt) to smuggle.

schmusen verb (PERF hat geschmust) to cuddle; Gabi hat mit Max geschmust Gabi cuddled Max.

Schmutz der dirt.

schmutzig adjective dirty.

Schmutzigkeit die dirtiness.

Schnabel der (PL die **Schnäbel**)
beak.

Schnalle die (PL die **Schnallen**)
buckle.

schnallen verb (PERF hat
geschnallt) **1** to fasten; **2** to
buckle.

schnarchen verb (PERF hat
geschnarcht) to snore.

Schnauze die (PL die **Schnauzen**)
1 muzzle; **eine kalte Schnauze** a
cold nose; **2 die Schnauze halten**
(informal) to keep your mouth
shut.

schnäuzen (PERF hat sich
geschnäuzt) **sich schnäuzen** to
blow your nose.

Schnecke die (PL die **Schnecken**)
snail.

Schnee der snow.

Schneeregen der sleet.

Schneesturm der (PL die
Schneestürme) blizzard.

Schneewehe die (PL die
Schneewehen) snow drift.

schneiden ◇verb (IMPERF schnitt,
PERF hat geschnitten) **1** to cut; **ich
kann dir die Haare schneiden** I
can cut your hair; **Evi hat sich die
Haare kurz schneiden lassen** Evi
had her hair cut short; **in Scheiben
schneiden** to slice; **2 sich
schneiden** to cut yourself; **ich
habe mich in den Finger
geschnitten** I've cut my finger;
3 sich schneiden to intersect;
4 Gesichter schneiden to pull
faces.

Schneider der (PL die **Schneider**)
tailor.

Schneiderin die (PL die
Schneiderinnen) dressmaker.

schneien verb (PERF hat
geschneit) to snow; **es schneit** it's
snowing.

schnell adjective quick, fast.

schnell adverb quickly; **mach
schnell!** hurry up!

Schnelligkeit die of speed.

Schnellimbiss der (PL die
Schnellimbisse) snack bar.

schnellstens adverb as quickly
as possible.

Schnellzug der (PL die
Schnellzüge) express (train).

schneuzen SEE schnäuzen.

Schnitt der (PL die **Schnitte**) **1** cut;
**er hat einen tiefen Schnitt im
Finger** he's got a deep cut in his
finger; **das Kostüm hat einen sehr
guten Schnitt** the suit is well cut;
2 cutting (of a film); **3 im Schnitt**
on average; **4** pattern.

schnitt SEE schneiden.

Schnittlauch der chives.

Schnitzel das (PL die **Schnitzel**)
1 escalope; **2** scrap.

schnitzen verb (PERF hat
geschnitzt) to carve.

Schnorchel der (PL die
Schnorchel) snorkel.

schnüffeln verb (PERF hat
geschnüffelt) **1** to sniff; **2** to snoop
around.

Schnuller der (PL die **Schnuller**)
dummy.

Schnupfen der (PL die **Schnupfen**) cold.

Schnur die (PL die **Schnüre**) 1 (piece of) string; 2 flex; 3 cord.

Schnurrbart der (PL die **Schnurrbärte**) moustache.

schnurren verb (PERF hat **geschnurrt**) to purr.

Schnurrhaar das (PL die **Schnurrhaare**) whisker.

Schnürsenkel der (PL die **Schnürsenkel**) shoelace.

schob SEE **schieben**.

Schock der (PL die **Schocks**) shock.

schockieren verb (PERF hat **schockiert**) to shock.

Schokolade die (PL die **Schokoladen**) chocolate.

schön adjective 1 beautiful; 2 nice; **schönes Wochenende!** have a nice weekend!; 3 good; **na schön** all right then; 4 **schönen Dank** thank you very much; **schöne Grüße** best wishes.

schon adverb 1 already ('schon' is often not translated); **schon wieder** again; **schon oft** often; **du wirst schon sehen** you'll see; **ja schon, aber ... well yes, but ...; nun geh schon!** go on then!; 2 yet; **hast du sie schon gesehen?** have you seen her yet?; **du weißt schon** you know; 3 even; 4 **komm schon!** come on!; 5 **schon deshalb** for that reason alone; 6 **das ist schon möglich** that's quite possible; 7 **er war schon mal da** he's been there before.

schonen verb (PERF hat **geschont**) 1 to look after; 2 **sich schonen** to take things easy.

Schönheit die (PL die **Schönheiten**) beauty.

Schornstein der (PL die **Schornsteine**) chimney, funnel.

schoss SEE **schießen**.

Schoß der (PL die **Schöße**) lap.

Schotte der (PL die **Schotten**) Scot, Scotsman.

Schottin die (PL die **Schottinnen**) Scot, Scotswoman.

schottisch adjective Scottish.

Schottland das Scotland.

schräg adjective 1 diagonal; 2 sloping.

schräg adverb **etwas schräg halten** to tilt something; **etwas schräg stellen** to put something at an angle.

Schrank der (PL die **Schränke**) 1 cupboard; 2 wardrobe.

Schranke die (PL die **Schranken**) barrier.

Schraube die (PL die **Schrauben**) screw.

schrauben verb (PERF hat **geschraubt**) to screw.

Schraubenschlüssel der (PL die **Schraubenschlüssel**) spanner.

Schraubenzieher der (PL die **Schraubenzieher**) screwdriver.

Schreck der fright; **jemandem einen Schreck einjagen** to give somebody a fright; **ich habe keinen Schreck bekommen** I got a fright.

schrecklich adjective terrible.

Schrei der (PL die **Schreie**) **1** cry, shout; **2** scream; **3** der letzte Schrei (informal) the latest thing.

Schreibblock der (PL die **Schreibblöcke**) writing pad.

schreiben ⋄verb (IMPERF schrieb, PERF hat geschrieben) **1** to write; David hat mir einen Brief geschrieben David wrote a letter to me; einen Test schreiben to do a test; **2** to spell; wie schreibt man das? how is it spelt?; **3** to type.

Schreibmaschine die (PL die **Schreibmaschinen**) typewriter.

Schreibpapier das writing paper.

Schreibtisch der (PL die **Schreibtische**) desk.

Schreibwaren plural noun stationery.

schreien ⋄verb (IMPERF schrie, PERF hat geschrien) **1** to cry, to shout; das Baby schreit the baby's crying; **2** to scream; vor Lachen schreien to scream with laughter; zum Schreien sein (informal) to be a scream.

Schreiner der (PL die **Schreiner**) joiner.

schrie SEE schreien.

schrieb SEE schreiben.

Schrift die (PL die **Schriften**) **1** writing; **2** type; **3** script.

schriftlich adjective written.

schriftlich adverb written; das lasse ich mir schriftlich geben I'll get that in writing; jemanden schriftlich einladen to send somebody a written invitation.

Schriftsteller der (PL die **Schriftsteller**) writer.

Schriftstellerin die (PL die **Schriftstellerinnen**) writer.

Schritt der (PL die **Schritte**) **1** step; **2** footstep.

schrumpfen verb (PERF ist geschrumpft) **1** to shrink; **2** to shrivel.

Schublade die (PL die **Schubladen**) drawer.

schubsen verb (PERF hat geschubst) to shove.

schüchtern adjective shy.

schuf SEE schaffen.

Schuh der (PL die **Schuhe**) shoe.

Schuhgröße die (PL die **Schuhgrößen**) shoe size.

Schularbeiten plural noun homework.

Schulaufgaben plural noun homework.

Schulbuch das (PL die **Schulbücher**) schoolbook.

Schuld die (PL die **Schulden**) **1** blame; Schuld haben to be to blame; jemandem Schuld geben to blame somebody; **2** fault; es war seine Schuld it was his fault; **3** guilt; **4** debt; Schulden haben to be in debt; Schulden machen to get into debt.

schuld adjective schuld sein to be to blame; du bist schuld daran it's your fault.

schulden verb (PERF hat geschuldet) to owe.

schuldig *adjective* **1** guilty; **2 jemandem etwas schuldig sein** to owe somebody something.

Schule die (PL die **Schulen**) school; **in die Schule gehen** to go to school.

schulen *verb* (PERF **hat geschult**) to train.

Schüler der (PL die **Schüler**) pupil, student.

Schülerin die (PL die **Schülerinnen**) pupil, student.

Schulferien *plural noun* school holidays.

schulfrei *adjective* **ein schulfreier Tag** a day off school; **wir haben heute schulfrei** there's no school today.

Schulfreund der (PL die **Schulfreunde**) schoolfriend.

Schulfreundin die (PL die **Schulfreundinnen**) schoolfriend.

Schulheft das (PL die **Schulhefte**) exercise book.

Schulhof der (PL die **Schulhöfe**) playground.

Schuljahr das (PL die **Schuljahre**) school year.

Schulschwänzer der (PL die **Schulschwänzer**) truant.

Schulschwänzerin die (PL die **Schulschwänzerinnen**) truant.

Schulstunde die (PL die **Schulstunden**) period.

Schultasche die (PL die **Schultaschen**) schoolbag.

Schulter die (PL die **Schultern**) shoulder.

schummeln *verb* (PERF **hat geschummelt**) to cheat.

Schuppe die (PL die **Schuppen**) **1** scale; **2 Schuppen** dandruff.

Schuppen der (PL die **Schuppen**) shed.

Schürze die (PL die **Schürzen**) apron.

Schuss der (PL die **Schüsse**) **1** shot; **2 dash** (*of brandy, vinegar*); **3** schuss (*in skiing*).

Schüssel die (PL die **Schüsseln**) bowl, dish.

Schuster der (PL die **Schuster**) shoemaker.

schütteln *verb* (PERF **hat geschüttelt**) **1** to shake; **2 sich schütteln** to shake yourself; **sich vor Ekel schütteln** to shudder.

schütten *verb* (PERF **hat geschüttet**) **1** to pour; **es schüttet** (*informal*) it's pouring (down); **2** to tip; **3** to spill.

Schutz der **1** protection; **2** shelter; **3** conservation.

Schutzbrille die (PL die **Schutzbrillen**) goggles.

Schütze der (PL die **Schützen**) **1** marksman; **2** Sagittarius; **Daniel ist Schütze** Daniel's Sagittarius.

schützen *verb* (PERF **hat geschützt**) **1** to protect; **die meisten Cremes schützen die Haut gegen Sonnenbrand** most creams protect the skin from sunburn; **2 gesetzlich geschützt** registered (*as a trade-mark*).

Schutzhütte die (PL die Schutzhütten) 1 mountain refuge; 2 shelter.

schwach adjective 1 weak; 2 dim (light); 3 poor (performance, memory).

Schwäche die (PL die Schwächen) weakness.

schwachsinnig adjective idiotic.

Schwager der (PL die Schwäger) brother-in-law.

Schwägerin die (PL die Schwägerinnen) sister-in-law.

Schwalbe die (PL die Schwalben) swallow.

Schwamm der (PL die Schwämme) sponge.

schwamm SEE schwimmen.

Schwan der (PL die Schwäne) swan.

schwanger adjective pregnant.

Schwangerschaft die (PL die Schwangerschaften) pregnancy.

schwanken verb (PERF hat geschwankt) 1 to sway; 2 to fluctuate; 3 to waver; 4 (PERF ist geschwankt) to stagger.

Schwanz der (PL die Schwänze) tail.

schwänzen verb (PERF hat geschwänzt) to skip, to skive off; **die Schule schwänzen** to play truant.

Schwarm der (PL die Schwärme) swarm.

schwarz adjective, adverb 1 black; **schwarz gekleidet** dressed in black; **ein schwarz gestreiftes**

Kleid a dress with black stripes; **das habe ich schwarz auf weiß** I have it in black and white; 2 **ins Schwarze treffen** to hit the nail on the head, to score a bull's eye; 3 **schwarz sehen** to be pessimistic; 4 **etwas schwarz machen** to do something illegally.

Schwarze der/die (PL die Schwarzen) black.

schwarzsehen SEE schwarz.

Schwarzwald der Black Forest.

schwätzen verb (PERF hat geschwätzt) to chatter.

Schwede der (PL die Schweden) Swede.

Schweden das Sweden.

Schwedin die (PL die Schwedinnen) Swede.

schwedisch adjective Swedish.

schweigen ◇verb (IMPERF schwieg, PERF hat geschwiegen) to be silent; **ganz zu schweigen von** ... not to mention ...

Schwein das (PL die Schweine) 1 pig; 2 pork; 3 **du Schwein!** (informal) you swine!; **Schwein haben** (informal) to be lucky.

Schweinefleisch das pork.

Schweinekotelett das (PL die Schweinekoteletts) pork chop.

Schweiß der sweat.

Schweiz die die Schweiz Switzerland.

Schweizer der (PL die Schweizer) Swiss.

Schweizerin die (PL die Schweizerinnen) Swiss.

a b c d e f g h i j k l m n o p q r s t u v w x y z

schweizerisch adjective Swiss.

Schwelle der (PL die Schwellen) threshold.

Schwellung die (PL die Schwellungen) swelling.

schwer adjective 1 heavy; zwei Pfund schwer sein to weigh two pounds; 2 difficult; 3 serious.

schwer adverb 1 heavily; 2 seriously; schwer krank seriously ill; 3 schwer arbeiten to work hard; jemandem schwer fallen to work hard for somebody; 4 sich mit etwas schwer tun to have difficulty with something.

schwerfallen SEE schwer.

schwerhörig adjective hard of hearing.

Schwert das (PL die Schwerter) sword.

schwertun SEE schwer.

Schwester die (PL die Schwestern) sister.

schwieg SEE schweigen.

Schwiegereltern plural noun parents-in-law.

Schwiegermutter die (PL die Schwiegermütter) mother-in-law.

Schwiegersohn der (PL die Schwiegersöhne) son-in-law.

Schwiegertochter die (PL die Schwiegertöchter) daughter-in-law.

Schwiegervater der (PL die Schwiegerväter) father-in-law.

schwierig adjective difficult.

Schwierigkeit die (PL die Schwierigkeiten) difficulty.

Schwimmbad das (PL die Schwimmbäder) swimming baths.

schwimmen ◇verb (IMPERF schwamm, PERF ist/hat geschwommen) 1 to swim; 2 to float.

Schwimmer der (PL die Schwimmer) swimmer.

Schwimmerbecken das (PL die Schwimmbecken) swimming pool (for experienced swimmers).

Schwimmerin die (PL die Schwimmerinnen) swimmer.

Schwimmweste die (PL die Schwimmwesten) life-jacket.

schwindlig adjective dizzy; mir ist schwindlig I feel dizzy.

Schwips der (PL die Schwipse) einen Schwips haben to be tipsy.

schwitzen verb (PERF hat geschwitzt) to sweat.

schwören ◇verb (IMPERF schwor, PERF hat geschworen) to swear.

schwül adjective close.

schwul adjective gay.

Schwule die (PL die Schwulen) gay.

Schwung der (PL die Schwünge) 1 swing; 2 drive; die Party in Schwung bringen to get the party going.

sechs number six.

sechster, sechste, sechstes adjective sixth.

sechzehn number sixteen.

sechzig number sixty.

See[1] der (PL die Seen) lake.

See[2] *die* sea.

Seehund *der* (PL die **Seehunde**) seal.

seekrank *adjective* seasick.

Seele *die* (PL die **Seelen**) soul.

Seemann *der* (PL die **Seeleute**) seaman, sailor.

Seetang *der* seaweed.

Segel *das* (PL die **Segel**) sail.

Segelboot *das* (PL die **Segelboote**) sailing boat.

Segelfliegen *das* gliding.

Segelflugzeug *das* (PL die **Segelflugzeuge**) glider.

Segellehrer *der* (PL die **Segellehrer**) sailing instructor.

Segellehrerin *die* (PL die **Segellehrerinnen**) sailing instructor.

segeln *verb* (PERF **ist gesegelt**) to sail.

sehen ◇*verb* (PRES **sieht**, IMPERF **sah**, PERF **hat gesehen**) 1 to see; **jemanden wieder sehen** to see somebody again; **mal sehen, ob** ... let's see if ...; 2 to look; 3 **eine Fernsehsendung sehen** to watch a television programme; 4 **gut/ schlecht sehen** to have good/bad eyesight; 5 **nach jemandem sehen** to look after somebody.

sehenswert *adjective* worth seeing.

Sehenswürdigkeiten *plural noun* sights.

Sehnsucht *die* longing; **Sehnsucht nach jemandem haben** to long to see somebody.

sehr *adverb* 1 very; **sehr gut** very good; 2 **danke sehr** thank you very much; 3 **ich habe Karin sehr gern** I like Karin a lot; 4 **Sehr geehrte Frau Huber** Dear Mrs Huber.

seid SEE **sein**.

Seide *die* (PL die **Seiden**) silk.

Seife *die* (PL die **Seifen**) soap.

Seil *das* (PL die **Seile**) 1 rope; 2 cable.

Seilbahn *die* (PL die **Seilbahnen**) cable railway.

sein[1] ◇*verb* (PRES **ist**, IMPERF **war**, PERF **ist gewesen**) 1 to be; **wir sind in der Küche** we're in the kitchen; **Rosi ist krank** Rosi is ill; **mir ist schlecht** I feel sick; **mir ist kalt/ heiß** I'm cold/hot; 2 **sie ist Lehrerin** she's a teacher; 3 **es ist drei Uhr** it's three o'clock; **Karl ist aus München** Karl's from Munich; **es war viel zu tun** there was a lot to be done; 4 **aus Seide sein** to be made of silk; 5 **etwas sein lassen** to stop something; **lass das sein!** stop it!; 6 **es sei denn, dass** ... unless ...; 7 *(used with certain verbs to form past tenses)* **ich bin nach Berlin gefahren** I went to Berlin; **wir sind kurz vor acht nach Hause gekommen** we got home shortly before eight o'clock; **er ist abgeholt worden** he's been collected.

sein[2] *adjective* 1 his; 2 *(of a thing or animal)* its; **der Hund ist in seiner Hütte** the dog is in its kennel; 3 *(after the pronoun 'man')* your, one's; **wenn man sich seine Eltern aussuchen könnte** if you could choose your parents.

a
b
c
d
e
f
g
h
i
j
k
l
m
n
o
p
q
r
s
t
u
v
w
x
y
z

seiner, seine, sein(e)s *pronoun* **1** his; **das ist nicht meine CD, das ist seine** it's not my CD, it's his; **du kannst seins nehmen** you can take his; **2** (*after the pronoun 'man'*) your own, one's own; **das Seine tun** to do one's share.

seinetwegen *adverb* **1** for his sake; **2** because of him; **3** on his account.

seinlassen SEE **sein**.

seins SEE **seiner**.

seit *preposition* (+ DAT) *conjunction* **1** since; **seit etwa einer Woche** since about a week; **seit du hier wohnst** since you've been living here; **seit wann?** since when?; **2 ich bin seit zwei Wochen hier** I've been here for two weeks; **seit einiger Zeit** for some time.

seitdem *adverb* since then; **ich habe sie seitdem nicht mehr gesehen** I haven't seen her since.

seitdem *conjunction* since.

Seite die (PL die **Seiten**) **1** side; **auf der einen Seite** on the one hand; **2** page; **das steht auf Seite zwanzig** it's on page twenty.

Seitenstechen das stich; **ich habe Seitenstechen** I've got a stitch.

Seitenstraße die (PL die **Seitenstraßen**) side street.

seither *adverb* since then.

Sekretär der (PL die **Sekretäre**) secretary.

Sekretärin die (PL die **Sekretärinnen**) secretary.

Sekt der (PL die **Sekte**) sparkling wine.

Sekte die (PL die **Sekten**) sect.

Sekunde die (PL die **Sekunden**) second.

selbst *pronoun* **1 ich selbst** I myself; **er selbst** he himself; **wir selbst** we ourselves; **Sie selbst** you yourself, you yourselves; **2 von selbst** by itself; **3 sie schneidet sich die Haare selbst** she cuts her own hair; **4** on one's own; **ich kann es selbst machen** I can do it on my own; **5 selbst gemacht** home-made.

selbst *adverb* even; **selbst wenn** even if.

selbständig SEE **selbstständig**.

Selbstbedienung die self-service.

selbstbewusst *adjective* self-confident.

Selbstbewusstsein das **1** self-confidence; **2** self-awareness.

selbstgemacht SEE **selbst**.

Selbstmord der (PL die **Selbstmorde**) suicide; **Selbstmord begehen** to commit suicide.

selbstsicher *adjective* self-confident.

selbstständig *adjective* **1** independent; **2** self-employed; **sich selbstständig machen** to set up on your own.

selbstverständlich *adjective* natural; **etwas für selbstverständlich halten** to take something for granted; **das ist**

selbstverständlich it goes without saying.

selbstverständlich *adverb* naturally, of course; **wir haben ihn selbstverständlich auf die Party eingeladen** of course we invited him to the party.

selten *adjective* rare.

selten *adverb* rarely.

seltsam *adjective* strange, odd.

Semester das (PL die **Semester**) semester, term.

Semikolon das (PL die **Semikolons**) semicolon.

Semmel die (PL die **Semmeln**) roll.

senden *verb* (PERF hat gesendet) **1** to send; **etwas an jemanden senden** to send something to somebody; **2** to broadcast; **seine Rede wird im ersten Programm gesendet** his speech will be broadcast on channel one; **3** to transmit.

Sendung die (PL die **Sendungen**) **1** programme; **2** consignment.

Senf der (PL die **Senfe**) mustard.

Senior der (PL die **Senioren**) **1** senior; **2 Senioren** senior citizens.

senkrecht *adjective* vertical.

Sensation die (PL die **Sensationen**) sensation, stir.

sensationell *adjective* sensational.

sensibel *adjective* sensitive.

sentimental *adjective* sentimental.

September der September.

Sequenz die (PL die **Sequenzen**) sequence (*in a film*).

Serie die (PL die **Serien**) **1** series; **2** serial.

Service¹ das (PL die **Service**) set (*of china, for example*).

Service² der service; **das Essen im Hotel ist gut, aber der Service ist furchtbar** the food in the hotel is good but the service is appalling.

servieren *verb* (PERF hat serviert) to serve.

Serviette die (PL die **Servietten**) napkin.

Sessel der (PL die **Sessel**) armchair.

Sessellift der (PL die **Sessellifte**) chair-lift.

setzen *verb* (PERF hat gesetzt) **1** to put; **ein Komma setzen** to put a comma; **vergiss nicht, deinen Namen auf die Liste zu setzen** don't forget to put your name on the list; **2** to move (*a counter in games*); **3 auf etwas setzen** to bet on something; **auf ein Pferd setzen** to back a horse; **4 sich setzen** to sit down; **sich auf einen Stuhl setzen** to sit down on a chair.

seufzen *verb* (PERF hat geseufzt) to sigh.

Seufzer der (PL die **Seufzer**) sigh.

Sex der sex; **Sex mit jemandem haben** to have sex with somebody.

Sexismus der sexism.

sexistisch *adjective* sexist.

sexuell *adjective* sexual.

a **Shampoo** das (PL die **Shampoos**) shampoo.

b **Shuttledienst** der (PL die **Shuttledienste**) shuttle service.

c **sich** pronoun 1 (with 'er/sie/es') himself/herself/itself; **sie hat sich eingeschlossen** she locked herself in; 2 (with plural 'sie') themselves; 3 (with 'Sie') yourself, yourselves (plural); 4 each other, one another; **sich kennen** to know each other; **Petra und Werner lieben sich** Petra and Werner love each other; 5 (not translated with certain verbs) **sich freuen** to be pleased; **sich wundern** to be surprised; 6 **Anita wäscht sich die Haare** Anita is washing her hair; **sich den Arm brechen** to break your arm; 7 **sich gut verkaufen** to sell well; 8 **von sich aus** of your own accord.

sicher adjective 1 safe; 2 certain; **bist du sicher?** are you sure?.

sicher adverb 1 safely; 2 certainly, surely; **sicher!** certainly!

Sicherheit die 1 safety; **zur Sicherheit** for safety's sake; **schnallen Sie sich zur Ihrer eigenen Sicherheit an** fasten your seat belt for your own safety; **etwas in Sicherheit bringen** to rescue something; **in Sicherheit sein** to be safe; 2 security; **die Sicherheit der Arbeitsplätze** job security; 3 certainty; **mit Sicherheit!** certainly! (as a reply).

Sicherheitsgurt der (PL die **Sicherheitsgurte**) seatbelt.

Sicherheitsnadel die (PL die **Sicherheitsnadeln**) safety pin.

sicherlich adverb certainly.

sichern verb (PERF **hat gesichert**) to secure; **jemandem etwas sichern** to secure something for somebody.

Sicherung die (PL die **Sicherungen**) 1 fuse; **die Sicherung ist durchgebrannt** the fuse has blown; 2 safeguard; **die Sicherung der Arbeitsplätze** safeguarding jobs; 3 safety catch.

Sicht die 1 view; **ich hatte eine gute Sicht auf den See** I had a good view of the lake; **auf lange Sicht** in the long term; 2 **aus meiner Sicht** as I see it; 3 visibility; **gute/schlechte Sicht** good/poor visibility.

sichtbar adjective visible.

sie pronoun 1 she; 2 her; **ich kenne sie** I know her; 3 it; **so eine hübsche Bluse, war sie teuer?** what a pretty blouse, was it expensive?; 4 they; **sie sind in der Küche** they're in the kitchen; 5 them; **ich habe sie gestern abgeschickt** I posted them yesterday.

Sie pronoun you; **kommen Sie herein!** come in!

Sieb das (PL die **Siebe**) 1 sieve; 2 strainer.

sieben number seven.

siebter, siebte, siebtes adjective seventh.

siebzehn number seventeen.

siebzig number seventy.

Siedlung die (PL die **Siedlungen**) 1 (housing) estate; 2 settlement.

Sieg der (PL die **Siege**) victory, win.

Siegel das (PL die **Siegel**) seal.

siegen verb (PERF **hat gesiegt**) to win.

Sieger der (PL die **Sieger**) winner.

Siegerin die (PL die **Siegerinnen**) winner.

sieht SEE **sehen**.

Silbe die (PL die **Silben**) syllable.

Silber das silver.

silbern adjective silver.

Silvester das New Year's Eve.

sind SEE **sein**.

Sinfonie die (PL die **Sinfonien**) symphony.

singen ◇verb (IMPERF **sang**, PERF **hat gesungen**) to sing.

sinken ◇verb (IMPERF **sank**, PERF **ist gesunken**) 1 to sink; 2 to go down.

Sinn der (PL die **Sinne**) 1 sense; 2 meaning; 3 point; **das hat keinen Sinn** there's no point.

sinnlos adjective pointless.

sinnvoll adjective 1 sensible; 2 meaningful.

Situation die (PL die **Situationen**) situation.

Sitz der (PL die **Sitze**) 1 seat; 2 fit (of clothes).

sitzen ◇verb (IMPERF **saß**, PERF **hat gesessen**) 1 to sit; **sitzen bleiben** to remain seated; 2 **sitzen bleiben** to have to repeat a year, to stay down (at school); 3 **er sitzt** (informal) he's in jail; 4 **jemanden sitzen lassen** (informal) to leave somebody in the lurch; 5 to fit (of

clothes); **der Mantel sitzt gut** the coat fits well.

Sitzplatz der (PL die **Sitzplätze**) seat.

Sitzung die (PL die **Sitzungen**) 1 meeting; 2 session.

Sizilien das Sicily.

Skandal der (PL die **Skandale**) scandal.

Skandinavien das Scandinavia.

skandinavisch adjective Scandinavian.

Skateboard der (PL die **Skateboards**) skateboard; **Skateboard fahren** to skateboard.

Skater der (PL die **Skater**) skater (on a skateboard).

Skelett das (PL die **Skelette**) skeleton.

skeptisch adjective sceptical.

Ski der (PL die **Ski(er)**) ski; **Ski fahren/laufen** to ski.

Skianzug der (PL die **Skianzüge**) ski suit.

Skibrille die (PL die **Skibrillen**) skiing goggles.

Skifahren das skiing.

Skifahrer der (PL die **Skifahrer**) skier.

Skifahrerin die (PL die **Skifahrerinnen**) skier.

Skilaufen das skiing.

Skiläufer der (PL die **Skiläufer**) skier.

Skiläuferin die (PL die **Skiläuferinnen**) skier.

a b c d e f g h i j k l m n o p q r s t u v w x y z

Skilehrer der (PL die **Skilehrer**) ski instructor.

Skizze die (PL die **Skizzen**) sketch.

Skooter der (PL die **Skooter**) bumper car, dodgem car.

Skorpion der (PL die **Skorpione**) 1 scorpion; 2 Scorpio.

Skulptur die (PL die **Skulpturen**) sculpture.

Slip der (PL die **Slips**) briefs, pants.

Slowake der (PL die **Slowaken**) Slovak.

Slowakei die Slovakia.

Slowakin die (PL die **Slowakinnen**) Slovak.

slowakisch adjective Slovak.

Slowenien das Slovenia.

Smoking der (PL die **Smokings**) dinner jacket.

SMS die (PL die **SMS**) text message.

so adverb 1 so; **nicht so viel** not so much; **und so weiter** and so on; 2 like this, like that; **so nicht** not like that; 3 as; **so bald wie** as soon as; 4 such; **so ein Zufall!** what a coincidence!; 5 **das kriegst du so** (informal) you get it for nothing; **6 so um zwanzig Euro** about twenty euros.

so conjunction **so dass** so that.

so exclamation right!, well!; **so?** really?

sobald conjunction as soon as.

Socke die (PL die **Socken**) sock.

Sofa das (PL die **Sofas**) sofa.

sofort adverb immediately.

sogar adverb even.

sogleich adverb at once.

Sohle die (PL die **Sohlen**) sole.

Sohn der (PL die **Söhne**) son.

Soja die soy.

solange conjunction as long as.

solch pronoun such; **solch einer/ eine/eins** one like that, somebody like that.

solcher, solche, solches adjective, pronoun 1 such; **ich habe solche Angst** I'm so frightened; 2 **ein solcher Mann** a man like that; **eine solche Frage** a question like that; **ein solches Haus** a house like that; 3 solche (plural) those; **solche wie die** people like that.

Soldat der (PL die **Soldaten**) soldier.

solide adjective 1 solid; 2 respectable.

Solist der (PL die **Solisten**) soloist.

Solistin die (PL die **Solistinnen**) soloist.

sollen ⋄verb (PRES **soll**, IMPERF **sollte**, PERF **hat gesollt**) 1 should; **sollte es regnen** if it should rain; 2 to be supposed to; **was soll das heißen?** what's that supposed to mean?; 3 **sagen Sie ihr, sie soll anrufen** tell her to ring; 4 **was soll ich machen?** what shall I do?; **soll ich?** shall I?; 5 **was soll's!** so what!

sollte, sollten, solltest, solltet SEE sollen.

Sommer der (PL die **Sommer**) summer.

sommerlich adjective summery, summer.

Sommersprossen *plural noun* freckles.

Sonderangebot *das* (PL *die* **Sonderangebote**) special offer; **im Sonderangebot** on special offer.

sonderbar *adjective* strange, odd.

sondern *conjunction* but; **nicht nur ..., sondern auch ...** not only ..., but also ...

Song *der* (PL *die* **Songs**) song.

Sonnabend *der* (PL *die* **Sonnabende**) Saturday.

sonnabends *adverb* on Saturdays.

Sonne *die* (PL *die* **Sonnen**) sun.

sonnen *verb* (PERF **hat sich gesonnt**) **sich sonnen** to sun yourself.

Sonnenaufgang *der* sunrise.

Sonnenbrand *der* sunburn.

Sonnenbrille *die* (PL *die* **Sonnenbrillen**) sunglasses.

Sonnencreme *die* (PL *die* **Sonnencremes**) suntan lotion.

Sonnenenergie *die* solar energy.

Sonnenmilch *die* suntan lotion.

Sonnenöl *das* suntan oil.

Sonnenschein *der* sunshine.

Sonnenstich *der* sunstroke.

sonnig *adjective* sunny.

Sonntag *der* (PL *die* **Sonntage**) Sunday.

sonntags *adverb* on Sundays.

sonst *adverb* **1** usually; **2** else; **wer sonst?** who else?; **was sonst?** what else?; **3 sonst noch etwas?** anything else?; **sonst noch**

jemand? anybody else?; **4 sonst wo** somewhere; **es kann sonst wo sein** it could be anywhere; **5** otherwise; **geh jetzt, sonst verpasst du den Bus** go now, otherwise you'll miss the bus.

sonstwo SEE **sonst**.

sooft *conjunction* whenever.

Sorge *die* (PL *die* **Sorgen**) worry; **sich Sorgen machen** to worry.

sorgen *verb* (PERF **hat gesorgt**) **1 für etwas sorgen** to take care of something; **für die Musik sorgen** to see to the music; **für jemanden sorgen** to look after somebody; **2 dafür sorgen, dass ...** to make sure that ...; **3 sich sorgen** to worry; **ich sorge mich um meine Eltern** I worry about my parents.

sorgfältig *adjective* careful.

Sorte *die* (PL *die* **Sorten**) **1** kind; **2** brand.

Soße *die* (PL *die* **Soßen**) **1** sauce; **2** gravy; **3** dressing.

Souvenir *das* (PL *die* **Souvenirs**) souvenir.

soviel *conjunction* as far as; **soviel ich weiß** as far as I know.

soviel *adverb* SEE **viel**.

soweit *conjunction* as far as; **soweit ich weiß, ist er in Ferien** as far as I know, he's on holiday.

soweit *adverb* SEE **weit**.

sowenig SEE **wenig**.

sowie *conjunction* **1** as well as; **2** as soon as.

sowieso *adverb* anyway.

a b c d e f g h i j k l m n o p q r s t u v w x y z

sowohl adverb sowohl ... als auch ... both ... and ...; sowohl er wie auch sein Freund both he and his friend.

sozial adjective social.

Sozialarbeiter der (PL die Sozialarbeiter) social worker.

Sozialarbeiterin die (PL die Sozialarbeiterinnen) social worker.

Sozialhilfe die social security.

Sozialismus der socialism.

sozialistisch adjective socialist.

Sozialkunde die social studies.

Sozialwohnung die (PL die Sozialwohnungen) council flat.

Soziologie die sociology.

sozusagen adverb so to speak.

Spalte die (PL die Spalten) 1 crack; 2 column (in text).

spalten verb (PERF hat gespalten) to split.

Spaniel der (PL die Spaniels) Spaniel.

Spanien das Spain.

Spanier der (PL die Spanier) Spaniard.

Spanierin die (PL die Spanierinnen) Spaniard.

spanisch adjective Spanish.

Spanisch das Spanish (language).

spann SEE spinnen.

spannend adjective exciting.

Spannung die (PL die Spannungen) 1 tension; 2 suspense (in a film or novel, for example); ich erwarte

seine Antwort mit Spannung I can't wait for his answer; 3 voltage.

Sparbüchse die (PL die Sparbüchsen) money box.

sparen verb (PERF hat gespart) 1 to save; auf etwas sparen to save up for something; 2 sich etwas sparen not to bother with something; sich die Mühe sparen to save yourself the trouble; 3 an etwas sparen to economize on something.

Spargel der asparagus.

Sparkasse die savings bank.

sparsam adjective 1 economical; 2 thrifty.

Sparschwein das (PL die Sparschweine) piggy bank.

Spaß der (PL die Späße) 1 fun; zum/ aus Spaß for fun; das macht Spaß it's fun; Segeln macht mir keinen Spaß I don't like sailing; 2 viel Spaß! have a good time!; 3 joke; er macht nur Spaß he's only joking.

spät adjective, adverb late; zu spät kommen to be late; wie spät ist es? what time is it?

Spaten der (PL die Spaten) spade.

später adjective later.

spätestens adverb at the latest.

Spatz der (PL die Spatzen) sparrow.

Spätzle plural noun noodles (South German dish).

spazieren verb (PERF ist spaziert) 1 to stroll; 2 spazieren gehen to go for a walk; hast du Lust, spazieren zu gehen? would you like to go for a walk?

spazierengehen SEE spazieren.

Spaziergang der (PL die Spaziergänge) walk; einen Spaziergang machen to go for a walk.

Speck der bacon.

Speiche die (PL die Speichen) spoke.

Speicher der (PL die Speicher) 1 loft, attic; 2 memory (in computing).

Speicherkapazität die storage capacity (on hard disk).

speichern verb (PERF hat gespeichert) 1 to store; 2 to save (in computing).

Speise die (PL die Speisen) 1 food; 2 dish.

Speisekarte die (PL die Speisekarten) menu.

Speisesaal der (PL die Speisesäle) 1 dining hall; 2 dining room.

Speisewagen der (PL die Speisewagen) dining car.

Spende die (PL die Spenden) donation.

spenden verb (PERF hat gespendet) 1 to donate; 2 to give.

spendieren verb (PERF hat spendiert) jemandem etwas spendieren to treat somebody to something.

Sperling der (PL die Sperlinge) sparrow.

Sperre die (PL die Sperren) 1 barrier; 2 ban.

sperren verb (PERF hat gesperrt) 1 to close; 2 to block (an entrance, access); 3 den Strom sperren to cut off the electricity; 4 einen Scheck sperren to stop a cheque; 5 ein Tier in einen Käfig sperren to shut an animal (up) in a cage.

spezialisieren verb (PERF hat spezialisiert) sich spezialisieren to specialize.

Spezialität die (PL die Spezialitäten) speciality.

speziell adjective special.

Spezies die (PL die Spezies) species.

Spiegel der (PL die Spiegel) mirror.

Spiegelbild das (PL die Spiegelbilder) reflection.

Spiegelei das (PL die Spiegeleier) fried egg.

spiegeln verb (PERF hat gespiegelt) 1 to reflect; 2 sich spiegeln to be reflected.

Spiel das (PL die Spiele) 1 game; 2 ein Spiel Karten a pack of cards; 3 es steht viel auf dem Spiel there's a lot at stake.

Spielautomat der (PL die Spielautomaten) gaming machine.

spielen verb (PERF hat gespielt) 1 to play; wir spielen morgen Fußball we're playing football tomorrow; 2 to gamble; 3 to act; das Stück war gut gespielt the play was well acted; 4 der Film spielt in Rom the film is set in Rome.

spielend adverb easily.

Spieler der (PL die Spieler) 1 player; 2 gambler.

Spielerin die (PL die **Spielerinnen**)
1 player; 2 gambler.

Spielfeld das (PL die **Spielfelder**)
pitch, field.

Spielhalle die (PL die **Spielhallen**)
amusement arcade.

Spielplatz der (PL die **Spielplätze**)
playground.

Spielverderber der (PL die
Spielverderber) spoilsport.

Spielverderberin die (PL die
Spielverderberinnen) spoilsport.

Spielwaren plural noun toys.

Spielzeug das 1 toy; 2 toys.

Spinat der spinach.

Spinne die (PL die **Spinnen**) spider.

spinnen ◇verb (IMPERF **spann**, PERF
hat **gesponnen**) 1 to spin; 2 du
spinnst! (informal) you're mad!

Spinnennetz das (PL die
Spinnennetze) 1 spider's web;
2 cobweb.

Spion der (PL die **Spione**) spy.

Spionage die spying, espionage.

spionieren verb (PERF hat
spioniert) to spy.

Spirituosen plural noun spirits
(alcohol).

spitz adjective pointed.

Spitze die (PL die **Spitzen**) 1 point;
2 top; **Schalke liegt jetzt an der
Spitze** Schalke is top of the league
at the moment; 3 peak; **von hier
kann man die schneebedeckten
Spitzen sehen** you can see the
snow-covered peaks from here;
4 front; **an der Spitze liegen** to be

in the lead; 5 lace; 6 **Spitze sein**
(informal) to be great.

spitzen verb (PERF hat **gespitzt**)
1 to sharpen; 2 **sich auf etwas
spitzen** (informal) to look forward
to something.

Spitzname der (PL die
Spitznamen) nickname.

Splitter der (PL die **Splitter**)
splinter.

splittern verb (PERF hat/ist
gesplittert) 1 to splinter; 2 to
shatter.

sponsern verb (PERF hat
gesponsert) to sponsor.

Sport der sport.

Sportgeschäft das (PL die
Sportgeschäfte) sports shop.

Sporthalle die (PL die **Sporthallen**)
sports hall.

Sportler der (PL die **Sportler**)
sportsman.

Sportlerin die (PL die
Sportlerinnen) sportswoman.

sportlich adjective 1 sporting;
2 sporty.

Sportplatz der (PL die **Sportplätze**)
sports field, sports ground.

Sportschuh der (PL die
Sportschuhe) trainer.

Sportverein der (PL die
Sportvereine) sports club.

Sportwagen der (PL die
Sportwagen) 1 sports car;
2 pushchair.

Sportzentrum das (PL die
Sportzentren) sports centre.

spotten verb (PERF hat gespottet) to mock.

sprach SEE **sprechen**.

Sprache die (PL die **Sprachen**) 1 language; 2 speech; **etwas zur Sprache bringen** to bring something up.

Sprachführer der (PL die **Sprachführer**) phrase-book.

sprachlos adjective speechless.

sprang SEE **springen**.

Sprechblase die (PL die **Sprechblasen**) speech bubble.

sprechen ✧verb (PRES **spricht**, IMPERF **sprach**, PERF **hat gesprochen**) 1 to speak; **Deutsch sprechen** to speak German; **mit wem spreche ich?** who's speaking? (on the phone); **jemanden sprechen** to speak to somebody; 2 **Frau Hahn ist nicht zu sprechen** Mrs Hahn is not available; 3 to talk; **mit jemandem über etwas sprechen** to talk to somebody about something; 4 to say (a word, sentence).

Sprecher der (PL die **Sprecher**) 1 spokesman; 2 (on TV) announcer; 3 (in a film) narrator; 4 speaker.

Sprecherin die (PL die **Sprecherinnen**) 1 spokeswoman; 2 (on TV) announcer; 3 (in a film) narrator; 4 speaker.

Sprechstunde die (PL die **Sprechstunden**) surgery.

spricht SEE **sprechen**.

Sprichwort das (PL die **Sprichwörter**) proverb.

springen ✧verb (IMPERF **sprang**, PERF **ist gesprungen**) 1 to jump; 2 to bounce (of a ball); 3 to dive; 4 to crack.

Spritze die (PL die **Spritzen**) 1 syringe; 2 injection; 3 hose.

spritzen verb (PERF hat gespritzt) 1 to inject; 2 to splash; **du hast mich nass gespritzt** you've splashed me; 3 to spray; 4 to spit (of fat); 5 (PERF **ist gespritzt**) to splash up.

Sprudel der (PL die **Sprudel**) sparkling mineral water.

sprühen verb (PERF hat gesprüht) 1 to spray; 2 to sparkle (of eyes); 3 (PERF **ist gesprüht**) to fly (of sparks); **die Funken sind in alle Richtungen gesprüht** sparks flew in all directions.

Sprung der (PL die **Sprünge**) 1 jump; 2 dive; 3 crack (in china, glass).

Sprungbrett das (PL die **Sprungbretter**) diving board.

spucken verb (PERF hat gespuckt) to spit.

Spülbecken das (PL die **Spülbecken**) sink.

spülen verb (PERF hat gespült) 1 to rinse; 2 to wash up; 3 to flush.

Spülmaschine die (PL die **Spülmaschinen**) dishwasher.

Spülmittel das (PL die **Spülmittel**) washing-up liquid.

Spültuch das (PL die **Spültücher**) dishcloth.

Spur die (PL die **Spuren**) 1 track; **auf der falschen Spur sein** to be on the wrong track; **jemandem auf die Spur kommen** to get on to somebody; **2** lane; **in der Spur bleiben** to keep in lane; **3** trail; **4** trace.

spüren *verb* (PERF **hat gespürt**) **1** to feel; **2** to sense.

Staat *der* (PL die **Staaten**) state.

staatlich *adjective* state; **eine staatliche Schule** a state school.

staatlich *adverb* by the state.

Staatsangehörigkeit *die* (PL die **Staatsangehörigkeiten**) nationality.

stabil *adjective* **1** stable; **2** sturdy.

stach SEE **stechen**.

Stachel *der* (PL die **Stacheln**) **1** spine; **2** spike; **3** sting.

Stachelbeere *die* (PL die **Stachelbeeren**) gooseberry.

Stacheldraht *der* barbed wire.

Stadion *das* (PL die **Stadien**) stadium.

Stadium *das* (PL die **Stadien**) stage.

Stadt *die* (PL die **Städte**) town, city.

städtisch *adjective* **1** urban; **2** municipal.

Stadtmitte *die* town centre.

Stadtplan *der* (PL die **Stadtpläne**) street map.

Stadtrand *der* outskirts (of town); **am Stadtrand von Lübeck** on the outskirts of Lübeck.

Stadtrat *der* (PL die **Stadträte**) town or city council.

Stadtrundfahrt *die* (PL die **Stadtrundfahrten**) sightseeing tour (*of a town*).

Stadtteil *der* (PL die **Stadtteile**) district.

Stahl *der* steel.

stahl SEE **stehlen**.

Stall *der* (PL die **Ställe**) **1** stable; **2** cowshed; **3** pigsty.

Stamm *der* (PL die **Stämme**) **1** trunk; **2** tribe; **3** stem (*of a word*).

Stammbaum *der* (PL die **Stammbäume**) family tree.

stammen *verb* (PERF **hat gestammt**) **aus Deutschland stammen** to come from Germany.

Stammgast *der* (PL die **Stammgäste**) regular customer (*in a pub or restaurant*).

stand SEE **stehen**.

Stand *der* (PL die **Stände**) **1** state; **etwas auf den neuesten Stand bringen** to bring something up to date; **2** score (*in a game*); **3** stall (*for a horse*); **4** stand (*in a fair*); **5** level (*of water, of a river*).

ständig *adjective* constant.

Standort *der* (PL die **Standorte**) position, location; **von ihrem Standort aus konnte sie nichts sehen** she couldn't see anything from where she was standing.

Stange *die* (PL die **Stangen**) **1** bar; **2** pole.

stank SEE **stinken**.

starb SEE **sterben**.

stark *adjective* **1** strong; **2** heavy (*rain, traffic*); **3** severe (*frost, pain*); **4** (*informal*) great; **das ist stark!** that's great!

Stärke die (PL die **Stärken**)
1 strength; 2 starch.

starrsinnig adjective obstinate.

Start der (PL die **Starts**) 1 start;
2 take-off.

Startbahn die (PL die **Startbahnen**)
runway.

starten verb (PERF **ist gestartet**)
1 (of a plane) to take off; 2 (PERF **hat gestartet**) to start, to launch (a campaign).

Station die (PL die **Stationen**)
1 station; 2 stop; **Station machen** to stop over; 3 ward (in hospital).

statt conjunction, preposition (+ GEN)
instead of; **statt zu arbeiten** instead of working; **sie ging statt ihrer Schwester** she went instead of her sister.

stattdessen conjunction instead.

stattfinden ◇verb (IMPERF **fand statt**, PERF **hat stattgefunden**) to take place.

Stau der (PL die **Staus**) 1 congestion;
2 traffic jam.

Staub der dust.

staubig adjective dusty.

staubsaugen verb (PERF **hat staubgesaugt**) to vacuum.

Staubsauger der (PL die **Staubsauger**) vacuum cleaner.

staunen verb (PERF **hat gestaunt**) to be amazed.

Steak das (PL die **Steaks**) steak.

stechen ◇verb (PRES **sticht**, IMPERF **stach**, PERF **hat gestochen**) 1 to prick; **sich in den Finger stechen** to prick your finger; 2 to sting, to

bite (of an insect); 3 **mit etwas in etwas stechen** to jab something into something.

Steckbrief der (PL die **Steckbriefe**) description (of a wanted person).

Steckdose die (PL die **Steckdosen**) socket.

stecken verb (PERF **hat gesteckt**)
1 to put; **du musst die Münze in den Schlitz stecken** put the coin into the slot; 2 to pin; 3 **wo steckt er?** where is he?; 4 **stecken bleiben** to get stuck; **den Schlüssel stecken lassen** to leave the key in the lock.

Stecker der (PL die **Stecker**) plug.

Stecknadel die (PL die **Stecknadeln**) pin.

Steckrübe die (PL die **Steckrüben**) turnip.

stehen ◇verb (IMPERF **stand**, PERF **hat gestanden**) 1 to stand; 2 to be; **es steht zwei zu zwei** the score is two all; **wie steht's?** what's the score?; 3 to have stopped (of a clock or a machine); 4 **es steht schlecht um ihn** he's in a bad way; **na, wie steht's?** how are you?; 5 **stehen bleiben** to stop; **die Uhr ist stehen geblieben** the clock has stopped;
6 **in der Zeitung steht, dass ...** it says in the paper that ...;
7 **jemandem (gut) stehen** to suit somebody; 8 **zu jemandem stehen** to stand by somebody; **na, wie steht's?** to be on good terms;
10 **zum Stehen kommen** to come to a standstill.

stehenbleiben SEE **stehen**.

a b c d e f g h i j k l m n o p q r s t u v w x y z

stehlen ◇*verb* (PRES **stiehlt**, IMPERF **stahl**, PERF **hat gestohlen**) to steal.

steif *adjective* stiff.

steigen *verb* (IMPERF **stieg**, PERF **ist gestiegen**) 1 to climb; **auf eine Leiter steigen** to climb up a ladder; **auf ein Fahrrad steigen** to get on a bike; **in den Bus steigen** to get on the bus; 2 to rise.

steil *adjective* steep.

Stein *der* (PL **die Steine**) stone.

Steinbock *der* (PL **die Steinböcke**) 1 ibex; 2 Capricorn; **Petra ist Steinbock** Petra's Capricorn.

Steinbruch *der* (PL **die Steinbrüche**) quarry.

Stelle *die* (PL **die Stellen**) 1 place, spot; **an deiner Stelle** in your place; **an dritter Stelle liegen** to be in third place; 2 job; **eine freie Stelle** a vacancy; 3 authority; 4 **auf der Stelle** immediately.

stellen *verb* (PERF **hat gestellt**) 1 to put; 2 to set (*a watch, task*); 3 **zur Verfügung stellen** to provide; 4 **lauter stellen** to turn up; **leiser stellen** to turn down; **die Heizung höher stellen** to turn the heating up; 5 **sich krank stellen** to pretend to be ill; 6 **sich stellen** to give yourself up; 7 **die Kinder stellten sich an die Wand** the children stood against the wall.

Stellenanzeige *die* (PL **die Stellenanzeigen**) job advertisement.

Stellplatz *der* (PL **die Stellplätze**) pitch (*for a tent*).

Stellung *die* (PL **die Stellungen**) position.

stellvertretend *adjective* 1 acting; 2 deputy; **der stellvertretende Feuerwehrhauptmann** the deputy chief fire officer.

Stellvertreter *der* (PL **die Stellvertreter**) 1 deputy; 2 representative.

Stellvertreterin *die* (PL **die Stellvertreterinnen**) 1 deputy; 2 representative.

Stempel *der* (PL **die Stempel**) 1 stamp; 2 postmark.

stempeln *verb* (PERF **hat gestempelt**) to stamp.

Steppdecke *die* (PL **die Steppdecken**) quilt.

sterben ◇*verb* (PRES **stirbt**, IMPERF **starb**, PERF **ist gestorben**) to die.

Stereoanlage *die* (PL **die Stereoanlagen**) stereo (system).

Stern *der* (PL **die Sterne**) star.

Sternzeichen *das* (PL **die Sternzeichen**) star sign; **was ist dein Sternzeichen?** what star sign are you?

Steuer[1] *das* (PL **die Steuer**) 1 (steering) wheel; 2 helm.

Steuer[2] *die* (PL **die Steuern**) tax.

steuern *verb* (PERF **hat gesteuert**) 1 to steer; 2 to control; 3 (PERF **ist gesteuert**) to head.

Stewardess *die* (PL **die Stewardessen**) stewardess, air hostess.

Stich der (PL die **Stiche**) 1 prick; 2 stab; 3 sting, bite (of an insect); 4 stitch; 5 trick (when playing cards); 6 engraving; 7 **jemanden im Stich lassen** to leave somebody in the lurch.

sticht SEE **stechen**.

sticken verb (PERF **hat gestickt**) to embroider.

Stickstoff der nitrogen.

Stiefbruder der (PL die **Stiefbrüder**) stepbrother.

Stiefel der (PL die **Stiefel**) boot.

Stiefkind das (PL die **Stiefkinder**) stepchild.

Stiefmutter die (PL die **Stiefmütter**) stepmother.

Stiefschwester die (PL die **Stiefschwestern**) stepsister.

Stiefvater der (PL die **Stiefväter**) stepfather.

stieg SEE **steigen**.

stiehlt SEE **stehlen**.

Stiel der (PL die **Stiele**) 1 handle; 2 stem.

Stier der (PL die **Stiere**) 1 bull; 2 Taurus; **Andrea ist Stier** Andrea's Taurus.

stieß SEE **stoßen**.

Stift der (PL die **Stifte**) 1 pencil; 2 crayon; 3 tack (nail).

Stil der (PL die **Stile**) style.

still adjective 1 quiet; 2 still.

stillen verb (PERF **hat gestillt**) 1 to quench; 2 to breast-feed.

stillhalten ◇verb (PRES **hält still**, IMPERF **hielt still**, PERF **hat stillgehalten**) to keep still.

Stimme die (PL die **Stimmen**) 1 voice; 2 vote.

stimmen verb (PERF **hat gestimmt**) 1 to be right; **stimmt das?** is that right?; 2 to vote; 3 to tune.

Stimmung die (PL die **Stimmungen**) 1 mood; 2 atmosphere.

stinken ◇verb (IMPERF **stank**, PERF **hat gestunken**) to smell, to stink.

Stipendium das (PL die **Stipendien**) 1 scholarship; 2 grant.

stirbt SEE **sterben**.

Stirn die (PL die **Stirnen**) forehead.

Stock[1] der (PL die **Stöcke**) stick.

Stock[2] der (PL die **Stock**) floor; **im ersten Stock** on the first floor.

Stockwerk das (PL die **Stockwerke**) floor.

Stoff der (PL die **Stoffe**) 1 material, fabric; 2 substance.

stöhnen verb (PERF **hat gestöhnt**) to groan.

stolpern verb (PERF **ist gestolpert**) 1 to stumble; 2 to trip; **ich bin über einen Stein gestolpert** I tripped on a stone.

stolz adjective proud.

stoppen verb (PERF **hat gestoppt**) to stop.

Stöpsel der (PL die **Stöpsel**) 1 plug; 2 stopper.

stören verb (PERF **hat gestört**) 1 to disturb; **Bitte nicht stören** please do not disturb; **2** to bother; **das stört mich nicht** that doesn't bother me; **3 stört es Sie, wenn ich das Fenster aufmache?** do you mind if I open the window?; **der Empfang ist gestört** there's interference (*on a TV*).

Störung die (PL die **Störungen**) **1** disturbance, interruption; **entschuldigen Sie die Störung** I'm sorry to bother you; **2** interference; **eine technische Störung** a technical fault.

Stoß der (PL die **Stöße**) **1** push; **2** pile; **ein Stoß Handtücher** a pile of towels.

stoßen ◇*verb* (PRES **stößt**, IMPERF **stieß**, PERF **hat gestoßen**) **1** to push; **2** to kick; **3 sich den Kopf stoßen** to hit your head; **ich habe mir den Kopf an dem Balken gestoßen** I hit my head on the beam; **sich stoßen** to bump yourself; **4 sich an etwas stoßen** to object to something; **5** (PERF **ist gestoßen**) **gegen etwas stoßen** to bump into something; **6** (PERF **ist gestoßen**) **auf etwas stoßen** to come across something.

Stoßstange die (PL die **Stoßstangen**) bumper.

Stoßzeit die (PL die **Stoßzeiten**) rush hour.

stottern *verb* (PERF **hat gestottert**) to stutter.

Strafe die (PL die **Strafen**) **1** punishment; **2** fine; **3** penalty.

Straftat die (PL die **Straftaten**) crime.

Strahl der (PL die **Strahlen**) **1** ray, beam; **2** jet.

strahlen *verb* (PERF **hat gestrahlt**) **1** to shine; **2** to beam.

Strahlung die (PL die **Strahlungen**) radiation.

Strand der (PL die **Strände**) beach.

Straße die (PL die **Straßen**) street, road; **in welcher Straße ist der Supermarkt?** which street is the supermarket in?; **über die Straße gehen** to cross the road; **jemanden auf die Straße setzen** (*informal*) to give somebody the sack; **mein Wirt hat mich einfach auf die Straße gesetzt** (*informal*) my landlord just turned me out (*of a flat or room*).

Straßenbahn die (PL die **Straßenbahnen**) tram; **mit der Straßenbahn fahren** to go by tram.

Straßenraub der **1** mugging; **2** street robbery.

Straßenräuber der (PL die **Straßenräuber**) mugger.

Straßenüberführung die (PL die **Straßenüberführungen**) **1** footbridge; **2** roadbridge.

Straßenunterführung die (PL die **Straßenunterführungen**) **1** subway; **2** underpass.

Strauch der (PL die **Sträucher**) bush.

Strauß[1] der (PL die **Sträuße**) bunch of flowers, bouquet.

Strauß[2] der (PL die **Strauße**) ostrich.

Streber der (PL die **Streber**) swot.

Strecke die (PL die **Strecken**)
1 distance; 2 route; 3 line (rail).

strecken verb (PERF hat
gestreckt) 1 to stretch (your arms,
legs); 2 sich strecken to stretch.

Streich der (PL die **Streiche**) trick.

streicheln verb (PERF hat
gestreichelt) to stroke.

streichen ◇verb (IMPERF **strich**,
PERF hat **gestrichen**) 1 to paint;
'frisch gestrichen' 'wet paint'; 2 to
spread (with butter); 3 to delete;
4 to cancel (a flight); 5 jemandem
über den Kopf streichen to stroke
somebody's head.

Streichholz das (PL die
Streichhölzer) match.

Streifen der (PL die **Streifen**)
1 stripe; 2 strip.

Streik der (PL die **Streiks**) strike.

streiken verb (PERF hat **gestreikt**)
to strike.

Streit der (PL die **Streite**) quarrel,
argument.

streiten ◇verb (IMPERF **stritt**, PERF
hat **gestritten**) 1 to quarrel, to
argue; 2 sich streiten to quarrel, to
argue.

streng adjective strict.

Stress der stress.

stressig adjective stressful.

streuen verb (PERF hat **gestreut**)
1 to spread; die Straßen streuen to
grit the roads; 2 to sprinkle.

Strich der (PL die **Striche**) 1 line;
2 stroke.

strich SEE **streichen**.

Strichpunkt der (PL die
Strichpunkte) semicolon.

stricken verb (PERF hat **gestrickt**)
to knit.

Strickjacke die (PL die
Strickjacken) cardigan.

stritt SEE **streiten**.

Stroh das straw.

Strohhalm der (PL die **Strohhalme**)
straw (for drinking).

Strom der (PL die **Ströme**) 1 river;
2 stream (of people or blood); es
regnet in Strömen it's pouring
with rain; 3 current.

Stromausfall der (PL die
Stromausfälle) power failure.

strömen verb (PERF ist **geströmt**)
to stream.

Strömung die (PL die **Strömungen**)
current.

Strudel der (PL die **Strudel**) strudel
(kind of Austrian cake).

Strumpf der (PL die **Strümpfe**)
1 stocking; 2 sock.

Strumpfhose die (PL die
Strumpfhosen) tights.

Stube die (PL die **Stuben**) room.

Stück das (PL die **Stücke**) 1 piece;
2 item; ein Euro das Stück one
euro each; 3 play.

Stückchen das (PL die **Stückchen**)
little piece.

Student der (PL die **Studenten**)
student.

Studentin die (PL die
Studentinnen) student.

studieren verb (PERF hat **studiert**)
to study; Horst studiert

a
b
c
d
e
f
g
h
i
j
k
l
m
n
o
p
q
r
s
t
u
v
w
x
y
z

Mathematik Horst is studying mathematics.

Studium das (PL die Studien) studies.

Stufe die (PL die Stufen) 1 step; 'Vorsicht Stufe' 'mind the step'; 2 stage (of development).

Stuhl der (PL die Stühle) chair.

stumm adjective 1 dumb; 2 silent.

stumpf adjective 1 blunt; 2 dull; 3 ein stumpfer Winkel an obtuse angle.

Stunde die (PL die Stunden) 1 hour; 2 lesson.

stundenlang adverb for hours.

Stundenplan der (PL die Stundenpläne) timetable.

stündlich adjective hourly.

stur adjective stubborn.

Sturm der (PL die Stürme) storm.

stürmisch adjective stormy.

Sturz der (PL die Stürze) 1 fall; 2 overthrow.

stürzen verb (PERF ist gestürzt) 1 to fall; 2 to rush (into a room); 3 (PERF hat gestürzt) to overthrow; 4 (PERF hat sich gestürzt) er hat sich aus dem Fenster gestürzt he threw himself out of the window; sich auf jemanden stürzen to pounce on somebody.

Sturzhelm der (PL die Sturzhelme) crash helmet.

stützen verb (PERF hat gestützt) to support; sich auf jemanden stützen to lean on somebody.

Subjekt das (PL die Subjekte) subject.

Substantiv das (PL die Substantive) noun.

subtil adjective subtle.

Subvention die (PL die Subventionen) subsidy.

subventionieren verb (PERF hat subventioniert) to subsidize.

Suche die (PL die Suchen) search.

suchen verb (PERF hat gesucht) 1 to look for; 'Zimmer gesucht' 'room wanted'; 2 to search.

süchtig adjective addicted.

Süchtige der/die (PL die Süchtigen) addict.

Südafrika das South Africa.

Südamerika das South America.

Süden der south.

südlich adjective 1 southern; 2 southerly.

südlich adverb, preposition (+ GEN) südlich von Wien to the south of Vienna; südlich der Stadt to the south of the town.

Südosten der south-east.

Südpol der South Pole.

Südwesten der south-west.

Summe die (PL die Summen) sum.

summen verb (PERF hat gesummt) 1 to hum; 2 to buzz.

Sünde die (PL die Sünden) sin.

super adjective (informal) great.

Supermarkt der (PL die Supermärkte) supermarket.

Suppe die (PL die Suppen) soup.

Surfen das surf.

surfen verb (PERF hat gesurft) to surf (in the sea, on the Internet); im

Internet surfen to surf the Internet.

Surfer der (PL die **Surfer**) surfer (on the sea and Internet).

Surferin die (PL die **Surferinnen**) surfer (on the sea and Internet).

süß adjective sweet.

Süßigkeit die (PL die **Süßigkeiten**) sweet.

Sweatshirt die (PL die **Sweatshirts**) sweatshirt.

symbolisch adjective symbolic.

sympathisch adjective likeable.

Symphonie die (PL die **Symphonien**) SEE **Sinfonie**.

Synagoge die (PL die **Synagogen**) synagogue.

synthetisch adjective synthetic.

System das (PL die **Systeme**) system.

Szene die (PL die **Szenen**) scene.

Tt

Tabak der (PL die **Tabake**) tobacco.

Tabelle die (PL die **Tabellen**) table.

Tablett das (PL die **Tabletts**) tray.

Tablette die (PL die **Tabletten**) tablet.

Tafel die (PL die **Tafeln**) 1 board, blackboard; **ein Wort an die Tafel schreiben** to write a word on the blackboard; 2 **eine Tafel Schokolade** a bar of chocolate.

Tag der (PL die **Tage**) day; **guten Tag** hello; **am Tag** in the daytime.

Tagebuch das (PL die **Tagebücher**) diary.

tagelang adverb for days.

Tagesanbruch der dawn.

Tagesausflug der (PL die **Tagesausflüge**) day trip.

Tageskarte die (PL die **Tageskarten**) 1 today's menu; 2 day ticket.

Tageslicht das daylight.

Tageslichtprojektor der (PL die **Tageslichtprojektoren**) overhead projector.

Tagesmutter die (PL die **Tagesmütter**) childminder.

Tagesschau die (PL die **Tagesschauen**) news (on television).

Tageszeitung die (PL die **Tageszeitungen**) daily paper.

täglich adjective daily; **sein täglicher Besuch** his daily visit.

täglich adverb daily; **zweimal täglich** twice daily, twice a day.

tagsüber adverb during the day.

Taille die (PL die **Taillen**) waist.

Takt der (PL die **Takte**) 1 tact; 2 time; **im Takt** in time to the music; 3 rhythm.

taktlos adjective tactless.

taktvoll adjective tactful.

Tal das (PL die **Täler**) valley.

Talent das (PL die **Talente**) talent.

Tampon der (PL die **Tampons**) tampon.

Tang der seaweed.

Tank der (PL die **Tanks**) tank.

a
b
c
d
e
f
g
h
i
j
k
l
m
n
o
p
q
r
s
t
u
v
w
x
y
z

tanken verb (PERF hat getankt) to fill up (with petrol) to get petrol.

Tanker der (PL die Tanker) tanker (on sea).

Tankstelle die (PL die Tankstellen) petrol station.

Tankwagen der (PL die Tankwagen) tanker (on road).

Tankwart der (PL die Tankwarte) petrol-pump attendant.

Tanne die (PL die Tannen) fir.

Tannenbaum der (PL die Tannenbäume) 1 fir tree; 2 Christmas tree.

Tante die (PL die Tanten) aunt.

Tanz der (PL die Tänze) dance.

tanzen verb (PERF hat getanzt) to dance.

Tänzer der (PL die Tänzer) dancer.

Tänzerin die (PL die Tänzerinnen) dancer.

Tapete die (PL die Tapeten) wallpaper.

tapezieren verb (PERF hat tapeziert) to (wall)paper.

tapfer adjective brave.

Tapferkeit die bravery.

Tarif der (PL die Tarife) 1 tariff; 2 rate.

Tasche die (PL die Taschen) 1 bag; 2 pocket; **er hat es aus eigener Tasche bezahlt** he paid for it out of his own pocket; **Max hat mir fünf Euro aus der Tasche gezogen** (informal) Max wangled five euros out of me.

Taschenbuch das (PL die Taschenbücher) paperback.

Taschendieb der (PL die Taschendiebe) pickpocket.

Taschengeld das pocket money.

Taschenlampe die (PL die Taschenlampen) torch.

Taschenmesser das (PL die Taschenmesser) penknife.

Taschenrechner der (PL die Taschenrechner) pocket calculator.

Taschentuch das (PL die Taschentücher) handkerchief.

Tasse die (PL die Tassen) cup.

Tastatur die (PL die Tastaturen) keyboard.

Taste die (PL die Tasten) 1 key; 2 button (on a phone or a machine).

tasten verb (PERF hat getastet) 1 to feel; 2 sich tasten to feel your way.

Tat die (PL die Taten) 1 action; 2 eine gute Tat a good deed; 3 crime; 4 in der Tat indeed.

tat SEE tun.

Täter der (PL die Täter) 1 culprit; 2 offender.

Täterin die (PL die Täterinnen) 1 culprit; 2 offender.

tätig adjective active.

Tätigkeit die (PL die Tätigkeiten) 1 activity; 2 job.

Tätigkeit die (PL die Tätigkeiten) activity.

Tätowierung die (PL die Tätowierungen) tattoo.

Tatsache die (PL die Tatsachen) fact.

tatsächlich *adjective* actual.

tatsächlich *adverb* 1 actually;
2 really.

Tau¹ *der* dew.

Tau² *das* (PL die **Taue**) rope.

taub *adjective* deaf.

Taube *die* (PL die **Tauben**) 1 pigeon;
2 dove.

tauchen *verb* (PERF **hat getaucht**)
1 to dip; 2 (PERF **hat/ist getaucht**)
(*'ist getaucht' is used when
movement is described*) to dive.

Taucher *der* (PL die **Taucher**) diver.

Taucherbrille *die* (PL die
Taucherbrillen) diving goggles.

Taucherin *die* (PL die
Taucherinnen) diver.

tauen *verb* (PERF **ist getaut**) 1 to
melt; 2 **es taut** it's thawing.

Taufe *die* (PL die **Taufen**)
christening.

taufen *verb* (PERF **hat getauft**) 1 to
christen; 2 to baptize.

taugen *verb* (PERF **hat getaugt**)
nichts taugen to be no good.

tauschen *verb* (PERF **hat
getauscht**) to exchange, to swap.

tausend *number* a thousand.

Taxi *das* (PL die **Taxis**) taxi.

Taxifahrer *der* (PL die **Taxifahrer**)
taxi driver.

Taxifahrerin *die* (PL die
Taxifahrerinnen) taxi driver.

Taxistand *der* (PL die **Taxistände**)
taxi rank.

Technik *die* (PL die **Techniken**)
1 technology; 2 technique.

Techniker *der* (PL die **Techniker**)
technician.

Technikerin *die* (PL die
Technikerinnen) technician.

technisch *adjective* 1 technical;
2 technological.

Technologie *die* technology.

technologisch *adjective*
technological.

Teddybär *der* (PL die **Teddybären**)
teddy bear.

Tee *der* (PL die **Tee(s)**) tea; **ein Tee
mit Zitrone** one lemon tea; **ein Tee
mit Milch** one tea with milk.

Teebeutel *der* (PL die **Teebeutel**)
tea bag.

Teekanne *die* (PL die **Teekannen**)
teapot.

Teelöffel *der* (PL die **Teelöffel**)
teaspoon.

Teenager *der* (PL die **Teenager**)
teenager.

Teich *der* (PL die **Teiche**) pond.

Teig *der* (PL die **Teige**) 1 dough;
2 pastry; 3 mixture.

Teigwaren *plural noun* pasta.

Teil¹ *der* (PL die **Teile**) 1 part; **der
zweite Teil** the second part; **zum
größten Teil** for the most part;
2 **zum Teil** partly; 3 share; **mein
Teil am Gewinn** my share of the
profit.

Teil² *das* (PL die **Teile**) 1 spare part;
2 part (*of a car, machine*); 3 unit (*of
furniture*).

teilen *verb* (PERF **hat geteilt**) 1 to
divide; 2 **sich etwas mit**

a
b
c
d
e
f
g
h
i
j
k
l
m
n
o
p
q
r
s
t
u
v
w
x
y
z

a

b

c

d

e

f

g

h

i

j

k

l

m

n

o

p

q

r

s

t

u

v

w

x

y

z

jemandem teilen to share something with somebody.

teilnehmen ◇*verb* (PRES **nimmt teil**, IMPERF **nahm teil**, PERF **hat teilgenommen**) **an etwas teilnehmen** to take part in something.

Teilnehmer der (PL die **Teilnehmer**) **1** participant; **2** competitor.

Teilnehmerin die (PL die **Teilnehmerinnen**) **1** participant; **2** competitor.

teils adverb partly.

Teilung die (PL die **Teilungen**) division.

Teilzeitarbeit die part-time work.

Telefax das (PL die **Telefax(e)**) fax.

Telefon das (PL die **Telefone**) telephone.

Telefonanruf der (PL die **Telefonanrufe**) phone call.

Telefonbuch das (PL die **Telefonbücher**) telephone directory, phone book.

Telefongespräch das (PL die **Telefongespräche**) telephone call.

Telefonhörer der (PL die **Telefonhörer**) receiver.

telefonieren verb (PERF **hat telefoniert**) to telephone, to make a phone call.

telefonisch adjective telephone.

telefonisch adverb by telephone; **er ist telefonisch nicht erreichbar** he can't be contacted by phone.

Telefonkarte die (PL die **Telefonkarten**) phone card.

Telefonnummer die (PL die **Telefonnummern**) telephone number.

Telefonzelle die (PL die **Telefonzellen**) phone box, call box.

Teleskop das (PL die **Teleskope**) telescope.

Teller der (PL die **Teller**) plate.

Temperatur die (PL die **Temperaturen**) temperature.

Tempo das (PL die **Tempos**) speed; **Tempo Tempo!** (*informal*) hurry up!

Tendenz die (PL die **Tendenzen**) **1** trend; **2** tendency.

tendieren verb (PERF **hat tendiert**) **zu etwas tendieren** to tend towards something.

Tennis das tennis.

Tennisplatz der (PL die **Tennisplätze**) tennis court.

Tennisschläger der (PL die **Tennisschläger**) tennis racket.

Tennisspieler der (PL die **Tennisspieler**) tennis player.

Tennisspielerin die (PL die **Tennisspielerinnen**) tennis player.

Teppich der (PL die **Teppiche**) **1** carpet; **2** rug.

Termin der (PL die **Termine**) **1** date; **einen Termin vereinbaren** to fix a date; **2** appointment; **3** der letzte **Termin** the deadline.

Terminal[1] der (PL die **Terminals**) terminal.

Terminal[2] das (PL die **Terminals**) (computer) terminal.

Terrasse die (PL die **Terrassen**) terrace.

Terror der terror.

Terrorismus der terrorism.

Terrorist der (PL die **Terroristen**) terrorist.

Terroristin die (PL die **Terroristinnen**) terrorist.

Tesafilm™ der Sellotape™.

Test der (PL die **Tests**) test; **ein Test zum Hörverständnis** a listening comprehension test.

testen verb (PERF **hat getestet**) to test.

teuer adjective expensive; **wie teuer?** how much?

Teufel der (PL die **Teufel**) devil.

Text der (PL die **Texte**) 1 text; 2 lyrics; 3 caption.

Textverarbeitung die word processing.

Theater das (PL die **Theater**) 1 theatre; 2 (informal) fuss.

Theaterstück das (PL die **Theaterstücke**) play.

Theke die (PL die **Theken**) 1 bar; 2 counter.

Thema das (PL die **Themen**) subject, topic.

Themenpark der (PL die **Themenparks**) theme park.

Themse die Thames.

theoretisch adjective theoretical.

theoretisch adverb in theory.

Theorie die (PL die **Theorien**) theory.

Therapie die (PL die **Therapien**) therapy.

Thermometer das (PL die **Thermometer**) thermometer.

Thron der (PL die **Throne**) throne.

Thunfisch der (PL die **Thunfische**) tuna.

Thymian der thyme.

tief adjective 1 deep; 2 low.

Tiefe die (PL die **Tiefen**) depth.

Tiefgarage die (PL die **Tiefgaragen**) underground car park.

Tiefkühlfach das (PL die **Tiefkühlfächer**) freezer compartment.

Tiefkühlkost die frozen food.

Tiefkühltruhe die (PL die **Tiefkühltruhen**) freezer.

Tiefsttemperatur die (PL die **Tiefsttemperaturen**) minimum temperature.

Tier das (PL die **Tiere**) animal.

Tierarzt der (PL die **Tierärzte**) vet.

Tierärztin die (PL die **Tierärztinnen**) vet.

Tiergarten der (PL die **Tiergärten**) zoo.

Tierkreis der zodiac.

Tierpark der (PL die **Tierparks**) zoo.

Tiger der (PL die **Tiger**) tiger.

Tinte die (PL die **Tinten**) ink.

Tintenfisch der (PL die **Tintenfische**) 1 octopus; 2 squid.

Tipp der (PL die **Tipps**) tip.

a b c d e f g h i j k l m n o p q r s t u v w x y z

tippen verb (PERF **hat getippt**) 1 to type; 2 to tap; 3 **auf etwas tippen** to bet on something; **ich tippe auf ihn** I'm tipping him to win; **im Lotto tippen** to do the lottery.

Tisch der (PL die **Tische**) 1 table; 2 **nach Tisch** after the meal.

Tischdecke die (PL die **Tischdecken**) tablecloth.

Tischler der (PL die **Tischler**) joiner, carpenter.

Tischtennis das table tennis.

Tischtuch das (PL die **Tischtücher**) tablecloth.

Titel der (PL die **Titel**) title.

Toast der (PL die **Toasts**) toast.

toben verb (PERF **hat getobt**) 1 to rage; 2 to go mad; 3 to charge about.

Tochter die (PL die **Töchter**) daughter.

Tod der (PL die **Tode**) death.

Todesstrafe die death penalty.

tödlich adjective 1 fatal; 2 deadly.

todmüde adjective (informal) dead tired.

todschick adjective (informal) trendy.

Toilette die (PL die **Toiletten**) toilet; **auf die Toilette gehen** to go to the toilet.

Toilettenpapier das toilet paper.

toll adjective (informal) brilliant.

Tollwut die rabies.

Tomate die (PL die **Tomaten**) tomato.

Tomatenmark das tomato purée.

Ton[1] der (PL die **Töne**) 1 sound; **er hat keinen Ton gesagt** he didn't make a sound; 2 **große Töne spucken** (informal) to talk big; 3 tone; **einen frechen Ton anschlagen** to adopt a cheeky tone; 4 note; 5 shade (of colour); 6 stress (in pronunciation).

Ton[2] der clay.

Tonband das (PL die **Tonbänder**) tape.

Tonbandgerät das (PL die **Tonbandgeräte**) tape recorder.

Tonne die (PL die **Tonnen**) 1 barrel; 2 bin (for rubbish); 3 tonne, ton.

Topf der (PL die **Töpfe**) 1 pot; 2 pan.

Töpferei die (PL die **Töpfereien**) pottery.

Tor das (PL die **Tore**) 1 gate; 2 goal; **mit 3 zu 2 Toren gewinnen** to win by 3 goals to 2.

Torte die (PL die **Torten**) 1 gateau; 2 cake.

Torwart der (PL die **Torwarte**) goalkeeper.

tot adjective dead.

total adjective complete.

total adverb completely; **du bist total verrückt** you're totally mad.

Tote der/die (PL die **Toten**) 1 dead man/woman; **die Toten** the dead; 2 fatality.

töten verb (PERF **hat getötet**) to kill.

totlachen verb (informal) (PERF **hat sich totgelacht**) **sich totlachen** to laugh your head off.

Tour die (PL die **Touren**) **1** tour; **2** trip; **3 auf diese Tour** (informal) in this way.

Tourismus der tourism.

Tourist der (PL die **Touristen**) tourist.

Touristeninformation die (PL die **Touristeninformationen**) **1** tourist information office; **2** tourist information.

Touristin die (PL die **Touristinnen**) tourist.

Tournee die (PL die **Tournees**) tour.

traben verb (PERF **ist getrabt**) to trot.

Tradition die (PL die **Traditionen**) tradition.

traditionell adjective traditional.

traf SEE **treffen**.

tragbar adjective **1** portable; **2** wearable.

tragen ◇verb (PRES **trägt**, IMPERF **trug**, PERF **hat getragen**) **1** to carry; **2** to wear; **sie trug ein weißes Kleid** she wore a white dress; **man trägt wieder kurz** short skirts are in fashion again; **3** to bear; **die Verantwortung für etwas tragen** to be responsible for something; **4** to support; **die Organisation trägt sich selbst** the organization is self-supporting.

Träger der (PL die **Träger**) **1** porter; **2** bearer (of a name, title); **3** strap (of a dress); **4** girder.

Tragetasche die (PL die **Tragetaschen**) carrier bag.

tragisch adjective tragic.

Tragödie die (PL die **Tragödien**) tragedy.

Trainer der (PL die **Trainer**) coach, trainer.

trainieren verb **hat trainiert**) **1** to coach; **2** to train.

Training das training.

Trainingsanzug der (PL die **Trainingsanzüge**) tracksuit.

Trainingsschuh der (PL die **Trainingsschuhe**) trainer (shoe).

Traktor der (PL die **Traktoren**) tractor.

trampen verb (PERF **ist getrampt**) to hitchhike.

Trampen das hitchhiking.

Tramper der (PL die **Tramper**) hitchhiker.

Tramperin die (PL die **Tramperinnen**) hitchhiker.

Träne die (PL die **Tränen**) tear.

trank SEE **trinken**.

Transplantation die (PL die **Transplantationen**) transplant.

Transport der (PL die **Transporte**) **1** transport; **2** consignment.

transportieren verb (PERF **hat transportiert**) to transport.

trat SEE **treten**.

Traube die (PL die **Trauben**) grape.

trauen verb (PERF **hat getraut**) **1** to trust; **jemandem trauen** to trust somebody; **2 sich trauen** to dare; **Ich trau mich nicht** I don't dare; **3** to marry.

Trauer die **1** grief; **2** mourning.

Traum der (PL die **Träume**) dream.

a b c d e f g h i j k l m n o p q r s t u v w x y z

a **träumen** verb (PERF **hat geträumt**) to dream.

b **traumhaft** adjective fabulous.

c **traurig** adjective sad.

d **Traurigkeit** die sadness.

Trauung die (PL die **Trauungen**) wedding.

e

f **Trauzeuge** der (PL die **Trauzeugen**) witness (at a wedding ceremony).

g

h **treffen** ◇verb (PRES **trifft**, IMPERF **traf**, PERF **hat getroffen**) 1 to hit; 2 to meet; 3 to make (arrangements, a decision); 4 **sich mit jemandem treffen** to meet somebody; 5 **sich gut treffen** to be convenient; 6 (PERF **ist getroffen**) **auf etwas treffen** to meet with (resistance, difficulties).

i

j

k

l

m **Treffen** das (PL die **Treffen**) meeting.

n **Treffer** der (PL die **Treffer**) 1 hit; 2 winner; 3 goal.

o **Treffpunkt** der (PL die **Treffpunkte**) meeting place.

p

q

r **treiben** ◇verb (IMPERF **trieb**, PERF **hat getrieben**) 1 to drive; 2 to do; **viel Sport treiben** to do a lot of sport; **Handel treiben** to trade; 3 **jemanden zur Eile treiben** to hurry somebody up; 4 **Unsinn treiben** to mess about; 5 (PERF **ist getrieben**) to drift.

s

t

u

v

w **Treibhaus** das (PL die **Treibhäuser**) hothouse.

x **Treibhauseffekt** der greenhouse effect.

y

z **Treibstoff** der fuel.

trennen verb (PERF **hat getrennt**) 1 to separate; 2 to divide (words, parts of a room); 3 **sich trennen** to separate; **wir haben uns getrennt** we've separated; **Jutta hat sich von ihm getrennt** Jutta has left him; 4 **sich von etwas trennen** to part with something.

Trennung die (PL die **Trennungen**) 1 separation; 2 division.

Treppe die (PL die **Treppen**) stairs; **eine Treppe** a flight of stairs.

Treppenhaus das stairwell; **im Treppenhaus** on the stairs.

treten ◇verb (PRES **tritt**, IMPERF **trat**, PERF **ist getreten**) 1 to step; 2 to tread; 3 to kick; 4 **mit jemandem in Verbindung treten** to get in touch with somebody.

treu adjective faithful.

Treuekarte die (PL die **Treuekarten**) loyalty card.

Tribüne die (PL die **Tribünen**) 1 stand (in a stadium); 2 platform.

Trick der (PL die **Tricks**) trick.

Trickfilm der (PL die **Trickfilme**) cartoon.

trieb SEE **treiben**.

trifft SEE **treffen**.

Trimm-dich-Pfad der (PL die **Trimm-dich-Pfade**) keep-fit trail.

trimmen verb (PERF **hat getrimmt**) 1 to trim; 2 **sich trimmen** to keep fit.

trinken ◇verb (IMPERF **trank**, PERF **hat getrunken**) to drink.

Trinkgeld das (PL die **Trinkgelder**) tip.

Trinkschokolade die drinking chocolate.

Trinkwasser das drinking water.

Tritt der (PL die **Tritte**) **1** step; **2** kick.

tritt SEE **treten**.

Triumph der (PL die **Triumphe**) triumph.

trocken adjective dry.

trockenlegen verb (PERF **hat trockengelegt**) to drain (a marsh, a pond).

trocknen verb (PERF **hat getrocknet**) to dry.

Trockner der (PL die **Trockner**) drier.

Trödel der (informal) junk.

Trödelmarkt der (PL die **Trödelmärkte**) flea market.

Trommel die (PL die **Trommeln**) drum.

trommeln verb (PERF **hat getrommelt**) to drum.

Trompete die (PL die **Trompeten**) trumpet.

Tropen (plural noun) die **Tropen** the tropics.

Tropfen der (PL die **Tropfen**) drop.

tropfen verb (PERF **hat getropft**) to drip.

Trophäe die (PL die **Trophäen**) trophy.

tropisch adjective tropical.

trösten verb (PERF **hat getröstet**) to console, to comfort.

trotz preposition (+ GEN) despite, in spite of.

trotzdem adverb nevertheless.

trüb adjective **1** dull, dismal; **2** cloudy (liquid).

trübsinnig adjective gloomy.

trug SEE **tragen**.

Truhe die (PL die **Truhen**) chest.

Trümmer plural noun ruins.

Trumpf der (PL die **Trümpfe**) **1** trump (card); **2** trumps.

Trunkenheit die drunkenness; **Trunkenheit am Steuer** drink-driving.

Truppen plural noun troops.

Truthahn der (PL die **Truthähne**) turkey.

Tscheche der (PL die **Tschechen**) Czech.

Tschechin die (PL die **Tschechinnen**) Czech.

tschechisch adjective Czech.

Tschechische Republik die Czech Republic.

tschüss exclamation bye!.

T-Shirt das (PL die **T-Shirts**) T-shirt.

Tube die (PL die **Tuben**) tube.

Tuberkulose die tuberculosis.

Tuch das (PL die **Tücher**) **1** cloth; **2** scarf.

tüchtig adjective **1** efficient; **2** competent.

Tüchtigkeit die **1** efficiency; **2** competence.

Tulpe die (PL die **Tulpen**) tulip.

Tumor der (PL die **Tumoren**) tumour.

tun ◇verb (PRES **tut**, IMPERF **tat**, PERF **hat getan**) **1** to do; **das tut man nicht** it isn't done; **das tut's**

a b c d e f g h i j k l m n o p q r s t u v w x y z

(*informal*) that'll do; **2** to put; **die Butter in den Kühlschrank tun** to put the butter in the fridge; **3** to pretend; **er tut nur so** he's only pretending; **4** to act; **freundlich tun** to act friendly; **5 jemandem etwas tun** to hurt somebody; **6 mit jemandem etwas zu tun haben** to have dealings with somebody; **das hat nichts damit zu tun** it's got nothing to do with it; **7 das tut nichts** it doesn't matter; **es hat sich viel getan** lots has happened.

Tunesien *das* Tunisia.

Tunesier *der* (PL **die Tunesier**) Tunisian.

Tunesierin *die* (PL **die Tunesierinnen**) Tunisian.

tunesisch *adjective* Tunisian.

Tunfisch *der* (PL **die Tunfische**) tuna.

Tunnel *der* (PL **die Tunnel**) tunnel.

Tupfen *der* (PL **die Tupfen**) dot.

tupfen *verb* (PERF **hat getupft**) to dab.

Tür *die* (PL **die Türen**) door.

Türke *der* (PL **die Türken**) Turk.

Türkei *die* Turkey.

Türkin *die* (PL **die Türkinnen**) Turk.

türkis *adjective* turquoise.

türkisch *adjective* Turkish.

Turm *der* (PL **die Türme**) **1** tower; **2** steeple; **3** rook, castle (*in chess*).

Turnanzug *der* (PL **die Turnanzüge**) leotard.

Turnen *das* **1** gymnastics; **2** physical education, PE.

turnen *verb* (PERF **hat geturnt**) to do gymnastics.

Turnhalle *die* (PL **die Turnhallen**) gymnasium, gym.

Turnier *das* (PL **die Turniere**) tournament.

Turnschuh *der* (PL **die Turnschuhe**) **1** trainer; **2** gym shoe.

Turnverein *der* (PL **die Turnvereine**) gymnastics club.

tuscheln *verb* (PERF **hat getuschelt**) to whisper.

tut SEE **tun**.

Tüte *die* (PL **die Tüten**) bag.

Typ *der* (PL **die Typen**) **1** type; **2** (*informal*) bloke.

typisch *adjective* typical.

Uu

U-Bahn *die* (PL **die U-Bahnen**) underground.

übel *adjective* **1** bad; **2 mir ist übel** I feel sick; **3 etwas übel nehmen** to take offence at something; **jemandem etwas übel nehmen** to hold something against somebody.

Übelkeit *die* nausea.

übelnehmen SEE **übel**.

üben *verb* (PERF **hat geübt**) to practise.

über *preposition* (+ DAT, *or* + ACC *with movement towards a place*) **1** over; **über Weihnachten** over Christmas; **2** above; **er wohnt über uns** he lives above us; **fünf Grad**

über Null five degrees above zero; **3** about; **über etwas schreiben** to write about something; **4** for; **ein Scheck über hundert Euro** a cheque for one hundred euros; **5** across (*a field, the street*); **6 über Frankfurt fahren** to go via Frankfurt; **7 über die Straße gehen** to cross the road.

über *adverb* **1 über und über** over and over; **2 jemandem über sein** to be better than somebody; **3 über sein** (*informal*) to be left over; **4 jemanden ist etwas über** (*informal*) somebody is fed up with something; **5 etwas über haben** (*informal*) to be fed up with something; **Nudeln habe ich über** I'm getting fed up with pasta.

überall *adverb* everywhere.

überarbeiten *verb* (PERF **hat überarbeitet**)) to revise (*a text*).

Überblick *der* (PL die **Überblicke**) **1 einen guten Überblick über etwas haben** to have a good view of something; **2** overall view; **den Überblick verlieren** to lose track of things; **3** summary.

überblicken *verb* (PERF **hat überblickt**) **1** to overlook; **2** to assess.

Überdosis *die* (PL die **Überdosen**) overdose.

Überdruss *der* **bis zum Überdruss** ad nauseam.

übereinander *adverb* **1** one on top of the other; **2 übereinander sprechen** to talk about each other.

übereinstimmen *verb* (PERF **hat übereingestimmt**) to agree.

überempfindlich *adjective* hypersensitive.

überfahren ◇*verb* (PRES **überfährt**, IMPERF **überfuhr**, PERF **hat überfahren**) to run over; **das Kind ist von einem Auto überfahren worden** the child was run over by a car.

Überfahrt *die* (PL die **Überfahrten**) crossing.

Überfall *der* (PL die **Überfälle**) **1** attack; **2** raid.

überfallen ◇*verb* (PRES **überfällt**, IMPERF **überfiel**, PERF **hat überfallen**) **1** to attack, to mug; **2** to raid; **3 jemanden mit Fragen überfallen** to bombard somebody with questions.

überfällig *adjective* overdue.

überflüssig *adjective* superfluous.

Überführung *die* (PL die **Überführungen**) **1** transfer; **2** flyover; **3** footbridge.

überfüllt *adjective* **1** crowded; **2** oversubscribed.

Übergang *der* (PL die **Übergänge**) **1** crossing; **2** transition.

übergeben ◇*verb* (PRES **übergibt**, IMPERF **übergab**, PERF **hat übergeben**) **1** to hand over; **2 sich übergeben** to be sick.

überhaben SEE **über**.

überhaupt *adverb* **1** in general; **2** anyway; **was will er überhaupt?** what does he want anyway?; **3 überhaupt nicht** not at all; **3 überhaupt nichts** nothing at all;

überhaupt keine Zeit haben to have no time at all.

überholen verb (PERF **hat überholt**) 1 to overtake; 2 to overhaul.

überholt adjective out-of-date.

überlassen ◇verb (PRES **überlässt**, IMPERF **überließ**, PERF **hat überlassen**) 1 **jemandem etwas überlassen** to let somebody have something; 2 **etwas jemandem überlassen** to leave something up to somebody (a decision, for example); **das bleibt dir überlassen** it's up to you.

überlaufen ◇verb (PRES **läuft über**, IMPERF **lief über**, PERF **ist übergelaufen**) to overflow.

überleben verb (PERF **hat überlebt**) to survive.

überlegen[1] verb (PERF **hat überlegt**) 1 to think; **sich etwas überlegen** to think something over; **ohne zu überlegen** without thinking; 2 **ich habe es mir anders überlegt** I've changed my mind.

überlegen[2] adjective 1 superior; **jemandem überlegen sein** to be superior to somebody; 2 convincing (victory).

überm = über dem.

übermäßig adjective excessive.

übermorgen adverb the day after tomorrow.

übernächster, übernächste, übernächstes adjective next but one; **übernächstes Jahr** the year after next.

übernachten verb (PERF **hat übernachtet**) to stay the night; **bei jemandem übernachten** to stay the night at somebody's house.

übernehmen ◇verb (PRES **übernimmt**, IMPERF **übernahm**, PERF **hat übernommen**) 1 to take over; 2 to take on; 3 **sich übernehmen** to take on too much.

überqueren verb (PERF **hat überquert**) to cross.

überraschen verb (PERF **hat überrascht**) to surprise.

Überraschung die (PL die **Überraschungen**) surprise.

überreden verb (PERF **hat überredet**) to persuade.

übers = über das.

Überschrift die (PL die **Überschriften**) heading.

überschüssig adjective surplus.

überschütten verb (PERF **hat überschüttet**) **jemanden mit etwas überschütten** to shower somebody with something.

Überschwemmung die (PL die **Überschwemmungen**) flood.

übersehen[1] ◇verb (PRES **übersieht**, IMPERF **übersah**, PERF **hat übersehen**) 1 to overlook; (informal) **einen Fehler übersehen** to overlook a mistake; 2 to assess (consequences, damages).

übersehen[2] ◇verb (PRES **sieht sich über**, IMPERF **sah sich über**, PERF **hat sich übersehen**) **sich etwas übersehen** (informal) to get fed up with seeing something.

übersetzen *verb* (PERF **hat übersetzt**) to translate.

Übersetzer *der* (PL *die* **Übersetzer**) translator.

Übersetzerin *die* (PL *die* **Übersetzerinnen**) translator.

Übersetzung *die* (PL *die* **Übersetzungen**) translation.

Übersicht *die* **1** overall view; **2** summary.

überspringen ◇*verb* (IMPERF **übersprang**, PERF **hat übersprungen**) **1** to jump (over); **2** to skip (*a chapter*).

überstehen ◇*verb* (IMPERF **überstand**, PERF **hat überstanden**) **1** to get over; **2** to survive.

Überstunden *plural noun* overtime; **Überstunden machen** to work overtime.

übertragen ◇*verb* (PRES **überträgt**, IMPERF **übertrug**, PERF **hat übertragen**) **1** to transfer; **2** to transmit; **3** to broadcast; **4** etwas ins Reine übertragen to make a fair copy of something; **5** sich auf jemanden übertragen to communicate itself to somebody (*of enthusiasm or nervousness*).

Übertragung *die* (PL *die* **Übertragungen**) **1** broadcast; **2** transmission.

übertreiben ◇*verb* (IMPERF **übertrieb**, PERF **hat übertrieben**) **1** to exaggerate; **2** to overdo.

Übertreibung *die* (PL *die* **Übertreibungen**) exaggeration.

überwältigend *adjective* overwhelming.

überweisen ◇*verb* (IMPERF **überwies**, PERF **hat überwiesen**) **1** to transfer; **2** to refer (*a patient*).

überzeugen *verb* (PERF **hat überzeugt**) **1** to convince; **2 sich selbst überzeugen** to satisfy yourself.

überzeugend *adjective* convincing.

Überzeugung *die* (PL *die* **Überzeugungen**) conviction.

überziehen[1] ◇*verb* (IMPERF **zog über**, PERF **hat übergezogen**) to put on (*a cardigan, jacket*).

überziehen[2] ◇*verb* (IMPERF **überzog**, PERF **hat überzogen**) **1** to overdraw; **2** to cover (*with icing, for example*).

üblich *adjective* usual.

U-Boot *das* (PL *die* **U-Boote**) submarine.

übrig *adjective* **1** remaining; **2 übrig sein** to be left over; **3 etwas übrig lassen** to leave something (over); **4 uns blieb nichts anderes übrig** we had no other choice; **5 alles Übrige** the rest; **die Übrigen** the others; **6 im Übrigen** besides.

übrigens *adverb* by the way.

übriglassen SEE **übrig**.

Übung *die* (PL *die* **Übungen**) **1** exercise; **2** practice; **aus der Übung sein** to be out of practice.

Ufer *das* (PL *die* **Ufer**) **1** bank (*of a river*); **2** shore.

Uhr *die* (PL *die* **Uhren**) **1** clock; **2** watch; **3** (*in time phrases*) es ist ein Uhr it's one o'clock; wie viel Uhr ist es? what's the time?; um

a
b
c
d
e
f
g
h
i
j
k
l
m
n
o
p
q
r
s
t
u
v
w
x
y
z

a

b **sechzehn Uhr** at four o'clock (in the afternoon).

Uhrzeiger der (PL die **Uhrzeiger**) hand (of a clock or watch).

c

d **Uhrzeigersinn** der im **Uhrzeigersinn** clockwise;

e **entgegen dem Uhrzeigersinn** anti-clockwise.

f **Uhrzeit** die time; **jemanden nach der Uhrzeit fragen** to ask somebody the time.

g

h **ulkig** adjective funny.

i **um** preposition (+ ACC) **1** round, around; **um das Haus herum** around the house; **2** at; **um fünf Uhr** at five o'clock; **3** around (about); **4** for; **um etwas bitten** to ask for something; **um seinetwillen** for his sake; **5 sich um jemanden sorgen** to worry about somebody; **6** by (indicating difference); **um vieles besser** better by far; **um so besser** so much the better.

j

k

l

m

n

o **um** adverb **1** about, around; **um die dreihundert Euro herum** about three hundred euros; **um Weihnachten** around Christmas; **2 um sein** (informal) to be over.

p

q

r

s **um** conjunction **um zu** (in order to); **er ist noch zu klein, um in die Schule zu gehen** he's too young to go to school.

t

u **umarmen** verb (PERF hat umarmt) to hug.

v **Umbau** der (PL die **Umbauten**) **1** renovation; **2** conversion.

w

x **umbinden** ◇verb (IMPERF band um, PERF hat umgebunden) to put on.

y

z

umblättern verb (PERF hat umgeblättert) to turn over.

umbringen ◇verb (IMPERF brachte um, PERF hat umgebracht) to kill.

umdrehen verb (PERF hat umgedreht) **1** to turn (round); **2 sich umdrehen** to turn round, to turn over.

umfallen ◇verb (PRES fällt um, IMPERF fiel um, PERF ist umgefallen) to fall down.

Umfrage die (PL die **Umfragen**) survey.

umgänglich adjective sociable.

Umgangsformen plural noun manners.

Umgangssprache die slang, colloquial language.

umgeben ◇verb (PRES umgibt, IMPERF umgab, PERF hat umgeben) to surround.

Umgebung die (PL die **Umgebungen**) **1** surroundings; **2** neighbourhood.

umgehen[1] ◇verb (IMPERF ging um, PERF ist umgegangen) **1** to go round (of a rumour, an illness); **2 mit jemandem streng umgehen** to treat somebody strictly; **3 er kann mit Geld nicht umgehen** he can't handle money; **mit seinen Sachen sorgfältig umgehen** to handle one's things carefully.

umgehen[2] ◇verb (IMPERF umging, PERF hat umgangen) to avoid.

Umgehungsstraße die (PL die **Umgehungsstraßen**) bypass.

umgekehrt adjective **1** opposite; **2** reverse (order); **3 es war**

umgekehrt it was the other way round.

umgekehrt *adverb* **1 und umgekehrt** and vice versa; **2** the other way round; **warum machst du es nicht umgekehrt?** why don't you do it the other way round?

umkehren *verb* (PERF **ist umgekehrt**) **1** to turn back; **nach zehn Minuten sind wir wieder umgekehrt** ten minutes later we turned back again; **2** to turn round (*a picture, book*); **3** to turn inside out (*a bag, for example*); **4 sie hat das ganze Zimmer umgekehrt** (*informal*) she turned the whole room upside down.

Umkleidekabine *die* (PL *die* **Umkleidekabinen**) changing cubicle.

Umkleideraum *der* (PL *die* **Umkleideräume**) changing room.

umkommen ◇*verb* (IMPERF **kam um**, PERF **ist umgekommen**) to be killed.

Umlaut *der* (PL *die* **Umlaute**) umlaut.

umlegen *verb* (PERF **hat umgelegt**) **1** to put on (*a scarf*); **2** to transfer (*a patient, call*); **3** jemanden umlegen (*informal*) to bump somebody off.

Umleitung *die* (PL *die* **Umleitungen**) diversion.

umrechnen *verb* (PERF **hat umgerechnet**) to convert.

Umrechnung *die* conversion.

Umrechnungskurs *der* exchange rate.

Umriss *der* (PL die **Umrisse**) outline.

umrühren *verb* (PERF **hat umgerührt**) to stir.

ums = **um das**.

umschalten *verb* (PERF **hat umgeschaltet**) **1** to turn over; **vom ersten aufs zweite Programm umschalten** to turn from channel one to channel two; **2 auf Rot umschalten** to change to red.

Umschlag *der* (PL *die* **Umschläge**) **1** envelope; **2** cover.

umsehen ◇*verb* (PRES **sieht sich um**, IMPERF **sah sich um**, PERF **hat sich umgesehen**) **sich umsehen** to look round.

umso *adverb* **umso besser** all the better; **je mehr, umso besser** the more the better.

umsonst *adverb* **1** in vain; **2** free, for nothing.

Umstand *der* (PL *die* **Umstände**) **1** circumstance; **unter diesen Umständen** under these circumstances; **2 unter Umständen** possibly; **3** jemandem Umstände machen to put somebody to trouble; **das macht gar keine Umstände** it's no trouble at all; **4 in anderen Umständen sein** to be pregnant.

umständlich *adjective* **1** laborious; **2** complicated.

umsteigen ◇*verb* (IMPERF **stieg um**, PERF **ist umgestiegen**) to change.

umstellen[1] *verb* (PERF **hat umgestellt**) **1** to rearrange; **2** to

a
b
c
d
e
f
g
h
i
j
k
l
m
n
o
p
q
r
s
t

v
w
x
y
z

a reset; **3** to change over; **4** sich
umstellen to adjust.

b
c umstellen² *verb* (PERF hat
umstellt) to surround.

d Umtausch *der* exchange.

e umtauschen *verb* (PERF hat
umgetauscht) to change, to

f exchange.

g unartig *adjective* naughty.

Umweg *der* (PL die Umwege)
detour.

h Umwelt *die* environment.

i umweltfeindlich *adjective*
environmentally unfriendly.

j umweltfreundlich *adjective*
environmentally friendly.

k
l Umweltschützer *der* (PL die
Umweltschützer)
environmentalist.

m Umweltschützerin *die* (PL die
Umweltschützerinnen)

n environmentalist.

Umweltverschmutzung *die*
o pollution.

p umwerfen ⬦ *verb* (PRES wirft um,
IMPERF warf um, PERF hat

q umgeworfen) **1** to knock over; **2** to
upset (*a plan*); das hat mich

r umgeworfen it's thrown me.

s umwerfend *adjective* fantastic.

umziehen ⬦ *verb* (IMPERF zog um,
u PERF ist umgezogen) **1** to move; sie
ziehen nächste Woche um they're

v moving next week; **2** (PERF hat
umgezogen) to change; **3** (PERF hat

w sich umgezogen) sich umziehen
to get changed.

x
y Umzug *der* (PL die Umzüge) **1** move;

z **2** procession.

unabhängig *adjective*
independent.

Unabhängigkeit *die*
independence.

unangenehm *adjective*
1 unpleasant; **2** embarrassing
(*question, situation*).

unartig *adjective* naughty.

unbedeutend *adjective*
insignificant.

unbedeutend *adverb* slightly.

unbedingt *adjective* absolute.

unbedingt *adverb* really; ich
muss ihn unbedingt sprechen I
really must talk to him; nicht
unbedingt not necessarily.

unbefriedigend *adjective*
unsatisfactory.

unbefriedigt *adjective*
unsatisfied.

unbegrenzt *adjective* unlimited.

unbehaglich *adjective*
1 uncomfortable; **2** uneasy.

unbekannt *adjective* unknown.

unbeliebt *adjective* unpopular.

unbequem *adjective*
uncomfortable.

unbestimmt *adjective*
1 indefinite; auf unbestimmte Zeit
for an indefinite period;
2 uncertain.

unbestimmt *adverb* vaguely;
etwas unbestimmt lassen to leave
something open.

unbewusst *adjective*
unconscious.

und *conjunction* and; und so weiter
and so on; na und? so what?

undankbar *adjective* ungrateful.

undeutlich *adjective* unclear.

undicht *adjective* leaking, leaky;
eine undichte Stelle a leak.

uneben *adjective* uneven.

unehrlich *adjective* dishonest.

unempfindlich *adjective* 1 hard-
wearing, easy-care; 2 immune;
gegen Kälte unempfindlich sein
not to feel the cold.

unentbehrlich *adjective*
indispensable.

unentschieden *adjective*
undecided; unentschieden spielen
to draw.

unerträglich *adjective*
unbearable.

unerwartet *adjective* unexpected.

unfähig *adjective* 1 incompetent;
2 unfähig sein, etwas zu tun to be
incapable of doing something.

unfair *adjective* unfair.

Unfall *der* (PL die **Unfälle**) accident.

unfreundlich *adjective*
unfriendly.

Unfug *der* 1 nonsense; 2 mischief;
Unfug machen to get up to
mischief.

Ungar *der* (PL die **Ungarn**)
Hungarian.

Ungarin *die* (PL die **Ungarinnen**)
Hungarian.

ungarisch *adjective* Hungarian.

Ungarn *das* Hungary.

Ungeduld *die* impatience.

ungeduldig *adjective* impatient.

ungeeignet *adjective* unsuitable.

ungefähr *adjective* approximate.

ungefähr *adverb* approximately,
about.

ungefährlich *adjective* safe,
harmless.

Ungeheuer *das* (PL die
Ungeheuer) monster.

ungeheuer *adjective* enormous.

ungehorsam *adjective*
disobedient.

ungelegen *adjective*
inconvenient.

ungemütlich *adjective*
uncomfortable.

ungenau *adjective* 1 inaccurate;
2 vague.

ungenießbar *adjective* 1 inedible;
2 undrinkable; 3 Bernd ist heute
aber ungenießbar (*informal*)
Bernd is quite unbearable today.

ungenügend *adjective*
1 insufficient; 2 unsatisfactory
(*mark at school*).

ungerade *adjective* eine
ungerade Zahl an odd number.

ungerecht *adjective* unjust.

ungern *adverb* reluctantly.

ungeschickt *adjective* clumsy.

ungesund *adjective* unhealthy.

ungewöhnlich *adjective*
unusual.

Ungeziefer *das* vermin.

ungezwungen *adjective*
1 informal; 2 natural.

unglaublich *adjective* incredible.

Unglück *das* (PL die **Unglücke**)
1 accident; 2 misfortune; 3 bad

a

b

c

d

e

f

g

h

i

j

k

l

m

n

o

p

q

r

s

t

u

v

w

x

y

z

luck; **das bringt Unglück** that's unlucky.

unglücklich *adjective* **1** unhappy; **2** unfortunate.

unglücklicherweise *adverb* unfortunately.

unheilbar *adjective* incurable.

unheimlich *adjective* eerie.

unheimlich *adverb* **1** eerily; **2** (*informal*) incredibly; **unheimlich viel** an incredible amount.

unhöflich *adjective* impolite.

Uniform *die* (PL *die* **Uniformen**) uniform.

uninteressant *adjective* uninteresting.

Universität *die* (PL *die* **Universitäten**) university.

Unkenntnis *die* ignorance.

unklar *adjective* unclear.

Unkosten *plural noun* expenses.

Unkraut *das* weed.

unleserlich *adjective* illegible.

unlogisch *adjective* illogical.

unmittelbar *adjective* immediate, direct.

unmodern *adjective* old-fashioned.

unmöglich *adjective* impossible.

Unmöglichkeit *die* impossibility.

unnötig *adjective* unnecessary.

unordentlich *adjective* untidy.

Unordnung *die* **1** disorder; **2** mess.

unpraktisch *adjective* impractical.

unpünktlich *adjective* unpunctual; **unpünktlich sein** to be late.

Unrecht *das* **1** wrong; **zu Unrecht** wrongly; **Unrecht haben** to be wrong; **2 jemandem Unrecht geben** to disagree with somebody.

unrecht *adjective* wrong; **jemandem unrecht tun** to do somebody an injustice.

unregelmäßig *adjective* irregular.

unreif *adjective* **1** unripe; **2** immature.

Unruhe *die* (PL *die* **Unruhen**) **1** restlessness; **2** agitation; **3 Unruhen** unrest.

Unruhestifter *der* (PL *die* **Unruhestifter**) troublemaker.

unruhig *adjective* restless.

uns *pronoun* **1** us; **gib es uns** give it to us; **sie kommen mit uns** they're coming with us; **2** ourselves; **wir waschen uns die Hände** we are washing our hands; **3** each other; **wir kennen uns** we know each other.

unscharf *adjective* blurred, indistinct.

unschuldig *adjective* innocent.

unser *pronoun* our.

unserer, unsere, unser(e)s *pronoun* ours.

unsertwegen *adverb* **1** for our sake; **2** because of us; **3** as far as we're concerned.

unsicher *adjective* **1** uncertain; **2** insecure.

unsicher adverb unsteadily.

unsichtbar adjective invisible.

Unsinn der nonsense.

unsrer SEE unserer.

unsympathisch adjective unpleasant; **er ist mir unsympathisch** I don't like Tobias.

unten adverb **1** at the bottom; **2** underneath; **3** downstairs; **hier unten** down here; **nach unten** down.

unter preposition (+ DAT or + ACC with movement towards a place) **1** under, below; **2** among; **unter anderem** among other things; **3 unter sich** by themselves; **unter uns gesagt** between ourselves; **4 unter der Woche** during the week.

Unterbewusstsein das subconscious.

unterbrechen ⋄verb (PRES unterbricht, IMPERF unterbrach, PERF hat unterbrochen) to interrupt.

Unterbrechung die (PL die Unterbrechungen) interruption.

unterbringen ⋄verb (IMPERF brachte unter, PERF hat untergebracht) **1** to put; **2** to put up (a guest).

untere SEE unterer.

untereinander adverb **1** among ourselves/yourselves/themselves; **2** one below the other.

unterer, untere, unteres adjective lower.

Unterführung die (PL die Unterführungen) subway.

untergehen ⋄verb (IMPERF ging unter, PERF ist untergegangen) **1** to set (of the sun); **2** to sink, to drown; **3** to come to an end.

Untergrundbahn die (PL die Untergrundbahnen) underground.

unterhalb preposition (+ GEN) below.

unterhalten ⋄verb (PRES unterhält, IMPERF unterhielt, PERF hat unterhalten) **1** to support; **2** to run (a hotel, leisure centre); **3** to entertain; **4 sich über etwas unterhalten** to talk about something; **5 sich unterhalten** to enjoy yourself.

unterhaltsam adjective entertaining.

Unterhaltung die (PL die Unterhaltungen) **1** conversation; **2** entertainment.

Unterhemd das (PL die Unterhemden) vest.

Unterhose die (PL die Unterhosen) underpants.

Unterkunft die (PL die Unterkünfte) accommodation.

Unterlagen plural noun documents, papers.

Untermieter der (PL die Untermieter) lodger.

Untermieterin die (PL die Untermieterinnen) lodger.

unternehmen ⋄verb (PRES unternimmt, IMPERF unternahm, PERF hat unternommen) **1** to undertake; **2 nichts unternehmen**

a b c d e f g h i j k l m n o p q r s t u v w x y z

a to do nothing; **was unternehmt ihr heute?** what are you doing today?

b **Unternehmen** das (PL die Unternehmen) **1** enterprise; **2** concern.

c **Unterricht** der **1** lessons; **heute haben wir keinen Unterricht** we've got no lessons today; **2** teaching.

d **unterrichten** verb (PERF hat unterrichtet) **1** to teach; **2** to inform; **3 sich unterrichten** to inform yourself.

e **Unterrichtsfach** das (PL die Unterrichtsfächer) subject.

f **Unterrock** der (PL die Unterröcke) slip.

g **unterscheiden** ◊verb (IMPERF unterschied, PERF hat unterschieden) **1** to distinguish, to tell apart; **2 sich unterscheiden** to differ.

h **Unterschied** der (PL die Unterschiede) difference.

i **unterschiedlich** adjective different; **das ist unterschiedlich** it varies.

j **unterschreiben** ◊verb (IMPERF unterschrieb, PERF hat unterschrieben) to sign.

k **Unterschrift** die (PL die Unterschriften) signature.

l **Unterseeboot** das (PL die Unterseeboote) submarine.

m **unterster, unterste, unterstes** adjective bottom, lowest.

n **unterstreichen** ◊verb (IMPERF unterstrich, PERF hat unterstrichen) to underline.

unterstützen verb (PERF hat unterstützt) to support.

Unterstützung die support.

untersuchen verb (PERF hat untersucht) **1** to examine; **2** to investigate.

Untersuchung die (PL die Untersuchungen) **1** examination, check-up; **2** investigation.

Untertasse die (PL die Untertassen) saucer.

Untertitel der (PL die Untertitel) subtitle.

Unterwäsche die underwear.

unterwegs adverb on the way; **den ganzen Tag unterwegs sein** to be out all day.

untreu adjective **1** unfaithful; **2** disloyal.

untüchtig adjective **1** inefficient; **2** incompetent.

ununterbrochen adjective uninterrupted.

unverbleit adjective unleaded.

unvergleichlich adjective incomparable.

unverheiratet adjective unmarried.

unverkäuflich adjective not for sale; **ein unverkäufliches Muster** a free sample.

unverschämt adjective impertinent.

unverständlich adjective incomprehensible.

unverzüglich adjective promptly; **bitte antworten Sie unverzüglich** please reply promptly.

unvorsichtig *adjective* careless.

unwahr *adjective* untrue.

unwahrscheinlich *adjective*
1 unlikely; **2** incredible.

unwahrscheinlich *adverb*
(*informal*) incredibly;
unwahrscheinlich schön
incredibly beautiful.

Unwetter *das* (PL *die* **Unwetter**)
storm.

unwichtig *adjective* unimportant.

unzählig *adjective* countless.

unzerbrechlich *adjective*
unbreakable.

unzertrennlich *adjective*
inseparable.

unzufrieden *adjective*
dissatisfied.

üppig *adjective* lavish.

uralt *adjective* ancient.

Urenkel *der* (PL *die* **Urenkel**) great-
grandson; **die Urenkel** the great-
grandchildren.

Urenkelin *die* (PL *die*
Urenkelinnen) great-
granddaughter.

Urkunde *die* (PL *die* **Urkunden**)
certificate.

Urlaub *der* (PL *die* **Urlaube**) holiday;
Urlaub haben to be on holiday; **auf/
im Urlaub** on holiday.

Urlauber *der* (PL *die* **Urlauber**)
holidaymaker.

Ursache *die* (PL *die* **Ursachen**)
cause; **keine Ursache!** don't
mention it!

Ursprung *der* (PL *die* **Ursprünge**)
origin.

ursprünglich *adjective* original.

ursprünglich *adverb* originally.

Urteil *das* (PL *die* **Urteile**)
1 judgement; **2** opinion; **3** verdict.

urteilen *verb* (PERF **hat geurteilt**)
to judge.

Urwald *der* (PL *die* **Urwälder**)
jungle.

USA *plural noun* USA.

usw. (*und so weiter*) etc.

Vv

vage *adjective* vague.

Vagina *die* (PL *die* **Vaginen**) vagina.

Valentinskarte *die* (PL *die*
Valentinskarten) valentine card.

Valentinstag *der* Valentine's Day.

Vanille *die* vanilla.

Variante *die* (PL *die* **Varianten**)
variety.

Vase *die* (PL *die* **Vasen**) vase.

Vater *der* (PL *die* **Väter**) father.

Vaterunser *das* Lord's Prayer.

Vati *der* (PL *die* **Vatis**) dad.

Veganer *der* (PL *die* **Veganer**)
vegan.

Vegetarier *der* (PL *die* **Vegetarier**)
vegetarian.

Vegetarierin *die* (PL *die*
Vegetarierinnen) vegetarian.

vegetarisch *adjective* vegetarian.

Veilchen *das* (PL *die* **Veilchen**)
violet.

Vene *die* (PL *die* **Venen**) vein.

Ventil das (PL die **Ventile**) valve.

Ventilator der (PL die **Ventilatoren**) fan.

verabreden verb (PERF hat verabredet) **1** to arrange; **was habt ihr verabredet?** what did you arrange?; **mit jemandem verabredet sein** to have arranged to meet somebody; **Laura ist mit Frank verabredet** Laura has a date with Frank; **2 sich mit jemandem verabreden** to arrange to meet somebody; **ich habe mich mit Oliver zum Tennis verabredet** I've arranged to play tennis with Oliver.

Verabredung die (PL die **Verabredungen**) **1** appointment; **2** date; **3** arrangement.

verabschieden verb (PERF hat verabschiedet) **1** to say goodbye to; **2 sich verabschieden** to say goodbye.

Verachtung die contempt.

verallgemeinern verb (PERF hat verallgemeinert) to generalize.

veralten verb (PERF ist veraltet) to become obsolete.

veränderlich adjective changeable.

verändern verb (PERF hat verändert) **1** to change; **2 sich verändern** to change.

Veränderung die (PL die **Veränderungen**) change.

veranstalten verb (PERF hat veranstaltet) to organize.

Veranstalter der (PL die **Veranstalter**) organizer.

Veranstaltung die (PL die **Veranstaltungen**) event.

verantwortlich adjective responsible.

Verantwortung die responsibility.

verantwortungsbewusst adjective responsible.

verantwortungslos adjective irresponsible.

verarbeiten verb (PERF hat verarbeitet) **1** to process; **etwas zu etwas verarbeiten** to make something into something; **2** to digest (food, information).

Verarbeitung die **1** use; **2** digestion; **3** processing of data.

verärgern verb (PERF hat verärgert) to annoy.

Verb das (PL die **Verben**) verb.

Verband der (PL die **Verbände**) **1** association; **sich zu einem Verband zusammenschließen** to form an associaton; **2** bandage, dressing; **einen Verband anlegen** to apply a dressing.

verband SEE **verbinden**.

verbergen ◇verb (PRES verbirgt, IMPERF verbarg, PERF hat verborgen) **1** to hide; **2 sich verbergen** to hide.

verbessern verb (PERF hat verbessert) **1** to improve; **2** to correct; **3 sich verbessern** to improve.

Verbesserung die (PL die **Verbesserungen**) **1** improvement; **2** correction.

verbiegen ◇*verb* (IMPERF **verbog**, PERF **hat verbogen**) **1** to bend; **2 sich verbiegen** to bend.

verbieten ◇*verb* (IMPERF **verbot**, PERF **hat verboten**) **1** to forbid; **sie hat ihm verboten, das Haus zu betreten** she forbade him to enter the house; **meine Eltern verbieten mir, am Abend wegzugehen** my parents don't allow me to go out in the evening; **2** to ban.

verbilligt *adjective* reduced.

verbinden ◇*verb* (IMPERF **verband**, PERF **hat verbunden**) **1** to connect, to join; **2** to combine; **3** to bandage, to dress (*a wound*); **jemandem die Augen verbinden** to blindfold somebody; **4 jemanden verbinden** to put somebody through (*on the phone*); **ich verbinde** I'm putting you through.

verbindlich *adjective* **1** friendly; **2** binding (*agreement, decision*).

Verbindung die (PL die **Verbindungen**) **1** connection; **2 gute Verbindungen haben** to have good contacts; **sich mit jemandem in Verbindung setzen** to get in touch with somebody; **3** combination; **4 eine chemische Verbindung** a chemical compound.

verbirgt SEE **verbergen**.

verbleit *adjective* leaded.

verblüffen *verb* (PERF **hat verblüfft**) to amaze.

verbog SEE **verbiegen**.

verbogen *adjective* hidden.

Verbot das (PL die **Verbote**) ban.

verbot SEE **verbieten**.

verboten *adjective* forbidden; **'Rauchen verboten'** 'no smoking'.

verbracht, **verbrachte** SEE **verbringen**.

verbrannt, **verbrannte** SEE **verbrennen**.

Verbrauch der consumption.

verbrauchen *verb* (PERF **hat verbraucht**) to use, to use up; **die Waschmaschine verbraucht nicht viel Strom** the washing machine doesn't use up much electricity.

Verbraucher der (PL die **Verbraucher**) consumer.

Verbrechen das (PL die **Verbrechen**) crime.

Verbrecher der (PL die **Verbrecher**) criminal.

verbreiten *verb* (PERF **hat verbreitet**) **1** to spread; **eine Krankheit verbreiten** to spread an illness; **2 eine Meldung über den Rundfunk verbreiten** to broadcast a message; **3 sich verbreiten** to spread; **die Neuigkeit hat sich schnell verbreitet** the news spread quickly.

verbreitet *adjective* widespread.

verbrennen ◇*verb* (IMPERF **verbrannte**, PERF **ist verbrannt**) **1** to burn; **2** (PERF **hat verbrannt**) to burn (*rubbish, leaves*); **3** (PERF **hat verbrannt**) to cremate; **4** (PERF **hat verbrannt**) **sich die Hand verbrennen** to burn your hand.

verbringen ◇*verb* (IMPERF **verbrachte**, PERF **hat verbracht**) to spend; **wir haben schöne Ferien in**

Bayern **verbracht** we spent a nice holiday in Bavaria.

verbunden SEE **verbinden**.

Verdacht der suspicion.

verdächtig *adjective* suspicious.

verdächtigen *verb* (PERF **hat verdächtigt**) to suspect.

verdammt *adjective, adverb* (*informal*) damned; **verdammt!** damn!

verdarb SEE **verderben**.

Verdauung die digestion.

verderben ◇*verb* (PRES **verdirbt**, IMPERF **verdarb**, PERF **hat verdorben**) **1** to spoil, to ruin; **das hat mir den Abend verdorben** it ruined the evening for me; **ich habe mir den Magen verdorben** I have an upset stomach; **2 es sich mit jemandem verderben** to get into somebody's bad books; **3** (PERF **ist verdorben**) to go off; **die Milch verdirbt, wenn du sie nicht in den Kühlschrank stellst** the milk will go off if you don't put it in the fridge.

verdienen *verb* (PERF **hat verdient**) **1** to earn; **2** to deserve.

Verdienst der (PL die **Verdienste**) **1** salary; **2** achievement.

verdirbt SEE **verderben**.

verdoppeln *verb* (PERF **hat verdoppelt**) **1** to double; **2 sich verdoppeln** to double.

verdorben SEE **verderben**.

verdünnen *verb* (PERF **hat verdünnt**) to dilute.

verehren *verb* (PERF **hat verehrt**) to worship.

Verehrer der (PL die **Verehrer**) admirer.

Verehrerin die (PL die **Verehrerinnen**) admirer.

Verein der (PL die **Vereine**) **1** society; **2** organization; **3** club.

vereinbaren *verb* (PERF **hat vereinbart**) to arrange.

Vereinbarung die (PL die **Vereinbarungen**) **1** agreement; **2** arrangement.

vereinfachen *verb* (PERF **hat vereinfacht**) to simplify.

vereinigen *verb* (PERF **hat vereinigt**) to unite; **ein Land wieder vereinigen** to reunify a country.

Vereinigte Staaten *plural noun* United States.

Vereinigung die (PL die **Vereinigungen**) organization.

verfahren ◇*verb* (PRES **verfährt**, IMPERF **verfuhr**, PERF **ist verfahren**) **1** to proceed; **2 ich habe mich verfahren** I've lost my way.

verfallen ◇*verb* (PRES **verfällt**, IMPERF **verfiel**, PERF **ist verfallen**) **1** to decay; **2** to expire (*of a passport or ticket*).

Verfallsdatum das (PL die **Verfallsdaten**) use-by date.

Verfassung die (PL die **Verfassungen**) **1** constitution; **2** state (*of a person*).

verfaulen *verb* (PERF **ist verfault**) to rot.

verfiel SEE **verfallen**.

verfolgen verb (PERF **hat verfolgt**) 1 to follow; 2 to persecute.

Verfolgung die (PL die **Verfolgungen**) 1 pursuit, hunt; 2 persecution.

verfügbar adjective available.

Verfügung die **jemandem etwas zur Verfügung stellen** to put something at somebody's disposal; **jemandem zur Verfügung stehen** to be at somebody's disposal.

verfuhr SEE **verfahren**.

verführen verb (PERF **hat verführt**) 1 to tempt; 2 to seduce.

Verführung die (PL die **Verführungen**) 1 temptation; 2 seduction.

vergab SEE **vergeben**.

vergangen verb SEE **vergehen**

vergangen adjective last.

Vergangenheit die 1 past; 2 past tense.

vergaß SEE **vergessen**.

vergeben ◇verb (PRES **vergibt**, IMPERF **vergab**, PERF **hat vergeben**) 1 to forgive; **jemandem etwas vergeben** to forgive somebody for something; 2 to give away, to award; 3 **vergeben sein** to be taken; **das Zimmer ist schon vergeben** the room's already taken.

vergeblich adverb in vain.

vergehen ◇verb (IMPERF **verging**, PERF **ist vergangen**) to pass.

vergessen ◇verb (PRES **vergisst**, IMPERF **vergaß**, PERF **hat vergessen**) to forget.

vergesslich adjective forgetful.

vergewaltigen verb (PERF **hat vergewaltigt**) to rape.

Vergewaltigung die (PL die **Vergewaltigungen**) rape.

vergibt SEE **vergeben**.

vergiften verb (PERF **hat vergiftet**) to poison.

verging SEE **vergehen**.

vergisst SEE **vergessen**.

Vergleich der (PL die **Vergleiche**) comparison.

vergleichen ◇verb (IMPERF **verglich**, PERF **hat verglichen**) to compare.

Vergnügen das (PL die **Vergnügen**) pleasure; **viel Vergnügen!** have fun!

vergnügen verb (PERF **hat sich vergnügt**) **sich vergnügen** to have fun.

vergnügt adjective cheerful.

vergrößern verb (PERF **hat vergrößert**) 1 to enlarge; 2 to increase; 3 to magnify; 4 to extend (a room, building); 5 **sich vergrößern** to expand, to grow bigger.

Vergrößerung die (PL die **Vergrößerungen**) 1 expansion; 2 enlargement (of a photograph).

verhaften verb (PERF **hat verhaftet**) to arrest; **er ist verhaftet worden** he was arrested.

a
b
c
d
e
f
g
h
i
j
k
l
m
n
o
p
q
r
s
t
u
v
w
x
y
z

verhalten ◇*verb* (PRES **verhält sich**, IMPERF **verhielt sich**, PERF **hat sich verhalten**) **sich verhalten** to behave.

Verhalten *das* behaviour.

Verhältnis *das* (PL die **Verhältnisse**) **1** relationship; **sie hat ein gutes Verhältnis zu ihren Eltern** she has a good relationship with her parents; **2** affair; **Gabi hat ein Verhältnis mit einem verheirateten Mann** Gabi is having an affair with a married man; **3** ratio (*in maths*); **4 in keinem Verhältnis zu etwas stehen** to be out of all proportion to something; **5 Verhältnisse** conditions; **über seine Verhältnisse leben** to live beyond your means.

verhältnismäßig *adverb* relatively.

verhandeln *verb* (PERF **hat verhandelt**) to negotiate; **über etwas verhandeln** to negotiate something.

Verhandlung *die* (PL die **Verhandlungen**) **1** negotiation; **2** hearing; **3** trial.

verhauen *verb* (PERF **hat verhauen**) **1** to beat up; **2 die Prüfung verhauen** (*informal*) to make a mess of the exam.

verheimlichen *verb* (PERF **hat verheimlicht**) to keep secret.

verheiratet *adjective* married.

verhext *adjective* bewitched.

verhielt SEE **verhalten**.

verhindern *verb* (PERF **hat verhindert**) **1** to prevent;

2 verhindert sein to be unable to make it; **Petra ist verhindert** Petra won't be able to make it.

verhungern *verb* (PERF **ist verhungert**) to starve.

Verhütungsmittel *das* (PL die **Verhütungsmittel**) contraceptive.

verirren *verb* (PERF **hat sich verirrt**) **sich verirren** to get lost.

verkam SEE **verkommen**.

Verkauf *der* (PL die **Verkäufe**) sale; **zum Verkauf** for sale.

verkaufen *verb* (PERF **hat verkauft**) to sell; **zu verkaufen** for sale.

Verkäufer *der* (PL die **Verkäufer**) **1** seller; **2** sales assistant.

Verkäuferin *die* (PL die **Verkäuferinnen**) **1** seller; **2** sales assistant.

Verkaufsautomat *der* (PL die **Verkauufsautomaten**) vending machine.

Verkehr *der* traffic.

Verkehrsampel *die* (PL die **Verkehrsampeln**) traffic lights.

Verkehrsamt *das* (PL die **Verkehrsämter**) tourist office.

Verkehrsinsel *die* (PL die **Verkehrsinseln**) traffic island.

Verkehrsunfall *der* (PL die **Verkehrsunfälle**) road accident.

Verkehrszeichen *das* (PL die **Verkehrszeichen**) traffic sign, road sign.

verkehrt *adjective* **1** wrong; **2 verkehrt herum** inside out, the wrong way round.

a
b
c
d
e
f
g
h
i
j
k
l
m
n
o
p
q
r
s
t
u
v
w
x
y
z

verklagen verb (PERF hat verklagt) to sue.

verkleiden verb (PERF hat sich verkleidet) sich verkleiden to dress up.

Verkleidung die (PL die Verkleidungen) disguise, fancy dress.

verkommen ◇verb (IMPERF verkam, PERF ist verkommen) 1 to go off (of food); 2 to become dilapidated (of a house); 3 to go to the bad.

verkratzt adjective scratched.

Verlag der (PL die Verlage) publisher's.

verlangen verb (PERF hat verlangt) 1 to ask for, to require; am Telefon verlangt werden to be wanted on the phone; 2 to demand; 3 to charge.

verlängern verb (PERF hat verlängert) 1 to extend; 2 to lengthen; 3 to renew (a passport, driving licence).

Verlängerung die (PL die Verlängerungen) 1 extension; 2 renewal; 3 extra time (in sport).

verlassen[1] ◇verb (PRES verlässt, IMPERF verließ, PERF hat verlassen) 1 to leave; jemanden verlassen to leave somebody; 2 sich auf etwas verlassen to rely on something; du kannst dich auf ihn verlassen you can rely on him.

verlassen[2] adjective deserted.

verlaufen ◇verb (PRES verläuft, IMPERF verlief, PERF ist verlaufen) 1 to go; es ist gut verlaufen it went well; 2 sich verlaufen to lose your way; 3 die Menge verlief sich schnell the crowd quickly dispersed.

verlegen[1] adjective embarrassed.

verlegen[2] verb (PERF hat verlegt) 1 to mislay; 2 to postpone; 3 to publish; 4 to lay (a carpet, cable).

Verlegenheit die embarrassment.

Verleih der (PL die Verleihe) 1 renting out, hiring out; 2 rental firm, hire shop.

verleihen ◇verb (IMPERF verlieh, PERF hat verliehen) 1 to hire out; 2 to lend; 3 to award.

verlernen verb (PERF hat verlernt) to forget.

verletzen verb (PERF hat verletzt) 1 to injure; 2 to hurt; 3 to violate (a law); 4 sich verletzen to hurt yourself.

Verletzte der/die (PL die Verletzten) 1 injured person; 2 casualty.

Verletzung die (PL die Verletzungen) injury.

verlieben verb (PERF hat sich verliebt) sich verlieben to fall in love.

verlief SEE verlaufen.

verlieh SEE verleihen.

verlieren ◇verb (IMPERF verlor, PERF hat verloren) to lose.

verließ SEE verlassen.

verloben verb (PERF hat sich verlobt) sich verloben to get engaged.

a
b
c
d
e
f
g
h
i
j
k
l
m
n
o
p
q
r
s
t
u
v
w
x
y
z

Verlobte der/die (PL die **Verlobten**) fiancé, fiancée.

Verlobung die (PL die **Verlobungen**) engagement.

verlocken verb (PERF hat **verlockt**) to tempt, to entice.

verlor, verloren SEE **verlieren**.

Verlosung die (PL die **Verlosungen**) prize draw.

Verlust der (PL die **Verluste**) loss.

vermeiden ◇ verb (IMPERF **vermied**, PERF hat **vermieden**) to avoid.

vermieten verb (PERF hat **vermietet**) 1 to rent out, to hire out; 2 to let; **Zimmer zu vermieten** rooms to let.

Vermieter der (PL die **Vermieter**) landlord.

Vermieterin die (PL die **Vermieterinnen**) landlady.

vermissen verb (PERF hat **vermisst**) to miss.

Vermittlung die (PL die **Vermittlungen**) 1 arrangement; 2 agency; 3 switchboard; 4 telephone exchange; 5 mediation.

Vermögen das (PL die **Vermögen**) fortune; **ein Vermögen machen** to make a fortune.

vermuten verb (PERF hat **vermutet**) to suspect.

vermutlich adjective probable.

vermutlich adverb probably.

vernachlässigen verb (PERF hat **vernachlässigt**) to neglect.

vernichten verb (PERF hat **vernichtet**) 1 to destroy; 2 to exterminate.

Vernunft die reason.

vernünftig adjective sensible.

verpacken verb (PERF hat **verpackt**) 1 to pack; 2 to wrap up.

Verpackung die (PL die **Verpackungen**) packaging.

verpassen verb (PERF hat **verpasst**) to miss.

verpesten verb, (PERF hat **verpestet**) to pollute.

Verpflegung die food; **Unterkunft und Verpflegung** board and lodging.

verpflichten verb (PERF hat **verpflichtet**) 1 sich verpflichten to promise; 2 sich vertraglich verpflichten to sign a contract; 3 verpflichtet sein, etwas zu tun to be obliged to do something; **jemandem zu Dank verpflichtet sein** to be obliged to somebody; 4 verpflichtend binding.

Verpflichtung die (PL die **Verpflichtungen**) 1 obligation; 2 commitment.

verprügeln verb (PERF hat **verprügelt**) to beat up.

verraten ◇ verb (PRES **verrät**, IMPERF **verriet**, PERF hat **verraten**) 1 to betray; 2 to give away; 3 to tell; 4 sich verraten to give yourself away.

verrechnen verb (PERF hat sich **verrechnet**) sich verrechnen to make a mistake.

verregnet adjective rainy.

verreisen verb (PERF **ist verreist**) to go away; **verreist sein** to be away.

verriet SEE **verraten**.

verrosten verb (PERF **ist verrostet**) to rust.

verrostet adjective rusty.

verrückt adjective mad, crazy.

Verrückte der/die (PL die **Verrückten**) maniac.

versagen verb (PERF **hat versagt**) to fail.

versammeln verb (PERF **hat versammelt**) 1 to assemble; 2 sich **versammeln** to assemble.

Versammlung die (PL die **Versammlungen**) meeting.

versäumen verb (PERF **hat versäumt**) to miss; es **versäumen, etwas zu tun** to fail to do something.

verschenken verb (PERF **hat verschenkt**) to give away.

verschieben ✧verb (IMPERF **verschob**, PERF **hat verschoben**) to postpone.

verschieden adjective 1 different; 2 various.

verschlafen ✧verb (PRES **verschläft**, IMPERF **verschlief**, PERF **hat verschlafen**) 1 to oversleep; 2 to sleep through (the day); 3 to miss (a date, the train).

verschlechtern verb (PERF **hat verschlechtert**) 1 to make worse; 2 sich **verschlechtern** to get worse.

verschlief SEE **verschlafen**.

verschließen ✧verb (IMPERF **verschloss**, PERF **hat verschlossen**) 1 to close (a tin, package); 2 to lock (a door, drawer).

verschlimmern verb (PERF **hat verschlimmert**) 1 to make worse; 2 sich **verschlimmern** to get worse.

verschloss SEE **verschließen**.

verschlucken verb (PERF **hat verschluckt**) 1 to swallow; 2 sich **verschlucken** to choke.

Verschluss der (PL die **Verschlüsse**) 1 fastener, clasp; 2 top (of a bottle).

verschmutzen verb (PERF **hat verschmutzt**) to soil; **die Umwelt verschmutzen** to pollute the environment.

Verschmutzung die pollution.

verschob SEE **verschieben**.

verschreiben ✧verb (IMPERF **verschrieb**, PERF **hat verschrieben**) 1 to prescribe; 2 sich **verschreiben** to make a mistake.

verschütten verb (PERF **hat verschüttet**) to spill.

verschwand SEE **verschwinden**.

verschwenden verb (PERF **hat verschwendet**) to waste.

Verschwendung die waste.

verschwinden ✧verb (IMPERF **verschwand**, PERF **ist verschwunden**) to disappear.

verschwommen adjective blurred.

a b c d e f g h i j k l m n o p q r s t u v w x y z

a

Versehen das (PL die **Versehen**) oversight; **aus Versehen** by mistake.

b

versehentlich adverb by mistake.

c

d

versetzen verb (PERF hat versetzt)
1 to move, to transfer (a person);
2 to move up (into the next class at school); **3** jemanden versetzen to stand somebody up; **4** jemandem einen Schreck versetzen to give somebody a fright; jemandem einen Tritt versetzen to kick somebody; **5** sich in jemandes Lage versetzen to put yourself in somebody's position.

e

f

g

h

i

j

verseuchen verb (PERF hat verseucht) to contaminate.

k

Verseuchung die (PL die **Verseuchungen**) contamination.

l

m

versichern verb (PERF hat versichert) **1** to insure; **2** to assert; jemandem versichern, dass ... to assure somebody that ....

n

o

Versicherung die (PL die **Versicherungen**) **1** insurance; **2** assurance.

p

q

r

Versicherungsgesellschaft die (PL die **Versicherungsgesell-schaften**) insurance company.

s

t

Versicherungsschein der (PL die **Versicherungsscheine**) insurance policy document.

u

v

versöhnen verb (PERF hat sich versöhnt) sich versöhnen to make up; sich mit jemandem versöhnen to make it up with somebody.

w

x

y

z

versorgen verb (PERF hat versorgt) **1** to supply; **2** to provide for; **3** to look after.

verspäten verb (PERF hat sich verspätet) sich verspäten to be late.

Verspätung die lateness, delay; **Verspätung haben** to be late.

versprechen ⬦verb (PRES verspricht, IMPERF versprach, PERF hat versprochen) **1** to promise; **2** sich viel von etwas versprechen to have high hopes of something; **3** sich versprechen to make a slip of the tongue.

Versprechen das (PL die **Versprechen**) promise.

Verstand der **1** mind; **den Verstand verlieren** to go out of your mind; **2** reason.

verstand SEE **verstehen**.

verstanden SEE **verstehen**.

verständigen verb (PERF hat verständigt) **1** to notify; **2** sich verständigen to communicate, to make yourself understood; **3** sich über etwas verständigen to agree on something.

Verständigung die **1** communication; **2** notification.

verständlich adjective **1** understandable; **jemandem etwas verständlich machen** to make something clear to somebody; **2** comprehensible.

Verständnis das (PL die **Verständnisse**) **1** comprehension; **2** understanding.

Verstärker der (PL die **Verstärker**)
amplifier.

verstauchen verb (PERF hat
verstaucht) to sprain; **sich den
Fuß verstauchen** to sprain your
ankle.

Versteck das (PL die **Verstecke**)
hiding place.

verstecken verb (PERF hat
versteckt) **1** to hide; **2 sich
verstecken** to hide.

verstehen ◇verb (IMPERF
verstand, PERF hat verstanden)
1 to understand; **etwas falsch
verstehen** to misunderstand
something; **2 sich gut verstehen** to
get on well; **3 das versteht sich
von selbst** that goes without
saying.

verstellbar adjective adjustable.

verstellen verb (PERF hat
verstellt) **1** to adjust; **2** to block;
3 to disguise; **4 sich verstellen** to
pretend.

verstimmt adjective **1** out of tune;
2 peeved; **3 ein verstimmter
Magen** an upset stomach.

verstopft adjective constipated.

Versuch der (PL die **Versuche**)
1 attempt; **2** experiment.

versuchen verb (PERF hat
versucht) to try.

verteidigen verb (PERF hat
verteidigt) to defend.

Verteidiger der (PL die
Verteidiger) **1** defender; **2** defence
counsel.

Verteidigung die defence.

verteilen verb (PERF hat verteilt)
to distribute.

Vertrag der (PL die **Verträge**)
1 contract; **2** treaty.

vertragen ◇verb (PRES **verträgt**,
IMPERF **vertrug**, PERF **hat vertragen**)
1 to stand, to take; **2 ich vertrage
keinen Kaffee** coffee disagrees
with me; **3 sich vertragen** to get
on; **sich wieder vertragen** to make
it up.

vertrat SEE vertreten.

Vertrauen das trust; **im Vertrauen**
in confidence.

vertrauen verb (PERF hat vertraut)
to trust.

vertraulich adjective
1 confidential; **2** familiar.

vertreten ◇verb (PRES **vertritt**,
IMPERF **vertrat**, PERF **hat vertreten**)
1 to stand in for; **2** to represent;
3 eine Meinung vertreten to hold
an opinion; **4 sich die Beine
vertreten** to stretch your legs.

Vertreter der (PL die **Vertreter**)
1 representative; **2** deputy.

Vertreterin die (PL die
Vertreterinnen) **1** representative;
2 deputy.

vertritt SEE vertreten.

vertrug SEE vertragen.

verunglücken verb (PERF ist
verunglückt) to have an accident.

verursachen verb (PERF hat
verursacht) to cause.

verurteilen verb (PERF hat
verurteilt) **1** to sentence; **2** to
condemn.

a **Verwaltung** die (PL die Verwaltungen) administration.

b **verwandt** adjective related.

c **Verwandte** der/die (PL die Verwandten) relative.

d **Verwandtschaft** die relatives.

e **verwechseln** verb (PERF hat verwechselt) to mix up, to confuse; **jemanden mit jemandem verwechseln** to mistake somebody for somebody; **ich verwechsele ihn mit seinem Bruder** I mistake him for his brother.

verwenden verb (PERF hat verwendet) to use.

Verwendung die use.

verwickelt adjective complicated.

verwirren verb (PERF hat verwirrt) 1 to confuse; 2 to tangle up.

verwirrt adjective confused.

verwöhnen verb (PERF hat verwöhnt) to spoil.

verwunden verb (PERF hat verwundet) to wound.

Verwundete der/die (PL die Verwundeten) casualty, injured person.

Verwundung die (PL die Verwundungen) injury, wound.

verzählen verb (PERF hat sich verzählt) sich verzählen to miscount.

Verzeichnis das (PL die Verzeichnisse) 1 list; 2 index.

verzeihen verb (IMPERF verzieh, PERF hat verziehen) to forgive; **verzeihen Sie, können Sie mir**

sagen ...? excuse me, could you tell me ...?

Verzeihung die forgiveness; **jemanden um Verzeihung bitten** to apologize to somebody; **Verzeihung!** sorry!

verzichten verb (PERF hat verzichtet) 1 to do without; **ich verzichte auf deine Hilfe** I can do without your help; 2 **auf etwas verzichten** to give up something (smoking or your share of something); to relinquish something (a right or privilege).

verzieh, verziehen SEE verzeihen.

verzögern verb (PERF hat verzögert) 1 to delay; 2 **sich verzögern** to be delayed.

Verzögerung die (PL die Verzögerungen) delay.

verzollen verb (PERF hat verzollt) to pay duty on; **haben Sie etwas zu verzollen?** have you anything to declare?

verzweifeln verb (PERF ist verzweifelt) to despair.

verzweifelt adjective desperate.

Verzweiflung die despair.

Vetter der (PL die Vettern) cousin.

Video das (PL die Videos) video.

Videokamera die (PL die Videokameras) video camera.

Videokassette die (PL die Videokassetten) video cassette.

Videorekorder der (PL die Videorekorder) video recorder.

Videospiel das (PL die Videospiele) video game.

Videothek die (PL die Videotheken) video shop.

Vieh das cattle.

viel adjective, pronoun **1** a lot of; **Erika hat viel Arbeit** Erika's got a lot of work; **2 viele** (plural) many, a lot of; **viele Leute** many people; **3** much, a lot; **wie viel?** how much?, how many?; **zu viel** too much; **vielen Dank** thank you very much; **viel Spaß!** have fun!; **viel Glück!** good luck!; **4 das viele Geld** all that money.

viel adverb **1** much, a lot; **viel weniger** much less; **so viel wie möglich** as much as possible; **sie redet viel** she talks a lot; **2 viel zu groß** far too big, much too big; **das dauert viel zu lange** it'll take far too long.

vielleicht adverb perhaps.

vielmals adverb danke vielmals thanks a lot.

vier number four.

Viereck das (PL die Vierecke) **1** rectangle; **2** square.

viereckig adjective **1** rectangular; **2** square.

vierte SEE vierter.

Viertel das (PL die Viertel) quarter; **es ist Viertel vor acht** it's quarter to eight.

viertel adjective quarter; **wir treffen uns um viertel acht** we'll meet at quarter past seven; **um drei viertel acht** at quarter to eight.

Viertelfinale das (PL die Viertelfinale) quarter finals.

Viertelstunde die (PL die Viertelstunden) quarter of an hour.

vierter, vierte, viertes adjective fourth.

vierzehn number fourteen.

vierzig number forty.

Villa die (PL die Villen) villa.

virtuell adjective virtual; **virtuelle Realität** virtual reality.

Virus das (PL die Viren) virus.

visuell adjective visual.

Visum das (PL die Visa) visa.

Vitamin das (PL die Vitamine) vitamin.

vitaminarm adjective low in vitamins.

vitaminreich adjective rich in vitamins.

Vogel der (PL die Vögel) bird.

Vogelbeobachter der (PL die Vogelbeobachter) birdwatcher.

Vogelbeobachterin die (PL die Vogelbeobachterinnen) birdwatcher.

Vogelscheuche die (PL die Vogelscheuchen) scarecrow.

Vokabel die (PL die Vokabeln) word; **Vokabeln** vocabulary.

Vokal der (PL die Vokale) vowel.

Volk das (PL die Völker) people.

Volkshochschule die adult education centre; **ein Kurs an der Volkshochschule** an adult education class.

a

Volkslied das (PL die **Volkslieder**) folk song.

b

Volkswirtschaft die economics.

c

voll adjective **1** full; **ein Korb voll Äpfel** a basket full of apples; **die volle Wahrheit** the whole truth; **2 etwas voll machen** to fill something up; **voll tanken** to fill up with petrol.

d

e

f

voll adverb **1** fully, completely; **voll und ganz** completely; **2 jemanden nicht für voll nehmen** (informal) not to take somebody seriously.

g

h

i

Volleyball der volleyball; **Volleyball spielen** to play volleyball.

j

k

völlig adjective complete.

l

völlig adverb completely.

m

vollkommen adjective **1** perfect; **2** complete.

n

vollkommen adverb completely.

o

Vollkornbrot das wholemeal bread.

p

vollmachen SEE **voll**.

q

Vollpension die full board.

vollständig adjective complete.

r

volltanken SEE **voll**.

s

vom = **von dem**.

t

u

von preposition (+ DAT) **1** from; **von heute an** from today; **von hier bis ... from here to ...**; **2** of; **eine Freundin von mir** a friend of mine; **3** about; **Peter hat mir von dem neuen Haus erzählt** Peter told me about the new house; **4** by; **ein Theaterstück von Brecht** a play by Brecht; **5 von mir aus** I don't mind.

v

w

x

y

z

voneinander adverb from each other; **sie sind voneinander abhängig** they depend on each other.

vor preposition (+ DAT or + ACC with movement towards a place) **1** in front of; **2** before; **Manfred war vor euch da** Manfred arrived before you; **kurz vor der Ampel** shortly before the lights; **3** with; **vor Angst zittern** to tremble with fear; **4** (with clock time) **zehn vor fünf** ten to five; **5** ago; **vor zwei Jahren** two years ago; **6 sich vor jemandem fürchten** to be frightened of somebody; **7 vor allen Dingen** above all; **8 vor sich hin summen** to hum to yourself.

vor adverb forward; **vor und zurück** backwards and forwards.

voraus adverb **1** ahead; **2 im Voraus** in advance.

vorausgehen ◇verb (IMPERF ging voraus, PERF ist vorausgegangen) **1** to go on ahead; **2** to precede.

voraussetzen verb (PERF hat vorausgesetzt) **1** to take for granted; **2** to require; **3 vorausgesetzt, dass ... provided that ...**

Voraussetzung die (PL die **Voraussetzungen**) **1** condition; **2** assumption.

vorbei adverb **1** past; **2** over; **vorbei sein** to be over.

vorbeifahren ◇verb (PRES fährt vorbei, IMPERF fuhr vorbei, PERF ist vorbeigefahren) to drive past, to pass.

vorbeigehen ✧*verb* (IMPERF **ging vorbei**, PERF **ist vorbeigegangen**) **1** to go past, to pass; **2** to drop in; **ich gehe bei Anne vorbei** I'll drop in on Anne.

vorbeikommen ✧*verb* (IMPERF **kam vorbei**, PERF **ist vorbeigekommen**) **1** to pass; **2** to get past; **3** to drop in.

vorbereiten *verb* (PERF **hat vorbereitet**) **1** to prepare; **2 sich vorbereiten** to prepare.

Vorbereitung *die* (PL *die* **Vorbereitungen**) preparation.

vorbeugen *verb* (PERF **hat vorgebeugt**) **1** to prevent; **2 sich vorbeugen** to lean forward.

Vorbild *das* (PL *die* **Vorbilder**) example.

vorderer, vordere, vorderes *adjective* front.

Vordergrund *der* foreground; **im Vordergrund** in the foreground.

Vorderseite *die* front.

vorderster, vorderste, vorderstes *adjective* front.

Vorfahr *der* (PL *die* **Vorfahren**) ancestor.

Vorfahrt *die* right of way; **'Vorfahrt beachten/gewähren'** 'give way'.

Vorfall *der* (PL *die* **Vorfälle**) incident.

Vorführung *die* (PL *die* **Vorführungen**) **1** performance; **2** demonstration.

Vorgänger *der* (PL *die* **Vorgänger**) predecessor.

Vorgängerin *die* (PL *die* **Vorgängerinnen**) predecessor.

vorgehen ✧*verb* (IMPERF **ging vor**, PERF **ist vorgegangen**) **1** to go on ahead; **2** to go forward; **3** to proceed; **4 die Uhr geht vor** the clock is fast; **5 was geht hier vor?** what's going on here?

Vorgehensweise *die* (PL *die* **Vorgehensweisen**) policy.

vorgestern *adverb* the day before yesterday.

vorhaben ✧*verb* (PRES **hat vor**, IMPERF **hatte vor**, PERF **hat vorgehabt**) **1** to intend; **2 etwas vorhaben** to have something planned.

Vorhang *der* (PL *die* **Vorhänge**) curtain.

Vorhängeschloss *das* (PL *die* **Vorhängeschlösser**) padlock.

vorher *adverb* beforehand, before.

Vorhersage *die* (PL *die* **Vorhersagen**) **1** forecast; **2** prediction.

vorhin *adverb* just now.

voriger, vorige, voriges *adjective* last.

vorkommen ✧*verb* (IMPERF **kam vor**, PERF **ist vorgekommen**) **1** to happen; **2** to occur; **3** to come forward; **4** to come out (*from behind somewhere*); **5** to seem; **jemandem bekannt vorkommen** to seem familiar to somebody; **6 sich alt vorkommen** to feel old.

Vorlauf *der* fast forward (*on video*).

vorläufig *adjective* temporary.

vorlesen ✧*verb* (PRES **liest vor**, IMPERF **las vor**, PERF **hat vorgelesen**)

a
b
c
d
e
f
g
h
i
j
k
l
m
n
o
p
q
r
s
t
u
v
w
x
y
z

a

1 to read (out); 2 jemandem
vorlesen to read to somebody.

b

vorletzter, vorletzte,
vorletztes *adjective* last but one;
vorletztes Jahr the year before
last.

c

d

Vormittag der (PL die **Vormittage**)
morning.

e

f

vormittags *adverb* in the
morning.

g

h

vorn *adverb* 1 at the front; **nach
vorn** to the front; 2 **von vorn** from
the beginning; **wieder von vorn
anfangen** to start again at the
beginning; **da vorn** over there.

i

j

k

Vorname der (PL die **Vornamen**)
first name.

l

vorne SEE **vorn.**

m

vornehm *adjective* 1 elegant;
2 distinguished.

n

o

vornehmen ◇*verb* (PRES **nimmt
vor,** IMPERF **nahm vor,** PERF **hat
vorgenommen**) 1 to carry out;
2 **sich vornehmen, etwas zu tun** to
plan to do something.

p

q

Vorort der (PL die **Vororte**) suburb.

r

Vorrat der (PL die **Vorräte**) supply,
stock.

s

Vorsatz der (PL die **Vorsätze**)
intention.

t

Vorschau die 1 preview; 2 trailer
(*of a film*).

u

v

Vorschlag der (PL die **Vorschläge**)
suggestion.

w

x

vorschlagen ◇*verb* (PRES **schlägt
vor,** IMPERF **schlug vor,** PERF **hat
vorgeschlagen**) to suggest.

y

z

Vorschrift die (PL die **Vorschriften**)
1 regulation; 2 instruction.

Vorschule die (PL die **Vorschulen**)
infant school.

vorsehen ◇*verb* (PRES **sieht sich
vor,** IMPERF **sah sich vor,** PERF **hat
sich vorgesehen**) **sich vorsehen**
to be careful.

Vorsicht die care; **Vorsicht!**
careful!, (*on a sign*) caution!

vorsichtig *adjective* careful.

vorsichtshalber *adverb* to be on
the safe side.

Vorsichtsmaßnahme die (PL die
Vorsichtsmaßnahmen)
precaution; **Vorsichtsmaßnahmen
gegen etwas ergreifen** to take
precautions against something.

Vorspeise die (PL die **Vorspeisen**)
starter.

Vorsprung der (PL die **Vorsprünge**)
1 ledge (*of a rock*); 2 lead (*over
somebody*).

vorstellen *verb* (PERF **hat
vorgestellt**) 1 to introduce; **darf
ich Ihnen Herrn Schulz
vorstellen?** may I introduce Mr
Schulz?; 2 **die Uhr vorstellen** to put
the clock forward; 3 **sich
vorstellen** to introduce yourself;
4 **sich beim Personalchef
vorstellen** to go for an interview
with the personnel manager;
5 **sich etwas vorstellen** to imagine
something; **stell dir vor!** can you
imagine?

Vorstellung die (PL die
Vorstellungen) 1 performance;

2 introduction; **3** interview *(for a job)*; **4** idea; **5** imagination.

Vorstellungsgespräch *das* (PL die **Vorstellungsgespräche**) interview.

Vorteil *der* (PL die **Vorteile**) advantage.

Vortrag *der* (PL die **Vorträge**) talk.

vorüber *adverb* **vorüber sein** to be over.

vorübergehend *adjective* temporary.

vorübergehend *adverb* temporarily.

Vorurteil *das* (PL die **Vorurteile**) prejudice.

Vorwahl *die* (PL die **Vorwahlen**) dialling code; **wählen Sie die Vorwahl 00 44 für Großbritannien** dial 00 44 for Britain.

vorwärts *adverb* forward(s).

vorwiegend *adverb* predominantly.

Vorwurf *der* (PL die **Vorwürfe**) reproach; **jemandem Vorwürfe machen** to reproach somebody.

vorzeigen *verb* (PERF hat **vorgezeigt**) to show.

vorziehen ⋄*verb* (PRES **zieht vor**, IMPERF **zog vor**, PERF **hat vorgezogen**) **1** to prefer; **2** to pull up *(a chair)*; **3** **den Vorhang vorziehen** to draw the curtain.

vorzüglich *adjective* excellent.

vulgär *adjective* vulgar.

Vulkan *der* (PL die **Vulkane**) volcano.

Ww

Waage *die* (PL die **Waagen**) **1** scales; **2** Libra; **Gabi ist Waage** Gabi's Libra.

waagerecht *adjective* horizontal.

wach *adjective* awake; **wach sein** to be awake; **wach werden** to wake up.

Wache *die* (PL die **Wachen**) **1** guard; **2** (police) station.

Wachhund *der* (PL die **Wachhunde**) guard dog.

Wachs *das* wax.

wachsen ⋄*verb* (PRES **wächst**, IMPERF **wuchs**, PERF **ist gewachsen**) to grow.

Wachstum *das* growth.

wackelig *adjective* wobbly.

wackeln *verb* (PERF hat **gewackelt**) to wobble.

Wade *die* (PL die **Waden**) calf.

Waffe *die* (PL die **Waffen**) weapon.

Waffel *die* (PL die **Waffeln**) waffle.

Waffenhandel *der* arms trade.

Wagen *der* (PL die **Wagen**) **1** car; **nimmst du den Wagen?** are you going by car?; **2** carriage *(of a train)*; **3** cart.

wagen *verb* (PERF hat **gewagt**) **1** to risk; **2** **es wagen, etwas zu tun** to dare to do something; **sich nicht irgendwohin wagen** not dare to go somewhere.

Wagenheber *der* (PL die **Wagenheber**) jack.

Wahl die (PL die **Wahlen**) **1** choice; **er hat die Wahl** it's his choice; **2** election; **die nächsten Wahlen sind im Herbst** the next election is in autumn.

wählen verb (PERF **hat gewählt**) **1** to choose; **zwischen zwei Möglichkeiten wählen** to choose between two possibilities; **2 haben Sie schon gewählt?** are you ready to order? (in a restaurant); **3** to elect; **4** to vote, to vote for; **sie wählt immer grün** she always votes green; **wählt Schröder!** vote for Schröder; **5** to dial; **ich muss die falsche Nummer gewählt haben** I must have dialled the wrong number.

Wahlfach das (PL die **Wahlfächer**) optional subject, option.

Wahnsinn der madness.

wahnsinnig adjective **1** mad; **wahnsinnig werden** to go mad; **2 wahnsinnigen Durst haben** to be terribly thirsty; **der Film war wahnsinnig gut** the film was incredibly good.

wahr adjective **1** true; **2 du kommst doch, nicht wahr?** you're coming, aren't you?

während preposition (+ GEN) during.

während conjunction **1** while; **2** whereas.

Wahrheit die (PL die **Wahrheiten**) truth.

Wahrsager der (PL die **Wahrsager**) fortune-teller.

Wahrsagerin die (PL die **Wahrsagerinnen**) fortune-teller.

wahrscheinlich adjective probable, likely.

wahrscheinlich adverb probably.

Währung die (PL die **Währungen**) currency.

Waise die (PL die **Waisen**) orphan; **er ist Waise** he's an orphan.

Wal der (PL die **Wale**) whale.

Wald der (PL die **Wälder**) wood, forest.

Waliser der (PL die **Waliser**) Welshman.

Waliserin die (PL die **Waliserinnen**) Welshwoman.

walisisch adjective Welsh.

Walkman™ der (PL die **Walkmans**) walkman™.

Walnuss die (PL die **Walnüsse**) walnut.

Wand die (PL die **Wände**) wall.

Wanderer der (PL die **Wanderer**) **1** hiker; **2** rambler.

Wanderin die (PL die **Wanderinnen**) **1** hiker; **2** rambler.

wandern verb (PERF **ist gewandert**) **1** to hike; **2** to go walking.

Wanderung das hiking.

Wanderung die (PL die **Wanderungen**) **1** hike; **2** walking tour.

Wandteppich der (PL die **Wandteppiche**) tapestry.

wann adverb when.

Wanne die (PL die Wannen) **1** tub; **2** bath.

war SEE sein.

warb SEE werben.

Ware die (PL die Waren) **1** article; **2** Waren goods.

waren SEE sein.

Warenhaus das (PL die Warenhäuser) department store.

warf SEE werfen.

warm adjective warm; eine warme Mahlzeit a hot meal; das Essen warm machen to heat up the food.

Wärme die warmth.

wärmen verb (PERF hat gewärmt) to warm, to heat.

Warndreieck das (PL die Warndreiecke) warning triangle.

warnen verb (PERF hat gewarnt) to warn; jemanden vor etwas warnen to warn somebody of something.

Warnung die (PL die Warnungen) warning.

warst, wart SEE sein.

Warteliste die (PL die Wartelisten) waiting list.

warten verb (PERF hat gewartet) **1** to wait; auf jemanden warten to wait for somebody; **2** auf sich warten lassen to take your time.

Wärter der (PL die Wärter) **1** keeper; **2** attendant; **3** warder.

Warteraum der (PL die Warteräume) waiting room.

Wärterin die (PL die Wärterinnen) **1** keeper; **2** attendant; **3** warder.

Wartezeit die wait; eine Stunde Wartezeit an hour's wait.

Wartezimmer das (PL die Wartezimmer) waiting room.

warum adverb why.

Warze die (PL die Warzen) wart.

was pronoun **1** what; was für ein/ eine ...? what kind of ...?; was für ein Fahrrad hast du? what kind of bike do you have?; was für ein Glück! what luck!; was kostet das? how much is it?; **2** that; alles, was wir brauchen all (that) we need; alles, was du willst all (that) you want; **3** (short for 'etwas') something; heute gibts was Gutes im Fernsehen there's something good on television today; **4** (short for 'etwas' in questions and negatives) anything; hast du was für mich? have you got anything for me?

Waschbecken das (PL die Waschbecken) washbasin.

Wäsche die **1** washing; **2** underwear.

waschen ◇ verb (PRES wäscht, IMPERF wusch, PERF hat gewaschen) **1** to wash; **2** sich waschen to have a wash; sich die Hände waschen to wash your hands.

Wäscheraum der (PL die Wäscheräume) laundry room.

Wäscherei die (PL die Wäschereien) laundry.

Waschlappen der (PL die Waschlappen) flannel.

Waschmaschine die (PL die Waschmaschinen) washing machine.

Waschpulver das (PL die Waschpulver) washing powder.

Waschsalon der (PL die Waschsalons) launderette.

Wasser das water.

wasserdicht adjective waterproof.

Wasserfall der (PL die Wasserfälle) waterfall.

Wasserfarbe die (PL die Wasserfarben) watercolour.

Wasserhahn der (PL die Wasserhähne) tap.

Wassermann der Aquarius; **Lisa ist Wassermann** Lisa's Aquarius.

Wassermelone die (PL die Wassermelonen) water melon.

Wasserskifahren das water-skiing.

Wassersport der water sport.

Wassertiefe die depth (of water); **Wassertiefe: 2 Meter** depth: 2 metres.

Watte die cotton wool.

wattiert adjective padded.

WC das (PL die WCs) WC, toilet.

weben verb (PERF hat gewebt) to weave.

Webseite die (PL die Webseiten) web page.

Website die (PL die Websites) web site.

Wechselkurs der (PL die Wechselkurse) exchange rate.

wechseln verb (PERF hat gewechselt) 1 to change; **kannst du mir zehn Euro wechseln?** have you got change for ten euros?; 2 to exchange (glances, letters).

Wechselstube die (PL die Wechselstuben) bureau de change.

wecken verb (PERF hat geweckt) to wake (up).

Wecker der (PL die Wecker) alarm clock; **Max geht mir auf den Wecker** (informal) Max gets on my nerves.

weder conjunction weder ... noch neither ... nor.

Weg der (PL die Wege) 1 way; **auf dem Weg nach Hause** on the way home; 2 path; 3 **sich auf den Weg machen** to set off; 4 **im Weg sein** to be in the way.

weg adverb 1 away; **geh weg!** go away!; **Hände weg!** hands off!; 2 gone; **der Ring ist weg** the ring's gone; **Heidi ist schon weg** Heidi's already gone.

wegen preposition (+ GEN) because of.

wegfahren ◇verb (PRES fährt weg, IMPERF fuhr weg, PERF ist weggefahren) 1 to leave; **sie fahren gerade weg** they are leaving just now; 2 (PERF hat weggefahren) to drive away (a car or things).

weggehen ◇verb (IMPERF ging weg, PERF ist weggegangen) 1 to go away; **2** to leave; **3** to go out; **wir gehen heute Abend weg** we're going out tonight; **4** to come out (of a stain).

weglassen ◇verb (PRES **lässt weg**, IMPERF **ließ weg**, PERF **hat weggelassen**) **1** to let go; **2** to leave out.

weglaufen ◇verb (PRES **läuft weg**, IMPERF **lief weg**, PERF **ist weggelaufen**) to run away.

weglegen verb (PERF **hat weggelegt**) **1** to put down; **2** to put away.

wegmachen verb (PERF **hat weggemacht**) to get rid of (a stain or wart, for example).

wegmüssen verb (informal) (PRES **muss weg**, IMPERF **musste weg**, PERF **hat weggemusst**) to have to go.

wegnehmen ◇verb (PRES **nimmt weg**, IMPERF **nahm weg**, PERF **hat weggenommen**) to take away.

wegräumen verb (PERF **hat weggeräumt**) to clear away.

wegschicken verb (PERF **hat weggeschickt**) **1** to send away; **2** to send off.

Wegweiser der (PL die **Wegweiser**) signpost.

wegwerfen ◇verb (PRES **wirft weg**, IMPERF **warf weg**, PERF **hat weggeworfen**) to throw away.

weh adjective **1** sore; **2 oh weh!** oh dear!; **3 es tut weh** it hurts.

wehen verb (PERF **hat geweht**) to blow.

Wehrdienst der military service.

wehren verb (PERF **hat sich gewehrt**) **sich wehren** to defend yourself.

wehrlos adjective defenceless.

wehtun ◇verb (PRES **tut weh**, IMPERF **tat weh**, PERF **hat wehgetan**) **1** to hurt; **mein Arm tut weh** my arm hurts; **jemandem wehtun** to hurt somebody; **2 sich wehtun** to hurt yourself.

Weibchen das (PL die **Weibchen**) female.

weiblich adjective **1** female; **2** feminine (noun).

weich adjective soft.

Weide die (PL die **Weiden**) **1** willow; **2** pasture.

weigern verb (PERF **hat sich geweigert**) **sich weigern** to refuse.

Weihnachten das (PL die **Weihnachten**) Christmas; **Frohe Weihnachten!** Merry Christmas!

Weihnachtskrippe die (PL die **Weihnachtskrippen**) Christmas crib scene.

Weihnachtslied das (PL die **Weihnachtslieder**) Christmas carol.

Weihnachtsmann der (PL die **Weihnachtsmänner**) Father Christmas.

Weihnachtstag der (PL die **Weihnachtstage**) Christmas Day; **zweiter Weihnachtstag** Boxing Day.

a b c d e f g h i j k l m n o p q r s t u v w x y z

a b c d e f g h i j k l m n o p q r s t u v w x y z

weil conjunction because.

Weile die while.

Wein der (PL die **Weine**) wine.

Weinberg der (PL die **Weinberge**) vineyard.

Weinbergschnecke die (PL die **Weinbergschnecken**) snail.

Weinbrand der (PL die **Weinbrände**) brandy.

weinen verb (PERF hat geweint) to cry.

Weinkarte die (PL die **Weinkarten**) wine list.

Weinkeller der (PL die **Weinkeller**) wine cellar.

Weinstube die (PL die **Weinstuben**) wine bar.

Weintraube die (PL die **Weintrauben**) grape.

Weise die (PL die **Weisen**) way; **auf diese Weise** in this way.

weise adjective wise.

Weisheit die (PL die **Weisheiten**) wisdom.

weiß¹ SEE wissen.

weiß² adjective white.

Weißwein der (PL die **Weißweine**) white wine.

weit adjective, adverb 1 wide, loose (clothes); 2 long; **eine weite Reise** a long journey; 3 far; **wie weit ist es?** how far is it?; **ist es noch weit?** is it much further?; **so weit wie möglich** as far as possible; **bei weitem** by far; 4 **von weitem** from a distance; 5 **ich bin so weit** I'm ready; 6 **weit verbreitet**

widespread; 7 **zu weit gehen** to go too far.

weiten verb (PERF hat sich geweitet) **sich weiten** to stretch.

weiter adjective, adverb 1 further; 2 in addition; 3 etwas weiter tun to go on doing something; **weiter nichts** nothing else; **weiter niemand** nobody else; 4 **und so weiter** and so on.

weiterer, weitere, weiteres adjective 1 further; 2 **ohne weiteres** just like that, easily; 3 **bis auf weiteres** for the time being.

weiterfahren ✧verb (PRES **fährt weiter**, IMPERF **fuhr weiter**, PERF **ist weitergefahren**) to go on.

weitergehen ✧verb (IMPERF **ging weiter**, PERF **ist weitergegangen**) to go on.

weiterhin adverb 1 still; 2 in future; 3 etwas weiterhin tun to go on doing something.

weitermachen verb (PERF hat weitergemacht) to carry on.

Weitsprung der long jump.

Weizen der wheat.

welcher, welche, welches adjective which; **welches Kleid?** which dress?; **um welche Zeit?** at what time?.

welches pronoun 1 which (one); 2 some; **brauchst du Briefmarken? ich habe welche** do you need stamps? I've got some; 3 any; **hast du welche?** have you got any?

Welle die (PL die **Wellen**) wave.

Wellensittich der (PL die **Wellensittiche**) budgerigar.

wellig *adjective* wavy.

Welt die (PL die **Welten**) world; **auf der ganzen Welt** in the whole world.

Weltall das universe.

Weltkrieg der (PL die **Weltkriege**) world war.

Weltmeister der (PL die **Weltmeister**) world champion.

Weltmeisterin die (PL die **Weltmeisterinnen**) world champion.

Weltmeisterschaft die (PL die **Weltmeisterschaften**) **1** world championship; **2 die Weltmeisterschaft** (*football*) the World Cup.

Weltraum der space.

Weltreise die (PL die **Weltreisen**) world tour.

wem *pronoun* to whom; **wem hat er das Geld gegeben?** who did he give the money to?

wen *pronoun* whom, who; **wen hast du eingeladen?** who did you invite?

Wende die **1** change; **2** reunification (*of Germany*).

wenig *pronoun, adjective* **1** little; **zu wenig** too little, not enough; **2** wenige few; **in wenigen Wochen** in a few weeks.

wenig *adverb* little; **so wenig wie möglich** as little as possible.

weniger *pronoun, adjective* less, fewer; **sie hat weniger Geschenke bekommen** she got fewer presents; **immer weniger Geld** less and less money; **immer weniger Häuser** fewer and fewer houses.

weniger *adverb, conjunction* less; **zehn weniger fünf** ten minus five.

wenigste SEE **wenigster**.

wenigstens *adverb* at least.

wenigster, wenigste, wenigstes *adjective, pronoun* least; **am wenigsten** least; **sein Geschenk hat mir am wenigsten gefallen** I liked his present least.

wenn *conjunction* **1** when; **wenn ich in München bin, schreibe ich dir** I'll write to you when I'm in Munich; **immer, wenn** whenever; **2** if; **wenn es regnet** if it rains; **3 außer wenn** unless.

wer *pronoun* who.

werben ◇*verb* (PRES **wirbt**, IMPERF **warb**, PERF **hat geworben**) **1** to advertise; **2** to recruit (*members*).

Werbespot der (PL die **Werbespots**) commercial, advert.

Werbung die **1** advertising; **in der Werbung arbeiten** to work in advertising; **2** advertisement; **im Fernsehen kommt viel Werbung** there are many advertisements on television; **Werbung für etwas machen** to advertise something.

werden ◇*verb* (PRES **wird**, IMPERF **wurde**, PERF **ist geworden**) **1** to become; **Arzt werden** to become a doctor; **2 müde werden** to get tired; **alt werden** to get old; **mir wird kalt** I'm getting cold; **3 mir wurde schlecht** I felt sick; **blass werden** to turn pale; **4 wach werden** to wake up; **5** (*used to form the future* *tense*) will, shall; **sie wird anrufen** she'll ring; **sie wird gleich da sein** she'll be here in a minute; **6** (*used to form the passive*) to be; **gerufen werden** to be called; **er wurde gefragt** he was asked; **7** (*used to form the conditional*) **sie würde kommen** she would come; **ich würde gern kommen, aber ...** I'd like to come but ....

werfen ✧*verb* (PRES **wirft**, IMPERF **warf**, PERF **hat geworfen**) to throw.

Werk *das* (PL die **Werke**) **1** work; **2** works (*a factory*).

Werken *das* handicraft.

Werkstatt *die* (PL die **Werkstätten**) workshop.

Werktag *der* (PL die **Werktage**) weekday.

werktags *adverb* on weekdays.

Werkzeug *das* (PL die **Werkzeuge**) tool.

Werkzeugkasten *der* (PL die **Werkzeugkästen**) tool box.

wert *adjective* **viel wert sein** to be worth a lot; **nichts wert sein** to be worthless.

Wert *der* (PL die **Werte**) **1** value; **im Wert von hundert Euro** worth one hundred euros; **2 auf etwas Wert legen** to attach importance to something; **3 es hat doch keinen Wert** there's no point.

wertlos *adjective* worthless.

wertvoll *adjective* valuable.

Wesen *das* (PL die **Wesen**) **1** nature, manner; **2** creature.

wesentlich *adjective* essential; **im Wesentlichen** essentially.

wesentlich *adverb* considerably.

weshalb *adverb* why.

Wespe *die* (PL die **Wespen**) wasp.

wessen *pronoun* whose.

Wessi *der* (*informal*) (PL die **Wessis**) West German.

Weste *die* (PL die **Westen**) waistcoat.

Westen *der* west.

Western *der* (PL die **Western**) western (*film*).

Westinder *der* (PL die **Westinder**) West Indian.

Westinderin *die* (PL die **Westinderinnen**) West Indian.

westlich *adjective* **1** western; **2** westerly.

westlich *adverb, preposition* (+ GEN) **westlich von Wien** west of Vienna; **westlich der Stadt** to the west of the town.

weswegen *adverb* why.

Wettbewerb *der* (PL die **Wettbewerbe**) competition, contest.

Wette *die* (PL die **Wetten**) bet; **mit jemandem um die Wette laufen** to race somebody.

wetten *verb* (PERF **hat gewettet**) to bet; **mit jemandem um etwas wetten** to bet somebody something.

Wetter *das* weather.

Wetterbericht *der* (PL die **Wetterberichte**) weather report.

Wettervorhersage *die* weather forecast.

Wettkampf *der* (PL die **Wettkämpfe**) contest.

Wettlauf *der* race.

wichtig *adjective* important; **das wichtigste Exportgut ist Wolle** the most important export is wool.

wickeln *verb* (PERF **hat gewickelt**) **1** to wind; **2 ein Kind wickeln** to change a baby.

Widder *der* (PL **die Widder**) **1** ram; **2** Aries; **Jan ist Widder** Jan's Aries.

widerlich *adjective* disgusting.

widersprechen ✧*verb* (PRES **widerspricht**, IMPERF **widersprach**, PERF **hat widersprochen**) to contradict.

Widerspruch *der* (PL **die Widersprüche**) contradiction.

Widerstand *der* resistance.

widerstehen ✧*verb* (IMPERF **widerstand**, PERF **hat widerstanden**) to resist.

widmen *verb* (PERF **hat gewidmet**) **1** to dedicate; **2** to devote; **3 sich einer Sache widmen** to devote yourself to something.

wie *adverb* **1** how; **wie geht's?** how are you?; **wie viel?** how much?, how many?; **wie viele Leute waren da?** how many people were there?; **um wie viel Uhr kommst du?** (at) what time are you coming?; **2 wie ist Ihr Name?** what is your name?; **wie ist das Wetter?** what's the weather like?; **3 wie bitte?** sorry?.

wie *conjunction* **1** as; **so schnell wie möglich** as quickly as possible; **2** like; **wie du** like you; **3 wie zum Beispiel** such as.

wieder *adverb* **1** again; **sie ist wieder da** she's back again; **2 jemanden wieder erkennen** to recognize somebody; **etwas wieder finden** to find something (again); **etwas wieder verwerten** to recycle something; **jemanden wieder beleben** to revive somebody.

wiederbekommen ✧*verb* (IMPERF **bekam wieder**, PERF **hat wiederbekommen**) to get back.

wiederbeleben *verb* (PERF **hat wiederbelebt**) SEE **wieder.**

wiedererkennen SEE **wieder.**

wiederfinden SEE **wieder.**

wiederholen *verb* (PERF **hat wiederholt**) **1** to repeat; **2** to bring back; **3** to revise (*schoolwork*); **4 sich wiederholen** to recur; **er hat sich wiederholt** he's repeated himself.

Wiederholung *die* (PL **die Wiederholungen**) **1** repetition; **2** repeat performance; **3** replay; **4** revision (*at school*).

Wiederhören *das* **auf Wiederhören!** (*said on the phone*) goodbye!

wiederkommen ✧*verb* (IMPERF **kam wieder**, PERF **ist wiedergekommen**) **1** to come back; **2** to come again.

Wiedersehen *das* (PL **die Wiedersehen**) **1** reunion; **2 auf Wiedersehen!** goodbye!

wiedersehen SEE **sehen.**

wiedervereinigen SEE **vereinigen.**

a b c d e f g h i j k l m n o p q r s t u v w x y z

Wiedervereinigung die reunification.

wiederverwerten SEE wieder.

Wiege die (PL die Wiegen) cradle.

wiegen ◇verb (IMPERF wog, PERF hat gewogen) to weigh.

Wiegenlied das (PL die Wiegenlieder) lullaby.

Wien das Vienna.

Wiese die (PL die Wiesen) meadow.

wieso adverb why.

wieviel SEE wie.

wievielmal adverb how often.

wievielter, wievielte, wievieltes adjective 1 which; 2 die wievielte Querstraße ist das von hier aus? how many roads is that from here?; der Wievielte ist heute? what's the date today?

wild adjective wild.

Wildleder das suede.

Wildpark der (PL die Wildparks) wildlife park.

Wildschwein das (PL die Wildschweine) wild boar.

will SEE wollen.

Wille der (PL die Willen); seinen Willen durchsetzen to get your own way.

willkommen adjective welcome.

willst SEE wollen.

Wimper die (PL die Wimpern) eyelash.

Wimperntusche die (PL die Wimperntuschen) mascara.

Wind der (PL die Winde) wind.

Windel die (PL die Windeln) nappy.

Windhund der (PL die Windhunde) greyhound.

windig adjective windy.

Windmühle die (PL die Windmühlen) windmill.

Windpark der (PL die Windparks) wind farm.

Windpocken plural noun chickenpox.

Windschutzscheibe die (PL die Windschutzscheiben) windscreen.

Windsurfen das windsurfing; Windsurfen gehen to go windsurfing.

Winkel der (PL die Winkel) 1 angle; 2 corner.

winken verb (PERF hat gewinkt) to wave.

Winter der (PL die Winter) winter.

winzig adjective tiny.

Wippe die (PL die Wippen) seesaw.

wir pronoun we; wir sind es it's us; wir alle all of us.

Wirbel der (PL die Wirbel) 1 whirl; 2 whirlwind; 3 whirlpool; 4 commotion.

Wirbelsäule die (PL die Wirbelsäulen) spine.

wirbt SEE werben.

wird SEE werden.

wirft SEE werfen.

wirken verb (PERF hat gewirkt) 1 to have an effect; 2 gegen etwas wirken to be effective against something; 3 to seem (sad, happy).

wirklich adjective real.

a b c d e f g h i j k l m n o p q r s t u v w x y z

wirklich adverb really.

Wirklichkeit die reality.

wirksam adjective effective.

Wirkung die (PL die **Wirkungen**) effect.

wirst SEE werden.

Wirt der (PL die **Wirte**) landlord.

Wirtin die (PL die **Wirtinnen**) landlady.

Wirtschaft die (PL die **Wirtschaften**) 1 economy; 2 pub.

wirtschaftlich adjective economic.

Wirtschaftswissenschaften plural noun business studies.

Wirtshaus das (PL die **Wirtshäuser**) pub.

wischen verb (PERF **hat gewischt**) to wipe.

wissen ⋄verb (PRES **weiß**, IMPERF **wusste**, PERF **hat gewusst**) to know; **ich weiß, dass er in London wohnt** I know he lives in London; **ich wüsste gern ...** I'd like to know ...; **von etwas wissen** to know about something; **weißt du was?** you know what?

Wissen das knowledge.

Wissenschaft die (PL die **Wissenschaften**) science.

Wissenschaftler der (PL die **Wissenschaftler**) scientist.

Wissenschaftlerin die (PL die **Wissenschaftlerinnen**) scientist.

wissenschaftlich adjective scientific.

Witwe die (PL die **Witwen**) widow.

Witwer der (PL die **Witwer**) widower.

Witz der (PL die **Witze**) joke.

witzig adjective funny.

wo adverb where; **wo seid ihr gewesen?** where have you been?; **in München, wo Markus seit einem Jahr lebt** in Munich, where Markus has been living for a year; **wo immer** wherever.

wo conjunction 1 seeing that; 2 although; **jetzt ist sie mir böse, wo ich doch so nett zu ihr war** now she's angry with me, although I've been so nice to her.

woanders adverb elsewhere.

Woche die (PL die **Wochen**) week.

Wochenende das (PL die **Wochenenden**) weekend.

wochenlang adverb for weeks.

Wochentag der (PL die **Wochentage**) weekday.

wochentags adverb on weekdays.

wöchentlich adjective weekly.

wofür adverb what ... for; **wofür brauchst du das Geld?** what do you need the money for?

wog SEE wiegen.

woher adverb where ... from; **woher ist er?** where does he come from?; **woher weißt du das?** how do you know?

wohin adverb where ... (to); **wohin geht ihr?** where are you going?

Wohl das 1 welfare, well-being; 2 **zu seinem Wohl** for his benefit; 3 **zum Wohl!** cheers!

a **wohl** *adverb* 1 well; **sich wohl fühlen** to feel well; **ich fühle mich heute nicht wohl** I don't feel well today; 2 **sich wohl fühlen** to be happy; **Anni fühlt sich in London wohl** Anni is happy in London; 3 **jemandem wohl tun** to do somebody good; 4 probably; **er hat den Zug wohl verpasst** he probably missed the train; **du bist wohl verrückt!** you must be mad!; 5 **wohl kaum** hardly.

wohlhabend *adjective* well-off.

wohltun SEE wohl.

wohnen *verb* (PERF **hat gewohnt**) 1 to live; 2 to stay (*for a short time*).

Wohngemeinschaft die (PL die **Wohngemeinschaften**) people sharing a flat/house; **wir wohnen in einer Wohngemeinschaft** we share a flat.

wohnhaft *adjective* resident.

Wohnheim das (PL die **Wohnheime**) 1 hostel; 2 home (*for old people*).

Wohnmobil das (PL die **Wohnmobile**) motor home.

Wohnort der (PL die **Wohnorte**) place of residence.

Wohnsitz der (PL die **Wohnsitze**) place of residence.

Wohnung die (PL die **Wohnungen**) flat, apartment.

Wohnwagen der (PL die **Wohnwagen**) caravan.

Wohnzimmer das (PL die **Wohnzimmer**) living room.

Wolf der (PL die **Wölfe**) wolf.

Wolke die (PL die **Wolken**) cloud.

Wolkenkratzer der (PL die **Wolkenkratzer**) skyscraper.

wolkig *adjective* cloudy.

Wolldecke die (PL die **Wolldecken**) blanket.

Wolle die wool.

wollen ◇*verb* (PRES **will**, IMPERF **wollte**, PERF **hat gewollt**) 1 to want; **Anne will einen Hund** Anne wants a dog; **ich will nach Hause** I want to go home; 2 **sie wollte gerade gehen** she was just about to go; 3 **ganz wie du willst** as you like.

womit *adverb* 1 what ... with; **womit hast du das gewaschen?** what did you wash it with?; 2 with which.

womöglich *adverb* possibly.

wonach *adverb* 1 what ... for; **wonach suchst du?** what are you looking for?; **wonach riecht es?** what does it smell of?; 2 after which, according to which; **eine Regelung, wonach wir eine Stunde mehr arbeiten müssen** a rule according to which we have to work an extra hour.

woran *adverb* what ... of 1 **woran denkst du?** what are you thinking of?; **woran hast du ihn erkannt?** how did you recognize him?; 2 on which, of which; **nichts, woran man sich verletzen könnte** nothing you could hurt yourself on.

worauf *adverb* 1 what ... on, what ... for; **worauf hast du die Vase gestellt?** what did you put the vase on?; **worauf wartet ihr?** what are you waiting for?; **2** on which, for which; **das Regal, worauf das Radio steht** the shelf the radio is on; **das Einzige, worauf ich mich freue** the only thing I'm looking forward to.

woraus *adverb* **1** what ... from, what ... of; **woraus ist das?** what's it made of?; **2** from which; **es gibt nichts, woraus wir trinken können** there isn't anything we can drink out of.

worin *adverb* **1** what ... in, in what; **2** in which; **die Punkte, worin ich mit dir übereinstimme** the points I agree with you on.

Wort *das* (PL **die Worte/Wörter**) word; **mir fehlen die Worte** I'm lost for words; **ich habe heute zwanzig neue Wörter gelernt** I've learnt twenty new words today.

Wörterbuch *das* (PL **die Wörterbücher**) dictionary.

wörtlich *adjective* word for word.

Wortschatz *der* vocabulary.

Wortspiel *das* (PL **die Wortspiele**) pun.

Wortstellung *die* word order.

worüber *adverb* **1** what ... over, what ... about; **worüber lacht ihr?** what are you laughing about?; **2** over which, about which.

worum *adverb* **1** about what; **worum geht es?** what's it about?; **worum hat sie dich gebeten?** what did she ask you for?; **2** for which; **3** round which.

wovon *adverb* **1** what ... from, what ... about; **wovon redet ihr?**

what are you talking about?; **2** from which, about which; **der Geruch, wovon mir schlecht geworden ist** the smell which made me feel sick.

wovor *adverb* **1** what ... of; **wovor hast du Angst?** what are you frightened of?; **2** in front of what; **3** of which; **4** in front of which; **der Turm, wovor wir stehen** the tower we are standing in front of.

wozu *adverb* **1** what ... for, why; **wozu brauchst du das?** what do you need it for?; **wozu?** what for?; **2** to which, for which; **wozu ich dir raten würde** which I would advise.

Wrack *das* (PL **die Wracks**) wreck.

Wuchs *der* growth.

wuchs SEE **wachsen**.

wund *adjective* sore.

Wunde *die* (PL **die Wunden**) wound.

Wunder *das* (PL **die Wunder**) miracle; **kein Wunder!** no wonder!

wunderbar *adjective* wonderful.

wundern *verb* (PERF **hat sich gewundert**) **sich wundern** to be surprised.

wunderschön *adjective* beautiful.

wundervoll *adjective* wonderful.

Wundschorf *der* (PL **die Wundschorfe**) scab.

Wunsch *der* (PL **die Wünsche**) wish; **auf Wunsch** on request; **haben Sie sonst noch einen Wunsch?** will there be anything else?

wünschen *verb* (PERF **hat gewünscht**) **1** to wish; **ich**

a
b
c
d
e
f
g
h
i
j
k
l
m
n
o
p
q
r
s
t
u
v
w
x
y
z

wünsche dir alles Gute zum Geburtstag I wish you a happy birthday; ich wünschte, ich könnte ... I wish I could ...; was wünschen Sie? can I help you?; 2 sich etwas wünschen to want something.

wünschenswert adjective desirable.

wurde, würde, wurden, würden, wurdest, würdest, wurdet, würdet SEE **werden**.

Wurf der (PL die **Würfe**) throw.

Würfel der (PL die **Würfel**) 1 dice (in games); 2 cube.

würfeln verb (PERF **hat gewürfelt**) to throw the dice.

Würfelspiel das (PL die **Würfelspiele**) game of dice.

Wurm der (PL die **Würmer**) worm.

Wurst die (PL die **Würste**) 1 sausage; 2 das ist mir Wurst (informal) I couldn't care less.

Würstchen das (PL die **Würstchen**) (little) sausage.

Wurzel die (PL die **Wurzeln**) root.

würzen verb (PERF **hat gewürzt**) to season.

würzig adjective spicy.

wusch SEE **waschen**.

wusste SEE **wissen**.

Wüste die (PL die **Wüsten**) desert.

Wut die rage; eine Wut auf jemanden haben to be furious with somebody.

wütend adjective furious.

Xx

x-beliebig adjective (informal) any; eine x-beliebige Zahl any number (you like).

x-mal adverb (informal) umpteen times; zum x-ten Mal for the umpteenth time.

Xylophon das (PL die **Xylophone**) xylophone.

Yy

Yoga das yoga.

Ypsilon das (PL die **Ypsilons**) Y.

Zz

zaghaft adjective 1 timid; 2 tentative.

zäh adjective tough.

Zahl die (PL die **Zahlen**) 1 number; 2 figure.

zahlen verb (PERF **hat gezahlt**) 1 to pay; hast du schon gezahlt? have you paid?; 2 to pay for; bitte zahlen! the bill please!

zählen verb (PERF **hat gezählt**) 1 to count; auf jemanden zählen to count on somebody; jemanden zu seinen Freunden zählen to count somebody among his friends; 2 zählen zu to be one of.

Zähler der (PL die **Zähler**) meter.

zahlreich *adjective* numerous.

Zahlung die (PL die Zahlungen) payment.

Zählung die (PL die Zählungen) 1 count; 2 census.

zahm *adjective* tame.

Zahn der (PL die Zähne) tooth.

Zahnarzt der (PL die Zahnärzte) dentist.

Zahnärztin die (PL die Zahnärztinnen) dentist.

Zahnbürste die (PL die Zahnbürsten) toothbrush.

Zahnfleisch das gums.

Zahnpasta die (PL die Zahnpasten) toothpaste.

Zahnschmerzen *plural noun* toothache.

Zange die (PL die Zangen) pliers.

zanken *verb* (PERF hat sich gezankt) **sich zanken** to squabble.

Zapfen der (PL die Zapfen) 1 cone; 2 icicle.

zappeln *verb* (PERF hat gezappelt) 1 to wriggle; 2 to fidget.

zart *adjective* 1 delicate, soft; 2 gentle; 3 tender.

zärtlich *adjective* affectionate.

Zauber der 1 magic; 2 spell.

Zauberer der (PL die Zauberer) magician, conjurer.

Zauberin die (PL die Zaubererinnen) magician, conjurer.

zauberhaft *adjective* enchanting.

zaubern *verb* (PERF hat gezaubert) to do magic.

Zaumzeug das (PL die Zaumzeuge) bridle.

Zaun der (PL die Zäune) fence.

z. B. (*zum Beispiel*) e.g.

Zebra das (PL die Zebras) zebra.

Zebrastreifen der (PL die Zebrastreifen) zebra crossing.

Zeh der (PL die Zehen) toe.

Zehe die (PL die Zehen) 1 toe; 2 clove (*of garlic*).

Zehenspitze die (PL die Zehenspitzen); **auf Zehenspitzen** on tiptoes.

zehn *number* ten.

Zehntel das (PL die Zehntel) tenth.

zehnter, zehnte, zehntes *adjective* tenth.

Zeichen das (PL die Zeichen) 1 sign; 2 signal.

Zeichentrickfilm der (PL die Zeichentrickfilme) cartoon film.

zeichnen *verb* (PERF hat gezeichnet) to draw.

Zeichnung die (PL die Zeichnungen) drawing.

Zeigefinger der (PL die Zeigefinger) index finger.

zeigen *verb* (PERF hat gezeigt) 1 to show; **Peter hat uns sein neues Auto gezeigt** Peter showed us his new car; 2 to point; **auf jemanden zeigen** to point at somebody; 3 **sich zeigen** to appear; 4 **es hat sich gezeigt, dass ...** it has become clear that ...; **es wird sich zeigen** time will tell.

Zeiger der (PL die Zeiger) hand.

Zeile die (PL die Zeilen) line.

a
b
c
d
e
f
g
h
i
j
k
l
m
n
o
p
q
r
s
t
u
v
w
x
y
z

Zeit die (PL die **Zeiten**) **1** time; **sich Zeit lassen** to take your time; **ich habe keine Zeit mehr** I haven't got any more time; **eine Zeit lang** for a time; **2 es hat Zeit** there's no hurry; **die erste Zeit** at first; **in nächster Zeit** in the near future.

Zeitalter das (PL die **Zeitalter**) age.

Zeitlang die SEE **Zeit**.

Zeitlupe die slow motion; **in Zeitlupe** in slow motion.

Zeitraum der (PL die **Zeiträume**) period.

Zeitschrift die (PL die **Zeitschriften**) magazine.

Zeitung die (PL die **Zeitungen**) newspaper.

Zeitungshändler der (PL die **Zeitungshändler**) newsagent.

Zeitverschwendung die waste of time.

zeitweise adverb at times.

Zelle die (PL die **Zellen**) **1** cell; **2** booth.

Zelt das (PL die **Zelte**) tent.

zelten verb (PERF **hat gezeltet**) to camp.

Zeltplatz der (PL die **Zeltplätze**) campsite.

Zement der cement.

Zentimeter der (PL die **Zentimeter**) centimetre.

Zentimetermaß das (PL die **Zentimetermaße**) tape measure.

zentral adjective central.

Zentrale die (PL die **Zentralen**) **1** central office, head office; **2** headquarters; **3** (telephone) exchange, switchboard.

Zentralheizung die central heating.

Zentrum das (PL die **Zentren**) centre.

zerbrechen ⋄verb (PRES **zerbricht**, IMPERF **zerbrach**, PERF **hat zerbrochen**) **1** to break; **Irene hat meine Vase zerbrochen** Irene broke my vase; **2** (PERF **ist zerbrochen**) to break; **die Untertasse ist zerbrochen** the saucer broke.

zerbrechlich adjective fragile.

Zerbrechlichkeit die fragility.

Zeremonie die (PL die **Zeremonien**) ceremony.

zerfallen verb (PRES **zerfällt**, IMPERF **zerfiel**, PERF **ist zerfallen**) to disintegrate, to decay.

zerreißen ⋄verb (IMPERF **zerriss**, PERF **hat zerrissen**) **1** to tear; **sie hat sich das Kleid zerrissen** she tore her dress; **2** to tear up; **Anna hat seinen Brief zerrissen** Anna tore up his letter; **3** (PERF **ist zerrissen**) to tear; **das Hemd ist in der Wäsche zerrissen** the shirt got torn in the washing.

zerschlagen ⋄verb (PRES **zerschlägt**, IMPERF **zerschlug**, PERF **hat zerschlagen**) **1** to smash, to smash up; **2 sich zerschlagen** to fall through (of plans); **meine Hoffnungen haben sich zerschlagen** my hopes were dashed.

zerschneiden verb (IMPERF **zerschnitt**, PERF **zerschnitten**) to cut up, to cut to pieces.

zerstören verb (PERF **hat zerstört**) to destroy.

Zerstörung die destruction.

zerstreuen verb (PERF **hat zerstreut**) 1 to scatter; 2 **jemanden zerstreuen** to entertain somebody; 3 **sich zerstreuen** to take your mind off things; 4 **die Menge hat sich zerstreut** the crowd's dispersed.

zerstreut adjective absent-minded.

Zettel der (PL die **Zettel**) 1 piece of paper; 2 note; 3 leaflet.

Zeug das (informal) 1 stuff; 2 things, gear; 3 **dummes Zeug** nonsense.

Zeuge der (PL die **Zeugen**) witness.

Zeugin die (PL die **Zeuginnen**) witness.

Zeugnis das (PL die **Zeugnisse**) 1 certificate; 2 report (at school).

Zickzack der (PL die **Zickzacke**) zigzag; **im Zickzack laufen** to zigzag.

Ziege die (PL die **Ziegen**) goat.

Ziegel der (PL die **Ziegel**) 1 brick; 2 tile.

ziehen ◇verb (IMPERF **zog**, PERF **hat gezogen**) 1 to pull; **an etwas ziehen** to pull on something; **einen Zahn ziehen** to pull out a tooth; 2 to draw; **einen Strich ziehen** to draw a line; **eine Niete ziehen** to draw a blank; 3 **die Bremse ziehen** to put on the brakes; 4 to grow (vegetables, flowers); 5 **sich ziehen** to run (of a path, road); 6 (PERF **ist gezogen**) to move; **sie sind nach Berlin gezogen** they've moved to Berlin.

Ziel das (PL die **Ziele**) 1 destination; 2 goal, aim; 3 finish (in sport).

zielen verb (PERF **hat gezielt**) to aim; **auf etwas zielen** to aim at something.

Zielscheibe die (PL die **Zielscheiben**) target.

zielstrebig adjective determined.

ziemlich adjective fair.

ziemlich adverb 1 quite; **ziemlich viel** quite a lot; 2 fairly; **ihre Eltern haben ein ziemlich großes Haus** her parents have a fairly large house.

zierlich adjective dainty.

Ziffer die (PL die **Ziffern**) figure.

Zifferblatt das (PL die **Zifferblätter**) face, dial.

zig adjective (informal) umpteen.

Zigarette die (PL die **Zigaretten**) cigarette.

Zigarre die (PL die **Zigarren**) cigar.

Zigeuner der (PL die **Zigeuner**) gypsy.

Zigeunerin die (PL die **Zigeunerinnen**) gypsy.

Zimmer das (PL die **Zimmer**) room; **Zimmer mit Frühstück** bed and breakfast; **'Zimmer frei'** 'vacancies'.

Zimmermädchen das (PL die **Zimmermädchen**) chambermaid.

Zimt der cinnamon.

a
b
c
d
e
f
g
h
i
j
k
l
m
n
o
p
q
r
s
t
u
v
w
x
y

Zink das zinc.

zirka adverb about.

Zirkel der (PL die **Zirkel**) pair of compasses.

Zirkus der (PL die **Zirkusse**) circus.

zischen verb (PERF **hat gezischt**) to hiss.

Zitat das (PL die **Zitate**) quotation.

zitieren verb (PERF **hat zitiert**) to quote.

Zitrone die (PL die **Zitronen**) lemon.

Zitronensaft der (PL die **Zitronensäfte**) lemon juice.

zittern verb (PERF **hat gezittert**) to tremble; **vor Kälte zittern** to shiver.

Zivildienst der community service.

Zivilisation die (PL die **Zivilisationen**) civilization.

zog SEE **ziehen**.

zögern verb (PERF **hat gezögert**) to hesitate.

Zoll der (PL die **Zölle**) 1 customs; **am Zoll** at customs; 2 duty; **Zoll auf etwas bezahlen** to pay duty on something.

Zollbeamte der (PL die **Zollbeamten**) customs officer.

Zollbeamtin die (PL die **Zollbeamtinnen**) customs officer.

zollfrei adjective duty-free.

Zollkontrolle die (PL die **Zollkontrollen**) customs check.

Zone die (PL die **Zonen**) zone.

Zoo der (PL die **Zoos**) Zoo.

Zoomobjektiv das (PL die **Zoomobjektive**) zoom lens.

Zopf der (PL die **Zöpfe**) plait.

Zorn der anger.

zornig adjective angry.

zu preposition (+ DAT) 1 to; **ich gehe zum Arzt** I'm going to the doctor's; **zu einer Party eingeladen sein** to be invited to a party; 2 **zu ... hin** towards; **zum Fenster hin** towards the window; **er kam zu dieser Tür herein** he came in through this door; 3 with; **das passt nicht zu meinem Mantel** it doesn't go with my coat; **es gab Wein zum Käse** there was wine with the cheese; 4 at; **zu Weihnachten** at Christmas; **zu Hause** at home; 5 **zu etwas werden** to turn into something; 6 **zu diesem Zweck** for this purpose; **was schenkst du Karin zum Geburtstag?** what are you giving Karin for her birthday?; **zum Spaß** for fun; **zum ersten Mal** for the first time; 7 **sich zu etwas äußern** to comment on something; **Papier zum Schreiben** paper to write on; 8 **nett zu jemandem sein** to be nice to somebody; 9 **sie waren zu zweit** there were two of them; **eine Marke zu achtzig Cent** an 80-Cent stamp; **es steht drei zu zwei** the score is 3-2; 10 **zu Fuß** on foot.

zu adverb 1 too; **zu groß** too big; 2 closed; **zu haben** to be closed; **Tür zu!** (informal) shut the door!; 3 **zu sein** to be closed; **alle Läden sind zu gewesen** the shops were all closed; 4 towards (indicating direction); 5 **mach zu!** (informal) hurry up!

zu *conjunction* to; **nichts zu essen** nothing to eat; **zu verkaufen** for sale.

zuallererst *adverb* first of all.

zuallerletzt *adverb* last of all.

Zubehör *das* accessories.

zubereiten *verb* (PERF **hat zubereitet**) to prepare; **sie bereitet das Essen zu** she's preparing the meal.

zubinden ✧*verb* (IMPERF **band zu**, PERF **hat zugebunden**) to tie, to tie up.

zubringen ✧*verb* (IMPERF **brachte zu**, PERF **hat zugebracht**) to spend; **sie bringt viel Zeit bei ihrem Freund zu** she spends a lot of time with her boyfriend.

Zucchini *plural noun* courgettes.

Zucht *die* (PL **die Zuchten**) **1** breed, species; **2** breeding (*of animals*); **3** breeding establishment.

züchten *verb* (PERF **hat gezüchtet**) to breed.

zucken *verb* (PERF **hat gezuckt**) to twitch.

Zucker *der* sugar.

Zuckerguss *der* icing.

zuckerkrank *adjective* diabetic.

zudecken *verb* (PERF **hat zugedeckt**) **1** to cover up, to cover; **2** to tuck up (*in bed*).

zueinander *adverb* **1** to one another; **lieb zueinander sein** to be nice to one another; **2** together; **zueinander passen** to go together; **zueinander halten** to stick together.

zuerst *adverb* **1** first; **2** at first.

Zufahrt *die* (PL **die Zufahrten**) **1** access; **2** drive(way).

Zufall *der* (PL **die Zufälle**) **1** chance; **durch Zufall** by chance; **2** coincidence; **so ein komischer Zufall** such a strange coincidence; **per Zufall traf ich ihn in der U-Bahn** by coincidence I met him in the tube.

zufällig *adjective* chance; **das war rein zufällig** it was purely by chance.

zufällig *adverb* by chance; **kannst du mir zufällig zehn Euro leihen?** could you lend me ten euros by any chance?

Zuflucht *die* refuge.

zufrieden *adjective* **1** content; **2** satisfied; **mit etwas zufrieden sein** to be satisfied with something.

zufrieden *adverb* **jemanden zufrieden lassen** to leave somebody in peace; **jemanden zufrieden stellen** to satisfy somebody.

zufriedenlassen, zufriedenstellen SEE **zufrieden**.

Zug *der* (PL **die Züge**) **1** train; **2** procession; **3** characteristic, trait; **4** move (*in games*); **5** swig (*when drinking*); **6** drag (*when smoking*); **7 in einem Zug** in one go.

Zugabe *die* (PL **die Zugaben**) **1** free gift; **2** encore.

a b c d e f g h i j k l m n o p q r s t u v w x y z

Zugang der (PL die **Zugänge**) access.

zugeben ◇verb (PRES **gibt zu**, IMPERF **gab zu**, PERF **hat zugegeben**) 1 to add; 2 to admit.

zugehen ◇verb (IMPERF **ging zu**, PERF **ist zugegangen**) 1 to close, to shut; **die Tür geht nicht zu** the door won't shut; 2 **auf etwas zugehen** to go towards something; **auf jemanden zugehen** to walk up to somebody; 3 **jemandem zugehen** to be sent to somebody; **4 auf der Party ging es lustig zu** the party was good fun; **5 dem Ende zugehen** to be nearing the end.

zügig adjective quick.

zugreifen ◇verb (IMPERF **griff zu**, PERF **hat zugegriffen**) 1 to grab it/them; 2 to help yourself; 3 to lend a hand.

zugunsten preposition (+ GEN) in favour of.

zuhaben SEE **zu**.

Zuhause das home.

zuhören verb (PERF **hat zugehört**) to listen.

Zuhörer der (PL die **Zuhörer**) listener.

Zuhörerin die (PL die **Zuhörerinnen**) listener.

zukleben verb (PERF **hat zugeklebt**) to seal (an envelope).

zukommen ◇verb (IMPERF **kam zu**, PERF **ist zugekommen**) 1 **auf jemanden zukommen** to come up to somebody; **nächstes Jahr kommt eine Menge Arbeit auf mich zu** I'm in for a lot of work next

year; 2 **jemandem etwas zukommen lassen** to give somebody something; 3 **etwas auf sich zukommen lassen** to take things as they come.

Zukunft die future.

zukünftig adjective future.

zulassen ◇verb (PRES **lässt zu**, IMPERF **ließ zu**, PERF **hat zugelassen**) 1 to allow; 2 to register (a car); 3 to leave closed.

Zulassung die (PL die **Zulassungen**) 1 registration; 2 admission.

zuletzt adverb 1 last; 2 in the end.

zum = zu dem; 1 **etwas zum Lesen** something to read; 2 **spätestens zum fünften März** by 5 March at the latest; 3 **er hat es zum Fenster hinausgeworfen** he threw it out of the window.

zumachen verb (PERF **hat zugemacht**) 1 to close, to shut; 2 to fasten.

zumindest adverb at least.

zunächst adverb 1 first (of all); 2 at first.

Zunahme die (PL die **Zunahmen**) increase.

Zuname der (PL die **Zunamen**) surname.

zunehmen ◇verb (PRES **nimmt zu**, IMPERF **nahm zu**, PERF **hat zugenommen**) 1 to increase; 2 to put on weight.

Zunge die (PL die **Zungen**) tongue.

zur = zu der.

zurechtkommen ◇*verb* (IMPERF **kam zurecht**, PERF **ist zurechtgekommen**) to cope, to manage.

zurechtlegen *verb* (PERF **hat zurechtgelegt**) 1 to put out ready; 2 **sich eine Ausrede zurechtlegen** to think up an excuse.

zurück *adverb* 1 back; 2 **Hamburg, hin und zurück** a return to Hamburg.

zurückbekommen ◇*verb* (IMPERF **bekam zurück**, PERF **hat zurückbekommen**) to get back; **zehn Pfennig zurückbekommen** to get 10 pfennigs change.

zurückbringen ◇*verb* (IMPERF **brachte zurück**, PERF **hat zurückgebracht**) 1 to bring back; 2 to take back.

zurückfahren ◇*verb* (PRES **fährt zurück**, IMPERF **fuhr zurück**, PERF **ist zurückgefahren**) 1 to go back; 2 to drive back; 3 (PERF **hat zurückgefahren**) to drive back; **jemanden zurückfahren** to drive somebody back.

zurückgeben ◇*verb* (PRES **gibt zurück**, IMPERF **gab zurück**, PERF **hat zurückgegeben**) to give back.

zurückgehen ◇*verb* (IMPERF **ging zurück**, PERF **ist zurückgegangen**) 1 to go back; **zurückgehen auf** to go back to; 2 to go down; 3 to decrease.

zurückhalten ◇*verb* (PRES **hält zurück**, IMPERF **hielt zurück**, PERF **hat zurückgehalten**) 1 to hold back; 2 **sich zurückhalten** to restrain yourself.

zurückkommen ◇*verb* (IMPERF **kam zurück**, PERF **ist zurückgekommen**) 1 to come back; **nach Hause zurückkommen** to return home; 2 to get back.

zurücklassen ◇*verb* (PRES **lässt zurück**, IMPERF **ließ zurück**, PERF **hat zurückgelassen**) to leave behind.

zurücklegen *verb* (PERF **hat zurückgelegt**) 1 to put back; 2 to keep, to put aside; 3 **Geld für etwas zurücklegen** to put money by for something; 4 to cover (*a distance*); 5 **sich zurücklegen** to lie back.

zurücknehmen ◇*verb* (PRES **nimmt zurück**, IMPERF **nahm zurück**, PERF **hat zurückgenommen**) to take back.

zurückrufen ◇*verb* (IMPERF **rief zurück**, PERF **hat zurückgerufen**) to call back.

zurücktreten ◇*verb* (PRES **tritt zurück**, IMPERF **trat zurück**, PERF **ist zurückgetreten**) 1 to step back; 2 to resign.

zurückzahlen *verb* (PERF **hat zurückgezahlt**) to pay back.

zurückziehen ◇*verb* (IMPERF **zog zurück**, PERF **hat zurückgezogen**) 1 to draw back; 2 to withdraw (*an offer*); 3 **sich zurückziehen** to withdraw, to retire.

zurzeit *adverb* at the moment.

Zusage *die* (PL **die Zusagen**) acceptance.

zusammen *adverb* 1 together; **zusammen sein** to be together; 2 altogether.

a b c d e f g h i j k l m n o p q r s t u v w x y

Zusammenarbeit die co-operation.

zusammenarbeiten verb (PERF hat zusammengearbeitet) to co-operate.

zusammenbleiben ◇verb (IMPERF blieb zusammen, PERF ist zusammengeblieben) to stay together.

zusammenbrechen ◇verb (PRES bricht zusammen, IMPERF brach zusammen, PERF ist zusammengebrochen) to collapse.

zusammenfassen verb (PERF hat zusammengefasst) to summarize.

Zusammenfassung die (PL die Zusammenfassungen) summary.

zusammenhalten ◇verb (PRES hält zusammen, IMPERF hielt zusammen, PERF hat zusammengehalten) 1 to hold together; 2 to keep together; 3 die Kinder haben zusammengehalten the children stuck together.

Zusammenhang der (PL die Zusammenhänge) 1 context; 2 connection.

zusammenkommen ◇verb (IMPERF kam zusammen, PERF ist zusammengekommen) 1 to meet; 2 to accumulate.

Zusammenkunft die (PL die Zusammenkünfte) meeting.

zusammenlegen verb (PERF hat zusammengelegt) 1 to put together; 2 to fold up; 3 to club together.

zusammennehmen ◇verb (PRES nimmt zusammen, IMPERF nahm zusammen, PERF hat zusammengenommen) 1 to gather up; 2 to summon up, to collect; 3 sich zusammennehmen to pull yourself together.

zusammenpassen verb (PERF hat zusammengepasst) 1 to match; 2 to be well matched (of people); 3 to fit together.

Zusammensein das get-together.

Zusammenstoß der (PL die Zusammenstöße) collision, crash.

zusammenstoßen ◇verb (PRES stößt zusammen, IMPERF stieß zusammen, PERF ist zusammengestoßen) to collide, to crash.

zusammenzählen verb (PERF hat zusammengezählt) to add up.

zusätzlich adjective additional, extra.

zusätzlich adverb in addition, extra.

zuschauen verb (PERF hat zugeschaut) to watch.

Zuschauer der (PL die Zuschauer) 1 spectator; 2 viewer; 3 die Zuschauer the audience.

Zuschauerin die (PL die Zuschauerinnen) 1 spectator; 2 viewer.

Zuschlag der (PL die Zuschläge) 1 surcharge; 2 supplement.

Zuschuss der (PL die Zuschüsse) 1 contribution; 2 grant.

zusehen ◇ *verb* (PRES **sieht zu**, IMPERF **sah zu**, PERF **hat zugesehen**) **1** to watch; **2 zusehen, dass** ... to see (to it) that ...

zusein SEE **zu**.

zusenden *verb* (PERF **hat zugesendet**) to send; **jemandem etwas zusenden** to send something to somebody.

Zustand *der* (PL die **Zustände**) **1** condition; **2** state.

zustande *adverb* **zustande bringen** to bring about; **zustande kommen** to come about.

zuständig *adjective* responsible.

Zustellung *die* (PL die **Zustellungen**) delivery.

zustimmen *verb* (PERF **hat zugestimmt**) to agree.

Zustimmung *die* (PL die **Zustimmungen**) **1** agreement; **2** approval.

zustoßen ◇ *verb* (PRES **stößt zu**, IMPERF **stieß zu**, PERF **ist zugestoßen**) to happen.

Zutat *die* (PL die **Zutaten**) ingredient.

zutreffen ◇ *verb* (PRES **trifft zu**, IMPERF **traf zu**, PERF **hat zugetroffen**) **auf etwas zutreffen** to apply to something.

Zutritt *der* entry; **Zutritt haben** to have access.

zuverlässig *adjective* reliable.

zuversichtlich *adjective* confident, optimistic.

Zuversichtlichkeit *die* confidence.

zuviel SEE **viel**.

zuvor *adverb* **1** before; **der Tag zuvor** the day before; **2** first.

zuwenig SEE **wenig**.

zuzahlen *verb* (PERF **hat zugezahlt**) to pay extra.

zuziehen ◇ *verb* (IMPERF **zog zu**, PERF **hat zugezogen**) **1** to pull tight; **2** to draw (*curtains*); **3** to call in (*an expert etc.*); **4** (PERF **ist zugezogen**) to move into an area; **5 sich eine Verletzung zuziehen** to sustain an injury; **sich eine Erkältung zuziehen** to catch a cold.

zuzüglich *preposition* (+ GEN) plus.

Zwang *der* (PL die **Zwänge**) **1** compulsion; **2** urge; **3** obligation.

zwang SEE **zwingen**.

zwängen *verb* (PERF **hat gezwängt**) to squeeze.

zwanglos *adjective* casual, informal.

zwar *adverb* **1** admittedly; **2 ich war zwar dabei, habe aber nichts gesehen** I was there, but I didn't see anything; **3 und zwar** to be exact.

Zweck *der* (PL die **Zwecke**) **1** purpose; **2** point; **es hat keinen Zweck** there's no point.

zwecklos *adjective* pointless.

zwei *number* two.

zweideutig *adjective* ambiguous.

zweifach *adjective* twice.

Zweifel *der* (PL die **Zweifel**) doubt.

zweifelhaft *adjective* **1** doubtful; **2** dubious.

zweifellos *adverb* undoubtedly.

zweifeln *verb* (PERF **hat gezweifelt**) to doubt; **an etwas zweifeln** to doubt something.

Zweig *der* (PL *die* **Zweige**) 1 branch; 2 twig.

zweihundert *number* two hundred.

zweimal *adverb* twice.

zweisprachig *adjective* bilingual.

zweispurig *adjective* two-track (*railway, recording, road*); **eine zweispurigen Straße** a dual carriageway.

zweit *adverb* **zu zweit** in twos; **wir sind zu zweit** there are two of us.

zweite SEE **zweiter.**

zweitens *adverb* secondly.

zweiter, zweite, zweites *adjective* second; **Mario kam als Zweiter** Mario was the second to arrive.

Zwerg *der* (PL *die* **Zwerge**) dwarf.

Zwiebel *die* (PL *die* **Zwiebeln**) 1 onion; 2 bulb.

Zwilling *der* (PL *die* **Zwillinge**) 1 twin; 2 **Zwillinge** Gemini; **Markus ist Zwilling** Markus is Gemini.

zwingen ◇*verb* (IMPERF **zwang**, PERF **hat gezwungen**) 1 to force; 2 **sich zwingen** to force yourself.

zwinkern *verb* (PERF **hat gezwinkert**) to wink.

zwischen *preposition* (+ DAT, or + ACC *with movement towards a place*) 1 between; 2 among (*a crowd*).

zwischendurch *adverb* 1 in between; 2 now and again.

Zwischenfall *der* (PL *die* **Zwischenfälle**) incident.

Zwischenlandung *die* (PL *die* **Zwischenlandungen**) stop-over.

Zwischenraum *der* (PL *die* **Zwischenräume**) gap, space.

Zwischenzeit *die* **in der Zwischenzeit** in the meantime.

zwo *number* two.

zwölf *number* twelve.

zwoter, zwote, zwotes *adjective* second.

VERB TABLES AND FORMS

On the following pages you will find forms for a regular German verb **machen** followed by the forms for a reflexive verb **sich wassen** and then the forms for the twelve most important irregular verbs in alphabetical order: **dürfen, essen, fahren, gehen, haben, kommen, können, müssen, sein, sollen, werden, wissen**.

After these are given the main forms for other irregular verbs. Note that the forms for the seperable verbs such as **aufstehen** are not given as they can be looked up under the base form (**stehen**).

1

machen
to do *or* to make

Imperative	**Past participle**
mach!	hat gemacht
macht!	
machen Sie!	

Present
ich mache
du machst
er* macht
wir machen
ihr macht
sie machen

Perfect
ich habe gemacht
du hast gemacht
er hat gemacht
wir haben gemacht
ihr habt gemacht
sie haben gemacht

Future
ich werde machen
du wirst machen
er wird machen
wir werden machen
ihr werdet machen
sie werden machen

Present subjunctive
ich mache
du machest
er mache
wir machen
ihr machet
sie machen

Imperfect
ich machte
du machtest
er machte
wir machten
ihr machtet
sie machten

Conditional
ich würde machen
du würdest machen
er würde machen
wir würden machen
ihr würdet machen
sie würden machen

* In these tables er *should be read as* er/sie/es

2

Imperative

wasch dich!
wascht euch!
waschen Sie sich!

Past participle

hat sich
gewaschen

sich waschen
to wash (oneself)

Present

ich	wasche mich
du	wäschst dich
er	wäscht sich
wir	waschen uns
ihr	wascht euch
sie	waschen sich

Perfect

ich	habe mich gewaschen
du	hast dich gewaschen
er	hat sich gewaschen
wir	haben uns gewaschen
ihr	habt euch gewaschen
sie	haben sich gewaschen

Future

ich	werde mich waschen
du	wirst dich waschen
er	wird sich waschen
wir	werden uns waschen
ihr	werdet euch waschen
sie	werden sich waschen

Present subjunctive

ich	wasche mich
du	waschest dich
er	wasche sich
wir	waschen uns
ihr	waschet euch
sie	waschen sich

Imperfect

ich	wusch mich
du	wuschst dich
er	wusch sich
wir	wuschen uns
ihr	wuscht euch
sie	wuschen sich

Conditional

ich	würde mich waschen
du	würdest dich waschen
er	würde sich waschen
wir	würden uns waschen
ihr	würdet euch waschen
sie	würden sich waschen

dürfen
to be allowed

Imperative	Past participle
—	hat gedurft

Present
ich darf
du darfst
er darf
wir dürfen
ihr dürft
sie dürfen

Perfect
ich habe gedurft
du hast gedurft
er hat gedurft
wir haben gedurft
ihr habt gedurft
sie haben gedurft

Future
ich werde dürfen
du wirst dürfen
er wird dürfen
wir werden dürfen
ihr werdet dürfen
sie werden dürfen

Present subjunctive
ich dürfe
du dürfest
er dürfe
wir dürfen
ihr dürfet
sie dürfen

Imperfect
ich durfte
du durftest
er durfte
wir durften
ihr durftet
sie durften

Conditional
ich würde dürfen
du würdest dürfen
er würde dürfen
wir würden dürfen
ihr würdet dürfen
sie würden dürfen

4

Imperative	**Past participle**	**essen**
iss!	hat gegessen	to eat
esst!		
essen Sie!		

Present

ich esse
du isst
er isst
wir essen
ihr esst
sie essen

Present subjunctive

ich esse
du essest
er esse
wir essen
ihr esset
sie essen

Perfect

ich habe gegessen
du hast gegessen
er hat gegessen
wir haben gegessen
ihr habt gegessen
sie haben gegessen

Imperfect

ich aß
du aßest
er aß
wir aßen
ihr aßt
sie aßen

Future

ich werde essen
du wirst essen
er wird essen
wir werden essen
ihr werdet essen
sie werden essen

Conditional

ich würde essen
du würdest essen
er würde essen
wir würden essen
ihr würdet essen
sie würden essen

fahren
to drive *or* to go

Imperative	**Past participle**
fahr!	ist gefahren
fahrt!	
fahren Sie!	

Present
ich fahre
du fährst
er fährt
wir fahren
ihr fahrt
sie fahren

Perfect
ich bin gefahren
du bist gefahren
er ist gefahren
wir sind gefahren
ihr seid gefahren
sie sind gefahren

Future
ich werde fahren
du wirst fahren
er wird fahren
wir werden fahren
ihr werdet fahren
sie werden fahren

Present subjunctive
ich fahre
du fahrest
er fahre
wir fahren
ihr fahret
sie fahren

Imperfect
ich fuhr
du fuhrst
er fuhr
wir fuhren
ihr fuhrt
sie fuhren

Conditional
ich würde fahren
du würdest fahren
er würde fahren
wir würden fahren
ihr würdet fahren
sie würden fahren

6

Imperative	**Past participle**	**gehen**
geh!	ist gegangen	to go
geht!		
gehen Sie!		

Present

ich gehe
du gehst
er geht
wir gehen
ihr geht
sie gehen

Present subjunctive

ich gehe
du gehest
er gehe
wir gehen
ihr gehet
sie gehen

Perfect

ich bin gegangen
du bist gegangen
er ist gegangen
wir sind gegangen
ihr seid gegangen
sie sind gegangen

Imperfect

ich ging
du gingst
er ging
wir gingen
ihr gingt
sie gingen

Future

ich werde gehen
du wirst gehen
er wird gehen
wir werden gehen
ihr werdet gehen
sie werden gehen

Conditional

ich würde gehen
du würdest gehen
er würde gehen
wir würden gehen
ihr würdet gehen
sie würden gehen

haben
to have

Imperative	**Past participle**
hab!	hat gehabt
habt!	
haben Sie!	

Present
ich habe
du hast
er hat
wir haben
ihr habt
sie haben

Perfect
ich habe gehabt
du hast gehabt
er hat gehabt
wir haben gehabt
ihr habt gehabt
sie haben gehabt

Future
ich werde haben
du wirst haben
er wird haben
wir werden haben
ihr werdet haben
sie werden haben

Present subjunctive
ich habe
du habest
er habe
wir haben
ihr habet
sie haben

Imperfect
ich hatte
du hattest
er hatte
wir hatten
ihr hattet
sie hatten

Imperfect subjunctive
ich hätte
du hättest
er hätte
wir hätten
ihr hättet
sie hätten

Conditional
ich würde haben
du würdest haben
er würde haben
wir würden haben
ihr würdet haben
sie würden haben

8

kommen
to come

Imperative	**Past participle**
komm!	ist gekommen
kommt!	
kommen Sie!	

Present

ich komme
du kommst
er kommt
wir kommen
ihr kommt
sie kommen

Present subjunctive

ich komme
du kommest
er komme
wir kommen
ihr kommet
sie kommen

Perfect

ich bin gekommen
du bist gekommen
er ist gekommen
wir sind gekommen
ihr seid gekommen
sie sind gekommen

Imperfect

ich kam
du kamst
er kam
wir kamen
ihr kamt
sie kamen

Future

ich werde kommen
du wirst kommen
er wird kommen
wir werden kommen
ihr werdet kommen
sie werden kommen

Conditional

ich würde kommen
du würdest kommen
er würde kommen
wir würden kommen
ihr würdet kommen
sie würden kommen

können
can *or* or to be able to

Imperative	Past participle
—	hat gekonnt
	hätte können

Present	Present subjunctive
ich kann	ich könne
du kannst	du könnest
er kann	er könne
wir können	wir können
ihr könnt	ihr könnet
sie können	sie können

Perfect	Imperfect
ich habe gekonnt	ich konnte
du hast gekonnt	du konntest
er hat gekonnt	er konnte
wir haben gekonnt	wir konnten
ihr habt gekonnt	ihr konntet
sie haben gekonnt	sie konnten

Future	Imperfect subjunctive
ich werde können	ich könnte
du wirst können	du könntest
er wird können	er könnte
wir werden können	wir könnten
ihr werdet können	ihr könntet
sie werden können	sie könnten

Conditional

ich würde können
du würdest können
er würde können
wir würden können
ihr würdet können
sie würden können

10

Imperative	Past participle	**müssen**
—	hat gemusst	must *or* to have to
	hätte müssen	

Present
- ich muss
- du musst
- er muss
- wir müssen
- ihr müsst
- sie müssen

Perfect
- ich habe gemusst
- du hast gemusst
- er hat gemusst
- wir haben gemusst
- ihr habt gemusst
- sie haben gemusst

Future
- ich werde müssen
- du wirst müssen
- er wird müssen
- wir werden müssen
- ihr werdet müssen
- sie werden müssen

Present subjunctive
- ich müsse
- du müssest
- er müsse
- wir müssen
- ihr müsset
- sie müssen

Imperfect
- ich musste
- du musstest
- er musste
- wir mussten
- ihr musstet*
- sie mussten

Imperfect subjunctive
- ich müsste
- du müsstest
- er müsste
- wir müssten
- ihr müsstet
- sie müssten

Conditional
- ich würde müssen
- du würdest müssen
- er würde müssen
- wir würden müssen
- ihr würdet müssen
- sie würden müssen

sein
to be

Imperative

sei!
seid!
seinen Sie!

Past participle

ist gewesen

Present	**Present subjunctive**
ich bin	ich sei
du bist	du seist/seiest
er ist	er sei
wir sind	wir seien
ihr seid	ihr seiet
sie sind	sie seien

Perfect	**Imperfect**
ich bin gewesen	ich war
du bist gewesen	du warst
er ist gewesen	er war
wir sind gewesen	wir waren
ihr seid gewesen	ihr wart
sie sind gewesen	sie waren

Future	**Imperfect subjunctive**
ich werde sein	ich wäre
du wirst sein	du wärst/wärest
er wird sein	er wäre
wir werden sein	wir wären
ihr werdet sein	ihr wärt/wäret
sie werden sein	sie wären

Conditional

ich würde sein
du würdest sein
er würde sein
wir würden sein
ihr würdet sein
sie würden sein

Imperative	**Past participle**	**sollen**
—	hat gesollt	should

Present

ich soll
du sollst
er soll
wir sollen
ihr sollt
sie sollen

Perfect

ich habe gesollt
du hast gesollt
er hat gesollt
wir haben gesollt
ihr habt gesollt
sie haben gesollt

Future

ich werde sollen
du wirst sollen
er wird sollen
wir werden sollen
ihr werdet sollen
sie werden sollen

Present subjunctive

ich solle
du sollest
er solle
wir sollen
ihr sollet
sie sollen

Imperfect

ich sollte
du solltest
er sollte
wir sollten
ihr solltet
sie sollten

Imperfect subjunctive

ich sollte
du solltest
er sollte
wir sollten
ihr solltet
sie sollten

Conditional

ich würde sollen
du würdest sollen
er würde sollen
wir würden sollen
ihr würdet sollen
sie würden sollen

13

werden
to become or to get

Imperative	Past participle
werde!	ist geworden
werde!	
werden Sie!	

Present
ich werde
du wirst
er wird
wir werden
ihr werdet
sie werden

Perfect
ich bin geworden
du bist geworden
er ist geworden
wir sind geworden
ihr seid geworden
sie sind geworden

Future
ich werde werden
du wirst werden
er wird werden
wir werden werden
ihr werdet werden
sie werden werden

Present subjunctive
ich werde
du werdest
er werde
wir werden
ihr werdet
sie werden

Imperfect
ich wurde
du wurdest
er wurde
wir wurden
ihr wurdet
sie wurden

Conditional
ich würde werden
du würdest werden
er würde werden
wir würden werden
ihr würdet werden
sie würden werden

14

Imperative	**Past participle**	**wissen**
wisse!	hat gewusst	to know
wisst!		
wissen Sie!		

Present

ich weiß
du weißt
er weiß
wir wissen
ihr wisst
sie wissen

Perfect

ich habe gewusst
du hast gewusst
er hat gewusst
wir haben gewusst
ihr habt gewusst
sie haben gewusst

Future

ich werde wissen
du wirst wissen
er wird wissen
wir werden wissen
ihr werdet wissen
sie werden wissen

Present subjunctive

ich wisse
du wissest
er wisse
wir wissen
ihr wisset
sie wissen

Imperfect

ich wusste
du wusstest
er wusste
wir wussten
ihr wusstet
sie wussten

Conditional

ich würde wissen
du würdest wissen
er würde wissen
wir würden wissen
ihr würdet wissen
sie würden wissen

German irregular verb forms

This list shows the main forms of other irregular verbs.

Infinitive	Present ich, du, er/sie/es	Imperfect er/sie/es	Perfect er/sie/es
bekommen	bekomme, bekommst, bekommt	bekam	hat bekommen
bergen	berge, birgst, birgt	barg	hat geborgen
besitzen	besitze, besitzt, besitzt	besaß	hat besessen
betrügen	betrüge, betrügst, betrügt	betrog	hat betrogen
biegen	biege, biegst, biegt	bog	hat *or* ist gebogen
bieten	biete, bietest, bietet	bot	hat geboten
binden	binde, bindest, bindet	band	hat gebunden
bitten	bitte, bittest, bittet	bat	hat gebeten
blasen	blase, bläst, bläst	blies	hat geblasen
bleiben	bleibe, bleibst, bleibt	blieb	ist geblieben
braten	brate, brätst, brät	briet	hat gebraten
brechen	breche, brichst, bricht	brach	hat *or* ist gebrochen
brennen	brenne, brennst, brennt	brannte	hat gebrannt
bringen	bringe, bringst, bringt	brachte	hat gebracht
denken	denke, denkst, denkt	dachte	hat gedacht
dürfen	darf, darfst, darf	durfte	hat gedurft
einladen	lade ein, lädst ein, lädt ein	lud ein	hat eingeladen
empfangen	empfange, empfängst, empfängt	empfing	hat empfangen
empfehlen	empfehle, empfiehlst, empfiehlt	empfahl	hat empfohlen
entscheiden	entscheide, entscheidest, entscheidet	entschied	hat entschieden
fahren	fahre, fährst, fährt	fuhr	ist *or* hat gefahren

Infinitive	Present ich, du, er/sie/es	Imperfect er/sie/es	Perfect er/sie/es
fallen	falle, fällst, fällt	fiel	ist gefallen
fangen	fange, fängst, fängt	fing	hat gefangen
fechten	fechte, fichtst, ficht	focht	hat gefochten
finden	finde, findest, findet	fand	hat gefunden
fliegen	fliege, fliegst, fliegt	flog	ist *or* hat geflogen
fliehen	fliehe, fliehst, flieht	floh	ist geflohen
fließen	fließe, fließt, fließt	floss	ist geflossen
fressen	fresse, frisst, frisst	fraß	hat gefressen
frieren	friere, frierst, friert	fror	hat *or* ist gefroren
geben	gebe, gibst, gibt	gab	hat gegeben
gefallen	gefalle, gefällst, gefällt	gefiel	hat gefallen
gehen	gehe, gehst, geht	ging	ist gegangen
gelingen	es gelingt mir/dir/ihm, ihr, ihm	gelang	ist gelungen
gelten	gelte, giltst, gilt	galt	hat gegolten
genießen	genieße, genießt, genießt	genoss	hat genossen
geraten	gerate, gerätst, gerät	geriet	ist geraten
geschehen	es geschieht	geschah	ist geschehen
gewinnen	gewinne, gewinnst, gewinnt	gewann	hat gewonnen
gießen	gieße, gießt, gießt	goss	hat gegossen
gleichen	gleiche, gleichst, gleicht	glich	hat geglichen
graben	grabe, gräbst, gräbt	grub	hat gegraben
greifen	greife, greifst, greift	griff	hat gegriffen
helfen	helfe, hilfst, hilft	half	hat geholfen
hinweisen	weise hin, weist hin, weist hin	wies hin	hat hingewiesen
kennen	kenne, kennst, kennt	kannte	hat gekannt
klingen	klinge, klingst, klingt	klang	hat geklungen
kneifen	kneife, kneifst, kneift	kniff	hat gekniffen

Infinitive	Present	Imperfect	Perfect
	ich, du, er/sie/es	er/sie/es	er/sie/es
kommen	komme, kommst, kommt	kam	ist gekommen
können	kann, kannst, kann	konnte	hat gekonnt
kriechen	krieche, kriechst, kriecht	kroch	ist gekrochen
lassen	lasse, lässt, lässt	ließ	hat gelassen
laufen	laufe, läufst, läuft	lief	ist gelaufen
leiden	leide, leidest, leidet	litt	hat gelitten
leihen	leihe, leihst, leiht	lieh	hat geliehen
lesen	lese, liest, liest	las	hat gelesen
liegen	liege, liegst, liegt	lag	hat gelegen
lügen	lüge, lügst, lügt	log	hat gelogen
mahlen	mahle, mahlst, mahlt	mahlte	hat gemahlen
meiden	meide, meidest, meidet	mied	hat gemieden
messen	messe, mißt, mißt	maß	hat gemessen
misslingen	misslinge, misslingst, misslingt	misslang	ist misslungen
mögen	mag, magst, mag	mochte	hat gemocht
müssen	muss, musst, muss	musste	hat gemusst
nehmen	nehme, nimmst, nimmt	nahm	hat genommen
nennen	nenne, nennst, nennt	nannte	hat genannt
pfeifen	pfeife, pfeifst, pfeift	pfiff	hat gepfiffen
raten	rate, rätst, rät	riet	hat geraten
reiben	reibe, reibst, reibt	rieb	hat gerieben
reißen	reiße, reißt, reißt	riss	hat or ist gerissen
reiten	reite, reitest, reitet	ritt	hat or ist geritten
rennen	renne, rennst, rennt	rannte	ist gerannt
riechen	rieche, riechst, riecht	roch	hat gerochen
rufen	rufe, rufst, ruft	rief	hat gerufen

Infinitive	Present	Imperfect	Perfect
	ich, du, er/sie/es	er/sie/es	er/sie/es
saufen	saufe, säufst, säuft	soff	hat gesoffen
schaffen	schaffe, schaffst, schafft	schuf	hat geschaffen
scheiden	scheide, scheidest, scheidet	schied	hat *or* ist geschieden
scheinen	scheine, scheinst, scheint	schien	hat geschienen
schieben	schiebe, schiebst, schiebt	schob	hat geschoben
schießen	schieße, schießt, schießt	schoss	hat *or* ist geschossen
schlafen	schlafe, schläfst, schläft	schlief	hat geschlafen
schlagen	schlage, schlägst, schlägt	schlug	hat geschlagen
schleichen	schleiche, schleichst, schleicht	schlich	ist geschlichen
schließen	schließe, schließt, schließt	schloss	hat geschlossen
schmeißen	schmeiße, schmeißt, schmeißt	schmiss	hat geschmissen
schmelzen	schmelze, schmilzt, schmilzt	schmolz	ist geschmolzen
schneiden	schneide, schneidest, schneidet	schnitt	hat geschnitten
schreiben	schreibe, schreibst, schreibt	schrieb	hat geschrieben
schreien	schreie, schreist, schreit	schrie	hat geschrien
schweigen	schweige, schweigst, schweigt	schwieg	hat geschwiegen
schwimmen	schwimme, schwimmst, schwimmt	schwamm	ist *or* hat geschwommen
schwören	schwöre, schwörst, schwört	schwor	hat geschworen
sehen	sehe, siehst, sieht	sah	hat gesehen
sein	bin, bist, ist	war	ist gewesen
singen	singe, singst, singt	sang	hat gesungen
sinken	sinke, sinkst, sinkt	sank	ist gesunken
sitzen	sitze, sitzt, sitzt	saß	hat gesessen
sollen	soll, sollst, soll	sollte	hat gesollt
spinnen	spinne, spinnst, spinnt	spann	hat gesponnen
springen	springe, springst, springt	sprang	ist gesprungen
stechen	steche, stichst, sticht	stach	hat gestochen
stehen	stehe, stehst, steht	stand	hat gestanden

Infinitive	Present	Imperfect	Perfect
	ich, du, er/sie/es	er/sie/es	er/sie/es
sprechen	spreche, sprichst, spricht	sprach	hat gesprochen
stehlen	stehle, stiehlst, stiehlt	stahl	hat gestohlen
steigen	steige, steigst, steigt	stieg	ist gestiegen
sterben	sterbe, stirbst, stirbt	starb	ist gestorben
stinken	stinke, stinkst, stinkt	stank	hat gestunken
stoßen	stoße, stößt, stößt	stieß	hat or ist gestoßen
streichen	streiche, streichst, streicht	strich	hat gestrichen
streiten	streite, streitest, streitet	stritt	hat gestritten
tragen	trage, trägst, trägt	trug	hat getragen
treffen	treffe, triffst, trifft	traf	hat getroffen
treiben	treibe, treibst, treibt	trieb	hat getrieben
treten	trete, trittst, tritt	trat	hat or ist getreten
trinken	trinke, trinkst, trinkt	trank	hat getrunken
tun	tue, tust, tut	tat	hat getan
überweisen	überweise, überweist, überweist	überwies	hat überwiesen
umziehen	ziehe um, ziehst um, zieht um	zog um	ist or hat umgezogen
verbieten	verbiete, verbietest, verbietet	verbot	hat verboten
verderben	verderbe, verdirbst, verdirbt	verdarb	hat or ist verdorben
vergessen	vergesse, vergißt, vergißt	vergaß	hat vergessen
verlieren	verliere, verlierst, verliert	verlor	hat verloren
verschwinden	verschwinde, verschwindest, verschwindet	verschwand	ist verschwunden
verzeihen	verzeihe, verzeihst, verzeiht	verzieh	hat verziehen
verstehen	verstehe, verstehst, versteht	verstand	hat verstanden

Infinitive	Present ich, du, er/sie/es	Imperfect er/sie/es	Perfect er/sie/es
wachsen	wachse, wächst, wächst	wuchs	ist gewachsen
waschen	wasche, wäscht, wäscht	wusch	hat gewaschen
werben	werbe, wirbst, wirbt	warb	hat geworben
werden	werde, wirst, wird	wurde	ist geworden
werfen	werfe, wirfst, wirft	warf	hat geworfen
wiegen	wiege, wiegst, wiegt	wog	hat gewogen
wissen	weiß, weißt, weiß	wusste	hatgewusst
wollen	will, willst, will	wollte	hat gewollt
ziehen	ziehe, ziehst, zieht	zog	hat *or* ist gezogen
zwingen	zwinge, zwingst, zwingt	zwang	hat gezwungen

Aa

a *indefinite article* **1** (*before a noun which is masculine in German*) ein; **a tree** ein Baum; **2** (*before a noun which is feminine in German*) eine; **a story** eine Geschichte; **3** (*before a noun which is neuter in German*) ein; **a dress** ein Kleid; **4** not a kein; **the party was not a success** die Party war kein Erfolg; **he didn't say a word** er hat kein Wort gesagt; **5 ten euros a metre** zehn Euro den Meter; **6 fifty kilometres an hour** fünfzig Stundenkilometer; **7 three times a day** dreimal täglich.

abandon *verb* **1** aufgeben ❖ SEP; **they abandoned the plan** sie gaben den Plan auf; **2** verlassen ❖; **they abandoned the city** sie verließen die Stadt.

abbey *noun* Abtei *die* (PL *die* Abteien).

abbreviation *noun* Abkürzung *die* (PL *die* Abkürzungen).

ability *noun* Fähigkeit *die* (PL *die* Fähigkeiten); **to have the ability to do something** etwas tun können.

able *adjective* fähig; **to be able to do something** etwas tun können; **she wasn't able to come** sie konnte nicht kommen.

abortion *noun* Abtreibung *die* (PL *die* Abtreibungen).

about *preposition* **1** über (+ ACC); **a film about space** ein Film über den Weltraum; **to talk about something/somebody** über etwas/ jemanden reden; **what is she talking about?** worüber redet sie?; **2** um (+ ACC); **to be about**

something um etwas gehen; **what's it about?** worum geht es?; **3 to know about something** von etwas (DAT) wissen; **she didn't know about the party** sie wusste nichts von der Party; **he knows nothing about it** er weiß nichts davon; **4 to think about something/somebody** an etwas/ jemanden (+ ACC) denken; **I'm thinking about you** ich denke an dich.

about *adverb* **1** (*approximately*) ungefähr; **about sixty people** ungefähr sechzig Leute; **in about a week** in ungefähr einer Woche; **2** (*when talking about time*) gegen; **about three o'clock** gegen drei Uhr; **3 to be about to do something** gerade etwas tun wollen; **I was (just) about to leave** ich wollte gerade gehen.

above *preposition* **1** über (+ DAT); **the lamp above the table** die Lampe über dem Tisch; **2 above all** vor allem.

abroad *adverb* im Ausland; **to live abroad** im Ausland leben; **to go abroad** ins Ausland fahren.

abscess *noun* Abszess *der* (PL *die* Abszesse).

abseiling *noun* Abseilen *das*.

absent *adjective* abwesend; **to be absent from school** in der Schule fehlen.

absent-minded *adjective* zerstreut.

absolute *adjective* absolut; **an absolute disaster** eine absolute Katastrophe.

absolutely *adverb* **1** wirklich; **it's absolutely dreadful** das ist wirklich furchtbar; **2** völlig; **you're absolutely right** du hast völlig Recht.

abuse *noun* **1** Missbrauch *der*; **drug abuse** Der Drogenmissbrauch; **2** (*insults*) Beschimpfungen (*plural*).

abuse *verb* **1 to abuse somebody** jemanden missbrauchen; **2** (*to insult*) beschimpfen.

accelerate *verb* beschleunigen.

accelerator *noun* Gaspedal *das* (PL die Gaspedale).

accent *noun* Akzent *der* (PL die Akzente); **to speak with a German accent** mit deutschem Akzent sprechen.

accept *verb* annehmen✧ SEP; **he accepted the invitation** er nahm die Einladung an.

acceptable *adjective* annehmbar.

access *noun* Zugang *der*.

access *verb* **to access data** auf Daten zugreifen.

accessory *noun* **1** Zubehörteil *das*; **accessories** Zubehör *das*; **2 accessories** (*fashion items*) Accessoires (*plural*).

accident *noun* **1** Unfall *der* (PL die Unfälle); **to have an accident** einen Unfall haben; **road accident** der Verkehrsunfall; **car accident** der Autounfall; **2** Zufall *der* (PL die Zufälle); **by accident** zufällig; **I found it by accident** ich habe es zufällig gefunden.

accidental *adjective* zufällig; **an accidental discovery** eine zufällige Entdeckung.

accidentally *adverb* **1** (*without meaning to*) versehentlich; **I accidentally threw it away** ich habe es versehentlich weggeworfen; **2** (*by chance*) zufällig; **I accidentally discovered that … ich habe zufällig herausgefunden, dass ….**

accident & emergency *noun* Notaufnahme *die*.

accommodation *noun* Unterkunft *die*; **accommodation is free** Unterkunft ist kostenlos; **I'm looking for accommodation** (*when looking for a room*) ich suche ein Zimmer.

accompany *verb* begleiten; **to accompany somebody** jemanden begleiten.

according *in phrase* **according to** laut (+ DAT); **according to Sophie** laut Sophie.

accordion *noun* Akkordeon *das* (PL die Akkordeons).

account *noun* **1** (*in a bank, shop, or post office*) Konto *das* (PL die Konten); **bank account** das Bankkonto; **to open an account** ein Konto eröffnen; **I have fifty pounds in my account** ich habe fünfzig Pfund auf meinem Konto; **2** (*an explanation*) Darstellung *die* (PL die Darstellungen); **I want to hear his account of what happened** ich möchte seine Darstellung der Ereignisse hören; **3 on account of** wegen (+ GEN); **4 to take something into account** etwas berücksichtigen.

accountant *noun* Buchhalter *der* (PL die Buchhalter), Buchhalterin die (PL die Buchhalterinnen); **she's an accountant** sie ist Buchhalterin.

accurate *adjective* genau.

accurately *adverb* genau.

accuse *verb* beschuldigen; **she accused me of stealing her pen** sie beschuldigte mich, ihren Kugelschreiber gestohlen zu haben.

ace *noun* Ass das (PL die Asse); **the ace of hearts** das Herzass.

ace *adjective* klasse (*informal*); **he's an ace drummer** er spielt klasse Schlagzeug.

ache *verb* schmerzen; **my head aches** mein Kopf schmerzt.

achieve *verb* **1** leisten; **she's achieved a great deal** sie hat eine Menge geleistet; **2** erreichen (*an aim*); **he achieved what he wanted** er hat erreicht, was er wollte.

achievement *noun* Leistung die (PL die Leistungen); **it's a great achievement** das ist eine große Leistung.

acid *noun* Säure die (PL die Säuren).

acne *noun* Akne die.

across *preposition* **1** (*over to the other side of*) über (+ ACC); **to run across the road** über die Straße laufen; **we walked across the park** wir sind durch den Park gegangen; **2** (*on the other side of*) auf der anderen Seite (+ GEN); **he lives across the river** er wohnt auf der anderen Seite des Flusses; **3 they live across the street** sie wohnen gegenüber.

act *noun* (*deed*) Tat die (PL die Taten).

act *verb* (*in a play or film*) spielen; **to act the part of the hero** die Rolle des Helden spielen.

action *noun* **1** Handlung die (PL die Handlungen); **2 to take action** etwas unternehmen.

action replay *noun* Wiederholung die (PL die Wiederholungen).

active *adjective* aktiv.

activity *noun* Aktivität die (PL die Aktivitäten).

actor *noun* Schauspieler der (PL die Schauspieler).

actress *noun* Schauspielerin die (PL die Schauspielerinnen).

actual *adjective* **what were his actual words?** was genau hat er gesagt?; **in actual fact** eigentlich.

actually *adverb* **1** (*in fact, as it happens*) eigentlich; **actually, I've changed my mind** ich habe mich eigentlich anders entschlossen; **2** (*really and truly*) wirklich; **did she actually say that?** hat sie das wirklich gesagt?

AD (*Anno Domini*) n. Chr. (*nach Christus*); **in 400 AD** 400 n. Chr.

ad *noun* **1** (*on TV*) Werbespot der (PL die Werbespots); **2** (*in a newspaper*) Anzeige die (PL die Anzeigen); **to put an ad in the paper** eine Anzeige in die Zeitung setzen; **the small ads** die Kleinanzeigen.

adapt *verb* **1 to adapt something** (*a book or film*) etwas bearbeiten; **2 to adapt to** sich anpassen SEP (+ DAT); **she's adapted to her new surroundings** sie hat sich an ihre neuen Umgebung angepasst.

adaptor *noun* **1** Adapter der (PL die Adapter); **2** (*for two plugs*)

a b c d e f g h i j k l m n o p q r s t u v w x y z

Doppelstecker der (PL die Doppelstecker).

add verb 1 hinzufügen SEP; **to add an introduction to something** etwas (DAT) eine Einleitung hinzufügen; 2 dazugeben✧ SEP; **add three eggs** geben Sie drei Eier dazu.

● **to add up** zusammenzählen SEP.

addict noun 1 (drug addict) Süchtige der/die (PL die Süchtigen); 2 **she's a telly addict** sie ist fernsehsüchtig; **he's a football addict** er ist ein Fußballnarr.

addicted adjective 1 **to become addicted to drugs** drogensüchtig werden; 2 **he's addicted to football** Fußball ist bei ihm zur Sucht geworden; 3 **I'm addicted to sweets** ich bin nach Süßigkeiten süchtig.

addition noun 1 (adding up) Addition die; 2 **in addition** außerdem; 3 **in addition to** zusätzlich zu (+ DAT).

additional adjective zusätzlich.

additive noun Zusatz der (PL die Zusätze).

address noun Adresse die (PL die Adressen); **do you know his address?** weißt du seine Adresse?; **to change address** die Adresse wechseln.

address book noun Adressbuch das (PL die Adressbücher).

adequate adjective angemessen.

adhesive noun Klebstoff der.

adhesive adjective adhesive tape der Klebstreifen.

adjective noun Adjektiv das (PL die Adjektive).

adjust verb 1 to adjust something etwas einstellen SEP; **he adjusted the set** er stellte das Gerät ein; **to adjust the distance** auf die (richtige) Entfernung einstellen; 2 **to adjust to something** sich an etwas (ACC) gewöhnen.

adjustable adjective verstellbar.

administration noun Verwaltung die.

admiration noun Bewunderung die.

admire verb bewundern.

admission noun Eintritt der; **'admission free'** 'Eintritt frei'.

admit verb 1 (confess, concede) zugeben✧ SEP; **she admits she lied** sie gibt zu, dass sie gelogen hat; 2 (allow to enter) hereinlassen✧ SEP; **to admit somebody to a restaurant** jemanden in ein Restaurant lassen; 3 **to be admitted to hospital** ins Krankenhaus eingeliefert werden.

adolescence noun Jugend die.

adolescent noun Jugendliche der/die (PL die Jugendlichen).

adopt verb adoptieren.

adopted adjective adoptiert.

adoption noun Adoption die (PL die Adoptionen).

adore verb lieben.

adult noun Erwachsene der/die (PL die Erwachsenen).

adult adjective the adult population Erwachsene (plural).

Adult Education noun Erwachsenenbildung die.

advance noun Fortschritt der (PL die Fortschritte); **advances in technology** technologische Fortschritte.

advance *verb* **1** (*make progress*) Fortschritte machen; **2** (*move forward*) (*of a group or an army*) vorrücken SEP (PERF *sein*).

advanced *adjective* fortgeschritten (*student, age*).

advantage *noun* **1** Vorteil *der* (PL die Vorteile); **there are several advantages** es gibt verschiedene Vorteile; **2 to take advantage of something** etwas ausnutzen SEP; **I always take advantage of the sales to buy myself some shoes** ich warte immer bis zum Schlussverkauf, um mir Schuhe zu kaufen; **3 to take advantage of somebody** (*unfairly*) jemanden ausnutzen SEP.

Advent *noun* Advent *der*.

adventure *noun* Abenteuer *das* (PL die Abenteuer).

adverb *noun* Adverb *das* (PL die Adverbien).

advert, advertisement *noun* **1** (*at the cinema or on television*) Werbespot *der* (PL die Werbespots); **2** (*in a newspaper for a job, article for sale, etc.*) Anzeige *die* (PL die Anzeigen); **she answered a job advertisement** sie meldete sich auf eine Stellenanzeige.

advertise *verb* **to advertise something in the newspaper** (*in the small ads*) etwas in der Zeitung inserieren; **I saw a bike advertised in the paper** ich habe ein Rad in der Zeitung inseriert gesehen.

advertising *noun* Werbung *die*.

advice *noun* Rat *der*; **to ask somebody's advice** jemanden um Rat fragen; **a piece of advice** ein Ratschlag.

advise *verb* raten✧ (+ DAT); **to advise somebody to do something** jemandem raten, etwas zu tun; **I advised him to stop** ich riet ihm anzuhalten; **I advised her not to buy the car** ich habe ihr geraten, das Auto nicht zu kaufen.

aerial *noun* Antenne *die* (PL die Antennen).

aerobics *noun* Aerobic *das*; **to do aerobics** Aerobic machen.

aeroplane *noun* Flugzeug *das* (PL die Flugzeuge).

aerosol *noun* **an aerosol can** eine Spraydose.

affair *noun* **1** Angelegenheit *die* (PL die Angelegenheiten); **international affairs** internationale Angelegenheiten; **current affairs** die Tagespolitik; **2 love affair** das Liebesverhältnis.

affect *verb* beeinflussen.

affectionate *adjective* liebevoll.

afford *verb* **to be able to afford something** (+ DAT) etwas leisten können; **we can't afford to go out much** wir können es uns nicht leisten, oft auszugehen; **I can't afford a new bike** ich kann mir kein neues Rad leisten.

afraid *adjective* **1 to be afraid of something** Angst vor etwas (DAT) haben; **she's afraid of dogs** sie hat Angst vor Hunden; **2 I'm afraid I can't help you** ich kann dir leider nicht helfen; **I'm afraid so** leider ja; **I'm afraid not** leider nicht.

Africa *noun* Afrika *das*; **to Africa** nach Afrika.

African *noun* Afrikaner *der* (PL die Afrikaner), Afrikanerin *die* (PL die Afrikanerinnen).

a
b
c
d
e
f
g
h
i
j
k
l
m
n
o
p
q
r
s
t
u
v
w
x
y
z

African *adjective* afrikanisch; **she is African** sie ist Afrikanerin.

after *preposition, adverb* **1** nach (+ DAT); **after 10 o'clock** nach zehn Uhr; **after lunch** nach dem Mittagessen; **after school** nach der Schule; **2 the day after tomorrow** übermorgen; **soon after** kurz danach; **3 to run after somebody** jemandem hinterherlaufen ⊹ SEP.

after *conjunction* nachdem; **after I'd finished my homework** nachdem ich meine Hausaufgaben gemacht hatte.

after all *adverb* schließlich; **after all, she's only six** sie ist schließlich erst sechs.

afternoon *noun* **1** Nachmittag *der* (PL die Nachmittage); **in the afternoon** am Nachmittag; **every afternoon** jeden Nachmittag; **2 this afternoon** heute Nachmittag; **on Sunday afternoon** am Sonntagnachmittag; **3 on Saturday afternoons** samstagsnachmittags; **at four o' clock in the afternoon** um vier Uhr nachmittags.

after-shave *noun* Rasierwasser *das* (PL die Rasierwasser).

afterwards *adverb* danach; **shortly afterwards** kurz danach.

again *adverb* **1** wieder; **she's ill again** sie ist wieder krank; **2 I saw her again yesterday** ich habe sie gestern wieder gesehen; **3 never again!** nie wieder!; **again and again** immer wieder; **4** (*one more time*) noch einmal; **try again** versuche es noch einmal; **you**

should ask her again du solltest sie noch einmal fragen.

against *preposition* gegen (+ ACC); **against the wall** gegen die Wand; **to lean against the wall** sich gegen die Wand lehnen; **I'm against the idea** ich bin gegen die Idee.

age *noun* **1** Alter *das*; **at the age of fifty** im Alter von fünfzig; **she's the same age as me** sie ist genauso alt wie ich; **to be under age** minderjährig sein; **2 I haven't seen Johnny for ages** ich habe Johnny schon ewig nicht mehr gesehen; **I haven't been to London for ages** ich bin schon ewig nicht mehr in London gewesen.

aged *adjective* alt; **a woman aged thirty** eine dreißigjährige Frau.

agent *noun* Vertreter *der* (PL die Vertreter), Vertreterin *die* (PL die Vertreterinnen); **an estate agent** ein Immobilienmakler; **a travel agent's** ein Reisebüro.

aggressive *adjective* aggressiv.

ago *adverb* vor (+ DAT); **an hour ago** vor einer Stunde; **three days ago** vor drei Tagen; **a long time ago** vor langer Zeit; **not long ago** vor kurzem; **how long ago was it?** wie lange ist das her?

agree *verb* **1 to agree with somebody** mit jemandem gleicher Meinung sein; **I agree with Laura** ich stimme Laura zu; **2 I agree** ich bin der gleichen Meinung; **I don't agree** ich bin anderer Meinung; **3 to agree that** ... zugeben ⊹ SEP, dass ...; **I agree that it's too late now** ich gebe zu, dass es jetzt zu spät ist; **4 to agree to something** mit etwas einverstanden sein;

Steve's agreed to help me Steve hat sich einverstanden erklärt, mir zu helfen; **5 coffee doesn't agree with me** Kaffee bekommt mir nicht.

agreement noun **1** (when sharing an opinion) Übereinstimmung die; **2** (contract) Abkommen das (PL die Abkommen).

agriculture noun Landwirtschaft die.

ahead adverb **1 go ahead!** bitte!; **2 straight ahead** geradeaus; **keep going straight ahead until you get to the crossroads** gehen Sie immer geradeaus bis zur Kreuzung; **3 our team was ten points ahead** unsere Mannschaft hatte zehn Punkte Vorsprung; **4 ahead of time** früher als geplant; **5 the people ahead of me** die Leute vor mir.

aid noun **1** Hilfe die; **aid to developing countries** die Entwicklungshilfe; **2 in aid of** zugunsten (+ GEN); **in aid of the homeless** zugunsten der Obdachlosen.

Aids noun Aids das; **to have Aids** Aids haben.

aim noun Ziel das (PL die Ziele); **their aim is to control pollution** ihr Ziel ist es, die Umweltverschmutzung unter Kontrolle zu bringen.

aim verb **1 to aim to do something** beabsichtigen, etwas zu tun; **we're aiming to finish it today** wir beabsichtigen, es heute fertig zu machen; **2 the campaign is aimed at young people** die Kampagne zielt auf junge Leute ab.

air noun **1** Luft die; **in the open air** im Freien; **to go out for a breath of air** frische Luft schöpfen gehen; **2 to travel by air** fliegen⬦ (PERF sein).

air-conditioned adjective klimatisiert.

air conditioning noun Klimaanlage die.

Air Force noun Luftwaffe die.

air hostess noun Stewardess die (PL die Stewardessen); **she's an air hostess** sie ist Stewardess.

airline noun Fluggesellschaft die (PL die Fluggesellschaften).

airmail noun **by airmail** per Luftpost.

air pollution noun Luftverschmutzung die.

airport noun Flughafen der (PL die Flughäfen).

alarm noun Alarm der (PL die Alarme); **fire alarm** der Feuermelder; **burglar alarm** die Alarmanlage.

alarm clock noun Wecker der (PL die Wecker).

album noun Album das (PL die Alben).

alcohol noun Alkohol der.

alcoholic noun Alkoholiker der (PL die Alkoholiker), Alkoholikerin die (PL die Alkoholikerinnen).

alcoholic adjective alkoholisch.

A levels noun Abitur das (Students take 'Abitur' at about 19 years of age. You can explain A levels briefly as follows: Diese Prüfungen werden in zwei Schritten abgelegt: AS und A2. AS Prüfungen finden nach einjähriger Vorbereitungszeit statt, und umfassen normalerweise vier

b
c
d
e
f
g
h
i
j
k
l
m
n
o
p
q
r
s
t
u
v
w
x
y
z

bis fünf Fächer. A2 Prüfungen macht man in weniger Fächern als man für die AS Prüfungen belegt hatte. AS und A2 Prüfungen werden benotet von A (beste Note) bis N (nicht bestanden). A levels stellen eine Zugangsberechtigung für die Universität dar) SEE **Abitur**.

alien noun 1 (foreigner) Ausländer der (PL die Ausländer), Ausländerin die (PL die Ausländerinnen); 2 (from outer space) Außerirdische der/die (PL die Außerirdischen).

alike adjective 1 gleich; 2 **they're all alike** sie sind alle gleich; 3 **to look alike** sich (DAT) ähnlich sehen; **the two brothers look alike** die beiden Brüder sehen sich ähnlich.

alive adjective 1 **to be alive** leben; **to stay alive** am Leben bleiben; 2 (lively) lebendig.

all adjective 1 (with a singular noun) ganz; **all the time** die ganze Zeit; **all day** den ganzen Tag; 2 (with a plural noun) alle; **all the knives** alle Messer; **all our friends** alle unsere Freunde.

all pronoun 1 (everything) alles; **they've eaten it all** sie haben alles aufgegessen; 2 (everybody) alle; **all of us** wir alle; **they're all there** sie sind alle da; 3 **not at all** gar nicht.

all adverb 1 ganz; **all alone** ganz allein; 2 **three all** drei beide.

all along adverb die ganze Zeit; **I knew it all along** ich habe es die ganze Zeit gewusst.

allergic adjective allergisch; **to be allergic to something** gegen etwas (ACC) allergisch sein.

allow verb 1 **to allow somebody to do something** jemandem erlauben, etwas zu tun; **the teacher allowed them to go home** der Lehrer erlaubte ihnen, nach Hause zu gehen; 2 **to be allowed to** dürfen◇; **I'm not allowed to go to the cinema during the week** ich darf während der Woche nicht ins Kino gehen.

all right adverb 1 (yes) ist gut, okay (informal); **'come round to my house around six' – 'all right'** 'komm um sechs bei mir vorbei' – 'okay'; 2 (fine) in Ordnung, okay (informal); **is everything all right?** ist alles okay?; **she's all right again** es geht ihr wieder gut; **it's all right by me** das geht in Ordnung; **is it all right if I come later?** ist es in Ordnung, wenn ich später komme?; 3 (not bad) gut, okay (informal); **the meal was all right** das Essen war okay; 4 **'how are you?' – 'I'm all right'** 'wie geht's dir?' – 'mir geht's gut'.

almost adverb fast; **almost every day** fast jeden Tag; **almost everybody** fast alle.

alone adjective 1 allein; **he lives alone** er lebt allein; 2 **leave me alone!** lass mich in Ruhe!

along preposition 1 entlang (+ ACC, or + DAT); **there are trees all along the river** am Fluss entlang stehen Bäume; **to go for a walk along the beach** am Strand entlang spazieren gehen; 2 (there is often no direct translation for 'along', so the sentence has to be expressed differently) **she lives along the road from me** sie wohnt in der gleichen Straße wie ich; **I'll bring it along** ich bringe es mit.

aloud adverb laut; **to read something aloud** etwas vorlesen✧ SEP.

alphabet noun Alphabet das (PL die Alphabete).

Alps plural noun **the Alps** die Alpen.

already adverb schon; **they've already left** sie sind schon weggegangen; **it's six o'clock already** es ist schon sechs Uhr.

Alsatian noun Schäferhund der (PL die Schäferhunde).

also adverb auch; **I've also invited Karen** ich habe Karen auch eingeladen.

alter verb 1 ändern (a report, a dress); 2 (to change) sich verändern.

alternative noun 1 Alternative die (PL die Alternativen); **there are several alternatives** es gibt mehrere Alternativen; 2 **we have no alternative** wir haben keine andere Wahl.

alternative adjective anderer/ andere/anderes (masculine/ feminine/neuter); **to find an alternative solution** eine andere Lösung finden.

alternative medicine noun Alternativmedizin die.

although conjunction obwohl; **although she's ill, she wants to help us** obwohl sie krank ist, will sie uns helfen.

altogether adverb 1 insgesamt; **I've spent thirty pounds altogether** habe ich insgesamt dreißig Pfund ausgegeben;

2 (completely) ganz; **I'm not altogether convinced** ich bin nicht ganz überzeugt.

always adverb immer; **I always leave at five** ich gehe immer um fünf (weg).

am verb SEE be.

a.m. abbreviation vormittags; **at 8 a.m.** um acht Uhr morgens.

amateur noun 1 Amateur der (PL die Amateure), Amateurin die (PL die Amateurinnen); 2 **amateur dramatics** das Laientheater.

amaze verb erstaunen; **what amazes me is** ... was mich erstaunt, ist ....

amazed adjective erstaunt; **I was amazed to see her** ich war erstaunt, sie zu sehen.

amazing adjective 1 (terrific) fantastisch; **they've got an amazing house** sie haben ein fantastisches Haus; 2 (extraordinary) erstaunlich; **she has an amazing number of friends** sie hat erstaunlich viele Freunde.

ambition noun Ehrgeiz der.

ambitious adjective ehrgeizig.

ambulance noun Krankenwagen der (PL die Krankenwagen).

America noun Amerika das; **in America** in Amerika; **to America** nach Amerika.

American noun Amerikaner der (PL die Amerikaner), Amerikanerin die (PL die Amerikanerinnen).

American adjective amerikanisch; **she's American** sie ist Amerikanerin.

among, amongst preposition 1 unter (+ DAT); **I found it amongst my books** ich habe das unter

a b c d e f g h i j k l m n o p q r s t u v w x y z

meinen Büchern gefunden; **amongst other things** unter anderem; **2** (*between*) among yourselves untereinander.

amount *noun* **1** Menge die (PL die Mengen); **a huge amount of work** eine Menge Arbeit; **2** (*of money*) Betrag der (PL die Beträge); **a large amount of money** ein sehr hoher Betrag.

amount *verb* **1 to amount to** sich belaufen◇; **the bill amounts to five hundred euros** die Rechnung beläuft sich auf fünfhundert Euro.

amp *noun* (*amplifier*) Verstärker der (PL die Verstärker).

amplifier *noun* Verstärker der (PL die Verstärker).

amuse *verb* amüsieren.

amusement arcade *noun* Spielhalle die (PL die Spielhallen).

amusing *adjective* amüsant.

an *article* SEE **a**.

anaesthetic *noun* Narkose die (PL die Narkosen).

analyse *verb* analysieren.

ancestor *noun* Vorfahr der (PL die Vorfahren).

anchovy *noun* Sardelle die (PL die Sardellen).

ancient *adjective* **1** alt; **ancient Greece** das alte Griechenland; **2** (*very old*) uralt; **an ancient pair of jeans** uralte Jeans.

and *conjunction* **1** und; **Rosie and I** Rosie und ich; **girls and boys** Mädchen und Jungen; **2 louder and louder** immer lauter; **3 try and come** versuche zu kommen.

angel *noun* Engel der (PL die Engel).

anger *noun* Zorn der.

angle *noun* Winkel der (PL die Winkel).

angrily *adverb* wütend.

angry *adjective* **to be angry** böse sein; **she was angry with me** sie war böse auf mich; **to get angry** böse werden.

animal *noun* Tier das (PL die Tiere).

ankle *noun* Knöchel der (PL die Knöchel).

anniversary *noun* **1** Jahrestag der (PL die Jahrestage); **2 our wedding anniversary** unser Hochzeitstag.

announce *verb* bekanntgeben ◇ SEP; **she announced her engagement** sie gab ihre Verlobung bekannt.

annoy *verb* **to be annoyed** verärgert sein; **to get annoyed with somebody** sich über jemanden ärgern; **she got annoyed about it** sie hat sich darüber geärgert.

annoying *adjective* ärgerlich.

annual *adjective* jährlich.

anorak *noun* Anorak der (PL die Anoraks).

anorexia *noun* Magersucht die.

another *adjective* **1** (*additional*) noch ein/noch eine/noch ein; **would you like another cup of tea?** möchtest du noch eine Tasse Tee?; **we need another three chairs** wir brauchen noch drei Stühle; **2** (*different*) ein anderer/eine andere/ein anderes; **we saw another film** wir haben einen anderen Film gesehen; **3 in another two years** in zwei weiteren Jahren.

answer noun **1** Antwort die (PL die
Antworten); **the right answer** die
richtige Antwort; **the wrong
answer** die falsche Antwort; **2 the
answer to a problem** die Lösung
eines Problems.

answer verb **1** antworten (+ DAT);
why don't you answer him?
warum antwortest du ihm nicht?;
2 beantworten (a letter, a question);
he hasn't answered our letter er
hat unseren Brief nicht
beantwortet.

answering machine noun
Anrufbeantworter der (PL die
Anrufbeantworter).

ant noun Ameise die (PL die
Ameisen).

anthem noun **the national anthem**
die Nationalhymne.

antibiotic noun Antibiotikum das
(PL die Antibiotika).

antique noun antiques
Antiquitäten (plural).

antique adjective antik; **an
antique table** ein antiker Tisch.

antique shop noun
Antiquitätengeschäft das (PL die
Antiquitätengeschäfte).

antiseptic noun Antiseptikum
das (PL die Antiseptika).

anxious adjective **1** (worried)
besorgt; **2** (keen) **she was anxious
to see him** sie wollte ihn unbedingt
sehen.

anxiously adverb ängstlich.

any adjective **1** irgendein; **if they
had any plan** wenn sie irgendeinen
Plan hätten; **2** (with plural nouns)
irgendwelche; **if they had any
plans** wenn sie irgendwelche Pläne

hätten; **3** (in questions 'any' is often
not translated) **have you got any
stamps?** haben Sie Briefmarken?;
have we got any milk? haben wir
Milch?; **4 not any** kein; **they
haven't made any plans** sie haben
nichts geplant; **we haven't got any
milk** wir haben keine Milch; **5** (no
matter which) jeder beliebige/jede
beliebige/jedes beliebige; **you can
have any colour** du kannst jede
beliebige Farbe haben.

any pronoun **1** (in questions,
replacing the noun) welcher/
welche/welches, (replacing a
plural noun) welche; **I need some
flour, have you got any?** ich
brauche Mehl, hast du welches?;
2 not any keiner/keine/keins,
(replacing a plural noun) keine; **I
don't want any** ich will keins
haben; **there aren't any** es gibt
keine; **3** (no matter which one)
irgendein; **'which chair can I
take?' – 'take any of them'**
'welchen Stuhl kann ich nehmen?'
– 'nimm irgendeinen'.

any adverb **1** (in questions) noch;
would you like any more?
möchtest du noch etwas?; **2** (with
negatives) **I can't see him any
more** ich kann ihn nicht mehr
sehen.

anybody, anyone pronoun **1** (in
questions) jemand; **does anybody
want some tea?** möchte jemand
Tee?; **is anybody in?** ist
irgendjemand da?; **2 not anybody**
niemand; **there isn't anybody in
the office** niemand ist im Büro;
3 (absolutely anybody) jeder;
anybody can do it das kann jeder.

a
b
c
d
e
f
g
h
i
j
k
l
m
n
o
p
q
r
s
t
u
v
w
x
y
z

anyhow adverb SEE **anyway**.

anyone pronoun SEE **anybody**.

anything pronoun 1 (in questions) irgendetwas; **is there anything I can do to help?** kann ich irgendwie helfen?; **2 not anything** nichts; **there isn't anything on the table** auf dem Tisch liegt nichts; 3 (anything at all) alles; **I'll do anything to help him** ich werde alles tun, um ihm zu helfen.

anyway, anyhow adverb 1 jedenfalls; **anyway, I'll ring you before I leave** jedenfalls ruf ich dich an, bevor ich fahre; 2 sowieso.

anywhere adverb 1 (in questions) irgendwo; **have you seen my keys anywhere?** hast du meine Schlüssel irgendwo gesehen?; **2 not anywhere** nirgends; **I can't find my keys anywhere** ich kann meine Schlüssel nirgends finden; 3 (to any place) irgendwohin; **are you going anywhere tomorrow?** fahrt ihr morgen irgendwohin?; **put your cases down anywhere** stell deine Koffer irgendwohin; 4 (in any place) überall; **you can get that anywhere** das kann man überall kriegen.

apart adjective, adverb 1 (separate) auseinander; **they've been apart for some time** sie sind schon lange auseinander; **2 to be two metres apart** zwei Meter auseinander liegen; 3 apart from außer (+ DAT); **apart from my brother everybody was there** außer meinem Bruder waren alle da.

apologize verb sich entschuldigen; **he apologized for**

his mistake er entschuldigte sich für seinen Fehler; **he apologized to Sam** er hat sich bei Sam entschuldigt.

apology noun Entschuldigung die (PL die Entschuldigungen).

apostrophe noun Apostroph der (PL die Apostrophe).

apparent adjective offensichtlich.

apparently adverb offensichtlich.

appeal noun Appell der (PL die Appelle).

appeal verb 1 to appeal for something um etwas (ACC) bitten◇; 2 to appeal to somebody sich an jemanden wenden◇; **horror films don't appeal to me** Horrorfilme sind nicht mein Geschmack.

appear verb 1 erscheinen◇ (PERF sein); **Mick appeared at breakfast** Mick erschien zum Frühstück; 2 to appear on television im Fernsehen auftreten◇ SEP (PERF sein); 3 (seem) scheinen◇; **it appears that somebody has stolen the key** es scheint, dass jemand den Schlüssel gestohlen hat.

appendicitis noun Blinddarmentzündung die.

appetite noun Appetit der; **it'll spoil your appetite** das verdirbt dir den Appetit.

applaud verb Beifall klatschen.

applause noun Beifall der.

apple noun Apfel der (PL die Äpfel).

apple tree noun Apfelbaum der (PL die Apfelbäume).

applicant noun Bewerber der (PL die Bewerber), Bewerberin die (PL die Bewerberinnen).

application form noun (for a job) Bewerbungsformular das (PL die Bewerbungsformulare).

application noun Bewerbung die (PL die Bewerbungen).

apply verb 1 to apply for a job sich um eine Stelle bewerben✧; 2 to apply for university sich um einen Studienplatz bewerben✧; 3 to apply for a passport einen Pass beantragen; 4 to apply to zutreffen✧ SEP auf (+ACC); that doesn't apply to students das trifft nicht auf Studenten zu.

appointment noun Termin der (PL die Termine); to make a dental appointment einen Zahnarzttermin vereinbaren; I've got a hair appointment at four ich habe um vier einen Friseurtermin.

appreciate verb I appreciate your advice ich bin dir für deinen Rat dankbar; I'd appreciate it if you could tidy up afterwards es wäre nett von dir, wenn du danach aufräumen würdest.

apprentice noun Lehrling der (PL die Lehrlinge).

apprenticeship noun Lehre die (PL die Lehren).

approach verb sich nähern (+DAT) (PERF sein); we were approaching the village wir näherten uns dem Dorf.

approve verb to approve of something mit etwas (DAT) einverstanden sein; they don't approve of her friends sie lehnen ihre Freunde ab.

approximate adjective ungefähr.

approximately adverb ungefähr; approximately fifty people ungefähr fünfzig Personen.

apricot noun Aprikose die (PL die Aprikosen).

April noun April der; in April im April.

April Fool noun (trick) Aprilscherz der (PL die Aprilscherze); April fool! April, April!

April Fool's Day noun der erste April.

apron noun Schürze die (PL die Schürzen).

aquarium noun Aquarium das (PL die Aquarien).

Aquarius noun Wassermann der; Sharon's Aquarius Sharon ist Wassermann.

Arab noun Araber der (PL die Araber), Araberin die (PL die Araberinnen).

Arab adjective arabisch; the Arab countries die arabischen Länder.

arch noun Bogen der (PL die Bogen).

archaeologist noun Archäologe der (PL die Archäologen), Archäologin die (PL die Archäologinnen); she's an archaeologist sie ist Archäologin.

archaeology noun Archäologie die.

architect noun Architekt der (PL die Architekten), Architektin die (PL die Architektinnen); he's an architect er ist Architekt.

architecture noun Architektur die.

are verb SEE BE.

area noun 1 (part of a town, a region) Gegend die (PL die

a b c d e f g h i j k l m n o p q r s t u v w x y z

Gegenden); **a nice area** eine nette Gegend; **in the Leeds area** in der Gegend von Leeds; **2 picnic area** der Picknickplatz.

argue verb sich streiten◇; **to argue about something** sich über etwas (ACC) streiten; **they're arguing about the result** sie streiten sich über das Ergebnis.

argument noun Streit der (PL die Streite); **to get into an argument with somebody** mit jemandem in Streit geraten◇; **to have an argument** sich streiten◇.

Aries noun Widder der; **Pauline's Aries** Pauline ist Widder.

arm noun Arm der (PL die Arme); **arm in arm** Arm in Arm; **to break your arm** sich (DAT) den Arm brechen.

armchair noun Sessel der (PL die Sessel).

armed adjective bewaffnet.

army noun **1** Heer das (PL die Heere); **2** (profession) Militär das; **to join the army** zum Militär gehen.

around preposition, adverb **1** (with time of day) gegen (+ ACC); **we'll be there around ten** wir werden gegen zehn da sein; **2** (with ages or amounts) etwa; **she's around fifteen** sie ist etwa fünfzehn; **we need around six kilos** wir brauchen etwa sechs Kilo; **3** (with dates) um (+ ACC herum); **around 10 August** um den 10. August herum; **4** (surrounding) um ... herum; **the countryside around Edinburgh** die Landschaft um Edinburgh herum; **5** (near) **is there a post office around here?** gibt es hier in der

Gegend eine Post?; **is Phil around?** ist Phil da?

arrange verb **to arrange something** etwas vereinbaren; **we've arranged to go to the cinema on Saturday** wir haben vereinbart, am Samstag ins Kino zu gehen.

arrest noun **to be under arrest** verhaftet sein.

arrest verb verhaften.

arrival noun Ankunft die (PL die Ankünfte).

arrive verb ankommen★ SEP (PERF sein); **they arrived at 3 p.m.** sie kamen um fünfzehn Uhr an.

arrow noun Pfeil der (PL die Pfeile).

art noun **1** Kunst die (PL die Künste); **modern art** moderne Kunst; **2** (school subject) Kunsterziehung die.

artery noun Arterie die (PL die Arterien).

art gallery noun Kunstgalerie die (PL die Kunstgalerien).

article noun **1** (in a newspaper or magazine) Artikel der (PL die Artikel); **2** (object) Stück das (PL die Stücke).

artificial adjective künstlich.

artist noun Künstler der, Künstlerin die (PL die Künstlerinnen); **he's an artist** er ist Künstler.

artistic adjective künstlerisch.

art school noun Kunsthochschule die (PL die Kunsthochschulen).

as conjunction, adverb **1** wie; **as you know** wie du weißt; **as usual** wie üblich; **as I told you** wie ich dir gesagt habe; **2** (because) da; **as there was no bus, we took a taxi**

da es keinen Bus gab, nahmen wir ein Taxi; **3** as ... as so ...wie; **he's as tall as his brother** er ist so groß wie sein Bruder; **come as quickly as possible** komm so schnell wie möglich; **4** as much ... as so viel ... wie; **you have as much time as I do** du hast so viel Zeit wie ich; **5 as many** ... as so viele ... wie; **we have as many problems as he does** wir haben genauso viele Probleme wie er; **6 as long as** vorausgesetzt; **we'll go tomorrow, as long as it's a nice day** wir gehen morgen, vorausgesetzt es ist schönes Wetter; **7 for as long as** solange; **you can stay for as long as you like** du kannst bleiben, solange du willst; **8 as soon as possible** so bald wie möglich; **9 to work as** arbeiten als; **he works as a waiter in the evenings** abends arbeitet er als Kellner; **as well** auch.

ash *noun* **1** Asche *die* (PL *die* Aschen); **2** (*tree*) Esche *die* (PL *die* Eschen).

ashamed *adjective* **to be ashamed of something** sich wegen etwas (DAT) schämen; **you should be ashamed of yourself!** du solltest dich schämen!

ashtray *noun* Aschenbecher *der* (PL *die* Aschenbecher).

Asia *noun* Asien *das*; **in Asia** in Asien.

Asian *noun* Asiate *der* (PL *die* Asiaten), Asiatin *die* (PL *die* Asiatinnen).

Asian *adjective* asiatisch.

ask *verb* **1** fragen; **to ask somebody something** jemanden nach etwas (DAT) fragen; **I asked him the way** ich fragte ihn nach dem Weg; **2 to ask something** um etwas (ACC) bitten; **to ask somebody a favour** jemanden um einen Gefallen bitten; **to ask somebody to do something** jemanden bitten, etwas zu tun; **ask Danny to give you a hand** bitte Danny, dir zu helfen; **3 to ask somebody a question** jemandem eine Frage stellen; **I asked him a few questions** ich habe ihm ein paar Fragen gestellt; **4** einladen◇ SEP; **they've asked us to a party** sie haben uns auf eine Party eingeladen; **Paul's asked Janie out on Friday** Paul hat Janie Freitag eingeladen; **5 to ask for** verlangen; **how much are they asking for the car?** wieviel verlangen sie für das Auto?

asleep *adjective* **to be asleep** schlafen◇; **the baby's asleep** das Baby schläft; **to fall asleep** einschlafen◇ SEP (PERF *sein*).

asparagus *noun* Spargel *der* (PL *die* Spargel).

aspirin *noun* Aspirin *das*.

assembly *noun* (*at school*) Morgenandacht *die* (PL *die* Morgenandachten).

assess *verb* beurteilen.

assignment *noun* (*at school*) Aufgabe *die* (PL *die* Aufgaben).

assist *verb* helfen (+ DAT) .

assistance *noun* Hilfe *die*.

assistant *noun* **1** Helfer *der* (PL *die* Helfer), Helferin *die* (PL *die* Helferinnen); **2** (*in school*) Assistent *der* (PL *die* Assistenten), Assistentin *die* (PL *die*

a

Assistentinnen); **3 shop assistant** der Verkäufer, die Verkäuferin.

b

association noun Verband der (PL die Verbände).

c

assorted adjective gemischt.

d

assortment noun Auswahl die.

assume verb annehmen✧ SEP; **I assume** ich nehme an.

e

asthma noun Asthma das.

f

astrology noun Astrologie die.

g

astronaut noun Astronaut der (PL die Astronauten), Astronautin die (PL die Astronautinnen).

h

astronomy noun Astronomie die.

i

at preposition **1** in (+ DAT); **at school** in der Schule; **at my office** in meinem Büro; **at the supermarket** im Supermarkt; **2** an (+ DAT); **at the station** am Bahnhof; **at the bus stop** an der Bushaltestelle; **3** bei (+ DAT); **at the dentist** beim Zahnarzt; **at Emma's** bei Emma; **she's at her brother's this evening** sie ist heute Abend bei ihrem Bruder; **at the hairdresser's** beim Friseur; **4 at a party** auf einer Party; **5 at home** zu Hause; **6** (talking about the time) um; **at eight o'clock** um acht Uhr; **7 at night** nachts; **at Christmas** zu Weihnachten; **at the weekend** am Wochenende; **8** (@ in e-mail addresses) Klammeraffe der; **john-dot-smith@easycom-dot-com** john-punkt-smith-Klammeraffe-easycom-punkt-com; **9 at last** endlich; **she's found a job at last** sie hat endlich einen Job gefunden.

j

k

l

m

n

o

p

q

r

s

t

u

v

w

x

athlete noun Athlet der (PL die Athleten), Athletin die (PL die Athletinnen).

y

z

athletic adjective sportlich.

athletics noun Leichtathletik die.

Atlantic noun **the Atlantic (Ocean)** der Atlantik.

atlas noun Atlas der (PL die Atlanten).

atmosphere noun Atmosphäre die (PL die Atmosphären).

atom noun Atom das (PL die Atome).

atomic adjective Atom-; **an atomic bomb** eine Atombombe.

attach verb befestigen.

attached adjective (emotionally) **to be attached to somebody/ something** an jemandem/etwas (DAT) hängen✧.

attachment noun **1** (in a letter) Anlage die (PL die Anlagen); **2** (in an email) Attachment das (PL die Attachments).

attack noun Angriff der (PL die Angriffe).

attack verb **1** angreifen✧ SEP; **2** (mug or raid) überfallen✧.

attempt noun Versuch der (PL die Versuche); **at the first attempt** beim ersten Versuch.

attempt verb **to attempt to do something** versuchen, etwas zu tun.

attend verb teilnehmen✧ SEP an (+ DAT); **to attend a meeting** an einer Besprechung teilnehmen; **to attend an evening class** einen Abendkurs besuchen.

attention noun

1 Aufmerksamkeit die; **to pay attention** aufpassen SEP; **I wasn't paying attention** ich habe nicht aufgepasst; **2 he wasn't paying attention to the teacher** er hörte dem Lehrer nicht zu.

attic noun Dachboden der (PL die Dachböden); **in the attic** auf dem Dachboden.

attitude noun 1 (way of thinking) Einstellung die; 2 (way of acting) Haltung die.

attract verb anziehen◇ SEP.

attraction noun 1 Anziehung die; 2 (a thing that attracts) Attraktion die (PL die Attraktionen); **the whale was a big attraction** der Wal war eine große Attraktion.

attractive adjective attraktiv.

au pair noun Aupairmädchen das (PL die Aupairmädchen); **I'm looking for a job as an au pair** ich suche eine Aupair-Stelle.

aubergine noun Aubergine die (PL die Auberginen).

audience noun Publikum das; **the television audience** die Fernsehzuschauer (plural).

August noun August der; **in August** im August.

aunt, auntie noun Tante die (PL die Tanten).

Australia noun Australien das; **to Australia** nach Australien.

Australian noun Australier der (PL die Australier), Australierin die (PL die Australierinnen).

Australian adjective australisch; **she's Australian** sie ist Australierin.

Austria noun Österreich das; **in Austria** in Österreich.

Austrian noun Österreicher der (PL die Österreicher), Österreicherin die (PL die Österreicherinnen).

Austrian adjective österreichisch; **he's Austrian** er ist Österreicher.

author noun Autor der (PL die Autoren), Autorin die (PL die Autorinnen).

autograph noun Autogramm das (PL die Autogramme).

automatic adjective automatisch.

automatically adverb automatisch.

autumn noun Herbst der (PL die Herbste); **in autumn** im Herbst.

available adjective (on sale) erhältlich.

average noun Durchschnitt der (PL die Durchschnitte); **on average** im Durchschnitt; **above average** über dem Durchschnitt.

average adjective durchschnittlich; **the average height** die durchschnittliche Größe.

avocado noun Avocado die (PL die Avocados).

avoid verb 1 vermeiden◇; **to avoid doing something** es vermeiden, etwas zu tun; **I avoid speaking to him** ich vermeide es, mit ihm zu reden; 2 (keep away from something or a place) meiden◇; **she avoids me** sie meidet mich.

awake adjective **to be awake** wach sein; **are you still awake?** bist du noch wach?

award noun Preis der (PL die Preise); **to win an award** einen Preis gewinnen.

aware adjective **to be aware of a problem** sich (DAT) eines Problems bewusst sein; **I'm aware of the danger** ich bin mir der Gefahr

b
c
d
e
f
g
h
i
j
k
l
m
n
o
p
q
r
s
t
u
v
w
x
y
z

a
b

bewusst; **as far as I'm aware** soweit ich weiß.

away *adverb* **1 to be away** nicht da sein; **I'll be away next week** ich bin nächste Woche nicht da; **2 to go away** verreisen (PERF *sein*); **Laura's gone away for a week** Laura ist auf eine Woche verreist; **go away!** geh weg!; **3 to run away** weglaufen◇ SEP (PERF *sein*); **the thieves ran away** die Diebe liefen weg; **4 the school is two kilometres away** die Schule ist zwei Kilometer entfernt; **how far away is it?** wie weit entfernt ist es?; **not far away** nicht weit entfernt; **5 to put something away** etwas wegräumen SEP; **I'm just putting my books away** ich räume gerade meine Bücher weg; **6 to give something away** etwas weggeben◇ SEP, (*as a present*) etwas verschenken; **she's given away all her cassettes** sie hat alle ihre Kassetten verschenkt.

away match *noun* Auswärtsspiel das (PL die Auswärtsspiele).

awful *adjective* furchtbar; **the film was awful** der Film war furchtbar; **I feel awful** (*ill*) ich fühle mich furchtbar; **I feel awful about it** es ist mir furchtbar unangenehm; **an awful lot of mistakes** furchtbar viele Fehler.

awkward *adjective* **1** schwierig; **it's an awkward situation** das ist eine schwierige Situation; **it's a bit awkward** das ist ein bisschen schwierig; **an awkward child** ein schwieriges Kind; **2 an awkward question** eine peinliche Frage.

axe *noun* Axt die (PL die Äxte).

Bb

baby *noun* Baby das (PL die Babys).

babysit *verb* babysitten.

babysitter *noun* Babysitter der (PL die Babysitter), Babysitterin die (PL die Babysitterinnen).

babysitting *noun* Babysitten das.

back *noun* **1** (*of a person or animal*) Rücken der (PL die Rücken); **he did it behind my back** er hat es hinter meinem Rücken getan; **2** (*of a piece of paper, cheque, or building*) Rückseite die (PL die Rückseiten); **on the back** auf der Rückseite; **3 the back of your hand** der Handrücken; **4 at the back** hinten; **at the back of the room** hinten im Zimmer; **we sat at the back** wir saßen hinten; **a garden at the back of the house** ein Garten hinter dem Haus; **5** (*of a chair or sofa*) Rückenlehne die (PL die Rückenlehnen); **6** (*in football or hockey*) Verteidiger der (PL die Verteidiger), Verteidigerin die (PL die Verteidigerinnen); **left back** der Linksverteidiger.

back *adjective* **1 a back seat** (*of a car*) der Rücksitz; **2 the back door** die Hintertür; **the back garden** der Garten hinter dem Haus.

back *adverb* **1** zurück; **there and back** hin und zurück; **to go back** (*on foot*) zurückgehen◇ SEP (PERF *sein*) (*in a vehicle*) zurückfahren◇ SEP (PERF *sein*); **2 to come back** zurückkommen◇ SEP (PERF *sein*); **they've come back from Italy** sie sind aus Italien zurückgekommen;

I'll be back at 8 o'clock ich bin um acht Uhr zurück; **Sue's not back yet** Sue ist noch nicht zurück; **3 to phone back** zurückrufen ◇ SEP; **I'll ring back later** ich rufe dich später zurück; **4 to give something back to somebody** jemandem etwas zurückgeben ◇ SEP; **give it back!** gib es zurück!

back verb (bet on) setzen auf (+ ACC).

● **to back up** (computing) sichern; **to back up a file** eine Sicherungskopie machen.

● **to back somebody up** jemanden unterstützen.

backache noun Rückenschmerzen (plural).

background noun 1 (of a person) Verhältnisse (plural); **she comes from a poor background** sie kommt aus ärmlichen Verhältnissen; 2 (in a picture, view, or situation) Hintergrund der (PL die Hintergründe); **background noise** Hintergrundgeräusche (plural); 3 (to events or problems) Hintergründe (plural).

backhand noun Rückhand die.

backing noun 1 (on sticky-back plastic, for example) Verstärkung die (PL die Verstärkungen); 2 (moral support) Unterstützung die; 3 (in music) Begleitung die; **a backing group** eine Begleitband.

backpack noun Rucksack der (PL die Rucksäcke).

backpack verb to go **backpacking** trampen (PERF sein).

back seat noun Rücksitz der (PL die Rücksitze).

backstroke noun Rückenschwimmen das.

back to front adverb verkehrt herum; **your jumper's back to front** du hast deinen Pullover verkehrt herum an.

backup noun 1 (support) Unterstützung die; 2 (in computing) Sicherungskopie die (PL die Sicherungskopien); **a backup disk** eine Sicherungsdiskette.

backwards adverb 1 rückwärts; 2 **to lean backwards** sich nach hinten lehnen; **to fall backwards** nach hinten fallen.

bacon noun Speck der; **bacon and eggs** Eier mit Speck.

bad adjective 1 (not good) schlecht; **a bad idea** eine schlechte Idee; **a bad meal** ein schlechtes Essen; **his new film's not bad** sein neuer Film ist nicht schlecht; **it's bad for your health** das ist ungesund; **I'm bad at physics** ich bin schlecht in Physik; 2 (serious) schlimm; **a bad mistake** ein schlimmer Fehler; **a bad cold** eine schlimme Erkältung; 3 **a bad accident** ein schwerer Unfall; 4 (rotten) schlecht; **to go bad** schlecht werden; 5 **a bad apple** ein fauler Apfel; 6 **bad language** Kraftausdrücke (plural); ★ **too bad!** schade!, so ein Pech!

badge noun Abzeichen das (PL die Abzeichen).

badly adverb 1 (poorly) schlecht; **he writes badly** er schreibt schlecht; **I slept badly** ich habe schlecht geschlafen; 2 (seriously) schwer; **they were badly injured** sie waren schwer verletzt; 3 (very much) dringend; **to need something badly** etwas dringend brauchen.

a
b
c
d
e
f
g
h
i
j
k
l
m
n
o
p
q
r
s
t
u
v
w
x
y
z

bad-mannered *adjective* to be bad-mannered schlechte Manieren haben.

badminton *noun* Badminton das.

bad-tempered *adjective* schlecht gelaunt; **a bad-tempered old man** ein schlecht gelaunter alter Mann.

bag *noun* 1 Tasche die (PL die Taschen); 2 *(made of paper or plastic)* Tüte die (PL die Tüten).

baggage *noun* Gepäck das.

bagpipes *plural noun* Dudelsack der (PL die Dudelsäke).

bags *plural noun* Gepäck das; **to pack your bags** (sein Gepäck) packen; ★ **to have bags under your eyes** Ringe unter den Augen haben *(informal)*.

bake *verb* 1 backen; **to bake a cake** einen Kuchen backen; **2 I'm baking** mir ist furchtbar heiß.

baked *adjective* 1 *(fish or fruit)* überbacken; **baked apples** Bratäpfel; **2 baked potatoes** die Ofenkartoffeln.

baked beans *plural noun* Bohnen in Tomatensoße.

baker *noun* Bäcker der (PL die Bäcker); **to go to the baker's** zum Bäcker gehen.

bakery *noun* Bäckerei die (PL die Bäckereien).

balance *noun* 1 Gleichgewicht das; **to lose your balance** das Gleichgewicht verlieren; **2** *(in a bank account)* Kontostand der.

balanced *adjective* ausgeglichen.

balcony *noun* Balkon der (PL die Balkons).

bald *adjective* 1 kahl; **2** *(of a person)* kahlköpfig; **to go bald** eine Glatze bekommen.

ball *noun* 1 *(for tennis, football, golf)* Ball der (PL die Bälle); **2** *(for billiards, croquet)* Kugel die (PL die Kugeln); **3** *(of string or wool)* Knäuel das (PL die Knäuel).

ballet *noun* Ballett das (PL die Ballette).

ballet dancer *noun* Balletttänzer der (PL die Balletttänzer), Balletttänzerin die (PL die Balletttänzerinnen).

balloon *noun* 1 Luftballon der (PL die Luftballons); **2** *(hot-air)* Ballon der (PL die Ballons).

ballpoint (pen) *noun* Kugelschreiber der (PL die Kugelschreiber).

ban *noun* Verbot das (PL die Verbote); **a ban on smoking** ein Rauchverbot.

ban *verb* verbieten✧; **to ban someone from smoking** jemandem verbieten zu rauchen.

banana *noun* 1 Banane die (PL die Bananen); **2 a banana yoghurt** ein Bananenjoghurt.

band *noun* 1 *(playing music)* Band die (PL die Bands); **rock band** die Rockband; **brass band** die Blaskapelle; **2 rubber band** das Gummiband.

bandage *noun* Verband der (PL die Verbände).

bandage *verb* verbinden✧.

bang *noun* *(noise)* Knall der (PL die Knalle).

bang *verb* 1 *(hit, knock)* schlagen✧; **he banged his fist on the table** er schlug mit der Faust auf den Tisch; **to bang on the door** gegen die Tür schlagen; **2 I**

basement

banged my head on the door ich
habe mir den Kopf an der Tür
gestoßen; **3 to bang into
something** gegen etwas (ACC)
knallen; **4** (*shut loudly*) zuknallen
SEP; **he banged the door** er knallte
die Tür zu.

bang *exclamation* peng!.

bank *noun* **1** (*for money*) Bank die
(PL die Banken); **I'm going to the
bank** ich gehe auf die Bank; **2** (*of a
river or lake*) Ufer das (PL die Ufer).

bank account *noun* Bankkonto
das (PL die Bankkonten).

bank balance *noun* Kontostand
der (PL die Kontostände).

bank card *noun* Scheckkarte die
(PL die Scheckkarten).

bank holiday *noun* gesetzliche
Feiertag der (PL die gesetzlichen
Feiertage).

banknote *noun* Geldschein der (PL
die Geldscheine).

bank statement *noun*
Kontoauszug der (PL die
Kontoauszüge).

bar *noun* **1** (*selling drinks*) Bar die
(PL die Bars); **Janet works in a bar**
Janet arbeitet in einer Bar;
2 (*counter*) Theke die (PL die
Theken); **on the bar** auf der Theke;
3 a bar of chocolate eine Tafel
Schokolade; **4 a bar of soap** ein
Stück Seife; **5** (*made of wood or
metal*) Stange die (PL die Stangen);
an iron bar eine Eisenstange; **6** (*in
music*) Takt der (PL die Takte).

barbecue *noun* **1** (*apparatus*)
Grill der (PL die Grills); **2** (*party*)
Grillfest das (PL die Grillfeste).

barbecue *verb* **to barbecue a
chicken** ein Hühnchen grillen;
barbecued chicken gegrilltes
Hühnchen.

bare *adjective* nackt.

barefoot *adjective* **to be barefoot**
barfuß sein; **to walk barefoot**
barfuß gehen.

bargain *noun* (*a good buy*) gute
Kauf der (PL die guten Käufe); **I got a
bargain** ich habe einen guten Kauf
gemacht; **it's a bargain!** das ist ein
Schnäppchen!

barge *noun* Kahn der (PL die
Kähne).

bark *noun* **1** (*of a tree*) Rinde die (PL
die Rinden); **2** (*of a dog*) Bellen das.

bark *verb* bellen.

barmaid *noun* Bardame die (PL die
Bardamen).

barman *noun* Barkeeper der (PL die
Barkeeper).

barn *noun* Scheune die (PL die
Scheunen).

barrel *noun* Fass das (PL die Fässer).

barrier *noun* Absperrung die (PL die
Absperrungen).

base *noun* (*bottom part*) Fuß der (PL
die Füße).

baseball *noun* Baseball der.

based *adjective* **1 to be based on**
basieren auf (+ DAT); **the film is
based on a true story** der Film
basiert auf einer wahren
Geschichte; **2 to be based in**
wohnen in (+ DAT); **he's based in
Bristol** er wohnt in Bristol.

basement *noun* Kellergeschoss
das (PL die Kellergeschosse).

a b c d e f g h i j k l m n o p q r s t u v w x y z

a
b
c
d
e
f
g
h
i
j
k
l
m
n
o
p
q
r
s
t
u
v
w
x
y
z

bash noun **1** Schlag der (PL die Schläge); **2** I'll have a bash ich probier's mal.

bash verb I bashed my head in ich habe mir den Kopf angestoßen.

basic adjective **1** grundlegend, Grund-; basic knowledge Grundkenntnisse (plural); her basic salary ihr Grundgehalt; **2** the basic problem das Hauptproblem; **3** (not luxurious) einfach.

basically adverb **1** grundsätzlich; it's basically all right grundsätzlich ist es okay; **2** basically, I don't want to come eigentlich will ich nicht kommen.

basics plural noun the basics das Wesentliche.

basin noun Becken das (PL die Becken).

basis noun **1** Basis die; **2** on a regular basis regelmäßig.

basket noun Korb der (PL die Körbe); a basket of apples ein Korb Äpfel; waste-paper basket der Papierkorb.

basketball noun Basketball der.

bass noun **1** Bass der (PL die Bässe); **2** double bass der Kontrabass.

bass guitar noun Bassgitarre die (PL die Bassgitarren).

bassoon noun Fagott das (PL die Fagotte).

bat noun **1** (for games) Schläger der (PL die Schläger); **2** (animal) Fledermaus die (PL die Fledermäuse).

bath noun **1** Bad das (PL die Bäder); to have a bath baden; **2** (tub) Badewanne die (PL die Badewannen).

bathroom noun Badezimmer das (PL die Badezimmer).

baths plural noun Badeanstalt die (PL die Badeanstalten).

bath towel noun Badetuch das (PL die Badetücher).

batter noun Teig der (PL die Teige); fish in batter ausgebackener Fisch.

battery noun Batterie die (PL die Batterien).

battle noun **1** (in war) Schlacht die (PL die Schlachten); **2** (contest) Kampf der (PL die Kämpfe).

Bavaria noun Bayern das.

bay noun **1** (on coast) Bucht die (PL die Buchten); **2** (in bus station) Haltebucht die (PL die Haltebuchten).

BC (before Christ) v.Chr. (vor Christus).

be verb **1** sein ♦ (PERF sein); Melanie is in the kitchen Melanie ist in der Küche; where is the butter? wo ist die Butter?; I'm tired ich bin müde; when we were in Germany als wir in Deutschland waren; **2** (with jobs and professions) sein ♦ (PERF sein); she's a teacher sie ist Lehrerin; he's a taxi driver er ist Taxifahrer; **3** (in clock times, days of the week, dates, and age) sein ♦ (PERF sein); it's three o'clock es ist drei Uhr; it's half past five es ist halb sechs; what day is it today? welcher Tag ist heute?; it's Tuesday today heute ist Dienstag; it's the twentieth of May heute ist der zwanzigste Mai; what's the date today? der Wievielte ist heute?; how old are you? wie alt bist du?; I'm fifteen ich bin fünfzehn; **4** (cold, hot, ill) sein ♦ (PERF sein);

I'm hot mir ist heiß; **I'm cold** mir ist kalt; **to be ill** krank sein; **5** (*weather*) sein◇ (PERF *sein*); **it's cold today** heute ist es kalt; **it's a nice day** es ist schönes Wetter; **it's raining** es regnet; **6 I'm hungry** ich habe Hunger; **she's thirsty** sie hat Durst; **7** (*saying how much something costs*) kosten; **how much are the bananas?** wie viel kosten die Bananen?; **8** (*go, come, or visit*) sein◇ (PERF *sein*); **I've never been to Berlin** ich war noch nie in Berlin gewesen; **have you been to England before?** warst du schon einmal in England?; **has the postman been?** war der Briefträger schon da?; **9** (*forming the passive*) werden◇ (PERF *sein*); **to be loved** geliebt werden; **he has been promoted** er ist befördert worden; **10 there is/are** es gibt; **is there a bank near here?** gibt es hier in der Nähe eine Bank?

beach *noun* Strand *der* (PL die Strände); **to go to the beach** zum Strand gehen; **on the beach** am Strand.

bead *noun* Perle *die* (PL die Perlen).

beak *noun* Schnabel *der* (PL die Schnäbel).

beam *noun* **1** (*of light*) Strahl *der* (PL die Strahlen); **2** (*for a roof*) Balken *der* (PL die Balken).

bean *noun* Bohne *die* (PL die Bohnen); **green beans** grüne Bohnen.

bear *noun* Bär *der* (PL die Bären).

bear *verb* **1** ertragen◇; **I can't bear the idea** ich kann den Gedanken nicht ertragen; **2 to bear something in mind** an etwas (ACC)

denken; **I'll bear it in mind** ich denke daran.

beard *noun* Bart *der* (PL die Bärte).

bearded *adjective* bärtig.

bearings *plural noun* **to get one's bearings** sich orientieren.

beast *noun* **1** (*animal*) Tier *das* (PL die Tiere); **2 you beast!** du Biest!

beat *noun* (*in music*) Takt *der*.

beat *verb* **1** (*defeat*) schlagen◇; **we beat them!** wir haben sie geschlagen; **2 you can't beat a good meal** es geht doch nichts über ein gutes Essen.

● **to beat somebody up** jemanden verprügeln.

beautiful *adjective* schön.

beauty *noun* **1** Schönheit *die* (PL die Schönheiten); **2 the beauty of it is that ...** das Schöne daran ist, dass ....

because *conjunction* **1** weil; **because it's cold** weil es kalt ist; **2 because of** wegen (+ GEN); **because of the accident** wegen des Unfalls; **because of you** deinetwegen.

become *verb* werden◇ (PERF *sein*); **she's become a painter** sie ist Malerin geworden.

bed *noun* **1** Bett *das* (PL die Betten); **double bed** das Doppelbett; **in bed** im Bett; **to go to bed** ins Bett gehen; **2** (*flower bed*) Beet *das* (PL die Beete).

bedclothes *plural noun* Bettwäsche *die*.

bedding *noun* Bettzeug *das*.

bedroom *noun* Schlafzimmer *das* (PL die Schlafzimmer); **bedroom furniture** Schlafzimmermöbel

a b c d e f g h i j k l m n o p q r s t u v w x y z

(*plural*); **my bedroom window** mein Schlafzimmerfenster.

bedside table noun Nachttisch der (PL die Nachttische).

bedsit, bedsitter noun möblierte Zimmer das (PL die möblierten Zimmer).

bedspread noun Tagesdecke die (PL die Tagesdecken).

bedtime noun Schlafenszeit die; **at bedtime** vor dem Schlafengehen.

bee noun Biene die (PL die Bienen).

beech noun Buche die (PL die Buchen).

beef noun Rindfleisch das; **we had roast beef** wir haben Rinderbraten gegessen.

beefburger noun Hamburger der (PL die Hamburger).

beer noun Bier das (PL die Biere); **two beers please** zwei Bier bitte; **beer can** die Bierdose.

beetle noun Käfer der (PL die Käfer).

beetroot noun Rote Bete die.

before preposition **1** vor (+ DAT); **before Monday** vor Montag; **he left before me** er ist vor mir gegangen; **the day before the wedding** am Tag vor der Hochzeit; **2 the day before** am Tag zuvor; **the day before yesterday** vorgestern; **the week before** in der Woche zuvor; **3** (*already*) schon einmal; **I've seen him before somewhere** ich habe ihn schon einmal irgendwo gesehen; **I had seen the film before** ich hatte den Film schon einmal gesehen.

before conjunction bevor; **I closed the windows before leaving** (or **before I left**) ich habe die Fenster zugemacht, bevor ich wegging;

before the train leaves bevor der Zug abfährt; **oh, before I forget ...** oh, bevor ich es vergesse ....

beforehand adverb (*ahead of time*) vorher; **phone beforehand** rufe vorher an.

beg verb **1** betteln; **to beg for money** um Geld betteln; **2** (*ask*) bitten◇; **he begged her not to say anything** er bat sie, nichts zu sagen; **3 I beg your pardon** entschuldigen Sie bitte.

begin verb anfangen◇ SEP, beginnen◇; **the meeting begins at ten** die Besprechung fängt um zehn an; **the words beginning with P** die Wörter, die mit P anfangen; **to begin to do something** anfangen, etwas zu tun; beginnen, etwas zu tun; **I'm beginning to understand why** ... ich beginne zu verstehen, warum ....

beginner noun Anfänger der (PL die Anfänger), Anfängerin die (PL die Anfängerinnen).

beginning noun Anfang der (PL die Anfänge); **at the beginning** am Anfang; **at the beginning of the holidays** am Anfang der Ferien.

behalf noun on behalf of im Namen von (+ DAT); **on behalf of Mr and Mrs Smith** im Namen von Herrn und Frau Smith.

behave verb **1** sich benehmen◇; **he behaved badly** er hat sich schlecht benommen; **2 to behave oneself** sich benehmen◇; **behave yourself!** benimm dich!

behaviour noun Benehmen das.

behind noun Hintern der (*informal*) (PL die Hintern).

behind preposition, adverb
1 hinter (+ DAT, or + ACC when there is movement towards a place); **behind the sofa** hinter dem Sofa; **behind them** hinter ihnen; **the car behind** das Auto hinter ihnen/uns; **2 to leave something behind** (belongings) etwas vergessen.

beige adjective beige.

Belgian noun Belgier der (PL die Belgier), Belgierin die (PL die Belgierinnen).

Belgian adjective belgisch; **he's Belgian** er ist Belgier.

Belgium noun Belgien das; **to Belgium** nach Belgien.

belief noun Glaube der (PL die Glauben); **his political beliefs** seine politische Überzeugung.

believe verb **1** glauben; **I believe so** ich glaube schon; **they believed what I said** sie glaubten, was ich sagte; **I don't believe you** das glaube ich dir nicht; **2 to believe in something** an etwas (ACC) glauben; **to believe in God** an Gott glauben.

bell noun **1** (in a church) Glocke die (PL die Glocken); **2** (on a door) Klingel die (PL die Klingeln); **to ring the bell** klingeln; **3** (for a cat or toy) Glöckchen das (PL die Glöckchen);
★ **that name rings a bell** der Name sagt mir etwas (literally: says something to me).

belong verb **1 to belong to** gehören (+ DAT); **that belongs to my mother** das gehört meiner Mutter; **2 to belong to a club** einem Klub angehören; **3** (go) gehören; **where does this vase belong?** wo gehört diese Vase hin?

belongings plural noun Sachen (plural); **all my belongings** alle meine Sachen.

below preposition unter (+ DAT, or + ACC when there is movement towards a place); **below the window** unter dem Fenster; **the flat below yours** die Wohnung unter dir.

below adverb **1** (further down) unten; **he called from below** er rief von unten herauf; **2 the flat below** die Wohnung darunter.

belt noun Gürtel der (PL die Gürtel).

bench noun Bank die (PL die Bänke).

bend noun **1** (in a road) Kurve die (PL die Kurven); **2** (in a river) Biegung die (PL die Biegungen).

bend verb **1** (make a bend in) biegen ❖ (a pipe or wire) beugen (your knee, arm, or head); **2** (curve) eine Biegung machen; **3 to bend down** sich bücken.

beneath preposition unter (+ DAT).

benefit noun **1** Vorteil der (PL die Vorteile); **2 unemployment benefit** die Arbeitslosenunterstützung.

bent adjective verbogen.

beret noun Baskenmütze die (PL die Baskenmützen).

beside preposition (next to) neben (+ DAT, or + ACC when there is movement towards a place); **she was sitting beside me** sie saß neben mir; **she sat down beside me** sie hat sich neben mich gesetzt; ★ **that beside the point** das hat nichts damit zu tun.

besides adverb (anyway) außerdem; **besides, it's too late** außerdem ist es zu spät; (as well)

a b c d e f g h i j k l m n o p q r s t u v w x y z

a
b
c
d
e
f
g
h
i
j
k
l
m
n
o
p
q
r
s
t
u
v
w
x
y
z

four dogs, and six cats besides vier Hunde und außerdem sechs Katzen.

best *adjective* 1 bester/beste/bestes; **she's my best friend** sie ist meine beste Freundin; 2 **she's the best at tennis** im Tennis ist sie die Beste; **it's best to wait** das Beste ist zu warten.

best *adverb* am besten; **he plays best** er spielt am besten; **I like Munich best** München gefällt mir am besten; **best of all** am allerbesten; **I like grapes best** ich mag Weintrauben am liebsten; ★ **all the best!** alles Gute!; ★ **to make the best of it** das Beste daraus machen; ★ **to do your best** sein Bestes tun;; **I did my best to help her** ich habe mein Bestes getan, um ihr zu helfen.

best man *noun* Trauzeuge der (PL die Trauzeugen).

bet *noun* Wette die (PL die Wetten).

bet *verb* wetten; **to bet on a horse** auf ein Pferd wetten; **I bet you'll forget it** ich wette mit dir, dass er es vergisst.

better *adjective, adverb* 1 besser; **she's found a better flat** sie hat eine bessere Wohnung gefunden; 2 **it works better than the other one** dieser geht besser als der andere; **even better** noch besser; **it's even better than before** das ist noch besser als vorher; 3 (*less ill*) I'm **better** es geht mir besser; **he's a bit better today** es geht ihm heute ein bisschen besser; **I feel better** ich fühle mich besser; 4 **to get better** besser werden; **my**

German is getting better mein Deutsch wird besser; 5 **so much the better** umso besser; **the sooner the better** je eher, desto besser.

better *adverb* **it's better to phone at once** es wäre besser, sofort anzurufen; **he'd better not go** er sollte besser nicht gehen; **I'd better go now** ich gehe jetzt besser.

better off *adjective* 1 (*richer*) besser gestellt; **they're better off than us** sie sind besser gestellt als wir; 2 (*more comfortable*) **to be better off** besser dran sein; **you'd be better off in bed** im Bett wärst du besser aufgehoben.

between *preposition* 1 zwischen (+ DAT, *or* + ACC *when there is movement towards a place*); **between London and Dover** zwischen London und Dover; **between Monday and Friday** zwischen Montag und Freitag; 2 (*sharing*) unter (+ DAT); **between ourselves** unter uns; **between the two of them** unter sich.

beyond *preposition* 1 (*in space*) jenseits (+ GEN); **beyond the border** jenseits (+ GEN) der Grenze; 2 (*in time*) nach (+ DAT); **beyond midnight** nach Mitternacht; 3 **it's beyond me!** das ist mir unverständlich.

Bible *noun* **the Bible** die Bibel.

bicycle *noun* Fahrrad das (PL die Fahrräder); **she rides a bicycle** sie fährt Rad.

bicycle lane *noun* Fahrradweg der (PL die Fahrradwege).

big *adjective* groß; **a big house** ein großes Haus; **my big sister** meine große Schwester; **a big mistake** ein großer Fehler; **it's too big for me** das ist mir zu groß.

big toe noun große Zehe die (PL die großen Zehen).

bike noun **1** (with pedals) Rad das (PL die Räder); **by bike** mit dem Rad; **2** (with motor) Motorrad das (PL die Motorräder).

bikini noun Bikini der (PL die Bikinis).

bilingual adjective zweisprachig.

bill noun Rechnung die (PL die Rechnungen); **can we have the bill, please?** die Rechnung bitte.

billiards noun Billard das; **to play billiards** Billard spielen.

billion noun Milliarde die (PL die Milliarden), Billion die (PL die Billionen); **two billion euros** zwei Milliarden Euro.

bin noun Mülleimer der (PL die Mülleimer).

binoculars plural noun Fernglas das (PL die Ferngläser).

biochemistry noun Biochemie die.

biology noun Biologie die.

bird noun Vogel der (PL die Vögel).

bird sanctuary noun Vogelschutzgebiet das (PL die Vogelschutzgebiete).

birdwatching noun das Beobachten von Vögeln; **to go birdwatching** Vögel beobachten.

Biro noun Kugelschreiber der (PL die Kugelschreiber).

birth noun Geburt die (PL die Geburten).

birth certificate noun Geburtsurkunde die (PL die Geburtsurkunden).

birthday noun Geburtstag der (PL die Geburtstage); **happy birthday!** herzlichen Glückwunsch zum Geburtstag!

birthday party noun Geburtstagsfeier die (PL die Geburtstagsfeiern).

biscuit noun Keks der (PL die Kekse).

bishop noun **1** (churchman) Bischof der (PL die Bischöfe); **2** (in chess) Läufer der (PL die Läufer).

bit noun **1** (piece) Stückchen das (PL die Stückchen); **a bit of chocolate** ein Stückchen Schokolade; **2** (a small amount) a bit of ein bisschen; **a bit of sugar** ein bisschen Zucker; **3** (in a book, film, etc.) Teil der (PL die Teile); **this bit is brilliant** dieser Teil ist hervorragend; **4 a bit** ein bisschen; **a bit too early** ein bisschen zu früh; **wait a bit!** warte ein bisschen!; **5 he's a bit of a show-off** er ist ein ziemlicher Angeber; **6 bit by bit** nach und nach.

bite noun **1** (snack) Happen der (PL die Happen); **we'll just have a bite before we go** wir essen noch einen kleinen Happen, bevor wir gehen; **2** (from an insect) Stich der (PL die Stiche); **mosquito bite** der Mückenstich; **3** (from a dog) Biss der (PL die Bisse).

bite verb **1** (person or dog) beißen✧; **2** (insect) stechen✧.

bitter adjective (taste) bitter.

black adjective **1** schwarz; **my black jacket** meine schwarze Jacke; **2 a black man** ein Schwarzer; **a black woman** eine Schwarze.

a

b

c

d

e

f

g

h

i

j

k

l

m

n

o

p

q

r

s

t

u

v

w

x

y

z

blackberry noun Brombeere die (PL die Brombeeren).

blackbird noun Amsel die (PL die Amseln).

blackboard noun Tafel die (PL die Tafeln).

blackcurrant noun Schwarze Johannisbeere die (PL die Schwarzen Johannisbeeren).

black pudding noun Blutwurst die (PL die Blutwürste).

blade noun Klinge die (PL die Klingen).

blame noun Schuld die; **to take the blame for something** die Schuld für etwas (ACC) auf sich (ACC) nehmen; **to put the blame on somebody** die Schuld auf jemanden schieben.

blame verb **to blame somebody for something** jemandem die Schuld an etwas (DAT) geben; **they blamed him for the accident** sie haben ihm die Schuld an dem Unfall gegeben; **she is to blame for it** sie ist daran schuld; **I blame the parents** ich gebe den Eltern Schuld; **I don't blame you** ich kann es dir nicht verdenken.

blank noun Lücke die (PL die Lücken).

blank adjective **1** (page) leer (tape or disk) unbespielt; **2 blank cheque** der Blankoscheck.

blanket noun Decke die (PL die Decken).

blaze noun Feuer das (PL die Feuer).

blaze verb brennen✧.

bleach noun Bleichmittel das (PL die Bleichmittel).

bleed verb bluten; **my nose is bleeding** meine Nase blutet.

blend verb mischen.

blender noun Mixer der (PL die Mixer).

bless verb segnen; **bless you!** (after a sneeze) Gesundheit!

blind noun (in a window) Rollo das (PL die Rollos).

blind adjective blind.

blink verb (mit den Augen) blinzeln.

blister noun Blase die (PL die Blasen).

blizzard noun Schneesturm der (PL die Schneestürme).

block noun (a building or buildings) Block der (PL die Blocks); **block of flats** der Wohnblock; **office block** das Bürohaus; **to drive round the block** um den Block fahren.

block verb **1** sperren (an exit or a road); **2 the sink's blocked** das Spülbecken ist verstopft.

blonde adjective blond.

blood noun Blut das.

blood test noun Blutprobe die (PL die Blutproben).

blouse noun Bluse die (PL die Blusen).

blow noun Schlag der (PL die Schläge).

blow verb **1** (a person) blasen✧; **2** (the wind) wehen; **3 the bomb blew the bridge to pieces** die Bombe hat die Brücke in die Luft gesprengt; **4 to blow your nose** sich (DAT) die Nase putzen.

● **to blow something out** etwas ausblasen✧ SEP.

● **to blow up** (*explode*) explodieren (PERF *sein*).

● **to blow something up** (*a tyre or balloon*) etwas aufblasen ◇ SEP, (*with explosives*) etwas sprengen.

blow-dry *noun* Föhnen *das*; **a cut and blow-dry** Schneiden und Föhnen.

blue *adjective* blau; **blue eyes** blaue Augen.

blunder *noun* Fehler *der* (PL die Fehler).

blunt *adjective* 1 (*a knife, pencil, or scissors*) stumpf; 2 (*a person or question*) direkt.

blurred *adjective* 1 (*not distinct*) verschwommen; 2 (*photo*) unscharf.

blush *verb* erröten (PERF *sein*).

board *noun* 1 (*plank, notice board, game*) Brett *das* (PL die Bretter); **chess board** das Schachbrett; 2 (*blackboard*) Tafel *die* (PL die Tafeln); 3 (*accommodation in a hotel*) **full board** die Vollpension; **half board** die Halbpension; **board and lodging** Unterkunft und Verpflegung.

boarder *noun* (*in a school*) Internatsschüler *der* (PL die Internatsschüler), Internatsschülerin *die* (PL die Internatsschülerinnen).

board game *noun* Brettspiel *das* (PL die Brettspiele).

boarding *noun* (*on a plane, train*) Einsteigen *das*.

boarding card *noun* Bordkarte *die* (PL die Bordkarten).

boarding school *noun* Internat *das* (PL die Internate).

boast *verb* prahlen; **he was boasting about his new bike** er prahlte mit seinem neuen Rad.

boat *noun* 1 Boot *das* (PL die Boote); **rowing boat** das Ruderboot; 2 (*larger boat*) Schiff *das* (PL die Schiffe); **to go by boat** mit dem Schiff fahren.

body *noun* 1 Körper *der* (PL die Körper); 2 (*corpse*) Leiche *die* (PL die Leichen).

bodybuilding *noun* Bodybuilding *das*.

bodyguard *noun* Leibwächter *der* (PL die Leibwächter).

body odour *noun* Körpergeruch *der*.

boil *noun* 1 **to bring the water to the boil** das Wasser zum Kochen bringen; 2 (*swelling*) Furunkel *der* (PL die Furunkel).

boil *verb* 1 kochen; **the water's boiling** das Wasser kocht; **to boil vegetables** Gemüse kochen; 2 (*put the kettle on*) **to boil some water** Wasser aufsetzen SEP.

● **to boil over** überkochen SEP (PERF *sein*).

boiled egg *noun* gekochte Ei *das* (PL die gekochten Eier).

boiled potato *noun* Salzkartoffel *die* (PL die Salzkartoffeln).

boiler *noun* (*for central heating*) Heizkessel *der* (PL die Heizkessel).

boiling *adjective* 1 (*water*) kochend; 2 **it's boiling hot today** heute ist es wahnsinnig heiß.

bolt *noun* (*on a door*) Riegel *der* (PL die Riegel).

a
b
c
d
e
f
g
h
i
j
k
l
m
n
o
p
q
r
s
t
u
v
w
x
y
z

bolt verb **1** (lock) verriegeln; **2** (gobble down) runterschlingen✧ SEP (informal).

bomb noun Bombe die (PL die Bomben).

bomb verb bombardieren.

bombing noun **1** (in war) Bombardierung die (PL die Bombardierungen); **2** (a terrorist attack) Bombenattentat das (PL die Bombenattentate).

bone noun **1** Knochen der (PL die Knochen); **2** (of a fish) Gräte die (PL die Gräten).

bonfire noun Feuer das (PL die Feuer).

bonnet noun **1** (of a car) Kühlerhaube die (PL die Kühlerhauben); **2** (clothing) Haube die (PL die Hauben).

boo verb ausbuhen SEP; **the crowd booed the referee** die Menge buhte den Schiedsrichter aus.

book noun **1** Buch das (PL die Bücher); **a book about dinosaurs** ein Buch über Dinosaurier; **my biology book** mein Biologiebuch; **2** (of stamps, tickets) Heft das (PL die Hefte); **3** exercise book das Heft; **cheque book** das Scheckbuch.

book verb **1** buchen (holiday, flight); **2** bestellen (a table, theatre, or cinema ticket); **I booked a table for 8 p.m.** ich habe einen Tisch für zwanzig Uhr bestellt.

bookcase noun Bücherregal das (PL die Bücherregale).

booking noun (for a flight or a holiday, for example) Buchung die (PL die Buchungen).

booking office noun **1** (at a train station) Fahrkartenschalter der (PL die Fahrkartenschalter); **2** (in a theatre or cinema) Kasse die (PL die Kassen).

booklet noun Broschüre die (PL die Broschüren).

bookshelf noun Bücherregal das (PL die Bücherregale).

bookshop noun Buchhandlung die (PL die Buchhandlungen).

boot noun **1** Stiefel der (PL die Stiefel); **2** (for football, walking, climbing, or skiing) Schuh der (PL die Schuhe); **football boots** Fußballschuhe; **3** (of a car) Kofferraum der (PL die Kofferräume).

border noun (between countries) Grenze die (PL die Grenzen); **at the border** an der Grenze.

bore noun **1** (a boring person) langweilige Mensch der (PL die langweiligen Menschen); **2** (a nuisance) **what a bore!** wie ärgerlich!

bored adjective **to be bored** sich langweilen; **I'm bored** ich langweile mich.

boring adjective langweilig.

born adjective geboren; **to be born** geboren werden; **she was born in Germany** sie ist in Deutschland geboren.

borrow verb sich (DAT) borgen; **can I borrow your bike?** kann ich mir dein Rad borgen?; **to borrow something from somebody** sich etwas von jemandem borgen; **I borrowed some money from Dad** ich habe mir Geld von Vati geborgt.

boss noun Chef der (PL die Chefs), Chefin die (PL die Chefinnen).

bossy adjective herrisch.

both pronoun beide; **they both came** sie kamen beide; **both my sisters were there** meine beiden Schwestern waren da; **both of us** wir beide; **they are both sold** beide sind verkauft.

both adverb **both at home and at school** sowohl zu Hause als auch in der Schule; **both in summer and in winter** sowohl im Sommer als auch im Winter.

bother noun **1** (minor trouble) Ärger der; **I've had a lot of bother with the car** ich hatte viel Ärger mit dem Auto; **2 if it isn't too much bother** wenn es nicht zu viel Mühe macht; **it's no bother** das ist kein Problem; **the children were no bother** die Kinder waren kein Problem; **without any bother** ohne irgendwelche Schwierigkeiten.

bother verb **1** (disturb) stören; **I'm sorry to bother you** es tut mir Leid, dich zu stören; **2** (worry) stören; **what's bothering you?** was stört dich?; **it doesn't bother me at all** das stört mich überhaupt nicht; **3** (take trouble) **don't bother to write** du brauchst nicht zu schreiben; **she didn't even bother to wait** sie hat nicht einmal gewartet; **don't bother!** lass es sein! (informal); **I can't be bothered** ich habe keine Lust.

bottle noun Flasche die (PL die Flaschen).

bottle bank noun Altglascontainer der (PL die Altglascontainer).

bottle opener noun Flaschenöffner der (PL die Flaschenöffner).

bottom noun **1** (of a bag, bottle, hole, or stretch of water) Boden der (PL die Böden); **at the bottom of the lake** am Boden des Sees; **at the bottom of the well** auf dem Grund des Brunnens; **2** (of a hill or building) Fuß der (PL die Füße); **at the bottom of the tower** am Fuß des Turms; **3** (of a garden, street, list) Ende das (PL die Enden); **at the bottom of the street** am Ende der Straße; **4 at the bottom of the page** unten auf der Seite; **5** (buttocks) Hintern der (informal) (PL die Hintern).

bottom adjective **1** unterster/unterste/unterstes; **the bottom shelf** das unterste Regalbrett; **2 the bottom flat** die Wohnung im Erdgeschoss.

bounce verb (jump) springen✧ (PERF sein).

bouncer noun Rausschmeißer der (PL die Rausschmeißer).

bound adjective (certain) **he's bound to be late** er kommt ganz bestimmt zu spät; **that was bound to happen** das musste so kommen.

boundary noun Grenze die (PL die Grenzen).

bow noun **1** (in a shoelace or ribbon) Schleife die (PL die Schleifen); **2** (for a violin or with arrows) Bogen der (PL die Bogen); **with bow and arrow** mit Pfeil und Bogen.

a
b
c
d
e
f
g
h
i
j
k
l
m
n
o
p
q
r
s
t
u
v
w
x
y
z

bowl noun 1 (large, for salad, mixing, or washing up) Schüssel die (PL die Schüsseln); 2 (smaller) Schale die (PL die Schalen).

bowler noun (in cricket) Werfer der (PL die Werfer), Werferin die (PL die Werferinnen).

bowling noun (tenpin) Bowling das; **to go bowling** kegeln gehen.

bow tie noun Fliege die (PL die Fliegen).

box noun 1 Schachtel die (PL die Schachteln); **a box of chocolates** eine Schachtel Pralinen; 2 **cardboard box** der Karton; 3 (on a form) Kästchen das (PL die Kästchen).

boxer noun Boxer der (PL die Boxer).

boxing noun 1 Boxen das; 2 **boxing match** der Boxkampf.

Boxing Day noun zweite Weihnachtsfeiertag der.

box office noun Kasse die (PL die Kassen).

boy noun Junge der (PL die Jungen); **a little boy** ein kleiner Junge.

boyfriend noun Freund der (PL die Freunde).

bra noun BH der (PL die BHs).

brace noun (for teeth) Spange die (PL die Spangen).

bracelet noun Armband das (PL die Armbänder).

bracket noun Klammer die (PL die Klammern); **in brackets** in Klammern.

brain noun Gehirn das (PL die Gehirne).

brainwave noun Geistesblitz der (PL die Geistesblitze).

brake noun Bremse die (PL die Bremsen).

brake verb bremsen.

branch noun 1 (of a tree) Ast der (PL die Äste); 2 (of a shop) Filiale die (PL die Filialen); 3 (of a bank) Zweigstelle die (PL die Zweigstellen).

brand noun Marke die (PL die Marken).

brand new adjective nagelneu.

brandy noun Weinbrand der (PL die Weinbrände).

brass noun 1 (metal) Messing das; 2 (in an orchestra) **the brass** die Blechbläser.

brass band noun Blaskapelle die (PL die Blaskapellen).

brave adjective tapfer.

bravery noun Tapferkeit die.

Brazilian adjective brasilianisch.

Brazilian noun Brasilianer der (PL die Brasilianer), Brasilianerin die (PL die Brasilianerinnen).

bread noun Brot das (PL die Brote); **a slice of bread** eine Scheibe Brot; **a piece of bread and butter** ein Butterbrot.

break noun 1 (a short rest or at school) Pause die (PL die Pausen); **ten minutes' break** eine Pause von zehn Minuten; **to take a break** Pause machen; **at break** in der Pause; 2 **the Christmas break** die Weihnachtsferien (plural).

break verb 1 zerbrechen◇, kaputtmachen SEP (informal); **he broke a glass** er hat ein Glas zerbrochen; **don't break the doll** mach die Puppe nicht kaputt; 2 (get damaged) zerbrechen◇ (PERF sein), kaputtgehen◇ SEP (informal) PERF sein); **the glass broke** das Glas zerbrach; **the eggs broke** die Eier sind kaputtgegangen; **3 to break your arm** sich (DAT) den Arm brechen; **4** brechen◇ (rules, promise); **to break one's promise** sein Versprechen brechen; **5 to break the record** den Rekord brechen◇; **6 to break the news that ...** melden, dass ....

● **to break down 1** (car) eine Panne haben; **the car broke down** das Auto hatte eine Panne; **2** (talks, negotiations) scheitern (PERF sein).

● **to break in** einbrechen◇ SEP (PERF sein).

● **to break up 1** (couple) sich trennen; **2** (crowd) sich auflösen SEP; **3 we break up on Thursday** die Ferien fangen Donnerstag an.

breakdown noun **1** (of a vehicle) Panne die (PL die Pannen); **we had a breakdown on the motorway** wir hatten eine Panne auf der Autobahn; **2** (in talks or negotiations) Scheitern das; **3** (a nervous collapse) Zusammenbruch der (PL die Zusammenbrüche); **to have a nervous breakdown** einen Nervenzusammenbruch haben.

breakdown truck noun Abschleppwagen der (PL die Abschleppwagen).

breakfast noun Frühstück das (PL die Frühstücke); **we have breakfast at eight** wir frühstücken um acht Uhr.

break-in noun Einbruch der (PL die Einbrüche).

breast noun Brust die (PL die Brüste).

breaststroke noun Brustschwimmen das.

breath noun Atem der; **out of breath** außer Atem; **to hold your breath** den Atem anhalten; **to get your breath back** wieder zu Atem kommen; **to take a deep breath** tief einatmen.

breathe verb atmen.

breathing noun Atmen das.

breed noun (of animal) Rasse die (PL die Rassen).

breeze noun Brise die (PL die Brisen).

brew verb **1** brauen (beer); **2** aufbrühen SEP (tea); **the tea's brewing** der Tee zieht noch.

brewery noun Brauerei die (PL die Brauereien).

brick noun Ziegel der (PL die Ziegel); **a brick wall** eine Ziegelmauer.

bride noun Braut die (PL die Bräute); **the bride and groom** das Brautpaar.

bridegroom noun Bräutigam der (PL die Bräutigame).

bridesmaid noun Brautjungfer die (PL die Brautjungfern).

bridge noun **1** (over a river) Brücke die (PL die Brücken); **2** (card game) Bridge das.

bridle noun Zaumzeug das (PL die Zaumzeuge).

brief adjective kurz.

briefcase noun Aktentasche die (PL die Aktentaschen).

briefly adverb kurz.

briefs plural noun Slip der (PL die Slips).

bright adjective **1** (colour) leuchtend; **bright green socks** leuchtend grüne Socken; **2** (eyes, sunshine) strahlend; **3** (light) hell; **4** (clever) intelligent; **she's not**

a
b
c
d
e
f
g
h
i
j
k
l
m
n
o
p
q
r
s
t
u
v
w
x
y
z

a
b
c
d
e
f
g
h
i
j
k
l
m
n
o
p
q
r
s
t
u
v
w
x
y
z

very bright sie ist nicht sehr intelligent; ★ **to look on the bright side** die Sache positiv sehen (*literally: to see things positively*).

brilliant *adjective* **1** (*very clever*) glänzend; **he's a brilliant surgeon** er ist ein glänzender Chirurg; **2** (*wonderful*) toll; **the party was brilliant!** die Party war toll!

bring *verb* **1** mitbringen ◇ SEP; **he brought a present** er brachte ein Geschenk mit; **bring your camera** bring deinen Fotoapparat mit; **2** (*to a place*) bringen ◇; **she's bringing the children home** sie bringt die Kinder nach Hause.

● **to bring somebody up** jemanden großziehen ◇ SEP; **he was brought up by his aunt** er wurde von seiner Tante großgezogen.

Britain *noun* Großbritannien *das*; **to Britain** nach Großbritannien.

British *plural noun* **the British** die Briten.

British *adjective* **1** britisch; **the British Isles** die Britischen Inseln; **2 he's British** er ist Brite; **she's British** sie ist Britin.

broad *adjective* **1** (*wide*) breit; **2** (*extensive*) weit.

broad bean *noun* dicke Bohne *die* (PL *die* dicken Bohnen).

broadcast *noun* Sendung *die* (PL *die* Sendungen).

broadcast *verb* senden.

broccoli *noun* Brokkoli *der* (PL *die* Brokkolis).

brochure *noun* Broschüre *die* (PL *die* Broschüren).

broke *adjective* **to be broke** pleite sein (*informal*).

broken *adjective* zerbrochen, kaputt (*informal*); **the window's broken** das Fenster ist kaputt; **to have a broken leg** ein gebrochenes Bein haben.

bronchitis *noun* Bronchitis *die*.

brooch *noun* Brosche *die* (PL *die* Broschen).

broom *noun* Besen *der* (PL *die* Besen).

brother *noun* Bruder *der* (PL *die* Brüder); **my mother's brother** der Bruder meiner Mutter.

brother-in-law *noun* Schwager *der* (PL *die* Schwäger).

brown *adjective* braun; **my brown shoes** meine braunen Schuhe; **light brown** hellbraun; **dark brown** dunkelbraun; **to go brown** (*suntanned*) braun werden.

brown bread *noun* Mischbrot *das* (PL *die* Mischbrote).

bruise *noun* **1** (*on a person*) blaue Fleck *der* (PL *die* blauen Flecken); **2** (*on fruit*) Druckstelle *die* (PL *die* Druckstellen).

brush *noun* **1** (*for your hair, clothes, nails, or shoes*) Bürste *die* (PL *die* Bürsten); **my hair brush** meine Haarbürste; **2** (*for sweeping*) Besen *der* (PL *die* Besen); **3** (*for paint*) Pinsel *der* (PL *die* Pinsel).

brush *verb* **1** bürsten; **to brush your hair** sich (DAT) die Haare bürsten; **I brushed my hair** ich habe mir die Haare gebürstet; **2 to brush your teeth** sich (DAT) die Zähne putzen.

Brussels *noun* Brüssel *das*.

Brussels sprout *noun* Rosenkohl *der*; **he likes Brussels sprouts** er mag Rosenkohl.

bubble *noun* Blase die (PL die Blasen).

bubble bath *noun* Badeschaum der.

bucket *noun* Eimer der (PL die Eimer).

buckle *noun* Schnalle die (PL die Schnallen).

Buddhism *noun* Buddhismus der.

Buddhist *noun* Buddhist der (PL die Buddhisten), Buddhistin die (PL die Buddhistinnen).

budget *noun* Budget das (PL die Budgets).

budgie *noun* Wellensittich der (PL die Wellensittiche).

buffet *noun* Büffet das (PL die Büffets).

buffet car *noun* Speisewagen der (PL die Speisewagen).

bug *noun* 1 (*insect*) Wanze die (PL die Wanzen); 2 (*germ*) Bazillus der (PL die Bazillen); **a stomach bug** eine Magengrippe; 3 **a computer bug** ein Programmierfehler.

build *verb* bauen.

builder *noun* Bauarbeiter der (PL die Bauarbeiter).

building *noun* Gebäude das (PL die Gebäude).

building site *noun* Baustelle die (PL die Baustellen).

building society *noun* Bausparkasse die (PL die Bausparkassen).

built-up *adjective* 1 bebaut; 2 **built-up area** das Wohngebiet.

bulb *noun* 1 (*lightbulb*) Glühbirne die (PL die Glühbirnen); 2 (*flower bulb*) Blumenzwiebel die (PL die Zwiebeln).

bull *noun* Bulle der (PL die Bullen).

bulldozer *noun* Planierraupe die (PL die Planierraupen).

bullet *noun* Kugel die (PL die Kugeln).

bulletin *noun* 1 (*written*) Bulletin das (PL die Bulletins); 2 (*on TV, radio*) **news bulletin** die Kurzmeldung.

bully *noun* 1 (*in school*) Rabauke der (PL die Rabauken); 2 (*adult*) Tyrann der (PL die Tyrannen).

bully *verb* schikanieren.

bum *noun* Hintern der (*informal*) (PL die Hintern).

bump *noun* 1 (*on a surface*) Unebenheit die (PL die Unebenheiten); **there are lots of bumps in the road** die Straße ist sehr uneben; 2 (*swelling*) Beule die (PL die Beulen); **a bump on the head** eine Beule am Kopf; 3 (*jolt*) Stoß der (PL die Stöße); 4 (*noise*) Bums der (PL die Bumse).

bump *verb* 1 (*bang*) stoßen✧; **I bumped my head** ich habe mir den Kopf gestoßen; **to bump into something** gegen etwas (ACC) stoßen; 2 **to bump into somebody** (*meet by chance*) jemanden zufällig treffen.

bumper *noun* Stoßstange die (PL die Stoßstangen).

bumpy *adjective* holperig.

bun *noun* 1 (*for a burger*) Brötchen das (PL die Brötchen), Semmel die (PL die Semmeln); 2 (*sweet*) süße Brötchen das (PL die süßen Brötchen).

bunch *noun* 1 (*of flowers*) Strauß der (PL die Sträuße); 2 (*of carrots, radishes*) Bund das (PL die Bunde); **a**

a b c d e f g h i j k l m n o p q r s t u v w x y z

bunch of keys ein Schlüsselbund; **3 a bunch of grapes** eine ganze Weintraube.

bundle noun Bündel das (PL die Bündel).

bungalow noun Bungalow der (PL die Bungalows).

bunk noun **1** (on a boat) Koje die (PL die Kojen); **2** (on a train) Bett das (PL die Betten).

bunk bed noun Etagenbett das (PL die Etagenbetten).

burger noun Hamburger der (PL die Hamburger).

burglar noun Einbrecher der (PL die Einbrecher), Einbrecherin die (PL die Einbrecherinnen).

burglar alarm noun Alarmanlage die (PL die Alarmanlagen).

burglary noun Einbruch der (PL die Einbrüche).

burn noun **1** (on the skin) Verbrennung die (PL die Verbrennungen); **2** (on fabric, object) Brandstelle die (PL die Brandstellen).

burn verb **1** verbrennen◇; **she burnt his letters** sie hat seine Briefe verbrannt; **2** (fire, candle) brennen◇; **3** (injure) verbrennen◇; **to burn yourself** sich verbrennen; **you'll burn your fingers!** du verbrennst dir die Finger!; **4** (cake, meat, etc.) anbrennen◇ SEP; **Mum's burnt the cake** Mutti hat den Kuchen anbrennen lassen.

burnt adjective **1** (papers, rubbish) verbrannt; **2** (cake, meat, etc.) angebrannt.

burst verb **1** platzen lassen (a balloon); **the tyre has burst** der Reifen ist geplatzt; **2 to burst out laughing** in Lachen ausbrechen◇ SEP (PERF sein); **to burst into tears** in Tränen ausbrechen◇ SEP (PERF sein); **3 to burst into flames** in Flammen aufgehen◇ SEP (PERF sein).

bury verb **1** begraben◇ (a dead person); **2** vergraben◇ (treasure or a bone).

bus noun Bus der (PL die Busse); **on the bus** im Bus; **by bus** mit dem Bus.

bus driver noun Busfahrer der (PL die Busfahrer), Busfahrerin die (PL die Busfahrerinnen).

bush noun Busch der (PL die Büsche).

business noun **1** (commercial dealings) Geschäfte (plural); **business is bad** die Geschäfte gehen schlecht; **he's in Leeds on business** er ist geschäftlich in Leeds; **2** (a line of business or profession) Branche die (PL die Branchen); **he's in the insurance business** er ist in der Versicherungsbranche; **3** (firm or company) Betrieb der (PL die Betriebe); **small businesses** kleine Betriebe; **4** (personal concern) Angelegenheit die (PL die Angelegenheiten); **mind your own business!** kümmere dich um deine eigenen Angelegenheiten!

businessman noun Geschäftsmann der (PL die Geschäftsleute).

a
b
c
d
e
f
g
h
i
j
k
l
m
n
o
p
q
r
s
t
u
v
w
x
y
z

business trip noun Geschäftsreise die (PL die Geschäftsreisen).

businesswoman noun Geschäftsfrau die (PL die Geschäftsfrauen).

bus pass noun Zeitkarte die (PL die Zeitkarten).

bus route noun Buslinie die (PL die Buslinien).

bus shelter noun Wartehäuschen das (PL die Wartehäuschen).

bus station noun Busbahnhof der (PL die Busbahnhöfe).

bus stop noun Bushaltestelle die (PL die Bushaltestellen).

bus ticket noun Busfahrkarte die (PL die Busfahrkarten).

busy adjective 1 beschäftigt; **he's busy** er ist beschäftigt; **she was busy packing** sie war mit Packen beschäftigt; 2 **to have a busy day** viel zu tun haben; 3 **the shops were busy** in den Läden war sehr viel los; 4 (phone) besetzt.

but conjunction 1 aber; **small but strong** klein aber stark; 2 (after a negative statement) sondern; **not Thursday but Friday** nicht Donnerstag, sondern Freitag; **not only ... but also** nicht nur ... sondern auch.

but preposition 1 außer (+ DAT); **everyone but Winston** alle außer Winston; **anything but that!** nur das nicht!; 2 **the last but one** der/die/das Vorletzte.

butcher noun 1 Fleischer der (PL die Fleischer), Fleischerin die (PL die Fleischerinnen), Metzger der (PL die Metzger), Metzgerin die (PL die Metzgerinnen); **he's a butcher** er

ist Fleischer, er ist Metzger; 2 **the butcher's** die Fleischerei, die Metzgerei.

butter noun Butter die.

butter verb buttern.

butterfly noun Schmetterling der (PL die Schmetterlinge).

button noun Knopf der (PL die Knöpfe); **the record button** die Aufnahmetaste.

buttonhole noun Knopfloch das (PL die Knopflöcher).

buy noun Kauf der (PL die Käufe); **a bad buy** ein schlechter Kauf.

buy verb kaufen; **I've bought the tickets** ich habe die Karten gekauft; **to buy something for somebody** jemandem etwas kaufen; **Sarah bought him a sweater** Sarah hat ihm einen Pullover gekauft.

buzz verb (a fly or bee) summen.

buzzer noun Summer der (PL die Summer).

by preposition 1 von (+ DAT); **I was bitten by a dog** ich bin von einem Hund gebissen worden; **by Mozart** von Mozart; 2 **by mistake** versehentlich; 3 (travel) mit (+ DAT); **to come by bus** mit dem Bus kommen; **to go by train** mit dem Zug fahren; **by bike** mit dem Rad; 4 (near) an (+ DAT); **by the sea** am Meer; **the stop by the school** die Haltestelle an der Schule; 5 (before) bis; **it'll be ready by Monday** es wird bis Montag fertig sein; **I'll be back by four** ich bin bis vier Uhr zurück; 6 **by now** inzwischen; 7 **by yourself** ganz allein; **I was by myself in the house** ich war ganz

a
b
d
e
f
g
h
i
j
k
l
m
n
o
p
q
r
s
t
u
v
w
x
y
z

allein im Haus; **she did it by herself** sie hat es ganz allein gemacht; **8 by the way** übrigens; **9 to go by** vorbeigehen✧ SEP (PERF sein).

bye *exclamation* tschüs! (*informal*).

bypass *noun* Umgehungsstraße die (PL die Umgehungsstraßen).

Cc

cab *noun* **1** Taxi das (PL die Taxis); **to call a cab** ein Taxi rufen; **2** (*on a lorry*) Führerhaus das (PL die Führerhäuser).

cabbage *noun* Kohl der.

cable *noun* Kabel das (PL die Kabel).

café *noun* Café das (PL die Cafés).

cage *noun* Käfig der (PL die Käfige).

cagoule *noun* Anorak der (PL die Anoraks).

cake *noun* Kuchen der (PL die Kuchen); **would you like a piece of cake?** möchtest du ein Stück Kuchen?

calculate *verb* berechnen.

calculation *noun* Rechnung die (PL die Rechnungen).

calculator *noun* Taschenrechner der (PL die Taschenrechner).

calendar *noun* Kalender der (PL die Kalender).

calf *noun* **1** (*animal*) Kalb das (PL die Kälber); **2** (*of your leg*) Wade die (PL die Waden).

call *noun* (*telephone*) Anruf der (PL die Anrufe); **I had several calls this morning** ich erhielt heute Morgen mehrere Anrufe; **thank**

you for your call danke für deinen Anruf; **a phone call** ein Telefonanruf.

call *verb* **1** rufen✧; **to call a taxi** ein Taxi rufen; **to call the doctor** einen Arzt rufen; **they called the police** sie riefen die Polizei; **2** (*phone*) anrufen✧ SEP; **call me later** ruf mich später an; **thank you for calling** danke für deinen Anruf; **I'll call you back later** ich rufe dich später zurück; **3** nennen✧; **they've called the baby Julie** sie haben das Baby Julie genannt; **4 to be called** heißen✧; **her brother is called Dan** ihr Bruder heißt Dan; **what's he called?** wie heißt er?

call box *noun* Telefonzelle die (PL die Telefonzellen).

calm *adjective* ruhig.

calm *verb* beruhigen.

● **to calm down** sich beruhigen; **he's calmed down a bit** er hat sich etwas beruhigt.

● **to calm somebody down** jemanden beruhigen; **I tried to calm her down** ich habe versucht, sie zu beruhigen.

calmly *adverb* ruhig.

calorie *noun* Kalorie die (PL die Kalorien).

camcorder *noun* Camcorder der (PL die Camcorder).

camel *noun* Kamel das (PL die Kamele).

camera *noun* **1** Fotoapparat der (PL die Fotoapparate); **2** (*film or video camera*) Kamera die (PL die Kameras).

camp *noun* Lager das (PL die Lager).

capable

camp verb campen, zelten.

campaign noun Kampagne die (PL die Kampagnen).

camper noun 1 (person) Camper der (PL die Camper), Camperin die (PL die Camperinnen); 2 (vehicle) Campingbus der (PL die Campingbusse).

camper van noun Wohnmobil das (PL die Wohnmobile).

camping noun Camping das; **to go camping** zelten; **we're going camping in Bavaria this summer** diesen Sommer zelten wir in Bayern.

campsite noun Campingplatz der (PL die Campingplätze).

can¹ noun 1 Dose die (PL die Dosen); **a can of tomatoes** eine Dose Tomaten; 2 (for petrol or oil) Kanister der (PL die Kanister).

can² verb 1 können◊; **I can't be there before ten** ich kann vor zehn Uhr nicht da sein; **can you open the door, please?** kannst du die Tür bitte aufmachen?; **can I help you?** kann ich Ihnen helfen?; **they couldn't come** sie konnten nicht kommen; **you could have told me** das hättest du mir wirklich sagen können; **I can't see him** ich kann ihn nicht sehen; **I can't remember it** ich kann mich nicht daran erinnern; **she can't drive** sich kann nicht Auto fahren; 2 (be allowed) dürfen◊; **you can't smoke here** Sie dürfen hier nicht rauchen.

Canada noun Kanada das; **to Canada** nach Kanada.

Canadian noun Kanadier der (PL die Kanadier), Kanadierin die (PL die Kanadierinnen).

Canadian adjective kanadisch; **he is Canadian** er ist Kanadier.

canal noun Kanal der (PL die Kanäle).

cancel verb absagen SEP; **the concert's been cancelled** das Konzert ist abgesagt worden.

cancer noun Krebs der; **to have lung cancer** Lungenkrebs haben.

Cancer noun Krebs der (PL die Krebse); **I'm Cancer** ich bin Krebs.

candidate noun Kandidat der (PL die Kandidaten), Kandidatin die (PL die Kandidatinnen).

candle noun Kerze die (PL die Kerzen).

candlestick noun Kerzenständer der (PL die Kerzenständer).

canned adjective in Dosen; **canned tomatoes** Tomaten in Dosen.

canoe noun Kanu das (PL die Kanus).

canoeing noun **to go canoeing** Kanu fahren◊ (PERF sein); **I like canoeing** ich fahre gerne Kanu.

can-opener noun Dosenöffner der (PL die Dosenöffner).

canteen noun Kantine die (PL die Kantinen).

canvas noun 1 (of a tent or bag) Segeltuch das; 2 (for painting on) Leinwand die.

cap noun 1 (hat) Kappe die (PL die Kappen); **baseball cap** Baseballkappe die; 2 (on a bottle or tube) Verschluss der (PL die Verschlüsse).

capable adjective fähig.

a
b
c
d
e
f
g
h
i
j
k
l
m
n
o
p
q
r
s
t
u
v
w
x
y
z

a
b
c
d
e
f
g
h
i
j
k
l
m
n
o
p
q
r
s
t
u
v
w
x
y
z

capital noun **1** (city) Hauptstadt die (PL die Hauptstädte); **Berlin is the capital of Germany** Berlin ist die Hauptstadt von Deutschland; **2** (letter) Großbuchstabe der (PL die Großbuchstaben); **in capitals** mit Großbuchstaben.

capitalism noun Kapitalismus der.

Capricorn noun Steinbock der (PL die Steinböcke); **Linda's Capricorn** Linda ist Steinbock.

captain noun Kapitän der (PL die Kapitäne).

capture verb festnehmen ◇ SEP.

car noun Auto das (PL die Autos); **to park the car** das Auto einparken; **we're going by car** wir fahren mit dem Auto; **car crash** der Autounfall.

caramel noun Karamell der (PL die Karamells).

caravan noun Wohnwagen der (PL die Wohnwagen).

card noun Karte die (PL die Karten); **card game** das Kartenspiel; **to have a game of cards** Karten spielen.

cardboard noun Pappe die.

cardigan noun Strickjacke die (PL die Strickjacken).

cardphone noun Kartentelefon das (PL die Kartentelefone).

care noun **1** Vorsicht die; **to take care crossing the road** beim Überqueren der Straße vorsichtig sein; **take care!** (be careful) sei vorsichtig!, (when saying goodbye) mach's gut!; **2** to take care to do something darauf achten, dass man etwas tut; **to take care of**

somebody auf jemanden aufpassen.

care verb **1** to care about something sich für etwas (ACC) interessieren; **she cares about the environment** die Umwelt liegt ihr am Herzen; **2** she doesn't care es ist ihr egal; **I couldn't care less!** das ist mir völlig egal!

career noun Karriere die (PL die Karrieren).

careful adjective vorsichtig; **a careful driver** ein vorsichtiger Fahrer, eine vorsichtige Fahrerin; **be careful!** sei vorsichtig!

carefully adverb **1** sorgfältig; **to read the instructions carefully** die Anweisungen sorgfältig lesen; **2** vorsichtig; **she put the vase down carefully** sie stellte die Vase vorsichtig hin; **drive carefully!** fahr vorsichtig!; **3** listen carefully! hören Sie gut zu!

careless adjective **1** he's very careless er ist sehr nachlässig; **this is careless work** das ist eine schlampige Arbeit; **2** a careless mistake ein Flüchtigkeitsfehler; **3** a careless driver ein leichtsinniger Fahrer.

car ferry noun Autofähre die (PL die Autofähren).

car hire noun Autovermietung die.

Caribbean noun the Caribbean (islands) die Karibik (singular).

carnation noun Nelke die (PL die Nelken).

carnival noun Karneval der (PL die Karnevale).

car park noun Parkplatz der (PL die Parkplätze), (multi-storey) Parkhaus das (PL die Parkhäuser).

carpenter noun Tischler der (PL die Tischler), Tischlerin die (PL die Tischlerinnen).

carpentry noun Tischlerhandwerk das.

carpet noun Teppich der (PL die Teppiche).

car phone noun Autotelefon das (PL die Autotelefone).

car radio noun Autoradio das (PL die Autoradios).

carriage noun (of a train) Abteil das (PL die Abteile).

carrier bag noun Tragetasche die (PL die Tragetaschen).

carrot noun Karotte die (PL die Karotten), Möhre die (PL die Möhren).

carry verb tragen; **she was carrying a case** sie trug einen Koffer.

● **to carry on** weitermachen SEP; **they carried on working** sie arbeiteten weiter.

carrycot noun Babytragetasche die (PL die Babytragetaschen).

carsick adjective **he gets carsick** ihm wird beim Autofahren schlecht.

carton noun 1 (of cream or yoghurt) Becher der (PL die Becher); 2 (of milk or orange) Tüte die (PL die Tüten).

cartoon noun 1 (a film) Zeichentrickfilm der (PL die Zeichentrickfilme); 2 (a comic strip) Cartoon der (PL die Cartoons); 3 (a drawing) Karikatur die (PL die Karikaturen).

cartridge noun (for a pen) Patrone die (PL die Patronen).

case[1] noun 1 (suitcase) Koffer der (PL die Koffer); **to pack a case** einen Koffer packen; 2 (a large wooden box) Kiste die (PL die Kisten); 3 (for spectacles or small things) Etui das (PL die Etuis).

case[2] noun 1 Fall der (PL die Fälle); **in that case** in dem Fall; **that's not the case** das ist nicht der Fall; **in case of fire** bei Feuer; 2 in case falls; **in case he comes** falls er kommt; 3 **just in case** für alle Fälle; 4 **in any case** sowieso; **in any case, it's too late** es ist sowieso zu spät.

cash noun 1 (money in general) Geld das; **I haven't any cash on me** ich habe kein Geld dabei; 2 (money rather than a cheque) Bargeld das; **to pay in cash** bar zahlen; **£50 in cash** fünfzig Pfund in bar.

cash card noun Bankkarte die (PL die Bankkarten).

cash desk noun Kasse die (PL die Kassen); **to pay at the cash desk** an der Kasse zahlen.

cash dispenser noun Geldautomat der (PL die Geldautomaten).

cashier noun Kassierer der (PL die Kassierer), Kassiererin die (PL die Kassiererinnen).

cash point noun Geldautomat der (PL die Geldautomaten).

cassette noun Kassette die (PL die Kassetten).

cassette recorder noun Kassettenrekorder der (PL die Kassettenrekorder).

cast noun (of a play) Besetzung die.

castle noun **1** Burg die (PL die Burgen); **2** (in chess) Turm der (PL die Türme).

casual adjective zwanglos.

casualty noun **1** (in an accident) Verletzte der/die (PL die Verletzten); **2** (hospital department) Unfallstation die (PL die Unfallstationen); he's in casualty er ist auf der Unfallstation.

cat noun Katze die (PL die Katzen), (tomcat) Kater der (PL die Kater); ★ it's raining cats and dogs es regnet in Strömen (literally: it's raining in streams).

catalogue noun Katalog der (PL die Kataloge).

catastrophe noun Katastrophe die (PL die Katastrophen).

catch noun **1** (on a door) Schnappriegel der (PL die Schnappriegel); **2** (a drawback) Haken der (PL die Haken); where's the catch? wo ist der Haken?

catch verb **1** fangen◇; Tom caught the ball Tom hat den Ball gefangen; she caught a fish sie hat einen Fisch gefangen; catch me! fang mich!; **2** to catch somebody doing something jemanden bei etwas (DAT) erwischen; he was caught stealing money er wurde beim Geldstehlen erwischt; **3** (be in time for) noch erreichen; did Tim catch his plane? hat Tim sein Flugzeug noch erreicht?; **4** (become ill with) bekommen◇; she's caught chickenpox sie hat die Windpocken bekommen; **5** verstehen◇ (what somebody says); I didn't catch your name ich habe Ihren Namen nicht verstanden.

● to catch up with somebody jemanden einholen SEP.

category noun Kategorie die (PL die Kategorien).

catering noun **1** (trade) Gastronomie die; **2** who's doing the catering? wer liefert das Essen und die Getränke?

caterpillar noun Raupe die (PL die Raupen).

cathedral noun Kathedrale die (PL die Kathedralen); Cologne cathedral der Kölner Dom.

Catholic noun Katholik der (PL die Katholiken), Katholikin die (PL die Katholikinnen).

Catholic adjective katholisch.

cattle plural noun Vieh das.

cauliflower noun Blumenkohl der; cauliflower cheese mit Käse überbackener Blumenkohl.

cause noun **1** Ursache die (PL die Ursachen); the cause of the accident die Unfallursache; **2** for a good cause für eine gute Sache.

cause verb verursachen; to cause difficulties Schwierigkeiten verursachen.

cave noun Höhle die (PL die Höhlen).

caving noun Höhlenforschung die; to go caving auf Höhlenforschung gehen.

CD noun CD die (PL die CDs).

CD player noun CD-Player der (PL die CD-Player).

CD-ROM noun CD-ROM die (PL die CD-ROMs).

chalet

ceiling noun Decke die (PL die Decken); **on the ceiling** an der Decke.

celebrate verb feiern; **he's celebrating his birthday** er feiert seinen Geburtstag.

celebrity noun Berühmtheit die (PL die Berühmtheiten).

celery noun Sellerie der (PL die Sellerie).

cell noun Zelle die (PL die Zellen).

cellar noun Keller der (PL die Keller).

cello noun Cello das (PL die Cellos); **to play the cello** Cello spielen.

cement noun Zement der.

cemetery noun Friedhof der (PL die Friedhöfe).

cent noun 1 (in euro system) Eurocent der (PL die Eurocents), Cent der (PL die Cents); **50 cents** 50 (Euro)cent; 2 (in dollar system) Cent der (PL die Cents); **25 cents** 25 Cent.

centigrade adjective Celsius; **ten degrees centigrade** zehn Grad Celsius.

centimetre noun Zentimeter der (PL die Zentimeter).

central adjective 1 zentral; **the office is very central** das Büro ist sehr zentral gelegen; 2 **in central London** im Zentrum von London.

Central Europe noun Mitteleuropa das.

central heating noun Zentralheizung die.

centre noun Zentrum das (PL die Zentren); **in the centre of** im Zentrum von (+ DAT); **in the town centre** im Stadtzentrum; a

shopping centre ein Einkaufszentrum.

century noun Jahrhundert das (PL die Jahrhunderte); **in the twentieth century** im zwanzigsten Jahrhundert.

cereal noun breakfast cereal Frühstücksflocken (plural).

ceremony noun Zeremonie die (PL die Zeremonien).

certain adjective 1 (definite) bestimmt; **a certain number of** eine bestimmte Zahl von (+ DAT); 2 (confident) sicher; **to be certain** sich (DAT) sicher sein; **are you certain of the address?** bist du sicher, dass das die richtige Adresse ist?; **I'm absolutely certain** ich bin mir ganz sicher; **to be certain that ...** sicher sein, dass ...; 3 **nobody knows for certain** niemand weiß es genau.

certainly adverb bestimmt; **certainly not** bestimmt nicht.

certificate noun 1 Bescheinigung die (PL die Bescheinigungen); 2 **birth certificate** die Geburtsurkunde; 3 (at school) Zeugnis das (PL die Zeugnisse).

chain noun Kette die (PL die Ketten).

chair noun 1 (upright) Stuhl der (PL die Stühle); **a kitchen chair** ein Küchenstuhl; 2 (with arms) Sessel der (PL die Sessel).

chair lift noun Sessellift der (PL die Sessellifte).

chalet noun 1 (in the mountains) Chalet das (PL die Chalets); 2 (in a holiday camp) Ferienhaus das (PL die Ferienhäuser).

a b c d e f g h i j k l m n o p q r s t u v w x y z

challenge noun Herausforderung die (PL die Herausforderungen).

champion noun Meister der (PL die Meister), Meisterin die (PL die Meisterinnen); **the world slalom champion** der Weltmeister im Slalom, die Weltmeisterin im Slalom.

chance noun 1 (opportunity) Gelegenheit die (PL die Gelegenheiten); **to have the chance to do something** die Gelegenheit haben, etwas zu tun; **if you have the chance to go to New York** wenn du die Gelegenheit hast, nach New York zu fahren; **I had no chance to speak to him** ich hatte keine Gelegenheit, mit ihm zu reden; 2 (likelihood) Aussicht die (PL die Aussichten); **he's got no chance of winning** er hat keine Aussicht zu gewinnen; 3 (luck) Zufall der; **by chance** zufällig; **do you have her address, by any chance?** hast du zufällig ihre Adresse?

change noun 1 (from one thing to another) Änderung die (PL die Änderungen); **a change of address** eine Adressänderung; **there's been a change of plan** der Plan ist geändert worden; 2 (alteration) Veränderung die (PL die Veränderungen); **they've made some changes to the house** sie haben im Haus ein paar Veränderungen vorgenommen; **a change in the weather** eine Wetterumschwung; 3 (for the sake of variety) **for a change, we could go to a restaurant** zur Abwechslung könnten wir in ein

Restaurant gehen; **it makes a change from hamburgers** das ist mal etwas anderes als Hamburger; **a change of clothes** etwas anderes zum Anziehen; 4 (cash) Wechselgeld das; **I haven't any change** ich habe kein Wechselgeld.

change verb 1 (make different) ändern; **you can't change her** du kannst sie nicht ändern; **to change your address** seine Adresse ändern; 2 (become different) sich verändern; **Liz has changed a lot** Liz hat sich sehr verändert; 3 (transform completely) verwandeln; **the prince changed into a frog** der Prinz verwandelte sich in einen Frosch; 4 (exchange in a shop) umtauschen SEP; **just change it for a larger size** tauschen Sie es einfach gegen eine Nummer größer um; 5 (change clothes) sich umziehen ◇ SEP; **Mike's just changing** Mike zieht sich gerade um; 6 (switch from one train or bus to another) umsteigen ◇ SEP (PERF sein); **we changed trains at Crewe** wir stiegen in Crewe um; 7 (switch one thing for another) wechseln; **I want to change my job** ich möchte meinen Arbeitsplatz wechseln; **they changed places** sie haben die Plätze gewechselt; 8 **to change your mind** sich anders entschließen ◇.

changing room noun (for sport or swimming) Umkleideraum der (PL die Umkleideräume).

channel noun 1 (on TV) Kanal der (PL die Kanäle); **to change channels** auf einen anderen Kanal umschalten; **2 the Channel** der Ärmelkanal.

Channel Tunnel noun Eurotunnel der.

chaos noun Chaos das; **it was chaos!** das war ein Chaos!

chapel noun Kapelle die (PL die Kapellen).

chapter noun Kapitel das (PL die Kapitel); **in chapter two** im zweiten Kapitel.

character noun **1** (personality) Charakter der; **2** (somebody in a book) Charakter der (PL die Charaktere); **3** (part in a play or film) Rolle die (PL die Rollen); **the main character** die Hauptrolle.

charcoal noun **1** (for burning) Holzkohle die; **2** (for drawing) Kohle die.

charge noun **1** (what you pay) Gebühr die (PL die Gebühren); **a booking charge** eine Buchungsgebühr; **an extra or additional charge** eine zusätzliche Gebühr; **there's no charge** das ist kostenlos; **2 to be in charge** für etwas (ACC) verantwortlich sein; **who's in charge of the children?** wer ist für die Kinder verantwortlich?; **3 to be on a charge of theft** wegen Diebstahls angeklagt sein.

charge verb **1** (ask to pay) berechnen; **they charge us fifteen pounds an hour** sie berechnen uns fünfzehn Pfund pro Stunde; **they didn't charge for delivery** sie haben die Lieferung nicht berechnet; **we won't charge you for it** wir berechnen Ihnen nichts dafür; **2 to charge somebody with**

something (+ GEN) jemanden wegen etwas anklagen SEP.

charity noun Wohltätigkeitsverein der (PL die Wohltätigkeitsvereine).

charming adjective reizend.

chart noun **1** (table) Tabelle die (PL die Tabellen); **2 the weather chart** die Wetterkarte; **3 the charts** die Hitparade.

charter flight noun Charterflug der (PL die Charterflüge).

chase noun Verfolgungsjagd die (PL die Verfolgungsjagden); **a car chase** eine Verfolgungsjagd mit dem Auto.

chase verb jagen.

chat noun Plauderei die (PL die Plaudereien); **to have a chat with somebody** mit jemandem plaudern.

chatroom noun Chatroom der (PL die Chatrooms).

chat show noun Talkshow die (PL die Talkshows).

chatter verb **1** (talk) schwatzen; **2 my teeth were chattering** ich klapperte mit den Zähnen.

cheap adjective billig; **cheap shoes** billige Schuhe; **that's very cheap** das ist sehr billig.

cheaply adverb billig; **to eat cheaply** billig essen.

cheap-rate adjective verbilligt; **a cheap-rate phone call** ein Gespräch zum Billigtarif.

cheat noun **1** Betrüger der (PL die Betrüger), Betrügerin die (PL die Betrügerinnen); **2** (in games) Mogler der (PL die Mogler), Moglerin die (PL die Moglerinnen).

a b c d e f g h i j k l m n o p q r s t u v w x y z

a
b
c
d
e
f
g
h
i
j
k
l
m
n
o
p
q
r
s
t
u
v
w
x
y
z

cheat verb **1** betrügen✧; **2** (in games) mogeln.

check noun **1** (in a factory or at a border control) Kontrolle die (PL die Kontrollen); **passport check** die Passkontrolle; **2** (in chess) **check!** Schach!

check verb **1** (make sure) prüfen; **he checked their statements** er prüfte ihre Aussagen; **2** (make sure by looking) nachsehen✧ SEP; **to check the time** auf die Uhr sehen; **check they're all back** sieh nach, ob alle wieder da sind; **3** (inspect) kontrollieren; **to check the tickets** die Fahrkarten kontrollieren.

● **to check in** sich anmelden SEP; **to check in at the airport** am Flughafen einchecken.

● **to check out** abreisen✧ SEP (PERF sein); **to check out of the hotel** das Hotel verlassen.

check-in noun Abfertigungsschalter der (PL die Abfertigungsschalter).

checkout noun Kasse die (PL die Kassen); **at the checkout** an der Kasse.

check-up noun Untersuchung die (PL die Untersuchungen).

cheek noun **1** (part of face) Backe die (PL die Backen); **2** (nerve) Frechheit die; **what a cheek!** so eine Frechheit!

cheeky adjective frech.

cheer noun **1** three cheers for Tom! ein dreifaches Hoch auf Tom!; **2** (when drinking) **cheers!** prost!

cheer verb **1** (shout hurray) Hurra schreien✧.

● **to cheer somebody up** jemanden aufmuntern SEP; **your visits always cheer me up** deine Besuche muntern mich immer auf; **cheer up!** Kopf hoch!.

cheerful adjective fröhlich.

cheese noun Käse der; **a cheese sandwich** ein Käsebrot.

chef noun Koch der (PL die Köche), Köchin die (PL die Köchinnen).

chemical noun Chemikalie die (PL die Chemikalien).

chemist noun **1** (in a pharmacy) Apotheker der (PL die Apotheker), Apothekerin die (PL die Apothekerinnen); **2 chemist's** (dispensing) Apotheke die (PL die Apotheken); **at the chemist's** in der Apotheke; **3** (scientist) Chemiker der (PL die Chemiker), Chemikerin die (PL die Chemikerinnen).

chemistry noun Chemie die.

cheque noun Scheck der (PL die Schecks); **to pay by cheque** mit Scheck bezahlen; **to write a cheque** einen Scheck ausstellen.

cheque book noun Scheckbuch das (PL die Scheckbücher).

cherry noun Kirsche die (PL die Kirschen).

chess noun Schach das; **to play chess** Schach spielen.

chessboard noun Schachbrett das (PL die Schachbretter).

chest noun **1** (part of the body) Brust die (PL die Brüste); **2** (box) Truhe die (PL die Truhen); **3 a chest of drawers** eine Kommode.

chestnut noun Esskastanie die (PL die Esskastanien).

chestnut tree noun 1 (horsechestnut) Rosskastanie die (PL die Rosskastanien); 2 (sweet chestnut) Edelkastanie die (PL die Edelkastanien).

chew verb kauen.

chewing gum noun Kaugummi der (PL die Kaugummis).

chicken noun Huhn das (PL die Hühner); **roast chicken** das Brathähnchen; **chicken breast** die Hühnerbrust.

chickenpox noun Windpocken (plural).

child noun Kind das (PL die Kinder); **when I was a child** ... als Kind ....

childish adjective kindisch.

childminder noun Tagesmutter die (PL die Tagesmütter).

chill noun 1 Kälte die; 2 **to have a chill** eine Erkältung haben.

chilled adjective gekühlt.

chilli noun Chili der.

chimney noun Schornstein der (PL die Schornsteine).

chimpanzee noun Schimpanse der (PL die Schimpansen).

chin noun Kinn das (PL die Kinne).

China noun China das.

china noun Porzellan das; **the china bowl** die Porzellanschüssel.

Chinese noun 1 **the Chinese** (people) die Chinesen; 2 (language) Chinesisch das.

Chinese adjective 1 chinesisch; **a Chinese man** ein Chinese; **a Chinese woman** eine Chinesin; 2 **to have a Chinese meal** chinesisch essen.

chip noun 1 (fried potato) **chips** Pommes frites (plural); **fish and chips** ausgebackener Fisch mit Pommes frites; 2 (microchip) Chip der (PL die Chips); 3 (in glass or china) angeschlagene Stelle die (PL die angeschlagenen Stellen).

chipped adjective angeschlagen.

chocolate noun 1 Schokolade die; **a box of chocolates** eine Schachtel Pralinen; 2 **chocolate ice cream** das Schokoladeneis; 3 **a cup of hot chocolate** eine Tasse Kakao.

choice noun 1 Wahl die (PL die Wahlen); **to make a good choice** eine gute Wahl treffen; 2 (variety) Auswahl die; **you have a choice of two flights** du hast zwei Flüge zur Auswahl.

choir noun Chor der (PL die Chöre).

choke noun (on a car) Choke der (PL die Chokes).

choke verb (by yourself) sich verschlucken; **she choked on a bone** sie hat sich an einer Gräte verschluckt.

choose verb 1 wählen; **you chose well** du hast gut gewählt; **it's hard to choose from all these colours** es ist schwer, unter allen diesen Farben zu wählen; 2 (select from a group of things) sich (DAT) aussuchen SEP; **Cathy chose the red skirt** Cathy suchte sich den roten Rock aus.

chop noun Kotelett das (PL die Koteletts); **a pork chop** ein Schweinekotelett.

chop verb hacken.

chord noun Akkord der (PL die Akkorde).

a
b
c
d
e
f
g
h
i
j
k
l
m
n
o
p
q
r
s
t
u
v
w
x
y
z

chorus noun **1** (when you all join in the song) Refrain der (PL die Refrains); **2** (a group of singers) Chor der (PL die Chöre).

Christ noun Christus der.

christening noun Taufe die (PL die Taufen).

Christian noun Christ der (PL die Christen), Christin die (PL die Christinnen).

Christian adjective christlich.

Christianity noun Christentum das.

Christian name noun Vorname der (PL die Vornamen).

Christmas noun Weihnachten das (PL die Weihnachten); **at Christmas** zu Weihnachten; **what did you get for Christmas?** was hast du zu Weihnachten bekommen?; **Happy Christmas!** Frohe Weihnachten!

Christmas card noun Weihnachtskarte die (PL die Weihnachtskarten).

Christmas carol noun Weihnachtslied das (PL die Weihnachtslieder).

Christmas cracker noun Knallbonbon der (PL die Knallbonbons).

Christmas Day noun erste Weihnachtstag der.

Christmas Eve noun Heiligabend der; **on Christmas Eve** Heiligabend.

Christmas present noun Weihnachtsgeschenk das (PL die Weihnachtsgeschenke).

Christmas tree noun Weihnachtsbaum der (PL die Weihnachtsbäume).

church noun Kirche die (PL die Kirchen); **to go to church** in die Kirche gehen.

chute noun (in a swimming pool or playground) Rutsche die (PL die Rutschen).

cider noun Apfelwein der (PL die Apfelweine).

cigar noun Zigarre die (PL die Zigarren).

cigarette noun Zigarette die (PL die Zigaretten).

cinema noun Kino das (PL die Kinos); **to go to the cinema** ins Kino gehen.

circle noun Kreis der (PL die Kreise); **to sit in a circle** im Kreis sitzen; **to go round in circles** sich im Kreis drehen.

circuit noun **1** (for athletes) Bahn die (PL die Bahnen); **2** (for cars) Rennbahn die (PL die Rennbahnen).

circumstance noun Umstand der (PL die Umstände); **under these circumstances** unter diesen Umständen.

circus noun Zirkus der (PL die Zirkusse).

citizen noun Bürger der (PL die Bürger), Bürgerin die (PL die Bürgerinnen).

city noun Stadt die (PL die Städte); **the city of Berlin** die Stadt Berlin.

city centre noun Stadtzentrum das (PL die Stadtzentren); **in the city centre** im Stadtzentrum, in der Innenstadt.

civil servant noun Beamte der (PL die Beamten), Beamtin die (PL die Beamtinnen); **she's a civil servant** sie ist Beamtin.

civilization noun Zivilisation die (PL die Zivilisationen).

claim verb behaupten; **he claims to know who** ... er behauptet zu wissen, wer ....

claim noun 1 (statement) Behauptung die (PL die Behauptungen); 2 (for compensation) Anspruch der (PL die Ansprüche); **to make a claim on insurance** seine Versicherungsansprüche geltend machen.

clap verb 1 klatschen; **everyone clapped** alle klatschten; 2 **to clap your hands** in die Hände klatschen.

clarinet noun Klarinette die (PL die Klarinetten); **to play the clarinet** Klarinette spielen.

clash noun (between two groups) Zusammenstoß der (PL die Zusammenstöße).

clash verb 1 (rival groups) zusammenstoßen❖ SEP; 2 (colours) sich beißen❖; **the curtains clash with the wallpaper** die Vorhänge passen farblich nicht zur Tapete.

class noun 1 (a group of students or pupils) Klasse die (PL die Klassen); **she's in my class** sie geht in meine Klasse; 2 (a lesson) Stunde die (PL die Stunden); **history class** die Geschichtsstunde; **in class** im Unterricht; 3 (category) Klasse die (PL die Klassen); **social class** die Gesellschaftsschicht.

classic adjective klassisch.

classical adjective klassisch; **classical music** die klassische Musik.

classroom noun Klassenzimmer das (PL die Klassenzimmer).

clay noun Ton der.

clean adjective sauber; **a clean shirt** ein sauberes Hemd; **my hands are clean** ich habe saubere Hände.

clean verb 1 putzen; **I cleaned the windows** ich habe die Fenster geputzt; 2 **to clean your teeth** sich (DAT) die Zähne putzen; **I'm going to clean my teeth** ich putze mir jetzt die Zähne.

cleaner noun 1 (cleaning lady) Putzfrau die (PL die Putzfrauen); 2 (in a public place) Reinigungskraft die (PL die Reinigungskräfte); 3 **dry cleaner's** die (chemische) Reinigung.

cleaning noun **to do the cleaning** putzen.

cleanser noun 1 (for the house) Reinigungsmittel das (PL die Reinigungsmittel); 2 (for your face) Reinigungsmilch die.

clear adjective 1 (that you can see through) klar; **clear water** klares Wasser; 2 (cloudless) klar; 3 (easy to understand) klar; **clear instructions** klare Anweisungen; **is that clear?** ist das klar? (informal); **to make something clear** etwas klar machen.

clear verb 1 räumen; **have you cleared your stuff out of your room?** hast du deine Sachen aus deinem Zimmer geräumt?; 2 **can I clear the table?** kann ich den Tisch abräumen SEP?; 3 **to clear your throat** sich räuspern.

● **to clear up** 1 (tidy up) aufräumen SEP; 2 (the weather) sich aufklären SEP; **the weather's**

clearing up a bit das Wetter klärt sich ein bisschen auf.

clearly adverb **1** (to think, speak, or hear) deutlich; **2** (obviously) eindeutig; **she was clearly better** sie war eindeutig besser.

clementine noun Klementine die (PL die Klementinen).

clever adjective **1** klug; **their children are all very clever** ihre Kinder sind alle sehr klug; **2** (ingenious) clever; **a clever idea** eine clevere Idee.

click noun **1** (noise) Klicken das; **2** (with mouse) Klick der (PL die Klicks); **a double click** ein Doppelklick.

click verb **to click on something** etwas anklicken SEP; **click on the icon twice** doppelklicken Sie das Icon!

client noun Klient der (PL die Klienten), Klientin die (PL die Klientinnen).

cliff noun Klippe die (PL die Klippen).

climate noun Klima das (PL die Klimata).

climb verb **1** (the stairs, a hill) hinaufgehen◊ SEP (PERF sein); **to climb a mountain** einen Berg besteigen◊ (PERF sein); **2** (a wall, tree, or rock) klettern (PERF sein), auf (+ ACC); **to climb a tree** auf einen Baum klettern.

climber noun Bergsteiger der (PL die Bergsteiger), Bergsteigerin die (PL die Bergsteigerinnen).

climbing noun Bergsteigen das; **they go climbing in Italy** sie gehen in Italien bergsteigen.

clinic noun Klinik die (PL die Kliniken).

clip noun **1** (from a film) Ausschnitt der (PL die Ausschnitte); **2** (for your hair) Klammer die (PL die Klammern).

cloakroom noun (for coats) Garderobe die (PL die Garderoben).

clock noun **1** Uhr die (PL die Uhren); **to put the clocks forward an hour** die Uhr eine Stunde vorstellen; **to put the clocks back** die Uhr zurückstellen; **2 an alarm clock** ein Wecker.

close¹ adjective, adverb **1** (result) knapp; **2** (friend, connection) eng; **3** (relation or acquaintance) nahe; **4** (near) in der Nähe; **the station's very close** der Bahnhof ist ganz in der Nähe; **she lives close by** sie wohnt in der Nähe; **5 close to** nahe, nah (informal) (+ DAT); **close to the cinema** nahe am Kino; **not very close** nicht sehr nah.

close² noun Ende das; **at the close** am Ende.

close verb zumachen SEP, schließen◊; **close your eyes!** mach die Augen zu!; **she closed the door** sie machte die Tür zu; **the post office closes at six** die Post macht um sechs zu, die Post schließt um sechs.

closed adjective geschlossen; **'closed on Mondays'** 'Montags geschlossen'.

closely adverb **1** (in distance) eng; **2** (carefully) genau; **to look at something closely** sich etwas genau ansehen.

closing date noun **the closing date for entries** (for a competition) der Einsendeschluss, (for a sporting event) der Meldeschluss.

closing time noun
1 Ladenschluss der; **2** (of a pub) Polizeistunde die.

cloth noun **1** (for drying up and polishing) Tuch das (PL die Tücher); **2** (for the floor) Lappen der (PL die Lappen); **3** (fabric) Stoff der (PL die Stoffe).

clothes plural noun **1** Kleider (plural); **2** to put your clothes on sich anziehen ◇ SEP; **to take your clothes off** sich ausziehen ◇ SEP; **to change your clothes** sich umziehen ◇ SEP.

clothes peg noun Wäscheklammer die (PL die Wäscheklammern).

clothing noun Kleidung die.

cloud noun Wolke die (PL die Wolken).

cloudy adjective bewölkt.

clown noun Clown der (PL die Clowns).

club noun **1** (association, for tennis-players, golfers) Klub der (PL die Klubs), (for footballers) Verein der (PL die Vereine); **a football club** ein Fußballverein; **2** (in cards) Kreuz das (PL die Kreuze); **the four of clubs** die Kreuz-Vier; **3** (golfing iron) Schläger der (PL die Schläger).

clue noun **1** Anhaltspunkt der (PL die Anhaltspunkte); **they have a few clues** sie haben ein paar Anhaltspunkte; **2** (in a crossword) Frage die (PL die Fragen); ★ **I haven't a clue** ich habe keine Ahnung.

clumsy adjective ungeschickt.

clutch noun (in a car) Kupplung die (PL die Kupplungen).

clutch verb **to clutch something** etwas festhalten ◇ SEP.

coach noun **1** (bus) Bus der (PL die Busse); **on the coach** im Bus; **to travel by coach** mit dem Bus fahren; **2** (sports trainer) Trainer der (PL die Trainer), Trainerin die (PL die Trainerinnen); **3** (railway carriage) Wagen der (PL die Wagen).

coach station noun Busbahnhof der (PL die Busbahnhöfe).

coach trip noun Busausflug der (PL die Busausflüge); **to go on a coach trip** einen Busausflug machen.

coal noun Kohle die (PL die Kohlen).

coarse adjective grob.

coast noun Küste die (PL die Küsten); **on the east coast** an der Ostküste.

coat noun **1** Mantel der (PL die Mäntel); **2 coat of paint** der Anstrich.

coat hanger noun Kleiderbügel der (PL die Kleiderbügel).

cobweb noun Spinnennetz das (PL die Spinnennetze).

cocaine noun Kokain das.

cock noun Hahn der (PL die Hähne).

cocoa noun Kakao der.

coconut noun Kokosnuss die (PL die Kokosnüsse).

cod noun Kabeljau der (PL die Kabeljaue).

code noun **1** (in law) Gesetzbuch das; **the highway code** die Straßenverkehrsordnung; **2 the dialling code for Hull** die Vorwahl für Hull.

coffee noun Kaffee der (PL die Kaffees); **a cup of coffee** eine Tasse Kaffee; **a black coffee,**

please einen Kaffee ohne Milch bitte; **a white coffee, please** einen Kaffee mit Milch bitte.

coffee break noun Kaffeepause die (PL die Kaffeepausen).

coffee cup noun Kaffeetasse die (PL die Kaffeetassen).

coffee machine noun Kaffeemaschine die (PL die Kaffeemaschinen).

coffin noun Sarg der (PL die Särge).

coin noun **1** Münze die (PL die Münzen); **she collects old coins** sie sammelt alte Münzen; **2 a pound coin** ein Einpfundstück.

coincidence noun Zufall der (PL die Zufälle).

Coke noun Cola die; **two Cokes please** zwei Cola bitte.

cold noun **1** (cold weather) Kälte die; **to be out in the cold** draußen in der Kälte sein; **2** (illness) Schnupfen der (PL die Schnupfen), Erkältung die (PL die Erkältungen); **to have a cold** Schnupfen haben; **Carol's got a cold** Carol hat Schnupfen; **a bad cold** eine schlimme Erkältung.

cold adjective **1** kalt; **your hands are cold** du hast kalte Hände; **cold milk** kalte Milch; **2** (weather, temperature) **it's cold today** heute ist es kalt; **3** (feeling) **I'm cold** mir ist kalt.

collapse verb **1** (a roof or wall) einstürzen SEP (PERF sein); **2** (a person) zusammenbrechen◇ SEP (PERF sein); **he collapsed in his office** er brach in seinem Büro zusammen.

collar noun **1** (on a garment) Kragen der (PL die Kragen); **2** (for an animal) Halsband das (PL die Halsbänder).

colleague noun Kollege der (PL die Kollegen), Kollegin die (PL die Kolleginnen).

collect verb **1** (as a hobby) sammeln; **do you collect stamps?** sammelst du Briefmarken?; **2** (fetch) abholen SEP; **she collects the children from school** sie holt die Kinder von der Schule ab; **3** **to collect up the exercise books** die Hefte einsammeln SEP.

collection noun (of stamps, CDs, money, etc.) Sammlung die (PL die Sammlungen).

collector noun Sammler der (PL die Sammler), Sammlerin die (PL die Sammlerinnen).

college noun **1** (for higher education) Hochschule die (PL die Hochschulen); **to go to college** studieren; **2** (a school) College das (PL die Colleges).

Cologne noun Köln das.

colour noun Farbe die (PL die Farben); **what colour is it?** welche Farbe hat es?; **do you have it in a different colour?** haben Sie es in einer anderen Farbe?

colour verb **1** (with paints or crayons) anmalen SEP; **to colour something red** etwas rot anmalen; **2** (with dye) färben.

colour blind adjective farbenblind.

colour film noun Farbfilm der (PL die Farbfilme).

colourful adjective bunt.

column noun **1** (of a building) Säule die (PL die Säulen); **2** (on a page) Spalte die (PL die Spalten).

comb noun Kamm der (PL die Kämme).

comb verb kämmen; **to comb your hair** sich (DAT) die Haare kämmen; **I'll just comb my hair** ich kämme mir nur die Haare.

come verb 1 kommen◇ (PERF sein); **come quick!** komm schnell!; **come here!** komm mal her!; **Nick came by car** Nick kam mit dem Auto; **can you come over for a coffee?** kannst du auf eine Tasse Kaffe kommen?; **did Jess come to school yesterday?** war Jess gestern in der Schule?; 2 (arrive) **coming!** ich komme schon!; **the bus is coming** der Bus kommt gerade; **come along!** komm schon!

● **to come back** zurückkommen ◇ SEP (PERF sein); **he's coming back to collect us** er kommt zurück, um uns abzuholen.

● **to come down** herunterkommen◇ SEP (PERF sein).

● **to come for** (collect) abholen SEP; **my father's coming for me** mein Vater holt mich ab.

● **to come in** hereinkommen ◇ SEP (PERF sein); **come in!** herein!; **she came into the kitchen** sie kam in die Küche.

● **to come off** (a button) abgehen ◇ SEP (PERF sein).

● **to come out** herauskommen ◇ SEP (PERF sein); **they came out when I called** als ich rief, kamen sie heraus; **the new CD's coming out soon** die neue CD kommt bald heraus.

● **to come up** heraufkommen ◇ SEP (PERF sein); **can you come up a moment?** kannst du eine Sekunde heraufkommen?

● **to come up to somebody** auf jemanden zukommen ◇ SEP (PERF sein).

comedian noun Komiker der (PL die Komiker), Komikerin die (PL die Komikerinnen).

comedy noun Komödie die.

comfortable adjective 1 bequem; **this chair's really comfortable** dieser Sessel ist wirklich bequem; 2 **to feel comfortable** (a person) sich wohl fühlen.

comfortably adverb bequem.

comic noun (magazine) Comicheft das (PL die Comichefte).

comic strip noun Comic der (PL die Comics).

comma noun Komma das (PL die Kommas).

command noun Befehl der (PL die Befehle).

comment noun (remark) Bemerkung die (PL die Bemerkungen); **he made some rude comments about my friends** er hat ein paar unhöfliche Bemerkungen über meine Freunde gemacht.

commentary noun Reportage die (PL die Reportagen); **the commentary on the soccer match** die Reportage über das Fußballspiel.

commentator noun Reporter der (PL die Reporter), Reporterin die (PL die Reporterinnen); **sports commentator** der Sportreporter.

commercial noun Werbespot der (PL die Werbespots).

commercial adjective kommerziell.

a
b
c
d
e
f
g
h
i
j
k
l
m
n
o
p
q
r
s
t
u
v
w
x
y
z

commit *verb* 1 begehen ◇ (*a crime*); 2 **to commit yourself to** sich festlegen SEP: auf (+ACC).

committee *noun* Ausschuss der (PL die Ausschüsse).

common *adjective* 1 häufig; **it's a common problem** das Problem kommt häufig vor; 2 **in common** gemeinsam; **they have nothing in common** sie haben nichts gemeinsam.

common sense *noun* gesunde Menschenverstand der.

communicate *verb* kommunizieren.

communication *noun* Verständigung die.

communion *noun* (*in a Catholic church*) Kommunion die, (*in a Protestant church*) Abendmahl das.

communism *noun* Kommunismus der.

community *noun* Gemeinschaft die (PL die Gemeinschaften); **the European Community** die Europäische Gemeinschaft.

commute *verb* **to commute between Oxford and London** zwischen Oxford und London pendeln (PERF sein).

commuter *noun* Pendler der (PL die Pendler), Pendlerin die (PL die Pendlerinnen).

compact disc *noun* Compactdisc die (PL die Compactdiscs).

compact disc player *noun* Compactdisc-Player der (PL die Compactdisc-Player).

company *noun* 1 (*business*) Gesellschaft die (PL die Gesellschaften); **an airline company** eine Fluggesellschaft;

she's set up a company hat eine Firma gegründet; 2 (*group*) Truppe die (PL die Truppen); **a theatre company** eine Theatertruppe; 3 **to keep somebody company** jemandem Gesellschaft leisten; **the dog keeps me company** der Hund leistet mir Gesellschaft.

compare *verb* vergleichen◇; **if you compare the German phrase with the English** wenn man den deutschen mit dem englischen Ausdruck vergleicht; **our house is small compared with yours** verglichen mit eurem ist unser Haus klein.

compartment *noun* Abteil das (PL die Abteile).

compass *noun* Kompass der (PL die Kompasse).

compatible *adjective* 1 zueinander passend; 2 (*in computing*) kompatibel.

compete *verb* 1 **to compete in something** (*race, event*) an etwas (DAT) teilnehmen◇ SEP; 2 **to compete with each other** miteinander konkurrieren; 3 **to compete for something** um etwas (ACC) kämpfen; **thirty people are competing for one job** dreißig Leute kämpfen um eine Stelle.

competent *adjective* fähig.

competition *noun* 1 (*a contest*) Wettbewerb der (PL die Wettbewerbe); 2 (*in a magazine*) Preisausschreiben das (PL die Preisausschreiben).

competitor *noun* Konkurrent der (PL die Konkurrenten),

Konkurrentin die (PL die Konkurrentinnen).

complain verb sich beschweren; **we complained about the meals** wir haben uns über das Essen beschwert.

complaint noun Beschwerde die (PL die Beschwerden); **to make a complaint** sich beschweren; **she made a complaint to the manager about the poor service** sie beschwerte sich bei dem Geschäftsführer über den schlechten Service.

complete adjective 1 (whole) vollständig; **the complete collection** die vollständige Sammlung; 2 (absolute) völlig; **a complete idiot** ein völliger Idiot (informal).

complete verb (to finish) beenden.

completely adverb völlig.

complexion noun Teint der (PL die Teints).

complicated adjective kompliziert.

compliment noun Kompliment das (PL die Komplimente); **to pay somebody a compliment** jemandem ein Kompliment machen.

composer noun Komponist der (PL die Komponisten), Komponistin die (PL die Komponistinnen).

comprehension noun Verständnis das; **a comprehension test** ein Test zum Textverständnis.

comprehensive school noun Gesamtschule die (PL die Gesamtschulen).

compulsory adjective 1 obligatorisch; 2 (at school)

compulsory subject das Pflichtfach.

computer noun Computer der (PL die Computer); **to work on a computer** am Computer arbeiten; **to have something on computer** etwas im Computer gespeichert haben.

computer engineer noun Computertechniker der (PL die Computertechniker), Computertechnikerin die (PL die Computertechnikerinnen).

computer game noun Computerspiel das (PL die Computerspiele).

computer program noun Computerprogramm das (PL die Computerprogramme).

computer programmer noun Programmierer der (PL die Programmierer), Programmiererin die (PL die Programmiererinnen).

computer science noun Informatik die.

computing noun Informatik die.

concentrate verb sich konzentrieren; **I can't concentrate** ich kann mich nicht konzentrieren; **I was concentrating on the film** ich konzentrierte mich auf den Film.

concentration noun Konzentration die.

concern verb (to affect) betreffen ◇; **this doesn't concern you** das betrifft Sie nicht; **as far as I'm concerned** was mich betrifft.

concert noun 1 Konzert das (PL die Konzerte); **to go to a concert** ins

a b **c** d e f g h i j k l m n o p q r s t u v w x y z

Konzert gehen; **2 concert ticket** die Konzertkarte.

conclusion *noun* Schluss der (PL die Schlüsse).

concrete *noun* Beton der; **the concrete floor** der Betonboden.

condemn *verb* verurteilen; **to condemn somebody to death** jemanden zum Tode verurteilen.

condition *noun* **1** Zustand der (PL die Zustände); **in good condition** in gutem Zustand; **weather conditions** die Wetterlage; **2** (*something you insist on*) Bedingung die (PL die Bedingungen); **on condition that you let me pay** unter der Bedingung, dass du mich zahlen lässt.

conditional *noun* Konditional das.

conditioner *noun* (*for your hair*) Spülung die (PL die Spülungen).

condom *noun* Kondom das (PL die Kondome).

conduct *noun* Benehmen das.

conduct *verb* dirigieren (*an orchestra or a piece of music*).

conductor *noun* (*of an orchestra*) Dirigent der (PL die Dirigenten), Dirigentin die (PL die Dirigentinnen).

cone *noun* **1** (*for ice cream*) Eistüte die (PL die Eistüten); **2** (*for traffic*) Verkehrshütchen das (PL die Verkehrshütchen).

conference *noun* Konferenz die (PL die Konferenzen).

confess *verb* gestehen✧.

confession *noun* Geständnis das (PL die Geständnisse).

confidence *noun* **1** (*self-confidence*) Selbstvertrauen das; **to be lacking in confidence** kein Selbstvertrauen haben; **2** (*faith in somebody else*) Vertrauen das; **to have confidence in somebody** jemandem vertrauen.

confident *adjective* **1** (*sure of yourself*) selbstbewusst; **2** (*sure that something will happen*) zuversichtlich.

confirm *verb* bestätigen; **he confirmed the date** er bestätigte das Datum.

confuse *verb* **1** verwirren (*a person*); **2 to confuse someone with somebody else** jemanden (mit jemandem anderem) verwechseln; **I confuse him with his brother** ich verwechsle ihn immer mit seinem Bruder.

confused *adjective* **1** wirr; **a confused story** eine wirre Geschichte; **2** durcheinander; **I'm confused about the holiday plans** ich bin mit den Ferienplänen durcheinander; **now I'm completely confused** jetzt bin ich völlig durcheinander.

confusing *adjective* verwirrend; **the instructions are confusing** die Anweisungen sind verwirrend.

confusion *noun* Verwirrung die.

congratulate *verb* gratulieren; **I congratulated Tim on passing his exam** ich gratulierte Tim zur bestandenen Prüfung.

congratulations *plural noun* Glückwünsche (*plural*); **congratulations on the baby!** herzlichen Glückwunsch zum Baby!

connect verb (to plug in to the mains) anschließen✧ SEP (a dishwasher or TV, for example).

connection noun 1 (between two ideas or events) Zusammenhang der (PL die Zusammenhänge); **there's no connection between his letter and my decision** es besteht kein Zusammenhang zwischen seinem Brief und meiner Entscheidung; **2** (between trains, planes, on phone, and electrical) Anschluss der (PL die Anschlüsse); **Sally missed her connection** Sally hat ihren Anschluss verpasst.

conscience noun Gewissen das; **to have a guilty conscience** ein schlechtes Gewissen haben.

conscious adjective bei Bewusstsein✧; **she is not fully conscious yet** sie ist noch nicht wieder bei vollem Bewusstsein; **I was conscious that he was a policeman** es war mir bewusst, dass er Polizist war.

conservation noun (of nature) Schutz der; **environmental conservation** der Umweltschutz.

conservative noun Konservative der/die (PL die Konservativen).

conservative adjective konservativ.

conservatory noun Wintergarten der (PL die Wintergärten).

consider verb 1 sich (DAT) überlegen (a suggestion or idea) **all things considered** alles in allem; **2** (think about (doing)) erwägen✧; **we are considering buying a flat** wir erwägen, eine Wohnung zu kaufen.

considerate adjective rücksichtsvoll.

considering preposition wenn man bedenkt; **considering her age** wenn man ihr Alter bedenkt; **considering he did it all himself** wenn man bedenkt, dass er es ganz allein gemacht hat.

consist verb to consist of bestehen✧ aus (+ DAT).

consonant noun Konsonant der (PL die Konsonanten).

constant adjective ständig.

constipated adjective verstopft.

construct verb bauen.

construction noun 1 (building) Gebäude das (PL die Gebäude); **a construction site** eine Baustelle; **2** (in grammar) Konstruktion die (PL die Konstruktionen).

consul noun Konsul der (PL die Konsuln).

consulate noun Konsulat das (PL die Konsulate).

consult verb konsultieren.

consumer noun Verbraucher der (PL die Verbraucher), Verbraucherin die (PL die Verbraucherinnen).

contact noun Kontakt der (PL die Kontakte); **to be in contact with somebody** mit jemandem in Kontakt sein; **we've lost contact** wir haben den Kontakt verloren; **Rob has contacts in the music business** Rob hat Kontakte zur Musikindustrie.

contact verb sich in Verbindung setzen mit (+ DAT); **I'll contact you tomorrow** ich setze mich morgen mit dir in Verbindung.

a b c d e f g h i j k l m n o p q r s t u v w x y z

contact lens noun Kontaktlinse die (PL die Kontaktlinsen).

contain verb enthalten✧.

container noun Behälter der (PL die Behälter).

contaminate verb verseuchen.

contemporary adjective
1 (around today) zeitgenössisch;
2 (modern) modern.

contents plural noun Inhalt der; **the contents of my suitcase** der Inhalt meines Koffers.

contest noun Wettbewerb der (PL die Wettbewerbe).

contestant noun Teilnehmer der (PL die Teilnehmer), Teilnehmerin die (PL die Teilnehmerinnen).

continent noun Kontinent der (PL die Kontinente).

continue verb 1 fortsetzen SEP; **we continued (with) our journey** wir setzten unsere Reise fort; 2 **to continue to do something** etwas weiter tun; **Jill continued talking** Jill redete weiter; 3 **'to be continued'** 'Fortsetzung folgt'.

continuous adjective ununterbrochen.

contraception noun Verhütung die.

contraceptive noun Verhütungsmittel das (PL die Verhütungsmittel).

contract noun Vertrag der (PL die Verträge).

contradict verb widersprechen✧ (+ DAT).

contradiction noun Widerspruch der (PL die Widersprüche).

contrary noun Gegenteil das; **on the contrary** im Gegenteil.

contrast noun Kontrast der (PL die Kontraste).

contribute verb beisteuern SEP (money).

contribution noun (to charity or an appeal) Spende die (PL die Spenden).

control noun (of a crowd or animals) Kontrolle die; **the police are in control of the situation** die Polizei hat die Situation unter Kontrolle; **keep your dogs under control** halten Sie Ihre Hunde unter Kontrolle; **everything's under control** alles ist unter Kontrolle; **to get out of control** außer Kontrolle geraten.

control verb **to control yourself** sich beherrschen.

convenient adjective 1 praktisch; **frozen food is very convenient** Tiefkühlkost ist sehr praktisch; 2 **to be convenient for somebody** jemandem passen; **whenever's convenient for you** wann immer es dir passt.

conventional adjective konventionell.

conversation noun Gespräch das (PL die Gespräche).

convert verb 1 umwandeln SEP; 2 (adapt a building) umbauen SEP; **we're going to convert the garage into a workshop** wir wollen die Garage zu einer Werkstatt umbauen.

convince verb überzeugen; **I'm convinced he's wrong** ich bin davon überzeugt, dass er sich irrt.

convincing adjective überzeugend.

cook noun Koch der (PL die Köche), Köchin die (PL die Köchinnen).

cook verb **1** kochen; **who's cooking tonight?** wer kocht heute Abend?; **I like cooking** ich koche gern; **to cook vegetables and pasta** Gemüse und Nudeln kochen; **cook the cabbage for five minutes** lass den Kohl fünf Minuten kochen; **2** (prepare for a meal) machen; **Fran's busy cooking supper** Fran macht gerade Abendessen; **how do you cook duck?** wie macht man Ente?; **3** (boil) kochen, (fry or roast) braten◇; **the potatoes are cooking** die Kartoffeln kochen; **the sausages are cooking** die Würstchen braten.

cooker noun Herd der (PL die Herde); **electric cooker** der Elektroherd; **gas cooker** der Gasherd.

cookery noun Kochen das.

cookery book noun Kochbuch das (PL die Kochbücher).

cooking noun **1** (preparing food) Kochen das; **cooking is fun** Kochen macht Spaß; **who's doing the cooking?** wer kocht?; **2** (food) Küche die; **Italian cooking** die italienische Küche.

cool noun **1** (coldness) Kühle die; **2** (calm) **to lose one's cool** durchdrehen SEP (PERF sein) (informal); **don't lose your cool!** dreh nicht durch!; **he kept his cool** er blieb gelassen.

cool adjective **1** (cold) kühl; **it's cool inside** drinnen ist es kühl; **2** (laid back) gelassen; **to stay cool** gelassen bleiben (PERF sein).

cool verb abkühlen SEP (PERF sein).

cop noun Polizist der (PL die Polizisten).

cope verb zurechtkommen◇ SEP (PERF sein); **she copes well** sie kommt gut zurecht; **to cope with the children** mit den Kindern zurechtkommen; **she's had a lot to cope with** sie musste mit viel fertig werden.

copy noun **1** (photocopy) Kopie die (PL die Kopien); **2** (of a book) Exemplar das (PL die Exemplare).

copy verb **1** (imitate) kopieren; **2** (make a copy of) abschreiben◇ SEP; **I copied (down) the address** ich habe die Adresse abgeschrieben; (in an exam) **to copy from somebody** bei jemandem abschreiben.

cord noun (for a blind, for example) Schnur die (PL die Schnüre).

cordless telephone noun schnurlose Telefon das (PL die schnurlosen Telefone).

core noun (of an apple or a pear) Kerngehäuse das (PL die Kerngehäuse).

cork noun **1** (in a bottle) Korken der (PL die Korken); **2** (material) Kork der.

corkscrew noun Korkenzieher der (PL die Korkenzieher).

corn noun **1** (wheat) Korn das; **2** (sweetcorn) Mais der.

corner noun **1** Ecke die (PL die Ecken); **at the corner of the street** an der Straßenecke; **it's just round the corner** es ist gleich um die Ecke; **2** (of mouth) Mundwinkel; **3** (of eye) Augenwinkel der (PL die

a
b
c
d
e
f
g
h
i
j
k
l
m
n
o
p
q
r
s
t
u
v
w
x
y
z

Augenwinkel; **out of the corner of your eye** aus den Augenwinkeln heraus; **4** (*bend in the road*) Kurve die (PL die Kurven); **5** (*in football*) Eckball der (PL die Eckbälle).

cornflakes plural noun die Cornflakes (*plural*).

corpse noun Leiche die (PL die Leichen).

correct adjective **1** richtig; **the correct answer** die richtige Antwort; **2 yes, that's correct** ja, das stimmt.

correct verb **1** verbessern; **2** (*teacher*) korrigieren; **the teacher has already corrected our homework** der Lehrer hat unsere Hausaufgaben schon korrigiert.

correction noun Verbesserung die (PL die Verbesserungen).

correctly adverb richtig; **have you filled in the form correctly?** hast du das Formular richtig ausgefüllt?

corridor noun Korridor der (PL die Korridore).

cosmetics plural noun Kosmetik die.

cost noun **1** Kosten (*plural*); **the cost of living** die Lebenshaltungskosten (*plural*); **2 the cost of a new computer** der Preis für einen neuen Computer.

cost verb kosten; **how much does it cost?** was kostet es?; **the tickets cost £10** die Karten kosten zehn Pfund; **it costs too much** das ist zu teuer.

costume noun Kostüm das (PL die Kostüme).

cosy adjective (*a room*) gemütlich.

cot noun Kinderbett das (PL die Kinderbetten).

cottage noun Häuschen das (PL die Häuschen).

cotton noun **1** (*fabric*) Baumwolle die; **cotton shirt** das Baumwollhemd; **2** (*thread*) Nähgarn das (PL die Nähgarne).

cotton wool noun Watte die.

couch noun Couch die (PL die Couchs).

cough noun Husten der; **a nasty cough** ein schlimmer Husten; **to have a cough** Husten haben.

cough verb husten.

could verb **1** (*the past tense of können is used to translate 'was able to'*) **I couldn't open it** ich konnte es nicht aufmachen; **they couldn't come** sie konnten nicht kommen; **she did all she could** sie hat getan, was sie konnte; **he couldn't drive** er konnte nicht Auto fahren; **she couldn't see anything** sie konnte überhaupt nichts sehen; **2** (*the past tense of dürfen is used to translate 'was allowed to'*) **they couldn't smoke there** sie durften dort nicht rauchen; **3** (*might*) (*the subjunctive of können is used to translate a wish or suggestion*) **could I speak to David?** könnte ich mit David sprechen?; **you could try phoning** du könntest versuchen anzurufen; **if he could pay** wenn er zahlen könnte; **he could be right** er könnte recht haben.

council noun Stadtrat der (PL die Stadträte).

count verb **1** (*reckon up*) zählen; **I counted my money** ich habe mein Geld gezählt; **2** (*include*) mitzählen

SEP; **thirty-five not counting the children** fünfunddreißig, die Kinder nicht mitgezählt.

counter noun 1 (in a shop) Ladentisch der (PL die Ladentische); 2 (in a post office or bank) Schalter der (PL die Schalter); 3 (in a bar or café) Theke die (PL die Theken); 4 (for board games) Spielmarke die (PL die Spielmarken).

country noun 1 (Germany, etc.) Land das (PL die Länder); **a foreign country** ein fremdes Land; **from another country** aus einem anderen Land; 2 (not town) Land das; **in the country** auf dem Land; **country road** die Landstraße.

country dancing noun Volkstanz der.

countryside noun 1 (not town) Land das; 2 (scenery) Landschaft die.

county noun Grafschaft die (PL die Grafschaften).

couple noun 1 (a pair) Paar das (PL die Paare); 2 **a couple of** ein paar; **a couple of times** ein paar Mal; **I've got a couple of things to do** ich habe ein paar Sachen zu tun.

courage noun Mut der.

courgette noun Zucchini die (PL die Zucchini).

courier noun 1 (for tourist group) Reiseleiter der (PL die Reiseleiter), Reiseleiterin die (PL die Reiseleiterinnen); 2 (delivery person) Kurier der (PL die Kuriere); **it will be delivered by courier** es wird mit Kurierdienst gebracht.

course noun 1 (lessons) Kurs der (PL die Kurse); **computer course** der Computerkurs; **to go on a course**

einen Kurs machen; 2 (part of a meal) Gang der (PL die Gänge); **the main course** der Hauptgang; 3 **golf course** der Golfplatz; 4 **of course** natürlich; **yes, of course!** ja, natürlich!; **he's forgotten, of course** er hat es natürlich vergessen.

court noun 1 (for playing sports) Platz der (PL die Plätze); 2 (law court) Gericht das; **to go to court** vor Gericht gehen.

cousin noun Cousin der (PL die Cousins), Kusine die (PL die Kusinen); **my cousin Sonia** meine Kusine Sonia.

cover noun 1 (of a book) Einband der (PL die Einbände); 2 (for a duvet or cushion) Bezug der (PL die Bezüge).

cover verb 1 (to cover up) zudecken SEP; **he covered her with a blanket** er hat sie mit einer Decke zugedeckt; 2 **he was covered in spots** er war mit Pickeln übersät; **the room was covered in dust** das Zimmer war völlig verstaubt; 3 (with leaves, snow, or for protection) bedecken; **the ground was covered with snow** der Boden war mit Schnee bedeckt; 4 (with fabric) beziehen✧.

cow noun Kuh die (PL die Kühe); **mad cow disease** der Rinderwahn.

coward noun Feigling der (PL die Feiglinge).

cowboy noun Cowboy der (PL die Cowboys).

crab noun Krabbe die (PL die Krabben).

crack noun 1 (in a glass or cup) Sprung der (PL die Sprünge); 2 (in

a b c d e f g h i j k l m n o p q r s t u v w x y z

wood or a wall) Riss der (PL die Risse); **3** *(a cracking noise)* Knacks der (PL die Knackse).

crack verb **1** *(to make a crack in)* anschlagen◇ SEP; **2** *(to break)* zerbrechen◇; **3** *(to make a noise) (a twig)* knacken.

cracker noun **1** *(biscuit)* Cracker der (PL die Cracker); **2** *(Christmas cracker)* Knallbonbon der (PL die Knallbonbons).

craft noun *(at school)* Werken das.

cramp noun Krampf der (PL die Krämpfe); **to have cramp in your leg** einen Krampf im Bein haben.

crane noun Kran der (PL die Kräne).

crash noun **1** *(an accident)* Unfall der (PL die Unfälle); **car crash** der Autounfall; **2** *(a noise)* Krachen das.

crash verb **1** *(a plane)* abstürzen SEP (PERF sein); **the plane crashed** das Flugzeug ist abgestürzt; **2** *(have a collision in a car)* einen Unfall haben; **3 to crash into something** gegen etwas (ACC) krachen (PERF sein); **the car crashed into a tree** das Auto krachte gegen einen Baum.

crash course noun Schnellkurs der (PL die Schnellkurse).

crash helmet noun Sturzhelm der (PL die Sturzhelme).

crate noun Kiste die (PL die Kisten).

crawl noun *(in swimming)* Kraulen das.

crawl verb **1** *(a person)* kriechen◇ (PERF sein), *(a baby)* krabbeln (PERF sein); **2** *(cars in a jam)* im Schneckentempo fahren◇ (PERF sein); **we were crawling along** wir fuhren im Schneckentempo.

crayon noun **1** *(wax)* Wachsmalstift der (PL die Wachsmalstifte); **2** *(coloured pencil)* Buntstift der (PL die Buntstifte).

craze noun Mode die; **the craze for rollerblades** die Inlinerwelle.

crazy adjective verrückt; **to be crazy for something** verrückt auf etwas (ACC) sein.

cream noun Sahne die; **strawberries and cream** Erdbeeren mit Sahne.

cream cheese noun Frischkäse der.

creased adjective zerknittert.

create verb (er)schaffen◇.

creative adjective kreativ.

creature noun Geschöpf das (PL die Geschöpfe).

crèche noun Kinderkrippe die (PL die Kinderkrippen).

credit noun Kredit der; **to buy something on credit** etwas auf Kredit kaufen.

credit card noun Kreditkarte die (PL die Kreditkarten).

cress noun Kresse die.

crew noun **1** *(on a ship or plane)* Besatzung die; **2 camera crew** das Kamerateam; **3** *(in water sports)* Mannschaft die (PL die Mannschaften).

crew cut noun Bürstenschnitt der (PL die Bürstenschnitte).

cricket noun **1** *(game)* Kricket das; **to play cricket** Kricket spielen; **2** *(insect)* Grille die (PL die Grillen).

cricket bat noun Kricketschläger der (PL die Kricketschläger).

crime noun **1** Verbrechen das (PL die Verbrechen); **theft is a crime** Diebstahl ist ein Verbrechen; **2** (criminality) Kriminalität die; **to fight crime** die Kriminalität bekämpfen.

criminal noun Kriminelle der/die (PL die Kriminellen).

criminal adjective kriminell.

crisis noun Krise die (PL die Krisen).

crisp noun Chip der (PL die Chips); **a packet of potato crisps** eine Tüte Kartoffelchips.

crisp adjective **1** (biscuit) knusprig; **2** (apple) knackig.

critical adjective **1** kritisch (remark, medical condition); **2** entscheidend (moment).

criticism noun Kritik die.

criticize verb kritisieren.

crocodile noun Krokodil das (PL die Krokodile).

crook noun (criminal) Gauner der (PL die Gauner), Gaunerin die (PL die Gaunerinnen).

crop noun Ernte die.

cross noun Kreuz das (PL die Kreuze).

cross adjective ärgerlich; **she was very cross** sie war sehr ärgerlich; **I'm cross with you** ich bin sehr ärgerlich auf dich.

cross verb **1** (to cross over) überqueren; **to cross the road** die Straße überqueren; **2 to cross your legs** die Beine übereinander schlagen❖; **3** (to cross each other) sich kreuzen; **the two roads cross here** die beiden Straßen kreuzen sich hier.

● **to cross out** durchstreichen❖ SEP.

cross-Channel adjective **a cross-Channel ferry** eine Fähre über den Ärmelkanal.

cross-country noun **1** Crosslauf der; **2 cross-country skiing** der Langlauf.

crossing noun **1** (from one place to another) Überquerung die (PL die Überquerungen); **2** (a sea journey) Überfahrt die (PL die Überfahrten); **Channel crossing** die Überfahrt über den Ärmelkanal; **3 pedestrian crossing** der Fußgängerübergang; **level crossing** der Bahnübergang.

crossroads noun Kreuzung die (PL die Kreuzungen); **at the crossroads** an der Kreuzung.

crossword noun Kreuzworträtsel das (PL die Kreuzworträtsel); **to do the crossword** ein Kreuzworträtsel machen.

crow noun Krähe die (PL die Krähen).

crow verb (a cock) krähen.

crowd noun **1** Menschenmenge die (PL die Menschenmengen); **in the crowd** in der Menschenmenge; **2** (spectators) **a crowd of five thousand** fünftausend Zuschauer (plural).

crowd verb **to crowd into or onto something** sich in etwas (ACC) drängen; **we all crowded into the train** wir drängten uns alle in den Zug.

crowded adjective überfüllt.

crown noun Krone die (PL die Kronen).

crude adjective **1** (rough and ready) primitiv; **2** (vulgar) ordinär.

cruel adjective grausam.

cruise noun Kreuzfahrt die (PL die Kreuzfahrten); **to go on a cruise** eine Kreuzfahrt machen.

crumb noun Krümel der (PL die Krümel).

crumpled adjective zerknittert.

crunchy adjective knusprig.

crush verb zerquetschen.

crust noun Kruste die (PL die Krusten).

crusty adjective knusprig.

crutch noun Krücke die (PL die Krücken); **to be on crutches** an Krücken gehen.

cry noun Schrei der (PL die Schreie).

cry verb **1** (weep) weinen; **2** (call out) schreien◇.

cub noun **1** (animal) Junge das (PL die Jungen); **2** (boy scout) Wölfling der (PL die Wölflinge).

cube noun Würfel der (PL die Würfel); **ice cube** der Eiswürfel.

cubic adjective (in measurements) Kubik-; **three cubic metres** drei Kubikmeter.

cubicle noun **1** (in a changing room) Kabine die; **2** (in a public lavatory) Toilette die (PL die Toiletten).

cuckoo noun Kuckuck der (PL die Kuckucke).

cucumber noun Gurke die (PL die Gurken).

cuddle noun **to give somebody a cuddle** jemanden in den Arm nehmen.

cuddle verb schmusen.

cue noun (billiards, pool, snooker) Queue das (PL die Queues).

cuff noun (on a shirt) Manschette die (PL die Manschetten).

cul-de-sac noun Sackgasse die (PL die Sackgassen).

culture noun Kultur die (PL die Kulturen).

cunning adjective listig.

cup noun **1** (for drinking) Tasse die (PL die Tassen); **a cup of tea** eine Tasse Tee; **2** (a trophy) Pokal der (PL die Pokale).

cupboard noun Schrank der (PL die Schränke); **in the kitchen cupboard** im Küchenschrank.

cup tie noun Pokalspiel das (PL die Pokalspiele).

cure noun Heilmittel das (PL die Heilmittel).

cure verb heilen.

curiosity noun Neugier die.

curious adjective neugierig.

curl noun Locke die (PL die Locken).

curl verb **1** locken (hair); **2** (of hair) sich locken.

currant noun Korinthe die (PL die Korinthen).

currency noun Währung die (PL die Währungen); **the Japanese currency** die japanische Währung; **foreign currencies** Devisen (plural).

current noun **1** (electricity) Strom der; **2** (in water or air) Strömung die (PL die Strömungen).

current adjective aktuell.

current affairs noun Tagespolitik die.

curriculum noun Lehrplan der (PL die Lehrpläne).

curry noun Curry das; **vegetable curry** das Gemüse in Currysoße.

cursor noun Cursor der (PL die Cursors).

curtain noun Vorhang der (PL die Vorhänge).

cushion noun Kissen das (PL die Kissen).

custard noun Vanillesoße die (PL die Vanillesoßen).

custom noun Brauch der (PL die Bräuche).

customer noun Kunde der (PL die Kunden), Kundin die (PL die Kundinnen); **customer services** Kundendienst der.

customs hall noun Zollabfertigung die.

customs officer noun Zollbeamte der (PL die Zollbeamten), Zollbeamtin die (PL die Zollbeamtinnen).

customs plural noun Zoll der; **to go through customs** durch den Zoll gehen.

cut noun 1 (injury) Schnittwunde die (PL die Schnittwunden); 2 (haircut) Schnitt der (PL die Schnitte).

cut verb 1 schneiden✧; **can you cut the bread please?** kannst du bitte das Brot schneiden?; **you'll cut yourself!** du schneidest dich!; **Kevin's cut his finger** Kevin hat sich in den Finger geschnitten; 2 **to cut the grass** den Rasen mähen; 3 **to get your hair cut** sich (DAT) die Haare schneiden lassen; **I had my hair cut** ich habe mir die Haare schneiden lassen; 4 **to cut prices** die Preise senken.

● **to cut down** 1 fällen (a tree); 2 **to cut down on cigarettes** seinen Zigarettenkonsum einschränken SEP.

● **to cut out something** 1 etwas ausschneiden✧ SEP (a shape, a newspaper article); 2 etwas streichen✧ (sugar, fatty food, holidays, for example).

● **to cut something up** etwas klein schneiden✧ (food).

cutlery noun Besteck das (PL die Bestecke).

CV noun Lebenslauf der (PL die Lebensläufe).

cycle noun (bike) Rad das (PL die Räder).

cycle verb Rad fahren✧ (PERF sein); **do you like cycling?** fährst du gerne Rad?; **we cycle to school** wir fahren mit dem Rad zur Schule.

cycle lane noun Fahrradweg die (PL die Fahrradwege).

cycle race noun Radrennen das (PL die Radrennen).

cycling noun Radfahren das.

cycling shorts noun Radlerhose die (PL die Radlerhosen).

cyclist noun Radfahrer der (PL die Radfahrer), Radfahrerin die (PL die Radfahrerinnen).

Dd

dad noun Vati der (PL die Vatis).

daffodil noun Osterglocke die (PL die Osterglocken).

a
b
c
d
e
f
g
h
i
j
k
l
m
n
o
p
q
r
s
t
u
v
w
x
y
z

daily adjective täglich; **his daily visit** sein täglicher Besuch.

daily adverb täglich; **she visits him daily** sie besucht ihn täglich.

dairy products plural noun Milchprodukte (plural).

daisy noun Gänseblümchen das (PL die Gänseblümchen).

dam noun Damm der (PL die Dämme).

damage noun Schaden der (PL die Schäden); **to do a lot of damage** großen Schaden anrichten.

damage verb beschädigen.

damn noun **I don't give a damn** das ist mir piepegal (informal).

damn exclamation **damn!** verdammt!

damp adjective feucht.

damp noun Feuchtigkeit die.

dance noun Tanz der (PL die Tänze); **a folk dance** ein Volkstanz.

dance verb tanzen; **I like dancing** ich tanze gerne.

dancer noun Tänzer der (PL die Tänzer), Tänzerin die (PL die Tänzerinnen).

dancing class noun Tanzstunde die (PL die Tanzstunden); **to go to dancing classes** in die Tanzstunde gehen.

dancing noun Tanzen das.

dandruff noun Schuppen (plural).

danger noun Gefahr die (PL die Gefahren); **to be in danger** in Gefahr sein.

dangerous adjective gefährlich; **it's dangerous to drive too fast** es ist gefährlich, zu schnell zu fahren.

Danish noun Dänisch das.

Danish adjective dänisch; **he's Danish** er ist Däne; **she's Danish** sie ist Dänin.

dare verb **1** wagen; **to dare to do something** es wagen, etwas zu tun; **I didn't dare suggest it** ich habe es nicht gewagt, das vorzuschlagen; **2 don't you dare tell her I'm here!** untersteh dich, ihr zu sagen, dass ich hier bin!; **3 I dare you!** du traust dich doch nicht!; **I dare you to tell him!** sag's ihm doch wenn du dich traust!

daring adjective gewagt; **that was a bit daring** das war etwas gewagt.

dark noun **in the dark** im Dunkeln; **after dark** nach Einbruch der Dunkelheit; **to be afraid of the dark** Angst im Dunkeln haben.

dark adjective **1** (colour) dunkel (adjectives ending in -el drop the e when followed by a vowel, which means that dunkel becomes dunkler/dunkle/dunkles); **a dark colour** eine dunkle Farbe; **it gets dark around five** es wird gegen fünf dunkel; **2 a dark blue skirt** ein dunkelblauer Rock; **she has dark brown hair** sie hat dunkelbraune Haare.

darkness noun Dunkelheit die; **in darkness** in der Dunkelheit.

darling noun Liebling der (PL die Lieblinge); **see you later, darling!** bis später, Liebling!

dart *noun* **1** Wurfpfeil der (PL die Wurfpfeile); **2** (*game*) Darts das; **to play darts** Darts spielen.

data *plural noun* Daten (*plural*).

database *noun* Datenbank die (PL die Datenbanken).

date *noun* **1** Datum das (PL die Daten); **what's the date today?** welches Datum haben wir heute?; **the date of the meeting** das Datum für das Treffen; **what date is he coming?** wann kommt er?; **2** Termin der (PL die Termine); **the last date for payment** letzte Zahlungstermin; **3 out of date** ungültig; **my passport's out of date** mein Pass ist ungültig; **4** (*appointment*) Verabredung die (PL die Verabredungen); **Laura's got a date with Frank** Laura ist mit Frank verabredet; **5** (*fruit*) Dattel die (PL die Datteln).

date of birth *noun* Geburtsdatum das (PL die Geburtsdaten).

daughter *noun* Tochter die (PL die Töchter); **Tina's daughter** Tinas Tochter.

daughter-in-law *noun* Schwiegertochter die (PL die Schwiegertöchter).

dawn *noun* Morgendämmerung die (PL die Morgendämmerungen).

day *noun* **1** Tag der (PL die Tage); **three days later** drei Tage später; **a few days ago** vor ein paar Tagen; **the day I went to London** an dem Tag, an dem ich nach London gefahren bin; **we spent the day in London** wir haben den Tag in London verbracht; **it rained all day** es hat den ganzen Tag geregnet; **the day after** am Tag danach; **the day**

deal

after the wedding am Tag nach der Hochzeit; **the day before** am Tag davor; **the day before the wedding** am Tag vor der Hochzeit; **2 the day after tomorrow** übermorgen; **my sister's arriving the day after tomorrow** meine Schwester kommt übermorgen an; **3 the day before yesterday** vorgestern; **my brother arrived the day before yesterday** mein Bruder kam vorgestern an; **4 during the day** tagsüber.

dead *adjective* tot; **her father's dead** ihr Vater ist tot.

dead *adverb* (*really*) irre (*informal*); **he's dead nice** er ist irre nett; **it was dead good** es war irre gut; **it was dead easy** es war kinderleicht; **you're dead right** du hast völlig Recht; **she arrived dead on time** sie kam auf die Minute pünktlich an.

dead end *noun* Sackgasse die (PL die Sackgassen).

deadline *noun* letzte Termin der (PL die letzten Termine).

deaf *adjective* taub.

deafening *adjective* ohrenbetäubend.

deal *noun* **1** (*involving money*) Geschäft das (PL die Geschäfte); **it's a good deal** das ist ein gutes Geschäft; **2** (*agreement*) Vereinbarung die (PL die Vereinbarungen); **to make a deal with somebody** mit jemandem eine Vereinbarung treffen; **it's a deal!** abgemacht!; **3 a great deal of** viel; **I don't have a great deal of time** ich habe nicht viel Zeit.

a
b
c
d
e
f
g
h
i
j
k
l
m
n
o
p
q
r
s
t
u
v
w
x
y
z

deal verb (in cards) geben; **it's you to deal** du gibst.

● **to deal with something** sich um etwas (ACC) kümmern; **Linda deals with the accounts** Linda kümmert sich um die Buchführung; **I'll deal with it as soon as possible** ich kümmere mich so schnell wie möglich darum.

dear adjective **1** lieb; **Dear Franz** Lieber Franz; **Dear Mr Smith** Sehr geehrter Herr Smith; **2** (expensive) teuer.

death noun Tod der; **after his father's death** nach dem Tod seines Vaters; **three deaths** drei Todesfälle; ★ **I was bored to death** ich habe mich zu Tode gelangweilt; ★ **I'm sick to death of it** ich habe es gründlich satt.

death penalty noun Todesstrafe die.

debate noun Debatte die (PL die Debatten).

debate verb debattieren.

debt noun (money owed) Schulden (plural); **to get into debt** in Schulden geraten.

decade noun Jahrzehnt das (PL die Jahrzehnte).

decaffeinated adjective koffeinfrei.

deceive verb betrügen✧.

December noun Dezember der (PL die Dezember); **in December** im Dezember.

decent adjective anständig; **a decent salary** ein anständiges Gehalt; **a decent meal** ein anständiges Essen.

decide verb **1** entscheiden✧, **to decide on something** sich für etwas (ACC) entscheiden; **he's decided against buying a new car** er hat sich entschieden, kein neues Auto zu kaufen; **2 to decide to do something** sich entschließen✧, etwas zu tun; **they've decided to buy a house** sie haben sich entschlossen, ein Haus zu kaufen.

decimal adjective Dezimal-; **decimal number** die Dezimalzahl.

decimal point noun Komma das (PL die Kommas).

decision noun Entscheidung die (PL die Entscheidungen); **to make a decision** eine Entscheidung treffen.

deckchair noun Liegestuhl der (PL die Liegestühle).

declare verb **1** erklären; **2** (at customs) **nothing to declare** nichts zu verzollen.

decorate verb **1** schmücken; **to decorate the Christmas tree** den Weihnachtsbaum schmücken; **2** (with paint) streichen✧, (with wallpaper) tapezieren; **we're decorating the kitchen this weekend** wir streichen dieses Wochenende die Küche.

decoration noun Verzierung die (PL die Verzierungen); **Christmas decorations** der Weihnachtsschmuck.

decrease noun Rückgang der (PL die Rückgänge); **a decrease in the number of accidents** ein Rückgang in der Anzahl der Unfälle.

decrease verb zurückgehen ⟡ SEP (PERF sein), abnehmen ⟡ SEP.

deep adjective tief; **a deep feeling of gratitude** ein tiefes Dankbarkeitsgefühl; **how deep is the swimming pool?** wie tief ist das Schwimmbecken?; **a hole two metres deep** ein zwei Meter tiefes Loch.

deep end noun Schwimmbecken das (PL die Schwimmbecken); **deep end: 2 metres** Wassertiefe: 2 Meter.

deep freeze noun Tiefkühltruhe die (PL die Tiefkühltruhen), (upright) Tiefkühlschrank der (PL die Tiefkühlschränke).

deeply adverb tief.

deer noun 1 Hirsch der (PL die Hirsche); 2 (roe deer) Reh das (PL die Rehe).

defeat noun Niederlage die (PL die Niederlagen).

defeat verb schlagen⟡.

defence noun Verteidigung die.

defend verb verteidigen.

defender noun Verteidiger der (PL die Verteidiger), Verteidigerin die (PL die Verteidigerinnen).

definite adjective 1 eindeutig; **a definite improvement** eine eindeutige Besserung; 2 (certain) sicher; **it's not definite yet** es ist noch nicht sicher; 3 (exact) klar; **a definite answer** eine klare Antwort.

definite article noun bestimmter Artikel der (PL die bestimmten Artikel).

definitely adverb 1 (when giving your opinion about something) eindeutig; **your German is definitely better than mine** dein Deutsch ist eindeutig besser als meins; 2 (without doubt) bestimmt; **she's definitely going to be there** sie wird bestimmt dort sein; **I'm definitely not coming** ich komme ganz bestimmt nicht; 3 **'are you sure you like this one better?' – 'definitely!'** 'gefällt dir diese wirklich besser?' - 'auf jeden Fall!'

definition noun Definition die (PL die Definitionen).

degree noun 1 Grad der (PL die Grade); **thirty degrees** dreißig Grad; 2 **a university degree** ein akademischer Grad.

delay noun Verspätung die (PL die Verspätungen); **a two-hour delay** eine zweistündige Verspätung.

delay verb 1 (hold up) aufhalten⟡ SEP; **she was delayed in the office** sie ist im Büro aufgehalten worden; 2 (train, plane) **to be delayed** Verspätung haben; **the flight was delayed by bad weather** der Flug hatte wegen des schlechten Wetters Verspätung; 3 (postpone) aufschieben⟡ SEP; **the decision has been delayed until Thursday** die Entscheidung wurde bis Donnerstag aufgeschoben.

delete verb 1 streichen⟡; 2 (in computing) löschen.

deliberate adjective absichtlich.

deliberately adverb absichtlich; **she did it deliberately** sie hat das absichtlich getan.

delicate adjective 1 (fabric, health) zart; 2 (situation, question) heikel; 3 (taste, smell) fein.

delicatessen noun
Feinkostgeschäft das (PL die
Feinkostgeschäfte).

delicious adjective köstlich.

delighted adjective hocherfreut;
to be delighted begeistert sein;
**they're delighted with their new
flat** sie sind von ihrer neuen
Wohnung begeistert; **I'm delighted
that you can come** ich freue mich
sehr, dass ihr kommen könnt.

deliver verb **1** liefern; **they're
delivering the washing machine
tomorrow** die Waschmaschine
wird morgen geliefert; **2** (mail,
newspapers) zustellen SEP.

delivery noun **1** Lieferung die (PL
die Lieferungen); **2** (of mail,
newspapers) Zustellung die (PL die
Zustellungen).

demand noun Nachfrage die (PL die
Nachfragen); **much in demand**
sehr gefragt.

demand verb verlangen.

demo noun (protest) Demo die
(informal) (PL die Demos).

democracy noun Demokratie die
(PL die Demokratien).

democratic adjective
demokratisch.

demolish verb abreißen ◇ SEP.

demonstrate verb **1** (a machine,
product, or technique) vorführen
SEP; **2** (protest) demonstrieren; **to
demonstrate against something**
gegen etwas (ACC) demonstrieren.

demonstration noun **1** (of a
machine, product, or technique)
Vorführung die (PL die
Vorführungen); **2** (protest)
Demonstration die (PL die
Demonstrationen).

demonstrator noun
Demonstrant der (PL die
Demonstranten), Demonstrantin
die (PL die Demonstrantinnen).

denim noun Jeansstoff der (PL die
Jeansstoffe); **a denim jacket** eine
Jeansjacke.

Denmark noun Dänemark das.

dental adjective **1** Zahn-; **dental
floss** die Zahnseide; **dental hygiene**
die Zahnpflege; **2 to have a dental
appointment** einen Zahnarzt
Termin haben.

dental surgeon noun Zahnarzt
der (PL die Zahnärzte), Zahnärztin
die (PL die Zahnärztinnen).

dentist noun Zahnarzt der (PL die
Zahnärzte), Zahnärztin die (PL die
Zahnärztinnen); **my mum's a
dentist** meine Mutter ist
Zahnärztin.

deny verb bestreiten ◇.

deodorant noun Deodorant das
(PL die Deodorants).

depart verb **1** (set out on a journey)
abreisen SEP (PERF sein); **2** (train,
coach) abfahren ◇ SEP (PERF sein);
3 (plane) abfliegen ◇ SEP (PERF sein).

department noun **1** (in a shop,
firm, or hospital) Abteilung die (PL
die Abteilungen); **the men's
department** die Herrenabteilung;
2 (of a university) Seminar das (PL
die Seminare); **the history
department** das Seminar für
Geschichte; **3** (in school)
Fachbereich der (PL die
Fachbereiche).

department store noun
Kaufhaus das (PL die Kaufhäuser).

departure noun **1** (of a person)
Abreise die; **2** (of a car, train)

Abfahrt die; **3** (*of a plane*) Abflug der.

departure lounge *noun* Abflughalle die (PL die Abflughallen).

depend *verb* **1 to depend on** abhängen✧ SEP von (+ DAT); **it depends on the price** das hängt vom Preis ab; **it depends on what you want** das hängt davon ab, was du willst; **2 it depends** es kommt darauf an.

deposit *noun* **1** (*when renting or hiring*) Kaution die (PL die Kautionen); **2** (*when booking a holiday or hotel room*) Anzahlung die (PL die Anzahlungen); **to pay a deposit** eine Anzahlung leisten; **3** (*on a bottle*) Pfand das.

depressed *adjective* deprimiert.

depressing *adjective* deprimierend.

depth *noun* Tiefe die.

deputy *noun* Stellvertreter der (PL die Stellvertreter), Stellvertreterin die (PL die Stellvertreterinnen); **the deputy headteacher** Konrektor der (PL die Konrektoren), Konrektorin die (PL die Konrektorinnen).

describe *verb* beschreiben✧.

description *noun* Beschreibung die (PL die Beschreibungen).

desert *noun* Wüste die (PL die Wüsten).

desert island *noun* verlassene Insel die (PL die verlassenen Inseln).

deserve *verb* verdienen.

design *noun* **1** Konstruktion die (PL die Konstruktionen); **the design of the plane** die Flugzeugkonstruktion; **2** (*artistic*

design) Design das (PL die Designs); **modern design** modernes Design; **3** (*pattern*) Muster das (PL die Muster); **a floral design** ein Blumenmuster; **4** (*sketch*) Entwurf der (PL die Entwürfe).

design *verb* **1** konstruieren (*a machine, plane, system*); **2** entwerfen✧ (*costumes, fabric, scenery*).

designer *noun* Designer der (PL die Designer), Designerin die (PL die Designerinnen).

desk *noun* **1** (*in an office or at home*) Schreibtisch der (PL die Schreibtische); **2** (*pupil's*) Pult das (PL die Pulte); **3 the reception desk** die Rezeption; **the information desk** die Auskunft.

despair *noun* Verzweiflung die.

despair *verb* **to despair of doing something** alle Hoffnung aufgeben✧ SEP, etwas zu tun.

desperate *adjective* **1** verzweifelt; **a desperate attempt** ein verzweifelter Versuch; **2 to be desperate to do something** etwas dringend tun müssen; **I'm desperate to speak to you** ich muss dich dringend sprechen; **to be desperate for something** etwas dringend brauchen.

dessert *noun* Nachtisch der (PL die Nachtische); **what's for dessert?** was gibts zum Nachtisch?

destination *noun* Ziel das (PL die Ziele).

destroy *verb* zerstören.

destruction *noun* Zerstörung die.

a b c d e f g h i j k l m n o p q r s t u v w x y z

detached house noun
Einfamilienhaus das (PL die
Einfamilienhäuser).

detail noun Einzelheit die (PL die
Einzelheiten).

detailed adjective ausführlich.

detective noun 1 (in the police)
Kriminalbeamte der (PL die
Kriminalbeamten),
Kriminalbeamtin die (PL die
Kriminalbeamtinnen); 2 private
detective der Detektiv, die
Detektivin.

detective story noun
Detektivgeschichte die (PL die
Detektivgeschichten).

detention noun 1 (at school)
Nachsitzen das; 2 (in prison) Haft
die.

detergent noun Waschmittel das
(PL die Waschmittel).

determined adjective
entschlossen; he's determined to
leave er ist fest entschlossen zu
gehen.

detour noun Umweg der (PL die
Umwege).

develop verb 1 entwickeln; to get
a film developed einen Film
entwickeln lassen; 2 sich
entwickeln; how children develop
wie Kinder sich entwickeln.

developing country noun
Entwicklungsland das (PL die
Entwicklungsländer).

development noun Entwicklung
die (PL die Entwicklungen).

devil noun Teufel der (PL die Teufel).

devoted adjective treu.

diabetes noun Zuckerkrankheit
die.

diabetic noun Diabetiker der (PL
die Diabetiker), Diabetikerin die (PL
die Diabetikerinnen).

diabetic adjective zuckerkrank; to
be diabetic zuckerkrank sein.

diagnosis noun Diagnose die (PL
die Diagnosen).

diagonal adjective diagonal.

diagram noun Diagramm das (PL
die Diagramme).

dial verb wählen; I dialled the
wrong number ich habe die falsche
Nummer gewählt; dial 00 49 for
Germany wählen Sie die Vorwahl
00 49 für Deutschland.

dialling tone noun Freizeichen
das.

dialogue noun Dialog der (PL die
Dialoge).

diamond noun 1 Diamant der (PL
die Diamanten), (gemstone) Brillant
der (PL die Brillanten); 2 (in cards)
Karo das; the jack of diamonds der
Karobube; 3 (shape) Raute die (PL
die Rauten).

diarrhoea noun Durchfall der.

diary noun 1 (for appointments)
Terminkalender der (PL die
Terminkalender); 2 Tagebuch das
(PL die Tagebücher); to keep a diary
ein Tagebuch führen.

dice noun Würfel der (PL die Würfel);
to throw the dice würfeln.

dictation noun Diktat das (PL die
Diktate).

dictionary noun Wörterbuch das
(PL die Wörterbücher).

did verb SEE do.

die verb 1 sterben ✧ (PERF sein); my
grannie died in January meine
Oma starb im Januar; 2 to be
dying to do something darauf

brennen, etwas zu tun; **I'm dying to meet her** ich brenne darauf, sie kennen zu lernen.

diesel noun **1** Dieselöl das; **2** diesel **engine** der Dieselmotor; **diesel car** der Diesel.

diet noun **1** Ernährung die; **a healthy diet** eine gesunde Ernährung; **2** (slimming or special) Diät die (PL die Diäten); **to be on a diet** Diät machen.

difference noun **1** Unterschied der (PL die Unterschiede); **I can't see any difference between the two** ich erkenne keinen Unterschied zwischen den beiden; **what's the difference between ...?** was ist der Unterschied zwischen ...?; **2 it makes a difference** es ist ein Unterschied; **it makes no difference** es ist egal; **it makes no difference what I say** es ist egal, was ich sage.

different adjective **1** verschieden; **the two sisters are very different** die beiden Schwestern sind sehr verschieden; **2 to be different from** anders sein als; **she's very different from her sister** sie ist ganz anders als ihre Schwester; **3** (separate) anderer/andere/ anderes; **she reads a different book every day** sie liest jeden Tag ein anderes Buch.

difficult adjective schwer; **it's really difficult** es ist sehr schwer; **he finds it difficult** es fällt ihm schwer.

difficulty noun Schwierigkeit die (PL die Schwierigkeiten); **to have difficulty doing something** Schwierigkeiten haben, etwas zu tun; **I had difficulty finding your house** ich hatte Schwierigkeiten, dein Haus zu finden.

dig verb graben❖; **to dig a hole** ein Loch graben.

digestion noun Verdauung die.

digital adjective digital; **digital watch** die Digitaluhr; **digital recording** die Digitalaufnahme.

dim adjective **1** schwach; **a dim light** ein schwaches Licht; **2** beschränkt; **she's a bit dim** sie ist ein bisschen beschränkt.

din noun Lärm der; **stop making such a din!** hör auf, so einen Lärm zu machen!

dinghy noun **1** sailing dinghy das Dingi; **2** rubber dinghy das Schlauchboot.

dining room noun Esszimmer das (PL die Esszimmer); **in the dining room** im Esszimmer.

dinner noun **1** (evening) Abendessen das (PL die Abendessen); **to invite somebody to dinner** jemanden zum Abendessen einladen; **2** (midday) Mittagessen das (PL die Mittagessen); **to have school dinner** in der Schulkantine zu Mittag essen.

dinner party noun Abendessen das (PL die Abendessen).

dinner time noun Essenszeit die.

dinosaur noun Dinosaurier der (PL die Dinosaurier).

diploma noun Diplom das (PL die Diplome).

direct adjective direkt; **a direct flight** ein Direktflug.

a b c d e f g h i j k l m n o p q r s t u v w x y z

direct *adverb* direkt; **the bus goes direct to the airport** der Bus fährt direkt zum Flughafen.

direct *verb* **1** to direct a film or a play bei einem Film oder einem Theaterstück Regie führen; **2** regeln (*traffic*).

direction *noun* **1** Richtung die (PL die Richtungen); **to go in the other direction** in die andere Richtung gehen; **2** to ask somebody for directions jemanden nach dem Weg fragen; **3** directions for use die Gebrauchsanweisung (*singular*).

directly *adverb* direkt; **directly afterwards** gleich danach.

director *noun* **1** (*of a company*) Direktor der (PL die Direktoren), Direktorin die (PL die Direktorinnen); **2** (*of a play, film*) Regisseur der (PL die Regisseure), Regisseurin die (PL die Regisseurinnen); **3** (*of a programme*) Leiter der (PL die Leiter), Leiterin die (PL die Leiterinnen).

directory *noun* Telefonbuch das (PL die Telefonbücher); **he's ex-directory** seine Nummer steht nicht im Telefonbuch.

dirt *noun* Schmutz der.

dirty *adjective* schmutzig; **my hands are dirty** ich habe schmutzige Hände; **to get something dirty** etwas schmutzig machen; **you'll get your dress dirty** du machst dir das Kleid schmutzig; **to get dirty** schmutzig werden; **the curtains get dirty quickly** die

Vorhänge werden sehr schnell schmutzig.

disability *noun* Behinderung die (PL die Behinderungen); **does he have a disability?** ist er behindert?

disabled *adjective* behindert; **disabled people** Behinderte (*plural*).

disadvantage *noun* **1** Nachteil der (PL die Nachteile); **2** to be at a disadvantage im Nachteil sein.

disagree *verb* **1** I disagree ich bin anderer Meinung; **2** to disagree with somebody mit jemandem nicht übereinstimmen SEP; **I disagree with James** ich stimme mit James nicht überein.

disappear *verb* verschwinden✧ (PERF sein).

disappearance *noun* Verschwinden das.

disappointed *adjective* enttäuscht; **I'm disappointed with my marks** ich bin über meine Noten enttäuscht.

disappointment *noun* Enttäuschung die (PL die Enttäuschungen).

disaster *noun* Katastrophe die (PL die Katastrophen); **it was a complete disaster** es war eine komplette Katastrophe.

disastrous *adjective* katastrophal.

disc *noun* **1** compact disc die Compactdisc; **2** tax disc (*for a vehicle*) die Steuerplakette; **3** slipped disc der Bandscheibenvorfall.

discipline *noun* Disziplin die.

disc-jockey *noun* Diskjockey der (PL die Diskjockeys).

disco noun **1** Disko die (PL die Diskos); **they're having a disco** sie veranstalten eine Disko; **2** (club) Disko die (PL die Diskos); **to go to a disco** in eine Disko gehen.

discount noun Rabatt der (PL die Rabatte).

discover verb entdecken.

discovery noun Entdeckung die (PL die Entdeckungen).

discreet adjective diskret.

discrimination noun Diskriminierung die; **discrimination against women** die Diskriminierung von Frauen; **racial discrimination** die Rassendiskriminierung.

discuss verb **to discuss something** etwas besprechen✧; **we'll discuss the problem tomorrow** wir besprechen das Problem morgen; **I'm going to discuss it with Phil** ich werde es mit Phil besprechen.

discussion noun Gespräch das (PL die Gespräche).

disease noun Krankheit die (PL die Krankheiten).

disguise noun Verkleidung die (PL die Verkleidungen); **to be in disguise** verkleidet sein.

disguise verb verkleiden; **disguised as a woman** als Frau verkleidet.

disgust noun Ekel der.

disgusted adjective **1** (filled with indignation) empört; **2** (nauseated) angeekelt.

disgusting adjective eklig.

dish noun **1** Schüssel die (PL die Schüsseln); **a large white dish** eine große weiße Schüssel; **satellite**

dish die Satellitenschüssel; **2** (type of food) Gericht das (PL die Gerichte); **risotto is my favourite dish** Risotto ist mein Lieblingsgericht; **3** (crockery) **the dishes** das Geschirr; **to do the dishes** Geschirr spülen.

dishcloth noun Spültuch das (PL die Spültücher).

dishonest adjective unehrlich.

dishonesty noun Unehrlichkeit die.

dishwasher noun Geschirrspülmaschine die (PL die Geschirrspülmaschinen).

disinfect verb desinfizieren.

disinfectant noun Desinfektionsmittel das.

disk noun Diskette die (PL die Disketten); **floppy disk** die Diskette; **hard disk** die Festplatte.

diskdrive noun Diskettenlaufwerk das (PL die Diskettenlaufwerke).

diskette noun Diskette die (PL die Disketten).

dismiss verb entlassen✧ (an employee).

disobedient adjective ungehorsam.

display noun **1** Ausstellung die (PL die Ausstellungen); **handicrafts display** die Handarbeitsausstellung; **to be on display** ausgestellt sein; **2** window display die Auslage; **3** firework display das Feuerwerk.

display verb ausstellen SEP.

disposable adjective Wegwerf-; **disposable towel** das Wegwerfhandtuch.

disqualify verb disqualifizieren.

a
b
c
d
e
f
g
h
i
j
k
l
m
n
o
p
q
r
s
t
u
v
w
x
y
z

disrupt verb stören.

dissolve verb auflösen SEP.

distance noun Entfernung die (PL die Entfernungen); **from this distance** aus dieser Entfernung; **from a distance** von weitem; **in the distance** in der Ferne; **it's within walking distance** es ist zu Fuß erreichbar.

distant adjective fern.

distinct adjective deutlich.

distinctly adverb **1** deutlich; **2 it's distinctly odd** es ist äußerst komisch.

distract verb ablenken SEP.

distribute verb verteilen.

district noun **1** (of a town) Stadtteil der (PL die Stadtteile); **a poor district of Berlin** ein ärmlicher Stadtteil von Berlin; **2** (in the country) Gebiet das (PL die Gebiete).

disturb verb stören; **sorry to disturb you** Entschuldigung, dass ich störe.

dive noun Kopfsprung der (PL die Kopfsprünge).

dive verb **1** einen Kopfsprung machen; **2** (swim underwater) tauchen (PERF sein).

diver noun **1** (underwater) Taucher der (PL die Taucher), Taucherin die (PL die Taucherinnen); **2** (from a diving board) Kunstspringer der (PL die Kunstspringer), Kunstspringerin die (PL die Kunstspringerinnen).

diversion noun (of traffic) Umleitung die (PL die Umleitungen).

divide verb teilen.

diving noun **1** (underwater) Tauchen das; **2** (from a diving board) Kunstspringen das.

diving board noun Sprungbrett das (PL die Sprungbretter).

division noun **1** Teilung die (PL die Teilungen); **2** (in maths) Division die (PL die Divisionen); **3** (sports league) Liga die (PL die Ligen).

divorce noun Scheidung die (PL die Scheidungen).

divorce verb sich scheiden lassen✧; **they divorced in May** sie haben sich im Mai scheiden lassen.

divorced adjective geschieden.

DIY noun **1** Heimwerken das; **2 to do DIY** heimwerken; **3 DIY shop** der Baumarkt (PL die Baumärkte).

dizzy adjective **I feel dizzy** mir ist schwindlig.

DJ noun DJ der (PL die DJs).

do verb **1** tun✧, machen; **what are you doing?** was machst du?; **I'm doing my homework** ich mache meine Hausaufgaben; **what have you done with the hammer?** was hast du mit dem Hammer gemacht?; **can you do me a favour?** kannst du mir einen Gefallen tun?; **do as I say** tu was ich sage; **do the cleaning** sie putzt; **I'll do the washing up** ich wasche ab; **I must do the shopping** ich muss einkaufen gehen; **3** (in questions) **do you like it?** gefällt es dir?; **when does the film start?** wann fängt der Film an?; **how do you open the door?** wie macht man die Tür auf?; **do you know him?** kennst du ihn?; **4** (in negative sentences) **I don't like mushrooms** ich mag keine Pilze; **Rosie doesn't like spinach** Rosie mag keinen Spinat; **you didn't shut the door** du hast die Tür nicht zugemacht; **it doesn't matter** das macht nichts; **5** (when it refers back to another verb, 'do' is not translated) **'do you live here?' – 'yes, I do'** 'wohnst du hier?' - 'ja'; **she has more money than I do** sie hat mehr Geld als ich; **'I live in Oxford' – 'so do I'** 'ich wohne in Oxford' - 'ich auch'; **'I didn't phone Gemma' – 'neither did I'** 'ich habe Gemma nicht angerufen' - 'ich auch nicht'; **6 don't you?, doesn't he?** nicht wahr?; **you know Helen, don't you?** du kennst Helen, nicht wahr?; **she left on Thursday, didn't she?** sie ist Donnerstag abgefahren, nicht wahr?; **7 that'll do** das reicht; **it'll do like that** das geht so.

● **to do something up 1** etwas zubinden◇ SEP (shoes); **2** etwas zumachen SEP (a cardigan, jacket); **3** etwas renovieren SEP (a house).

● **to do without something** ohne etwas (ACC) auskommen◇ SEP (PERF sein); **we can do without knives** wir können ohne Messer auskommen.

doctor noun Arzt der (PL die Ärzte), Ärztin die (PL die Ärztinnen); **her mother's a doctor** ihre Mutter ist Ärztin.

document noun Dokument das (PL die Dokumente).

documentary noun Dokumentarfilm der (PL die Dokumentarfilme).

dodgems plural noun **the dodgems** Autoskooter der (PL die Autoskooter).

dog noun Hund der (PL die Hunde).

do-it-yourself noun Heimwerken das.

dole noun Arbeitslosengeld das; **to be on the dole** arbeitslos sein.

doll noun Puppe die (PL die Puppen).

dollar noun Dollar der (PL die Dollars).

dolphin noun Delfin der (PL die Delfine).

domino noun **1** Dominostein der (PL die Dominosteine); **2** (game) **dominoes** Domino das; **to play dominoes** Domino spielen.

donkey noun Esel der (PL die Esel).

don't SEE do.

door noun Tür die (PL die Türen); **to open the door** die Tür aufmachen; **to shut the door** die Tür zumachen.

doorbell noun Türklingel die (PL die Türklingeln); **to ring the doorbell** klingeln.

dot noun **1** Punkt der (PL die Punkte); **at ten on the dot** Punkt zehn Uhr; **2** (small dot on fabric) Pünktchen das (PL die Pünktchen).

double adjective, adverb **1** doppelt; **a double helping** eine doppelte Portion; **double the size** doppelt so groß; **double the time** doppelt so viel Zeit; **at double the price** zum doppelten Preis; **2 double room** das Doppelzimmer; **3 double bed** das Doppelbett.

double bass noun Kontrabass der (PL die Kontrabässe).

double-decker bus noun Doppeldeckerbus der (PL die Doppeldeckerbusse).

doubles noun (in tennis) Doppel das (PL die Doppel).

a
b
c
d
e
f
g
h
i
j
k
l
m
n
o
p
q
r
s
t
u
v
w
x
y
z

doubt noun Zweifel der (PL die Zweifel); **there's no doubt about it** es besteht kein Zweifel daran; **I have my doubts** ich habe gewisse Zweifel.

doubt verb to doubt something etwas bezweifeln; **I doubt it** das bezweifle ich; **I doubt that …** ich bezweifle, dass …; **I doubt they'll buy it** ich bezweifle, dass sie es kaufen.

doubtful adjective **1** fraglich; **it's doubtful** es ist fraglich; **2 to be doubtful about doing something** Bedenken haben, ob man etwas tun soll; **I'm doubtful about inviting them together** ich habe Bedenken, ob ich sie zusammen einladen soll.

dough noun Teig der.

doughnut noun Krapfen der (PL die Krapfen).

down adverb, preposition **1** unten; **he's down in the cellar** er ist unten im Keller; **it's down there** es ist da unten; **2 down the road** (nearby) in der Nähe; **there's a chemist's just down the road** eine Apotheke ist ganz in der Nähe; **3 to go down** nach unten gehen; **I went down to open the door** ich ging nach unten, um die Tür aufzumachen; **to walk down the street** die Straße entlanggehen SEP (PERF sein); **to run down the stairs** die Treppe runterrennen SEP (PERF sein) (informal); **4 to come down** herunterkommen✧ SEP (PERF sein); **she came down into the kitchen** sie kam in die Küche herunter; **5 to sit down** sich setzen; **she sat down on the chair** sie setzte sich auf den Stuhl; **6 to write something down** etwas aufschreiben✧ SEP.

downstairs adverb **1** unten; **she's downstairs** sie ist unten; **2** (with movement) nach unten; **to go downstairs** nach unten gehen; **3 in Erdgeschoss**; **the flat downstairs** die Wohnung im Erdgeschoss.

doze verb dösen.

dozen noun Dutzend das (PL die Dutzende).

drag noun **1 what a drag!** so'n Mist! (informal); **2 what a drag she is!** Mann, ist die langweilig! (informal).

drag verb schleppen.

dragon noun Drache der (PL die Drachen).

drain noun **1** (outlet pipe) Abflussrohr das (PL die Abflussrohre); **2 the drains:** Kanalisation die (PL die Kanalisationen).

drain verb abgießen ✧ SEP (vegetables); trockenlegen SEP (fields, land).

drama noun **1** (play) Drama das (PL die Dramen); **he made a big drama out of it** er hat ein großes Drama daraus gemacht (informal); **2** (dramatic nature) Dramatik die.

dramatic adjective dramatisch.

draught noun Luftzug der; **there's a draught in here** hier zieht es.

draughts noun Damespiel das; **to play draughts** Dame spielen.

draw noun **1** (in a match) Unentschieden das; **to end in a draw** mit einem Unentschieden enden; **2** (*lottery*) Ziehung *die* (PL *die* Ziehungen).

draw *verb* **1** zeichnen; **she can draw really well** sie kann wirklich sehr gut zeichnen; **2 to draw the curtains** (*open*) die Vorhänge aufziehen✧ SEP, (*close*) die Vorhänge zuziehen✧ SEP; **3** (*in a match*) unentschieden spielen; **we drew three all** wir haben drei zu drei unentschieden gespielt.

drawer *noun* Schublade *die* (PL *die* Schubladen).

drawing *noun* Zeichnung *die* (PL *die* Zeichnungen).

drawing pin *noun* Reißzwecke *die* (PL *die* Reißzwecken).

dreadful *adjective* furchtbar.

dreadfully *adverb* furchtbar; **I'm dreadfully late** ich habe mich furchtbar verspätet; **I'm dreadfully sorry** es tut mir furchtbar Leid.

dream *noun* Traum *der* (PL *die* Träume); **to have a dream** einen Traum haben.

dream *verb* träumen; **to dream about something** von etwas (DAT) träumen.

dress *noun* Kleid *das* (PL *die* Kleider).

dress *verb* **to dress a child** ein Kind anziehen✧ SEP.

● **to dress up** sich verkleiden; **to dress up as a vampire** sich als Vampir verkleiden.

dressed *adjective* **1** angezogen; **is Tom dressed yet?** ist Tom schon angezogen?; **2 she was dressed in black trousers and a yellow shirt** sie trug eine schwarze Hose und ein gelbes Hemd; **3 to get dressed**

sich anziehen✧ SEP; **I got dressed quickly** ich zog mich schnell an.

dressing gown *noun* Morgenrock *der* (PL *die* Morgenröcke).

dressing table *noun* Frisierkommode *die* (PL *die* Frisierkommoden).

drier *noun* **hair drier** der Föhn; **tumble drier** der Wäschetrockner.

drill *noun* Bohrer *der* (PL *die* Bohrer).

drink *noun* Getränk *das* (PL *die* Getränke) **1 to have a drink** etwas trinken; **would you like a drink of water?** möchtest du etwas Wasser trinken?; **2** (*an alcoholic drink*) Drink *der* (PL *die* Drinks); **they've invited us round for drinks** sie haben uns auf einen Drink eingeladen; **let's have a drink!** trinken wir einen! (*informal*).

drink *verb* trinken✧; **he drank a glass of water** er trank ein Glas Wasser.

drive *noun* **1 to go for a drive** eine Autofahrt machen; **2** (*in front of a house*) Einfahrt *die* (PL *die* Einfahrten).

drive *verb* **1** fahren✧ (PERF *sein*); **she drives very fast** sie fährt sehr schnell; **to drive a car** Auto fahren; **I'd like to learn to drive** ich möchte Autofahren lernen; **can you drive?** kannst du Auto fahren?; **2 we drove to Berlin** wir sind mit dem Auto nach Berlin gefahren; **3 to drive somebody** (*to a place*) jemanden (irgendwohin) fahren (PERF *haben*); **Mum drove me to the station** Mutti hat mich zum Bahnhof gefahren; **to drive**

a b c d e f g h i j k l m n o p q r s t u v w x y z

a somebody home jemanden nach Hause fahren; ★ she drives me
b mad! sie macht mich verrückt!.
driver noun 1 Fahrer der (PL die
c Fahrer), Fahrerin die (PL die Fahrerinnen); 2 (of a locomotive)
d Lokomotivführer der (PL die Lokomotivführer),
e Lokomotivführerin die (PL die Lokomotivführerinnen).
f **driving instructor** noun
g Fahrlehrer der (PL die Fahrlehrer), Fahrlehrerin die (PL die
h Fahrlehrerinnen).
driving lesson noun Fahrstunde
i die (PL die Fahrstunden).
j **driving licence** noun Führerschein der (PL die
k Führerscheine).
driving test noun Fahrprüfung
l die; to take your driving test die
m Fahrprüfung machen; Jenny's passed her driving test Jenny hat
n die Fahrprüfung bestanden.
drop noun Tropfen der (PL die
o Tropfen).
p **drop** verb 1 to drop something etwas fallen lassen; I dropped my
q glasses ich habe meine Brille fallen lassen; 2 drop it! lass das!;
r 3 I'm going to drop history next year nächstes Jahr lege ich
s Geschichte ab; 4 absetzen SEP (a person); could you drop me at the
t station? könntest du mich am Bahnhof absetzen?
u **drought** noun Dürre die (PL die
v Dürren).
w **drown** verb ertrinken ✧ (PERF sein); she drowned in the lake sie
x ertrank im See.

drug noun 1 (medicine)
Medikament das (PL die Medikamente); 2 (illegal) drugs
Drogen (plural).

drug abuse noun
Drogenmissbrauch der.

drug addict noun
Drogenabhängige der/die (PL die Drogenabhängigen).

drug addiction noun
Drogenabhängigkeit die.

drum noun 1 Trommel die (PL die Trommeln); 2 drums das
Schlagzeug; to play drums
Schlagzeug spielen.

drummer noun Schlagzeuger der (PL die Schlagzeuger),
Schlagzeugerin die (PL die Schlagzeugerinnen).

drunk noun Betrunkene der/die (PL die Betrunkenen).

drunk adjective betrunken; to get drunk sich betrinken ✧.

dry adjective trocken.

dry verb 1 trocknen; to let something dry etwas trocknen lassen; to dry your hair sich (DAT) die Haare trocknen; to dry the washing die Wäsche trocknen; 2 to dry your hands sich (DAT) die Hände abtrocknen SEP; I dried my feet ich trocknete mir die Füße ab; to dry the dishes das Geschirr abtrocknen.

dry cleaner's noun chemische Reinigung die.

dryer noun SEE drier.

dual carriageway noun zweispurige Straße die (PL die zweispurigen Straßen).

dubbed adjective a dubbed film ein synchronisierter Film.

duck noun Ente die (PL die Enten).

due adjective, adverb 1 to be due to do something etwas tun müssen; **Paul's due back soon** Paul muss bald zurück sein; **we're due to leave on Thursday** wir müssen Donnerstag abfahren; **2 due to** wegen (+ GEN); **due to bad weather** wegen schlechten Wetters.

dull adjective 1 dull weather trübes Wetter; it's a dull day today heute ist ein trüber Tag; **2** (boring) langweilig.

dumb adjective 1 stumm; **2** (stupid) dumm; **he asked some dumb questions** er hat ein paar dumme Fragen gestellt.

dump verb 1 abladen◇ SEP (rubbish); **2** (put down) hinwerfen◇ SEP; **he dumped it in the rubbish** er hat es in den Müll geworfen; **3** abschieben◇ SEP (a person) (informal); **she's dumped her boyfriend** sie hat ihren Freund abgeschoben.

dungarees plural noun Latzhose die (PL die Latzhosen).

during preposition während (+ GEN); **during the night** während der Nacht; **I saw her during the holidays** ich habe sie während der Ferien gesehen.

dusk noun Dämmerung die (PL die Dämmerungen); **at dusk** bei Einbruch der Dunkelheit.

dust noun Staub der.

dust verb 1 abstauben SEP (furniture, objects); **2** (in a room) Staub wischen; **she's dusting** sie wischt Staub.

dustbin noun Mülltonne die (PL die Mülltonnen).

dustman noun Müllmann der (PL die Müllmänner).

dusty adjective staubig.

Dutch noun 1 (language) Holländisch das; **2 the Dutch** (people) die Holländer.

Dutch adjective holländisch; **he's Dutch** er ist Holländer; **she's Dutch** sie ist Holländerin.

duty noun 1 Pflicht die (PL die Pflichten); **to have a duty to do something** die Pflicht haben, etwas zu tun; **you have a duty to inform us** du hast die Pflicht, uns zu benachrichtigen; **2 to be on duty** Dienst haben; **to be on night duty** Nachtdienst haben; **I'm off duty tonight** ich habe heute Abend keinen Dienst.

duty-free adjective zollfrei; **duty-free shop** der Dutyfreeshop; **duty-free goods** zollfreie Waren (plural).

duvet noun Bettdecke die (PL die Bettdecken).

duvet cover noun Bettbezug der (PL die Bettbezüge).

dye noun Färbemittel das (PL die Färbemittel).

dye verb färben; **to dye your hair** sich die Haare färben; **I'm going to dye my hair black** ich werde mir die Haare schwarz färben; **I'm going to have my hair dyed pink** ich lasse mir die Haare rosa färben.

dynamic adjective dynamisch.

dyslexia noun Legasthenie die.

dyslexic adjective legasthenisch; **to be dyslexic** Legastheniker sein, Legasthenikerin sein.

Ee

each adjective, pronoun **1** jeder/ jede/jedes; **each Sunday** jeden Sonntag; **each time** jedes Mal; **at the beginning of each year** am Anfang jedes Jahres; **we each have an invitation** jeder von uns hat eine Einladung; **my sisters each have a computer** jede meiner Schwestern hat einen Computer; **she gave us an apple each** sie hat jedem von uns einen Apfel gegeben; **each of you** jeder von euch/jede von euch; **we each got a present** jeder Einzelne hat ein Geschenk bekommen; **2 the tickets cost ten pounds each** die Karten kosten je zehn Pfund; **£5 each** (per person) fünf Pfund pro Person, (per item) fünf Pfund pro Stück.

each other pronoun ('each other' is usually translated using a reflexive pronoun) **they love each other** sie lieben sich; **we know each other** wir kennen uns; **do you see each other often?** seht ihr euch oft?

eagle noun Adler der (PL die Adler).

ear noun Ohr das (PL die Ohren).

earache noun **to have earache** Ohrenschmerzen haben.

earlier adverb **1** (a while ago) vor kurzem; **your brother phoned earlier** dein Bruder hat vor kurzem angerufen; **2** (not as late) früher; **we should have started earlier** wir hätten früher anfangen sollen.

early adverb **1** (in the morning) früh; **to get up early** früh aufstehen; **it's too early** es ist zu früh; **2** (for an appointment) **to be early** (zu) früh dran sein; **we're early, the train doesn't leave until ten** wir sind früh dran, der Zug fährt erst um zehn Uhr ab.

early adjective **1** (one of the first) **in the early months** während der ersten Monate; **I'm getting the early train** ich nehme den früheren Zug; **2 to have an early lunch** früh zu Mittag essen; **Jan's having an early night** Jan geht früh zu Bett; **3 in the early afternoon** am frühen Nachmittag; **in the early hours** in den frühen Morgenstunden.

earn verb verdienen; **Richard earns five pounds an hour** Richard verdient fünf Pfund die Stunde.

earring noun Ohrring der (PL die Ohrringe).

earth noun Erde die; **life on earth** das Leben auf der Erde; ★ **what on earth are you doing?** was in aller Welt machst du da?

earthquake noun Erdbeben das (PL die Erdbeben).

easily adverb leicht; **he's easily the best** er ist mit Abstand der Beste.

east noun Osten der; **in the east** im Osten.

east adjective, adverb östlich, Ost-; **the east side** die Ostseite; **an east wind** ein Ostwind; **east of Munich** östlich von München.

Easter noun Ostern das (PL die Ostern); **they're coming at Easter** sie kommen zu Ostern; **Happy Easter!** Frohe Ostern.

Easter Day noun Ostersonntag der (PL die Ostersonntage).

Easter egg noun Osterei das (PL die Ostereier).

Eastern Europe noun Osteuropa das.

easy adjective leicht; **it's easy!** das ist leicht!; **it was easy to decide** die Entscheidung fiel uns leicht.

eat verb 1 essen✧; **he was eating a banana** er aß eine Banane; **we're going to have something to eat** wir essen jetzt etwas; **2 to eat your breakfast** frühstücken.

EC noun EG die (Europäische Gemeinschaft).

echo noun Echo das (PL die Echos).

echo verb wiederholen.

ecological adjective ökologisch.

ecology noun Ökologie die.

economical adjective sparsam.

economics noun Wirtschaftswissenschaften (plural).

economy noun Wirtschaft die.

edge noun 1 Kante die (PL die Kanten); **the edge of the table** die Tischkante; **2** (of a road, sheet of paper, or cliff) Rand der (PL die Ränder); **at the edge of the forest** am Waldrand.

edible adjective essbar.

edit verb redigieren.

editor noun 1 (of a newspaper or magazine) Chefredakteur der (PL die Chefredakteure), Chefredakteurin die (PL die Chefredakteurinnen); **2** (of a book) Redakteur der (PL die Redakteure), Redakteurin die (PL die Redakteurinnen).

educate verb erziehen✧.

education noun Ausbildung die.

effect noun 1 Wirkung die (PL die Wirkungen); **the effect of the explosion was horrific** die Wirkung der Explosion war entsetzlich; **2 to have an effect on something** eine Auswirkung auf etwas (ACC) haben; **it had a good effect on the whole family** es hatte eine gute Auswirkung auf die ganze Familie; **3** (in a film) Effekt der (PL die Effekte); **special effects** die Specialeffekte.

effective adjective effektiv.

efficient adjective 1 (person) tüchtig; **2** (machine or organization) leistungsfähig.

effort noun 1 Mühe die (PL die Mühen); **2 to make an effort** sich bemühen; **Toya made an effort to help us** Toya hat sich bemüht, uns zu helfen; **he didn't even make the effort to apologize** er hat sich nicht einmal die Mühe gemacht, sich zu entschuldigen.

e.g. abbreviation z.B. (zum Beispiel).

egg noun Ei das (PL die Eier); **a fried egg** ein Spiegelei; **a hard-boiled egg** ein hart gekochtes Ei.

egg-cup noun Eierbecher der (PL die Eierbecher).

a
b
c
d
e
f
g
h
i
j
k
l
m
n
o
p
q
r
s
t
u
v
w
x
y
z

eggshell noun Eierschale die (PL die Eierschalen).

egg-white noun Eiweiß das (PL die Eiweiße).

egg-yolk noun Eigelb das (PL die Eigelbe).

eight number acht; **Maya's eight** Maya ist acht; **at eight o'clock** um acht Uhr.

eighteen number achtzehn; **Jason's eighteen** Jason ist achtzehn.

eighth number achter/achte/ achtes; **on the eighth of July** am achten Juli.

eighty number achtzig; **eighty-five** fünfundachtzig.

either pronoun **1** (one or the other) einer von beiden/eine von beiden/ eins von beiden; **take either (of them)** nimm einen von beiden/ eine von beiden/eins von beiden; **I don't like either (of them)** ich mag keinen von beiden/keine von beiden/keins von beiden; **2** (both) beide (plural); **either is possible** beide sind möglich; **on either side** auf beiden Seiten.

either conjunction **1** either ... or entweder ... oder; **either Susie or Judy** entweder Susie oder Judy; **2** (with a negative) either ... or weder ... noch; **he didn't ring either Sam or Emma** er hat weder Sam noch Emma angerufen; **3 I don't know them either** ich kenne sie auch nicht.

elastic noun Gummiband das (PL die Gummibänder).

elastic band noun Gummiband das (PL die Gummibänder).

elbow noun Ellbogen der (PL die Ellbogen).

elder adjective älterer/ältere/ älteres; **her elder brother** ihr älterer Bruder.

elderly adjective alt; **the elderly** ältere Menschen (plural).

eldest adjective ältester/älteste/ ältestes; **her eldest brother** ihr ältester Bruder.

elect verb wählen; **she has been elected** sie ist gewählt worden.

election noun Wahl die (PL die Wahlen); **in the election** bei den Wahlen; **to call an election** allgemeine Wahlen ausrufen SEP.

electric adjective elektrisch.

electrical adjective elektrisch, Elektro-; **electrical equipment** Elektrogeräte (plural).

electrician noun Elektriker der (PL die Elektriker), Elektrikerin die (PL die Elektrikerinnen).

electricity noun Strom der.

electronic adjective elektronisch.

electronics noun Elektronik die.

elegant adjective elegant.

elephant noun Elefant der (PL die Elefanten).

eleven number elf; **Josh is eleven** Josh ist elf; **at eleven o'clock** um elf Uhr; **a football eleven** eine Fußballelf.

eleventh number elfter/elfte/ elftes; **the eleventh of September** der elfte September; **on the eleventh floor** im elften Stock.

else adverb **1** (in addition) sonst; **who else?** wer sonst?; **did you see anyone else?** hast du sonst noch jemanden gesehen?; **nothing else** sonst nichts; **I don't want anything**

else ich will sonst nichts; **2 would you like something else?** möchten Sie sonst noch etwas?; **3** (*instead or different*) anderer/andere/anderes; **somewhere else** irgendwo anders; **everyone else** alle anderen; **somebody else** jemand anders; **something else** etwas anderes; **4 or else** sonst; **hurry up, or else we'll be late** beeil dich, sonst kommen wir zu spät.

email *noun* E-Mail *die* (PL die E-Mails).

embarrassed *adjective* verlegen; **he was very embarrassed** er war ganz verlegen.

embarrassing *adjective* peinlich.

embassy *noun* Botschaft *die* (PL die Botschaften); **the German Embassy** die Deutsche Botschaft.

emergency exit *noun* Notausgang *der* (PL die Notausgänge).

emergency *noun* Notfall *der* (PL die Notfälle).

emotion *noun* Gefühl *das* (PL die Gefühle).

emotional *adjective* **1** (*person*) emotional; **2** (*speech or occasion*) emotionsgeladen.

emperor *noun* Kaiser *der* (PL die Kaiser).

emphasize *verb* betonen; **he emphasized that it was voluntary** er betonte, dass es freiwillig war.

empire *noun* Reich *das* (PL die Reiche); **the Roman Empire** das Römische Reich.

employ *verb* **1** (*have working for you*) beschäftigen; **2** (*take on a worker*) einstellen SEP.

employee *noun* Angestellte *der/die* (PL die Angestellten).

employer *noun* Arbeitgeber *der* (PL die Arbeitgeber), Arbeitgeberin *die* (PL die Arbeitgeberinnen).

employment *noun* Arbeit *die*.

empty *adjective* leer; **an empty bottle** eine leere Flasche.

empty *verb* **1** (*empty out*) ausleeren SEP; **2** (*pour*) schütten.

enclose *verb* (*in a letter*) beilegen SEP; **please find enclosed a cheque** ein Scheck liegt bei.

encourage *verb* ermutigen; **to encourage somebody to do something** jemanden (dazu) ermutigen, etwas zu tun; **Mum encouraged me to try again** Mutti hat mich dazu ermutigt, es noch einmal zu versuchen.

encouragement *noun* Ermutigung *die* (PL die Ermutigungen).

encouraging *adjective* ermutigend.

encyclopedia *noun* Lexikon *das* (PL die Lexika).

end *noun* **1** Ende *das* (PL die Enden); **'The End'** 'Ende'; **at the end of the film** am Ende des Films; **by the end of the lesson** als die Stunde zu Ende war; **in the end I went home** schließlich bin ich nach Hause gegangen; **Sally's coming at the end of June** Sally kommt Ende Juni; **I read to the end of the page** ich habe die Seite zu Ende gelesen; **hold the other end** halte das andere Ende fest; **at the end of the street** am Ende der Straße; **2** (*in sports*) Spielfeldhälfte *die* (PL

die Spielfeldhälften); **to change
ends** die Seiten wechseln.

end verb **1** (to put an end to)
beenden; **they've ended the strike**
sie haben den Streik beendet; **2** (to
come to an end) enden; **the day
ended with a meal** der Tag endete
mit einem Essen.

• **to end up 1 to end up doing
something** am Ende etwas tun; **we
ended up taking a taxi** am Ende
haben wir ein Taxi genommen; **2
to end up somewhere** irgendwo
landen (PERF sein) (informal); **Rob
ended up in Berlin** Rob landete
schließlich in Berlin.

endangered adjective gefährdet;
an endangered species eine von
Aussterben bedrohte Art.

ending noun **1** Ende das (PL die
Enden); **2** (in grammar) Endung
die (PL die Endungen).

endless adjective endlos (day or
journey, for example).

enemy noun Feind der (PL die
Feinde); **to make enemies** sich
(DAT) Feinde machen.

energetic adjective
energiegeladen.

energy noun Energie die.

engaged adjective **1** (to be
married) verlobt; **they're engaged**
sie sind verlobt; **to get engaged**
sich verloben; **2** (a phone or toilet)
besetzt; **it's engaged, I'll ring later**
es ist besetzt, ich rufe später an.

engagement noun (to marry)
Verlobung die (PL die Verlobungen).

engagement ring noun
Verlobungsring der (PL die
Verlobungsringe).

engine noun **1** (in a car) Motor der
(PL die Motoren); **2** (pulling a train)
Lokomotive die (PL die
Lokomotiven).

engineer noun **1** (who comes for
repairs) Techniker der (PL die
Techniker), Technikerin die (PL die
Technikerinnen); **2** (who builds
roads and bridges) Ingenieur der (PL
die Ingenieure), Ingenieurin die (PL
die Ingenieurinnen).

England noun England das; **I'm
from England** ich bin Engländer,
ich bin Engländerin.

English noun **1** (the language)
Englisch das; **do you speak
English?** sprechen Sie Englisch?;
he answered in English er hat auf
Englisch geantwortet; **2** (the
people) the English die Engländer.

English adjective **1** (of or from
England) englisch; **the English
team** die englische Mannschaft;
he's English er ist Engländer; **she's
English** sie ist Engländerin; **2 an
English lesson** eine
Englischstunde; **our English
teacher** unser Englischlehrer,
unsere Englischlehrerin.

English Channel noun the
English Channel der Ärmelkanal.

Englishman noun Engländer der
(PL die Engländer).

Englishwoman noun
Engländerin die (PL die
Engländerinnen).

enjoy verb **1 did you enjoy the
party?** hat dir die Party gefallen?;
we really enjoyed the concert das
Konzert hat uns wirklich gut
gefallen; **2 to enjoy doing
something** etwas gerne tun✧; **I**

enjoy reading ich lese gerne; **do you enjoy living in York?** wohnst du gerne in York?; **3 to enjoy oneself** sich gut amüsieren; **we really enjoyed ourselves** wir haben uns richtig gut amüsiert; **enjoy yourself!** viel Vergnügen!; **did you enjoy yourself?** hast du dich gut amüsiert?

enjoyable *adjective* nett.

enormous *adjective* riesig.

enough *adverb, adjective, pronoun* **1** genug; **there's enough for everyone** es gibt genug für alle; **big enough** groß genug; **have we got enough bread?** haben wir genug Brot?; **2 that's enough** das reicht.

enquire *verb* to enquire about sich erkundigen nach (+ DAT); **I'm going to enquire about the trains** ich werde mich nach den Zügen erkundigen.

enrol *verb* sich anmelden SEP; **I want to enrol on the course** ich möchte mich zu dem Kurs anmelden.

enter *verb* **1** (*to go inside*) gehen ◇ PERF *sein*) in (+ ACC) (*a room or a building*); **we all entered the church** wir gingen alle in die Kirche hinein; **2** (*in computing*) eingeben ◇ SEP; **3 to enter for** sich anmelden SEP zu (+ DAT) (*an exam or a race*); **to enter for a competition** an einem Preisausschreiben teilnehmen ◇ SEP.

entertain *verb* **1** (*to keep amused*) unterhalten ◇; **2** (*to have people round*) Gäste haben ◇; **they don't entertain much** sie haben selten Gäste.

entertainment *noun* (*fun*) Unterhaltung *die*; **there wasn't much entertainment in the evenings** abends war wenig Unterhaltung geboten.

enthusiasm *noun* Begeisterung *die*.

enthusiast *noun* **1** Enthusiast *der* (PL die Enthusiasten), Enthusiastin *die* (PL die Enthusiastinnen); **2** (*for sports*) Fan *der* (PL die Fans); **he's a rugby enthusiast** er ist ein Rugbyfan.

enthusiastic *adjective* begeistert.

entire *adjective* ganz; **the entire class** die ganze Klasse.

entirely *adverb* ganz.

entrance *noun* **1** (*fee*) Eintritt *der*; **2** (*way in*) Eingang *der* (PL die Eingänge).

entry *noun* **1** (*way in*) Eingang *der* (PL die Eingänge), (*for cars*) Einfahrt *die* (PL die Einfahrten); **2 'no entry'** 'Zutritt verboten', (*to cars*) 'Einfahrt verboten'.

entry phone *noun* Sprechanlage *die* (PL die Sprechanlagen).

envelope *noun* Briefumschlag *der* (PL die Briefumschläge).

environment *noun* Umwelt *die*.

environmental *adjective* Umwelt-; **environmental pollution** die Umweltverschmutzung.

environment-friendly *adjective* umweltfreundlich.

epidemic *noun* Epidemie *die* (PL die Epidemien).

epileptic *adjective* epileptisch.

episode *noun* **1** (*an event*) Episode *die* (PL die Episoden); **2** (*on TV or radio*) Folge *die* (PL die Folgen).

a
b
c
d
e
f
g
h
i
j
k
l
m
n
o
p
q
r
s
t
u
v
w
x
y
z

equal *adjective* gleich; **milk and water in equal quantities** gleich viel Milch und Wasser.

equal *verb* gleichen✧ (+ DAT).

equality *noun* Gleichberechtigung die.

equalize *verb* ausgleichen✧ SEP; **they equalized in the last minute** sie haben in der letzten Minute ausgeglichen.

equally *adverb* (to share) gleichmäßig; **we divided it equally** wir haben es gleichmäßig verteilt.

equator *noun* Äquator der.

equip *verb* ausrüsten SEP; **well equipped for the hike** für die Wanderung gut ausgerüstet; **equipped with rucksacks** mit Rucksäcken ausgerüstet.

equipment *noun* 1 (for sport) Ausrüstung die (PL die Ausrüstungen); 2 Ausstattung die (PL die Ausstattungen); **laboratory equipment** die Laborausstattung; 3 (something needed for an activity) Geräte (plural); **recording equipment** Aufnahmegeräte.

equivalent *adjective* gleichwertig; **to be equivalent to** etwas (DAT) entsprechen; **1 litre is equivalent to about 1.75 pints** ein Liter entspricht ungefähr 1,75 Pints.

error *noun* 1 (in spelling, typing, on a computer, or in maths) Fehler der (PL die Fehler); **spelling error** der Rechtschreibfehler; 2 (wrong opinion) Irrtum der (PL die Irrtümer).

error message *noun* Fehlermeldung die (PL die Fehlermeldungen).

escalator *noun* Rolltreppe die (PL die Rolltreppen).

escape *noun* (from prison) Ausbruch der (PL die Ausbrüche).

escape *verb* 1 (from prison) ausbrechen✧ SEP (PERF sein); 2 entkommen✧ (PERF sein); **to escape from somebody** jemandem entkommen.

especially *adverb* besonders.

essay *noun* Aufsatz der (PL die Aufsätze); **an essay on German reunification** ein Aufsatz über die deutsche Wiedervereinigung.

essential *adjective* unbedingt erforderlich; **it's essential to reply quickly** es ist unbedingt erforderlich, sofort zu antworten.

estate *noun* 1 (a housing estate) Wohnsiedlung die (PL die Wohnsiedlungen); 2 (a big house and grounds) Landsitz der (PL die Landsitze).

estate agent *noun* Immobilienmakler der (PL die Immobilienmakler), Immobilienmaklerin die (PL die Immobilienmaklerinnen).

estate car *noun* Kombiwagen der (PL die Kombiwagen).

estimate *noun* 1 (a quote for work) Kostenvoranschlag der (PL die Kostenvoranschläge); 2 (a rough guess) Schätzung die (PL die Schätzungen).

estimate *verb* schätzen.

etc. *abbreviation* usw. (und so weiter).

ethnic *adjective* ethnisch; **an ethnic minority** eine ethnische Minderheit.

a
b
c
d
e
f
g
h
i
j
k
l
m
n
o
p
q
r
s
t
u
v
w
x
y
z

EU noun EU die (*Europäische Union*).

euro noun Euro der (PL die Euros); **the euro is divided into 100 cents** ein Euro hat 100 Cent.

Europe noun Europa das.

European noun Europäer der (PL die Europäer), Europäerin die (PL die Europäerinnen).

European adjective europäisch.

European Union noun Europäische Union die.

eurozone noun Euroland das

even[1] adverb **1** sogar; **even Lisa is coming** sogar Lisa kommt; **2 not even** nicht einmal; **I don't like animals, not even dogs** ich mag keine Tiere, nicht einmal Hunde; **3 without even asking** ohne wenigstens zu fragen; **4 even if** selbst wenn; **even if they arrive late** selbst wenn sie spät ankommen; **5** (*with a comparison*) (*sogar*) noch; **even bigger** sogar noch größer; **even faster** noch schneller; **even better than** sogar noch besser als; **the song is even better than their last one** das Lied ist sogar noch besser als ihr letztes; **6 even so** trotzdem; **even so, we had a good time** trotzdem haben wir uns gut amüsiert.

even[2] adjective **1** (*surface or layer*) eben; **2** (*number*) gerade; **six is an even number** sechs ist eine gerade Zahl; **3** (*equal*) gleich (*distance, value*); **the score is even** das Punktzahl ist gleich; **4 to get even with somebody** es jemandem heimzahlen.

evening noun **1** Abend der (PL die Abende); **in the evening** am Abend;

this evening heute Abend; tomorrow evening morgen Abend; on Monday evening am Montagabend; every Thursday evening jeden Donnerstagabend; the evening before am Abend zuvor; the evening meal das Abendessen; **2 at six o'clock in the evening** um sechs Uhr abends; the other evening neulich abends; I work in the evening(s) ich arbeite abends.

evening class noun Abendkurs der (PL die Abendkurse).

event noun **1** (*a happening*) Ereignis das (PL die Ereignisse); **2** (*in athletics*) Disziplin die (PL die Disziplinen).

eventually adverb schließlich.

ever adverb **1** (*at any time*) je; **have you ever noticed that?** hast du das je bemerkt?; **more than ever** mehr denn je; **colder than ever** kälter denn je; **he drove more slowly than ever** er fuhr langsamer als je zuvor; **2 not ever** nie; **nobody ever came** es kam nie jemand; **hardly ever** fast nie; **3** (*always*) immer; **as cheerful as ever** so vergnügt wie immer; **the same as ever** so wie immer; **4 ever since** seitdem; **and it's been raining ever since** und seitdem regnet es.

every adjective **1** jeder/jede/jedes; **every house has a garden** jedes Haus hat einen Garten; **every day** jeden Tag; **every Monday** jeden Montag; **every time** jedes Mal; **2 every few days** alle paar Tage; **every ten kilometres** alle zehn Kilometer; **3 every one** jeder Einzelne/jede Einzelne/jedes

Einzelne; **I've seen every one of his films** ich habe jeden Einzelnen seiner Filme gesehen; **4 every now and then** ab und zu.

everybody, everyone *pronoun* **1** alle *(plural)*; **everybody knows that ...** alle wissen, dass ...; **everyone else** alle anderen; **2** *(each one)* jeder; **not everybody can afford it** das kann sich nicht jeder leisten.

everything *pronoun* alles; **everything is ready** es ist alles fertig; **everything's fine** es ist alles okay *(informal)*; **everything else** alles andere; **he gets everything he wants** er bekommt alles, was er will.

everywhere *adverb* **1** überall; **there was dirt everywhere** überall war Dreck; **she went everywhere** sie ist überall hingegangen; **everywhere else** sonst überall; **2 everywhere she went** wohin sie auch ging.

evidently *adverb* offensichtlich.

evil *noun* Böse *das*.

evil *adjective* böse.

exact *adjective* genau; **the exact fare** das genaue Fahrgeld; **it's the exact opposite** das ist das genaue Gegenteil.

exactly *adverb* genau; **they're exactly the right age** sie sind genau im richtigen Alter; **yes, exactly!** ja, genau!

exaggerate *verb* übertreiben✧.

exaggeration *noun* Übertreibung *die* (PL die Übertreibungen).

exam *noun* Prüfung *die* (PL die Prüfungen); **history exam** die

Geschichtsprüfung, **to sit an exam** eine Prüfung machen; **to pass an exam** eine Prüfung bestehen; **to fail an exam** durch eine Prüfung fallen.

examination *noun* Prüfung *die* (PL die Prüfungen).

examine *verb* **1** *(at school or university)* prüfen; **2** *(at the doctor's)* untersuchen.

examiner *noun* Prüfer *der* (PL die Prüfer), Prüferin *die* (PL die Prüferinnen).

example *noun* Beispiel *das* (PL die Beispiele); **for example** zum Beispiel; **to set a good example** ein gutes Beispiel geben.

excellent *adjective* ausgezeichnet.

except *preposition* **1** außer (+ DAT); **every day except Tuesday** täglich außer Dienstag; **we play except when it rains** wir spielen, außer wenn es regnet; **except in March** außer März; **2 except for** außer (+ DAT); **except for the children** außer den Kindern.

exception *noun* Ausnahme *die* (PL die Ausnahmen); **without exception** ohne Ausnahme; **with the exception of** mit Ausnahme von (+ DAT).

exchange *noun* **1** Austausch *der*; **the students are coming to London on an exchange** die Schüler kommen auf einen Schüleraustausch nach London; **exchange student** der Austauschstudent, *die* Austauschstudentin; **an exchange of pupils** ein Schüleraustausch;

2 in exchange for his help für seine Hilfe.

exchange *verb* umtauschen SEP; **can I exchange this shirt for a smaller one?** kann ich dieses Hemd gegen ein kleineres umtauschen?

exchange rate *noun* Wechselkurs *der* (PL die Wechselkurse).

excite *verb* **1** (*thrill*) begeistern; **2** (*agitate*) aufregen SEP.

excited *adjective* aufgeregt; **the children are excited** die Kinder sind aufgeregt; **the dogs get excited when they hear the car** die Hunde geraten in Aufregung, wenn sie das Auto hören; **2** (*annoyed or angry*) **to get excited** sich aufregen SEP.

exciting *adjective* aufregend; **a very exciting film** ein sehr aufregender Film.

exclamation mark *noun* Ausrufezeichen *das* (PL die Ausrufezeichen).

excursion *noun* Ausflug *der* (PL die Ausflüge).

excuse *noun* Entschuldigung *die* (PL die Entschuldigungen).

excuse *verb* (*apologizing*) **excuse me!** Entschuldigung!

exercise *noun* **1** Übung *die* (PL die Übungen); **a maths exercise** eine Matheübung; **2 physical exercise** körperliche Bewegung; **to get exercise** sich Bewegung verschaffen.

exercise bike *noun* Heimtrainer *der* (PL die Heimtrainer).

exercise book *noun* Heft *das* (PL die Hefte); **my German exercise book** mein Deutschheft.

exhaust (pipe) *noun* Auspuff *der* (PL die Auspuffe).

exhaust fumes *noun* Abgase *die* (plural).

exhausted *adjective* erschöpft.

exhibition *noun* Ausstellung *die* (PL die Ausstellungen); **the Dürer exhibition** die Dürer-Ausstellung.

exist *verb* existieren.

exit *noun* **1** Ausgang *der* (PL die Ausgänge); **2** (*from a motorway*) Ausfahrt *die* (PL die Ausfahrten).

expect *verb* **1** erwarten (*guests or a baby*); **we're expecting thirty visitors** wir erwarten dreißig Besucher; **2** (*require something*) **to expect somebody to do something** erwarten, dass er etwas tut; **3** rechnen mit (+ DAT) (*something to happen*); **I didn't expect that** damit habe ich nicht gerechnet; **I didn't expect it at all** damit habe ich überhaupt nicht gerechnet; **4** (*suppose*) glauben; **I expect she'll bring her boyfriend** ich glaube, sie bringt ihren Freund mit; **yes, I expect so** ich glaube ja.

expedition *noun* Expedition *die* (PL die Expeditionen).

expel *verb* **to be expelled** (*from school*) von der Schule verwiesen werden.

expensive *adjective* teuer; **those shoes are too expensive for me** diese Schuhe sind mir zu teuer; **the most expensive CDs** die teuersten CDs.

a b c d e f g h i j k l m n o p q r s t u v w x y z

a
b
c
d
e
f
g
h
i
j
k
l
m
n
o
p
q
r
s
t
u
v
w
x
y
z

experience noun **1** Erfahrung die (PL die Erfahrungen); **2** (an event) Erlebnis das (PL die Erlebnisse).

experienced adjective erfahren.

experiment noun Experiment das (PL die Experimente); **to do an experiment** ein Experiment machen.

expert noun Experte der (PL die Experten), Expertin die (PL die Expertinnen); **he's a computer expert** er ist ein Computerexperte.

expire verb ablaufen✧ SEP (PERF sein).

expiry date noun Verfallsdatum das (PL die Verfallsdaten).

explain verb erklären.

explanation noun Erklärung die (PL die Erklärungen).

explode verb explodieren (PERF sein).

explore verb erforschen.

explosion noun Explosion die (PL die Explosionen).

export noun Export der (PL die Exporte); **the chief export is wool** das wichtigste Exportgut ist Wolle.

export verb exportieren; **Russia exports a lot of oil and timber** Russland exportiert viel Öl und Holz.

exposure noun (of a film) Belichtung die; **a 24-exposure film** ein Film mit 24 Aufnahmen.

express noun (train) Schnellzug der (PL die Schnellzüge).

express verb **1** ausdrücken SEP; **2 to express yourself** sich ausdrücken.

expression noun Ausdruck der (PL die Ausdrücke).

extend verb **1** verlängern; **2** ausbauen SEP (a house).

extension noun **1** (to a house) Anbau der (PL die Anbauten); **2** (telephone) Apparat der (PL die Apparate); **can I have extension 2347 please?** bitte verbinden Sie mich mit Apparat 2347 (note that in spoken German telephone numbers are usually broken down into groups of two figures); **3** (electrical) Verlängerung die (PL die Verlängerungen).

extension number noun Apparatnummer die (PL die Apparatnummern).

exterior adjective äußerer/ äußere/äußeres.

extinct adjective **1** (animal) ausgestorben; **2** (volcano) erloschen.

extinguish verb **1** löschen (a fire); **2 to extinguish a cigarette** eine Zigarette ausmachen SEP.

extinguisher noun Feuerlöscher der (PL die Feuerlöscher).

extra adjective **1** zusätzlich, extra (informal) (extra never has an ending); **extra homework** zusätzliche Hausaufgaben; **wine is extra** Wein kostet extra; **you have to pay extra** das wird extra berechnet; **2 at no extra charge** ohne Aufschlag.

extra adverb **1** besonders; **he was extra careful** er war besonders vorsichtig; **2 extra large** extragroß.

extraordinary adjective außerordentlich.

extra time noun (in football) Verlängerung die (PL die

Verlängerungen); **to go into extra time** in die Verlängerung gehen.

extravagant adjective verschwenderisch (person).

extreme noun Extrem das (PL die Extreme); **to go from one extreme to another** von einem Extrem ins andere fallen.

extreme adjective extrem.

extremely adverb äußerst; **extremely fast** äußerst schnell.

eye noun Auge das (PL die Augen); **a girl with blue eyes** ein Mädchen mit blauen Augen; **shut your eyes!** mach die Augen zu!; ★ **to keep an eye on something** auf etwas (ACC) aufpassen SEP.

eyebrow noun Augenbraue die (PL die Augenbrauen).

eyelash noun Augenwimper die (PL die Augenwimpern).

eyelid noun Augenlid das (PL die Augenlider).

eyeliner noun Eyeliner der (PL die Eyeliner).

eye shadow noun Lidschatten der (PL die Lidschatten).

eyesight noun **to have good eyesight** gute Augen haben; **to have bad eyesight** schlechte Augen haben.

Ff

fabric noun (cloth) Stoff der (PL die Stoffe).

fabulous adjective phantastisch.

face noun **1** (of a person) Gesicht das (PL die Gesichter); **to pull a face**

eine Grimasse schneiden; **2** (of a clock or watch) Zifferblatt das (PL die Zifferblätter).

face verb **1** gegenüberstehen◇ SEP (PERF sein) (+ DAT); **she was facing him** sie stand ihm gegenüber; **2 the house faces the park** das Haus befindet sich gegenüber dem Park; **3** (to stand the idea of) verkraften; **I can't face going back** es bringe es nicht über mich zurückzugehen; **4 to face up to something** sich etwas (DAT) stellen.

facilities plural noun **1 the school has good sports facilities** die Schule hat gute Sportanlagen; **2 the flat has no cooking facilities** die Wohnung hat keine Kochgelegenheit.

fact noun Tatsache die (PL die Tatsachen); **the fact is that ...** Tatsache ist, dass ...; **in fact** tatsächlich; **is that a fact?** Tatsache?

factory noun Fabrik die (PL die Fabriken).

fade verb **1** (fabric) ausbleichen◇ SEP (PERF sein); **faded jeans** ausgebleichte Jeans; **2** (a colour or memory) verblassen (PERF sein); **the colours have faded** die Farben sind verblasst.

fail verb **1** nicht bestehen◇ (a test or an exam); **I failed my driving test** ich habe meine Fahrprüfung nicht bestanden; (in a test or an exam) durchfallen◇ SEP (PERF sein); **three students failed** drei Studenten sind durchgefallen; **3 to fail to do something** etwas nicht tun; **he failed to inform us** er hat uns nicht benachrichtigt; ★ **without fail** auf jeden Fall;; **ring me without fail** ruf mich auf jeden Fall an.

failure noun **1** Misserfolg der (PL die Misserfolge); **it was a terrible failure** es war ein schrecklicher Misserfolg; **2** (of equipment) Ausfall der (PL die Ausfälle); **a power failure** ein Stromausfall.

faint adjective **1** (slight) leicht; **a faint smell of gas** ein leichter Gasgeruch; **I haven't the faintest idea** ich habe nicht die blasseste Ahnung (informal); **2** (voice or sound) leise.

faint verb ohnmächtig werden; **Lisa fainted** Lisa wurde ohnmächtig.

fair noun Jahrmarkt der (PL die Jahrmärkte).

fair adjective **1** (not unfair) gerecht; **2** (hair) blond; **he's fair-haired** er ist blond; **3** (skin) hell; **fair-skinned** hellhäutig; **4** (fairly good) ganz gut (chance, condition, or performance); **5** (weather) schön; **if it's fair tomorrow** wenn es morgen schön ist.

fairground noun Jahrmarkt der (PL die Jahrmärkte).

fairly adverb (quite) ziemlich.

fairy noun Fee die (PL die Feen).

fairy tale noun Märchen das (PL die Märchen).

faith noun **1** (trust) Vertrauen das; **to have faith in somebody** Vertrauen zu jemandem haben; **2** (religious belief) Glaube der (PL die Glauben).

faithful adjective treu; **to be faithful to somebody** jemandem treu sein.

faithfully adverb **Yours faithfully** Hochachtungsvoll.

fake noun **1** Imitation die (PL die Imitationen); **the diamonds were fakes** die Brillanten waren eine Imitation; **2** (a painting or money) Fälschung die (PL die Fälschungen).

fake adjective gefälscht; **a fake passport** ein gefälschter Pass.

fall noun Fall der (PL die Fälle); **to have a fall** stürzen (PERF sein).

fall verb **1** fallen◇ (PERF sein); **mind, you'll fall** pass auf, dass du nicht hinfällst; **Tony fell off his bike** Tony ist vom Rad gefallen; **she fell down the stairs** sie ist die Treppe hinuntergefallen; **2** (of temperature, prices) sinken◇ (PERF sein).

false adjective falsch; **a false alarm** ein falscher Alarm.

fame noun Ruhm der.

familiar adjective bekannt; **his face is familiar** sein Gesicht kommt mir bekannt vor.

family noun Familie die (PL die Familien); **a family of six** eine sechsköpfige Familie; **Ben's one of the family** Ben gehört zur Familie; **the Morris family** Familie Morris.

famous adjective berühmt.

fan noun **1** (a supporter) Fan der (PL die Fans); **Will's a Chelsea fan** Will ist ein Fan von Chelsea; **2** (electric, for cooling) Ventilator der (PL die Ventilatoren); **3** (hand-held) Fächer der (PL die Fächer).

fanatic noun Fanatiker der (PL die Fanatiker), Fanatikerin die (PL die Fanatikerinnen).

fancy noun **to take somebody's fancy** jemandem gefallen◇; **the picture took his fancy** das Bild hat es ihm angetan.

fancy adjective (equipment) ausgefallen.

fancy verb **1** (to want) (do you) **fancy a coffee?** hast du Lust auf einen Kaffee?; **do you fancy going to the cinema?** hast du Lust, ins Kino zu gehen?; **2 I really fancy him** ich stehe total auf ihn; **3** (just) **fancy that!** stell dir vor!; **fancy you being here!** na so was, dich hier zu treffen!

fancy dress noun **in fancy dress** verkleidet; **fancy-dress party** das Kostümfest.

fantastic adjective fantastisch; **really? that's fantastic!** wirklich? das ist ja fantastisch!; **a fantastic holiday** fantastische Ferien.

far adverb, adjective **1** weit; **it's not far** es ist nicht weit; **is it far to Carlisle?** ist es weit nach Carlisle?; **how far is it to Bristol?** wie weit ist es bis nach Bristol?; **2 he took us as far as Newport** er hat uns bis Newport mitgenommen; **3 by far** bei weitem; **the prettiest by far** bei weitem das hübscheste; **4** (much) viel; **far better** viel besser; **far faster** viel schneller; **far too many people** viel zu viele Leute; **5 so far** bis jetzt; **so far everything's going well** bis jetzt läuft alles gut; **6 as far as I know** soweit ich weiß.

fare noun **1** (on a bus, train, or the underground) Fahrpreis der (PL die Fahrpreise); **2** (on a plane) Flugpreis der (PL die Flugpreise);

half fare der halbe Fahrpreis; **full fare** der volle Fahrpreis.

Far East noun der Ferne Osten, Fernost das.

farm noun Bauernhof der (PL die Bauernhöfe).

farmer noun Bauer der (PL die Bauern), Bäuerin die (PL die Bäuerinnen).

farming noun Landwirtschaft die.

fascinating adjective faszinierend.

fashion noun Mode die (PL die Moden); **in fashion** in Mode; **to go out of fashion** aus der Mode kommen.

fashionable adjective modisch.

fashion model noun Mannequin das (PL die Mannequins).

fashion show noun Modenschau die (PL die Modenschauen).

fast adjective **1** schnell; **a fast car** ein schnelles Auto; **2** (of a clock or watch) **to be fast** vorgehen◇ SEP (PERF sein); **my watch is fast** meine Uhr geht vor; **you're ten minutes fast** deine Uhr geht zehn Minuten vor.

fast adverb **1** schnell; **he swims fast** er schwimmt schnell; **2 to be fast asleep** fest schlafen.

fast food noun Fastfood das.

fast forward noun Vorlauf der.

fat noun Fett das (PL die Fette).

fat adjective **1** (meat) fett; **2** (person) dick, fett (informal); **a fat man** ein dicker Mann; **to get fat** fett werden (informal).

fatal adjective tödlich.

father noun Vater der (PL die Väter); **my father's office** das Büro von meinem Vater.

Father Christmas noun der Weihnachtsmann.

father-in-law noun Schwiegervater der (PL die Schwiegerväter).

fault noun 1 (when you are responsible) Schuld die; **it's Stephen's fault** Stephen ist schuld; **it's not my fault** es ist nicht meine Schuld; 2 (in tennis) double fault der Doppelfehler.

favour noun 1 (a kindness) Gefallen der (PL die Gefallen); **to do somebody a favour** jemandem einen Gefallen tun; **can you do me a favour?** kannst du mir einen Gefallen tun?; **to ask a favour of somebody** jemanden um einen Gefallen bitten; 2 **to be in favour of something** für etwas (ACC) sein.

favourite adjective Lieblings-; **my favourite band** meine Lieblingsband.

fax noun Fax das (PL die Faxe).

fax verb faxen.

fear noun Angst die (PL die Ängste).

fear verb fürchten.

feather noun Feder die (PL die Federn).

feature noun 1 (of your face) Gesichtszug der (PL die Gesichtszüge); **to have delicate features** feine Gesichtszüge haben; 2 (of a car or a machine) Merkmal das (PL die Merkmale).

February noun Februar der; **in February** im Februar.

fed up adjective 1 **I'm fed up** ich habe die Nase voll (informal); **he's fed up with her** er hat die Nase voll von ihr; 2 **to be fed up with something** etwas (ACC) satt haben (informal); **I'm fed up with working every day** ich habe es satt, jeden Tag zu arbeiten.

feed verb füttern; **have you fed the dog?** hast du den Hund gefüttert?

feel verb 1 sich fühlen; **I don't feel well** ich fühle mich nicht gut; 2 spüren; **I didn't feel a thing** ich habe nichts gespürt; 3 **I feel tired** ich bin müde; **I feel cold** mir ist kalt; 4 **to feel afraid** Angst haben; **to feel thirsty** Durst haben; 5 **to feel like doing something** Lust haben, etwas zu tun; **I feel like going to the cinema** ich habe Lust, ins Kino zu gehen; 6 (touch) fühlen; 7 (to the touch) sich anfühlen SEP; **to feel soft** sich weich anfühlen.

feeling noun 1 Gefühl das (PL die Gefühle); **to show your feelings** seine Gefühle zeigen; **a dizzy feeling** ein Schwindelgefühl; **I have the feeling James doesn't like me** ich habe das Gefühl, dass James mich nicht mag; 2 **to hurt somebody's feelings** jemanden verletzen.

felt-tip (pen) noun Filzstift der (PL die Filzstifte).

female noun (animal) Weibchen das (PL die Weibchen).

female adjective weiblich.

feminine adjective weiblich.

feminist noun Feministin die (PL die Feministinnen), Feminist der (PL die Feministen).

feminist *adjective* feministisch.

fence *noun* Zaun *der* (PL die Zäune).

ferry *noun* Fähre *die* (PL die Fähren).

fertilizer *noun* Dünger *der*.

festival *noun* (*of films, art, or music*) Festspiele (*plural*).

fetch *verb* 1 (*collect*) abholen SEP; Tom's fetching the children Tom holt die Kinder ab; 2 holen; fetch me the other knife hol mir das andere Messer.

fever *noun* Fieber *das*.

few *adjective, pronoun* 1 wenige; few people know that ... wenige Leute wissen, dass ...; 2 a few (*several*) ein paar (*ein paar never changes*); a few weeks ein paar Wochen; in a few minutes in ein paar Minuten; have you got any tomatoes? we want a few for the salad haben Sie Tomaten? wir brauchen ein paar für den Salat; 3 quite a few eine ganze Menge; there were quite a few questions es gab eine ganze Menge Fragen.

fewer *adjective* weniger; there are fewer mosquitoes this year dieses Jahr gibt es weniger Mücken.

fiancé *noun* Verlobte *der* (PL die Verlobten).

fiancée *noun* Verlobte *die* (PL die Verlobten).

field *noun* 1 (*with grass or crops*) Feld *das* (PL die Felder); a field of wheat ein Kornfeld; 2 (*for sport*) Spielfeld *das* (PL die Spielfelder).

fierce *adjective* 1 wild (*animal or person*); 2 heftig (*storm or battle*).

fifteen *number* fünfzehn.

fifth *number* fünfter/fünfte/fünftes; the fifth of January der

fünfte Januar; on the fifth floor im fünften Stock.

fifty *number* fünfzig.

fig *noun* Feige *die* (PL die Feigen).

fight *noun* 1 (*a scuffle*) Schlägerei *die* (PL die Schlägereien); 2 (*in boxing or against illness*) Kampf *der* (PL die Kämpfe).

fight *verb* 1 (*to have a fight*) sich prügeln; they were fighting sie haben sich geprügelt; 2 (*to quarrel*) sich streiten◊; they're always fighting sie streiten sich immer; 3 (*struggle against*) kämpfen gegen (+ ACC) (*poverty or a disease*).

figure *noun* 1 (*number*) Zahl *die* (PL die Zahlen); a four-figure number eine vierstellige Zahl; 2 (*body shape*) Figur *die*; good for your figure gut für die Figur; 3 (*a person*) Gestalt *die* (PL die Gestalten).

figure *verb* to figure something out etwas herausfinden◊ SEP (*the answer or reason*).

file *noun* 1 (*for records of a person or case*) Akte *die* (PL die Akten); 2 (*ring binder or folder*) Ordner *der* (PL die Ordner); 3 (*on a computer*) Datei *die* (PL die Dateien); 4 a nail file eine Nagelfeile.

file *verb* 1 ablegen SEP (*documents*); 2 to file your nails sich (DAT) die Nägel feilen.

fill *verb* 1 füllen (*a container*); she filled my glass sie füllte mein Glas; 2 to be filled with people voller Menschen sein; filled with smoke voller Rauch.

● **to fill in** ausfüllen SEP (*a form*).

a b c d e f g h i j k l m n o p q r s t u v w x y z

a
b
c
d
f
g
h
i
j
k
l
m
n
o
p
q
r
s
t
u
v
w
x
y
z

filling noun **1** (of a pie) Füllung die (PL die Füllungen); **2** (in a tooth) Füllung die (PL die Füllungen).

film noun (in a cinema and for a camera) Film der (PL die Filme); **shall we go and see the new film about Freud?** wollen wir uns den neuen Film über Freud ansehen?; **to make a film** einen Film drehen; **a 24-exposure colour film** ein Farbfilm mit 24 Aufnahmen.

film star noun Filmstar der (PL die Filmstars).

filter noun Filter der (PL die Filter).

filthy adjective dreckig.

final noun (in sport) Endspiel das (PL die Endspiele).

final adjective letzter/letzte/letztes; **the final instalment** die letzte Folge; **the final result** das Endergebnis.

finally adverb schließlich.

find verb finden◇; **did you find your passport?** hast du deinen Pass gefunden?; **I can't find my keys** ich kann meine Schlüssel nicht finden.

● **to find out 1** (to enquire) sich informieren; **I don't know, I'll find out** das weiß ich nicht, ich werde mich informieren; **2 to find something out** etwas (ACC) herausfinden◇ SEP (the facts or an answer); **when she found out the truth** als sie die Wahrheit herausfand.

fine noun Bußgeld das (PL die Bußgelder) (for parking or speeding).

fine adjective **1** (in good health) gut; **'how are you?' – 'fine, thanks'** 'wie

gehts?' - 'danke, gut'; **I'm fine** mir geht es gut; **2** (convenient) in Ordnung; **ten o'clock? yes, that's fine** zehn Uhr? ja, in Ordnung!; **Friday will be fine** Freitag geht in Ordnung; **3** (sunny) schön; (weather or day) **if it's fine** wenn es schön ist; **in fine weather** bei schönem Wetter; **4** (not coarse or thick) fein.

finely adverb fein (chopped or grated).

finger noun Finger der (PL die Finger); ★ **I'll keep my fingers crossed for you** ich drücke dir den Daumen.

fingernail noun Fingernagel der (PL die Fingernägel).

finish noun **1** (end) Schluss der (PL die Schlüsse); **2** (in a race) Ziel das (PL die Ziele).

finish verb **1** beenden (a conversation or quarrel); **to finish a discussion** ein Gespräch beenden; **to be finished with something** mit etwas (DAT) fertig sein (work or a project); **have you finished your homework?** bist du mit den Hausaufgaben fertig?; **wait, I haven't finished!** warte, ich bin noch nicht fertig!; **2** (to finish off) **to finish doing something** etwas zu beenden; **have you finished (reading) the letter?** hast du den Brief zu Ende gelesen?; **he hasn't yet finished (writing) the report** er hat den Bericht noch nicht zu Ende geschrieben; **3** (come to an end) zu Ende sein, aus sein (informal) (a meeting or performance); **the film finishes at ten o'clock** der Film ist um zehn

Uhr zu Ende; **when does school finish?** wann ist die Schule aus?

● **to finish with** (*complete your use of*) nicht mehr brauchen; **when you've finished with these clothes, give them back to me** wenn du die Sachen nicht mehr brauchst, gib sie mir zurück; **have you finished with the computer?** brauchen Sie den Computer noch?

Finland noun Finnland das.

Finnish noun (*the language*) Finnisch das.

Finnish adjective finnisch; **he's Finnish** er ist Finne; **she's Finnish** sie ist Finnin.

fire noun **1** (*in a grate*) Kaminfeuer das (PL die Kaminfeuer); **to light the fire** das Feuer im Kamin anmachen; **2** (*accidental*) Feuer das (PL die Feuer); **to catch fire** (*fabric, furnishings*) Feuer fangen; **3** (*in a building or forest*) Brand der (PL die Brände); **to set fire to a factory** eine Fabrik in Brand stecken; **4** **to be on fire** brennen✧.

fire verb **1** (*with a gun*) schießen✧; **to fire at somebody** auf jemanden schießen; **2** abfeuern SEP (*a gun*).

fire alarm noun Feuermelder der (PL die Feuermelder).

fire brigade noun Feuerwehr die.

fire engine noun Feuerwehrauto das (PL die Feuerwehrautos).

fire escape noun Feuertreppe die (PL die Feuertreppen).

fire extinguisher noun Feuerlöscher der (PL die Feuerlöscher).

firefighter noun Feuerwehrmann der (PL die Feuerwehrleute).

fireplace noun Kamin der (PL die Kamine).

fire station noun Feuerwache die (PL die Feuerwachen).

firework noun Feuerwerkskörper der (PL die Feuerwerkskörper); **firework display** das Feuerwerk.

firm noun (*business*) Firma die (PL die Firmen).

firm adjective **1** fest; **2** (*strict*) streng.

first adjective erster/erste/erstes; **the first of May** der erste Mai; **for the first time** zum ersten Mal; **I was the first to arrive** ich kam als Erster/Erste an; **Susan was first** Susan war die Erste; **to come first in the 100 metres** beim Hundertmeterlauf Erster/Erste werden.

first adverb **1** (*to begin with*) zuerst; **first, I'm going to make some tea** zuerst mache ich Tee; **2** **at first** zuerst; **at first he was shy** er war zuerst schüchtern.

first aid noun erste Hilfe die.

first class adjective (*ticket, carriage, or hotel*) erster Klasse; **a first-class hotel** ein Hotel erster Klasse; **he always travels first class** er reist immer erster Klasse; **a first-class compartment** ein Erste-Klasse-Abteil.

first floor noun erste Stock der; **on the first floor** im ersten Stock.

firstly adverb zunächst.

first name noun Vorname der (PL die Vornamen).

fir tree noun Tanne die (PL die Tannen).

a b c d e f g h i j k l m n o p q r s t u v w x y z

fish noun Fisch der (PL die Fische).

fish verb fischen, (with a rod) angeln.

fish and chips noun ausgebackener Fisch mit Pommes frites.

fisherman noun Fischer der (PL die Fischer).

fishing noun Fischen das, (with a rod) Angeln das; **to go fishing** fischen/angeln gehen.

fishing rod noun Angel die (PL die Angeln).

fishing tackle noun Angelausrüstung die.

fist noun Faust die (PL die Fäuste).

fit noun 1 (of rage) Anfall der (PL die Anfälle); **your dad'll have a fit when he sees your hair** dein Vater kriegt bestimmt einen Anfall, wenn er deine Haare sieht; **2 an epileptic fit** ein epileptischer Anfall.

fit adjective (healthy) fit; **I feel really fit** ich fühle mich richtig fit; **to keep fit** fit bleiben.

fit verb 1 (be the right size for) (of shoes or a garment) passen (+ DAT); **this skirt doesn't fit me** der Rock passt mir nicht; **2** (be able to be put into) passen in (+ ACC); **will my cases all fit in the car?** passen meine Koffer alle in das Auto?; **the key doesn't fit in the lock** der Schlüssel passt nicht ins Schloss; **3** (install) einbauen SEP.

fitted carpet noun Teppichboden der (PL die Teppichböden).

fitted kitchen noun Einbauküche die (PL die Einbauküchen).

fitting room noun Umkleidekabine die (PL die Umkleidekabinen).

five number fünf; **it's five o'clock** es ist fünf Uhr.

fix verb 1 (repair) reparieren; **Mum's fixed the computer** Mutti hat den Computer repariert; **2** (decide on) festlegen◇ SEP; **to fix a date** einen Termin festlegen; **3** machen (a meal); **I'll fix supper** ich mache Abendessen.

fizzy adjective sprudelnd; **fizzy water** das Sprudelwasser.

flag noun Fahne die (PL die Fahnen).

flame noun Flamme die (PL die Flammen).

flan noun Torte die (PL die Torten); **fruit flan** die Obsttorte.

flap verb (of a bird) to flap its wings mit den Flügeln schlagen◇.

flash noun (on a camera) Blitz der (PL die Blitze); **flash of lightning** der Blitz.

flash verb 1 (a light) aufleuchten SEP, (repeatedly) blinken; **2 to flash by** or **past** vorbeiflitzen SEP (informal).

flashback noun Rückblende die (PL die Rückblenden).

flat noun Wohnung die (PL die Wohnungen); **a third-floor flat** eine Wohnung im dritten Stock.

flat adjective 1 flach; **flat shoes** flache Schuhe; **a flat landscape** eine flache Landschaft; **2 a flat tyre** ein platter Reifen.

flatmate noun Mitbewohner der (PL die Mitbewohner), Mitbewohnerin die (PL die Mitbewohnerinnen).

flatter *noun* schmeicheln (+ DAT).

flavour *noun* **1** Geschmack *der* (PL die Geschmäcke); **the sauce has a bitter flavour** die Soße hat einen bitteren Geschmack; **strawberry flavour** Erdbeergeschmack; **2** (*of drinks, coffee, or tea*) Aroma *das* (PL die Aromen).

flavour *verb* würzen; **vanilla-flavoured** mit Vanillegeschmack.

flea *noun* Floh *der* (PL die Flöhe).

flesh *noun* Fleisch *das*.

flex *noun* Kabel *das* (PL die Kabel).

flight *noun* **1** Flug *der* (PL die Flüge); **the flight was delayed** der Flug hatte Verspätung; **charter flight** Charterflug; **the flight from Munich to London takes an hour and a half** die Flugzeit von München nach London beträgt eineinhalb Stunden; **2 flight of stairs** die Treppe.

flight attendant *noun* Flugbegleiter *der* (PL die Flugbegleiter), Flugbegleiterin *die* (PL die Flugbegleiterinnen).

flipper *noun* Flosse *die* (PL die Flossen).

flirt *verb* flirten.

float *verb* **1** (*on water*) treiben◇; **2** (*in the air*) schweben.

flood *noun* **1** (*of water*) Überschwemmung *die* (PL die Überschwemmungen); **2 to be in floods of tears** in Tränen aufgelöst sein; **3** (*of letters or complaints*) Flut *die*.

flood *verb* überschwemmen.

floodlight *noun* Flutlicht *das*.

floor *noun* **1** Boden *der* (PL die Böden); **your glasses are on the floor** deine Brille liegt auf dem Boden; **2 to sweep the floor** fegen; **to sweep the kitchen floor** die Küche fegen; **3** (*a storey*) Stock *der* (PL die Stock); **on the second floor** im zweiten Stock.

floppy disk *noun* Diskette *die* (PL die Disketten).

florist *noun* Blumenhändler *der* (PL die Blumenhändler), Blumenhändlerin *die* (PL die Blumenhändlerinnen).

flour *noun* Mehl *das*.

flow *verb* fließen◇ (PERF sein).

flower *noun* Blume *die* (PL die Blumen); **bunch of flowers** der Blumenstrauß.

flower *verb* blühen.

flu *noun* Grippe *die* (PL die Grippen); **to have flu** die Grippe haben.

fluent *adjective* **she speaks fluent Italian** sie spricht fließend Italienisch.

fluently *adverb* fließend.

flute *noun* Flöte *die* (PL die Flöten); **to play the flute** Flöte spielen.

fly *noun* Fliege *die* (PL die Fliegen).

fly *verb* **1** fliegen◇ (PERF sein); **we flew to Berlin** wir sind nach Berlin geflogen; **2** steigen lassen (*a kite*); **3** fliegen◇ (PERF haben) (*a plane or helicopter*); **4** (*to pass quickly*) schnell vergehen◇ (PERF sein).

foam *noun* **1** (*foam rubber*) Schaumgummi *der*; **foam mattress** die Schaumgummimatratze; **2** (*on a drink*) Schaum *der*.

focus *noun* Brennpunkt *der* (PL die Brennpunkte) **to be in focus** scharf sein; **to be out of focus** unscharf sein.

a b c d e f g h i j k l m n o p q r s t u v w x y z

focus verb scharf stellen (a camera).

fog noun Nebel der.

foggy adjective neblig.

foil noun (kitchen foil) Alufolie die.

fold noun 1 (in fabric or skin) Falte die (PL die Falten); 2 (in paper) Falz der (PL die Falze).

fold verb falten; **to fold something up** etwas zusammenfalten SEP.

folder noun Mappe die (PL die Mappen).

follow verb 1 folgen (+ DAT); **follow me!** folgen Sie mir!; 2 **do you follow me?** verstehst du, was ich meine?

following adjective folgend; **the following evening** am folgenden Abend.

fond adjective **to be fond of somebody** jemanden gern haben; **I'm very fond of him** ich habe ihn sehr gern.

food noun 1 Essen das; **I have to buy some food** ich muss noch etwas zu essen einkaufen; 2 **I like German food** ich mag die deutsche Küche; 3 (stocks) Lebensmittel (plural); **we bought food for the holiday** wir haben Lebensmittel für die Ferien eingekauft.

food poisoning noun Lebensmittelvergiftung die.

fool noun Dummkopf der (PL die Dummköpfe).

foot noun Fuß der (PL die Füße); **Lucy came on foot** Lucy ist zu Fuß gekommen.

football noun Fußball der (PL die Fußbälle); **to play football** Fußball spielen.

footballer noun Fußballspieler der (PL die Fußballspieler), Fußballspielerin die (PL die Fußballspielerinnen).

footpath noun Fußweg der (PL die Fußwege).

footprint noun Fußabdruck der (PL die Fußabdrücke).

footstep noun Schritt der (PL die Schritte).

for preposition 1 für (+ ACC); **a present for my mother** ein Geschenk für meine Mutter; **what's it for?** wofür ist das?; 2 (for a particular occasion or event) zu (+ DAT); **sausages for lunch** Würstchen zum Mittagessen; **Sam got a bike for Christmas** Sam hat zu Weihnachten ein Rad bekommen; **what for?** wozu?; 3 (time expressions in the past but continuing in the present) seit (+ DAT); **I've been waiting here for an hour** (and I'm still waiting) ich warte hier seit einer Stunde; **my brother's been living in Berlin for three years** (and he still lives there) mein Bruder wohnt seit drei Jahren in Berlin; 4 (time expressions in the past or the future) **I studied French for six years** (but I no longer do) ich habe sechs Jahre lang Französisch gelernt; **I'll be away for four days** ich werde vier Tage nicht da sein; 5 (with a price) für (+ ACC); **I sold my bike for fifty pounds** ich habe mein Rad für fünfzig Pfund verkauft; 6 **what's the German for 'bee'?** wie heißt 'bee' auf Deutsch?

foul

forbid *verb* verbieten◇; **to forbid somebody to do something** jemandem verbieten, etwas zu tun.

forbidden *adjective* verboten.

force *noun* Kraft die (PL die Kräfte).

force *verb* zwingen◇; **to force somebody to do something** jemanden zwingen, etwas zu tun.

forecast *noun* Vorhersage die (PL die Vorhersagen).

foreground *noun* Vordergrund der; **in the foreground** im Vordergrund.

forehead *noun* Stirn die (PL die Stirnen).

foreign *adjective* **1** ausländisch; **in a foreign country** im Ausland; **from a foreign country** aus dem Ausland; **2 foreign language** die Fremdsprache.

foreigner *noun* Ausländer der (PL die Ausländer), Ausländerin die (PL die Ausländerinnen).

forest *noun* Wald die (PL die Wälder).

forever *adverb* **1** immer; **I'd like to stay here forever** ich möchte für immer hier bleiben; **2** (*non-stop*) ständig; **he's forever asking questions** er fragt ständig.

forget *verb* vergessen◇; **to forget about something** etwas vergessen; **we've forgotten the bread** wir haben das Brot vergessen; **to forget to do something** vergessen, etwas zu tun; **I forgot to phone** ich habe vergessen anzurufen.

forgive *verb* verzeihen◇ (+ DAT) **to forgive somebody** jemandem verzeihen; **I forgave him** ich habe ihm verziehen; **to forgive somebody for doing something**

jemandem verzeihen, dass er/sie etwas getan hat; **I forgave her for losing my ring** ich habe ihr verziehen, dass sie meinen Ring verloren hat.

fork *noun* Gabel die (PL die Gabeln).

form *noun* **1** Formular das (PL die Formulare); **to fill in a form** ein Formular ausfüllen; **2** (*shape or kind*) Form die (PL die Formen); **in the form of** in Form von; **to be on form** gut in Form sein; **3** (*in school*) Klasse die (PL die Klassen).

form *verb* bilden.

formal *adjective* formell (*invitation, event*).

format *noun* Format das (PL die Formate).

former *adjective* ehemalig; **a former pupil** ein ehemaliger Schüler, eine ehemalige Schülerin.

fortnight *noun* vierzehn Tage (*plural*); **we're going to Spain for a fortnight** wir fahren vierzehn Tage nach Spanien.

fortunately *adverb* glücklicherweise.

fortune *noun* Vermögen das (PL die Vermögen); **to make a fortune** ein Vermögen machen.

forty *number* vierzig.

forward *noun* (*in sport*) Stürmer der (PL die Stürmer).

forward *adverb* (*to the front*) nach vorn; **to move forward** vorrücken SEP (PERF *sein*); **a seat further forward** ein Platz weiter vorn.

foster child *noun* Pflegekind das (PL die Pflegekinder).

foul *noun* (*in sport*) Foul das (PL die Fouls).

foul *adjective* scheußlich; **the weather's foul** das Wetter ist scheußlich.

fountain *noun* Brunnen *der* (PL die Brunnen).

fountain pen *noun* Füllfederhalter *der* (PL die Füllfederhalter).

four *number* vier; **it's four o'clock** es ist vier Uhr; ★ **on all fours** auf allen vieren.

fourteen *number* vierzehn.

fourth *number* vierter/vierte/ viertes; **the fourth of July** der vierte Juli; **on the fourth floor** im vierten Stock.

fox *noun* Fuchs *der* (PL die Füchse).

fragile *adjective* zerbrechlich.

frame *noun* **1** Rahmen *der* (PL die Rahmen); **2** (*of spectacles*) Gestell *das* (PL die Gestelle).

franc *noun* **1** (*Swiss*) Franken *der* (PL die Franken); **a fifty-franc note** ein Fünfzig-Franken-Schein; **2** (*former French and Belgian currencies*) Franc *der* (PL die Francs).

France *noun* Frankreich *das*; **to France** nach Frankreich.

frantic *adjective* **1** (*very upset*) **to be frantic** außer sich (DAT) sein; **I was frantic with worry** ich war außer mir vor Sorge; **2** (*desperate*) fieberhaft (*effort or search*).

freckle *noun* Sommersprosse *die* (PL die Sommersprossen).

free *adjective* **1** (*when you don't pay*) kostenlos; **a free ride** eine kostenlose Fahrt; **a free ticket** eine Freikarte; **2** (*without charge*) umsonst; **to do something for free** etwas umsonst machen; **3** (*not*

occupied) frei; **are you free on Thursday?** haben Sie am Donnerstag Zeit?; **4** sugar-free ohne Zucker; **lead-free** bleifrei.

free *verb* befreien.

freedom *noun* Freiheit *die*.

free gift *noun* Werbegeschenk *das* (PL die Werbegeschenke).

free kick *noun* Freistoß *der* (PL die Freistöße).

freeze *verb* **1** (*in a freezer*) einfrieren ✧ SEP; **to freeze raspberries** Himbeeren einfrieren; **2** (*in cold weather*) frieren ✧; **it's freezing** es friert; **3** (*become covered with ice*) zufrieren ✧ SEP (PERF sein); **the pond is frozen** der Teich ist zugefroren.

freezer *noun* Gefrierschrank *der* (PL die Gefrierschränke).

freezing *noun* below freezing unter Null; **three degrees above freezing** drei Grad über Null.

freezing *adjective* **1 I'm freezing** ich friere sehr; **2 it's freezing outside** es ist eiskalt draußen.

French *noun* **1** (*the language*) Französisch *das*; **2** (*the people*) **the French** die Franzosen.

French *adjective* **1** französisch; **Jean-Marc is French** Jean-Marc ist Franzose; **2** (*teacher or lesson*) Französisch-; **the French class** der Französischunterricht.

French bean *noun* grüne Bohne *die* (PL die grünen Bohnen).

French dressing *noun* Vinaigrette *die*.

French fries *plural noun* Pommes frites (*plural*).

Frenchman noun Franzose der (PL die Franzosen).

French window noun Terrassentür die (PL die Terrassentüren).

Frenchwoman noun Französin die (PL die Französinnen).

frequent adjective häufig.

fresh adjective frisch; **fresh eggs** frische Eier; **I'm going out for some fresh air** ich gehe ein bisschen frische Luft schnappen.

Friday noun 1 Freitag der (PL die Freitage); **next Friday** nächsten Freitag; **last Friday** letzten Freitag; **on Friday (am)** Freitag; **I'll phone you on Friday evening** ich rufe dich Freitagabend an; **every Friday** jeden Freitag; **Good Friday** Karfreitag; 2 **on Fridays** freitags; **closed on Fridays** freitags geschlossen.

fridge noun Kühlschrank der (PL die Kühlschränke); **put it in the fridge** stell es in den Kühlschrank.

friend noun 1 Freund der (PL die Freunde), Freundin die (PL die Freundinnen); **a friend of mine** ein Freund von mir; 2 **to make friends** sich anfreunden; **he made friends with Danny** er hat sich mit Danny angefreundet; **he is friends with Danny** er ist mit Danny befreundet.

friendly adjective freundlich.

friendship noun Freundschaft die (PL die Freundschaften).

fries plural noun Pommes frites (plural).

fright noun 1 Schreck der (PL die Schrecke); **to have** or **get a fright** einen Schreck bekommen; 2 **you**

gave me a fright! du hast mich erschreckt!

frighten verb 1 (of an explosion or shot) erschrecken; 2 (scare or threaten) **to frighten somebody** jemandem Angst machen.

frightened adjective **to be frightened** Angst haben; **Martin's frightened of snakes** Martin hat Angst vor Schlangen.

frightening adjective beängstigend.

fringe noun 1 (hairstyle) Pony der (PL die Ponys); 2 (on clothes or a curtain) Fransen (plural).

frog noun Frosch der (PL die Frösche).

from preposition 1 von (+ DAT); **ten metres from the cinema** zehn Meter vom Kino; **a letter from Tom** ein Brief von Tom; **from Monday to Friday** von Montag bis Freitag; **from now on** von jetzt an; 2 aus (+ DAT); **he comes from Dublin** er kommt aus Dublin; **the train from London** der Zug aus London; 3 **from seven o'clock onwards** ab sieben Uhr; **from then on** von da ab.

front noun 1 (of a cupboard, card, or envelope) Vorderseite die (PL die Vorderseiten), (of a building) Vorderfront die (PL die Vorderfronten); 2 (of a garment or in an interior) Vorderteil das (PL die Vorderteile); 3 (at the seaside) Strandpromenade die (PL die Strandpromenaden); 4 (of a car) **to sit in (the) front** vorne sitzen; 5 (of a train or queue) vordere Ende das; 6 (of a procession or in a race) Spitze die; 7 **in/at the front** vorne;

in/at the front of vorne in (+ DAT, or + ACC *with movement towards a place*); **there are still seats at the front of the train** es gibt hin Plätze vorne im Zug; **we got on at the front of the train** wir sind vorne in den Zug eingestiegen; **8 in front of** vor (+ DAT, or + ACC *with movement towards a place*); **in front of the TV** vor dem Fernseher; **in front of me** vor mir.

front *adjective* **1** vorderer/vordere/ vorderes; **in the front rows** in den vorderen Reihen; **2** Vorder-; **front seat** (*of a car*) der Vordersitz; **front wheel** das Vorderrad.

front door *noun* Haustür die (PL die Haustüren).

frontier *noun* Grenze die (PL die Grenzen).

frost *noun* Frost der.

frosty *adjective* frostig.

frown *verb* die Stirn runzeln; **he frowned at us** er blickte uns mit gerunzelter Stirn an.

frozen *adjective* (*in a freezer*) tiefgekühlt; **a frozen pizza** eine Tiefkühlpizza.

fruit *noun* **1** (*a single fruit or type of fruit*) Frucht die (PL die Früchte); **2** (*various fruits*) Obst das; **we bought cheese and fruit** wir haben Käse und Obst gekauft.

fruit juice *noun* Fruchtsaft der (PL die Fruchtsäfte).

fruit machine *noun* Spielautomat der (PL die Spielautomaten).

fruit salad *noun* Obstsalat der (PL die Obstsalate).

frustrated *adjective* frustriert.

fry *verb* braten◇; **we fried fish** wir haben Fisch gebraten; **fried potatoes** Bratkartoffeln; **fried egg** das Spiegelei.

frying pan *noun* Bratpfanne die (PL die Bratpfannen).

fuel *noun* (*for a car*) Kraftstoff der.

full *adjective* **1** voll; **the glass is full** das Glas ist voll; **I'm full** ich bin voll (*informal*); **2 full of** voller (+ GEN); **the train was full of tourists** der Zug war voller Touristen; **3 at full speed** in voller Fahrt; **4 to write something out in full** etwas voll ausschreiben.

full stop *noun* Punkt der (PL die Punkte).

full-time *adjective* **a full-time job** eine Ganztagsstelle.

fully *adverb* völlig.

fun *noun* **1** Spaß der; **have fun!** viel Spaß!; **we had fun catching the ponies** die Ponys einzufangen machte uns Spaß; **skiing is fun** Skifahren macht Spaß; **I do it for fun** ich mache es aus Spaß; **2 to have fun** sich amüsieren; **★ to make fun of somebody** sich über jemanden lustig machen.

funds *plural noun* Geldmittel (*plural*).

funeral *noun* Beerdigung die (PL die Beerdigungen).

funfair *noun* Jahrmarkt der (PL die Jahrmärkte).

funny *adjective* **1** (*amusing*) lustig; **a funny story** eine lustige Geschichte; **he's so funny** er ist so witzig; **2** (*strange*) komisch; **a funny noise** ein komisches Geräusch; **that's funny, I'm sure I**

paid das ist komisch, ich bin mir sicher, dass ich gezahlt habe.

fur noun **1** (on an animal) Fell das (PL die Felle); **2** (for a coat) Pelz der (PL die Pelze); **fur coat** der Pelzmantel.

furious adjective wütend; **she was furious with Steve** sie war wütend auf Steve.

furniture noun Möbel (plural); **to buy some furniture** Möbel kaufen; **piece of furniture** das Möbelstück.

further adverb weiter; **further than the station** weiter als der Bahnhof; **ten kilometres further on** zehn Kilometer weiter; **further off** weiter entfernt; **further forward** weiter vorn; **further back** weiter hinten.

fuse noun Sicherung die (PL die Sicherungen).

fuss noun Theater das; **to make a fuss** ein Theater machen; **to make a big fuss about the bill** ein großes Theater um die Rechnung machen.

fussy adjective **to be fussy about something** wählerisch in etwas (DAT) sein (food, for example).

future noun Zukunft die; **in future** in Zukunft.

Gg

gadget noun Gerät das (PL die Geräte).

gain verb **1** gewinnen✧; **in order to gain time** um Zeit zu gewinnen; **2** profitieren; **to gain by something** von etwas profitieren.

gale noun Sturm der (PL die Stürme).

gallery noun Galerie die (PL die Galerien).

gamble verb spielen (for money).

game noun **1** Spiel das (PL die Spiele); **game of chance** das Glücksspiel; **board game** das Brettspiel; **2 to have a game of cards** eine Partie Karten spielen; **3 to have a game of football** Fußball spielen; **4 games** (at school) Sport der.

gang noun Bande die (PL die Banden); **all the gang were there** die ganze Bande war da.

gap noun **1** (hole) Lücke die (PL die Lücken); **2** (in time) Pause die (PL die Pausen); **a two-hour gap** eine zweistündige Pause; **3 age gap** der Altersunterschied.

gap year noun Orientierungsjahr das (PL die Orientierungsjahre).

garage noun **1** (for keeping your car) Garage die (PL die Garagen); **2** (for repairing cars) Autowerkstatt die (PL die Autowerkstätten); **3** (for petrol) Tankstelle die (PL die Tankstellen).

garden noun Garten der (PL die Gärten).

gardener noun Gärtner der (PL die Gärtner), Gärtnerin die (PL die Gärtnerinnen).

gardening noun Gartenarbeit die.

garlic noun Knoblauch der.

garment noun Kleidungsstück das (PL die Kleidungsstücke).

gas noun Gas das.

gas cooker noun Gasherd der (PL die Gasherde).

a b c d e f g h i j k l m n o p q r s t u v w x y z

gas fire noun Gasofen der (PL die Gasöfen).

gas meter noun Gaszähler der (PL die Gaszähler).

gate noun 1 (in garden) Pforte die (PL die Pforten); 2 (in field) Gatter das (PL die Gatter); 3 (at an airport) Flugsteig der (PL die Flugsteige).

gather verb 1 (of people) sich versammeln; 2 sammeln (fruit, vegetables, flowers); 3 as far as I can gather soweit ich weiß.

gay adjective (homosexual) schwul (informal).

gaze verb to gaze at something etwas anstarren SEP.

GCSEs noun plural (You can explain GCSEs briefly as follows: Dies sind Prüfungen, die im Alter von ca 16 Jahren in bis zu 12 Fächern abgelegt werden. Sie werden von A* (beste Note) bis N (nicht bestanden) benotet. Viele Schüler und Schülerinnen machen nach den GCSEs weiter und legen die A-level Prüfungen ab) SEE A levels.

gear lever noun Schalthebel der (PL die Schalthebel).

gear noun 1 (in a car) Gang der (PL die Gänge); to change gear schalten; 2 (equipment) Ausrüstung die; camping gear die Campingausrüstung; 3 (things) Sachen (plural); I've left all my gear at Gary's ich habe alle meine Sachen bei Gary gelassen.

gel noun Gel das (PL die Gele).

Gemini noun Zwillinge (plural); Steph's Gemini Steph ist Zwilling.

gender noun (of a word) Geschlecht das (PL die Geschlechter); what is the gender of 'Haus'? welches Geschlecht hat 'Haus'?

general noun General der (PL die Generäle).

general adjective allgemein; in general im Allgemeinen; the general election die allgemeinen Wahlen.

general knowledge noun Allgemeinwissen das.

generally adverb im Allgemeinen.

generation noun Generation die (PL die Generationen).

generator noun Generator der (PL die Generatoren).

generous adjective großzügig.

genetics noun Genetik die.

Geneva noun Genf das; Lake Geneva der Genfer See.

genius noun Genie das (PL die Genies); Lisa, you're a genius! Lisa, du bis ein Genie!

gentle adjective sanft.

gentleman noun Herr der (PL die Herren); ladies and gentlemen! meine Damen und Herren!

gently adverb sanft.

gents noun (lavatory) Herrentoilette die (PL die Herrentoiletten); (on a sign) 'Gents' 'Herren'; where's the gents? wo ist die Herrentoilette?

genuine adjective 1 (real, authentic) echt; a genuine diamond ein echter Brillant; 2 aufrichtig (person); she's very genuine sie ist sehr aufrichtig.

geography noun Geographie die, (at school) Erdkunde die.

germ *noun* **1** Keim *der* (PL die Keime); **2** *(causing a cold)* germs Bazillen *(plural)*.

German *noun* **1** *(person)* Deutsche *der/die* (PL die Deutschen); **2** *(language)* Deutsch *das*; **in German** auf Deutsch.

German *adjective* deutsch; **he is German** er ist Deutscher; **she is German** sie ist Deutsche; **our German teacher** unser Deutschlehrer, unsere Deutschlehrerin.

Germany *noun* Deutschland *das*; **to Germany** nach Deutschland; **from Germany** aus Deutschland.

get *verb* **1** *(obtain, receive)* bekommen✧, kriegen *(informal)*; **I got a bike for my birthday** ich habe ein Rad zum Geburtstag bekommen; **Fred got the job** Fred hat die Stelle bekommen; **she got a shock** sie hat einen Schreck gekriegt; **I got a good mark for my German homework** ich habe auf meine Deutschhausaufgaben eine gute Note bekommen; **2** *he's got lots of money* er hat viel Geld; **she's got long hair** sie hat lange Haare; **3** *(fetch)* holen; **I'll get some bread** ich hole Brot; **I'll get your bag for you** ich hole dir deine Tasche; **4** *to have got to do something* etwas tun müssen✧; **I've got to phone before midday** ich muss vor Mittag anrufen; **5** *to get (to) somewhere* irgendwo ankommen✧ SEP (PERF *sein*); **when I got to London** als ich in London ankam; **we got here this morning**

wir sind heute Morgen angekommen; **what time did they get there?** wann sind sie angekommen; **6** *(become)* werden✧ (PERF *sein*); **it's getting late** es wird spät; **it's getting dark** es wird dunkel; **7** *to get something done* etwas machen lassen✧; **I'm getting my hair cut today** ich lasse mir heute die Haare schneiden.

● **to get back** zurückkommen✧ SEP (PERF *sein*); **Mum gets back at six** Mutti kommt um sechs zurück.

● **to get something back** etwas zurückbekommen✧ SEP, etwas zurückkriegen SEP *(informal)*; **did you get your books back?** hast du deine Bücher zurückbekommen?

● **to get into something** *(a vehicle)* in etwas (ACC) einsteigen✧ SEP (PERF *sein*); **he got into the car** er ist ins Auto eingestiegen.

● **to get off something** *(a vehicle)* aus etwas (DAT) aussteigen✧ SEP (PERF *sein*); **I got off the train at Banbury** ich bin in Banbury aus dem Zug ausgestiegen.

● **to get on: how's Amanda getting on?** wie gehts Amanda?

● **to get on something** *(a vehicle)* in etwas (ACC) einsteigen✧ SEP (PERF *sein*); **she got on the train at Reading** sie ist in Reading in den Zug eingestiegen.

● **to get on with somebody** sich mit jemandem verstehen✧; **she doesn't get on with her brother** sie versteht sich nicht mit ihrem Bruder.

get

a
b
c
d
e
f
g
h
i
j
k
l
m
n
o
p
q
r
s
t
u
v
w
x
y
z

a
b
c
d
e
f
g
h
i
j
k
l
m
n
o
p
q
r
s
t
u
v
w
x
y
z

ghost

• **to get out of something** (*a vehicle*) aussteigen◇ SEP (PERF *sein*); **Laura got out of the car** Laura ist aus dem Auto ausgestiegen.

• **to get together** sich wieder sehen◇ SEP; **we must get together soon** wir müssen uns bald mal wieder sehen.

• **to get up** aufstehen◇ SEP (PERF *sein*); **I get up at seven** ich stehe um sieben auf.

ghost *noun* Geist *der* (PL die Geister).

giant *noun* Riese *der* (PL die Riesen).

giant *adjective* riesig; **a giant lorry** ein riesiger Lastwagen.

gift *noun* **1** Geschenk *das* (PL die Geschenke); **a Christmas gift** ein Weihnachtsgeschenk; **2** Begabung *die*; **to have a gift for something** für etwas (ACC) begabt sein; **Jo has a real gift for languages** Jo ist wirklich sprachbegabt.

gigabyte *noun* Gigabyte *das* (PL die Gigabytes); **a fifty gigabyte hard disk** eine Festplatte mit fünfzig Gigabyte Speicherkapazität.

gigantic *adjective* riesig.

gin *noun* Gin *der* (PL die Gins).

ginger *noun* Ingwer *der* (PL die Ingwer).

gipsy *noun* Zigeuner *der* (PL die Zigeuner), Zigeunerin *die* (PL die Zigeunerinnen).

giraffe *noun* Giraffe *die* (PL die Giraffen).

girl *noun* Mädchen *das* (PL die Mädchen); **three boys and four girls** drei Jungen und vier Mädchen; **when I was a little girl I**

had ... als kleines Mädchen hatte ich ....

girlfriend *noun* Freundin *die* (PL die Freundinnen).

give *verb* **1** geben◇; **to give something to somebody** jemandem etwas geben; **I'll give you my address** ich gebe dir meine Adresse; **give me the key** gib mir den Schlüssel; **Yasmin's dad gave her the money** Yasmins Vater hat ihr das Geld gegeben; **2** (*give as a gift*) schenken; **to give somebody a present** jemandem etwas schenken.

• **to give something away** etwas weggeben◇ SEP; **she's given away all her books** sie hat alle ihre Bücher weggegeben.

• **to give something back to somebody** jemandem etwas zurückgeben◇ SEP; **I gave her back the keys** ich habe ihr die Schlüssel zurückgegeben.

• **to give in** nachgeben◇ SEP; **my mum said no but she gave in in the end** meine Mutti hat nein gesagt, aber schließlich hat sie nachgegeben.

• **to give up** aufgeben◇ SEP; **I give up!** ich gebe auf!

• **to give up doing something** etwas aufgeben◇ SEP; **she's given up smoking** sie hat das Rauchen aufgegeben.

glad *adjective* froh; **I'm glad to hear he's better** ich bin froh, dass es ihm besser geht; **I'm glad to be back** ich bin froh, dass ich wieder zurück bin.

glass noun Glas das (PL die Gläser); **a glass of water** ein Glas Wasser; **a glass table** ein Glastisch.

glasses plural noun Brille die (PL die Brillen); **to wear glasses** eine Brille tragen.

glider noun Segelflugzeug das (PL die Segelflugzeuge).

global warming noun globale Temperaturanstieg der.

glove noun Handschuh der (PL die Handschuhe); **a pair of gloves** ein Paar Handschuhe.

glove compartment noun Handschuhfach das (PL die Handschuhfächer).

glue noun Klebstoff der (PL die Klebstoffe).

go noun 1 (in a game) **whose go is it?** wer ist dran?; **it's my go** ich bin dran; 2 **to have a go at doing something** versuchen, etwas zu tun; **I'll have a go at mending it** ich versuche, es zu reparieren.

go verb 1 (on foot) gehen ✧ (PERF sein); **to go to school** in die Schule gehen; **Mark's gone to the dentist's** Mark ist zum Zahnarzt gegangen; **to go shopping** einkaufen gehen; 2 (in a vehicle) fahren ✧ (PERF sein); **we're going to London** wir fahren nach London; **we're planning to go early** wir wollen früh losfahren; **to go on holiday** in die Ferien fahren; 3 (by plane) fliegen ✧ (PERF sein); 4 **to go for a walk** spazieren gehen ✧ SEP (PERF sein); 5 (with another verb) **I'm going to do it** ich werde es tun; **I'm going to make some tea** ich mache Tee; **he was going to phone you** er wollte dich anrufen;

6 (leave) gehen ✧ (PERF sein); **Pauline's already gone** Pauline ist schon gegangen; 7 (on a journey) abfahren ✧ SEP (PERF sein); **when does the train go?** wann fährt der Zug ab?; 8 (turn out) verlaufen ✧ (PERF sein) (event); **how did your evening go?** wie ist dein Abend verlaufen?; **the party went well** die Party war gut.

● **to go away** 1 weggehen ✧ SEP (PERF sein); **go away!** geh weg!; 2 (on holiday) verreisen (PERF sein).

● **to go back** 1 zurückgehen ✧ SEP (PERF sein); **I'm going back to Germany in March** ich werde im März nach Deutschland zurückkehren; **I'm not going back there again!** ich gehe da nicht wieder zurück!; 2 **I went back home** ich bin nach Hause gegangen.

● **to go down** 1 hinuntergehen ✧ SEP (PERF sein); **she's gone down to the kitchen** sie ist in die Küche hinuntergegangen; **to go down the stairs** die Treppe hinuntergehen; 2 (price, temperature) fallen ✧ (PERF sein); 3 (tyre, balloon, airbed) Luft verlieren ✧.

● **to go in** hineingehen ✧ SEP (PERF sein); **he went in and shut the door** er ist hineingegangen und hat die Tür zugemacht.

● **to go into** 1 (person) gehen in (+ ACC) PERF sein); **Fran went into the kitchen** Fran ging in die Küche; 2 (object) passen in (+ ACC); **this book won't go into my bag** dieses Buch passt nicht in meine Tasche.

● **to go off** 1 (bomb) explodieren

a
b
c
d
e
f
g
h
i
j
k
l
m
n
o
p
q
r
s
t
u
v
w
x
y
z

(PERF *sein*); **2** (*alarm clock*) klingeln; **my alarm clock went off at six** mein Wecker hat um sechs geklingelt; **3** (*fire or burglar alarm*) losgehen♦ SEP (PERF *sein*); **the fire alarm went off** der Feuermelder ging los.

● **to go on 1 what's going on?** was ist los?; **2 to go on doing something** weiter etwas tun; **she went on talking** sie hat weitergeredet; **3 to go on about something** stundenlang von etwas (DAT) reden; **he's always going on about his dog** er redet stundenlang von seinem Hund.

● **to go out 1** (*for an evening*) ausgehen♦ SEP, weggehen♦ SEP (PERF *sein*) (*informal*); **we're going out tonight** wir gehen heute Abend aus; **2** (*leave*) **she went out of the kitchen** sie ist aus der Küche gegangen; **3 to be going out with somebody** mit jemandem gehen♦ (PERF *sein*) (*informal*); **she's going out with my brother** sie geht mit meinem Bruder; **4** (*light, fire*) ausgehen♦ SEP (PERF *sein*); **the light went out** das Licht ist ausgegangen.

● **to go past something** an etwas (DAT) vorbeigehen♦ SEP; **we went past your house** wir sind an eurem Haus vorbeigegangen.

● **to go round: to go round to somebody's house** jemanden besuchen; **we went round to Fred's last night** wir haben gestern Abend Fred besucht.

● **to go round something 1** um etwas (ACC) herumgehen♦ SEP (PERF

sein) (*building, park, garden*); **2** besichtigen (*museum, monument*).

● **to go through 1 the train goes through Cologne** der Zug fährt durch Köln; **2 to go through a room** durch ein Zimmer gehen; **3** (*search*) durchsuchen.

● **to go up 1** (*person*) hinaufgehen♦ SEP (PERF *sein*); **she's gone up to her room** sie ist in ihr Zimmer hinaufgegangen; **to go up the stairs** die Treppe hinaufgehen; **2** (*prices*) steigen♦ (PERF *sein*); **the price of petrol has gone up** die Benzinpreise sind gestiegen.

goal noun Tor das (PL die Tore); **to score a goal** ein Tor schießen; **to win by 3 goals to 2** mit 3 zu 2 Toren gewinnen.

goalkeeper noun Torwart der (PL die Torwarte), Torfrau die (PL die Torfrauen).

goat noun Ziege die (PL die Ziegen).

God noun Gott der; **to believe in God** an Gott glauben.

god noun Gott der (PL die Götter).

godchild noun Patenkind das (PL die Patenkinder).

goddaughter noun Patentochter die (PL die Patentöchter).

goddess noun Göttin die (PL die Göttinnen).

godfather noun Pate der (PL die Paten).

godmother noun Patin die (PL die Patinnen).

godson noun Patensohn der (PL die Patensöhne).

goggles plural noun Schutzbrille die (PL die Schutzbrillen); **swimming**

goggles Schwimmbrille die (PL die Schwimmbrillen); **skiing goggles** Skibrille die (PL die Skibrillen).

gold noun Gold das; **a gold bracelet** ein Goldarmband.

goldfish noun Goldfisch der (PL die Goldfische).

golf noun Golf das; **to play golf** Golf spielen.

golf club noun 1 (place) Golfklub der (PL die Golfklubs); 2 (iron) Golfschläger der (PL die Golfschläger).

golf course noun Golfplatz der (PL die Golfplätze).

golfer noun Golfspieler der (PL die Golfspieler), Golfspielerin die (PL die Golfspielerinnen).

good adjective 1 gut; **she's a good teacher** sie ist eine gute Lehrerin; **the cherries are very good** die Kirschen sind sehr gut; **2 to be good for you** gesund sein; **tomatoes are good for you** Tomaten sind gesund; **3 good at** gut in (+ DAT); **she's good at maths** sie ist gut in Mathe; **he's good at drawing** er kann gut zeichnen; **4** (well-behaved) brav; **be good!** sei brav!; **5** (kind) nett; **she's been very good to me** sie ist sehr nett zu mir gewesen; **6 for good** endgültig; **I've stopped smoking for good** ich habe das Rauchen endgültig aufgegeben.

good afternoon exclamation guten Tag!

goodbye exclamation auf Wiedersehen!

good evening exclamation guten Abend!.

Good Friday noun Karfreitag der (PL die Karfreitage).

good-looking adjective gut aussehend.

good morning exclamation guten Morgen!

goodness exclamation meine Güte!; **for goodness sake!** um Himmels willen!

good night exclamation gute Nacht!

goods plural noun Waren (plural).

goods train noun Güterzug der (PL die Güterzüge).

goose noun Gans die (PL die Gänse).

gorgeous adjective herrlich; **it's a gorgeous day** es ist ein herrlicher Tag.

gorilla noun Gorilla der (PL die Gorillas).

gosh exclamation Mensch!

gossip noun 1 (person) Klatschbase die (PL die Klatschbasen); 2 (scandal) Klatsch der.

gossip verb klatschen.

government noun Regierung die (PL die Regierungen).

grab verb 1 packen; **she grabbed my arm** sie packte mich am Arm; **2 to grab something from somebody** jemandem etwas (ACC) entreißen❖; **he grabbed the book from me** er hat mir das Buch entrissen.

grade noun (mark) Note die (PL die Noten); **to get good grades** gute Noten bekommen.

gradual adjective allmählich.

gradually adverb allmählich; **the weather got gradually better** das Wetter wurde allmählich besser.

a b c d e f g h i j k l m n o p q r s t u v w x y z

a

graffiti plural noun Graffiti (plural).

b

grain noun Korn das (PL die Körner).

c

gram noun Gramm das; **100 grams of salami** hundert Gramm Salami.

d

grammar noun Grammatik die.

e

grammar school noun Gymnasium das (PL die Gymnasien).

f

g

grammatical adjective grammatikalisch; **a grammatical error** eine Grammatikfehler.

h

gran noun Oma die (PL die Omas).

i

grandchildren plural noun Enkelkinder (plural).

j

granddad noun Opa der (PL die Opas).

k

granddaughter noun Enkelin die (PL die Enkelinnen).

l

grandfather noun Großvater der (PL die Großväter).

m

grandma noun Oma die (PL die Omas).

n

grandmother noun Großmutter die (PL die Großmütter).

o

grandpa noun Opa der (PL die Opas).

p

grandparents plural noun Großeltern (plural).

q

grandson noun Enkel der (PL die Enkel).

r

s

granny noun Omi die (PL die Omis).

t

grape noun Weintraube die (PL die Weintrauben); **a grape** eine Weintraube; **to buy some grapes** Weintrauben kaufen; **do you like grapes?** magst du Weintrauben?; **a bunch of grapes** eine ganze Weintraube.

u

v

w

x

grapefruit noun Grapefruit die (PL die Grapefruits).

y

z

graph noun Grafik die (PL die Grafiken).

grasp verb festhalten◇ SEP.

grass noun 1 Gras das; **to lie on the grass** im Gras liegen; 2 (lawn) Rasen der (PL die Rasen); **to cut the grass** den Rasen mähen.

grasshopper noun Heuschrecke die (PL die Heuschrecken).

grate verb reiben◇; **grated cheese** geriebener Käse.

grateful adjective dankbar; **to be grateful to somebody** jemandem dankbar sein.

grater noun Reibe die (PL die Reiben).

grave noun Grab das (PL die Gräber).

graveyard noun Friedhof der (PL die Friedhöfe).

gravy noun Soße die (PL die Soßen).

grease noun Fett das.

greasy adjective 1 fettig; **to have greasy skin** fettige Haut haben; 2 (food) fett.

great adjective 1 groß; **a great poet** ein großer Dichter; 2 (terrific) großartig; **it was a great party** das war eine großartige Party; **great!** großartig!, prima! (informal); 3 **a great deal of** sehr viel; **a great many** sehr viele.

Great Britain noun Großbritannien das.

Greece noun Griechenland das.

greedy adjective gierig, (with food) gefräßig.

Greek noun 1 (person) Grieche der (PL die Griechen), Griechin die (PL die Griechinnen); 2 (language) Griechisch das.

Greek adjective griechisch; **she's Greek** sie ist Griechin.

green noun **1** (colour) Grün das; **a pale green** ein Hellgrün; **2 the Greens** (ecologists) die Grünen.

green adjective **1** grün; **a green door** eine grüne Tür; **2 the Green Party** die Grünen (plural).

greengrocer noun Obst- und Gemüsehändler der (PL die Obst- und Gemüsehändler).

greenhouse noun Gewächshaus das (PL die Gewächshäuser).

greenhouse effect noun Treibhauseffekt der.

greetings plural noun Grüße (plural); **Season's Greetings** fröhliche Weihnachten und ein glückliches neues Jahr.

greetings card noun Glückwunschkarte die (PL die Glückwunschkarten).

grey adjective grau.

greyhound noun Windhund der (PL die Windhunde).

grid noun **1** (grating) Gitter das (PL die Gitter); **2** (network) Netz das (PL die Netze).

grief noun Trauer die.

grill noun Grill der (PL die Grills).

grill verb grillen; **I'm going to grill the sausages** ich grille die Würstchen.

grim adjective grauenvoll.

grin verb grinsen.

grind verb mahlen.

grip verb (hold on to) festhalten✧ SEP.

groan noun Stöhnen das.

groan verb stöhnen.

grocer noun Lebensmittelhändler der (PL die Lebensmittelhändler).

groceries plural noun Lebensmittel (plural).

grocer's noun Lebensmittelgeschäft das (PL die Lebensmittelgeschäfte).

groom noun Bräutigam der (PL die Bräutigame); **the bride and groom** das Brautpaar.

gross adjective **1 a gross injustice** eine schreiende Ungerechtigkeit; **2** grob; **a gross error** ein grober Fehler; **3** (disgusting) ekelhaft; **the food was gross!** das Essen war ekelhaft!

ground noun **1** Boden der; **to sit on the ground** auf dem Boden sitzen; **2** (for sport) Sportplatz der (PL die Sportplätze); **football ground** der Fußballplatz.

ground adjective gemahlen; **ground coffee** gemahlener Kaffee.

ground floor noun Erdgeschoss das; **they live on the ground floor** sie wohnen im Erdgeschoss.

group noun Gruppe die (PL die Gruppen).

grow verb (get bigger) **1** wachsen✧ (PERF sein); **your hair grows very quickly** deine Haare wachsen sehr schnell; **my little sister's grown quite a bit this year** meine kleine Schwester ist dieses Jahr ein ganzes Stück gewachsen; **the number of students is still growing** die Zahl der Studenten wächst noch; **2** anbauen SEP (fruit, vegetables); **3 to grow a beard** sich (DAT) einen Bart wachsen lassen; **4** (become) werden✧ (PERF sein); **to grow old** alt werden.

a
b
c
d
e
f
g
h
i
j
k
l
m
n
o
p
q
r
s
t
u
v
w
x
y
z

- **to grow up 1** erwachsen werden; **the children are growing up** die Kinder werden erwachsen; **2** aufwachsen✧ SEP (PERF *sein*); **she grew up in Scotland** sie ist in Schottland aufgewachsen.

growl *verb* knurren.

grown-up *noun* Erwachsene der/die (PL die Erwachsenen).

growth *noun* Wachstum *das*.

grudge *noun* **to bear a grudge against somebody** etwas gegen jemanden haben; **she bears me a grudge** sie hat etwas gegen mich.

grumble *verb* **1** murren; **he's always grumbling** er murrt immer; **2 to grumble about something** sich über etwas (ACC) beklagen; **what's she grumbling about?** worüber beklagt sie sich?

guarantee *noun* Garantie die (PL die Garantien); **a year's guarantee** ein Jahr Garantie.

guarantee *verb* garantieren.

guard *noun* **1 prison guard** der Gefängniswärter, die Gefängniswärterin; **2** (*on a train*) Zugführer der (PL die Zugführer), Zugführerin die (PL die Zugführerinnen); **3 security guard** der Wächter, die Wächterin.

guard *verb* bewachen.

guard dog *noun* Wachhund der (PL die Wachhunde).

guess *noun* **have a guess!** rate mal!; **it's a good guess** gut geraten.

guess *verb* **1** raten✧; **guess who I saw last night** rate mal, wen ich gestern Abend gesehen habe; **2** (*guess something correctly*) es

erraten✧; **you'll never guess!** du errätst es nie!

guest *noun* Gast der (PL die Gäste); **we've got guests coming tonight** wir haben heute Abend Gäste; **a paying guest** ein zahlender Gast.

guide *noun* **1** (*person*) Führer der (PL die Führer), Führerin die (PL die Führerinnen); **2** (*book*) Reiseführer der (PL die Reiseführer); **3** (*girl guide*) Pfadfinderin die (PL die Pfadfinderinnen).

guidebook *noun* **1** Reiseführer der (PL die Reiseführer); **2** (*to a museum or monument*) Handbuch das (PL die Handbücher).

guide dog *noun* Blindenhund der (PL die Blindenhunde).

guideline *noun* Richtlinie die (PL die Richtlinien).

guilty *adjective* **1** schuldig; **2 to feel guilty** ein schlechtes Gewissen haben; **I felt guilty about the noise** ich hatte ein schlechtes Gewissen wegen des Lärms.

guinea pig *noun* **1** (*pet*) Meerschweinchen das (PL die Meerschweinchen); **2** (*in an experiment*) Versuchskaninchen das (PL die Versuchskaninchen).

guitar *noun* Gitarre die (PL die Gitarren); **to play the guitar** Gitarre spielen.

gum *noun* **1** (*in your mouth*) Zahnfleisch das; **2** (*chewing gum*) Kaugummi der (PL die Kaugummi).

gun *noun* **1** Pistole die (PL die Pistolen); **2** (*rifle*) Gewehr das (PL die Gewehre).

gutter *noun* **1** (*in the street*) Rinnstein der (PL die Rinnsteine);

2 (*on roof*) *edge*) Dachrinne *die* (PL *die* Dachrinnen).

guy *noun* Typ *der* (PL *die* Typen) (*informal*); **he's a nice guy** er ist ein netter Typ; **that guy from Newcastle** der Typ aus Newcastle.

gym *noun* **1** (*school lesson*) Turnen *das*; **2** (*building*) Turnhalle *die* (PL *die* Turnhallen); **3** (*health club*) Fitnesscenter *das* (PL *die* Fitnesscenter); **to go to the gym** ins Fitnesscenter gehen.

gym shoe *noun* Turnschuh *der* (PL *die* Turnschuhe).

gymnasium *noun* Turnhalle *die* (PL *die* Turnhallen).

gymnast *noun* Turner *der* (PL *die* Turner), Turnerin *die* (PL *die* Turnerinnen).

gymnastics *noun* Turnen *das*.

Hh

habit *noun* Gewohnheit *die* (PL *die* Gewohnheiten); **it's a bad habit** es ist eine schlechte Gewohnheit.

haddock *noun* Schellfisch *der*; **smoked haddock** geräucherter Schellfisch.

hail *noun* Hagel *der*.

hailstone *noun* Hagelkorn *das* (PL *die* Hagelkörner).

hailstorm *noun* Hagelschauer *der* (PL *die* Hagelschauer).

hair *noun* Haare (*plural*); **to comb your hair** sich (DAT) die Haare kämmen; **to wash your hair** sich (DAT) die Haare waschen; **to have your hair cut** sich (DAT) die Haare schneiden lassen; **she's had her hair cut** sie hat sich die Haare schneiden lassen; **2 a hair** ein Haar.

hairbrush *noun* Haarbürste *die* (PL *die* Haarbürsten).

haircut *noun* **1** Haarschnitt *der* (PL *die* Haarschnitte); **2 to have a haircut** sich (DAT) die Haare schneiden lassen.

hairdresser *noun* Friseur *der* (PL *die* Friseure), Friseurin *die* (PL *die* Friseurinnen); **at the hairdresser's** beim Friseur.

hair drier *noun* Föhn *der* (PL *die* Föhne).

hair gel *noun* Haargel *das* (PL *die* Haargele).

hairgrip *noun* Haarklemme *die* (PL *die* Haarklemmen).

hairslide *noun* Haarspange *die* (PL *die* Haarspangen).

hairspray *noun* Haarspray *das* (PL *die* Haarsprays).

hairstyle *noun* Frisur *die* (PL *die* Frisuren).

hairy *adjective* behaart.

half *noun* **1** Hälfte *die* (PL *die* Hälften); **half of** die Hälfte von (+ DAT); **I gave him half of the money** ich habe ihm die Hälfte von dem Geld gegeben; **half of it** die Hälfte davon; **2 half an apple** ein halber Apfel; **3 to cut something in half** etwas halbieren; **4** (*as a fraction*) halb; **three and a half** dreieinhalb; **5** (*in time*) halb; **half an hour** eine halbe Stunde; **an hour and a half** anderthalb Stunden; **it's half past three** es ist halb vier (*literally: half on the way to four*);

a b c d e f **g** **h** i j k l m n o p q r s t u v w x y z

6 (*in weights and measures*) halb; **half a litre** ein halber Liter.

half hour *noun* halbe Stunde die; **every half hour** jede halbe Stunde.

half price *adjective, adverb* zum halben Preis; **half-price CDs** CDs zum halben Preis.

half-time *noun* Halbzeit die; **at half-time the score is 0-0** zur Halbzeit steht es null zu null.

halfway *adverb* **1** auf halbem Weg; **halfway to Frankfurt** auf halbem Weg nach Frankfurt; **2 to be halfway through doing something** mit etwas halb fertig sein; **I'm halfway through my homework** ich bin mit meinen Hausaufgaben halb fertig.

hall *noun* **1** (*in a house*) Diele die (PL die Dielen); **2** (*public*) Saal der (PL die Säle); **village hall** der Gemeindesaal; **concert hall** der Konzertsaal.

Hallowe'en *noun* der Tag vor Allerheiligen (*in Germany there are no particular customs for this date*).

ham *noun* Schinken der; **a ham sandwich** ein Schinkenbrot.

hamburger *noun* Hamburger der (PL die Hamburger).

hammer *noun* Hammer der (PL die Hammer).

hamster *noun* Hamster der (PL die Hamster).

hand *noun* **1** Hand die (PL die Hände); **to have something in your hand** etwas in der Hand haben; **to hold somebody's hand** jemandes Hand halten; **2 to give somebody a hand** jemandem helfen✧; **can you give me a hand**

to move the table into the corner? kannst du mir helfen, den Tisch in die Ecke zu rücken?; **do you need a hand?** kann ich dir helfen?; **3 on the other hand ...** andererseits ...; **4** (*of a watch or clock*) Zeiger der (PL die Zeiger); **the hour hand** der Stundenzeiger.

hand *verb* **to hand something to somebody** jemandem etwas geben✧; **I handed him the keys** ich gab ihm die Schlüssel.

● **to hand something in** etwas abgeben✧ SEP; **hand in your homework** gebt eure Hausaufgaben ab.

● **to hand something out** etwas austeilen SEP.

handbag *noun* Handtasche die (PL die Handtaschen).

handcuffs *plural noun* Handschellen (*plural*).

handful *noun* **a handful of** eine Hand voll.

handicapped *adjective* behindert.

handkerchief *noun* Taschentuch das (PL die Taschentücher).

handle *noun* **1** (*of a door, drawer, bag, or knife*) Griff der (PL die Griffe); **2** (*on a cup, jug, or basket*) Henkel der (PL die Henkel); **3** (*of a frying pan or broom*) Stiel der (PL die Stiele).

handle *verb* **1** erledigen; **Gina handles the correspondence** Gina erledigt die Korrespondenz; **2** umgehen✧ SEP (PERF *sein*) mit; **she's good at handling people** sie kann gut mit Menschen umgehen; **3** fertig werden ✧PERF *sein*) mit; **he**

can't handle problems er kann mit Problemen nicht fertig werden.

handlebars plural noun Lenkstange die (PL die Lenkstangen).

hand luggage noun Handgepäck das.

handmade adjective handgemacht.

handsome adjective gut aussehend; **he's a handsome guy** er ist ein gut aussehender Typ.

handwriting noun Handschrift die (PL die Handschriften).

handy adjective 1 praktisch; **this little knife's very handy** dieses kleine Messer ist sehr praktisch; 2 griffbereit; **I always keep a notebook handy** ich habe immer ein kleines Notizbuch griffbereit.

hang verb 1 hängen◇; **there was a mirror hanging on the wall** an der Wand hing ein Spiegel; 2 aufhängen SEP; **to hang a mirror on the wall** einen Spiegel an der Wand aufhängen.

● **to hang around** rumhängen◇ SEP (PERF sein) (informal); **we were hanging around outside the cinema** wir haben vor dem Kino rumgehangen.

● **to hang on** warten; **hang on a second!** warten Sie einen Moment!

● **to hang up** (on the phone) auflegen SEP; **she hung up on me** sie hat einfach aufgelegt.

● **to hang something up** etwas aufhängen SEP.

hang-gliding noun Drachenfliegen das; **to go hang-gliding** Drachenfliegen gehen.

hangover noun Kater der (PL die Kater).

happen verb 1 passieren (PERF sein); **what happened?** was ist passiert?; **it happened in June** es ist im Juni passiert; 2 **what's happening?** was ist los?; **what's happened to Jill?** was ist mit Jill los?; 3 **what's happened to the can-opener?** wo ist der Dosenöffner?; 4 **if you happen to see him** wenn du ihn zufällig triffst; **Leila happened to be there** Leila war zufällig da.

happily adverb 1 glücklich; 2 (willingly) gerne; **I'll happily do it for you** ich tu es gerne für dich.

happiness noun Glück das.

happy adjective glücklich; **a happy child** ein glückliches Kind; **Happy Birthday** herzlichen Glückwunsch zum Geburtstag.

harbour noun Hafen der (PL die Häfen).

hard adjective 1 hart; 2 (difficult) schwer; **a hard question** eine schwere Frage; **it's hard to say** es ist schwer zu sagen.

hard adverb 1 **to work hard** hart arbeiten; 2 **to try hard** sich sehr bemühen.

hard disk noun Festplatte die (PL die Festplatten).

hardly adverb 1 kaum; **I can hardly hear him** ich kann ihn kaum hören; **there was hardly anybody there** es war kaum jemand da; **we've got hardly any milk** wir haben kaum Milch; **hardly anything** kaum etwas; **he ate hardly anything** er hat kaum etwas gegessen; 2 **hardly ever** fast nie; **I**

a b c d e f g h i j k l m n o p q r s t u v w x y z

a

hardly ever see him ich sehe ihn fast nie.

b

hard up *adjective* **to be hard up** knapp bei Kasse sein.

c

hare *noun* Hase der (PL die Hasen).

d

harm *noun* **it won't do any harm** es kann nichts schaden.

e

harm *verb* **1 to harm somebody** jemandem etwas tun; **they didn't harm him** sie haben ihm nichts getan; **2** schaden (+ DAT) *(health, environment, reputation)*; **a cup of coffee won't harm you** eine Tasse Kaffee schadet nicht.

f

g

h

harmful *adjective* schädlich.

i

harmless *adjective* unschädlich.

j

harvest *noun* Ernte die (PL die Ernten); **to get the harvest in** die Ernte einbringen.

k

hat *noun* Hut der (PL die Hüte).

l

hate *verb* hassen; **I hate geography** ich hasse Erdkunde.

m

hatred *noun* Hass der.

n

have *verb* **1** haben✧; **Anna has three brothers** Anna hat drei Brüder; **how many sisters do you have?** wie viele Schwestern hast du?; **2 what have you got in your hand?** was hast du in der Hand?; **he has (got) flu** er hat die Grippe; **3** *(to form past tenses, some verbs in German take 'haben' and others 'sein')* **I've finished** ich bin fertig; **have you seen the film?** hast du den Film gesehen?; **Rosie hasn't arrived yet** Rosie ist noch nicht angekommen; **4 to have to do something** etwas tun müssen✧; **I have to phone my mum** ich muss meine Mutter anrufen; **5** *('have' is often translated by a more special German verb)* **we had a coffee** wir

o

p

q

r

s

t

u

v

w

x

y

z

haben einen Kaffee getrunken; **what will you have?** was nehmen Sie?; **I'll have an omelette** ich nehme ein Omelett; **I'm going to have a shower** ich dusche jetzt; **to have lunch** zu Mittag essen; **to have dinner** *(in the evening)* zu Abend essen; **6** *(get)* bekommen✧; **Emma had a letter from Sam yesterday** gestern bekam Emma einen Brief von Sam; **she had a baby** sie hat ein Baby bekommen; **7 to have something done** etwas machen lassen✧; **I'm going to have my hair cut** ich lasse mir die Haare schneiden; **8 to have on** *(be wearing)* anhaben✧ SEP; **to have nothing on** nichts anhaben.

hawk *noun* Habicht der (PL die Habichte).

hay *noun* Heu das.

hay fever *noun* Heuschnupfen der.

hazelnut *noun* Haselnuss die (PL die Haselnüsse).

he *pronoun* er; **he lives in Manchester** er wohnt in Manchester.

head *noun* **1** Kopf der (PL die Köpfe); **he shook his head** er schüttelte den Kopf; **2** *(of a school)* Direktor der (PL die Direktoren), Direktorin die (PL die Direktorinnen); **3** *(of a firm)* Chef der (PL die Chefs), Chefin die (PL die Chefinnen); **4** *(when tossing a coin)* **'heads or tails?'** 'Kopf oder Zahl?'

● **to head for something** auf etwas (ACC) zusteuern SEP (PERF sein); **Liz headed for the door** Liz steuerte auf die Tür zu.

headache noun Kopfschmerzen (plural); **I've got a headache** ich habe Kopfschmerzen.

headlight noun Scheinwerfer der (PL die Scheinwerfer).

headline noun Schlagzeile die (PL die Schlagzeilen).

headmaster noun Direktor der (PL die Direktoren).

headmistress noun Direktorin die (PL die Direktorinnen).

headphones noun Kopfhörer der (PL die Kopfhörer).

headteacher noun Direktor der (PL die Direktoren), Direktorin die (PL die Direktorinnen).

health noun Gesundheit die.

health centre noun Ärztezentrum das (PL die Ärztezentren).

healthy adjective gesund.

heap noun Haufen der (PL die Haufen); **I've got heaps of work** ich habe einen Haufen Arbeit (informal).

hear verb hören; **I can't hear anything** ich kann überhaupt nichts hören; **I hear you've bought a dog** ich habe gehört, dass ihr einen Hund gekauft habt.

● **to hear about something** von etwas (DAT) hören; **have you heard about the concert?** hast du von dem Konzert gehört?

● **to hear from somebody** von jemandem hören.

hearing aid noun Hörgerät das (PL die Hörgeräte).

heart noun **1** Herz das (PL die Herzen); **2 to learn something by heart** etwas auswendig lernen;

3 (in cards) Herz das; **the jack of hearts** der Herzbube.

heart attack noun Herzinfarkt der (PL die Herzinfarkte).

heat noun Hitze die.

heat verb **1** to heat something etwas heiß machen; **I'll go and heat the soup** ich mache die Suppe heiß; **2** the soup's heating die Suppe wird warm; **3** heizen (a room).

● **to heat something up** etwas aufwärmen SEP; **I'm heating the sauce up** ich wärme die Soße auf.

heater noun Heizgerät das (PL die Heizgeräte).

heather noun Heidekraut das.

heating noun Heizung die.

heatwave noun Hitzewelle die (PL die Hitzewellen).

heaven noun Himmel der.

heavy adjective **1** schwer; **my rucksack's really heavy** mein Rucksack ist sehr schwer; **2** (busy) **I've got a heavy day tomorrow** ich habe morgen viel zu tun; **3** (in quantity) stark; **heavy rain** starker Regen.

hectic adjective hektisch; **a hectic day** ein hektischer Tag.

hedge noun Hecke die (PL die Hecken).

hedgehog noun Igel der (PL die Igel).

heel noun **1** (of foot or sock) Ferse die (PL die Fersen); **2** (of a shoe) Absatz der (PL die Absätze).

height noun **1** (of a person) Größe die; **what height are you?** wie groß bist du?; **2** (of a building, mountain) Höhe die; **what height is it?** wie hoch ist es?

a
b
c
d
e
f
g
h
i
j
k
l
m
n
o
p
q
r
s
t
u
v
w
x
y
z

a

helicopter noun Hubschrauber der (PL die Hubschrauber).

b

hell noun Hölle die; **hell!** verdammt! (informal).

c

hello exclamation **1** (polite) guten Tag!; **2** (informal, and on the phone) hallo!

d

e

helmet noun Helm der (PL die Helme).

f

help noun Hilfe die; **do you need any help?** kann ich dir helfen?, (in a shop) kann ich Ihnen behilflich sein?

g

h

help verb **1** helfen✧ (+ DAT); **to help somebody (to) do something** jemandem helfen, etwas zu tun; **can you help me lay the table?** kannst du mir helfen, den Tisch zu decken?; **2** to help yourself to something nimm dir Gemüse; **help yourself to vegetables** nimm dir Gemüse; **help yourself!** greif zu!; **3 help!** Hilfe!; **4** he can't help it er kann nichts dafür.

i

j

k

l

m

helper noun Helfer der (PL die Helfer), Helferin die (PL die Helferinnen).

n

helpful adjective (person) hilfsbereit.

o

helping noun Portion die (PL die Portionen); **would you like a second helping?** möchtest du eine zweite Portion?

p

q

r

hem noun Saum der (PL die Säume).

s

hen noun Henne die (PL die Hennen).

t

her pronoun (in German this pronoun changes according to the function it has in the sentence or the preposition it follows) **1** (as a direct object in the accusative) sie; **I know her** ich kenne sie; **I saw her last**

u

v

w

x

y

z

week ich habe sie letzte Woche gesehen; **2** (after prepositions + ACC) sie; **without her** ohne sie; **we've heard a lot about her** wir haben viel über sie gehört; **3** (as an indirect object or after verbs that take the dative) ihr; **I gave her my address** ich habe ihr meine Adresse gegeben; **we helped her** wir haben ihr geholfen; **4** (after prepositions + DAT) ihr; **with her** mit ihr; **5** (in comparisons) sie; **he's older than her** er ist älter als sie; **6** (in the nominative) sie; **it was her** sie war es.

her adjective **1** (before a masculine noun) ihr; **her brother** ihr Bruder; **2** (before a feminine noun) ihre; **her sister** ihre Schwester; **3** (before a neuter noun) ihr; **her house** ihr Haus; **4** (before a plural noun) ihre; **her children** ihre Kinder; **5** (with parts of the body) der/die/das, die (plural); **she had a glass in her hand** sie hatte ein Glas in der Hand; **she's washing her hands** sie wäscht sich die Hände.

herb noun Kraut das (PL die Kräuter).

herd noun (of cattle, goats) Herde die (PL die Herden).

here adverb **1** (in or at this place) hier; **not far from here** nicht weit von hier; **here's my address** hier ist meine Adresse; **I want to stay here** ich möchte hier bleiben; **2** (to this place) hierher; **when Peter came here** als Peter hierher kam; **3 here they are!** da sind sie!; **Tom isn't here at the moment** Tom ist im Moment nicht da.

hero noun Held der (PL die Helden).

heroin *noun* Heroin *das*.

heroine *noun* Heldin *die* (PL *die* Heldinnen).

herring *noun* Hering *der* (PL *die* Heringe).

hers *pronoun* **1** (*for a masculine noun*) ihrer; **my coat is blue and hers is red** mein Mantel ist blau und ihrer ist rot; **I took my hat and she took hers** ich nahm meinen Hut und sie nahm ihren; **2** (*for a feminine noun*) **I gave Ann my address and she gave me hers** ich habe Ann meine Adresse gegeben und sie hat mir ihre gegeben; **3** (*for a neuter noun*) ihr(e)s; **my bike is new but hers is old** mein Rad ist neu, aber ihrs ist alt; **4** (*for masculine/ feminine/ neuter plural nouns*) ihre; **I showed Emma my photos and she showed me hers** ich habe Emma meine Fotos gezeigt und sie hat mir ihre gezeigt; **5 the CDs are hers** die CDs gehören ihr; **it's hers** das gehört ihr.

herself *pronoun* **1** (*reflexive*) sich; **she's hurt herself** sie hat sich wehgetan; **2** (*stressing something*) selbst; **she said it herself** sie hat es selbst gesagt; **3 she did it by herself** sie hat es ganz allein gemacht.

hesitate *verb* zögern.

heterosexual *adjective* heterosexuell.

heterosexual *noun* Heterosexuelle *der/die* (PL *die* Heterosexuellen).

hi *exclamation* hallo!.

hiccups *plural noun* **to have the hiccups** einen Schluckauf haben.

hidden *adjective* verborgen.

hide *verb* **1** sich verstecken; **she hid behind the door** sie hat sich hinter die Tür versteckt; **2 to hide something** etwas verstecken.

hi-fi *noun* Hi-Fi-Anlage *die* (PL *die* Hi-Fi-Anlagen).

high *adjective* **1** hoch; **how high is the wall?** wie hoch ist die Mauer?; **the wall is two metres high** die Mauer ist zwei Meter hoch; **the shelf is too high** das Regal ist zu hoch; (*the adjective 'hoch' loses its c when it has an ending, becoming hoher/hohe/hohes*) **a high tower** ein hoher Turm; **a high wall** eine hohe Mauer; **at high speed** mit hoher Geschwindigkeit; **a high voice** eine hohe Stimme; **2 high winds** starker Wind.

high *adverb* hoch.

Highers, Advanced Highers *noun plural* Abitur *das* ((*Students take 'Abitur' at about 19 years of age. You can explain Highers briefly as follows: Highers werden im vorletzten Jahr der Sekundarstufe in bis zu fünf Fächern abgelegt. Manche Schüler legen zusätzlich Advanced Highers in ihrem letzten Schuljahr ab. Advanced Highers werden in bis zu drei Fächern, die bereits für Highers belegt wurden, abgelegt. Beide Qualifikationen werden von A bis C benotet und sind Hochschulzugangsberechtigungen*)) SEE Abitur.

high-heeled *adjective* hochhackig.

high jump *noun* Hochsprung *der*.

hijack *verb* **to hijack a plane** ein Flugzeug entführen.

a
b
c
d
e
f
g
h
i
j
k
l
m
n
o
p
q
r
s
t
u
v
w
x
y
z

hijacker noun Entführer der (PL die Entführer).

hijacking noun Entführung die (PL die Entführungen).

hike noun Wanderung die (PL die Wanderungen).

hiker noun Wanderer der (PL die Wanderer), Wanderin die (PL die Wanderinnen).

hiking noun Wandern das

hilarious adjective lustig.

hill noun 1 (large hill) Berg der (PL die Berge); **you can see the hills** man kann die Berge sehen; 2 (smaller) Hügel der (PL die Hügel); **to walk up the hill** den Hügel hinaufgehen; 3 (hillside) Hang der (PL die Hänge); **the house on the hill** das Haus am Hang.

him pronoun (in German this pronoun changes according to the function it has in the sentence or the preposition it follows) 1 (as a direct object in the accusative) ihn; **I know him** ich kenne ihn; **I saw him last week** ich habe ihn letzte Woche gesehen; 2 (after prepositions + ACC) ihn; **he fought against him** er hat gegen ihn gekämpft; **without him** ohne ihn; 3 (as an indirect object or after verbs that take the dative) ihm; **I gave him my address** ich habe ihm meine Adresse gegeben; **you must help him** du musst ihm helfen; 4 (after prepositions + DAT) ihm; **with him** mit ihm; 5 (in comparisons) er; **she's older than him** sie ist älter als er; 6 (in the nominative) er; **it was him** er war es.

himself pronoun 1 (reflexive) sich; **he's hurt himself** er hat sich wehgetan; 2 (stressing something) selbst; **he said it himself** er hat es selbst gesagt; 3 **he did it by himself** er hat es ganz allein gemacht.

Hindu adjective hinduistisch.

hip noun Hüfte die (PL die Hüften).

hippie noun Hippie der (PL die Hippies).

hippopotamus noun Nilpferd das (PL die Nilpferde).

hire noun 1 Vermietung die; **car hire** die Autovermietung; 2 **for hire** zu vermieten.

hire verb mieten.

his adjective 1 (before a masculine noun) sein; **his brother** sein Bruder; 2 (before a feminine noun) seine; **his sister** seine Schwester; 3 (before a neuter noun) sein; **his house** sein Haus; 4 (before a plural noun) seine; **his children** seine Kinder; 5 (with parts of the body) der/die/das, die (plural); **he had a glass in his hand** er hatte ein Glas in der Hand; **he's washing his hands** er wäscht sich (DAT) die Hände.

his pronoun 1 (for a masculine noun) seiner; **my hat is red and his is blue** mein Hut ist rot und seiner ist blau; 2 (for a feminine noun) seine; **I gave him my address and he gave me his** ich habe ihm meine Adresse gegeben und er hat mir seine gegeben; 3 (for a neuter noun) sein(e)s; **my book is new but his is old** mein Buch ist neu, aber seins ist alt; 4 (for masculine/feminine/ neuter plural nouns) seine; **I've invited my parents and Steve's invited his** ich habe meine Eltern eingeladen und Steve hat seine eingeladen; **5 the green car's his** das grüne Auto gehört ihm; **it's his** das gehört ihm.

historic *adjective* historisch.

history *noun* Geschichte *die*.

hit *noun* **1** Hit *der* (PL die Hits); **their latest hit** ihr neuester Hit; **2** (*success*) Erfolg *der* (PL die Erfolge); **the film is a huge hit** der Film ist ein großer Erfolg.

hit *verb* **1** treffen◇; **to hit the ball** den Ball treffen; **2 to hit your head on something** sich (DAT) den Kopf an etwas (DAT) stoßen; **I hit my head on the door** ich habe mir den Kopf an der Tür gestoßen; **3** prallen gegen (+ACC) (PERF *sein*); **the car hit a wall** das Auto ist gegen eine Wand geprallt; **4 to be hit by a car** von einem Auto angefahren werden.

hitch *noun* Problem *das* (PL die Probleme); **there's been a slight hitch** ein kleines Problem ist aufgetaucht.

hitch *verb* **to hitch a lift** per Anhalter fahren◇ (PERF *sein*).

hitchhike *verb* per Anhalter fahren◇ (PERF *sein*); **we hitchhiked to Heidelberg** wir sind per Anhalter nach Heidelberg gefahren.

hitchhiker *noun* Anhalter *der* (PL die Anhalter), Anhalterin *die* (PL die Anhalterinnen).

hitchhiking *noun* Trampen *das*.

HIV-negative *adjective* HIV-negativ.

HIV-positive *adjective* HIV-positiv.

hobby *noun* Hobby *das* (PL die Hobbys).

hockey *noun* Hockey *das*.

hockey stick *noun* Hockeyschläger *der* (PL die Hockeyschläger).

hold *verb* **1** halten◇; **to hold something in your hand** etwas in der Hand halten; **can you hold the torch?** kannst du die Taschenlampe halten?; **2** (*be able to contain*) fassen; **the jug holds a litre** der Krug fasst einen Liter; **3 to hold a meeting** eine Versammlung abhalten◇ SEP; **4 can you hold the line, please?** bleiben Sie bitte am Apparat; **5 hold on!** (*wait*) warten Sie! (*on the phone*) bleiben Sie am Apparat.

● **to hold on to something** (*to stop yourself from falling*) sich an etwas (DAT) festhalten◇ SEP.

● **to hold somebody up** (*delay*) jemanden aufhalten◇ SEP; **I was held up at the dentist's** ich bin beim Zahnarzt aufgehalten worden.

● **to hold something up** (*raise*) etwas hochhalten◇ SEP.

hold-up *noun* **1** Verzögerung *die* (PL die Verzögerungen); **2** (*traffic jam*) Stau *der* (PL die Staus); **3** (*robbery*) Überfall *der* (PL die Überfälle).

hole *noun* Loch *das* (PL die Löcher).

holiday *noun* **1** Ferien (*plural*) Urlaub *der* (PL die Urlaube) (*students, schoolchildren, and families usually have 'Ferien'; people in paid employment usually have 'Urlaub'*); **where are you going for your holiday?** wo fahrt

a b c d e f g h i j k l m n o p q r s t u v w x y z

ihr in den Ferien hin?'; **have a good holiday!** schöne Ferien!, schönen Urlaub!; **to be away on holiday** auf Urlaub sein, in den Ferien sein; **to go on holiday** in Urlaub fahren, in die Ferien fahren; **the school holidays** die Schulferien; 2 (*day off work*) freie Tag *der* (PL die freien Tage); **I'm taking two days' holiday next week** ich nehme mir nächste Woche zwei Tage frei; 3 public holiday *der* Feiertag; **Monday's a holiday** Montag ist ein Feiertag.

holiday home *noun* Ferienhaus *das* (PL die Ferienhäuser).

Holland *noun* Holland *das*.

hollow *adjective* hohl.

holy *adjective* heilig.

home *noun* 1 **I was at home** ich war zu Hause; **to stay at home** zu Hause bleiben; 2 **make yourself at home** mach es dir bequem.

home *adverb* 1 (*to home*) nach Hause; **Susie's gone home** Susie ist nach Hause gegangen; **on my way home** auf dem Weg nach Hause; **to get home** nach Hause kommen; **we got home at midnight** wir sind um Mitternacht nach Hause gekommen; 2 (*at home*) zu Hause; **I'll be home in the afternoon** ich bin am Nachmittag zu Hause.

homeless *adjective* obdachlos; **the homeless** die Obdachlosen.

homemade *adjective* selbst gemacht; **homemade biscuits** selbst gebackene Kekse.

homeopathic *adjective* homöopathisch.

homesick *adjective* **to be homesick** Heimweh haben.

homework *noun* Hausaufgaben (*plural*); **I did my homework** ich habe meine Hausaufgaben gemacht; **my German homework** meine Deutschhausaufgaben.

homosexual *adjective* homosexuell.

homosexual *noun* Homosexuelle *der/die* (PL die Homosexuellen).

honest *adjective* ehrlich.

honestly *adverb* ehrlich.

honesty *noun* Ehrlichkeit *die*.

honey *noun* Honig *der* (PL die Honige).

honeymoon *noun* Flitterwochen *die* (*plural*); **they're going to Italy on their honeymoon** sie fahren nach Italien in die Flitterwochen.

honour *noun* Ehre *die*.

hood *noun* 1 Kapuze *die* (PL die Kapuzen); 2 (*on a car*) Verdeck *das* (PL die Verdecke).

hook *noun* 1 Haken *der* (PL die Haken); 2 **to take the phone off the hook** das Telefon aushängen SEP.

hooligan *noun* Hooligan *der* (PL die Hooligans).

hooray *exclamation* hurra!.

Hoover *noun* Staubsauger *der* (PL die Staubsauger).

hoover *verb* saugen; **I hoovered my bedroom** ich habe mein Schlafzimmer gesaugt.

hope *noun* Hoffnung *die* (PL die Hoffnungen); **to give up hope** die Hoffnung aufgeben.

hope *verb* 1 hoffen; **we hope you'll be able to come** wir hoffen, ihr könnt kommen; **I'm hoping to see you on Friday** ich hoffe, dich am Freitag zu sehen; **2 I hope so** hoffentlich; **I hope not** hoffentlich nicht.

hopefully adverb hoffentlich; **hopefully, the film won't have started** hoffentlich hat der Film noch nicht angefangen.

hopeless adjective miserabel (informal); **I'm hopeless at geography** ich bin miserabel in Erdkunde.

horizontal adjective horizontal, waagrecht; **the flag has three horizontal bars** die Flagge hat drei waagrechte Streifen.

horn noun **1** (of an animal, instrument) Horn das (PL die Hörner); **2** (of a car) Hupe die (PL die Hupen).

horoscope noun Horoskop das (PL die Horoskope).

horrible adjective **1** furchtbar; **the weather was horrible** das Wetter war furchtbar; **2** (person) gemein; **she's really horrible** sie ist richtig gemein; **he was really horrible to me** er war richtig gemein zu mir.

horror noun Entsetzen das.

horror film noun Horrorfilm der (PL die Horrorfilme).

horse noun Pferd das (PL die Pferde).

horse chestnut noun (tree and nut) Rosskastanie die (PL die Rosskastanien).

horseshoe noun Hufeisen das (PL die Hufeisen).

hose noun Schlauch der (PL die Schläuche).

hosepipe noun Schlauch der (PL die Schläuche).

hospital noun Krankenhaus das (PL die Krankenhäuser); **in hospital** im Krankenhaus; **to be taken into hospital** ins Krankenhaus kommen.

hospitality noun Gastfreundschaft die.

host noun **1** Gastgeber der (PL die Gastgeber); **2** (on a TV programme) Moderator der (PL die Moderatoren).

hostage noun Geisel die (PL die Geiseln).

hostel noun **youth hostel** die Jugendherberge.

hostess noun **1** Gastgeberin die (PL die Gastgeberinnen); **2** (on a TV programme) Moderatorin die (PL die Moderatorinnen); **3 air hostess** die Stewardess.

hot adjective **1** heiß; **be careful, the plates are hot** sei vorsichtig, die Teller sind heiß; **it's hot today** heute ist es heiß; **2** (person) **I'm very hot** mir ist sehr heiß; **3** (spicy) scharf; **the curry's too hot for me** das Curry ist mir zu scharf; **4 a hot meal** ein warmes Essen.

hot dog noun Hotdog das (or) der (PL die Hotdogs).

hotel noun Hotel das (PL die Hotels).

hour noun Stunde die (PL die Stunden); **two hours later** zwei Stunden später; **we waited for two hours** wir haben zwei Stunden lang gewartet; **I've been waiting for hours** ich warte schon seit Stunden; **two hours ago** vor zwei Stunden; **to be paid by the hour** pro Stunde bezahlt werden; **every hour** jede Stunde; **half an hour** eine

a b c d e f g h i j k l m n o p q r s t u v w x y z

a

halbe Stunde; **a quarter of an hour** eine Viertelstunde; **an hour and a half** anderthalb Stunden.

b

house noun **1** Haus das (PL die Häuser); **2 at somebody's house** bei jemandem; **I'm at Judy's house** ich bin bei Judy; **I'm going to Sid's house tonight** ich gehe heute Abend zu Sid; **I phoned from Jill's house** ich habe von Jill aus angerufen.

c

d

e

f

g

housewife noun Hausfrau die (PL die Hausfrauen).

h

housework noun Hausarbeit die; **he does the housework** er macht den Haushalt (informal).

i

j

k

hovercraft noun Luftkissenfahrzeug das (PL die Luftkissenfahrzeuge).

l

m

how adverb **1** wie; **how did you do it?** wie hast du das gemacht?; **how are you?** wie geht es dir?; **how many?** wie viele?; **how many brothers do you have?** wie viele Brüder hast du?; **how old are you?** wie alt bist du?; **how far is it?** wie weit ist es?; **how far is it to York?** wie weit ist es bis York?; **how long will it take?** wie lange dauert es?; **how long have you known her?** wie lange kennst du sie?; **2 how much?** wie viel?; **how much money do you have?** wie viel Geld hast du?; **how much is it?** wie viel kostet das?

n

o

p

q

r

s

t

u

v

however adverb **1** jedoch; **2** (in questions) however did she do it? wie hat sie das nur gemacht?; **3 however famous he is** wie berühmt er auch sein mag.

w

x

y

z

hug noun to give somebody a hug jemanden umarmen; **she gave me a hug** sie hat mich umarmt.

huge adjective riesig.

hum verb summen.

human adjective menschlich.

human being noun Mensch der (PL die Menschen).

humour noun Humor der; **to have a sense of humour** Humor haben.

hundred number hundert; **two hundred** zweihundert; **two hundred and ten** zweihundertzehn; **a hundred people** hundert Menschen; **about a hundred** um die hundert; **hundreds of people** hunderte von Menschen.

Hungary noun Ungarn das.

hunger noun Hunger der.

hungry adjective to be hungry Hunger haben; **I'm hungry** ich habe Hunger.

hunt verb **1** jagen (an animal); **2** suchen (a person).

hunting noun Jagd die; **fox-hunting** die Fuchsjagd.

hurry noun to be in a hurry es eilig haben; **I'm in a hurry** ich habe es eilig; **there's no hurry** es eilt nicht.

hurry verb **1** sich beeilen; **I must hurry** ich muss mich beeilen; **hurry up!** beeil dich!; **2 he hurried home** er ging schnell nach Hause.

hurt verb **1** to hurt somebody jemandem wehtun◇ SEP; **you're hurting me!** du tust mir weh!; **that hurts!** das tut weh!; **my arm hurts** der Arm tut mir weh; **3** to hurt yourself sich (DAT) wehtun◇ SEP; **did you hurt yourself?** hast du dir wehgetan?

hurt adjective **1** (in an accident) verletzt; **three people were hurt** drei Menschen wurden verletzt; **2** (in feelings) gekränkt; **she felt hurt** sie fühlte sich gekränkt.

husband noun Ehemann der (PL die Ehemänner).

hygienic adjective hygienisch.

hymn noun Kirchenlied das (PL die Kirchenlieder).

hypermarket noun Großmarkt der (PL die Großmärkte).

hyphen noun Bindestrich der (PL die Bindestriche).

Ii

I pronoun ich; **I have two sisters** ich habe zwei Schwestern.

ice noun Eis das.

ice cream noun Eis das; **two chocolate ice creams** zwei Schokoladeneis.

ice hockey noun Eishockey das.

ice rink noun Eisbahn die (PL die Eisbahnen).

ice-skating noun **to go ice-skating** Schlittschuh laufen✧ (PERF sein).

icy adjective **1** vereist (road); **2** (very cold) eiskalt.

idea noun **1** Idee die (PL die Ideen); **what a good idea!** was für eine gute Idee!; **2** **I've no idea** ich habe keine Ahnung.

ideal adjective ideal.

identical adjective identisch.

identification noun
1 Identifizierung die; **2** (proof of identity) Ausweispapiere (plural).

identity card noun Personalausweis der (PL die Personalausweise).

idiot noun Idiot der (PL die Idioten).

idiotic adjective idiotisch.

i.e. abbreviation d. h. (das heißt).

if conjunction **1** wenn; **if it rains** wenn es regnet; **if I won the lottery** wenn ich in der Lotterie gewinnen sollte; **if not** wenn nicht; **if only** wenn nur; **if only you'd told me** wenn du mir das nur gesagt hättest; **2** **even if** selbst wenn; **even if it snows** selbst wenn es schneit; **3** **if I were you** an deiner Stelle; **4** (whether) ob; **I wonder if he'll come** ich bin gespannt, ob er kommt; **as if** als ob.

ignore verb **1** ignorieren; **2** überhören (what somebody says).

ill adjective krank; **to fall ill, to be taken ill** krank werden; **I feel ill** ich fühle mich krank.

illegal adjective illegal.

illness noun Krankheit die (PL die Krankheiten).

illusion noun Illusion die (PL die Illusionen).

illustration noun Illustration die (PL die Illustrationen).

image noun Bild das (PL die Bilder); ★ **he's the spitting image of his father** er ist das Ebenbild seines Vaters.

imagination noun Phantasie die.

imaginative adjective phantasievoll.

imagine verb sich (DAT) vorstellen; **imagine that you're very rich** stell

a
b
c
d
e
f
g
h
i
j
k
l
m
n
o
p
q
r
s
t
u
v
w
x
y
z

dir vor, du bist sehr reich; **you can't imagine how hard it was** du kannst dir nicht vorstellen, wie schwer es war.

imitate *verb* nachahmen SEP.

immediate *adjective* **1** (*without delay*) unmittelbar; **2 the immediate family** die engste Familie.

immediately *adverb* **1** sofort; **I rang them immediately** ich habe sie sofort angerufen; **2 immediately before** unmittelbar davor; **immediately after** unmittelbar danach.

immigrant *noun* Einwanderer *der* (PL die Einwanderer), Einwanderin *die* (PL die Einwanderinnen).

immigration *noun* Einwanderung *die*.

impatience *noun* Ungeduld *die*.

impatient *adjective* **1** ungeduldig; **2 to be impatient with somebody** ungeduldig mit jemandem sein.

impatiently *adverb* ungeduldig.

imperfect *noun* (*verb tense*) Imperfekt *das*; **"ich schlug" is in the imperfect** "ich schlug" steht im Imperfekt.

import *noun* Import *der* (PL die Importe).

import *verb* importieren.

importance *noun* Wichtigkeit *die*.

important *adjective* wichtig.

impossible *adjective* unmöglich; **it's impossible to find a telephone** es ist unmöglich, ein Telefon zu finden.

impressed *adjective* beeindruckt; **to be impressed by something** von etwas (DAT) beeindruckt sein.

impression *noun* Eindruck *der* (PL die Eindrücke); **to make a good impression on somebody** einen guten Eindruck auf jemanden machen; **I got the impression he was hiding something** ich hatte den Eindruck, dass er etwas verheimlichte.

impressive *adjective* eindrucksvoll.

improve *verb* **1 to improve something** etwas verbessern; **2** (*get better*) besser werden; **the weather is improving** das Wetter wird besser.

improvement *noun* Verbesserung *die* (PL die Verbesserungen).

in *preposition* **1** in (+ DAT *or*; *with movement into*, + ACC); **it is in my pocket** es ist in meiner Tasche; (*with movement*) **he put it in his pocket** er hat es in die Tasche gesteckt; **she sat in the sun** sie saß in der Sonne; **I read it in the newspaper** ich habe es in der Zeitung gelesen; **in Oxford** in Oxford; **in Germany** in Deutschland; **2 the biggest city in the world** die größte Stadt der Welt; **a house in the country** ein Haus auf dem Land; **in the street** auf der Straße; **3** (*wearing and with colours*) in (+ DAT); **the girl in the pink shirt** das Mädchen im rosa Hemd; **4 in German** auf Deutsch; **5** (*time expressions*) in (+ DAT); **in May** im Mai; **in 1994** (im Jahre) 1994; **in winter** im Winter; **in summer** im Sommer; **in the night** in der Nacht; **I'll phone you in ten minutes** ich rufe dich in zehn

Minuten an; **she was ready in five minutes** sie war in fünf Minuten fertig; **6 in the morning** am Morgen; **at eight in the morning** um acht Uhr morgens; **7** (*among people or in literature*) bei (+ DAT); **it's rare in children** das ist selten bei Kindern; **in Shakespeare** bei Shakespeare; **in the army** beim Militär; **8 in time** rechtzeitig.

in *adverb* **1** (*inside*) hinein-, herein-, rein- (*informal*) (*Herein-, hinein-, and rein- form prefixes to separable verbs. 'Herein-' is used with verbs like kommen, which have the sense of moving towards the speaker. 'Hinein-' is used with verbs like gehen, which have the sense of going away from the speaker. The informal 'rein-' can be used with either movement*); **to come in** hereinkommen✧ SEP (PERF *sein*); **to go in** hineingehen✧ SEP (PERF *sein*); **he was not allowed to go into the room** er durfte nicht ins Zimmer reingehen; **to run in** reinlaufen✧ SEP (PERF *sein*) (*informal*); **2 to be in** da sein; **Mick's not in at the moment** Mick ist im Moment nicht da; **3** (*at home*) zu Hause; **4** (*indoors*) drinnen; **in here** hier drinnen; **in there** da drinnen.

include *verb* einschließen✧ SEP; **service is included in the price** die Bedienung ist im Preis inbegriffen.

including *preposition* **1** einschließlich (+ GEN); **everyone, including the children** alle, einschließlich der Kinder; **£50 including postage** fünfzig Pfund einschließlich Porto; **including Sundays** einschließlich sonntags;

2 not including Sundays außer sonntags.

income *noun* Einkommen *das* (PL *die* Einkommen).

income tax *noun* Einkommenssteuer *die* (PL *die* Einkommenssteuern).

increase *noun* Erhöhung *die* (PL *die* Erhöhungen) (*in price, for example*).

increase *verb* **1** steigen✧ (PERF *sein*); **the price has increased by £10** der Preis ist um zehn Pfund gestiegen; **2** erhöhen (*salary*).

incredible *adjective* unglaublich.

incredibly *adverb* (*very*) unglaublich; **the film's incredibly boring** der Film ist unglaublich langweilig.

indeed *adverb* **1** (*to emphasize*) wirklich; **she's very pleased indeed** sie hat sich wirklich sehr gefreut; **2** (*certainly*) natürlich; **'can you hear the radio?' – 'indeed I can!'** 'kannst du das Radio hören?' – 'ja, natürlich!'; **3 thank you very much indeed** vielen herzlichen Dank.

indefinite article *noun* unbestimmter Artikel *der* (PL *die* umbestimmten Artikel).

independence *noun* Unabhängigkeit *die*.

independent *adjective* unabhängig; **independent school** *die* Privatschule.

index *noun* Register *das* (PL *die* Register).

India *noun* Indien *das*.

Indian *noun* **1** Inder *der* (PL *die* Inder), Inderin *die* (PL *die* Inderinnen); **2** (*a Native American*)

Indian Indianer der (PL die Indianer), Indianerin die (PL die Indianerinnen).

Indian adjective **1** indisch; **he's Indian** er ist Inder; **2** (Native American) indianisch; **she's Indian** sie ist Indianerin.

indicate verb **1** zeigen auf (+ ACC) (a person or a thing); **2** (of a car or driver) blinken.

indigestion noun Magenverstimmung die (PL die Magenverstimmungen).

individual noun Einzelne der/die (PL die Einzelnen).

individual adjective **1** einzeln (serving, contribution); **2** **individual tuition** der Einzelunterricht.

indoor adjective **an indoor swimming pool** ein Hallenbad; **indoor games** Spiele im Haus, (in sports) Hallenspiele.

indoors adverb drinnen; **it's cooler indoors** drinnen ist es kühler; **to go indoors** ins Haus gehen.

industrial adjective industriell.

industrial estate noun Industriegebiet das (PL die Industriegebiete).

industry noun Industrie die (PL die Industrien); **the car industry** die Autoindustrie.

inefficient adjective uneffektiv.

inevitable adjective unvermeidlich.

inevitably adverb zwangsläufig.

inexperienced adjective unerfahren.

infant school noun Vorschule die (PL die Vorschulen).

infection noun Infektion die (PL die Infektionen); **eye infection** die Augeninfektion; **throat infection** die Halsentzündung.

infectious adjective ansteckend.

infinitive noun Infinitiv der (PL die Infinitive).

inflammable adjective leicht entflammbar.

inflatable adjective **inflatable mattress** die Luftmatratze; **inflatable boat** das Schlauchboot.

inflate verb aufblasen ◇ SEP (a mattress or boat).

inflation noun Inflation die (PL die Inflationen).

influence noun Einfluss der (PL die Einflüsse); **to be a good influence on somebody** einen guten Einfluss auf jemanden haben.

influence verb beeinflussen.

inform verb informieren; **to inform somebody of something** jemanden über etwas (ACC) informieren.

informal adjective **1** zwanglos (meal or event); **2** ungezwungen (language, tone).

information noun Auskunft die; **where can I get information about flights to Berlin?** wo kann ich Auskunft über Flüge nach Berlin bekommen?

information desk, **information office** noun Auskunftsbüro das (PL die Auskunftsbüros).

information technology noun Informatik die.

ingredient noun Zutat die (PL die Zutaten).

inhabitant noun Einwohner der (PL die Einwohner), Einwohnerin die (PL die Einwohnerinnen).

initials plural noun Initialen (plural).

initiative noun Initiative die (PL die Initiativen); **you must use your initiative** du musst die Initiative ergreifen.

injection noun Spritze die (PL die Spritzen).

injure verb verletzen.

injury noun Verletzung die (PL die Verletzungen).

ink noun Tinte die (PL die Tinten).

in-laws noun Schwiegereltern (plural).

inner adjective inner.

innocent adjective unschuldig.

insane adjective 1 geisteskrank; 2 (foolish) wahnsinnig.

insect noun Insekt das (PL die Insekten); **insect bite** der Insektenstich.

insect repellent noun Insektenvertilgungsmittel das.

inside noun on the inside innen; **the inside of the oven is black** innen ist der Herd schwarz.

inside preposition in (+ DAT, or, with movement towards a place, + ACC); **inside the cinema** im Kino; **to go inside (the house)** ins Haus gehen.

inside adverb drinnen; **she's inside, I think** ich glaube, sie ist drinnen.

inside out adjective, adverb (clothing) links.

insist verb darauf bestehen◇; **if you insist** wenn du darauf bestehst; **to insist on doing something** darauf bestehen, etwas zu tun; **he insists on paying** er besteht darauf zu zahlen; **to insist that ...** darauf bestehen, dass ...; **Ruth insisted I was wrong** Ruth hat darauf bestanden, dass ich Unrecht hatte.

inspector noun 1 (on a bus or train) Kontrolleur der (PL die Kontrolleure), Kontrolleurin die (PL die Kontrolleurinnen); 2 (in the police) Kommissar der (PL die Kommissare), Kommissarin die (PL die Kommissarinnen).

install verb installieren.

instalment noun (of a story or serial) Folge die (PL die Folgen).

instance noun for instance zum Beispiel.

instant noun Augenblick der (PL die Augenblicke); **come here this instant!** komm sofort her!.

instant adjective 1 Instant- (coffee, tea); 2 (immediate) sofortig.

instantly adverb sofort.

instead adverb 1 Ted couldn't come, so I came instead (of him) Ted konnte nicht kommen, also bin ich an seiner Stelle gekommen; 2 instead of statt (+ GEN or + DAT); **he bought a bike instead of a car** statt eines Autos hat er ein Fahrrad gekauft; **instead of cake I had cheese** statt Kuchen habe ich Käse genommen; **instead of playing tennis we went swimming** statt Tennis zu spielen, sind wir schwimmen gegangen.

instinct noun Instinkt der (PL die Instinkte).

institute noun Institut das (PL die Institute).

a b c d e f g h i j k l m n o p q r s t u v w x y z

a
b
c
d
e
f
g
h
i
j
k
l
m
n
o
p
q
r
s
t
u
v
w
x
y
z

instructions *plural noun* Anweisung die (PL die Anweisungen); **follow the instructions on the packet** befolgen Sie die Anweisung auf der Packung; **'instructions for use'** 'Gebrauchsanweisung'.

instructor *noun* Lehrer der (PL die Lehrer), Lehrerin die (PL die Lehrerinnen); **my skiing instructor** mein Skilehrer.

instrument *noun* Instrument das (PL die Instrumente); **to play an instrument** ein Instrument spielen.

insulin *noun* Insulin das.

insult *noun* Beleidigung die (PL die Beleidigungen).

insult *verb* beleidigen.

insurance *noun* Versicherung die (PL die Versicherungen); **travel insurance** die Reiseversicherung; **do you have holiday medical insurance?** bist du urlaubskrankenversichert?

intelligence *noun* Intelligenz die.

intelligent *adjective* intelligent.

intend *verb* beabsichtigen; **as I intended** wie beabsichtigt; **to intend to do something** beabsichtigen, etwas zu tun; **we intend to spend the night in Rome** wir beabsichtigen, in Rom zu übernachten.

intensive care *noun* Intensivpflege die; **he's now in intensive care** er ist jetzt auf der Intensivstation.

intention *noun* Absicht die (PL die Absichten); **I have no intention of paying** ich habe nicht die Absicht zu zahlen.

interest *noun* **1** Interesse das (PL die Interessen); **to have lots of interests** viele Interessen haben; **he has an interest in jazz** er hat Interesse an Jazz; **2** (*financial*) Zinsen (*plural*).

interest *verb* interessieren; **that doesn't interest me** das interessiert mich nicht.

interested *adjective* **to be interested in something** sich für etwas (ACC) interessieren; **Sean's interested in cooking** Sean interessiert sich für Kochen.

interesting *adjective* interessant.

interfere *verb* **1 to interfere with something** (*to fiddle with it*) sich (DAT) an etwas (DAT) zu schaffen machen; **don't interfere with my computer!** mach dir nicht an meinem Computer zu schaffen!; **2 to interfere in something** sich in etwas (ACC) einmischen SEP (*somebody else's affairs*).

interior designer *noun* Innenarchitekt der (PL die Innenarchitekten), Innenarchitektin die (PL die Innenarchitektinnen).

international *adjective* international.

Internet *noun* Internet das; **on the Internet** im Internet.

Internet cafe *noun* Internetcafé das (PL die Internetcafés); **where is there an Internet cafe?** wo gibt es hier ein Internetcafé?

interpret *verb* (*act as an interpreter*) dolmetschen.

interpreter *noun* Dometscher der (PL die Dolmetscher),

Dolmetscherin die (PL die Dometscherinnen).

interrupt verb unterbrechen✧.

interruption noun
Unterbrechung die (PL die Unterbrechungen).

interval noun (in a play or concert)
Pause die (PL die Pausen).

interview noun 1 (for a job)
Vorstellungsgespräch das (PL die Vorstellungsgespräche); **to go for an interview** sich vorstellen SEP; **2** (in a newspaper, on TV, or radio)
Interview das (PL die Interviews).

interview verb interviewen (on TV, radio).

interviewer noun Interviewer der (PL die Interviewer), Interviewerin die (PL die Interviewerinnen).

into preposition 1 in (+ ACC); **he's gone into the garden** er ist in den Garten gegangen; **I put the ball into the bag** ich habe den Ball in die Tasche getan; **we all got into the car** wir sind alle ins Auto gestiegen; **to go into town** in die Stadt gehen; **to get into bed** ins Bett gehen; **to translate into German** ins Deutsche übersetzen; **to change pounds into euros** Pfund in Euro wechseln; **2** (against) gegen (+ ACC); **he drove into the wall** er ist gegen die Wand gefahren; **3 to be into jazz** auf Jazz abfahren✧ SEP (PERF sein) (informal).

introduce verb vorstellen SEP; **she introduced me to her brother** sie hat mich ihrem Bruder vorgestellt; **she introduced her brother to me** sie hat mir ihren Bruder vorgestellt; **can I introduce you to**

my mother? darf ich Sie meiner Mutter vorstellen?

introduction noun (in a book)
Einleitung die (PL die Einleitungen).

invade verb einfallen✧ SEP in (PERF sein) (+ ACC).

invalid noun Kranke der/die (PL die Kranken).

invent verb erfinden✧.

invention noun Erfindung die (PL die Erfindungen).

inverted commas plural noun
Anführungszeichen (plural); **in inverted commas** in Anführungszeichen.

investigation noun
Untersuchung die (PL die Untersuchungen); **an investigation into the incident** eine Untersuchung des Vorfalls.

invisible adjective unsichtbar.

invitation noun Einladung die (PL die Einladungen); **an invitation to dinner** eine Einladung zum Abendessen.

invite verb einladen✧ SEP; **Kirsty invited me to lunch** Kirsty hat mich zum Mittagessen eingeladen; **he's invited me out on Tuesday** er hat mich eingeladen, Dienstag mit ihm auszugehen; **they invited us round** sie haben uns zu sich eingeladen.

inviting adjective verlockend.

involve verb 1 erfordern; **it involves a lot of time** es erfordert viel Zeit; **2** (include) beteiligen; **the game will involve everybody** alle können sich an dem Spiel beteiligen; **to be involved in something** an etwas (DAT) beteiligt sein; **I am involved in the new**

a
b
c
d
e
f
g
h
i
j
k
l
m
n
o
p
q
r
s
t
u
v
w
x
y
z

project ich bin an dem neuen Projekt beteiligt; **3** (*implicate*) verwickeln; **to get involved in something** in etwas (ACC) verwickelt werden; **two cars were involved in the accident** zwei Autos waren in den Unfall verwickelt; **4 to get involved with somebody** sich mit jemandem einlassen✧ SEP.

Iran noun Iran der.

Iraq noun Irak der.

Ireland noun Irland das; **the Republic of Ireland** die Republik Irland.

Irish noun **1** (*the language*) Irisch das; **2** (*the people*) die Iren die.

Irish adjective irisch; **he's Irish** er ist Ire; **she's Irish** sie ist Irin.

Irishman noun Ire der (PL die Iren).

Irish Sea noun Irische See die.

Irishwoman noun Irin die (PL die Irinnen).

iron noun **1** (*for clothes*) Bügeleisen das (PL die Bügeleisen); **2** (*the metal*) Eisen das.

iron verb bügeln.

ironing noun Bügeln das; **to do the ironing** bügeln.

ironing board noun Bügelbrett das (PL die Bügelbretter).

ironmonger's noun Haushaltswarengeschäft das (PL die Haushaltswarengeschäfte).

irregular adjective unregelmäßig.

irritable adjective reizbar.

irritate verb ärgern.

irritating adjective ärgerlich.

Islam noun Islam der.

Islamic adjective islamisch.

island noun Insel die (PL die Inseln).

isolated adjective **1** (*remote*) abgelegen; **2** (*single*) einzeln; **isolated cases** Einzelfälle.

Israel noun Israel das.

Israeli noun Israeli der/die (PL die Iraelis).

Israeli adjective israelisch.

issue noun **1** (*something you discuss*) Frage die (PL die Fragen); **a political issue** eine politische Frage; **2** (*of a magazine*) Ausgabe die (PL die Ausgaben).

issue verb (*hand out*) ausgeben✧ SEP.

it pronoun **1** (*as the subject*) er (*standing for a masculine noun*), sie (*standing for a feminine noun*), es (*standing for a neuter noun*); **'where's my key?' – 'it's in the kitchen'** wo ist mein Schlüssel?' – 'er ist in der Küche'; **'where's my bag?'– 'it's in the living-room'** wo ist meine Tasche?' – 'sie ist im Wohnzimmer'; **'how old is your car?' – 'it's five years old'** wie alt ist dein Auto?' – 'es ist fünf Jahre alt'; **2** (*as the direct object, in the accusative*) ihn (*standing for a masculine noun*), sie (*standing for a feminine noun*), es (*standing for a neuter noun*); **'where's your umbrella?' –'I've lost it'** wo ist dein Regenschirm?'- 'ich habe ihn verloren'; **have you seen my bag?' -'I saw it in the kitchen'** hast du meine Tasche gesehen?' - 'ich habe sie in der Küche gesehen'; **have you read his new book?' - 'I've just bought it'** hast du sein neues Buch gelesen?' - 'ich habe es gerade gekauft'; **3 to it** ihm (*masculine*),

ihr (feminine), ihm (neuter); **4 yes,
it's true** ja, das stimmt; **it doesn't
matter** das macht nichts; **5 who is
it?** wer ist da?; **it's me** ich bins;
what is it? was ist los?; **6 it's
raining** es regnet; **it's Monday** es ist
Montag; **it's two o'clock** es ist zwei
Uhr; **7 of it** davon; **8 out of it**
daraus.

Italian noun **1** (the language)
Italienisch das; **2** (person) Italiener
der (PL die Italiener), Italienerin die
(PL die Italienerinnen).

Italian adjective **1** italienisch;
Italian food die italienische Küche;
2 my Italian class mein
Italienischunterricht.

italics noun Kursivschrift die; **in
italics** kursiv.

Italy noun Italien das.

itch verb **1 my back's itching** mein
Rücken juckt; **2 this jumper itches**
dieser Pullover kratzt.

item noun **1** Gegenstand der (PL die
Gegenstände); **2** (for sale in a shop)
Artikel der (PL die Artikel).

its adjective **1** sein (for a masculine
noun), ihr (for a feminine noun),
sein (for a neuter noun); **the dog
has lost its collar** der Hund hat
sein Halsband verloren; **the cat's
in its basket** die Katze ist in ihrem
Korb; **the horse is brown and its
mane is black** das Pferd ist braun
und seine Mähne ist schwarz;
2 (for a plural noun) seine
(standing for a feminine noun),
(standing for a masculine noun)
ihre, seine (standing for a neuter
noun); **its toys** seine Spielsachen,
ihre Spielsachen.

itself pronoun **1** (reflexive) sich; **the
cat's washing itself** die Katze putzt
sich; **2 he left the dog by itself** er
hat den Hund allein gelassen.

ivy noun Efeu der.

Jj

jack noun **1** (in cards) Bube der (PL
die Buben); **the jack of clubs** der
Kreuzbube; **2** (for a car)
Wagenheber der (PL die
Wagenheber).

jacket noun Jacke die (PL die
Jacken).

jacket potatoes noun in der
Schale gebackenen Kartoffeln.

jackpot noun Jackpot der (PL die
Jackpots); **to win the jackpot** den
Hauptgewinn bekommen; **to hit
the jackpot** das große Los ziehen.

jam noun **1** Marmelade die (PL die
Marmeladen); **raspberry jam** die
Himbeermarmelade; **2 traffic jam**
der Stau.

January noun Januar der; **in
January** im Januar.

Japan noun Japan das.

Japanese noun **1** (the language)
Japanisch das; **2** (person) Japaner
der (PL die Japaner), Japanerin die
(PL die Japanerinnen); **the
Japanese** die Japaner.

Japanese adjective japanisch.

jar noun **1** (small) Glas das (PL die
Gläser); **a jar of jam** ein Glas
Marmelade; **2** (large) Topf der (PL
die Töpfe).

a b c d e f g h i j k l m n o p q r s t u v w x y z

javelin noun Speer der (PL die Speere).

jaw noun Kiefer der (PL die Kiefer).

jazz noun Jazz der.

jealous adjective eifersüchtig; **to be jealous of somebody** eifersüchtig auf jemanden sein.

jeans plural noun Jeans (plural); **my jeans** meine Jeans; **a pair of jeans** ein Paar Jeans.

jelly noun 1 Gelee das (PL die Gelees); 2 (dessert) Götterspeise die (PL die Götterspeisen).

jellyfish noun Qualle die (PL die Quallen).

jersey noun 1 (jumper) Pullover der (PL die Pullover); 2 (for football) Trikot das (PL die Trikots).

Jesus noun Jesus der; **Jesus Christ** Jesus Christus.

jet noun (a plane) Jet der (PL die Jets).

jet lag noun Jetlag der.

Jew noun Jude der (PL die Juden), Jüdin die (PL die Jüdinnen).

jewel noun Edelstein der (PL die Edelsteine).

jeweller noun Juwelier der (PL die Juweliere).

jeweller's noun Juweliergeschäft das.

jewellery noun Schmuck der.

Jewish adjective jüdisch.

jigsaw noun Puzzlespiel das (PL die Puzzlespiele).

job noun 1 (paid work) Stelle die (PL die Stellen), Job der (PL die Jobs) (informal); **a job as a secretary** eine Stelle als Sekretärin; 2 (a task) Arbeit die (PL die Arbeiten); **it's not an easy job** das ist keine leichte Arbeit; 3 **she made a good job of it** sie hat es gut gemacht.

jobless adjective arbeitslos.

jog verb joggen◊ (PERF sein).

join verb 1 (become a member of) beitreten◊ SEP (+ DAT) (PERF sein); **I've joined the tennis club** ich bin dem Tennisklub beigetreten; 2 (to meet up with) treffen◊; **I'll join you later** ich treffe euch später.

● **to join in** 1 mitmachen SEP; **Kylie never joins in** Kylie macht nie mit; 2 **to join in something** bei etwas (DAT) mitmachen SEP; **won't you join in the game?** willst du bei dem Spiel nicht mitmachen?

joint noun 1 (of meat) Braten der (PL die Braten); **a joint of beef** ein Rinderbraten; 2 (in your body) Gelenk das (PL die Gelenke).

joke noun Witz der (PL die Witze); **to tell a joke** einen Witz erzählen.

joke verb Witze machen; **you must be joking!** du machst wohl Witze!

joker noun (in cards) Joker der (PL die Joker).

journalism noun Journalismus der.

journalist noun Journalist der (PL die Journalisten), Journalistin die (PL die Journalistinnen); **Sean's a journalist** Sean ist Journalist.

journey noun 1 (a long one) Reise die (PL die Reisen); **on our journey to Italy** auf unserer Reise nach Italien; 2 (shorter; to work or school) Fahrt die (PL die Fahrten); **bus journey** die Busfahrt.

joy noun Freude die (PL die Freuden).

joystick noun (for computer games) Joystick der (PL die Joysticks).

Judaism noun Judentum das.

judge noun **1** (in court) Richter der (PL die Richter); **2** (in sporting events) Schiedsrichter der (PL die Schiedsrichter); **3** (in a competition) Preisrichter der (PL die Preisrichter).

judge verb schätzen (time or distance).

judo noun Judo das; **he does judo** er macht Judo.

jug noun Krug der (PL die Krüge).

juice noun Saft der; **two orange juices please** zwei Orangensaft bitte.

juicy adjective saftig.

jukebox noun Jukebox die (PL die Jukeboxes).

July noun Juli der; **in July** im Juli.

jumble sale noun Basar der (PL die Basare).

jump noun Sprung der (PL die Sprünge); **parachute jump** der Fallschirmsprung.

jump verb springen ◇ (PERF sein).

jumper noun Pullover der (PL die Pullover).

junction noun **1** (of roads) Kreuzung die (PL die Kreuzungen); **2** (on railway) Gleisanschluss der (PL die Gleisanschlüsse).

June noun Juni der; **in June** im Juni.

jungle noun Dschungel der.

junior adjective jünger; **junior school** die Grundschule; **the juniors** (at primary school) die Grundschüler, die Grundschülerinnen.

junk noun Trödel der.

junk food noun ungesunde Essen das.

just adverb **1** (very recently) gerade; **to have just done something** gerade etwas getan haben; **Tom has just arrived** Tom ist gerade angekommen; **2 to be just doing something** gerade dabei sein, etwas zu tun; **I'm just doing the food** ich bin gerade dabei, Essen zu machen; **3 just before midday** kurz vor Mittag; **just after 4 o'clock** kurz nach vier Uhr; **4** (only) nur; **just for fun** nur zum Vergnügen; **he's just a child** er ist doch nur ein Kind; **just me and Justine are coming** nur ich und Justine kommen; **5 just a minute!** einen Moment!; **6 just coming!** ich komme schon!; **7** (exactly) **just as** genauso wie. **he's got just as many friends** er hat genauso viele Freunde.

justice noun Gerechtigkeit die.

Kk

kangaroo noun Känguru das (PL die Kängurus).

karate noun Karate das.

karting noun Gokarten das; **to go go-karting** Gokarten fahren.

kebab noun Kebab der (PL die Kebabs).

keen adjective **1** (enthusiastic or committed) begeistert; **he's a keen photographer** er ist ein begeisterter Fotograf; **you don't seem too keen** du scheinst nicht gerade begeistert zu sein; **2 to be keen on** mögen ◇; **I'm not keen on**

a b c d e f g h i j k l m n o p q r s t u v w x y z

fish ich mag Fisch nicht; **3 to be keen on doing** (or **to do**) **something** etwas gerne tun.

keep verb **1** behalten✧; **you can keep the book** du kannst das Buch behalten; **to keep a secret** ein Geheimnis für sich behalten; **2 will you keep my seat?** können Sie meinen Platz freihalten?; **3 to keep somebody waiting** jemanden warten lassen; **4** (store) aufbewahren SEP; **can I keep my watch in your desk?** kann ich meine Uhr in deinem Schreibtisch aufbewahren?; **where do you keep saucepans?** wo sind die Töpfe?; **5** (not throw away) aufheben✧ SEP; **I kept all his letters** ich habe alle seine Briefe aufgehoben; **6 to keep on doing something** etwas weiter tun; **she kept on talking** sie hat weitergeredet; **can I keep my watch** straight on weiter geradeaus gehen; **7 to keep on doing something** (time after time) dauernd etwas tun; **he keeps on ringing me up** er ruft mich dauernd an; **8** (maintain) halten✧; **to keep the food warm** das Essen warm halten; **to keep a promise** ein Versprechen halten; **9** (stay) bleiben✧ (PERF sein); **to keep calm** ruhig bleiben; **to keep out of the sun** im Schatten bleiben.

kennel noun **1** (for one dog) Hundehütte die (PL die Hundehütten); **2** (for boarding) **kennels** Hundepension die (PL die Hundepensionen).

kerb noun Randstein der.

kettle noun Kessel der (PL die Kessel); **to put the kettle on** Wasser aufsetzen.

key noun **1** (for a lock) Schlüssel der (PL die Schlüssel); **bunch of keys** der Schlüsselbund; **2** (on a piano or keyboard) Taste die.

keyboard noun (for a computer) Tastatur die (PL die Tastaturen).

keyring noun Schlüsselring der (PL die Schlüsselringe).

kick noun **1** (from a person or a horse) Tritt der (PL die Tritte); **to give somebody a kick** jemandem einen Tritt geben; **2** (in football) Schuss der (PL die Schüsse); ★ **to get a kick out of doing something** etwas leidenschaftlich gerne tun.

kick verb **1 to kick somebody** jemandem einen Tritt geben; **2 to kick the ball** den Ball schießen.

● **to kick off** anstoßen✧ SEP.

kick-off noun Anstoß der.

kid noun (child) Kind das (PL die Kinder); **Dad's looking after the kids** Vati passt auf die Kinder auf.

kidnap verb entführen.

kidnapper noun Entführer der (PL die Entführer), Entführerin die (PL die Entführerinnen).

kidney noun Niere die (PL die Nieren).

kill verb **1** töten (an animal); **2** (murder) umbringen✧ SEP; **he killed the girl** er brachte das Mädchen um; **3 she was killed in a car accident** sie kam bei einem Autounfall ums Leben.

killer noun Mörder der (PL die Mörder), Mörderin die (PL die Mörderinnen).

kilo noun Kilo das (PL die Kilo); **a kilo of sugar** ein Kilo Zucker; **two euros a kilo** zwei Euro den Kilo.

kilogram noun Kilogramm das (PL die Kilogram).

kilometre noun Kilometer der (PL die Kilometer).

kilt noun Kilt der (PL die Kilts).

kind noun 1 (for newspapers or snacks) Art die (PL die Arten); **this kind of book** diese Art Buch; **all kinds of people** alle möglichen Leute; 2 (brand) Sorte die (PL die Sorten).

kind adjective nett; **she was very kind to me** sie war sehr nett zu mir.

kindness noun Freundlichkeit die.

king noun König der (PL die Könige); **the king of hearts** der Herzkönig.

kingdom noun Königreich das (PL die Königreiche); **the United Kingdom** das Vereinigte Königreich.

kiosk noun 1 (for newspapers or snacks) Kiosk das (PL die Kioske); 2 (for a phone) Telefonzelle die (PL die Telefonzellen).

kipper noun Räucherhering der (PL die Räucherheringe).

kiss noun Kuss der (PL die Küsse); **to give somebody a kiss** jemandem einen Kuss geben.

kiss verb küssen; **kiss me!** küss mich!; **we kissed each other** wir haben uns geküsst.

kit noun 1 (of tools) Werkzeug das; 2 (in a box) **a tool kit** ein Werkzeugkasten; 3 (clothes) Sachen (plural); **where's my football kit?** wo sind meine Fußballsachen?; 4 (for making a model, a piece of furniture, etc.) Bausatz der (PL die Bausätze).

kitchen noun Küche die (PL die Küchen); **the kitchen table** der Küchentisch.

kitchen foil noun Alufolie die.

kitchen roll noun Küchenrolle die (PL die Küchenrollen).

kite noun Drachen der; **to fly a kite** einen Drachen steigen lassen.

kitten noun Kätzchen das (PL die Kätzchen).

kiwi fruit noun Kiwi die (PL die Kiwis).

knee noun Knie das (PL die Knie); **on (your) hands and knees** auf allen vieren.

kneel verb knien◇; **to kneel (down)** sich hinknien SEP.

knickers plural noun Schlüpfer der (PL die Schlüpfer); **two pairs of knickers** zwei Schlüpfer.

knife noun Messer das (PL die Messer).

knife verb einstechen◇ SEP auf (+ ACC), (kill) erstechen◇.

knight noun (in chess) Springer der (PL die Springer).

knit verb stricken.

knitting noun Strickerei die.

knob noun 1 (on a door or walking stick) Knauf der (PL die Knäufe); 2 (control on a radio or machine) Knopf der (PL die Knöpfe); 3 **knob of butter** das kleine Stückchen Butter.

knock noun Schlag der (PL die Schläge); **a knock on the head** ein Schlag auf den Kopf; **a knock at the door** ein Klopfen an der Tür.

knock verb 1 (to bang) stoßen◇; **I knocked my arm on the table** ich

a b c d e f g h i j k l m n o p q r s t u v w x y z

habe mir den Arm am Tisch gestoßen; **2 to knock on something** an etwas (ACC) klopfen.

● **to knock down 1** (*in a traffic accident*) anfahren✧ SEP (*a person*); **2** (*to demolish*) abreißen✧ SEP (*an old building*).

● **to knock out 1** (*to make unconscious*) bewusstlos schlagen✧; **2** (*in sport, to eliminate*) k.o. schlagen✧.

knot noun Knoten der (PL die Knoten); **to tie a knot** einen Knoten machen.

know verb **1** (*know a fact*) wissen✧; **do you know where Tim is?** weißt du, wo Tim ist?; **I know they've moved house** ich weiß, dass sie umgezogen sind; **yes, I know** ja, weiß ich; **you never know!** man kann nie wissen!; **I know how to get to town** ich weiß, wie man in die Stadt kommt; **2** (*be personally acquainted with*) kennen✧; **do you know the Jacksons?** kennst du die Jacksons?; **all the people I know** alle Leute, die ich kenne; **I don't know his mother** ich kenne seine Mutter nicht; **3 to know how to do something** wissen, wie man etwas macht; **Steve knows how to make potato salad** Steve kann Kartoffelsalat machen; **Liz knows how to mend it** Liz kann es reparieren; **4 to know about** Bescheid wissen über (+ ACC) (*items in the news*); **5 to know about** sich auskennen✧ SEP mit (*machines, cars, etc.*); **Lindy knows about computers** Lindy kennt sich mit Computern aus; **6 to get to know**

somebody jemanden kennen lernen.

knowledge noun Wissen das.

Koran noun Koran der.

kosher adjective koscher.

LI

lab noun Labor das (PL die Labors).

label noun Etikett das (PL die Etikette).

laboratory noun Labor das (PL die Labors).

lace noun **1** (*for a shoe*) Schnürsenkel der (PL die Schnürsenkel); **to tie your laces** sich (DAT) die Schnürsenkel binden; **2** (*fabric or trimming*) Spitze die.

ladder noun **1** (*for climbing*) Leiter die (PL die Leitern); **2** (*in your tights*) Laufmasche die (PL die Laufmaschen).

ladies noun (*lavatory*) Damentoilette die (PL die Damentoiletten); (*on a sign*) '**Ladies**' 'Damen'.

lady noun Dame die (PL die Damen); **ladies and gentlemen** meine Damen und Herren.

ladybird noun Marienkäfer der (PL die Marienkäfer).

lager noun helle Bier das (PL die hellen Biere), Helle das (PL die Hellen) (*informal*); **a lager, please** ein Helles bitte.

laid-back adjective gelassen.

lake noun See der (PL die Seen); **Lake Geneva** der Genfer See.

landlady noun **1** (of a house or room) Vermieterin die (PL die Vermieterinnen); **2** (of a pub) Gastwirtin die (PL die Gastwirtinnen).

landlord noun **1** (of a house or room) Vermieter der (PL die Vermieter); **2** (of a pub) Gastwirt der (PL die Gastwirte).

lane noun **1** (small road) Weg der (PL die Wege); **2** (of a motorway) Spur die (PL die Spuren).

language noun **1** (German, Italian, etc.) Sprache die (PL die Sprachen); **foreign language** die Fremdsprache; **2** (way of speaking) Ausdrucksweise die; **bad language** Kraftausdrücke (plural).

lap noun **1** Schoß der (PL die Schöße); **2** (in races) Runde die (PL die Runden).

laptop noun Laptop der (PL die Laptops).

larder noun Speisekammer die (PL die Speisekammern).

large adjective groß.

laser noun Laser der (PL die Laser).

laser beam noun Laserstrahl der (PL die Laserstrahlen).

laser printer noun Laserdrucker der (PL die Laserdrucker).

laser surgery noun Laseroperation die (PL die Laseroperationen).

last adjective letzter/letzte/letztes; **last week** letzte Woche; **for the last time** zum letzten Mal; **last night** letzte Nacht.

last adverb **1** (in final position) als Letzter/als Letzte/als Letztes; **Rob arrived last** Rob kam als Letzter an; **2** **at last!** endlich!; **3** (most

recently) zuletzt; **I last saw him in May** ich habe ihn zuletzt im Mai gesehen.

last verb dauern; **the film lasted two hours** der Film dauerte zwei Stunden.

late adjective, adverb **1** spät; **I'm late** ich bin spät dran; **we were five minutes late** wir haben uns fünf Minuten verspätet; **they arrived late** sie sind zu spät angekommen; **to be late for something** zu spät zu etwas (DAT) kommen; **we were late for the party** wir kamen zu spät zur Party; **2** (of a bus or train) Verspätung haben; **the train was an hour late** der Zug hatte eine Stunde Verspätung; **3** (late in the day) spät; **we got up late** wir sind spät aufgestanden; **the chemist is open late** die Apotheke hat bis spät auf; **late last night** gestern spät in der Nacht; **too late!** zu spät!

lately adverb in letzter Zeit.

later adverb später; **I'll explain later** ich erkläre es später; **see you later!** bis später!

latest adjective **1** neuester/ neueste/neuestes; **the latest news** die neuesten Nachrichten; **the latest in audio equipment** das Neueste an Audioausrüstung; **2** **at the latest** spätestens.

Latin noun Latein das.

laugh noun Lachen das; **to do something for a laugh** etwas aus Spaß machen.

laugh verb **1** lachen; **everybody laughed** alle haben gelacht; **to laugh about something** über etwas (ACC) lachen; **2** **to laugh at**

a b c d e f g h i j k l m n o p q r s t u v w x y z

a somebody jemanden auslachen
SEP; **they'll only laugh at me** sie
b lachen mich bestimmt aus.

c **launch** noun **1** (of a ship)
Stapellauf der ; **2** (of a product)
d Einführung die; **3** (of a spacecraft)
Abschuss der.

e **launch** verb **1** auf den Markt
f bringen✧ (a product); **2** ins All
schiessen✧ (a spacecraft); **3** zu
g Wasser lassen ✧ (a ship).

h **launderette** noun Waschsalon
der (PL die Waschsalons).

i **lavatory** noun Toilette die (PL die
Toiletten); **to go to the lavatory** auf
j die Toilette gehen.

k **lavender** noun Lavendel der.

l **law** noun **1** Gesetz das (PL die
Gesetze); **to break the law** gegen
m das Gesetz verstoßen; **2 it's against
the law** das ist verboten; **3** (subject
n of study) Jura die (no plural).

o **lawn** noun Rasen der (PL die Rasen).

lawnmower noun Rasenmäher
p der (PL die Rasenmäher).

q **lawyer** noun Rechtsanwalt der (PL
die Rechtsanwälte),
r Rechtsanwältin die (PL die
Rechtsanwältinnen).

s **lay** verb **1** (put) legen; **she laid the
cards on the table** sie legte die
t Karten auf den Tisch; **2 to lay the
table** den Tisch decken.

u **lay-by** noun Parkplatz der (PL die
v Parkplätze).

w **layer** noun Schicht die (PL die
Schichten).

x **lazy** adjective faul.

y **lead**¹ noun **1** (when you are ahead)
Führung die; **to be in the lead** in
z Führung liegen; **Baxter's in the
lead** Baxter liegt in Führung; **to**

take the lead in Führung gehen;
2 (electric) Kabel das (PL die Kabel);
3 (for a dog) Leine die (PL die
Leinen); **on a lead** an der Leine;
4 (role) Hauptrolle die (PL die
Hauptrollen); **5** (an actor)
Hauptdarsteller der (PL die
Hauptdarsteller),
Hauptdarstellerin die (PL die
Hauptdarstellerinnen).

lead verb **1** führen; **the path leads
to the sea** der Weg führt zum Meer;
to lead by three points mit drei
Punkten führen; **2 to lead the way**
vorangehen✧ SEP (PERF sein); **3 to
lead to something** zu etwas (DAT)
führen (an accident or problems, for
example).

lead² noun (metal) Blei das.

lead singer noun Leadsänger der
(PL die Leadsänger), Leadsängerin
die (PL die Leadsängerinnen).

leader noun **1** (of a political party)
Vorsitzende der/die (PL die
Vorsitzenden); **2** (of an expedition
or group) Leiter der (PL die Leiter),
Leiterin die (PL die Leiterinnen);
3 (in a competition) Erste der/die (PL
die Ersten); **4** (of a gang) Anführer
der (PL die Anführer), Anführerin
die (PL die Anführerinnen).

leaf noun Blatt das (PL die Blätter).

leaflet noun **1** (with instructions)
Merkblatt das (PL die Merkblätter);
2 (for advertising) Reklameblatt
das (PL die Reklameblätter).

leak noun **1** (in a roof, tent)
undichte Stelle die (PL die
undichten Stellen); **2 gas leak** die
undichte Gasleitung; **3** (in a boat)
Leck das (PL die Lecks).

leak *verb* (*bottle or roof*) undicht sein.

leak *adjective* (*meat*) mager.

lean *verb* **1 to lean on something** sich an etwas (ACC) lehnen; **he leaned against the door** er hat sich gegen die Tür gelehnt; **2** sich lehnen; **she was leaning out of the window** sie lehnte sich aus dem Fenster; **3 to lean forward** sich fahren vorbeugen SEP.

leap year *noun* Schaltjahr *das* (PL die Schaltjahre).

learn *verb* lernen; **to learn German** Deutsch lernen; **to learn (how) to drive** Autofahren lernen.

learner *noun* Lerner *der* (PL die Lerner); **to be a fast learner** schnell lernen; **2** (*beginner*) Anfänger *der* (PL die Anfänger), Anfängerin *die* (PL die Anfängerinnen).

least *adjective, pronoun* **1** wenigster/wenigste/wenigstes; **to have least time** am wenigsten Zeit haben; **Tony has the least money** Tony hat das wenigste Geld; **2** (*the slightest*) geringster/ geringste/geringstes; **I haven't the least idea** ich habe nicht die geringste Ahnung.

least *adverb* **1** am wenigsten; **I like the blue shirt least** ich mag das blaue Hemd am wenigsten; **2 the least expensive hotel** das billigste Hotel; **3 at least** (*at a minimum*) mindestens; **at least twenty people** mindestens zwanzig Leute; **4 at least** (*at any rate*) wenigstens; **she's a teacher, at least I think**

she is sie ist Lehrerin, glaube ich wenigstens.

leather *noun* Leder *das*; **leather jacket** die Lederjacke.

leave *noun* Urlaub *der*; **three days' leave** drei Tage Urlaub.

leave *verb* **1** (*go away*) gehen◇ (PERF *sein*), (*by car*) fahren◇ SEP (PERF *sein*), (*a train or bus*) abfahren◇ SEP (PERF *sein*); **they're leaving tomorrow evening** sie fahren morgen Abend; **we left at six** wir sind um sechs Uhr gegangen; **the train leaves Munich at ten** der Zug fährt um zehn Uhr von München ab; **2** (*go away from or go out of*) verlassen◇; **I left the office at five** ich habe das Büro um fünf verlassen; **he left his wife** er hat seine Frau verlassen; **3** (*deposit or allow to remain in the same state*) lassen◇; **you can leave your coats in the hall** Sie können Ihre Mäntel in der Diele lassen; **to leave the door open** die Tür offen lassen; **leave it until tomorrow** lass es bis morgen; **4 to leave somebody something** jemandem etwas hinterlassen◇ (*a message or money*); **he didn't leave a message** er hat keine Nachricht hinterlassen; **5** (*not do*) stehen lassen◇; **leave the washing up** lass den Abwasch stehen; **6** (*forget*) vergessen◇; **he left his umbrella on the train** er hat seinen Regenschirm im Zug vergessen; **7 be left** übrig sein (PERF *sein*); **there are two pancakes left** zwei Pfannkuchen sind noch übrig; **I don't have any money left** ich habe kein Geld mehr übrig; **we have ten**

a
b
c
d
e
f
g
h
i
j
k
l
m
n
o
p
q
r
s
t
u
v
w
x
y
z

minutes left wir haben noch zehn Minuten Zeit.

lecture noun **1** (at university) Vorlesung die (PL die Vorlesungen); **2** (public) Vortrag der (PL die Vorträge).

leek noun Lauch der.

left noun **on the left** links; **to drive on the left** links fahren; **on my left** links von mir.

left adverb links; **turn left at the church** an der Kirche links abbiegen.

left adjective linker/linke/linkes; **his left foot** sein linker Fuß.

left-click noun Klick der (mit der linken Maustaste).

left-click verb **left-click the icon** das Icon mit der linken Maustaste anklicken.

left-hand adjective **the left-hand side** die linke Seite.

left-handed adjective linkshändig.

left-luggage office noun Gepäckaufbewahrung die (PL die Gepäckaufbewahrungen).

leg noun **1** Bein das (PL die Beine); **my left leg** mein linkes Bein; **to break your leg** sich (DAT) das Bein brechen; **2** (in cooking) Keule die (PL die Keulen); **leg of lamb** die Lammkeule; ✱ **to pull somebody's leg** jemanden auf den Arm nehmen.

legal adjective gesetzlich.

leggings plural noun Leggings (plural).

leisure noun Freizeit die; **in my leisure time** in meiner Freizeit.

lemon noun Zitrone die (PL die Zitronen).

lemonade noun Limonade die (PL die Limonaden).

lemon juice noun Zitronensaft der.

lend verb leihen✧; **to lend something to somebody** jemandem etwas leihen; **I lent Judy my bike** ich habe Judy mein Rad geliehen; **will you lend it to me?** kannst du es mir leihen?

length noun Länge die (PL die Längen).

lens noun **1** (in a camera) Objektiv das (PL die Objektive); **2** (in spectacles) Brillenglas das (PL die Brillengläser); **3 contact lenses** Kontaktlinsen (plural).

Lent noun Fastenzeit die.

lentil noun Linse die (PL die Linsen).

Leo noun Löwe der (PL die Löwen); **I'm a Leo** ich bin Löwe.

leotard noun Turnanzug der (PL die Turnanzüge).

lesbian adjective lesbisch.

less pronoun, adjective, adverb weniger ('weniger' never changes); **Ben eats less** Ben isst weniger; **less time** weniger Zeit; **less than** weniger als; **less than three hours** weniger als drei Stunden; **you spent less than me** du hast weniger als ich ausgegeben; **less and less** immer weniger.

lesson noun (class) Stunde die (PL die Stunden); **German lesson** die Deutschstunde; **driving lesson** die Fahrstunde.

let[1] verb **1** (allow) lassen✧; **to let somebody do something** jemanden etwas tun lassen; **she**

lets me drive her car sie lässt mich mit ihrem Auto fahren; **the police let us through** die Polizei hat uns durchgelassen; **let me in** lass mich hinein; 2 (*as a suggestion or a command*) **let's go!** gehen wir!; **let's not talk about it** reden wir nicht mehr darüber; **let's eat out** essen wir im Restaurant.

● **to let off** 1 abfeuern◇ (*fireworks*); 2 (*to excuse from*) befreien von (+DAT) (*homework*).

let[2] *verb* (*to rent out*) vermieten; **'flat to let'** 'Wohnung zu vermieten'.

letter box *noun* Briefkasten der (PL die Briefkästen).

letter *noun* 1 Brief der (PL die Briefe); **a letter for you from Delia** ein Brief für dich von Delia; 2 (*of the alphabet*) Buchstabe der (PL die Buchstaben).

lettuce *noun* Salat der; **two lettuces** zwei Salatköpfe.

leukaemia *noun* Leukämie die.

level *noun* Höhe die; **at eye level** in Augenhöhe.

level *adjective* 1 eben (*ground or floor*); 2 (*horizontal*) waagerecht (*shelf*); 3 (*at the same height*) auf gleicher Höhe; **to be level with the ground** auf gleicher Höhe mit dem Boden sein.

level crossing *noun* Bahnübergang der (PL die Bahnübergänge).

lever *noun* Hebel der (PL die Hebel).

liar *noun* Lügner der (PL die Lügner), Lügnerin die (PL die Lügnerinnen).

liberal *adjective* 1 tolerant; 2 (*in politics*) liberal; **the Liberal Democrats** die Liberaldemokraten.

Libra *noun* Waage die; **Sean's Libra** Sean ist Waage.

librarian *noun* Bibliothekar der (PL die Bibliothekare), Bibliothekarin die (PL die Bibliothekarinnen).

library *noun* Bibliothek die (PL die Bibliotheken); **public library** die öffentliche Bücherei.

licence *noun* 1 (*for a TV*) Genehmigung die (PL die Genehmigungen); 2 (*driving licence*) Führerschein der (PL die Führerscheine).

lick *verb* lecken.

lid *noun* Deckel der (PL die Deckel).

lie *noun* Lüge die (PL die Lügen); **to tell a lie** (or **lies**) lügen◇.

lie *verb* 1 (*to be stretched out*) liegen◇; **he's lying on the sofa** er liegt auf dem Sofa; **my coat lay on the bed** mein Mantel lag auf dem Bett; 2 (*to lie down*) (*for a rest*) sich hinlegen SEP; **I'm going to lie down for a little** ich lege mich ein bisschen hin; 3 (*tell lies*) lügen◇.

lie-in *noun* **to have a lie-in** ausschlafen◇ SEP.

life *noun* Leben das (PL die Leben); **all her life** ihr ganzes Leben lang; **full of life** voller Leben; **that's life!** so ist das Leben!

lifeboat *noun* Rettungsboot das (PL die Rettungsboote).

lifeguard *noun* Rettungsschwimmer der (PL die Rettungsschwimmer), Rettungsschwimmerin die (PL die Rettungsschwimmerinnen); **is there a lifeguard at the pool?** gibt

life jacket

es einen Bademeister im Schwimmbad?

life jacket noun Schwimmweste die (PL die Schwimmwesten).

life-style noun Lebensstil der (PL die Lebensstile).

lift noun 1 Aufzug der (PL die Aufzüge); **let's take the lift** fahren wir mit dem Aufzug; 2 (a ride) to **give somebody a lift to the station** jemanden zum Bahnhof mitnehmen✧ SEP; **Khaled's giving me a lift** Khaled nimmt mich mit; **would you like a lift?** möchtest du mitfahren?

lift verb hochheben✧ SEP; **he lifted the box** er hob die Kiste hoch.

light noun 1 Licht das; **will you turn the light on?** kannst du das Licht anmachen?; **to turn off the light** das Licht ausmachen; **are your lights on?** hast du das Licht an?; 2 (in the street) Straßenlampe die (PL die Straßenlampen); 3 (a lamp) Lampe die (PL die Lampen); 4 **traffic lights** der Ampel (singular); **the lights are green** die Ampel ist grün; 5 (for a cigarette) **have you got a light?** hast du Feuer?

light adjective 1 (not dark) hell; **a light blue dress** ein hellblaues Kleid; **it gets light at six** es wird um sechs hell; 2 (not heavy) leicht; **a light coat** ein leichter Mantel; **a light breeze** eine leichte Brise.

light verb 1 anzünden SEP (the fire, a match, the gas); **we lit a fire** wir zündeten ein Feuer an; 2 **to light a cigarette** sich (DAT) eine Zigarette anzünden.

light bulb noun Glühbirne die (PL die Glühbirnen).

lighter noun Feuerzeug das (PL die Feuerzeuge).

lighthouse noun Leuchtturm der (PL die Leuchttürme).

lightning noun Blitz der; **flash of lightning** der Blitz; **to be struck by lightning** vom Blitz getroffen werden.

like[1] preposition, conjunction 1 wie; **like me** wie ich; **like a duck** wie eine Ente; **like I said** wie gesagt; **what's it like?** wie ist es?; **what was the weather like?** wie war das Wetter?; 2 **like this/that** so; 3 ähnlich + (DAT) 1 **to look like somebody** jemandem ähnlich sehen; **Cindy looks like her father** Cindy sieht ihrem Vater ähnlich.

like[2] verb 1 mögen✧; **I like vegetables** ich mag Gemüse; **I don't like meat** ich mag kein Fleisch; **I like Dürer best** ich mag Dürer am liebsten; **2 to like doing something** etwas gerne tun; **Mum likes reading** Mutti liest gerne; 3 **I would like ...** ich möchte gerne ...; **would you like a coffee?** möchten Sie einen Kaffee?; **what would you like to eat?** was möchten Sie essen?; **yes, if you like** ja, wenn du willst; **4 I like the dress** das Kleid gefällt mir; **how do you like it?** wie gefällt es dir?

likely adjective wahrscheinlich; **she's likely to phone** wahrscheinlich ruft sie an.

lime noun Kalk der.

limit noun Grenze die (PL die Grenzen); **speed limit** die Geschwindigkeitsbeschränkung.

limp noun to have a limp hinken.

line noun 1 Linie die (PL die Linien); **a straight line** eine gerade Linie; **to draw a line** eine Linie ziehen; 2 (in writing) Zeile die (PL die Zeilen); **six lines of text** sechs Zeilen Text; 3 (railway) Bahnlinie die (PL die Bahnlinien) (from one place to another); **on the line** (on the track) auf der Strecke; 4 (a queue of people or cars) Schlange die (PL die Schlangen); **to stand in line** Schlange stehen; 5 (telephone) Leitung die (PL die Leitungen); **the line's bad** die Verbindung ist schlecht; **hold the line, please** bitte bleiben Sie am Apparat.

line verb füttern (a coat).

linen noun Leinen das; **a linen jacket** eine Leinenjacke.

lining noun Futter das (PL die Futter).

link noun Verbindung die (PL die Verbindungen); **what's the link between the two?** was für eine Verbindung besteht zwischen den beiden?

link verb verbinden✧ (two places); **the two towns are linked by a railway line** die beiden Städte sind durch eine Bahnlinie miteinander verbunden.

lion noun Löwe der (PL die Löwen).

lip noun Lippe die (PL die Lippen).

lip-read verb von den Lippen lesen✧.

lipstick noun Lippenstift der (PL die Lippenstifte).

liquid noun Flüssigkeit die (PL die Flüssigkeiten).

liquid adjective flüssig.

liquidizer noun Mixer der (PL die Mixer).

list noun Liste die (PL die Listen).

listen verb 1 zuhören SEP; **I wasn't listening** ich habe nicht zugehört; **to listen to somebody** jemandem zuhören; **you're not listening to me** du hörst mir nicht zu; 2 **to listen to something** etwas (ACC) hören; **to listen to the radio** Radio hören.

listener noun (to the radio) Hörer der (PL die Hörer), Hörerin die (PL die Hörerinnen).

literature noun Literatur die (PL die Literaturen).

litre noun Liter der (PL die Liter); **a litre of milk** ein Liter Milch.

litter noun (rubbish) Abfall der.

litter bin noun Abfalleimer der (PL die Abfalleimer).

little adjective, pronoun 1 (small) klein; **a little boy** ein kleiner Junge; **a little break** eine kleine Pause; 2 (not much) wenig; **we have very little time** wir haben sehr wenig Zeit; 3 **a little** ein wenig; **we have a little left** wir haben ein wenig übrig; 4 **just a little, please** nur ein bisschen, bitte; **it's a little late** es ist ein bisschen spät; **a little more** ein bisschen mehr; **a little less** ein bisschen weniger; ★ **little by little** nach und nach.

little finger noun kleine Finger der (PL die kleinen Finger).

live[1] verb 1 (in a house or town) wohnen; **she lives in York** sie wohnt in York; **we live in a flat** wir wohnen in einer Wohnung; 2 (be or stay alive, spend one's life) leben;

a b c d e f g h i j k l m n o p q r s t u v w x y z

we're living in the country now wir leben jetzt auf dem Land; **they live on fruit** sie leben von Obst; **they live apart** sie leben getrennt.

live² *adjective, adverb* **1** live (*broadcast*); **a live programme** eine Livesendung; **live music** die Livemusik; **a broadcast live from Wembley** eine Liveübertragung aus Wembley; **to broadcast a concert live** ein Konzert live senden; **2** (*alive*) lebend.

lively *adjective* lebhaft.

liver *noun* Leber die (PL die Lebern).

living *noun* Lebensunterhalt der; **to earn a living** sich (DAT) seinen Lebensunterhalt verdienen.

living room *noun* Wohnzimmer das (PL die Wohnzimmer).

lizard *noun* Eidechse die (PL die Eidechsen).

load *noun* **1** (*on a lorry*) Ladung die (PL die Ladungen); **a (lorry-)load of bricks** eine Ladung Ziegelsteine; **2 a bus-load of tourists** ein Bus voll Touristen; **3 loads of** massenhaft (*informal*); **loads of tourists** massenhaft Touristen; **they've got loads of money** sie haben einen Haufen Geld (*informal*).

load *verb* **1** beladen ◇ (*a vehicle*); **2 to load a camera** einen Film einlegen SEP.

loaf *noun* Brot das (PL die Brote); **a loaf of white bread** ein Weißbrot.

loan *noun* **1** (*from a person*) Leihgabe die (PL die Leihgaben); **2** (*by a bank*) Kredit der (PL die Kredite).

loan *verb* leihen ◇.

loathe *verb* hassen, **I loathe getting up early** ich hasse es, früh aufzustehen.

local *noun* **1** (*a pub*) Stammkneipe die (PL die Stammkneipen); **2 the locals** (*people*) die Einheimischen.

local *adjective* **1** hiesig; **the local library** die hiesige Bücherei; **2 local newspaper** die Lokalzeitung.

lock *noun* Schloss das (PL die Schlösser).

lock *verb* abschließen ◇ SEP (*a door, room, or bicycle*); **have you locked the door?** hast du abgeschlossen?

lodger *noun* Untermieter der (PL die Untermieter), Untermieterin die (PL die Untermieterinnen).

loft *noun* Dachboden der (PL die Dachböden).

log *noun* **1** Baumstamm der (PL die Baumstämme); **2** (*as firewood*) Holzscheit das (PL die Holzscheite); **a log fire** ein offenes Feuer.

lollipop *noun* Lutscher der (PL die Lutscher).

London *noun* London das.

Londoner *noun* Londoner der (PL die Londoner), Londonerin die (PL die Londonerinnen).

lonely *adjective* einsam; **to feel lonely** sich einsam fühlen.

long *adjective, adverb* **1** lang; **a long film** ein langer Film; **a long day** ein langer Tag; **it's five metres long** es ist fünf Meter lang; **the film is an hour long** der Film dauert eine Stunde; **2 a long time** lange; **he stayed for a long time** er ist lange geblieben; **I've been here for a long time** ich bin schon lange hier; **a long time ago** vor langer Zeit; **this won't take long** das dauert nicht lange; **3 how long?** wie lange?; **how long have you been here?** wie lange sind Sie schon hier?; **long ago** vor langer Zeit; **4 a long way** weit; **it's a long way to the cinema** bis zum Kino ist es weit; **5 all night long** die ganze Nacht; **6 no longer** nicht mehr; **he doesn't work here any longer** er arbeitet nicht mehr hier.

long verb **to long to do something** sich danach sehnen, etwas zu tun; **I'm longing to see you** ich verlange mich danach, dich zu sehen.

long-distance call noun (within the country) Ferngespräch das (PL die Ferngespräche).

long jump noun Weitsprung der.

longlife milk noun H-Milch die.

loo noun Klo das (PL die Klos) (informal).

look noun **1** (a glance) Blick der (PL die Blicke); **to take a look at somebody** einen Blick auf jemanden werfen; **2** (a tour) **to have a look at the school** sich (DAT) die Schule ansehen; **to have a look round the town** sich (DAT) die Stadt ansehen; **3 to have a look for** suchen.

look verb **1** sehen◇; **to look out of the window** aus dem Fenster sehen; **I wasn't looking** ich habe nicht hingesehen; **2 to look at** ansehen◇ SEP; **he looked at the girl** er hat das Mädchen angesehen; **to look at something** sich (DAT) etwas ansehen; **I'm looking at the photos** ich sehe mir

die Fotos an; **3** (to seem) **aussehen**◇ SEP; **she looks sad** sie sieht traurig aus; **the salad looks delicious** der Salat sieht köstlich aus; **to look like** aussehen wie; **what does the house look like?** wie sieht das Haus aus?; **4** (resemble) **to look like somebody** jemandem ähnlich sehen; **she looks like her aunt** sie sieht ihrer Tante ähnlich; **they look like each other** sie sehen sich ähnlich.

● **to look after 1** sich kümmern um (+ ACC); **Dad's looking after the children** Vati kümmert sich um die Kinder; **2** aufpassen SEP auf (+ ACC) (luggage).

● **to look for** suchen; **I'm looking for my keys** ich suche meine Schlüssel.

● **to look forward to** sich freuen auf (+ ACC) (a party or a trip, for example).

● **to look out** (to be careful) aufpassen SEP; **look out, it's hot!** pass auf, das ist heiß!

● **to look up** nachschlagen◇ SEP (in a dictionary or directory); **he's looking it up in the dictionary** er schlägt es im Wörterbuch nach.

loose adjective **1** (screw or knot) locker; **2** (garment) weit; **3 loose change** das Kleingeld; ★ **I'm at a loose end** ich habe nichts zu tun.

lorry noun Lastwagen der (PL die Lastwagen).

lorry driver noun Lastwagenfahrer der (PL die Lastwagenfahrer),

a b c d e f g h i j k l m n o p q r s t u v w x y z

Lastwagenfahrerin die (PL die Lastwagenfahrerinnen).

lose *verb* 1 verlieren◇; **we lost** wir haben verloren; **we lost the match** wir haben das Spiel verloren; **Sam's lost his watch** Sam hat seine Uhr verloren; 2 **to get lost** sich verlaufen◇; **we got lost in the woods** wir haben uns im Wald verlaufen; 3 **to lose weight** abnehmen◇ SEP.

loss *noun* Verlust der (PL die Verluste).

lost property *noun* Fundsachen (*plural*).

lot *noun* 1 **a lot** viel; **Wilbur eats a lot** Wilbur isst viel; **I spent a lot** ich habe viel ausgegeben; **he's a lot better** es geht ihm viel besser; **a lot of** viel; **a lot of coffee** viel Kaffee; 2 (*many*) **a lot of** viele; **a lot of books** viele Bücher; 3 **lots of** eine Menge (*informal*); **lots of people** eine Menge Leute.

lottery *noun* Lotterie die (PL die Lotterien); **to win the lottery** in der Lotterie gewinnen.

loud *adjective* 1 laut; **in a loud voice** mit lauter Stimme; 2 **to say something out loud** etwas laut sagen.

loudly *adverb* laut.

loudspeaker *noun* Lautsprecher der (PL die Lautsprecher).

lounge *noun* 1 (*in a house*) Wohnzimmer das (PL die Wohnzimmer); 2 (*in a hotel or an airport*) Halle die (PL die Hallen); **departure lounge** die Abflughalle.

love *noun* 1 Liebe die; **for love** aus Liebe; 2 **to be in love with somebody** in jemanden verliebt

sein; **she's in love with Jake** sie ist in Jake verliebt; 3 **Gina sends her love** Gina lässt grüßen; **with love from Charlie** herzliche Grüße von Charlie; 4 (*in tennis*) null.

love *verb* 1 lieben (*a person*); **I love you** ich liebe dich; 2 sehr gerne mögen◇ (*a place or food*); **she loves London** sie mag London sehr gerne; **Wayne loves chocolate** Wayne mag Schokolade sehr gerne; 3 **to love doing something** etwas sehr gerne tun; **I love dancing** ich tanze sehr gerne; 4 **I'd love to come** ich würde sehr gerne kommen.

lovely *adjective* schön; **a lovely dress** ein schönes Kleid; **we had lovely weather** wir hatten schönes Wetter; **we had a lovely day** der Tag war sehr schön.

low *adjective* 1 niedrig; **a low table** ein niedriger Tisch; **at a low price** zu einem niedrigen Preis; 2 (*not loud*) leise; **in a low voice** mit leiser Stimme.

lower *adjective* (*not as high*) tiefer.

lower *verb* senken.

loyalty *noun* Loyalität die (PL die Loyalitäten).

loyalty card *noun* Treuekarte die (PL die Treuekarten).

luck *noun* 1 Glück das; **good luck!** viel Glück!; **with a bit of luck** wenn wir Glück haben; 2 **bad luck!** so ein Pech!

luckily *adverb* zum Glück; **luckily for them** zu ihrem Glück.

lucky *adjective* 1 **to be lucky** Glück haben; **we were lucky** wir haben Glück gehabt; 2 **to be lucky**

(bringing luck) Glück bringen; **it's supposed to be lucky** es soll Glück bringen; **my lucky number** meine Glückszahl.

luggage noun Gepäck das; **my luggage is in the boot** mein Gepäck ist im Kofferraum.

lump noun 1 Klumpen der (PL die Klumpen); 2 *(of sugar or butter)* Stück das (PL die Stücke).

lunch noun Mittagessen das (PL die Mittagessen); **to have lunch** zu Mittag essen; **we had lunch in Oxford** wir haben in Oxford zu Mittag gegessen.

lunch break noun Mittagspause die (PL die Mittagspausen).

lunch hour, lunch time noun Mittagszeit die.

lung noun Lungenflügel der; **lungs** die Lunge (singular).

luxurious adjective luxuriös.

lyrics plural noun Text der.

Mm

mac noun Regenmantel der (PL die Regenmäntel).

macaroni noun Makkaroni (plural).

machine noun 1 Maschine die (PL die Maschinen); 2 *(a slot machine)* Automat der (PL die Automaten).

machinery noun die Maschinen (plural).

mackerel noun Makrele die (PL die Makrelen).

mad adjective 1 verrückt; **she's completely mad!** sie ist total

verrückt!; 2 *(angry)* wütend; **to be mad at somebody** wütend auf jemanden sein; 3 **to be mad about something** ganz verrückt auf etwas (ACC) sein; **she's mad about horses** sie ist ganz verrückt auf Pferde.

madman noun Verrückte der (PL die Verrückten).

madness noun Wahnsinn der.

magazine noun 1 Zeitschrift die (PL die Zeitschriften), *(with mostly photos)* Magazin das (PL die Magazine).

magic noun Zauber der, *(conjuring tricks)* Zauberei die.

magic adjective 1 Zauber-; **magic wand** der Zauberstab; 2 *(great)* super *(informal)*.

magician noun 1 *(wizard)* Zauberer der (PL die Zauberer); 2 *(conjurer)* Zauberkünstler der (PL die Zauberkünstler).

magnificent adjective wundervoll.

magnifying glass noun Lupe die (PL die Lupen).

maiden name noun Mädchenname der (PL die Mädchennamen).

mail noun Post die.

mail order noun Bestellung per Post die; **to buy something by mail order** etwas bei einem Versandhaus bestellen; **mail order catalogue** der Versandhauskatalog.

main adjective Haupt-; **main entrance** der Haupteingang.

main course noun Hauptgericht das (PL die Hauptgerichte).

mainly adverb hauptsächlich.

main road noun Hauptstraße die (PL die Hauptstraßen).

maize noun Mais der.

major adjective 1 (important) groß; 2 (serious) schwer; **a major accident** ein schwerer Unfall.

Majorca noun Mallorca das.

majority noun Mehrheit die.

make noun Marke die (PL die Marken); **the make of a car** die Automarke.

make verb 1 machen; **to make a meal** Essen machen; **I made breakfast** ich habe Frühstück gemacht; **she made her bed** sie hat ihr Bett gemacht; **to make somebody happy** jemanden glücklich machen; **it makes you tired** das macht einen müde; 2 herstellen SEP; **they make computers** sie stellen Computer her; **'made in Germany'** 'in Deutschland hergestellt'; 3 **he made me wait** er ließ mich warten; **she makes me laugh** sie bringt mich zum Lachen; 4 verdienen; **he makes forty pounds a day** er verdient vierzig Pfund pro Tag; **to make a living** seinen Lebensunterhalt verdienen; 5 (force) zwingen✧; **to make somebody do something** jemanden zwingen, etwas zu tun; **she made him give the money back** sie hat ihn gezwungen, das Geld zurückzugeben; 6 (the verb 'make' is often translated by a more specific verb) **to make a cake** einen Kuchen backen; **to make a phone call** telefonieren; **to make a dress** ein Kleid nähen; 7 **to make friends with somebody** sich mit

jemandem anfreunden SEP; 8 **I can't make it tonight** ich kann heute Abend nicht kommen; 9 **two and three make five** zwei und drei ist fünf.

● **to make something up** 1 etwas erfinden✧; **she made up an excuse** sie hat eine Ausrede erfunden; 2 **to make it up** (after a quarrel) sich versöhnen; **they've made it up again** sie haben sich wieder versöhnt.

make-up noun 1 Make-up das; **I don't wear make-up** ich trage kein Make-up; 2 **to put on your make-up** sich schminken; **Jo's putting on her make-up** Jo schminkt sich.

male adjective 1 männlich; **male voice** die Männerstimme; 2 **male animal** das Männchen; **male rat** das Rattenmännchen; 3 **male student** der Student.

male chauvinist noun Chauvinist der (PL die Chauvinisten).

man noun 1 Mann der (PL die Männer); **an old man** ein alter Mann; 2 (the human race) der Mensch.

manage verb 1 leiten (a business, team); **she manages a travel agency** sie leitet ein Reisebüro; 2 (cope) zurechtkommen✧ SEP (PERF sein); **I can manage** ich komme schon zurecht; 3 **to manage to do something** es schaffen, etwas zu tun; **he managed to push the door open** er hat es geschafft, die Tür aufzustoßen; **I didn't manage to get in touch with her** ich habe es nicht geschafft, sie zu erreichen.

management noun
1 Management das (PL die Managements); **management course** der Managementkurs;
2 Leitung die.

manager noun 1 (of a company or bank) Direktor der (PL die Direktoren), Direktorin die (PL die Direktorinnen), 2 (of a shop or restaurant) Geschäftsführer der (PL die Geschäftsführer), Geschäftsführerin die (PL die Geschäftsführerinnen); 3 (in football) Trainer der (PL die Trainer), Managerin die (PL die Managerinnen), Trainerin die (PL die Trainerinnen); 4 (in entertainment) Manager der (PL die Manager), Managerin die (PL die Managerinnen).

manageress noun (of a shop or restaurant) Geschäftsführerin die (PL die Geschäftsführerinnen).

mania noun Manie die (PL die Manien).

maniac noun Wahnsinnige der/die (PL die Wahnsinnigen); **she drives like a maniac** sie fährt wie eine Wahnsinnige.

man-made adjective man-made fibre die Kunstfaser.

manner noun 1 in a manner of speaking mehr oder weniger; 2 **manners** Manieren (plural); **to have good manners** gute Manieren haben; **it's bad manners to talk like that** es gehört sich nicht, so zu reden.

mantelpiece noun Kaminsims der (PL die Kaminsimse).

manual noun Handbuch das (PL die Handbücher).

manufacture verb herstellen SEP.

manufacturer noun Hersteller der (PL die Hersteller).

many adjective, pronoun viele; **does she have many friends?** hat sie viele Freunde?; **we didn't see many people** wir haben nicht viele Leute gesehen; **not many** nicht viele; **many of them forgot** viele haben es vergessen; **there were too many people** es waren zu viele (Leute) da; **how many?** wie viele?; **how many were there?** wie viele waren da?; **how many sisters have you got?** wie viele Schwestern hast du?; **how many are there left?** wie viele sind übrig geblieben?; **I've never had so many presents** ich habe noch nie so viele Geschenke bekommen; 2 (a lot) so many so viel; **I have so many things to do** ich habe so viel zu tun; 3 (as much as) as many as so viel wie; **take as many as you like** nimm so viel wie du willst; 4 (too much) that's far too many das ist viel zu viel.

map noun 1 Karte die (PL die Karten); 2 (of a town) Stadtplan (PL die Stadtpläne).

marathon noun Marathonlauf der (PL die Marathonläufe).

marble noun 1 Marmor der; 2 (for playing) Murmel die (PL die Murmeln); **to play marbles** Murmeln spielen.

march noun Marsch der (PL die Märsche).

march verb marschieren (PERF sein).

March noun März der; **in March** im März.

mare noun Stute die (PL die Stuten).

a b c d e f g h i j k l m n o p q r s t u v w x y z

margarine noun Margarine die.

margin noun Rand der (PL die Ränder).

marijuana noun Marihuana das.

mark noun **1** (at school) Note die (PL die Noten); **I got a good mark in German** ich habe eine gute Note in Deutsch bekommen; **2** (stain) Fleck der (PL die Flecke); **3** (German currency until replaced by the euro; one hundred marks = 51.13 euros) Mark die (PL die Mark).

mark verb **1** korrigieren; **the teacher marks our homework** die Lehrerin korrigiert unsere Hausaufgaben; **2** (in sports) decken.

market noun Markt der (PL die Märkte).

marketing noun Marketing das.

marmalade noun Orangenmarmelade die.

maroon adjective kastanienbraun.

marriage noun **1** Ehe die; **2** (wedding) Hochzeit die (PL die Hochzeiten).

married adjective **1** verheiratet; **they've been married for twenty years** sie sind seit zwanzig Jahren verheiratet; **2** married couple das Ehepaar.

marry verb **1** to marry somebody jemanden heiraten; **she married a Frenchman** sie hat einen Franzosen geheiratet; **2** to get married heiraten; **they got married in July** sie haben im Juli geheiratet.

marvellous adjective wunderbar.

marzipan noun Marzipan das.

mascara noun Wimperntusche die.

masculine noun (in German and other grammars) männlich.

mash verb stampfen.

mashed potatoes plural noun Kartoffelbrei der (singular).

mask noun Maske die (PL die Masken).

mass noun **1** a mass of eine Menge; **2** masses of massenhaft (informal); **they've got masses of money** sie haben massenhaft Geld; **there's masses left over** es ist massenhaft übrig geblieben; **3** (religious) Messe die (PL die Messen); **to go to mass** zur Messe gehen.

massage noun Massage die (PL die Massagen).

massive adjective riesig.

master verb **1** meistern; **2** to master a language eine Sprache beherrschen.

masterpiece noun Meisterwerk das (PL die Meisterwerke).

mat noun **1** (doormat) Matte die (PL die Matten); **2** (to put under a hot dish) Untersetzer der (PL die Untersetzer); **3** table mat das Platzdeckchen.

match noun **1** (for lighting) Streichholz das (PL die Streichhölzer); **box of matches** die Streichholzschachtel; **2** (in sports) Spiel das (PL die Spiele); **football match** das Fußballspiel; **to watch the match** das Spiel sehen; **to win the match** das Spiel gewinnen; **to lose the match** das Spiel verlieren.

match verb passen zu (+ DAT); **the jacket matches the skirt** die Jacke passt zu dem Rock.

mate noun Freund der (PL die Freunde); **I'm going to the pub with my mates** ich gehe mit meinen Freunden in die Kneipe.

material noun 1 (*fabric, also information*) Stoff der (PL die Stoffe); 2 (*substance*) Material das (PL die Materialien).

mathematics noun Mathematik die.

maths noun Mathe die (*informal*); **I like maths** ich mag Mathe gerne; **Anna's good at maths** Anna ist gut in Mathe.

matter noun **what's the matter?** was ist los?.

matter verb 1 **that's what matters most** das ist am wichtigsten; **it matters a lot to me** es ist mir sehr wichtig; **does it really matter?** ist das wirklich so wichtig?; 2 **it doesn't matter** es macht nichts; **it doesn't matter if it rains** es macht nichts, wenn es regnet; 3 **you can write it in German or English, it doesn't matter** du kannst es auf Deutsch oder Englisch schreiben, das ist egal; 4 **to matter to somebody** jemandem etwas ausmachen SEP; **does it matter to you if I leave earlier?** macht es dir etwas aus, wenn ich früher gehe?

mattress noun Matratze die (PL die Matratzen).

maximum noun Maximum das (PL die Maxima); **the maximum number/speed possible is 200** die Höchstzahl/ Höchstgeschwindigkeit ist 200.

maximum adjective maximal; **the maximum temperature** die Höchsttemperatur; **she got the maximum points** sie erreichte die Höchstpunktzahl.

may verb 1 **she may be ill** vielleicht ist sie krank; **we may go to Spain** wir fahren vielleicht nach Spanien; 2 (*expressing permission*) dürfen✧; **may I close the door?** darf ich die Tür zumachen?

May noun Mai der; **in May** im Mai.

maybe adverb vielleicht; **maybe they've got lost** vielleicht haben sie sich verlaufen.

May Day noun der Erste Mai.

mayonnaise noun Majonäse die.

mayor noun Bürgermeister der (PL die Bürgermeister), Bürgermeisterin die (PL die Bürgermeisterinnen).

me pronoun (*in German this pronoun changes according to the function it has in the sentence or the preposition it follows*) 1 (*as a direct object in the accusative*) mich; **she knows me** sie kennt mich; 2 (*after a preposition that takes the accusative*) mich; **they left without me** sie sind ohne mich losgefahren; **wait for me!** warte auf mich!; 3 (*as an indirect object or following a verb that takes the dative*) mir; **can you give me your address?** kannst du mir deine Adresse geben?; **he helped me** er hat mir geholfen; 4 (*after a preposition that takes the dative*) mir; **she never talks to me** sie redet nie mit mir; 5 (*in comparisons*) than me als ich; **she's older than me** sie ist älter als ich; 6 (*in the nominative*) ich; **it's me** ich bin's; **not me** ich nicht.

meadow noun Wiese die (PL die Wiesen).

meal noun 1 Essen das (PL die Essen); **to cook a meal** Essen kochen; 2 **to go for a meal** essen gehen.

mean verb 1 (signify) bedeuten; **what does that mean?** was bedeutet das?; 2 (intend to say) meinen; 3 **what do you mean?** was meinst du?; **that's not what I meant** das habe ich nicht gemeint; 4 **to mean to do something** etwas tun wollen; **I meant to phone my mother** ich wollte meine Mutter anrufen; 5 **to be meant to do something** etwas tun sollen; **she was meant to be here at six** sie sollte um sechs hier sein.

mean adjective 1 (with money) geizig; 2 (unkind) gemein; **she's really mean to her brother** sie ist richtig gemein zu ihrem Bruder; **what a mean thing to do!** das ist gemein!

meaning noun Bedeutung die (PL die Bedeutungen).

means noun 1 Mittel das (PL die Mittel); **means of transport** das Verkehrsmittel; 2 **a means of** eine Möglichkeit; **a means of earning money** eine Möglichkeit, Geld zu verdienen; 3 **by means of** mit Hilfe (+ GEN); 4 **by all means!** selbstverständlich!

meantime adverb **for the meantime** einstweilen; **in the meantime** in der Zwischenzeit.

meanwhile adverb in der Zwischenzeit; **meanwhile she was waiting at the station** in der Zwischenzeit wartete sie am Bahnhof.

measles noun Masern (plural).

measure verb messen❖.

measurements plural noun Maße (plural); **the measurements of the room** die Maße des Zimmers; **my measurements** meine Maße.

meat noun Fleisch das; **I don't like meat** ich mag kein Fleisch.

mechanic noun Mechaniker der (PL die Mechaniker), Mechanikerin die (PL die Mechanikerinnen).

mechanical adjective mechanisch.

medal noun Medaille die (PL die Medaillen); **the gold medal** die Goldmedaille.

media noun **the media** die Medien (plural).

medical noun 1 ärztliche Untersuchung die (PL die ärztlichen Untersuchungen); 2 **to have a medical** sich untersuchen lassen.

medical adjective 1 medizinisch; 2 ärztlich (examination, treatment).

medicine noun 1 (drug) Medikament das (PL die Medikamente); 2 (subject of study) Medizin die; **she's studying medicine** sie studiert Medizin; 3 **alternative medicine** die Alternativmedizin.

Mediterranean noun **the Mediterranean (Sea)** das Mittelmeer.

medium adjective mittlerer/ mittlere/mittleres.

medium-sized adjective mittelgroß.

meet verb **1** (by chance) treffen◇; **I met Rosie at the baker's** ich habe Rosie beim Bäcker getroffen; **2** (by appointment) sich treffen mit (+ DAT); **I'll meet you outside the cinema** ich treffe mich mit dir vor dem Kino; **3** sich treffen; **we're meeting at six** wir treffen uns um sechs; **4** (get to know) kennen lernen; **I met a German girl last week** ich habe letzte Woche eine Deutsche kennen gelernt; **5 I've never met Oskar** ich kenne Oskar nicht; **6** (off a train or bus, for example) abholen SEP; **my dad's meeting me at the station** mein Vater holt mich vom Bahnhof ab.

meeting noun **1** (by arrangement) Treffen das (PL die Treffen); **2** (in business) Besprechung die (PL die Besprechungen); **she's in a meeting** sie ist in einer Besprechung; **3** (by chance, in sports) Begegnung die (PL die Begegnungen).

megabyte noun Megabyte das (PL die Megabytes).

melon noun Melone die (PL die Melonen).

melt verb **1** schmelzen◇ (PERF sein); **the snow has melted** der Schnee ist geschmolzen; **2** (in cookery) zerlassen◇ (butter, fat); **melt the butter in a saucepan** Butter im Topf zerlassen.

member noun Mitglied das (PL die Mitglieder).

Member of Parliament noun Abgeordnete der/die (PL die Abgeordneten).

membership noun Mitgliedschaft die.

membership card noun Mitgliedskarte die (PL die Mitgliedskarten).

membership fee noun Mitgliedsbeitrag der (PL die Mitgliedsbeiträge).

memorial noun Denkmal das (PL die Denkmäler); **a war memorial** ein Kriegsdenkmal.

memorize verb **to memorize something** etwas auswendig lernen.

memory noun **1** (of a person) Gedächtnis das; **you have a good memory** du hast ein gutes Gedächtnis; **2** (of the past) Erinnerung die (PL die Erinnerungen); **I have good memories of our stay in Italy** ich habe schöne Erinnerungen an unseren Urlaub in Italien; **3** (of a computer) Speicher der.

mend verb **1** reparieren; **2** (by sewing) ausbessern SEP.

meningitis noun Hirnhautentzündung die.

mental adjective **1** geistig; **2 mental illness** die Geisteskrankheit; **mental hospital** die psychiatrische Klinik.

mention verb erwähnen.

menu noun **1** (in a restaurant) Speisekarte die (PL die Speisekarten); **is there a set menu?** gibt es ein Menü?; **2** (in computing) Menü das (PL die Menüs).

meringue noun Baiser das (PL die Baisers).

merit noun **1** Verdienst das (PL die Verdienste); **2** (good feature or

a b c d e f g h i j k l m n o p q r s t u v w x y z

advantage) Vorzug der (PL die Vorzüge).

merry *adjective* **1** fröhlich; **Merry Christmas** fröhliche Weihnachten; **2** (*from drinking*) angeheitert.

merry-go-round *noun* Karussell das (PL die Karussells).

mess *noun* **1** Durcheinander das; **my papers are in a complete mess** meine Unterlagen sind ein einziges Durcheinander; **what a mess!** was für ein Durcheinander!; **2** to make a mess eine Unordnung machen; **3** to clear up the mess aufräumen SEP.

● **to mess about** herumalbern SEP; **stop messing about!** hör auf herumzualbern!

● **to mess about with something** mit etwas (DAT) herumspielen SEP; **it's dangerous to mess about with matches** es ist gefährlich, mit Streichhölzern herumzuspielen.

● **to mess something up 1** etwas durcheinander bringen ❖; **you've messed up all my papers** Sie haben meine Unterlagen völlig durcheinander gebracht; **2** (*make dirty*) etwas schmutzig machen; **3** (*botch*) etwas verpfuschen.

message *noun* **1** Nachricht die (PL die Nachrichten); **a telephone message** eine telefonische Nachricht; **2** to give somebody a message jemandem etwas ausrichten SEP.

messy *adjective* **1** (*dirty*) **it's a messy job** das ist eine schmutzige Arbeit; **2 he's a messy eater** er bekleckert sich beim Essen; **3 her**

writing's really messy sie hat eine furchtbare Schrift; **4** (*untidy*) **she's very messy** sie ist sehr unordentlich.

metal *noun* Metall das (PL die Metalle).

meter *noun* **1** (*electricity, gas, taxi*) Zähler der (PL die Zähler); **to read the meter** den Zähler ablesen ❖ SEP; **2 parking meter** die Parkuhr.

method *noun* Methode die (PL die Methoden).

Methodist *noun* Methodist der (PL die Methodisten), Methodistin die (PL die Methodistinnen).

metre *noun* Meter der (PL die Meter).

metric *adjective* metrisch.

microchip *noun* Mikrochip der (PL die Mikrochips).

microphone *noun* Mikrofon das (PL die Mikrofone).

microscope *noun* Mikroskop das (PL die Mikroskope).

microwave (oven) *noun* Mikrowellenherd der (PL die Mikrowellenherde).

midday *noun* Mittag der; **at midday** mittags.

middle *noun* **1** Mitte die; **in the middle of the room** in der Mitte des Zimmers; **in the middle of June** Mitte Juni; **in the middle of the night** mitten in der Nacht; **2** to be in the middle of doing something gerade dabei sein, etwas zu tun; **when she phoned I was in the middle of washing my hair** als sie anrief, war ich gerade dabei, mir die Haare zu waschen.

middle-aged *adjective* mittleren Alters; **a middle-aged lady** eine Dame mittleren Alters.

middle-class *adjective* der Mittelschicht; **a middle-class family** eine Familie der Mittelschicht.

Middle-East *noun* **the Middle East** der Nahe Osten.

midge *noun* Mücke die (PL die Mücken).

midnight *noun* Mitternacht die; **at midnight** um Mitternacht.

Midsummer's Day *noun* Sommersonnenwende die.

might *verb* **1** 'are you going to phone him?' — 'I might' 'rufst du ihn an?' — 'vielleicht'; **I might invite Jo** vielleicht lade ich Jo ein; **he might have forgotten** vielleicht hat er es vergessen; **2 she might be right** sie könnte Recht haben.

migraine *noun* Migräne die.

mike *noun* (*microphone*) Mikro das (PL die Mikros) (*informal*).

mild *adjective* mild.

mile *noun* **1** Meile die (PL die Meilen) (*Germans use kilometres for distances; to convert miles to kilometres, multiply by 8 and divide by 5*); **it's ten miles to Oxford** es sind sechzehn Kilometer bis Oxford; **2 it's miles better** das ist viel besser.

military *adjective* militärisch.

milk *noun* Milch die; **full-cream milk** die Vollmilch; **skimmed milk** die Magermilch; **semi-skimmed milk** die fettarme Milch.

milk *verb* melken.

milk chocolate *noun* Milchschokolade die.

milkman *noun* Milchmann der (PL die Milchmänner).

milk shake *noun* Milchshake der (PL die Milchshakes).

millennium *noun* Jahrtausend das (PL die Jahrtausende).

millimetre *noun* Millimeter der (PL die Millimeter).

million *noun* Million die (PL die Millionen); **a million people** eine Million Menschen; **two million people** zwei Millionen Menschen.

millionaire *noun* Millionär der (PL die Millionäre), Millionärin die (PL die Millionärinnen).

mimic *verb* nachmachen SEP.

mince *noun* Hackfleisch das.

mind *noun* **1** Sinn der; **it never crossed my mind to ask them for help** es kam mir überhaupt nicht in den Sinn, sie um Hilfe zu bitten; **2** Meinung die; **to change your mind** seine Meinung ändern; **I've changed my mind** ich habe meine Meinung geändert; **3 to make up your mind to do something** sich entschließen ◊, etwas zu tun; **I can't make up my mind which dress to wear** ich kann mich nicht entschließen, welches Kleid ich anziehe; **4 I've made up my mind** ich habe mich entschieden.

mind *verb* **1** aufpassen SEP (+ ACC); **can you mind my bag for me?** können Sie auf meine Handtasche aufpassen?; **could you mind the baby for ten minutes?** könntest du zehn Minuten auf das Baby aufpassen?; **2 do you mind closing the door?** würden Sie bitte die Tür zumachen?; **3 do you mind if ...?** würde es Ihnen etwas ausmachen SEP, wenn ...?; **do you mind if I open the window?** würde es Ihnen etwas ausmachen, wenn ich das Fenster aufmache?; **I don't mind** es macht mir nichts aus; **I don't mind the heat** die Hitze macht mir nichts aus; **4 never mind** macht nichts.

mine[1] noun Bergwerk das (PL die Bergwerke); **coal mine** das Kohlenbergwerk.

mine[2] pronoun **1** (for a masculine noun) mein; **she took her coat and I took mine** sie hat ihren Mantel genommen und ich habe meinen genommen; **2** (for a feminine noun) meine; **she gave me her address and I gave her mine** sie hat mir ihre Adresse gegeben und ich habe ihr meine gegeben; **3** (for a neuter noun) meins; **her dress is red and mine is blue** ihr Kleid ist rot und meins ist blau; **4** (for masculine/feminine/neuter plural nouns) meine; **she showed me her photos and I showed her mine** sie hat mir ihre Fotos gezeigt und ich habe ihr meine gezeigt; **5 a friend of mine** ein Freund von mir; **it's mine** das gehört mir.

miner noun Bergarbeiter der (PL die Bergarbeiter).

mineral water noun Mineralwasser das.

miniature noun Miniatur die (PL die Miniaturen).

miniature adjective Miniatur-; **miniature model** Miniaturmodell das.

minibus noun Kleinbus der (PL die Kleinbusse).

minimum noun Minimum das (PL die Minima); **a minimum of** ein Minimum von.

minimum adjective Mindest-; **the minimum age** das Mindestalter; **minimum wage** der Mindestlohn.

miniskirt noun Minirock der (PL die Miniröcke).

minister noun **1** (in government) Minister der (PL die Minister), Ministerin die (PL die Ministerinnen); **2** (of a church) Geistliche der/die (PL die Geistlichen).

ministry noun Ministerium das (PL die Ministerien).

minor adjective kleiner.

minority noun Minderheit die (PL die Minderheiten).

mint noun **1** (herb) Minze die (PL die Minzen); **2** (sweet) Pfefferminzbonbon der (PL die Pfefferminzbonbons).

minus preposition minus (+ GEN); **seven minus three is four** sieben minus drei ist vier; **it was minus ten this morning** es war minus zehn heute Morgen.

minute[1] noun **1** Minute die (PL die Minuten); **I'll be ready in two minutes** ich bin in zwei Minuten fertig; **it's five minutes' walk from here** es ist fünf Minuten zu Fuß von hier; **2** Moment der; **just a minute!** einen Moment bitte!; **3 in a minute** gleich.

minute[2] adjective winzig; **the bedrooms are minute** die Schlafzimmer sind winzig.

miracle noun Wunder das (PL die Wunder).

mirror *noun* Spiegel der (PL die Spiegel); **he looked at himself in the mirror** er hat sich im Spiegel betrachtet.

misbehave *verb* sich schlecht benehmen✧.

miserable *adjective* **1** elend; **he was miserable without her** ohne sie fühlte er sich elend; **2 I feel really miserable today** ich fühle mich heute richtig elend; **3** mies; **it's miserable weather** das Wetter ist mies; **she gets paid a miserable salary** sie bekommt ein mieses Gehalt.

Miss *noun* Fräulein das; **Miss Jones** Fräulein Jones, Frau Jones (*adult women are usually addressed as 'Frau', whether or not they are married*).

miss *verb* **1** verpassen; **she missed her train** sie hat ihren Zug verpasst; **I missed the film** ich habe den Film verpasst; **to miss an opportunity** eine Gelegenheit verpassen; **2** nicht treffen✧; **the stone missed me** der Stein hat mich nicht getroffen; **the ball missed the goal** der Schuss ging am Tor vorbei; **missed!** nicht getroffen!; **3** versäumen; **he's missed his classes** er hat den Unterricht versäumt; **4** vermissen (*a person or thing*); **I miss you** ich vermisse dich; **she's missing her sister** sie vermisst ihre Schwester; **I miss England** ich vermisse England.

missing *adjective* **1** fehlend; **she's found the missing pieces** sie hat die fehlenden Teile gefunden; **the missing link** das fehlende Glied;

2 to be missing fehlen; **there's a plate missing** ein Teller fehlt; **there are three forks missing** drei Gabeln fehlen; **3 to go missing** verschwinden✧ (PERF sein); **several things have gone missing lately** mehrere Sachen sind kürzlich verschwunden; **4 three children are missing** drei Kinder werden vermisst.

missionary *noun* Missionar der (PL die Missionare), Missionarin die (PL die Missionarinnen).

mist *noun* Nebel der.

mistake *noun* **1** Fehler der (PL die Fehler); **spelling mistake** der Rechtschreibfehler; **you've made lots of mistakes** du hast viele Fehler gemacht; **2 to make a mistake** (*be mistaken*) sich irren; **sorry, I made a mistake** Entschuldigung, ich habe mich geirrt; **3 by mistake** aus Versehen.

mistake *verb* **I mistook you for your brother** ich habe dich mit deinem Bruder verwechselt.

mistaken *adjective* **to be mistaken** sich täuschen; **you're mistaken** du täuschst dich.

mistletoe *noun* Mistel die (PL die Misteln).

misty *adjective* dunstig; **a misty morning** ein dunstiger Morgen.

misunderstand *verb* missverstehen✧; **I misunderstood** ich habe es missverstanden.

misunderstanding *noun* Missverständnis das (PL die Missverständnisse); **there's been a misunderstanding** da liegt ein Missverständnis vor.

mix noun Mischung die (PL die Mischungen); **a good mix** eine gute Mischung; **cake mix** die Backmischung.

mix verb **1** vermischen; **mix the ingredients together** die Zutaten vermischen; **mix the cream into the sauce** die Sahne in die Soße rühren; **2 to mix with** verkehren mit (+ DAT); **she mixes with lots of interesting people** sie verkehrt mit vielen interessanten Leuten.

● **to mix up 1** durcheinander bringen✧; **you've mixed up all the papers** du hast alle Unterlagen durcheinander gebracht; **you've got it all mixed up** du hast alles durcheinander gebracht; **2** (confuse) verwechseln; **I get him mixed up with his brother** ich verwechsele ihn mit seinem Bruder.

mixed adjective **1** bunt; **a mixed programme** ein buntes Programm; **2** gemischt; **a mixed salad** ein gemischter Salat.

mixture noun Mischung die (PL die Mischungen); **it's a mixture of jazz and rock** es ist eine Mischung aus Jazz und Rock.

moan verb (complain) jammern; **stop moaning!** hör auf zu jammern!

mobile home noun Wohnwagen der (PL die Wohnwagen).

mobile phone noun Handy das (PL die Handys).

mock noun (mock exam) Übungsprüfung die (PL die Übungsprüfungen).

mock verb sich lustig machen über (+ ACC); **stop mocking me** hör auf, dich über mich lustig zu machen.

model noun **1** Modell das (PL die Modelle); **his car is the latest model** sein Auto ist das neueste Modell; **a model of Westminster Abbey** ein Modell von der Westminsterabtei; **2** (fashion model) Mannequin das (PL die Mannequins); **she's a model** sie ist Fotomodell.

model aeroplane noun Modellflugzeug das (PL die Modellflugzeuge).

model railway noun Modelleisenbahn die (PL die Modelleisenbahnen).

modem noun Modem der (PL die Modems).

modern adjective modern.

modernize verb modernisieren.

modern languages noun neuere Sprachen (plural).

modest adjective bescheiden.

modify verb abändern SEP.

moisture noun Feuchtigkeit die.

moisturizer noun Feuchtigkeitscreme die.

mole noun **1** (animal) Maulwurf der (PL die Maulwürfe); **2** (on the skin) Leberfleck der (PL die Leberflecke).

molecule noun Molekül das (PL die Moleküle).

molehill noun Maulwurfshügel der (PL die Maulwurfshügel).

moment noun **1** Moment der (PL die Momente); **at any moment** jeden Moment; **at the moment** im Moment, im Augenblick; **at the right moment** im richtigen

a
b
c
d
e
f
g
h
i
j
k
l
n
o
p
q
r
s
t
u
v
w
x
y
z

Moment; **2** Augenblick der (PL die Augenblicke); **wait a moment!** einen Augenblick!; **3 he'll be ready in a moment** er ist gleich fertig.

monarchy noun Monarchie die.

monastery noun Kloster das (PL die Klöster).

Monday noun **1** Montag der; **on Monday** am Montag; **I'm going to see him on Monday** ich sehe ihn am Montag; **see you on Monday!** bis Montag!; **every Monday** jeden Montag; **last Monday** letzten Montag; **next Monday** nächsten Montag; **2 on Mondays** montags; **the museum is closed on Mondays** das Museum ist montags geschlossen.

money noun Geld das; **I don't have enough money** ich habe nicht genug Geld; **to make money** Geld verdienen.

money box noun Sparbüchse die (PL die Sparbüchsen).

monitor noun (of a computer) Monitor der (PL die Monitoren).

monk noun Mönch der (PL die Mönche).

monkey noun Affe der (PL die Affen).

monotonous adjective eintönig.

monster noun Ungeheuer das (PL die Ungeheuer).

month noun Monat der; **in the month of May** im Mai; **this month** diesen Monat; **next month** nächsten Monat; **last month** letzten Monat; **for three months** drei Monate lang; **every month** jeden Monat; **every three months** alle drei Monate; **in two months'**

time in zwei Monaten; **at the end of the month** am Monatsende.

monthly adjective monatlich; **monthly payment** die monatliche Zahlung; **monthly ticket** die Monatskarte.

monument noun Denkmal das (PL die Denkmäler).

mood noun **1** Laune die (PL die Launen); **to be in a good mood** gute Laune haben; **to be in a bad mood** schlechte Laune haben; **2 I'm not in the mood** ich habe keine Lust dazu; **I'm not in the mood for working** ich habe keine Lust zum Arbeiten.

moon noun Mond der (PL die Monde); **by the light of the moon** im Mondschein; ★ **to be over the moon** im siebten Himmel sein (literally: to be in seventh heaven).

moonlight noun Mondschein der; **by moonlight** im Mondschein.

moped noun Moped das (PL die Mopeds).

moral noun Moral die; **the moral of the story** die Moral der Geschichte.

moral adjective moralisch.

morals noun Moral die.

more adverb **1** (followed by an adjective) (in German the ending '-er' is added to the adjective to show the comparative) **more interesting** interessanter; **the book's more interesting than the film** das Buch ist interessanter als der Film; **more difficult** schwieriger; **more slowly** langsamer; **more easily** einfacher; **books are getting more and more expensive** Bücher werden immer teurer; **2 not any**

more (*no longer*) nicht mehr; **she doesn't live here any more** sie wohnt nicht mehr hier.

more *adjective* **1** mehr (*'mehr' never changes*); **more friends** mehr Freunde; **more ... than** mehr ... als; **they have more money than we do** sie haben mehr Geld als wir; **2 no more** kein; **there's no more milk** es ist keine Milch mehr da; **3** (*of something you have already*) noch; **would you like some more cake?** möchtest du noch etwas Kuchen?; **a few more glasses** noch ein paar Gläser.

more *pronoun* **1** mehr; **he eats more than me** er isst mehr als ich; **no more, thank you** nichts mehr, danke; **2** (*of something you have already*) noch; **we need three more** wir brauchen noch drei; **any more?** noch etwas?; **3 more and more** immer mehr; **it takes more and more time** es beansprucht immer mehr Zeit; **4 more or less** mehr oder weniger; **it's more or less finished** es ist mehr oder weniger fertig.

morning *noun* **1** Morgen *der* (PL die Morgen); **in the morning** am Morgen; **this morning** heute Morgen; **tomorrow morning** morgen früh; **yesterday morning** gestern Morgen; **on Friday morning** am Freitagmorgen; **2 in the morning** (*regularly*) morgens; **she doesn't work in the morning** sie arbeitet morgens nicht; **on Friday mornings** freitagmorgens; **at six o'clock in the morning** um sechs Uhr morgens; **3** (*as opposed to afternoon*) Vormittag *der* (PL die Vormittage); **I spent the whole morning waiting for him** ich habe den ganzen Vormittag auf ihn gewartet.

Moscow *noun* Moskau *das*.

Moslem *noun* Moslem *der* (PL die Moslems), Moslemin *die* (PL die Mosleminnen).

mosque *noun* Moschee *die* (PL die Moscheen).

mosquito *noun* Mücke *die* (PL die Mücken); **mosquito bite** *der* Mückenstich.

most *adjective, pronoun* **1** (*followed by a plural noun*) meisten; **most children like chocolate** die meisten Kinder mögen Schokolade; **most of my friends** die meisten meiner Freunden; **2** (*followed by a singular noun*) der meiste/die meiste/das meiste; **they've eaten most of the ice-cream** sie haben das meiste Eis gegessen; **3 the most** (*followed by a noun or a verb*) am meisten; **I've got the most time** ich habe am meisten Zeit; **4 most of the time** die meiste Zeit; **most of them** die meisten.

most *adverb* **1** (*followed by an adjective*) (*in German the ending '-(e)st' is added to the adjective to show the superlative*) **the most interesting film** der interessanteste Film; **the most exciting story** die spannendste Geschichte; **the most boring book** das langweiligste Buch; **2 am meisten**; **I've got the most time** ich habe am meisten Zeit; **the noise bothers me most** der Lärm stört mich am meisten; **3** (*very*) höchst; **it's most**

a b c d e f g h i j k l **m** n o p q r s t u v w x y z

unlikely es ist höchst unwahrscheinlich.

moth noun **1** Nachtfalter der (PL die Nachtfalter); **2** (clothes moth) Motte die (PL die Motten).

mother noun Mutter die (PL die Mütter); **Kate's mother** Kates Mutter.

mother-in-law noun Schwiegermutter die (PL die Schwiegermütter).

Mother's Day noun Muttertag der (PL die Muttertage).

motivation noun Motivation die.

motor noun Motor der (PL die Motoren).

motorbike noun Motorrad das (PL die Motorräder).

motorcyclist noun Motorradfahrer der (PL die Motorradfahrer), Motorradfahrerin die (PL die Motorradfahrerinnen).

motorist noun Autofahrer der (PL die Autofahrer), Autofahrerin die (PL die Autofahrerinnen).

motor racing noun Autorennsport der.

motorway noun Autobahn die (PL die Autobahnen).

mouldy adjective schimmelig.

mountain noun Berg der (PL die Berge); **in the mountains** in den Bergen.

mountain bike noun Mountainbike das (PL die Mountainbikes).

mountaineer noun Bergsteiger der (PL die Bergsteiger), Bergsteigerin die (PL die Bergsteigerinnen).

mountaineering noun Bergsteigen das; **to go mountaineering** Bergsteigen gehen.

mountainous adjective gebirgig.

mouse noun Maus die (PL die Mäuse) (also for a computer).

mousse noun Mousse die (PL die Mousses).

moustache noun Schnurrbart der (PL die Schnurrbärte).

mouth noun **1** (of a person) Mund der (PL die Münder); **2** (of an animal) Maul das (PL die Mäuler); **3** (of a river) Mündung der (PL die Mündungen).

mouthful noun (food) Bissen der (PL die Bissen) (informal).

mouth organ noun Mundharmonika die (PL die Mundharmonikas); **to play the mouth organ** Mundharmonika spielen.

move noun **1** (to a different house) Umzug der (PL die Umzüge); **2** (in a game) Zug der (PL die Züge); **your move!** du bist am Zug!

move verb **1** sich bewegen; **she didn't move** sie hat sich nicht bewegt; **2 to move up** vorrücken SEP (PERF sein); **move up a bit** rücken Sie etwas vor; **3** wegnehmen✧ SEP; **can you move your bag, please?** können Sie Ihre Handtasche bitte wegnehmen?; **4 to move something somewhere else** etwas woandershin stellen; **I've moved the chest into the cellar** ich habe die Truhe in den Keller gestellt; **5** (car) fahren✧ (PERF sein); **6** (traffic) vorwärtskommen✧ SEP (PERF sein);

a
b
c
d
e
f
g
h
i
j
k
l
n
o
p
q
r
s
t
u
v
w
x
y
z

7 (*driver*) wegfahren✧ SEP; **could you move your car, please?** würden Sie bitte Ihr Auto wegfahren?; **8 to move forward** (*person*) vorrücken SEP (PERF *sein*) (*vehicle*) vorwärts fahren✧ (PERF *sein*); **9** (*move house*) umziehen✧ SEP (PERF *sein*); **we're moving on Tuesday** wir ziehen am Dienstag um; **they've moved to London** sie sind nach London umgezogen.

● **to move away** wegziehen SEP (PERF *sein*).

● **to move in** einziehen SEP (PERF *sein*); **she's moving in with friends** sie zieht bei Freunden ein.

● **to move out** ausziehen SEP (PERF *sein*); **we're moving out next week** wir ziehen nächste Woche aus.

movement *noun* Bewegung *die* (PL die Bewegungen).

movie *noun* Film *der* (PL die Filme); **to go to the movies** ins Kino gehen.

moving *adjective* **1** fahrend; **a moving car** ein fahrendes Auto; **2** (*emotionally*) ergreifend.

mow *verb* mähen.

mower *noun* Rasenmäher *der* (PL die Rasenmäher).

MP *noun* Abgeordnete *der/die* (PL die Abgeordneten).

Mr *noun* Herr *der*; (*in an address*) **Mr Angus Brown** Herrn Angus Brown; (*in a letter*) **Dear Mr Brown** Sehr geehrter Herr Brown.

Mrs *noun* Frau *die*; **Mrs Mary Hendry** Frau Mary Hendry; (*in a letter*) **Dear Mrs Hendry** Sehr geehrte Frau Hendry.

Ms *noun* Frau *die* (*there is no direct equivalent to 'Ms' in German, but 'Frau' may be used whether the woman is married or not*).

much *adjective, adverb, pronoun* **1** viel; **she doesn't eat much for breakfast** sie isst nicht viel zum Frühstück; **much more** viel mehr; **much quicker** viel schneller; **we don't have much time** wir haben nicht viel Zeit; **2 not much** nicht viel; **'do you have a lot of work?' – 'no, not much'** 'hast du viel Arbeit?' – ' 'nein, nicht viel'; **3 so much** so viel; **I have so much to do** ich habe so viel zu tun; **you shouldn't have given me so much** du hättest mir nicht so viel geben sollen; **4 as much as** so viel; **take as much as you like** nimm so viel du willst; **5 too much** zu viel; **she gets too much money from her parents** sie bekommt zu viel Geld von ihren Eltern; **that's far too much** das ist viel zu viel; **6 how much? wie viel?; how much is it?** wie viel kostet es?; **how much do you want?** wie viel möchten Sie?; **how much money do you need?** wie viel Geld brauchst du?; **7** (*greatly*) sehr; **he loved her very much** er hat sie sehr geliebt; **too much** zu sehr; **so much** (so) sehr; **we liked it so much** es hat uns sehr gefallen; **8** (*often*) oft; **I don't watch television much** ich sehe nicht oft fern; **we don't go out much** wir gehen nicht oft aus; **9 thank you very much** vielen Dank.

mud *noun* Schlamm *der*.

muddle *noun* **1** Durcheinander das; **2 to be in a muddle** durcheinander sein.

mug *noun* Becher der (PL die Becher); **a mug of milk** ein Becher Milch.

mug *verb* **to mug somebody** jemanden überfallen✧; **to be mugged** überfallen werden.

mugging *noun* Straßenraub der.

multiplication *noun* Multiplikation die.

multiply *verb* multiplizieren; **six multiplied by four** sechs multipliziert mit vier.

mum, mummy *noun* Mutti die (PL die Muttis); **Tom's mum** Toms Mutti; **I'll ask my mum** ich frage Mutti.

mumps *noun* Mumps der.

Munich *noun* München das.

murder *noun* Mord der (PL die Morde).

murder *verb* ermorden.

murderer *noun* Mörder der (PL die Mörder), Mörderin die (PL die Mörderinnen).

muscle *noun* Muskel der (PL die Muskeln).

muscular *adjective* muskulös.

museum *noun* Museum das (PL die Museen); **to go to the museum** ins Museum gehen.

mushroom *noun* Pilz der (PL die Pilze), Champignon der (PL die Champignons); **mushroom salad** der Champignonsalat.

music *noun* Musik die; **pop music** die Popmusik; **classical music** die klassische Musik.

musical *noun* Musical das (PL die Musicals).

musical *adjective* **1** musical instrument das Musikinstrument; **2 they're a very musical family** sie sind eine sehr musikalische Familie.

musician *noun* Musiker der (PL die Musiker), Musikerin die (PL die Musikerinnen).

Muslim *noun* Muslem der (PL die Muslim), Muslimin die (PL die Musliminnen).

mussel *noun* Muschel die (PL die Muscheln).

must *verb* **1** müssen✧; **we must leave now** wir müssen jetzt gehen; **you must learn the vocabulary** du musst die Vokabeln lernen; **2** (with a negative) dürfen✧; **you mustn't do that** das darfst du nicht tun; **3** (expressing probability) müssen✧; **you must be tired** ihr müsst müde sein; **it must be five o'clock** es muss fünf Uhr sein; **he must have forgotten** er muss es vergessen haben.

mustard *noun* Senf der (PL die Senfe).

mutter *verb* murmeln.

my *adjective* **1** (before a masculine noun) mein; **my brother** mein Bruder; **they don't like my dog** sie mögen meinen Hund nicht; **2** (before a feminine noun) meine; **my sister** meine Schwester; **3** (before a neuter noun) mein; **that's my new car** das ist mein neues Auto; **we can go in my car** wir können mit meinem Auto fahren; **4** (before masculine/feminine/neuter plural nouns)

a
b
c
d
e
f
g
h
i
j
k
l
m
n
o
p
q
r
s
t
u
v
w
x
y
z

meine; **my children** meine Kinder;
5 (*with parts of the body*) der/die/
das; **I had a glass in my hand** ich
hatte ein Glas in der Hand; **I'm
washing my hands** ich wasche mir
die Hände.

myself *pronoun* **1** (*reflexive and
after a preposition taking the
accusative*) mich; **I've cut myself**
ich habe mich geschnitten; **I've
addressed the letter to myself** ich
habe den Brief an mich adressiert;
2 (*reflexive and after a preposition
taking the dative*) mir; **I've hurt
myself** ich habe mir wehgetan; **I
said to myself** ich habe mir gesagt;
3 (*stressing something*) selbst; **I
said it myself** ich habe es selbst
gesagt; **4 by myself** allein.

mysterious *adjective* rätselhaft.

mystery *noun* **1** Rätsel *das* (PL die
Rätsel); **2** (*book*) Krimi *der* (PL die
Krimis) (*informal*).

myth *noun* Mythos *der* (PL die
Mythen).

mythology *noun* Mythologie *die*
(PL die Mythologien).

Nn

nail *noun* (*on your finger or toe, also
metal*) Nagel *der* (PL die Nägel).

nail *verb* nageln.

nailbrush *noun* Nagelbürste *die*
(PL die Nagelbürsten).

nailfile *noun* Nagelfeile *die* (PL die
Nagelfeilen).

nail polish *noun* Nagellack *der*.

nail polish remover *noun*
Nagellackentferner *der*.

naked *adjective* nackt.

name *noun* **1** Name *der* (PL die
Namen); **I've forgotten her name**
ich habe ihren Namen vergessen;
what's your name? wie heißt du?;
my name's Joy ich heiße Joy; **2** (*of
a book or film*) Titel *der* (PL die Titel).

napkin *noun* Serviette *die* (PL die
Servietten).

nappy *noun* Windel *die* (PL die
Windeln).

narrow *adjective* schmal; **a narrow
street** eine schmale Straße.

nasty *adjective* **1** (*mean*) gemein;
that was a nasty thing to do das
war gemein; **2** (*unpleasant, bad*)
scheußlich; **that's a nasty job das
ist eine scheußliche Arbeit; a nasty
smell** ein scheußlicher Geruch.

nation *noun* Nation *die* (PL die
Nationen).

national *adjective* national.

national anthem *noun*
Nationalhymne *die* (PL die
Nationalhymnen).

nationality *noun* Nationalität *die*
(PL die Nationalitäten).

national park *noun*
Nationalpark *der* (PL die
Nationalparks).

natural *adjective* natürlich.

naturally *adverb* natürlich.

nature *noun* Natur *die*.

nature reserve *noun*
Naturschutzgebiet *das* (PL die
Naturschutzgebiete).

naughty *adjective* unartig.

navy *noun* Marine *die*; **my uncle's
in the navy** mein Onkel ist bei der
Marine.

navy-blue *adjective* marineblau.

near *adjective* 1 nah(e); 2 (*the superlative of nah(e) is der/die/das nächste*) the nearest park der nächste Park; **the nearest bank** die nächste Bank; **the nearest shop** das nächste Geschäft.

near *preposition* nahe an (+ DAT); **near (to) the station** nahe am Bahnhof.

near *adverb* 1 nah(e) (*in spoken German 'nah' is more common*); **they live quite near** sie wohnen ganz nah; 2 **to come nearer** näher kommen.

nearby *adverb* nahe gelegen; **there's a park nearby** hier in der Nähe ist ein Park.

nearly *adverb* fast; **nearly empty** fast leer.

neat *adjective* 1 (*well organized, tidy*) ordentlich; **a neat room** ein ordentliches Zimmer; 2 adrett (*clothes or the way you look*).

necessarily *adverb* not necessarily nicht unbedingt.

necessary *adjective* nötig; **if necessary** falls nötig.

neck *noun* 1 (*of a person*) Hals der (PL die Hälse); 2 (*of a garment*) Kragen der (PL die Kragen).

necklace *noun* Halskette die (PL die Halsketten).

need *noun* there's no need, I've already done it das ist nicht nötig, ich habe es schon gemacht; **there's no need to wait** du brauchst nicht zu warten.

need *verb* 1 brauchen; **we need bread** wir brauchen Brot; **everything you need** alles, was

man braucht; 2 (*to have to*) müssen◇; **I need to go to the bank** ich muss zur Bank gehen; 3 (*with a negative*) **you needn't wait** du brauchst nicht zu warten.

needle *noun* Nadel die (PL die Nadeln).

negative *noun* (*of a photo*) Negativ das (PL die Negative).

neglected *adjective* vernachlässigt.

neighbour *noun* Nachbar der (PL die Nachbarn), Nachbarin die (PL die Nachbarinnen); **we're going round to the neighbours'** wir besuchen die Nachbarn.

neighbourhood *noun* Nachbarschaft die; **in our neighbourhood** in unserer Nachbarschaft.

neither *conjunction* 1 neither ... nor ... noch; **I have neither the time nor the money** ich habe weder die Zeit noch das Geld; 2 **neither do I** ich auch nicht; **'I don't like fish' – 'neither do I'** 'ich mag keinen Fisch' – 'ich auch nicht'; **'I didn't like the film' – 'neither did Kirsty'** 'mir hat der Film nicht gefallen' – 'Kirsty hat er auch nicht gefallen'.

neither *pronoun* keiner von beiden/keine von beiden/keins von beiden; **'which do you like?' – 'neither'** 'welches gefällt dir?' – 'keins von beiden'.

nephew *noun* Neffe der (PL die Neffen).

nerve *noun* 1 Nerv der (PL die Nerven); 2 **to lose your nerve** die Nerven verlieren; **you've got a nerve!** du hast Nerven! (*informal*);

a b c d e f g h i j k l m n o p q r s t u v w x y z

3 what a nerve! so eine Frechheit!
★ **he gets on my nerves** er geht mir auf die Nerven (*informal*).

nervous *adjective* **1** (*afraid*) ängstlich; **to feel nervous about something** Angst vor etwas (DAT) haben; **2** (*highly strung*) nervös (*person*).

nest *noun* Nest das (PL die Nester).

net *noun* Netz das (PL die Netze).

Netherlands *noun* Niederlande (*plural*); **in the Netherlands** in den Niederlanden.

nettle *noun* Nessel die (PL die Nesseln).

network *noun* Netzwerk das (PL die Netzwerke).

neutral *noun* (*neutral gear*) Leerlauf der; **to be in neutral** im Leerlauf sein.

neutral *adjective* neutral.

never *adverb* **1** nie; **Ben never smokes** Ben raucht nie; **I've never told him** ich habe es ihm nie gesagt; **never again** nie wieder; **2** noch nie; **'have you ever been to Spain?'** – **'no, never'** 'warst du schon mal in Spanien?' – 'nein, noch nie'; **3 never mind** macht nichts.

new *adjective* neu; **have you seen their new house?** hast du ihr neues Haus gesehen?

news *noun* **1** (*new information*) Nachricht die (PL die Nachrichten); **I've got good news** ich habe gute Nachrichten; **2 a piece of news** eine Neuigkeit; **any news?** was gibt es Neues?; **3** (*on TV or the radio*) Nachrichten (*plural*); **we saw it on the news** wir haben es in den Nachrichten gesehen.

newsagent *noun* Zeitungshändler der (PL die Zeitungshändler).

newspaper *noun* Zeitung die (PL die Zeitungen).

newsreader *noun* Nachrichtensprecher der (PL die Nachrichtensprecher), Nachrichtensprecherin die (PL die Nachrichtensprecherinnen).

New Year *noun* Neujahr das; **Happy New Year!** ein gutes neues Jahr!

New Year's Day *noun* Neujahr das.

New Year's Eve *noun* Silvester der.

New Zealand *noun* Neuseeland das.

next *adjective* **1** nächster/nächste/ nächstes; **the next train leaves at ten** der nächste Zug fährt um zehn ab; **next week** nächste Woche; **next Thursday** nächsten Donnerstag; **next year** nächstes Jahr; **next time I see you** nächstes Mal, wenn ich dich sehe; **2** (*following*) nächste; **next please!** der Nächste bitte/die Nächste bitte; **the next thing** das Nächste; **the next day** am nächsten Tag; **the letter arrived the next day** der Brief kam am nächsten Tag an; **3** the week after next übernächste Woche; **4** (*next-door*) nebenan; **I'm in the next room** ich bin nebenan.

next *adverb* **1** (*afterwards*) danach; **what did he say next?** was hat er danach gesagt?; **2** (*now*) als Nächstes; **what shall we do next?** was machen wir als Nächstes?; **3 next to** neben (+ DAT, *or* + ACC *with* *movement towards a place);* **the house next to the baker's** das Haus neben dem Bäcker; **I sat down next to her** ich habe mich neben sie gesetzt.

next door *adverb* nebenan; **they live next door** sie wohnen nebenan; **the girl next door** das Mädchen von nebenan.

nice *adjective* **1** *(pleasant)* schön; **we had a nice evening** wir haben einen schönen Abend verbracht; **Brighton's a nice town** Brighton ist eine schöne Stadt; **we had nice weather** wir hatten schönes Wetter; **2 to have a nice time** sich amüsieren; **have a nice day!** viel Spaß!; **3** *(attractive to look at)* hübsch; **that's a nice dress** das ist ein hübsches Kleid; **4** *(kind, friendly)* nett *(person)*; **she's really nice** sie ist wirklich nett; **5 to be nice to somebody** nett zu jemandem sein; **she's been very nice to me** sie war sehr nett zu mir; **6** *(tasting good)* gut; **it tastes nice** es schmeckt gut.

nickname *noun* Spitzname *der* (PL die Spitznamen).

niece *noun* Nichte *die* (PL die Nichten).

night *noun* **1** *(after bedtime)* Nacht *die* (PL die Nächte); **during the night** während der Nacht; **Sunday night** Sonntag Nacht; **it's cold at night** nachts ist es kalt; **to stay the night** über Nacht bleiben; **I stayed the night at Emma's** ich habe bei Emma übernachtet; **2** *(before you go to bed)* Abend *der* (PL die Abende); **what are you doing tonight?** was macht ihr heute Abend?; **one night** eines Abends; **tomorrow night** morgen Abend; **I met Greg last night** ich habe Greg gestern Abend getroffen; **on Friday night** am Freitagabend; **see you tonight!** bis heute Abend!

night club *noun* Nachtklub *der* (PL die Nachtklubs).

nightie *noun* Nachthemd *das* (PL die Nachthemden).

nightmare *noun* Albtraum *der* (PL die Albträume).

nil *noun* *(in sport)* null; **they won four-nil** sie haben vier zu null gewonnen.

nine *number* neun.

nineteen *number* neunzehn.

ninety *number* neunzig.

ninth *number* neunter/neunte/ neuntes; **on the ninth floor** im neunten Stock; **on the ninth of June** am neunten Juni.

no *adverb* nein; **I said no** ich habe nein gesagt; **no thank you** nein danke.

no *adjective* **1** kein; **we've got no bread** wir haben kein Brot; **no problem!** kein Problem!; **2** *(on a notice)* **'no smoking'** 'Rauchen verboten'; **'no parking'** 'Parken verboten'.

nobody *pronoun* niemand; **'who's there?' - 'nobody'** 'wer ist da?' - 'niemand'; **there's nobody in the kitchen** es ist niemand in der Küche; **nobody was at home** niemand war zu Hause.

nod *verb* nicken; **he nodded in agreement** er hat zustimmend genickt.

noise *noun* Lärm *der*; **to make a noise** Lärm machen.

noise pollution *noun* Lärmbelästigung *die*

noisy *adjective* laut.

none *pronoun* **1** (*not one*) keiner/ keine/keins; **none of us** keiner von uns/ keine von uns; **'how many students failed the exam?' – 'none'** 'wie viele Schüler sind durch die Prüfung gefallen?' – 'keine'; **none of the boys knows him** keiner der Jungen kennt ihn; **2 there's none left** es ist nichts mehr übrig.

nonsense *noun* Unsinn *der*; **to talk nonsense** Unsinn reden; **nonsense!** Unsinn!

non-smoker *noun* Nichtraucher *der* (PL *die* Nichtraucher) Nichtraucherin *die* (PL *die* Nichtraucherinnen).

non-stop *adjective* durchgehend (*train*), Nonstop- (*flight*).

non-stop *adverb* ununterbrochen; **she talks non-stop** sie redet ununterbrochen.

noodles *plural noun* Nudeln *die* (*plural*).

noon *noun* Mittag *der*; **at (twelve) noon** um zwölf (Uhr mittags).

no-one *pronoun* niemand; **'who's there?' – 'no-one'** 'wer ist da?' – 'niemand'; **there's no-one in the kitchen** es ist niemand in der Küche; **no-one was at home** niemand war zu Hause.

nor *conjunction* **1** neither ...nor weder ...noch; **I have neither the time nor the money** ich habe weder die Zeit noch das Geld; **2 nor do I** ich auch nicht; **'I don't like fish' – 'nor do I'** 'ich mag keinen

Fisch' - 'ich auch nicht'; **nor do we** wir auch nicht.

normal *adjective* normal.

normally *adverb* **1** (*usually*) normalerweise; **2** (*in a normal way*) normal.

north *noun* Norden *der*; **in the north** im Norden.

north *adjective* nördlich, Nord-; **the north side** die Nordseite; **north wind** *der* Nordwind.

north *adverb* **1** (*towards the north*) nach Norden; **to travel north** nach Norden fahren; **2 north of London** nördlich von London.

North America *noun* Nordamerika *das*.

North American *noun* Nordamerikaner *der* (PL *die* Nordamerikaner), Nordamerikanerin *die* (PL *die* Nordamerikanerinnen).

North American *adjective* nordamerikanisch.

northeast *noun* Nordosten *der*.

northeast *adjective* **in northeast England** in Nordostengland.

Northern Ireland *noun* Nordirland *das*.

North Pole *noun* Nordpol *der*.

North Sea *noun* **the North Sea** die Nordsee.

northwest *noun* Nordwesten *der*.

northwest *adjective* **in northwest England** in Nordwestengland.

Norway *noun* Norwegen *das*.

Norwegian *noun* **1** (*person*) Norweger *der* (PL *die* Norweger), Norwegerin *die* (PL *die* Norwegerinnen); **2** (*language*) Norwegisch *das*.

Norwegian *adjective* norwegisch.

nose *noun* Nase *die* (PL die Nasen); **to blow your nose** sich (DAT) die Nase putzen.

not *adverb* **1** nicht; **not on Sundays** sonntags nicht; **not all alone!** nicht ganz allein!; **not bad** nicht schlecht; **not at all** überhaupt nicht; **not yet** noch nicht; **Sam didn't phone** Sam hat nicht angerufen; **I hope not** hoffentlich nicht; **2 not a** kein/keine; **he's not a specialist** er ist kein Fachmann; **not a bit** kein bisschen.

note *noun* **1** (*a short letter*) Zettel *der* (PL die Zettel), (*informal*) Brief *der* (PL die Briefe); **2** (*in a class*) Notiz *die* (PL die Notizen); **to take notes** sich (DAT) Notizen machen; **3** (*a banknote*) Schein *der* (PL die Scheine); **a ten-pound note** ein Zehnpfundschein; **4** (*in music*) Note *die* (PL die Noten).

notebook *noun* Notizbuch *das* (PL die Notizbücher).

notepad *noun* Notizblock *der* (PL die Notizblöcke).

nothing *pronoun* nichts; **'what did you say?' – 'nothing'** 'was hast du gesagt?' – 'nichts'; **nothing special** nichts Besonderes; **nothing new** nichts Neues; **I saw nothing** ich habe nichts gesehen; **there's nothing left** es ist nichts mehr übrig.

notice *noun* **1** (*a sign*) Schild *das* (PL die Schilder); **2** (*an advertisement*) Anzeige *die* (PL die Anzeigen); **3** (*advance warning*) Ankündigung *die*; **4 don't take any notice of her** nimm keine Notiz von ihr; **5 at short notice** kurzfristig.

notice *verb* bemerken; **I didn't notice anything** ich habe nichts bemerkt.

notice board *noun* Anschlagbrett *das* (PL die Anschlagbretter).

nought *noun* Null *die* (PL die Nullen).

noun *noun* Substantiv *das* (PL die Substantive).

novel *noun* Roman *der* (PL die Romane).

novelist *noun* Romanautor *der* (PL die Romanautoren), Romanautorin *die* (PL die Romanautorinnen).

November *noun* November *der*; **in November** im November.

now *adverb* **1** jetzt; **where is he now?** wo ist er jetzt?; **from now on** von jetzt an; **2 he just now** er ist gerade eben gegangen; **I saw her just now in the corridor** ich habe sie gerade eben im Gang gesehen; **3 do it right now!** mach es sofort!; **4 now and then** hin und wieder.

nowadays *adverb* heutzutage; **nowadays they are quite common** heutzutage sind sie ziemlich häufig.

nowhere *adjective* nirgends; **there's nowhere to park** man kann nirgends parken.

nuclear *adjective* Kern-; **nuclear power** *die* Kernenergie; **nuclear power station** *das* Kernkraftwerk.

nude *noun* **in the nude** nackt.

nude *adjective* nackt.

a b c d e f g h i j k l m n o p q r s t u v w x y z

nuisance *noun* it's a nuisance das ist ärgerlich; **what a nuisance!** wie ärgerlich!

numb *adjective* **1** (*with cold*) gefühllos; **2** (*emotionally*) benommen.

number plate *noun* Nummernschild *das* (PL die Nummernschilder).

number *noun* **1** (*of a house, telephone, or account*) Nummer *die* (PL die Nummern); **I live at number five** ich wohne in der Nummer fünf; **my new phone number** meine neue Telefonnummer; **2** (*a written figure*) Zahl *die* (PL die Zahlen); **3** (*amount*) Anzahl *die*; **the number of visitors** die Anzahl der Besucher.

nun *noun* Nonne *die* (PL die Nonnen).

nurse *noun* **1** (*female*) Krankenschwester *die* (PL die Krankenschwestern); **Janet's a nurse** Janet ist Krankenschwester; **2** (*male*) Krankenpfleger *der* (PL die Krankenpfleger).

nursery *noun* **1** (*for children*) Kindertagesstätte *die* (PL die Kindertagesstätten); **2** (*for plants*) Gärtnerei *die* (PL die Gärtnereien).

nursery school *noun* Kindergarten *der* (PL die Kindergärten).

nut *noun* **1** Nuss *die* (PL die Nüsse); **2** (*for a bolt*) Mutter *die* (PL die Muttern).

nylon *noun* Nylon *das*.

Oo

oak *noun* Eiche *die* (PL die Eichen).

oar *noun* Ruder *das* (PL die Ruder).

oats *noun* Hafer *der*; **porridge oats** Haferflocken (*plural*).

obedient *adjective* gehorsam.

obey *verb* **1** gehorchen (+ DAT); **to obey somebody** jemandem gehorchen; **2 to obey the rules** sich an die Vorschriften halten✧.

object *noun* **1** (*thing*) Gegenstand *der* (PL die Gegenstände); **2** (*aim*) Zweck *der*; **3** (*in grammar*) Objekt *das* (PL die Objekte).

object *verb* etwas dagegen haben✧; **if you don't object** wenn Sie nichts dagegen haben.

objection *noun* Einwand *der* (PL die Einwände).

oboe *noun* Oboe *die* (PL die Oboen); **to play the oboe** Oboe spielen.

obscene *adjective* obszön.

observe *verb* beobachten.

obsessed *adjective* besessen; **she's really obsessed with her diet** sie ist von ihrer Schlankheitskur ganz besessen.

obstacle *noun* Hindernis *das* (PL die Hindernisse).

obstinate *adjective* starrsinnig.

obtain *verb* erhalten✧.

obvious *adjective* eindeutig.

obviously *adverb* **1** (*of course*) natürlich; **2** (*looking at something*) offensichtlich; **the house is obviously empty** das Haus steht offensichtlich leer.

occasion *noun* Gelegenheit *die* (PL die Gelegenheiten); **on special**

a
b
c
d
e
f
g
h
i
j
k
l
m
n
p
q
r
s
t
u
v
w
x
y
z

occasions zu besonderen Gelegenheiten.

occasionally *adverb* gelegentlich.

occupation *noun* Beruf *der* (PL die Berufe).

occupied *adjective* **1** (taken) besetzt; **the seat is occupied** der Platz ist besetzt; **2** (lived in) bewohnt.

occur *verb* **1** to occur to somebody jemandem einfallen✧ SEP (PERF sein); **it occurs to me that ...** mir fällt ein, dass ...; **2 it never occurred to me** darauf wäre ich nie gekommen; **3** (happen) sich ereignen.

ocean *noun* Ozean *der* (PL die Ozeane).

o'clock *adverb* **at ten o'clock** um zehn Uhr; **it's three o'clock** es ist drei Uhr.

October *noun* Oktober *der*; **in October** im Oktober.

octopus *noun* Tintenfisch *der* (PL die Tintenfische).

odd *adjective* **1** (strange) komisch; **that's odd, I'm sure I heard the bell** das ist komisch, ich habe es bestimmt klingeln gehört; **2** (number) ungerade; **three is an odd number** drei ist eine ungerade Zahl; **3 the odd one out** die Ausnahme.

odds and ends *plural noun* Kleinkram *der*.

of *preposition* **1** von (+ DAT); (instead of translating of with 'von', the genitive case can be used) **the parents of the children** die Eltern von den Kindern, die Eltern der Kinder; **the name of the flower** der

Name der Blume; **it's very kind of you** das ist sehr nett von Ihnen; **2** (with quantities 'of' is not translated) **a kilo of tomatoes** ein Kilo Tomaten; **a bottle of milk** eine Flasche Milch; **the three of us** wir drei; **3 of it/them** davon (things); **of them** von ihnen (people); **how many of them didn't pay?** wie viele von ihnen haben nicht gezahlt?; **Ray has four cars but he's selling three of them** Ray hat vier Autos, aber er verkauft drei davon; **half of it** die Hälfte davon; **we ate a lot of it** wir haben viel davon gegessen; **4 the sixth of June** der sechste Juni; **5 made of** aus; **a bracelet made of silver** ein Armband aus Silber.

off *adverb, adjective, preposition* **1** (switched off) aus; **is the telly off?** ist der Fernseher aus?; **to turn off the lights** das Licht ausmachen SEP; **2** (electricity, water, gas) abgestellt; **the gas and electricity were off** Gas und Strom waren abgestellt; **to turn off the tap** den Wasserhahn zudrehen SEP; **3 to be off** (to leave) gehen✧ (PERF sein), (in a vehicle) fahren✧ (PERF sein); **I must be off** ich muss gehen; **4 on my day off** an meinem freien Tag; **to take three days off work** sich (DAT) drei Tage frei nehmen; **we were given two days off school** wir hatten zwei Tage schulfrei; **to be off sick** wegen Krankheit fehlen; **Maya's off school today** Maya fehlt heute in der Schule; **5** (cancelled) abgesagt; **the match is off** das Spiel ist abgesagt worden; **6 '20% off shoes'** 'Schuhe 20% reduziert'.

offence noun 1 (*crime*) Straftat die (PL die Straftaten); 2 to take offence beleidigt sein; he takes offence easily er ist schnell beleidigt.

offer noun 1 Angebot das (PL die Angebote); job offer das Stellenangebot; 2 on special offer im Sonderangebot.

offer verb anbieten ◇ SEP (*a present, a reward, or a job*); he offered her a chair er bot ihr einen Stuhl an; to offer to do something anbieten, etwas zu tun; he offered to drive me to the station er hat angeboten, mich zum Bahnhof zu fahren.

office noun Büro das (PL die Büros); he's still at the office er ist noch im Büro.

office block noun Bürohaus das (PL die Bürohäuser).

officer noun Offizier der (PL die Offiziere).

official adjective offiziell.

off-licence noun Wein- und Spirituosenhandlung die (PL die Wein- und Spirituosenhandlungen).

often adverb 1 oft; he's often late er kommt oft zu spät; how often? wie oft?; 2 more often öfter; couldn't you come more often? könntest du nicht öfter kommen?

oil noun 1 (*crude oil*) Öl das; 2 olive oil das Olivenöl; suntan oil das Sonnenöl.

oil slick noun Ölteppich der (PL die Ölteppiche).

ointment noun Salbe die (PL die Salben).

okay adjective 1 okay (*informal*); tomorrow at ten, okay? morgen

um zehn, okay?; is it okay if I don't come till Friday? ist es okay, wenn ich erst Freitag komme?; 2 (*person*) in Ordnung; Daisy's okay Daisy ist in Ordnung; 3 (*nothing special, not ill*) ganz gut; the film was okay der Film war ganz gut; I've been ill but I'm okay now ich war krank, aber jetzt geht es mir ganz gut; 'how are you?' – 'okay' 'wie geht's?' – 'ganz gut'; 4 it's okay by me mir ist es recht.

old adjective 1 (*not young, not new, previous*) alt; an old man ein alter Mann; an old lady eine alte Dame; an old tree ein alter Baum; old people alte Leute; bring some old clothes bring ein paar alte Sachen mit; I've only got their old address ich habe nur ihre alte Adresse; 2 (*talking about age*) how old are you? wie alt bist du?; ten years old James ist zehn Jahre alt; a two-year-old child ein zweijähriges Kind; 4 my older sister meine ältere Schwester; she's older than me sie ist älter als ich; he's a year older than me er ist ein Jahr älter als ich.

old age noun Alter das.

old age pensioner noun Rentner der (PL die Rentner), Rentnerin die (PL die Rentnerinnen).

old-fashioned noun altmodisch.

olive noun Olive die (PL die Oliven).

olive oil noun Olivenöl das (PL die Olivenöle).

Olympic Games, Olympics plural noun Olympische Spiele (plural).

omelette noun Omelett das (PL die Omelette); **a cheese omelette** ein Käseomelett.

on preposition **1** auf (+ DAT, or + ACC with movement towards a place); **it's on the desk** es ist auf dem Schreibtisch; **2** (attached to) an (+ DAT, or + ACC with movement towards a place); **on the wall** an der Wand; **3 on the beach** am Strand; **on the right/left** rechts/links; **4** (in expressions of time) **on March 21st** am 21. März; **he's arriving on Tuesday** er kommt am Dienstag an; **it's shut on Sundays** es ist sonntags geschlossen; **on rainy days** an Regentagen; **5** (for buses, trains, etc.) **to go on the bus** mit dem Bus fahren; **I met Jackie on the train** ich habe Jackie im Zug getroffen; **let's go on our bikes** fahren wir mit dem Rad; **6 on TV** im Fernsehen; **on the radio** im Radio; **on video** auf Video; **7 on holiday** in den Ferien.

on adjective **1** (switched on) **to be on** an sein; **the lights are on** das Licht ist an; **is the radio on?** ist das Radio an?; **2** (happening) **what's on TV?** was gibts im Fernsehen?; **what's on this week at the cinema?** was läuft diese Woche im Kino?

once adverb **1** einmal; **I've tried once already** ich habe es schon einmal versucht; **try once more** versuch es noch einmal; **once a day** einmal täglich; **once upon a time ...** es war einmal ...; **2 more than once** mehrmals; **3 at once** (immediately) sofort; **the doctor came at once** der Arzt kam sofort;

4 at once (at the same time) gleichzeitig; **I can't do two things at once** ich kann nicht zwei Sachen gleichzeitig machen.

one number (when counting) eins, (with a noun) ein; **one son** ein Sohn; **one apple** ein Apfel; **if you want a biro I've got one** falls du einen Kugelschreiber brauchst, habe ich einen; **at one o'clock** um ein Uhr.

one pronoun **1** einer/eine/eins; **I saw the photos, can I have one of them?** ich habe die Fotos gesehen, kann ich eins davon haben?; **2 this one** dieser/diese/dieses; **I'd prefer that bike, but this one's cheaper** ich würde lieber das Rad haben, aber dieses ist billiger; **3 that one** der da/die da/das da; **'which video?' – 'that one'** 'welches Video?' – 'das da'; **4 which one?** welcher/welche/welches?; **'my foot's hurting' – 'which one?'** 'mir tut der Fuß weh' – 'welcher?'; **'she borrowed a skirt from me' – 'which one?'** 'sie hat sich einen Rock von mir geliehen' – 'welchen?'; **5** (you) man; **one never knows** man kann nie wissen.

one's adjective sein/seine/sein; **one pays for one's car** man zahlt für sein Auto.

oneself pronoun **1** (reflexive) sich; **to wash oneself** sich waschen; **2** (stressing something) selbst; **one has to do everything oneself** man muss alles selbst machen.

one-way street noun Einbahnstraße die (PL die Einbahnstraßen).

a
b
c
d
e
f
g
h
i
j
k
l
m
n
o
p
q
r
s
t
u
v
w
x
y
z

a

onion noun Zwiebel die (PL die Zwiebeln).

b

only adjective 1 einziger/einzige/ einziges; **the only free seat** der einzige freie Platz; **the only thing you could do** das Einzige, was du machen könntest; 2 **an only child** ein Einzelkind.

c

d

e

f

only adverb, conjunction 1 nur; **they've only got two bedrooms** sie haben nur zwei Schlafzimmer; **Anne's only free on Fridays** Anne hat nur freitags Zeit; **there are only three left** es sind nur noch drei übrig; **I'd walk, only it's raining** ich würde zu Fuß gehen, nur regnet es; 2 (very recently) gerade erst; **he's only just got the message** er hat die Nachricht gerade erst bekommen; **we've only just made it on time** wir sind gerade noch rechtzeitig angekommen.

g

h

i

j

k

l

m

o

onto preposition auf (+ ACC).

p

open noun **in the open** im Freien.

open adjective 1 offen; **the door's open** die Tür is offen; **the baker's is not open** die Bäckerei ist nicht geöffnet; 2 **in the open air** im Freien.

q

r

s

open verb 1 aufmachen SEP; **can you open the door for me?** kannst du mir die Tür aufmachen?; **the bank opens at nine** die Bank macht um neun auf; 2 (open up) sich öffnen; **the door opened slowly** die Tür öffnete sich langsam.

t

u

v

w

opera noun Oper die (PL die Opern).

x

operate verb 1 (medically) operieren; **will they have to**

y

z

operate (on him/her)? werden sie ihn/sie operieren müssen?; 2 bedienen (a machine).

operation noun 1 Operation die (PL die Operationen); 2 **to have an operation** operiert werden.

opinion noun Meinung die (PL die Meinungen); **in my opinion** meiner Meinung nach.

opinion poll noun Meinungsumfrage die (PL die Meinungsumfragen).

opponent noun Gegner der (PL die Gegner), Gegnerin die (PL die Gegnerinnen).

opportunity noun Gelegenheit die (PL die Gelegenheiten); **to have the opportunity of doing something** die Gelegenheit haben, etwas zu tun.

opposite noun Gegenteil das (PL die Gegenteile); **no, quite the opposite** nein, ganz im Gegenteil.

opposite adjective 1 entgegengesetzt (direction); **she went off in the opposite direction** sie ging in die entgegengesetzte Richtung; 2 (facing) gegenüberliegend; **in the house opposite** in dem gegenüberliegenden Haus.

opposite adverb gegenüber; **they live opposite** sie wohnen gegenüber.

opposite preposition gegenüber (+ DAT); **opposite the station** gegenüber dem Bahnhof.

optician noun Optiker der (PL die Optiker), Optikerin die (PL die Optikerinnen).

optimistic *adjective*
zuversichtlich, optimistisch.

option *noun* Wahl *die*; **we have no option** wir haben keine andere Wahl.

optional *adjective* auf Wunsch erhältlich; **optional subject** *das* Wahlfach.

or *conjunction* **1** oder; **English or German?** Englisch oder Deutsch?; **today or Tuesday?** heute oder Dienstag?; **2** (*in negatives*) noch; **I don't have a cat or a dog** ich habe weder eine Katze noch einen Hund; **not in June or July** weder im Juni noch im Juli; **3** (*or else*) sonst; **phone Mum, or she'll worry** ruf Mutti an, sonst macht sie sich Sorgen.

oral *noun* (*an exam*) Mündliche *das* (*informal*); **my German oral** meine mündliche Deutschprüfung.

orange *noun* (*the fruit*) Orange *die* (PL *die* Orangen); **orange juice** *der* Orangensaft.

orange *adjective* orange ('*orange*' *never changes*); **my orange socks** meine orange Socken.

orchestra *noun* Orchester *das* (PL *die* Orchester).

order *noun* **1** (*sequence*) Reihenfolge *die* (PL *die* Reihenfolgen); **in the right order** in der richtigen Reihenfolge; **in the wrong order** in der falschen Reihenfolge; **in alphabetical order** in alphabetischer Reihenfolge; **2** (*in a restaurant, café, or shop*) Bestellung *die* (PL *die* Bestellungen); **3** '**out of order**' 'außer Betrieb'; **4** **in order to** um etwas zu tun.

order *verb* **1** (*in a restaurant or a shop*) bestellen; **we ordered soup** wir haben Suppe bestellt; **have you ordered?** haben Sie schon bestellt?; **2** bestellen (*a taxi*).

ordinary *adjective* normal.

organ *noun* **1** (*the instrument*) Orgel *die* (PL *die* Orgeln); **2** (*of the body*) Organ *das* (PL *die* Organe).

organic *adjective* Bio- (*food*); **organic food** *die* Biokost.

organization *noun* Organisation *die* (PL *die* Organisationen).

organize *verb* **1** organisieren; **2** veranstalten (*a conference or festival*).

orienteering *noun* Orientierungslauf *der*

original *adjective* **1** ursprünglich; **the original plan was better** der ursprüngliche Plan war besser; **2** originell; **it's a really original novel** das ist ein wirklich origineller Roman.

originally *adverb* ursprünglich; **originally we wanted to go by car** ursprünglich wollten wir mit dem Auto fahren.

orphan *noun* Waise *die* (PL *die* Waisen); **he is an orphan** er ist Waise.

ostrich *noun* Strauß *der* (PL *die* Strauße).

other *adjective* **1** anderer/andere/anderes; **we took the other road** wir haben die andere Straße genommen; **where are the others?** wo sind die anderen?; **the other two cars** die anderen beiden Autos; **2** give me the other one** gib mir den anderen/die andere/das andere (*the translation of 'the other*

a
b
c
d
e
f
g
h
i
j
k
l
m
n
o
p
q
r
s
t
u
v
w
x
y
z

one' depends on the gender of the noun it refers to); **3 the other day** neulich; **4 every other week** jede zweite Woche; **5 somebody or other** irgendjemand; **something or other** irgendetwas; **somewhere or other** irgendwo; **6 any other questions?** sonst noch Fragen?

otherwise *adverb, conjunction* sonst.

ought *verb ('ought' is usually translated by the subjunctive of 'sollen')* **I ought to go** ich sollte eigentlich gehen; **they ought to have known the address** sie hätten die Adresse kennen sollen; **you oughtn't to have any problems** du solltest keine Probleme haben.

our *adjective* **1** *(before a masculine noun)* unser; **our father** unser Vater; **2** *(before a feminine noun)* unsere; **our mother** unsere Mutter; **3** *(before a neuter noun)* unser; **our house** unser Haus; **4** *(before masculine/feminine/neuter plural nouns)* unsere; **our parents** unsere Eltern; **5** *(with parts of the body)* der/die/das *(plural: die)* ; **we'll go and wash our hands** wir waschen uns die Hände.

ours *pronoun* **1** *(for a masculine noun)* unserer; **their garden's bigger than ours** ihr Garten ist größer als unserer; **2** *(for a feminine noun)* unsere; **their kitchen is smaller than ours** ihre Küche ist kleiner als unsere; **3** *(for a neuter noun)* unseres; **their child is younger than ours** ihr Kind ist jünger als unseres; **4** *(for plural nouns)* unsere; **they've invited**

their friends and we've invited ours sie haben ihre Freunde eingeladen und wir haben unsere eingeladen; **5 the green car is ours** das grüne Auto gehört uns; **it's ours** es gehört uns; **a friend of ours** ein Freund von uns.

ourselves *pronoun* **1** *(reflexive)* uns; **we introduced ourselves** wir haben uns vorgestellt; **2** *(for emphasis)* selbst; **in the end we did it ourselves** schließlich haben wir es selbst gemacht.

out *adverb* **1** *(outside)* draußen; **it's cold out there** es ist kalt da draußen; **they're out in the garden** sie sind draußen im Garten; **2 to go out** hinausgehen◇ SEP (PERF *sein*), rausgehen◇ SEP (PERF *sein*) *(informal)*; **to go out shopping** einkaufen gehen; **3 get out!** raus! *(informal)*; **4 the ball is out** der Ball ist aus; **5** *(absent)* **to be out** nicht da sein; **Mr Barnes is out** Herr Barnes ist nicht da; **6 to go out** *(for an evening or to the theatre or cinema)* ausgehen◇ SEP (PERF *sein*), weggehen◇ SEP (PERF *sein*) *(informal)*; **are you going out this evening?** gehst du heute Abend weg?; **to be going out with somebody** mit jemandem gehen; **Alison's going out with Danny now** Alison geht jetzt mit Danny; **7 to ask somebody out** jemanden einladen◇ SEP; **he's asked me out** er hat mich eingeladen; **8** *(light, fire)* aus; **4 the ball is out** das Licht aus?

out *preposition* **out of** aus (+ DAT); **to go out of the room** aus dem Zimmer gehen; **he threw it out of**

the window er hat es aus dem Fenster geworfen; **to drink out of a glass** aus einem Glas trinken; **she took the photo out of her bag** sie hat das Foto aus der Tasche genommen.

outdoor adjective (activity or sport) im Freien; **outdoor games** Spiele im Freien.

outdoors adverb draußen; **to go outdoors** nach draußen gehen.

outing noun Ausflug der (PL die Ausflüge); **to go on an outing** einen Ausflug machen.

outline noun (of an object) Umriss der (PL die Umrisse).

out-of-date adjective **1** (no longer valid) ungültig; **my passport's out of date** mein Pass ist ungültig; **2** (old-fashioned) altmodisch (clothes, music).

outside noun Außenseite die; **it's blue on the outside** außen ist es blau.

outside adjective Außen-.

outside adverb draußen; **it's cold outside** es ist kalt draußen.

outside preposition vor (+ DAT); **I'll meet you outside the cinema** ich treffe mich vor dem Kino mit dir.

outskirts plural noun Stadtrand der; **on the outskirts of Lübeck** am Stadtrand von Lübeck.

oven noun Ofen der (PL die Öfen); **to put something in the oven** etwas in den Ofen tun.

over preposition **1** (above) über (+ DAT); **there's a mirror over the sink** über dem Waschbecken hängt ein Spiegel; **2** (involving movement) über (+ ACC); **he threw**

the ball over the wall er hat den Ball über die Mauer geworfen; **3 over here** hier drüben; **the food is over here** das Essen ist hier drüben; **4 over there** da drüben; **she's over there** sie ist da drüben; **5** (more than) über; **it will cost over a hundred pounds** es wird über hundert Pfund kosten; **he's over sixty** er ist über sechzig; **6** (during) über (+ ACC); **over Christmas** über Weihnachten; **over the weekend** übers Wochenende; **7** (finished) zu Ende; **when the meeting's over** wenn die Besprechung zu Ende ist; **it's all over** es ist vorbei; **8 over the phone** am Telefon; **to ask someone over** jemanden einladen ◇ SEP; **to come over** herüberkommen ◇ SEP; **come over on Saturday** komm am Samstag zu uns herüber; **9 all over the place** überall; **I've been looking for it all over** ich habe überall danach gesucht.

overdose noun Überdosis die (PL die Überdosen).

overtake verb überholen.

overtime noun **to work overtime** Überstunden machen.

overweight adjective **to be overweight** Übergewicht haben.

owe verb schulden; **I owe him ten pounds** ich schulde ihm zehn Pfund.

owing adjective **1** (outstanding) ausstehend; **there's five pounds owing** fünf Pfund stehen aus; **2 owing to** wegen (+ GEN); **owing to the snow** wegen des Schnees.

owl noun Eule die (PL die Eulen).

a b c d e f g h i j k l m n o p q r s t u v w x y z

own adjective **1** eigen; **my own computer** mein eigener Computer; **I've got my own room** ich habe mein eigenes Zimmer; **2 on your own** allein; **Annie did it on her own** Annie hat es allein gemacht.

own verb besitzen✧.

owner noun Besitzer der (PL die Besitzer), Besitzerin die (PL die Besitzerinnen).

oxygen noun Sauerstoff der.

oyster noun Auster die (PL die Austern).

ozone layer noun Ozonschicht die.

Pp

pace noun **1** (a step) Schritt der (PL die Schritte); **2** (the speed you walk at) Tempo das (PL die Tempos).

Pacific noun **the Pacific (Ocean)** der Pazifik.

pack noun **1** Packung die (PL die Packungen); **2 pack of cards** das Kartenspiel.

pack verb **1** packen (your case); **I haven't packed yet** ich habe noch nicht gepackt; **I'll pack my case tonight** ich packe meinen Koffer heute Abend; **2** einpacken SEP (clothes, shoes, etc.); **have you packed my red shirt?** hast du mein rotes Hemd eingepackt?

package noun Paket das (PL die Pakete).

package holiday noun Pauschalurlaub der (PL die Pauschalurlaube).

packed lunch noun Lunchpaket das (PL die Lunchpakete).

packet noun **1** Päckchen das (PL die Päckchen); **a packet of tea** ein Päckchen Tee; **2** (box) Schachtel die (PL die Schachteln); **3** (bag) Tüte die (PL die Tüten); **a packet of crisps** eine Tüte Chips.

pad noun (of paper) Block der (PL die Blöcke).

paddle noun (for a canoe) Paddel das (PL die Paddel).

paddle verb **1** (at the seaside) plauschen (PERF sein); **to go paddling** plauschen gehen; **2** (a canoe) paddeln.

padlock noun Vorhängeschloss das (PL die Vorhängeschlösser).

page noun Seite die (PL die Seiten); **on page seven** auf Seite sieben.

pain noun Schmerz der (PL die Schmerzen); **to be in pain** Schmerzen haben; **I've got a pain in my leg** ich habe Schmerzen im Bein; ★ **Eric's a real pain (in the neck)** Eric geht einem richtig auf den Wecker (informal).

painful adjective schmerzhaft.

painkiller noun Schmerzmittel das (PL die Schmerzmittel).

paint noun Farbe die (PL die Farben); **'wet paint'** 'frisch gestrichen'.

paint verb malen (a picture), streichen✧ (a room); **to paint a room pink** ein Zimmer rosa streichen.

paintbrush noun Pinsel der (PL die Pinsel).

painter *noun* (*picture*) Maler der (PL die Maler), Malerin die (PL die Malerinnen).

painting *noun* (*picture*) Gemälde das (PL die Gemälde); **a painting by Picasso** ein Gemälde von Picasso.

pair *noun* 1 Paar das (PL die Paare); **a pair of socks** ein Paar Socken; **2 a pair of scissors** eine Schere; **3 a pair of trousers** eine Hose; **a pair of knickers** eine Unterhose; **4 to work in pairs** paarweise arbeiten.

Pakistan *noun* Pakistan das.

palace *noun* Palast der (PL die Paläste).

pale *adjective* blass; **to turn pale** blass werden; **pale green** zartgrün.

palm *noun* 1 (*of your hand*) Handfläche die (PL die Handflächen); **2** (*a palm tree*) Palme die (PL die Palmen).

pan *noun* 1 (*saucepan*) Topf der (PL die Töpfe); **a pan of water** ein Topf Wasser; **2** (*frying-pan*) Pfanne die (PL die Pfannen).

pancake *noun* Pfannkuchen der (PL die Pfannkuchen).

panel *noun* 1 (*for a discussion*) Diskussionsrunde die, (*for a quiz*) Rateteam das; **2** (*a piece of wood*) Tafel die (PL die Tafeln).

panic *noun* Panik die.

panic *verb* in Panik geraten◇; **don't panic!** keine Panik!

pantomime *noun* Märchenvorstellung die (PL die Märchenvorstellungen).

pants *plural noun* Unterhose die (PL die Unterhosen).

paper *noun* 1 Papier das; **a sheet of paper** ein Blatt Papier; **2 paper hanky** das Papiertaschentuch;

3 paper cup der Pappbecher; **4** (*newspaper*) Zeitung die (PL die Zeitungen); **it was in the paper** es stand in der Zeitung; **5 papers** (*documents*) Unterlagen (*plural*).

paperback *noun* Taschenbuch das (PL die Taschenbücher).

paperclip *noun* Büroklammer die (PL die Büroklammern).

paper towel *noun* Papierhandtuch das (PL die Papierhandtücher).

parachute *noun* Fallschirm der (PL die Fallschirme).

parade *noun* Umzug der (PL die Umzüge).

paraffin *noun* Petroleum das .

paragraph *noun* Absatz der (PL die Absätze); **'new paragraph'** 'Absatz'.

parallel *adjective* parallel.

paralysed *adjective* gelähmt.

parcel *noun* Paket das (PL die Pakete).

pardon *noun* **I beg your pardon** (*as an apology*) Entschuldigung!; **pardon?** wie bitte?

parent *noun* Elternteil der; **parents** Eltern (*plural*); **my parents live in Germany** meine Eltern wohnen in Deutschland; **parents' evening** der Elternabend.

park *noun* 1 Park der (PL die Parks); **theme park** der (thematische) Freizeitpark; **2 car park** der Parkplatz.

park *verb* 1 parken; **you can park outside the house** du kannst vor dem Haus parken; **2 to find somewhere to park** einen Parkplatz finden.

parking *noun* Parken das; **'no parking'** 'Parken verboten'.

a
b
c
d
e
f
g
h
i
j
k
l
m
n
o
p
q
r
s
t
u
v
w
x
y
z

a

parking meter noun Parkuhr die (PL die Parkuhren).

b

parking space noun Parklücke die (PL die Parklücken).

c

parking ticket noun Strafzettel der (PL die Strafzettel).

d

parliament noun Parlament das (PL die Parlamente).

e

parrot noun Papagei der (PL die Papageien).

f

parsley noun Petersilie die.

g

part noun 1 Teil der (PL die Teile); **part of the garden** Teil des Gartens; **the last part of the book** der letzte Teil des Buches; 2 that's **part of your job** das gehört dazu; 3 **to take part in something** an etwas (DAT) teilnehmen SEP; 4 (spare part) Teil das (PL die Teile) (for a machine or an engine); 5 (a role in a play) Rolle die (PL die Rollen).

h

i

j

k

particular adjective besonderer/ besondere/besonderes; **nothing in particular** nichts Besonderes.

l

particularly adverb besonders; **not particularly interesting** nicht besonders interessant.

m

n

parting noun 1 (in your hair) Scheitel der (PL die Scheitel); 2 (departure) Abschied der (PL die Abschiede).

o

p

partly adverb teilweise.

q

partner noun Partner der (PL die Partner), Partnerin die (PL die Partnerinnen).

r

s

part-time adjective Teilzeit-; **part-time work** die Teilzeitarbeit.

t

part-time adverb **to work part-time** Teilzeit arbeiten.

u

v

party noun 1 (small, private) Party die (PL die Partys), Feier die (PL die Feiern); **a Christmas party** eine Weihnachtsfeier; **to have a birthday party** eine Geburtstagsparty machen; 2 (more formal, in the evening) Gesellschaft die (PL die Gesellschaften); **we've been invited to a party at the Smiths' house** wir sind zu einer Gesellschaft bei Smiths eingeladen worden; 3 (group) Gruppe die (PL die Gruppen); **a party of schoolchildren** eine Gruppe Schulkinder; 4 (in politics) Partei die (PL die Parteien).

w

x

y

z

party game noun Gesellschaftsspiel das (PL die Gesellschaftsspiele).

pass noun 1 (to let you in) Ausweis der (PL die Ausweise); 2 **bus pass** die Buskarte; 3 (over the mountains) Pass der (PL die Pässe); 4 (in an exam) **to get a pass in maths** die Mathematikprüfung bestehen.

pass verb 1 (walk past) vorbeigehen SEP (PERF sein) an (+ DAT) (a place or building); **we passed your house** wir sind an deinem Haus vorbeigegangen; 2 (drive past) vorbeifahren SEP (PERF sein) an (+ DAT) (a place or building); 3 (overtake) überholen (a car); 4 (give) reichen; **could you pass me the sugar please?** könnten Sie mir bitte den Zucker reichen?; 5 (time) vergehen (PERF sein); **the time passed slowly** die Zeit verging langsam; 6 bestehen (an exam); **to pass an exam** eine Prüfung bestehen; **did you pass in German?** hast du die Deutschprüfung bestanden?

passage noun **1** (*corridor*) Gang der (PL die Gänge); **2** (*a piece of text*) Passage. die (PL die Passagen).

passenger noun **1** (*in a plane or ship*) Passagier der (PL die Passagiere); **2** (*in a train or bus*) Fahrgast der (PL die Fahrgäste); **3** (*in a car*) Mitfahrer der (PL die Mitfahrer).

passive noun Passiv das,

passive adjective passiv.

Passover noun Passah das.

passport noun Reisepass der (PL die Reisepässe), Pass der (PL die Pässe).

password noun **1** (*to gain entry*) Kennwort das (PL die Kennwörter); **2** (*for access to data*) Passwort das (PL die Passwörter); **to give the password** das Passwort eingeben.

past noun Vergangenheit die; **in the past** in der Vergangenheit.

past adjective **1** (*recent*) letzter/letzte/letztes; **in the past few weeks** in den letzten paar Wochen; **2** (*over*) vorbei; **winter is past** der Winter ist vorbei.

past preposition, adverb **1** **to walk past something** an etwas (DAT) vorbeigehen◇ SEP (PERF sein); **we went past the school** wir sind an der Schule vorbeigegangen; **to go past** vorbeifahren◇ (PERF sein); **2** (*after*) nach (+ DAT); **it's just past the post office** es ist kurz nach der Post; **3** (*talking about time*) **ten past six** zehn nach sechs; **half past four** halb fünf; **a quarter past two** Viertel nach zwei.

pasta noun Nudeln (*plural*); **I don't like pasta** ich mag keine Nudeln.

pastry noun **1** (*for baking*) Teig der, **2** (*cake*) Gebäck das.

patch noun **1** (*for mending*) Flicken der (PL die Flicken); **2** (*of snow or ice*) Stelle die (PL die Stellen); **3** (*of blue sky*) Stückchen das (PL die Stückchen).

path noun Weg der (PL die Wege), (*very narrow*) Pfad der (PL die Pfade).

pathetic adjective (*useless, hopeless*) jämmerlich.

patience noun **1** Geduld die; **2** (*card game*) Patience die.

patient noun Patient der (PL die Patienten), Patientin die (PL die Patientinnen).

patient adjective geduldig.

patiently adverb geduldig.

patio noun Terrasse die (PL die Terrassen).

pattern noun **1** (*on wallpaper or fabric*) Muster das (PL die Muster); **2** (*dressmaking, knitting*) Schnitt der (PL die Schnitte).

pause noun Pause die (PL die Pausen).

pavement noun Bürgersteig der (PL die Bürgersteige); **on the pavement** auf dem Bürgersteig.

paw noun Pfote die (PL die Pfoten).

pawn noun (*in chess*) Bauer der (PL die Bauern).

pay noun (*wage*) Lohn der (PL die Löhne), (*salary*) Gehalt das (PL die Gehälter).

pay verb **1** zahlen; **I'm paying** ich zahle; **to pay cash** bar zahlen; **to pay by credit card** mit Kreditkarte zahlen; **they pay £8 an hour** sie zahlen acht Pfund die Stunde; **to**

a b c d e f g h i j k l m n o p q r s t u v w x y z

pay phone 510 **ENGLISH - GERMAN**

pay by cheque mit Scheck zahlen;
2 bezahlen ('*bezahlen' is used when you pay a person, a bill or for something*); **to pay for something** etwas bezahlen; **Tony paid for the drinks** Tony hat die Getränke bezahlt; **it's all paid for** es ist alles bezahlt; **3 to pay somebody back** (*money*) jemandem Geld zurückzahlen SEP; **4 to pay attention** aufpassen SEP; **5 to pay a visit to somebody** jemanden besuchen.

pay phone noun
Münzfernsprecher der (PL die Münzfernsprecher).

payment noun **1** Bezahlung die (*of sum, bill, debt, or fine*); **2** Zahlung die (PL die Zahlungen) (*of interest, tax, or fee*).

PC noun (*computer*) PC der (PL die PC).

pea noun Erbse die (PL die Erbsen).

peace noun Frieden der.

peaceful adjective friedlich.

peach noun Pfirsich der (PL die Pfirsiche).

peacock noun Pfau der (PL die Pfauen).

peak period (*for holidays*) Hauptferienzeit die (PL die Hauptferienzeiten).

peak rate noun (*for phoning*) Höchsttarif der (PL die Höchsttarife).

peak time noun (*for traffic*) Stoßzeit die (PL die Stoßzeiten).

peanut noun Erdnuss die (PL die Erdnüsse).

peanut butter noun Erdnussbutter die.

pear noun Birne die (PL die Birnen).

pearl noun Perle die (PL die Perlen).

pebble noun Kieselstein der (PL die Kieselsteine).

peculiar adjective komisch.

pedal noun Pedal das (PL die Pedale).

pedal verb (*on a bike*) **to pedal off** (mit dem Rad) wegfahren ◇ (PERF sein).

pedestrian noun Fußgänger der (PL die Fußgänger), Fußgängerin die (PL die Fußgängerinnen).

pedestrian crossing noun Fußgängerüberweg der (PL die Fußgängerüberwege).

pedestrian precinct noun Fußgängerzone die (PL die Fußgängerzonen).

pee noun **to have a pee** pinkeln (*informal*).

peel noun Schale die (PL die Schalen).

peel verb schälen (*fruit, vegetables*).

peg noun **1** (*hook*) Haken der (PL die Haken); **2 clothes peg** die Wäscheklammer (PL die Wäscheklammern); **3** (*for a tent*) Hering der (PL die Heringe).

pen noun (*ball-point*) Kugelschreiber der (PL die Kugelschreiber); **felt pen** der Filzstift.

penalty noun **1** (*a fine*) Geldstrafe die (PL die Geldstrafen); **2** (*in football*) Elfmeter der (PL die Elfmeter).

pence plural noun Pence (*plural*).

pencil noun Bleistift der (PL die Bleistifte); **to write in pencil** mit Bleistift schreiben.

pencil case noun
Federmäppchen das (PL die
Federmäppchen).

pencil sharpener noun
Bleistiftanspitzer der (PL die
Bleistiftanspitzer).

penfriend noun Brieffreund der
(PL die Brieffreunde), Brieffreundin
die (PL die Brieffreundinnen); **my
German pen-friend is called Heidi**
meine deutsche Brieffreundin
heißt Heidi.

penguin noun Pinguin der (PL die
Pinguine).

penis noun Penis der (PL die
Penisse).

penknife noun Taschenmesser das
(PL die Taschenmesser).

penny noun Penny der (PL die
Pence).

pension noun Rente die (PL die
Renten).

pensioner noun Rentner der (PL die
Rentner), Rentnerin die (PL die
Rentnerinnen).

people plural noun **1** Leute
(plural), Menschen (plural)
('Menschen' is used in a more formal
context); **most people round here**
die meisten Leute hier; **several
people** verschiedene Leute; **nice
people** nette Leute; **all the people
in the world** alle Menschen auf der
Welt; **a crowd of people**
Menschenmenge die; **2** (when you're
counting them) Personen (plural);
for ten people für zehn Personen;
**how many people have you
invited?** wie viele Personen hast
du eingeladen?; **3 people say that
...** man sagt, dass ....

pepper noun **1** (spice) Pfeffer der;
2 (vegetable) Paprikaschote die (PL
die Paprikaschoten).

peppermill noun Pfeffermühle
die (PL die Pfeffermühlen).

peppermint noun (plant)
Pfefferminze die; **peppermint tea**
der Pfefferminztee.

per preposition pro (+ ACC); **ten
pounds per person** zehn Pfund pro
Person.

per cent adverb Prozent das; **sixty
per cent of students** sechzig
Prozent der Studenten.

percentage noun Prozentsatz der
(PL die Prozentsätze).

percussion noun Schlagzeug das;
to play percussion Schlagzeug
spielen.

perfect adjective **1** perfekt; **she
speaks perfect English** sie spricht
perfekt Englisch; **2** (ideal) herrlich
(day or weather).

perfectly adverb **1** (absolutely)
vollkommen; **2** (faultlessly)
perfekt.

perform verb **1** spielen (a piece of
music or a part); **2** singen ◇ (a
song); **3 to perform a play** ein
Theaterstück aufführen SEP.

performance noun **1** (playing or
acting) Darstellung die (PL die
Darstellungen); **his performance
as Hamlet** seine Darstellung des
Hamlet; **2** (show or film)
Vorstellung die (PL die
Vorstellungen); **the performance
starts at eight** die Vorstellung
fängt um acht Uhr an; **3** (of a play
or opera) Aufführung die (PL die
Aufführungen).

a
b
c
d
e
f
g
h
i
j
k
l
m
n
o
p
q
r
s
t
u
v
w
x
y
z

a | b | c | d | e | f | g | h | i | j | k | l | m | n | o | **p** | q | r | s | t | u | v | w | x | y | z

performer noun Künstler der (PL die Künstler), Künstlerin die (PL die Künstlerinnen).

perfume noun Parfüm das (PL die Parfüme).

perhaps adverb vielleicht; **perhaps he's missed the train** vielleicht hat er den Zug verpasst.

period noun 1 (length of time) Zeit die (PL die Zeiten); **trial period** die Probezeit; **2** (a portion of time) Zeitraum der; **a two-year period** ein Zeitraum von zwei Jahren; **3** (in school) Stunde die (PL die Stunden); **4** (menstruation) Periode die (PL die Perioden).

perm noun Dauerwelle die (PL die Dauerwellen).

permanent adjective **1** ständig; **2** fest (job or address, for example).

permanently adverb **1** dauernd; **2 to be permanently employed** fest angestellt sein.

permission noun Erlaubnis die; **to get permission to do something** Erlaubnis zu etwas (DAT) erhalten.

permit noun Genehmigung die (PL die Genehmigungen).

permit verb **1** erlauben; **to permit somebody to do something** jemandem erlauben, etwas zu tun; **smoking is not permitted** Rauchen ist nicht gestattet; **2 weather permitting** bei entsprechendem Wetter.

person noun **1** Person die (PL die Personen); **there's still room for one more person** wir haben noch Platz für eine Person; **2 in person** persönlich.

personal adjective persönlich.

personality noun Persönlichkeit die (PL die Persönlichkeiten).

personally adverb persönlich; **personally, I'm against it** ich persönlich bin dagegen.

perspiration noun Schweiß der.

persuade verb überreden; **to persuade somebody to come** jemanden überreden zu kommen.

pessimistic adjective pessimistisch.

pest noun **1** (greenfly, for example) Schädling der (PL die Schädlinge); **2** (annoying person) Nervensäge die (PL die Nervensägen) (informal).

pet noun **1** Haustier das (PL die Haustiere; **do you have a pet?** habt ihr Haustiere?; **a pet dog** ein Hund; **2 Julie is teacher's pet** Julie ist der Liebling des Lehrers.

petrol noun Benzin das (PL die Benzine); **to fill up with petrol** tanken; **to run out of petrol** kein Benzin mehr haben.

petrol station noun Tankstelle die (PL die Tankstellen).

pharmacy noun Apotheke die (PL die Apotheken).

pheasant noun Fasan der (PL die Fasane).

philosophy noun Philosophie die (PL die Philosophien).

phone noun Telefon das (PL die Telefone); **she's on the phone** sie telefoniert; **I was on the phone to Sophie** ich habe mit Sophie telefoniert; **you can book by phone** du kannst telefonisch buchen.

phone verb **1** telefonieren; **while I was phoning** während ich telefonierte; **2 to phone somebody**

jemanden anrufen❖ SEP; **I'll phone you tonight** ich rufe dich heute Abend an.

phone book noun Telefonbuch das (PL die Telefonbücher).

phone box noun Telefonzelle die (PL die Telefonzellen).

phone call noun **1** Anruf der (PL die Anrufe); **to get a phone call** einen Anruf erhalten; **2 to make a phone call** ein Telefongespräch führen; **phone calls are free** Telefongespräche sind gebührenfrei.

phone card noun Telefonkarte die (PL die Telefonkarten).

phone number noun Telefonnummer die (PL die Telefonnummern).

photo noun Foto das (PL die Fotos); **to take a photo** ein Foto machen; **to take a photo of somebody** ein Foto von jemandem machen.

photocopier noun Fotokopiergerät das (PL die Fotokopiergeräte).

photocopy noun Fotokopie die (PL die Fotokopien).

photocopy verb fotokopieren.

photograph noun Fotografie die (PL die Fotografien); **to take a photograph** ein Foto machen.

photograph verb fotografieren.

photographer noun Fotograf der (PL die Fotografen), Fotografin die (PL die Fotografinnen).

photography noun Fotografie die.

phrase noun Phrase die (PL die Phrasen); **an idiomatic phrase** eine Redewendung.

phrase-book noun Sprachführer der (PL die Sprachführer).

physical adjective körperlich.

physics noun Physik die.

physiotherapist noun Physiotherapeut der (PL die Physiotherapeuten), Physiotherapeutin die (PL die Physiotherapeutinnen).

physiotherapy noun Physiotherapie die.

piano noun Klavier das (PL die Klaviere); **to play the piano** Klavier spielen; **piano lesson** Klavierstunde.

pick noun **to take your pick** sich (DAT) etwas aussuchen SEP.

pick verb **1** (to select) wählen; **he picked his words carefully** er wählte seine Worte mit Bedacht; **2** (choose for oneself) sich (DAT) aussuchen SEP; **pick any book** such dir irgendein Buch aus; **3 to pick a team** eine Mannschaft aufstellen; **4** pflücken (fruit); **to pick strawberries** Erdbeeren pflücken.

● **to pick up 1** (lift) (in die Hand) nehmen❖; **he picked up the papers** er nahm die Unterlagen; **2** (collect) abholen SEP; **I'll pick you up at six** ich hole dich um sechs Uhr ab; **I'll pick up the keys tomorrow** ich hole die Schlüssel morgen ab.

pickpocket noun Taschendieb der (PL die Taschendiebe).

picnic noun Picknick das (PL die Picknicke); **to have a picnic** ein Picknick machen.

picture noun **1** Bild das (PL die Bilder); **2 to go to the pictures** (the cinema) ins Kino gehen.

a
b
c
d
e
f
g
h
i
j
k
l
m
n
o
p
q
r
s
t
u
v
w
x
y
z

pie noun 1 (*sweet*) Kuchen der (PL die Kuchen); **apple pie** der Apfelkuchen; 2 (*savoury*) Pastete die (PL die Pasteten).

piece noun 1 (*a bit*) Stück das (PL die Stücke); **a big piece of cheese** ein großes Stück Käse; 2 (*that you fit together*) Teil das (PL die Teile); **the pieces of a jigsaw** die Teile von einem Puzzle; **to take something to pieces** etwas in Einzelteile zerlegen; 3 **piece of furniture** das Möbelstück; **a piece of information** eine Information; **a piece of luck** ein Glücksfall; 4 (*coin*) Stück das (PL die Stücke); **a five-pence piece** ein Fünf-Pence-Stück.

pierce verb 1 durchstechen◇ SEP; 2 **to have pierced ears** Löcher in den Ohrläppchen haben.

pig noun Schwein das (PL die Schweine).

pigeon noun Taube die (PL die Tauben).

piggy bank noun Sparschwein das (PL die Sparschweine).

pigtail noun Zopf der (PL die Zöpfe).

pile noun 1 (*a neat stack*) Stapel der (PL die Stapel); **a pile of plates** ein Stapel Teller; 2 (*a heap*) Haufen der (PL die Haufen).

● **to pile something** (*neatly*) etwas aufstapeln SEP, (*in a heap*) etwas auftürmen SEP.

pill noun Pille die (PL die Pillen).

pillar noun Säule die (PL die Säulen).

pillow noun Kopfkissen das (PL die Kopfkissen).

pilot noun Pilot der (PL die Piloten), Pilotin die (PL die Pilotinnen).

pimple noun Pickel der (PL die Pickel).

pin noun 1 (*for sewing*) Stecknadel die (PL die Stecknadeln); 2 **a three-pin plug** ein dreipoliger Stecker.

● **to pin up** 1 hochstecken SEP (*a hem*); 2 anschlagen◇ SEP (*a notice*).

PIN noun (*personal identification number*) Geheimnummer die.

pinball noun Flippern das; **to play pinball** flippern; **pinball machine** der Flipper.

pinch noun (*of salt, for example*) Prise die (PL die Prisen).

pinch verb 1 kneifen◇; **she pinched my arm** sie hat mich in den Arm gekniffen; 2 (*to steal*) klauen; **somebody's pinched my bike** jemand hat mein Rad geklaut.

pine noun Kiefer die (PL die Kiefern); **pine furniture** Kiefernmöbel (plural).

pineapple noun Ananas die (PL die Ananas).

pine cone noun Kiefernzapfen der (PL die Kiefernzapfen).

ping-pong noun Tischtennis das; **to play ping-pong** Tischtennis spielen.

pink adjective rosa ('rosa' never changes); **pink hats** rosa Hüte.

pip noun (*in a fruit*) Kern der (PL die Kerne).

pipe noun 1 (*for gas or water*) Rohr das (PL die Rohre); 2 (*for smoking*) Pfeife die (PL die Pfeifen); **he smokes a pipe** er raucht Pfeife.

pirate noun Pirat der (PL die Piraten).

Pisces noun Fische (*plural*); **Amanda is Pisces** Amanda ist Fisch.

pitch *noun* Platz der (PL die Plätze); **football pitch** der Fußballplatz.

pitch *verb* **to pitch a tent** ein Zelt aufstellen SEP.

pity *noun* **1** *(feeling sorry for somebody)* Mitleid das; **2 what a pity!** wie schade!; **it would be a pity to miss the beginning** es wäre schade, den Anfang zu verpassen.

pity *verb* **to pity somebody** jemanden bemitleiden.

pizza *noun* Pizza die (PL die Pizzas).

place *noun* **1** Ort der (PL die Orte); **Salzburg is a wonderful place** Salzburg ist ein sehr schöner Ort; **in place** an Ort und Stelle; **2 all over the place** überall; **3** *(a space)* Platz der (PL die Plätze); **a place for the car** ein Platz für das Auto; **is there a place for me?** ist Platz für mich?; **will you keep my place?** kannst du mir den Platz freihalten?; **to change places** die Plätze tauschen; **4** *(spot)* Stelle die (PL die Stellen); **this is a good place to stop** das ist eine gute Stelle zum Halten; **5** *(in a race)* Platz der (PL die Plätze); **to gain first place** den ersten Platz belegen; **6 at your place** bei dir; **we'll go round to Zafir's place** wir gehen zu Zafir; **7 to take place** stattfinden ◇ SEP; **the competition will take place at four** der Wettbewerb findet um vier Uhr statt.

place *verb* *(upright)* stellen, *(lying flat)* legen.

plain *noun* Ebene die (PL die Ebenen).

plain *adjective* **1** einfach; **plain food** einfaches Essen; **2** *(unflavoured)* Natur-; **plain yoghurt** der Naturjoghurt; **3** *(not patterned)* einfarbig; **plain curtains** einfarbige Vorhänge.

plait *noun* Zopf der (PL die Zöpfe).

plan *noun* Plan der (PL die Pläne); **we've made plans for the summer** wir haben Pläne für den Sommer gemacht; **to go according to plan** nach Plan gehen; **everything went according to plan** alles ging nach Plan.

plan *verb* **1 to plan to do something** etwas vorhaben ◇ SEP; **we're planning to leave at eight** wir haben vor, um acht abzufahren; **2** *(make plans for, organize, design)* planen; **she's planning a trip to Italy** sie plant eine Reise nach Italien.

plane *noun* Flugzeug das (PL die Flugzeuge); **we went by plane** wir sind geflogen.

planet *noun* Planet der (PL die Planeten).

plant *noun* Pflanze die (PL die Pflanzen); **a house plant** eine Topfpflanze.

plant *verb* pflanzen.

plaster *noun* **1** *(sticking plaster)* Pflaster das (PL die Pflaster); **2** *(for walls)* Verputz der; **3** Gips der; **to have your leg in plaster** das Bein in Gips haben.

plastic *noun* Plastik das; **plastic bag** die Plastiktüte.

plate *noun* Teller der (PL die Teller).

platform *noun* **1** *(in a station)* Bahnsteig der (PL die Bahnsteige); **2 the train is arriving at platform six** der Zug fährt auf Gleis sechs

a
b
c
d
e
f
g
h
i
j
k
l
m
n
o
p
q
r
s
t
u
v
w
x
y
z

play noun (in the theatre) Stück das (PL die Stücke); **television play** das Fernsehspiel; **we are putting on a play by Brecht at school** wir führen ein Stück von Brecht in der Schule auf.

play verb **1** spielen; **the children are playing with a ball** die Kinder spielen Ball; **they play the piano and the guitar** sie spielen Klavier und Gitarre; **who's playing Hamlet?** wer spielt Hamlet?; **to play tennis** Tennis spielen; **they were playing cards** sie haben Karten gespielt; **2** (in sport) **to play somebody** gegen jemanden spielen; **Italy are playing Germany** Italien spielt gegen Deutschland; **3** spielen (a tape, CD, or record); **play your new CD** spiel mal deine neue CD.

player noun **1** Spieler der (PL die Spieler), Spielerin die (PL die Spielerinnen); **football player** der Fußballspieler; **2** (in the theatre) Schauspieler der (PL die Schauspieler), Schauspielerin die (PL die Schauspielerinnen).

playground noun Spielplatz der (PL die Spielplätze); **school playground** der Schulhof.

playgroup noun Spielgruppe die (PL die Spielgruppen).

playing field noun Sportplatz der (PL die Sportplätze).

pleasant adjective angenehm.

please adverb bitte; **two coffees, please** zwei Kaffee bitte; **could you turn the TV off, please?** könntest du bitte den Fernseher ausmachen?

pleased adjective **1** erfreut; **I'm really pleased!** das freut mich wirklich!; **2 she was pleased with her present** sie hat sich über ihr Geschenk gefreut; **3 pleased to meet you!** freut mich!

pleasure noun **1** (amusement) Vergnügen das; **2** (joy) Freude die; **to get a lot of pleasure out of something** viel Freude an etwas (DAT) haben.

plenty pronoun **1** (lots) viel; **he's got plenty of money** er hat viel Geld; **2** (enough) genug; **that's plenty!** das ist genug!; **we've got plenty of time left** wir haben noch genug Zeit.

plot noun (of a film or novel) Handlung die.

plough noun Pflug der (PL die Pflüge).

plough verb pflügen.

plug noun **1** (electrical) Stecker der (PL die Stecker); **2** (in a bath or sink) Stöpsel der (PL die Stöpsel); **to pull out the plug** den Stöpsel herausziehen.

plum noun Pflaume die (PL die Pflaumen); **plum tart** der Pflaumenkuchen.

plumber noun Installateur der (PL die Installateure).

plural noun Mehrzahl die Plural der; **in the plural** in der Mehrzahl, im Plural.

plus preposition plus (+ DAT); **three children plus a baby** drei Kinder und ein Baby.

p.m. abreviation nachmittags (for times up to 6 p.m.), abends (for times *after 6 p.m.*); **at two p.m.** um zwei Uhr nachmittags, um vierzehn Uhr; **at nine p.m.** um neun Uhr abends, um einundzwanzig Uhr (*in German you usually express times after midday in terms of the 24-hour clock*).

pocket *noun* Tasche *die* (PL *die* Taschen).

pocket money *noun* Taschengeld *das*.

poem *noun* Gedicht *das* (PL *die* Gedichte).

poet *noun* Dichter *der* (PL *die* Dichter), Dichterin *die* (PL *die* Dichterinnen).

poetry *noun* Dichtung *die*.

point *noun* 1 (*tip*) Spitze *die* (PL *die* Spitzen); **the point of a nail** die Spitze eines Nagels; 2 (*a tiny mark or dot*) Punkt *der* (PL *die* Punkte); 3 (*in time*) Zeitpunkt *der* (PL *die* Zeitpunkte); **at that point** zu diesem Zeitpunkt; **to be on the point of doing something** gerade etwas tun wollen; 4 **that's not the point** darum geht es nicht; **there's no point phoning, he's out** es hat keinen Sinn anzurufen, er ist nicht da; **what's the point?** wozu?; 5 **that's a good point!** das stimmt!; **the point is ...** es geht darum ...; 6 **point of view** der Standpunkt; **from my point of view** von meinem Standpunkt aus; 7 **her strong point** ihre Stärke; 8 (*in scoring*) Punkt *der* (PL *die* Punkte); **to win by fifteen points** mit fünfzehn Punkten Vorsprung gewinnen; 9 (*in decimals*) **6 point 4** sechs Komma vier (*in German, a*

comma is used for the decimal point).

point *verb* 1 hinweisen ✧ SEP auf (+ ACC); **a notice pointing to the station** ein Schild, das in Richtung Bahnhof zeigt; 2 (*with your finger*) zeigen auf (+ ACC); **he pointed at Tom** er zeigte auf Tom.

pointless *adjective* sinnlos; **it's pointless to keep on ringing** es ist sinnlos, dauernd zu klingeln.

poison *noun* Gift *das* (PL *die* Gifte).

poison *verb* vergiften.

poisonous *adjective* giftig.

Poland *noun* Polen *die*.

polar bear *noun* Eisbär *der* (PL *die* Eisbären).

pole *noun* 1 (*for a tent*) Stange *die* (PL *die* Stangen); 2 (*for skiing*) Stock *der* (PL *die* Stöcke); 3 **the North Pole** der Nordpol.

Pole *noun* (*a Polish person*) Pole *der* (PL *die* Polen), Polin *die* (PL *die* Polinnen).

police *noun* **the police** die Polizei; **the police are coming** die Polizei kommt.

police car *noun* Streifenwagen *der* (PL *die* Streifenwagen).

policeman *noun* Polizist *der* (PL *die* Polizisten).

police station *noun* Polizeiwache *die* (PL *die* Polizeiwachen).

policewoman *noun* Polizistin *die* (PL *die* Polizistinnen).

policy *noun* 1 (*plan of action*) Vorgehensweise *die* (PL *die* Vorgehensweisen); **the policy on immigration** die Einwanderungspolitik;

a b c d e f g h i j k l m n o p q r s t u v w x y z

2 (*document*) Versicherungsschein der (PL die Versicherungsscheine).

polish noun 1 (*for furniture*) Politur die; 2 (*for shoes*) Schuhcreme die; 3 (*for the floor*) Bohnerwachs das.

polish verb 1 polieren (*furniture, silver*); 2 to polish your shoes seine Schuhe putzen.

Polish noun (*language*) Polnisch das.

Polish adjective polnisch.

polite adjective höflich; to be polite to somebody höflich zu jemandem sein.

political adjective politisch.

politician noun Politiker der (PL die Politiker), Politikerin die (PL die Politikerinnen).

politics noun Politik die.

pollen noun Pollen der; the pollen count for today is ... die Pollenzahl heute ist ....

polluted adjective verschmutzt.

pollution noun Umweltverschmutzung die.

polo-necked adjective Rollkragen-; a polo-necked jumper ein Rollkragenpullover.

pond noun Teich der (PL die Teiche).

pony noun Pony das (PL die Ponys).

ponytail noun Pferdeschwanz der (PL die Pferdeschwänze).

poodle noun Pudel der (PL die Pudel).

pool noun 1 (*swimming pool*) Schwimmbecken das (PL die Schwimmbecken); 2 (*pond*) Tümpel der (PL die Tümpel); 3 (*puddle*) Lache die (PL die Lachen); 4 (*game*) Poolbillard das; 5 the

football pools das Toto; to do the pools Toto spielen.

poor adjective 1 arm; a poor country ein armes Land; a poor family eine arme Familie; 2 poor Tanya's failed her exam die arme Tanya ist durch die Prüfung gefallen; 3 (*bad*) schlecht; that's a poor result das ist ein schlechtes Ergebnis; the weather was pretty poor das Wetter war ziemlich schlecht.

pop noun Popmusik die; pop concert das Popkonzert; pop star der Popstar; pop song das Popsong.

● to pop into: I'll just pop into the bank ich gehe kurz auf die Bank.

popcorn noun Popcorn das.

pope noun Papst der (PL die Päpste).

poppy noun Mohn der.

popular adjective beliebt.

population noun Bevölkerung die.

porch noun Vorbau der (PL die Vorbauten).

pork noun Schweinefleisch das; pork chop das Schweinekotelett.

porridge noun Haferbrei der.

port noun 1 Hafen der (PL die Häfen); 2 (*wine*) Portwein der (PL die Portweine).

porter noun 1 (*at a station or an airport*) Gepäckträger der (PL die Gepäckträger); 2 (*in a hotel*) Portier der (PL die Portiers).

portion noun (*of food*) Portion die (PL die Portionen).

portrait noun Porträt das (PL die Porträts).

Portugal noun Portugal das.

Portuguese noun 1 (*language*) Portugiesisch das; 2 (*a person*) Portugiese der (PL die Portugiesen),

Portuguesin die (PL die Portugiesinnen).

Portuguese adjective portugiesisch.

posh adjective vornehm; **a posh area** eine vornehme Gegend.

position noun 1 Platz der (PL die Plätze); 2 (situation) Lage die (PL die Lagen); 3 (status, job) Stellung die (PL die Stellungen).

positive adjective 1 (sure) sicher; **I'm positive he's left** ich bin mir sicher, dass er gegangen ist; 2 (enthusiastic) positiv; **her reaction was very positive** ihre Reaktion war sehr positiv.

possess verb besitzen◆.

possessions plural noun Sachen (plural); **all my possessions are in the flat** alle meine Sachen sind in der Wohnung.

possibility noun Möglichkeit die (PL die Möglichkeiten).

possible adjective möglich; **it's possible** es ist gut möglich; **if possible** wenn möglich; **as quickly as possible** so schnell wie möglich.

possibly adverb 1 (maybe) möglicherweise; '**will you be at home at midday?**' – '**possibly**' 'bist du mittags zu Hause?' – 'möglicherweise'; 2 **how can you possibly believe that?** wie kannst du das nur glauben?; **I can't possibly arrive before Thursday** ich kann unmöglich vor Donnerstag ankommen.

post noun 1 Post die; **to send something by post** etwas per Post schicken; (letters) **is there any post for me?** ist Post für mich gekommen?; 2 (a pole) Pfosten der

(PL die Pfosten); 3 (a job) Stelle die (PL die Stellen).

post verb **to post a letter** einen Brief abschicken SEP.

postbox noun Briefkasten der (PL die Briefkästen).

postcard noun Postkarte die (PL die Postkarten).

postcode noun Postleitzahl die (PL die Postleitzahlen).

poster noun 1 (for decoration) Poster das (PL die Poster); **I've bought an Oasis poster** ich habe ein Poster von Oasis gekauft; 2 (advertising) Plakat das (PL die Plakate); **I saw a poster for the concert** ich habe ein Plakat für das Konzert gesehen.

postman noun Briefträger der (PL die Briefträger).

post office noun Post die; **the post office is on the right** die Post ist auf der rechten Seite.

postpone verb verschieben◆; **we've postponed the meeting until next week** wir haben die Besprechung auf nächste Woche verschoben.

postwoman noun Briefträgerin die (PL die Briefträgerinnen).

pot noun 1 (jar) Topf der (PL die Töpfe); **a pot of honey** ein Topf Honig; 2 (teapot) Kanne die (PL die Kannen); 3 **the pots and pans** die Töpfe und Pfannen.

potato noun Kartoffel die (PL die Kartoffeln); **fried potatoes** Bratkartoffeln (plural); **mashed potatoes** der Kartoffelbrei.

potato crisps plural noun Kartoffelchips (plural).

a
b
c
d
e
f
g
h
i
j
k
l
m
n
o
p
q
r
s
t
u
v
w
x
y
z

pottery noun **1** (*craft*) Töpferei die; **2** (*objects*) Töpferwaren (*plural*).

pound noun **1** (*money*) Pfund das (PL die Pfunde); **fourteen pounds** vierzehn Pfund; **1.6 euros to the pound** 1,6 Euro für ein Pfund; **a five pound note** ein Fünfpfundschein; **2** (*in weight*) Pfund das; **two pounds of apples** zwei Pfund Äpfel.

pour verb **1** gießen◇ (*liquid*); **he poured milk into the pan** er hat Milch in den Topf gegossen; **2** eingießen◇ SEP (*a drink*); **to pour the tea** den Tee eingießen; **I poured him a drink** ich habe ihm etwas zu trinken eingeschenkt; **3** (*with rain*) **it's pouring** es gießt.

poverty noun Armut die.

powder noun **1** Pulver das (PL die Pulver); **2** (*for face or body*) Puder der (PL die Puder).

power noun **1** (*electricity*) Strom der; **a power cut** eine Stromsperre; **2** (*energy*) Energie die; **nuclear power** die Kernenergie; **3** (*strength*) Kraft die; **4** (*over other people*) Macht die; **to be in power** an der Macht sein.

power point noun Steckdose die (PL die Steckdosen).

power station noun Kraftwerk das (PL die Kraftwerke).

powerful adjective (*strong*) stark, (*influential*) mächtig.

practical adjective praktisch.

practically adverb fast.

practice noun **1** (*for sport*) Training das; **hockey practice** das Hockeytraining; **2** Übung die; **to do your piano practice** Klavier üben;

to be out of practice aus der Übung sein.

practise verb **1** üben (*an instrument, exercise, or skill*); **to practise the piano** Klavier üben; **2** anwenden SEP (*a language*); **a week in Berlin to practise my German** eine Woche in Berlin, um mein Deutsch anzuwenden; **3** (*in sport*) trainieren; **the team practises on Wednesday** die Mannschaft trainiert mittwochs.

praise verb loben; **to praise somebody for something** jemanden für etwas (ACC) loben.

pram noun Kinderwagen der (PL die Kinderwagen).

prawn noun Garnele die (PL die Garnelen).

pray verb beten.

prayer noun Gebet das (PL die Gebete).

precaution noun Vorsichtsmaßnahme die (PL die Vorsichtsmaßnahmen); **to take precautions against something** Vorsichtsmaßnahmen gegen (+ ACC) etwas ergreifen.

precinct noun **shopping precinct** das Einkaufszentrum; **pedestrian precinct** die Fußgängerzone.

precisely adverb genau; **at eleven o'clock precisely** um genau elf Uhr.

prefer verb **1** vorziehen◇ SEP; **I prefer Anna to her sister** ich mag Anna lieber als ihre Schwester; **2 to prefer to do something** etwas lieber tun; **I prefer to stay at home** ich bleibe lieber zu Hause.

pregnant adjective schwanger.

prejudice noun Vorurteil das (PL die Vorurteile); **to fight against racial prejudice** gegen Rassenvorurteile ankämpfen.

prejudiced adjective **to be prejudiced** voreingenommen sein.

prep noun Hausaufgaben (plural); **my English prep** meine Englischhausaufgaben.

prep school noun private Grundschule die.

preparation noun Vorbereitung die (PL die Vorbereitungen); **in preparation for something** in Vorbereitung für etwas (ACC); **our preparations for Christmas** unsere Weihnachtsvorbereitungen.

prepare verb **1** vorbereiten SEP; **to prepare somebody for something** jemanden auf etwas (ACC) vorbereiten; **2 to be prepared for the worst** sich auf das Schlimmste gefasst machen.

prepared adjective bereit; **I'm prepared to pay half** ich bin bereit, die Hälfte zu zahlen.

preposition noun Präposition die (PL die Präpositionen).

prescription noun Rezept das (PL die Rezepte); **on prescription** auf Rezept.

presence noun Anwesenheit die; **he admitted it in my presence** er gab es in meiner Anwesenheit zu.

present noun **1** (a gift) Geschenk das (PL die Geschenke); **to give somebody a present** jemandem ein Geschenk machen; **2** (the time now) Gegenwart die; **in the present (tense)** im Präsens; **3 that's all for the present** das ist vorläufig alles.

present adjective **1** (attending) anwesend; **Mr Blair is not present** Herr Blair ist nicht anwesend; **to be present at something** (DAT) anwesend sein; **fifty people were present at the funeral** fünfzig Personen waren bei der Beerdigung anwesend; **2** (existing now) gegenwärtig; **the present situation** die gegenwärtige Lage; **3 at the present time** zur Zeit.

present verb **1** überreichen (a prize); **2** (introduce) vorstellen SEP; **3** (on TV, radio) moderieren (a programme).

presenter noun (on TV) Moderator der (PL die Moderatoren), Moderatorin die (PL die Moderatorinnen).

presently adverb **1** (now) momentan; **2** (soon) bald.

president noun Präsident der (PL die Präsidenten), Präsidentin die (PL die Präsidentinnen).

press noun **the press** die Presse.

press verb **1** (to push) drücken; **press here!** hier drücken!; **2** drücken auf (+ ACC) (a button or switch); **she pressed the button** sie hat auf den Knopf gedrückt.

press conference noun Pressekonferenz die (PL die Pressekonferenzen).

pressure noun Druck der; **to put pressure on somebody** jemanden unter Druck setzen.

pressure gauge noun Druckluftmesser der (PL die Druckluftmesser).

pressure group noun Interessengruppe die (PL die Interessengruppen).

pretend verb to pretend that ... so tun, als ob ...; **he's pretending not to hear** er tut so, als ob er nicht hört.

pretty adjective hübsch; **a pretty dress** ein hübsches Kleid.

pretty adverb ziemlich; **it was pretty silly** das war ziemlich blöd.

prevent verb to prevent somebody from doing something jemanden daran hindern, etwas zu tun; **there's nothing to prevent you from leaving** niemand kann dich daran hindern zu gehen.

previous adjective 1 (earlier) früher (years, opportunity, or job); 2 (immediately preceding) vorig; **on the previous Tuesday** am vorigen Dienstag.

price noun Preis der (PL die Preise); **the price per kilo** der Preis pro Kilo; **CDs have gone up in price** CDs sind im Preis gestiegen; **what is the price of this?** was kostet das?

price list noun Preisliste die (PL die Preislisten).

price ticket noun Preisschild das (PL die Preisschilder).

prick verb stechen✧; **to prick your finger** sich in den Finger stechen.

pride noun Stolz der.

priest noun Priester der (PL die Priester).

primary school noun Grundschule die (PL die Grundschulen).

primary (school) teacher noun Grundschullehrer der (PL die Grundschullehrer),

Grundschullehrerin die (PL die Grundschullehrerinnen).

prime minister noun Premierminister der (PL die Premierminister), Premierministerin die (PL die Premierministerinnen).

prince noun Prinz der (PL die Prinzen).

princess noun Prinzessin die (PL die Prinzessinnen).

principal noun (of a college) Direktor der (PL die Direktoren), Direktorin die (PL die Direktorinnen).

principal adjective (main) Haupt-.

principle noun Prinzip das (PL die Prinzipien); **on principle** im Prinzip; **that's true in principle** im Prinzip stimmt das.

print noun 1 (letters) Druck der; **in small print** klein gedruckt; 2 (a photo) Abzug der (PL die Abzüge); **colour print** der Farbabzug.

printer noun (for a computer) Drucker der (PL die Drucker).

print-out noun Ausdruck der (PL die Ausdrucke).

prison noun Gefängnis das (PL die Gefängnisse); **in prison** im Gefängnis.

prisoner noun Gefangene der/die (PL die Gefangenen).

private adjective 1 Privat-, privat; **private school** die Privatschule; **private property** das Privateigentum; **to have private lessons** Privatstunden nehmen; 2 **in private** privat.

prize noun Preis der (PL die Preise); **to win a prize** einen Preis gewinnen.

prize-giving noun Preisverleihung die (PL die Preisverleihungen).

prizewinner noun Gewinner der (PL die Gewinner), Gewinnerin die (PL die Gewinnerinnen).

probable adjective wahrscheinlich.

probably adverb wahrscheinlich.

problem noun Problem das (PL die Probleme); **it's a serious problem** das ist ein ernstes Problem; **no problem!** kein Problem!

process noun 1 (in parade) Prozess der (PL die Prozesse); **2 to be in the process of doing something** dabei sein, etwas zu tun.

procession noun 1 (in parade) Umzug der (PL die Umzüge); **2** (at religious festival) Prozession die (PL die Prozessionen).

produce noun (food) Erzeugnisse (plural).

produce verb 1 herstellen SEP (goods, food); **2** vorzeigen SEP (a ticket, document); **I produced my passport** ich habe meinen Pass vorgezeigt; **3** erzeugen (interest, tension); **it produces heat** es erzeugt Wärme; **4 to produce a film** einen Film produzieren; **5 to produce a play** ein Theaterstück inszenieren.

producer noun (of a film or programme) Produzent der (PL die Produzenten).

product noun Produkt das (PL die Produkte).

production noun 1 (of a film or an opera) Produktion die (PL die Produktionen); **2** (of a play) Inszenierung die (PL die Inszenierungen); **a new production of Hamlet** eine neue Inszenierung von Hamlet; **3** (by a factory) Produktion die.

profession noun Beruf der (PL die Berufe).

professional noun 1 (a trained person) Fachmann der (PL die Fachleute); **2** (in sport) Profi der (PL die Profis).

professional adjective 1 professionell (work, sportsman); **a professional footballer** ein professioneller Fußballer; **2** beruflich (career, success); **she's a professional singer** sie ist Sängerin von Beruf.

professor noun Professor der (PL die Professoren), Professorin die (PL die Professorinnen).

profile noun Profil das (PL die Profile).

profit noun Gewinn der (PL die Gewinne).

profitable adjective rentabel.

program noun computer program das Programm.

programme noun 1 (for a play or an event) Programm das (PL die Programme); **2** (on TV or radio) Sendung die (PL die Sendungen).

programmer noun Programmierer der (PL die Programmierer), Programmiererin die (PL die Programmiererinnen).

progress noun 1 Fortschritt der (PL die Fortschritte); **to make progress** Fortschritte machen; **2 to be in progress** im Gange sein.

project noun 1 (at school) Arbeit die (PL die Arbeiten); **2** (a plan)

Projekt das (PL die Projekte); **a project to build a bridge** ein Brückenbauprojekt.

promise noun Versprechen das (PL die Versprechen); **to make somebody a promise** jemandem ein Versprechen geben; **to keep a promise** ein Versprechen halten; **it's a promise!** versprochen!

promise verb **to promise something** etwas versprechen◊; **I've promised to ring my mother** ich habe versprochen, meine Mutter anzurufen.

promote verb **to be promoted** (in football) aufsteigen◊ SEP (PERF sein), (at work) befördert werden.

promotion noun 1 Beförderung die; 2 (in football) Aufstieg der; 3 (in advertising) Werbung die.

promptly adverb 1 (at once) sofort; **he promptly fell off again** er fiel sofort wieder herunter; 2 (quickly) schnell; **please reply promptly** bitte antworten Sie unverzüglich; 3 (punctually) pünktlich; **they left promptly at five o'clock** sie fuhren pünktlich um 5 Uhr ab.

pronoun noun Pronomen das (PL die Pronomen).

pronounce verb aussprechen◊ SEP; **you don't pronounce the 'c'** das 'c' spricht man nicht aus.

pronunciation noun Aussprache die.

proof noun Beweis der (PL die Beweise); **there's no proof that ...** es gibt keine Beweise dafür, dass ....

propaganda noun Propaganda die.

propeller noun Propeller der (PL die Propeller).

proper adjective 1 (correct, real, genuine) richtig; **the proper answer** die richtige Antwort; **he's not a proper doctor** er ist kein richtiger Arzt; 2 (decent) anständig; **I need a proper meal** ich brauche ein anständiges Essen; 3 **in its proper place** an den richtigen Ort.

properly adverb 1 richtig; 2 (decent) anständig.

property noun 1 (your belongings) Eigentum das; 2 (land, premises) Besitz der; **'private property'** 'Privatbesitz'; 3 (house) Haus das (PL die Häuser).

propose verb 1 (suggest) vorschlagen◊ SEP; 2 (marriage) **he proposed to her** er hat ihr einen Heiratsantrag gemacht.

protect verb schützen; **to protect somebody from something** jemanden vor etwas (DAT) schützen.

protection noun Schutz der.

protein noun Protein das (PL die Proteine).

protest noun 1 Beschwerde die (PL die Beschwerden); **to make a protest** eine Beschwerde einlegen SEP; 2 (disapproval) Protest der (PL die Proteste); **in protest against something** aus Protest gegen etwas (ACC).

protest verb protestieren; **to protest about something** gegen etwas (ACC) protestieren.

protest march noun Protestmarsch der (PL die Protestmärsche).

Protestant noun Protestant der (PL die Protestanten), Protestantin die (PL die Protestantinnen).

Protestant adjective protestantisch.

proud adjective stolz; **to be proud about something** stolz auf etwas (ACC) sein.

prove verb beweisen ◇.

proverb noun Sprichwort das (PL die Sprichwörter).

provide verb zur Verfügung stellen.

provided, providing conjunction vorausgesetzt; **provided it doesn't rain** vorausgesetzt, es regnet nicht.

prune noun Backpflaume die (PL die Backpflaumen).

psychiatrist noun Psychiater der (PL die Psychiater), Psychiaterin die (PL die Psychiaterinnen).

psychological adjective psychologisch.

psychologist noun Psychologe der (PL die Psychologen), Psychologin die (PL die Psychologinnen).

psychology noun Psychologie die.

PTO abbreviation b.w. (bitte wenden).

pub noun Kneipe die (PL die Kneipen) (informal).

public noun **the public** die Öffentlichkeit; **in public** in aller Öffentlichkeit.

public adjective öffentlich.

public holiday noun gesetzliche Feiertag der (PL die gesetzlichen Feiertage); **January 1st is a public holiday** der erste Januar ist ein gesetzlicher Feiertag.

publicity noun **1** Publicity die; **2** (advertising) Werbung die.

public school noun Privatschule die (PL die Privatschulen).

public transport noun öffentliche Verkehrsmittel (plural).

publish verb veröffentlichen.

publisher noun **1** Verleger der (PL die Verleger), Verlegerin die (PL die Verlegerinnen); **2** (company) Verlag der (PL die Verlage).

pudding noun (dessert) Nachtisch der (PL die Nachtische); **for pudding we've got strawberries** zum Nachtisch gibt es Erdbeeren.

puddle noun Pfütze die (PL die Pfützen).

puff noun (of smoke) Wölkchen das (PL die Wölkchen).

puff pastry noun Blätterteig der.

pull verb **1** ziehen ◇; **to pull a cart** einen Wagen ziehen; **2** ziehen an (+ DAT); **to pull a rope** an einem Seil ziehen; **he pulled a letter out of his pocket** er hat einen Brief aus der Tasche gezogen; ★ **he's pulling your leg!** er nimmt dich auf den Arm (literally: he's picking you up in his arms).

● **to pull down 1** herunterziehen ◇ SEP; **2** (demolish) abreißen ◇ SEP (a building).

● **to pull in** (at the roadside) an den Straßenrand fahren ◇ (PERF sein).

pullover noun Pullover der (PL die Pullover).

pulse noun Puls der; **the doctor took my pulse** der Arzt maß meinen Puls.

a b c d e f g h i j k l m n o p q r s t u v w x y z

a

pump noun Pumpe die (PL die
Pumpen); **bicycle pump** die
Fahrradpumpe.

b

c

pump verb pumpen.

● **to pump up** aufpumpen SEP.

d

pumpkin noun Kürbis der (PL die
Kürbisse).

e

f

punch noun 1 (in boxing)
Faustschlag der (PL die
Faustschläge); 2 (drink) Bowle die
(PL die Bowlen).

g

h

punch verb 1 **he punched me in
the stomach** er hat mich in den
Magen geboxt; 2 lochen (a ticket).

i

j

punctual adjective pünktlich.

punctuation noun
Zeichensetzung die.

k

l

punctuation mark noun
Satzzeichen das (PL die
Satzzeichen).

m

puncture noun (flat tyre)
Reifenpanne die (PL die
Reifenpannen).

n

o

punish verb bestrafen.

p

punishment noun Strafe die (PL die
Strafen).

q

pupil noun Schüler der (PL die
Schüler), Schülerin die (PL die
Schülerinnen).

r

s

puppet noun Puppe die (PL die
Puppen).

t

u

puppy noun junge Hund der (PL die
jungen Hunde); **a boxer puppy** ein
junger Boxer.

v

pure adjective rein.

w

purple adjective lila ('lila' never
changes).

x

y

purpose noun 1 Zweck der (PL die
Zwecke); **what's the purpose of it?**
was hat das für einen Zweck?; 2 on

z

purpose absichtlich; **she did it on
purpose** das hat sie absichtlich
getan; **he closed the door on
purpose** er hat die Tür absichtlich
zugemacht.

purr verb schnurren.

purse noun Portemonee das (PL die
Portemonees).

push noun **to give something a
push** etwas schieben✧.

push verb 1 schubsen; **he pushed
me** er hat mich geschubst; 2 (to
press) drücken auf (+ ACC) (a bell or
button); 3 **to push somebody to do
something** jemanden zu etwas
drängen; **his teacher is pushing
him to sit the exam** sein Lehrer
drängt ihn, die Prüfung zu
machen; 4 **to push your way
through the crowd** sich durch die
Menge drängeln.

● **to push something away**
etwas wegschieben✧ SEP; **she
pushed her plate away** sie schob
ihren Teller weg.

pushchair noun Sportwagen der
(PL die Sportwagen).

put verb 1 (place generally) tun✧;
put some milk in your tea tu etwas
Milch in den Tee; **you can put the
butter in the fridge** du kannst die
Butter in den Kühlschrank tun;
2 (lay flat) legen; **she put the
pencil on the desk** sie hat den
Bleistift auf den Schreibtisch
gelegt; 3 (place upright) stellen;
where did you put my bag? wo
hast du meine Handtasche
hingestellt?; 4 (write) schreiben✧;
put your address here schreiben
Sie Ihre Adresse hierhin.

● **to put away** wegräumen SEP; **put**

away your things räume deine Sachen weg.

● **to put back 1** zurücktun SEP, zurücklegen SEP, zurückstellen SEP *(the translation of 'put back' depends on the way it is done: if it's placed lying down, use 'zurücklegen', if placed upright use 'zurückstellen' and if it could be either, use 'zurücktun')*; **I put it back in the drawer** ich habe es in die Schublade zurückgetan; **2** *(postpone)* verschieben◇; **the meeting has been put back until Thursday** die Besprechung ist auf Donnerstag verschoben worden.

● **to put down** *(lying down)* hinlegen SEP, hinstellen SEP; **where can I put the vase down?** wo kann ich die Vase hinstellen?

● **to put off 1** *(postpone)* verschieben◇; **he's put off my lesson till Thursday** er hat meine Stunde auf Donnerstag verschoben; **2** *(turn off)* ausmachen SEP; **don't forget to put off the lights** vergiss nicht, das Licht auszumachen; **3 to put somebody off something** jemandem die Lust an etwas *(DAT)* verderben◇; **it really put me off my food** das hat mir wirklich den Apetitt verdorben; **4 to put somebody off doing something** jemanden davon abbringen◇ SEP, etwas zu tun; **don't be put off** lass dich nicht davon abbringen.

● **to put on 1** anziehen◇ SEP *(clothes)*; **I'll just put my shoes on** ich ziehe nur schnell meine Schuhe

an; **2** auflegen SEP *(a CD or record)*; **I'm putting on Oasis** ich lege Oasis auf; **3** *(switch on)* anmachen SEP *(a light or the heating)*; **could you put the lamp on?** kannst du die Lampe anmachen?

● **to put out 1** *(put outside)* nach draußen tun◇, raustun◇ SEP *(informal)*; **have you put the rubbish out?** hast du den Müll rausgebracht?; **2** ausmachen SEP *(a light or cigarette)*; **I've put the lights out** ich habe das Licht ausgemacht; **3 to put out your hand** die Hand ausstrecken SEP.

● **to put up 1** heben◇ *(your hand)*; **2** aufhängen SEP *(a picture or poster)*; **I've put up some posters in my room** ich habe ein paar Poster in meinem Zimmer aufgehängt; **3** anschlagen◇ SEP *(a notice)*; **4** erhöhen *(the price)*; **they've put up the fare** sie haben den Fahrpreis erhöht; **5** *(for the night)* **friends put me up** ich habe bei Freunden übernachtet; **can you put me up on Friday?** kannst du Freitag bei euch übernachten?

● **to put up with something** etwas aushalten◇ SEP; **I don't know how she puts up with it** ich weiß nicht, wie sie das aushält.

puzzle noun *(jigsaw)* Puzzle das *(PL die Puzzles)*.

puzzled adjective verdutzt.

pyjamas plural noun Schlafanzug der *(PL die Schlafanzüge)*; **a pair of pyjamas** ein Schlafanzug; **where are my pyjamas?** wo ist mein Schlafanzug?

Qq

qualification noun **1** (*ability, experience*) Qualifikation die (PL die Qualifikationen); **2** (*on paper*) Zeugnis das (PL die Zeugnisse).

qualified adjective **1** ausgebildet; **she's a qualified ski instructor** sie ist eine ausgebildete Skilehrerin; **2** (*having a degree or a diploma*) Diplom-; **a qualified engineer** ein Diplomingenieur.

qualify verb **1** (*to be eligible*) berechtigt sein; **we don't qualify for a reduction** wir bekommen keine Ermäßigung; **2** (*in sport*) sich qualifizieren; **they qualified for the third round** sie haben sich für die dritte Runde qualifiziert.

quality noun Qualität die; **good quality products** Waren von guter Qualität.

quantity noun Menge die (PL die Mengen).

quarrel noun Streit der (PL die Streite); **to have a quarrel** Streit haben.

quarrel verb sich streiten◇; **they're always quarrelling** sie streiten sich dauernd.

quarry noun Steinbruch der (PL die Steinbrüche).

quarter noun **1** Viertel das (PL die Viertel); **a quarter of the price** ein Viertel des Preises; **three quarters of the class** drei Viertel der Klasse; **it's a quarter past ten** es ist Viertel nach zehn; **it's a quarter to ten** es ist Viertel vor zehn; **2 we meet at quarter to eight** wir treffen uns um Viertel vor acht; **3 a quarter of an**

hour eine Viertelstunde; **4 three quarters of an hour** eine Dreiviertelstunde; **5 an hour and a quarter** eineinviertel Stunden.

quarter finals noun Viertelfinale das (PL die Viertelfinale).

queen noun **1** Königin die (PL die Königinnen); **2** (*in chess, cards*) Dame die (PL die Damen).

query noun Frage die (PL die Fragen); **are there any queries?** gibt es irgendwelche Fragen?

question noun Frage die (PL die Fragen); **to ask somebody a question** jemandem eine Frage stellen; **I asked her a question** ich habe ihr eine Frage gestellt; **it's out of the question** das kommt nicht in Frage.

question verb befragen (*a person*).

question mark noun Fragezeichen das (PL die Fragezeichen).

questionnaire noun Fragebogen der (PL die Fragebögen).

queue noun (*of people, cars*) Schlange die (PL die Schlangen); **to stand in a queue** Schlange stehen; **a queue of cars** eine Autoschlange.

quick adjective schnell; **to have a quick lunch** schnell etwas zu Mittag essen; **it's quicker on the motorway** auf der Autobahn geht es schneller; **to have a quick look at something** sich (DAT) etwas schnell ansehen; **be quick!** mach schnell!

quickly adverb schnell; **I'll just quickly phone my mother** ich rufe nur schnell meine Mutter an.

quiet adjective **1** (*silent*) still;
to keep quiet still sein; **please
keep quiet** sei bitte still; **2** (*not
loud*) leise; **the children are very
quiet** die Kinder sind ganz leise;
in a quiet voice mit leiser
Stimme; **3** (*peaceful*) ruhig;
a quiet street eine ruhige
Straße.

quietly adverb **1** (*speak, move*)
leise; **he got up quietly** er ist leise
aufgestanden; **2** (*read or play*)
ruhig; **to sit quietly** ruhig sitzen.

quilt noun Steppdecke die (PL die
Steppdecken).

quite adverb **1** (*fairly*) ziemlich; **it's
quite cold outside** es ist ziemlich
kalt draußen; **quite often** ziemlich
oft; **quite a few** ziemlich viele;
quite a few of our friends came
ziemlich viele unserer Freunde
sind gekommen; **quite a few
people** ziemlich viele Leute; **that's
quite a good idea** das ist eine ganz
gute Idee; **2** (*completely*) völlig; **it
was quite amazing** es war einfach
fantastisch; **not quite** nicht ganz;
she's not quite ready sie ist noch
nicht ganz fertig; **3** genau; **I don't
quite know what he wants** ich weiß
nicht genau, was er will; **quite!**
genau!

quiz noun Quiz das (PL die Quiz).

quotation noun (*from a book*) Zitat
das (PL die Zitate).

quotation marks plural noun
Anführungszeichen (*plural*); **in
quotation marks** in
Anführungszeichen.

quote noun **1** (*from a book*) Zitat
das (PL die Zitate); **2** (*estimate*)

Kostenvoranschlag der (PL die
Kostenvoranschläge).

quote verb zitieren.

Rr

rabbi noun Rabbi der (PL die Rabbis).

rabbit noun Kaninchen das (PL die
Kaninchen).

rabies noun Tollwut die.

race noun **1** (*a sports event*) Rennen
das (PL die Rennen); **cycle race** das
Radrennen; **2 to have a race**
(*running*) um die Wette laufen✧
(PERF *sein*), (*swimming*) um die
Wette schwimmen✧ (PERF *sein*);
3 (*an ethnic group*) Rasse die (PL die
Rassen).

racetrack noun Rennbahn die (PL
die Rennbahnen).

racial adjective rassisch, Rassen-;
racial discrimination die
Rassendiskriminierung.

racing car noun Rennwagen der
(PL die Rennwagen), Rennfahrerin
die (PL die Rennfahrerinnen).

racing driver noun Rennfahrer
der (PL die Rennfahrer).

racism noun Rassismus der.

racist noun Rassist der (PL die
Rassisten), Rassistin die (PL die
Rassistinnen).

racist adjective rassistisch.

racket noun **1** (*for tennis*) Schläger
der (PL die Schläger); **my tennis
racket** mein Tennisschläger;
2 (*noise*) Krach der.

radiation noun Strahlung die (PL
die Strahlungen).

a

radiator noun Heizkörper der (PL die Heizkörper).

b

radio noun Radio das (PL die Radios); **to listen to the radio** Radio hören; **to hear something on the radio** etwas im Radio hören.

c

d

radioactive adjective radioaktiv.

radio-controlled adjective ferngesteuert.

e

f

radio station noun Rundfunkstation die (PL die Rundfunkstationen).

g

h

radish noun Radieschen das (PL die Radieschen).

i

rag noun Lumpen der (PL die Lumpen).

j

k

rage noun Wut die; **to fly into a rage** in Wut geraten◇ (PERF sein); **she's in a rage** sie ist wütend; ★ **it's all the rage** das ist der letzte Schrei (literally: it's the last scream).

l

m

rail noun 1 (for a train) Schiene die (PL die Schienen); 2 (the railway) **to go by rail** mit der Bahn fahren; 3 (on a balcony, bridge, or stairs) Geländer das (PL die Geländer).

n

o

p

rail card noun Bahnpass der (PL die Bahnpässe).

q

railing(s) noun Geländer das (PL die Geländer).

r

s

railway noun 1 (the system) Bahn die; **the railways** die Bahn; 2 **railway line** (from one place to another) die Bahnstrecke; 3 **on the railway line** (the track) auf dem Gleis.

t

u

v

railway carriage noun Eisenbahnwagen der (PL die Eisenbahnwagen).

w

x

railway station noun Bahnhof der (PL die Bahnhöfe).

y

z

rain noun Regen der; **in the rain** im Regen.

rain verb regnen; **it's raining** es regnet; **it's going to rain** es wird regnen.

rainbow noun Regenbogen der (PL die Regenbogen).

raincoat noun Regenmantel der (PL die Regenmäntel).

rainy adjective regnerisch.

raise verb 1 (lift up) hochheben◇ SEP; 2 (increase) erhöhen (prices); 3 **to raise money for something** Geld für etwas aufbringen◇ SEP.

raisin noun Rosine die (PL die Rosinen).

rake noun Rechen der (PL die Rechen).

rally noun 1 (a meeting) Versammlung die (PL die Versammlungen); 2 (for cars) Rallye die (PL die Rallyes); 3 (in tennis) Ballwechsel der (PL die Ballwechsel).

rambler noun Wanderer der (PL die Wanderer), Wanderin die (PL die Wanderinnen).

rambling noun Wandern das.

range noun 1 (a choice) Auswahl die; **a wide range of travel brochures** eine große Auswahl an Reiseprospekten; 2 **a range of subjects** verschiedene Fächer; **in a range of colours** in verschiedenen Farben; 3 **a computer in this price range** ein Computer in dieser Preislage; **that's out of my price range** das kann ich mir nicht leisten.

rap noun Rap der (music).

rape noun Vergewaltigung die (PL die Vergewaltigungen).

ready

rape verb vergewaltigen.

rare adjective **1** selten; **a rare bird** ein seltener Vogel; **2** englisch gebraten (steak).

rarely adverb selten.

rash noun Ausschlag der (PL die Ausschläge).

rash adjective voreilig.

raspberry noun Himbeere die (PL die Himbeeren); **raspberry jam** die Himbeermarmelade.

rat noun Ratte die (PL die Ratten).

rate noun **1** (a charge) Gebühren (plural); **postage rates** Postgebühren; **2 are there special rates for children?** gibt es Sonderpreise für Kinder?; **at reduced rates** zu ermäßigten Preisen; **3 rate of exchange** der Wechselkurs; **4 rate of pay** der Lohnsatz; **5** (a level) Rate die (PL die Raten); **a high cancellation rate** eine hohe Absagerate; **6 at any rate** auf jeden Fall.

rather adverb **1** lieber; **I'd rather wait** ich warte lieber; **I'd rather you didn't go** es wäre mir lieber, wenn du nicht gingest; **2** ziemlich; **I'm rather busy** ich habe ziemlich viel zu tun; **I've got rather a lot of shopping to do** ich muss noch ziemlich viel einkaufen; **3 rather than** eher als; **in summer rather than winter** eher im Sommer als im Winter.

rave noun (party) Fete die (PL die Feten) (informal).

raw adjective roh.

razor noun Rasierapparat der (PL die Rasierapparate).

razor blade noun Rasierklinge die (PL die Rasierklingen).

RE noun Religionsunterricht der.

reach noun Reichweite die; **out of reach** außer Reichweite; **within reach** leicht erreichbar; **to be within easy reach of Munich** von München aus leicht erreichbar sein.

reach verb **1** ankommen◇ SEP (PERF sein) an (+ DAT) a place or point, ankommen◇ SEP (PERF sein) in (+ DAT) (a town or country); **when you reach the station** wenn du am Bahnhof ankommst; **2** kommen◇ (PERF sein) zu (+ DAT) (an agreement, a conclusion); **to reach a decision** zu einer Entscheidung kommen; **3 to reach for something** nach etwas (DAT) greifen◇.

react verb reagieren.

reaction noun Reaktion die (PL die Reaktionen).

read verb **1** lesen◇; **what are you reading at the moment?** was liest du zur Zeit?; **I'm reading a detective novel** ich lese einen Krimi; **2 to read out** vorlesen◇ SEP; **he read out the list to the students** er hat die Liste den Studenten vorgelesen.

reading noun **1** (action) Lesen das; **2** (reading matter) Lektüre die; **some easy reading for the holidays** eine leichte Lektüre für die Ferien.

ready adjective **1** fertig; **supper's not ready yet** das Essen ist noch nicht fertig; **we are not quite ready** wir sind noch nicht ganz fertig; **are you ready to leave?** seid ihr fertig?, (on a journey) seid ihr

a
b
c
d
e
f
g
h
i
j
k
l
m
n
o
p
q
r
s
t
u
v
w
x
y
z

reisefertig?; **to get ready** sich fertig machen; **I'm getting ready to play tennis** ich mache mich zum Tennisspielen fertig; **I was getting ready for bed** ich war gerade dabei, ins Bett zu gehen; **2 to get something ready** (*complete*) etwas fertig machen, etwas vorbereiten SEP (*a room or food*); **I'll get your room ready** ich bereite dein Zimmer vor.

real *adjective* **1** (*genuine*) echt; **it's a real diamond** das ist ein echter Brillant; **he's a real coward** er ist ein echter Feigling; **2** (*true*) richtig; **is that her real name?** ist das ihr richtiger Name?; **3** (*not imagined*) wirklich; **it's a real pity you can't come** es ist wirklich schade, dass du nicht kommen kannst.

realistic *adjective* realistisch.

reality *noun* Wirklichkeit die; **a reality show** eine Reality-Show.

realize *verb* wissen✧; **I hadn't realized** das wusste ich nicht; **I didn't realize he was French** ich wusste nicht, dass er Franzose ist; **do you realize what time it is?** weißt du, wie viel Uhr es ist?

really *adverb* **1** wirklich; **the film was really good** der Film war wirklich gut; **really?** wirklich?; **2 not really** eigentlich nicht.

reason *noun* Grund der (PL die Gründe); **for that reason** aus diesem Grund; **the reason why I phoned** der Grund meines Anrufs.

reasonable *adjective* vernünftig.

receipt *noun* Quittung die (PL die Quittungen).

receive *verb* erhalten✧.

receiver *noun* Hörer der (PL die Hörer); **to pick up the receiver** den Hörer abnehmen✧ SEP.

recent *adjective* **1** kürzlich erfolgter/kürzlich erfolgte/kürzlich erfolgtes; **the recent closure** die kürzlich erfolgte Schließung; **2 in recent years** in den letzten Jahren.

recently *adverb* **1** (*at a time not long ago*) kürzlich; **2** (*over the recent period*) in letzter Zeit.

reception *noun* **1** Rezeption die (PL die Rezeptionen); **he's waiting at reception** er wartet an der Rezeption; **2** Empfang der (PL die Empfänge); **a big wedding reception** ein großer Hochzeitsempfang; **3 to get a good reception** gut aufgenommen werden.

receptionist *noun* **1** Empfangsdame die (PL die Empfangsdamen); **2** (*in a doctor's surgery*) Sprechstundenhilfe die (PL die Sprechstundenhilfen).

recipe *noun* Rezept das (PL die Rezepte).

reckon *verb* glauben; **I reckon it's a good idea** ich glaube, das ist eine gute Idee.

recognize *verb* erkennen✧.

recommend *verb* empfehlen✧; **can you recommend a dentist?** kannst du mir einen Zahnarzt empfehlen?; **I recommend the fish soup** ich empfehle die Fischsuppe.

record *noun* **1** Rekord der (PL die Rekorde); **it's a world record** das ist ein Weltrekord; **record sales** Verkaufsrekorde; **2** (*of events*) Aufzeichnung die (PL die

Aufzeichnungen); **on record** aufgezeichnet; **to keep a record of something** über etwas Buch führen; **3** (*music*) Platte die (PL die Platten); **a Miles Davis record** eine Platte von Miles Davis; **4 records** (*office files*) Unterlagen (*plural*); **I'll just check your records** ich prüfe nur Ihre Unterlagen.

record *verb* (*on tape*) aufnehmen◇ SEP; **I'm recording it on cassette** ich nehme es auf Kassette auf.

recorder *noun* **1** Blockflöte die (PL die Blockflöten); **to play the recorder** Blockflöte spielen; **2 cassette recorder** der Kassettenrekorder; **video recorder** der Videorekorder.

recording *noun* (*on tape or CD*) Aufnahme die (PL die Aufnahmen), (*on video*) Aufzeichnung die (PL die Aufzeichnungen).

record player *noun* Plattenspieler der (PL die Plattenspieler).

recover *verb* sich erholen; **she's recovered now** sie hat sich wieder erholt.

recovery *noun* (*from an illness*) Erholung die; **to make a good recovery** sich gut erholen.

rectangle *noun* Rechteck das (PL die Rechtecke).

rectangular *adjective* rechteckig.

recycle *verb* recyceln.

red *adjective* rot; **a red car** ein rotes Auto; **to go red** rot werden; **to have red hair** rote Haare haben.

Red Cross *noun* **the Red Cross** das Rote Kreuz.

redcurrant *noun* Johannisbeere die (PL die Johannisbeeren);

redcurrant jelly das Johannisbeergelee.

redecorate *verb* (*with paint*) neu streichen◇, (*with wallpaper*) neu tapezieren; **they've redecorated the kitchen** sie haben die Küche neu gestrichen.

redo *verb* noch einmal machen.

reduce *verb* **1 to reduce prices** die Preise herabsetzen SEP; **2 to reduce speed** die Geschwindigkeit verringern.

reduction *noun* **1** (*in price*) Ermäßigung die (PL die Ermäßigungen); **2** (*in speed or number*) Reduzierung die.

redundant *adjective* **to be made redundant** entlassen werden.

referee *noun* (*in sport*) Schiedsrichter die (PL der Schiedsrichter), Schiedsrichterin die (PL die Schiedsrichterinnen).

reference *noun* Referenz die (PL die Referenzen), (*for a job*) she gave me a good reference sie hat mir eine gute Referenz gegeben.

reference book *noun* Nachschlagewerk das (PL die Nachschlagewerke).

refill *verb* nachfüllen SEP.

reflect *verb* spiegeln; **to be reflected** sich spiegeln.

reflection *noun* **1** (*in a mirror or on water*) Spiegelung die (PL die Spiegelungen); **to see your reflection in the mirror** sich im Spiegel sehen; **2** (*thought*) Überlegung die; **on reflection** nach nochmaliger Überlegung.

reflexive *adjective* **a reflexive verb** ein reflexives Verb.

refreshing *adjective* erfrischend.

a
b
c
d
e
f
g
h
i
j
k
l
m
n
o
p
q
r
s
t
u
v
w
x
y
z

refreshment noun Erfrischung die (PL die Erfrischungen).

refrigerator noun Kühlschrank der (PL die Kühlschränke).

refuge noun Zuflucht die; **a mountain refuge** eine Schutzhütte; **to take refuge in** sich flüchten in (+ DAT).

refugee noun Flüchtling der (PL die Flüchtlinge).

refund noun Rückzahlung die (PL die Rückzahlungen).

refund verb zurückerstatten SEP.

refusal noun 1 Weigerung die (PL die Weigerungen); 2 (for a job) Absage die (PL die Absagen); **to get a refusal** eine Absage bekommen.

refuse noun (rubbish) Abfall der.

refuse verb sich weigern; **I refused** ich habe mich geweigert; **he refuses to help** er weigert sich zu helfen.

regards plural noun Grüße (plural); **regards to your parents** viele Grüße an deine Eltern; **Nat sends his regards** Nat lässt grüßen.

reggae noun Reggae der.

region noun Gebiet das (PL die Gebiete).

regional adjective regional.

register noun (in school) Anwesenheitsliste die (PL die Anwesenheitslisten).

register verb 1 eintragen ✧ SEP (a name); 2 (report) anmelden SEP.

registered letter noun Einschreiben das (PL die Einschreiben).

registration number noun Autonummer die (PL die Autonummern).

regret verb bedauern.

regular adjective regelmäßig; **regular visits** regelmäßige Besuche.

regularly adverb regelmäßig.

regulation noun Vorschrift die (PL die Vorschriften).

rehearsal noun Probe die (PL die Proben).

rehearse verb proben.

reheat verb aufwärmen SEP.

reject verb ablehnen SEP.

related adjective verwandt; **we're not related** wir sind nicht verwandt.

relation noun Verwandte der/die (PL die Verwandten).

relationship noun Beziehung die (PL die Beziehungen); **I have a good relationship with my parents** ich habe eine gute Beziehung zu meinen Eltern.

relative noun Verwandte der/die (PL die Verwandten).

relatively adverb relativ.

relax verb entspannen; **I'm going to relax and watch telly tonight** heute Abend entspanne ich mich und sehe fern.

relaxed adjective entspannt.

relaxing adjective entspannend.

relay race noun Staffel die (PL die Staffeln).

release noun (a film, CD, or book) 1 Neuerscheinung die (PL die Neuerscheinungen); **this week's new releases** die neuen Filme der Woche; 2 (of a prisoner or hostage)

Freilassung die (PL die
Freilassungen).

release verb **1** herausbringen✧
SEP (a record, film, or video);
2 freilassen✧ SEP (a person).

reliable adjective zuverlässig.

relief noun Erleichterung die; **what
a relief!** da bin ich aber erleichtert!

relieve verb stillen (pain).

relieved adjective erleichtert; **I
was relieved to hear you'd arrived**
ich war erleichtert zu hören, dass
du angekommen bist.

religion noun Religion die (PL die
Religionen).

religious adjective religiös.

rely verb **1** (trust) **to rely on
somebody** sich auf jemanden
verlassen✧; **I'm relying on your
help for Saturday** ich verlasse
mich darauf, dass du mir am
Samstag hilfst; **2** (be dependent on)
to rely on angewiesen sein auf
(+ ACC).

remain verb (be left over) übrig
bleiben✧ (PERF sein); (stay)
bleiben✧ (PERF sein).

remark noun Bemerkung die (PL die
Bemerkungen); **to make remarks
about something** Bemerkungen
über etwas (ACC) machen.

remarkable adjective
bemerkenswert.

remarkably adverb
bemerkenswert.

remember verb **1** sich erinnern
an (+ ACC) (a person or an occasion);
I don't remember daran kann ich
mich nicht erinnern; **do you
remember the holiday in Italy?**
erinnerst du dich noch an die
Ferien in Italien?; **2 I can't**

remember his number seine
Nummer fällt mir nicht ein; **3 to
remember to do something** daran
denken✧, etwas zu tun; **remember
to lock the door** denk daran
abzuschließen; **I remembered to
bring the CDs** ich habe daran
gedacht, die CDs mitzubringen.

remind verb **1** erinnern; **to remind
somebody to do something**
jemanden daran erinnern, etwas
zu tun; **remind your mother to pick
me up** erinnere deine Mutter
daran, mich abzuholen; **he
reminds me of my brother** er
erinnert mich an meinen Bruder;
2 oh, that reminds me ... dabei fällt
mir ein ....

remote adjective abgelegen.

remote control noun **1** (for a car
or plane) Fernsteuerung die (PL die
Fernsteuerungen); **2** (for TV or
video) Fernbedienung die (PL die
Fernbedienungen).

remove verb **1** entfernen (a stain,
mark, or obstacle); **2** ausziehen✧
SEP (clothes).

renew verb verlängern (a passport
or licence).

rent noun Miete die (PL die Mieten).

rent verb mieten; **Simon's rented a
flat** Simon hat eine Wohnung
gemietet.

reorganize verb umorganisieren.

repair noun Reparatur die (PL die
Reparaturen).

repair verb reparieren; **to get
something repaired** etwas
reparieren lassen; **we've had the
television repaired** wir haben

unseren Fernseher reparieren lassen.

repay verb zurückzahlen SEP.

repeat noun Wiederholung die (PL die Wiederholungen).

repeat verb wiederholen.

repeatedly adverb wiederholt.

repetitive adjective eintönig.

replace verb ersetzen.

reply noun Antwort die (PL die Antworten); **I didn't get a reply to my letter** ich habe keine Antwort auf meinen Brief bekommen; **there's no reply** niemand antwortet.

reply verb antworten; **I still haven't replied to the letter** ich habe immer noch nicht auf den Brief geantwortet.

report noun 1 (of an event) Bericht der (PL die Berichte); 2 (school report) Zeugnis das (PL die Zeugnisse).

report verb 1 melden (a problem or an accident); **we've reported the theft** wir haben den Diebstahl gemeldet; 2 sich melden; **I had to report to reception** ich musste mich an der Rezeption melden; 3 (in the news) berichten; **to report on the strike** über den Streik berichten.

reporter noun Reporter der (PL die Reporter), Reporterin die (PL die Reporterinnen).

represent verb 1 darstellen SEP (a word, a thing, an idea); 2 vertreten ◊ (a group or company).

representative noun Vertreter der (PL die Vertreter), Vertreterin die (PL die Vertreterinnen).

reproduction noun 1 (process) Fortpflanzung die (PL die Fortpflanzungen); 2 (of sound etc) Wiedergabe die ; 3 (copy) Reproduktion. die (PL die Reproduktionen).

republic noun Republik die (PL die Republiken).

reputation noun 1 Ruf der; **to have a good reputation** einen guten Ruf haben; 2 **she has a reputation for honesty** sie gilt als ehrlich.

request noun Bitte die (PL die Bitten); **at my mother's request** auf Bitte meiner Mutter.

request verb bitten ◊; **to request something** um etwas (ACC) bitten.

rescue noun Rettung die; **rescue operation** die Rettungsaktion; **to come to somebody's rescue** jemandem zu Hilfe kommen.

rescue verb retten; **they rescued the dog** sie haben den Hund gerettet.

rescue party noun Rettungsmannschaft die (PL die Rettungsmannschaften).

research noun 1 Forschung die; **for research into Aids** für die Aidsforschung; 2 **to do research** forschen.

research verb **to research into something** etwas erforschen.

resemblance noun Ähnlichkeit die (PL die Ähnlichkeiten).

reservation noun (a booking) Reservierung die (PL die Reservierungen); **to make a reservation (for a room)** (ein Zimmer) reservieren lassen.

reserve noun **1** Reserve die (PL die Reserven); **we have a few in reserve** wir haben ein paar in Reserve; **2 nature reserve** das Naturschutzgebiet; **3** (for a match) Reservespieler der (PL die Reservespieler), Reservespielerin die (PL die Reservespielerinnen).

reserve verb reservieren; **this table is reserved** dieser Tisch ist reserviert.

reservoir noun Reservoir das (PL die Reservoirs).

resident noun Bewohner der (PL die Bewohner), Bewohnerin die (PL die Bewohnerinnen).

residential adjective Wohn-; **a residential area** eine Wohngegend.

resign verb **1** (from your job) kündigen; **2** (from an official post) zurücktreten ✧ SEP.

resignation noun **1** Kündigung die (PL die Kündigungen); **2** (from an official post) Rücktritt der.

resist verb widerstehen ✧ (+ DAT) (an offer or temptation).

resit verb wiederholen (an exam).

resort noun **1** (for holidays) holiday resort der Urlaubsort; **ski resort** der Wintersportsort; **seaside resort** das Seebad; **2 as a last resort** als letzter Ausweg.

respect noun Respekt der.

respect verb respektieren.

respectable adjective anständig.

responsibility noun Verantwortung die (PL die Verantwortungen).

responsible adjective **1** verantwortlich; **he was responsible for the accident** er

war für den Unfall verantwortlich; **I'm responsible for booking the rooms** ich bin für die Zimmerreservierung verantwortlich; **2** (reliable) verantwortungsbewusst; **he's not very responsible** er ist nicht sehr verantwortungsbewusst.

rest noun **1** the rest der Rest; **the rest of the day** der Rest des Tages; **the rest of the bread** der Brotrest, der Rest von dem Brot; **2** (the others) **the rest** die Übrigen; **the rest have gone home** die Übrigen sind nach Hause gegangen; **3** Erholung die; **he's going to the mountains for a rest** er fährt zur Erholung ins Gebirge; **ten days' rest** zehn Tage Erholung; **to have a rest** sich ausruhen SEP; **4** (a short break) Pause die (PL die Pausen); **to stop for a rest** eine Pause machen.

rest verb (have a rest) sich ausruhen SEP.

restaurant noun Restaurant das (PL die Restaurants).

restful adjective erholsam.

restless adjective unruhig.

restrain verb zurückhalten ✧ SEP.

result noun **1** Ergebnis das (PL die Ergebnisse); **the exam results** die Prüfungsergebnisse; **2 as a result** infolgedessen; **as a result we missed the train** infolgedessen haben wir den Zug verpasst.

retire verb **1** (from work) in den Ruhestand gehen ✧; (civil servant, teacher, soldier) in Pension gehen ✧; **she retires in June** sie geht im Juni in Pension; **2 to be retired** im Ruhestand sein ✧.

a b c d e f g h i j k l m n o p q r s t u v w x y z

retirement noun Ruhestand der; since his retirement seitdem er in den Ruhestand gegangen ist.

return noun 1 (coming back) Rückkehr die; the return journey die Rückreise; 2 by return of post postwendend; 3 in return for für; in return for his help für seine Hilfe; 4 in return dafür; ★ many happy returns! herzlichen Glückwunsch zum Geburtstag.

return verb 1 (come back) zurückkommen◇ SEP (PERF sein); he returned ten minutes later er kam zehn Minuten später zurück; to return from holiday aus den Ferien zurückkommen; 2 (go back) zurückgehen◇ SEP (PERF sein), (drive) zurückfahren◇ SEP (PERF sein); we are planning to return in the evening wir wollen am Abend zurückfahren; 3 (to give back) zurückgeben◇ SEP; Gemma's never returned the video Gemma hat das Video nie zurückgegeben.

return fare noun Preis für eine Rückfahrkarte der, (for a flight) Preis für einen Rückflugschein der.

return ticket noun Rückfahrkarte die (PL die Rückfahrkarten); (for a flight) Rückflugticket das (PL die Rückflugtickets).

reveal verb enthüllen.

reverse verb 1 (in a car) rückwärts fahren◇ SEP (PERF sein); 2 to reverse the charges ein R-Gespräch führen.

review noun (of a book, play, or film) Kritik die (PL die Kritiken).

review verb rezensieren (a book, play, or film).

revise verb 1 lernen (for an exam); Tessa's busy revising for her exams Tessa lernt jetzt für ihre Prüfung; 2 wiederholen; to revise maths Mathe wiederholen.

revision noun Wiederholung die.

revive verb 1 (a person) wiederbeleben SEP; 2 (to recover) sich erholen.

revolting adjective eklig.

revolution noun Revolution die (PL die Revolutionen).

reward noun Belohnung die (PL die Belohnungen).

reward verb belohnen.

rewind verb zurückspulen SEP (a cassette or video).

rhinoceros noun Nashorn das (PL die Nashörner).

rhubarb noun Rhabarber der.

rhyme noun Reim der (PL die Reime).

rhythm noun Rhythmus der (PL die Rhythmen).

rib noun Rippe die (PL die Rippen).

ribbon noun Band das (PL die Bänder).

rice noun Reis der; rice pudding der Milchreis.

rich adjective 1 reich; they are very rich sie sind sehr reich; 2 the rich die Reichen.

rid adjective to get rid of something etwas loswerden◇ SEP (PERF sein) (informal); we got rid of the car wir sind das Auto losgeworden.

riddle noun Rätsel das (PL die Rätsel).

ride noun Fahrt die (PL die Fahrten); **to go for a ride (on a bike)** eine Fahrt machen; **to go for a ride (on a horse)** reiten gehen✧ (PERF sein).

ride verb 1 **to ride a bike** Rad fahren✧ (PERF sein); **can you ride a bike?** kannst du Rad fahren?; **I've never ridden a bike** ich bin noch nie Rad gefahren; 2 **to ride (a horse)** reiten✧ (PERF sein); **I've never ridden a horse** ich bin noch nie auf einem Pferd geritten.

rider noun 1 (on a horse) Reiter der (PL die Reiter), Reiterin die (PL die Reiterinnen); 2 (on a bike) Radler der (PL die Radler), Radlerin die (PL die Radlerinnen); 3 (on a motorbike) Fahrer der (PL die Fahrer), Fahrerin die (PL die Fahrerinnen).

ridiculous adjective lächerlich.

riding noun Reiten das; **to go riding** reiten gehen✧.

riding school noun Reitschule die (PL die Reitschulen).

rifle noun Gewehr das (PL die Gewehre).

right noun 1 (not left) rechte Seite die; **on the right** auf der rechten Seite; **on my right** rechts von mir; 2 (to do something) Recht das (PL die Rechte); **to have the right to something** ein Recht auf etwas (ACC) haben; **the right to work** das Recht auf Arbeit; **you have no right to say that** du hast kein Recht, das zu sagen.

right adjective 1 (not left) rechter/ rechte/rechtes; **my right hand** meine rechte Hand; 2 (correct) richtig; **the right answer** die

richtige Antwort; **is this the right address?** ist das die richtige Adresse?; 3 **to be right** (of a person) Recht haben; **you see, I was right** siehst du, ich hatte Recht; 4 **you were right not to say anything** du hattest Recht, nichts zu sagen; 5 **the clock is right** die Uhr geht richtig; 6 **yes, that's right** ja, das stimmt; **is that right?** stimmt das?

right adverb 1 (direction) rechts; **turn right at the lights** biege an der Ampel rechts ab; 2 (correctly) richtig; **you're not doing it right** du machst das nicht richtig; 3 (completely) ganz; **right at the bottom** ganz unten; **right at the beginning** ganz am Anfang; 4 (exactly) genau; **right in the middle** genau in der Mitte; 5 **right now** sofort; 6 (okay) gut; **right, let's go** gut, gehen wir.

right-click noun Klick der mit der rechten Maustaste (PL die Klicks mit der rechten Maustaste).

right-hand adjective **on the right-hand side** rechts.

right-handed adjective rechtshändig.

ring noun 1 (on the phone) **to give somebody a ring** jemanden anrufen✧ SEP; 2 (for your finger) Ring der (PL die Ringe); 3 (circle) Kreis der (PL die Kreise); 4 **there was a ring at the door** es hat geklingelt.

ring verb 1 (a bell or phone) klingeln; **the phone rang** das Telefon klingelte; 2 (phone) anrufen✧ SEP; **I'll ring you**

a b c d e f g h i j k l m n o p q r s t u v w x y z

tomorrow ich rufe dich morgen an; **3 to ring for a taxi** ein Taxi rufen.

● **to ring back** zurückrufen ✧ SEP; **I'll ring you back later** ich rufe dich später zurück.

● **to ring off** auflegen SEP.

ring road noun Ringstraße die (PL die Ringstraßen).

rinse verb spülen.

riot noun Aufstand der (PL die Aufstände).

rioting noun Unruhen (plural).

rip verb zerreißen ✧.

ripe adjective reif; **are the tomatoes ripe?** sind die Tomaten reif?

rip-off noun **it's a rip-off** das ist Nepp (informal).

rise noun **1** Anstieg der; **a rise in temperature** ein Temperaturanstieg; **2 pay rise** die Gehaltserhöhung.

rise verb **1** (the sun) aufgehen ✧ SEP (PERF sein); **2** (prices) steigen ✧ (PERF sein).

risk noun Risiko das (PL die Risiken); **to take a risk** ein Risiko eingehen.

risk verb riskieren; **he risks losing his job** er riskiert es, seine Stelle zu verlieren.

river noun Fluss der (PL die Flüsse).

road noun **1** Straße die (PL die Straßen); **the road to London** die Straße nach London; **2 the baker's is on the other side of the road** die Bäckerei ist auf der anderen Straßenseite; **3 across the road** gegenüber; **they live across the**

road from us sie wohnen bei uns gegenüber.

road accident noun Verkehrsunfall der (PL die Verkehrsunfälle).

road map noun Straßenkarte die (PL die Straßenkarten).

roadside noun **by the roadside** am Straßenrand.

road sign noun Straßenschild das (PL die Straßenschilder).

roadworks plural noun Straßenarbeiten (plural).

roast noun Braten der (PL die Braten).

roast adjective gebraten; **roast potatoes** Bratkartoffeln; **roast beef** der Rinderbraten.

rob verb **1** berauben (a person); **2** ausrauben SEP (a bank).

robber noun Räuber der (PL die Räuber).

robbery noun Raub der (PL die Raube); **bank robbery** der Bankraub.

robot noun Roboter der (PL die Roboter).

rock climbing noun Klettern das; **to go rock climbing** (zum) Klettern gehen.

rock noun **1** (a big stone) Felsen der (PL die Felsen); **2** (the material) Fels der; **3** (music) Rock der; **rock band** die Rockband; **to dance rock and roll** Rock 'n' Roll tanzen.

rocket noun Rakete die (PL die Raketen).

rock music noun Rockmusik die.

rock star noun Rockstar der (PL die Rockstars).

rocky adjective felsig.

rod noun **a fishing rod** eine Angel.

role noun Rolle die (PL die Rollen); **to play the role of Hamlet** die Rolle des Hamlet spielen.

roll noun 1 Rolle die (PL die Rollen); **a roll of film** eine Rolle Film; **a toilet roll** eine Rolle Toilettenpapier; 2 **bread roll** das Brötchen, die Semmel (South German).

roll verb rollen (PERF sein).

roller noun 1 (for hair) Lockenwickler der (PL die Lockenwickler); 2 (for paint) Rolle die (PL die Rollen).

rollerblades plural noun Inlineskates (plural), Inliners (plural).

rollercoaster noun Achterbahn die (PL die Achterbahnen).

roller skates plural noun Rollschuhe (plural).

Roman Catholic adjective römisch-katholisch.

romantic adjective romantisch.

roof noun Dach das (PL die Dächer).

roof rack noun Gepäckträger der (PL die Gepäckträger).

rook noun 1 (in chess) Turm der (PL die Türme); 2 (bird) Saatkrähe die (PL die Saatkrähen).

room noun 1 Zimmer das (PL die Zimmer); **she's in the other room** sie ist im anderen Zimmer; **a three-room flat** eine Dreizimmerwohnung; 2 (space) Platz der; **enough room for two** genug Platz für zwei; **very little room** wenig Platz; **to make room** Platz machen.

root noun Wurzel die (PL die Wurzeln).

rope noun Seil das (PL die Seile).

rose noun Rose die (PL die Rosen).

rot verb verfaulen (PERF sein).

rotten adjective verfault.

rough adjective 1 (scratchy) rau; 2 (vague) grob (plan or estimate); 3 **a rough idea** eine vage Vorstellung; 4 (stormy) stürmisch; **a rough sea** eine stürmische See; 5 (difficult) **to have a rough time** es schwer haben; 6 **to sleep rough** im Freien schlafen.

roughly adverb (approximately) ungefähr; **roughly ten per cent** ungefähr zehn Prozent; **it takes roughly three hours** es dauert ungefähr drei Stunden.

round noun Runde die (PL die Runden); **a round of talks** eine Gesprächsrunde; **a round of drinks** eine Runde.

round adjective rund; **a round table** ein runder Tisch.

round preposition 1 um (+ ACC); **round the city** um die Stadt; **round my arm** um meinen Arm; **they were sitting round the table** sie haben um den Tisch gesessen; **it's just round the corner** es ist gleich um die Ecke; 2 **to go round a museum** ein Museum besuchen.

round adverb 1 **to go round to somebody's house** jemanden besuchen (+ DAT); 2 **to invite somebody round** jemanden zu sich (DAT) einladen ✧ SEP; **we invited Sally round for lunch** wir haben Sally zum Mittagessen eingeladen; 3 **to look round the shops** sich in den Geschäften umsehen ✧ SEP; 4 **all the year round** das ganze Jahr hindurch.

b
c
d
e
f
g
h
i
j
k
l
m
n
o
p
q
r
s
t
u
v
w
x
y
z

...undabout noun **1** (for traffic) Kreisverkehr der; **2** (in a fairground) Karussell das (PL die Karussells).

route noun **1** (that you plan) Route die (PL die Routen); **the best route is via Calais** die beste Route führt über Calais; **2 bus route** die Buslinie.

routine noun Routine die (PL die Routinen).

row¹ noun **1** Reihe die (PL die Reihen); **in the front row** in der ersten Reihe; **in the back row** in der letzten Reihe; **2 in a row** hintereinander; **four times in a row** viermal hintereinander.

row verb (in a boat) rudern (PERF sein), (a boat, a person) rudern (PERF haben); **we rowed across the lake** wir sind über den See gerudert; **he rowed us across the lake** er hat uns über den See gerudert.

row² noun **1** (a quarrel) Krach der (informal) (PL die Kräche); **to have a row** Krach haben; **they've had a row** sie haben Krach gehabt; **I had a row with my parents** ich habe Krach mit meinen Eltern gehabt; **2** (noise) Krach der; **they were making a terrible row** sie haben einen furchtbaren Krach gemacht.

rowing noun Rudern das; **to go rowing** rudern gehen.

rowing boat noun Ruderboot das (PL die Ruderboote).

royal adjective königlich; **the royal family** die königliche Familie.

rub verb reiben✧; **to rub your eyes** sich (DAT) die Augen reiben.

● **to rub something out** etwas ausradieren SEP.

rubber noun **1** (an eraser) Radiergummi der (PL die Radiergummis); **2** (material) Gummi der; **rubber soles** Gummisohlen.

rubbish noun **1** (for the bin) Müll der, **2** (nonsense) Quatsch der (informal); **you're talking rubbish!** du redest Quatsch.

rubbish adjective schlecht; **the film was rubbish** der Film war schlecht; **they're a rubbish band** sie sind eine lausige Band.

rubbish bin noun Mülleimer der (PL die Mülleimer).

rucksack noun Rucksack der (PL die Rucksäcke).

rude adjective **1** unhöflich; **that's rude** das ist unhöflich; **2** unanständig; **a rude joke** ein unanständiger Witz.

rug noun **1** Teppich der (PL die Teppiche); **2** (a blanket) Decke die (PL die Decken).

rugby noun Rugby das.

ruin noun (remains) Ruine die (PL die Ruinen); **in ruins** in Trümmern.

ruin verb **1** ruinieren; **you'll ruin your jacket** du ruinierst dir die Jacke; **2** verderben✧ (day, holiday); **it ruined my evening** das hat mir den Abend verdorben.

rule noun **1** Regel die (PL die Regeln); **the rules of the game** die Spielregeln; **as a rule** in der Regel; **2** (administrative) Vorschrift die (PL die Vorschriften); **according to the school rules** nach den Schulvorschriften.

ruler noun Lineal das (PL die Lineale); **I've lost my ruler** ich habe mein Lineal verloren.

rum noun Rum der.

rumour noun Gerücht das (PL die Gerüchte).

run noun 1 (in games, sport, and for fitness) Lauf der (PL die Läufe); **to go for a run** laufen gehen (PERF sein), joggen gehen (PERF sein); 2 (of a play) Laufzeit die; 3 (in skiing) Abfahrt die (PL die Abfahrten); 4 **in the long run** auf lange Sicht.

run verb 1 laufen✧ (PERF sein); **I ran ten kilometres** ich bin zehn Kilometer gelaufen; **he ran across the pitch** er ist über das Spielfeld gelaufen; 2 (run fast) rennen✧ (PERF sein); **Kitty ran for the bus** Kitty rannte, um den Bus zu kriegen; 3 (drive) fahren✧; **I'll run you home later** ich fahre dich später nach Hause; 4 (organize) veranstalten (a course or competition); **who's running this competition?** wer veranstaltet diesen Wettbewerb?; 5 (manage) leiten (a business); **she's been running the firm for years** sie leitet die Firma schon seit Jahren; **to run a shop** ein Geschäft leiten; 6 (a train or a bus) fahren✧ (PERF sein); **the buses don't run on Sundays** sonntags fahren keine Busse; 7 **to run a bath** ein Bad einlaufen lassen.

● **to run away** weglaufen✧ SEP (PERF sein).

● **to run into something** gegen etwas (ACC) fahren✧ (PERF sein); **the car ran into a tree** das Auto ist gegen einen Baum gefahren.

● **to run out of something: we've run out of bread** wir haben kein Brot mehr; **I'm running out of money** ich habe kaum noch Geld.

● **to run somebody over** jemanden überfahren✧; **he nearly got run over** er ist beinahe überfahren worden.

runner noun Läufer der (PL die Läufer), Läuferin der (PL die Läuferinnen).

runner-up noun Zweite der/die (PL die Zweiten).

running noun (for exercise) Laufen das, Jogging das.

running adjective 1 **running water** fließendes Wasser; 2 **three days running** drei Tage hintereinander; **to win three times running** dreimal hintereinander gewinnen.

runway noun 1 (for take-off) Startbahn die (PL die Startbahnen); 2 (for landing) Landebahn die (PL die Landebahnen).

rush noun (a hurry) **to be in a rush** in Eile sein; **sorry, I'm in a rush** Entschuldigung, ich bin in Eile.

rush verb 1 (hurry) sich beeilen; **I must rush!** ich muss mich beeilen; 2 (run) hetzen (PERF sein); **she rushed out** sie stürmte raus (informal); 3 **Louise was rushed to hospital** Louise ist schnellstens ins Krankenhaus gebracht worden.

a
b
c
d
e
f
g
h
i
j
k
l
m
n
o
p
q
r
s
t
u
v
w
x
y
z

rush hour noun Stoßzeit die (PL die Stoßzeiten); **in the rush hour** während der Stoßzeit.

Russia noun Russland das.

Russian noun 1 (a person) Russe der (PL die Russen), Russin die (PL die Russinnen); 2 (the language) Russisch das.

Russian adjective russisch; **he's Russian** er ist Russe.

rust noun Rost der.

rusty adjective rostig.

rye noun Roggen der.

Ss

Sabbath noun 1 (Jewish) Sabbat der (PL die Sabbate); 2 (Christian) Sonntag der (PL die Sonntage).

sack noun 1 Sack der (PL die Säcke); 2 **to get the sack** rausgeschmissen werden (informal).

sack verb **to sack somebody** jemanden rausschmeißen ◇ SEP (informal).

sad adjective traurig.

saddle noun Sattel der (PL die Sättel).

saddlebag noun Satteltasche die (PL die Satteltaschen).

sadly adverb 1 traurig; **she looked at me sadly** sie hat mich traurig angesehen; 2 (unfortunately) leider.

safe adjective 1 (out of danger) sicher; **to feel safe from something** sich vor etwas (DAT) sicher fühlen; 2 **she's safe** sie ist in

Sicherheit; 3 (not dangerous) ungefährlich; **the path is safe** der Weg ist ungefährlich; **it's not safe** das ist gefährlich.

safety noun Sicherheit die.

safety belt noun Sicherheitsgurt der (PL die Sicherheitsgurte).

safety pin noun Sicherheitsnadel die (PL die Sicherheitsnadeln).

Sagittarius noun Schütze der; **Kylie's Sagittarius** Kylie ist Schütze.

sail noun Segel das (PL die Segel).

sailing noun Segeln das; **to go sailing** segeln.

sailing boat noun Segelboot das (PL die Segelboote).

sailor noun Seemann der (PL die Seeleute).

saint noun Heilige der/die (PL die Heiligen).

sake noun 1 **for your mother's sake** deiner Mutter zuliebe; 2 **for heaven's sake** um Gottes willen.

salad noun Salat der (PL die Salate); **tomato salad** der Tomatensalat.

salad dressing noun Salatsoße die (PL die Salatsoßen).

salami noun Salami die (PL die Salamis).

salary noun Gehalt das (PL die Gehälter).

sale noun 1 (selling) Verkauf der (PL die Verkäufe); **the sale of the house** der Verkauf des Hauses; **'for sale'** 'zu verkaufen'; 2 **the sales** der Ausverkauf; **I bought it in the sales** ich habe es im Ausverkauf gekauft.

sales assistant noun Verkäufer der (PL die Verkäufer), Verkäuferin die (PL die Verkäuferinnen).

salesman noun Verkäufer der (PL die Verkäufer).

saleswoman noun Verkäuferin die (PL die Verkäuferinnen).

salmon noun Lachs der (PL die Lachse).

salt noun Salz das.

salty adjective salzig.

same adjective **the same** der gleiche/die gleiche/das gleiche; **she said the same thing** sie hat das gleiche gesagt; **her birthday's the same day as mine** sie hat am gleichen Tag Geburtstag wie ich; **at the same time** zur gleichen Zeit; **their car's the same as ours** sie haben das gleiche Auto wie wir.

same adverb **1 the same** gleich; **the two bikes look the same** die beiden Fahrräder sehen gleich aus; **2 all the same** trotzdem.

sample noun Muster das (PL die Muster); **a free sample** ein unverkäufliches Muster, eine Warenprobe.

sand noun Sand der.

sandal noun Sandale die (PL die Sandalen); **a pair of sandals** ein Paar Sandalen.

sandpaper noun Sandpapier das (PL die Sandpapiere).

sandwich noun Sandwich das (PL die Sandwichs), belegte Brot das (PL die belegten Brote); **ham sandwich** das Schinkenbrot.

sanitary towel noun Damenbinde die (PL die Damenbinden).

Santa Claus noun der Weihnachtsmann.

sarcastic adjective sarkastisch.

sardine noun Sardine die (PL die Sardinen).

SARS noun SARS das.

satchel noun Ranzen der (PL die Ranzen).

satellite noun Satellit der (PL die Satelliten).

satellite dish noun Satellitenschüssel die (PL die Satellitenschüsseln).

satellite television noun Satellitenfernsehen das.

satisfactory adjective befriedigend.

satisfied adjective zufrieden.

satisfy verb befriedigen.

satisfying adjective **1** befriedigend; **2 a satisfying meal** ein sättigendes Essen.

Saturday noun **1** Samstag der (PL die Samstage), Sonnabend der (North German) (PL die Sonnabende); **on Saturday** am Sonnabend/am Samstag; **I'm going out on Saturday** ich gehe Sonnabend aus; **see you on Saturday!** bis Samstag!; **every Saturday** jeden Samstag; **last Saturday** vorigen Sonnabend; **next Saturday** nächsten Sonnabend; **2 on Saturdays** samstags, sonnabends (North German); **the museum is closed on Saturdays** das Museum ist sonnabends/ samstags geschlossen; **to have a Saturday job** sonnabends/ samstags arbeiten.

sauce noun Soße die (PL die Soßen).

saucepan noun Kochtopf der (PL die Kochtöpfe).

saucer noun Untertasse die (PL die Untertassen).

a
b
c
d
e
f
g
h
i
j
k
l
m
n
o
p
q
r
s
t
u
v
w
x
y
z

sausage *noun* Wurst *die* (PL *die* Würste).

save *verb* **1** retten (*life*); **to save somebody's life** jemandem das Leben retten; **the doctors saved his life** die Ärzte haben ihm das Leben gerettet; **2** sparen (*money*); **I've saved £60** ich habe sechzig Pfund gespart; **I cycle to school to save money** ich fahre mit dem Rad zur Schule, um Geld zu sparen; **we'll take a taxi to save time** um Zeit zu sparen, nehmen wir ein Taxi; **3** (*on a computer*) speichern; **4** (*stop*) abwehren SEP (*a shot*); **to save a penalty** einen Elfmeter abwehren.

● **to save up** sparen; **I'm saving up for a car** ich spare auf ein Auto.

savings *plural noun* Ersparnisse (*plural*).

savoury *adjective* (*not sweet*) pikant.

saw *noun* Säge *die* (PL *die* Sägen).

sax *noun* Saxophon *das* (PL *die* Saxophone).

saxophone *noun* Saxophon *das* (PL *die* Saxophone); **to play the saxophone** Saxophon spielen.

say *verb* **1** sagen; **what did you say?** was hast du gesagt?; **she says she's tired** sie sagt, dass sie müde ist; **he said to wait here** er hat gesagt, wir sollen hier warten; **they say** man sagt; **2** to say something again etwas wiederholen; **3** that's to say das heißt.

saying *noun* Redensart *die* (PL *die* Redensarten); **it's just a saying** das ist so eine Redensart; **as the saying goes** wie man so sagt.

scab *noun* Wundschorf *der* (PL *die* Wundschorfe).

scale *noun* **1** (*of a map or model*) Maßstab *der* (PL *die* Maßstäbe); **2** (*extent*) Ausmaß *das* (PL *die* Ausmaße); **the scale of the disaster** das Ausmaß der Katastrophe; **3** (*in music*) Tonleiter *die* (PL *die* Tonleitern).

scales *noun* Waage *die* (PL *die* Waagen); **bathroom scales** die Personenwaage.

scandal *noun* **1** Skandal *der* (PL *die* Skandale); **2** (*gossip*) Klatsch *der* (*informal*).

Scandinavia *noun* Skandinavien *das*.

Scandinavian *adjective* skandinavisch.

scanner *noun* Scanner *der* (PL *die* Scanner).

scar *noun* Narbe *die* (PL *die* Narben).

scarce *adjective* knapp.

scare *noun* **1** Schrecken *der* (PL *die* Schrecken); **to give somebody a scare** jemandem einen Schrecken einjagen SEP; **2** (*general alarm*) Panik *die* (PL *die* Paniken); **to cause a scare** eine Panik auslösen; **3 bomb scare** die Bombendrohung.

scare *verb* **to scare somebody** jemanden erschrecken; **you scared me!** du hast mich erschreckt!

scarecrow *noun* Vogelscheuche *die* (PL *die* Vogelscheuchen).

scared *adjective* **1** to be scared Angst haben; **I'm scared** ich habe Angst; **to be scared of something** vor etwas (DAT) Angst haben; **he's scared of dogs** er hat vor Hunden Angst; **2** to be scared of doing something sich nicht trauen, etwas zu tun; **I'm scared of telling him the truth** ich traue mich nicht, ihm die Wahrheit zu sagen.

scarf noun **1** (silky) Tuch das (PL die Tücher); **2** (long, warm) Schal der (PL die Schals).

scary adjective unheimlich.

scene noun **1** (of an incident or event) Schauplatz der (PL die Schauplätze); **to be on the scene** am Schauplatz sein; **the scene of the crime** der Tatort; **2** (world) **the music scene** die Musikszene; **on the fashion scene** in der Modewelt; **3** (argument) Szene die (PL die Szenen); **to make a scene** eine Szene machen.

scenery noun **1** (landscape) Landschaft die; **2** (in the theatre) Bühnenbild das.

schedule noun Programm das (PL die Programme).

scheduled flight noun Linienflug der (PL die Linienflüge).

scheme noun Projekt das (PL die Projekte).

scholarship noun Stipendium das (PL die Stipendien).

school noun Schule die (PL die Schulen); **at school** in der Schule; **to go to school** zur Schule gehen.

schoolbook noun Schulbuch das (PL die Schulbücher).

schoolboy noun Schüler der (PL die Schüler).

schoolchildren plural noun Schulkinder (plural).

schoolfriend noun Schulfreund der (PL die Schulfreunde), Schulfreundin die (PL die Schulfreundinnen).

schoolgirl noun Schülerin die (PL die Schülerinnen).

science noun Wissenschaft die (PL die Wissenschaften).

science fiction noun Sciencefiction die.

scientific adjective wissenschaftlich.

scientist noun Wissenschaftler der (PL die Wissenschaftler), Wissenschaftlerin die (PL die Wissenschaftlerinnen).

scissors plural noun Schere die (PL die Scheren); **a pair of scissors** eine Schere.

scoop noun **1** (implement) Eisportionierer der (PL die Eisportionierer); **2** (quantity) Eiskugel die (PL die Eiskugeln); **how many scoops would you like?** wieviele Kugeln Eis möchtest du?; **3** (in journalism) Knüller der (PL die Knüller).

scooter noun **1** (motor scooter) Motorroller der (PL die Motorroller); **2** (for a child) Roller der (PL die Roller).

score noun Spielstand der (PL die Spielstände); **the score was three two** es stand drei zu zwei.

score verb **1 to score a goal** ein Tor schießen◇; **2 to score three points** drei Punkte erzielen; **3** (keep score) zählen.

Scorpio noun Skorpion der; **Neil is Scorpio** Neil ist Skorpion.

Scot noun Schotte der (PL die Schotten), Schottin die (PL die Schottinnen); **the Scots** die Schotten.

Scotland noun Schottland das; **from Scotland** aus Schottland.

a b c d e f g h i j k l m n o p q r **s** t u v w x y z

Pauline's from Scotland Pauline kommt aus Schottland; **to Scotland** nach Schottland.

Scots *adjective* schottisch.

Scotsman *noun* Schotte der (PL die Schotten).

Scotswoman *noun* Schottin die (PL die Schottinnen).

Scottish *adjective* schottisch; **he's Scottish** er ist Schotte.

scout *noun* Pfadfinder der (PL die Pfadfinder).

scrambled eggs *noun* Rührei das.

scrap *noun* Stück das (PL die Stücke); **a scrap of paper** ein Stück Papier.

scrapbook *noun* Sammelalbum das (PL die Sammelalben).

scrape *verb* **1** schaben (*potatoes or carrots*); **2** (*remove dirt or paint*) abkratzen SEP; **3** (*damage*) schrammen.

scratch *noun* (*on your skin or a surface*) Kratzer der (PL die Kratzer); ★ **to start from scratch** von vorn anfangen◇ SEP.

scratch *verb* (*scratch yourself*) sich kratzen; **to scratch your head** sich am Kopf kratzen.

scream *noun* Schrei der (PL die Schreie).

scream *verb* schreien◇.

screen *noun* **1** Bildschirm der (PL die Bildschirme); (*of a TV or computer*); **on the screen** auf dem Bildschirm; **2** (*in the cinema*) Leinwand die (PL die Leinwände).

screw *noun* Schraube die (PL die Schrauben).

screw *verb* schrauben.

screwdriver *noun* Schraubenzieher der (PL die Schraubenzieher).

scribble *verb* kritzeln.

scrub *verb* scheuern (*a saucepan or the floor*); **to scrub your nails** sich (DAT) die Nägel bürsten.

scuba diving *noun* Gerätetauchen das.

sculptor *noun* Bildhauer der (PL die Bildhauer), Bildhauerin die (PL die Bildhauerinnen); **Rebecca's a sculptor** Rebecca ist Bildhauerin.

sculpture *noun* Skulptur die (PL die Skulpturen).

sea *noun* Meer das (PL die Meere), See die; **by the sea** am Meer, an der See.

seafood *noun* Meeresfrüchte (*plural*); **I love seafood** ich esse Meeresfrüchte sehr gern.

seagull *noun* Möwe die (PL die Möwen).

seal *noun* (*animal*) Robbe die (PL die Robben), Seehund der (PL die Seehunde).

seal *verb* zukleben SEP (*an envelope*).

search *verb* **1** absuchen SEP; **I've searched my desk but I can't find the letter** ich habe meinen Schreibtisch abgesucht, aber ich kann den Brief nicht finden; **2** durchsuchen; **they searched the building for him** sie haben das Gebäude nach ihm durchsucht; **3** suchen; **to search for something** nach etwas (DAT) suchen; **I've been searching everywhere for my scissors** ich habe überall nach meiner Schere gesucht.

seashell noun Muschel die (PL die Muscheln).

seasick adjective to be seasick seekrank sein.

seaside noun at the seaside am Meer.

season noun 1 Jahreszeit die (PL die Jahreszeiten); the four seasons die vier Jahreszeiten; 2 (period of social or sporting activity) Saison die (PL die Saisons); the tennis season die Tennissaison; off-season prices Preise außerhalb der Saison; 3 strawberries are not in season at the moment jetzt ist nicht die richtige Zeit für Erdbeeren.

season ticket noun Dauerkarte die (PL die Dauerkarten).

seat noun 1 Sitz der (PL die Sitze); the front seat (in a car) der Vordersitz; the back seat der Rücksitz; take a seat nehmen Sie Platz (formal), setz dich (informal); 2 (on a bus, in the theatre, etc.) Platz der (PL die Plätze); to book a seat einen Platz reservieren; can you keep my seat? kannst du mir meinen Platz freihalten?

seatbelt noun Sicherheitsgurt der (PL die Sicherheitsgurte).

seaweed noun Tang der.

second noun Sekunde die (PL die Sekunden); can you wait a second? kannst du eine Sekunde warten?

second adjective 1 zweiter/zweite/zweites; for the second time zum zweiten Mal; 2 the second of July der zweite Juli.

secondary school noun 1 weiterführende Schule die (PL die weiterführenden Schulen) (Germans define the type of secondary school); 2 Gymnasium das (PL die Gymnasien) (grammar school, from age 10 to 19 when Abitur is taken); 3 Realschule die (PL die Realschulen) (from age 10 to 16, less academic than a Gymnasium).

secondhand adjective, adverb gebraucht; a secondhand bike ein gebrauchtes Fahrrad; secondhand car der Gebrauchtwagen; I bought it secondhand ich habe es gebraucht gekauft.

secondly adverb zweitens.

secret noun Geheimnis das (PL die Geheimnisse); to tell somebody a secret jemandem ein Geheimnis verraten; in secret heimlich.

secret adjective geheim; a secret plan ein geheimer Plan; to keep something secret etwas geheim halten.

secretary noun Sekretär der (PL die Sekretäre), Sekretärin die (PL die Sekretärinnen); the secretary's office das Sekretariat.

secretly adverb heimlich.

sect noun Sekte die (PL die Sekten).

section noun Teil der (PL die Teile).

security noun Sicherheit die.

security guard noun Wächter der (PL die Wächter), Wächterin die (PL die Wächterinnen).

see verb 1 sehen◇; I saw Lindy yesterday ich habe Lindy gestern gesehen; have you seen the film? hast du den Film gesehen?; I can't see anything ich kann überhaupt nichts sehen; 2 to go and see nachsehen◇ SEP; I'll go and see ich

a
b
c
d
e
f
g
h
i
j
k
l
m
n
o
p
q
r
s
t
u
v
w
x
y
z

sehe nach; **3** (*visit*) besuchen; **why don't you come and see us in the summer?** warum besucht ihr uns nicht im Sommer?; **4 to see somebody home** jemanden nach Hause begleiten; **5 see you!** tschüs! (*informal*); **see you on Saturday!** bis Samstag!; **see you soon!** bis bald!

● **to see to something** sich um etwas (ACC) kümmern; **Jo's seeing to the drinks** Jo kümmert sich um die Getränke.

seed *noun* Samen *der* (PL die Samen).

seem *verb* **1** scheinen✧; **his story seems odd to me** seine Geschichte kommt mir komisch vor; **he seems shy** er scheint schüchtern zu sein; **the museum seems to be closed** das Museum scheint geschlossen zu sein; **2 it seems (that)** ... anscheinend ...; **it seems he's left** anscheinend ist er weggegangen; **it seems that there are problems** anscheinend gibt es Probleme.

seesaw *noun* Wippe *die* (PL die Wippen).

select *verb* auswählen SEP.

self-confidence *noun* Selbstbewusstsein *das*; **she doesn't have much self-confidence** sie hat sehr wenig Selbstbewusstsein.

self-employed *adjective* **to be self-employed** selbstständig sein; **my parents are self-employed** meine Eltern sind selbstständig.

selfish *adjective* egoistisch.

self-service *adjective* **a self-service restaurant** ein Selbstbedienungsrestaurant.

sell *verb* **1** verkaufen; **to sell something to somebody** jemandem etwas verkaufen; **I sold him my bike** ich habe ihm mein Rad verkauft; **the house sold for a million** das Haus wurde für eine Million verkauft; **2 the concert's sold out** das Konzert ist ausverkauft; **the tickets sold out very quickly** die Karten waren schnell ausverkauft.

sell-by date *noun* Verfallsdatum *das* (PL die Verfallsdaten).

Sellotape™ *noun* Tesafilm *der*.

sellotape *verb* **to sellotape something** etwas mit Tesafilm kleben.

semi *noun* Doppelhaushälfte *die* (PL die Doppelhaushälften).

semicircle *noun* Halbkreis *der* (PL die Halbkreise).

semicolon *noun* Strichpunkt *der* (PL die Strichpunkte).

semi-detached house *noun* Doppelhaushälfte *die* (PL die Doppelhaushälften).

semi-final *noun* Halbfinale *das* (PL die Halbfinale).

send *verb* schicken; **to send something to somebody** jemandem etwas schicken; **I sent her a present for her birthday** ich habe ihr zum Geburtstag ein Geschenk geschickt.

● **to send somebody back** jemanden zurückschicken SEP.

● **to send something back** etwas zurückschicken SEP.

sender *noun* Absender *der* (PL die Absender).

senior citizen noun Senior der (PL die Senioren), Seniorin die (PL die Seniorinnen).

sensation noun 1 (feeling) Gefühl das; 2 (impact) Sensation die (PL die Sensationen); **she caused a sensation** sie erregte viel Aufsehen.

sensational adjective sensationell.

sense noun 1 (common sense) Verstand der; 2 (faculty) Sinn der (PL die Sinne); **sense of smell** der Geruchssinn; **sense of touch** der Tastsinn; **to have a sense of humour** Humor haben; **she has no sense of humour** sie hat keinen Sinn für Humor; 3 (meaning) Sinn der; **this sentence makes no sense** dieser Satz ergibt keinen Sinn; **it doesn't make sense to do that** es ist Unsinn, das zu machen; **it makes sense to collect her first** es ist sinnvoll, sie erst abzuholen.

sensible adjective vernünftig; **be sensible** sei vernünftig; **that's a sensible suggestion** das ist ein vernünftiger Vorschlag.

sensitive adjective empfindlich; **for sensitive skin** für empfindliche Haut.

sentence noun 1 (words) Satz der (PL die Sätze); 2 (prison) Strafe die (PL die Strafen); **the death sentence** die Todesstrafe.

sentence verb verurteilen; **to be sentenced to death** zum Tode verurteilt werden; **to sentence somebody to a year in prison** jemanden zu einem Jahr Gefängnis verurteilen.

sentimental adjective sentimental.

separate adjective 1 extra ('extra' never has an ending); **a separate pile** ein extra Stapel; **she wrote it on a separate sheet of paper** sie hat es auf ein anderes Blatt Papier geschrieben; **the drinks are separate** die Getränke gehen extra; 2 (different) verschieden; **two separate problems** zwei verschiedene Probleme; 3 **they have separate rooms** sie haben getrennte Zimmer.

separate verb 1 trennen; 2 (a couple) sich trennen.

separately adverb 1 extra; 2 getrennt; **they live separately** sie leben getrennt.

separation noun Trennung die (PL die Trennungen).

September noun September der; **in September** im September.

sequel noun Folge die (PL die Folgen).

sequence noun 1 (series) Reihe die (PL die Reihen); **a sequence of events** eine Reihe von Ereignissen; **in sequence** in der richtigen Reihenfolge; 2 (in a film) Sequenz die (PL die Sequenzen).

sergeant noun 1 (in the police) Polizeimeister der (PL die Polizeimeister), Polizeimeisterin die (PL die Polizeimeisterinnen); 2 (in the army) Feldwebel der (PL die Feldwebel).

serial noun 1 Fortsetzungsgeschichte die (PL die Fortsetzungsgeschichten); 2 (on TV or radio) Serie die (PL die Serien).

a
b
c
d
e
f
g
h
i
j
k
l
m
n
o
p
q
r
s
t
u
v
w
x
y
z

a

series noun Serie die (PL die Serien); **television series** die Fernsehserie.

b

serious adjective **1** ernst; a **serious discussion** eine ernste Unterhaltung; **to be serious about something** etwas ernst nehmen; **are you serious?** ist das dein Ernst?; **2** schwer (accident or mistake).

c

d

e

seriously adverb **1** im Ernst; **seriously, I have to go now** im Ernst, ich muss jetzt gehen; **seriously?** im Ernst?; **2 to take somebody seriously** jemanden ernst nehmen; **3** (gravely) schwer; **she is seriously ill** sie ist schwer krank.

f

g

h

i

j

k

servant noun Bedienstete der / die (PL die Bediensteten).

l

m

serve noun (in tennis) Aufschlag der (PL die Aufschläge); **it's my serve** ich habe Aufschlag.

n

serve verb **1** (in tennis) aufschlagen✧ SEP; **Becker is serving** Becker schlägt auf; **2** servieren; **can you serve the vegetables, please?** können Sie bitte das Gemüse servieren? ★ **it serves him right** das geschieht ihm recht.

o

p

q

r

s

service noun **1** (in a restaurant, shop, etc.) Bedienung die; **service is included** inklusive Bedienung; **2** (from a company or firm to a customer) Service der; **3** the **emergency services** der Notdienst; **4** (church service) Gottesdienst der (PL die Gottesdienste); **5** (of a car or machine) Wartung die (PL die Wartungen).

t

u

v

w

x

y

z

service area noun Raststätte die (PL die Raststätten).

service charge noun Bedienung die; **there is no service charge** die Bedienung wird nicht extra berechnet.

service station noun Tankstelle die (PL die Tankstellen).

serviette noun Serviette die (PL die Servietten).

session noun Sitzung die (PL die Sitzungen).

set noun **1** (for playing a game) Spiel das (PL die Spiele); **chess set** das Schachspiel; **2 train set** die Spielzeugeisenbahn; **3** (in tennis) Satz der (PL die Sätze).

set adjective **1** fest (hours, habits); a **set date** ein festes Datum; **at a set time** zu einer festgesetzten Zeit; **2 set menu** das Menü.

set verb **1** festlegen SEP (a date, time); **2** aufstellen SEP (a record); **3 to set the table** den Tisch decken; **to set an alarm clock** einen Wecker stellen; **I've set my alarm for seven** ich habe meinen Wecker auf sieben gestellt; **4 to set your watch** eine Uhr richtig stellen; **5** (sun) untergehen✧ SEP.

● **to set off** aufbrechen✧ SEP (PERF sein); **we're setting off at ten** wir brechen um zehn auf; **they set off for Vienna yesterday** sie sind gestern nach Wien aufgebrochen.

● **to set off something 1** etwas auslösen SEP (an alarm, reaction); **2** etwas abbrennen✧ SEP (a firework); **3** etwas explodieren lassen (a bomb).

● **to set out** aufbrechen◇ SEP (PERF *sein*); **they set out for Hamburg at ten** sie sind um zehn nach Hamburg aufgebrochen.

settee *noun* Sofa das (PL die Sofas).

settle *verb* 1 bezahlen (*a bill*); 2 lösen (*a problem*); 3 beilegen SEP (*an argument*).

seven *number* sieben; **Rosie's seven** Rosie ist sieben.

seventeen *number* siebzehn; **I'm seventeen** ich bin siebzehn.

seventh *adjective* siebter/siebte/siebtes; **on the seventh floor** im siebten Stock; **the seventh of July** der siebte Juli.

seventies *plural noun* **the seventies** die Siebzigerjahre; **in the seventies** in den Siebzigerjahren.

seventieth *adjective* siebzigster/siebzigste/siebzigstes; **it's her seventieth birthday** es ist ihr siebzigster Geburtstag.

seventy *number* siebzig; **my granny's seventy** meine Oma ist siebzig.

several *adjective, pronoun* 1 mehrere; **I've read several of her novels** ich habe mehrere ihrer Romane gelesen; 2 **I've seen her several times** ich habe sie mehrmals gesehen.

sew *verb* nähen.

sewing *noun* Nähen das; **I like sewing** ich nähe gern.

sewing machine *noun* Nähmaschine die (PL die Nähmaschinen).

sex *noun* 1 (*gender*) Geschlecht das (PL die Geschlechter); 2 (*intercourse*) Sex der; **to have sex with someone** mit jemandem Sex haben.

sex education *noun* Aufklärungsunterricht der.

sexism *noun* Sexismus der.

sexist *adjective* sexistisch; **sexist remarks** sexistische Bemerkungen.

sexual *adjective* sexuell.

sexual harassment *noun* sexuelle Belästigung die.

sexuality *noun* Sexualität die.

sexy *adjective* sexy.

shabby *adjective* schäbig.

shade *noun* 1 Ton der (PL die Töne); **a shade of green** ein Grünton; 2 Schatten der; **in the shade** im Schatten.

shadow *noun* Schatten der (PL die Schatten).

shake *verb* 1 (*tremble*) zittern; **I was shaking with fear** ich zitterte vor Angst; 2 **to shake something** etwas schütteln; **to shake your head** (*meaning no*) den Kopf schütteln; 3 **to shake hands with somebody** jemandem die Hand geben◇; **she shook hands with me** sie hat mir die Hand gegeben; **we shook hands** wir gaben uns die Hand.

shaken *adjective* erschüttert; **I was shaken by the news** die Nachricht hat mich erschüttert.

shall *verb* **shall I come with you?** soll ich mitkommen?; **shall we stop now?** sollen wir jetzt aufhören?

shallow *adjective* flach; **stay in the shallow end of the pool** bleib am flachen Ende des Beckens.

a
b
c
d
e
f
g
h
i
j
k
l
m
n
o
p
q
r
s
t
u
v
w
x
y
z

shambles noun Chaos das; **it was a total shambles!** es war ein völliges Chaos!

shame noun 1 Schande die; **the shame of it!** was für eine Schande!; **2 what a shame!** wie schade!; **it's a shame she can't come** schade, dass sie nicht kommen kann.

shampoo noun Shampoo das (PL die Shampoos); **I bought some shampoo** ich habe Shampoo gekauft.

shamrock noun Klee der.

shandy noun Radler der (PL die Radler) (South German), Alsterwasser das (PL die Alsterwasser) (North German).

shape noun Form die (PL die Formen).

share noun 1 Anteil der (PL die Anteile); **your share of the money** dein Anteil am Geld; **he paid his share** er hat seinen Anteil gezahlt; **2** (in a company) Aktie die (PL die Aktien).

share verb teilen; **I'm sharing a room with Lucy** ich teile ein Zimmer mit Lucy.

shark noun Hai der (PL die Haie), Haifisch der (PL die Haifische).

sharp adjective 1 (knife) scharf; **this knife isn't very sharp** dieses Messer ist nicht sehr scharf; **2** (pointed) spitz; **a sharp pencil** ein spitzer Bleistift; **3 a sharp bend** eine scharfe Kurve; **4** (clever) clever.

shave verb 1 (have a shave) sich rasieren; **2 to shave your legs** sich (DAT) die Beine rasieren; **3 to shave off your beard** den Bart abrasieren SEP.

shaver noun Rasierapparat der (PL die Rasierapparate); **electric shaver** der Elektrorasierer.

shaving cream noun Rasiercreme die (PL die Rasiercremes).

shaving foam noun Rasierschaum der.

she pronoun sie; **she's a student** sie ist Studentin; **she's a very good teacher** sie ist eine sehr gute Lehrerin.

shed noun Schuppen der (PL die Schuppen).

sheep noun Schaf das (PL die Schafe).

sheepdog noun Schäferhund der (PL die Schäferhunde).

sheer adjective rein; **it's sheer stupidity** das ist reine Dummheit.

sheet noun 1 (for a bed) Laken das (PL die Laken); **2 a sheet of paper** ein Blatt Papier; **a blank sheet** ein leeres Blatt; **3** (of glass or metal) Platte die (PL die Platten); ★ **to be as white as a sheet** leichenblass sein.

shelf noun 1 (in the home or a shop) Regal das (PL die Regale); **a set of shelves** ein Regal; **2** (in an oven) Schiene die (PL die Schienen).

shell noun 1 (of an egg or a nut) Schale die (PL die Schalen); **2** (seashell) Muschel die (PL die Muscheln).

shellfish noun 1 Schalentier das (PL die Schalentiere); **2** (in cookery) Meeresfrüchte (plural).

shelter noun Schutz der; **in the shelter of** im Schutz (+ GEN); **to take shelter from the rain** sich unterstellen SEP.

shepherd noun Schäfer der (PL die Schäfer).

sherry noun Sherry der (PL die Sherrys).

Shetland Islands noun Shetlandinseln (plural).

shield noun Schild der (PL die Schilde).

shift noun Schicht die (PL die Schichten); **the night shift** die Nachtschicht; **to be on night shift** Nachtschicht haben.

shift verb **to shift something** etwas verrücken.

shifty adjective verschlagen; **he looks shifty** er sieht verschlagen aus; **a shifty-looking guy** ein verschlagener Typ.

shin noun Schienbein das (PL die Schienbeine).

shine verb scheinen◊; **the sun is shining** die Sonne scheint.

shiny adjective glänzend.

ship noun Schiff das (PL die Schiffe).

shipyard noun Werft die (PL die Werften).

shirt noun **1** (man's) Hemd das (PL die Hemden); **2** (woman's) Bluse die (PL die Blusen).

shiver verb zittern.

shock noun **1** Schock der (PL die Schocks); **to get a shock** einen Schock bekommen; **it gave me a shock** das hat mir einen Schock versetzt; **2 electric shock** der elektrische Schlag.

shock verb (upset) erschüttern; (cause scandal) schockieren.

shocked adjective schockiert.

shocking adjective schockierend.

shoe noun Schuh der (PL die Schuhe); **a pair of shoes** ein Paar Schuhe.

shoelace noun Schnürsenkel der (PL die Schnürsenkel).

shoe polish noun Schuhcreme die (PL die Schuhcremes).

shoe shop noun Schuhgeschäft das (PL die Schuhgeschäfte).

shoot verb **1** (fire) schießen◊; **to shoot at somebody** auf jemanden schießen; **she shot him in the leg** sie hat ihm ins Bein geschossen; **he was shot in the arm** er wurde am Arm getroffen; **2** (kill, execute) erschießen◊; **he was shot by terrorists** er wurde von Terroristen erschossen; **3** (in football, hockey) schießen◊; **4 to shoot a film** einen Film drehen.

shop noun Geschäft das (PL die Geschäfte), Laden der (PL die Läden); **shoe shop** das Schuhgeschäft; **to go round the shops** einen Einkaufsbummel machen.

shop assistant noun Verkäufer der (PL die Verkäufer), Verkäuferin die (PL die Verkäuferinnen).

shopkeeper noun Ladenbesitzer der (PL die Ladenbesitzer), Ladenbesitzerin die (PL die Ladenbesitzerinnen).

shoplifter noun Ladendieb der (PL die Ladendiebe), Ladendiebin die (PL die Ladendiebinnen).

shoplifting noun Ladendiebstahl der.

shopping noun **1** Einkäufe (plural); **can you put the shopping away?** kannst du die Einkäufe wegräumen?; **2** (activity)

a b c d e f g h i j k l m n o p q r s t u v w x y z

a
b
c
d
e
f
g
h
i
j
k
l
m
n
o
p
q
r
s
t
u
v
w
x
y
z

shopping trolley *noun* Einkaufen *das*; **shopping is fun** Einkaufen macht Spaß; **to go shopping** einkaufen gehen✧.

shopping trolley *noun* Einkaufswagen *der* (PL *die* Einkaufswagen).

shop window *noun* Schaufenster *das* (PL *die* Schaufenster).

short *adjective* **1** kurz; **a short dress** ein kurzes Kleid; **she has short hair** sie hat kurze Haare; **2 a short break** eine kurze Pause; **to go for a short walk** einen kurzen Spaziergang machen; **it's a short walk from the bus stop** es ist nicht weit zu Fuß von der Bushaltestelle; **3 to be short of something** knapp mit etwas (DAT) sein; **we're a bit short of money at the moment** wir sind im Moment etwas knapp bei Kasse; **we're getting short of time** die Zeit wird uns knapp.

shortage *noun* Mangel *der*.

shortbread *noun* Buttergebäck *das*.

shortcrust pastry *noun* Mürbeteig *der*.

short cut *noun* Abkürzung *die* (PL *die* Abkürzungen).

shortly *adverb* gleich; **shortly before I left** kurz bevor ich ging; **shortly after** kurz danach.

shorts *plural noun* Shorts (*plural*); **a pair of shorts** ein Paar Shorts; **my red shorts** meine roten Shorts.

short-sighted *adjective* kurzsichtig; **I'm short-sighted** ich bin kurzsichtig.

shot *noun* **1** (*from a gun*) Schuss *der* (PL *die* Schüsse); **2** (*a photo*) Aufnahme *die* (PL *die* Aufnahmen).

should *verb* **1** sollen✧ (*'should' is usually translated by the imperfect subjunctive of 'sollen'*); **you should ask Simon** du solltest Simon fragen; **the potatoes should be ready now** die Kartoffeln sollten jetzt fertig sein; **2** (*'should have' is translated by 'hätte sollen'*) **you should have told me** du hättest es mir sagen sollen; **I shouldn't have stayed** ich hätte nicht bleiben sollen; **you shouldn't have said that** das hättest du nicht sagen sollen; **3** (*'should would' is translated by 'würde'*) **I should forget it if I were you** an deiner Stelle würde ich es vergessen; **4 I should think** ich würde sagen; **I should think he's forgotten** ich würde sagen, er hat's vergessen; **5 this should be enough** das müsste eigentlich reichen.

shoulder *noun* Schulter *die* (PL *die* Schultern).

shoulder bag *noun* Umhängetasche *die* (PL *die* Umhängetaschen).

shout *noun* Schrei *der* (PL *die* Schreie).

shout *verb* **1** schreien✧; **stop shouting!** hör auf zu schreien!; **2** (*call*) rufen✧; **he shouted at us to come back** er rief uns zu, wir sollten zurückkommen.

shovel *noun* Schaufel *die* (PL *die* Schaufeln).

show *noun* **1** (*on stage*) Show *die* (PL *die* Shows); **we went to see a show** wir haben eine Show gesehen; **2** (*on TV, radio*) Sendung *die* (PL *die* Sendungen); **3** (*exhibition*) Ausstellung *die* (PL die Ausstellungen); **fashion show** die Modenschau.

show *verb* 1 zeigen; **to show something to somebody** jemandem etwas zeigen; **I'll show you my photos** ich zeige dir meine Fotos; **to show somebody how something works** jemandem zeigen, wie etwas funktioniert; **he showed me how to make pancakes** er hat mir gezeigt, wie man Pfannkuchen macht; **2 it shows!** das sieht man!

● **to show off** angeben◇ SEP.

shower *noun* 1 (*in a bathroom*) Dusche die (PL die Duschen); **to have a shower** duschen; **2** (*of rain*) Schauer der (PL die Schauer).

show-jumping *noun* Springreiten das.

show-off *noun* Angeber der (PL die Angeber), Angeberin die (PL die Angeberinnen).

shriek *verb* kreischen.

shrimp *noun* Krabbe die (PL die Krabben).

shrink *verb* 1 schrumpfen (PERF sein); **2** (*clothes*) einlaufen◇ SEP (PERF sein); **my sweater has shrunk** mein Pullover ist eingelaufen.

Shrove Tuesday *noun* Fastnachtsdienstag der.

shrug *verb* **to shrug your shoulders** mit den Achseln zucken.

shuffle *verb* **to shuffle the cards** die Karten mischen.

shut *adjective* zu; **the shops are shut** die Geschäfte haben zu.

shut *verb* zumachen SEP; **can you shut the door please?** kannst du die Tür bitte zumachen?; **the**

shops shut at six die Geschäfte machen um sechs zu.

● **to shut up** den Mund halten◇ (*informal*); **shut up!** halt den Mund!.

shuttlecock *noun* Federball der (PL die Federbälle).

shuttle service *noun* Pendelverkehr der; **there's a shuttle service from the airport** es gibt einen Shuttledienst vom Flughafen.

shy *adjective* schüchtern.

shyness *noun* Schüchternheit die.

Sicily *noun* Sizilien das.

sick *adjective* 1 (*ill*) krank; **2 to be sick** (*vomit*) sich übergeben◇; **I was sick several times** ich habe mich mehrmals übergeben; **3 I feel sick** mir ist schlecht; **4** übel; **this joke** ein übler Witz; **5 to be sick of something** etwas satt haben; **I'm sick of staying at home every day** ich habe es satt, jeden Tag zu Hause zu sitzen.

sickness *noun* Krankheit die (PL die Krankheiten).

side *noun* 1 Seite die (PL die Seiten); **on the other side of the street** auf der anderen Straßenseite; **on the wrong side** auf der falschen Seite; **I'm on your side** (*I agree with you*) ich bin auf deiner Seite; **2** (*edge*) Rand der (PL die Ränder) (*of a pool, river*); **at the side of the road** am Straßenrand; **3** (*team*) Mannschaft die (PL die Mannschaften); **the winning side** die siegreiche Mannschaft; **she plays on our side** sie spielt bei uns; **4 to take sides** Partei ergreifen◇; **he always takes sides against her** er ergreift immer gegen sie Partei; **5 side by side** nebeneinander.

sideboard noun Anrichte die (PL die Anrichten).

sideburns noun Koteletten (plural).

side-effect noun Nebenwirkung die (PL die Nebenwirkungen).

side street noun Seitenstraße die (PL die Seitenstraßen).

sieve noun Sieb das (PL die Siebe).

sigh noun Seufzer der (PL die Seufzer).

sigh verb seufzen.

sight noun **1** Anblick der; **it was a marvellous sight** es war ein herrlicher Anblick; **2 at first sight** auf den ersten Blick; **3** (eyesight) **to have poor sight** schlechte Augen haben; **to know somebody by sight** jemanden vom Sehen kennen; **out of sight** außer Sicht; **to lose sight of somebody** jemanden aus den Augen verlieren; **4 the sights** die Sehenswürdigkeiten; **to see the sights** die Sehenswürdigkeiten besichtigen.

sightseeing noun Sightseeing das; **to do some sightseeing** einige Sehenswürdigkeiten besichtigen.

sign noun **1** (notice) Schild das (PL die Schilder); **there's a sign on the door** da ist ein Schild an der Tür; **2** (trace, indication) Zeichen das (PL die Zeichen); **3** (of the zodiac) Sternzeichen das (PL die Sternzeichen); **what sign are you?** was für ein Sternzeichen bist du?

sign verb **1** unterschreiben✧; **to sign a cheque** einen Scheck unterschreiben; **2** (using sign

language) sich durch Zeichensprache verständigen.

● **to sign on** sich arbeitslos melden.

signal noun Signal das (PL die Signale).

signature noun Unterschrift die (PL die Unterschriften).

significant adjective bedeutend.

sign language noun Zeichensprache die (PL die Zeichensprachen).

signpost noun Wegweiser der (PL die Wegweiser).

silence noun Stille die.

silent adjective still.

silk noun Seide die.

silk adjective Seiden-; **a silk blouse** eine Seidenbluse.

silky adjective seidig.

silly adjective dumm; **it was a really silly thing to do** das war wirklich dumm.

silver noun Silber das.

silver adjective Silber-; **a silver medal** eine Silbermedaille.

similar adjective ähnlich; **it looks similar to my old bike** es sieht so ähnlich wie mein altes Rad aus.

similarity noun Ähnlichkeit die (PL die Ähnlichkeiten).

simple adjective einfach.

simply adverb einfach.

sin noun Sünde die (PL die Sünden).

since preposition **1** seit (+ DAT) (notice that German uses the present tense for an action starting in the past and still going on in the present); **I have been in Berlin since Saturday** ich bin seit Samstag in Berlin; **since when?**

seit wann?; **2** (*with a negative the perfect tense is used*) **I haven't seen her since Monday** ich habe sie seit Montag nicht gesehen.

since *conjunction* **1** seit; **since I have known him** seit ich ihn kenne; **since I've been learning German** seitdem ich Deutsch lerne; **2** (*because*) da; **since it was raining, the match was cancelled** da es regnete, wurde das Spiel abgesagt.

since *adverb* seitdem; **I haven't seen him since** ich habe ihn seitdem nicht mehr gesehen.

sincere *adjective* aufrichtig.

sincerely *adverb* **Yours sincerely** Mit freundlichen Grüßen.

sing *verb* singen❖.

singer *noun* Sänger *der* (PL die Sänger), Sängerin *die* (PL die Sängerinnen).

singing *noun* **1** Singen *das*; **a singing lesson** eine Singstunde; **2** **I like singing** ich singe gern.

single *noun* **1** (*ticket*) einfache Fahrkarte *die* (PL die einfachen Fahrkarten); **a single to Munich, please** eine einfache Fahrkarte nach München bitte; **2** (*record, CD*) Single *die* (PL die Singles).

single *adjective* **1** (*not married*) allein stehend; **a single woman** eine allein stehende Frau, (*on forms*) ledig; **2** (*just one*) einzig; **I haven't had a single reply** ich habe keine einzige Antwort bekommen; **3** **not a single one** kein Einziger/ keine Einzige/kein Einziges; **4** **single room** das Einzelzimmer; **single bed** das Einzelbett.

single parent *noun* allein Erziehende *der/die* (PL die allein Erziehenden); **she's a single parent** sie ist allein erziehende Mutter; **a single-parent family** eine Einelternfamilie.

singles *plural noun* (*in tennis*) Einzel *das* (PL die Einzel); **the women's singles** das Dameneinzel; **the men's singles** das Herreneinzel.

singular *noun* Einzahl *die*; **in the singular** in der Einzahl.

sink *noun* Spülbecken *das* (PL die Spülbecken).

sink *verb* sinken❖ (PERF *sein*).

sir *noun* Herr *der* (PL die Herren); (*in German,' Sir' is usually not translated*) **would you like another one, sir?** möchten Sie noch eins?; **yes, sir** ja, mein Herr.

sister *noun* Schwester *die* (PL die Schwestern); **my sister's ten** meine Schwester ist zehn.

sister-in-law *noun* Schwägerin *die* (PL die Schwägerinnen).

sit *verb* **1** (*to sit down*) sich setzen; **you can sit on the sofa** ihr könnt euch aufs Sofa setzen; **sit on the floor** setz dich auf den Boden; **2** (*to be sitting*) sitzen❖; **Leila was sitting on the sofa** Leila saß auf dem Sofa; **to sit on the floor** auf dem Boden sitzen; **3** **to sit an exam** eine Prüfung machen.

● **to sit down** sich setzen; **he sat down on the chair** er setzte sich auf den Stuhl; **do sit down** setzen Sie sich.

sitcom *noun* Situationskomödie *die* (PL die Situationskomödien).

a b c d e f g h i j k l m n o p q r s t u v w x y z

site noun **1 building site** die Baustelle; **2 camping site** der Campingplatz; **3 archaeological site** die archäologische Stätte.

sitting room noun Wohnzimmer das (PL die Wohnzimmer).

situated adjective **to be situated** sich befinden◇; **the house is situated in a small village** das Haus befindet sich in einem kleinen Dorf.

situation noun **1** (location) Lage die (PL die Lagen); **2** (circumstances) Situation die (PL die Situationen).

six number sechs; **Harry's six** Harry ist sechs.

sixteen number sechzehn; **Alice is sixteen** Alice ist sechzehn.

sixth adjective sechster/sechste/ sechstes; **on the sixth floor** im sechsten Stock; **on the sixth of July** am sechsten Juli.

sixty number sechzig; **she's sixty** sie ist sechzig.

size noun **1** Größe die (PL die Größen); **it depends on the size of the house** es kommt auf die Größe des Hauses an; **2 what size is the window?** wie groß ist das Fenster?; **3** (in clothes) Größe die (PL die Größen); **what size do you take?** welche Größe haben Sie?; **4** (of shoes) Schuhgröße die (PL die Schuhgrößen); **I take a size thirty-eight** ich habe Schuhgröße achtunddreißig.

skate noun **1** (an ice skate) Schlittschuh der (PL die Schlittschuhe); **2** (a roller skate) Rollschuh der (PL die Rollschuhe).

skate verb **1** (ice-skate) Schlittschuh laufen◇ (PERF sein);

2 (roller-skate) Rollschuh laufen◇ (PERF sein).

skateboard noun Skateboard das (PL die Skateboards).

skateboarding noun Skateboardfahren das; **to go skateboarding** Skateboard fahren◇ (PERF sein).

skater noun **1** (on rollerskates) Rollschuhfahrer der (PL die Rollschuhfahrer), Rollschuhfahrerin die (PL die Rollschuhfahrerinnen); **2** (on ice) Eisläufer der (PL die Eisläufer), Eisläuferin die (PL die Eisläuferinnen); **3** (on a skateboard) Skater der (PL die Skater).

skating noun **1** (on ice) Schlittschuhlaufen das; **to go skating** Schlittschuh laufen◇ (PERF sein); **2** (roller-skating) Rollschuhlaufen das; **to go roller-skating** Rollschuh laufen◇ (PERF sein).

skating rink noun **1** (ice rink) Eisbahn die (PL die Eisbahnen); **2** (for roller-skating) Rollschuhbahn die (PL die Rollschuhbahnen).

skeleton noun Skelett das (PL die Skelette).

sketch noun **1** Skizze die (PL die Skizzen); **2** (comedy routine) Sketch der (PL die Sketche).

ski noun Ski der (PL die Skier).

ski verb Ski fahren◇ (PERF sein); **he can ski** er kann Ski fahren.

ski boot noun Skistiefel der (PL die Skistiefel).

skid *verb* schleudern (PERF *sein*); **the car skidded** das Auto kam ins Schleudern.

skier *noun* Skifahrer der (PL die Skifahrer), Skifahrerin die (PL die Skifahrerinnen).

skiing *noun* Skifahren das; **to go skiing** Ski fahren◇ (PERF *sein*).

ski lift *noun* Skilift der (PL die Skilifte).

ski suit *noun* Skianzug der (PL die Skianzüge).

skimmed milk *noun* fettarme Milch die.

skin *noun* Haut die (PL die Häute).

skinhead *noun* Skinhead der (PL die Skinheads).

skinny *adjective* dünn.

skip *noun* (*for rubbish*) Container der (PL die Container).

skip *verb* **1** auslassen◇ SEP (*a meal, part of a book*); **I skipped a few chapters** ich ließ ein paar Kapitel aus; **2 to skip a lesson** eine Stunde schwänzen (*informal*).

skirt *noun* Rock der (PL die Röcke); **a long skirt** ein langer Rock; **a tight skirt** ein enger Rock; **a mini-skirt** ein Minirock.

skittles *plural noun* Kegeln das.

skull *noun* Schädel der (PL die Schädel).

sky *noun* Himmel der (PL die Himmel).

skyscraper *noun* Wolkenkratzer der (PL die Wolkenkratzer).

slam *verb* zuknallen SEP; **she slammed the door** sie hat die Tür zugeknallt; **the door slammed** die Tür ist zugeknallt.

slang *noun* Slang der (PL die Slangs).

slap *noun* Klaps der (PL die Klapse), (*in the face*) Ohrfeige die (PL die Ohrfeigen).

slap *verb* **to slap somebody** (*across the face*) jemanden ohrfeigen, (*on the bottom*) jemandem einen Klaps geben.

sledge *noun* Schlitten der (PL die Schlitten).

sledging *noun* **to go sledging** Schlitten fahren◇ (PERF *sein*).

sleep *noun* Schlaf der; **you need more sleep** du brauchst mehr Schlaf; **I had a good sleep** ich habe gut geschlafen; **to go to sleep** einschlafen◇ SEP (PERF *sein*); **he's gone back to sleep** er ist wieder eingeschlafen.

sleep *verb* schlafen◇; **she's sleeping** sie schläft.

sleeping bag *noun* Schlafsack der (PL die Schlafsäcke).

sleeping pill *noun* Schlaftablette die (PL die Schlaftabletten).

sleepy *adjective* **to be sleepy** schläfrig sein; **he was getting sleepy** er wurde schläfrig.

sleet *noun* Schneeregen der.

sleeve *noun* Ärmel der (PL die Ärmel); **a long-sleeved jumper** ein Pullover mit langen Ärmeln; **a short-sleeved shirt** ein Hemd mit kurzen Ärmeln; **to roll up your sleeves** die Ärmel hochkrempeln.

slice *noun* Scheibe die (PL die Scheiben); **a slice of bread** eine Scheibe Brot.

slice *verb* **to slice something** etwas in Scheiben schneiden◇.

slide *noun* **1** (*photo*) Dia das (PL die Dias); **2** (*hairslide*) Haarspange die

a b c d e f g h i j k l m n o p q r s t u v w x y z

(PL die Haarspangen); **3** (for sliding down) Rutschbahn die (PL die Rutschbahnen).

slight adjective klein; **there is a slight problem** es gibt ein kleines Problem.

slightly adverb etwas.

slim adjective schlank.

slim verb abnehmen ◇ SEP; **I'm slimming** ich mache eine Schlankheitskur.

sling noun Schlinge die (PL die Schlingen); **to have your arm in a sling** den Arm in der Schlinge haben.

slip noun **1** (mistake) Fehler der (PL die Fehler); **2** (petticoat) Unterrock der (PL die Unterröcke).

slip verb **1** (slide) ausrutschen SEP (PERF sein); **2 it slipped my mind** es ist mir entfallen.

● **to slip up** einen Fehler machen.

slipper noun Hausschuh der (PL die Hausschuhe).

slippery adjective glatt.

slope noun Hang der (PL die Hänge).

slot noun Schlitz der (PL die Schlitze).

slot machine noun **1** (vending machine) Automat der (PL die Automaten); **2** (games machine) Spielautomat der (PL die Spielautomaten).

slow adjective **1** langsam; **the service is a bit slow** die Bedienung ist etwas langsam; **2** (of a clock or watch) **to be slow** nachgehen ◇ SEP (PERF sein); **my watch is slow** meine Uhr geht nach.

● **to slow down** langsamer werden.

slowly adverb langsam; **he got up slowly** er ist langsam aufgestanden; **can you speak more slowly, please?** können Sie bitte etwas langsamer sprechen?

slug noun Nacktschnecke die (PL die Nacktschnecken).

sly adjective gerissen (a person); ★ **on the sly** heimlich.

smack noun Klaps der (PL die Klapse).

smack verb **to smack somebody** jemandem einen Klaps geben ◇.

small adjective klein; **a small dog** ein kleiner Hund.

smart adjective **1** (well-dressed, posh) elegant; **a smart restaurant** ein elegantes Restaurant; **2** (clever) clever.

smash noun (collision) Zusammenstoß der (PL die Zusammenstöße).

smash verb **1** (break) zerschlagen ◇; **they smashed a window pane** sie haben eine Fensterscheibe zerschlagen; **2** (get broken) zerbrechen ◇ (PERF sein); **the plate smashed** der Teller ist zerbrochen.

smashing adjective klasse (informal).

smell noun Geruch der (PL die Gerüche); **a nasty smell** ein scheußlicher Geruch; **a smell of gas** ein Gasgeruch.

smell verb **1** riechen ◇; **I can't smell anything** ich kann nichts riechen; **to smell of perfume** nach Parfüm riechen; **2** (smell bad) stinken◆; **the drains smell** der Abfluss stinkt.

smelly *adjective* **1** stinkend; **her smelly dog** ihr stinkender Hund; **2 to be smelly** stinken◆.

smile *noun* Lächeln *das*.

smile *verb* lächeln; **to smile at somebody** jemanden anlächeln SEP.

smoke *noun* Rauch *der*.

smoke *verb* rauchen; **she doesn't smoke** sie raucht nicht.

smoked *adjective* geräuchert; **smoked salmon** Räucherlachs *der*.

smoker *noun* Raucher *der* (PL die Raucher), Raucherin *die* (PL die Raucherinnen).

smoking *noun* 'no smoking' 'Rauchen verboten'; **to give up smoking** mit dem Rauchen aufhören.

smooth *adjective* **1** glatt; **a smooth surface** eine glatte Oberfläche; **2** (*person*) aalglatt.

smug *adjective* selbstgefällig.

smuggle *verb* **to smuggle something** etwas schmuggeln.

smuggler *noun* **1** Schmuggler *der* (PL die Schmuggler), Schmugglerin *die* (PL die Schmugglerinnen); **2 drugs smuggler** *der* Drogenschmuggler.

snack *noun* Snack *der* (PL die Snacks).

snail *noun* Schnecke *die* (PL die Schnecken).

snake *noun* Schlange *die* (PL die Schlangen).

snap *noun* (*card game*) Schnippschnapp *das* (PL die Schnippschnapp).

snap *verb* **1** (*break*) brechen◆ (PERF sein); **2 to snap something** zerbrechen◆; **3 to snap your fingers** mit den Fingern schnalzen.

snapshot *noun* Schnappschuss *der* (PL die Schnappschüsse).

snarl *verb* knurren.

snatch *verb* **1** entreißen◆; **to snatch something from somebody** jemandem etwas entreißen; **she had her bag snatched** man hat ihr die Handtasche entrissen; **2 he snatched it out of my hand** er hat es mir aus der Hand gerissen.

sneak *verb* **1 to sneak in** sich hineinschleichen◆ SEP; **to sneak out** sich hinausschleichen◆ SEP; **2 to sneak on somebody** jemanden verpetzen (*informal*).

sneeze *verb* niesen.

sniff *verb* schnüffeln.

snob *noun* Snob *der* (PL die Snobs).

snobbery *noun* Snobismus *der*.

snooker *noun* Snooker *das*.

snooze *verb* Nickerchen *das* (PL die Nickerchen); **to have a snooze** ein Nickerchen machen.

snore *verb* schnarchen.

snow *noun* Schnee *der*.

snow *verb* schneien; **it's snowing** es schneit.

snowball *noun* Schneeball *der* (PL die Schneebälle).

snow drift *noun* Schneewehe *die* (PL die Schneewehen).

snowman *noun* Schneemann *der* (PL die Schneemänner).

so *conjunction, adverb* **1** so; **he's so lazy** er ist so faul; **not so** nicht so; **our house is a bit like yours, but**

not so big unser Haus ist so ähnlich wie eures, aber nicht so groß; **2 so much** so sehr; **I hate it so much** ich hasse es so sehr; **3 so much** so viel; **I have so much work** ich habe so viel Arbeit; **4 so many** so viele; **we've got so many problems** wir haben so viele Probleme; **5** (therefore) also; **he got up late, so he missed his train** er ist zu spät aufgestanden und hat deshalb den Zug verpasst; **so what shall we do?** also, was machen wir?; **6 so what?** na und?; **7** (also) so do I, so did I ich auch; **'I live in Leeds'– 'so do I'** 'ich wohne in Leeds'– 'ich auch'; **I liked the film and so did he** ich fand den Film gut und er auch; **so am I** ich auch; **so do we** wir auch; **8 I think so** ich glaube schon; **9 I hope so** hoffentlich.

soak verb einweichen SEP.

soaked adjective patschnass; ★ **to be soaked to the skin** patschnass sein.

soap noun **1** Seife, die (PL die Seifen); **2** (soap opera) Seifenoper die (PL die Seifenopern).

soap powder noun Seifenpulver das.

sober adjective nüchtern.

• **to sober up** nüchtern werden✧ (PERF sein).

soccer noun Fußball der.

social adjective **1** sozial; **social problems** soziale Probleme; **2** gesellschaftlich (engagement, ambition); **social engagements** gesellschaftliche Verpflichtungen; **social class** die gesellschaftliche

Schicht; **3** (sociable) gesellig (evening, person).

socialism noun Sozialismus der.

socialist noun Sozialist der (PL die Sozialisten), Sozialistin die (PL die Sozialistinnen).

social security noun
1 Sozialhilfe die; **to be on social security** Sozialhilfe bekommen; **2** (the system) Sozialversicherung die.

social worker noun Sozialarbeiter der (PL die Sozialarbeiter), Sozialarbeiterin die (PL die Sozialarbeiterinnen).

society noun Gesellschaft die (PL die Gesellschaften).

sociology noun Soziologie die.

sock noun Socke die (PL die Socken); **a pair of socks** ein Paar Socken.

socket noun (power point) Steckdose die (PL die Steckdosen).

sofa noun Sofa das (PL die Sofas).

sofa bed noun Schlafcouch die (PL die Schlafcouchs).

soft adjective **1** weich; **2 a soft option** eine bequeme Lösung; ★ **to have a soft spot for somebody** eine Schwäche für jemanden haben.

soft drink noun alkoholfreie Getränk das (PL die alkoholfreien Getränke).

soft toy noun Stofftier das (PL die Stofftiere).

software noun Software die.

soil noun Erde die.

solar energy noun Sonnenenergie die.

soldier noun Soldat der (PL die Soldaten).

solicitor noun **1** (*dealing with lawsuits*) Rechtsanwalt der (PL die Rechtsanwälte), Rechtsanwältin die (PL die Rechtsanwältinnen); **2** (*dealing with property or documents*) Notar der (PL die Notare), Notarin die (PL die Notarinnen).

solid adjective **1** (*not flimsy*) stabil; **a solid structure** ein stabiler Bau; **2** massiv; **a table made of solid oak** ein Tisch aus massiver Eiche; **solid silver** massives Silber.

solo noun Solo das (PL die Solos); **guitar solo** das Gitarrensolo.

solo adjective Solo-; **a solo act** eine Solonummer.

solo adverb solo.

soloist noun Solist der (PL die Solisten), Solistin die (PL die Solistinnen).

solution noun Lösung die (PL die Lösungen).

solve verb lösen.

some adjective, adverb **1** (*followed by a singular noun*) etwas; **would you like some salad?** möchtest du etwas Salat?; **can you lend me some money?** kannst du mir etwas Geld leihen?; **have you got some bread?** (*some is often not translated*) hast du Brot?; **2** (*followed by a plural noun*) (*a few*) ein paar; **I've bought some apples** ich habe ein paar Äpfel gekauft; **3** (*followed by a plural noun*) (*a certain number but not all*) einige; **some of his films are too violent** einige von seinen Filmen sind zu brutal; **4** (*referring to something that has been mentioned*) 'would

you like tea?' — 'thanks, I've got some' 'möchten Sie Tee?' — 'nein danke, ich habe schon welchen'; **he's eaten some of it** er hat etwas davon gegessen; **I'd like some** ich möchte etwas; (*with a plural noun*) ich möchte welche; **5** (*certain people or things*) manche; **some people think he's right** manche Leute glauben, dass er Recht hat; **6** **some day** eines Tages.

somebody, someone pronoun jemand; **there's somebody in the garden** da ist jemand im Garten.

somehow adverb irgendwie; **I've got to finish this essay somehow** ich muss diesen Aufsatz irgendwie fertig schreiben.

something pronoun **1** etwas; **there's something I've got to tell you** ich muss dir etwas erzählen; **something new** etwas Neues; **something interesting** etwas Interessantes; **there's something wrong** irgendetwas stimmt nicht; **2 their house is really something!** ihr Haus ist einfach Klasse!

sometime adverb irgendwann; **give me a ring sometime next week** ruf mich irgendwann nächste Woche an.

sometimes adverb manchmal; **I sometimes take the train** manchmal fahre ich mit der Bahn.

somewhere adverb **1** (*in a place*) irgendwo; **I've left my bag somewhere here** ich habe meine Handtasche hier irgendwo liegen lassen; **2** (*to a place*) irgendwohin; **I'd like to go somewhere warm** ich möchte irgendwohin fahren, wo es warm ist.

a
b
c
d
e
f
g
h
i
j
k
l
m
n
o
p
q
r
s
t
u
v
w
x
y
z

son noun Sohn der (PL die Söhne).

song noun Lied das (PL die Lieder).

son-in-law noun Schwiegersohn der (PL die Schwiegersöhne).

soon adverb **1** bald; **we'll soon be on holiday** wir haben bald Ferien; **see you soon!** bis bald!; **2 as soon as she arrives** sobald sie ankommt; **as soon as possible** so bald wie möglich; **3 it's too soon** es ist zu früh.

sooner adverb **1** früher; **we should have started sooner** wir hätten früher anfangen sollen; **sooner or later** früher oder später; **2 I'd sooner wait** ich würde lieber warten.

soprano noun Sopran der (PL die Soprane).

sore noun wunde Stelle die (PL die wunden Stellen).

sore adjective **1** (inflamed) wund; **to have a sore throat** Halsschmerzen haben; **2 he has a sore leg** ihm tut das Bein weh; **my arm's sore** mir tut der Arm weh; ★ **it's a sore point** es ist ein wunder Punkt.

sorry adjective **1 I'm really sorry** es tut mir wirklich Leid; **sorry to disturb you** es tut mir Leid, dass ich dich störe; **I'm sorry I forgot your birthday** es tut mir Leid, dass ich deinen Geburtstag vergessen habe; **I'm sorry, we're closing** es tut mir Leid, aber wir machen jetzt zu; **2 sorry!** Entschuldigung!; **3 sorry?** wie bitte?; **4 I feel sorry for him** er tut mir Leid.

sort noun Art die (PL die Arten); **a sort of dance music** eine Art Tanzmusik; **what sort of car have you got?** was für ein Auto hast

du?; **all sorts of people** alle möglichen Leute; **for all sorts of reasons** aus allen möglichen Gründen.

● **to sort something out**
1 Ordnung schaffen◇ in (+ DAT) (papers, desk, room, possessions); **I must sort out my room tonight** ich muss heute Abend in meinem Zimmer Ordnung schaffen; **2** klären (a problem, arrangement); **Liz is sorting it out** Liz klärt es.

so-so adjective so lala (informal); **'how was the film?'— 'so-so'** 'wie war der Film?'— 'mittelmäßig'.

soul noun **1** Seele die (PL die Seelen); **2** (music) Soul der.

sound noun **1** (noise) Geräusch das (PL die Geräusche); **2** (of voices, laughter, bell) Klang der; **the sound of her voice** der Klang ihrer Stimme; **I can hear the sound of voices** ich kann Stimmen hören; **3 without a sound** lautlos; **4** (volume) Lautstärke die; **to turn the sound down** leiser stellen.

sound verb **1 it sounds easy** es hört sich einfach an; **2 it sounds as if she's happy** sie scheint glücklich zu sein.

sound asleep adverb **to be sound asleep** fest schlafen◇.

sound effect noun Geräuscheffekt der (PL die Geräuscheffekte).

soundtrack noun Soundtrack der (PL die Soundtracks).

soup noun Suppe die (PL die Suppen); **mushroom soup** die Pilzsuppe.

soup plate noun Suppenteller der (PL die Suppenteller).

soup spoon *noun* Suppenlöffel der (PL die Suppenlöffel).

sour *adjective* sauer.

south *noun* Süden der; **in the south** im Süden.

south *adjective* Süd-, südlich; **the south side** die Südseite; **south wind** der Südwind.

south *adverb* Süden der; **south of Berlin** südlich von Berlin; **they went south** sie sind nach Süden gefahren.

South Africa *noun* Südafrika das.

South America *noun* Südamerika das.

southeast *noun* Südosten der.

southeast *adjective* **in southeast England** in Südostengland.

South Pole *noun* Südpol der.

southwest *noun* Südwesten der.

southwest *adjective* **in southwest England** in Südwestengland.

souvenir *noun* Souvenir das (PL die Souvenirs).

soya *noun* Soja die.

space *noun* 1 (*room*) Platz der; **there's enough space** es ist genug Platz; **we've got enough space for two** wir haben genug Platz für zwei; 2 (*gap*) Zwischenraum der (PL die Zwischenräume); **to leave a large space between lines** viel Platz zwischen den Zeilen lassen; 3 (*parking*) space der Parklücke; 4 (*outer space*) Weltraum der; **in space** im Weltraum.

spacecraft *noun* Raumschiff das (PL die Raumschiffe).

spade *noun* 1 Spaten der (PL die Spaten); 2 (*in cards*) Pik das; **the queen of spades** die Pikdame.

Spain *noun* Spanien das; **from Spain** aus Spanien; **to Spain** nach Spanien.

Spaniard *noun* Spanier der (PL die Spanier), Spanierin die (PL die Spanierinnen).

spaniel *noun* Spaniel der (PL die Spaniels).

Spanish *noun* 1 (*language*) Spanisch das; **I'm learning Spanish** ich lerne Spanisch; 2 **the Spanish** (*people*) die Spanier.

Spanish *adjective* spanisch; **Pedro is Spanish** Pedro ist Spanier.

spanner *noun* Schraubenschlüssel der (PL die Schraubenschlüssel).

spare *adjective* Extra-; **we have a spare ticket** wir haben eine Karte übrig.

spare *verb* to have time to spare Zeit haben; **can you spare a moment?** hast du einen Moment Zeit?

spare part *noun* Ersatzteil das (PL die Ersatzteile).

spare room *noun* Gästezimmer das (PL die Gästezimmer).

spare time *noun* Freizeit die; **in my spare time** in meiner Freizeit.

spare wheel *noun* Reserverad das (PL die Reserveräder).

sparkling *adjective* sparkling mineral water Mineralwasser mit Kohlensäure; **sparkling wine** der Schaumwein.

sparrow *noun* Spatz der (PL die Spatzen).

speak *verb* 1 sprechen✧; **do you speak German?** sprechen Sie Deutsch?; **spoken German**

gesprochenes Deutsch; **to speak to somebody about something** mit jemandem über etwas (ACC) sprechen; **she's speaking to Mike about it** sie spricht mit Mike darüber; **2 who's speaking?** (on the phone) wer ist am Apparat?

speaker noun **1** (on a music system) Lautsprecher der (PL die Lautsprecher); **2** (at a public lecture) Redner der (PL die Redner), Rednerin die (PL die Rednerinnen).

special adjective **1** besonderer/besondere/besonderes; **on special occasions** bei besonderen Anlässen; **2 special offer** das Sonderangebot.

specialist noun Fachmann der (PL die Fachleute), Fachfrau die (PL die Fachfrauen).

specialize verb sich spezialisieren auf (+ ACC); **to specialize in I'm specializing in business studies** ich spezialisiere mich auf Wirtschaftswissenschaften.

specially adverb **1** besonders; **not specially** nicht besonders; **it's specially good for babies** es ist besonders gut für Babys; **2** (specifically) speziell; **I made this cake specially for you** ich habe diesen Kuchen speziell für dich gebacken.

species noun Art die (PL die Arten).

spectacles noun Brille die (PL die Brillen).

spectacular adjective spektakulär.

spectator noun Zuschauer der (PL die Zuschauer), Zuschauerin die (PL die Zuschauerinnen).

speech noun Rede die (PL die Reden); **to make a speech** eine Rede halten.

speechless adjective sprachlos; **to be speechless: she was speechless with rage** sie war sprachlos vor Wut.

speed noun **1** Geschwindigkeit die (PL die Geschwindigkeiten); **at top speed** mit Höchstgeschwindigkeit; **what speed was he doing?** wie schnell ist er gefahren?; **2** (gear) Gang der (PL die Gänge); **a twelve-speed bike** ein Rad mit zwölf Gängen.

● **to speed up 1** beschleunigen (a car); **2** (of a person, car) schneller werden.

speeding noun zu schnelle Fahren das; **he was fined for speeding** er hat wegen zu schnellen Fahrens ein Bußgeld bekommen.

speed limit noun Geschwindigkeitsbeschränkung die.

spell noun **1** (of time) Weile die; **for a spell** eine Weile; **2 cold spell** die Kälteperiode; **sunny spells** sonnige Abschnitte.

spell verb **1** (in writing) schreiben✧; **how do you spell it?** wie schreibt man das?; **how do you spell your surname?** wie schreibt man Ihren Nachnamen?; **2** (out loud) buchstabieren.

spell checker noun Rechtschreibprogramm das (PL die Rechtschreibprogramme).

spelling noun Rechtschreibung die; **spelling mistake** der Rechtschreibfehler.

spend verb 1 ausgeben✧ SEP (money); **I've spent all my money** ich habe mein ganzes Geld ausgegeben; 2 verbringen✧ (time); **we spent three days in Munich** wir haben drei Tage in München verbracht; **she spends her time reading** sie verbringt ihre Zeit mit Lesen.

spice noun Gewürz das (PL die Gewürze).

spicy adjective scharf; **he doesn't like spicy food** er mag kein scharfes Essen.

spider noun Spinne die (PL die Spinnen).

spill verb verschütten; **I've spilled my wine on the carpet** ich habe meinen Wein auf dem Teppich verschüttet.

spinach noun Spinat der.

spine noun Wirbelsäule die (PL die Wirbelsäulen).

spire noun Kirchturm der (PL die Kirchtürme).

spirit noun 1 (energy) Energie die; 2 **in the right spirit** mit der richtigen Einstellung.

spirits noun 1 (alcohol) Spirituosen (plural); **2 to be in good spirits** guter Laune sein.

spit verb 1 spucken; **2 to spit something out** etwas ausspucken SEP; **spit it out!** spuck es aus!

spite noun 1 **in spite of** trotz (+ GEN); **we decided to go in spite of the rain** wir beschlossen trotz des Regens zu gehen; 2 (nastiness) Boshaftigkeit die; **to do something out of spite** etwas aus Boshaftigkeit tun.

spiteful adjective gehässig.

splash noun 1 (noise) Platsch der; **2 splash of colour** der Farbfleck.

splash verb bespritzen.

splendid adjective herrlich.

splinter noun Splitter der (PL die Splitter).

split verb 1 (with an axe or a knife) spalten; **to split wood** Holz spalten; 2 (come apart) zerreißen✧ (PERF sein); **the lining has split** das Futter ist zerrissen; 3 (divide up) teilen; **they split the money between them** sie haben das Geld untereinander geteilt.

● **to split up 1** (a group or crowd) sich auflösen SEP; **2** (a couple) sich trennen; **she's split up with her husband** sie hat sich von ihrem Mann getrennt; **she's split up with Sam** sie hat mit Sam Schluss gemacht (informal).

spoil verb verderben✧; **it completely spoiled our evening** das hat uns den Abend völlig verdorben; **to spoil somebody's fun** jemandem den Spaß verderben.

spoiled adjective verwöhnt; **a spoiled child** ein verwöhntes Kind.

spoilsport noun Spielverderber der (PL die Spielverderber), Spielverderberin die (PL die Spielverderberinnen).

spoke noun (of a wheel) Speiche die (PL die Speichen).

spokesman noun Sprecher der (PL die Sprecher).

spokeswoman noun Sprecherin die (PL die Sprecherinnen).

sponge noun Schwamm der (PL die Schwämme).

sponge cake noun Rührkuchen der (PL die Rührkuchen).

a
b
c
d
e
f
g
h
i
j
k
l
m
n
o
p
q
r
s
t
u
v
w
x
y
z

a

sponsor noun Sponsor der (PL die Sponsoren).

b

sponsor verb sponsern.

c

spooky adjective gruselig; **a spooky story** eine gruselige Geschichte.

d

spoon noun Löffel der (PL die Löffel); **a spoon of sugar** ein Löffel Zucker; **soup spoon** der Suppenlöffel; **teaspoon** der Teelöffel.

e

f

g

spoonful noun Löffel der (PL die Löffel).

h

sport noun 1 Sport der; **to be good at sport** gut im Sport sein; **my favourite sport** mein Lieblingssport; 2 (in games) **to be a good sport** ein guter Verlierer sein.

i

j

k

sports bag noun Sporttasche die (PL die Sporttaschen).

l

sports car noun Sportwagen der (PL die Sportwagen).

m

sports centre noun Sportzentrum das (PL die Sportzentren).

n

o

sports club noun Sportverein der (PL die Sportvereine).

p

sportsman noun Sportler der (PL die Sportler).

q

r

sportswear noun Sportbekleidung die.

s

sportswoman noun Sportlerin die (PL die Sportlerinnen).

t

sporty adjective sportlich; **she's very sporty** sie ist sehr sportlich.

u

spot noun 1 (pattern in fabric) Punkt der (PL die Punkte); **a red shirt with black spots** ein rotes Hemd mit schwarzen Punkten; 2 (on your skin) Pickel der (PL die Pickel); **I've got spots** ich habe Pickel; **to be covered in spots**

v

w

x

y

z

völlig verpickelt sein; 3 (stain) Fleck der (PL die Flecke); **you've got a spot on your shirt** du hast einen Fleck auf dem Hemd; 4 (spotlight) Scheinwerfer der (PL die Scheinwerfer); (in the home) Spot der (PL die Spots); 5 **on the spot** (immediately) auf der Stelle; **we'll do it for you on the spot** wir machen es Ihnen auf der Stelle; 6 (at hand) **on the spot** zur Stelle; 7 (at the same place) **on the spot** an Ort und Stelle.

spot verb entdecken; **he spotted his friend in the crowd** er entdeckte seinen Freund in der Menge.

spotlight noun 1 Scheinwerfer der (PL die Scheinwerfer); 2 (in the home) Spot der (PL die Spots).

spotty adjective (pimply) pickelig.

spouse noun 1 (male) Ehemann der (PL die Ehemänner); 2 (female) Ehefrau die (PL die Ehefrauen).

sprain noun Verstauchung die (PL die Verstauchungen).

sprain verb **to sprain your ankle** sich (DAT) den Fuß verstauchen.

spray noun (spray can) Spray das (PL die Sprays).

spray verb sprühen.

spread noun Brotaufstrich der; **cheese spread** der Streichkäse.

spread verb 1 (of news or a disease) sich verbreiten; 2 streichen◆ (butter, jam, glue).

spreadsheet noun (on a computer) Tabellenkalkulation die.

spring noun 1 (the season) Frühling der (PL die Frühlinge); **in the spring** im Frühling; **spring**

flowers Frühlingsblumen; **2** (*made of metal*) Feder die (PL die Federn); **3** (*providing water*) Quelle die (PL die Quellen).

springtime noun Frühjahr das; **in springtime** im Frühjahr.

spring water noun Quellwasser das.

sprint noun Sprint der (PL die Sprints).

sprint verb rennen✧ (PERF sein).

sprinter noun Sprinter der (PL die Sprinter), Sprinterin die (PL die Sprinterinnen).

sprout noun (*Brussels sprout*) Rosenkohl der; **he likes sprouts** er mag Rosenkohl.

spy noun Spion der (PL die Spione), Spionin die (PL die Spioninnen).

spy verb **to spy on somebody** jemandem nachspionieren SEP; **he's spying on me** er spioniert mir nach.

squabble verb sich zanken.

square noun **1** (*shape*) Quadrat das (PL die Quadrate); **2** (*in a town or village*) Platz der (PL die Plätze); **the village square** der Dorfplatz.

square adjective quadratisch; **a square box** eine viereckige Schachtel; **three square metres** drei Quadratmeter; **the room is four metres square** das Zimmer ist vier mal vier Meter; ★ **to go back to square one** noch einmal von vorn anfangen.

squash noun **1** (*drink*) Saft der; **orange squash** der Orangensaft; **2** (*sport*) Squash das.

squash verb zerquetschen.

squeak verb **1** (*door; hinge*) quietschen; **2** (*person, animal*) quieken.

squeeze verb **1** drücken; **to squeeze somebody's hand** jemandem die Hand drücken; **2** drücken (*toothpaste*).

squirrel noun Eichhörnchen das (PL die Eichhörnchen).

stab verb stechen✧; **to stab somebody** (*kill*) jemanden erstechen✧.

stable noun Stall der (PL die Ställe).

stable adjective stabil.

stack noun **1** Stapel der (PL die Stapel); **2 stacks of** ein Haufen; **she's got stacks of CDs** sie hat einen Haufen CDs.

stadium noun Stadion das (PL die Stadien).

staff noun **1** (*of a company*) Personal das; **2** (*in a school*) Lehrkräfte (*plural*).

stage noun **1** (*for a performance*) Bühne die (PL die Bühnen); **on stage** auf der Bühne; **2** (*phase*) Phase die (PL die Phasen); **at this stage of the project** in dieser Phase des Projekts; **at this stage it's hard to say** im Augenblick ist es schwer zu sagen.

staggered adjective (*amazed*) verblüfft.

stain noun Fleck der (PL die Flecke).

stain verb beflecken.

stainless steel noun Edelstahl der; **a stainless steel sink** ein Spülbecken aus Edelstahl.

stair noun **1** (*step*) Stufe die (PL die Stufen); **2 the stairs** die Treppe (*singular*); **I met her on the stairs**

a
b
c
d
e
f
g
h
i
j
k
l
m
n
o
p
q
r
s
t
u
v
w
x
y
z

ich habe sie auf der Treppe getroffen.

staircase noun Treppe die (PL die Treppen).

stale adjective alt.

stalemate noun (in chess) Patt das (PL die Patts).

stall noun 1 (at a market or fair) Stand der (PL die Stände); 2 (in a theatre) **the stalls** das Parkett.

stammer noun **to have a stammer** stottern.

stamp noun Briefmarke die (PL die Briefmarken).

stamp verb 1 frankieren (a letter); 2 **to stamp your foot** mit dem Fuß aufstampfen.

stamp album noun Briefmarkenalbum das (PL die Briefmarkenalben).

stamp collection noun Briefmarkensammlung die (PL die Briefmarkensammlungen).

stand[1] verb 1 stehen◇; **several people were standing** viele Leute standen; **we stood outside the cinema** wir haben vor dem Kino gestanden; **I can't stand her** ich kann sie nicht ausstehen; **I can't stand waiting** ich kann es nicht ausstehen, wenn man warten muss; **3** (keep going) aushalten◇ SEP; **I can't stand it any longer** ich halte es nicht mehr aus.

stand noun (in a stadium) Tribüne die (PL die Tribünen).

● **to stand for something** (be short for) bedeuten; **UN stands for United Nations** UN bedeutet United Nations.

● **stand up** aufstehen◇ SEP (PERF sein); **everybody stood up** alle standen auf.

stand[2] noun 1 (in a stadium) Tribüne die (PL die Tribünen); 2 (in fair) Stand der (PL die Stände).

standard noun 1 (level) Niveau das; **of high standard** von hohem Niveau; 2 **standard of living** der Lebensstandard; 3 **she sets herself high standards** sie stellt hohe Ansprüche an sich selbst.

standard adjective normal; **the standard size** die Normalgröße.

Standard grades noun plural (You can explain Standard grades as follows: Diese Prüfungen werden im Alter von ca 16 Jahren in sechs oder sieben Fächern abgelegt. Sie werden von 1 (beste Note) bis 7 (Kurs abgeschlossen) benotet. Viele Schüler machen nach Standard Grades weiter, und legen Highers und Advanced Highers ab) SEE Highers.

staple noun Heftklammer die (PL die Heftklammern).

staple verb heften; **to staple the pages together** die Seiten zusammenheften.

stapler noun Hefter der (PL die Hefter).

star noun 1 (in the sky) Stern der (PL die Sterne); 2 (person) Star der (PL die Stars); **he's a film star** er ist ein Filmstar.

star verb **to star in a film** in einem Film die Hauptrolle spielen; **starring ... in der Hauptrolle ....**

stare verb 1 starren; **what are you staring at?** was starrst du so?; **2 to**

stare at somebody jemanden anstarren SEP; **he's staring at the wall** er starrt die Wand an.

start noun 1 Anfang der; **at the start** am Anfang; **at the start of the film** am Anfang des Films; **from the start** von Anfang an; **we knew from the start that it was dangerous** wir wussten von Anfang an, dass es gefährlich war; **2 to make a start on something** mit etwas (DAT) anfangen✧ SEP; **I've made a start on my homework** ich habe mit meinen Hausaufgaben angefangen; **3** (of a race) Start der (PL die Starts).

start verb 1 anfangen✧ SEP; **the film starts at eight** der Film fängt um acht an; **I've started the book** ich habe das Buch angefangen; **to start doing something** anfangen, etwas zu tun; **I've started learning Spanish** ich habe angefangen, Spanisch zu lernen; **to start crying** anfangen zu weinen; **2 to start a business** ein Geschäft gründen; **3 to start a car** ein Auto starten; **she started the car** sie hat das Auto gestartet; **4 the car won't start** das Auto springt nicht an.

starter noun (first course) Vorspeise die (PL die Vorspeisen).

starve verb verhungern; **I'm starving!** ich bin schon am Verhungern!

state noun 1 Zustand der (PL die Zustände); **the house is in a very bad state** das Haus ist in einem sehr schlechten Zustand; **2** (country) Staat der (PL die Staaten); **the state** der Staat; **3 the States** (USA) die Staaten; **they live**

in the States sie leben in den Staaten.

state verb 1 erklären (intention, reason); **2** angeben✧ SEP (an address, income, a reason).

stately home noun herrschaftliche Anwesen das (PL die herrschaftlichen Anwesen).

statement noun Erklärung die (PL die Erklärungen).

station noun 1 Bahnhof der (PL die Bahnhöfe); **at the railway station** am Bahnhof; **bus station** der Busbahnhof; **2 police station** der Polizeiwache; **3 radio station** der Rundfunksender.

stationer's noun Schreibwarengeschäft das (PL die Schreibwarengeschäfte).

statistics noun (subject) Statistik die; **the statistics** (figures) die Statistik.

statue noun Statue die (PL die Statuen).

stay noun Aufenthalt der (PL die Aufenthalte); **our stay in Cologne** unser Aufenthalt in Köln; **enjoy your stay!** einen schönen Aufenthalt!

stay verb 1 bleiben✧ (PERF sein); **I'll stay here** ich bleibe hier; **how long are you staying?** wie lange bleibst du?; **2** (spend the night) **you can stay with us** du kannst bei uns übernachten; **to stay the night with friends** bei Freunden übernachten; **3** (be temporarily lodged) wohnen; **where are you staying?** wo wohnst du?; **I'm staying in a hotel** ich wohne im Hotel; **4** (be on a visit) sein✧ (PERF

a
b
c
d
e
f
g
h
i
j
k
l
m
n
o
p
q
r
s
t
u
v
w
x
y
z

sein); **I'm going to stay with my sister this weekend** ich bin am Wochenende bei meiner Schwester; **I stayed in Munich for a couple of days** ich war ein paar Tage in München.

● **to stay in** zu Hause bleiben✧ (PERF *sein*); **I'm staying in tonight** heute Abend bleibe ich zu Hause.

steady *adjective* **1** fest; **a steady job** eine feste Stelle; **2** gleichmäßig; **at a steady pace** mit gleichmäßiger Geschwindigkeit; **3** (*hand, voice*) ruhig; **to hold something steady** etwas ruhig halten; **4** (*dependable*) zuverlässig.

steak *noun* Steak das (PL die Steaks); **steak and chips** Steak mit Pommes frites.

steal *verb* stehlen✧.

steam *noun* Dampf der.

steel *noun* Stahl der.

steep *adjective* steil; **a steep slope** ein steiler Hang.

steeple *noun* (*spire*) Kirchturm der (PL die Kirchtürme).

steering wheel *noun* Lenkrad das (PL die Lenkräder).

step *noun* **1** Schritt der (PL die Schritte); **to take a step forwards** einen Schritt nach vorn machen; **to take a step backwards** einen Schritt zurück machen; **2** (*stair*) Stufe die (PL die Stufen).

● **to step back** zurücktreten✧ SEP (PERF *sein*).

● **to step forward** vortreten✧ SEP (PERF *sein*).

stepbrother *noun* Stiefbruder der (PL die Stiefbrüder).

stepdaughter *noun* Stieftochter die (PL die Stieftöchter).

stepfather *noun* Stiefvater der (PL die Stiefväter).

stepladder *noun* Trittleiter die (PL die Trittleitern).

stepmother *noun* Stiefmutter die (PL die Stiefmütter).

stepsister *noun* Stiefschwester die (PL die Stiefschwestern).

stepson *noun* Stiefsohn der (PL die Stiefsöhne).

stereo *noun* Stereoanlage die (PL die Stereoanlagen).

sterling *noun* Sterling der; **in sterling** in Pfund (Sterling).

stew *noun* Eintopf der (PL die Eintöpfe).

steward *noun* Steward der (PL die Stewards).

stewardess *noun* Stewardess die (PL die Stewardessen).

stick *noun* **1** Stock der (PL die Stöcke); **2** hockey stick ein Hockeyschläger.

stick *verb* **1** (*with glue*) kleben; **2** (*put*) tun✧; **stick them on my desk** tu sie auf meinen Schreibtisch.

sticker *noun* Aufkleber der (PL die Aufkleber).

sticky tape *noun* Klebestreifen der.

sticky *adjective* **1** klebrig; **I've got sticky hands** ich habe klebrige Hände; **2** **a sticky label** ein Aufkleber.

stiff *adjective* **1** steif; **to feel stiff** steif sein, (*after exercise*)

Muskelkater haben; **to have a stiff neck** einen steifen Hals haben; **2 to be bored stiff** sich zu Tode langweilen; **3 to be scared stiff** furchtbare Angst haben.

still *adjective* **1 sit still!** sitz still!; **keep still!** halt still!; **2 still mineral water** Mineralwasser ohne Kohlensäure.

still *adverb* **1** noch; **do you still live in London?** wohnst du noch in London?; **I've still not finished** ich bin immer noch nicht fertig; **he's still working** er arbeitet noch; **2** (*nevertheless*) trotzdem; **I told her not to, but she still did it** ich habe es ihr verboten, aber sie hat es trotzdem gemacht; **3 better still** noch besser.

sting *noun* Stich der (PL die Stiche).

sting *verb* stechen✧.

stink *noun* Gestank der.

stink *verb* stinken✧; **it stinks of fish in here** es stinkt hier nach Fisch.

stir *verb* rühren.

stitch *noun* **1** (*in sewing, surgical*) Stich der (PL die Stiche); **2** (*in knitting*) Masche die (PL die Maschen); **3** (*pain*) Seitenstechen das.

stock *noun* **1** (*in a shop*) Warenbestand der; **to have something in stock** etwas auf Lager haben; **to be out of stock** ausverkauft sein; **2** (*supply*) Vorrat der (PL die Vorräte); **I always have a stock of pencils** ich habe immer einen Bleistiftvorrat; **3** (*for cooking*) Brühe die; **chicken stock** die Hühnerbrühe.

stock *verb* (*in a shop*) führen; **they don't stock books** sie führen keine Bücher.

stock cube *noun* Brühwürfel der (PL die Brühwürfel).

stock exchange *noun* Börse die (PL die Börsen).

stocking *noun* Strumpf der (PL die Strümpfe).

stomach *noun* Magen der (PL die Mägen).

stomach-ache *noun* Magenschmerzen (*plural*); **to have stomach-ache** Magenschmerzen haben.

stone *noun* Stein der (PL die Steine); **stone wall** die Steinmauer.

stool *noun* Hocker der (PL die Hocker).

stop *noun* Haltestelle die (PL die Haltestellen); **bus stop** die Bushaltestelle.

stop *verb* **1** halten✧; **does the train stop in Stuttgart?** hält der Zug in Stuttgart?; **2 to stop somebody/ something** jemanden/etwas anhalten✧ SEP; **the police stopped the car** die Polizei hielt den Wagen an; **3** (*cease*) aufhören SEP; **the noise has stopped** der Lärm hat aufgehört; **to stop doing something** aufhören, etwas zu tun; **he's stopped smoking** er hat aufgehört zu rauchen; **she never stops asking questions** sie hört nie auf, Fragen zu stellen; **stop it!** hör auf!; **4 to stop somebody doing something** jemanden daran hindern, etwas zu tun; **I can't stop her ringing him** ich kann sie nicht daran hindern, ihn anzurufen;

a
b
c
d
e
f
g
h
i
j
k
l
m
n
o
p
q
r
s
t
u
v
w
x
y
z

a
b
c
d
e
f
g
h
i
j
k
l
m
n
o
p
q
r
s
t
u
v
w
x
y
z

5 (*prevent*) verhindern (*an accident, a crime*).

stopwatch *noun* Stoppuhr die (PL die Stoppuhren).

store *noun* (*shop*) Geschäft das (PL die Geschäfte); **department store** das Kaufhaus.

store *verb* **1** aufbewahren SEP, (*in a warehouse*) lagern; **2** (*on a computer*) speichern.

storey *noun* Stockwerk das (PL die Stockwerke); **a four-storey house** ein vierstöckiges Haus.

storm *noun* **1** Sturm der (PL die Stürme); **2** (*thunderstorm*) Gewitter das (PL die Gewitter).

stormy *adjective* stürmisch.

story *noun* Geschichte die (PL die Geschichten); **to tell a story** eine Geschichte erzählen.

stove *noun* (*cooker*) Herd der (PL die Herde).

straight *adjective* **1** gerade; **a straight line** eine gerade Linie; **2 to have straight hair** glatte Haare haben.

straight *adverb* **1** (*in direction*) straight ahead geradeaus; **to go straight ahead** geradeaus gehen; **2** (*immediately, directly*) sofort; **straight away** sofort; **he went straight to the doctor's** er ging sofort zum Arzt.

straightforward *adjective* einfach.

strain *noun* Stress der; **the strain of the last few weeks** der Stress in den letzten Wochen; **to be a strain** anstrengend sein.

strain *verb* **1** zerren (*a muscle*); **2** verrenken (*your arm, back*); **he's**

strained his back er hat sich (DAT) den Rücken verrenkt.

strange *adjective* seltsam; **his strange behaviour** sein seltsames Verhalten.

stranger *noun* Fremde der/die (PL die Fremden).

strangle *verb* erwürgen.

strap *noun* **1** (*on a case, bag, camera*) Riemen der (PL die Riemen); **2** (*on a garment*) Träger der (PL die Träger); **3** (*of a watch*) Armband das (PL die Armbänder).

strapless *adjective* trägerlos.

straw *noun* **1** (*for drinking*) Strohhalm der (PL die Strohhalme); **2** (*the material*) Stroh das; **straw hat** der Strohhut.

strawberry *noun* Erdbeere die (PL die Erdbeeren); **strawberry jam** die Erdbeermarmelade.

stray *adjective* **a stray dog** ein streunender Hund.

stream *noun* Bach der (PL die Bäche).

street *noun* Straße die (PL die Straßen); **I met Simon in the street** ich habe Simon auf der Straße getroffen.

streetlamp *noun* Straßenlaterne die (PL die Straßenlaternen).

street map *noun* Stadtplan der (PL die Stadtpläne).

streetwise *adjective* gewieft.

strength *noun* Kraft die (PL die Kräfte).

stress *noun* Stress der.

stress *verb* betonen; **to stress the importance of something** die Wichtigkeit von etwas betonen.

stretch *verb* **1** (*garment, shoes*) sich dehnen; **this jumper has**

stretched der Pullover hat sich gedehnt; **2 to stretch your legs** sich (DAT) die Beine vertreten❖.

stretcher noun Trage die (PL die Tragen).

stretchy adjective elastisch.

strict adjective streng.

strike noun Streik der (PL die Streiks); **to go on strike** in den Streik treten❖; (PERF sein); **to be/go on strike** streiken.

strike verb **1** (hit) schlagen❖; **the clock struck six** die Uhr schlug sechs; **2** (be/go on strike) streiken.

striker noun **1** (in football) Stürmer der (PL die Stürmer), Stürmerin die (PL die Stürmerinnen); **2** (person on strike) Streikende der/die (PL die Streikenden).

string noun **1** (for tying) Schnur die (PL die Schnüre); **2** (on a musical instrument) Saite die (PL die Saiten).

strip noun Streifen der (PL die Streifen).

strip verb **1** (undress) sich ausziehen❖ SEP; **2** (remove paint from) abbeizen SEP.

strip cartoon noun Comicstrip der (PL die Comicstrips).

stripe noun Streifen der (PL die Streifen).

striped adjective gestreift.

stroke noun **1** (style of swimming) Stil der (PL die Stile); **2** (medical) Schlaganfall der (PL die Schlaganfälle); **to have a stroke** einen Schlaganfall bekommen; ★ **a stroke of luck** ein Glücksfall; **to have a stroke of luck** Glück haben.

stroke verb streicheln.

strong adjective **1** (person, drink, feeling) stark; **2** (sturdy) stabil (furniture); **strong shoes** feste Schuhe.

strongly adverb **1** (believe, oppose) fest; **2** (support) nachdrücklich; **3** (advise, recommend) dringend; **4 she smelt strongly of garlic** sie hat stark nach Knoblauch gerochen.

struggle noun Kampf der (PL die Kämpfe); **the struggle for freedom** der Kampf für die Freiheit; **it's been a struggle** es war ein Kampf.

struggle verb **1** (to obtain something) kämpfen; **to struggle to do something** kämpfen, um etwas zu tun; **she struggled for a place** sie kämpfte um einen Platz; **2** (physically, in order to escape or reach something) sich wehren; **3** (have difficulty in doing something) sich abmühen SEP; **they are struggling to pay the rent** sie mühen sich ab, ihre Miete zu zahlen; **he's struggling with his homework** er müht sich mit seinen Hausaufgaben ab.

stub noun cigarette stub die Kippe.

● **to stub out** ausdrücken SEP.

stubborn adjective stur.

stuck adjective **1** (jammed) **it's stuck** es klemmt; **the drawer's stuck** die Schublade klemmt; **2 to get stuck** (person) stecken bleiben❖ (in a lift, traffic jam, or place).

stud noun **1** (on clothes) Niete die (PL die Nieten); **2** (on a boot) Stollen der

(PL die Stollen); **3** (earring) Ohrstecker der (PL die Ohrstecker).

student noun **1** (at college or university) Student der (PL die Studenten), Studentin die (PL die Studentinnen); **2** (at school) Schüler der (PL die Schüler), Schülerin die (PL die Schülerinnen).

studio noun **1** (film, TV) Studio das (PL die Studios); **2** (artist's) Atelier das (PL die Ateliers).

study verb **1** lernen; he's busy studying for his exams er lernt fleißig für seine Prüfung; **2** studieren; she's studying medicine sie studiert Medizin.

stuff noun (things, personal belongings) Zeug das (informal); we can put all that stuff in the attic wir können das ganze Zeug auf den Dachboden bringen; you can leave your stuff at my house du kannst dein Zeug bei mir lassen.

stuff verb **1** (shove) stopfen; she stuffed some things into a suitcase sie hat ein paar Sachen in einen Koffer gestopft; **2** füllen (vegetables, turkey); stuffed peppers gefüllte Paprikaschoten.

stuffing noun (in cooking) Füllung die (PL die Füllungen).

stuffy adjective (airless) stickig.

stumble verb stolpern (PERF sein).

stunned adjective sprachlos.

stunning adjective toll (informal).

stunt noun (in a film) Stunt der (PL die Stunts).

stuntman noun Stuntman der (PL die Stuntmen).

stupid adjective dumm; that was really stupid das war wirklich dumm; I did something stupid ich habe etwas Blödes gemacht.

stutter noun to have a stutter stottern.

stutter verb stottern.

style noun **1** Stil der (PL die Stile); style of living der Lebensstil; he has his own style er hat seinen eigenen Stil; **2** (fashion) Mode die; it's the latest style das ist die neueste Mode.

subject noun **1** Thema das (PL die Themen); the subject of my talk das Thema meiner Rede; **2** (at school) Fach das (PL die Fächer); my favourite subject is biology mein Lieblingsfach ist Biologie.

submarine noun Unterseeboot das (PL die Unterseeboote), U-Boot das (PL die U-Boote).

subscription noun Abonnement das (PL die Abonnements); to take out a subscription to a magazine eine Zeitschrift abonnieren.

subsidize verb subventionieren.

subsidy noun Subvention die (PL die Subventionen).

substance noun Substanz die (PL die Substanzen).

substitute noun (in sport) Ersatzspieler der (PL die Ersatzspieler), Ersatzspielerin die (PL die Ersatzspielerinnen).

substitute verb ersetzen.

subtitled adjective mit Untertiteln.

subtitles plural noun Untertitel (plural).

subtle adjective subtil.

subtract verb abziehen ⬧ SEP.

suburb noun Vorort der (PL die Vororte); a suburb of Edinburgh ein Vorort von Edinburgh; in the suburbs of London in den Londoner Vororten.

suburban adjective Vorort-; a suburban train ein Vorortzug.

subway noun (underpass) Unterführung die (PL die Unterführungen).

succeed verb gelingen ⬧ (PERF sein); we've succeeded in contacting her es ist uns gelungen, sie zu erreichen.

success noun Erfolg der (PL die Erfolge); a great success ein großer Erfolg.

successful adjective
1 erfolgreich; he's a successful writer er ist ein erfolgreicher Schriftsteller; 2 to be successful in doing something etwas mit Erfolg tun.

successfully adverb mit Erfolg.

such adjective, adverb 1 so; they're such nice people das sind so nette Leute; I've had such a busy day ich habe so einen hektischen Tag gehabt; it's such a long way es ist so weit; it's such a pity es ist so schade; 2 such a lot of (followed by a singular noun) so viel; they've got such a lot of money sie haben so viel Geld; 3 such a lot of (followed by a plural noun) so viele; she's got such a lot of problems sie hat so viele Probleme; 4 such as wie; in big cities such as Glasgow in großen Städten wie Glasgow; 5 there's no such thing so etwas gibt es nicht.

suck verb lutschen; to suck your thumb am Daumen lutschen.

sudden adjective plötzlich; ★ all of a sudden plötzlich.

suddenly adverb plötzlich; he suddenly started to laugh plötzlich hat er angefangen zu lachen; suddenly the light went out plötzlich ging das Licht aus.

suede noun Wildleder das; suede jacket die Wildlederjacke.

suffer verb leiden ⬧; to suffer from asthma an Asthma leiden.

sufficiently adverb genug.

sugar noun Zucker der; do you take sugar? nimmst du Zucker?

suggest verb vorschlagen ⬧ SEP; he suggested I should speak to you about it er hat vorgeschlagen, dass ich mit dir darüber sprechen soll.

suggestion noun Vorschlag der (PL die Vorschläge); to make a suggestion einen Vorschlag machen.

suicide noun Selbstmord der (PL die Selbstmorde); to commit suicide Selbstmord begehen.

suit noun 1 (man's) Anzug der (PL die Anzüge); 2 (woman's) Kostüm das (PL die Kostüme).

suit verb 1 (be convenient) passen (+ DAT); does Monday suit you? passt Ihnen Montag?; 2 (look good on) stehen ⬧ (+ DAT); hats suit her ihr stehen Hüte.

suitable adjective 1 geeignet; to be suitable for something für etwas geeignet sein; it's suitable for children es ist für Kinder geeignet; 2 (convenient) passend; at a suitable time zur passenden Zeit;

Saturday is the most suitable day for me Samstag passt mir am besten; **3** (*for a social occasion*) angemessen (*clothes*).

suitcase *noun* Koffer der (PL die Koffer).

sulk *verb* schmollen.

sum *noun* **1** Summe die (PL die Summen); **a sum of money** eine Geldsumme; **2** (*calculation*) Rechenaufgabe die (PL die Rechenaufgaben).

● **to sum up** zusammenfassen SEP.

summarize *verb* zusammenfassen SEP.

summary *noun* Zusammenfassung die (PL die Zusammenfassungen).

summer *noun* Sommer der (PL die Sommer); **in summer** im Sommer; **summer clothes** die Sommerkleidung; **the summer holidays** die Sommerferien.

summertime *noun* Sommer der; **in summertime** im Sommer.

summit *noun* Gipfel der (PL die Gipfel).

sun *noun* Sonne die (PL die Sonnen); **in the sun** in der Sonne.

sunbathe *verb* sich sonnen.

sunblock *noun* Sunblocker der (PL die Sunblocker).

sunburn *noun* Sonnenbrand der (PL die Sonnenbrände).

sunburned *adjective* **to get sunburned** einen Sonnenbrand bekommen.

Sunday *noun* **1** Sonntag der (PL die Sonntage); **on Sunday** am Sonntag; **I'm going to the cinema on Sunday** ich gehe (am) Sonntag ins Kino; **see you on Sunday!** bis Sonntag!; **every Sunday** jeden Sonntag; **last Sunday** vorigen Sonntag; **next Sunday** nächsten Sonntag; **2 on Sundays** sonntags; **the museum is closed on Sundays** das Museum ist sonntags geschlossen.

sunflower *noun* Sonnenblume die (PL die Sonnenblumen); **sunflower oil** das Sonnenblumenöl.

sunglasses *plural noun* Sonnenbrille die (PL die Sonnenbrillen).

sunlight *noun* Sonnenlicht das.

sunny *adjective* sonnig; **a sunny day** ein sonniger Tag; **sunny intervals** sonnige Abschnitte.

sunrise *noun* Sonnenaufgang der (PL die Sonnenaufgänge).

sunroof *noun* Schiebedach das (PL die Schiebedächer).

sunscreen *noun* Sonnenschutzcreme die (PL die Sonnenschutzcremes).

sunset *noun* Sonnenuntergang der (PL die Sonnenuntergänge).

sunshine *noun* Sonnenschein der.

sunstroke *noun* Sonnenstich der (PL die Sonnenstiche); **to get sunstroke** einen Sonnenstich bekommen.

suntan *noun* Bräune die; **to have a suntan** braun sein; **to get a suntan** braun werden.

suntan lotion *noun* Sonnenmilch die.

suntan oil *noun* Sonnenöl das.

super *adjective* klasse (*informal*) (*'klasse' never changes*); **we had a super time** es war wirklich klasse.

supermarket noun Supermarkt der (PL die Supermärkte).

supernatural adjective übernatürlich.

superstitious adjective abergläubisch.

supervise verb beaufsichtigen.

supervisor noun Aufseher der (PL die Aufseher), Aufseherin die (PL die Aufseherinnen).

supper noun Abendessen das (PL die Abendessen); **I had supper at Sandy's** ich war bei Sandy zum Abendessen.

supplement noun 1 (to newspaper) Beilage die (PL die Beilagen); 2 (to fare) Zuschlag der (PL die Zuschläge).

supplies plural noun Vorrat der (PL die Vorräte).

supply noun 1 (stock) Vorrat der (PL die Vorräte); 2 to be in short supply knapp sein.

supply verb 1 stellen; **the school supplies the books** die Schule stellt die Bücher; 2 (deliver) liefern; **to supply somebody with something** jemandem etwas liefern.

supply teacher noun Aushilfslehrer der (PL die Aushilfslehrer), Aushilfslehrerin die (PL die Aushilfslehrerinnen).

support noun Unterstützung die; **in support** zur Unterstützung.

support verb 1 (back up), unterstützen; **her teachers have really supported her** die Lehrer haben sie sehr unterstützt; **to support somebody financially** jemanden finanziell unterstützen;

2 **Will supports Chelsea** Will ist ein Chelsea-Fan; **what team do you support?** für welche Mannschaft bist du?; 3 (keep, provide for) ernähren; **to support a family** eine Familie ernähren.

supporter noun 1 Fan der (PL die Fans); **she's a Manchester United supporter** sie ist ein Manchester-United-Fan; 2 (of a party or cause) Anhänger der (PL die Anhänger), Anhängerin die (PL die Anhängerinnen).

suppose verb annehmen ✦ SEP; **I suppose she's forgotten** ich nehme an, sie hat es vergessen.

supposed adjective to be supposed to do something etwas tun sollen; **you were supposed to be here at six** du solltest um sechs hier sein.

sure adjective 1 sicher; **are you sure?** bist du sicher?; **are you sure you saw her?** bist du sicher, dass du sie gesehen hast?; 2 **sure!** klar!

surely adverb doch sicherlich; **surely she hasn't forgotten** sie hat es doch sicherlich nicht vergessen.

surf noun Surfen das,

surf verb **to surf the Net/Web** im Internet surfen.

surface noun Oberfläche die (PL die Oberflächen).

surfboard noun Surfbrett das (PL die Surfbretter).

surfer noun (on the sea and Internet) Surfer der (PL die Surfer), Surferin die (PL die Surferinnen).

surfing noun Surfen das.

surgeon noun Chirurg der (PL die Chirurgen), Chirurgin die (PL die Chirurginnen).

a b c d e f g h i j k l m n o p q r s t u v w x y z

surgery noun **1** to have surgery operiert werden; **2** (doctor's) Praxis die (PL die Praxen); **the dentist's surgery** die Zahnarztpraxis; **3** (surgery hours) Sprechstunde die.

surname noun Nachname der (PL die Nachnamen).

surprise noun Überraschung die (PL die Überraschungen); **what a surprise!** was für eine Überraschung!

surprised adjective überrascht; **I was surprised to see her** ich war überrascht, sie zu sehen.

surprising adjective überraschend.

surround verb umgeben; **surrounded by** umgeben von (+ DAT); **she was surrounded by friends** sie war von Freunden umgeben.

survey noun Umfrage die (PL die Umfragen).

survive verb überleben.

survivor noun Überlebende der/die (PL die Überlebenden).

suspect noun Verdächtige der/die (PL die Verdächtigen).

suspect adjective verdächtig.

suspect verb verdächtigen.

suspend verb **1** to be suspended (from school) vom Unterricht ausgeschlossen werden; **2** (from a team) sperren; **to suspend a player for four weeks** einen Spieler für vier Wochen sperren.

suspense noun Spannung die.

suspicious adjective **1** misstrauisch; **to be suspicious of somebody** jemandem

misstrauen; **2** (suspicious looking) verdächtig.

swallow noun (bird) Schwalbe die (PL die Schwalben).

swallow verb schlucken.

swan noun Schwan der (PL die Schwäne.

swap verb tauschen; **do you want to swap?** willst du tauschen?; **he swapped his bike for a computer** er hat sein Rad gegen einen Computer getauscht; **we swapped seats** wir tauschten die Plätze.

swear verb (use bad language) fluchen.

swearword noun Kraftausdruck der (PL die Kraftausdrücke).

sweat noun Schweiß der.

sweat verb schwitzen.

sweater noun Pullover der (PL die Pullover).

Swede noun Schwede der (PL die Schweden), Schwedin die (PL die Schwedinnen).

swede noun Kohlrübe die (PL die Kohlrüben).

Sweden noun Schweden das; **from Sweden** aus Schweden; **to Sweden** nach Schweden.

Swedish noun (the language) Schwedisch das.

Swedish adjective schwedisch; **he's Swedish** er ist Schwede; **she's Swedish** sie ist Schwedin.

sweep verb fegen.

sweet noun **1** Bonbon der (PL die Bonbons); **2** (dessert) Nachtisch der (PL die Nachtische).

sweet adjective **1** süß; **I try not to eat sweet things** ich versuche nichts Süßes zu essen; **she looks**

really sweet in that hat mit dem Hut sieht sie richtig süß aus; **2** (*kind*) lieb; **she's a really sweet person** sie ist wirklich ein sehr lieber Mensch; **how sweet of him** wie lieb von ihm.

sweetcorn *noun* Mais *der.*

swell *verb* (*part of the body*) anschwellen✧ SEP (PERF *sein*).

swelling *noun* Schwellung *die* (PL *die* Schwellungen).

swim *noun* **to go for a swim** schwimmen gehen✧ (PERF *sein*).

swim *verb* schwimmen✧ (PERF *sein*); **can he swim?** kann er schwimmen?; **to swim across a lake** an die gegenüberliegende Seite des Sees schwimmen.

swimmer *noun* Schwimmer *der* (PL *die* Schwimmer), Schwimmerin *die* (PL *die* Schwimmerinnen); **she's a strong swimmer** sie ist eine gute Schwimmerin.

swimming *noun* Schwimmen *das*; **to go swimming** schwimmen gehen✧.

swimming cap *noun* Badekappe *die* (PL *die* Badekappen).

swimming costume *noun* Badeanzug *der* (PL *die* Badeanzüge).

swimming pool *noun* Schwimmbecken *das* (PL *die* Schwimmbecken).

swimming trunks *noun* Badehose *die* (PL *die* Badehosen).

swimsuit *noun* Badeanzug *der* (PL *die* Badeanzüge).

swindle *noun* Betrug *der* (PL *die* Betrüge); **what a swindle!** was für ein Betrug!

swindle *verb* betrügen.

swing *noun* Schaukel *die* (PL *die* Schaukeln).

Swiss *noun* (*person*) Schweizer *der* (PL *die* Schweizer), Schweizerin *die* (PL *die* Schweizerinnen); **the Swiss** die Schweizer.

Swiss *adjective* schweizerisch; **she is Swiss** sie ist Schweizerin.

switch *noun* (*for a light, radio, etc.*) Schalter *der* (PL *die* Schalter).

switch *verb* (*change*) wechseln; **to switch places** die Plätze wechseln.

● **to switch something off** etwas ausschalten SEP.

● **to switch something on** etwas anschalten SEP.

Switzerland *noun* die Schweiz; **from Switzerland** aus der Schweiz; **in Switzerland** in der Schweiz; **to Switzerland** in die Schweiz.

swollen *adjective* geschwollen.

swop *verb* SEE **swap.**

sword *noun* Schwert *das* (PL *die* Schwerter).

syllabus *noun* Lehrplan *der* (PL *die* Lehrpläne); **to be on the syllabus** auf dem Lehrplan stehen.

symbol *noun* Symbol *das* (PL *die* Symbole).

symbolic *adjective* symbolisch.

sympathetic *adjective* verständnisvoll.

sympathize *verb* **to sympathize with somebody** mit jemandem mitfühlen SEP; **I sympathize with you** ich kann mit Ihnen mitfühlen.

sympathy *noun* Mitleid *das.*

symphony *noun* Sinfonie *die* (PL *die* Sinfonien).

a b c d e f g h i j k l m n o p q r s t u v w x y z

symptom noun Symptom das (PL die Symptome).

synagogue noun Synagoge die (PL die Synagogen).

synthesizer noun Synthesizer der (PL die Synthesizer).

synthetic adjective synthetisch.

syringe noun Spritze die (PL die Spritzen).

system noun System das (PL die Systeme).

Tt

table noun Tisch der (PL die Tische); **to lay the table** den Tisch decken; **to clear the table** den Tisch abräumen SEP.

tablecloth noun Tischdecke die (PL die Tischdecken).

tablespoon noun Esslöffel der (PL die Esslöffel); **a tablespoon of flour** ein Esslöffel Mehl.

table tennis noun Tischtennis das.

tablet noun Tablette die (PL die Tabletten).

tackle verb 1 (in football or hockey) angreifen◇ SEP; 2 angehen◇ SEP (PERF sein) (a job or a problem).

tact noun Takt der.

tactful adjective taktvoll; **that wasn't very tactful** das war nicht sehr taktvoll.

tadpole noun Kaulquappe die (PL die Kaulquappen).

tail noun 1 Schwanz der (PL die Schwänze); 2 'heads or tails?' — 'tails' 'Kopf oder Zahl?'— 'Zahl'.

take verb 1 nehmen◇; **he took a sweet** er nahm einen Bonbon; **take my hand** nimm meine Hand; **I took the bus** ich habe den Bus genommen; **do you take sugar?** nimmst du Zucker?; 2 (with time) dauern; **it takes two hours** es dauert zwei Stunden; 3 (react to) aufnehmen◇ SEP; **he took the news calmly** er hat die Nachricht gelassen aufgenommen; 4 (take to a place) bringen◇; **I'm taking Jake to my parents** ich bringe Jake zu meinen Eltern; **I must take the car to the garage** ich muss das Auto in die Werkstatt bringen; **to take somebody home** jemanden nach Hause bringen; 5 **to take something up(stairs)** etwas hinaufbringen◇ SEP; **could you take the towels up?** könntest du die Handtücher heraufbringen?; 6 **to take something down(stairs)** etwas hinunterbringen◇ SEP; **Cheryl's taken the cups down** Cheryl hat die Tassen heruntergebracht; 7 (carry with you) mitnehmen◇ SEP; **she's taken some of the files home** sie hat einige der Akten mit nach Hause genommen; **I'm taking my Walkman** ich nehme meinen Walkman mit; **I'll take him next time** nächstes Mal nehme ich ihn mit; 8 nehmen◇ SEP (a credit card or a cheque); **do you take cheques?** nehmen Sie Schecks?; 9 machen (an exam, a holiday, or a photo); **she's taking her driving test tomorrow** sie macht morgen ihre Fahrprüfung; **to take a holiday** Ferien machen; 10 (need) brauchen; **it takes a lot of courage** dazu braucht man viel Mut; **it takes me at least two hours to read it** ich brauche mindestens zwei Stunden, um es zu lesen; **11 take**◇ (*clothes size*); **what size do you take?** welche Größe haben Sie?

● **to take something apart** etwas auseinander nehmen◇.

● **to take something back** etwas zurückbringen◇ SEP.

● **to take off 1** (*plane*) abfliegen◇ SEP (PERF *sein*); **2** ausziehen◇ SEP (*clothes, shoes*); **take your jacket off** zieh die Jacke aus; **to take your clothes off** sich ausziehen; **3** abziehen◇ SEP (*money*); **he took five pounds off the price** er hat fünf Pfund vom Preis abgezogen.

● **to take out something** (*from a bag or pocket*) etwas herausnehmen◇ SEP; **Eric took out his wallet** Eric nahm seine Brieftasche heraus.

● **to take somebody out** jemanden ausführen SEP; **to take somebody out for a meal** jemanden zum Essen in ein Restaurant einladen◇ SEP.

takeaway *noun* **1** (*meal*) Essen zum Mitnehmen *das* (PL *die* Essen zum Mitnehmen); **an Indian takeaway** ein indisches Essen zum Mitnehmen; **2** (*where you buy it*) Restaurant mit Straßenverkauf *das* (PL *die* Restaurants mit Straßenverkauf).

take-off *noun* (*of a plane*) Abflug *der* (PL *die* Abflüge).

talent *noun* Talent *das* (PL *die* Talente); **to have a talent for painting** ein Talent zum Malen haben.

talented *adjective* talentiert; **he's really talented** er ist wirklich talentiert.

talk *noun* **1** (*a chat*) Gespräch *das* (PL *die* Gespräche); **we had a serious talk about it** wir hatten ein ernstes Gespräch darüber; **2** Vortrag *der* (PL *die* Vorträge); **she's giving a talk on Hungary** sie hält einen Vortrag über Ungarn.

talk *verb* **1** reden; **to talk to somebody** mit jemandem reden; **we talked about football** wir haben über Fußball geredet; **what's he talking about?** wovon redet er?; **we'll talk about it later** darüber reden wir später; **they're always talking** sie reden immer; **2 to talk to somebody on the phone** mit jemandem telefonieren.

tall *adjective* **1** groß; **she's very tall** sie ist sehr groß; **I'm 1.7 metres tall** ich bin ein Meter siebzig groß; **2** hoch (*building or tree*).

tame *adjective* zahm.

tampon *noun* Tampon *der* (PL *die* Tampons).

tan *noun* Bräune *die*; **to have a tan** braun sein; **to get a tan** braun werden.

tank *noun* **1** (*for petrol or water*) Tank *der* (PL *die* Tanks); **2** (*for fish*) Aquarium *das* (PL *die* Aquarien); **3** (*military*) Panzer *der* (PL *die* Panzer).

tanker *noun* **1** (*on sea*) Tanker *der* (PL *die* Tanker); **2** (*on the road*) Tankwagen *der* (PL *die* Tankwagen).

a b c d e f g h i j k l m n o p q r s t u v w x y z

tanned *adjective* braun.

tap *noun* Wasserhahn *der* (PL die Wasserhähne); **to turn on the tap** den Wasserhahn aufdrehen SEP; **to turn off the tap** den Wasserhahn zudrehen SEP; **the hot tap** der Warmwasserhahn.

tap *verb* klopfen; **to tap on the door** an die Tür klopfen.

tap-dancing *noun* Stepptanzen *das*.

tape *noun* **1** Kassette *die* (PL die Kassetten); **my tape of the Stones** meine Kassette von den Stones; **I've got it on tape** ich habe es auf Kassette; **2 sticky tape** *der* Klebestreifen.

tape *verb* aufnehmen ✧ SEP; **I want to tape the film** ich will den Film aufnehmen.

tape measure *noun* Metermaß *das* (PL die Metermaße).

tape recorder *noun* Tonbandgerät *das* (PL die Tonbandgeräte).

tapestry *noun* Wandteppich *der* (PL die Wandteppiche).

target *noun* Ziel *das* (PL die Ziele).

tart *noun* Kuchen *der* (PL die Kuchen); **apple tart** der Apfelkuchen.

tartan *adjective* Schotten-; **a tartan skirt** ein Schottenrock.

task *noun* Aufgabe *die* (PL die Aufgaben).

taste *noun* **1** Geschmack *der* (PL die Geschmäcke); **a taste of onions** ein Zwiebelgeschmack; **she's got no taste** sie hat keinen Geschmack; **2 in bad taste** geschmacklos.

taste *verb* **1** schmecken; **the soup tastes horrible** die Suppe schmeckt furchtbar; **2 to taste of something** nach etwas (DAT) schmecken; **it tastes of garlic** es schmeckt nach Knoblauch; **3** (*try a little*) probieren; **do you want to taste?** möchtest du mal probieren?

tasty *adjective* schmackhaft.

tattoo *noun* Tätowierung *die* (PL die Tätowierungen); **he's got a tattoo on his arm** er hat eine Tätowierung am Arm.

Taurus *noun* Stier *der*; **Josephine's Taurus** Josephine ist (ein) Stier.

tax *noun* Steuer *die* (PL die Steuern) (*on goods, income*).

taxi *noun* Taxi *das* (PL die Taxis); **to go by taxi** mit dem Taxi fahren; **to take a taxi** ein Taxi nehmen.

taxi driver *noun* Taxifahrer *der* (PL die Taxifahrer), Taxifahrerin *die* (PL die Taxifahrerinnen).

taxi rank *noun* Taxistand *der* (PL die Taxistände).

tea *noun* **1** Tee *der* (PL die Tees); **a cup of tea** eine Tasse Tee; **to have tea** Tee trinken; **2** (*evening meal*) Abendessen *das* (PL die Abendessen).

teabag *noun* Teebeutel *der* (PL die Teebeutel).

teach *verb* **1** beibringen ✧ SEP; **she's teaching me to drive** sie bringt mir das Autofahren bei; **2 to teach yourself something** sich (DAT) etwas beibringen ✧ SEP; **I taught myself Italian** ich habe mir Italienisch beigebracht; **3 that'll teach you!** das wird dir eine Lehre sein!; **4** unterrichten; **her mum**

teaches maths ihre Mutter unterrichtet Mathematik.

teacher noun Lehrer der (PL die Lehrer), Lehrerin die (PL die Lehrerinnen).

teaching noun Unterrichten das.

team noun Mannschaft die (PL die Mannschaften); **football team** die Fußballmannschaft.

teapot noun Teekanne die (PL die Teekannen).

tear¹ noun (a rip) Riss der (PL die Risse).

tear verb 1 zerreißen◇; **she tore up my letter** sie hat meinen Brief zerrissen; 2 reißen◇ (PERF sein); **the net has torn** das Netz ist gerissen; **be careful, it tears easily** sei vorsichtig, es reißt leicht.

tear² noun (when you cry) Träne die (PL die Tränen); **to be in tears** in Tränen aufgelöst sein; **to burst into tears** in Tränen ausbrechen.

tease verb 1 necken (a person); 2 quälen (an animal).

teaspoon noun Teelöffel der (PL die Teelöffel); **a teaspoon of vinegar** ein Teelöffel Essig.

teatime noun (evening meal) Abendessenszeit die; **it's teatime!** es gibt Abendessen!

tea towel noun Geschirrtuch das (PL die Geschirrtücher).

technical adjective technisch.

technical college noun Fachhochschule die (PL die Fachhochschulen).

technician noun Techniker der (PL die Techniker), Technikerin die (PL die Technikerinnen).

technique noun Technik die (PL die Techniken).

techno noun (music) Techno der.

technological adjective technologisch.

technology noun 1 Technologie die; 2 **information technology** die Informatik.

teddy bear noun Teddybär der (PL die Teddybären).

teenage adjective 1 Teenage-; 2 **they have a teenage son** sie haben einen Sohn im Teenageralter; 3 (films, magazines, etc.) für Teenager; **a teenage magazine** eine Jugendzeitschrift.

teenager noun Teenager der (PL die Teenager); **a group of teenagers** eine Gruppe von Teenagern.

teens plural noun **the teens** die Teenagerjahre; **he's in his teens** er ist ein Teenager.

tee-shirt noun T-Shirt das (PL die T-Shirts).

telephone noun Telefon das (PL die Telefone); **on the telephone** am Telefon.

telephone verb anrufen◇ SEP; **I'll telephone the bank** ich rufe die Bank an.

telephone box noun Telefonzelle die (PL die Telefonzellen).

telephone call noun Telefongespräch das (PL die Telefongespräche).

telephone directory noun Telefonbuch das (PL die Telefonbücher).

telephone number noun Telefonnummer die (PL die Telefonnummern).

telescope noun Fernrohr das (PL die Fernrohre), Teleskop das (PL die Teleskope).

a
b
c
d
e
f
g
h
i
j
k
l
m
n
o
p
q
r
s
t
u
v
w
x
y
z

televise verb im Fernsehen übertragen◇; **they're televising the match** sie übertragen das Spiel im Fernsehen.

television noun 1 Fernsehen das; **I saw it on television** ich habe es im Fernsehen gesehen; 2 **to watch television** fernsehen◇ SEP; **I'm watching television** ich sehe fern.

television programme noun Fernsehsendung die (PL die Fernsehsendungen).

tell verb 1 sagen; **to tell somebody something** jemandem etwas sagen; **if she asks, tell her** sag's ihr, wenn sie fragt; 2 **to tell somebody to do something** jemandem sagen, er/sie soll etwas tun; **he told me to do it myself** er hat mir gesagt, ich soll es selbst machen; **she told me not to wait** sie sagte mir, ich solle nicht warten; 3 (explain) **can you tell me how to do it?** kannst du mir sagen, wie man das macht? 4 erzählen (a story); **tell me about your holiday** erzähl mir von deinen Ferien; 5 (to see) sehen◇; **you can tell it's old** man sieht, dass es alt ist; **I can't tell them apart** ich kann sie nicht unterscheiden.

telly noun 1 (set) Fernseher der (PL die Fernseher); 2 **to watch telly** fernsehen◇ SEP; **I saw her on telly** ich habe sie im Fernsehen gesehen.

temp noun Aushilfskraft die (PL die Aushilfskräfte).

temper noun **to lose your temper** wütend werden.

temperature noun 1 Temperatur die (PL die Temperaturen); **what is the temperature?** wie viel Grad sind es? 2 **to have a temperature** Fieber haben.

temporary adjective vorübergehend.

temptation noun Versuchung die (PL die Versuchungen).

tempted adjective versucht; **I'm really tempted to come** ich würde am liebsten kommen.

tempting adjective verlockend.

ten number zehn; **Harry's ten** Harry ist zehn.

tend verb **to tend to do something** dazu neigen, etwas zu tun.

tender adjective 1 (loving) zärtlich; 2 (painful) empfindlich.

tennis noun Tennis das; **to play tennis** Tennis spielen.

tennis ball noun Tennisball der (PL die Tennisbälle).

tennis court noun Tennisplatz der (PL die Tennisplätze).

tennis player noun Tennisspieler der (PL die Tennisspieler), Tennisspielerin die (PL die Tennisspielerinnen).

tennis racket noun Tennisschläger der (PL die Tennisschläger).

tenor noun Tenor der (PL die Tenöre).

tenpin bowling noun Bowling das.

tense noun Zeit die; **the present tense** das Präsens; **in the future tense** im Futur.

tense adjective gespannt.

tent noun Zelt das (PL die Zelte).

tenth number zehnter/zehnte/zehntes; **on the tenth floor** im zehnten Stock; **the tenth of April** der zehnte April.

term noun 1 (in school) Halbjahr das (PL die Halbjahre), (at university) Semester das (PL die Semester).

terminal noun 1 (at an airport) Terminal der (PL die Terminals); 2 **bus terminal** die Endstation; 3 (computer terminal) Terminal das (PL die Terminals).

terrace noun 1 (outside a house) Terrasse die (PL die Terrassen); 2 (row of houses) Häuserreihe die (PL die Häuserreihen); 3 **the terraces** (at a stadium) die Ränge (plural).

terrible adjective furchtbar.

terribly adverb 1 (very) sehr; **not terribly clean** nicht sehr sauber; 2 (badly) furchtbar; **I played terribly** ich habe furchtbar gespielt.

terrific adjective 1 irre (informal); **a terrific amount** eine irre Menge; 2 **terrific!** super! (informal).

terrified adjective verängstigt; **to be terrified** furchtbare Angst haben.

terrorism noun Terrorismus der.

terrorist noun Terrorist der (PL die Terroristen), Terroristin der (PL die Terroristinnen).

test noun 1 (in school) Klassenarbeit die (PL die Klassenarbeiten); **we've got a maths test tomorrow** wir schreiben morgen eine Mathearbeit; 2 (medical check,

trial) Test der (PL die Tests); **eye test** der Sehtest; **blood test** die Blutprobe; 3 **driving test** die Fahrprüfung; **she's taking her driving test on Friday** sie macht am Freitag ihre Fahrprüfung; **he passed his driving test** er hat seine Fahrprüfung bestanden.

test verb (in school) prüfen; **can you test me?** kannst du mich abfragen?

test tube noun Reagenzglas das (PL die Reagenzgläser).

text noun Text der (PL die Texte).

textbook noun Lehrbuch das (PL die Lehrbücher).

text message noun SMS die (PL die SMS).

Thames noun the Thames die Themse.

than conjunction als; **they have more money than we do** sie haben mehr Geld als wir; **more than forty** mehr als vierzig; **more than thirty years** mehr als dreißig Jahre.

thank verb 1 **to thank somebody for something** sich bei jemandem für etwas (ACC) bedanken; 2 **thank you** danke; **thank you for looking after the children** danke, dass du auf die Kinder aufgepasst hast.

thanks plural noun 1 Dank der; **thanks a lot!** vielen Dank!; **many thanks** vielen Dank; 2 **no thanks** nein danke; **thanks for your letter** danke für deinen Brief; 3 **thanks to** dank (+ DAT); **it was thanks to him that we made it** dank ihm haben wir es geschafft.

thank you *adverb* danke; **thank you very much for the cheque** herzlichen Dank für den Scheck; **no thank you** nein danke; **a thank-you letter** ein Dankbrief.

that *adjective* **1** dieser/diese/dieses; **that boy** dieser Junge; **that woman** diese Frau; **that house** dieses Haus; **2** that one der da/die da/das da; **'which cake would you like?' – 'that one, please'** 'welchen Kuchen möchten Sie?' – 'den da, bitte; **I like all the dresses but I'm going to buy that one** mir gefallen alle Kleider, aber ich kaufe das da.

that *adverb* so; **it's not that easy** es ist nicht so einfach.

that *pronoun* **1** das; **what's that?** was ist das?; **who's that?** wer ist das?; **where's that?** wo ist das?; **is that Mandy?** ist das Mandy?; **2** das; **did you see that?** hast du das gesehen?; **that's my bedroom** das ist mein Schlafzimmer; **3** (*in relative clauses*) der/die/das (*depending on the gender of the noun 'that' refers to*); **the train that's leaving now** der Zug, der jetzt abfährt; **the flower that I picked** die Blume, die ich gepflückt habe; **the car that's red** das Auto, das rot ist.

that *conjunction* dass; **I knew that he was lying** ich wußte, dass er log.

the *definite article* **1** der/die/das (*the article changes according to the gender of the noun*); (*before a masculine noun*) **the dog** der Hund; (*before a feminine noun*) **the cat** die Katze; (*before a neuter noun*) **the car** das Auto; **2** (*before all plural*

nouns) die; **the windows** die Fenster.

theatre *noun* Theater *das* (PL die Theater); **to go to the theatre** ins Theater gehen.

theft *noun* Diebstahl *der* (PL die Diebstähle).

their *adjective* ihr, (*plural*) ihre; **their son** ihr Sohn; **their daughter** ihre Tochter; **their car** ihr Auto; **their presents** ihre Geschenke.

theirs *pronoun* **1** ihrer (*when standing for a masculine noun*); **our garden's smaller than theirs** unser Garten ist kleiner als ihrer; **2** ihre (*when standing for a feminine noun*); **your flat is bigger than theirs** deine Wohnung ist größer als ihre; **3** ihrs (*when standing for a neuter noun*); **our car was cheaper than theirs** unser Auto war billiger als ihrs; **4** ihre (*when standing for a plural noun*); **our children are older than theirs** unsere Kinder sind älter als ihre; **5 the yellow car's theirs** das gelbe Auto gehört ihnen; **it's theirs** das gehört ihnen.

them *pronoun* **1** (*as a direct object in the accusative*) sie; **I know them** ich kenne sie; **I don't know them** ich kenne sie nicht; **2** (*after prepositions + ACC*) sie; **it's for them** das ist für sie; **3** (*as an indirect object or following a verb that takes the dative*) ihnen; **I told them a story** ich habe ihnen eine Geschichte erzählt; **4** (*to them*) ihnen; **I gave them my address** ich habe ihnen meine Adresse gegeben; **5** (*after prepositions + DAT*) ihnen; **I'll go with them** ich gehe mit ihnen mit; **6** (in comparisons) he's older than them er ist älter als sie.

theme noun Thema das (PL die Themen).

theme park noun Themenpark der (PL die Themenparks).

themselves pronoun **1** sich; **they** enjoyed themselves sie haben sich amüsiert; **2** (for emphasis) selbst; **the boys can do it themselves** die Jungen können es selbst machen.

then adverb **1** (next) dann; **I get up and then I make the bed** ich stehe auf und dann mache ich das Bett; **I went to the post office and then the bank** ich bin zur Post und dann auf die Bank gegangen; **2** (at that time) damals; **we were living in York then** wir haben damals in York gewohnt; **3** (in that case) dann; **then why worry?** warum machst du dir dann Sorgen?; **4** since then seitdem; **5** from then on von da an.

theory noun **1** Theorie die (PL die Theorien); **2** in theory theoretisch.

there adverb **1** (in a fixed location) da; **up there** da oben; **down there** da unten; **in there** da drin; **stay there** bleib da; **2** over there da drüben; **she's over there with Mark** sie ist da drüben mit Mark; **3** (with movement to a place) dahin; **put it there** leg es dahin; **we're going there on Tuesday** wir fahren am Dienstag dahin; **4** (further away) dort; **I've seen photos of Oxford but I've never been there** ich habe Fotos von Oxford gesehen, aber ich war noch

nie dort; **5** there is (there exists) da ist, es ist; **there's a cat in the garden** da ist eine Katze im Garten; **there's enough bread** es ist genug Brot da; **no, there's not enough** nein, es ist nicht genug da; **there is es gibt; there's only one hospital in this town** in dieser Stadt gibt es nur ein Krankenhaus; **there are** da sind, es sind; **there were lots of people in town** es waren viele Leute in der Stadt; **there are** (there exist) es gibt; **there are lots of museums here** es gibt hier viele Museen; **9** (when drawing attention) da; **there they are!** da sind sie!; **there's the bus coming!** da kommt der Bus!

therefore adverb deshalb.

thermometer noun Thermometer das (PL die Thermometer).

these adjective diese; **these glasses** diese Gläser.

these pronoun die; **these are cheaper** die sind billiger.

they pronoun **1** sie; **'where are the knives?' – 'they're in the drawer'** 'wo sind die Messer?' – 'sie sind in der Schublade'; **2** man; **they say** man sagt.

thick adjective dick; **a thick layer of butter** eine dicke Schicht Butter.

thief noun Dieb der (PL die Diebe), Diebin die (PL die Diebinnen).

thigh noun Oberschenkel der (PL die Oberschenkel).

thin adjective dünn.

thing noun **1** (an object) Ding das (PL die Dinge); **they have lots of**

a b c d e f g h i j k l m n o p q r s t u v w x y z

nice things sie haben viele schöne Dinge; **she told me some strange things** sie hat mir ein paar seltsame Dinge erzählt; **that thing next to the hammer** das Ding da neben dem Hammer; **2 things** (*belongings*) Sachen (*plural*); **you can leave your things in my room** du kannst deine Sachen in meinem Zimmer lassen; **3 the best thing to do is ...** am besten wäre es ...; **4** (*subject, affair*) Sache *die* (PL *die* Sachen); **the thing is, I've lost her address** ist die, ich habe ihre Adresse verloren; **5 how are things?** wie geht's?

think *verb* **1** (*believe*) glauben; **do you think they'll come?** glaubst du, sie kommen?; **no, I don't think so** nein, ich glaube nicht; **I think so** ich glaube schon; **I think he's already paid** ich glaube, er hat schon gezahlt; **2** denken◇; **I'm thinking about you** ich denke an dich; **what are you thinking about?** woran denkst du?; **3 what do you think of that?** was halten Sie davon?; **I don't think much of her proposal** ich halte nicht viel von ihrem Vorschlag; **4 what do you think of my new jacket?** wie findest du meine neue Jacke?; **5** (*remember*) **to think to do something** daran denken, etwas zu tun; **he didn't think of locking the door** er hat nicht daran gedacht, die Tür abzuschließen; **6** (*to think carefully*) nachdenken◇ SEP; **he thought for a moment** er hat einen Moment lang nachgedacht; **think about it!** denk darüber nach!; **7 I've**

thought it over carefully ich habe es mir genau überlegt; **8** (*imagine*) sich (DAT) vorstellen SEP; **just think, we'll soon be in Spain!** stell dir vor, bald sind wir in Spanien!; **I never thought it would be like this** so habe ich es nie vorgestellt, dass es so sein würde.

third *noun* Drittel *das* (PL *die* Drittel); **a third of the population** ein Drittel der Bevölkerung.

third *adjective* dritter/dritte/ drittes; **on the third floor** im dritten Stock; **on the third of March** am dritten März.

thirdly *adverb* drittens.

Third World *noun* Dritte Welt *die*.

thirst *noun* Durst *der*.

thirsty *adjective* durstig; **to be thirsty** Durst haben; **I'm thirsty** ich habe Durst; **we were all thirsty** wir hatten alle Durst.

thirteen *number* dreizehn; **Ahmed's thirteen** Ahmed ist dreizehn.

thirty *number* dreißig.

this *adjective* **1** dieser/diese/ dieses; **this boy** dieser Junge; **this flower** diese Blume; **this car** dieses Auto; **at the end of this week** Ende dieser Woche; **2 this morning** heute Morgen; **this evening** heute Abend; **this afternoon** heute Nachmittag; **this one** der/die/ das, (*with more emphasis*) dieser/ diese/dieses; **if you need a pen** you can have this one wenn du einen Kugelschreiber brauchst, kannst du den haben; **I'll take this one** ich nehme diesen.

this *pronoun* **1** das; **can you hold this?** kannst du das festhalten?; **what's this?** was ist das?; **2 this is my sister Carla** (*in introductions*) das ist meine Schwester Carla; **3 this is Tracy speaking** (*on the phone*) hier spricht Tracy.

thistle *noun* Distel die (PL die Disteln).

thorn *noun* Dorn der (PL die Dornen).

those *adjective* diese; **those books** diese Bücher.

those *pronoun* die da; **if you need more knives you can take those** wenn du mehr Messer brauchst, kannst du die da nehmen.

though *conjunction* obwohl; **though it's cold** obwohl es kalt ist.

though *adverb* dennoch; **it was a good idea, though** es war dennoch eine gute Idee.

thought *noun* Gedanke der (PL die Gedanken).

thousand *number* **1** tausend; **a thousand** eintausend; **three thousand** dreitausend; **2 thousands of** Tausende von; **there were thousands of tourists in Venice** Tausende von Touristen waren in Venedig.

thread *noun* Faden der (PL die Fäden).

thread *verb* einfädeln (*a needle*).

threat *noun* Drohung die (PL die Drohungen); **is that a threat?** soll das eine Drohung sein?

threaten *verb* drohen (+ DAT); **he threatened her** er hat ihr gedroht;

to threaten to do something damit drohen, etwas zu tun.

three *number* drei; **Oskar's three** Oskar ist drei.

three-quarters *noun* drei Viertel die.

three-quarters *adverb* **three-quarters full** drei viertel voll.

thrilled *adjective* **to be thrilled** sich wahnsinnig freuen.

thriller *noun* Thriller der (PL die Thriller).

thrilling *adjective* spannend.

throat *noun* Hals der (PL die Hälse); **to have a sore throat** Halsschmerzen haben.

through *preposition* **1** (*across, via*) durch (+ ACC); **through the forest** durch den Wald; **the train goes through Leeds** der Zug fährt durch Leeds; **through the window** durch das Fenster; **2 to let somebody through** jemanden durchlassen ✧ SEP; **the police let us through** die Polizei ließ uns durch; **3 I know them through my cousin** ich kenne sie über meinen Vetter.

throw *verb* **1** werfen ✧; **I threw the letter in the bin** ich habe den Brief in den Mülleimer geworfen; **2 to throw something to somebody** jemandem etwas zuwerfen ✧ SEP; **throw me the ball** wirf mir den Ball zu; **to throw something at somebody** etwas nach jemandem werfen.

• **to throw something away** etwas wegwerfen ✧ SEP; **I'm throwing away the old newspapers** ich werfe die alten

Zeitungen weg.

- **to throw somebody out** jemanden rauswerfen ◇ SEP.
- **to throw something out** etwas wegwerfen ◇ SEP (*rubbish*).

thumb noun Daumen der (PL die Daumen).

thump verb schlagen ◇, auf (+ ACC); **he thumped the radio to see if it would work** er schlug auf das Radio, um zu sehen ob es dann funktionierte.

thunder noun Donner der; **peal of thunder** der Donnerschlag.

thunderstorm noun Gewitter das (PL die Gewitter).

thundery adjective gewittrig.

Thursday noun 1 Donnerstag der (PL die Donnerstage); **on Thursday** (am) Donnerstag; **I'm leaving on Thursday** ich fahre am Donnerstag ab; **see you on Thursday** bis Donnerstag; **every Thursday** jeden Donnerstag; **last Thursday** vorigen Donnerstag; **next Thursday** nächsten Donnerstag; 2 **on Thursdays** donnerstags; **the museum is closed on Thursdays** das Museum ist donnerstags geschlossen.

thyme noun Thymian der.

tick verb 1 (*clock, watch*) ticken; 2 (*on paper*) abhaken SEP.

ticket noun 1 (*for an exhibition, theatre, or cinema*) Karte die (PL die Karten); **two tickets for the concert** zwei Karten für das Konzert; 2 (*for the underground, a bus, or a train*) Fahrkarte die (PL die Fahrkarten); **a plane ticket** ein Flugschein, ein Ticket; 3 (*for left luggage, parking*) Zettel der (PL die Zettel); 4 (*for a lottery or raffle*) Los das (PL die Lose); 5 **parking ticket** der Strafzettel.

ticket inspector noun Schaffner der (PL die Schaffner), Schaffnerin die (PL die Schaffnerinnen).

ticket office noun (*at a station*) Fahrkartenschalter der (PL die Fahrkartenschalter).

tickle verb kitzeln.

tide noun 1 (*high*) Flut die (Fluten); **at high tide** bei Flut; 2 (*low*) Ebbe die (PL die Ebben); **the tide is out** es ist Ebbe.

tidy adjective ordentlich.

tidy verb aufräumen SEP; **I'll tidy (up) the kitchen** ich räume die Küche auf.

tie noun 1 (*necktie*) Krawatte die (PL die Krawatten); 2 (*in a match*) Unentschieden das.

tie verb 1 binden ◇; **to tie your shoelaces** sich (DAT) die Schnürsenkel binden; 2 **to tie a knot in something** einen Knoten in etwas (ACC) machen; 3 (*in a match*) **we tied two all** wir haben zwei zu zwei gespielt.

tiger noun Tiger der (PL die Tiger).

tight adjective (*close-fitting*) eng; **the skirt's a bit tight** der Rock ist etwas eng; **these shoes are too tight** diese Schuhe sind zu eng; **she was wearing tight jeans** sie hatte enge Jeans an.

tighten verb anziehen ◇ SEP (*a screw, knot*); **he tightened his belt** er schnallte seinen Gürtel enger;

he tightened his grip er griff fester zu.

tightly *adverb* fest.

tights *plural noun* Strumpfhose die (PL die Strumpfhosen); **a pair of purple tights** eine lila Strumpfhose.

tile *noun* **1** (*on a floor*) Fliese die (PL die Fliesen); **2** (*on a wall*) Kachel die (PL die Kacheln); **3** (*on a roof*) Ziegel der (PL die Ziegel).

till[1] *preposition, conjunction* **1** bis; **they're staying till Sunday** sie bleiben bis Sonntag; **till then** bis dann; **till now** bis jetzt; **2** (*when 'till' is followed by a noun it is usually translated as 'bis zu' + DAT*) **till the evening** bis zum Abend; **3** not till erst**; **she won't be back till ten** sie kommt erst um zehn zurück; **we won't know till Monday** wir werden erst am Montag Bescheid wissen.

till[2] *noun* Kasse die (PL die Kassen); **please pay at the till** bitte zahlen Sie an der Kasse.

time *noun* **1** (*on the clock*) Zeit die; **it's time for breakfast** es ist Zeit zum Frühstücken; **2 what time is it?** wie viel Uhr ist es?; **at what time does it start?** um wie viel Uhr fängt es an?; **ten o'clock German time** zehn Uhr, deutsche Zeit; **3 on time** pünktlich; **4** (*an amount of time*) Zeit die; **we've got lots of time** wir haben viel Zeit; **I haven't got time now** ich habe jetzt keine Zeit; **there's no time left to do it** dafür bleibt keine Zeit mehr; **from time to time** von Zeit zu Zeit; **for a long time** lange; **5** (*moment*) Moment der

(PL die Momente); **this isn't a good time to discuss it** das ist kein guter Moment, um darüber zu sprechen; **at the right time** im richtigen Moment; **for the time being** im Moment; **any time now** jeden Moment; **6 at times** manchmal; **7** (*in a series*) Mal das (PL die Male); **eight times** achtmal; **for the first time** zum ersten Mal; **the first time I saw you** das erste Mal, als ich dich sah; **three times a year** dreimal jährlich; **8 three times two is six** drei mal zwei ist sechs; **9 to have a good time** sich amüsieren; **we had a really good time** wir haben uns richtig gut amüsiert; **have a good time!** viel Vergnügen!

timetable *noun* **1** (*in school*) Stundenplan der (PL die Stundenpläne); **2** (*for trains or buses*) Fahrplan der (PL die Fahrpläne); **bus timetable** der Busfahrplan.

tin *noun* Dose die (PL die Dosen); **a tin of tomatoes** eine Dose Tomaten.

tinned *adjective* in Dosen; **tinned peas** Erbsen in Dosen.

tin opener *noun* Dosenöffner der (PL die Dosenöffner).

tiny *adjective* winzig.

tip *noun* **1** (*end*) Spitze die (PL die Spitzen); **2** (*money*) Trinkgeld das; **3** (*useful hint*) Tipp der (PL die Tipps) (*informal*).

tip *verb* (*give money*) ein Trinkgeld geben ◊ (+ DAT); **we tipped the waiter** wir haben dem Kellner ein Trinkgeld gegeben.

tiptoe noun on tiptoe auf Zehenspitzen.

tired adjective **1** müde; I'm tired ich bin müde; you look tired du siehst müde aus; **2** to be tired of something etwas satt haben; I'm tired of London ich habe London satt; I'm tired of watching TV every evening ich habe es satt, jeden Abend fernzusehen.

tiring adjective ermüdend.

tissue noun (a paper hanky) Papiertaschentuch das (PL die Papiertaschentücher).

tissue paper noun Seidenpapier das.

title noun Titel der (PL die Titel).

to preposition **1** (to a country or town) nach; to go to London nach London fahren; the motorway to Italy die Autobahn nach Italien; they're going to Switzerland sie fahren in die Schweiz; **2** (to the cinema, theatre, school, office) in (+ ACC); I'm going to school ich gehe in die Schule; she's gone to the office sie ist ins Büro gegangen; we want to go to town wir wollen in die Stadt gehen; **3** (to a wedding, party, university, the toilet) auf (+ ACC); she's gone to the toilet sie ist auf die Toilette gegangen; **4** (addressed or attached to) an (+ ACC); a letter to my parents ein Brief an meine Eltern; **5** give the book to her gib ihr das Buch; he said to me that ... er hat mir gesagt, dass ...; **6** (to somebody's house, a particular place, or person) zu (+ DAT); I went round to Paul's house ich bin zu Paul nach Hause

gegangen; we're going to the Browns' for supper wir gehen zu Browns zum Abendessen; I'm going to the dentist tomorrow morgen gehe ich zum Zahnarzt; **7** (talking about the time) it's ten to nine es ist zehn vor neun; from eight to ten von acht bis zehn; from Monday to Friday von Montag bis Freitag; **8** (in order to) um ... zu (+ infinitive); he gave me some money to buy a sandwich er hat mir Geld gegeben, um ein Sandwich zu kaufen; **9** (in verbal phrases with the infinitive) zu; I have nothing to do ich habe nichts zu tun; have you got something to eat? hast du etwas zu essen?

toast noun **1** Toast der (PL die Toasts); two slices of toast zwei Scheiben Toast; **2** (to your health) Toast der (PL die Toasts); to drink a toast to somebody auf jemanden trinken.

toaster noun Toaster der (PL die Toaster).

tobacco noun Tabak der.

tobacconist's noun Tabakladen der (PL die Tabakläden).

today adverb heute; today's her birthday ist heute Geburtstag.

toe noun Zeh der (PL die Zehen).

toffee noun Karamell der.

together adverb **1** zusammen; we did it together wir haben es zusammen gemacht; **2** (at the same time) gleichzeitig; they all left together sie sind alle gleichzeitig weggegangen.

toilet noun Toilette die (PL die Toiletten); **she's gone to the toilet** sie ist auf die Toilette gegangen.

toilet paper noun Toilettenpapier das.

toilet roll noun Rolle Toilettenpapier die (PL die Rollen Toilettenpapier).

token noun 1 (for a machine or game) Marke die (PL die Marken); 2 (voucher) Gutschein der (PL die Gutscheine); **gift token** der Geschenkgutschein.

tolerant adjective tolerant.

toll noun 1 (payment) Gebühr die (PL die Gebühren); 2 (number) Zahl die; **the death toll has risen to 25** die Zahl der Todesopfer ist jetzt bei 25.

tomato noun Tomate die (PL die Tomaten); **tomato salad** der Tomatensalat; **tomato sauce** die Tomatensoße.

tomorrow adverb 1 morgen; **I'll do it tomorrow** ich mache es morgen; **tomorrow afternoon** morgen Nachmittag; **tomorrow morning** morgen früh; **tomorrow night** morgen Abend; 2 **the day after tomorrow** übermorgen.

tone noun (on an answerphone, of a voice, or letter) Ton der (PL die Töne).

tongue noun Zunge die (PL die Zungen); **to stick your tongue out at somebody** jemandem die Zunge herausstrecken; ★ **it's on the tip of my tongue** es liegt mir auf der Zunge.

tonic noun Tonic das (PL die Tonics); **a gin and tonic** ein Gin Tonic.

tonight adverb 1 (this evening) heute Abend; **I'm going out with my friends tonight** ich gehe heute Abend mit meinen Freunden weg; 2 (after bedtime) heute Nacht.

tonsillitis noun Mandelentzündung die; **Ahlem's got tonsillitis** Ahlem hat eine Mandelentzündung.

too adverb 1 zu; **it's too expensive** es ist zu teuer; **too often** zu oft; **2 too much** zu viel; **I've spent too much** ich habe zu viel ausgegeben; **too many** zu viele; 3 (as well) auch; **Karen's coming too** Karen kommt auch; **me too!** ich auch!

tool noun Werkzeug das (PL die Werkzeuge).

tool box noun Werkzeugkasten der (PL die Werkzeugkästen).

tool kit noun Werkzeug das.

tooth noun Zahn der (PL die Zähne); **to brush your teeth** sich (DAT) die Zähne putzen.

toothache noun Zahnschmerzen (plural).

toothbrush noun Zahnbürste die (PL die Zahnbürsten).

toothpaste noun Zahnpasta die (PL die Zahnpasten).

top noun 1 (highest part) Spitze die (PL die Spitzen) (of a tree); 2 **at the top of** oben auf (+ DAT); **at the top of the ladder** oben auf der Leiter; **it's on top of the chest of drawers** es liegt oben auf der Kommode; 3 **at the top** oben; **there are four rooms at the top** oben sind vier Zimmer; **from top to bottom** von oben bis unten; 4 (of a container, jar, or box)

Deckel der (PL die Deckel); **5** (of a mountain) Gipfel der (PL die Gipfel); **6** (a lid) Kappe die (PL die Kappen) (of a pen), Verschluss der (PL die Verschlüsse) (of a bottle); **7** (of a garment) Oberteil das (PL die Oberteile); **8** (in sport) **the top of the table** die Tabellenspitze; ★ **and on top of all that** obendrein; ★ **it was a bit over the top** es war leicht übertrieben.

top adjective oberster/oberste/oberstes (step or floor); **on the top floor** im obersten Stockwerk.

topic noun Thema das (PL die Themen).

topping noun Belag der (PL die Beläge); **which topping would you like?** welchen Belag hättest du gerne?

torch noun Taschenlampe die (PL die Taschenlampen).

torn adjective zerrissen.

tortoise noun Schildkröte die (PL die Schildkröten).

torture noun **1** Folter die (PL die Foltern); **2 the exam was torture** die Prüfung war die Hölle (informal).

torture verb quälen.

Tory noun Konservative der/die (PL die Konservativen).

total noun **1** (number) Gesamtzahl die (PL die Gesamtzahlen); **2** (result of addition) Summe die (PL die Summen).

total adjective gesamt.

totally adverb völlig.

touch noun **1** (contact) **to get in touch with somebody** sich mit

jemandem in Verbindung setzen; **to stay in touch with somebody** mit jemandem Kontakt halten; **2 we've lost touch** wir haben keinen Kontakt mehr; **I've lost touch with Peter** ich habe keinen Kontakt mehr zu Peter; **3** (a little bit) **a touch of salt** eine Spur Salz; **it was a touch embarrassing** es war ein bisschen peinlich.

touch verb **1** berühren; **2** (get hold of) anfassen SEP; **don't touch that** fass das nicht an.

touched adjective gerührt.

touching adjective rührend.

tough adjective **1** hart; **she's had a tough time** sie hat eine harte Zeit hinter sich; **a tough guy** ein harter Kerl; **2** zäh; **the meat's tough** das Fleisch ist zäh; **3** fest (material, shoes, etc.); **4** tough luck! Pech!; **tough, you're too late** so'n Pech, du bist zu spät dran.

tour noun **1** Besichtigung die (PL die Besichtigungen); **a tour of the city** eine Stadtbesichtigung; **we did a tour of the castle** wir haben das Schloss besichtigt; **2 guided tour** die Führung; **3 package tour** die Pauschalreise; **4** (by a band or theatre group) Tournee die (PL die Tournees); **to go on tour** auf Tournee gehen.

tour verb (performer) auf Tournee sein✧ (PERF sein); **they're touring America** sie sind auf Tournee in Amerika.

tour guide noun Reiseleiter der (PL die Reiseleiter), Reiseleiterin die (PL die Reiseleiterinnen).

tourism noun Tourismus der.

tourist noun Tourist der (PL die Touristen), Touristin die (PL die Touristinnen).

tourist information office noun Fremdenverkehrsbüro das (PL die Fremdenverkehrsbüros).

tournament noun Turnier das (PL die Turniere); **tennis tournament** das Tennisturnier.

tow verb **to be towed away** abgeschlept werden ✧ (PERF sein).

towards preposition zu (+ DAT); **she went off towards the lake** sie ist zum See gegangen; **to come towards somebody** auf jemanden zukommen✧ SEP (PERF sein).

towel noun Handtuch das (PL die Handtücher).

tower noun Turm der (PL die Türme).

tower block noun Hochhaus das (PL die Hochhäuser).

town noun Stadt die (PL die Städte); **to go into town** in die Stadt gehen.

town centre noun Stadtmitte die (PL die Stadtmitten).

town hall noun Rathaus das (PL die Rathäuser).

toy noun Spielzeug das.

toyshop noun Spielzeuggeschäft das (PL die Spielzeuggeschäfte).

trace noun Spur die (PL die Spuren); **there was no trace of the thieves** es fehlte jede Spur von den Dieben.

trace verb **1** (find) finden✧; **2** (follow) verfolgen; **3** (copy) durchpausen SEP.

tracing paper noun Pauspapier das.

track noun **1** (for sport) Bahn die (PL die Bahnen); **cycling track** die Radrennbahn; **racing track** (for cars) die Rennstrecke; **2** (a path) Weg der (PL die Wege); **3** (song) Stück das (PL die Stücke); **this is my favourite track** das ist mein Lieblingsstück.

track suit noun Trainingsanzug der (PL die Trainingsanzüge).

tractor noun Traktor der (PL die Traktoren).

trade noun **1** (a profession) Gewerbe das; **2** (skill, craft) Handwerk das; **to learn a trade** ein Handwerk erlernen.

trade union noun Gewerkschaft die (PL die Gewerkschaften).

tradition noun Tradition die (PL die Traditionen).

traditional adjective traditionell.

traffic noun Verkehr der.

traffic island noun Verkehrsinsel die (PL die Verkehrsinseln).

traffic jam noun Stau der (PL die Staus).

traffic lights plural noun Ampel die (PL die Ampeln).

traffic warden noun Verkehrsüberwacher der (PL die Verkehrsüberwacher), Politesse die (PL die Politessen).

tragedy noun Tragödie die (PL die Tragödien).

tragic adjective tragisch.

trail noun (a path) Pfad der (PL die Pfade); **a nature trail** ein Naturlehrpfad.

a b c d e f g h i j k l m n o p q r s t u v w x y z

trailer noun Anhänger der (PL die Anhänger).

train noun Zug der (PL die Züge); **he's coming by train** er kommt mit dem Zug; **I met her on the train** ich habe sie im Zug getroffen; **the train for York** der Zug nach York.

train verb 1 (for a career) ausbilden SEP; 2 **she's training to be a nurse** sie macht eine Ausbildung zur Krankenschwester; 3 (in sport) trainieren; **the team trains on Wednesdays** die Mannschaft trainiert mittwochs.

trainee noun Auszubildende der/die (PL die Auszubildenden).

trainer noun 1 (of an athlete or horse) Trainer der (PL die Trainer), Trainerin die (PL die Trainerinnen); 2 **trainers** Turnschuhe (plural).

training noun 1 (for a career) Ausbildung die; 2 (for sport) Training das.

train ticket noun Zugfahrkarte die (PL die Zugfahrkarten).

train timetable noun Bahnfahrplan der (PL die Bahnfahrpläne).

tram noun Straßenbahn die (PL die Straßenbahnen).

tramp noun Landstreicher der (PL die Landstreicher), Landstreicherin die (PL die Landstreicherinnen).

transfer noun Abziehbild das (PL die Abziehbilder).

transform verb verwandeln.

transistor noun Transistor der (PL die Transistoren).

translate verb übersetzen; **to translate something into German** etwas ins Deutsche übersetzen.

translation noun Übersetzung die (PL die Übersetzungen).

translator noun Übersetzer der (PL die Übersetzer), Übersetzerin die (PL die Übersetzerinnen).

transparent adjective durchsichtig.

transplant noun Transplantation die (PL die Transplantationen).

transport noun Transport der (PL die Transporte); **the transport of goods** der Warentransport; **public transport** öffentliche Verkehrsmittel (plural).

trap noun Falle die (PL die Fallen).

travel noun Reisen das; **foreign travel** Auslandsreisen (plural).

travel verb reisen (PERF sein).

travel agency noun Reisebüro das (PL die Reisebüros).

travel agent's noun Reisebüro das (PL die Reisebüros).

traveller noun 1 Reisende der/die (PL die Reisenden); 2 (gypsy) Zigeuner der (PL die Zigeuner), Zigeunerin die (PL die Zigeunerinnen).

traveller's cheque noun Reisescheck der (PL die Reiseschecks).

travel-sick adjective reisekrank; **I get travel-sick** ich werde reisekrank.

tray noun Tablett das (PL die Tabletts).

tread *verb* to tread on something auf etwas (ACC) treten ◇ (PERF *sein*); **she trod on my foot** sie ist mir auf den Fuß getreten.

treasure *noun* Schatz der (PL die Schätze).

treat *noun* 1 I took them to the circus as a treat ich habe ihnen eine besondere Freude gemacht und sie in den Zirkus eingeladen; 2 (*food*) Leckerbissen der (PL die Leckerbissen).

treat *verb* 1 behandeln; **he treats his dog well** er behandelt seinen Hund gut; **the doctor who treated you** der Arzt, der dich behandelt hat; 2 to treat somebody to something jemandem etwas spendieren; **I'll treat you to an ice cream** ich spendiere euch ein Eis.

treatment *noun* Behandlung die (PL die Behandlungen).

tree *noun* Baum der (PL die Bäume).

tremble *verb* zittern.

trend *noun* 1 (*a fashion*) Trend der (PL die Trends); 2 (*a tendency*) Tendenz die (PL die Tendenzen).

trendy *adjective* modern.

trial *noun* (*in court*) Prozess der (PL die Prozesse).

triangle *noun* Dreieck das (PL die Dreiecke).

trick *noun* 1 (*a joke*) Streich der (PL die Streiche); **to play a trick on somebody** jemandem einen Streich spielen; 2 (*a knack or by a conjuror*) Trick der (PL die Tricks); **there must be a trick to it** da muss ein Trick dabei sein.

trick *verb* hereinlegen SEP; **he tricked me!** er hat mich hereingelegt!

tricky *adjective* verzwickt; **it's a tricky situation** das ist eine verzwickte Situation.

tricycle *noun* Dreirad das (PL die Dreiräder).

trim *verb* schneiden ◇ (*hair*).

trip *noun* 1 Reise die (PL die Reisen); **a trip to Florida** eine Reise nach Florida; **he's going on a business trip** er macht eine Geschäftsreise; 2 (*a day out*) Ausflug der (PL die Ausflüge); **a day trip to France** ein Tagesausflug nach Frankreich.

trip *verb* (*to stumble*) stolpern (PERF *sein*); **Nicky tripped over a stone** Nicky ist über einen Stein gestolpert.

triumph *noun* Triumph der (PL die Triumphe).

trolley *noun* 1 (*for shopping*) Einkaufswagen der (PL die Einkaufswagen); 2 (*for luggage*) Kofferkuli der (PL die Kofferkulis).

trombone *noun* Posaune die (PL die Posaunen).

troops *plural noun* Truppen (*plural*).

trophy *noun* Trophäe die (PL die Trophäen), (*in competitions*) Pokal der (PL die Pokale).

trot *verb* traben (PERF *sein*).

trouble *noun* 1 (*general difficulties*) Ärger der; **to make trouble** Ärger machen; **to get into trouble** Ärger bekommen; **we had trouble with the travel agency** wir hatten Ärger mit dem Reisebüro;

a b c d e f g h i j k l m n o p q r s t u v w x y z

2 (*problem*) Problem das (PL die Probleme); **the trouble is, I've lost his phone number** das Problem ist, dass ich seine Telefonnummer verloren habe; **Steph's in trouble** Steph hat Probleme; **what's the trouble?** was ist los?; **it's no trouble!** das ist kein Problem; **3** (*difficulty, effort*) Mühe die; **to have trouble doing something** Mühe haben, etwas zu tun; **I had trouble finding a seat** ich hatte Mühe, einen Platz zu finden; **it's not worth the trouble** das ist nicht der Mühe wert.

trousers plural noun Hose die (PL die Hosen); **my old trousers** meine alte Hose; **a new pair of trousers** eine neue Hose.

trout noun Forelle die (PL die Forellen).

truant noun Schulschwänzer der (PL die Schulschwänzer), Schulschwänzerin die (PL die Schulschwänzerinnen); **she's playing truant** sie schwänzt die Schule.

truck noun Lastwagen der (PL die Lastwagen).

true adjective **1** wahr; **a true story** eine wahre Geschichte; **2 is that true?** stimmt das?; **it's true she's absent-minded** das stimmt, sie ist sehr vergesslich.

trump noun Trumpf der (PL die Trümpfe); **hearts are trumps** Herz ist Trumpf.

trumpet noun Trompete die (PL die Trompeten).

trunk noun **1** (*of a tree*) Stamm der (PL die Stämme); **2** (*of an elephant*) Rüssel der (PL die Rüssel).

trunks plural noun **swimming trunks** Badehose die (PL die Badehosen).

trust noun Vertrauen das.

trust verb **1** (*believe*) **to trust somebody** jemandem vertrauen; **2** (*rely on*) **you can trust him** man kann sich auf ihn verlassen.

truth noun Wahrheit die.

try noun Versuch der (PL die Versuche); **it's my first try** es ist mein erster Versuch; **to have a try** es versuchen; **give it a try!** versuch's doch mal!.

try verb **1** versuchen; **to try to do something** versuchen, etwas zu tun; **I'm trying to open the door** ich versuche, die Tür aufzumachen; **2** (*taste*) probieren.
● **to try something on** etwas anprobieren SEP (*a garment*).

T-shirt noun T-Shirt das (PL die T-Shirts).

tube noun **1** Tube die (PL die Tuben); **2** (*the Underground*) **the Tube** die U-Bahn.

tuberculosis noun Tuberkulose die.

Tuesday noun **1** Dienstag der (PL die Dienstage); **on Tuesday** (am) Dienstag; **I'm going to the cinema on Tuesday** ich gehe Dienstag ins Kino; **see you on Tuesday!** bis Dienstag!; **every Tuesday** jeden Dienstag; **last Tuesday** vorigen Dienstag; **next Tuesday** nächsten Dienstag; **2 on Tuesdays**

dienstags; **the museum is closed on Tuesdays** das Museum ist dienstags geschlossen.

tuition noun **1** Unterricht der; **piano tuition** der Klavierunterricht; **2 extra tuition** Nachhilfestunden (plural).

tulip noun Tulpe die (PL die Tulpen).

tumble-drier noun Wäschetrockner der (PL die Wäschetrockner).

tumbler noun Becherglas das (PL die Bechergläser).

tuna noun Thunfisch der.

tune noun Melodie die (PL die Melodien).

tunnel noun Tunnel der (PL die Tunnel); **the Channel Tunnel** der Eurotunnel.

turkey noun Pute die (PL die Puten).

Turkey noun die Türkei; **from Turkey** aus der Türkei; **in Turkey** in der Türkei; **to Turkey** in die Türkei.

Turkish noun (language) Türkisch das.

Turkish adjective türkisch; **he is Turkish** er ist Türke; **she is Turkish** sie ist Türkin.

turn noun **1** (in a game) **it's your turn** du bist an der Reihe; **whose turn is it?** wer ist an der Reihe?; **it's Jane's turn** Jane ist an der Reihe; **2 to take turns** sich abwechseln; **to take it in turns to do something** abwechselnd etwas tun; **3** (in a road) Kurve die (PL die Kurven); **to take a right/left turn** nach rechts/links abbiegen.

turn verb **1** drehen; **turn the key to the right** dreh den Schlüssel nach rechts; **turn your chair round** dreh deinen Stuhl herum; **2** (person, car) abbiegen ◇ SEP (PERF sein); **turn left at the next set of lights** biegen Sie an der nächsten Ampel links ab; **3** (become) werden ◇ (PERF sein); **she turned red** sie wurde rot.

● **to turn back** umkehren SEP (PERF sein).

● **to turn off 1** (from a road) abbiegen ◇ SEP (PERF sein); **2** (switch off) ausmachen SEP (a light, an oven, a TV, or radio), zudrehen SEP (a tap), abstellen SEP (gas, electricity, or water), ausschalten SEP (an engine).

● **to turn on** anmachen SEP (a TV, radio, or light), aufdrehen SEP (a tap), anschalten SEP (an oven), anlassen ◇ SEP (an engine).

● **to turn out 1 to turn out well** gut ausgehen ◇ SEP (PERF sein); **the discussions turned out badly** die Gespräche sind schlecht ausgegangen; **it all turned out all right in the end** am Ende ging alles gut aus; **2 it turned out that I was right** es stellte sich heraus, dass ich Recht hatte.

● **to turn up 1** (to arrive) aufkreuzen SEP (PERF sein); **they turned up an hour later** sie sind eine Stunde später aufgekreuzt; **2** (to make louder) lauter machen.

turning noun Abzweigung die (PL die Abzweigungen); **take the third turning on the right** nimm die dritte Abzweigung rechts.

a b c d e f g h i j k l m n o p q r s t u v w x y z

a **turnip** noun Steckrübe die (PL die Steckrüben).

b **turquoise** adjective türkis.

c **turtle** noun Schildkröte die (PL die Schildkröten).

d **TV** noun Fernsehen das; **I saw her on TV** ich habe sie im Fernsehen gesehen.

e **tweezers** noun Pinzette die (PL die Pinzetten).

f **twelfth** number zwölfter/zwölfte/zwölftes; **on the twelfth floor** im zwölften Stock; **the twelfth of May** der zwölfte Mai.

g **twelve** number **1** zwölf; **Tara's twelve** Tara ist zwölf; **2 at twelve o'clock** um zwölf Uhr.

h **twenty** number zwanzig; **Marie's twenty** Marie ist zwanzig; **twenty-one** einundzwanzig.

i **twice** adverb **1** zweimal; **I've asked him twice** ich habe ihn zweimal gefragt; **twice a day** zweimal täglich; **2 twice as much** doppelt so viel.

j **twig** noun Zweig der (PL die Zweige).

k **twin** noun Zwilling der (PL die Zwillinge); **Helen and Tim are twins** Helen und Tim sind Zwillinge; **her twin sister** ihre Zwillingsschwester.

l **twin** verb **Richmond is twinned with Konstanz** Richmond und Konstanz sind Partnerstädte.

m **twist** verb **1** (bend out of shape) verbiegen✧; **2** verdrehen (words, meaning); **3 to twist your ankle** sich den Knöchel verrenken.

n **two** number zwei; **Ben's two** Ben ist zwei; **two by two** zu zweit.

type noun Art die; **what type of computer is it?** welche Art Computer ist es?.

type verb (on a typewriter) Schreibmaschine schreiben✧, tippen (informal); **I'm learning to type** ich lerne Schreibmaschine schreiben; **I'm just typing some letters** ich tippe gerade ein paar Briefe.

typewriter noun Schreibmaschine die (PL die Schreibmaschinen).

typical adjective typisch.

tyre noun Reifen der (PL die Reifen).

Uu

ugly adjective hässlich.

UK noun (United Kingdom) Vereinigte Königreich das.

ulcer noun Geschwür das (PL die Geschwüre).

Ulster noun Ulster; **from Ulster** aus Ulster, aus Nordirland.

umbrella noun Regenschirm der (PL die Regenschirme).

umpire noun Schiedsrichter der (PL die Schiedsrichter), Schiedsrichterin die (PL die Schiedsrichterinnen).

UN noun (United Nations) UN (plural).

unable adjective **to be unable to do something** etwas nicht tun können; **he's unable to come** er kann nicht kommen.

unavoidable *adjective* unvermeidlich.

unbearable *adjective* unerträglich.

unbelievable *adjective* unglaublich.

uncertain *adjective* **1** (*not sure*) **to be uncertain whether** ... sich (DAT) nicht sicher sein, ob ...; **2** (*unpredictable*) ungewiss (*future or result*).

uncle *noun* Onkel *der* (PL die Onkel).

uncomfortable *adjective* **1** unbequem (*shoes, chair, or journey*); **2** unangenehm (*situation, heat*).

unconscious *adjective* (*out cold*) bewusstlos.

under *preposition* **1** (*underneath*) unter (+ DAT, *or* + ACC *when there is movement towards a place*); **the dog's under the bed** der Hund ist unter dem Bett; **the ball rolled under the bed** der Ball ist unter das Bett gerollt; **2 under there** da drunter; **perhaps it's under there** vielleicht ist es da drunter; **3** (*less than*) unter (+ DAT); **under £20** unter zwanzig Pfund; **children under five** Kinder unter fünf.

under-age *adjective* **to be under-age** minderjährig sein.

underclothes *plural noun* Unterwäsche *die*.

undercooked *adjective* nicht gar.

underestimate *verb* unterschätzen.

underground *noun* (*railway*) U-Bahn *die* (PL die U-Bahnen); **I saw her on the underground** ich habe

sie in der U-Bahn gesehen; **shall we go by underground?** fahren wir mit der U-Bahn?

underground *adjective* unterirdisch (*cave*); **underground car park** die Tiefgarage.

underline *verb* unterstreichen◇.

underneath *preposition* unter (+ DAT, *or* + ACC *when there is movement towards a place*); **it's underneath the newspaper** es ist unter der Zeitung; **I put it underneath the newspaper** ich habe es unter die Zeitung gelegt.

underneath *adverb* darunter; **check underneath** sieh darunter nach.

underpants *plural noun* Unterhose *die* (PL die Unterhosen); **my underpants** meine Unterhose.

underpass *noun* Unterführung *die* (PL die Unterführungen).

understand *verb* verstehen◇; **do you understand?** verstehst du?; **I couldn't understand what he was saying** ich konnte ihn nicht verstehen; **I can't understand why she doesn't want to see him** ich kann nicht verstehen, warum sie ihn nicht sehen will.

understandable *adjective* **that's understandable** das ist verständlich.

understanding *noun* Verständnis *das*.

understanding *adjective* verständnisvoll.

underwear *noun* Unterwäsche *die*.

undo *verb* aufmachen SEP.

a
b
c
d
e
f
g
h
i
j
k
l
m
n
o
p
q
r
s
t
u
v
w
x
y
z

undone adjective **to come undone** aufgehen◇ SEP (PERF sein).

undress verb **to get undressed** sich ausziehen◇ SEP.

unemployed noun **the unemployed** die Arbeitslosen (plural).

unemployed adjective arbeitslos.

unemployment noun Arbeitslosigkeit die.

uneven adjective uneben (surface); **her pulse is uneven** ihr Puls ist unregelmäßig; **your writing is very uneven** deine Schrift ist sehr ungleichmäßig; **the icing is uneven** diese Kuchenglasur ist nicht glatt.

unexpected adjective unerwartet.

unexpectedly adverb (to happen, arrive) überraschend.

unfair adjective unfair; **it's unfair on young people** es ist jungen Leuten gegenüber unfair.

unfashionable adjective unmodern.

unfasten verb aufmachen SEP.

unfit adjective nicht fit; **I'm terribly unfit** ich bin nicht sehr fit.

unfold verb **1** (a map) ausbreiten SEP; **2** (to develop) spielen; **the story unfolds in Africa** die Geschichte spielt in Afrika.

unfortunate adjective unglücklich.

unfortunately adverb leider.

unfriendly adjective unfreundlich.

ungrateful adjective undankbar.

unhappy adjective **1** unglücklich; **2** (not satisfied) unzufrieden; **to be unhappy about something** mit etwas unzufrieden sein.

unhealthy adjective ungesund.

uniform noun Uniform die (PL die Uniformen).

union noun (trade union) Gewerkschaft die (PL die Gewerkschaften).

Union Jack noun **the Union Jack** die britische Nationalflagge.

unique adjective einzigartig.

unit noun **1** (for measuring, for example) Einheit die (PL die Einheiten); **2** (in a kitchen) Einbauschrank der (PL die Einbauschränke); **3** (a department) Abteilung die (PL die Abteilungen); **the research unit** die Forschungsabteilung.

United Kingdom noun Vereinigtes Königreich das.

United Nations noun Vereinte Nationen (plural).

United States (of America) plural noun Vereinigte Staaten (von Amerika) (plural).

universe noun Universum das, Weltall das.

university noun Universität die (PL die Universitäten); **to go to university** auf die Universität gehen.

unkind adjective unfreundlich.

unknown adjective unbekannt.

unleaded petrol noun bleifreie Benzin das.

unless *conjunction* es sei denn; **unless he does it** es sei denn, er macht es; **unless you write** es sei denn, du schreibst.

unlike *adjective* **1** im Gegensatz zu (+ DAT); **unlike me, she hates dogs** im Gegensatz zu mir hasst sie Hunde; **2 it's unlike her to be late** es sieht ihr gar nicht ähnlich, zu spät zu kommen.

unlikely *adjective* unwahrscheinlich.

unlimited *adjective* unbegrenzt.

unload *verb* **1** ausladen✧ SEP (*luggage, car*); **2** entladen✧ (*lorry*).

unlock *verb* aufschließen✧ SEP.

unlucky *adjective* **1 to be unlucky** (*person*) Pech haben; **I was unlucky, the shop was shut** ich hatte Pech, das Geschäft war zu; **2** (*bringing bad luck*) Unglücks-; **thirteen is an unlucky number** dreizehn ist eine Unglückszahl; **it's unlucky** es bringt Unglück.

unmarried *adjective* ledig.

unnecessary *adjective* unnötig.

unpack *verb* auspacken SEP; **I'm just unpacking my rucksack** ich packe gerade meinen Rucksack aus; **I'll just unpack and then come down** ich packe nur noch aus und dann komme ich runter.

unpaid *adjective* unbezahlt.

unpleasant *adjective* unangenehm.

unplug *verb* **to unplug the lamp** den Stecker der Lampe herausziehen✧ SEP.

unpopular *adjective* unbeliebt.

unreasonable *adjective* uneinsichtig; **he's being really unreasonable** er ist so uneinsichtig.

unrecognizable *adjective* nicht wieder zu erkennen.

unreliable *adjective* unzuverlässig; **he's unreliable** er ist unzuverlässig.

unsafe *adjective* gefährlich (*wiring, for example*).

unsatisfactory *adjective* unbefriedigend.

unscrew *verb* aufschrauben SEP.

unshaven *adjective* unrasiert.

unsuccessful *adjective* **1** erfolglos; **an unsuccessful attempt** ein erfolgloser Versuch; **2 to be unsuccessful** keinen Erfolg haben; **I tried, but I was unsuccessful** ich habe es versucht, aber ich hatte keinen Erfolg.

unsuitable *adjective* unpassend.

untidy *adjective* unordentlich; **the house is always untidy** das Haus ist immer unordentlich.

until *preposition, conjunction* **1** bis; **until Monday** bis Montag; **until now** bis jetzt; **until then** bis dahin; **2** (*when 'until' is followed by a noun it is usually translated as 'bis zu'* + DAT) **until the tenth** bis zum Zehnten; **until the morning** bis zum Morgen; **3 not until** erst; **not until September** erst im September; **it won't be finished until Friday** es wird erst Freitag fertig sein.

unusual *adjective* ungewöhnlich; **an unusual face** ein ungewöhnliches Gesicht.

a b c d e f g h i j k l m n o p q r s t u v w x y z

unwilling adjective **to be unwilling to do something** etwas nicht tun wollen.

unwrap verb auspacken SEP.

up preposition, adverb **1** (out of bed) **to be up** auf sein◇ (PERF sein); **Liz isn't up yet** Liz ist noch nicht auf; **I was up late last night** ich war gestern bis spät auf; **2 to get up** aufstehen◇ SEP (PERF sein); **we got up at six** wir sind um sechs aufgestanden; **3** (higher up) auf (+ DAT, or + ACC when there is movement towards a place); **up on the roof** auf dem Dach; **4 up here** hier oben; **up there** da oben; **to go up** (upstairs) nach oben gehen; **I went up** ich bin nach oben gegangen; **5 to go up the road** die Straße entlanggehen◇ SEP (PERF sein); **it's further up the road** es ist weiter die Straße entlang; **6 to go up the hill** (on foot) hinaufgehen◇ SEP (PERF sein), (in a vehicle) hinauffahren◇ SEP (PERF sein); (in spoken German the prefix 'rauf-' is most common) **does the bus go up the hill?** fährt der Bus den Berg rauf?; **7 to come up** herauskommen◇ SEP (PERF sein), raufkommen◇ SEP (PERF sein) (informal); **8** (wrong) **what's up?** was ist los?; (informal) **what's up with him?** was ist mit ihm los?; **9 up to** bis, **up to here** bis hier; **up to last week** bis zur letzten Woche; **10 she came up to me** sie kam auf mich zu; **11 what's she up to?** was hat sie vor?; **12 it's up to you** (it's for you to decide) das hängt von dir ab; (it concerns only you) das ist

deine Sache; ★ **time's up!** die Zeit ist um.

up-date noun Aktualisierung die (PL die Aktualisierungen); **here's an up-date on our plans** dies ist der neueste Stand unserer Pläne.

up-date verb **1** (to revise) überarbeiten (timetables, information); **2** (to modernize) auf den neuesten Stand bringen ◇ (styles, furnishings).

upheaval noun Unruhe die (PL die Unruhen).

upper-class adjective der Oberschicht; **an upper-class family** eine Familie der Oberschicht.

upright adjective aufrecht; **put it upright** stell es aufrecht; **to stand upright** aufrecht stehen.

upset noun **stomach upset** die Magenverstimmung.

upset adjective **1** (annoyed) ärgerlich; **he's upset** er ist ärgerlich; **2** (distressed) bestürzt, (sad) betrübt.

upset verb **to upset somebody** (hurt) jemanden kränken, (annoy) jemanden ärgern.

upside down adjective verkehrt herum.

upstairs adverb **1** oben; **Mum's upstairs** Mutti ist oben; **2** (with movement) nach oben; **to go upstairs** nach oben gehen.

up-to-date adjective **1** (in fashion) modern; **2** (information) aktuell.

upwards adjective nach oben.

urgent adjective dringend.

us *pronoun* uns; **she knows us** sie kennt uns; **they saw us** sie haben uns gesehen; **with us** mit uns.

US *noun* USA (*plural*).

USA *noun* USA (*plural*).

use *noun* 1 Gebrauch *der*; **instructions for use** die Gebrauchsanweisung (*singular*); 2 **it's no use** es hat keinen Zweck; **it's no use phoning** es hat keinen Zweck anzurufen.

use *verb* benutzen; **we used the dictionary** wir haben das Wörterbuch benutzt; **to use something to do something** etwas zu etwas (DAT) benutzen; **I used a towel to dry myself** ich habe ein Handtuch zum Abtrocknen benutzt.

● **to use up** 1 aufbrauchen SEP (*food*); 2 verbrauchen (*money*).

used *adjective* 1 **to be used to something** an etwas (ACC) gewöhnt sein; **I'm used to cats** ich bin an Katzen gewöhnt; **I'm not used to it!** das bin ich nicht gewohnt!; **I'm not used to eating in restaurants** ich bin nicht daran gewöhnt, in Restaurants zu essen; 2 **to get used to something** sich an etwas (ACC) gewöhnen; **you'll soon get used to the new car** du wirst dich schnell an das neue Auto gewöhnen; **I've got used to living here** ich habe mich daran gewöhnt, hier zu wohnen; **you'll get used to it** du wirst dich schon daran gewöhnen.

used *verb* **they used to live in the country** sie haben früher auf dem Land gewohnt; **she used to smoke** sie hat früher geraucht.

useful *adjective* nützlich.

useless *adjective* 1 unbrauchbar; **this knife's useless** dieses Messer ist unbrauchbar; **you're completely useless!** du bist wirklich zu nichts zu gebrauchen!; 2 nutzlos (*advice, information, or facts, for example*); **useless knowledge** nutzloses Wissen; 3 (*pointless*) zwecklos.

user *noun* Benutzer *der* (PL die Benutzer), Benutzerin *die* (PL die Benutzerinnen).

user-friendly *adjective* benutzerfreundlich.

usual *adjective* 1 üblich; **it's the usual problem** es ist das übliche Problem; **as usual** wie üblich; 2 **it's colder than usual** es ist kälter als gewöhnlich.

usually *adjective* normalerweise; **I usually leave at eight** normalerweise gehe ich um acht weg.

Vv

vacancy *noun* 1 (*in a hotel*) 'vacancies' 'Zimmer frei'; 'no vacancies' 'belegt'; 2 **job vacancy** die freie Stelle.

vacant *adjective* frei.

vaccinate *noun* impfen.

vaccination *noun* Impfung *die* (PL die Impfungen).

a
b
c
d
e
f
g
h
i
j
k
l
m
n
o
p
q
r
s
t
u
v
w
x
y
z

vacuum verb saugen; **I'm going to vacuum my room** ich sauge mein Zimmer.

vacuum cleaner noun Staubsauger der (PL die Staubsauger).

vagina noun Vagina die (PL die Vaginen).

vague adjective vage.

vain adjective eitel; **in vain** vergeblich.

valentine card noun Valentinskarte die (PL die Valentinskarten).

Valentine's Day noun Valentinstag der (PL die Valentinstage).

valid adjective gültig.

valley noun Tal das (PL die Täler).

valuable adjective wertvoll.

value noun Wert der (PL die Werte).

value verb schätzen.

van noun Lieferwagen der (PL die Lieferwagen).

vandal noun Rowdy der (PL die Rowdys).

vandalism noun Vandalismus der.

vandalize verb mutwillig zerstören.

vanilla noun Vanille die; **vanilla ice cream** das Vanilleeis.

vanish verb verschwinden✧ (PERF sein).

variety noun **1** Abwechslung die (in a routine, diet, or style); **for the sake of variety** zur Abwechslung; **2** (kind) Sorte die (PL die Sorten); **a new variety of apple** eine neue

Apfelsorte; **3** (assortment) Auswahl die.

various adjective verschieden; **there are various ways of doing it** man kann es auf verschiedene Art und Weise machen.

vary verb **1** (become different) sich ändern; **2 it varies a lot** es ist sehr unterschiedlich; **3** (make different) ändern (a programme or method).

vase noun Vase die (PL die Vasen).

VAT noun Mehrwertsteuer die.

VCR noun Videorekorder der (PL die Videorekorder).

VDU noun Bildschirm der (PL die Bildschirme).

veal noun Kalbfleisch das.

vegan noun Veganer der (PL die Veganer), Veganerin die (PL die Veganerinnen).

vegetable noun Gemüse das; **fresh vegetables** frisches Gemüse.

vegetarian noun Vegetarier der (PL die Vegetarier), Vegetarierin die (PL die Vegetarierinnen).

vegetarian adjective vegetarisch.

vehicle noun Fahrzeug das (PL die Fahrzeuge).

vein noun Vene die (PL die Venen).

velvet noun Samt der.

vending machine noun Automat der (PL die Automaten).

verb noun Verb das (PL die Verben).

verdict noun Urteil das (PL die Urteile).

verge noun **1** (roadside) Bankett das (PL die Banketten); **2 to be on the verge of doing something** im Begriff sein, etwas zu tun; **I was on

the verge of leaving ich war im Begriff zu gehen.

version noun Version die (PL die Versionen).

versus preposition gegen (+ ACC); **Arsenal versus Chelsea** Arsenal gegen Chelsea.

vertical adjective senkrecht.

very adverb sehr; **it's very difficult** es ist sehr schwer; **very much** sehr viel; **very little** sehr wenig.

very adjective **1 the very person I need!** genau der Mann, den ich brauche, genau die Frau, die ich brauche; **the very thing he's looking for** genau das, was er sucht; **in the very middle** genau in der Mitte; **2 at the very end** ganz am Ende; **at the very front** ganz vorne.

vest noun Unterhemd das (PL die Unterhemden).

vet noun Tierarzt der (PL die Tierärzte), Tierärztin die (PL die Tierärztinnen); **she's a vet** sie ist Tierärztin.

via preposition über (+ ACC); **we're going to Frankfurt via Brussels** wir fahren über Brüssel nach Frankfurt.

vicar noun Pfarrer der (PL die Pfarrer).

vicious adjective **1** bösartig (dog); **2** brutal (attack).

victim noun Opfer das (PL die Opfer).

victory noun Sieg der (PL die Siege).

video noun **1** (film, cassette) Video das (PL die Videos); **to watch a video** ein Video ansehen; **I've got it**

on video ich habe es auf Video; **it's out on video** das gibts als Video; **2** (video recorder) Videorekorder der (PL die Videorekorder).

video verb aufzeichnen SEP; **I'll video it for you** ich zeichne es für dich auf.

video camera noun Videokamera die (PL die Videokameras).

video cassette noun Videokassette die (PL die Videokassetten).

video game noun Videospiel das (PL die Videospiele).

video recorder noun Videorekorder der (PL die Videorekorder).

video shop noun Videothek die (PL die Videotheken).

Vienna noun Wien das; **to Vienna** nach Wien.

view noun **1** Aussicht die; **a room with a view of the lake** ein Zimmer mit Aussicht auf den See; **2** (opinion) Meinung die (PL die Meinungen); **in my view** meiner Meinung nach; **point of view** der Standpunkt.

viewer noun Zuschauer der (PL die Zuschauer), Zuschauerin die (PL die Zuschauerinnen).

vile adjective ekelhaft.

villa noun Villa die (PL die Villen).

village noun Dorf das (PL die Dörfer).

vine noun Weinrebe die (PL die Weinreben).

vinegar noun Essig der.

a
b
c
d
e
f
g
h
i
j
k
l
m
n
o
p
q
r
s
t
u
v
w
x
y
z

vineyard noun Weinberg der (PL die Weinberge).

violence noun Gewalt die.

violent adjective 1 gewalttätig (person, film, behaviour); 2 heftig (jolt, punch).

violin noun Geige die (PL die Geigen); **to play the violin** Geige spielen.

violinist noun Geiger der (PL die Geiger), Geigerin die (PL die Geigerinnen).

virgin noun Jungfrau die (PL die Jungfrauen).

Virgo noun Jungfrau die; **Robert's Virgo** Robert ist Jungfrau.

virtual reality noun virtuelle Realität die.

virus noun (in medicine and IT) Virus der (PL die Viren); **anti-virus software** Antivirenprogramm das (PL die Antivirenprogramme).

visa noun Visum das (PL die Visa).

visible adjective sichtbar.

visit noun Besuch der (PL die Besuche); **I was in Berlin on a visit to friends** ich war in Berlin bei Freunden zu Besuch; **my last visit to Germany** mein letzter Deutschlandbesuch.

visit verb 1 besuchen (a person); 2 besichtigen (a building, town).

visitor noun 1 Besucher der (PL die Besucher), Besucherin die (PL die Besucherinnen); 2 **we've got visitors tonight** wir haben heute Abend Besuch; 3 (in a hotel) Gast der (PL die Gäste).

visual adjective visuell.

vital adjective unbedingt erforderlich; **it's vital to book** man muss unbedingt buchen.

vitamin noun Vitamin das (PL die Vitamine).

vivid adjective lebhaft (colours, memory); **to have a vivid imagination** eine lebhafte Phantasie haben.

vocabulary noun Wortschatz der.

vocational adjective beruflich.

vodka noun Wodka der (PL die Wodkas).

voice noun Stimme die (PL die Stimmen).

volcano noun Vulkan der (PL die Vulkane).

volleyball noun Volleyball der; **to play volleyball** Volleyball spielen.

volume noun 1 Lautstärke die; **could you turn down the volume?** könntest du etwas leiser stellen?; 2 (book) Band der (PL die Bände).

voluntary adjective 1 freiwillig; **a voluntary worker** ein freiwilliger Helfer, eine freiwillige Helferin; 2 **to do voluntary work** für einen wohltätigen Zweck arbeiten.

volunteer noun Freiwillige der/die (PL die Freiwilligen).

volunteer verb **to volunteer to do something** sich bereit erklären, etwas zu tun.

vomit verb sich übergeben ◇.

vote verb wählen; **to vote for somebody** jemanden wählen; **she always votes Green** sie wählt immer die Grünen.

a b c d e f g h i j k l m n o p q r s t u v w x y z

voucher *noun* Gutschein *der* (PL *die* Gutscheine).

vowel *noun* Vokal *der* (PL *die* Vokale).

vulgar *adjective* vulgär.

Ww

waffle *noun* Waffel *die* (PL *die* Waffeln).

wage(s) *noun* Lohn *der* (PL *die* Löhne).

waist *noun* Taille *die* (PL *die* Taillen).

waistcoat *noun* Weste *die* (PL *die* Westen).

waist measurement *noun* Taillenweite *die*.

wait *noun* Wartezeit *die*; **an hour's wait** eine Stunde Wartezeit.

wait *verb* **1** warten; **they're waiting in the car** sie warten im Auto; **she kept me waiting** sie hat mich warten lassen; **2 to wait for somebody** auf jemanden warten; **wait for me** warten auf mich; **to wait for something** auf etwas (ACC) warten; **we waited for a taxi** wir haben auf ein Taxi gewartet; **3 to wait for somebody to do something** darauf warten, dass jemand etwas tut; **I'm waiting for him to ring** ich warte darauf, dass er anruft; **4 I can't wait to open it** ich kann's kaum erwarten, es aufzumachen.

waiter *noun* Kellner *der* (PL *die* Kellner); **waiter!** Herr Ober!

waiting list *noun* Warteliste *die* (PL *die* Wartelisten).

waiting room *noun* Wartezimmer *das* (PL *die* Wartezimmer), (*at a station*) Warteraum *der* (PL *die* Warteräume).

waitress *noun* Kellnerin *die* (PL *die* Kellnerinnen); **waitress!** Fräulein!

wake *verb* **1** wecken (*somebody*); **Jess woke me at six** Jess hat mich um sechs geweckt; **2** aufwachen SEP (PERF *sein*); **I woke (up) at six** ich bin um sechs aufgewacht; **wake up!** wach auf!

Wales *noun* Wales *das*; **from Wales** aus Wales; **to Wales** nach Wales.

walk *noun* **1** Spaziergang *der* (PL *die* Spaziergänge); **to go for walk** einen Spaziergang machen; **we'll go for a little walk round the village** wir machen einen kleinen Spaziergang durchs Dorf; **2 to take the dog for a walk** mit dem Hund spazieren gehen ✧ (PERF *sein*); **3 it's about five minutes' walk from here** es ist ungefähr fünf Minuten zu Fuß von hier.

walk *verb* **1** (*go, not run*) gehen ✧ (PERF *sein*); **he walks very slowly** er geht sehr langsam; **I'll walk to the bus stop with you** ich gehe mit dir zur Bushaltestelle; **2** (*on foot rather than by car or bus*) zu Fuß gehen ✧ (PERF *sein*); **it's not far, we can walk** es ist nicht weit, wir können zu Fuß gehen; **3** (*walk around*) spazieren gehen ✧ (PERF *sein*); **we walked around the old town** wir sind in der Altstadt spazieren gegangen; **4** (*move on foot*) laufen ✧ (PERF *sein*);

a
b
c
d
e
f
g
h
i
j
k
l
m
n
o
p
q
r
s
t
u
v
w
x
y
z

to learn to walk laufen lernen; **the child can't walk yet** das Kind kann noch nicht laufen.

walking distance noun **to be within walking distance** zu Fuß zu erreichen sein; **it's within walking distance of the sea** man kann das Meer zu Fuß erreichen.

walking noun (*hiking*) Wandern das; **to go walking** wandern (PERF sein).

walkman noun Walkman der (PL die Walkmen).

wall noun **1** (*inside a building*) Wand die (PL die Wände); **there's a picture on every wall** an jeder Wand hängt ein Bild; **2** (*outside*) Mauer die (PL die Mauern).

wallet noun Brieftasche die (PL die Brieftaschen).

wallpaper noun Tapete die (PL die Tapeten).

walnut noun Walnuss die (PL die Walnüsse).

wander verb **to wander around town** durch die Stadt bummeln (PERF sein); **to wander off** weggehen◇ SEP (PERF sein).

want verb **1** wollen◇; **do you want to come?** willst du mitkommen?; **what do you want to do?** was willst du machen?; **I don't want to bother him** ich will ihn nicht stören; **2** (*more polite*) mögen◇ ('*ich möchte' is much politer than 'ich will*'); **do you want some more coffee?** möchtest du noch Kaffee?; **I want two pounds of apples please** ich möchte gern zwei Pfund

Äpfel ('*möchte gern' is particularly used when shopping*).

war noun Krieg der (PL die Kriege).

ward noun Station die (PL die Stationen).

wardrobe noun Kleiderschrank der (PL die Kleiderschränke).

warm adjective **1** warm; **a warm coat** ein warmer Mantel; **it's warm today** heute ist es warm; **I'll keep your dinner warm** ich halte dir das Essen warm; **it's warm inside** drinnen ist es warm; **I am warm** mir ist warm; **2** (*friendly*) herzlich; **a warm welcome** ein herzlicher Empfang.

warm verb wärmen; **to warm the plates** die Teller wärmen.

● **to warm up 1** (*weather*) warm werden; **2** (*an athlete*) sich aufwärmen SEP; **3** (*to heat up*) aufwärmen SEP; **I'll warm the soup up for you** ich wärme dir die Suppe auf.

warmth noun Wärme die.

warn verb **1** warnen; **I warn you, it's expensive** ich warne dich, es ist teuer; **to warn somebody not to do something** jemanden davor warnen, etwas zu tun; **she warned me not to let him drive** sie hat mich davor gewarnt, ihn fahren zu lassen; **2** he warned me to lock the car er hat mich ermahnt, das Auto abzuschließen.

warning noun Warnung die (PL die Warnungen).

wart noun Warze die (PL die Warzen).

wash *noun* **to give something a wash** etwas waschen◇; **to have a wash** sich waschen.

wash *verb* **1** waschen◇; **I've washed your jeans** ich habe deine Jeans gewaschen; **2** (*have a wash*) sich waschen◇; **to get washed** sich waschen◇; **3 to wash your hands** sich (DAT) die Hände waschen; **I washed my hands** ich habe mir die Hände gewaschen; **to wash your hair** sich (DAT) die Haare waschen; **4 to wash the dishes** abwaschen◇ SEP.

● **to wash up** abwaschen◇ SEP.

washbasin *noun* Waschbecken das (PL die Waschbecken).

washing *noun* Wäsche die; **to do the washing** Wäsche waschen.

washing machine *noun* Waschmaschine die (PL die Waschmaschinen).

washing powder *noun* Waschpulver das.

washing-up liquid *noun* Spülmittel das (PL die Spülmittel).

washing-up *noun* Abwasch der; **to do the washing-up** den Abwasch machen.

wasp *noun* Wespe die (PL die Wespen).

waste *noun* Verschwendung die; **it's a waste of time** das ist eine Zeitverschwendung.

waste *verb* verschwenden.

waste-bin *noun* Mülltonne die (PL die Mülltonnen).

waste-paper basket *noun* Papierkorb der (PL die Papierkörbe).

watch *noun* Uhr die (PL die Uhren); **my watch is fast** meine Uhr geht vor; **my watch is slow** meine Uhr geht nach.

watch *verb* **1** (*to look at*) sich (DAT) ansehen◇ SEP; **I was watching a film** ich habe mir einen Film angesehen; **2** (*keep a check on, look after*) achten auf (+ ACC); **watch the children** achte auf die Kinder; **4** (*to be careful*) aufpassen SEP; **watch you don't spill it** pass auf, dass du es nicht verschüttest; **watch out!** pass auf!; **5** (*observe*) beobachten; **they were being watched** sie wurden beobachtet.

water *noun* Wasser das.

water *verb* gießen◇ (*plants*).

waterfall *noun* Wasserfall der (PL die Wasserfälle).

watering can *noun* Gießkanne die (PL die Gießkannen).

water melon *noun* Wassermelone die (PL die Wassermelonen).

waterproof *adjective* wasserdicht.

water-skiing *noun* Wasserskifahren das; **to go water-skiing** Wasserski fahren◇.

water sports *plural noun* Wassersport der.

wave *noun* **1** (*in the sea*) Welle die (PL die Wellen); **2** (*with your hand*) **to give somebody a wave** jemandem zuwinken SEP; **she gave him a wave from the bus** sie winkte ihm vom Bus zu.

a
b
c
d
e
f
g
h
i
j
k
l
m
n
o
p
q
r
s
t
u
v
w
x
y
z

wave verb **1** (*with your hand*) winken; **2** (*flap*) schwenken (*a flag, for example*).

wax noun Wachs das.

way noun **1** (*a route or road*) Weg der (PL die Wege); **the way to town** der Weg in die Stadt; **we asked the way to the station** wir haben gefragt, wie man zum Bahnhof kommt; **on the way back** auf dem Rückweg; **on the way** unterwegs; **to be in the way** im Weg sein; **to be in somebody's way** jemandem im Weg sein; **to get out of the way** aus dem Weg gehen; **2 to lose your way** sich verlaufen✧, (*in a car*) sich verfahren✧; **3 'way in'** 'Eingang'; **'way out'** 'Ausgang'; **4** (*direction*) Richtung die (PL die Richtungen); **which way did he go?** in welche Richtung ist er gegangen?; **this way** in diese Richtung; **5** (*side*) **the right way up** richtig herum; **the wrong way round** falsch herum; **the other way round** andersherum; **6** (*distance*) **it's a long way** es ist weit weg; **we still had a little way to go** wir mussten noch ein kleines Stück gehen; **7** (*manner*) Art und Weise die; **my way of learning German** meine Art und Weise, Deutsch zu lernen; **he does it his way** er macht es auf seine Art und Weise; **I've done it the wrong way** ich habe es falsch gemacht; **in a way** gewisser Weise; **8 no way!** keinen Fall!; **9 by the way** übrigens.

we pronoun wir; **we're going to the cinema tonight** wir gehen heute Abend ins Kino.

weak adjective **1** (*feeble*) schwach; **in a weak voice** mit schwacher Stimme; **2** dünn (*coffee or tea*).

wealthy adjective reich.

weapon noun Waffe die (PL die Waffen); **weapons of mass destruction** Massenvernichtungswaffen die (*plural*).

wear noun **children's wear** die Kinderkleidung; **sports wear** die Sportkleidung.

wear verb tragen✧, anhaben✧ SEP (*informal*); **she often wears red** sie trägt oft Rot; **Tamsin's wearing her jeans** Tamsin hat ihre Jeans an.

weather noun **1** Wetter das; **what's the weather like?** wie ist das Wetter?; **in fine weather** bei schönem Wetter; **the weather is terrible** das Wetter ist furchtbar; **2 in wet weather** wenn es regnet; **the weather was cold** es war kalt.

weather forecast noun Wettervorhersage die; **the weather forecast says it will rain** der Wettervorhersage zufolge soll es regnen.

web noun **1** (*spider's*) Spinnennetz das (PL die Spinnennetze); **2 the Web** Netz das.

web page noun Webseite die (PL die Webseiten).

web site noun Website die (PL die Websites).

wedding noun Hochzeit die (PL die Hochzeiten).

Wednesday noun **1** Mittwoch der (PL die Mittwoche); **on Wednesday** (am) Mittwoch; **I'm going to the**

cinema on Wednesday ich gehe Mittwoch ins Kino; **see you on Wednesday!** bis Mittwoch!; **every Wednesday** jeden Mittwoch; **last Wednesday** vorigen Mittwoch; **next Wednesday** nächsten Mittwoch; **2 on Wednesdays** mittwochs; **the museum is closed on Wednesdays** das Museum ist mittwochs geschlossen.

weed *noun* Unkraut *das*.

week *noun* Woche *die* (PL *die* Wochen); **last week** vorige Woche; **next week** nächste Woche; **this week** diese Woche; **for weeks** wochenlang; **a week today** heute in einer Woche; **in three weeks' time** in drei Wochen.

weekday *noun* **on weekdays** wochentags.

weekend *noun* Wochenende *das* (PL *die* Wochenenden); **last weekend** voriges Wochenende; **next weekend** nächstes Wochenende; **they're coming for the weekend** sie kommen übers Wochenende; **I'll do it at the weekend** ich mache es am Wochenende; **have a nice weekend!** (ein) schönes Wochenende!

weigh *verb* **1** wiegen ◊; **to weigh something** etwas wiegen; **to weigh yourself** sich wiegen; **2 how much do you weigh?** wie viel wiegst du?; **I weigh 50 kilos** ich wiege fünfzig Kilo.

weight *noun* **1** Gewicht *das* (PL *die* Gewichte); **2 to put on weight** zunehmen ◊ SEP; **3 to lose weight** abnehmen ◊ SEP.

weird *adjective* seltsam.

welcome *noun* **1 they gave us a warm welcome** sie haben uns herzlich empfangen; **2 welcome to Oxford!** herzlich willkommen in Oxford!

welcome *adjective* willkommen; **you're welcome any time** du bist immer willkommen; **'thank you!' – 'you're welcome!'** 'danke!' – 'bitte!'.

welcome *verb* begrüßen; **to welcome somebody** jemanden begrüßen.

well¹ *adverb* **1 to be well** gesund sein; **I'm very well, thank you** danke, es geht mir gut; **get well soon!** gute Besserung!; **2 gut; Terry played well** Terry hat gut gespielt; **it's well paid** es wird gut bezahlt; **well done!** gut gemacht!; **3 as well** auch; **Kevin's coming as well** Kevin kommt auch; **4 na ja; well, never mind** na ja, macht nichts; **5 gut; it may well be that ...** es ist gut möglich, dass ...; **very well then, you can go** also gut, du kannst gehen.

well² *noun* Brunnen *der* (PL *die* Brunnen).

well-behaved *adjective* artig.

well-done *adjective* durchgebraten (*steak*).

wellington (boot) *noun* Gummistiefel *der* (PL *die* Gummistiefel).

well-known *adjective* bekannt.

well-off *adjective* wohlhabend.

Welsh *noun* **1 the Welsh** (*people*) die Waliser (*plural*); **2** (*language*) Walisisch *das*.

a
b
c
d
e
f
g
h
i
j
k
l
m
n
o
p
q
r
s
t
u
v
x
y
z

a
b
c
d
e
f
g
h
i
j
k
l
m
n
o
p
q
r
s
t
u
v
w
x
y
z

Welsh adjective walisisch; **he's Welsh** er ist Waliser; **she's Welsh** sie ist Waliserin.

Welshman noun Waliser der (PL die Waliser).

Welshwoman noun Waliserin die (PL die Waliserinnen).

west noun Westen der; **in the west** im Westen.

west adjective West-; **the west side** die Westseite; **west wind** der Westwind; **west of** westlich von; **it's west of Munich** es liegt westlich von München.

west adverb nach Westen.

western noun (film) Western der (PL die Western).

West Indian noun Westinder der (PL die Westinder), Westinderin die (PL die Westinderinnen).

West Indian adjective westindisch.

West Indies plural noun die Westindischen Inseln (plural); **in the West Indies** auf den Westindischen Inseln.

wet adjective 1 nass; **we got wet** wir sind nass geworden; 2 **a wet day** ein regnerischer Tag.

whale noun Wal der (PL die Wale).

what pronoun, adjective 1 (in questions) was; **what did you say?** was hast du gesagt?; **what's she doing?** was macht sie?; **what did you buy?** was hast du gekauft?; **what is it?** was ist das?; **what's the matter?** was ist los?; **what's happened?** was ist passiert?; **what?** was?; 2 **what's your address?** wie ist Ihre Adresse?;

what's her name? wie heißt sie?; **what was it like?** wie war's?; 3 (asking for an amount) wie viel; **at what time?** um wie viel Uhr?; 4 (that which) was (relative pronoun); **she told me what had happened** sie hat mir gesagt, was passiert ist; **do what I tell you** tu, was ich dir sage; 5 (which) welcher/welche/welches; **what country is it in?** in welchem Land ist es?; **what colour is it?** welche Farbe hat es?; **what make is it?** welche Marke ist es?; 6 **what for?** wozu?

wheat noun Weizen der.

wheel noun Rad das (PL die Räder); **the spare wheel** das Reserverad; **the steering wheel** das Lenkrad.

wheelbarrow noun Schubkarre die (PL die Schubkarren).

wheelchair noun Rollstuhl der (PL die Rollstühle).

when adverb wann; **when is she arriving?** wann kommt sie an?; **when's your birthday?** wann hast du Geburtstag?

when conjunction 1 (with the past) als; **I was out shopping when you rang** ich war beim Einkaufen, als du anriefst; 2 (with the present or future) wenn; **when she comes I'll ring** wenn sie kommt, rufe ich an.

where adverb, conjunction wo; **where do you live?** wo wohnst du?; **where are you going?** wo gehst du hin?; **I don't know where they live** ich weiß nicht, wo sie wohnen.

whether conjunction ob; **I don't know whether he's back** ich weiß nicht, ob er schon zurück ist.

which adjective, pronoun
1 welcher/welche/welches; **which CD did you buy?** welche CD hast du gekauft?; **2 which (one)** welcher/welche/welches (depending on the gender of the noun the question refers back to); **'I met your brother' – 'which one?'** 'ich habe deinen Bruder getroffen' – 'welchen?'; **'I met your sister' – 'which one?'** 'ich habe deine Schwester getroffen' – 'welche?'; **'have you seen my book?' – 'which one?'** 'hast du mein Buch gesehen?' – 'welches?'; **3** (relative pronoun) der/die/das (depending on the gender of the noun 'which' refers to), (plural) die; **the film which is showing now** der Film, der gerade läuft; **the lamp which is on the table** die Lampe, die auf dem Tisch steht; **the book which I lent you** das Buch, das ich dir geliehen habe; **the books which I've read** die Bücher, die ich gelesen habe.

while noun **for a while** eine Weile; **she worked here for a while** sie hat eine Weile hier gearbeitet; **after a while** nach einer Weile.

while conjunction während; **you can make some coffee while I'm finishing my homework** du kannst Kaffee kochen, während ich meine Hausaufgaben fertig mache.

whip noun Peitsche die (PL die Peitschen).

whip verb schlagen✧ (cream); **whipped cream** die Schlagsahne.

whisker noun Schnurrhaar das (PL die Schnurrhaare).

whisky noun Whisky der (PL die Whiskys).

whisper noun Flüstern das; **in a whisper** im Flüsterton.

whisper verb flüstern.

whistle noun Pfeife die (PL die Pfeifen).

whistle verb pfeifen✧.

white noun Weiß das; **egg white** das Eiweiß.

white adjective weiß; **a white shirt** ein weißes Hemd.

white coffee noun Kaffee mit Milch der (PL die Kaffees mit Milch).

Whitsun noun Pfingsten das (PL die Pfingsten).

who pronoun **1** (in questions) wer; **who wants some chocolate?** wer möchte Schokolade?; **2** (in the accusative) wen; **who did you ring?** wen hast du angerufen?; **3** (in the dative) wem; **who did you give it to?** wem hast du es gegeben?; **4** (relative pronoun) der/die/das (depending on the gender of the noun 'who' refers to), (plural) die; **my boy friend who lives in Liverpool** mein Freund, der in Liverpool wohnt; **my girl friend who lives in Berlin** meine Freundin, die in Berlin wohnt; **the child who's staying with us** das Kind, das bei uns wohnt; **the friends who are coming to see us tonight** die Freunde, die heute Abend zu Besuch kommen.

whole noun **the whole of the class** die ganze Klasse; **the whole**

a b c d e f g h i j k l m n o p q r s t u v w x y z

of Germany ganz Deutschland; **on the whole** im Großen und Ganzen.

whole adjective ganz; **the whole family** die ganze Familie; **the whole morning** den ganzen Morgen; **the whole time** die ganze Zeit; **the whole world** die ganze Welt.

wholemeal adjective Vollkorn-; **wholemeal bread** das Vollkornbrot.

whom pronoun 1 den/die/das, (plural) die; **the man whom I saw** der Mann, den ich sah; **the woman whom I saw** die Frau, die ich sah; **the child whom I saw** das Kind, das ich sah; 2 (in the dative) dem/der/dem, (plural) denen; **the girl to whom I wrote** das Mädchen, dem ich geschrieben habe; 3 (in questions) wen; **whom did you see?** wen haben Sie gesehen?; 4 **to whom did you give it?** wem haben Sie es gegeben?

whose pronoun, adjective 1 (in questions) wessen; **whose is this jacket?** wessen Jacke ist das?; **whose shoes are these?** wessen Schuhe sind das?; 2 **whose is it?** wem gehört das?; **I know whose it is** ich weiß, wem es gehört; 3 (as a relative pronoun) dessen/deren/dessen (depending on the gender of the noun 'whose' refers to), (plural) deren; **the man whose car I'm buying** der Mann, dessen Auto ich kaufe; **the woman whose bag I found** die Frau, deren Tasche ich gefunden habe; **the girl whose sister I know** das Mädchen, dessen Schwester ich kenne; **the people**

whose children he teaches die Leute, deren Kinder er unterrichtet.

why adverb 1 warum; **why did she phone?** warum hat sie angerufen?; **why not?** warum nicht?; 2 **that's why I don't want to come** deswegen will ich nicht kommen.

wicked adjective 1 (bad) böse; 2 (brilliant) geil (informal).

wide adjective 1 breit; **it's a very wide road** es ist eine sehr breite Straße; **the shelf is 30 cm wide** das Regal ist dreißig Zentimeter breit; **wide screen** das Breitbild; 2 groß; **a wide range** eine große Auswahl.

wide adverb **the door was wide open** die Tür stand weit offen.

wide awake adjective hellwach.

widow noun Witwe die (PL die Witwen).

widower noun Witwer der (PL die Witwer).

width noun Breite die.

wife noun Ehefrau die (PL die Ehefrauen).

wig noun Perücke die (PL die Perücken).

wild adjective 1 wild; **wild animals** wilde Tiere; 2 (crazy) verrückt (idea, party, person); 3 **to be wild about something** scharf auf etwas (ACC) sein.

wildlife noun Tierwelt die; **a programme on wildlife in Africa** eine Sendung über die afrikanische Tierwelt.

wildlife park noun Wildpark der (PL die Wildparks).

will *verb* **1** (*in German the present tense is often used to express future actions and intentions*) **I'll wait for you at the bus stop** ich warte an der Bushaltestelle auf dich; **he'll be pleased to help you** er hilft dir gern; **that won't be a problem** das ist kein Problem; **I'll phone them at once** ich rufe sie sofort an; **2** (*the German future tense is used when firm intention is stressed, when referring to the more distant future and when some doubt about the future is expressed*) werden⬦; **he will definitely come** er wird ganz bestimmt kommen; **she'll probably ring before leaving** sie wird wahrscheinlich anrufen, bevor sie geht; **3** (*in questions and requests*) **will you have some more tea?** möchten Sie noch Tee?; **will you help me?** hilfst du mir?; **'will you write to me?' — 'of course I will!'** 'schreibst du mir?' — 'ja, natürlich'; **'he won't like it' — 'yes he will'** 'es wird ihm nicht gefallen' — 'doch', 4 wollen⬦; **he won't help us** er will uns nicht helfen; **the car won't start** das Auto will nicht anspringen.

willing *adjective* **to be willing to do something** bereit sein, etwas zu tun; **I'm willing to pay half** ich bin bereit, die Hälfte zu zahlen.

willingly *adverb* gern.

willow *noun* Weide *die* (PL die Weiden).

win *noun* Sieg *der* (PL die Siege); **our win over Everton** unser Sieg über Everton.

win *verb* **1** gewinnen⬦; **we won!** wir haben gewonnen!; **2 to win a prize** einen Preis bekommen.

wind[1] *noun* Wind *der* (PL die Winde).

wind[2] *verb* **1** wickeln (*a wire or rope, for example*); **2** aufziehen⬦ SEP (*a clock*).

wind farm *noun* Windpark *der* (PL die Windparks).

wind instrument *noun* Blasinstrument *das* (PL die Blasinstrumente).

window *noun* **1** Fenster *das* (PL die Fenster); **to look out of the window** aus dem Fenster sehen; **2** (*in a shop*) Schaufenster *das* (PL die Schaufenster).

windscreen *noun* Windschutzscheibe *die* (PL die Windschutzscheiben).

windscreen wiper *noun* Scheibenwischer *der* (PL die Scheibenwischer).

windsurfing *noun* Windsurfen *das*; **to go windsurfing** windsurfen gehen.

windy *adjective* windig; **it's windy today** heute ist es windig.

wine *noun* Wein *der* (PL die Weine); **a glass of white wine** ein Glas Weißwein.

wing *noun* Flügel *der* (PL die Flügel).

wink *verb* **to wink at somebody** jemandem zuzwinkern SEP.

winner *noun* Sieger *der* (PL die Sieger), Siegerin *die* (PL die Siegerinnen).

winning *adjective* siegreich.

winnings *plural noun* Gewinn *der*.

a b c d e f g h i j k l m n o p q r s t u v w x y z

winter noun Winter der (PL die Winter); **in winter** im Winter.

wipe verb 1 abwischen SEP; **I'll just wipe the table** ich wische schnell den Tisch ab; **to wipe your nose** sich (DAT) die Nase abwischen; **2 to wipe the floor** den Boden wischen; **3 to wipe your feet** sich (DAT) die Schuhe abtreten SEP.
● **to wipe up** abtrocknen SEP (dishes).

wire noun Draht der (PL die Drähte); **electric wire** die Leitung.

wise adjective weise.

wish noun 1 Wunsch der (PL die Wünsche); **to make a wish** sich (DAT) etwas wünschen; **make a wish!** wünsch dir was!; **2 best wishes on your birthday** alles Gute zum Geburtstag; **3** (in a letter) **with best wishes** mit freundlichen Grüßen.

wish verb 1 **I wish she were here** ich wünschte, sie wäre hier; **2 to wish for something** sich (DAT) etwas wünschen; **3 to wish somebody a happy Christmas** jemandem frohe Weihnachten wünschen; **I wished him happy birthday** ich habe ihm alles Gute zum Geburtstag gewünscht.

wit noun Geist der.

with preposition 1 mit (+ DAT); **with me** mit mir; **with pleasure** mit Vergnügen; **he went on holiday with his friends** er ist mit seinen Freunden in die Ferien gefahren; **a girl with red hair** ein Mädchen mit roten Haaren; **2** (at the house of) bei (+ ACC); **we're staying the night with friends** wir übernachten bei

Freunden; **3** vor (+ DAT); **to shiver with cold** vor Kälte zittern; **to tremble with fear** vor Angst zittern; **4 I haven't got any money with me** ich habe kein Geld dabei.

without preposition ohne (+ ACC); **without you** ohne dich; **without a sweater** ohne einen Pullover; **without knowing** ohne zu wissen.

witness noun Zeuge der (PL die Zeugen), Zeugin die (PL die Zeuginnen).

witty adjective geistreich.

wolf noun Wolf der (PL die Wölfe).

woman noun Frau die (PL die Frauen); **a woman friend** eine Freundin; **a woman doctor** eine Ärztin.

wonder noun Wunder das (PL die Wunder); **it's no wonder you're tired** es ist kein Wunder, dass du müde bist.

wonder verb 1 sich fragen; **I wonder why she did that** ich frage mich, warum sie das getan hat; **2 I wonder who?** wer wohl?; **I wonder where Jake is** wo Jake wohl ist?; **3** (in polite requests) **I wonder if you could tell me ...?** könnten Sie mir vielleicht sagen ...?

wonderful adjective wunderbar.

wood noun Holz das; **the lamp is made of wood** die Lampe ist aus Holz.

wooden adjective Holz-, hölzern; **wooden toys** das Holzspielzeug.

woodwork noun (craft) Tischlerei die.

wool noun Wolle die.

word noun **1** Wort das (PL die Wörter) *(the plural 'Wörter' is used when the words are unrelated)*; **a long word** ein langes Wort; **what's the German word for 'window'?** wie heißt 'window' auf Deutsch?; **I've learned ten German words today** ich habe heute zehn deutsche Wörter gelernt; **words in the dictionary** Wörter im Wörterbuch; **2** Wort das (PL die Worte) *(the plural 'Worte' is used when the words are connected in a text or conversation)*; **he wanted to say a few words** er wollte ein paar Worte sagen; **in other words** mit anderen Worten; **to have a word with somebody** mit jemandem sprechen; **3** *(promise)* Wort das; **to keep your word** sein Wort halten; **he broke his word** er hat sein Wort gebrochen; **4 the words of a song** der Text von einem Lied.

word processing noun Textverarbeitung die.

word processor noun Textverarbeitungssystem das (PL die Textverarbeitungssysteme).

work noun Arbeit die; **I enjoy my work** meine Arbeit macht mir Spaß; **she's looking for work** sie sucht Arbeit; **I've got some work to do** ich habe noch etwas Arbeit; **he's out of work** er hat keine Arbeit; **to be off work** nicht arbeiten; **Ben's off work** *(sick)* Ben ist krank; **to go to work on the tube** mit der U-Bahn zur Arbeit fahren.

work verb **1** arbeiten; **she works in an office** sie arbeitet in einem Büro; **Mum works as a dentist** Mutti ist Zahnärztin; **he works part-time** er arbeitet halbtags; **2** *(to operate)* sich auskennen ⟡ SEP mit; **can you work the video?** kennst du dich mit dem Videorekorder aus?; **3** *(function)* funktionieren; **the washing machine's not working** die Waschmaschine funktioniert nicht; **4** *(a plan or idea)* klappen; **that worked really well** das hat prima geklappt.

● **to work out 1** *(understand)* verstehen ⟡; **I can't work out why** ich kann nicht verstehen, warum; **2** *(exercise)* trainieren; **3** *(go well)* klappen; **4** *(calculate)* ausrechnen SEP *(a sum)*; **I'll work out how much it would cost** ich rechne aus, wie viel es kosten würde; **5** *(solve)* lösen *(a problem)*.

worker noun Arbeiter der (PL die Arbeiter), Arbeiterin die (PL die Arbeiterinnen).

work experience noun Praktikum das (PL die Praktika); **to do work experience** ein Praktikum machen.

working-class adjective der Arbeiterschicht; **a working-class family** eine Familie der Arbeiterschicht.

work of art noun Kunstwerk das (PL die Kunstwerke).

workshop noun Werkstatt die (PL die Werkstätten).

world noun Welt die; **the biggest tree in the world** der größte Baum der Welt; **all over the world** auf der

a
b
c
d
e
f
g
h
i
j
k
l
m
n
o
p
q
r
s
t
u
v
w
x
y
z

ganzen Welt; **the Western world** die westliche Welt.

World Cup noun **the World Cup** die Weltmeisterschaft.

world war noun Weltkrieg der (PL die Weltkriege); **the Second World War** der Zweite Weltkrieg.

worm noun Wurm der (PL die Würmer).

worn out adjective **1** (person) erschöpft; **2** (clothes or shoes) abgetragen.

worried adjective **1** besorgt; **his worried parents** seine besorgten Eltern; **2 to be worried about somebody** sich (DAT) um jemanden Sorgen machen; **we're worried about Susan** wir machen uns um Susan Sorgen.

worry noun Sorge die (PL die Sorgen).

worry verb sich (DAT) Sorgen machen; **don't worry!** keine Sorge!; **don't worry about it** mach dir darum keine Sorgen.

worrying adjective beunruhigend.

worse adjective **1** (more unpleasant) schlimmer (problem, pain, illness); **things couldn't be worse** es kann nicht schlimmer kommen; **2** (less good) schlechter; **it was even worse than the last time** es war noch schlechter als letztes Mal; **to get worse** schlechter werden; **the weather's getting worse** das Wetter wird schlechter; **she's getting worse** (in health) es geht ihr schlechter.

worst adjective **1** (most unpleasant) schlimmster/schlimmste/

schlimmstes; **the worst** der/die/das schlimmste; **it was the worst day of my life** es war der schlimmste Tag meines Lebens; **if the worst comes to the worst** wenn es zum Schlimmsten kommt; **2** (least good) schlechtester/schlechtste/schlechtestes; **it's his worst film** das ist sein schlechtester Film; **French is my worst subject** in Französisch bin ich am schlechtesten.

worth adjective **to be worth** wert sein; **how much is it worth?** wie viel ist es wert?; **it's worth buying** das lohnt sich zu kaufen; **it's worth it** das lohnt sich; **it's not worth it** es lohnt sich nicht.

would verb **1 would you like something to eat?** möchtest du etwas essen?; **what would you like?** was möchten Sie?; **2 I wouldn't do it** ich würde das nicht machen; **I would buy it, but I haven't got any money at the moment** ich würde es kaufen, aber ich habe zur Zeit kein Geld; **I'd like to go to the cinema** ich würde gern ins Kino gehen; **she said she'd help us** sie hat gesagt, sie würde uns helfen; **3 that would be a good idea** das wäre ein gute Idee; **if we had asked her she would have helped us** wenn wir sie gefragt hätten, hätte sie uns geholfen; **4 he wouldn't answer** er wollte nicht antworten; **the car wouldn't start** das Auto wollte nicht anspringen.

wound *noun* Wunde *die* (PL *die* Wunden).

wound *verb* verwunden.

wrap *verb* einwickeln SEP; **I'm going to wrap (up) my presents** ich wickele meine Geschenke ein; **could you wrap it for me please?** können Sie es bitte in Geschenkpapier einwickeln?

wrapping paper *noun* Geschenkpapier *das*.

wreck *noun* 1 Wrack *das* (PL *die* Wracks); **2 I feel a wreck** ich bin völlig kaputt.

wreck *verb* 1 zerstören (*a building or machinery*); **2** kaputtfahren◆ SEP (*a car*); **3** verderben◆ (*a party, holidays*); **it completely wrecked my evening** das hat mir den Abend völlig verdorben; **4** zunichte machen (*plans*).

wrestler *noun* Ringer *der* (PL *die* Ringer), Ringerin *die* (PL *die* Ringerinnen).

wrestling *noun* Ringen *das*.

wrist *noun* Handgelenk *das* (PL *die* Handgelenke).

write *verb* schreiben◆; **to write to somebody** jemandem schreiben; **I'll write her a letter** ich schreibe ihr einen Brief; **to write to a firm** an eine Firma schreiben.

● **to write down** aufschreiben◆ SEP; **I wrote down her name** ich schrieb ihren Namen auf; **she wrote it down for me** sie hat es mir aufgeschrieben.

writer *noun* Schriftsteller *der* (PL *die* Schriftsteller), Schriftstellerin *die* (PL *die* Schriftstellerinnen).

writing *noun* Schrift *die*.

wrong *adjective* 1 (*not correct*) falsch; **the wrong answer** die falsche Antwort; **it's the wrong address** das ist die falsche Adresse; **2 you've got the wrong number** Sie haben sich verwählt; **3 to be wrong** (*be mistaken*) sich irren; **I must have been wrong** ich muss mich geirrt haben; **4** (*out of order*) **to be wrong** nicht stimmen; **there's something wrong** etwas stimmt nicht; **5** (*dishonest*) nicht richtig; **it's wrong to make him pay for it** es ist nicht richtig, dass er dafür zahlen muss; **he's wrong** er hat Unrecht; **you're quite wrong there**, cars pollute the environment da haben Sie aber Unrecht, Autos verschmutzen die Umwelt; **6 what's wrong?** was ist los?

wrong *adverb* 1 (*false*) falsch; **he's got it wrong** er hat es falsch gemacht; **2 to go wrong** (*break*) kaputtgehen◆ SEP (PERF *sein*) (*informal*); **3 to go wrong** schief gehen◆ (*plan*).

Xx

xerox *noun* Fotokopie *die* (PL *die* Fotokopien).

xerox *verb* fotokopieren.

X-ray *noun* Röntgenaufnahme *die* (PL *die* Röntgenaufnahmen); **to have an X-ray** geröntgt werden◆ (PERF *sein*).

a b c d e f g h i j k l m n o p q r s t u v w x y z

X-ray verb röntgen; **they X-rayed her ankle** sie haben ihren Knöchel geröntgt.

Yy

yacht noun 1 (sailing boat) Segelboot das (PL die Segelboote); 2 (large luxury boat) Jacht die (PL die Jachten).

yawn verb gähnen.

year noun 1 Jahr das (PL die Jahre); **six years ago** vor sechs Jahren; **the whole year** das ganze Jahr; 2 **they lived in Moscow for years** sie haben jahrelang in Moskau gewohnt; 3 **to be seventeen years old** siebzehn Jahre alt sein; **a two-year-old child** ein zweijähriges Kind; 4 (in school) Klasse die (PL die Klassen) (in German secondary schools the years go from the 'fünfte Klasse' to the 'dreizehnte Klasse'); **I'm in Year 10** (in Britain) ich gehe in die zehnte Klasse; **he'll be in Year 11** (in Britain) er kommt in die elfte Klasse.

yell verb schreien✧.

yellow adjective gelb.

yes adverb 1 ja; **yes please** ja bitte; **'is Tom in his room?' – 'yes, he is'** 'ist Tom im Zimmer?' - 'ja'; 2 (answering a negative) doch; **'you don't want to come with us, do you?' – 'yes, I do!'** 'du willst nicht mitkommen?' - 'doch!'; **'you haven't finished, have you?' – 'yes, I have'** 'Sie sind noch nicht fertig, oder?' - 'doch!'.

yesterday adverb 1 gestern; **I saw her yesterday** ich habe sie gestern gesehen; **yesterday afternoon** gestern Nachmittag; **yesterday morning** gestern früh; 2 **the day before yesterday** vorgestern.

yet adverb 1 **not yet** noch nicht; **it's not ready yet** es ist noch nicht fertig; 2 (in questions) schon; **has she mentioned it yet?** hat sie es schon erwähnt?

yoghurt noun Joghurt der (PL die Joghurt).

yolk noun Eigelb das (PL die Eigelbe).

you pronoun 1 (as the subject of the sentence and in comparisons) du (familiar form, singular), Sie (polite form, singular and plural); ('du' is the familiar way of talking to family members, close friends, and people of your own age; 'Sie' is more polite) **do you want to go to the cinema tonight?** möchtest du heute Abend ins Kino gehen?; **can you tell me where the station is, please?** können Sie mir bitte sagen, wo der Bahnhof ist?; **he's older than you** er ist älter als du, er ist älter als Sie; 2 (the object form of 'du' and 'Sie', in the dative) dir (familiar form, singular), Ihnen (polite form, singular and plural); **I'll lend you my bike** ich leihe dir mein Rad; **I'll write to you** ich schreibe Ihnen; **I'll come with you** ich komme mit Ihnen mit; 3 (the object form of 'du' and 'Sie', in the accusative) dich (familiar form, singular), Sie (polite form, singular and plural); **I saw you** ich habe

dich gesehen, ich habe Sie gesehen;
4 (*as the subject of the sentence*) ihr
(*familiar form, plural*); **do you all
want to come?** wollt ihr alle
kommen?; **5** (*the object form, in the
accusative and the dative*) euch; **I'll
invite you all!** ich lade euch alle
ein!; **I'll give it to you later** ich gebe
es euch später.

young *adjective* jung; **young
people** junge Leute; **he's younger
than me** er ist jünger als ich;
**Tessa's two years younger than
me** Tessa ist zwei Jahre jünger als
ich.

your *adjective* **1** (*familiar form,
singular*) dein (*this is the familiar
way of talking to family members,
close friends, and people of your own
age; 'Ihr' is more polite*); **I met your
brother** ich habe deinen Bruder
getroffen; **I met your sister** ich
habe deine Schwester getroffen; **I
drove your car** ich bin mit deinem
Auto gefahren; **I know your
brothers** ich kenne deine Brüder;
2 (*familiar form, plural*) euer; **your
brother** euer Bruder; **your sister**
eure Schwester; **your car** euer
Auto; **your friends are waiting
downstairs** eure Freunde warten
unten; **3** (*polite form, singular and
plural*) Ihr; **your brother** Ihr
Bruder; **your sister** Ihre
Schwester; **your car is in the
garage** Ihr Auto ist in der Garage;
you can all bring your friends Sie
können alle Ihre Freunde
mitbringen.

yours *pronoun* **1** (*familiar form,
singular*) deiner/deine/deins (*this*

*is the familiar way of talking to
family members, close friends, and
people of your own age, 'Ihrer/Ihre/
Ihrs' is more polite*); **my brother's
younger than yours** mein Bruder
ist jünger als deiner; **my sister is
older than yours** meine Schwester
ist älter als deine; **I enjoyed that
book - is it yours?** das Buch hat
mir gefallen - ist es deins?; **my
shoes are more expensive than
yours** meine Schuhe sind teurer als
deine; **2** (*familiar form, plural*)
euer/eure/eures; **my children are
younger than yours** meine Kinder
sind jünger als eure; **3** (*polite form,
singular and plural*) Ihrer/Ihre/
Ihrs; **his father must be older
than yours** sein Vater muss älter
als Ihrer sein; **4** **she's a friend of
yours** sie ist eine Freundin von
Ihnen; **these books are yours**
diese Bücher gehören Ihnen; **5** (*in
letters*) **Yours sincerely** Mit
freundlichen Grüßen.

yourself *pronoun* **1** (*when
translated by a reflexive verb in
German*) dich, (*formal*) sich; **ask
yourself** frage dich, fragen Sie sich;
2 (*as a reflexive dative pronoun*)
dir, (*formal*) sich; **did you hurt
yourself?** hast du dir wehgetan?,
haben Sie sich wehgetan?; **3** (*for
emphasis*) selbst; **did you do it
yourself?** hast du es selbst
gemacht?; **4 all by yourself** ganz
allein.

yourselves *pronoun* **1** euch,
(*formal*) sich; **make yourselves
comfortable** macht es euch
gemütlich, machen Sie es sich

a
b
c
d
e
f
g
h
i
j
k
l
m
n
o
p
q
r
s
t
u
v
w
x
y
z

gemütlich; **2** (*for emphasis*) selbst; **did you do it yourselves?** habt ihr es selbst gemacht?; **3 by yourselves** allein.

youth *noun* **1** (*stage in life*) Jugend die; **2** (*young people*) die Jugendlichen; **today's youth** die Jugend von heute; **3** (*young male*) Jugendliche der (PL die Jugendlichen).

youth hostel *noun* Jugendherberge die (PL die Jugendherbergen).

Yugoslavia *noun* Jugoslawien das; **in the former Yugoslavia** im ehemaligen Jugoslawien.

Zz

zany *adjective* verrückt.

zebra *noun* Zebra das (PL die Zebras).

zebra crossing *noun* Zebrastreifen der (PL die Zebrastreifen).

zero *noun* Null die (PL die Nullen).

zigzag *verb* **1** im Zickzack laufen✧ (PERF sein); **2** (*in a car*) im Zickzack fahren✧ (PERF sein).

zip *noun* Reißverschluss der (PL die Reißverschlüsse).

zodiac *noun* Tierkreis der; **the signs of the zodiac** die Sternzeichen (*plural*).

zone *noun* Zone die (PL die Zonen).

zoo *noun* Zoo der (PL die Zoos).

zoom lens *noun* Zoomobjektiv das (PL die Zoomobjektive).

GERMAN LIFE AND CULTURE

The year in Germany 631

Food and drink.. 632

Life at School. 333

On holiday in Germany 634

Life in Germany 636

Did you know ... ? 637

Numbers. 638

Dates. .. .. ,. .. 639

Important Dates 640

Days, Months, Seasons.. 641

Map of Germany 644

The year in Germany

Neujahr
New Year's Day, a public holiday.

Id-al-Fitr
The date of this Muslim festival varies from year to year. It is celebrated mainly by the Turkish population, the largest Muslim group in Germany.

Heilige Drei Könige
Feast of the Three Kings: 6th January. This and some other days are public holidays only in Roman Catholic parts of Germany.

Valentinstag
St Valentine's Day: 14th February. The custom of people sending a special message to someone they love is growing in Germany.

Fastnacht
Carnival, celebrated in February or March with fancy dress parties, and elaborate processions in cities like Mainz and Köln. In Bavaria, *Fastnacht* is called *Fasching*.

Ostern
Easter. Children hunt for chocolate eggs in the garden, and many families decorate their dining room with intricately painted eggs. Good Friday (*Karfreitag*) and Easter Monday (*Ostermontag*) are both public holidays.

der 1. Mai
1st May: a public holiday.

Christi Himmelfahrt
Ascension Day, a public holiday at the end of May.

Pfingstmontag
Whit Monday. A public holiday, usually at the beginning of June.

Tag der Deutschen Einheit
3rd October. A public holiday that commemorates the reuniting of East and West Germany in 1989.

Reformationstag
Reformation Day, 31st October. A public holiday in the Protestant parts of Germany.

Allerheiligen
1st November: All Saints Day. A public holiday in most Roman Catholic parts of Germany.

Sankt Nikolaus
6th December. On the night before St Nicholas' day, children put a shoe outside their bedroom. In the morning, it is filled with chocolates, nuts and maybe a small present.

Heiligabend
Christmas Eve: 24th December. Most families have a real Christmas tree, and put their presents under it. The main celebration is in the evening. People exchange presents and often light real candles on the tree. Many later go to midnight mass.

1. Weihnachtstag
Christmas Day: 25th December. People often have a lie-in after the celebrations of the night before. They have a big midday meal, and often visit family. The 26th December is a public holiday, too.

Silvester
31st December. It is traditional to see the New Year in with fireworks.

Food and drink

Apfelstrudel
This apple pie, originally from Austria, has a very thin pastry.

Bäckerei
A baker's shop, which usually sells many different types of bread, e.g. some with whole cereal seeds. They also sell rolls, called *Brötchen* in the north of Germany, and *Semmel* in the south.

Bretzen
Salted rolls in the shape of an 8, they are a speciality of the south of Germany.

Café
A German café serves coffee, cakes and small meals. Coffee and hot chocolate are sold by the cup (*Tasse*) or the pot (*Kännchen*).

chips
Crisps. Chips, French fries, are called *Pommes frites*.

Eis
Ice cream. Flavours may include e.g.
- Kirsch (*cherry*),
- Pistazzien (*pistachio nut*),
- Stracciatella (*vanilla with chocolate chips*),
- Zitrone (*lemon*),
and many others.

Emmental
A Swiss cheese.

Kalb
Veal, the meat from a calf, is widely available in Germany.

Käsefondue
Cheese fondue. It is made from cheese melted in white wine, and is eaten by dipping bread into a communal pot.

Konditorei
A cake shop, which will sell a wide range of cakes (*Kuchen*) and gateaux (*Torten*).

Milch
Milk. Full cream milk is called *Vollmilch. Buttermilch*, similar to a runny yoghurt, is widely available.

Sauerkraut
Sauerkraut is boiled, pickled cabbage. It is often eaten with sausages.

Schwarzwälderkirschtorte
Black Forest Gateau, made with chocolate, cherries, and fresh whipped cream.

Spezi
A refreshing drink made from lemonade and cola.

Stollen
A rich bread-like cake, often enhanced with marzipan, and eaten at Christmas.

Türkische Spezialitäten
Turkish specialities. There are many Turkish restaurants and shops, as Turks are one of the largest ethnic groups in Germany.

Wurst
Sausage. Germany has a huge range of sausages which can be boiled (*Bockwurst*), fried or grilled (*Bratwurst*), or served cold like salami.

Life at School

Abitur

The end-of-school exam taken by pupils who have stayed at school to the age of 18 or 19.

Gymnasium

Grammar school. At the age of 10, pupils move from primary school (*Grundschule*) to one of four types of secondary school, depending on their ability at school:

- *Gymnasium* which requires the most academic work,
- *Realschule* or *Hauptschule*, in which work is a bit easier,
- *Sonderschule*, for pupils with learning difficulties.

There are only very few comprehensive schools (*Gesamtschulen*) in Germany.

hitzefrei

"heat free". In many schools, pupils are sent home early if the thermometer reaches 27° C.

Klasse

As most German pupils begin school when they are six, they are usually in Klasse 6 at the age of 11:

Klasse 6 = *Year 7*

Klasse 7 = *Year 8*

Klasse 8 = *Year 9*

Klasse 9 = *Year 10*

Noten

School marks. There is a set system of marks from 1 – 6 throughout Germany:

Note 1 is the best mark,
Note 6 is the lowest.
Pupils with too many low marks can be required to repeat a year (*sitzen bleiben*) instead of going on to a higher class.

die Schulferien

German school holidays can vary considerably from year to year, because different parts of Germany have their summer holidays at different times, in an effort to reduce traffic jams at peak holiday periods. There may be:

- one or two weeks in October / November
- two weeks at Christmas
- one or two weeks in February
- two weeks at Easter
- a week at Whitsun
- six or seven weeks in summer

The overall length of school holidays is much as in Britain.

Schultag

School day. The German school day is usually from 8.00 a.m. to 1 p.m. for younger pupils, with older pupils often having afternoon classes on one or more afternoons a week.

Wandertag

Trip day: a day on which school classes go on class trips. It is often the pupils who suggest where they should go.

On holiday in Germany

die Alpen
The Alps cover much of Austria and Switzerland, and stretch along the southern border of Germany. They are a popular holiday area in both summer and winter. The highest points in the three countries are:
Germany: *Zugspitze* 2964m
Austria: *Groß Glockner* 3797m
Switzerland: *Monte Rosa* 4634m

Autobahn
Motorway. Germany has an impressive network of free motorways. Motorway services are called *Raststätte* or *Autohof*.

Bayern
Bavaria, Germany's biggest *Land*, or province, is in the south, with the Alps along its southern border. Its capital is Munich. Bavaria is famous for its big wooden farmhouses and its many local beers.

Brandenburger Tor
This gateway, built in 1791, is Berlin's most famous landmark, and it is where Berliners celebrated the reunification of Germany in 1989.

Berliner Mauer
The Berlin Wall. East Germany (*DDR*) was separated from West Germany, and governed by a Communist government, from 1948 to 1989. In Berlin, the Communists built a wall around West Berlin, to prevent people from East Germany fleeing to the West. The wall was taken down after the two parts of Germany were re-united in 1989.

Donau
River Danube, which begins in Germany and reaches the Black Sea in Romania. Barges bring freight to and from Eastern Europe into Austria and Germany. A canal connects the Danube to the Rhine.

Fremdenzimmer
You see this sign outside houses which offer Bed & Breakfast accommodation. Holiday flats have the sign *Ferienwohnung*.

Hauptbahnhof
In towns which have several railway stations, the main railway station is nearly always called the *Hauptbahnhof*.

ICE
InterCity Express. These are Germany's fastest trains. You pay a supplement to travel in them, and have to book a seat.

Liechtenstein
A tiny country of 160 km^2 bordering Switzerland. It has its own government and issues its own stamps, but uses Swiss francs.

Neuschwanstein
The ultimate fairy-tale castle, *Neuschwanstein* was built in a dramatic Alpine setting to the orders of King Ludwig II of Bavaria. It was completed after his death in 1886.

Oktoberfest
A popular festival in Munich, with fun fairs and beer tents. It actually begins in September.

Ostsee

Baltic Sea. With large sandy beaches, this is a popular holiday area, especially as it is within easy reach of Berlin.

Rathaus

Town hall. It is often a grand building in the main square.

Reichstag

Built in 1894, the Reichstag was the seat of the German parliament. Destroyed by fire in 1933, it was rebuilt following the reunification of Germany in 1989, and the German parliament now sits there again.

Rhein

River Rhine. It cuts through the hills in a deep valley, with vines on the hillsides and castles on the tops. Barges carry goods to and from Holland, France, etc

Skiferien

Skiing holidays. Switzerland, Austria and Germany have established ski resorts, and winter sports are popular in all three countries.

Straßenbahn

Tram. Many German cities have trams as well as buses. Buy your tickets from the machine at the stop (it's cheaper than from the driver) and cancel them once you are on the tram. The same tickets can be used on buses and underground trains, too.

Südtirol

South Tyrol. Part of Italy, in the Alps, where people speak both German and Italian.

U-Bahn

Underground trains. The trains serving the suburbs are called *S-Bahn*.

Weihnachtsmarkt

Christmas market. Decorated with greenery and smelling of mulled wine and roast chestnuts, these markets are a beautiful setting for buying Christmas gifts.

Wien

Vienna, the capital of Austria. Known for its music, its museums and cafes, the white horses in the Spanish Riding School and the *Riesenrad*, an enormous Ferris wheel built in 1897.

Life in Germany

Biergarten
'Beer gardens' are common especially in the south of Germany, where people of all generations relax on summer afternoons and evenings. Coffee, cake, soft drinks, and small meals can be ordered, as well as beer.

Bundestag
The German 'House of Commons'. Members of Parliament (*Abgeordnete*) are elected every four years.

Feiertag
Public holiday. Germany has more public holidays than most countries in Europe, but if a public holiday falls on a Saturday or Sunday, it's 'lost', i.e. the following Monday is a working day as usual.

Freibad
Outdoor swimming pool. These are very popular, as summers are hot. People often swim in lakes, too.

Hochdeutsch
High German, or 'standard German', as spoken e.g. on TV. Each area of German, Austria and German-speaking Switzerland has its own – often quite marked – dialect.

Kaffee und Kuchen
When, in mid-afternoon, Germans, Swiss and Austrians say it's time for 'coffee', they often mean it's time for a slice of cake as well. All three countries are justifiably famous for their mouth-watering cakes.

Kanton
Switzerland is divided into 26 provinces called *Kantonen*.

Kanzler
The German prime minister is called the *Kanzler* (Chancellor).

Land
Germany is divided into 16 provinces, each called a Land. The largest is Bavaria (*Bayern*), the Land with the largest population is *Nordrhein-Westfalen*. Three cities are *Länder* in their own right: Berlin, Hamburg, and Bremen.

Marktplatz
At the centre of most towns is the 'market square', often lined with gabled houses.

Olympia-Stadion
A big stadium in Munich, home to the football team, *Bayern München*.

Personalausweis
Identity card, which can be used instead of a passport for travel within the EU.

Postleitzahl
Postcode. German postcodes have five figures and no letters.

Republik
Germany is a republic, with a president (*Präsident*) at its head.

Did you know...?

★ that you can be fined if you cross the road when the traffic light (*Ampel*) is red for pedestrians?

★ that a *Berliner* is a doughnut, a *Bitburger* a beer, a *Homburger* a hat, a *Wiener* a sausage, and a *Hamburger*, of course, a hamburger?

★ that German letter boxes (*Briefkästen*) are yellow?

★ that cars from Switzerland have the letters *CH* and stamps have the name *Helvetia*?

★ that, in Austria, potatoes are often called *Erdäpfel* (apples of the earth) and tomatoes *Paradeiser* (fruits of paradise)?

★ that more people in the EU (*Europäische Union*) have German as their mother tongue than English, French, or any other language?

★ that the wooden beams of half-timbered houses (*Fachwerkhäuser*) are red, not black, because they used to be preserved with bull's blood?

★ that people who live in the south of Germany get more public holidays (*Feiertage*) than those who live in the north?

★ that Germany's biggest airport (*Flughafen*) is Frankfurt, and its busiest seaport is Hamburg?

★ that the usual way of greeting people is:
Guten Tag in northern Germany,
Grüß Gott in southern Germany,
Grüezi in Switzerland,
Servus in Austria,
but you can also say *Hallo* everywhere?

★ that the biggest city in Switzerland is Zürich, but the capital city (*Hauptstadt*) is Bern?

★ that the name *Köln* comes from the Roman word 'colonia', because the city was a Roman colony?

★ that Switzerland's most famous mountain, the *Matterhorn* (4478m), is not its highest; the highest is the *Monte Rosa* (4634m)?

★ that until 1918, Austria (*Österreich*) was at the centre of an empire that included Hungary, Slovakia, Czech Republic, and parts of Poland, Ukraine and Italy?

★ that officers in the German police (*Polizei*) wear a green uniform and are armed?

★ that a minority of Swiss people speak *Romansch*, a language derived from Latin?

★ that to travel on Swiss or Austrian motorways, you have to buy a sticker called a *Vignette*, and display the sticker on the car windscreen?

NUMBERS

null	0	einundzwanzig	21
eins	1	zweiundzwanzig	22
zwei	2	dreiundzwanzig	23
drei	3	vierundzwanzig	24
vier	4	fünfundzwanzig	25
fünf	5	sechsundzwanzig	26
sechs	6	siebenundzwanzig	27
sieben	7	achtundzwanzig	28
acht	8	neunundzwanzig	29
neun	9		
zehn	10	dreißig	30
elf	11	vierzig	40
zwölf	12	fünfzig	50
dreizehn	13	sechzig	60
vierzehn	14	siebzig	70
fünfzehn	15	achtzig	80
sechzehn	16	neunzig	90
siebzehn	17		
achtzehn	18	hundert	100
neunzehn	19	tausend	1000
zwanzig	20	eine Million	1 000 000

DATES

am ersten Januar	on January 1st
der erste Januar	the 1st of January
zweite (2.)	2nd
dritte (3.)	3rd
vierte (4.)	4th
fünfte	5th
sechste	6th
siebte	7th
achte	8th
neunte	9th
zehnte	10th
elfte	11th
zwölfte	12th
dreizehnte	13th
vierzehnte	14th
fünfzehnte	15th
sechzehnte	16th
siebzehnte	17th
achtzehnte	18th
neunzehnte	19th
zwanzigste	20th
einundzwanzigste	21st
dreißigste	30th

IMPORTANT DATES

Feiertag	public holiday
Fasching/Fastnacht	carnival time
Heiligabend	Christmas Eve
Karfreitag	Good Friday
Maifeiertag	May Day
Neujahr	New Year
Ostern	Easter
Pfingsten	Whitsun
Silvester	New Year's Eve
Weihnachten	Christmas
1.Weihnachtstag	Christmas Day
2. Weihnachtstag	Boxing Day

DAYS

Montag	Monday
Dienstag	Tuesday
Mittwoch	Wednesday
Donnerstag	Thursday
Freitag	Friday
Samstag/Sonna-bend	Saturday
Sonntag	Sunday

MONTHS

Januar	January
Februar	February
März	March
April	April
Mai	May
Juni	June
Juli	July
August	August
September	September
Oktober	October
November	November
Dezember	December

SEASONS

der Winter	winter
der Frühiing	spring
der Sommer	summer
der Herbst	autumn

MAP

Deutschland

DEUTSCHLAND	GERMANY
Bundesland	**State**
Baden-Württemberg	Baden-Württemberg
Bayern	Bavaria
Berlin	Berlin
Brandenburg	Brandenburg
Bremen	Bremen
Hamburg	Hamburg
Hessen	Hessen
Mecklenburg-Vorpommern	Mecklenburg-West Pomerania
Niedersachsen	Lower Saxony
Nordrhein-Westfalen	North Rhine-Westphalia
Rheinland-Pfalz	Rhineland-Palatinate
Saarland	Saarland
Sachsen	Saxony
Sachsen-Anhalt	Saxony-Anhalt
Schleswig-Holstein	Schleswig-Holstein
Thüringen	Thuringia

NOTES

NOTES

NOTES

NOTES

NOTES